GLOBAL MARKETING MANAGEMENT

KU-306-052

FOURTH EDITION

Masaaki Kotabe
Temple University

Kristiaan Helsen
Hong Kong University of Science and Technology

BICENTENNIAL
1807
WILEY
2007
BICENTENNIAL

JOHN WILEY & SONS, INC.

DEDICATION

To Sylvia Donnelly-Kotabe
—MK

To my mother and Vu
—KH

ASSOCIATE PUBLISHER	Judith Joseph
SENIOR ACQUISITIONS EDITOR	Jayme Heffler
ASSOCIATE EDITOR	Jennifer Conklin
EDITORIAL ASSISTANT	Carissa Marker
EXECUTIVE MARKETING MANAGER	Christopher Ruel
SENIOR PRODUCTION EDITOR	Patricia McFadden
DESIGNER	Michael St. Martine
PRODUCTION MANAGEMENT SERVICES	Pinetree Composition Services
COVER PHOTO	Photo Disk, Inc./Getty Images

This book was set in 10/12 TimesTen Roman by Laserwords, Inc and printed and bound by Courier Companies. The cover was printed by Courier Companies.

This book is printed on acid free paper. ∞

Copyright © 2008 John Wiley & Sons, Inc. All rights reserved.

No part of this publication may be reproduced, stored in a retrieval system or transmitted in any form or by any means, electronic, mechanical, photocopying, recording, scanning or otherwise, except as permitted under Sections 107 or 108 of the 1976 United States Copyright Act, without either the prior written permission of the Publisher, or authorization through payment of the appropriate per-copy fee to the Copyright Clearance Center, Inc. 222 Rosewood Drive, Danvers, MA 01923, (978) 750-8400, fax (978) 750-4470. Requests to the Publisher for permission should be addressed to the Permissions Department, John Wiley & Sons, Inc., 111 River Street, Hoboken, NJ 07030, (201)748-6011, fax (201)748-6008, E-Mail: PERMREQ@WILEY.COM. To order books or for customer service please call 1-800-CALL WILEY (225-5945).

ISBN   978-0-47175527-2

Printed in the United States of America

10 9 8 7 6 5 4

DUBLIN BUSINESS SCHOOL
LIBRARY
RECEIVED
1 5 OCT 2008

ABOUT THE AUTHORS

Masaaki "Mike" Kotabe holds the Washburn Chair Professorship in International Business and Marketing and is Director of Research at the Institute of Global Management Studies at the Fox School of Business and Management at Temple University. Prior to joining Temple University in 1998, he was Ambassador Edward Clark Centennial Endowed Fellow and Professor of Marketing and International Business at the University of Texas at Austin. Dr. Kotabe also served as the Vice President of the Academy of International Business in the 1997–1998 term. He received his Ph.D. in Marketing and International Business from Michigan State University. Dr. Kotabe teaches international marketing, global sourcing strategy, and Asian business practices at the undergraduate and MBA levels and theories of international business at the doctoral level. He has lectured widely at various business schools around the world. For his research, he has worked closely with leading companies such as AT&T, NEC, Nissan, Philips, Sony, and Ito-Yokado (parent of 7-Eleven stores), and served as adviser to the United Nations' and World Trade Organization's Executive Forum on National Export Strategies.

Dr. Kotabe has written many scholarly publications. His research has appeared in numerous journals including *Journal of Marketing, Journal of International Business Studies, Strategic Management Journal,* and *Academy of Management Journal.* His books include *Global Sourcing Strategy: R&D Manufacturing, Marketing Interfaces* (1992), *Japanese Distribution System* (1993), *Anticompetitive Practices in Japan* (1996), *MERCOSUR and Beyond* (1997), *Marketing Management* (2001), *Market Revolution in Latin America: Beyond Mexico* (2001), and *Emerging Issues in International Business Research* (2002).

He currently serves as the Editor of the *Journal of International Management* and is or has been on the editorial boards of numerous other journals. He also serves as an Adviser to the Institute of Industrial Policy Studies (IPS) National Competitiveness Report.

In the 1997 issue of *Journal of Teaching in International Business,* Dr. Kotabe was ranked the most prolific international marketing researcher in the world in the last 10 years. He has been recently elected a Fellow of the Academy of International Business for his significant contribution to international business research and education. He is also an elected member of the New York Academy of Sciences.

Kristiaan Helsen has been Associate Professor of Marketing at the Hong Kong University of Science and Technology (HKUST) since 1995. Prior to joining HKUST, he was on the faculty of the University of Chicago for five years. He has lectured at Nijenrode University (Netherlands), Purdue University, the Catholic University of Lisbon, and CEIBS (Shanghai). Dr. Helsen received his Ph.D. in Marketing from the Wharton School of the University of Pennsylvania.

His research areas include promotional strategy, competitive strategy, and hazard rate modeling. His articles have appeared in journals such as *Marketing Science, Journal of Marketing, Journal of Marketing Research,* and *European Journal of Operations Research,* among others. Dr. Helsen is on the editorial boards of the *International Journal of Research in Marketing* and the *Journal of Marketing.*

PREFACE

◆ ◆ ◆ ◆ ◆ ◆ ◆ ◆

THREE FUNDAMENTAL ISSUES ADDRESSED IN THE FOURTH EDITION

We have received quite a few letters and e-mails as well as comments on Amazon.com from instructors and business executives around the world who used the previous editions of our *Global Marketing Management*. Their comments have been unanimously favorable. Thanks to the increased desire in many parts of the world for access to our book in their own languages, it has been translated into Chinese, Japanese, Portuguese, and Spanish. However, we just cannot sit on the laurel. As the world around us has been constantly changing, the content and context of our book also must change to reflect the *climate of the time*. In our mind, the role of a textbook is not only to describe today's realities but also to extrapolate logically from them how the future will unfold. After all, that is how marketing executives have to act and make *correct* decisions based on the facts they have gathered. Today's realities are a product of past realities, and the future will be an uncharted course of events lying ahead of us. We constantly strive to help you better understand state-of-the-art marketing practices on a global basis with relevant historical background, current marketing environments, and logical explanations based on a massive amount of knowledge generated by marketing executives as well as by academic researchers from around the world.

The fourth edition of our book builds on three major changes that took place in the last decade or so. First, the landscape of the global economy changed drastically in this period. The Asian and Latin American financial crises, the further expansion of the European Union (EU), the economic recovery of Japan from its decade-long recession, and the emergence of China and India as economic superpowers, have occurred during the this period. For example, until the mid-1990s, it seemed certain that the Asian economy would grow at a fairly fast pace as it had done in the last 40 years. However, to everyone's surprise, the Asian economic miracle was brought to a screeching halt by the region's financial crisis toward the end of 1998. The ramifications of the Asian financial crisis are not limited to Asian countries and their trading partners. Another epoch-making event was the introduction of a common European currency, known as the *euro,* on January 1, 1999. China's role as the world's factory is well established, and India's increased role in information technology development is obvious.

Second, the explosive growth of information technology tools, including the Internet and electronic commerce (e-commerce), has had a significant effect on the way we do business internationally. This is a relatively new phenomenon that we need to look at carefully. On one hand, everyone seems to agree that business transactions will be faster and more global early on. And it is very true. As a result, marketing management techniques such as customer relationship management and global account management have become increasingly feasible. However, on the other hand, the more deeply we have examined this issue, the more convinced we have become that certain things would not change or could even become more local as a result of the globalization that the Internet and e-commerce bestowed on us.

Third, it is an underlying human tendency to desire to be different when there are economic and political forces of convergence (often referred to as *globalization*). When the globalization argument (and movement) became fashionable in the 1980s and 1990s, many of us believed that globalization would make global marketing easier. As we explain later in the text, marketing beyond national borders has indeed become easier, but it does not necessarily mean that customers want the same products in countries around the world. For example, many more peoples around the world try to emphasize cultural and ethnic differences as well as accept those differences than ever before. Just think about many new countries being born around the world as well as regional unifications taking place at the same time. Another example is that while e-commerce promotion on the Internet goes global, product delivery may need to be fairly local to address local competition and exchange rate fluctuations as well as the complexities of international physical distribution (export declarations, tariffs, and nontariff barriers). From a supply-side point of view, globalization has brought us more products from all corners of the world. However, from a demand-side (marketing-side) point of view, customers have a much broader set of goods and services from which to *choose*. In other words, marketers now face even more divergent customers with divergent preferences—far from a homogeneous group of customers.

Indeed, these changes we have observed in the last decade or so are more than extraordinary. In this fourth edition, we have expanded on issues related to them in all chapters where relevant. We have added many new examples that have occurred in this period. However, we do not sacrifice logical depth in favor of new examples. This revision required a significant amount of work, as it has in the past. It was well worth the effort however because we are confident that readers like you will become satisfied and enlightened.

We strongly believe that cases provide students not only with lively discussions of what goes on with many companies but also with in-depth understanding of many marketing-related concepts and tools as used by those companies. In this revision, we added many new cases as well as several cases from the earlier edition that were voted as *favorites* by our textbook users and their students. This edition has a total of 35 cases. They represent many products and services and many regions and countries as well as many nationalities. Six of them are included in the book itself, and the rest are placed on the textbook Web site for easy download at www.wiley.com/college/kotabe.

Many users of previous editions continue to comment that our book is probably the most academically rigorous and conceptually sound text, yet it is full of lively examples that students can easily identify with in order to drive home important points. We combine the academic rigor and relevance (and fun of reading) of materials to meet both undergraduate and MBA educational requirements. We keep this tradition in our fourth edition.

OUR PEDAGOGICAL ORIENTATION ◆ ◆ ◆ ◆ ◆ ◆ ◆ ◆

Marketing in the global arena is a very dynamic discipline. Today, there are many international or global marketing management books vying for their respective niches in the market. The current market is a mature one. As you will learn in our book, in a mature market, firms tend to focus closely—perhaps too closely—on immediate product features for sources of differentiation and may inadvertently ignore the fundamental changes that may be reshaping the industry. Often, those fundamental changes come from outside the industry. The same logic applies to the textbook market. Whether existing textbooks are titled international marketing or global marketing, they continue to be bound by the traditional bilateral (international) view of competition. Any new textbook must embrace the traditional coverage of existing textbooks, but we emphasize the multilateral (global) nature of marketing throughout our book.

Some textbooks have replaced the word international with global. Such a change amounts to a repackaging of an existing product we often see in a mature product market, and it does not necessarily make a textbook globally oriented. We needed some paradigm shift to accomplish the task of adding truly global dimensions and complex realities to a textbook. You might ask, "What fundamental changes are needed for a paradigm shift?" and then, "Why do we need fundamental changes to begin with?"

Our answer is straightforward. Our ultimate objective is to help you prepare for the new 21st century and become an effective manager overseeing global marketing activities in an increasingly competitive environment. You may or may not choose marketing for your career. If you do, what you will learn in our book will have direct relevance and help you understand how you, as a marketing manager, can affect other business functions for effective corporate performance on a global basis. If you choose other functional areas of business for your career, our book will help you understand how you can work effectively with marketing people for the same corporate goal. Our book is organized as shown in the flowchart.

We believe that our pedagogical orientation not only embraces existing marketing knowledge and methods but also sets itself apart from the competition in a number of fundamental ways as discussed in the following section.

Global Orientation

As we indicated at the outset, the word *global* epitomizes the competitive pressure and market opportunities from around the world and the firm's need to optimize its market performance on a global basis. Whether a company operates domestically or across national boundaries, it can no longer avoid competitive pressure and market opportunities. For optimal market performance, a company should also be ready and willing to take advantage of resources on a global basis while responding to the different needs and wants of consumers. In a way, global marketing is a constant struggle with economies of scale and scope needs of the firm and its responsiveness and sensitivity to different market conditions. While some people call it a "glocal" orientation, we use the term *global* to emphasize marketing flexibility on a global basis.

Let's look at a hypothetical U.S. company exporting finished products to Europe and Japan. Traditionally, this export phenomenon has been treated as a bilateral business transaction between a U.S. company and foreign customers. However, in reality this export transaction may be nothing more to the executives of the U.S. company, than the last phase of the company's activities they manage. Indeed, this company procures certain components from long-term suppliers in Japan and Mexico, other components in a business-to-business (B2B) transaction on the Internet with a supplier in Korea, and its domestic sources in the United States and assembles a finished product in its Singapore plant for export to Europe and Japan as well as back to the United States. The Japanese supplier of critical components is a joint venture majority owned by this U.S. company whereas the Mexican supplier has a licensing agreement with the U.S. company that provides most of the technical know-how. A domestic supplier in the United States is in fact a subsidiary of a German company. In other words, this particular export transaction by the U.S. company involves a joint venture, a licensing agreement, a B2B transaction, a subsidiary operation, local assembly, and R&D, all managed directly or indirectly by the U.S. company. Add the realities of market complexities arising from diverse customer preferences in European, Japanese, and North American markets. Think about how these arrangements could affect the company's decisions over product policy, pricing, promotion, and distribution channels.

Many existing textbooks have focused on each of these value-adding activities as if they could be investigated independently. Obviously, in reality, they are not independent of each other and cannot be. We emphasize this multilateral realism by examining these value-adding activities as holistically as possible.

Interdisciplinary Perspective

To complement our global orientation, we offer an interdisciplinary perspective in all relevant chapters. We believe strongly that you cannot become a seasoned marketing executive without understanding how other functional areas interface with marketing. The reverse is also true for nonmarketing managers. Some of the exemplary areas in

Globalization

1. Globalization Imperative

Global Marketing Environment

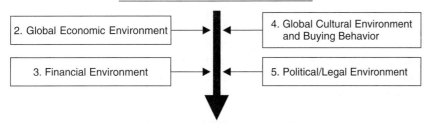

2. Global Economic Environment

3. Financial Environment

4. Global Cultural Environment and Buying Behavior

5. Political/Legal Environment

Development of Competitive Strategy

6. Global Marketing Research

7. Global Segmentation and Positioning

8. Global Marketing Strategies

9. Global Market Entry Strategies

10. Global Sourcing Strategy

Global Marketing Strategy Development

11. Product Development
12. Marketing Products and Services

14. Communicating with the World Consumer
15. Sales Management

13. Global Pricing

16. Global Logistics and Distribution
17. Export/Import Management

Managing Global Operations

18. Planning, Organization, and Control of Global Marketing Operations

19. Global Marketing and the Internet

which such a broad understanding of the interface issues is needed are product innovation, designing for manufacturability, standardization of product/components, and product positioning. In particular, Japanese competition has made us aware of the importance of these issues, and leading-edge business schools have increasingly adopted such an integrated approach to business education. Our book strongly reflects this state-of-the-art orientation.

Proactive Orientation

Market orientation is a fundamental philosophy of marketing. It is an organizational culture that puts customers' interest first in developing a long-term profitable enterprise. In essence, market orientation symbolizes that a market-driven firm is willing to constantly update its strategies using signals from the marketplace. Thus, marketing managers take market cues from the expressed needs and wants of customers. Consequently, the dominant orientation is that of a firm reacting to forces in the marketplace to differentiate itself from its competitors. This reactive "outside-in" perspective is reflected in the typical marketing manager's reliance on marketing intelligence, forecasting, and market research.

While recognizing this traditional market orientation, we also believe that marketing managers should adopt an "inside-out" perspective and capabilities to shape or drive markets. This aspect of the link between strategic planning and marketing implementation has not been sufficiently treated in existing textbooks. For example, recent trends in technology licensing indicate that it is increasingly used as a conscious, proactive component of a firm's global product strategy. We believe that it is important for marketers to influence actions of the firm that are some distance away from the customer in the value chain because such actions have considerable influence on the size of the market and customer choice in intermediate and end-product markets.

Cultural Sensitivity

A book could not be written devoid of its authors' background, expertise, and experiences. Our book represents an amalgam of our truly diverse backgrounds, expertise, and experiences across North and South America, Asia, and Western and Eastern Europe. Given our upbringing and work experience in Asia, Western Europe, and Latin America, as well as our educational background in the United States, we have been sensitive not only to cultural differences and diversities but also to similarities.

Realistically speaking, there are more similarities than differences across many countries. In a number of cases, most of us tend either to focus too much on cultural differences rather than on similarities or completely ignore them. If you look only at cultural differences, you will be led to believe that country markets are uniquely different, thus requiring marketing strategy adaptations. If, on the other hand, you do not care about, or care to know about, cultural differences, you may be extending a culture-blind, ethnocentric view of the world. Either way, you may not benefit from the economies of scale and scope accruing from exploiting cultural similarities—and differences.

Over the years, two fundamental counteracting forces have shaped the nature of marketing in the international arena. The same counteracting forces have been revisited at different times by many authors in such terms as *standardization versus adaptation* (1960s), *globalization versus localization* (1970s), *global integration versus local responsiveness* (1980s), *scale versus sensitivity* (1990s), and more recently—let us add our own—*online scale versus offline market sensitivity*. Terms have changed, but the quintessence of the strategic dilemma that multinational companies (MNCs) face today has not changed and will probably remain unchanged for years to come. However, the two fundamental issues are no longer an either/or issue. Forward-looking, proactive firms have the ability and willingness to accomplish both tasks simultaneously. As we explain in the text, for example, Honda, developed its Accord model to satisfy universal customer needs for reliability, drivability, and comfort but marketed it as a family sedan in Japan, as a commuter car in the United States, and as an inexpensive sports car in Germany. By doing so, it addressed cultural differences in the way people of different nationalities perceive and drive what is essentially the same car.

With our emphasis on global and proactive orientations, however, we will share our ideas with you on how to hone your expertise to be both culturally sensitive and able to see how to benefit from cultural similarities and differences.

We strongly believe that theory is useful to the extent that it helps practices. There are many useful theories for international marketing practices. Some of the practical theories are a logical extension of generic marketing theories you may have encountered in a marketing course. Others are, however, unique to the international environment.

Many people believe—rather erroneously—that international or global marketing is just a logical extension of domestic marketing and that if you have taken a generic marketing course, you would not need to learn anything international. The international arena is like a Pandora's box. Once you move into it you need to learn many more facts, concepts, and frameworks than you ever thought of to become a seasoned marketing manager working globally. To assist you in acquiring this new knowledge, various theories provide the conceptual tools that enable you to abstract, analyze, understand, predict phenomena, and formulate effective decisions. Theories also provide an effective means to convey your logic to your peers and bosses with strong, convincing, power.

We apply those theories in our own extensive international work, advising corporate executives in the design of effective global strategies and teaching our students at various business schools around the world. Our role as educators is to convey sometimes complex theories in everyday languages, and our textbook reflects this. This leads to our next orientation.

Research Orientation

This book is designed not only to be user friendly but also to emphasize practice. We believe in experiential learning and practical applications. Rote learning of facts, concepts, and theories is not sufficient. A good marketing manager should be able to put these to practice. We use many examples and anecdotes as well as our own observations and experiences to vividly portray practical applications. This book also contains real-life, lively cases so that you can further apply your newly acquired knowledge to practice and experience for yourself what it takes to be an effective international marketing manager.

Therefore, this book has been written for both upper-level undergraduate and MBA students who wish to learn practical applications of marketing and related logic and subsequently work internationally. Although we overview foundation materials in this book, we expect that students have completed a basic marketing course.

Practical Orientation

As stated earlier, we extensively address the implications of the Internet and e-commerce in global marketing activities. E-commerce is very promising, but various environmental differences—particularly cultural, legal, and consumer needs differences—are bound to prevent it from becoming an instantaneous free-wheeling tool for global marketing. What you need to learn is how to manage *online scale and scope economies* and *offline sensitivities to different market requirements*. We try our best to help you become Internet-savvy. All chapters discuss these elements when relevant. In particular, Chapter 19 provides an in-depth analysis of global marketing issues in the age of the Internet. We admit that the impact of the Internet on global marketing activities has many more unknowns than knowns. That is why we point out areas in which the Internet is likely to affect the way we do business and have you think seriously about the imminent managerial issues that you will have to deal with upon graduation. Chapter 19 serves not as an epilogue to the fourth edition but as a prologue to your exciting career ahead of you.

In addition to being user friendly, the book also emphasizes practice. We believe in instructor support materials. To accomplish our stated goals and orientations, we

Internet Implications

have made a major effort to provide practical theories and their explanations using examples, anecdotes, and cases to maximize the student's learning experience.

Some of the specific features follow:

- **The Global Perspectives** which are in every chapter, bring concrete examples from the global marketing environment into the classroom. They highlight some of the hottest global topics that students should be aware of and may actually act on in their career. The instructor can use these inserts to exemplify theory or use them as minicases for class discussion.

- **Long cases** are designed to challenge students with real and current business problems and issues. They require in-depth analysis and discussion of various topics covered in the chapters and help students experience how the knowledge they have gained can be applied in real-life situations. A total of 35 cases cover various aspects of marketing situations as well as products, regions, and nationalities of firms. Six of them are included in the text and the rest are placed on the textbook Web site for easy download.

- **Short cases** at the end of each chapter are designed to address various specific issues explained in the chapters. These cases are useful in showing students how relevant the newly learned subject matter is and for open class discussion with the students.

- **Maps** provide economic geography of the world. Students should know about where various economic resources are available and how they shape the nature of trade and investment and thus the nature of global competition. Global marketing cannot be appreciated without an understanding of economic geography.

- **Review Questions** help students test themselves on the facts, concepts, theories, and other chapter materials in their own words. We strongly believe that by doing so, students will gain active working knowledge rather than passive knowledge by rote learning.

- **Discussion Questions** are designed to serve as minicases to which students apply the specific knowledge they learned in each chapter to actual business situations. Most of the issues presented in these questions are problems facing multinational marketing managers and have been adopted from recent issues of leading business newspapers and magazines.

Instructor Resources

- **The Instructor's Manual** provides major assistance while allowing flexibility in course scheduling and teaching emphasis. The materials in the manual include the following:

  - **Teaching Plans:** Alternative teaching plans and syllabi are included to accommodate the instructor's preferred course structure and teaching schedules. Alternative teaching schedules are developed for the course to be taught in a semester format, on a quarter basis or as an executive seminar.
  - **Discussion Guidelines:** Specific teaching objectives and guidelines for each chapter are developed to help stimulate classroom discussion.
  - **Exercises Using Various Web Sites:** The explosion of information available on the Internet has changed the milieu for intelligence gathering for business decision making. Students need to be well versed in this new information technology. We strongly believe that actual hands-on use of materials on the Internet to solve business problems will provide students a systematic opportunity to learn how to find and how to use available information for competitive advantage.

- **Test Bank:** A test bank consists of short essay questions and multiple choice questions. This test bank is also computerized and available to adopters on IBM-compatible computer diskettes.
- **PowerPoint Slides:** Available on the Web to assist the instructor in preparing presentation materials.
- **Video Materials:** Videos allow students to visualize critical issues discussed in the text.

- **Home Page on the Web:** Make sure to visit our Web site http://www.wiley.com/ college/kotabe/for useful instructional information.

- **Global Marketing Management System Online, 2.0 (GMMSO2),** developed by Dr. Basil J. Janavaras, professor of International Business at Minnesota State University, is a Web-based global marketing management research and planning program. As a bonus, each student who purchases the fourth edition of *Global Marketing Management* will receive a complimentary registration code that will provide access to the software. This practical, realistic program guides students through the systematic and integrative process of gathering, evaluating, and using certain types of information to help them to determine which markets to enter with a particular product or service and to create a marketing plan for the country with the optimal market environment for penetration. It is both interactive and experiential. More specifically, the program enables students to do the following:

  - Perform a situation analysis of a company in a global context.
  - Research global markets.
  - Identify high potential country markets for selected products or services.
  - Conduct in-depth market and competitive analysis.
  - Determine the best entry mode strategies.
  - Develop international marketing plans and strategies.

This system addition requires virtually no preparation time of the instructor beyond becoming familiar with the Web-based navigation. A Student Guide, Glossary, and targeted Web-based resources are provided in sample student projects as models to guide first-time users through the GMMSO process.

An Instructor's Manual is also available to those who use the GMMSO. It includes the following:

- Frequently asked questions/answers/suggestions.
- Schedules for quarters and semester modules.
- Table that correlates the software content with the content in the text.
- Outlines for the presentation and the final paper.
- PowerPoint presentation of the entire GMMSO for instructional purposes.

Because this is a Web-based product, it involves no administrative work for the instructor. Additional benefits for Instructors:

- Monitor student progress and review completed projects online.
- Integrate knowledge from this and other courses.
- Bridge the gap between theory and the real world of business.
- Obtain technical support.

In addition, it can be used from anywhere in the world.

If you are interested in using the GMMSO class project, register online at www.gmmso2.com or contact your local Wiley representative for details at: www.wiley .com/college/rep

Finally, we are delighted to share our teaching experience with you through this book. Our teaching experience is an amalgam of our own learning and knowledge gained through our continued discussion with our colleagues, our students, and our executive friends. We would also like to learn from you, the instructors and the students, who use our book. We are certain that you can learn from our book, and we believe that there are many more things that we can learn from you. We sincerely welcome your comments and questions.

ACKNOWLEDGMENTS

This book would not have materialized without the guidance, assistance, and encouragement of many of our mentors, colleagues, students, and executives with whom we have worked and from whom we have learned from over the years. We are truly indebted to each one of them. We also thank the many reviewers for their constructive comments and suggestions, which helped us improve our argument and clarity and increase the quality of our book. For this fourth edition, we'd like to thank:

Susan Douglas
New York University

H. Rika Houston
California State University, Los Angeles

Miguel Morales
Saint Mary's University

Alphonso Ogbuehi
Bryant University

Scott Roberts
Roger Williams University

Jan-Benedict E.M. SteenKamp
Tilburg University

Masaaki Kotabe extends his thanks to his colleagues around the world. Dean Moshe Porat at Temple University's Fox School of Business and Management is acknowledged for emphasizing international business education and research as the school's primary focus of excellence, providing enormous opportunities to meet leading practioners and executives of international business and discuss with them those emerging issues that are shaping and reshaping the way business is conducted around the world. Dr. Kotabe also credits Crytal Jiang and Sonia Ketkar for providing so many fascinating business examples and cases from around the world throughout the revision process.

Various colleagues outside Temple University have helped in the writing process. Tim Wilkinson (Montana State University) offered an interesting insight into the workings of the European Union and its marketing peculiarities. Amal Karunaratha (University of Adelaide, Australia) assisted in providing interesting examples from Down Under. Taro Yaguchi (Omori & Yaguchi Law Firm, Philadelphia) offered an interesting insight into the workings of the European Union and its marketing peculiarities. Amal Karunaratna (University of Adelaide, Australia) assisted in providing interesting examples from the Down Under. Taro Yaguchi (Omori & Yaguchi Law Firm, Philadelphia) offered an update on ever-changing laws and treaties that affect firms marketing internationally. Sae-Woon Park (Changwon National University, Korea), who has many years of export management and export financing practices, assisted in documenting the most up-to-date and state-of-the-art export practices in use today.

Kristiaan Helsen would like to extend his thanks to MBA students at the University of Chicago, Nijenrode University, Hong Kong University of Science and Technology, and MIM students at Thammassat University (Bangkok), Particularly Joe Giblin and Vincent Chan (Baxter) for assisting with two of the case studies, Wiebeke Vuursteen (now with Nestlé), and Edmund Wong and Philip Cheung (now with IBM) for their help with some of the exhibits. He also acknowledges the valuable comments in Chapter 14 from Chris Beaumont and John Mackay, both with McCann-Erickson, Japan. Thanks are also due to the Executive MBA students at Purdue University's AT&T/Lucent Technology program. A word of gratitude for their feedback and encouragement is given to two colleagues who spent their sabbatical at HKUST Jerry Albaum (University of Oregon) and Al Shocker (University of Minnesota).

We would also like to thank some of the day-to-day "warriors" in the global marketing arena for sharing their insights and experiences with us, in particular: Doug Barrie (Wrigley Company), Mark Boersma (Blistex), Keith Aim (formerly Sara Lee), F. J. Thompson (Heineken), Monika Sturm (Siemens Hong Kong), Bill Hicks and Jim Austin (Baxter Healthcare), and Olivia Kan (formerly PepsiCo China).

The textbook becomes ever more useful when accompanied by good resources for instructors and students. Preparing a good resource guide is no small task. Syed Anwar (West Texas A&M University) deserves special credit not only for preparing the excellent Resource Guide and Test Bank to go with the book but also for providing useful examples and insights throughout the revision process. We'd also like to thank Lawrence K. Duke of Drexel University for his work on the PowerPoint presentations.

A very special word of appreciation goes to the staff of John Wiley & Sons, Inc., particularly Jayme Heffler and Jennifer Conklin for their continued enthusiasm and support throughout the course of this project.

Finally and most importantly, we are deeply grateful to you, the professors, students, and professionals, for using this book. We stand by our book and sincerely hope that it adds to your knowledge and expertise. Thank you!

BRIEF CONTENTS

CONTENTS

DUBLIN BUSINESS SCHOOL LIBRARY

GLOBALIZATION IMPERATIVE

 HAPTER OVERVIEW

1. WHY GLOBAL MARKETING IS IMPERATIVE

2. GLOBALIZATION OF MARKETS: CONVERGENCE AND DIVERGENCE

3. EVOLUTION OF GLOBAL MARKETING

4. APPENDIX: THEORIES OF INTERNATIONAL TRADE AND THE MULTINATIONAL ENTERPRISE

Marketing products and services around the world, transcending national and political boundaries, is a fascinating phenomenon. The phenomenon, however, is not entirely new. Products have been traded across borders throughout recorded civilization, extending back beyond the Silk Road that once connected East with West from Xian to Rome on land and the recently excavated sea trade route between the Roman Empire and India that existed 2,000 years ago.[1] However, since the end of World War II, the world has experienced a spectacular economic growth never seen before in human history, led by large U.S. companies in the 1950s and 1960s, then by European and Japanese companies in the 1970s and 1980s, and most recently by the emergence of new emerging market superpowers, such as China and India since the 1990s. In particular, competition coming recently from emerging markets in Asia and Latin America has given the notion of global competition a touch of extra urgency and significance that you see almost daily in print media such as *Wall Street Journal, Financial Times, Nikkei Shimbun,* and *Folha de São Paulo,* as well as TV media such as the BBC, NBC, and CNN. With a few exceptions, such as Korea's Samsung Electronics (consumer electronics) and China's Haier (home appliances), these emerging-market multinational companies are not yet household names in the industrialized world, but from India's Infosys Technologies (IT services) to Brazil's Embraer (light jet aircrafts) and from Taiwan's Acer (computers) to Mexico's Cemex (building materials), a new class of formidable competitors is rising.[2]

---

[1] "Archaeologists Find Silk Road Equal: Dig Shows Extensive Roman Sea Trade with India," CNN.com, June 12, 2002.

[2] "A New Threat to America Inc," *Business Week,* July 25, 2005, p. 114; also read Martin Roll, *Asian Brand Strategy: How Asia Builds Strong Brands* (New York: Palgrave Macmillan, 2006).

In this chapter, we will introduce you to the complex and constantly evolving realities of global marketing. The objective is to make you think beyond exporting and importing. As you will learn shortly, despite wide media attention to them, exporting and importing represent a relatively small portion of what constitutes international business. We are not saying, however, that exporting and importing are not important. Global trade and output growth in 2004 were the strongest since 2000. Total trade value, including merchandise trade and commercial services trade, reached almost $11 trillion in 2004, compared to $7.6 trillion in 2000.[3] The Asian financial crisis in 1997, followed by a recession in the United States exacerbated by the September 11 terrorist attacks on the United States in 2001 and Argentina's financial crisis that was worsened in 2002, sent the world economy into a global slowdown. Particularly, the effect of the recession in the United States was felt literally throughout the world. As a result, world merchandise exports in 2001 dipped 1 percent in volume and contracted 4 percent in value to $6 trillion compared with that of 2000. Commercial services exports also slipped slightly by 1.5 percent to $1.4 trillion. For example, although the neighboring Canadian economy escaped recession in 2001, its GDP growth was down to a mere 1.5 percent in 2001, compared with 4.5 percent in 2000 and 5.4 percent in 1999. This slowdown mostly reflects the bursting of the investment bubble in high-tech and information technology industries on both sides of the U.S.–Canada border and the sharp contraction in U.S. demand for Canadian goods and services. Similarly, even geographically distant countries, such as Australia, equally felt the meltdown in those U.S. industries.[4] The improved market conditions in the United States and Europe as well as a strong recovery in Asia have slowly but steadily improved the world economy since 2002. At the time of this writing, however, the aftermath of the U.S.-led war against Iraq, high oil prices, and deadly bird flu scare around the world, among other things, continue to curb the world economy from a full-fledged recovery. Although sometimes bumpy, the drive for globalization continues to be promoted through more free trade; more Internet commerce; more networking of businesses, schools, and communities; and more advanced technologies.[5]

◆ ◆ ◆ ◆ ◆ ◆ ◆ ◆ ◆ WHY GLOBAL MARKETING IS IMPERATIVE

We frequently hear terms such as *global markets, global competition, global technology,* and *global competitiveness.* In the past, we heard similar words with *international* or *multinational* instead of *global* attached to them. What has happened since the 1980s? Are these terms just fashionable concepts of the time without some deep meanings? Or has something inherently changed in our society?

Saturation of Domestic Markets. First and at the most fundamental level, the saturation of domestic markets in the industrialized parts of the world forced many companies to look for marketing opportunities beyond their national boundaries. The economic and population growths in developing countries also gave those companies an additional incentive to venture abroad. Now companies from emerging economies, such as Korea's Samsung and Hyundai and Mexico's Cemex and Grupo Modelo, have made inroads into the developed markets around the world. The same logic applies

---

[3]*World Trade Report 2005: Exploring the Link between Trade, Standards, and the WTO* (Geneva: World Trade Organization, 2005).

[4]"The Economy" *Australia Country Profile,* Business Source Premier, 2002, pp. 15–23; and "The Economy" *Canada Country Profile,* Business Source Premier, 2002, pp. 26–35.

[5]The reader needs to be cautioned that there may be limits to the benefit of globalization for two primary reasons. First, firms in poor countries with very weak economic and financial infrastructure may not be able to (afford to) adjust fast enough to the forces of globalization. Second, poor countries could be made worse off by trade liberalization because trade tends to be opened for high-tech goods and services exported by rich countries—such as computers and financial services—but remains protected in areas where those poor countries could compete, such as agricultural goods, textiles, or construction. See, for example, "Globalization Gets Mixed Grades in U.S. Universities," *Wall Street Journal,* December 2, 2002, pp. A1 and A14.

equally to companies from developed countries, such as Australia and New Zealand, geographically isolated from the other major industrialized parts of the world. For example, unbeknownst to most Americans, Dôme Coffees Australia is building a multinational coffee shop empire by expanding into Asia and the Middle East. Sooner or later, the day will come when Starbucks from the United States and Dôme Coffees from Australia may be competing head-on for global dominance.[6]

Global Competition. Second, we believe something profound has indeed happened in our view of competition around the world. About 30 years ago, the world's greatest automobile manufacturers were General Motors, Ford, and Chrysler. Today, companies such as Toyota, Honda, BMW, Renault, and Huyndai, among others, stand out as competitive nameplates in the global automobile market. Now with a 15 percent market share in the United States, Toyota's market share is larger than Ford's 14 percent. At the time of this writing, Toyota is expected to boost its global automobile production to more than 9.2 million units in 2006, making it almost certain that the Japanese auto giant will surpass General Motors to become the world's largest automaker in terms of worldwide output.[7] Similarly, the term *personal computer* was almost synonymous with IBM, which dominated the PC business around the world. Today, the computer market is crowded with Dell and Hewlett-Packard (HP) from the United States, Sony and Toshiba from Japan, Samsung from Korea, Acer from Taiwan,[8] and so on. Indeed, Lenovo, a personal computer company from China, acquired the IBM PC division in 2005 and now sells Thinkpad series under the Lenovo brand. The deal not only puts Lenovo into the industry's third place but also challenges the world's top players, Dell and HP/Compaq, respectively.[9] Nike is a U.S. company with a truly all-American shoe brand, but its shoes are all made in foreign countries and exported to many countries. Pillsbury (known for its Betty Crocker's recipes and Häagen-Dazs ice cream brand) and 7-Eleven convenience stores are two American institutions owned and managed, respectively, by Diageo from the United Kingdom and Ito-Yokado from Japan. On the other hand, the world of media, led by U.S. media giants, has become equally global in reach. MTV has 35 channels worldwide targeting teenagers around the world, with 15 of them in Europe, and large parts of its local channel contents are made in each local area. CNN has 22 different versions. In 1996, 70 percent of the English-language version of CNN International was American; today that share has shrunk to about 8 percent.[10] The video game industry has been truly global from day one; Sony's Playstation 2, Microsoft's Xbox, and Nintendo's GameCube now vie for customers in the Triad regions (i.e., North America, Western Europe, and Japan) simultaneously.[11]

Need for Global Cooperation. Third, global competition also brings about global cooperation. This is most obvious in the information technology industry. Japan's Toshiba and Sony and U.S. computer maker IBM agreed to jointly develop advanced semiconductor processing technologies for the next generation of chips. As part of the project, IBM will transfer its latest technologies to Sony and Toshiba, and the partner companies will each send engineers to IBM's research center in New York to work on the joint project.[12] Toshiba and South Korea's Samsung also agreed to work together to produce dynamic random access memory (DRAM) chips for business-use

---

[6]"Bean Countess," *Australian Magazine,* December 9–10, 2000, p. 50+.

[7]"Toyota on Track to Unseat GM as World's Top Auto Maker," *NikkeiNet Interactive,* http://www.nni.nikkei.co.jp/, October 26, 2005.

[8]"Why Taiwan Matters: The Global Economy Couldn't Function without It, but Can It Really Find Peace with China?" *Business Week,* May 16, 2005, pp. 74–81.

[9]"Can China's Lenovo Brand in the Land of Dell?" *B to B,* October 10, 2005, pp. 1 and 45.

[10]"Think Global," *Economist,* April 11, 2002.

[11]"The Next Wave of Videogames," *Wall Street Journal,* May 12, 2005, pp. D1 and D4.

[12]Toshiba, Sony, IBM to Develop New Chip-Making Technologies," *Nikkei Interactive Net,* www.nni.nikkei.co.jp, April 2, 2002.

and high-speed network applications.[13] Beginning in 1982, Japan's Fujitsu and IBM battled each other for 15 years in such areas as software copyright. In October 2001, however, they began discussing a comprehensive tie-up involving the joint development of software and the mutual use of computer technology. IBM was considering sharing its PC server technology with Fujitsu, and the Japanese company was thinking about supplying routers to IBM.[14] Cooperation also happens in the auto industry. French carmaker Renault SA took a 36.8 percent stake in Japanese carmaker Nissan Motor Corp. in 1999. The two companies began producing cars on joint platforms in 2005. To help pave the way for that, the two car makers decided in March 2001 that they would combine their procurement operations in a joint-venture company that would eventually handle 70 percent of the companies' global purchasing. The joint venture will be headquartered in Paris, with offices in Japan and the United States.[15]

Internet Revolution. Fourth, another profound change in the last decade is the proliferation of the Internet and electronic commerce (**e-commerce**). According to an International Data Corporation report, the total global e-commerce volume increased more than sevenfold from $358 billion in 2000 to $2.58 trillion in 2004. The U.S. share of e-commerce grew from $162 billion (45 percent of world total) to $991 billion (38 percent of world total).[16] These data clearly indicate that e-commerce has spread significantly more outside the United States, indicating a further globalization of e-commerce. In the same time period, the number of Internet users rose from 367 million in 2000 to 817 million in 2004.[17] Developing countries' share in the Internet population of the world grew by nearly 50 percent between 2000 and 2003. However, Internet users in the developing world are concentrated in a relatively small number of countries. China, Korea, India, Brazil, and Mexico alone account for more than 60 percent of them.[18] E-commerce sales totaled $150 billion in 2004—a 56 percent increase over $96 billion of sales a year earlier.[19] These statistics clearly demonstrate the rapid growth of Internet use and e-commerce around the world.

Compared to business-to-consumer (B2C) e-commerce, business-to-business (B2B) e-commerce is larger, growing faster, and has less unequal geographical distribution globally.[20] Increases in the freedom of the movements of goods, services, capital, technology, and people coupled with rapid technological development resulted in an explosion of global B2B e-commerce. The share of the global B2B e-commerce that a country is likely to receive, on the other hand, depends on country-level factors such as income and population size; the availability of credit, venture capital, and telecom and logistical infrastructure; tax and other incentives; tariff/nontariff barriers; government emphasis on the development of human capital; regulations to influence firms' investment in R&D; organizational level politics; language; and the activities of international agencies.[21]

Who could have anticipated today's e-commerce companies including Amazon, eBay, and Yahoo in the United States; QXL ricardo and Kelkoo in Europe; and

---

[13]"Toshiba, Samsung Unite DRAMs," *Japan Times Online,* www.japantimes.co.jp, May 9, 2002.

[14]"Fujitsu, IBM Negotiate Comprehensive Tie-up," *Nikkei Interactive Net,* http://www.nni.nikkei.co.jp, October 18, 2001.

[15]A WSJ.com News Roundup, "Renault and Nissan Will Combine Buying Operations in Joint Venture, http://www.WSJ.com, March 13, 2001.

[16]IDC, Internet Commerce Market Model, Version 8.3, International Data Corporation, www.idc.com, 2004.

[17]Datamonitor, "Global Internet Software & Services: Industry Profile," http://www.datamonitor.com, May 2005.

[18]*E-Commerce and Development Report 2004* (Geneva: United Nations Trade and Development, 2004).

[19]VISA News Releases, "Visa International Projects US$150 Billion in 2004 Global E-commerce Sales," http://www.corporate.visa.com/, accessed March 15, 2006.

[20]B2B and B2C, among others, have become trendy business terms in recent years. However, they are fundamentally the same as the more conventional terms *consumer marketing* and *industrial marketing,* respectively, except that B2B and B2C imply the use of the Internet, Intranet, customer relationship management software, and other information technology expertise. In this book, we will not use use these trendy terms unless they are absolutely necessary in making our point.

[21]Nikhilesh Dholakia, "Determinants of the Global Diffusion of B2B E-commerce," *Electronic Markets,* 12 (March 2002), pp. 120–29.

Rakuten and 7dream in Japan? The Internet opened the gates for companies to sell directly to consumers easily across national boundaries. Many argue that e-commerce is less intimate than face-to-face retail, but it could actually provide more targeted demographic and psychographic information. Today the Internet has profoundly changed consumer behavior. For example, eBay seized an astonishing $24 billion worth of trade in 2003. InterActiveCorp (IAC), the owner of expedia.com and hotels.com, achieved $10 billion worth of travel revenue in 2003.[22]

Manufacturers that traditionally sell through the retail channel may benefit the most from e-commerce. Most important, the data allow for the development of relevant marketing messages aimed at important customers and initiate loyal relationships on a global basis.[23] With the onset of satellite communications, consumers in developing countries are as familiar with global brands as consumers in developed countries, and as a result, there is tremendous pent-up demand for products marketed by multinational companies (which we also refer to as *MNCs*).[24]

What's more, the Internet builds a platform for a two-way dialogue between manufacturers and consumers, allowing consumers to design and order their own products from the manufacturers. The customized build-to-order business model is already an established trend. Dell Computer is a pioneer that does business globally by bypassing traditional retail channels. It accepts orders by phone, fax, or on the Internet.[25] General Motors started providing a build-to-order Web service for its Brazilian customers in 2000. Mazda's Web Tune Factory site, being one of the first Japanese auto build-to-order models, allows consumers to choose their own engine specifications, transmission type, body color, wheel design, and other interior and exterior equipment.[26] However, as presented in Global Perspective 1-1, we would also like to stress as a caveat that the proliferation of e-commerce and satellite communications does not necessarily mean that global marketing activities are going culture and human contact free. Learning foreign languages probably remains as important as ever.

An examination of the *Fortune Global 100* largest companies in the world also vividly illustrates the profound changes in the competitive milieu and provides a faithful mirror image of broad economic trends that we have seen over the past 30 some years (see Exhibit 1-1). Particularly, the last decade was characterized by the long-term recession in Japan and a resurgence of the U.S. economy that had been battered by foreign competition in the 1980s. Consider Japan, which has suffered several recessions since 1995 and many political changes, as an example. The number of Japanese companies on the list of the largest 100 companies fell from 23 in 2000 to 13 in 2005. The number of U.S. and European firms has stayed relatively stable since 1990. Although the United States boasts the largest number of firms in the top 100 list, the list of countries with large firms is becoming more decentralized. One of the biggest changes since 1990 has been the emergence of China.[27] As economic reform progressed and Chinese companies improved their accounting standards, their presence grew steadily. Four Chinese companies are on the 2005 *Fortune Global 100* list. The current world economy has changed drastically from what it was merely a decade ago.

The changes observed in the past 30 years simply reflect that companies from other parts of the world have grown in size relative to those of the United States despite

---

[22]"A Perfect Market," *Economist,* May 13, 2004, p. 3.

[23]Andrew Degenholtz, "E-Commerce Fueling the Flame for New Product Development," *Marketing News,* March 29, 1999, p. 18.

[24]D. J. Arnold and J. Quelch, "New Strategies in Emerging Markets," *Sloan Management Review,* 40(1), 1998, pp. 7–20.

[25]However, Dell's direct sales on the Internet fails to work in some emerging markets, particularly where customers want to see products before they buy. Such is the case in small cities in China. See "Dell May Have to Reboot in China," *Business Week,* November 7, 2005, p. 46.

[26]Setsuko Kamiya, "Mazda Lets Buyers Fine-Tune Roadster," *The Japan Times Online,* http://www.hapantimes.co.jp, January 5, 2002.

[27]See "The China Price," *Business Week,* December 6, 2004, pp. 102–20; and "How China Runs the World Economy," *Economist,* July 30, 2005, p. 11.

◆ ◆

𝒢LOBAL PERSPECTIVE 1-1

THE INTERNET WORLD AND CULTURAL AND HUMAN ASPECTS OF GLOBAL MARKETING

Cultural differences greatly affect business relationships in the world of e-commerce, but they are often underestimated, especially in international team-building efforts. The problem is not only language issues. Foreign companies need acceptance by the local market and understanding of the local business culture. The Internet's awesome communications power can be turned into a conduit for miscommunication if such cultural factors are ignored. Knowing what level of communication is appropriate for a certain level of trust is particularly important in a Web-based environment where face-to-face contact may be more limited.

Think, for example, of a typical mid-size manufacturer in, say, Taiwan, China, or Thailand. Would it enter into a strategic business relationship with companies and people that it encounters only through computerized interactions? The short answer is yes; it will enter into such relationships. However, we qualify our positive reply by adding that the initial courtship ritual must continue to have personal face-to-face, one-to-one, or what we feel is becoming a new "screen-to-screen" relationship dimension as with the traditional business model.

However, after the initial mating ritual, you can and already do see tremendous transactional business-to-business activity in these countries. There is nothing to say that e-commerce can or should replace the human element to relationship building. In fact, e-commerce is a new form of personalized relationship building in which even the highest context cultures engage. eBay and the other online auction companies are perfect examples of such new electronic relationship and trust

building. Even in Eastern cultures, we see numerous gambling sites springing up where the only aspects of the relationship are anonymous e-commerce related.

The critical factor will be the Web site evolving into the first step in developing the personal international business relationship. Unless the Web site makes the first connection based on sensitivity to the cross-cultural aspects of interface design; human factors; navigation currency, time, and date conventions; localization; internationalization; and so on, the ability to "connect" will be stilted.

In the information technology sector, one can look at Dell and Gateway, both of which do very strong business in the Asia/Pacific region. The networking company Cisco Systems serves as an example of the morphing of electronic and personal relationships. While they have done a tremendous job of building global relationships and partnerships on an in-country face-to-face level, almost 90 percent of their business (i.e., sales transactions) is conducted over the Web.

Has the Web replaced the need for the personal business courtship? Absolutely not. Has it added a new element to the same relationship after the bonds are formed? Most definitely. Will there be new electronic forms of relationship building that replace the old face-to-face model in a karaoke bar ...? Yes, it is happening already, starting with video/teleconferences in the boardroom and expanding downward to Microsoft NetMeeting using a minicam on the desktop.

Just think that one decade or so ago very few of us would hardly dream that most Web-enabled adolescents communicate more on AOL Instant Messenger than they do over the phone or in person. In 10 years, technology will give us HDTV screen quality with real time audio and video bandwidth. This surely will not completely replace face-to-face interaction among global sellers and buyers. But it will certainly offer a viable substitute for those who grew up chatting online.

Sources: Frank Cutitta, GINLIST@LIST.MSU.EDU, April 17, 1999; Ken Cottrill, "The World According to Hollywood," *Traffic World,* November 6, 2002; and Nitish Singh, Vikas Kumar, and Daniel Baack, "Adaptation of Cultural Content: Evidence from B2C E-Commerce Firms," *European Journal of Marketing,* 39 (1/2, 2005), pp. 71–86.

---

the resurgence of the U.S. economy in the 1990s. In other words, today's environment is characterized not only by much more competition from around the world but also by more fluid domestic and international market conditions than in the past. As a result, many U.S. executives are feeling much more competitive urgency in product development, materials procurement, manufacturing, and marketing around the world. It does not necessarily mean that U.S. companies have lost their competitiveness, however. The robust economy in the United States in the late 1990s met a slowdown in 2000 due to the crash of the dot.com's bubble economy and was worsened by the terrorist attacks on September 11, 2001. The strong consumer demand has saved its economy, however. On the other hand, many Asian countries have recovered from the 1997 Asian financial crisis. (See Chapter 3 for detail).

The same competitive pressure equally applies to executives of foreign companies. For example, while its Japanese home market was the incredible shrinking market in the 1990s, Toyota's new strategy has been to de-Japanize its business and make the U.S. market its corporate priority. By 2001, Toyota had already accomplished its goal

EXHIBIT 1-1

CHANGE IN THE WORLD'S 100 LARGEST COMPANIES
AND THEIR NATIONALITIES

Country	1970	1980	1990	2000*	2005*
United States**	64	45	33	36	35
Japan	8	8	16	23	13
Germany**	8	13	12	10	14
France	3	12	10	7	9
Switzerland	2	3	3	4	3
Netherlands**	4	5	3	6	4
Britain**	9	7	8	6	10
Italy**	3	4	4	3	4
Belgium	0	1	1	1	1
Venezuela	0	1	1	1	0
China	0	0	0	3	4
South Korea	0	0	2	0	2
Spain	0	0	2	1	1
Sweden	0	0	2	0	0
Brazil	0	1	1	0	0
Mexico	0	1	1	1	1
Austria	0	0	1	0	0
Finland	0	0	1	0	0
South Africa	0	0	1	0	0
Canada	0	2	0	0	1
Australia	1	0	0	0	0
Total	102	103	102	103	102

Source: Fortune, various issues up to 2005.

Fortune Global 500 criteria changed to include services firms (including retailing and trading)

**Includes joint nationality of firms (joint nationality has been counted for both the countries), so the total may exceed 100.

by selling more vehicles in the United States (1.74 million) than in Japan (1.71 million), with almost two-thirds of the company's operating profit coming from the U.S. market. Now Toyota's top U.S. executives are increasingly local hires. As Mark Twain once said, "if you stand still, you will get run over." This analogy holds true in describing such competitive pressure in this era of global competition.

It is not only this competitive force that is shaping global business today. Particularly in the past several years, many political and economic events have affected the nature of global competition. The demise of the Soviet Union, the establishment of the European Union and the North American Free Trade Agreement, deregulation, and privatization of state-owned industries have also changed the market environments around the world. Furthermore, the emerging markets of Eastern Europe and the rapidly reemerging markets of Southeast Asia also add promises to international businesses.

The fluid nature of global markets and competition makes the study of global marketing not only interesting but also challenging and rewarding. The term *global* epitomizes both the competitive pressure and the expanding market opportunities all over the world. It does not mean, however, that all companies have to operate globally like IBM, Sony, Philips, or Samsung. Whether a company operates domestically or across national boundaries, it can no longer avoid competitive pressure from around the world. Competitive pressure can also come from competitors at home. When Weyerhaeuser, a forest products company headquartered in Seattle, Washington, began exporting newspaper rolls to Japan, it had to meet the exacting quality standard that Japanese newspaper publishers demanded—and it did. As a result, this Seattle company now boasts the best newspaper rolls and outperforms other domestic companies in the U.S. market as well. Even smaller firms could benefit from exacting foreign market requirements. When Weaver Popcorn Co. of Van Buren, Indiana, started to export popcorn to Japan, Japanese distributors demanded better quality and fewer imperfections. This led to improvements in Weaver's processing equipment and product, which helped its domestic as well as international sales.[28] Furthermore, e-commerce comes in handy to those smaller firms with international marketing ambitions. For example, LaPebbles.com, a small hand-crafted jewelry maker based in the northeastern part of the United States, can tap into potentially large global markets. So can small firms based in foreign countries looking to the U.S. market. Therefore, even purely domestic companies that have never sold anything abroad cannot be shielded from international competitive pressure. The point is that when we come across the term *global,* we should be made aware of both this intense competitive pressure and the expanding market opportunities on a global basis.

◆ ◆ ◆ ◆ ◆ ◆ ◆ ◆   ## GLOBALIZATION OF MARKETS: CONVERGENCE AND DIVERGENCE

When a country's per capita income is less than $10,000, much of it is spent on food and other necessities, and very little disposable income remains. However, once per capita income reaches $20,000 or so, the disposable portion of income increases dramatically because the part of the income spent on necessities does not rise nearly as fast as income increases. As a result, people around the world with per capita income of $20,000 and above have considerable purchasing power. With this level of purchasing power, people, regardless of their nationality, tend to enjoy similar educational levels, academic and cultural backgrounds, and access to information. As these cultural and social dimensions begin to resemble each other in many countries, people's desire for material positions, ways of spending leisure time, and aspirations for the future become increasingly similar. Even the deeply rooted cultures have begun to converge.[29] In other words, from a marketing point of view, those people have begun to share a similar "choice set" of goods and services originating from many parts of the world. What does this mean?

In one sense, we see young people jogging, wearing Nike shoes (an American product made in China), listening to System of a Down (an Armenian rock band) or Thalia Sodi (a Mexican pop singer) on Apple Computer's iPod (a U.S. product) in Hong Kong, Philadelphia, São Paulo, Sydney, and Tokyo. Similarly, yuppies (young urban professionals) in Amsterdam, Chicago, Osaka, and Dallas share a common lifestyle, driving a BMW (a German car assembled in Toluca, Mexico) to the office listening to Sumi Jo's and Sissel Kyrkjebø's new CD albums (purchased on their business trips to Korea and Norway, respectively), using a Dell notebook computer (a U.S. product made by Quanta, a Taiwanese company) at work, calling their colleagues with a Nokia cellular phone (a Finnish product), signing important documents with an exquisite Parker Pen (made by a French-based company owned by a U.S. company), and having a nice seafood buffet at Mövenpick (a Swiss restaurant chain) on a Friday. In the evenings, these people spend their spare time browsing around various Web sites using Google search engine (a U.S. Internet company) to do some "virtual" window-shopping on their PCs (powered by a microprocessor made in Malaysia by Intel, a U.S. company). The convergence of consumer needs in many parts of the world translates into tremendous business opportunities for companies willing to risk venturing abroad.

The *convergence* of consumer needs at the macro level may be true, but it does not necessarily mean that individual consumers will adopt all of the products from around the world. Globalization does not suffocate local cultures but liberates

---

[28]Doug LeDuc, "Overseas Markets Spur Growth for Van Buren, Ind.-Based Popcorn Maker," *The News-Sentinel,* April 19, 1999.

[29]For an excellent story about global cultural convergence, read "Global Culture" and "A World Together," *National Geographic,* 196 (August 1999), pp. 2–33.

them from the ideological conformity of nationalism.[30] As a result, we have become ever more selective. Therefore, you could find one of your friends at school in the United States driving a Toyota Tacoma (a compact Japanese truck made by General Motors and Toyota in Fremont, California), enjoying Whoppers at a Burger King fast-food restaurant (an ex-British but now U.S. company), and practicing capoeira (a 400-year-old Brazilian martial art) and another friend in Austria driving a Peugeot 107 (a French car made by Toyota in the Czech Republic; also marketed as the Citroën 1 as well as the Toyota Aygo), enjoying sushi at a sushi restaurant (a Japanese food), and practicing karate (an ancient Japanese martial art), as well as a cousin of yours driving a Ford Escape (a U.S. sports utility vehicle), munching on pizzas (a U.S. food of Italian origin), and practicing soccer (a sport of English origin, known as *football* outside the United States and some few other countries). In other words, thanks to market globalization, we have not only become more receptive to new things, but also we have a much wider, more divergent "choice set" of goods and services to choose from to shape our own individual preferences and lifestyles. This is true whether you live in a small town in the United States or a big city in Europe. In other words, the *divergence* of consumer needs is taking place at the same time. For example, Pollo Campero, a Latin American fried chicken chain from Guatemala that offers a crunchy bite of chicken with a Latin service in a Latin American environment, has been catching on quietly in the United States, the land of KFC, to cater to Americans' increased appetite for a different kind of chicken.[31] From a marketing point of view, it is becoming more difficult—not easier—to pinpoint consumers' preferences in any local market around the world, the more globalized the markets become.

As presented in Global Perspective 1-2, the European Union (EU) offers a vivid example of how market forces of convergence and divergence are at work. One thing is clear. There is no such a thing as a static market in an era of globalization.

◆ ◆

$\mathcal{G}$LOBAL PERSPECTIVE 1-2

MARKET CONVERGENCE AND DIVERGENCE AT WORK IN THE EUROPEAN UNION (EU)

Will Euroland survive? Rejection of the proposed EU Constitution by France and The Netherlands in 2005 caused anguish for political and EU economic elites. An "ever closer union" had been seen—until the no vote called it into question (see Chapter 2 for details)—as the European answer to globalization, political security, and economic growth. European leaders are not the only ones concerned. Insightful U.S. and Japanese business managers are also worried because, contrary to popular belief, the chief economic beneficiaries of European integration are U.S. and Japanese multinational corporations.

Historically, Europe, due to its national and cultural differences, had heterogenous and fragmented markets. These markets produced small to mid-size firms capable of adapting to, and prospering in, highly differentiated environments. Even the largest European companies tended to operate at the national, rather than pan-European, level, avoiding the many encumbrances of functioning across borders where market conditions were so dissimilar. For instance, for many years

Unilever sold a fabric softener in 10 countries under seven different brand names, using a variety of marketing strategies and bottle shapes.

Typical European firms pursued niche strategies, emphasizing craftsmanship, specialization, and networks of relationships. Europe, with its myriad laws, languages, and customs, historically constituted a market environment with significant entry and operating barriers. Foreign firms could not use economies of scale or scope inherent in large homogenous markets; they were unable to compete on the basis of low cost or low price. High labor costs, heavy taxation to support welfare states, and high expectations of European retailers and consumers all worked together to shape an environment that favored the creation of specialized, premium products rather than mass consumption products. This put U.S. multinationals in Europe at a competitive disadvantage.

The traditional European advantage was based on the notion that a less homogenous marketplace requires a more individualized marketing strategy. This approach is at odds

---

[30]Mario Vargas Llosa, "The Culture of Liberty," *Foreign Affairs,* 122 (January/February 2001), pp. 66–71.

[31]"From Guatemala with Love," *Chain Leader,* September/October 2005, pp. 28–32.

with the strategy of many U.S. firms: the ability to reduce costs through economies of scale and scope. Historically, market fragmentation shielded Europe from U.S. competition. Such fragmentation constituted location-specific advantages that were either costly to overcome or simply impenetrable for many smaller U.S. companies. However, the creation of the European Union changed the rules of the game.

One major purpose of the EU is to create extensive homogeneous markets in which large European firms are able to take advantage of economies of scale and therefore are better able to compete with their U.S. counterparts. EU reformers hope to create an economy analogous to that of the United States, in which low inflation coexists with high growth, thereby leading to low unemployment.

The formation of the EU has resulted in extremely large levels of U.S. and Japanese foreign direct investment (FDI) in Europe. Why? First, it was feared that the EU would become "Fortress Europe" through the implementation of significant protectionist measures against firms from outside it. Under these circumstances, FDI constitutes tariff jumping in anticipation of negative actions that may or may not occur in the future. Second, the elimination of internal borders creates a single market amenable to the large economies of scale and scope preferred by U.S. and Japanese multinationals.

Numbers tell the story. The average foreign direct investment inflows into the European Community (as the EU was known until November 1, 1993) amounted to $65,629 million from 1985–1995. The inflow in 1999 (the year the euro, a new currency adopted by 11 EU member countries, was launched) was $479,372 million—a 700 percent increase. By 2000 Japanese investment in the EU was roughly six times more than EU investment in Japan. In 1980, the total FDI stock of the European Community was $216,296 million, and

by 2003, it was $3,335,454 million. Finally, FDI stock as a percent of GDP was 8.5 percent in 1987 (the year that that plans for the Maastricht Treaty were presented). In 2002, the year in which euro notes and coins replaced local currencies, it was 34.6 percent.

Four decades ago, the French intellectual J.J. Servan-Schreiber complained bitterly about the U.S. presence in Europe in the best-selling book, *The American Challenge* (1967). The Europeans now face similar competitive dynamics. Ironically, in their quest for economic competitiveness, they may have made themselves more vulnerable to the ambitions of U.S. and Japanese multinationals.

What can European firms do to cope with the onslaught of U.S. and Japanese multinationals? Large European firms can counter U.S. competitors by exporting or investing directly in the United States and other markets. Red Bull, the Austrian company that created the energy drink category, expanded throughout Europe after the Maastricht Treaty came into force in 1993. In 1997 it was big enough to take on the U.S. market, and by 1999, its sales were $75 million. Mergers and acquisitions resulting from unification also enhance the ability of EU firms to enter the United States. For example, in June 2000, the French firm Publicis Group acquired Saatchi & Saatchi, the U.K.-based advertising firm, as a means of strengthening its position in the U.S. market.

Smaller European firms are likely to consider pursuing a universal niche market strategy. For instance, Iona Technologies PLC, an Irish software firm, has successfully internationalized by pursuing a global niche market strategy.

Finally, there remain EU customers who continue to prefer the more expensive, high-quality European products. Keeping this market segment from being eroded by U.S. and Japanese competitors is key in retaining the viability of the EU market. The irony is that, if the failure of the EU Constitution is just the first event in a cascade of reversals for the integrationists, the newly refragmented markets may once again play a major role in strengthening the competitive position of smaller European firms.

Source: Based on Lance Eliot Brouthers and Timothy J. Wilkinson, "Is the EU Destroying European Competitiveness?" *Business Horizons*, 45 (July-August 2002), pp. 37–42; updated by Professor Timothy J. Wilkinson in July 2005.

International Trade versus International Business

The United States, which enjoys one of the highest per capita income levels in the world, has long been the most important single market for both foreign and domestic companies. As a result of its insatiable demand for foreign products, the United States has been running a trade deficit since 1973—for more than three consecutive decades (more on this in 2). The popular press have often portrayed the trade deficits as a declining competitiveness of the United States. This assumes—rather erroneously—that U.S. companies engaged only in exports and imports and that international trade takes place between independent buyers and sellers across national boundaries. In order to appreciate the complexities of global competition, the nature of international trade and international business have to be clarified first, followed by a discussion of who manages international trade.

First of all, we have to understand the distinction between international trade and international business. Indeed, **international trade** consists of exports and imports, say, between the United States and the rest of the world. If U.S. imports exceed U.S. exports, then the nation registers a trade deficit. If the opposite were the case, the United States registers a trade surplus. On the other hand, **international business** is a broader concept and includes international trade and foreign production. U.S. companies typically market their products in three ways. First, they can export their products from the United States, which is recorded as a U.S. export. Second, they can invest in their foreign production on their own and manufacture those products abroad for sale there. This transaction does not show up as a U.S. export, however. Third, they can contract out manufacturing in whole or part to a company in a foreign country, either by way of licensing or joint venture agreement. Of course, not all companies engage in all three forms of international transaction. Nonetheless, foreign manufacture on their own or on a contractual basis is a viable alternative means to exporting products abroad. Although it is not widely known, foreign production constitutes a much larger portion of international business than international trade.

The extensive international penetration of U.S. and other companies has been referred to as *global reach.*[32] Since the mid-1960s, U.S.-owned subsidiaries located around the world have produced and sold three times the value of all U.S. exports. Although more recent statistics are not available, this 3:1 ratio of foreign manufacture to international trade remained largely unchanged in the 1980s and 1990s, and it becomes much more conspicuous if we look at U.S. business with the European Union, where U.S.-owned subsidiaries sold more than six times the total U.S. exports in 1990. Similarly, European-owned subsidiaries operating in the United States sold five times as much as U.S. imports from Europe.[33] This suggests that experienced companies tend to manufacture overseas much more than they export. On the other hand, Japanese companies did not expand their foreign manufacturing activities in earnest until about 20 years ago. According to one estimate, more than 90 percent of all cases of Japanese foreign direct investment have taken place since 1985.[34] Despite their relative inexperience in international expansion, Japanese subsidiaries registered two-and-a-half times as much foreign sales as all Japanese exports worldwide by 1990.[35]

Who Manages International Trade?

As just discussed, international trade and foreign production are increasingly managed on a global basis. Furthermore, international trade and foreign production are also intertwined in a complex manner. Think about Honda Motors, a Japanese automobile manufacturer. Honda initially exported its Accords and Civics to the United States in the 1970s. By the mid-1980s, the Japanese company began manufacturing those cars in Marysville, Ohio, in the United States. The company currently exports U.S.-made Accord models to Japan and elsewhere and boasts that it is the largest exporter of U.S.-made automobiles in the United States. Recently Honda announced that it will start manufacturing its "world car" in Thailand, Brazil, and probably China due to the low cost and then export it mainly to Europe and Japan. It is expected that all Honda cars in Japan will eventually be produced and imported from aboard.[36] Similarly, Texas Instruments has a large semiconductor manufacturing plant in Japan, not only marketing its semiconductor chips in Japan but also exporting them from Japan to the United States and elsewhere. In addition to traditional exporting from their home base, those companies manufacture their products in various foreign countries both for local sale and further exporting to the rest of the world, including their respective home countries. In other words, multinational companies (MNCs) are increasingly managing the international trade flow within themselves. This phenomenon is called **intrafirm trade.**

---

[32] Richard J. Barnet and R. E. Muller, *Global Reach: The Power of the Multinational Corporations* (New York: Simon and Schuster, 1974).

[33] Peter J. Buckley and R. D. Pearce, "Overseas Production and Exporting by the World's Largest Enterprises," *International Executive,* 22 (Winter 1980), pp. 7–8; and Dennis J. Encarnation, "Transforming Trade and Investment, American, European, and Japanese Multinationals Across the Triad," paper presented at the Academy of International Business Annual Meetings, November 22, 1992.

[34] Masaaki Kotabe, "The Promotional Roles of the State Government and Japanese Manufacturing Direct Investment in the United States," *Journal of Business Research,* 27 (June 1993), pp. 131–46.

[35] Encarnation (see fn 33).

[36] "Honda to Re-Important 'World Car' Produced in Thailand," *Nikkei Interactive Net,* http://www.nni.nikkei.co.jp, December 18, 2001; and "Honda Could Bring a Small Car to Europe from Thailand," *Automotive News Europe,* December 13, 2004, p. 3.

Intrafirm trade makes trade statistics more complex to interpret because part of the international flow of products and components is taking place between affiliated companies within the same corporate system, transcending national boundaries. Although statistical information is scarce, one official report by the United Nations shows that in 1999, 34 percent of world trade was intrafirm trade between MNCs and their foreign affiliates and between those affiliates, and that an additional 33.3 percent of world trade represented exports by those MNCs and their affiliates. In other words, two-thirds of world trade is managed one way or another by MNCs.[37] These trade ratios have been fairly stable over time.[38]

Although few statistics are available, service industries are going through the same evolution as manufacturing industries on a global basis. Indeed, some similarities in intrafirm trade of services exist. In 2004, $2.1 trillion worth of commercial services was traded globally. Among the top global service exporters and importers, the United States was ranked the largest exporter, providing $319 billion of services to the rest of the world in 2004. The United States was also the top importer of services, receiving $259 billion worth of services.[39] Today, approximately 16 percent of the total value of U.S. exports and imports of services were conducted across national boundaries on an intrafirm basis.[40] Government deregulation and technological advancement have facilitated the tradability of some services globally and economically.

◆ ◆ ◆ ◆ ◆ ◆ ◆ ◆   **EVOLUTION OF GLOBAL MARKETING**

What is Marketing?   Marketing is essentially a creative corporate activity involving the planning and execution of the conception, pricing, promotion, and distribution of ideas, products, and services in an exchange that not only *satisfies* customers' current needs but also *anticipates* and *creates* their future needs at a profit.[41] Marketing is much broader than selling; it also encompasses the entire company's *market orientation* toward customer satisfaction in a competitive environment. In other words, marketing strategy requires close attention to both customers and competitors.[42] Quite often marketers have focused excessively on satisfying customer needs while ignoring competitors. In the process, competitors have outmaneuvered them in the marketplace with better, less expensive products. It is widely believed that in many cases, U.S. companies have won the battle of discovering and initially filling customer needs only to be defeated in the competitive war by losing the markets they pioneered to European and Japanese competitors.[43]

---

[37] Khalil Hamdani, "The Role of Foreign Direct Investment in Export Strategy," paper presented at 1999 Executive Forum on National Export Strategies, International Trade Centre, the United Nations, September 26–28.

[38] United Nations Center on Transnational Corporations, *Transnational Corporations in World Development: Trends and Perspectives* (New York: United Nations, 1988); "Organization for Economic Cooperation and Development," *Intra-Firm Trade* (Paris, OECD, 1993); and William J. Zeile, "U.S. Affiliates of Foreign Companies," *Survey of Current Business,* August 2005, pp.198–214.

[39] *World Trade Report 2005: Exploring the Link between Trade, Standards, and the WTO* (Geneva: World Trade Organization, 2005).

[40] Janet Y. Murray and Masaaki Kotabe, "Sourcing Strategies of U.S. Service Companies: A Modified Transaction-Cost Analysis," *Strategic Management Journal,* 20, (September 1999), pp. 791–809; Masaaki Kotabe and Janet Y. Murray, "Global Procurement of Service Activities by Service Firms," *International Marketing Review,* 21(6), 2004, pp. 615–633; and for detailed statistics, see Michael A. Mann, Laura L. Brokenbaugh, and Sylvia E. Bargas, "U.S. International Services," Survey of Current Business, 80 (October 2000), pp. 119–61.

[41] This definition is modified from the American Marketing Association's definition of *marketing* and is strongly influenced by Drucker's conception of two entrepreneurial functions—marketing and innovation—that constitute business. Recent thinking about marketing also suggests that the task of the marketer is not only to satisfy the current needs and wants of customers but also to innovate on products and services, anticipating and even creating their future needs and wants. See Peter F. Drucker, *The Practice of Management* (New York: Harper & Brothers, 1954), pp. 37–39; and Frederick E. Webster, Jr., "The Changing Role of Marketing in the Corporation," *Journal of Marketing,* 56 (October 1992), pp. 1–16.

[42] Aysegül Özsomer and Bernard Simonin, "Antecedents and Consequences of Market Orientation in a Subsidiary Context," *Enhancing Knowledge Development in Marketing,* 1999 American Marketing Association Educators' Proceedings, Summer 1999, p. 68.

[43] Robert M. Peterson, Clay Dibrell, and Timothy L. Pett, "Whose Market Orientation Is Longest: A Study of Japan, Europe, and the United States," *Enhancing Knowledge Development in Marketing,* 1999 American Marketing Association Educators' Proceedings, Summer 1999, p. 69.

It is increasingly difficult for companies to avoid the impact of competition from around the world and the convergence of the world's markets. As a result, an increasing number of companies are drawn into marketing activities outside their home country. However, as previously indicated, various companies approach marketing around the world very differently. For example, Michael Dell established Dell Computer because he saw a burgeoning market potential for IBM-compatible personal computers in the United States. After his immediate success at home, he realized a future growth potential would exist in foreign markets. Then his company began exporting Dell PCs to Europe and Japan. In a way, this was a predictable pattern of foreign expansion. On the other hand, not all companies go through this predictable pattern. Think about a notebook-size Macintosh computer, the PowerBook 100, that Apple Computer introduced in 1991. In 1989, Apple enlisted Sony, the Japanese consumer electronics giant, to design and manufacture this notebook computer for both U.S. and Japanese markets.[44] Sony has world-class expertise in miniaturization and has been a supplier of disk drives, monitors, and power supplies to Apple for various Macintosh models. In an industry such as personal computers in which technology changes quickly and the existing product becomes obsolete in a short period of time, a window of business opportunity is naturally limited. Therefore, Apple's motivation was to introduce the notebook computer on the markets around the world as soon as it could before competition picked up.

Companies generally develop different marketing strategies depending on the degree of experience and the nature of operations in international markets. Companies tend to evolve over time, accumulating international business experience and learning the advantages and disadvantages associated with complexities of manufacturing and marketing around the world.[45] As a result, many researchers have adopted an evolutionary perspective of internationalization of the company just like the evolution of the species over time. In the following pages, we formally define and explain five stages characterizing the evolution of global marketing. Of course, not all companies go through the complete evolution from a purely domestic marketing stage to a purely global marketing stage. An actual evolution depends also on the economic, cultural, political, and legal environments of various country markets in which the company operates as well as the nature of the company's offerings. A key point here is that many companies are constantly under competitive pressure to move forward both *reactively* (responding to the changes in the market and competitive environments) and *proactively* (anticipating the change). Remember that "If you stand still, you will get run over...."

Therefore, knowing the dynamics of the evolutionary development of international marketing involvement is important for two reasons. First, it helps to understand how companies learn and acquire international experience and how they use it to gain competitive advantage over time. This may help an executive to be better prepared for the likely change needed in the company's marketing strategy. Second, with this knowledge, a company may be able to compete more effectively by predicting its competitors' likely marketing strategy in advance.

Domestic Marketing

As shown in Exhibit 1-2, the evolution of marketing across national boundaries has five identifiable stages.[46] The first stage is **domestic marketing.** Before entry into international markets, many companies focus solely on their domestic market. Their marketing strategy is developed based on information about domestic customer needs and wants, industry trends, and economic, technological, and political environments at home.

[44]"Apple's Japanese Ally," *Fortune,* November 4, 1991, pp. 151–52.

[45]Anna Shaojie Cui, David A. Griffith, and S. Tamer Cavusgil, "The Influence of Competitive Intensity and Market Dynamism on Knowledge Management Capabilities of Multinational Corporation Subsidiaries," *Journal of International Marketing,* 13(3), 2005, pp. 32–53.

[46]This section draws from Balaj S. Chakravarthy and Howard V. Perlmutter, "Strategic Planning for a Global Business," *Columbia Journal of World Business* (Summer 1985), pp. 3–10; and Susan P. Douglas and C. Samuel Craig, "Evolution of Global Marketing Strategy: Scale, Scope and Synergy," *Columbia Journal of World Business* 24 (Fall 1989), pp. 47–59.

EXHIBIT 1-2
EVOLUTION OF GLOBAL MARKETING

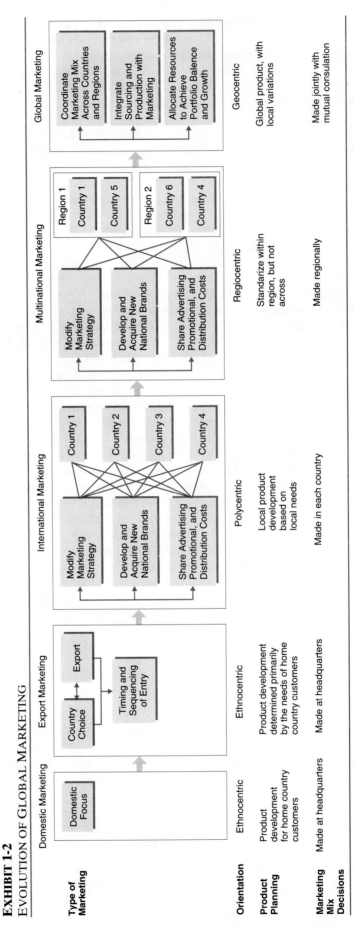

Source: Constructed from Susan P. Douglas and C. Samuel Craig, "Evolution of Global Marketing Strategy: Scale, Scope and Synergy," *Columbia Journal of World Business,* 24 (Fall 1985), p. 50; and Balai S. Chakravarthy and Howard V. Perlmutter, "Strategic Planning for a Global Business," *Columbia Journal of World Business,* 20 (Summer 1985), p. 6.

When those companies consider competition, they essentially look at domestic competition. Today, it is highly conceivable that domestic competition is made up of both domestic competitors and foreign competitors marketing their products in the home market. Domestic marketers tend to be *ethnocentric* and pay little attention to changes taking place in the global marketplace, such as changing lifestyles and market segments, emerging competition, and better products that have yet to arrive in their domestic market. *Ethnocentrism* is defined here as the predisposition of a firm to be predominantly concerned with its viability worldwide and legitimacy only in its home country[47]—that is, where all strategic actions of a company are tailored to domestic responses under similar situations. As a result, these companies may be vulnerable to the sudden changes forced on them from foreign competition. U.S. automobile and consumer electronics manufacturers suffered from this ethnocentrism in the 1960s and 1970s as a result of their neglect of imminent competition from Japanese low-cost manufacturers.

The second stage is **export marketing,** which usually begins with unsolicited orders from foreign customers. When a company receives an order from abroad, it may reluctantly fill the order initially, but it gradually learns the benefit of marketing overseas. In general, in the early stage of export marketing involvement, the internationalization process is a consequence of incremental adjustments to the changing conditions of the company and its environment rather than a result of its deliberate strategy. Such a pattern is due to the consequence of increased uncertainty in international business, increased costs of information, and the lack of technical knowledge about international marketing activities. At this early export marketing stage, exporters tend to engage in *indirect exporting* by relying on export management companies or trading companies to handle their export business.

Export Marketing

Some companies progress to a more involved stage of internationalization by *direct exporting,* once three internal conditions have been satisfied. First, company management obtains favorable expectations of the attractiveness of exporting based on experience. Second, the company has access to key resources necessary for undertaking additional export-related tasks. Such availability of physical, financial, and managerial resources is closely associated with firm size. Particularly, small companies may have few trained managers and little time for long-term planning because they are preoccupied with day-to-day operational problems and consequently find it difficult to become involved in exporting. Third, management is willing to commit adequate resources to export activities.[48] The company's long-term commitment to export marketing depends on how successful management is in overcoming various barriers encountered in international marketing activities. An experienced export marketer has to deal with difficulties in maintaining and expanding export involvement. These difficulties include import/export restrictions, cost and availability of shipping, exchange rate fluctuations, collection of money, and development of distribution channels, among others. Overall, favorable experience appears to be a key component in getting companies involved in managing exports directly without relying on specialized outside export handlers. To a large degree, an appropriate measure of favorableness for many companies consists of profits. An increase in profits due to a certain activity is likely to increase the company's interest in such activity.[49]

External pressures also prod companies into export marketing activities. Saturated domestic markets may make it difficult for a company to maintain sales volume in an increasingly competitive domestic market; it will become much more serious when foreign competitors begin marketing products in the domestic market. Export marketers begin paying attention to technological and other changes in the global marketplace that domestic marketers tend to ignore. However, export marketers still

---

[47]Chakravarthy and Perlmutter, "Strategic Planning," pp. 3–10.

[48]S. Tamer Cavusgil, "On the Internationalization Process of Firms," *European Research,* 8 (November 1980), pp. 273–79.

[49]Masaaki Kotabe and Michael R. Czinkota, "State Government Promotion of Manufacturing Exports: A Gap Analysis," *Journal of International Business Studies,* 23 (Fourth Quarter 1992), pp. 637–58.

tend to take an *ethnocentric* approach to foreign markets as being an extension of their domestic market and export products developed primarily for home country customers with limited adaptation to foreign customers' needs.

International Marketing

Once export marketing becomes an integral part of the company's marketing activity, it will begin to seek new directions for growth and expansion. We call this stage **international marketing.** A unique feature of international marketing is its *polycentric* orientation with emphasis on product and promotional adaptation in foreign markets whenever necessary.[50] *Polycentric orientation* refers to a firm's predisposition to the existence of significant local cultural differences across markets, necessitating the operation in each country to be viewed independently, "that is, all strategic decisions are thus tailored to suit the cultures" of the concerned country. As the company's market share in a number of countries reaches a certain point, it becomes important for the company to defend its position through local competition. Because of local competitors' proximity to and familiarity with local customers, they tend to have an inherent "insider" advantage over foreign competition. To strengthen its competitive position, the international marketer begins to adapt products and promotion, if necessary, to meet the needs and wants of local customers in two alternative ways. First, the company may allocate a certain portion of its manufacturing capacity to its export business. Second, because of transportation costs, tariffs, and other regulations as well as the availability of human and capital resources in the foreign markets, the company may even begin manufacturing in the foreign market. BMW has been exporting its cars to the United States for many years. The German company has invested in a manufacturing plant in South Carolina to be more adaptive to changing customer needs in this important market and to take advantage of rather inexpensive resources as a result of the dollar depreciation against the euro. Accordingly, BMW South Carolina has become part of BMW Group's global manufacturing network and is the exclusive manufacturing plant for all Z4 roadster and X5 sports activity vehicles.[51]

If international marketing is taken to the extreme, a company may establish an independent foreign subsidiary in each and every foreign market and have each subsidiary operate independently of each other without any measurable headquarters control. This special case of international marketing is known as **multidomestic marketing.** Product development, manufacturing, and marketing are all executed by each subsidiary for its own local market. As a result, different product lines, product positioning, and pricing may be observed across those subsidiaries. Few economies of scale benefits can be obtained. However, multidomestic marketing is useful when customer needs are so different across different national markets that no common product or promotional strategy can be developed. Even Coca-Cola, which once practiced a globally standardized marketing strategy, changed its strategy when it found that its structure had become too cumbersome and that it was insensitive to local markets. In 2000, the company decided to return to a more multidomestic marketing approach and to give more freedom to local subsidiaries. Local marketing teams are now permitted to develop advertising to local consumers and even launch new local brands.[52]

Multinational Marketing

Now the company markets its products in many countries around the world. We call this stage **multinational marketing.** Company management comes to realize the benefit of economies of scale in product development, manufacturing, and marketing by consolidating some of its activities on a regional basis. This *regiocentric* approach suggests that product planning may be standardized *within* a region (e.g., a group of contiguous and similar countries), such as Western Europe, but not *across* regions. Products may be manufactured regionally as well. Similarly, advertising, promotional,

---

[50]Warren J. Keegan, "Multinational Product Planning: Strategic Alternatives," *Journal of Marketing,* 33 (January 1969), pp. 58–62.

[51]http://www.bmwusa.com/about/, accessed January 27, 2006.

[52]Isabelle Schuiling and Jean-Noë Kapferer, "Real Differences between Local and International Brands: Strategic Implications for International Marketers," *Journal of International Marketing,* 12(4), 2004, pp. 97–112.

and distribution costs may be shared by subsidiaries in the region. In order for the company to develop its regional image in the marketplace, it may develop and acquire new regional brands to beef up its regional operations. General Motors has a regional subsidiary, Opel (headquartered in Germany), to market both GM and Opel cars with a strong European distinction. In more recent years, GM, unable to sell its way into Japan for a long time, quietly formed a network of equity alliances with Japanese automakers to expand into this once impenetrable market and serve as a platform for its Asian expansion. Even when having difficulty occupying a market, a firm may think out of box regarding alliance or partnership that can lead it into the market.

While enabling the consolidation of operations within countries or regions, the international (country-by-country) or multinational (region-by-region) orientation will nonetheless tends to result in market fragmentation worldwide. Operational fragmentation leads to higher costs. As many Japanese companies entered the world markets as low-cost manufacturers of reliable products in the 1970s, well-established U.S. and European multinational companies were made acutely aware of the vulnerability of being high-cost manufacturers. Levitt, an arduous globalization proponent, argues:

Global Marketing

> Gone are accustomed differences in national or regional preference. Gone are the days when a company could sell last year's models—or lesser versions of advanced products—in the less developed world.... The multinational and the global corporation are not the same thing. The multinational corporation operates in a number of countries, and adjusts its products and practices in each—at high relative costs. The global corporation operates with resolute constancy—at low relative cost—as if the entire world (or major regions of it) were a single entity; it sells the same things in the same way everywhere.[53]

Global marketing refers to marketing activities by companies that emphasize the following:

1. *Standardization Efforts*—Standardizing marketing programs across different countries particularly with respect to product offering, promotional mix, price, and channel structure. Such efforts increase opportunities for the transfer of products, brands, and other ideas across subsidiaries and help address the emergence of global customers.

2. *Coordination across Markets*—Reducing cost inefficiencies and duplication of efforts among their national and regional subsidiaries.

3. *Global Integration*—Participating in many major world markets to gain competitive leverage and effective integration of the firm's competitive campaigns across these markets by being able to subsidize operations in some markets with resources generated in others and responding to competitive attacks in one market by counterattacking in others.[54]

Although Levitt's view is somewhat extreme, many researchers agree that global marketing does not necessarily mean that products, promotion, pricing, and distribution are standardized worldwide but that a company is proactively willing to adopt a global perspective instead of country-by-country or region-by-region perspective in developing a marketing strategy. Although not all companies adopt global marketing, an increasing number of companies are proactively trying to find commonality in their marketing strategy among national subsidiaries (See Global Perspective 1-3). For example, Black & Decker, a U.S. hand tool manufacturer, adopted a global perspective by standardizing and streamlining components such as motors and rotors while maintaining a wide range of product lines and created a universal image for

[53]Theodore Levitt, "The Globalization of Markets," *Harvard Business Review,* 61 (May–June 1983), pp. 92–102.
[54]Shaoming Zou and S. Tamer Cavusgil, "The GMS: A Broad Conceptualization of Global Marketing Strategy and its Effect on Firm Performance," *Journal of Marketing,* 66 (October 2002), pp. 40–56.

◆ ◆

𝒢LOBAL PERSPECTIVE 1-3
GLOBALIZING THE BUSINESS TERMS BEFORE GLOBALIZING THE FIRM

International was the first word that William Hudson, president and CEO of AMP Inc., Harrisburg, Pennsylvania, told his corporate colleagues to cut from their business vocabularies. Why? The term creates a "Chinese wall" that divides a globalizing company into "domestic" and "international" sides, he explained to a meeting of A. T. Kearney Inc. officers in Chicago. "It's almost as if you don't jump over that wall" to work or team together, he said.

Another banished word: *subsidiary.* It conveys "a parent/child relationship," said Mr. Hudson. Headquarters tends

to lord its power over foreign and domestic operations and "make them feel like inferior souls." Revising the business lexicon is not easy, Mr. Hudson readily admitted. "Every now and then [one of the words] shows up on a ... slide when somebody makes a presentation. And I've got to put up my hand and say: 'Erase that word.'"

Next, what is the difference between internationalization and globalization? In the mind of many people they are separate concepts, and many prefer *globalization* over *internationalization. Internationalization* takes place between individual nations, between individual companies operating in different countries, and between individual citizens of different countries. *Globalization,* however, increasingly ignores national boundaries.

Source. Industry Week, June 7, 1993, pp. 51–53; and Jon Erlendsson, "Globalization and Innovation," http://www.hi.is/~joner/eaps/cq_globi.htm, accessed December 15, 2005.

---

its products. In this case, it was not standardization of products per se but the company's effort at standardizing the key components and the product design for manufacturability in the manufacturing industry and core and supplementary services in the service industry to achieve global leadership in cost and value.

The Impact of Economic Geography and Climate on Global Marketing

Global marketing does not necessarily mean that products can be developed anywhere on a global basis. The economic geography, climate, and culture, among other things, affect the way in which companies develop certain products and consumers want them. First, the availability of resources is a major determinant of industry location. The U.S. automobile industry was born at the dawn of the 20th century as a result of Henry Ford's decision to locate his steel-making foundry in Detroit midway between sources of iron ore in the Mesabi range in Minnesota and sources of bituminous coal in Pennsylvania. Similarly, in the last quarter of the 20th century, Silicon Valley in and around Palo Alto, California, and Silicon Hill in Austin, Texas, emerged as high-tech meccas as a result of abundant skilled human resources (thanks to leading universities in the areas) aided by warm, carefree environments—a coveted atmosphere conducive to creative thinking. For the same reason, Bangalore, India, has emerged as an important location for software development. Brazil boasts automobiles with flex-fuel engines, powered by ethanol or gasoline or any combination of both, on its roads, thanks to an abundant supply of ethanol produced from subsidized sugar cane. Even bananas are produced in abundance in Iceland, thanks to nature-provided geothermal energy tapped in greenhouses.[55] Because Germans consume the largest amount of bananas in the European Union—about 33 lbs (or 15 kg)—on a per capita basis, Iceland could become an exporter of bananas to Germany![56]

Obviously, the availability of both natural and human resources is important in primarily determining industry location as those resources, if unavailable, could become a bottleneck. It is to be stressed that consumer needs are equally important as a determinant of industry location.[57] As the Icelandic banana example shows, the

---

[55] "Iceland Information," http://www.vjv.com/information/country/europe_west/iceland_info.html, accessed December 15, 2005.

[56] Paul Sutton, "The Banana Regime of the European Union, the Caribbean, and Latin America," *Journal of Interamerican Studies and World Affairs,* 39 (Summer 1997), pp. 5–36.

[57] Michael E. Porter, *The Competitive Advantage of Nations* (New York: Free Press, 1990).

fact that Germans consume a large amount of bananas gives Icelandic growers a logistical advantage. Ask yourself why cellular phones have been most widely adopted in Finland and fax machines and bubble-jet printers in Japan. Finland and other Scandinavian countries have heavy snows in the winter, but the snow is very damp owing to the warm Gulf Stream moderating what could otherwise be a frigid climate. The heavy, damp snow frequently brings down power lines. Thus, Scandinavians always wished for a mobile method of communication such as CB radio and cellular phones. Companies such as Nokia in Finland and Ericsson in Sweden have become world-class suppliers of cellular technology.[58] Similarly, Japanese consumers always wanted machines that could easily produce and reproduce the complex characters in their language. Thus, Japanese companies such as Canon, Epson (a subsidiary of Seiko Watch), and Fujitsu have emerged as major producers of fax and bubble-jet printers in the world. For outdoor-activity-loving Australians, surfing is a national sport. No wonder that Quicksilver, an Australian company that knows functional as well as aesthetic designs for sportswear quite well, has conquered the European market from stake boarders beneath the Eiffel Tower to snowboarders in the Swiss Alps and surfers in Spain.[59] Similarly, Billabong, another Australian surfing goods retailer with a keen eye on what outdoor sports lovers want to wear, is expanding into the U.S. market with a broad range of leisure-related products following the acquisition of Element, a U.S. skateboarding clothing company, and Von Zipper, a U.S. sunglasses and snow goggles brand.[60] Indeed, as the old proverb says, "Necessity is the mother of invention."

The point is that what companies can offer competitively may be determined by either the availability of natural and human resources or the unique consumer needs in different countries or regions or by both. Global marketers are willing to exploit their local advantages for global business opportunities. Then ask yourself another question about an emerging societal need around the world, environmental protection. Where are formidable competitors likely to originate in the near future? We think it is Germany. Germans have long been concerned about their environmental quality represented by the cleanliness of the Rhine River. When the Rhine was polluted by phosphorus—a major whitening agent in laundry detergent—the German government became the first in the world to ban the agent. Now German companies are keen on developing products that are fully recyclable. Recyclable products will become increasingly important in a not distant future. Naturally, marketing executives need to have an acute understanding of not only the availability of various resources but also emerging consumer and societal needs on a global basis.

So far we have focused on complex realities of international trade and investment that have characterized our global economy in the past 20 years. Some vital statistics have been provided. The more statistics we see, the more befuddled we become by the sheer complexities of our global economy. It even seems as though there were not a modicum of orderliness in our global economy like a jungle. Naturally, we wish the world had been much simpler. In reality, it is becoming ever more complex. Luckily enough, however, economists and business researchers have tried over the years to explain the ever-increasing complexities of the global economy in simpler terms. A simplified yet logical view of the world is called a **theory.** Indeed, there are many different ways—theories—of looking at international trade and investment taking place in the world. For those of you interested in understanding some orderliness in the complex world of international trade and investment, we encourage you to read the appendix to this chapter. Some theoretical understanding will help you not only appreciate the competitive world in which we live but also make better strategy decisions for a company you may join shortly or a company you may own.

---

[58]Lilach Nachum, "Does Nationality of Ownership Make Any Difference and If so Under What Circumstances," *Journal of International Management,* 9 (2003).

[59]"Global Surfin' Safari: Quiksilver Rides Wave In Europe and Far East," *Women's Wear Daily,* June 30, 2005, pp. 1–8.

[60]"Skateboarding Springs into Billabong," *The Australian,* July 4, 2001, p. 21.

SUMMARY ◆

The amount of world trade grew from $200 billion to more than $11 trillion in the last 30 years. Although world trade volume is significant in and of itself, international business is much more than trade statistics show. Companies from Western Europe, the United States, and Japan collectively produce probably more than three times as much in their foreign markets as they export. About one-third of their exports and imports is transacted on an intrafirm basis between their parent companies and their affiliated companies abroad or between the affiliated companies themselves.

What this all means is that it is almost impossible for domestic company executives to consider their domestic markets and domestic competition alone. If they fail to look beyond their national boundaries, they may unknowingly lose marketing opportunities to competitors that do. Worse yet, foreign competitors will encroach on their hard-earned market position at home so fast that it may be too late for them to respond. International markets are so intertwined that separating international from domestic business may be a futile mental exercise.

Historically, international expansion has always been a strategy consideration after domestic marketing and has therefore been reactionary to such things as a decline in domestic sales and increased domestic competition. Global marketing is a proactive response to the intertwined nature of business opportunities and competition that know no political boundaries. However, global marketing does not necessarily mean that companies should market the same product in the same way around the world as world markets are converging. To the extent feasible, they probably should. Nonetheless, global marketing requires a company's willingness to adopt a global perspective instead of country-by-country or region-by-region perspective in developing a marketing strategy for growth and profit.

What companies can offer competitively may be determined either by the availability of natural and human resources or by the unique consumer needs in different countries or regions or by both. Global marketers should be willing to exploit their local advantages for global marketing opportunities. The proliferation of e-commerce on the Internet accelerates such global marketing opportunities.

KEY TERMS ◆

Domestic marketing
e-commerce (electronic commerce)

Export marketing
Global marketing
International business

International marketing
International trade
Intrafirm trade

Multidomestic marketing
Multinational marketing
Theory Triad regions

REVIEW QUESTIONS ◆

1. Discuss the reasons why international business is much more complex today than it was 20 years ago.
2. What is the nature of global competition?
3. Does international trade accurately reflect the nature of global competition?
4. Why are consumption patterns similar across industrialized countries despite cultural differences?

5. How is global marketing different from international marketing?
6. Why do you think a company should or should not market the same product in the same way around the world?
7. What is *proactive standardization?*
8. How is the Internet reshaping the nature of global marketing?

DISCUSSION QUESTIONS ◆

1. The United States and Japan, which are the two largest economies in the world, are also the largest importers and exporters of goods and services. However, imports and exports put together comprise only 20 to 30 percent of their gross domestic products. This percentage has not changed much over the last three decades for both of these countries. Does this imply that the corporations and the media may be overemphasizing globalization? Discuss why you agree or do not agree with the last statement.

2. Merchandise trade today accounts for less than 2 percent of all foreign exchange transactions around the world. Can one deduce that merchandise plays an insignificant role in today's economies? Why or why not?

3. A major cereal manufacturer produces and markets standardized breakfast cereals to countries around the world. Minor modifications in attributes such as sweetness of the product are made to cater to local needs. However, the core products and brands are standardized. The company entered

the Chinese market a few years ago and was extremely satisfied with the results. The company's sales continue to grow at a rate of around 50 percent a year in China. Encouraged by its marketing success in China and other Asian countries and based on the market reforms taking place, the company started operations in India by manufacturing and marketing its products. Initial response to the product was extremely encouraging, and within one year, the company was thinking in terms of rapidly expanding its production capacity. However, after a year, sales tapered off and started to fall. Detailed consumer research seemed to suggest that while the upper-middle social class, especially families in which both spouses were working and to whom this product was targeted, adopted the cereals as an alternative meal (i.e., breakfast) for a short time, they eventually returned to the traditional Indian breakfast. The CEOs of some other firms in the food industry in India have stated that non-Indian snack products and restaurant business are the areas in which multinational companies (MNCs) can hope for success. Trying to replace a full meal with a non-Indian product has less a chance of succeeding. You are a senior executive in the international division of this food MNC with experience of operating in various countries in a product management function. The CEO plans to send you to India on a fact-finding mission to determine answers to these specific questions. What, in your opinion, would be the answers to these questions:

    a. Was entering the market with a standardized product a mistake?

    b. Was the problem caused by the product or the way it was positioned?

    c. Given the advantages to be gained through leveraging brand equity and product knowledge on a global basis and the disadvantages of differing local tastes, what would be your strategy for entering new markets?

4. Globalization involves the organizationwide development of a global perspective, which requires globally thinking managers. Although the benefits of globalization have received widespread attention, the difficulties in developing managers who think globally has received scant attention. Some senior managers consider this to be a significant stumbling block in companies's globalization efforts. Do you agree with the concerns of these managers? Would the lack of truly globally thinking managers cause problems for implementing a global strategy? How does the proliferation of e-commerce affect the way these managers conduct business?

5. The e-commerce business in China has entered a golden period with transaction volume of online trading reaching 21.86 billion yuan (US$2.64 billion) in 2004. With 94 million Internet users, more than 40 million people conducted transactions on the Internet in 2004, compared with 10.7 million in 2001, and more than 60 percent of people expressed their willingness to try online trading in 2005. Among net citizens, roughly 20 million people have had the experience of playing games online. China's largest e-game operator, Shanda Interactive Entertainment Limited, has accumulated a huge amount of wealth in just a couple of years. In May 2004, Shanda was listed on the NASDAQ and generated US$373 million in the online games market; 39.3 percent of this market is from China. Now the company is shifting its business focus from the computer platform to the TV platform—including games, music, and literature—through a set-top box to penetrate those 340 million households that already own a television. With 1.4 billion in population, the Chinese market is inviting to both online and offline businesses. In terms of online businesses, what do you foresee as opportunities and threats to multinational corporations, especially in emerging economies?

SHORT CASES

CASE 1-1

VODAFONE GROUP: GLOBAL MARKETING REQUIRES A VERY LOCAL ATTENTION

After four years of struggling in Japan, Vodafone Group, a British company and the world's largest cellular carrier in terms of market capitalization, may have finally learned a valuable lesson. Global marketing does not necessarily mean that the company can treat all markets the same way. In essence, think globally, but act locally.

Since entering the Japanese market in 2001 by taking over J-Phone Co., a local cellular provider, the company has seen its reputation slip with its handsets being viewed as dull and its service second rate. Vodafone was focused on building a global brand and cutting costs by procuring large numbers of handsets to sell throughout the world. In Japan, however, this came at the expense of products and services to suit the nation's finicky and tech-savvy consumers. Vodafone ended up being slower than Japanese rivals to roll out flashy new handsets and competitive pricing plans. It has thus failed to gain market share, coming in last among Japan's three major cellular carriers NTT, DoCoMo and KDDI. In July 2004, Vodafone's unit in Japan, Vodafone KK, became the first of the three carriers to report a monthly net loss of customers from the period one year earlier. Vodafone's struggle in Japan shows that it is not always an advantage to act like a big global player.

Vodafone's Japan revenue represents 20 percent of the company's revenues overall. As such, its success in Japan is vital to Vodafone's global operations. Now Vodafone KK is trying to revive a business dogged by paltry subscriber growth and a tendency to be behind the curve in Japan's cutting-edge cell phone market. Vodafone KK has been used to getting management directives from its London headquarters. Now the Japanese unit vows that more ideas will originate in Japan, and instead of trying so hard to make European handsets fly in the Japanese market, the company will focus more on making phones that are unique to Japan.

Source: "Vodafone Pins Japan Recovery on Tailoring Products to Locals," *Wall Street Journal,* November 17, 2005, p. B3.

Reviving Vodafone in Japan will not be easy. Worse, time is running out. If Vodafone KK cannot turn its operations around in a year, it will probably never be able to do it because Japan's intensely competitive cellular market is about to get even tougher with new government rules that will let people keep their phone number when changing carriers—potentially setting off a flow of customers from the weakest to the strongest. Competition will intensify further when new players who have just received government licenses enter the Japanese market.

The company now realizes that handsets are the key to grabbing Japanese consumers. It underestimated the importance that the Japanese customer places on the functionality, user interface, and manufacturer's brand itself. The company is now launching a wider variety of handsets, such as ones that look and act like digital music players or function as mobile wallets. It plans to pick up the pace of its launches in the next several months. Vodafone also is pulling back from its strategy of saving costs by marketing the same types of handsets in Japan as it sells in other countries. Those handsets flopped because they were not as advanced or easy to use as the ones Vodafone's Japanese rivals were offering.

DISCUSSION QUESTIONS

1. Why do firms such as Vodafone need to have a global marketing strategy although its product development, as well as the rest of its marketing strategy, needs to be localized for tech-savvy consumers in Japan?
2. What alternative strategy could Vodafone have used to regain its market position in Japan? For the future, how could Vodafone tap into the convergence among global consumers?

CASE 1-2

CHRYSLER: STILL TRYING TO MAKE A COMEBACK

In some industries, global competition is so intense that firms eventually have to respond to the global marketing imperative. One such notable example is the automobile industry. Once-American-owned Chrysler has had a very bumpy ride down the annals of the global auto industry but has so far managed to survive the cutthroat competition among the industry players. The Daimler-Benz (German)—Chrysler (U.S.) merger was a momentous one for the global auto

industry in general and the U.S. auto industry in particular, which witnessed one of its Big Three fall into foreign hands.

Daimler-Benz, owner of the prestigious Mercedes brand of cars that are perceived the world over as a status symbol, maintains a global image for its Mercedes models. As for Chrysler, the company underwent several changes soon after the merger, an important one being its reinvention as a global brand from a home grown U.S. one. A significant part of this transformation was the evolving global marketing strategy at Chrysler that was reflected in a change in structure and marketing campaigns. Prior to the changes, Chrysler's sales and marketing operations were organized with separate sales and marketing divisions for its home market (i.e., United States), Mexico, Canada, and one for its other foreign markets. Chrysler combined these domestic and international sales and marketing divisions into a single unit.

The company also reset its objectives to achieve a goal of increased sales from outside the United States. At the time, around 20 percent of its total sales were from foreign operations. On the media front, Chrysler began working with some of Mercedes' media partners. The personnel shake-up included hiring one communications manager for each of its brands for both domestic and international affairs as opposed to its earlier strategy of having separate managers for each brands at both the domestic and the international levels.

Just over a year after the merger, Chrysler introduced its first "global product", the unique 1930s style new car, the PT Cruiser, which was its first product to boast a global marketing campaign. Publicity for the car was first launched in the U.S.

market in April and in the European market two months later and soon after in the rest of the world. Chrysler developed the global marketing campaign for the car after careful collaboration with its national and international offices from all around the globe. In keeping with the global brand image for the car, Chrysler maintained the same content for its advertisements, the only difference being the different languages used in the commercials in different countries. On the production side, the only difference in the cars sold in various markets was the steering wheel, depending on whether mandated local laws left-hand or right-hand drive. Chrysler invented the minivan over 20 years ago, and the Voyager Minivan remained its highest selling model. As part of its new global marketing, Chrysler developed a global campaign for this brand also. It will be interesting to see how far this new strategy takes Chrysler.

DISCUSSION QUESTIONS

1. Will the new global strategy work for Chrysler? Why?
2. Should auto firms have global strategies? Discuss your point of view.

FURTHER READING

"A Survey of Globalization: Globalization and Its Critics". *Economist*, September 29, 2001, pp. 1–30.

Bhagwati, Jagdish. "The Globalization Guru". *Finance & Development*, 42 (September 2005), pp. 4–7.

de La Torre, José, and Richard W. Moxon. "Introduction to the Symposium E-Commerce and Global Business: The Impact of the Information and Communication Technology Revolution on the Conduct of International Business". *Journal of International Business Studies*, 32 (4th Quarter 2001), pp. 617–39.

Dunning, John H., ed. *Making Globalization Good: The Moral Challenges of Global Capitalism*. New York: Oxford University Press, 2003.

Eden, Lorraine, and Stefanie Lenway. "The Janus Face of Globalization". *Journal of International Business Studies*, 32 (Third Quarter 2001), pp. 383–400.

Eroglu, Sevgin. "Does Globalization Have Staying Power?" *Marketing Management*, 11 (March/April 2002), pp. 18–3.

Fleenor, Debra. "The Coming and Going of the Global Corporation". *Columbia Journal of World Business*, 28 (Winter 1993), pp. 6–16.

Friedman, Thomas L. *The Lexus and the Olive Tree*, rev. ed. New York: Farrar, Straus & Giroux, 2000.

Gwynne, Peter. "The Myth of Globalization?" *Sloan Management Review*, 44 (Winter 2003), p. 11.

Jain, Subhash C. *Toward a Global Business Confederation: A Blueprint for Globalization*. Westport, CT: Praeger, 2003.

Kogut, Bruce. "What Makes a Company Global?" *Harvard Business Review*, 77 (January–February 1999), p. 165–70.

Luo, Xueming, K. Sivakumar, and Sandra S. Liu. "Globalization, Marketing Resources, and Performance: Evidence From China". *Journal of the Academy of Marketing Science*, 33 (Winter 2005), pp. 50–65.

"Measuring Globalization". *Foreign Affairs*, 122 (January/February 2001), pp. 56–65.

Roll, Martin. *Asian Brand Strategy: How Asia Builds Strong Brands*. New York: Palgrave Macmillan, 2006.

Speier, Cheri, Michael G. Harvey, and Jonathan Palmer. "Virtual Management of Global Marketing Relationships". *Journal of World Business*, 33 (Fall 1998), pp. 263–76.

Tétreault Mary Ann, and Robert A. Denemark, ed. *Gods, Guns, and Globalization: Religious Radicalism and International Political Economy*. London: Lynne Rienner Publishers, 2004.

APPENDIX: THEORIES OF INTERNATIONAL TRADE AND THE MULTINATIONAL ENTERPRISE

Theories are simplifications of the complex realities one way or another. A few important theories will be explained here. Each of the theories provides a number of fundamental principles with which you cannot only appreciate why international trade and investment occur but also prepare

for the next impending change you will probably see in the not-so-distant future. These theories are arranged chronologically so that you can better understand what aspect of the ever-increasing complexities of international business each theory was designed to explain.

Comparative Advantage Theory. At the aggregate level, countries trade with each other for fundamentally the same reasons that individuals exchange products and services for mutual benefit. By doing so, we all benefit collectively. *Comparative advantage theory* is an arithmetic demonstration made by the English economist David Ricardo almost 190 years ago that a country can gain from engaging in trade even if it has an absolute advantage or disadvantage. In other words, even if the United States is more efficient in the production of everything than China, both countries will benefit from trade between them by specializing in what each country can produce relatively more efficiently.

Let us demonstrate the comparative advantage theory in its simplest form: The world is made up of two countries (the United States and China) and two products (personal computers and desks). We assume that there is only one PC model and only one type of desk. We further assume that labor is the only input to produce both products. Transportation costs are also assumed to be zero. The production conditions and consumption pattern in the two countries before and after trade are presented in Exhibit 1-3. As shown, U.S. labor is assumed to be more productive absolutely in the production of both personal computers (PC) and desks than Chinese labor.

Intuitively, you might argue that since the United States is more productive in both products, U.S. companies will export both PCs and desks to China, and Chinese companies cannot compete with U.S. companies in either product category. Furthermore, you might argue that because China cannot sell anything to the United States, China cannot pay for imports from the United States. Therefore, these two countries cannot engage in trade. This is essentially the **absolute advantage** argument. Is this argument true? The answer is no.

If you closely look at labor productivity of the two industries, you see that the United States can produce PCs more efficiently than desks compared to the situation in China. The United States has a 3:1 advantage in PCs but only a 2:1

advantage in desks over China. In other words, the United States can produce three PCs instead of a desk (or as few as one-third of a desk per PC), while China can produce two PCs for a desk (or as many as one-half of a desk per PC). Relatively speaking, the United States is comparatively more efficient in making PCs (at a rate of three PCs per desk) than China (at a rate of two PCs per desk). However, China is comparatively more efficient in making desks (at a rate of one-half a desk per PC) than the United States (at a rate of one-third of a desk per PC). Therefore, we say that the United States has a **comparative advantage** in making PCs while China has a comparative advantage in making desks.

Comparative advantage theory suggests that the United States should specialize in the production of PCs while China should specialize in the production of desks. As shown in Exhibit 1-3, the United States produced and consumed 100 PCs and 20 desks, and China produced and consumed 40 PCs and 30 desks. As a whole, the world (the United States and China combined) produced and consumed 140 PCs and 50 desks. Now as a result of specialization, the United States concentrates all of its labor resources on PC production while China allocates all labor resources to desk production. The United States can produce 60 more PCs by giving up 20 desks it used to produce (at a rate of three PCs per desk), resulting in a total production of 160 PCs and no desks. Similarly, China can produce 20 more desks by moving its labor from PC production to desk production (at a rate of one-half of a desk per PC), with a total production of 50 desks and no PCs. Now the world as a whole produces 160 PCs and 50 desks.

Before trade occurs, U.S. consumers are willing to exchange as many as three PCs for each desk, while Chinese consumers are willing to exchange as few as two PCs for each desk, given their labor productivity, respectively. Therefore, the price of a desk acceptable to both U.S. and Chinese consumers should be somewhere between two and three PCs. Let us assume that the mutually acceptable price, or **commodity**

EXHIBIT 1-3
COMPARATIVE ADVANTAGE AT WORK

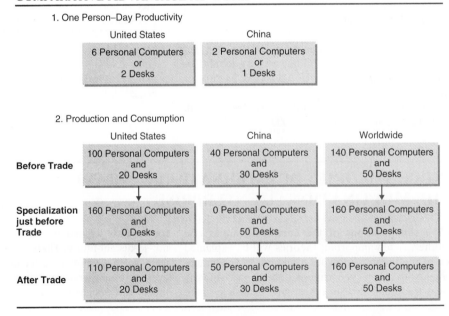

1. One Person–Day Productivity

	United States	China
	6 Personal Computers or 2 Desks	2 Personal Computers or 1 Desks

2. Production and Consumption

	United States	China	Worldwide
Before Trade	100 Personal Computers and 20 Desks	40 Personal Computers and 30 Desks	140 Personal Computers and 50 Desks
Specialization just before Trade	160 Personal Computers and 0 Desks	0 Personal Computers and 50 Desks	160 Personal Computers and 50 Desks
After Trade	110 Personal Computers and 20 Desks	50 Personal Computers and 30 Desks	160 Personal Computers and 50 Desks

terms of trade (a price of one good in terms of another), is 2.5 PCs per desk. Now let the United States and China engage in trade at the commodity terms of trade of 2.5 PCs per desk. To simplify our argument, further assume that the United States and China consume the same number of desks after trade as they did before trade, that is, 20 desks and 30 desks, respectively. In other words, the United States has to import 20 desks from China in exchange for 50 PCs (20 desks times a price of a desk in terms of PCs), which are exported to China from the United States. As a result of trade, the United States consumes 110 PCs and 20 desks, while China consumes 50 PCs and 30 desks. Given the same amount of labor resources, both countries respectively consume 10 more PCs while consuming the same number of desks. Obviously, specialization and trade have benefited both countries.

In reality, we rarely exchange one product for another. We use foreign exchange instead. Let us assume that the price of a desk is $900 in the United States and 6,300 yuan in China. Based on the labor productivity in the two countries, the price of a PC should be $300 (at a rate of one-third of a desk per PC) in the United States and 3,150 yuan (at a rate of one-half desk per PC) in China. As we indicated earlier, U.S. consumers are willing to exchange as many as three PCs for each desk worth $900 in the United States. Three PCs in China are worth 9,450 yuan. Therefore, U.S. consumers are willing to pay as much as 9,450 yuan to import a $900 desk from China. Similarly, Chinese consumers are willing to import a minimum of two PCs (worth 6,300 yuan in China) for each desk they produce (worth $900 in the United States). Therefore, the mutually acceptable exchange rate should be:

$$6,300 \text{ yuan} \leq \$900 \leq 9,450 \text{ yuan},$$

$$\text{or } 7.0 \text{ yuan} \leq \$1 \leq 10.5 \text{ yuan}.$$

An actual exchange rate also will be affected by consumer demands and money supply situations in the two countries. Nonetheless, it is clear that exchange rates are primarily determined by international trade.

From this simple exercise, we can make a few general statements or principles of international trade.

Principle 1. Countries benefit from international trade.

Principle 2. International trade increases worldwide production by specialization.

Principle 3. Exchange rates are determined primarily by traded goods.

By now you might have wondered why U.S. workers are more productive than Chinese workers. So far we have assumed that labor is the only input in economic production. In reality, we do not produce anything with manual labor alone. We use machinery, computers, and other capital equipment (capital for short) to help us produce efficiently. In other words, our implicit assumption was that the United States has more abundant capital relative to labor than China does. Naturally, the more capital we have relative to our labor stock, the less expensive a unit of capital should be relative to a unit of labor. The less expensive a unit of capital relative to a unit of labor, the more capital we tend to use and specialize in industry that requires a large amount of capital. In other words, the capital: labor endowment ratio affects what type of industry a country tends to specialize in. In general, a capital-abundant country (e.g., the United States) tends to specialize in capital-intensive industry and export capital-intensive products (personal computers) and import labor-intensive products (desks). Conversely, a labor-abundant country (China) tends to specialize in labor-intensive industry and export labor-intensive products (desks), and import capital-intensive products (personal computers). This refined argument is known as the **factor endowment theory** of comparative advantage.

The factor endowment theory can be generalized a bit further. For example, the United States is abundant not only with capital but also abundant with a highly educated (i.e., skilled) labor force. Therefore, it is easy to predict that the United States has comparative advantage in skill-intensive industries such as computers and biotechnology and exports a lot of computers and genetically engineered ethical drugs around the world, and it imports manual labor-intensive products such as textiles and shoes from labor-abundant countries such as China and Brazil. Global Perspective 1-4 clearly shows that

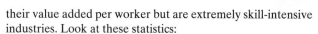

GLOBAL PERSPECTIVE 1-4

It is correct to say that the best way to improve living standards is to encourage investment in sophisticated industries like computers and aerospace. Is it correct to say that the best way to improve living standards is to encourage investment in industries that provide high value added per worker? The real high-value industries in the United States are extremely capital-intensive sectors such as cigarettes and oil refining. High-tech sectors that everyone imagines are the keys to the future, such as aircraft and electronics, are only average in

their value added per worker but are extremely skill-intensive industries. Look at these statistics:

Value Added per Worker	Thousands
Cigarettes	$823
Petroleum refining	270
Automobile	112
Tires and inner tubes	101
Aerospace	86
Electronics	74
All manufacturing	73

Source: Adapted from Paul Krugman, "Competitiveness: Does It Matter?" *Fortune,* March 7, 1994, pp. 109–15.

labor productivity alone shows a very erroneous impression of industry competitiveness.

Now you might have begun wondering how comparative advantage arguments will help businesspeople in the real world. Suppose that you work as a strategic planner for Nike. Shoe manufacturing is extremely labor intensive, while shoe designing is becoming increasingly hi-tech (i.e., skill intensive). The United States is a relatively skill-abundant and labor-scarce country. Therefore, the country has a comparative advantage in skill-intensive operations but has a comparative disadvantage in labor-intensive operations. There are two ways to use your knowledge of comparative advantage arguments. First, it is easy to predict where competition comes from. Companies from countries such as China and Brazil will have a comparative advantage in shoe manufacturing over Nike in the United States. Second, you can advise Nike to establish shoe-manufacturing plants in labor-abundant countries instead of in the labor-scarce United States. As mentioned, shoe designing has become increasingly hi-tech, involving computer-aided designing and development of light, shock-absorbent material, which requires an extremely high level of expertise. Therefore, based on the comparative advantage argument, you suggest that product designing and development be done in the United States, where required expertise is relatively abundant. Indeed, that is what Nike does as a result of global competitive pressure, and it has exploited various countries' comparative advantage to its advantage (no pun intended). Nike has product designing, development, and special material development conducted in the United States and has manufacturing operations in labor-abundant countries such as China and Brazil.

The comparative advantage theory is useful in explaining interindustry trade, say computers and desks, between countries that have very different factor endowments. It suggests efficient allocation of limited resources across national boundaries by specialization and trade but hardly explains business competition because computer manufacturers and desk manufacturers do not compete directly. Furthermore, this theory fails to explain the expansion of trade among the industrialized countries with similar factor endowments. Trade among the 20 or so industrialized countries now constitutes almost 60 percent of world trade, and much of it is intraindustry in nature. In other words, similar products are differentiated either physically or only in the customers' minds and traded across countries. Thus, BMW exports its sports cars to Japan while Honda exports its competing models to Germany. BMW and Honda compete directly within the same automobile industry. This type of intraindustry competition cannot be explained by comparative advantage theory.

International Product Cycle Theory.

When business practitioners think of competition, they usually refer to intraindustry competition. Why and how does competition tend to evolve over time and across national boundaries in the same industry? Then how does a company develop its marketing strategy in the presence of competitors at home and abroad? **International product cycle theory** addresses all of these questions.

Several speculations have been made.[61] First, a large domestic market such as that in the United States makes it possible for U.S companies to enjoy **economies of scale** in mass production and mass marketing, enabling them to become lower-cost producers than their competition in foreign countries. Therefore, those low-cost producers can market their products in foreign markets and still remain profitable. In addition, an **economies of scope** argument augments an economies of scale argument. Companies from a small country can still enjoy economies of scale in production and marketing by extending their business scope beyond their national boundary. For example, Nestlé, a Swiss food company, can enjoy economies of scale by considering European, U.S., and Japanese markets together as its primary market. Second, technological innovation can provide an innovative company a competitive advantage, or **technological gap,** over its competitors both at home and abroad. Until competitors learn about and imitate the innovation, the original innovator company enjoys a temporary monopoly power around the world. Therefore, it is technological innovators that tend to market new products abroad. Third, it is generally the per capita income level that determines consumers' **preference similarity,** or consumption patterns, regardless of nationality. Preference similarity explains why intraindustry trade has grown tremendously among the industrialized countries with similar income levels.

Combining these forces with the earlier comparative advantage theory, international product cycle theory was developed in the 1960s and 1970s to explain a realistic, dynamic change in international competition over time and place.[62] This comprehensive theory describes the relationship between trade and investment over the product life cycle.

One of the key underlying assumptions in the international product cycle theory is that "necessity is the mother of invention." In the United States, where personal incomes and labor costs were the highest in the world particularly in the 1960s and 1970s, consumers desired products that would save their labor and time and satisfy materialistic needs. Historically, U.S. companies developed and introduced many products that were labor and time saving or responded to high-income consumer needs, including dishwashers, microwave ovens, automatic washers and dryers, personal computers, and so on. Similarly, companies in Western Europe tend to innovate on material- and capital-saving products and processes to meet their local consumers' needs and lifestyle orientation. Small and no-frill automobiles and recyclable products are such examples. Japanese companies stress products that conserve not only material and capital but also space to address their

[61]Mordechai E. Kreinin, *International Economics: A Policy Approach,* 5th ed. (New York: Harcourt Brace Jovanovich, 1987), pp. 276–78.

[62]See, for example, Raymond Vernon, "International Investment and International Trade in the Product Cycle," *Quarterly Journal of Economics,* 80 (May 1966), pp. 190–207; "The Location of Economic Activity," *Economic Analysis and the Multinational Enterprise,* John H. Dunning, ed. (London: George Allen and Unwin, 1974), pp. 89–114; and "The Product Cycle Hypothesis in a New International Environment," Oxford *Bulletin of Economics and Statistics,* 41 (November 1979), pp. 255–67.

[63]Vernon, 1979. (see 62)

EXHIBIT 1-4
INTERNATIONAL PRODUCT CYCLE

	Introduction	*Growth*	*Maturity*	*Decline*
Demand structure	Nature of demand not well understood Consumers willing to pay premium price for a new product	Price competition begins Product standard emerging	Competition based on price and product differentiation	Mostly price competition
Production	Short runs, rapidly changing techniques Dependent on skilled labor	Mass production	Long runs with stable techniques Capital intensive	Long runs with stable techniques Lowest cost production needed either by capital intensive production or by massive use of inexpensive labor
Innovator company marketing strategy	Sales mostly to home-country (e.g., U.S.) consumers Some exported to other developed countries (e.g., Europe and Japan)	Increased exports to the other developed countries (e.g., Europe and Japan)	Innovator company (e.g., U.S.) begins production in Europe and Japan to protect its foreign competition	Innovator company (U.S.) may begin production in developing countries
International competition	A few competitors at home (e.g., U.S.)	Competitors in developed countries (e.g., Europe and Japan) begin production for their domestic markets They also begin exporting to the United States	European and Japanese companies increase exports to the United States They begin exporting to developing countries	European and Japanese competitors may begin production in developing countries Competitors from developing countries also begin exporting to the world

Source: Expanded on Louis T. Wells Jr., "International Trade: The Product Life Cycle Approach," in Reed Moyer, ed., *International Business: Issues and Concepts* (New York: Wiley, 1984), pp. 5–22.

local consumers' acute concern about space limitation. Therefore, Japanese companies excel in developing and marketing small energy-efficient products of all kinds.[63]

International product cycle theory suggests that new products are developed primarily to address the needs of the local consumers, only to be demanded later by foreign consumers who have similar needs with a similar purchasing power. As the nature of new products and their manufacturing processes becomes widely disseminated over time, the products eventually become mass-produced standard products around the world. At that point, the products' cost competitiveness becomes a determinant of success and failure in global competition. Your knowledge of comparative advantage theory helps your company identify where strong low-cost competitors tend to appear and how the company should plan production locations.

As presented in Exhibit 1-4, the pattern of evolution of the production and marketing process explained in the international product cycle consists of four stages: introduction, growth, maturity, and decline. Let us explain the international

product cycle from a U.S. point of view. It is to be remembered, however, that different kinds of product innovations also occur in countries (mostly developed) other than the United States. If so, a similar evolutionary pattern of development will begin from those other industrialized countries.

In the *introductory stage,* a U.S. company innovates on a new product to meet domestic consumers' needs in the U.S. market. A few other U.S. companies may introduce the same product. At this stage, competition is mostly domestic among U.S. companies. Some of those companies may begin exporting the product to a few European countries and Japan where they can find willing buyers similar to U.S. consumers. Product standards are not likely to be established yet. As a result, competing product models or specifications may exist on the market. Prices tend to be high. In the *growth stage,* product standards emerge and mass production becomes feasible. Lower prices spawn price competition. U.S. companies increase exports to Europe and Japan as those foreign markets expand. However, European and Japanese companies also begin producing the product in their own local markets and even begin exporting it to the United States. In the *maturity stage,* many U.S. and foreign companies vie for market share in the international markets. They try to lower prices and differentiate their products to outbid their competition. U.S. companies that have carved out market share in Europe and Japan by exporting decide to make a direct investment in production in those markets to protect their market position there. U.S. and foreign companies also begin to export to developing countries because more consumers in those developing countries can afford the product as its price falls. Then, in the *decline stage,* companies in the developing countries also begin producing the product and marketing it in the rest of the world. U.S., European, and Japanese companies may also begin locating their manufacturing plants in those developing countries to take advantage of inexpensive labor. The United States eventually begins to import what was once a U.S. innovation.

The international product cycle argument holds true as long as we can assume that innovator companies are not informed about conditions in foreign markets, whether in other industrialized countries or in the developing world. As we amply indicated in the body of this chapter, such an assumption has become very iffy. Nor can it be safely assumed that U.S. companies are exposed to a very different home environment from European and Japanese companies. Indeed, the differences among the industrialized countries are reduced to trivial dimensions. Seeking to exploit global scale economies, an increasing number of companies are likely to establish various plants in both developed countries and developing countries and to crosshaul between plants for the manufacture of final products. As an explanation of international business behavior, international product cycle theory has limited explanatory power. It does describe the initial international expansion (exporting followed by direct investment) of many companies, but the mature globe-trotting companies of today have succeeded in developing a number of other strategies for surviving in global competition.

Internalization/Transaction Cost Theory. Now that many companies have established plants in various countries, they have to manage their corporate activities across national boundaries. Those companies are conventionally called *multinational companies* (MNCs). It is inherently much more complex and difficult to manage corporate activities and market products across national boundaries rather than from a domestic base. Then why do those MNCs invest in foreign manufacturing and marketing operations instead of just exporting from their home base? International product cycle theory explains that companies invest abroad reactively when their foreign market positions are threatened by local competitors. Thus, the primary objective of foreign direct investment for the exporting companies is to keep their market positions from being eroded. Are there any proactive reasons for companies to invest overseas?

To address this issue, a new strand of theory has been developed. It is known as **internalization** or **transaction cost theory.** Any company has some proprietary expertise, that makes it different from its competitors. Without such expertise no company can sustain its competitive advantage. Such expertise may be reflected in a new product, unique product design, efficient production technique, or even brand image

itself. As in the international product cycle argument, a company's expertise may eventually become common knowledge as a result of competitors copying it or reverse engineering its product. Therefore, it is sometimes to an innovator company's advantage to keep its expertise to itself as long as possible in order to maximize the economic value of the expertise. A company's unique expertise is just like any information. Once information is let out, it becomes a "public good"—and free.

In other words, the MNC can be considered an organization that uses its internal market to produce and distribute products in an efficient manner in situations where the true value of its expertise cannot be assessed in ordinary external business transactions. Generating expertise or knowledge requires the company to invest in research and development. In most circumstances, it is necessary for the company to overcome this appropriability problem by creating of a monopolistic internal market (i.e., internalization) when the knowledge advantage can be developed and explored in an optimal manner on a global basis.[64] The motive to internalize knowledge is generally strong when the company needs to invest in business assets (e.g., manufacturing and marketing infrastructure) that have few alternative uses, employs those assets frequently, and faces uncertainty in negotiating, monitoring, and enforcing a contract. Such a situation suggests a high level of transaction costs due to specific assets and contractual uncertainty involved.[65]

The company's expertise can be channeled through three routes to garner competitive advantage: appropriability regime, dominant design, and manufacturing/marketing ability.[66] **Appropriability regime** refers to aspects of the commercial environment that govern a company's ability to retain its technological advantage. It depends on the efficacy of legal mechanisms of protection, such as patents, copyrights, and trade secrets. However, in today's highly competitive market, legal means of protecting proprietary technology have become ineffective as new product innovations are relatively easily reverse engineered, improved on, and invented around by competitors without violating patents and other proprietary protections bestowed on them. It is widely recognized that the most effective ways of securing maximum returns from a new product innovation are through lead time and moving fast down the experience curve (i.e., quickly resorting to mass production).[67] Obviously, the value of owning technology has lessened drastically in recent years as the inventor company's temporary monopoly over its technology has shortened.

Dominant design is a narrow class of product designs that begins to emerge as a "standard" design. A company that

[64] Alan M. Rugman, ed., *New Theories of the Multinational Enterprise* (London: Croom Helm, 1982).

[65] Oliver E. Williamson, "The Economics of Organization: The Transaction Cost Approach," *American Journal of Sociology,* 87 (1981), pp. 548–77.

[66] David J. Teece, "Capturing Value from Technological Innovation: Integration, Strategic Partnering, and Licensing Decisions," in Bruce R. Guile and Harvey Brooks, eds., *Technology and Global Industry: Companies and Nations in the World Economy* (Washington, D.C.: National Academy Press), pp. 65–95.

[67] Richard C. Levin, Alvin K. Klevorick, Richard R. Nelson, and Sidney G. Winter, "Appropriating the Returns from Industrial Research and Development," *Brookings Papers on Economic Activity,* 3 (1987), pp. 783–831.

has won a dominant design status has an absolute competitive advantage over its competition. In an early stage of product development, many competing product designs exist. After considerable trial and error in the marketplace, a product standard tends to emerge. A good example is Sony's Betamax format and Matsushita's VHS format for VCRs. The Betamax format was technologically superior with better picture quality than the VHS format but could not play as long to record movies as the VHS could. Although the Sony system was introduced slightly earlier than the Matsushita system, the tape's capability to record movies turned out to be fatal to Sony as the VHS tape was increasingly used for home movie rental and home recording of movies. Thus, the VHS has emerged as the worldwide standard for videocassette recording.

Was it simply the act of the "invisible hand" in the marketplace? The answer is clearly no. Matsushita actively licensed its VHS technology to Sanyo, Sharp, and Toshiba for production and supplied VHS-format videocassette recorders to RCA, Magnavox, and GTE Sylvania for resale under their respective brand names.[68] When Philips introduced a cassette tape recorder, a similar active licensing strategy had been employed for a quick adoption as a dominant standard around the world. Despite various government hurdles to stall the Japanese domination of emerging HDTV technology, Sony is currently trying to make its format a standard by working its way into Hollywood movie studios. It is clear that a wide adoption of a new product around the world, whether autonomous or deliberated, seems to guarantee it a dominant design status.

Manufacturing and marketing ability is in almost all cases required for successful commercialization of a product innovation. The issue here is to what extent this ability is specialized to the development and commercialization of a new product. Indeed, many successful companies have highly committed their productive assets to closely related areas without diversifying into unrelated businesses. This commitment is crucial. Take semiconductor production, for example. A director at SEMATECH (a U.S. government-industry semiconductor manufacturing technology consortium established in Austin, Texas, to regain U.S. competitive edge in semiconductor manufacturing equipment from Japanese competition) admits that despite and because of a rapid technological turnover, any serious company wishing to compete on a state-of-the-art computer chip with the Japanese will have to invest a minimum of $1 billion in a semiconductor manufacturing equipment and facility. General Motors invested more than $5 billion for its Saturn project to compete with the Japanese in small car production and marketing. A massive retooling is also necessary for any significant upgrade in both industries. Furthermore, the software side of the manufacturing ability may be even more difficult to match because it involves such specialized operational aspects as just-in-time (JIT) manufacturing management, quality control, and components sourcing relationships. Regardless of nationality, those multinational companies that are successful in global markets tend to excel not only in product innovative ability but also in manufacturing and marketing competencies.[69] It is clear that innovative companies committed to manufacturing and marketing excellence will likely remain strong competitors in industry.

These three sources of competitive advantage are not independent of each other. Given the relative ease of learning about competitors' proprietary knowledge without violating patents and other legal protections, many companies resort to mass production and mass marketing to drive down the cost along the experience curve. To do so requires enormous investment in manufacturing capacity. As a result, the efficacy of an appropriability regime depends highly on investment in manufacturing and marketing ability. Similarly, a wide acceptance of a product is most likely necessary for the product to become a dominant design in the world for the product's next generation. Thus, mass production and marketing on a global scale are likely to be a necessary, if not sufficient, condition for a company to attain a dominant design status for its product.

It is apparent that patents, copyrights, and trade secrets are not necessarily optimal means of garnering competitive advantage unless they are strongly backed by strengths in innovative manufacturing and marketing on a global basis. Likewise, companies strong in manufacturing without innovative products also suffer from competitive disadvantage. In other words, it takes such an enormous investment to develop new products and to penetrate new markets that few companies can go it alone anymore. Thus, to compete with integrated global competitors, an increasing number of companies have entered into strategic alliances to complement their competitive weaknesses with their partner's competitive strengths.

[68]Richard S. Rosenbloom and Michael A. Cusumano, "Technological Pioneering and Competitive Advantage: The Birth of VCR Industry," *California Management Review,* 29 (Summer 1987), pp. 51–76.

[69]Masaaki Kotabe, "Corporate Product Policy and Innovative Behavior of European and Japanese Multinationals: An Empirical Investigation," *Journal of Marketing,* 54 (April 1990), pp. 19–33.

SUMMARY

Three theories that cast some insight into the workings of international business have been reviewed. These theories are not independent of each other. Rather, they supplement each other. Comparative advantage theory is useful when we think broadly about the nature of industrial development and international trade around the world. International product cycle theory helps explain why and how a company initially extends its market horizons abroad and how foreign competitors shape global competition over time and place. Internalization or transaction cost theory provides some answers to how to manage multinational operations in a very competitive world.

Other theories supplement our understanding of international business. However, they are beyond the scope of this textbook and are probably unnecessary. Now you can appreciate how international business has expanded in scope over time. With an understanding of these theories, we hope you can better understand the rest of the book.

KEY TERMS

Absolute advantage
Appropriability regime
Commodity terms of trade
Comparative advantage
Dominant design

Economies of scale
Economies of scope
Factor endowment theory
Internalization theory

International product cycle
   theory
Manufacturing and
   marketing ability
Preference similarity

Principles of international
   trade
Technological gap
Transaction cost theory

ECONOMIC ENVIRONMENT

 HAPTER OVERVIEW

1. INTERTWINED WORLD ECONOMY

2. COUNTRY COMPETITIVENESS

3. EMERGING ECONOMIES

4. EVOLUTION OF COOPERATIVE GLOBAL TRADE AGREEMENTS

5. INFORMATION TECHNOLOGY AND THE CHANGING NATURE OF COMPETITION

6. REGIONAL ECONOMIC ARRANGEMENTS

7. MULTINATIONAL CORPORATIONS

At no other time in economic history have countries been more economically interdependent than they are today. Although the second half of the 20th century had the highest ever sustained growth rates in **gross domestic product** (GDP) in history, the growth in international flows in goods and services (called *international trade*) has consistently surpassed the growth rate of the world economy. Simultaneously, the growth in international financial flows—which include foreign direct investment, portfolio investment, and trading in currencies—has achieved a life of its own. Thanks to trade liberalization heralded by the General Agreement on Tariffs and Trade (GATT) and the World Trade Organization (WTO), the GATT's successor, the barriers to international trade and financial flows keep getting lower. From 1990 to 2004, global GDP grew some 40 percent, while total global merchandise exports increased by almost 120 percent.[1]

However, the beginning of the 21st century was beset with a recessionary world economy. For example, growth in the value of U.S. trade decelerated throughout 2001. Western Europe's merchandise exports and imports values increased by about 2 percent during the same period. Overall, the year 2001 witnessed the first decline

---

[1]Computed from *World Trade Report 2005: Exploring the Link between Trade, Standards, and the WTO* (Geneva: World Trade Organization, 2005).

in the volume of world merchandise trade since 1982 and the first decrease in world merchandise output since 1991. On the other hand, the transition economies recorded an outstanding trade growth performance in an adverse global environment. A further strengthening of trade and investment links between the European Union and Central and Eastern Europe contributed largely to this outcome. Africa and the Middle East also expanded their imports despite a fall in prices of oil and other commodities in 2001. Overall, global GDP growth edged up only by about 1 percent due chiefly to a more resilient services sector.[2] Since then, however, the world economy has continued to recover. The world economy grew at 4 percent in 2004, the strongest annual growth rate in more than a decade. This economic recovery is largely credited to the improved economic situation in North America and Asia. Global merchandise trade rose by 9 percent in real terms in 2004, also the best annual growth rate since 2000.[3]

Expanding world markets are a key driving force for the 21st century economy. Although the severe slump in Asia in the late 1990s, the renewed financial crisis in South America, and the slump in the U.S. and European economies in 2001 point up the vulnerabilities to the global marketplace, the long-term trends of fast-rising trade and rising world incomes still remain in place.

Since the second half of the 1990s, there have been some strong antiglobalization movements for various reasons including economics, environmental concern, and U.S. cultural hegemony, among others. Let us focus just on economics here. Some in developed countries argue that globalization would result in increased competition from low-income countries, thus threatening to hold down wages, say, in the United States. However, real wages in the United States increased at a 1.3 percent annual rate in the 1990s, much faster than the 0.2 percent annual gain of the 1980s.[4]

Antiglobalization sentiment aside, and short of war, continued terrorism on the scale of the September 11, 2001 terrorist attacks in the United States, a bird flu epidemic, or market-closing, inward-turning policies, most countries in the 21st century are likely to keep pursuing globalization. The global annual trade in goods and services amounted to almost $11 trillion, or 27 percent of global GDP, in 2004.[5] World trade's share of GDP in 1980 was no more than 9 percent. As a consequence, even a firm that is operating in only one domestic market is not immune to the influence of economic activities external to that market. The net result of these factors has been the increased interdependence of countries and economies, increased competitiveness, and the concomitant need for firms to keep a constant watch on the international economic environment.

◆ ◆ ◆ ◆ ◆ ◆ ◆ ◆ INTERTWINED WORLD ECONOMY

There is no question that the global economy is becoming more intertwined. Countries are more interdependent of each other. For example, on August 7, 2002, to respond the economic chaos in South America that was triggered by the financial crisis in Argentina, the International Monetary Fund's announced a $30 billion financial rescue package for Brazil. The IMF action resonated through the global markets, the region, and Brazilian politics. It sent a jolt across global emerging markets, pushing various currencies higher as investors welcomed both the vote of confidence in Brazil and the broader implications of the loan announcement for emerging market assets.[6]

Despite the increasingly intertwined world economy, the United States is still relatively more insulated from the global economy than other nations. The United States imports about 80 percent more than it exports. In an $11.7 trillion economy in

[2]WTO News: 2002 Press Release, "Disappointing Trade Figures Underscore Importance of Accelerating Trade Talks," October 7, 2002, http://www.wto.org/, Accessed November 12, 2002.

[3]*World Trade Report 2005.*

[4]"Restating the '90s," *Economist,* April 1, 2002, pp. 51–58.

[5]*World Trade Report 2005.*

[6]"Lifelines for Brazil and Uruguay," *Economist,* August 10, 2002, pp. 33–34.

EXHIBIT 2-1

TOP 10 PURCHASERS OF U.S. EXPORTS AND SUPPLIERS OF U.S. IMPORTS
IN GOODS, 2004

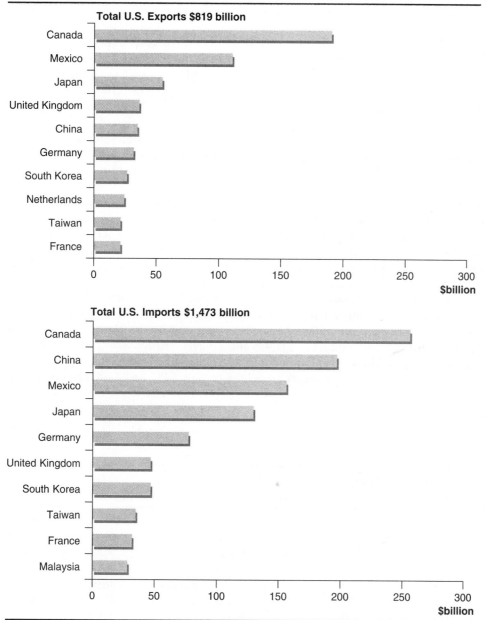

Source: U.S. Bureau of Economic
Analysis, International Economic
Accounts database, up to 2005.

2004, its trade deficit of $666 billion is about 6 percent of the GDP. About 88 percent
of what Americans consume is produced in the United States (measured as the ratio
of the country's imports to its GDP)—which implies that in the absence of a chain
reaction from abroad, the United States is relatively more insulated from external
shocks than Britain or Taiwan. The imports/GDP ratios for Britain and Thailand are
about 22 percent and 51 percent, respectively. Nonetheless, the U.S. economy, too, is
getting increasingly intertwined with the rest of the world economy. The dollar value of
international trade in goods and services in 2004 for the United States was $2.92 trillion.[7]
Most of the trade in goods was with a few major trading partners, as shown in Exhibit 2-1.

---

[7]Computed from trade statistics in Word Trade Organization, *International Trade Statistics 2005,* http://www.
wto.org/english/res_e/statis_e/its2005_e/its05_overview_e.htm, accessed February 20, 2006.

The importance of international trade and investment cannot be overemphasized for any country. In general, *the larger the country's domestic economy, the less dependent it tends to be on exports and imports relative to its GDP.*[8] Let's compute trade dependency ratios (total trade/GDP) using the available statistics. For the United States (GDP = $11.7 trillion in 2004), international trade in goods (sum of exports and imports) rose from 10 percent of the GDP in 1970 to 20 percent in 2004. For Japan (GDP = $4.6 trillion), with slightly less than half of the U.S. GDP, forms 22 percent in 2004. For Germany (GDP = $2.7 trillion or a little over half the GDP of Japan), trade forms about 60 percent of the GDP. For the Netherlands (GDP = $577 billion), trade value exceeds GDP for as high as 117 percent of GDP (due to re-export); and for Singapore (GDP = $107 billion), trade is more than 320 percent of its GDP![9] These trade statistics are relative to the country's GDP. In absolute dollar terms, however, a small relative trade percentage of a large economy still translates into large volumes of trade (see Exhibit 2-2). As shown in the last column for exports and imports in Exhibit 2-2, the per capita amount of exports and imports is another important statistic for marketing purposes because it represents, on average, how much involved or dependent each individual is on international trade.

For instance, individuals (consumers and companies) in the United States and Japan—the world's two largest economies—tend to be able to find domestic sources for their needs since their economies are diversified and extremely large. The U.S. per capita values of exports and imports are $2,795 and $5,206, respectively. For Japan, the values are relatively similar to those of the United States, with $4,445 and $3,570, respectively. On the other hand, individuals in smaller and rich economies tend to rely more heavily on international trade, as illustrated by the Netherlands with the per capita exports and imports of $21,975 and $19,589, respectively. Although China's overall exports and imports amounted to $593.3 billion and $561.2 billion, respectively, the per capita exports and imports amounted to only $457 and $432, respectively, in

EXHIBIT 2-2
LEADING EXPORTERS AND IMPORTERS IN WORLD TRADE IN GOODS, 2004

Rank	Exporters	Value ($billion)	Value per capita ($)	Rank	Importers	Value ($billion)	Value per capita ($)
1	Germany	912.3	11,071	1	United States	1525.5	5,206
2	United States	818.8	2,795	2	Germany	716.9	8,700
3	China	593.3	457	3	China	561.2	432
4	Japan	565.8	4,445	4	France	465.5	7,707
5	France	448.7	7,429	5	United Kingdom	463.5	7,687
6	Netherlands	358.2	21,975	6	Japan	454.5	3,570
7	Italy	349.2	6,010	7	Italy	351.0	6,041
8	United Kingdom	346.9	5,753	8	Netherlands	319.3	19,589
9	Canada	316.5	9,738	9	Belgium	285.5	27,718
10	Belgium	306.5	29,757	10	Canada	279.8	8,609

Source: Computed from trade statistics in World Trade Organization, *International Trade Statistics 2005*, http://www.wto.org/english/res_e/statis_e/ its2005_e/its05_overview_e.htm, accessed February 20, 2006; and population statistics in Central Intelligence Agency, *World Factbook 2004*, Washington, D.C.: U.S. Government, 2004.

[8]In other words, smaller economies are more susceptible than larger economies to various external shocks in the world economy, such as the recession in the Unite States that would import less, sudden oil price surge, and exchange rate fluctuations. Read "Restoring the Balance: The World Economy Is Still Growing Rapidly, but Is Also out of Kilter," *Economist*, September 24, 2005, p. 13.

[9]Based on GDP information from World Bank, Key Development and Statistics, http://web.worldbank.org/ WBSITE/EXTERNAL/DATASTATISTICS/0,contentMDK:20535285~menuPK:1390200~pagePK:64133150~ piPK:64133175~theSitePK:239419,00.html, and trade statistics from World Trade Organization, *International Trade Statistics 2005*, http://www.wto.org/english/res_e/statis_e/its2005_e/its05_overview_e.htm.

2004.[10] One implication of these figures is that the higher the per capita trade, the more closely intertwined is that country's economy with the rest of the world. Intertwining economies by the process of specialization due to international trade leads to job creation in both the exporting country and the importing country.

However, beyond the simple figure of trade as a rising percentage of a nation's GDP lies the more interesting question of what rising trade does to the economy of a nation. A nation that is a successful trader (i.e., it makes goods and services that other nations buy and it buys goods and services from other nations) displays a natural inclination to be competitive in the world market. The threat of a possible foreign competitor is a powerful incentive for firms and nations to invest in technology and markets in order to remain competitive. Also, apart from trade flows, foreign direct investment, portfolio investment, and daily financial flows in the international money markets profoundly influence the economies of countries that may be seemingly completely separate.

Foreign direct investment—which means investment in manufacturing and service facilities in a foreign country with an intention to engage actively in managing them—is another facet of the increasing integration of national economies. As shown in Exhibit 2-3, the overall world inflow of foreign direct investment (FDI) increased in the last two decades 25 times fold and in 2000, the inflow of FDI reached a record high of $1.39 trillion. In 2000, developed countries represented more than three-quarters of world FDI inflow, with developing countries reaching only $249 billion in the same year. However, global inflows of FDI declined three years in a row from 2001 to 2003 before picking up in 2004, which was prompted again by a fall in FDI inflows to developed countries. In particular, the FDI inflows to the United States fell more than 50 percent during this period due primarily to the aftermath of the September 11, 2001, terrorist attacks but has picked up again since. Only developing countries—most of them from Asia, Africa and Pacific—witnessed a relatively consistent increase.[11]

Two things should be noted. In the past, foreign direct investment was considered as an alternative to exports to avoid tariff barriers. However, these days, foreign direct

Foreign Direct Investment

EXHIBIT 2-3
FOREIGN DIRECT INVESTMENT INFLOWS, 1980-2004

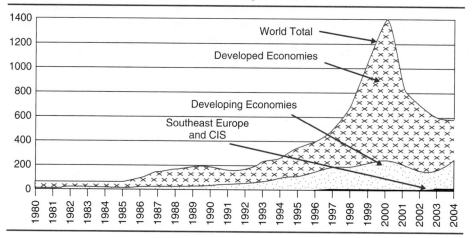

Source: UNCTAD, FDI/TNC database, www.unctad.org/fdistatistics). Note: CIS = Commonwealth of Independent States (Russia, Central Asia, and Caucasus states).

---

[10]It is to be noted that although China's per capita exports and imports are much smaller than those in the developed economies, they both increased as much as 60 percent from 2001 to 2004. The rapid rise of the Chinese economy is clearly visible.

[11]United Nations Conference on Trade and Development, *World Investment Report 2005* (Geneva: United Nations, 2005).

investment and international trade have become complementary.[12] For example, Dell Computer uses a factory in Ireland to supply personal computers in Europe instead of exporting from Austin, Texas. Similarly, Honda, a Japanese automaker with a major factory in Marysville, Ohio, is the largest exporter of automobiles from the United States. As firms invest in manufacturing and distribution facilities outside their home countries to expand into new markets around the world, they have added to the stock of foreign direct investment. Second, although not shown in the exhibit, the composition of FDI has shifted from manufacturing to services in all regions. FDI in services increased from being one-quarter of the world FDI stock in 1970s to about 60 percent of the world FDI in the early 2000s. FDI inflows in services were valued at some $500 billion during the period 2001–2002. Most notably, FDI outflows in services are no longer dominated by firms from the United States. By 2002, Japan and the European Union (EU) had emerged as significant sources and developing countries' outward FDI in services sectors also began to grow evidently from the 1990s.

The increase in foreign direct investment is also promoted by efforts of many national governments to woo multinationals and by the leverage that the governments of large potential markets such as China and India have in granting access to multi-nationals. For example, in 2002, China's FDI inflow reached $53 billion. Meanwhile, China gradually became a source of FDI by contributing to an accumulated book value of at least $35 billion of outward FDI at the end of 2002.[13] Sometimes trade friction can also promote foreign direct investment. Investment in the United States by Japanese companies is, to an extent, a function of the trade imbalances between the two nations and by the consequent pressure applied by the U.S. government on Japan to do something to reduce the bilateral trade deficit. Because most of the U.S. trade deficit with Japan is attributed to Japanese cars exported from Japan, Japanese automakers, such as Honda, Toyota, Nissan, and Mitsubishi, have expanded their local production by setting up production facilities in the United States. In 1986, Japanese automakers exported 3.43 million cars from Japan and assembled only 0.62 million cars in the United States. By 1992, the number of exported cars equaled the number of U.S.-built Japanese cars at 1.7 million cars each. Since then, Japanese automakers have manufactured more cars in the United States than they have exported from Japan. In 1997, they produced 2.31 million cars in the United States and imported 1.27 million cars from Japan. During the period 1986–1999, Japanese automakers also increased their purchases of U.S.-made components almost 13 times from $2.5 billion in 1986 to 31.9 billion in 1999.[14] Today Toyota has 46 plants in 26 countries. It has design centers in California and in France on the Côte d'Azur and its engineering centers located in the Detroit area and in Belgium and Thailand.[15] This localization strategy reduced Japanese automakers' vulnerability to political retaliation by the United States under the Super 301 laws of the **Omnibus Trade and Competitiveness Act of 1988.**

Portfolio Investment

An additional facet to the rising integration of economies has to do with **portfolio investment** (or **indirect investment**) in foreign countries and with money flows in the international financial markets. *Portfolio investment* refers to investments in foreign countries that can be withdrawn at short notice, such as investment in foreign stocks and bonds. In the international financial markets, the borders between nations have, for all practical purposes, disappeared.[16] The enormous amounts of money traded on a daily basis have assumed a life of their own. When trading in foreign currencies began, it was as an adjunct transaction to an international trade transaction in goods

---

[12]"Trade by Any Other Name," *Economist,* October 3, 1998, pp. 10–14.

[13]*World Investment Report 2005.*

[14]"JAMA Members Set New Records in Their Purchase of U.S.-Made Auto Part," Japan Auto Trends, *Today's JAMA,* March 2000, http://www.jamaserv.jama.or.jp/e_press/index.html, accessed October 30, 2002.

[15]"The Car Company in Front," *Economist,* January 27, 2005, pp. 65–67.

[16]Kenichi Ohmae, *The Borderless World* (New York: Harper Collins Books, 1990).

and services—banks and firms bought and sold currencies to complete the export or import transaction or to hedge the exposure to fluctuations in the exchange rates in the currencies of interest in the trade transaction. However, in today's international financial markets, traders trade currencies most of the time without an underlying trade transaction. They trade on the accounts of the banks and financial institutions they work for, mostly on the basis of daily news on inflation rates, interest rates, political events, stock and bond market movements, commodity supplies and demand, and so on. As mentioned earlier, the weekly volume of international trade in currencies exceeds the annual value of the trade in goods and services.

The effect of this proverbial tail wagging the dog is that all nations with even partially convertible currencies are exposed to the fluctuations in the currency markets. A rise in the value of the local currency due to these daily flows vis-à-vis other currencies makes exports more expensive (at least in the short run) and can add to the trade deficit or reduce the trade surplus. A rising currency value also deters foreign investment in the country and encourages outflow of investment.[17] It may also encourage a decrease in the interest rates in the country if the central bank of that country wants to maintain the currency exchange rate and a decrease in the interest rate would spur local investment. An interesting example is the Mexican meltdown in early 1995 and the massive devaluation of the peso, which was exacerbated by the withdrawal of money by foreign investors. More recently, the massive depreciation of many Asian currencies in the period 1997–1999, known as the *Asian financial crisis,* is also an instance of the influence of these short-term movements of money.[18] Implications of the Asian financial crisis are explained in detail in Chapter 3. Unfortunately, the influences of these short-term money flows are today far more powerful determinants of exchange rates than an investment by a Japanese or German automaker.

Another example involves Brazil, which was a largely protected market until 1995. Liberalization is on the way as a result of the formation in 1994 of the Southern Common Market (Mercado Común del Sur, or MERCOSUR) (to be explained later in the chapter). Since the debt crisis of 1982, Brazil had suffered a chronic hyperinflation that ruined its economy and competitiveness. Brazil's new currency, the real, was launched in 1994 both as the instrument and as the symbol of a huge effort for Brazil to catch up with the developed world. Financial markets first attacked the Brazilian real in March 1995 in the wake of Mexico's peso devaluation. Brazil responded by adopting a pegged exchange rate, under which the real devalued by 7.5 percent a year against the U.S. dollar. Then the Asian financial crisis and the crash of many Asian currencies (with as much as 75 percent in the case of Indonesian currency, rupiah, in a matter of a few months) in 1998 reverberated in Brazil and Mexico because portfolio investors started viewing all emerging markets with a jaundiced eye. Worse yet, in 2002, Argentina caused another financial crisis in Latin America, triggered by one of the largest government debt defaults ever. The Brazilian real was under pressure, falling from R1/US$ in July 1994 to R3.63/US$ in October 2002—a whopping 72 percent depreciation since its introduction. The central bank had to sell dollars and buy *real* to shore up its value. This led to a credit crunch, causing a slowdown in export growth only to be temporarily stabilized by the International Monetary Fund's $30 billion rescue loan to Brazil in 2002.[19] There were also adverse effects on the Indian stock markets. The point is that, at least in the short run, these daily international flows of money have dealt a blow to the notion of economic independence and nationalism.

---

[17]"Beware of Hot Money," *Business Week,* April 4, 2005, pp. 52–53.

[18]Masaaki Kotabe, "The Four Faces of the Asian Financial Crisis: How to Cope with the Southeast Asia Problem, the Japan Problem, the Korea Problem, and the China Problem," *Journal of International Management,* 4 (1), 1998, 1S–6S.

[19]"A Matter of Faith—Will a Big Bail-Out Led by the IMF Allow Brazil to Avoid Defaulting?" *Economist,* August 15, 2002; the Brazilian economy has since stabilized and started growing again, which is reflected in the real's appreciation of the *real* to R2.28/US$ as of late 2005.

◆ ◆ ◆ ◆ ◆ ◆ ◆ ◆   COUNTRY COMPETITIVENESS

Country competitiveness refers to a country's productiveness, which is represented by its firms' domestic and international productive capacity. Human, natural, and capital resources of a country primarily shape the nature of corporate productive capacity in the world and, thus, the nature of international business. As explained in the Appendix to Chapter 1, a country's relative endowment in those resources shapes its competitiveness.

Changing Country Competitiveness

Country competitiveness is not a fixed thing. The dominant feature of the global economy is the rapid change in the relative status of various countries' economic output. In 1830, China and India alone accounted for about 60 percent of the manufactured output of the world. Since then, the share of the world manufacturing output produced by the 20 or so countries that are today known as the rich industrial economies moved from about 30 percent in 1830 to almost 80 percent by 1913.[20] In the 1980s, the U.S. economy was characterized as "floundering" or even "declining," and many pundits predicted that Asia, led by Japan, would become the leading regional economy in the 21st century. Then the 1997–1999 Asian financial crisis changed the economic milieu of the world (to be explained in detail in Chapter 3). Since the September 11th, 2001, terrorist attacks, the U.S. economy has grown faster than that of any other developed countries at an annual rate of 3 to 4 percent. However, even the U.S. economic growth rate pales in comparison to that of China and India, two leading emerging economic powers in the last decade or so. China and India have grown at an annual rate of 7 to 10 percent and 4 to 7 percent, respectively, since the dawn of the 21st century.[21] Obviously, a decade is a long time in the ever-changing world economy, and, indeed, no single country has sustained its economic performance continuously.

Human Resources and Technology

Although wholesale generalizations should not be made, the role of human resources has become increasingly important as a primary determinant of industry and country competitiveness as the level of technology has advanced. As shown in Exhibit 2-4, World Economic Forum's *Global Competitiveness Report* placed two Asian Tigers (Taiwan and Singapore) among the world's top 10 economies along with Finland,

EXHIBIT 2-4
GLOBAL COMPETITIVENESS RANKING

Country	Score	Rank	Country	Score	Rank	Country	Score	Rank	Country	Score	Rank
Finland	5.94	1	Netherlands	5.21	11	Austria	4.95	21	Belgium	4.63	31
United States	5.81	2	Japan	5.18	12	Portugal	4.91	22	Slovenia	4.59	32
Sweden	5.65	3	United Kingdom	5.11	13	Chile	4.91	23	Kuwait	4.58	33
Denmark	5.65	4	Canada	5.1	14	Malaysia	4.9	24	Cyprus	4.54	34
Taiwan	5.58	5	Germany	5.1	15	Luxembourg	4.9	25	Malta	4.54	35
Singapore	5.48	6	New Zealand	5.09	16	Ireland	4.86	26	Thailand	4.5	36
Iceland	5.48	7	South Korea	5.07	17	Israel	4.84	27	Bahrain	4.48	37
Switzerland	5.46	8	United Arab Emirates	4.99	18	Hong Kong	4.83	28	Czech Republic	4.42	38
Norway	5.4	9	Qatar	4.97	19	Spain	4.8	29	Hungary	4.38	39
Australia	5.21	10	Estonia	4.95	20	France	4.78	30	Tunisia	4.32	40

Source: World Economic Forum, *Global Competitiveness Report 2005–2006,* http://www.weforum.org/.

---

[20] Paul Bairoch, "International Industrialization Levels from 1750 to 1980," *Journal of European Economic History,* 11 (1982), pp. 36–54.

[21] United Nations Conference on Trade and Development, *Trade and Development Report 2005.*

the United States, Sweden, Denmark, Iceland, Switzerland, Norway, and Australia. These two Asian countries have virtually no natural resources to rely on for building their competitiveness. Clearly, human resources are crucial for the long-term economic vitality of natural resource-poor countries. All the top 10-ranked countries, with the exception of the United States and Canada, are scarce in natural resources.

In this country competitiveness report in 2005 to 2006, 5 of the top 10 countries are Nordic countries, led by Finland. Nordic countries share a number of characteristics that make them extremely competitive, such as very healthy macroeconomic environments and highly transparent and efficient public institutions with general agreement within society on the spending priorities to be met by the government budget. While the business communities in the Nordic countries point to high tax rates as a potential problem area, there is no evidence that these rates are adversely affecting the ability of these countries to compete effectively in world markets or to provide their respective populations some of the highest standards of living in the world. Indeed, the high levels of government tax revenue have delivered world-class educational establishments, an extensive safety net, and a highly motivated and skilled labor force.[22]

Although the United States ranked second after Finland, the prognosis for the future U.S. competitiveness might not be as good as it currently appears. Seemingly contradictory to the current U.S. situation, the U.S. Council on Competitiveness[23] reported in 1999 that the U.S. technological competitiveness had peaked in 1985 and that the United States may be living off its historical assets that are not being renewed (see Exhibit 2-5 showing the change in the innovative capability of leading countries

EXHIBIT 2-5
CHANGE IN COUNTRY INNOVATIVENESS:
A KEY TO A COUNTRY'S LONG-TERM COMPETITIVENESS

Year Rank	1980	1986	1993	1995	1999	2005 (expected)
1	Switzerland	Switzerland	Switzerland	U.S.A.	Japan	Japan
2	U.S.A.	U.S.A.	Japan	Switzerland	Switzerland	Finland
3	Germany	Japan	U.S.A.	Japan	U.S.A.	Switzerland
4	Japan	Germany	Germany	Sweden	Sweden	Denmark
5	Sweden	Sweden	Sweden	Germany	Germany	Sweden
6	Canada	Canada	Denmark	Finland	Finland	U.S.A.
7	France	Finland	France	Denmark	Denmark	Germany
8	Netherlands	Netherlands	Canada	France	France	France
9	Finland	Norway	Finland	Canada	Norway	Norway
10	U.K.	France	Australia	Norway	Canada	Canada
11	Norway	Denmark	Netherlands	Netherlands	Australia	Australia
12	Denmark	U.K.	Norway	Australia	Netherlands	Austria
13	Austria	Australia	U.K.	Austria	Austria	Netherlands
14	Australia	Austria	Austria	U.K.	U.K.	U.K.
15	Italy	Italy	New Zealand	New Zealand	New Zealand	New Zealand
16	New Zealand	New Zealand	Italy	Italy	Italy	Spain
17	Spain	Spain	Spain	Spain	Spain	Italy

Source: Adapted from Michael E. Porter and Scott Stern, *The New Challenge to America's Prosperity: Findings from the Innovation Index,* Washington, D.C.: Council on Competitiveness, 1999, pp. 34–35.

[22]"Nordic Countries and East Asian Tigers Top the Rankings in the World Econo{-\break}mic Forum's 2005 Competitiveness Rankings," Press Release, World Economic Forum, http://www.weforum.org/site/homepublic.nsf/Content/Nordic+countries+and+East+Asian+tigers+top+the+rankings+in+the+World+Economic+Forum'+2005+competitiveness+rankings, accessed January 20, 2006.

[23]Michael E. Porter and Scott Stern, *The Challenge to America's Prosperity: Findings from the Innovation Index* (Washington, DC: Council on Competitiveness, 1999).

over the years). Although a more recent country innovativeness report is not available, this report clearly pointed to the rise of Finland as a technological powerhouse. Other conclusions include that although the United States and Switzerland had been the most innovative in the last three decades, other OECD nations have been increasingly catching up to the U.S. and Swiss levels. In particular, Denmark and Sweden have registered major gains in innovative capacity since the mid-1980s. Another interesting observation is that despite its economic slowdown in the 1990s, Japan has maintained its innovative capacity over the years without little sign of weakening. The recent strong recovery of the Japanese economy seems to underscore its technological strengths, among other things.[24] Finally, although not shown in Exhibit 2-5, Singapore, Taiwan, South Korea, India, Israel, and Ireland have upgraded their innovative capacity over the past decade, becoming new centers of innovative activity.[25]

One major lesson here is that we should not be misled by mass media coverage of the current economic situations of various countries. While mass media coverage is factual and near-term focused, it may inadvertently cloud our strategic thinking. In other words, the current stellar performance of the U.S. economy should not erroneously lull us into believing that U.S. companies are invincible in the global economy.[26] Information technology (IT) characterizes one of the most dynamic and turbulent industries today. As presented in Global Perspective 2-1, no one can be sure of the U.S. dominance even for the next decade.

◆ ◆ ◆ ◆ ◆ ◆ ◆ ◆ EMERGING ECONOMIES

Large economies and large trading partners have been located mostly in the **Triad Regions** of the world (North America, Western Europe, and Japan, collectively producing more than 80 percent of world GDP with 20 percent of the world's population) in much of the 20th century.[27] However, in the next 10 to 20 years, the greatest commercial opportunities are expected to be found increasingly in 10 **big emerging markets** (BEMs): the Chinese Economic Area (CEA: including China, Hong Kong region, and Taiwan), India, Commonwealth of Independent States (Russia, Central Asia, and Caucasus states), South Korea, Mexico, Brazil, Argentina, South Africa, Central European countries,[28] Turkey, and the Association of Southeast Asian Nations (ASEAN: including Indonesia, Brunei, Malaysia, Singapore, Thailand, the Philippines, and Vietnam). For instance, in the past 20 years, China's real annual GDP growth rate has averaged 9.5 percent a year while India's has been 5.7 percent, compared to the average 3 percent GDP growth in the United States. Accordingly, an increasing number of competitors are also expected to originate from those emerging economies. According to a trade report published by World Trade Organization in 2005,[29] the world's nine largest exporting countries accounted for almost half of the world trade in 2004: Germany ($915 billion), the United States ($619 billion), China ($593 billion), Japan ($565 billion), France ($451 billion), United Kingdom ($346 billion), Italy ($346 billion), Canada ($322 billion), and Mexico ($189 billion). A few notable recent changes attest to the globalization of the markets. First, Germany overtook the United States as the largest exporting country for the first time. Second, China surged to become the second largest exporting country, surpassing Japan. Third, Mexico has emerged as one of the major exporting countries. Clearly, the milieu of the world economy has changed significantly.

[24]"The Viagra Economy, A Survey of the World Economy," *Economist,* September 24, 2005, pp. 12–14; and "Japan: The Sun Also Rises," *Economist,* October 6, 2005, pp. 3–6.

[25]Porter and Stern, *The Challenge to America's Prosperity,"* p. 7.

[26]Paul Krugman, "America the Boastful," *Foreign Affairs,* 77 (May/June 1998), pp. 32–45.

[27]Lowell Bryan, *Race for the World: Strategies to Build A Great Global Firm,* (Boston, MA: Harvard Business School Press, 1999).

[28]Poland, Czech Republic, Slovakia, Slovenia, Hungary, Estonia, Latvia, Lithuania, Romania, and Bulgaria. See an excellent article, "The Rise of Central Europe," *Business Week,* December 12, 2005, pp. 50–56.

[29]*World Trade Report 2005.*

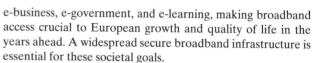

$\mathcal{G}$LOBAL PERSPECTIVE 2-1

INFORMATION TECHNOLOGY COMPETITIVENESS OF THE UNITED STATES, THE EUROPEAN UNION, JAPAN, AND BEYOND

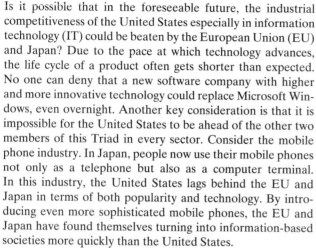

Is it possible that in the foreseeable future, the industrial competitiveness of the United States especially in information technology (IT) could be beaten by the European Union (EU) and Japan? Due to the pace at which technology advances, the life cycle of a product often gets shorter than expected. No one can deny that a new software company with higher and more innovative technology could replace Microsoft Windows, even overnight. Another key consideration is that it is impossible for the United States to be ahead of the other two members of this Triad in every sector. Consider the mobile phone industry. In Japan, people now use their mobile phones not only as a telephone but also as a computer terminal. In this industry, the United States lags behind the EU and Japan in terms of both popularity and technology. By introducing even more sophisticated mobile phones, the EU and Japan have found themselves turning into information-based societies more quickly than the United States.

The EU launched its ambitious plan, called *eEurope,* in 2002. It aims to develop modern public services and a dynamic environment for e-business through widespread availability of broadband access at competitive prices and a secure information infrastructure. Its primary goal is the development and delivery of services and applications such as e-health,

Sources: Thomas Bleha, "Down to the Wire," *Foreign Affairs,* 84 (May/June 2005), pp. 111–24; "Widespread and Affordable Broadband Access Is Essential to Realize the Potential of the Information Society," *eEurope,* http://europa.eu.int/information_society/eeurope/2005/all_about/broadband/index_en.htm, accessed December 15, 2005.

e-business, e-government, and e-learning, making broadband access crucial to European growth and quality of life in the years ahead. A widespread secure broadband infrastructure is essential for these societal goals.

The Japanese government has also launched a similar plan to realize an information-oriented society. For example, by May 2003, a higher percentage of homes in Japan than in the United States had broadband, and Japan had moved well beyond the basic connections still in use in the United States. Today, nearly all Japanese have access to "high-speed" broadband with an average connection speed 16 times faster than that in the United States—for only about $20 a month. Even faster "ultra-high-speed" broadband, which runs through fiber-optic cable, became available throughout Japan for $30 to $40 a month at the end of 2005. That is to say that nothing of Internet access through mobile phones, an area in which Japan is even further ahead of the United States.

It is now clear that Japan and its neighbors will lead the charge in high-speed broadband over the next several years. South Korea already has the world's highest percentage of broadband users, and in 2004 the absolute number of broadband users in urban China surpassed that in the United States. These countries' progress will have serious economic implications. By dislodging the United States from the lead it commanded not so long ago, Japan and its neighbors as well as Europe have positioned themselves to be the first states to reap the benefits of the broadband era: economic growth, increased productivity, technological innovation, and an improved quality of life.

As a result, over the next two decades, the markets that hold the greatest potential for dramatic increases in U.S. exports are not the traditional trading partners in Europe and Japan, which now account for the overwhelming bulk of the international trade of the United States but will be the BEMs. Already, there are signs that in the future, the biggest trade headache for the United States may not be Japan but China and India.[30] China's trade surplus with the United States ballooned from $86 billion in 2000 to $162 billion in 2004; it had already surpassed Japan's trade surplus position with the United States by 2000.[31] India has increasingly become a hotbed as sources of information technology (IT), communications, software development, and call centers, particularly for many U.S. multinationals. Russia is extremely rich in natural resources, including oil and natural gas, that are dwindling in the rest of the word, has gradually warmed up to international commerce, and will potentially become a major trading nation. Because these three leading emerging economies, among others, are likely to reshape the nature of international business in the next decade, we profile these countries here. (See Exhibit 2-6 for country profile.)

---

[30]The economic role of smaller emerging economies cannot be ignored. Read, for example, "Good Morning, Vietnam: Intel's Deal to Build a Factory is Likely to Spur More Western Investment," *Business Week,* March 13, 2006, pp. 50–51.

[31]"U.S. Presses China on Goods Piracy," *Wall Street Journal* May, 2, 2005.

EXHIBIT 2-6
COUNTRY PROFILE IN 2005

	China	India	Russia
Population	1,306 million	1,080 million	143 million
Population Growth Rate	.58%	1.4%	−.37%
GDP in current US$	$1,909.7 billion	$746.1 billion	$772.1 billion
GDP in current US$ based on purchasing power parity	$8.09 trillion	$3.60 trillion	$1.59 trillion
GDP per capita based on purchasing power parity	$6,193	$3,315	$11,209
GDP real growth rate	9.1%	6.2%	6.7%
Inflation rate	3.0%	3.9%	12.8%
Current account balance	$115.6 billion	−$13.5 billion	$101.8 billion
Current account balance/GDP	6.1%	−1.8%	13.2%

Source: Compiled from IMF statistics and U.S. Central Intelligence Agency, *The World Factbook 2005*, http://www.odci.gov/cia/publications/factbook/index.html.

China[32] ***Economy.*** The People's Republic of China (China) was founded in 1949 by the Chinese Communist Party. Starting in 1978, China's president introduced economic reforms to the country. Since then, China's leaders have pursued economic liberalization and sustainable economic growth alongside enduring communist political control. As a new member of the World Trade Organization (WTO) in 2001, China has become one of the world's emerging giants, along with India, Brazil, and Russia. Unlike other emerging economies, China has recently received much attention due to its greater participation in the global economy. China has a population of 1.3 billion people with its nominal GDP of US$1.9 trillion in 2005. However, according to the purchasing power parity-adjusted estimate, China's real purchasing power could now exceed US$8 trillion, while Japan's purchasing power is estimated at around US$4 trillion. The United States, as the largest economy, stands at a total purchasing power of about $12 trillion. In other words, in terms of real purchasing power, China could now rank as the second largest economy in the world after the United States.

However, China's purchasing power is not distributed evenly throughout the country. It is mainly concentrated in major cities, such as Shanghai, Beijing, Shenzhen, and Dalian. Consumers from the top 10 cities account for only 4 percent of the total population but represent 22.6 percent of the total purchasing power. Another phenomenon in China is the increasing income inequality. Generally, a large part of China's growing income has been represented by a small share of the population living in costal areas. In China, two-thirds of the population of 1.3 billion lives in the countryside or in rural areas without rural retirement pension and unemployment benefits. The impact of foreign direct investment (FDI) on the country's economic development has been recognized; however, most of it flows to the locations around the coastal areas with little impact on the inland areas. Even today, nearly 30 million Chinese people live below the poverty line, and the gap between China's richest and poorest is among the widest in Asia. The Chinese central government has even realized that raising living standards of the rural poor is essential to maintain the country's social stability. With growing economic development, the income gap widens from region to region. As a result, people in developed areas, such as the East Coast, gained higher income than those in developing and underdeveloped areas (inland China), thus

---

[32]This section draws from the following articles: "The Other Side of China's Success Story," *Financial Times*, January 19, 2003; "The Struggle of the Champions," *Economist*, January 6, 2005; "U.S. Presses China on Goods Piracy," *Wall Street Journal*, www.wsj.com, accessed May 2, 2005; "The Myth of China Inc.," *Economist*, September 1, 2005, "The Frugal Giant," *Economist*, September 22, 2005; and "A Billion Tough Sells," *Business Week*, March 20, 2006, pp. 44–45.

making the income disparity between coastal and inland as well as urban and rural areas and within regions more obvious.

Industry. China had no private companies in the 1970s. During the 1980s, the structure of China's industry changed fundamentally. After two decades of reform and privatization, roughly only one-third of China's economy is still controlled by the government through state-owned enterprises (SOEs), but they are concentrated in key sectors including defense and utilities. Although many of the biggest SOEs have publicly quoted subsidiaries on international stock markets, the government retains ultimate ownership. For example, the top 190 or so SOEs are directly controlled by the State Assets Supervision and Administration Commission (SASAC), which was set up in 2003 to restructure these often moribund firms. Unlike the Japanese government whose officials coordinated the country's domestic development before launching foreign expansion, Chinese firms are not guided by one single, controlling legislative body. Nevertheless, a study by the Organization for Economic Co-operation and Development (OECD) found that, in 2003, private companies in China accounted for 63 percent of business-sector output (which represents 94 percent of GDP). China has been developing formidable capabilities in technology production, and the entire nation is embracing a great leap forward in modern technology. Some automobile, steel, and telecommunication companies have reported revenue growth in excess of 30 percent.

For example, Haier, China's leading manufacturer of home appliances, has built a commanding domestic market share of 20 to 70 percent for most home appliances with offices in more than 100 countries and overseas revenues of over $1 billion. Recently, the company unsuccessfully attempted to make a bid for Maytag Corp to further extend its competitive advantage to foreign countries. Similarly, Whirlpool, a leading U.S. manufacturer of home appliances, has to face competition from Haier and Guangdong Kelon, two major Chinese competitors, whose technology is nearly as good as Whirlpool's but with lower prices and a better distribution channel. By 1997, Whirlpool had to close down its refrigerator and air conditioner plants and devote its microwave factory to exports. Now Whirlpool's only surviving washing machine factory makes appliances under contract for Kelon under Kelon's own brand—a reversal of the usual hierarchy between western and Chinese firms. Ericsson, Lucent, and other equipment makers also had to accept the reality of losing ground to China's domestic telecoms firms such as Huawei.

It is important to note that China is on its way to becoming the world's largest Internet community. The Central Intelligence Agency estimated that in 2004, China had 94 million Internet users. Fueling this tremendous growth of the Internet are younger consumers with a thirst for fun, knowledge, and communication with the outside world. The Internet facilitates prepurchase information searches, product comparisons, and sharing product experience with others. Chinese youths are becoming more pragmatic, educated, and cosmopolitan. eBay, for example, is adding about 1 million users per quarter, totaling 11.6 million registered users during three years' investment in China. In 2004, the e-commerce business in China entered a golden period, with transaction volume of online trading reaching 21.86 billion yuan (US$2.64 billion). Among the 94 million Internet users, more than 40 million people conducted transactions on the Internet in 2004. Without a doubt, with a 1.3 billion population, the Chinese market is inviting online businesses to achieve great prospects for years to come.

China is also challenged by its troublesome banking system, the lack of a transparent legal system, corruption, the risk of social and political conflicts, and severe environmental pollution. One major issue that international managers must manage in the growing market is corruption. According to Passau University's calculation on the Corruption Perception Index (CPI) for 2004, corruption issues cost productivity losses totaled a whopping $4 trillion, which is roughly 12 percent of the World's GDP. China is still one of the countries (ranked 77 out of 146 countries, with 146th being the most corrupt) that has a high CPI score.[33] Accordingly, China's relatively high corruption discourages FDI by a significant amount. Moreover, inexplicit regulatory burden in China also discourages investors from venturing into the promising market. After all, it is not easy to understand different China's legislative bodies, namely the central provincial, and municipal governments.

In addition to corruption and other factors, China's lack of intellectual property protection and weak enforcement of contracts are troublesome. Poor telecommunications, inadequate infrastructure, and the country's vast size compound the problem with intellectual property protection. Some domestic companies must fight with counterfeit goods as well as legitimate goods from famous Western companies. China is by far the world's leading producer of counterfeit goods, from up-scale designer-brand clothing to pirated films and books, to imitation consumer electronic and aircraft parts. Most Chinese buy pirated products, such as software, motion pictures, and music CDs because they are so much cheaper than their legitimate counterparts. For instance, pirated Microsoft Office software can cost as little as $1 on the black market in contrast to the legitimate software's cost of roughly the entire monthly income for most middle-class Chinese. The majority of counterfeit products is sold from mobile stores, so it is difficult for local governments to crack down on these illegal activities. It has been estimated that $16 billion worth of goods sold each year in China are counterfeit. This illegal market costs legitimate companies billions of dollars in lost sales annually. For example, Procter & Gamble has determined that it loses 10 to 15 percent of its revenue in China annually to counterfeit products. It appears that only those companies willing to bring their price closer to the black market price or offer differentiated services can secure a large market in the long run.[34]

Market.   In general, business in China is taking off, but its conduct is quite different from business in the West. Companies must meet the challenge of serving hard-to-reach, price-sensitive consumers who typically have more stringent requirements than their counterparts in the developed world. On the one hand, China has roughly 10 percent of the population, or 10 to 13 million consumers, who prefer luxury goods. Most of those consumers who prefer luxury brands are entrepreneurs and young professionals working for multinational firms with much higher salaries than the majority of people. With higher education and higher purchasing power, the young generations are brand and status conscious and consider luxury goods as personal achievements and high social status. As stated earlier, they live in major cities on the country's eastern coast, where luxury brands are considered prominent logos for the high-income clientele. Many luxury brands such as Armani, Prada, and Louis Vuitton have been introduced to the east coast of China in recent years, and business has been booming. According to Louis Vuitton, China is its fourth-largest market in terms of sales worldwide. No wonder many high-end firms label Chinese shoppers as the "new Japanese"—a potentially huge group of status-conscious, increasingly wealthy people hungry for brands and fanatical about spending.

On the other hand, with an average GDP per capita (based on purchasing power parity) of $6,200 in 2005, a majority of Chinese consumers are extremely price sensitive. Therefore, to attract both status-conscious and highly price-sensitive consumers, many domestic and foreign companies are readjusting their marketing strategies based on demand predictions. General Motors, for example, has an extremely well-developed range of brands and cars to target different market segments. To lure China's newly rich consumers, the company offers Cadillac SRX sport-utility vehicles for $75,000 plus and CTS sedans $55,000. The $30,000 Buick Regal is positioned to the cost-conscious entrepreneurs who want a prestigious car. Furthermore, $15,000–$20,000 Buick Excelle is offered to mid-level consumers. As for young urban consumers eager to have their

[33]Transparency International, Corruption Perceptions Index Score, http://www.icgg.org/. 2004.

[34]"Imitating Property is Theft," *Economist*, May 15, 2003.

first car, the company promotes mini, hatchback, and other models ranging from $5,700 to $12,000. To sell to the three-fourth of China's population in the country, GM offers the Wuling, which goes for $4,000 to $6,500. In 2004, 25 percent of GMs profit came from China's market, and that percentage is expected to grow in the future. GM counts its sustainable growth in China as a critical factor for the company's development in the global market. Statistics from the China Ministry of Commerce revealed that more than 5 million cars were sold in the Chinese market in 2004, and the country boasted 27.1 million cars at the end of 2004, making it the third largest auto market in the world. Apparently, understanding that China is not a homogeneous market is imperative to win different customer segments.

After all, China is a country with a population of 1.3 billion people of 56 ethnic groups that speak more than 100 dialects. Accordingly, what people prefer to have differs greatly from north to south, east to west, rich to poor, young to old, and city to country. Proctor & Gamble, for instance, has won inland consumers with a relatively inexpensive detergent, Tide Clean White, while it promotes the more expensive brand Tide Triple Action to city consumers. It has developed differentiated marketing strategies to meet the desires and needs of people from all over the country. P&G introduced a 320-gram bag of Tide Clean White for 23¢, compared with 33¢ for 350 grams of Tide Triple Action. Clean White does not offer benefits such as stain removal and fragrance and contains less advanced cleaning enzymes, but it costs less to make and, according to P&G, outperforms every other brand at that price level. Without a doubt, the tiered pricing initiative helps the company compete against less expensive local brands while protecting the value of its global brands. Moreover, to reach China's urban consumers, P&G has sponsored *Absolute Challenge,* a popular reality TV show, which has featured contestants competing to win a product representative position for multinational companies. To reach the inland consumers, P&G has blanketed village kiosks and corner shops with advertising materials emphasizing the value offered by Tide Clean White and other low-end products.

What P&G and other multinational companies learned in China is that it is no longer enough simply to cater to big cities. Although it was once good enough for companies to focus on such major metropolitan areas as Beijing and Shanghai, more and more companies are offering differentiated products tailored to different segments of the population in exchange for market share. An example is Wahaha, the largest domestic beverage producer. The company has successfully developed distribution channels in both urban and rural areas. It not only actively sponsors prime time TV programs to target the urban population but also paints the company's logo on village walls to reach the mass rural population. Like P&G, many multinational companies find distribution to rural Chinese area a huge challenge. Motorola, for example, found that in China's lower-tier cities, the young people not only consider a cell phone's value but also tend to be very individualistic in taste. As a result, the company has designed its least expensive phones with MP3 downloading and customized ring tones to promote to the lower-tier market segment. Today Motorola is capable of getting the right handsets to each location with less expensive phones in rural areas and snazzier ones in cities. Since it entered China in 1987, Motorola has witnessed substantial sales growth in both major metropolitan and rural areas largely due to the increasing demand for mobile phones.

Multinationals are now competing with local companies for the more discerning Chinese consumers. More domestic products now on the market are similar to those of MNCs. Consequently, consumers are more likely to be attracted by low prices or promotions rather than brand reputation and product quality. In automobile industry, most consumers prefer affordable small cars and are most likely to purchase cars priced under $12,000. One popular Chinese automaker, Chery, priced its QQ model between $5,500 and $7,500 and Xiali, another aggressive domestic automaker followed the suit. Foreign automakers, such as Honda, General Motors, and Volkswagen face the fact that although the Chinese market is lucrative with a growing demand, they cannot compete with the Chinese automakers' competitive prices in attracting price-conscious

Chinese consumers. As a result, some foreign automakers are sacrificing profits for sales volume in the growing market.

Competition in China is brutal. Consider mobile phones as an example. The inviting Chinese market had a total of 368 million mobile phone subscribers in 2004. The country's shops offered more than 700 types of mobile phones produced by over 30 companies. Foreign mobile phone manufacturers face fierce competition from domestic manufacturers, which tend to use price (low cost) as their main differentiator. In such a volatile environment, market shares can be transformed seemingly overnight.

Many foreign giants have found it increasingly difficult to generate profits in China's market. In the dairy industry, especially the liquid-milk sector, the market is dogged by price wars and dominated by local brands, so foreign companies such as Dannon, Kraft, and Friesland Coberco have quit dairy production in China. Some foreign companies find it difficult to sell their products, especially when they look similar to competitors', because their marketing and pricing strategies do not cater to Chinese consumers. Accordingly, only those companies that develop core technology with advanced management and marketing expertise excel in the volatile market. To mitigate marketing disadvantages, many multinational companies must buy their way into the Chinese market by taking an equity interest in leading domestic companies or forming joint ventures with established local brands. They agreed to offer their capital and technology expertise in exchange for market penetration in China.

Apparently, multinational firms cannot simply assume that they have first-mover advantages to enter the promising Chinese market through brand recognition and established distribution channels with prominent market share. Price-conscious Chinese consumers are far more unpredictable than expected, and the bureaucratic issues they must deal with at different administrative levels present problems. Consequently, firms should consider China as a long-term investment—longer than expected—to achieve positive cash flows.

Moreover, some foreign companies have found it difficult to take their investments out of China. Doing so successfully requires not only selling or liquidating the foreign investor's stake in the venture in a tax-efficient manner from both a Chinese and home country tax perspective but also navigating through a potentially difficult path of administrative procedures through China's foreign exchange controls. Both making and withdrawing an investment in China requires careful planning. To achieve the optimal result, foreign investors should give due attention to exit planning as part of the evaluation process before making an investment.

India[35]   *Economy.*   India gained independence in 1947 after two centuries of British colonial rule. It is now the second most populous country in the world (with 1 billion people) behind China. With nominal gross domestic product (GDP) of US $746 billion in 2005, India has the world's 10th largest economy. Its real GDP grew by an average of 5.6 percent a year in the 1980s and achieved 8.5 percent, 6.9 percent, and 6.7 percent, respectively, from 2003 to 2005. India's trade has been growing rapidly with its two-way trade amounting to $150 billion in 2005. India's foreign direct investment inflow amounted to $3.4 billion during the same time. Information technology and IT-enabled services output has grown rapidly, owning largely to India's reputation and cost advantages in these sectors. In its own way, India has climbed the economic ladder and has become the world's key process outsourcing center. Roughly 40 percent of *Fortune* 500 companies are estimated to have outsourced services from India.

---

[35]This section draws an the following articles: "Marketing Gurus Say: In India, Think Cheap, Lose the Cold Cereal," *Wall Street Journal,* October 11, 1996; Devesh Kapur and Ravi Ramamurti, "India's Emerging Competitive Advantage in Services," *Academy of Management Executive,* 15(2), 2001, pp. 20–32; C.K. Prahalad and Kenneth Lieberthal, "The End of Corporate Imperialism," *Harvard Business Review,* 81(8), 2003, pp. 109–117; Jayashree Dubey and Rajni Patel, "Small Wonders of the Indian Market," *Journal of Consumer Behaviour,* 4(2), 2004, pp. 145–51; and "The Great Divide," *Economist,* March 3, 2005.

Meanwhile, its software exports amounted to $7.6 billion in the period 2001 to 2002. All of these factors indicate that technical and process outsourcing will continue to be a key component of India's mainstream economy.

India's key exporting commodities include gems, jewelry, cotton, fabric, and pharmaceutical and petroleum products. Its key trading partners for exports are the United States, the United Arab Emirates, and the United Kingdom. In particular, the United States accounts for 22 percent of India's total merchandise exports. It is estimated that almost 200 of the blue-chip firms on the *Fortune* 500 list outsource at least some of their software requirements to India's software ventures. The United States, the European Union (EU), and China are its major partners for imports. Imports from the EU account for 22 percent of the total. India's trade deficit rose to an estimated $22.7 billion in 2004 from $8.9 billion in 2003. Although exports performed strongly, rising by 13.5 percent to $67.3 billion, imports soared by 32 percent to $90 billion in the same period.

India is a two-tier economy composed of a cutting-edge and globally competitive knowledge-driven service sector that employs the brightest of the middle classes and a large agricultural sector that employs the majority of the numerous poorly educated people. With a reputation for low-quality products, India's manufacturing sector has traditionally been underdeveloped. Currently, agricultural sector represents 20 percent of GDP, services 53 percent, and manufacturing 27 percent. Apparently, the service area, particularly the software industry, is the most dynamic growth sector.

India's rigid labor laws are the main obstacle to an increased role for manufacturing. A large proportion of heavy industry is still publicly owned. After liberalization, India gradually reduced its antiexport bias, and more resources have been moved into labor-intensive industries. Historically, a policy of import substitution in the decades after independence encouraged the development of a broad industrial base, but a lack of competition contributed to poor product quality and inefficiencies in production. Several sectors have now been opened to foreign participation under India's liberalizing reform program.

In the early 1990s, India initiated economic reforms that have been slow and patchy when compared to these in other rapidly growing emerging economies. Economic development has spread unevenly across states. Nevertheless, India has a large number of highly qualified professionals, as well as several internationally established industrial groups. Gradually, the country has become a prodigious exporter of remote services ranging from skilled software coders, accentless call center representatives, long-distance salespeople, invisible insurance clerks, medical record transcribers, and patient number crunchers. Aiming to become the back office for the world's banks, India wants to climb up the value chain by offering more sophisticated services to foreign companies.

Industry. India's software industry has been growing at 50 percent annually. According to a study by McKinsey & Company, the output of the country's software and service industries will rise to $87 billion in 2008, of which $50 billion will be exported. Two-thirds of the increase is projected to generate from new growth opportunities in IT-enabled services, including call center operations and transcription, design, and engineering services. It is estimated that roughly 2.2 million people will be employed in the software and IT-related industries. India is on its way to becoming a major exporter of software services based on its large well-educated workforce including people with accentless English and others who have engineering skills. Moreover, India is revealing strength in skill-intensive tradeable services, ranging from software development, information technology–enabled services, and product/project engineering and design to biotechnology, pharmaceuticals, media, entertainment and health care. Many world-famous companies are building their research and development centers in clusters, such as these in Bangalore and Hyderabad. Thus, international competitiveness and opportunities for MNCs in India differ from emerging economies, such as China, that have emerged as manufacturing powerhouses. Rapid technological change in IT industries indicates that India is not locked into lower-level manufacturing activities but could move up the value chain to export value-deepening services, such as consulting, project management and research and development.

India has also attracted many IT-enabled projects from foreign financial firms and other service sectors. GE Capital International Services, for example, employs more than 13,000 people in India in various departments including finance, accounting, and remote marketing. Similarly, Citigroup's e-Serve employs more than 3,000 people in Mumbai and Chennai. MNCs today are transferring more complex processes to India. Consequently, many investment banks, accountants, and consulting firms are outsourcing their work to India-based subcontractors.

Some restrictions of the Indian government have become barriers for foreign investors to overcome as they have in other emerging economies. One example is Press Note 18 that requires any investor with previous or existing joint ventures or technology agreements to seek approval from the Foreign Investment Promotion Board (FIPB) for new direct investments in the same or related field. Applicants must prove that the new proposal will not jeopardize the interest of the existing joint venture or technology partners. The Press Note 18 is intended to protect the interests of shareholders, public financial institutions, and workers. Government officials have been reluctant to abandon the guideline because they believe that their domestic industry is not strong enough to face direct competition from foreign firms in selected sectors. Under the guidelines, Suzuki must include Maruti Udvog, its existing joint venture, in its plans to make new investments for a car assembly plant and a diesel engine plant. According to Suzuki, Indian governmental regulations have become a tool of the Indian partners to demand unrealistic and opportunistic exit valuations or to create more barriers for foreign competitors.

It is imperative for MNCs to assess the political power of their domestic competitors before committing to a significant investment in India. After all, even though India's legal system is relatively impartial, free, and fair, they are notoriously slow. Disputes often take decades to be resolved and, as a result, many foreign companies build in clauses allowing for international arbitration of disputes. The regulatory system, which is not immune to policy reversals due to pressures from vested interests and interministry rivalries, makes the situation worse. Fortunately, in recent years, more transparent regulatory systems are being introduced in previously under-regulated sectors.

Still, tariff and nontariff barriers continue to be used in the country to protect its domestic industry. India's removal of its remaining import quotas in April 2001 was expected to lead to a surge in imports. However, this did not happen because the government compensated by introducing high tariffs on some products. Customs duties on agricultural goods were raised, and the total duty on second-hand cars is now more than 180 percent. Well-connected companies or lobby groups have consistently been able to counteract many of India's World Trade Organization (WTO) liberalization measures. In general, foreign companies should assess the political power of their domestic competitors before proceeding with a significant investment.

As they must in other developing countries, international managers investing in India must deal with corruption. In 2004, India ranked 90th of 146 countries (with the 146th being the most corrupt) in an international corruption evaluation. Even though India's intellectual property protection is far better than that in China, its weak legal regime has ambiguous rules toward patent products. GlaxoSmithKline (GSK), one of the world's biggest drug firms, for instance, has long aspired to do more drug development in India. However, the company must combat in India with companies that specialize in making copycat drugs and then selling them cheaply to India's vast domestic market. Recently, GSK was disappointed to find that even under new legislation and the WTO's patent regulations, the Indian government still ignores its need to protect patented products so that domestic firms cannot make or market the same drug using the data released with the product.

Market. Having been attracted by its vast market potential, many MNCs have made longer than expected commitment to market expansion in India. For example, Coca-Cola tried for decades to enter the promising market. Initially, the company was India's leading soft drink producer. In 1977, the company was ordered by a new government to dilute its stake in its Indian unit and turn over Coke's secret formula. As a result, Coca-Cola had to exit the market. When the Indian government began to attract foreign investment, Coca-Cola returned in 1993. Even though the company quickly gained a lead in the market by buying famous local brands, it has spent millions of dollars to fight legal and legislative battles all across India, in particular dealing with campaigns of nongovernmental organizations (NGO). Basically, the company was accused of stealing water, poisoning land, and selling drinks laced with dangerous pesticides. Moreover, the company suffered financially due to its lack of understanding that affordable prices are essential to win the hearts of Indian consumers. Unlike Unilever, an Anglo-Dutch consumer goods conglomerate that successfully adopted the low-margin/high-volume business model for India, Coca-Cola raised prices on certain products only to accept a failed market. In 2004, Coca-Cola re-introduced its 200 ml bottles and reduced prices to Rs5 (just under 11 cents) to secure its market in India.

Although consumers in emerging markets are much more affluent than they were a decade ago, they are not affluent by Western standards. In India, the top marketing tier consists of a small number (2 million) of consumers who are willing to accept Western brands and can afford them. The second tier has a much larger group (60 million) of people, but is less attracted to international brands. The massive group, the third tier (the rest of the population) is loyal to local customs, habits, and often brands. The market pyramid in India can well explain why U.S. automakers failed to penetrate the emerging markets in the last decade. For example, Ford's recent introduction of the Escort, priced at more than $21,000, is in the luxury segment. Remember that in India, the most popular car, the Maruti Suzuki, sells for $10,000 or less. Apparently, Ford ignored Tier 2 of the pyramid with its market positioning, it is no wonder then that despite almost a decade in India, Ford still lags far behind some competitors that came to India at about the same time. Today, both Ford and GM are small players in India's car market with a meager 3 percent market share. Their Korean competitor, Hyundai, has snatched a 17 percent market share by selling its tiny Santro. It appears that U.S. automakers are bringing their existing products and marketing strategies to India without properly accounting for the country's market pyramids. Many companies, therefore, become high-end niche players. In India, only 7 million people have purchasing power of more than US$20,000 dollars. It should have been no surprise that when Revlon introduced its beauty products to India, only the top tier could afford its products. These companies have learned that to survive the fierce competition, they must tailor their products to local tastes and needs with affordable prices. After all, in India, roughly 63 million of the population has the purchasing power between $10,000 and $20,000. Although the rapidly growing emerging market will make a significant contribution to the future performance of worldwide businesses, MNCs will have to reconfigure their resource bases, readjust their cost structures, redesign their product development processes, and challenge their assumptions about existing business models.

In India, the median household income is about $480; however, the private savings rate is an impressive 24 percent. Most people are worried about their social security system, so frugality has deep historical roots in the country. For example, although India is the world's largest market for razor blades, it is not a market for disposable shavers. Fewer than 1 percent of the blades bought in cities are attached to a plastic handles. The logic is simple. People cannot stand the waste of throwing away the razor blades. Sanitary napkin manufacturers face the same dilemma when they enter the country with 1 billion in population. Companies found that most Indian women recycle old cotton sheets. As a result, less than 2 percent of all Indian women and just 23 percent of adult urban women use sanitary napkins. Generally speaking, Indian consumers are very sensitive about the price/quality equation, which greatly provides low-cost local competitors the edge in the rapidly growing market. MNCs cannot duplicate their successful business models in other developed countries to the Indian market. They must learn to turn these price sensitivity characteristics to their advantage by offering customers good prices with global standards.

In the past decade, many companies learned that goods packaged in family-size quantities are not easy to promote in India, whether they are detergents, shampoos, or tea leaves. On the contrary, small packs give consumers the satisfaction of using branded products at low costs and are more affordable to the lower income group and rural masses. Now MNCs try to promote products such as detergents, shampoos, ready-to-eat food products, tea, coffee, nail polish, and toothpaste in packages of small quantity. Surprisingly, the small packaged products make up to 20 percent to 30 percent of the market share. What multinational companies gradually learned in India is that small package size is more efficient to target the urban, semiurban, and rural markets from the middle and lower classes. Companies, domestic or international, dealing in the fast-moving consumer goods industry and durables have recognized that price is the greatest determinant of perceived value for Indian consumers and are enjoying success with "small consumption-small price tag" logic. An example is Coca-Cola's re-introduction of its 200 ml cola bottles for only Rs5 (11 cents). The low price strategy has accounted for half of the revenues of its cola products. To secure its market share, Coca-Cola has also introduced its returnable 200 ml glass bottle in the same price range. The efforts have paid off, and 80 percent of new sales now come from the rural markets. Similarly, Nestlé has not only secured the market with small packs of its products such as its Chocostick with a Rs2 (4 cents) price but also has successfully localized its products and appeased price-conscious housewives. To win these price-sensitive consumers, Nestlé has created an Indian-style instant coffee, Sunrise, blended with chicory to produce a strong and familiar flavor to Indian consumers at an affordable price. The company also promotes a mint flavored with the local betel nut and mixes for traditional Indian desserts. More than half of Nestlé's products sold in India cost less than 70 cents. When Nestlé cut the price of its Maggi noodles from 19 cents to 14 cents, for example, sales volume tripled. Increasingly, MNCs realize that to offer competitive pricing, localization in India is a must. Today, many automakers have learned to rely on Asian sources for price and suitability of components to meet the demand of India's price-sensitive consumers.

It is also imperative for MNCs to reconsider their branding strategy in India. Branding in India is more complex than many companies expected largely due to the complexity and variances of culture and people across the Indian subcontinent. When MNCs do not have enough knowledge about the end users and fail to effectively segment the market into accessible groups, they would find it difficult to increase their market share with their already established global branding strategies. Coca-Cola, for example, overvalued the pull of its brand among Tier-2 consumers. The company originally based its advertising strategy on its worldwide image, which failed. Coca-Cola purchased the local brand, Thums Up in 1993 but failed for years to realize the importance of localized branding in terms of local consumers. Now Coca-Cola is positioning itself by using local heroes in its advertising and promoting Thums Up. Many companies, such as Hindustan Lever and Pepsi, have developed effective brand operations and thus achieved huge success.

Multinational companies have gradually realized that India's consumption boom has been fueled by price wars for everything, whether cars or shampoo products. For instance, Hindustan Lever Ltd., the Indian subsidiary of consumer-goods giant Unilever, and rival Procter & Gamble Co. have long been locked in a bitter price war. Following rival Unilever's huge lead by developing an Avon-style direct sales force, P&G is countering with its own van sales program to reach rural areas. P&G has also followed Unilever by introducing low-cost, single-use sachets of its laundry detergent brands. The two famous MNCs are still trying to capture the largest segment of the market. Similarly, with the dramatic increase of cell phone subscriptions in the past five years, the competition among phone companies has been fierce, both from domestic and international manufacturers. To grasp a market share of the emerging economy, MNCs have been discounting their products to maintain a stable market share. Some auto companies have decreased their prices about 20 percent to secure their leading market position. Moreover, it may also take longer than expected for MNCs to generate profits in India. For example, Johnson & Johnson, one of the most successful consumer products multinationals, has entered India some 35 years ago, but its turnover of $50 million is only equivalent to its sales in Malaysia, home to just 19 million people. Many new entrants must sit tight through years of losses before they make profits. The market for consumable and luxury products is much less than expected in this country of more than 1 billion people.

Without a doubt, India has caught the world's attention in terms of fostering genuine entrepreneurship in some industries by favoring domestic over foreign investment. Some IT firms, such as Infosys, Wipro, and Tata Consultancy Services, are now among the world's best. Outside the IT industry, unfortunately, many firms still retain bad habits and feuding often afflicts family firms. To enter the vast emerging market, MNCs must realize that the country's economy and industrialization are far from homogeneous or uniform. Consequently, MNCs should think strategically and selectively about which states or regions, rather than India as a whole, to enter. Furthermore, MNCs should establish and maintain informal ties with all important political parties given the fact that political power changes hands rapidly in India at both the federal and state levels. Eventually, many MNCs found it beneficial to set up joint ventures with a native partner for assistance in such delicate situations that call for tact, diplomacy, and public relations savvy.

Currently, foreign investment in some sectors of the Indian economy, such as insurance and the media, is limited to a minority stake, and in the retail sector, it is banned altogether. Companies such as McDonald's Corp. of the United States and Italy's Benetton Group have opened in the subcontinent but usually through franchising agreements in which Indian partners dominate and make most key decisions. That may explain why investors have not found India, which received $4 billion in FDI in 2004, as attractive as the Chinese market. Nonetheless, the government of the world's second-most-populous country has become more accommodating to foreign investment; India offers much growth potential for foreign companies.

Economy. With a population of 143 million people and a current GDP of $772 **Russia**[36] billion (or $1.59 trillion in purchasing power parity) in 2005, Russia is one of the largest markets in the world. Many multinational companies (MNCs) have come to Russia since 1986 when Soviet President Gorbachev encouraged foreign investors to seek joint ventures with Soviet partners. Since the financial crisis of 1998, the country has experienced six straight years of growth, averaging 6.5 percent annually, thanks largely to rising oil prices. Russia currently is considered the next economic superpower of the world. Foreign direct investment hit a record high of $9.4 billion in 2004 with a 39 percent increase from the previous year. Shifting to a market economy, Russia presents many opportunities for foreign companies. Its international financial position has improved since the 1998 financial crisis as witnessed by the reduction of its foreign debt from 90 percent of the GDP to around 28 percent in 2005. However, the country's economy largely depends on oil, natural gas, metals, and timber, representing more than 80 percent of exports, leaving the country vulnerable to swings in world commodity prices. High oil prices are expected to put strong upward pressure on

[36]This section draws from the following articles: "Young and Restless," *Business Russia,* Economist Intelligence Unit, 1998, pp. 4–5; "Brand Aid," *Country Monitor,* Economist Intelligence Unit, 1999, p. 3; "Suspicious Behavior," *Business Russia,* Economist Intelligence Unit, 2002, p. 5; Gary Anders and Danila Usachev, "Strategic Elements of Eastman Kodak's Successful Market Entry in Russia," *Thunderbird International Business Review,* 45 (March/April 2003), pp. 171–83; Tarun Khanna, Krishna G. Palepu, and Jayant Sinha, "Strategies That Fit Emerging Markets, " *Harvard Business Review,* 83 (6), 2005, pp 63–76; and "Russia: Shoppers Gone Wild," *Business Week,* February 20, 2006.

the real exchange rate, undermining the cost competitiveness of the industrial sector and dampening growth in the medium term. Accordingly, Russia must rejuvenate its manufacturing sector if the country is to achieve broad-based economic growth. At present, the country's per capita purchasing power is about 35 percent of the developed EU level and 25 percent of that of the United States.

Russia's improved competitiveness and higher oil prices greatly facilitated its dramatic turnaround in the external current account, from a deficit of around half of 1 percent of GDP in 1998 to a surplus of 12 percent of GDP in 1999. This surplus increased during 2000 to an estimated 17 percent of GDP.

In spite of its recent economic upturn, the Russian economy is facing some serious problems. One of the most significant is the continued impact of corruption in both the public and private sectors. The country also suffers from a weak banking system, a poor business climate that discourages both domestic and foreign investors, and widespread lack of trust in institutions. Even though tax reforms and the newly established political and economic stability have improved the investment climate, the country still needs to improve its enforcement and implementation of policies to reduce operational risks for businesses. For foreign investors, investing in Russia still requires a long-term commitment and patient cultivation. Hence, it is imperative for MNCs to fully understand local rules and regulations before they locate their operations and further align their expertise with local partners.

Industry. Despite these problems, FDI inflows have increased strongly, as have other forms of capital inflow. FDI inflows averaged $3 billion annually during the period 1998 to 2002 and then picked up remarkably to $8 billion in 2003 and $11.7 billion in 2004. Many large-scale investments were concentrated in natural resources sector (i.e., oil and gas). Meanwhile, the fast-growing retail and consumer goods sectors have also attracted many foreign companies. Largely due to the country's high tariff on foreign imports, many firms have been motivated to build plants in Russia. In the past, Russia's attractions of an underdeveloped but fast-growing market size of 143 million people, abundant natural resources (with one-third of the world's gas reserves or around 8 percent of proven oil reserves), and a low-cost and relatively skilled workforce had been more than offset by serious deficiencies of the institutional environment. Recent political and economic reforms have greatly enhanced the country's investment situation. For example, the government initiated a new law on foreign investment in 1999 and amended it later to guarantee national treatment (i.e., same treatment as given to domestic companies), repatriation of profits, and compensation in the case of nationalization.

Despite its continuous growth in FDI inflows since 2003, the country remains below potential. In other words, its economic growth still lags behind the country's potential, especially compared to other emerging economies, such as China's $50 billion FDI inflows during the same period. Russia's cumulative FDI inflows are one of the lowest among all 27 transition economies and one-fifth of the average penetration ratio into east-central Europe.

One of the major barriers for foreign investors entering the country is its overall complex institutional environment. On the one hand, political and macroeconomic stabilization have occurred recently, and the business environment has improved. On the other hand, the country's overall business environment remains difficult and unpredictable. The recent attack on Yukos Oil Company has highlighted institutional deficiencies, which demonstrates that property rights still ultimately depend on the will of the state. The concentration of economic power in a few massive conglomerates impedes competition in an economy. Although the government is trying to reduce the regulatory burden on business, will continue to hinder policy implementation an inefficient and cumbersome bureaucracy.

According to Passau University's Corruption Perception Index, Russia's corruption perceptions index in 2004 ranked 90 out of 146 countries (with 146 as the most corrupt country). The government's control of corruption is much lower than that of China and India. The country's high levels of official corruption, crumbling legal system, and inadequate laws covering the enforcement of property rights combine to discourage foreign and domestic investment.

Accordingly, the inefficient controls of bureaucracy compound the issue of investment uncertainty. Investors in the natural resource and metals sectors, in particular, face considerable uncertainty as Russia defines which assets it considers strategic and thus open to foreign majority control. Many foreign companies form alliances to gain access to government and local inputs instead of considering Greenfield investments and acquisitions. Although the Russian government has urged legislation to clarify the situation and delineate which areas will be subject to restricted access, government policy remains confusing and uncertain.

Nevertheless, recent survey indicates that foreign investment in Russia on average yields higher returns than that in China or India. Many foreign companies have developed the skills and local knowledge to navigate the Russian business environment. Although corruption tops the list of foreign investors' concerns, it does not appear to be an insuperable barrier to doing business in Russia. Hence, many businesses were satisfied with their business success in Russia and planned to expand their investments there.

Despite the continuing problems of the business environment and the regulatory uncertainty affecting the natural resources sector, macroeconomic fundamentals remain strong and market opportunities are inviting. When compared to other emerging economies, such as China and India, Russia has yet to diversify its industrial performance beyond the oil, gas, and minerals sector. Nevertheless, the country's growth of both consumer spending and domestic investment has been incredible. Judging from 2005 economic data, consumer consumption and fixed investment represent 5.8 percent and 2.8 percent, respectively of its 7.1 percent GDP growth. The fixed investment by domestic businesses in Russia is much smaller than that of its foreign counterparts. For instance, Russian businesses invested 17 percent of GDP in themselves last year, compared with the 20 percent investment of GDP in and 50 percent in Chinese.

Market. Nevertheless, in recent years the general economic improvement in Russia has led to increased consumer spending and demand for consumable products. One of the driving forces for increased consumer spending has been the growing Russian middle class, especially in Moscow. Russia has the third largest number of billionaires on *Forbes Magazine*'s list of richest people after the United States and Germany; more billionaires live in Moscow than in New York (33 compared with 31). Growth of consumer expenditure has also benefited from the impact of real disposable incomes on continuing utilities and housing subsidies.

Imported goods made heavy inroads into the Russian market throughout most of the 1990s. Until the 1998 financial crisis, imported goods were stimulated by real appreciation of the ruble and the advertising-enhanced power of Western brand names. In the wake of the 1998 ruble devaluation, many of these imports were crowding out of the market, which in turn helped revive domestic production across the full range of consumer goods industries. Since 2000, with the help of the recovery in income and ruble appreciation, consumers again are consuming foreign brands in many categories.

Apparently, the new free market offers Russian consumers options and alternatives that were unavailable during the Soviet era. With the liberalized market, Russian consumers have more choices between domestic and imported products. Although most consumers may prefer certain domestic brands, such as chocolates and vodka, to foreign brands, Russian products in general cannot compete with Western and Asian imports because their product quality standards have been lower than those of these importers. Consequently, consumers prefer global brands in automobiles and high-technology products, whereas local brands succeed in the food and beverage industries.

Like other emerging economies, Russia has extremely wide income disparities. According to the government's official data, the richest 10 percent of the population receive around 30 percent of national income whereas the poorest 10 percent receive only 2 percent. The richest 10 percent also have incomes that are nearly 15 times higher than the poorest 10 percent.

Currently, young Russian consumers (ages 5 to 18) represent more than 20 percent of the population. Some 5 percent of Russia's high-income earners are under age 20, making $500 per month or more. MNCs, such as Reebok, Nike, and Coca-Cola have targeted Russian teens with aggressive advertising. Unlike teenagers in China who prefer to buy products from U.S., European, and Japanese companies, Russian teenagers love both domestic and foreign products as long as product quality meets their expectations. That is to say, they buy Western products simply because products are better, not because of the country of origin. Moreover, MNCs have learned that companies cannot judge Russia's young generations by Western standards. Russian youth are yearning for self-expression, yet they like to dress in the same style. The New Soviets and New Cosmopolitans among Russian consumers have demonstrated polarized consumption styles. Both segments are eager to try new things, but the New Soviets are deeply rooted in the past and thus are more "Russian" and accept only new ideas that make them comfortable. New Cosmopolitans, on the other hand, are more experienced, better educated, emotionally stronger, more likely to accept new things. To grab the hearts of young consumers, properly understanding their unique characteristics is crucial. After all, the youth market is worth battling for even though it is as fickle as the Western one.

It is imperative for MNCs to carefully examine their advertising strategy in Russia. Toyota learned the hard way the importance of carefully selecting an advertising agency and controlling its marketing campaign. To launch its $50,000 to $100,000 Lexus model to the Russian rich, the company advertised it with the opening of the U.S. sci-fi film *Minority Report*. Toyota hired a local advertising agency to design a strategy to send out invitations to the opening. The advertising company designed an invitation, saying "you are under suspicion" to match the marketing campaign's theme. The attendance was impressive; three-quarters of those invited attended the film, but the public relations effect was unfavorable. The ad company received worried phone calls from the security services of 40 of the targeted companies. Obviously, local and global ad agencies are available in Russia, but foreign companies need to pay close attention to the conduct of their marketing campaigns.

In general, Russian consumers are suspicious of marketing campaigns and are not responsive to TV and outdoor advertising, but a friend's recommendation (word-of-mouth advertising) works well. As a result, foreign investors have to rethink appropriate marketing techniques to penetrate the Russian market. Eastman Kodak, for instance, allocated 20 percent to 30 percent of its annual budget to promotions of its brand name by organizing and sponsoring various public events and to its advertising campaigns. To date, Kodak has gradually established consumer acceptance through open and frequent communications with its consumers. Reebok, a manufacturer and distributor of footwear and other clothing products successfully created public good will by donating $50,000 worth of products to public schools and the Russian Olympic team. Accordingly, Kodak and Reebok have had a successful market entry in Russia.

As they have in other emerging economies, MNCs found that consumers in Russia are not highly loyal to brands. As they did in India, MNCs found in Russia that small packaged products offer consumers the satisfaction of using branded products at low costs and are therefore more affordable to the mass population. Unilever followed that logic with small packages of Brooke Bond, Lipton's, and Beseda teas. The company also introduced trial sachets of its Sunsilk shampoos. Similarly, to penetrate the vast market, Eastman Kodak Company increased diversification by offering new lines specifically for local demand. It introduced a number of inexpensive products that the average Russian could generally afford. So far the company's most successful product launched in Russia has been Kodak Color Plus film. It is not on the cutting edge of consumer imaging technology like Kodak Gold film, but this product with well-balanced quality, costs approximately $1 per roll. The introduction of Kodak Color Plus in Russia strengthened the company's competitiveness in the price-sensitive market.

To target those consumers that do not display preference for foreign brands, foreign companies have tried to promote their products by emphasizing local roots. Mars, the U.S. candy giant, has presented itself as a semi-Russian company since 1996. The company has strongly established itself by advertising the extent of its local production in its marketing campaigns. Although all categories of consumer goods imports have witnessed a plunge in market share in Russia, Mars brand management has won numerous consumers and become one of the country's top five sellers in the confectionary business.

Many foreign companies entering the Russian market in the 1990s learned to be extremely cautious about their capital investment. The Russian financial crisis in 1998 demonstrated how crucial it is for companies to quickly pull corporate funds out of a sinking economy. Some foreign investors still prefer minimum capital investment to avoid potential problems. There may be a short-term difference in approach to established and potential new investors with the latter being more sensitive to recent developments. Most companies that are already in place, in contrast, seem to be gearing up for more investments. General global conditions for FDI also appear favorable after several relatively lean years. Recently, Toyota announced its plan to build a $140 million automobile manufacturing plant in St. Petersburg. A week earlier, LG Electronics unveiled plans to build a $100 million plan, to make flat-screen televisions, refrigerators, washing machines, and audio equipment. In 2004, Alcoa of the United States acquired two fabricating facilities. Coca-Cola also acquired Russia's largest juice maker for an estimated $600 million. More interesting, the German company BASF has entered the gas field by taking a 50 percent-minus-one-share stake. FDI reached a record $11.7 billion in 2004, up from $8 billion in 2003; inflows in the first quarter 2006 already amounted to $5.4 billion.

All in all, Russia's rapidly growing consumer market and further economic opening resulting from WTO membership will make it comparatively attractive for foreign companies. Although the country has gradually enhanced its competitive position, in the long run, Russia needs institutional and structural reforms to effectively utilize its human capital and develop other manufacturing sectors to sustain its competitiveness.

EVOLUTION OF COOPERATIVE GLOBAL TRADE AGREEMENTS

◆ ◆ ◆ ◆ ◆ ◆ ◆ ◆

General Agreements on Tariffs and Trade

In the aftermath of World War II, the then-major powers negotiated the establishment of the **International Trade Organization (ITO)** to ensure free trade among nations through negotiated lowering of trade barriers. ITO would have been an international organization operating under the umbrella of the United Nations with statutory powers to enforce agreements. However, when the U.S. government announced in 1950 that it would not seek congressional approval of the organization, the ITO was effectively dead. Instead, to keep the momentum of increasing trade through the lowering of trade barriers alive, the signatories to ITO agreed to operate under the informal aegis of the **General Agreements on Tariffs and Trade (GATT).** GATT provided a forum for multilateral discussion among countries to reduce trade barriers. Nations met periodically to review the status of world trade and to negotiate mutually agreeable reductions in trade barriers.

The main operating principle of GATT is the concept of **normal trade relations** (NTR) status (formerly known as **most favored nation,** or MFN, status). The NTR status meant that any country that was a member state to a GATT agreement and that extended a reduction in tariff to another nation would have to automatically extend the same benefit to all members of GATT. However, there was no enforcement mechanism, and over time many countries negotiated bilateral agreements, especially for agricultural products, steel, textiles, and automobiles. GATT was successful in lowering trade barriers to a substantial extent (e.g., developed countries' average tariffs on manufactured goods from around 40 percent down to a mere 4 percent) during its existence from 1948 to 1994. However, some major shortcomings limited its potential and effectiveness. The initial rounds of GATT concentrated only on lowering tariff barriers. As trade in services expanded faster than the trade in goods and GATT concentrated on merchandise trade, more and more international trade came to be outside the purview of GATT. Second, GATT tended to concentrate mostly on tariffs, and many nations used nontariff barriers, such as quota and onerous customs procedures, to get around the spirit of GATT when they could not increase tariffs. Finally, as developed nations moved from manufacturing-based economies to services- and knowledge-based economies, they felt the need to bring intellectual property within the purview of international agreement because that was where the competitive advantage lay for firms in the developed nations.

World Trade Organization

The **World Trade Organization (WTO)** was created in the eighth round of GATT talks—called the **Uruguay Round**—that lasted from 1986 to 1994. The WTO took effect on January 1, 1995. It has statutory powers to adjudicate trade disputes among nations to oversee the smooth functioning of the multilateral trade accords agreed on under the Uruguay Round. *Its main function is to ensure that trade flows as smoothly, predictably, and freely as possible.* As of December 11, 2005, the WTO had 149 member countries.[37] This round was successful in bringing many agricultural products and textiles under the purview of GATT. The Uruguay Round created an environment in which a global body of customs and trade law is developing. In particular, the Uruguay Round ensured the ultimate harmonization of the overall customs process and the fundamental determinations that are made for all goods crossing an international border: admissibility, classification, and valuation.[38] It also included provisions for trade in intellectual property for the first time and provided for many services.

Then, the ninth and latest round—called the **Doha Development Agenda (Doha Round,** for short)—was launched in Doha, Qatar, in November 2001. Most notably, the inaugural meeting at the Doha Round also paved the way for China and Taiwan to obtain full membership in the WTO[39] (See Global Perspective 2-2 on China's accession to the WTO.) However, the WTO's latest round of multilateral trade talks did not make much progress in other areas. (Exhibit 2-7 gives an idea of the "intended" scope of the Doha Round). This new round places the needs and interests of developing countries at the heart of its work. For example, it is estimated that two-thirds of the world's poorest people depend on agriculture. Tariffs on agricultural products are five times higher on average than those for industrial products, undermining the ability of developing countries to trade their way out of poverty. The United States currently spends up to $19.1 billion on farm-production subsidies, which heavily distort trade. The EU spends over $75 billion.[40] The reluctance of some of the world's richest countries to substantially reduce high farm tariff and nontariff barriers had long

---

[37]Several new members during recent years are Albania, China, Croatia, Georgia, Jordan, Lithuania, Moldova, the Sultanate of Oman, and Taiwan. At the time of writing this chapter, the application of 24 countries were being considered for accession: Algeria, Andorra, Armenia, Azerbaijan, the Bahamas, Belarus, Bhutan, Bosnia Herzegovina, Cambodia, Cape Verde, Kazakhstan, Lao People's Democratic Republic, Lebanon, Macedonia, the Russian Federation, Samoa, Saudi Arabia, Seychelles, Sudan, Tajikistan, Tonga, Ukraine, Uzbekistan, Vietnam, Yemen, and Serbia-Montegegro (known as Yugoslavia until February 2003).

[38]Paulsen K. Vandevert, "The Uruguay Round and the World Trade Organization: A New Era Dawns in the Private Law of International Customs and Trade," *Case Western Reserve Journal of International Law,* 31 (Winter 1999), pp. 107-18.

[39]Anne McGuirk, "The Doha Development Agenda," *Finance & Development,* 39 (September 2002), pp. 4–7.

[40]"A Stopped Clock Ticks Again," *Economist,* October 13, 2005, pp. 76–79.

Exhibit 2-7

AGENDA FOR THE DOHA ROUND

- Implementation-related issues and concerns
- Agriculture
- Services
- Market access for nonagricultural products
- Trade-related aspects of intellectual property rights (TRIPS)
- Relationship between trade and investment
- Interaction between trade and competition policy
- Transparency in government procurement
- Trade facilitation
- WTO rules: antidumping
- WTO rules: subsidies
- WTO rules: regional trade agreements
- Dispute settlement understanding
- Trade and environment
- Electronic commerce
- Small economies
- Trade, debt, and finance
- Trade and transfer of technology
- Technical cooperation and capacity building
- Least-developed countries
- Special and differential treatment

Source: World Trade Organization, http://www.wto.org/, accessed February 15, 2006.

stymied the opportunity to secure other reforms that would deliver huge benefits to the world trading regime. Unfortunately, the gulf separating the negotiators was so wide that the trade negotiations collapsed on July 23, 2006 during a meeting among ministers from the U.S., the European Union, Brazil, India, Japan, and Australia with no time table set for restarting or concluding the talks. However, the apparent collapse could prove temporary, as in previous rounds of trade talks that took eight years or more to conclude.[41] The agenda also includes new trade talks, an action program to resolve developing countries' complaints about the implementation of Uruguay Round agreements and an accord on Trade-related aspects of intellectual property rights (TRIPS) ensuring that patent protection does not block developing countries' access to affordable medicines.

Incidentally, the WTO is not simply an extension of GATT. The GATT was a multilateral agreement with no institutional foundations. It was applied on a provisional basis in strict legal terms. The WTO is a permanent institution with its own secretariat. WTO commitments are full and permanent and legally binding under international law. Although GATT was restricted to trade in merchandise goods, WTO includes trade in services and trade-related aspects of intellectual property. It is to be noted that GATT lives on within WTO. Some of the major issues and agendas in WTO are highlighted in the following sections.

Dispute Settlement Mechanism. The WTO dispute settlement mechanism is faster, more automatic, and therefore much less susceptible to blockages than the old GATT system. Once a country indicates to the WTO that it has a complaint about the trade practices of another country, an automatic schedule kicks in. The two countries have three months for mutual "consultations" to iron out their differences. If the disputants cannot come to a mutually satisfactory settlement, the dispute is referred to the dispute settlement mechanism of WTO, under which a decision has to be rendered

---

[41] "Doha Round Talks Break Down on Farm Support, Trade Barriers," *Wall Street Journal,* July 24, 2006.

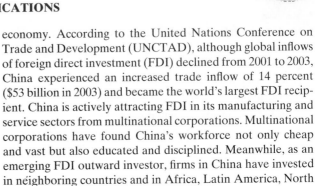

$\mathscr{G}$LOBAL PERSPECTIVE 2-2

CHINA'S ACCESSION TO THE WTO AND ITS IMPLICATIONS

After 15 years of arduous negotiation, China joined the World Trade Organization (WTO) in December 2001. The United States reached a bilateral agreement with China on WTO accession that secures broad-ranging, comprehensive, one-way trade concession on China's part in which China made specific commitments to open its market to U.S. exports of industrial goods, services, and agricultural products to a degree unprecedented in the modern era. For example, China promised to reduce import tariffs from an average of 24.6 percent to 9.4 percent within three to five years. The United States also offered extension of permanent normal trade relations (NTR) to China as China entered the WTO. The vote of the U.S. House of Representatives was called one of the most important trade and foreign policy decisions the United States had made in many years. Because of the accession, the markets of WTO members were also opened to China.

Trade officials from the United States, Europe, and Japan have portrayed China's entry into the WTO as an antidote to their growing trade deficits with China. The reality, however, is that China's agreement to reduce tariffs, phase out import quotas, open new sectors of its economy to foreign investment, and otherwise follow WTO rules will not reverse this imbalance in trade. China's accession to the WTO has begun to boost the economic reforms in the world's most populous nation. There is no doubt that China and its 1.3 billion people benefit tremendously from its WTO accession. It has allowed China to expand trade, attract foreign investment, and give private firms a greater role in the economy, but, more important, it has increasingly integrated China with the rest of the world

Sources: "Analysis: Chinese Threat to Japan Manufacturers," *Nikkei Net Interactive,* May 29, 2001; Nicholas R. Lardy, "Sweet and Sour Deal," *Foreign Policy,* March/April 2002, pp. 20–21; Bill Powell, "It's All Made in China Now," *Fortune,* March 4, 2002; "Tilting at Dragons," *Economist,* October 25, 2003, pp. 65–66; and "The China Price," *Business Week,* December 6, 2004, pp. 102–24.

economy. According to the United Nations Conference on Trade and Development (UNCTAD), although global inflows of foreign direct investment (FDI) declined from 2001 to 2003, China experienced an increased trade inflow of 14 percent ($53 billion in 2003) and became the world's largest FDI recipient. China is actively attracting FDI in its manufacturing and service sectors from multinational corporations. Multinational corporations have found China's workforce not only cheap and vast but also educated and disciplined. Meanwhile, as an emerging FDI outward investor, firms in China have invested in neighboring countries and in Africa, Latin America, North America, and Europe to access natural resources, markets, and strategic assets such as technology and brand names. In 2002, China's outward investment flows exceeded $35 billion, reaching more than 160 countries.

Entry into the WTO membership followed Beijing's winning the right to host the 2008 Olympic games and Shanghai's hosting the Asia Pacific Economic Cooperation (APEC) leaders' summit. Driven by its government's open policy to foreign investment since 1980s and accession by WTO as an important trade partner to the world, China is emerging as the virtual factory of the world, driving a profound shift in global investment flows.

How will this affect other economies such as these in the United States, Japan, and Europe? With China's increased trade surplus with the United States, the deflationary crisis in Tokyo, and European manufacturers becoming vulnerable to the "Made in China" shock, should China be blamed for the rich countries' economic problems? On the one hand, China has presented business opportunities for firms to offshore manufacturing and services jobs with a low-wage, skilled workforce and lowered its import tariffs since its entry into the WTO; on the other hand, China has caused some firms to lose global market share and job opportunities by conducting cheap-currency strategy.

---

within six months of setting up a panel to resolve the dispute. The decision of the panel is supposed to be legally binding. However, trade experts have revealed deep ambivalence about the WTO's experiment with binding adjudication, and there is little clear sense of where the system should go from here. Litigation draws on different skills, resources, and even cultural attitudes than does diplomacy, with the possibility of placing certain nations at a real disadvantage.[42] As Global Perspective 2-3 shows, the United States frequently violates the WTO principles and resorts to unilateral trade sanctions against foreign trading partners.

Finally, although WTO is a global institutional proponent of free trade, it is not without critics. In December 1999, WTO launched what would have become the beginning of a ninth Round of negotiations inaugurated in Seattle, the United States. However, its Seattle meeting was only to be greeted by jeers and riots triggered by

---

[42]Susan Esserman and Robert Howse, "The TWO on Trial," *Foreign Affairs,* 82 (January/February 2003), pp. 130–40.

$\mathcal{G}$LOBAL PERSPECTIVE 2-3

TRADE BARRIERS AND POLITICS

The United States thinks of itself as a leading exponent of free trade and frequently brings actions against other nations as unfair trading partners. On March 20, 2002, President George W. Bush announced that the United States would impose tariffs of up to 30 percent on most steel imports as a way to save the domestic steel industry. This temporary steel tariff has set a dangerous precedent for the others, however, by opening the floodgates on new tariffs by other World Trade Organization (WTO) members. In response to the U.S. action, the European Union (EU) immediately filed a complaint with the WTO and decided to impose six-month protective tariffs of 14.9 percent to 26 percent on 15 kinds of steel imports that exceed current quotas. Japan also notified the WTO of its plans to impose 100 percent retaliatory tariffs on U.S. steel imports. China is also preparing to erect new trade barriers in retaliation for the steep U.S. tariffs. In May 2002, the Chinese government announced its plan to levy tariff-rate quotas on imports of nine steel products, which would impose tariffs ranging from 7 percent to 26 percent once imports of those products exceed a designated amount. Furthermore, if the WTO panel rules that the U.S. steel tariffs conflict with WTO agreements, China

Sources: Campion Walsh, "EU's Lamy Warns US Steel Tariffs a Dangerous Example," *Dow Jones Newswires,* May 21, 2002; Owen Brown, "EU, China Discuss Campaign against US Steel Tariffs," *Dow Jones Newswires,* April 4, 2002; Andrew Batson, "China Prepares Retaliation against US Steel Tariffs," *Dow Jones Newswires,* May 21, 2002; "WTO Approves EU Bid for Panel on US Steel Tariff Hikes," *Dow Jones Newswire,* June 3, 2002; Dan Bilefsky and Edward Alden, "Test for Bush as EU Retaliates on Gluten Tariffs," *Financial Times,* January 21, 2001; "U.S. Puts Tariff on Canadian Lumber amid Allegations of Unfair Subsidies," *Wall Street Journal,* March 22, 2002; and "Steel, Rolled," *Economist,* August 31, 2002, p. 54.

says it will impose 24 percent tariffs on a list of U.S. products including wastepaper, bean oil, and electric compressors.

The WTO agreed to step into the escalating dispute, agreeing to the EU's request for a panel to rule on the legality of the U.S. decision. The panel could take up to a year to rule on the tariffs' legality, and either side can appeal the ruling, but a decision by the appellate body would then be final. The U.S. argument is the safeguard practice: Under WTO rules, countries can impose temporary increases in tariffs to give time for a domestic industry to restructure to improve competitiveness. According to the EU, Japan, China, and South Korea, however, the U.S. action breaks WTO rules: There was no overall increase in steel imports—a precondition for a safeguard action—and some of the moves target the wrong steel products. Although the U.S. government decided to take back some of its earlier tariffs under pressure from the EU, the U.S. protectionism on its steel industry remains a volatile trade dispute.

The U.S. protectionism is considered a major setback for the world trade system, but it is not new. In January 2001, the European Commission announced it would retaliate against U.S. restriction on wheat gluten imports in 1998 by imposing a tariff on corn gluten feed exported from the United States, which could cost U.S. exporters up to $29.1 million a year. A WTO panel ruled that the United States had failed to establish a causal link between wheat gluten imports and losses being suffered by U.S. companies. Thus, the EU is allowed to offset the damage with similar restriction on imports from the United States. In March 2002, the U.S. government levied tariffs averaging 29 percent on a popular type of Canadian lumbers, but this was said to be an act of retaliation for Canada's "unfair trade practices."

---

labor unions, environmentalists, and other on-lookers who were opposed to free trade for various reasons. As a result, the meeting was postponed until 2001 under so much uncertainty, which resulted in the Doha Round mentioned earlier. Indeed, contrary to the globalization forces at work, anti-globalization sentiment has been building over the years (See Global Perspective 2-4).

Trade-Related Aspects of Intellectual Property Rights (TRIPS). **The Trade-Related Aspects of Intellectual Property Rights** (TRIPS) agreement, concluded as part of the GATT Uruguay Round, mandates that each member country accord to the nationals of other member countries the same treatment as its nationals with regard to intellectual property protection. (See Chapter 5 for details.) However, it is not an international attempt to create a universal patent system. In March 2002, the WTO's TRIPS Council started its work on a list of issues developed at the November 2001 Ministerial Conference in Doha. These include specific aspects of TRIPS and public health, geographical indications, protecting plant and animal inventions, biodiversity, traditional knowledge, the general review of the TRIPS agreement, and technology transfer. One hot issue is to find a solution to the problems countries may face in using compulsory licensing if they have too little or no pharmaceutical

$\mathcal{G}$LOBAL PERSPECTIVE 2-4

ANTIGLOBALIZATION MOVEMENT

Oppositions to corporate and economic globalization have been growing for many years but have received media attention only since the late 1990s. The antiglobalization movement, launched by a French farmer, quickly spread the to other parts of the world. The growing trend toward antiglobalization activism is directed, first, against multinational corporate power and, second, global agreements on economic growth made by international trade institutions, such as the World Trade Organization (WTO), the World Bank, and the International Monetary Fund (IMF).

The movement is often described as "multigenerational, multiclass, and multi-issue." Participants protest against

Sources: Konstantin Lezhandr, "The Future of Europe's Anti-globalization Activists," *Itogi,* April 24, 2002, p. 26; "Anti-Globalization: A Spreading Phenomenon," *Perspectives* (Canadian Security Intelligence Report # 2000/08), http://www.csis-scrs.gc.ca/eng/miscdocs/200008_e.html; Sean Higgins, "Anti-Globalization Protesters Discover New Enemy: Israel," *Investor's Business Daily,* April 23, 2002, p. A16; James Petras, "Porto Alegre 2002: A Tale of Two Forums—Correspondence; Anti-Globalization Social Forum," *Monthly Review,* 53 (April 1, 2002), p. 56; and Julian Nundy, "Fire Destroy McDonald's Site in France; Police Suspect Arson," *Bloomberg News,* May 7, 2002.

capitalism, free trade, international investment (especially from the West to the Third World), cultural and economic globalization, wars, and Western politics. During the last few years, massive antiglobalization protests have accompanied international meetings in cities such Seattle, Quebec City, Genoa, and Washington. The movement became a front-page story when its protesters gathered during the WTO meeting in Seattle in late 1999, almost disrupting the meeting. Later protests focused on the World Bank and IMF. The main slogan is "Here, another world is possible."

Two types of people join this movement: reformists and radicals. Reformists are often engaged in a serious exchange of ideas and proposals on socioeconomic and environmental changes that ask for a broader international participation in decision making. Protests organized by radicals often become violent and disruptive. Campaigners cyberattacked international businesses' Web sites, burned their properties, and destroyed international meetings. Multinational companies are often accused of social injustice, unfair labor practices—including slave labor wages, living, and working conditions—and a lack of concern for the environment, mismanagement of natural resources, and ecological damage.

---

manufacturing capacity. During a special session, WTO members have also embarked on a two-phase program for completing negotiations on a multilateral registration system for geographical indications for wines and spirits.[43]

Global E-Commerce. Due to an explosive use of the Internet, a global effort to regulate international e-commerce has become increasingly necessary (see Chapter 19 for the impact of the Internet on various marketing activities). Nielsen/NetRatings Internet audience survey results show that 888 million people around the world used the Internet as of March 2005, a 146 percent increase from 2000 to 2005.[44] To address this issue, the WTO's Work Program on Electronic Commerce has been working to define the trade-related aspects of electronic commerce that would fall under the parameters of WTO mandates. The Work Program submitted a report to the organization's General Council on March 31, 1999, in which it sought to define such services as intellectual barriers to trade in the context of electronic commerce. Probably the best thing the WTO can do to assist the development of electronic commerce in global trade is to meet its stated goal of assisting in the creation of an environment in which electronic commerce can flourish. According to WTO documents, such an environment requires liberalized market policies and predictable trade regimes that encourage the massive investments in technology that is required for electronic commerce to work.[45]

The United States is taking the lead in bringing e-commerce-related issues to the table. A U.S. document presented to the Work Program's general meeting on March 22,

---

[43] Compiled from TRIPS Material on the WTO Web site, http://www.wto.org/english/tratop_e/trips_e/trips_e.htm; "Patently Problematic," *Economist,* September 14, 2002, pp.75–76; and Donald Richards, "Trade-Related Intellectual Property Rights," *Review of International Political Economy,* 12 (August 2005), pp. 535–51.

[44] Internet World Stats, http://www.internetworldstats.com/stats.htm, accessed December 20, 2005.

[45] David Biederman, "E-Commerce and World Trade," *Traffic World,* 258 (April 26, 1999), p. 22.

1999, clearly outlined both the issues raised by the introduction of e-commerce in international trade and the importance of e-commerce to the global economy. The United States also proposed that the WTO examine services that may emerge as more viable in terms of international trade through e-commerce. For example, with the widespread use of the Internet, has the notion of retailing across borders—previously inhibited by different time zones and the high cost of international communications—now become commercially viable? Now that networked appliances increasingly are used, will remote monitoring, testing, and diagnostics of such devices become increasingly important? Much has yet to be clarified and resolved.

INFORMATION TECHNOLOGY AND THE CHANGING NATURE OF COMPETITION

◆ ◆ ◆ ◆ ◆ ◆ ◆ ◆ ◆

As the nature of value-adding activities in developed nations shifts more and more to information creation, manipulation, and analysis, the developed nations are taking an increased interest in international intellectual property protection measures. Imagine a farmer in the nineteenth century headed into the twentieth century. The intrinsic value of food will not go away in the new century, but as food becomes less and less expensive to produce, the share of the economy devoted to agriculture will shrink (in the United States, agriculture contributes less than 3 percent to the GDP) and so will the margins for the farmer. It would be advisable to move into manufacturing or at least into food processing to maintain margins.

An analogous situation faces a content maker for **information-related products** such as software, music, movies, newspapers, magazines, and education in the late 20th century headed into the 21st century. Until now, content has always been manifested physically: first in people who knew how to do things; then in books, sheet music, records, newspapers, loose-leaf binders, and catalogs; and most recently in tapes, discs, and other electronic media. At first, information could not be "copied": It could only be re-implemented or transferred. People could build new machines or devices that were copies of or improvements on the original; people could tell each other things and share wisdom or techniques to act upon. (Re-implementation was cumbersome and reuse did not take away from the original, but the process of building a new implementation—a new machine or a trained apprentice—took considerable time and physical resources.)

Later, with symbols, paper, and printing presses, people could copy knowledge, and it could be distributed in "fixed" media; performances could be transcribed and recreated from musical scores or scripts. Machines could be mass produced. With such mechanical and electronic media, intellectual value could easily be reproduced, and the need (or demand from creators) to protect intellectual property arose. New laws enabled owners and creators to control the production and distribution of copies of their works. Although reproduction was easy, it was still mostly a manufacturing process, not something an individual could do easily. It took time and money. Physical implementation contributed a substantial portion of the cost.

With the advent of the Information Age, firms face a new situation; not only is it easy for individuals to make duplicates of many works or to reuse their content in new works, but also the physical manifestation of content is almost irrelevant. Over the Internet, any piece of **electronically represented intellectual property** can be almost instantly copied anywhere in the world. Because more and more of value creation in the developed nations is coming from the development and sale of such information-based intellectual property, it is no surprise that developed nations are highly interested in putting strong international intellectual property laws in place. For instance, a recent survey of more than 200 of the largest firms in United Kingdom disclosed that 83 percent of those firms had experienced different types of cyber crime in 2003. Furthermore,

Value of Intellectual Property in Information Age

according to an international specialist in computer forensics, roughly 70 percent of U.K. business professionals have stolen corporate intellectual property through personal e-mails when leaving their employers. Obviously, it is costly for corporations to protect their intellectual property and to adjust for losses in productivity and perceived damage to corporate brand and share price.[46] The U.S. insistence on the inclusion of provisions relating to intellectual property in WTO's TRIPS Agreement is a direct consequence, which is understandable because cyber crime affects all parties with intellectual property. Technology-based protection of electronic information through hardware, software, or a combination thereof in the form of encryption and digital signatures has been suggested as the means of circumventing the problem of unauthorized copying.[47]

Controlling copies (once created by the author or by a third party), however, becomes a complex challenge. A firm can either control something very tightly, limiting distribution to a small, trusted group, or it can rest assured that eventually its product will find its way to a large nonpaying audience—if anyone cares to have it in the first place. Creators of content on the Internet, however, still face the eternal problem: The value of their work generally will not receive recognition without wide distribution. Only by attracting broad attention can an artist or creator hope to attract high payment for copies. Thus, on the Internet, the creators give first performances or books (or whatever) away widely in hopes of recouping with subsequent works, but the breadth of distribution lessens the creator's control of who gets copies and what they do with them. In principle, it should be possible to control and charge for such widely disseminated works, but this will become more and more difficult. People want to pay only for what is perceived as scarce: a personal performance or a custom application or some tangible manifestation that cannot easily be reproduced (by nature or by fiat; that is why the art world has numbered lithographs, for example).

The trick may be to control not the copies of the firm's information product but instead a relationship with the customers: subscriptions or membership. That is often what customers want because they see the relationship as an assurance of a continuing supply of reliable, timely content. Thus, the role of marketing may be expected to assume increasing importance. A firm can, of course, charge a small amount for mass copies. Metering schemes will allow vendors to charge—in fractions of a penny, if desired—according to usage or users rather than copies. However, this scheme will not much change the overall approaching-zero trend of content pricing. At best, it will make charging those low prices much easier.

There are other hurdles for content creators with the emergence of e-commerce. One is the rise of a truly efficient market for information. Content used to be **unfungible:** It was difficult to replace one item with another. Most information is not unique, however, although its creators like to believe it is. There are now specs for content such as stock prices, search criteria, movie ratings, and classifications. In the world of software, for instance, it is becoming easier to define and create products equivalent to a standard. Unknown vendors who can guarantee functionality will squeeze the prices of the market leaders. Of course the leaders (such as Microsoft) can use almost-free content to sell ancillary products or upgrades because they are the leaders and because they have re-invested in loyal distribution channels. The content is advertising for the dealers who resell as well as for the vendors who create. This transformation in the form of value creation and ease of dissemination implies a jump in economic integration as nations become part of an international electronic commerce network. Not only money but also products and services will flow faster.

The other consequence of fungible content, information products, and electronic networks is an additional assault on the power of national governments to regulate international commerce. Ford uses a product design process whereby designers at

---

[46]DeeDee Doke, "Sniffing Out the Evidence," *Personnel Today,* May 11, 2004, pp. 20–22.

[47]Ravi Kalaktota and Andrew B. Whinston, *Frontiers of Electronic Commerce* (Reading, MA: Addison Wesley, 1996). See Chapter 15.

Dearborn, Michigan, pass on their day's work in an electronic form to an office in Japan, which then passes it to designers in Britain, who pass it back to Dearborn the next day. When the information represented in the design crosses borders, how do the governments of the United States, Japan, and Britain treat this information? How will such exchanges be regulated? Less-open societies such as China and Malaysia, recognizing the power of electronic networks, are already attempting to regulate the infrastructure of and access to the electronic network.

Proliferation of E-Commerce and Regulations

A similar problem applies to electronic commerce. The rapid proliferation of e-commerce led by Internet and e-commerce providers, such as AOL, Yahoo, and Amazon.com as well as by traditional marketers that have gone into e-commerce, such as Dell Computer, Victoria's Secret, and Nokia, has spawned a type of international commerce and transactions with which countries' regulations have not kept pace. In terms of e-commerce, how do countries control online purchases and sales? If one looks at Europe, each country has different tax laws and Internet regulations, as well as consumer protection laws. In addition, import and export formalities still apply to goods bought electronically. How to monitor electronic commerce transactions remains a problem for most national governments.[48]

One such example is illustrated by the launch of Viagra by Pfizer in 1998. The company celebrated the most successful drug launch in history with the introduction of Viagra, the first pill that offered effective oral treatment for men who suffer from erectile dysfunction (impotence). Since that time, the name Pfizer has become a synonym for Viagra and vice versa, due to a media hype that arose after this launch of the first of so-called lifestyle drugs to treat undesired symptoms that suppress quality of life. The Internet attracted the portion of patients from all over the world who are not willing to talk about their problem even to their doctors. The Internet quickly filled with "virtual" pharmacies that promised to supply Viagra via a mouse click. Internet pharmacies sometimes try to conceal their location, are set up in offshore places, and sell their items in a gray area of business. Customers who are not willing to disclose their erectile dysfunction can easily order Viagra without consultation of their physician but run the risk of becoming victims of fraud. Internet pharmacies that are selling genuine Viagra pills have found a way to get around the lack of prescription by their customers' physicians in the following way: An online-consultation form can be filled out within a few minutes (at a consultation fee of $65 to $75). The pharmacy's physician then will issue the prescription based on the information ("honestly") given by the customer.[49] This procedure allows the customer to retain a high degree of anonymity while the pharmacy fulfills the obligation to distribute Viagra only after a physician's consultation.

Pfizer and counterfeiting experts have warned the public not to buy from Internet pharmacies.[50] Cases of fraud usually do not occur at reputable pharmacies, but there are many other fraudulent Web sites that will exploit the patient's unwillingness to talk about impotence. The Federal Trade Commission (FTC) is in charge of dealing with entities trying to mislead potential customers and commit fraud. The FTC sent out some warnings about products that claim to be related to Viagra but require no prescription. The warnings advise people to check the credentials of suppliers. Reports of Internet fraud indicate that businesses set up to sell counterfeit pills managed to have about 150,000 customers in about a year. The owner of these "enterprises" advertised pills under names similar to Viagra, such as Viagrae. Pfizer sued, and the FTC was able to find that this name was only one small part in a larger fraud to distribute large amounts of phony pills.[51]

---

[48]Kim Viborg Andersen, Roman Beck, Rolf T. Wigand, Niels Bjùrn-Andersen, and Eric Brousseau, "European e-Commerce Policies in the Pioneering Days, the Gold Rush and the Post-Hype Era," *Information Polity,* 9 (3/4), 2004, pp. 217–232.

[49]See, for example, www.qualitymed.com, www.medservices.com, or www.MDHealthline.com.

[50]"Black Market Filled Phony Viagra Tablets," article at www.cafecrowd.com, accessed August 10, 1999.

[51]See "FTC: Watch for Viagra Knock-Offs," at www.msnbc.com/news/2090, accessed August 10, 1999.

Regulating international e-commerce obviously requires cross-border cooperation. The rising problems have resulted in rendered in numerous international treaties. For example, in May 2001, the Council of Europe, working with Canada, Japan, South Africa, and the United States, approved the 27th draft of the convention on cyber crime, the first international treaty on crime in cyberspace. The treaty requires participating countries to create laws regarding various issues including digital copyrights and computer-related fraud. It offers international businesses the best hope for legal recourse if they become the victim of cyber crime in e-commerce. The United Nations Commission on International Trade Law (UNCITRAL), the core legal body within the United Nations system in the field of international trade law, has also formed a Working Group on Electronic Commerce to reexamine these treaties.[52]

◆ ◆ ◆ ◆ ◆ ◆ ◆ ◆   # REGIONAL ECONOMIC ARRANGEMENTS

An evolving trend in international economic activity is the formation of multinational trading blocs. These blocs take the form of a group of countries (usually contiguous) that decide to have common trading policies for the rest of the world in terms of tariffs and market access but give preferential treatment to one another. Organizational form varies among market regions, but the universal reason for the formation of such groups is to ensure the economic growth and benefit of the participating countries. Regional cooperative agreements have proliferated since the end of World War II. There are already more than 120 regional free trade areas worldwide. Among the more well-known ones existing today are the European Union and the North American Free Trade Agreement. Some of the lesser-known ones include the MERCOSUR (Southern Cone Free Trade Area) and the Andean Group in South America, the Gulf Cooperation Council in the Arabian Gulf region (GCC), the South Asian Agreement for Regional Cooperation in South Asia (SAARC), and the Association of South East Asian Nations (ASEAN). The existence and growing influence of these multinational groupings implies that nations need to become part of such groups to remain globally competitive. To an extent, the regional groupings reflect the countervailing force to the increasing integration of the global economy; they are efforts by governments to control the pace of the integration.

Market groups take many forms, depending on the degree of cooperation and interrelationships, which lead to different levels of integration among the participating countries. There are five levels of formal cooperation among member countries of these regional groupings, ranging from free trade area to the ultimate level of integration, political union.

Before the formation of a regional group of nations for freer trade, some governments agree to participate jointly in projects that create an economic infrastructure (such as dams, pipelines, roads) and that decrease the levels of barriers from a level of little or no trade to substantial trade. Each country can make a commitment to financing part of the project, as India and Nepal did for a hydroelectric dam on the Gandak River. Alternatively, they can share expertise on rural development and poverty alleviation programs and lower trade barriers in selected goods as did SAARC, which comprises India, Pakistan, Sri Lanka, Bangladesh, Nepal, Maldives, and Bhutan. This type of loose cooperation is considered a precursor to a more formal trade agreement.

Free Trade Area   A **free trade area** has a higher level of integration than loosely formed regional cooperation and is a formal agreement among two or more countries to reduce or eliminate customs duties and nontariff trade barriers among partner countries. However, member countries are free to maintain individual tariff schedules for countries that do not

---

[52]Bill Wall, "An Imperfect Cybercrime Treaty," *CIO,* February 15, 2002; and Jason R. Boyarski, "United Nations Working Group Focuses on E-Commerce," *Intellectual Property & Technology Law Journal,* 13 (October 2001).

belong to the free trade group. One fundamental problem with this arrangement is that a free trade area can be circumvented by nonmember countries that can export to the nation having the lowest external tariff in a free trade area and then transport the goods to the destination country in the free trade area without paying the higher tariff applicable if it had gone directly to the destination country. To stem foreign companies from benefiting from this tariff-avoiding method of exporting, *local content laws* are usually introduced. These laws require that for a product to be considered "domestic" and thus not subject to import duties, a certain percentage or more of the value of the product should be sourced within the free trade area. Thus, local content laws are designed to encourage foreign exporters to set up their manufacturing locations in the free trade area.

The North American Free Trade Agreement (NAFTA) is the free trade agreement among Canada, the United States, and Mexico. It eliminates all tariffs on industrial products traded between Canada, Mexico, and the United States within a period of 10 years from the date of implementation of the NAFTA agreement—January 1, 1994. NAFTA was preceded by the free trade agreement between Canada and the United States, which went into effect in 1989. The United States also has a free trade area agreement with Israel. Canada signed a trade deal with the Andean Group in 1999 as a forerunner to a possible free trade agreement.[53] Mexico also established a formal trans-Atlantic free trade area agreement with the European Union without U.S. involvement in 2000[54] and with Japan in 2005.[55] The United States also reached a free trade agreement with Chile on December 11, 2002,[56] and most recently formed the Central American-Dominican Republic Free Trade Agreement (CAFTA-DR) with Costa Rica, the Dominican Republic, El Salvador, Guatemala, Honduras, and Nicaragua, which was effective January 1, 2006.[57]

Another free trade group is the European Free Trade Association (EFTA) consisting of Iceland, Liechtenstein, Norway, and Switzerland. Although Austria, Finland, and Sweden used to be EFTA member countries, they have joined the European Union (EU), and Switzerland has been negotiating with EU to become a member.[58] It appears that some, if not all of, the remaining EFTA members may gradually merge into the European Union (discussed later). In the meantime, Singapore and EFTA also agreed to form a free trade area effective on January 1, 2003.[59] MERCOSUR is a free trade area consisting of consisting of Brazil, Argentina, Uruguay, Paraguay and Venezuela with Chile, Bolivia, and Peru, as associate members[60] with the intention to lower internal trade barriers and the ultimate goal of the creation of a customs union.[61]

One probably most ambitious free trade area plan is also in the works. The Free Trade Area of the Americas (FTAA) was proposed in December 1994, by 34 countries in the region as an effort to unite the economies of the Western Hemisphere into a single free trade agreement, which was originally planned to have been completed by January 2005. Because of political opposition and reluctance from some major countries, such as Brazil and Venezuela, the negotiations for the agreement were

---

[53]"Canadian Companies Get Andean Boost," *World Trade,* 12 (September 1999), p. 14.

[54]"Mexico Turns To Europe," *Europe,* July/August 2001, pp. 18–19.

[55]Joseph P. Whitlock, "US Has Stake in Japan-Mexico FTA," *Journal of Commerce,* 6 (23), June 6, 2005, pp. 34–34.

[56]"U.S. and Chile Reach Free Trade Accord," *New York Times,* http://www.nytimes.com, December 11, 2002.

[57]"CAFTA-DR to Build Options over Time," *Marketing News,* February 1, 2006, pp. 13–14.

[58]Sieglinde Gstöhl, "Scandinavia and Switzerland: Small, Successful and Stubborn towards the EU," *Journal of European Public Policy,* 9 (August 2002), pp. 529–49.

[59]"Singapore-EFTA Agreement Sets New Standards," *Managing Intellectual Property,* (July/August 2002), pp. 11–12.

[60]Venezuela became a fifth permanent member of MERCOSUR on July 4, 2006. See "Chavez, Castro May Push Mercosur Meeting Leftward," *New York Times,* July 20, 2006.

[61]Maria Cecilia Coutinho de Arruda and Masaaki Kotabe, "MERCOSUR: An Emergent Market in South America," in Masaaki Kotabe, *MERCOSUR and Beyond: The Imminent Emergence of the South American Markets* (Austin, TX: The University of Texas at Austin, 1997).

stalled even at the most recent Summit of the Americas, November 4–5, 2005.[62] If completed, however, the FTAA agreement would encompass an area from the Yukon to Tierra del Fuego with 800 million people and about $13 trillion in production of goods and services, making it the most significant regional trade initiative presently pursued by the United States. Regional cooperative agreements in the 1990s such as NAFTA and MERCOSUR have made trading within the continent much easier, but the South American markets are still less open than those of East Asia. Despite the fact that many doubted the U.S. government's power to stand up to domestic industries crying for protection, many are seeing FTAA as more than a remote hypothesis and are already preparing for it. Brazil, a member of MERCOSUR and that is South America's largest economy, is not sure about FTAA but cannot afford the loss if the rest of the Americas join without it.[63]

Japan had not been keen on regional free trade area agreements because it has preferred a broader multilateral free trade regime as espoused by WTO. However, under pressure from an increasing number of successful regional trade agreements, Japan aiming to offset the economic challenges posed by the EU and the NAFTA zones, has formed a free trade agreement with Singapore, another with Mexico,[64] and resumed free trade area talks with ASEAN[65] (see Global Perspective 2-5 on Japan's push for free trade areas in Asia).

◆ ◆

$\mathcal{G}$LOBAL PERSPECTIVE 2-5

FREE TRADE AREAS IN ASIA

The global trend of forming strategic trade blocs is accelerating, given the success of the EU and the NAFTA. The United States already has NAFTA under its belt and is now creating a pan-American trade area. Because the United States and European countries now have entered the final stages of creating huge economic zones, Japan figured that it is time to catch up.

In January 2002, the Japanese government, having criticized and opposed free trade agreements (FTAs) for years, had its first-ever FTA with Singapore. Now it is proposing an East Asia Free-Trade Area no later than 2012. The grouping, dubbed by Japanese officials as "ASEAN plus five," would represent one-third of the world's population and would cover the 10 member Association of Southeast Asian Nations (ASEAN) as well as Japan, mainland China, South Korea, Hong Kong, and Taiwan. With progress in ASEAN-India

Sources: Yoshikuni Sugiyama, "Economic Forum—Japan Does About-Face on Asia FTAs," *Yomiuri Shimbun,* September 11, 2001; Hatakeyama Noboru, "What Is the ASEAN Economic Community?" *Economy, Culture & History Japan Spotlight Bimonthly,* 24 (May/June 2005), p. 2; and "Japan to Reopen Trade Pact Talks with ASEAN in April," *NikkeiNet Interactive,* http://www.nni.nikkei.co.jp, March 11, 2006.

economic ties also being under way, the establishment of a pan-Asian economic zone covering a wide area from East Asia to South Asia is possible. As a result, the creation of a pan-Asian economic zone would include "ASEAN plus five," and India is being advocated.

Japan believes that the integration should take place well ahead of 2012, the deadline for Japan and other industrial members of the Asia-Pacific Economic Cooperation forum to liberalize trade under the so-called Bogor Declaration. Japan's aggressive pursuit of bilateral FTAs with Asian countries could eventually lead to an expanded Japan-led economic bloc in the region. In the future, the area could be extended to Australia and New Zealand, according to the official. The partnership would involve a comprehensive economic integration in terms of free trade and cross-border investment, services trade, and harmonization of economic policies and systems. China and ASEAN, meanwhile, held the first meeting of senior officials in May 2002 to draw up a blueprint for the free-trade area that their leaders agreed in 2001 to set up within 10 years. Because ASEAN invited Japan, China, and South Korea to its annual summit in 1997, ASEAN has already evolved into "ASEAN-plus-three".

---

[62]"Hemisphere Meeting Ends without Trade Consensus," *New York Times,* November 6, 2005.

[63]"Overview of the FTAA Process," www.ftaa-alca.org/View_e.asp, Accessed December 15, 2002; and "A Really Big Gree-Trade Zone," *Business Week,* December 23, 2002, p. 40.

[64]Joseph P. Whitlock, "US Has Stake in Japan–Mexico FTA," *Journal of Commerce,* 6 (23), June 6, 2005, pp. 34–34.

[65]"Japan to Reopen Trade Pact Talks with ASEAN in April," *NikkeiNet Interactive,* http://www.nni.nikkei.co.jp, March 11, 2006.

Customs Union

The inherent weakness of the free trade area concept could lead to its gradual disappearance in the future, although it could continue to be an attractive stepping-stone to a higher level of integration. When members of a free trade area add common external tariffs to the provisions of the free trade agreement, the free trade area becomes a **customs union.**

Therefore, members of a customs union have not only reduced or eliminated tariffs among themselves but also a common external tariff with countries that are not members of the customs union. This prevents nonmember countries from exporting to member countries that have low external tariffs with the goal of sending the exports to a country that has a higher external tariff through the first country that has a low external tariff. The ASEAN (Brunei, Cambodia, Indonesia, Laos, Malaysia, Myanmar, the Philippines, Singapore, Thailand, and Vietnam) is a good example of a current functional customs union with the goal of a common market. The Treaty of Rome of 1958, which formed the European Economic Community, created a customs union between West Germany, France, Italy, Belgium, the Netherlands, and Luxembourg.

Common Market

As cooperation increases among the countries of a customs union, they can form a **common market,** which eliminates all tariffs and other barriers to trade among its members, adopts a common set of external tariffs for nonmembers, and removes all restrictions on the flow of capital and labor among member nations. The 1958 Treaty of Rome that created the European Economic Community had the ultimate goal of the creation of a common market, a goal that was substantially achieved in the early 1990s in Western Europe.

The **Maastricht Treaty,** which succeeded the Treaty of Rome, became effective on November 1, 1993, calling for the creation of a union (and hence the change in name to *European Union*). At a historic summit on December 13, 2002, the EU agreed to add 10 new member countries, creating the 25-member **European Union** effective on May 1, 2004, with a total economy larger than that of the United States.[66] Those 10 new members are mostly Eastern and Central European countries once part of the former Soviet Union. Now German banks can freely open branches in Poland, and Portuguese workers can live and work in Luxembourg.

Monetary Union

The Maastricht Treaty in January 1999 also laid down rules for, and accomplished, the creation of a **monetary union** with the introduction of the euro, a new European currency that began its circulation in January 2002. As per the Maastricht Treaty, the EU's 12 member countries[67] have adopted the euro so far. A monetary union represents the fourth level of integration with a single common currency among politically independent countries. In strict technical terms, a monetary union does not require the existence of a common market or a customs union, a free trade area, or a regional cooperation for development. However, it is the logical next step to a common market because it requires the next higher level of cooperation among member nations.

Political Union

The culmination of the process of integration is the creation of a **political union,** which can be another name for a nation that truly achieves the levels of integration described

---

[66] As of the beginning of 2006, the European Union consisted of 25 countries: Austria, Belgium, Cyprus, Czech Republic, Denmark, Estonia, Finland, France, Germany, Greece, Hungary, Ireland, Italy, Latvia, Lithuania, Luxembourg, Malta, Poland, Portugal, Slovakia, Slovenia, Spain, Sweden, the Netherlands, and the United Kingdom.

[67] The euro member countries are Belgium, Germany, Greece, Spain, France, Ireland, Italy, Luxembourg, the Netherlands, Austria, Portugal, and Finland. It is to be noted that two large EU member countries—the United Kingdom and Sweden—have not joined the euro monetary region.

here on a voluntary basis. The ultimate stated goal of the Maastricht Treaty is the formating a political union through the adoption of a constitution for an enlarged European Union. However, the member countries have varying levels of concern about ceding any part of their sovereignty to an envisaged political union. In May 2005, France shocked Europe by voting against the EU constitution with a decisive margin. In June, the Dutch voted more strongly against the constitution. According to analysts, the rejection by the Dutch and French is a terrible blow to the morale of true believers in a political union for the EU. For the constitution to become effective, all 25 EU members must ratify it. Because France has always been politically central to the EU as one of its six founders and one of the 12 members that accepted the European currency, it is extremely difficult for the EU to handle the current crisis. Previously, some political leaders urged voters to approve the constitution to make Europe more efficient, dynamic, and democratic. However, the French consider the constitution as a means for the EU members to impose "Anglo-Saxon" free market policies on them. They voted against the constitution to protect their jobs, employment rights, and social benefits from low-cost, low-tax, deregulated countries.[68]

◆ ◆ ◆ ◆ ◆ ◆ ◆ ◆ ## MULTINATIONAL CORPORATIONS

Although no steadfast definition of **multinational corporation** (MNC) exists, the U.S. government defines it for statistical purposes as a company that owns or controls 10 percent or more of the voting securities or the equivalent of at least one foreign business enterprise. Many large multinationals have numerous subsidiaries and affiliates in many parts of the world. In the early 1970s, Howard Perlmutter, a professor at the Wharton School of the University of Pennsylvania, predicted that by 1985, around 80 percent of the noncommunist world's productive assets would be controlled by just 200 to 300 companies. Now some 70,000 multinational companies have 690,000 affiliates in foreign countries. In 2003, foreign affiliates employed about 53 million people around the world, compared to 24 million in 1990. The stock of outward foreign direct investment (FDI) increased from $1.7 trillion in 1990 to $8.2 trillion in 2003. Foreign affiliates' sales account for 23 percent of world GDP. Although FDI stock in manufacturing experienced a consecutive decline from 2000 to 2003, FDI stock in services climbed from 43 percent of the region's total inward stock in 1995 to 60 percent in 2003, with an estimated value of $4 trillion. During the same period, FDI stock in manufacturing fell to 44 percent. Outward FDI in services continues to be dominated by developed countries, although FDI is more evenly distributed among them. By 2002, Japan and the European Union had emerged as significant sources of outward FDI in service sectors. Developing countries' outward FDI in services has also grown gradually since the 1990s.[69]

The forces of economies of scale, lowering trade, and investment barriers, needs to be close to markets, internalization of operations within the boundaries of one firm, and the diffusion of technology will continue to increase multinationals' influence in international trade and investment. The sovereignty of nations will perhaps continue to weaken because of MNCs and the increasing integration of economies. Some developing countries harbor negative feelings about the sense of domination by large MNCs, but the threat to sovereignty may not assume the proportions alluded to by some researchers.[70] Although the sheer size established MNCs appears hegemonic and have some monopolistic power in smaller economies, MNCs have yet to solve

---

[68]"Dead, but Not Yet Buried," *Economist,* June 4, 2005, pp. 47–48.

[69]United Nations Conference on Trade and Development, *World Investment Report 2004* and *World Investment Report 2005* (Geneva: United Nations, 2004 and 2005).

[70]Raymond Vernon, *Sovereignty at Bay* (New York: Basic Books, 1971).

the problem associated with their large size. Current trends indicate that beyond a certain size, firms tend to become complacent and slow and falter against competition. They are no longer able to remain focused on their businesses and lack the drive, motivation, and can-do attitude that permeates smaller firms. Those firms that do focus on their core businesses shed unrelated businesses that tend to be less profitable or even incur losses.[71] For example, Novartis, the Swiss pharmaceutical group, recently sold off its Swedish Wasa biscuits and crackers subsidiary to the Italian food company Barilla to concentrate on its health science products.[72] Thus, the nation-state, while considerably weaker than its nineteenth century counterpart, is likely to remain alive and well.

Currency movements, capital surpluses, faster growth rates, and falling trade and investment barriers have helped MNCs from many countries join the cross-border scene. In today's world, it is not unusual for a start-up firm to become global at its inception. Those firms are known as *born global*.[73] It is now easier than ever for small firms to be in international business through exports, imports, and e-commerce. A major survey of companies with fewer than 500 employees conducted by Arthur Andersen & Co. and National Small Business United, a trade group, found that exporters averaged $3.1 million in revenue compared with $2.1 million for all companies in the survey in 1996 and reported that exporters' profits increased 4.4 percent while the overall average was 2.6 percent. Exporters are also more technology savvy: 92 percent have computers (versus 79 percent overall), and 70 percent use the Internet (versus 44 percent overall).[74]

SUMMARY ❖

The world economy is becoming increasingly intertwined, and virtually no country that has a steadily rising standard of living is independent of the economic events in the rest of the world. It is almost as if participation in the international economy is a *sine qua non* of economic growth and prosperity—a country must participate in the world economy to grow and prosper—but participation is not without its risks. Events outside one country can have detrimental effects on the economic health of that country. The Asian financial crisis that started in 1997 with a precipitous depreciation of Thailand's baht, Indonesia's rupiah, Malaysia's ringgit, and Korea's won, among others, was a situation in which the withdrawal of funds by portfolio investors caused a severe economic crisis. In effect, participating in the international economy imposes its own discipline on a nation, independent of the policies of that nation's government, This is not to suggest that countries should stay outside the international economic system because of the risks. Those countries that have elected to stay outside the international economic system—autarkies such as Burma and North Korea—continue to fall farther behind the rest of the world in terms of living standards and prosperity.

Various forces are responsible for the increased integration. Major emerging economies have begun to reshape the nature of international trade and investment. Growth in international trade continuously outpaces the rise in national outputs. Transportation and communications are becoming faster, less expensive, and more widely accessible. The nature of value-adding activities is changing in the advanced countries from manufacturing to services and information manipulation. Such changes are a result of and a force behind the rapid advancement in telecommunications and computers. Even developing nations, regardless of their political colors, have realized the importance of telecommunications and e-commerce and are attempting to improve their infrastructure. The capital markets of the world are already integrated for all practical purposes, and this integration affects exchange rates, interest rates, investments, employment, and growth across the world. Multinational corporations have truly become the global operations in name and spirit that they were envisaged to be. Even smaller companies are leapfrogging the gradual expansion pattern of traditional multinational companies by adopting e-commerce that has no national boundaries. In short, to repeat an old maxim, the world is becoming a global village. When Karl Marx said in 1848 that the world was becoming a smaller place, he could not have imagined how small it truly has become.

[71] John A. Doukas and L.H.P. Lang, "Foreign Direct Investment, Diversification and Firm Performance," *Journal of International Business Studies,* 34 (March 2003), pp. 153–72.

[72] Paul Betts, "Barilla Pays SFr475m for Wasa Biscuits," *Financial Times,* April 27, 1999, p.33.

[73] Alex Rialp, Josep Rialp, and Gary A. Knight, "The Phenomenon of Early Internationalizing Firms: What Do We Know after a Decade (1993–2003) of Scientific Inquiry?" *International Business Review,* 14 (April 2005), pp. 147–66.

[74] "Export Energy," *Business Week,* November 17, 1997.

KEY TERMS ◆

Big emerging markets (BEMs)

Common market

Country competitiveness

Customs union

Doha Development Agenda (Doha Round)

Electronically represented intellectual property

European Union

Foreign direct investment

Free trade area

General Agreements on Tariffs and Trade (GATT)

Gross Domestic Product (GDP)

Intellectual-related products

International Trade Organization (ITO)

Maastricht Treaty

Monetary union

Multinational corporation (MNC)

Normal trade relations (NTR) status [formerly most favored nation (MFN) status]

Omnibus Trade and Competitiveness Act of 1988

Political union

Portfolio (indirect) investment

Trade-related aspects of intellectual property rights (TRIPS) agreement

Triad regions

Uruguay Round

World Trade Organization (WTO)

Unfungible

REVIEW QUESTIONS ◆ ◆ ◆ ◆ ◆ ◆ ◆ ◆ ◆ ◆ ◆ ◆ ◆ ◆ ◆ ◆ ◆

1. What are some of the visible signs of the current increased economic interdependence among countries? What are some reasons for this growth in interdependence and for the rise in global integration?

2. What is GATT, and what is its role in international transactions?

3. How is the WTO different from GATT? What functions is WTO expected to perform?

4. In what ways have U.S. foreign direct investment and trade patterns changed over the past decade?

5. Cooperative interrelationships between countries (regional groupings) can be classified into five broad categories.

What are these categories, and how does each differ from the others?

6. Do current measures of balance of payments accurately reflect a country's transactions with the rest of the world? What are the concerns?

7. What challenges do the content creators and information providers face due to the advent and popularity of the electronic media? Are there current mechanisms to protect their rights? What are the macroeconomic implications for industrialized countries?

8. What are some of the forces influencing the increase in size of multinational corporations? Are any forces influencing them to downsize?

DISCUSSION QUESTIONS ◆ ◆ ◆ ◆ ◆ ◆ ◆ ◆ ◆ ◆ ◆ ◆ ◆ ◆ ◆

1. Recently in response to a dispute with both the U.S. and the European Union concerning their possible action of imposing tariffs on cheap textile products from China, China took countermeasure actions to exclude those products from the existing export tariffs to ward off damages to its economy. To resolve the issue, in June 2005, the EU signed an agreement with China imposing new quotas on 10 categories of textile goods, limiting growth in those categories to between 8 percent and 12.5 percent a year. The agreement was made in hope of providing EU's domestic manufacturers time to adjust to a world of unfettered competition, but for most retailers in Europe, which had already placed orders for mountains of new goods from China, it turned out to be a disaster when 10s of millions of garments piled up in warehouses and customs checkpoints, after Chinese textile manufacturers exceeded their quotas right after the restriction. As a matter of fact, less than a month after the agreement, men's trousers hit their import quota, followed rapidly by blouses, bras, T-shirts, and flax yarn. It is estimated that France lost about one-third of its jobs in the sector between 1993 and 2003. Italy has also seen its firms suffer since the euro transition. Nevertheless, it is not

clear as to how the quota restriction on Chinese goods would help domestic producers, especially when there are so many low-cost firms in low-wage countries such as Bangladesh and Costa Rica waiting to take up any Chinese slack. According to an EU official, the action against China was designed to help workers in those very countries in that the EU also considered the effect the Chinese market share was having on other developing countries that have historically been dependent on our market. Who will protect jobs in Tunisia and Morocco? While large retailers will probably be able to find new sources for their autumn and winter lines under the quota restriction, it seems that smaller stores may be driven into bankruptcy as the clothes they have bought were buried in warehouses around Europe. Do you think the EU textile war with China will eventually save the EU's domestic businesses? Should the United States follow the EU to impose textile quota on Chinese imports to protect its domestic businesses? Why or why not?

2. A justification of developing countries against product patents for pharmaceutical products has been that if they were enforced, life-saving drugs would be out of reach for all but the very rich. A similar argument is being used in

a populist move in the U.S Senate for reducing the patent lives of innovative drugs in a bid to reduce health care costs. Some senators and the pharmaceutical industry leaders claim that this move would discourage medical innovation and slow the development of drugs for the cure of such diseases as AIDS and cancer, and thereby increase the costs of caring for current and future patients. How would you react to the arguments and counterarguments for reducing patent lives, and what would be your stance on this issue? In your opinion, what would be the international repercussions if this bill were to pass? How do you think other developed and developing countries would react?

3. In 1990, Robert Reich, an ex-Harvard professor (and Labor Secretary in the Clinton administration) stated that multinational corporations (MNCs) have become so internationally oriented that what is good for U.S. multinationals may no longer be good for the United States. Therefore, the U.S. government should not treat U.S. MNCs any differently than foreign corporations' subsidiaries in the United States. Laura Tyson, then a professor at the University of California, Berkeley (and the chairperson of the Council of Economic Advisers in the Clinton administration), countered this by stating that U.S. MNCs still remain overwhelmingly American in terms of their highest-value production and that economic and national security considerations required U.S. policy makers to differentiate between U.S.- and foreign-owned corporations. Whom would you agree with, and why? According to the International Automobile Manufacturers Association, foreign-owned auto plants in the United States contributed to 500,000 jobs and U.S.$10 billion in investments. Would this information influence your previous answer? How?

4. Information technology is having significant effects on the globalization activities of corporations. Texas Instruments is now developing sophisticated chips in India. Motorola has set up programming and equipment design centers in China, India, Singapore, Hong Kong, Taiwan, and Australia. Similarly, a large number of U.S. and European corporations are looking at ways to transfer activities such as preparing tax returns, account statements, insurance claims, and other information processing work to Asia. Although until now only blue-collar employees in the industrialized countries faced the threat of competition from low-wage countries (which could be countered to some extent through direct and indirect trade barriers), this new trend in movement of white-collar tasks may be a cause for concern to industrialized countries as the sophistication of these tasks increases. This movement of white-collar jobs could be a cause for social concern in the near future. Do you foresee social pressures in developed countries having the potential of reversing the trend of movement of white-collar tasks to developing countries? Given the intangibility of information, are there any effective ways of controlling the movement of information across borders?

5. The effects of the formation of regional trade blocs on international trade could be interpreted in two ways. One way is to view regional blocs as one step forward in the process of ensuring completely free trade among countries on a global basis. On the other hand, the formation of regional blocs could be seen as a step backward toward an era of greater protectionism and greater trade tensions between the regions. Which view would you agree with, and why?

6. Electronic commerce (e-commerce) blurs the distinction between a good and a service. Under WTO, goods tend to be subject to tariffs; services are not, but trade in services is limited by restrictions on "national treatment" or quantitative controls on access to foreign markets. For example, a compact disc sent from one country to another is clearly a good, and will be subject to an import tariff as it crosses the national border. But if the music on the disc is sent electronically from a computer in one country to one in another country via the Internet, is it a good or a service? Customized data and software, which can be put on CD, are usually treated as services. What confusion would you expect with the WTO overseeing increased transaction on the Internet?

SHORT CASES

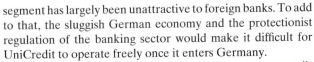

CASE 2-1

A TRULY EUROPEAN BANK—UNICREDIT HVB

Until recently, cross-border mergers between service firms were almost unheard of in the European Union due to the national protectionist sentiment that persisted in European business. Industry analysts had been predicting this trend for several years, but the coming years are expected to actually witness more mergers between banks in Europe on the heels of the biggest banking merger so far in European history between Italy's UniCredit (formerly UniCredito Italiano) and Germany's HVB (Hypovereinsbank) Group. The merger created the fourth largest European bank with a market capitalization of over 41 billion euros. UniCredit offered five of its own shares for one share of HVB, valuing HVB at 15.4 billion euros.

In 2005, Milan-based UniCredit made a bid to merge with HVB. It was rumored that France's PNB Paribas and other major banks were also eyeing the unprofitable German bank. The primary motivation for the merger is supposed to be Bank Austria, majority owned by HVB. UniCredit, which already owned banks in Croatia, Poland, Czech Republic, and Turkey had been on the lookout to expand its operations in Eastern Europe. With the addition of Eastern European economies into the European Union some months earlier, this move was just in time. The emerging Central and Eastern European area offers great growth opportunities for the merged bank, in that only about 50 percent of the total population in the area owns a bank account with only a small percentage of those owning savings accounts.

With the completion of the merger, UniCredit HVB became the largest bank in Central and Eastern Europe in terms of assets and number of branches, more than twice the size of the second largest bank in the region. It also becomes the leader in Italy, Austria, and Germany.

However, for UniCredit, entering the German market is going to be easier attempted than done. The German banking regulation is notorious for its three-tier structure that disallows mergers between public savings banks, private bodies, and cooperative lenders. As a result, the German banking

segment has largely been unattractive to foreign banks. To add to that, the sluggish German economy and the protectionist regulation of the banking sector would make it difficult for UniCredit to operate freely once it enters Germany.

As for European business in general, the merger entails employee layoffs in excess of 9,000 employees, most of them in the Central and Eastern region. The merger also comes in the wake of criticism of Italy's policies by the European Union's regulatory bodies because Italy's central bank initially prevented Dutch ABN Amro and other European banks from taking over two of Italy's banks. The Italian government gave in and stepped aside a few months later when it received a warning from the European Union's internal markets commissioner. Italy, however, commended UniCredit's purchase of Germany's HVB.

The news of the merger between UniCredit and HVB has significant implications for the unconsolidated European banking sector and it is already creating a disturbance among other banks. More European integration taking place and relaxing of regulation have provoked erstwhile shy European banks to pursue growth opportunities beyond their national borders. In addition, the passing of a new Europewide banking regulation, know as *Basel II,* is expected to benefit cross-border mergers within Europe. In the past, European banks restricted themselves to domestic mergers, which sat better with shareholders than foreign mergers that did not bring about sufficient synergies. Brussels waits and watches for that wave of consolidation in Europe's banking industry.

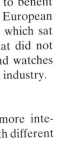

DISCUSSION QUESTIONS

1. Although the European Union is becoming more integrated, it is still made up of distinct nation states with different governments. What does this mean for "cross-border" marketing after the cross-border merger?

2. Why have mergers between manufacturing companies in Europe been more common that those between service firms?

3. How does the addition of 10 new states in the EU's territory affect European business in general and the strategies of existing European multinationals in particular?

Source: "UniCredit Advances—but Must Stay on its Toes," *Euromoney,* September 2005, pp. 284–288, and various other sources.

CASE 2-2

BOEING VERSUS AIRBUS? OR THE U. S. VERSUS THE EU? LET THE WTO DECIDE!

So who gets to decide which party wins when two of the world's largest aircraft manufacturers engage in a trade war? Well, apparently, it is the World Trade Organization (WTO),

which in 2005 received its biggest international trade petition since its establishment in 1995: the case to settle the dispute between U.S.-based Boeing and European Airbus. Airbus is jointly owned by European aerospace company EADS and BAE Systems.

The dispute is not new. It dates back to the 1980s when the two behemoths went head on against each other in the market for civil aircraft. In 1992, the two rivals attempted to reach a settlement. Airbus had largely relied on "launch aid" from European governments such as those of France, Germany, and the United Kingdom (UK) while Boeing received subsidies from U.S. government agencies, mainly the Department of Defense and the National Aeronautics and Space Administration (NASA). Airbus' launch aid consisted of loans for product development that were written off if the products failed in the market. However, if the product was a success, the governments would continue to receive royalties from it even after the loans were paid off. Under the bilateral settlement in 1992, the companies and the countries involved agreed that Boeing's aid from external parties would not exceed 4 percent of its revenues and Airbus's loans would be maintained at 33 percent of its development costs for an aircraft.

The new found peace in 1992 did not last too long. Both parties remained suspicious that the other was breaking the terms of the bilateral contract. What exacerbated the situation was the Airbus launch of five new products after the 1992 agreement, its final blow to Boeing being its most recent A380 model. Boeing meanwhile managed to introduce only one new product in the same time period. Furthermore, Airbus became a profitable company and was on par with Boeing's market position and therefore, according to Boeing, Airbus no longer needed help from the European governments. In May 2004, U.S. Trade Representative Robert E. Zoellick met with Pascal Lamy, European Commissioner for Trade, to suggest that both parties agree to rule out the use of new subsidies for aircraft, but the Europeans refused to make any promises. In fact, Airbus continued to seek launch aid from the government. And so the discussions went on.

In October 2004, the United States filed a complaint with the WTO against Airbus, and the EU retaliated by immediately filing a countersuit with the WTO against Boeing. Their reasons remained the same: EU government aid versus U.S. subsidies. To avoid an expensive legal encounter, once again the two parties decided to engage in bilateral negotiations with the expectation that they would reach a settlement by April 11, 2005, but it was not meant to be. Boeing and its supporters

Source: "In the Race," *Aviation Week & Space Technology,* October 10, 2005, pp. 22–23, and various other sources.

maintained their stance against Airbus, which instead insisted that Boeing's Japanese suppliers had obtained soft loans from their government and therefore Boeing benefited from these indirect subsidies as well. Finally, in June 2005, both parties reapproached the WTO.

The WTO's trade agreement on Subsidies and Countervailing Measures disallows government subsidies or subsidies from public bodies to a particular company or industry. The U.S. side of the appeal to the WTO includes its claim that Airbus breached these WTO rules when it accepted around $15 billion in loans from the EU governments. On the other hand, the EU claims that Boeing broke the WTO rules when it received around $23 billion in subsidies. It will be interesting to see who wins the case, Boeing or Airbus, and, since their respective governments are solidly intertwined with the companies, the United States or the European Union.

The last time the WTO adjudicated a similar case was in the 1990s, the case being Brazil's Embraer versus Canada's Bombardier, both medium-size jet manufacturers. However, in that case, even though the WTO gave a "guilty" verdict to both parties, there was no special action taken by either party. Their governments continued to grant subsidies to the companies. According to experts, it is likely that the WTO would find both parties guilty in the Boeing-Airbus case as well, which may once again lead the firms to pursue another bilateral agreement.

While the outcome of the WTO's decision might chart out the course of future competition between Boeing and Airbus, the importance of the case sheds light on the role of the WTO in world trade negotiations and policy. Even though many countries still have bilateral trade agreements, more countries are turning to the WTO to arbitrate their disputes. With a growing membership that rests at 149 in 2006, the WTO's authority on trade matters is being recognized and its world trade rules supersede bilateral and other similar trade pacts. In the meantime, Boeing and Airbus wait for a verdict.

DISCUSSION QUESTIONS

1. On one hand, the WTO's role in international trade is becoming more significant. On the other hand, its verdict on the case of Brazil's Embraer versus Canada's Bombardier did not seem to solve the problem. Discuss.

2. Why does the Boeing–Airbus case, a dispute between two firms, extend to their governments?

3. What issues should the WTO consider before making a decision? How should the WTO make a decision?

FURTHER READING ◆

Bezmen, Trisha L, and David D. Selover. "Patterns of Economic Interdependence in Latin America." *International Trade Journal,* 19 (Fall 2005), pp. 217–67.

Johansson, Johny K. *In Your Face: How American Marketing Excess Fuels Anti-Americanism.* Upper Saddle River, NJ: Financial Times Prentice Hall, 2004.

Kotler, Philip, Somkid Jatusripitak, and Suvit Maesincee. *The Marketing of Nations: A Strategic Approach to Building National Wealth.* New York: Free Press, 1997.

"Latin America: A Time of Transition." *Finance and Development,* 42 (4), December 2005.

Rugman, Alan. *The Regional Multinationals.* Cambridge: Cambridge University Press, 2005.

Montealegre, Ramiro. "Four Visions of E-Commerce in Latin America in the Year 2010." *Thunderbird International Business Review,* 43 (6) (2002), pp. 717–35.

Moore, Mike, ed. *Doha and Beyond: The Future of the Multilateral Trading System.* New York: Cambridge University Press, 2004.

Schulz, Michael, Fredrik Soderbaum, and Joakim Ojendal, ed. *Regionalization in a Globalizing World: A Comparative Perspective on Forms, Actors, and Processes.* New York: Zed Books, 2001.

Shenkar, Oded. *The Chinese Century: The Rising Chinese Economy and Its Impact on the Global Economy, the Balance of Power, and Your Job.* Upper Saddle River, NJ: Wharton School Publishing, 2005.

Sohn, Byeong Hae. "Regionalization of Trade and Investment in East Asia and Prospects for Further Regional Integration." *Journal of the Asia Pacific Economy,* 7 (June 2002), pp. 160–81.

"The China Price." *Business Week,* December 6, 2004, pp. 102–24.

"The Tiger in Front: A Survey of India and China." *Economist,* March 5, 2005.

The European Union: A Guide for Americans. Washington, DC: Delegation of the European Commission, 2002.

Vachani, Sushil. "Mavericks and Free Trade: Chile's Pivotal Role in the Formation of the FTAA." *Thunderbird International Business Review,* 46 (May/June 2004), pp. 237–53.

FINANCIAL ENVIRONMENT

CHAPTER OVERVIEW

1. HISTORICAL ROLE OF THE U.S. DOLLAR

2. DEVELOPMENT OF THE CURRENT INTERNATIONAL MONETARY SYSTEM

3. FIXED VERSUS FLOATING EXCHANGE RATES

4. FOREIGN EXCHANGE AND FOREIGN EXCHANGE RATES

5. BALANCE OF PAYMENTS

6. ECONOMIC AND FINANCIAL TURMOIL AROUND THE WORLD

7. MARKETING IN EURO-LAND

When international transactions occur, *foreign exchange* is the monetary mechanism allowing the transfer of funds from one nation to another. The existing international monetary system always affects companies as well as individuals whenever they buy or sell products and services across national boundaries. The dollar's strengths vis-à-vis other major currencies at the dawn of this new century affected not only foreign but also U.S. companies. For example, in the fourth-quarter of 2001, Amazon.com posted its first-ever profit of US$5.1 million, thanks to reduced U.S. dollar payments on its euro-denominated debt.[1] Similarly, due to the weaker yen compared to the U.S. dollar in 2005, Japanese multinational corporations, such as Toyota, were able to post higher profit as these companies' overseas businesses in the United States collect sales in U.S. dollars but report profit in Japanese yen. Every 1 yen drop in the Japanese currency is expected to lift Toyota's operating profit by around 25 billion yen (which would amount to a whopping $212 million at 118 yen/$ as of November 7, 2005).[2] It is obvious that the current international monetary system has a profound impact not only on individuals and companies but also on the U.S. balance of payments at the aggregate level.

---

[1] Raizel Robin, "New Age Profit," *Canadian Business,* February 18, 2002.
[2] "Weaker Yen to Buoy Japanese Exporters' Profits," *Nikkei Net Interactive,* July 5, 2005.

This chapter examines international trade in monetary terms. In fact, the international monetary system has changed rather drastically over the years. Given the drastic realignment in recent years of the exchange rates of major currencies, including the U.S. dollar, the European euro, and the Japanese yen, the current international monetary system may well be in for a major change. The adoption of the euro as a common currency in the European Union in 1999 is just one example of the many changes to come. Although international marketers have to operate in a currently existing international monetary system for international transactions and settlements, they should understand how the scope and nature of the system has changed and how it has worked over time. Forward-looking international marketers need to be aware of the dynamics of the international monetary system.

The last decade—particularly, the second half of the last decade—of the 20th century proved to be one of the most turbulent periods in recent history. The seemingly unstoppable rapid economic growth of Asia came to a screeching halt in 1997, and the introduction of the euro in the European Union in 1999 drastically changed the European economic environment. The beginning of the 21st century has not been smooth, either. As described in Chapter 2, the financial crisis in South America and the slump in the U.S. and European economies since 2001 have also indicated how vulnerable the global economy can be. These events profoundly affect international marketing practices. We are convinced that these epoch-making events need your special attention and that your understanding of them will allow you to become seasoned marketing decision makers in crucial areas such as product development, brand management, and pricing, when you develop marketing strategy on a global basis. It is another way to tell you that you have to be up-to-the-minute with ever-changing events that could affect your understanding of the class material, let alone your future career. In this chapter, we also provide a special detailed examination of the implications of the Asian and South American financial crises and marketing in Euro-Land.

◆ ◆ ◆ ◆ ◆ ◆ ◆ ◆ HISTORICAL ROLE OF THE U.S. DOLLAR

Each country has its own currency through which it expresses the value of its products. An international monetary system is necessary because each country has a different monetary unit or currency that serves as a medium of exchange and store of value. The absence of a universal currency means that we must have a system that allows for the transfer of purchasing power between countries with different national currencies. For international trade settlements, the various currencies of the world must be exchanged from one to another. This is accomplished through foreign exchange markets.

Periodically, a country must review the status of its economic relations with the rest of the world in terms of its exports and imports, its exchange of various kinds of services, and its purchase and sale of different types of capital assets and other international payments, receipts, and transfers. In the post-World War II period, a number of institutions came into existence to monitor and assist countries as necessary in keeping their international financial commitments. As a result, a new system of international monetary relations emerged to promote increased international trade through the 1950s and 1960s. In the early 1970s, however, a weakening U.S. dollar caused the existing system to show strains and eventually break down.

The U.S. trade deficit has pushed the value of the U.S. dollar downward in the last 40 years. Since 1960, the dollar has fallen by approximately two-thirds against the euro (using Germany's currency as a proxy before 1999) and the Japanese yen.[3] Despite this long-term trend, the value of the dollar also fluctuates significantly in the short and intermediate terms and remains stronger than commonly expected. Whether a strong dollar is in the best interest of the United States or not is debatable, but a strong dollar certainly reflects global confidence in U.S. economic leadership. However, the

---

[3]"The Passing of the Buck?" *Economist*, December 4, 2004. pp. 71–73.

dollar could become an overvalued currency and make the current account deficits unsustainably large. A sharp downward shift of dollar value could have an enormous impact on global economy. During the annual G8 Summit meetings in June 2002, one of the most urgent issues was whether enough had been done to cushion against a collapse of the dollar.[4]

For example, within two years after the euro's introduction in 1999, the dollar had appreciated 20 percent against the euro. However, from 2001 to 2005, the dollar kept depreciating against the euro by as much as 30 percent (and roughly 17 percent against a broad basket of currencies) because of the weak U.S. economy, increased fear of rising U.S. inflation rates, uncertainty about the aftermath of a U.S.-led war with Iraq, and rising oil prices.[5] Despite the recent recovery in the U.S. economy since 2002, the persistent U.S. trade deficits suggest that the dollar is more likely to depreciate than appreciate in the long run, although some short-term fluctuations are possible.

DEVELOPMENT OF THE CURRENT INTERNATIONAL MONETARY SYSTEM

◆ ◆ ◆ ◆ ◆ ◆ ◆ ◆

The Bretton Woods Conference

Post-World War II developments had long-range effects on international financial arrangements, the role of gold, and the problems of the adjustment of balance of payments disequilibria. Following World War II, there was a strong desire to adhere to goals that would bring economic prosperity and hopefully a long-term peace to the world. The negotiations to establish the postwar international monetary system took place at the resort of Bretton Woods in New Hampshire in 1944. The negotiators at the **Bretton Woods Conference** recommended the following:

1. Each nation should be at liberty to use macroeconomic policies for full employment.

2. Free floating exchange rates would not work. Their ineffectiveness had been demonstrated in the interwar years. The extremes of both permanently fixed and floating rates should be avoided.

3. A monetary system was needed that would recognize that exchange rates were both a national and international concern.[6]

To avoid both the rigidity of a fixed exchange rate system and the chaos of freely floating exchange rates, the Bretton Woods Agreement provided for an adjustable peg. Under this system, currencies were to establish par values in terms of gold, but there was to be little, if any, convertibility of the currencies into gold. Each government was responsible for monitoring its own currency to see that it did not float beyond 1 percent above or below its established par value. As a nation's currency attained or approached either limit, its central bank intervened in the world financial markets to prevent the rate from passing the limit.

Under this system, a country experiencing a balance-of-payments deficit would normally experience devaluation pressure on its current value. The country's authorities would defend its currency by using its foreign currency reserves, primarily U.S. dollars, to purchase its own currency on the open market to push its value back up to its par value. A country experiencing a balance-of-payments surplus would do the opposite and sell its currency on the open market. An institution called the **International Monetary Fund (IMF)** was established at Bretton Woods to oversee the newly agreed-upon monetary system. If a country experienced a fundamental or long-term disequilibrium in its balance of payments, it could alter its peg by up to 10 percent from its initial par

---

[4]Jesper Koll, "Dangers of a Falling Dollar," *Wall Street Journal,* June 12, 2002.

[5]"Running out of Puff?" *Economist,* April 16, 2005, pp. 63–64,

[6]Carlo Cottarelli and Curzio Giannini, *Credibility without Rules? Monetary Framework in the Post-Bretton Woods Era* (Washington, DC: International Monetary Fund, 1997).

value without approval from the International Monetary Fund. Adjustment beyond 10 percent required IMF approval.

In the 1960s, the United States began to experience sequential balance of payments deficits, resulting in downward pressure on the dollar. Because the U.S. government was obligated to maintain the dollar at its par value, it had to spend much of its gold and foreign currency reserves to purchase dollars on the world financial markets. In addition, the U.S. dollar was the reserve currency, convertible to gold under the Bretton Woods Agreement; the U.S. Treasury was obligated to convert dollars to gold upon demand by foreign central banks.

Furthermore, many central banks engaged in massive dollar purchases on the foreign exchange markets to counteract the downward pressure on the dollar and related upward pressure on their own currencies. The continued defense of the dollar left central banks around the world with massive amounts of dollars. These countries, knowing that the dollars they held were in fact convertible to gold with the U.S. Treasury, attempted to hold back, demanding gold in exchange. However, it became clear by 1971 that the dollar was quite overvalued, and devaluation of the dollar versus gold was inevitable. Central banks increasingly presented U.S. dollar balances to the U.S. Treasury for conversion to gold, and gold flowed out of the U.S. vaults at an alarming rate.

This situation led President Richard Nixon to suspend the convertibility of the dollar to gold on August 15, 1971. This effectively ended the exchange rate regime begun at Bretton Woods more than 25 years earlier.

The International Monetary Fund

The International Monetary Fund (IMF) oversees the international monetary system. The IMF is a specialized agency within the United Nations established to promote international monetary cooperation and to facilitate the expansion of trade and to contribute to increased employment and improved economic conditions in all member countries.

Its purposes are as follows:

1. To promote international monetary cooperation through a permanent institution, providing the machinery for consultations and collaboration on international monetary problems.

2. To facilitate the expansion and balanced growth of international trade, and to contribute thereby to the promotion and maintenance of high levels of employment and real income, and to the development of the productive resources of all members as primary objectives of economic policy.

3. To promote exchange stability, to maintain orderly exchange arrangements among members, and to avoid competitive exchange depreciation.

4. To assist in the establishment of a multilateral system of payments in respect to current transactions between members and in the elimination of foreign exchange restrictions that hamper the growth of world trade.

5. To give confidence to members by making the general resources of the fund temporarily available to them under adequate safeguards, thus providing them with the opportunity to correct maladjustments in their balance of payments without resorting to measures destructive of national or international prosperity.

6. In accordance with the above, to shorten the duration and lessen the degree of disequilibrium in the international balance of payments to members.[7]

Today the IMF has 184 members.[8] Its accomplishments include sustaining a rapidly increasing volume of trade and investment and displaying flexibility in adapting

---

[7]International Monetary Fund, *The Role and Function of the International Monetary Fund* (Washington, DC: International Monetary Fund, 1985).

[8]International Monetary Fund Homepage, http://www.imf.org/, accessed December 20, 2005.

to changes in international commerce. To an extent, the IMF serves as an international central bank to help countries during periods of temporary balance of payments difficulties by protecting their rates of exchange. This has helped countries avoid the placement of foreign exchange controls and other trade barriers.

As time passed, it became evident that the IMF's resources for providing short-term accommodation to countries in monetary difficulties were not sufficient. To resolve the situation and to reduce upward pressure on the U.S. dollar by countries holding dollar reserves, the fund created special drawing rights in 1969. **Special drawing rights (SDRs)** are special account entries on the IMF books designed to provide additional liquidity to support growing world trade. The value of SDRs is determined by a weighted average of a basket of four currencies: the U.S. dollar, the Japanese yen, the European Union's euro, and the British pound. Although SDRs are a form of fiat money and not convertible to gold, their gold value is guaranteed, which helps to ensure their acceptability.

Participant nations may use SDRs as a source of currency in a spot transaction, a loan for clearing a financial obligation, security for a loan, and a swap against a currency or in a forward exchange operation. A nation with a balance of payment problems may use its SDRs to obtain usable currency from another nation designated by the fund. By providing a mechanism for international monetary cooperation, working to reduce restrictions to trade and investment flows, and helping members with their short-term balance of payment difficulties, the IMF makes a significant and unique contribution to economic stability and improved living standards throughout the world.

In the wake of the 1997–1998 Asian financial crisis, the IMF has worked on policies to overcome or even prevent future crisis. After 1997, the external payments situation was stabilized through IMF-led aid programs, and financial packages were being geared to encourage the adoption of policies that could prevent crises in selected developing countries. Backed by an quota increase of $90 billion, the IMF would make a contingent short-term line of credit available before a crisis occurs but only if a country adopts certain policies that would limit its vulnerability. The line of credit is expected to be of short-term and charges interest rates above market rates to discourage misuse.[9] Most recently, the IMF announced $30 billion in emergency loans to Brazil, which was battered by the financial crisis in Argentina in 2002. The announcement pushed various developing market currencies higher as investors welcomed both the vote of confidence in Brazil and the broader implications of the loan announcement for emerging market assets. These loans sent a message that international organizations have a commitment to countries with major financial problems.[10]

Another creation of the Bretton Woods Agreement was the International Bank for Reconstruction and Development, known as the **World Bank.** Although the International Monetary Fund was created to aid countries in financing their balance of payment difficulties and maintaining a relatively stable currency, the World Bank was initially intended to finance postwar reconstruction and development and later for infrastructure building projects in the developing world. More recently, the World Bank has begun to participate actively with the IMF to resolve debt problems of the developing world, and it may also play a major role in bringing a market economy to the former members of the Eastern bloc. Each year the World Bank lends between US$15–20 billion to developing country governments to support projects for economic development and poverty reduction. The World Bank is the largest external fund provider for education and HIV/AIDS programs, strongly supports debt relief, and is responding to the voices of the poor. The organization greatly supports developing

The International Bank for Reconstruction and Development

[9]Suk H. Kim and Mahfuzul Haque, "The Asian Financial Crisis of 1997: Causes and Policy Response," *Multinational Business Review,* 10 (Spring 2002), pp. 37–44; and Ramon Moreno, "Dealing with Currency Crises," *FRBSF Economic Letter,* Number 99–11, (April 2, 1999).

[10]"Special Summary of Stories on IMF $30B Package for Brazil," *Dow Jones Newswire,* August 8, 2002; "IMF Improves Terms on Emergency Aid," *Finance & Development,* 42 (March 2005), p. 3.

country governments to build schools and health centers, provide water and electricity, fight disease, and protect the environment.[11]

Fixed versus Floating Exchange Rates

Since the 1970s, all major nations have had their currencies floating rather than fixed. An IMF meeting in Jamaica in 1976 reached consensus on amendments to the IMF Articles of Agreement that accepted floating rates as the basis for the international monetary system. The amended agreement recognized that real rate stability can be achieved only through stability in underlying economic and financial conditions. Exchange rate stability cannot be imposed by adoption of pegged exchange rates and official intervention in the foreign exchange markets.

There are two kinds of currency floats, referred to as *free* or *clean* or as *managed* or *dirty*. The **free (clean) float** is the closest approximation to perfect competition because it requires no government intervention and billions of units of currency are being traded by buyers and sellers. Buyers and sellers may change sides on short notice as information, rumors, or moods change, or as their clients' needs differ.

A **managed (dirty) float** allows for a limited amount of government intervention to soften sudden swings in the value of a currency. If a nation's currency enters into a rapid ascent or decline, that nation's central bank may wish to sell or buy that currency on the open market in a countervailing movement to offset the prevailing market tendency. This is for the purpose of maintaining an orderly, less volatile foreign exchange market.

In March 1973, the major currencies began to float in the foreign exchange markets. The advocates for floating exchange regime argued that it would end balance of payments disequilibria because the value of each currency would float up or down to a point where supply equaled demand. It has not worked that way, at least in part due to the reluctance of governments to permit extreme changes in the value of their currencies. Governments have intervened in the currency markets to moderate or prevent value changes. In reality, however, the supposed benefits of floating exchange rates have not been exhibited to date. For example,

1. Floating exchange rates were supposed to facilitate balance of payments adjustments. However, imbalances not only have not disappeared, but have become worse, as attested to by the recent Asian and Latin American financial crises.

2. Currency speculation was expected to be curtailed, but speculation has been greater than ever. Similarly, short-term speculations worsened the Asian and Latin financial crisis.

3. Market forces left to their own devices were expected to determine the correct foreign exchange rate balance. However, imbalances have become greater than ever, as have fluctuations in rates.

4. Autonomy in economic and monetary policy was hoped to be preserved, allowing each country the free choice of its monetary policy and rate of inflation, but this has also not materialized.

As a result, international marketers have had to cope with the ever-fluctuating exchange rates (see Exhibit 3-1). Refer to the enormous change in Toyota's operating profits as a result of a small change in the yen/dollar exchange rate illustrated in the opening paragraph of this chapter. Even a small fluctuation in exchange rates cannot be ignored because it has an enormous impact on a company's operating profit.

Currency Blocs

Although currencies of most countries float in value against one another, those of many developing countries are pegged (or fixed) to one of the major currencies or to a basket of major currencies such as the U.S. dollar, SDRs or some specially chosen currency

---

[11]The World Bank, http://www.worldbank.org/, accessed December 20, 2005.

EXHIBIT 3-1
FOREIGN EXCHANGE RATE FLUCTUATIONS 1980–2005
(FOREIGN CURRENCY UNITS/U.S. DOLLAR)

Year	Deutsche Mark	French Franc	Japanese Yen	Swiss Franc	British Pound
1980	1.96	4.55	203	1.76	0.42
1985	2.46	7.56	201	2.08	0.69
1990	1.49	5.13	134	1.30	0.52
1991	1.52	5.18	125	1.36	0.53
1992	1.61	5.51	125	1.46	0.66
1993	1.73	5.90	112	1.48	0.68
1994	1.55	5.35	100	1.31	0.64
1995	1.43	4.90	103	1.15	0.65
1996	1.50	5.12	94	1.24	0.64
1997	1.73	5.84	121	1.45	0.64
1998	1.82	6.10	139	1.53	0.60
1999		0.94 euro*	108	1.69	0.66
2000		1.08	108	1.69	0.66
2001		1.12	122	1.69	0.69
2002		1.06	125	1.55	0.67
2003		0.88	116	1.35	0.61
2004		0.80	108	1.24	0.55
2005		0.80	116	1.24	0.55

Source: International Monetary Fund, *Balance of Payments Statistics Yearbook,* various issues, (Washington, DC: U.S. Government Printing Office).

*The euro was introduced in 1999 and completely replaced the currencies of member countries in 2002.

mix. In general, developing countries that depend on their trading relationships with a major country, such as the United States, for economic growth tend to use the currency of the major country.

For example, the Chinese currency, renminbi (yuan), had been pegged to the U.S. dollar for a decade at 8.28 yuan/$. Based on its growing trade surplus with the United States as well as its sustained real GDP growth in the past 20 years of 9.5 percent, China has been accused of pursuing a cheap-yuan policy and has been pressured to revalue its currency. In the past, to prevent the yuan from rising against the dollar, the Chinese central bank has had to buy huge amounts of U.S. Treasury securities. The Chinese government has believed that the fixed exchange rate provides stability to the Chinese economy because it relies so much on trade with the United States. However, as the dollar continued to fall, the Chinese central bank decided on July 21, 2005, to abandon the yuan's peg to the dollar in favor of a link to a basket of several currencies, including the euro and the yen, and revalued the yuan by 2.1 percent against the dollar. On September 23, 2005, the Chinese central bank further decided to let the yuan float against the major currencies but only to a limited extent. Then the yuan would be allowed to fluctuate by up to 3 percent a day against the euro, yen, and other nondollar currencies, compared with 1.5 percent previously. Daily movements against the dollar, meanwhile, remain limited to only 0.3 percent.[12]

Today, the global economy is increasingly dominated by three major **currency blocs.** Each of the U.S. dollar, the EU's euro, and the Japanese yen represents its "sphere of influence" on the currencies of other countries in the respective regions (i.e., North and South America, Europe, and East Asia, respectively).[13] After its launch,

---

[12]"Yuan Step at a Time," *Economist,* January 22, 2005, p. 74; and "Patching the Basket," *Economist,* October 1, 2005, p. 71.

[13]Michael H. Moffett, Arthur I. Stonehill, and David K. Eiteman, *Fundamentals of Multinational Finance,* 2nd ed. Reading, Mass.: Addison-Wesley, 2006.

the euro immediately became the world's second leading international currency. The U.S. dollar is still likely to remain the dominant international currency for the time being, but due to the large size of the euro-area economy, the stability attached to the euro, and the ongoing integration of national financial markets in Europe into broad, deep, and liquid pan-European financial markets, the euro is gradually becoming an international currency.[14] Although the U.S. dollar has lost some of its role as the international transaction currency, it remains a currency of choice that many Latin American companies use for operating purposes. The Japanese yen has increasingly become a regional transaction currency in Asia. In other words, U.S. companies will find it easier to do business with companies in Latin America as business planning and transactions are increasingly conducted in dollar denominations. On the other hand, those U.S. companies will increasingly have to accept yen-denominated business transactions in Asia and euro-denominated transactions in Europe, thus being susceptible to exchange rate fluctuations. Considering increased trade volumes with Asian and European countries as well as with Latin American countries, it has become more important for U.S. marketing executives to understand the dynamic forces that affect exchange rates and predict the exchange rate fluctuations.

◆ ◆ ◆ ◆ ◆ ◆ ◆ ◆ ◆ FOREIGN EXCHANGE AND FOREIGN EXCHANGE RATES

Foreign exchange, as the term implies, refers to the exchange of one country's money for that of another country. When international transactions occur, foreign exchange is the monetary mechanism allowing the transfer of funds from one nation to another. In this section, we explore the factors that influence exchange rates over time and the way the exchange rates are determined.

Purchasing Power Parity

One of the most fundamental determinants of the exchange rate is **purchasing power parity (PPP),** by which the exchange rate between the currencies of two countries makes the purchasing power of both currencies equal. In other words, the value of a currency is determined by what it can buy.

The following formula represents the relationship between inflation rates and the exchange rate:

$$R_t = R_0 \times \frac{(1 + \text{Infl}_{\text{Brt}})}{(1 + \text{Infl}_{\text{US}})}$$

where

$$
\begin{aligned}
R &= \text{the exchange rate quoted in £/\$} \\
\text{Infl} &= \text{inflation rate} \\
t &= \text{time period}
\end{aligned}
$$

For example, if British inflation were 5 percent a year and U.S. inflation were 2 percent a year, the value of the dollar would be expected to rise by the difference of 3 percent, so that the real prices of goods in the two countries would remain fairly similar. If the current exchange rate (R_0) is 0.551 British pounds to the dollar (£0.551 $), then

$$R_t = 0.551 \times \frac{(1 + 0.05)}{(1 + 0.02)} = £0.566/\$$$

In other words, the dollar is expected to appreciate from £0.551/$ to £0.566/$ in a year. The U.S. dollar will be able to buy slightly more British pounds.

In fact, the *Economist* publishes a PPP study every year based on McDonald's Big Mac hamburger sold all over the world. It is known as the *Big Mac Index* to show whether currencies are at their "correct" exchange rate. Look at the recent Big Mac Index to see how actual exchange rates "deviate" from the Big Mac Index (See

---

[14]"The Passing of the Buck?" *Economist*, December 4, 2004. pp. 71–73.

EXHIBIT 3-2

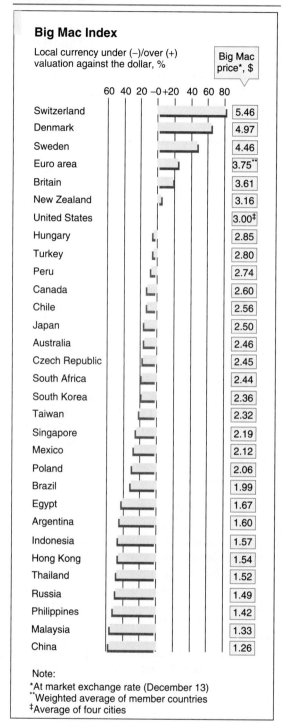

Big Mac Index

Local currency under (–)/over (+) valuation against the dollar, %

Big Mac price*, $

Switzerland	5.46
Denmark	4.97
Sweden	4.46
Euro area	3.75**
Britain	3.61
New Zealand	3.16
United States	3.00‡
Hungary	2.85
Turkey	2.80
Peru	2.74
Canada	2.60
Chile	2.56
Japan	2.50
Australia	2.46
Czech Republic	2.45
South Africa	2.44
South Korea	2.36
Taiwan	2.32
Singapore	2.19
Mexico	2.12
Poland	2.06
Brazil	1.99
Egypt	1.67
Argentina	1.60
Indonesia	1.57
Hong Kong	1.54
Thailand	1.52
Russia	1.49
Philippines	1.42
Malaysia	1.33
China	1.26

Note:
*At market exchange rate (December 13)
**Weighted average of member countries
‡Average of four cities

Source: "Big Mac Index," *Economist,* December 16, 2004. © 2004 The Economist Newspaper Ltd. All rights reserved. Reprinted with permission.www.economist.com

Exhibit 3-2). For example, the lowest cost burger in the chart is in China, at $1.26, compared with an average price of $3 in the United States. This implies that the yuan is 58 percent undervalued relative to the U.S. dollar based on the Big Mac dollar-PPP. On the same basis, the euro is 25 percent overvalued, the Swiss franc a whopping 82 percent overvalued, and the yen 17 percent undervalued.[15] Overall, most of the

---

[15]"Big Mac Index," *Economist,* December 16, 2004.

emerging-market currencies are more than 30 percent undervalued. Theoretically, over the long run, exchange rates tend to go toward the direction of the PPP index. If the dollar is overvalued relative to a foreign currency (i.e., the foreign currency is undervalued relative to the dollar), people using that foreign currency will find it more expensive to buy goods from the United States. Conversely, people living in the United States will find it cheaper to import goods from a country with an undervalued currency.

Forecasting Exchange Rate Fluctuation

Actual exchange rates can be very different from the expected rates. Those deviations are not necessarily a random variation. As summarized in Exhibit 3-3, many interrelated factors influence the value of a floating currency. In particular, the nation's inflation rate relative to its trading partners, its balance of payments situation, and world political events are the three most fundamental factors.

Although accurately predicting the actual exchange rate fluctuations is not possible and it is not related directly to marketing executives' jobs, seasoned marketers can benefit from the knowledge. Exchange rate fluctuations have an enormous direct impact on a company's bottom line—profitability.

Coping with Exchange Rate Fluctuations

When the fast-food operator KFC opens new restaurants in Mexico, for example, it often imports some of the kitchen equipment, including fryers, roasters, stainless steel counters, and other items for its stores from U.S. suppliers.

To pay for these imports, the Mexican KFC subsidiary must purchase U.S. dollars with Mexican pesos through its bank in Mexico City. This is necessary because the Mexican peso is not readily accepted currency in the United States. Most likely, KFC–Mexico will pay for the imported merchandise via a bank cashier's check denominated in U.S. dollars from its local bank in Mexico City. If the exchange rate on the date of purchase is 10.19 Mexican pesos per U.S. dollar and the debt is $10,000 dollars, then KFC–Mexico must pay 101,900 pesos, plus a commission to the bank, for the dollars it sends to the U.S. supplier. The bank in Mexico acquires the dollars on the open foreign exchange market or through other banks for the purpose of satisfying the foreign exchange needs of its customers.

This is the case when currency is freely convertible with minimal government foreign exchange controls, as has been true in Mexico. However, this is not always the case. Governments have often limited the amount of domestic currency that can leave a country to avoid capital flight and decapitalization. One example of this was South Africa in the 1980s where it was illegal to buy foreign currency or take domestic currency out of the country without government approval. If a company in South Africa required foreign manufactured goods, it had to solicit authorization for the purchase of foreign exchange through the national treasury to make payment.

Prior to the fall of communism, even more rigid exchange controls existed in the former Soviet Union and other Eastern bloc countries where trade in foreign currency was a crime meriting harsh punishment. The problem with such tight exchange controls is that often they promote a black market in unauthorized trade in the controlled currency. In such cases, the official rate of exchange for a currency tends to be overvalued, or in other words, possessing an officially stated value that does not reflect its true worth. The black market will more likely reflect its true worth on the street.

Another issue affecting foreign exchange concerns fluctuation in the rates of exchange by which currencies either appreciate or depreciate with respect to one another. Since the 1970s, most of the world's currencies have been on a floating system, often fluctuating with wide variations. For example, in 1976, the Mexican peso traded at an exchange rate of 12.5 per dollar, but in 1993 it had fallen to 3,200 pesos per dollar.

This peso depreciation reflected much higher inflation in Mexico compared to that in the United States, and the fear of political/financial instability in Mexico prompted Mexican residents to buy dollars for security. In 1993, the Mexican government dropped three zeroes off the currency, creating a new peso (nuevo peso) worth 3.2 pesos per

EXHIBIT 3-3
FACTORS INFLUENCING FOREIGN EXCHANGE RATES

MACROECONOMIC FACTORS

1. *Relative inflation.* A country suffering relatively higher inflation rates than other major trading partners will experience depreciation of its currency.

2. *Balance of payments.* Improvement (deterioration) in the balance of payments for goods and services is an early sign of a currency appreciation (depreciation).

3. *Foreign exchange reserves.* A government may intervene in the foreign exchange markets to either push up or push down the value of its currency. The central bank can support (depreciate) the domestic currency by selling its foreign currency reserves to buy its own currency (selling its domestic currency to buy foreign currency).

4. *Economic growth.* If the domestic economy is growing fast relative to that of major trading partners, the country's imports tend to rise faster than exports, resulting in a deterioration of the trade balance and thus depreciation of its currency. However, if the domestic economic growth attracts a large amount of investment from abroad, it could offset the negative trade effect, thus potentially resulting in the appreciation of the domestic currency.

5. *Government spending.* An increase in government spending, particularly if financed through deficit spending, causes increased inflationary pressures on the economy. Inflation leads to domestic currency depreciation (as in 1).

6. *Money supply growth.* Many countries' central banks attempt to stave off recession by increasing money supply to lower domestic interest rates for increased consumption and investment. Increase in money supply usually leads to higher inflation rates and subsequently currency depreciation.

7. *Interest rate policy.* As in 6, the central bank may also control its discount rate (interest rate charged to banks) to raise domestic lending rates to control inflation. Higher interest rates discourage economic activity and tend to reduce inflation and attract investment from abroad. Reduced inflation and increased investment from abroad both lead to currency appreciation.

POLITICAL FACTORS

1. *Exchange rate control.* Some governments have an explicit control on the exchange rate. The official rate for domestic currency is artificially overvalued, thereby discouraging foreign companies from exporting to such a country. However, as long as there is a genuine domestic demand for imported products, the black market for foreign currency tends to appear. Black market exchange rates for a domestic currency tend to be much lower than the government-imposed artificial rate. Thus, a wide spread between the official exchange rate and the black market rate indicates potential pressures leading to domestic currency devaluation.

2. *Election year or leadership change.* Expectations about imminent government policy change influence exchange rates. In general, pro-business government policy tends to lead to domestic currency appreciation as foreign companies are willing to accept that currency for business transactions.

RANDOM FACTORS

Unexpected and/or unpredicted events in a country, such as the assassination of political figures and sudden stock market crash, can cause its currency to depreciate for fear of uncertainty. Similarly, events such as sudden discovery of huge oil reserves and gold mines tend to push up the currency value.

Source: Developed from a discussion in Chapter 3 of David K. Eiteman, Arthur I. Stonehill, and Michael H. Moffett, *Multinational Business Finance,* 9th ed. (New York: Addison-Wesley, 2001).

dollar. This rate climbed again with the depreciation that began in December 1994 to the 11 pesos per dollar range by 2004. Since then, the peso has begun to appreciate a little against the U.S. dollar as the dollar has weakened. On the other hand, in the early 1980s, the Japanese yen traded at approximately 250 yen per dollar, but by 1996 had appreciated to 94 yen per dollar (before losing value slightly to approximately 116 yen per dollar in 2005). This long-term depreciation of the dollar against the yen reflected continuing U.S. trade deficits with Japan as well as a higher level of inflation in the United States relative to Japan.

Many countries attempt to maintain a lower value for their currency to encourage exports. The reason for this is that if the dollar depreciates against the Japanese yen, for example, U.S. manufactured goods should become cheaper to the Japanese consumers, who find that their supply of yen suddenly purchases a larger quantity of dollars, and Japanese and other foreign goods are more expensive to Americans. The depreciation of the U.S. dollar should then help to reduce the U.S. deficit with its trading partners by increasing exports and reducing imports in the absence of other countervailing factors.

Directly related to the issue of floating currency is the concept of transaction gain or loss on the import or export of merchandise. Returning to the example of KFC–Mexico's import of $10,000 in kitchen equipment, if that company ordered the equipment in January 2003 (when the exchange rate was 10 pesos per dollar) for payment in June 2004 (when the exchange rate had fallen to 11.5 pesos per dollar), KFC–Mexico would incur a foreign exchange transaction loss. This happens because the company would have to buy dollars for payment in the month of June at a depreciated rate, thus paying more pesos for every dollar purchased. Only if it had the foresight (or good luck) to buy the dollars in January 2003 at the more favorable rate could they avoid this foreign exchange loss. A more detailed illustration follows:

Cost of imported equipment in pesos at exchange rate in effect at order date (10 pesos per dollar)	100,000 pesos
Cost of imported equipment in pesos at exchange rate in effect at payment date (11.5 pesos per dollar)	115,000 pesos
Foreign exchange loss in pesos	15,000 pesos

Conversely, if the peso were to appreciate prior to the payment date, KFC–Mexico would have a transaction gain in foreign exchange.

Spot versus Forward Foreign Exchange

If payment on a transaction is to be made immediately, the purchaser has no choice other than to buy foreign exchange on the **spot (current) market** for immediate delivery. However, if payment is to be made at some future date, as was the case in the KFC–Mexico example, the purchaser has the option to buy foreign exchange on the spot market or on the **forward market** for delivery at some future date. The advantage of the forward market is that the buyer can lock in an exchange rate and avoid the risk of currency fluctuations; this is called **currency hedging,** or protecting oneself against potential loss.[16]

The sound management of foreign exchange in an environment of volatile floating rates requires an astute corporate treasurer and effective coordination with the purchasing or marketing functions of the business.[17] If a business sees its national currency or the currency of one of its subsidiaries declining, it may purchase a stronger foreign currency as a reserve for future use. Often, if the corporation's money managers are savvy enough, significant income can be generated through foreign exchange transactions beyond that of normal company operations.[18] However, in recent years, many companies seem to be reducing their hedging because exchange rate fluctuations have become so erratic and unpredictable. According to a survey conducted by the University of Pennsylvania's Wharton School and the Canadian Imperial Bank of

---

[16]Alternatively, there is **operational hedging,** which is to shift production and procurement abroad to match revenues in foreign currency when exchange rate fluctuations are very difficult to predict (i.e., successful currency hedging is increasingly difficult). For example, by producing abroad all of the products a company sells in foreign markets, this company has created an "operational hedge" by shielding itself from fluctuating exchange rates. See, for example, Christos Pantzalis, Betty J. Simkins, Paul A. Laux, "Operational Hedges and the Foreign Exchange Exposure of U.S. Multinational Corporations," *Journal of International Business Studies,* 32 (4), 2001, pp. 793–812.

[17]Raj Aggarwal and Luc A. Soenen, "Managing Persistent Real Changes in Currency Values: The Role of Multinational Operating Strategies," *Columbia Journal of World Business* (Fall 1989), pp. 60–67.

[18]Stephen D. Makar and Stephen P. Huffman, "Foreign Currency Risk Management Practices in U.S. Multinationals," *Journal of Applied Business Research,* 13 (Spring 1997), pp. 73–86.

Commerce, only one-third of large U.S. companies engage in some kind of foreign currency hedging.[19]

For example, Merck, a pharmaceutical giant, hedges some of its foreign cash flows using one- to five-year options to sell the currencies for dollars at fixed rates. Merck argues that it can protect adverse currency moves by exercising its options or enjoy favorable moves by not exercising them. In contrast, many well-established companies see no strong need to hedge for protection against currency risk. The reason is that fluctuations in the underlying business can spoil the hedge's effectiveness. For companies with a strong belief in hedging, the sustained rise in the dollar over the past several years proved a serious test. Coca-Cola hopes to limit the negative impact of unfavorable currency swings on earnings to 3 percent annually over the long term. However, Coca-Cola's profits from foreign sales decreased by 10 percent due to the stronger dollar in 1998 instead. Eastman Kodak once used aggressive hedging strategy but abandoned such practice recently as it realized that hedging was not necessary since the ups and downs of currencies would even out in the long run.[20]

However, it does not necessarily mean that currency hedging is less important to any company. Who should consider financial hedging more seriously? For an export-oriented economy that depends heavily on the export of dollar-based products, such as Norway, currency hedging strategies remain vital.[21] While more young companies have begun to be involved with international imports or exports, currency hedging has also become more accessible to them thanks to a growing number of services offered by large banks as well as business-to-business Web sites. Currency hedging allows small business owners to greatly reduce or eliminate the uncertainties attached to any foreign currency transaction.

Forward currency markets exist for the strongest currencies, including the EU's euro, British pound, Canadian dollar, Japanese yen, Swiss franc, and U.S. dollar. The terms of purchase are usually for delivery of the foreign currency in either 30, 60, or 90 days from the date of purchase. These aforementioned currencies are often called *hard currencies* because they are the world's strongest and represent the world's leading economies.

Traditionally weaker currencies, such as the Indian rupee or the Colombian peso, are rarely used in forward currency markets, because there is no worldwide demand for such a market; nearly all international transactions are expressed in terms of a hard currency. Exhibit 3-4 illustrates the daily quotes for foreign exchange on the spot and forward markets. In the second column, the foreign currency is expressed in terms of how many dollars it takes to buy one unit of foreign currency. The third column indicates the inverse, or how many units of a foreign currency it would take to purchase one dollar. For example, on July 21, 2006, 1 Japanese yen was worth $0.008607; or more conventionally, the value of the yen was expressed as 116.18 yen per dollar. Similarly, on the same day, one euro was worth $1.2697; or conversely, 1 U.S. dollar could buy 0.7876 euro.

The dramatic swings in the value of the dollar since the early 1980s have made it clear that foreign companies charge different prices in the United States than in other markets.[22] When the dollar appreciated against the Japanese yen and the German mark in the 1980s, Japanese cars were priced fairly low in the United States, justified by the cheaper yen, while German cars became far more expensive in the United States

Exchange Rate Pass-Through

[19]Peter Coy, De'Ann Weimer, and Amy Barrett, "Perils of the Hedge Highwire," *Business Week,* October 26, 1998, p. 74.

[20]Ibid.

[21]Ranga Nathan and Nils E. Joachim Hoegh-Krohn, "Norwegian Institutional Investors: Currency Risk," *Derivatives Quarterly,* 6 (Fall 1999), pp. 59–63.

[22]Terry Clark, Masaaki Kotabe, and Dan Rajaratnam, "Exchange Rate Pass-Through and International Pricing Strategy: A Conceptual Framework and Research Propositions," *Journal of International Business Studies,* 30 (Second Quarter 1999), pp. 249–68.

EXHIBIT 3-4
FOREIGN EXCHANGE RATES

The following New York foreign exchange mid-range rates apply to trading among banks in amounts of $1 million and more, as quoted at 4 p.m. U.S. Eastern time by Reuters and other sources. Retail transactions provide fewer units of foreign currency per dollar.

Country	U.S. $ equivalent	Currency per U.S. $	Country	U.S. $ equivalent	Currency per U.S. $
Argentina (Peso)	0.3245	3.0817	Norway (Krone)	0.1601	6.2461
Australia (Dollar)	0.7522	1.3294	New Zealand (Dollar)	0.6242	1.6021
Bahrain (Dinar)	2.6525	0.3770	Mexico (Peso)	0.09117	10.969
Brazil (Real)	0.4548	2.1988	Pakistan (Rupee)	0.01658	60.314
Canada (Dollar)	0.8785	1.1383	Peru (New Sol)	0.3085	3.2415
1 Month Forward	0.8793	1.1373	Philippines (Peso)	0.01918	52.138
3 Months Forward	0.8811	1.1349	Poland (Zloty)	0.3212	3.1133
6 Months Forward	0.8837	1.1316	Russia (Ruble)	0.03722	26.867
Chile (Peso)	0.001847	541.42	Saudi Arabia (Riyal)	0.2666	3.7509
China (Renminbi)	0.1253	7.9828	Singapore (Dollar)	0.6317	1.5830
Colombia (Peso)	0.0004049	2,469.7	Slovak Republic (Koruna)	0.03304	30.266
Czech Republic (Koruna)	0.04467	22.386	South Africa (Rand)	0.1419	7.0472
Commercial Rate			South Korea (Won)	0.001053	949.94
Denmark (Krone)	0.1702	5.8754	Sweden (Krona)	0.1372	7.2886
Ecuador (US Dollar)	1.0000	1.0000	Switzerland (Frane)	0.8088	1.2364
Egypt (Pound)	0.1741	5.7438	1 Month Forward	0.8116	1.2321
Hong Kong (Dollar)	0.1286	7.7757	3 Months Forward	0.8169	1.2241
Hungary (Forint)	0.004588	217.96	6 Months Forward	0.8245	1.2129
India (Rupee)	0.02140	46.729	Taiwan (Dollar)	0.03054	32.744
Indonesia (Rupiah)	0.0001093	9,149.1	Thailand (Baht)	0.02637	37.922
Israel (Shekel)	0.2238	4.4683	Turkish (Lira)	0.6443	1.5520
Japan (Yen)	0.008607	116.18	U.K. (Pound)	1.8590	0.5379
1 Months Forward	0.008644	115.69	1 Month Forward	1.8602	0.5376
3 Months Forward	0.008719	114.69	3 Months Forward	1.8628	0.5368
6 Months Forward	0.008831	113.24	6 Months Forward	1.8661	0.5359
Jordan (Dinar)	1.4104	0.7090	United Arab Emirates (Dirham)	0.2723	3.6724
Kuwait (Dinar)	3.4579	0.2892	Uruguay (Peso) Financial	0.04180	23.923
Lebanon (Pound)	0.0006634	1,507.4	Venezuela (Bolivar)	0.0004660	2,145.9
Malaysia (Ringitt)	0.2718	3.6792	Special Drawing Rights	1.4782	0.6765
Malta (Lira)	2.9602	0.3378	Euro	1.2697	0.7876

Note: Special Drawing Rights (SDR) are based on exchange rates for the U.S., British, and Japanese currencies.
Source: Wall Street Journal, July 21, 2006, and The International Monetary Fund.

than in Europe. In the 1990s, when the dollar began depreciating against the yen and the mark, Japanese and German auto makers had to increase their dollar prices in the United States. Japanese automakers did not raise their prices nearly as much as German competitors. Obviously, they "price to market."[23] As a result, Japanese car makers did not lose as much U.S. market share as did German car makers.

One of the success factors for many Japanese companies in the U.S. markets seems to be in the way they used dollar-yen exchange rates to their advantage, known as the **target exchange rate.** Japanese companies, in particular, are known to employ a very unfavorable target exchange rate (i.e., hypothetically appreciated yen environment) for their costing strategy to make sure they will not be adversely affected should the yen appreciate. Therefore, despite close to a twofold appreciation of the yen vis-à-vis the dollar from 240 yen/$ to 110 yen/$ in a decade, the dollar prices of Japanese

---

[23] "Pricing Paradox: Consumers Still Find Imported Bargains Despite Weak Dollar," *Wall Street Journal* (October 7, 1992), p. A6.

products have not increased nearly as much. The extent to which a foreign company changes dollar prices of its products in the U.S. market as a result of exchange rate fluctuations is called **exchange rate pass-through.** Although accurately estimating the average increase in dollar prices of Japanese products is almost impossible, our estimate suggests that about a 30 percent price increase, or pass-through, occurs over the same period. If this estimate is accurate, Japanese companies must have somehow absorbed more than 70 percent of the price increase. This cost absorption could result from smaller profit margins and cost reductions as well as effective use of the unfavorable target exchange rate for planning purposes. According to Morgan Stanley Japan Ltd.'s estimate in the 1990s,[24] Toyota could break even at an unheard of 52 yen to the dollar. In other words, as long as the Japanese currency does not appreciate all the way to 52 yen to the dollar, Toyota is expected to earn windfall operating profits.

The emergence of the Internet as a global purchasing tool also brings a whole new aspect to the concept of pass-through, particularly at the retail setting. Now that retailers can sell to the world through one Web site, it is increasingly difficult for them to set different prices for each country. One can see this with software purchased and downloaded over the Internet. Consumers in England will not pay 120 pounds for a software program that they know sells for $100 in the United States. Online commerce will limit price flexibility in foreign markets.

This pass-through issue will be elaborated on in Chapter 13 when we discuss global pricing issues.

BALANCE OF PAYMENTS

The balance of payments of a nation summarizes all transactions that have taken place between its residents and the residents of other countries over a specified time period, usually a month, quarter, or year. The transactions contain three categories: current account, capital account, and official reserves. There is also an extra category for statistical discrepancy. Exhibit 3-5 shows the balance of payments for the United States 1990–2003.

The balance of payments record is made on the basis of the rules of credits (transaction that result in an inflow of money) and debits (transactions that result in an outflow of money), similar to those in business accounting. Exports, like sales, are outflows of goods, and are entered as credits to merchandise trade. Imports, or inflows of goods, are represented by debits to the same account. These exports and imports are most likely offset by an opposite entry to the capital account, reflecting the receipt of cash or the outflow of cash for payment.

When a German tourist visits the United States and spends money on meals and lodging, this results in a credit to the U.S. trade in services balance reflecting the rendering of a U.S. service to a foreign resident. On the other hand, this transaction would represent a debit to the trade in services account of Germany, reflecting the receipt of a service from a U.S. resident (or company) by a resident of Germany. If the foreign resident's payment is made in cash, the credit to trade in services is offset by a debit (inflow) to short-term capital. On the other hand, if a foreign resident purchases land in the United States, paying cash, this is represented on the U.S. balance of payments as a debit to short-term capital (representing the inflow of payment for the land) and a credit to long-term capital (representing the outflow of ownership of real estate).

This concept is based on the principle of double-entry accounting, so theoretically every debit must be offset by a credit to some other account within the balance of payments statement. In other words, the balance of payments statement must always

[24]Valerie Reitman, "Toyota Names a Chief Likely to Shake Up Global Auto Business," *Wall Street Journal* (August 11, 1995), pp. A1, A5.

EXHIBIT 3-5
U.S. BALANCE OF PAYMENTS, 1990–2003

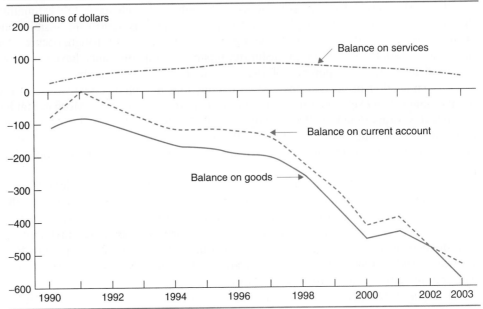

Source: Statistical Abstract of the United States 2004–2005 (Washington, DC: U.S. Census Bureau, 2005).

balance because total debits must equal total credits. A deficit (debit balance) in one account will then be offset by a surplus (credit balance) in another account. If the statement does not balance, an entry must be made as a statistical discrepancy. In reality, however, there is no national accountant making accounting entries for every international transaction. In the United States, the Department of Commerce, which prepares the balance of payments statement, must gather information from a variety of sources, including banks and other business entities, concerning the inflow and outflow of goods, services, gifts, and capital items.

The **balance of payments on goods** (also know as **trade balance**) shows trade in currently produced goods. Trade balance is the most frequently used indicator of the health of a country's international trade position. The **balance of payments on services** shows trade in currently transacted services. The **balance of payments in current account (current account balance,** for short) shows trade in currently produced goods and services, as well as unilateral transfers including private gifts and foreign aid. The goods or merchandise account deals with tangibles such as autos, grain, machinery, and equipment that can be seen and felt as well as exported and imported. The services account deals with intangibles that are sold or bought internationally. Examples include dividends or interest on foreign investments, royalties on trademarks or patents abroad, food or lodging (travel expenses), and transportation. Unilateral transfers are transactions with no *quid pro quo;* some of these transfers are made by private individuals and institutions and some by the government. These gifts are sometimes for charitable, missionary, or educational purposes, and other times they consist of funds wired home by migrant workers to their families in their country of origin. The largest unilateral transfers are aid, either in money or the form of goods and services, from developed to developing countries.

Although not shown in Exhibit 3-5, the mirror image of the balance of payments in the current account (goods, services, and unilateral transfers), as a result of double-entry accounting, is the capital account. The balance of payments in **capital account** summarizes financial transactions and is divided into two sections, short- and long-term capital accounts. Long-term capital includes any financial asset maturing in a period exceeding one year, including equities. Subaccounts under long-term capital are direct investment and portfolio investment.

Direct investments are those investments in enterprises or properties that are effectively controlled by residents of another country. Whenever 10 percent or more of the voting shares in a U.S. company are held by foreign investors, the company is classified as a U.S. affiliate of a foreign company and therefore a foreign direct investment.[25] Similarly, if U.S. investors hold 10 percent or more of the voting shares of a foreign company, the entity is considered a foreign affiliate of a U.S. company.

Portfolio investment includes all long-term investments that do not give the investors effective control over them. Such transactions typically involve the purchase of stocks or bonds of foreign investors for investment. These shares are normally bought for investment, not control, purposes.

Short-term capital includes only those items maturing in less than one year, including cash. The official reserves account registers the movement of funds to and from central banks.

A key point to remember here is that the deficit or surplus is calculated based not on the aggregate of all transactions in the balance of payments but on the net balance for certain selected categories.

There are three particularly important balances to identify on the balance of payments statement of a country, including the balance of the *merchandise trade account,* the *current account* (including merchandise trade, trade in services, and unilateral transfers), and the *basic balance* (the current account and long-term capital). Everyone knows about the U.S. deficit in merchandise trade, but what is less commonly known is that the U.S. regularly runs a surplus in trade in services. This surplus offsets a small part of the deficit in the merchandise account (see Global Perspective 3-1).

Many observers have commented that in the period of the 1980s to 1990s, the United States was able to continue its import binge via the sale of long-term investments, including real estate and ownership in companies. This belief was heightened by the high-profile sale of U.S. companies such as Chrysler and Columbia Records to foreign investors. These foreigners invested in U.S. capital assets, paying in cash that was then recycled in payment for merchandise imports by U.S. residents. The criticism was made that the U.S. was selling off capital assets for short-term merchandise imports like a wealthy heir who sells off the family jewels to finance a profligate lifestyle. Meanwhile, others viewed the increase in foreign investment in the United States as proof of the nation's vitality and long-term attractiveness to investors.

According to the theory of international trade and balance of payments, a surplus or deficit in a country's basic balance should be self-correcting to some extent. This self-correction is accomplished through the internal and external market adjustments. The market adjustment mechanisms bring a nation's deficit or surplus within the basic balance back into equilibrium. This is a natural event in which the economy of a nation corrects its prior excesses by moving back toward the middle.[26]

The **internal market adjustment** refers to the movement of prices and incomes in a country. The following is a hypothetical example of such an adjustment process in the case of a current account surplus country, such as Japan.

The Internal and External Adjustments

1. As Japan continues to export more than it imports, resulting in a surplus in the current account, its internal money supply grows, the result of receiving payment from foreigners for their purchases of goods, services, and investments originating in Japan. The payments are made to Japanese residents and may be deposited in banks in either Japan or abroad in either yen or foreign currency. But wherever and however payment is made, it becomes an asset of a Japanese resident.

---

[25] Department of Commerce, *U.S. Direct Investment Abroad* (Washington, DC: Bureau of Economic Analysis, 2004).

[26] Mordechai E. Kreinin, *International Economics: A Policy Approach* (Mason, OH: Thomson South-Western, 2006), pp. 241–52.

GLOBAL PERSPECTIVE 3-1

BALANCE OF PAYMENTS AND COMPETITIVENESS OF A NATION

The Information Age characterizes the world we live in today, but some people do not seem to recognize it. Each time U.S. trade statistics are reported, we hear the dismal news of a trade deficit such as the $707 billion deficit in 2004. But when it comes to U.S. balance of payments, many people do not look beyond the "trade" statistics.

Trade statistics refer to exports and imports of goods; they do not include trade of services. When the United States incurred a $707 billion trade deficit in goods in 2004, its trade deficit was partly—albeit weakly—offset by a $60 billion trade surplus in services. Such services, the hallmark of the Information Age, include telecommunications, education, financial services, and a host of other intangibles.

These and other services have not had only one good year. Around the world, service companies are expanding rapidly, ringing up sales at a fast pace. Indeed, worldwide, services now account for more than $2 trillion in international trade.

Why, then, does this important development go unnoticed? It is primarily because many of people still measure their economic performance based on the facts of an earlier era, which meant apples, steel, sneakers and the like—tangible merchandise and nothing else. Many just do not realize a new day has dawned—one in which advertising exports can mean as much as auto exports.

Sources: Based on Daniel J. Connors, Jr. and Douglas S. Heller, "The Good Word in Trade Is 'Services,'" *New York Times,* September 19, 1993, p. B1; Stephen S. Cohen and John Zysman, *Manufacturing Matters: The Myth of the Post-Industrial Economy* (New York: Basic Books, 1987); and *World Trade Report 2005: Exploring the Links between Trade, Standards, and the WTO* (Geneva: World Trade Organization, 2005).

The Department of Commerce collects U.S. trade data. It keeps track of more than 10,000 different kinds of tangible goods. But when it comes to services, the agency collects trade data for only a few service categories. Services excluded from or addressed only partially by Department of Commerce data include such significant ones as public relations, management consulting, legal services, and many financial- and information-related services. Although accurate estimates are difficult, it is believed that exports of services are 70 percent higher than reported in Department of Commerce trade data.

What is wrong with underplaying the importance of services? First, it misleads the public about the nation's true competitiveness. Second, it induces government officials to develop trade policy on mistaken premises. Third, and worst of all, the growth of services could be thwarted because many nontariff barriers to trade in services—such as discriminatory licensing and certification rules and bans of the use of internationally known company names—do not receive as much policy attention as do tariffs on goods and thus could harm U.S. service companies trying to sell various services abroad.

There is also a word of caution, however. The increased importance of services in the U.S. balance of payments does not necessarily mean that the United States can ignore manufacturing businesses. First, exports of services have been historically too small to offset the staggering trade deficits in goods. Second, if the United States loses mastery and control of manufacturing, the high-paying and thus important service jobs that are directly linked to manufacturing—such as product design, engineering, accounting, finance and insurancing, and transportation—may also wither away. Manufacturing and those services are tightly linked and may not be separable.

---

2. As Japan's money supply increases, domestic residents of Japan spend more because they have more money available to spend. Japan's money supply is increasing because foreigners are buying Japanese goods in larger quantities than Japanese are buying foreign goods.

3. As local residents in Japan spend more (i.e., have greater demand for products and services), domestic prices rise. In other words, inflation occurs.

4. As domestic prices increase, Japanese residents find that foreign goods are relatively cheaper.

5. Because the Japanese find foreign goods cheaper, they import more goods from abroad. This begins to reduce Japan's current account surplus and bring it back into balance.

The **external market adjustment** concerns exchange rates or a nation's currency and its value with respect to the currencies of other nations. The following is a hypothetical description of the application of the external adjustment to a surplus nation, in this case again, Japan:

1. Japan exports more than it imports, resulting in a surplus in its current account, so foreigners must pay Japanese residents for the goods they purchase from Japan. Payment will likely be made in Japanese yen.

2. Because Japanese residents export more than they import, there is more demand for yen by foreigners than demand for dollars by Japanese residents. This excess in relative demand for yen causes it to appreciate in value with respect to other currencies. Remember that it appreciates because foreigners must pay Japanese suppliers for their goods and services.

3. The appreciated yen causes Japanese goods, services, and investments to be more expensive to foreign residents who convert prices quoted in yen to their local currencies.

4. All other things being equal, this should cause foreigners to buy fewer Japanese goods and thus shrink Japan's trade surplus.

However, other factors, such as a country's taste for foreign goods and general habits of consumption, as well as the quality and reputation of its manufactured goods must be considered. Many other factors beyond domestic prices and foreign exchange values affect Japan's trade balance with the United States, and these factors have become a topic of serious discussion between the governments of these two nations.

ECONOMIC AND FINANCIAL TURMOIL AROUND THE WORLD

◆ ◆ ◆ ◆ ◆ ◆ ◆ ◆

Since the last few years of the 20th century some unprecedented economic and financial crises in some parts of the world have caused significant slowdowns in the growth of the world economy and international trade and investment. Excessive borrowing by companies, households, or governments lie at the root of almost every economic crisis of the past two decades from East Asia to Russia and to South America, and from Japan to the United States. In this section to illustrate the global ripple effect of regional economic downturn, we highlight the Asian financial crisis of 1997–1998 and the South American financial crisis of 2002 that spread from Argentina to other parts of South America.

Asian Financial Crisis and Its Aftermath

Chronologically speaking, China's devaluation of its currency, yuan, from 5.7 yuan/$ to 8.7 yuan/$ in 1994, set the stage for the ongoing saga of the Asian financial crisis. The mechanism of how the Asian financial crisis occurred is summarized in Exhibit 3-6.

The currency devaluation made China's exports cheaper in Southeast Asia where most currencies were virtually pegged to the U.S. dollar. According to Lawrence Klein, a Nobel Laureate in economics, the Southeast Asian countries' strict tie to the U.S. dollar cost them between 10 and 20 percent of export loss spread over three or four years.[27]

Separately, Japan's postbubble recession caused its currency to depreciate from 99.7 yen/$ in 1994 to 126.1 yen/$ in 1997, resulting in two pronged problems for Southeast Asian countries. First, recession-stricken Japan reduced imports from its Asian neighbors; second, the depreciated yen helped Japanese companies increase their exports to the rest of Asia. Consequently, Southeast Asian countries' trade deficits with China and Japan increased abruptly in a relatively short period. Southeast Asian countries' trade deficits were paid for by their heavy borrowing from abroad, leaving their financial systems vulnerable and making it impossible to maintain their

---

[27]"Panel Discussion One: An Overview of the Crisis," *Journal of International Management,* Supplement, 4 (1), 1998, pp. 7S–17S.

EXHIBIT 3-6
MECHANISM OF THE ASIAN FINANCIAL CRISIS

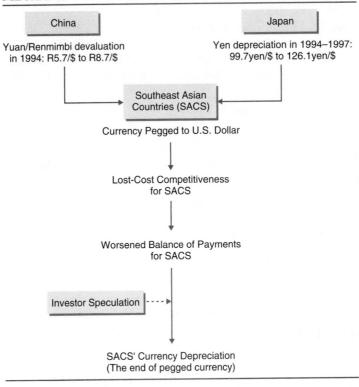

currency exchange rates vis-à-vis the U.S. dollar. The end result was the sudden currency depreciation by the end of 1997. For example, Thailand lost almost 60 percent of its baht's purchasing power in dollar terms in 1997. Malaysian ringgit lost some 40 percent of its value in the same period. The Korean won was similarly hit toward the end of 1997 and depreciated 50 percent against the U.S. dollar in less than two months. The worst case was Indonesia, whose rupiah lost a whopping 80 percent of its value in the last quarter of 1997. In a way, this would amount to a U.S. dollar bill becoming worth only 20 cents in three months!

The Asian financial crisis in the latter half of the 1990s had escalated into the biggest threat to global prosperity since the oil crisis of the 1970s. The region's once booming economies were fragile, liquidity problems hurt regional trade, and losses from Asian investments eroded profits for many Japanese companies. Similarly, among Western companies, quite a few U.S. companies that had large investments in Asia reported less than expected earnings. Others feared that the Asian crisis would wash ashore to the seemingly unrelated regions of the world, including the United States and Europe.[28] For example, the unsettling ups and downs of the Dow Jones Industrial Average reflected the precarious nature of U.S. investments in Asia. Economists blamed Asia for nipping the world's economic growth by one percentage point in 1998–1999.[29]

The Asian market's recovery from the crisis began at the beginning of this century. The acceleration of Asia's economic growth since 2000 can be largely credited to the recovery of the Japanese economy.[30] In 2003, Asia's GDP grew at 3.5 percent, exceeding

---

[28]"Europeans, Despite Big Stakes Involved, Follow U.S. Lead in Asia Financial Crisis," *Wall Street Journal,* January 16, 1998, p. A11.

[29]This section builds on Masaaki Kotabe, "The Four Faces of the Asian Financial Crisis: How to Cope with the Southeast Asia Problem, the Japan Problem, the Korea Problem, and the China Problem," *Journal of International Management,* 4 (1), 1998, 1S–6S.

[30]"The Sun Also Rises," *Economist,* October 8, 2005, pp. 3–6.

the average growth rate for the 1990s. Furthermore, Asian developing countries' GDP growth continued to exceed 5 percent. Asia's merchandise trade growth was realized primarily by intraregional trade, which rose by 20 percent to $950 billion in 2003. In addition, China's surging import demand and increased purchase of investment goods, semimanufactured goods, and machinery parts have sustained output and exports in many East Asian economies. According to the Asian Development Bank, Asia's developing economies will sustain robust growth into 2008 boosted by strong domestic demand, regional trade, and a steady inflow of investment. The GDP for Asia, excluding Japan, is expected to grow between 6.5 percent and 6.9 percent annually over the next few years. As the rest of developing Asia integrates more strongly with China and India, the region will witness a vigorous growth in intraregional trade. However, emerging Asian economies face many obstacles to sustain its growth. Southeast Asia is warned to be at risk from surging oil prices, epidemics, terror attacks, and sizable U.S. external imbalances. China is challenged by its troublesome banking system, the lack of a transparent legal system, corruption, the risk of social and political conflicts, and severe environmental pollution.[31]

Starting at the end of 2001, we witnessed the largest debt default in Argentina. Unlike the Asian financial crisis, Argentina's problems took a long time to develop and gave signs to investors and analysts.[32] However, the trouble has turned out to be much worse than anyone would have imagined. By April 2002, Argentine currency had lost nearly 40 percent of its value following the government's freeing it from the dollar in December 2001. The unemployment rate reached about 25 percent, and bank accounts remained frozen. Several presidents failed to slow down the recession. The economy contracted by 1 percent in 2001 and a whopping 8 percent in 2002.[33] In December 2001, the government stopped payment on much of its $141 billion in foreign debt—the largest government default in history. Thousands of commercial establishments were closed in a week.

> ## The South American Financial Crisis and Its Aftermath

The first cause for the crisis lies in Argentina's own monetary system. For a decade, the Argentine government fixed the peso at one U.S. dollar, which overvalued the currency and caused a lack of competitiveness when other currencies depreciated. Three months after peso was freed from the dollar, the rate became 3 pesos to the dollar, with a depreciation of 67 percent.[34] The second cause is an almost unbelievable government debt. Argentina had years of chronic government deficit spending. The debt sent the interest rate up and caused many businesses to close. As more companies were closed and more people were laid off, the government's tax income shrank and increased its debt burden. Finally, when the IMF refused to make an advance payment on a previously agreed loan to allow Argentine to make its next debt payment, the economy became paralyzed. The Argentine crisis inevitably hurt its neighbors, such as Brazil, South America's largest economy that conducted nearly one-third of its trade with Argentina. The Mexican peso weakened 5 percent within two months after the end of March 2002. The Brazilian real retreated 6.4 percent over the same period, and several other regional currencies had also slid while their counterparts from Asia and Europe were in their 12-month high. After the Argentine crisis, both international bank loans and capital inflows to Latin America declined. International financial flows to Latin America have declined substantially since the crisis in Argentina.[35]

---

[31] World Trade Report 2005: Exploring the Links between Trade, Standards, and the WTO (Geneva: World Trade Organization, 2005) "The Real Great Leap Forward," *Economist*, October 2, 2005, pp. 6–8; and "World Bank Warns Global Recovery Has Peaked," *Wall Street Journal*, April 7, 2005, p. A2.

[32] Martin Crutsinger, "Shock Waves from Argentina Crisis Could Yet Reach U.S. Economy," *AP Newswire*, April 28, 2002.

[33] Terry L. Mccoy, "Argentine Meltdown Threatens to Derail Latin Reforms," *The Orlando Sentinel*, April 22, 2002, p. A15.

[34] Ian Campbell, "As IMF Fiddles, Argentina Burns," *United Press International*, March 28, 2002.

[35] Patricia Alvarez-Plata and Mechthild Schrooten, "Latin America after the Argentine Crisis: Diminishing Financial Market Integration," *Economic Bulletin*, 40 (December 2003), pp. 431–36.

Financial Crises in Perspective

There is some commonality across the recent financial problems facing Asian and South American countries and in how they affected businesses and consumers in the region. The Asian financial crisis must be placed in a proper perspective because the "economic miracles" of the East and Southeast Asian countries have already shifted the pendulum of international trade from cross-Atlantic to cross-Pacific in the last decade. Companies from the United States and Japan, in particular, have been helping shape the nature of the cross-Pacific bilateral and multilateral trade and investment. Today, as a result, North America's trade with five Asian countries alone exceeds its trade with the European union by more than of 20 percent. The trend is irreversible. Although the recent stock market turmoil and the subsequent depreciation of the foreign exchange rates of many Asian countries may have set back their economic progress temporarily, their fundamental economic forces are likely to remain intact.

However, for these countries to sustain their strong economic performance, the importance of several necessary conditions needs to be stressed. They include strong financial institutions (commercial and investment banks, stock exchanges); transparency in the way the institutions do business; financial reporting systems consistent with free markets where capital and goods flow competitively; and supply of a managerial pool to shepherd these economies through very difficult transitional periods. While the Asian countries remain strong and attractive with respect to their "economic" fundamentals, the recent events have demonstrated that the institutional environment of the countries needs reforms.

Responses to the Regional Financial Crises

Given its economic significance, let us use the Asian financial crisis of 1997–1998 and explain how domestic and foreign companies coped with the sudden recessionary environment brought about by the crisis.

Reeling from the initial shock of the financial crisis, marketing executives have begun to cope with the realities of marketing their products in a completely changed world—from one that was once believed to keep growing with ever-increasing prosperity to one that has decimated the burgeoning middle class by snapping more than 50 percent of the consumers' spending power. Marketers are facing two dire consequences of the crisis: declining markets and increased competition from existing competitors. Their major task is to figure out how to keep current customers and gain new ones and maintain profitability in the long run.

Although Asia's current recession caused by its financial crisis is a serious one, other countries or regions have also experienced economic slumps over the years. *Recession* is usually defined as an economic situation in which a country's GDP has shrunk for two consecutive quarters. Based on this definition, the United States has experienced 29 recessions since 1894, approximately once every four to five years. We first examine how consumers react to an economic slump and then show different ways in which competing companies cope with recession and changed consumer needs.

Consumer Response to the Recession. As we all know from our own personal experiences, consumers tend to become more selective in choosing products and stay away from impulse buying in a recessionary period. In other words, we begin to spend our money more wisely and emphasize value for our money. We may consume less of some products but we may consume more of certain other products. General changes in the consumption pattern in an economic downturn are summarized in Exhibit 3-7.

Although a recession alters the mood of a country, it does not necessarily affect consumption of all products in the same way. If you were to travel today to any major city in Asia, such as Kuala Lumpur in Malaysia, you will hardly notice any change in shopping behavior at first glance. Finding a parking spot at One Utama, a large shopping mall on the outskirts of Kuala Lumpur, is as difficult now as it was a year ago. Young Malaysian couples shop for groceries and kitchenware while moviegoers flock to a cinema multiplex showing Sony Pictures' *DaVinci Code*. The coffee houses such as Starbucks are successful as ever, teeming with trendy customers, and high-tech

EXHIBIT 3-7
CHANGES IN THE CONSUMPTION PATTERN DURING A RECESSION

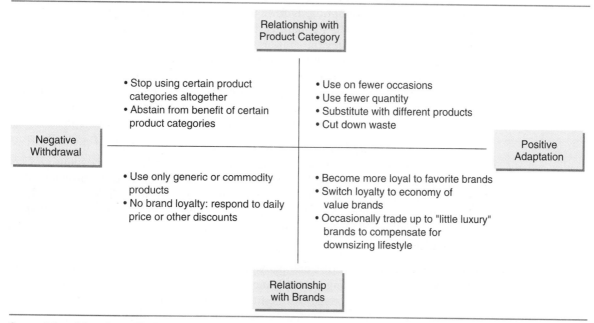

Source: Adapted from James Chadwick, "Communicating through Tough Times," *Economic Bulletin,* August 1998, p. 27

aficionados are trying out the latest PalmPilots. In sharp contrast, if you visit the huge upscale Meladas Casa Mobili store, you will see few middle-class families buying its exquisite Italian furniture. Indeed, the most susceptible to a recessionary downturn usually are big-ticket items, such as cars, home furnishings, large appliances, and travel. Those relatively unaffected are alcohol, tobacco, small appliances, packaged goods, and computer items.[36]

Corporate Response to the Recession. Various companies react differently to the recession based on their different corporate objectives. In general, there are short-term and long-term orientations in crisis management. *Short-term orientation* dictates that the corporate goal is to maximize year-to-year profit (or minimize loss), whereas *long-term orientation* tolerates some short-term loss for the benefit of future gains. Although any definitive value judgment should not be made of the two different orientations, short-term orientation tends to serve stockholders' speculative needs while long-term orientation tends to cater to customer needs. A short-term oriented solution is to pull out of the market, at least as long as the markets remain in a recession. Long-term oriented solutions are to modify marketing strategies in various ways to address the fact that consumer needs completely change during a recession.

• *Pull out.* Pulling out of the market is an easy way out financially at least in the short run. Immediately after Indonesia's rupiah depreciated by almost 80 percent in several months, J.C. Penney and Wal-Mart simply left the Indonesian market. Similarly, Daihatsu, a small Japanese automobile manufacturer, decided to pull out of Thailand. While pullout strategy may be the least painful option in the short run, it could cause some irreparable consequences in the long run, particularly in many Asian countries where long-term, trustworthy, and loyal relationships are a vital part of doing business and short-term financial sacrifices are revered as an honorable act. A better strategy would be to cut the planned production volume and maintain corporate presence in the market as General Motors did in Thailand.[37]

---

[36]James Chadwick, "Communicating through Tough Times in Asia," *Economic Bulletin,* August 1998, pp. 25–29.
[37]"Asia's Sinking Middle Class," *Far Eastern Economic Review,* April 9, 1998, p. 12.

- *Emphasize a product's value.* Weary consumers become wiser consumers. In a prosperous time, middle-class consumers may have resorted to some impulse buying and conspicuous consumption. During a recession, however, they want to maintain their current lifestyle and standard of living, but they want to feel vindicated that the product or service they purchase is worth the money they pay for it. Marketers must develop a promotion that emphasizes the value contained in the product. For example, Procter & Gamble's new Pantene shampoo line, which sells for $2.20 to $7.30, is one of the most expensive shampoos available in Hong Kong. Its advertising campaign promoted Pantene's extra moisturizers and other high-tech ingredients to clearly communicated the benefits of Pantene over other less expensive brands.[38]

  Another way to add value is to enhance a product's perceived quality image. For example, in Thailand, an advertising campaign for a relatively inexpensive Clan MacGregor scotch whiskey made locally under license emphasized the product value: "Even if you have to buy something cheap, you are getting something of real value." This is stated in reference to the three times more expensive imported Johnnie Walker Black Label whiskey. This ad helped enhance Clan MacGregor's quality image in the minds of consumers.[39]

- *Change the product mix.* If a company has a wide array of product lines, it can shift the product mix by pushing relatively inexpensive product lines while de-emphasizing expensive lines. This strategy is suited to ride over a slump by generating sufficient cash flow not only to cover the fixed costs of business operations but also to maintain the corporate presence on the market. Particularly in Asia, a company's dedication to the market as perceived by local customers will win it many favorable points in the long run. For example, Burberry's, a British fashion retailer, replaced its expensive jackets in window displays with relatively inexpensive T-shirts, stressing that everyone can still afford some luxury even in hard times.[40]

- *Repackage the goods.* As stated earlier, middle-class consumers want to maintain their lifestyle and quality of life as much as possible. It means that they will keep buying what they have been buying but consume less of it. Companies like Unilever are repackage their products to suit consumers' declining purchasing power. Unilever reduced the size of its Magnum brand ice cream packs and made it cheaper, offered giveaways on its Lux soaps (buy six, get one free), and marketed its detergents in smaller and less expensive refillable packs.[41]

- *Maintain stricter inventory.* Japanese companies have long taught us that their just-in-time (JIT) inventory management practices not only reduce unnecessary inventory but also improve their product assortment by selling only what customers want at the moment. Even if companies are not practicing JIT inventory management, it makes a lot of sense to keep inventory low. Essentially, inventory ties up capital in unsold merchandise that can be costly to the company. For example, the Kuala Lumpur store of Swedish furniture retailer Ikea did not restock certain slow-selling items.[42]

- *Look outside the region for expansion opportunities.* Asia's recession is still a regional problem although there is some risk that it will bring down the rest of the world with it to cause a global economic crisis. Nevertheless, market opportunities can be found outside the recession-stricken part of Asia. This strategy is not only a part of geographical diversification to spread out the market risk but also an effective way to take advantage of cheaper Asian currencies that translate to lower prices in other foreign countries. For instance, Esprit, the Hong Kong–based retailer,

---

[38]"Multinationals Press On in Asia despite Perils of Unstable Economies," *Asian Wall Street Journal*, September 4–5, 1998, p. 12.

[39]"Asia's Sinking Middle Class," p. 12.

[40]Ibid., p. 13.

[41]Ibid., p. 12.

[42]Ibid., p. 13.

marketed aggressively in Europe. Despite the Asian slump, its revenues increased 52 percent during fiscal 1998 with most of the gain coming from the European market.[43] Hewlett-Packard and Dell Computer, among others, that depend heavily on less expensive components made in Asia, trimmed the prices of their products.[44]

• *Increase advertising in the region.* It sounds somewhat antithetical to the preceding strategy, but there is also a strong incentive to introduce new products. It is a buyer's market for advertising space. Television stations maintain advertising rates but give bonus airtime, effectively cutting advertising costs. As a result, Unilever could better afford to reach the large middle-class market segment in Hong Kong that its SunSilk shampoo targets. American Express launched its Platinum card for the first time in Malaysia, it targeted the highest income consumers whose wealth was cushioned by investment overseas.[45]

Historical evidence also suggests that it is usually a mistake to cut advertising budgets during a recession.[46] For example, Oxy, a South Korean household products manufacturer, like many other hard-hit companies, slashed its advertising budget by one-third while its competitors halted their advertising completely. Before the slump, Oxy had commanded an 81 percent of the closet dehumidifier market with its Thirsty Hippo model. Instead of losing sales, Oxy boosted its market share to 94 percent at the expense of its rivals.[47]

• *Increase local procurement.* Many foreign companies operating in Asian countries tend to procure certain crucial components and equipment from their parent companies. When Asian currencies depreciated precipitously, the process of those imported components and equipment went up enormously in local currencies. Companies with localized procurement were not were affected easily by fluctuating exchange rates. As a result, many companies scurried to speed steps toward making their operations in Asian countries more local. Japanese companies seemed to be one step ahead of U.S. and European competitors in this localization strategy. Since the yen's sharp appreciation in the mid-1980s, Japanese manufacturers have moved to build an international production system less vulnerable to currency fluctuations by investing in local procurement.[48]

MARKETING IN EURO-LAND   ◆ ◆ ◆ ◆ ◆ ◆ ◆

Historical Background

Initially, the European Union (formerly, European Economic Community) consisted of 6 countries, including Belgium, Germany, France, Italy, Luxembourg and the Netherlands. Denmark, Ireland and the United Kingdom joined in 1973; Greece in 1981; Spain and Portugal in 1986; Austria, Finland and Sweden in 1995. The European Union consisted of 15 developed European countries until 2004, when 10 more countries joined the European Union—Cyprus, the Czech Republic, Estonia, Hungary, Latvia, Lithuania, Malta, Poland, Slovakia, and Slovenia. Today the European Union consists of 25 countries. These 10 central and eastern European countries are, in general, less developed than the previous 15 countries. Hence, due to the great differences in per capita income and historic national animosities, the European Union faces difficulties in devising and enforcing common policies.

On January 1, 1999, the 11 countries (those countries indicated in dark blue except Greece) listed in Exhibit 3-8 of the so-called euro zone embarked on a venture that

---

[43]"With Asia in Collapse, Esprit Pushes Aggressively into Europe," *Asian Wall Street Journal,* January 4, 1999, p. 2.

[44]"Asia Crisis May Benefit U.S. Companies," *New York Times on the Web,* January 19, 1998, at www.nytimes.com.

[45]"Multinationals Press On in Asia despite Perils of Unstable Economies," p. 12.

[46]Chadwick, "Communicating through Tough Times in Asia," pp. 26–28.

[47]Karene Witcher, "Marketing Strategies Help Asian Firms Beat a Downturn," *Asian Wall Street Journal,* December 7, 1998, p. 9.

[48]"Manufacturers Reshape Asian Strategies," *Nikkei Weekly,* January 12, 1998, pp. 1 and 5.

EXHIBIT 3-8
EURO ZONE COUNTRIES

created the world's second largest economic zone after the United States. The seeds for the euro were laid almost exactly three decades ago. In 1969, Pierre Werner, a former prime minister of Luxembourg, chaired a think-tank on how a European monetary union (EMU) could be achieved by 1980. The Werner report published in October 1970 outlined a three-phase plan that was very similar to the blueprint ultimately adopted in the Maastricht Treaty, signed on February 7, 1992. Like the Maastricht Treaty, the plan envisioned the replacement of local currencies by a single currency. However, EMU was put on hold following the monetary chaos created by the first oil crisis of 1973. The next step on the path to monetary union was the creation of the European monetary system (EMS) in the late 1970s. Except for the United Kingdom, all member states of the European Union joined the Exchange rate mechanism (ERM). The ERM determined bilateral currency exchange rates. Currencies of the then-nine member states could still fluctuate but movements were limited to a margin of 2.25 percent. The EMS also led to the European currency unit (ECU), in some sense the predecessor of the euro. Note that this newly bred currency never became a physical currency.

The foundations for monetary union were laid at the Madrid summit in 1989 when the EU member states undertook steps that would lead to free movement of capital. The Maastricht Treaty signed shortly after spelled out the guidelines toward creation of the EMU. Monetary union was to be capped by the launch of a single currency by 1999. This treaty also set norms in terms of government deficits, government debt, and inflation that applicants had to meet to qualify for EMU membership. All applicants, with the exception of Greece, originally met the norms, although in some cases (e.g., Belgium, Italy) the rules were bent rather liberally. These 11 countries forming the euro zone surrendered their right to issue their own money starting January 1999. Greece subsequently joined the euro zone in 2001, raising the total euro zone membership to 12. Monetary policy for this group of countries is now run by the European Central

Bank headquartered in Frankfurt, Germany. Three of the developed EU member states, the United Kingdom (not surprisingly), Sweden, and Denmark, decided to opt out of the surrender of their currencies. The new EU members may choose to adopt the euro in the future when they meet the EU's fiscal and monetary standards and the member states' agreement. Of those 15 developed European nations, 12 countries form the current euro zone. The euro zone economies, with a population of roughly 300 million people, combined represent about one-third of the world's gross domestic product and 20 percent of overall international trade. Each of these countries has committed itself to adopt a single currency, the **euro,** designated by the € symbol. Euro bank notes and coins are shown in Exhibit 3-9.

On January 1, 2002, the euro notes and coins (see Exhibit 3-10 for some spelling rules) began to replace the German mark, the Dutch guilder, and scores of other currencies. By July 1, 2002, the local currencies ceased to exist. Those of you who traversed Europe before 2002 may remember the financial strains of exchanging one European currency for another one. This hassle has become a thing of the past. The creation of the euro has been described as "the most far-reaching development in Europe since the fall of the Berlin Wall."[49] According to the Economic and Monetary

EXHIBIT 3-9
THE EURO-BANK NOTES AND COINS

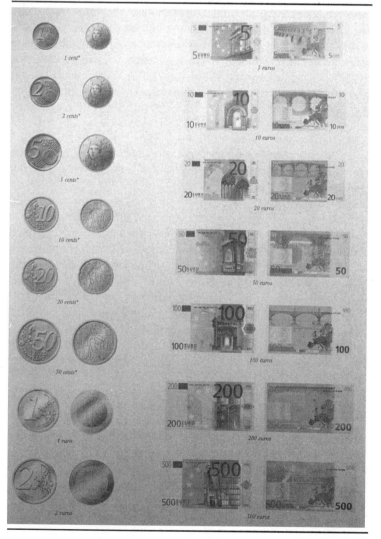

Source: Courtesy Forestier Yves/Corbis Sygma.

[49]"The Long and Arduous Ascent of Euro-Man," *Financial Times,* December 15, 1998, p. 4.

EXHIBIT 3-10

THE EURO—OFFICIAL SPELLING RULES

One indication of the confusion surrounding the euro is the spelling of the word. Here are the "official" rules:

- Question 1: Upper case or lower case?

   Answer: lower case. In English but also in almost all other official EU languages, the spelling should always be lower case, that is, euro, not Euro. One notable exception is Denmark—one of the four euro-out countries—where it is spelled Euro.

- Question 2: Plural: euros or euro?

   Answer: euro. This rule sounds puzzling, but that is the official plural form in English (and in Dutch and Italian, for example). Some of the Community languages (e.g., French, Spanish) add an "s".

Source: The European Union's Server at http://www. europa.eu.int

Union (EMU), it has already helped create a new culture of economic stability in Europe, to weather the recent slowdown in the world economy, and to avoid the kind of damaging intra-European exchange rate tension. With the euro in place, the citizens of euro area countries are now experiencing the benefits of increased price transparency, more intense competition in the market place, and greater financial integration in Europe.[50] Although some of the benefits of the euro to firms and consumers are clear, many policy questions are still unanswered.

To protect all member states, the EU has made agreements to maintain economic stability within the euro zone and avoid any financial crisis. For example, under the Europe's Stability and Growth pact, the EU's executive body would recommend issuing public warnings to any country that fell foul of European deficit control agreements. Some countries, such as France, complain that there was too much stress on budget stability and not enough on growth, thus seeking to loosen the constraints imposed on national budgets.[51]

Ramifications of the Euro for Marketers

Will the euro be the final stage leading to a "United States of Europe"? What opportunities does the euro create for firms operating in the euro zone? What are the possible threats? Answers to these and many other euro-related questions are murky at best (See Global Perspective 3-2).

What is clear is that the switch to the euro has had a wide-ranging impact on companies doing business in the euro zone. It has been accompanied by gains but also plenty of pain. Massive investments in computer infrastructure and logistical expenses have been needed for the changeover. For example, Allianz, the German insurance group, spent $124 million in euro-related data processing and devoted the equivalent of 342 years' worth of extra personnel into its euro-changeover enterprise. DaimlerChrysler pumped $120 million in its euro-conversion projects.[52] A consensus estimate was that the euro switch could have cost companies around $65 billion.[53] In addition to these upfront investments was the cost of lost revenues from price harmonization within the euro zone. Apart from these immediate bottom-line effects, the EMU also has a strategic impact on companies' operations. For marketers, the key challenges include these:

- *Price transparency.* Before the introduction of the euro, drug prices varied as much as 250 percent within Europe, and German cars in Italy cost up to 30 percent less than in their home market.[54] Conventional wisdom says that prices will slide down to the same level throughout the euro zone. The reason for that is that the single currency makes markets more transparent for consumers and corporate purchasing

---

[50]"Three and a Half Years on the Benefits of the Single Currency are Evident," The European Commission, Brussels, June 19, 2002, http://europa.eu.int/.

[51]"France Challenges EU Deficit Pact," *CNN News,* http://www.cnn.com/, June 18, 2002.

[52]"The Euro. Are You Ready?" *Business Week,* December 14, 1998, p. 35.

[53]Ibid.

[54]"When the Walls Come Down," *Economist,* July 5, 1997, p. 69.

$\mathcal{G}$LOBAL PERSPECTIVE 3-2

THE EURO PROBLEM

In 2005, many countries in the European Union were grumbling about the euro, complaining that it had weakened the financial advantages that firms previously had in stable economies. The euro area's three largest economies in France, Germany, and Italy were struggling with how to stimulate economic growth. Germany, for example, was battling unfriendly growth rates and double-digit unemployment; Italy entered its second recession in two years in the first quarter of 2005; and France voiced its complains by rejecting the European constitution. According to a government minister in Italy, the euro should be blamed for Italy's poor economic performance, and he even advocated re-introducing the lira.

What is wrong with the euro which was once believed would create "the most far-reaching development in Europe since the fall of the Berlin wall"? Can the currency be unified across the EU? Ideally, currency zones should be solid and homogenous enough to exhibit little regional variation in business cycles. One potential problem for the one-size-fits-all monetary policy is that it would make some countries in the region linger in

Sources: "Three and a Half Years on the Benefits of the Single Currency are Evident," The European Commission, Brussels, June 19, 2002, http://europa.eu.int/; and "Can This Union Be Saved?" *Economist,* Global Agenda, June 3, 2005, http://www.economist.com/agenda/displayStory.cfm?story_id=4051116.

recession while others experience rapid growth. This is exactly what happened in the EU region with a few countries, such as Ireland, growing rapidly while its large economies, such as Germany and Italy, stagnating.

In Europe, the lack of an adjustment mechanism from the European Central Bank to mitigate imbalances across different regions pushes the EU into a survival situation instead of creating a new culture of economic stability. Wide differences in social insurance and retirement programs across the region, as well as the language and cultural barriers, do not seem to easily drive convergence of the labor market. Furthermore, policy makers were recently unsuccessful in forcing fiscal policies into rough alignment, and strong public resistance has made government unwilling, or unable, to implement some structural reforms.

When growth in the euro area is weak and business confidence is declining, what are the disadvantages of the euro's weak position for its member countries? How would less productive economies cope with competition in the euro area when devaluation is no longer an option? Would a single interest rate for different economies cause problems? Finally, unlike the United States, which has central controls on its national budget, how could Europe survive with a single currency without effective controls on national budgets?

---

departments. Now that retailers in different euro zone member states display their prices in euro, price differentials have become clear to the consumer. Customers can then easily compare prices of goods across countries.[55] Savvy shoppers will bargain hunt across borders or search the Internet for the best deal. Significant price gaps will also open arbitrage opportunities leading to parallel imports from low-priced to high-priced markets. Ultimately, manufacturers will be forced to make their prices more uniform. While the logic of this argument sounds strong, there is some skepticism about whether the greater transparency achieved via the euro will really push prices downward. For one thing, one could argue that anyone capable of browsing the Internet or handling a pocket calculator already enjoys the benefits of full price transparency. Hence, whether a single currency will enlighten shoppers a great deal is debatable. For many goods and services, cross-border transaction costs (e.g., shipping bulky goods), cost differentials (e.g., labor, energy), standard differences (e.g., televisions in France), and different tax regimes will still justify significant price gaps. Shrewd companies can also find ways to "localize" their products by offering different features or product configurations. One important point to remember is that transparency is a two-way thing. For many firms, the cost of both their end-product and of supplies sourced from within the euro zone will become more comparable.[56] In fact, in a 1997 survey of 2,100 companies within the European Union, 65 percent of the respondents viewed "greater price transparency" as one of the key areas of cost saving (ranked second behind "reduction of exchange risks or costs").[57] Pricing implications of the euro will be discussed further in Chapter 13.

---

[55]John Paul Quinn, "The Euro: See-Through Pricing Arrives," *Electrical Wholesaling,* April 2002, pp. 22–24.

[56]"US Sop Giants' Million-$ Chances to Score," *Financial Times,* December 16, 1998, p. 4.

[57]www.euro.fee.be/Newsletter.

- *Intensified competitive pressure.* Many analysts predicted competitive pressure to intensify in scores of industries following the launch of the euro. Pressure to lower prices has increased. Most likely, the single currency spurs the pace of cross-border competition. But then intensified competition should be seen as the outcome of an ongoing process of which the euro is one single step. The euro plays a role but it is surely not the sole driver that accelerates rivalry within the European Union. To prepare their defenses, several companies took measures to lower their costs. This desire to cut costs has also spurred a wave of mergers and acquisitions to build up economies of scale. The Dutch supermarket chain Ahold, for example, is scouting opportunities in Britain, France, Germany, and Italy. By building up muscle, Ahold will be able to negotiate better prices with its suppliers.

- *Streamlined supply chains.* Another consequence of the euro is that companies will attempt to further streamline their supply channels. When prices are quoted in euro, singling out the most efficient supplier becomes far easier. Cutting back the number of suppliers is one trend. Numerous firms also plan to build up partnerships with their suppliers. Xerox, for instance, is cutting its supplier base by a factor of 10.[58]

- *New opportunities for small and medium-size companies.* The euro is most likely a boon for small and medium-size enterprises (SMEs). So far, many SMEs have limited their operations to their home markets. One motivation for being provincial has often been the huge costs and hassle of dealing with currency fluctuations. According to one study, currency volatility has deterred almost one-third of German SMEs from doing business abroad.[59]

- *Adaptation of internal organizational structures.* The euro also provides multinational companies (MNCs) an incentive to rethink their organizational structure. In the past, firms maintained operations in each country to match supply and demand within that country, often at the expense of scale economies. Given that currency volatility, one of the factors behind such setups, has significantly lessened with the introduction of the euro, many MNCs doing business on the continent are trimming their internal operations.[60] For instance, Michelin, the French tire maker, closed 90 percent of its 200 European distribution sites. The pharmaceutical concern Novartis streamlined its European production and eliminated overlapping operations.[61] In the long run, firms like Michelin and Novartis should enjoy tremendous benefits of economies of scale. Once again, the euro should be viewed as a catalyst stimulating a trend that has been ongoing for a number of years rather than a trigger.

- *EU regulations crossing national boundaries.* As the EU matures and the member governments expand its authority, Europeans have found that it has increasingly become a force for social regulation that crosses ethnic and national boundaries. Its officials are regulating what people can eat, how they can travel, and even how they incinerate their trash. Through a series of "infringement" suits in the European Court of Justice, the EU took Belgium, Germany, Austria, Ireland, Italy, Portugal and Spain to task for inappropriately awarding private contracts, burning waste, dumping sludge, bailing out failing businesses, and blocking independently made television programs. As of August 7, 2000, some 3,580 cases were pending for national violations of EU farming, fishing, educational, fiscal, consumer, transportation, taxation, and environmental policies. Countries stand accused of failing to enact laws that conform to EU policies or of failing to enforce such laws.[62]

---

[58]"Business Performance Will Need Sharper Edge," *Financial Times,* November 5, 1998, p. VIII; and John K. Ryans, "Global Marketing in the New Millennium," *Marketing Management,* 8 (Winter 1999), pp. 44–47.

[59]"When the Walls Come Down," p. 70.

[60]"Faster Forward," *Economist,* November 28, 1998, p. 84.

[61]"The Euro," *Business Week,* April 27, 1998, p. 38.

[62]Jeffrey Smith, "EU Rules Leave a Bad Taste in Italians' Mouths," *Washington Post,* August 7, 2000, p. A01.

SUMMARY

The international financial environment is constantly changing as a result of income growth, the balance of payments position, inflation, exchange rate fluctuations, and unpredictable political events in various countries. The International Monetary Fund and World Bank assist in the economic development of many countries, particularly developing countries, and promote stable economic growth in many parts of the world. In most cases, the change in a county's balance of payments position is an immediate precursor to its currency rate fluctuation and subsequent instability in the international financial market.

Thanks to the huge domestic economy and the international transaction currency role of the U.S. dollar, many U.S. companies have been shielded from the changes in the international financial market during much of the post-World War II era. However, as the U.S. economy depends increasingly on international trade and investment for its livelihood, few companies can ignore the changes.

Having depended more on foreign business, many European and Japanese companies have honed their international financial expertise as a matter of survival, particularly since the early 1970s. Accordingly, European countries and Japan have been better able to cope with foreign exchange rate fluctuations than the United States.

International marketers should be aware of the immediate consequences of exchange rate fluctuations on pricing. Because increased cost pressure is a factor in an era of global competition, cost competitiveness has become an extremely important strategic issue to many companies. Astute companies have even employed an adverse target exchange rate for cost accounting and pricing purposes. Although accurate prediction is not possible, international marketers should be able to "guesstimate" the direction of exchange rate movements in major currencies. Some tools are available.

The chapter highlighted Asian and South American financial crises and the introduction of the euro in the European Union (EU). We do not mean to imply that other issues, such as the collapse of the Russian economy, the recessions in the United States and the EU, and global warming are not equally important and do not have many business implications. We are sure that you are convinced of the importance of keeping constantly abreast of events around you to understand and cope with the ever-changing nature of international business.

We expect that companies from various Asian countries will become ever-leaner and more astute competitors in many different ways. South America is also expected to recover.[63] U.S. and other foreign companies doing business in Asia and South America should not pull out of those markets simply because it is very difficult to do business there. Doing so will likely damage corporate reputation and customer trust. U.S. and other foreign companies should have a longer-term orientation in dealing with Asian and South American consumers and competitors by developing strategies that emphasize value and reducing operational costs, thereby reducing susceptibility to occasional financial upheavals.

On the other hand, the EU is going through a different economic and political metamorphosis. Its relatively new common currency, the euro, has begun to change the way companies do business in Europe. Price comparison across European countries has become easier than ever before. The ease of doing business across countries permits small and medium-size companies to go "international" in the region. Competitive pressure has increased. European companies also enjoy broader economies of scale and scope, making themselves more competitive in and outside the EU. Again, U.S. and other foreign companies should not take for granted the changing face of the EU market and competition originating from it.

---

[63] Masaaki Kotabe and Ricardo Leal, *Market Revolution in Latin America: Beyond Mexico*, (New York: Elsevier Science, 2001).

KEY TERMS

Balance of payments on current account
Balance of payments on goods
Balance of payments on services
Bretton Woods Conference
Capital account
Current account balance
Currency bloc
Currency hedging

Direct investment
Euro
Exchange rate pass-through
External market adjustment
Fixed exchange rate
Forward market
Free (clean) float
Internal market adjustment
International Monetary Fund (IMF)

Managed (dirty) float
Operational hedging
Portfolio investment
Purchasing power parity (PPP)
Special drawing rights (SDRs)
Spot (current) market
Target exchange rate
Trade balance
World Bank

REVIEW QUESTIONS

1. How did the U.S. dollar become the international transaction currency in the post–World War II era?

2. Which international currency or currencies are likely to assume an increasing role as the international transaction currency in international trade? Why?

3. Why is a fixed exchange rate regime that promotes the stability of the currency value inherently unstable?

4. Discuss the primary roles of the International Monetary Fund and World Bank.

5. What is the managed float?

6. How does a currency bloc help a multinational company's global operations?

7. Describe in your own words how knowledge of the spot and forward exchange rate market helps international marketers.

8. Why is the exchange rate pass-through usually less than perfect (i.e., less than 100 percent)?

9. Define the four types of balance of payments measures.

10. Describe the sequence of events that took place to cause the Asian financial crisis in the late 1990s.

11. What are the advantages and disadvantages of having the euro as a common currency in the European Union?

DISCUSSION QUESTIONS

1. The Big Mac Index of the *Economist* was introduced in the popular press as a guide to whether currencies are at their "correct" exchange rate. Although the merits of this index have been mentioned, this index has various defects. Identify and explain the defects associated with this index.

2. Fujitsu, a Japanese computer manufacturer, has been quoted as taking various steps to prevent wild foreign exchange fluctuations from affecting the company's business. One step it took is the balancing of export and import contracts. In 2001, the company entered into $3.4 billion of export contracts and $3.2 billion of import contracts. For the year 2002, these figures were expected to be balanced. Explain how this measure would help Fujitsu. What are the advantages and disadvantages of this measure? Are there any alternate courses of action that would give the same end results?

3. In a referendum in September 2000, citizens in Denmark voted to reject the Europe's single currency, the euro. The result was close, with 53.1 percent of voters rejecting the membership and 46.9 percent favoring adoption. Many feared that rejection would deepen divisions within the European Union, leaving Denmark out of the integration and cooperation; others believe that a single currency would erode Danish sovereignty. Do you believe that rejection of membership will create a "two-speed" Europe?

4. In July 2005, China dropped its decade-long currency peg to the U.S. dollar and repegged to a basket of currencies. China reevaluated yuan to make the currency effectively 2.1 percent stronger against the U.S. dollar. Under the new currency system, China has not yet surrendered control of the currency. It has moved away from a fixed exchange rate but not all the way to a flexible or free-floating one. U.S. manufacturers and labor unions hope the yuan's revaluation will help U.S. factory sales and jobs by making U.S. goods more affordable abroad. The currency move will make Chinese exports a little more expensive abroad. Many Asian countries have been trying to compete with China's low-cost manufacturing, and after China's yuan revaluation, Malaysia announced it would drop its peg to the U.S. dollar as well. In the short run, the change in China's currency management system could be almost unnoticeable. In the longer run, however, the impact on trade and on the world financial system could be huge. Based on what you learned from this chapter, what would be the impacts on the world's economy if China and other Asian countries truly allowed their currencies to float, or instead keep holding them within narrow bands against the dollar?

5. As presented in Global Perspective 3-2, many countries in the European Union are complaining that the euro has weakened the financial advantages that firms previously had in stable economies. The euro area's three largest economies, France, Germany, and Italy are now struggling to stimulate economic growth. Germany, for example, is battling with unfriendly growth rates and double-digit unemployment; Italy entered its second recession in two years in the first quarter of 2005; and France expressed its complaints by rejecting the European constitution. According to a government minister in Italy, the euro should be blamed for Italy's poor economic performance; he even advocated reintroducing the lira. So the question is whether the united currency can be unified across the EU. Ideally, currency zones should be solid and homogenous enough to exhibit little regional variation in business cycles. However, the current one-size-fits-all monetary policy could make some countries in the region linger in recession while others experience rapid growth. Witnessing the rapid growth of a few countries, such as Ireland, while other large economies, such as those of Germany and Italy, stagnate, should the EU make any changes to its currency system? Or what needs to be done to adjust the EU problem?

SHORT CASES ◆ ◆ ◆ ◆ ◆ ◆ ◆ ◆

◆ ◆

*C*ASE 3-1

SAMSUNG'S SURVIVAL OF THE ASIAN FINANCIAL CRISIS

The Asian financial crisis severely affected the South Korean economy, reflecting on its currency and balance of payments situation. Several South Korean companies went bankrupt in its aftermath, the epicenter of which occurred in the year 1997. Others such as Daewoo and Hyundai are still struggling to hang on eight years after the crisis. Among those that survived is the successful South Korean *chaebol* (conglomerate) Samsung with revenues of more than $50 billion and over 60 related and unrelated divisions under its umbrella. Samsung is known all over the world for its flat screen liquid display panels and superior memory chips as well as finished products such as cell phones and other consumer electronics. The company's electronics division Samsung Electronics is now one of the largest technology companies in Asia, competing head on with older Japanese electronics firms such as Sony and Matsushita for global market share.

Samsung rose to global fame in the late 1980s and early 1990s when it introduced its DRAM (dynamic random access memory) chips in the West and developments in chip technology soon led it to present its 1 megabit chip, the first in the world and a technological breakthrough at the time. Samsung went on to later introduce upgrades on its chips in the years that led up to the crisis of 1997 and even though it was successful in chip manufacturing, it was losing out to its competitors in consumer electronics and white goods. When the Asian financial crisis hit, many companies shut down, but Samsung steeled itself and persevered among falling prices for chips and its other products. To boost profitability, the company laid off around 30 percent of its workforce after the crisis but continued to invest in innovation to bring it out of the red. How did Samsung make a turnaround? It turned to the huge North American and Western European markets, known for their penchant for technologically advanced products and greater purchasing power among consumers compared with that of Asian consumers.

Samsung had to work hard to gain market share in these markets. In the years after the crisis, it set up subsidiaries in Western countries. One of its main targets was the large U.S. market. The company realized that to succeed in the U.S.

and the global arena, key factors would include better design to be able to charge premium prices and therefore generate increased revenues. The company set out and did just that. It focused on research in digital technology, design, and utility and brought in designers from the best design schools in the Western hemisphere. Their designers were sent all over the world to draw inspiration for electronics architecture. Thus, Samsung sought to differentiate itself from its global rivals through superior design. Its efforts paid off. By 2005, Samsung had captured the high-end TV market in the United States, and its brand was the best selling in such items in the country. It also is the largest maker of DRAMs and LCD monitors. Every year, the company increases its design staff and budget. Its design staff evaluates consumer tastes and advises engineers on products. Since 2000, the company won more than 100 citations at design competitions and in 2004 alone, it became the first Asian company to win five citations in the Industrial Design Excellence Awards, more than any of its Western competitors.

In a way, the Asian financial crisis proved to be an indirect blessing for the company. Because of the crisis, the South Korean government stepped in to revive the industry, enabling firms like Samsung to take the necessary measures to get back to profitability such as laying off workers, which in South Korea is a contentious issue due to its highly unionized workers. Also, the crisis pushed the company to look at larger markets. Somewhere in the midst of all the chaos that surrounded companies during and after the Asian financial crisis, the company made a big decision to transform itself from a "me-too" producer of electronics to one of the most innovative companies and leading brands in the world. In 2005, it is known for its "cool" products. Between 1998 and 2004, the company doubled R&D expenditures to more than $3 billion. Today, the company that could have easily sunk in the crisis has brand equity worth more than $10 billion, and its market capitalization is greater than that of Sony and other Japanese electronics leaders that have been around much longer than Samsung.

DISCUSSION QUESTIONS

1. What did Samsung do differently from other firms that also faced the Asian financial crisis?

2. What should Samsung do to continue to bring in profits in the future?

3. What can global firms do to reduce vulnerability to financial crises?

Source: Seung-Ho Kwon, Dong-Khee Ree, and Chung-Sok Sub, "Globalization Strategies of South Korean Electronics Companies after the 1997 Asian Financial Crisis," *Asia Pacific Business Review,* 10 (Spring/Summer 2004), pp. 422–440; "A Perpetual Crisis Machine," *Fortune,* September 19, 2005, pp. 58–76; and "The Lessons for Sony at Samsung," *Business Week,* October 10, 2005 pp. 37–38.

CASE 3-2

EMERSON ELECTRIC IN EUROPE

Western European countries have always been a hotbed for U.S. foreign investment for a variety of reasons such as geographical proximity and cultural similarity compared to Asian countries. Recently, however, several U.S. firms have cut back their Western European operations in favor of other regions in the world. On one hand, this practice is not new because even in the past, firms abandoned high-cost manufacturing in Western Europe to move to low-cost Asian countries. At the same time, they maintained marketing and sales divisions in Europe. Today, however, many U.S. multinationals are scaling back in Western Europe almost completely. One such firm is U.S. electrical manufacturer Emerson Electric.

Emerson Electric, which has been in existence for 125 years, rose to fame in U.S. industry for its wide range of electrical products from air conditioner compressors to garbage disposal systems—everything but the kitchen sink! The company also boasts a low-cost manufacturing strategy and has made its mark in the list of the top U.S. companies with its record of increased earnings for 43 years in a row—until its winning streak came to a screeching halt in 2001 when profits fell by more than 27 percent for the first time! However, the company bounced back to profitability quickly with serious cost-cutting measures. The company closed several factories and laid off more than 15,000 employees and moved operations to low-wage countries.

Emerson Electric also reduced its Western European operations, like so many other U.S. firms that realized that Western European investment was merely dragging down profitability. Emerson Electric's operations in the region represented around 15 percent of its total assets and brought in a quarter of the company's revenues. Needless to say, it was an important foreign market, but the company was getting more and more disenchanted with Western Europe. Apart from the high cost of labor in the region, Western Europe was just no longer worth investing in for the firm. The Western European economy had been stagnating for almost five years with growth of less than 1.5 percent and a significant lowering in consumer spending. Furthermore, with the introduction of the euro, spending U.S. dollars in Europe was expensive. The protective European governments not only frowned on employee firings but also made it prohibitively expensive to do so.

So Emerson Electric did what it could. It reduced new investment in Western Europe, shifting toward Central and Eastern Europe instead, a long-term move from the West in the sense that the company did not fill job vacancies left due to the job cuts, indicating that the company did not expect an economic recovery in the area anytime soon. As a result of such moves by several multinational firms, foreign direct investment in the euro zone before the addition of its newest members fell by almost 50 percent in the year 2004.

Some U.S. firms are still hanging on to their European operations, but others like Emerson Electric are not prepared to let Western Europe bring down its profitability. With more than 350 million plus consumers in the area, however, it is worthwhile to wait and see just how far the company is willing to pull back.

DISCUSSION QUESTIONS

1. What can the European governments do to ensure that their countries remain attractive to foreign investors?

2. Was it a good decision for Emerson Electric to reduce its investment in Western Europe? Why?

3. What strategies should Emerson Electric have in place for its European operations in terms of the the company future?

Source: "Time to Cut their Losses," *Business Week,* May 23, 2005, p. 56, and various other sources.

FURTHER READING

Beaverstock, Jonathan V., Michael Hoyler, Kathryn Pain, and Peter J. Taylor, "Demystifying the Euro in European Financial Centre Relations: London and Frankfurt, 2000–2001," *Journal of Contemporary European Studies,* 13, August 2005, pp. 143–157.

Cogue, Dennis E. "Globalization: First We Kill All the Currency Traders." *Journal of Business Strategy,* 17 (2) (March/April 1996): 12–13.

Dhanani, Alpa, "The Management of Exchange-Rate Risk: A Case from the Manufacturing Industry," *Thunderbird International Business Review,* 46 (May/June 2004): 317–338.

Genberg, Hans. *The International Monetary System: Its Institutions and Its Future.* New York: Springer, 1995.

"In Search of Elusive Domestic Demand," *Economist,* October 15, 2005: 44–45.

Knox, Andrea, "Pricing in Euroland," *World Trade,* January 1999: 52–56.

Kotabe, Masaaki, and Ricardo Leal, *Market Revolution in Latin America: Beyond Mexico,* New York: Elsevier Science, 2001.

Lazer, William, and Eric H. Shaw, "Global Marketing Management: At the Dawn of the New Millennium," *Journal of International Marketing,* 8 (1), 2000: 65–77.

Miller, Kent D., and Jeffrey J. Reuer, "Firm Strategy and Economic Exposure to Foreign Exchange Rate Movements," *Journal of International Business Studies,* 29 (Third Quarter 1998): 493–513.

Mudd, Shannon, Robert Grosse, and John Mathis, "Dealing with Financial Crises in Emerging Markets," *Thunderbird International Business Review,* 44 (May-June 2002): 399–430.

Trichet, Jean-Claude, "The Euro after Two Years," *Journal of Common Market Studies,* 39 (March 2001): 1–13.

GLOBAL CULTURAL ENVIRONMENT AND BUYING BEHAVIOR

4

HAPTER OVERVIEW

1. DEFINITION OF CULTURE

2. ELEMENTS OF CULTURE

3. CROSS-CULTURAL COMPARISONS

4. ADAPTATION TO CULTURES

5. CULTURE AND THE MARKETING MIX

6. ORGANIZATIONAL CULTURES

7. GLOBAL ACCOUNT MANAGEMENT (GAM)

8. GLOBAL CUSTOMER RELATIONSHIP MANAGEMENT (CRM)

Buyer behavior and consumer needs are largely driven by cultural norms. Managers running a company in a foreign country need to interact with people from different cultural environments. Conducting global business means that you must deal with consumers, strategic partners, distributors, and competitors with different cultural mindsets. Cultures often provide the cement for members of the same society. A given country could be an economic basket case compared to the rest of the world, but its cultural heritage often provides pride and self-esteem to its citizens. Foreign cultures also intrigue. A stroll along Hong Kong's Nathan Road, Singapore's Orchard Road, or Shanghai's Nanjing Road reveals the appeal of Western cuisine and dress codes among Asian citizens. At the same time, cultures may also foster resentment, anxiety, or even division. When plans for Euro-Disney were revealed, French intellectuals referred to the planned theme park as a "cultural Chernobyl."[1] Many Japanese sumo-wrestling fans resent the rising prominence of foreigners like the Bulgarian Malhlyanov, better known by his sumo name of Kotooshu, meaning "Zither of Europe."[2]

---

[1] In contrast, the Hong Kong government actively pursued Disney in the hope of setting up a Disney theme park in the territory. Hong Kong Disneyland, Disney's second theme park in Asia, opened in September 2005, http://www.disney.com.hk/en.

[2] "Big in Bulgaria, Huge in Japan," *Financial Times,* December 30/31, 2005, p. W3.

To be able to grasp the intricacies of foreign markets, people must have a deeper understanding of cultural differences. From a global marketing perspective, the cultural environment matters for two main reasons. First and foremost, cultural forces are a major factor in shaping a company's global marketing mix program. Global marketing managers constantly face the thorny issue of the degree to which cultural differences should force adaptations of the firm's marketing strategy. Cultural blunders can easily become a costly affair for multinational corporations (MNCs). Some of the possible liabilities of cultural gaffes include embarrassment, lost customers, legal consequences, missed opportunities, huge costs in damage control, and tarnished brand or corporate reputations.[3] Second, cultural analysis often pinpoints market opportunities. Companies that meet cultural needs that their competitors have so far ignored often gain a competitive edge. For instance, several Japanese diaper makers were able to steal market share away from Procter & Gamble by selling diapers that were much thinner than the ones marketed by P&G, thereby better meeting the desires of Japanese mothers.[4] (Japanese homes have less space than most European or U.S. houses.)

Evolving trends, as mapped out by changes in cultural indicators, also lead to market opportunities that savvy marketers can leverage. Consider for a moment the opportunities created by the "little emperors and empresses" in China, who altogether provide a market of around 300 million children. Children in China impact consumption patterns in three ways: (1) they have spending power, (2) they have "pester power," and (3) they act as change agents. Giving pocket money to children is increasingly common in China. Chinese children—who are most often an only child because of China's one-child policy—also have a tremendous amount of "pester power." Finally, children are important change agents for scores of new products because they are often the first ones to be exposed (via friends, television) to the innovation. Capitalizing on these trends, Pepsi-Cola launched a fruit drink (Fruit Magix) in China that targeted children.[5]

Within a given culture, consumption processes can be described via a sequence of four stages: access, buying behavior, consumption characteristics, and disposal (see Exhibit 4-1):

- *Access.* Does the consumer have physical and/or economic access to the product/service?
- *Buying behavior.* How do consumers make the decision to buy in the foreign market?
- *Consumption characteristics.* What factors drive the consumption patterns?
- *Disposal.* How do consumers dispose of the product (in terms of resale, recycling, etc.)?[6]

Each of these stages is heavily influenced by the culture in which the consumer thrives.

This chapter deals with the cultural environment of the global marketplace. First we describe the concept of culture, and then we explore various elements of culture. Cultures differ a great deal, but they also have elements in common. We will discuss several schemes that can be used to compare cultures. Cultural mishaps are quite likely to occur when conducting global business. As a global business manager, you should be aware of your own cultural norms and other people's cultural mindset. To that end, we will discuss several ways to adapt to foreign cultures. Cultural forces shape a company's marketing mix. The chapter will also discuss the influence of culture on a firm's marketing mix policy. This chapter will primarily consider national cultures. However,

[3]Tevfik Dalgic and Ruud Heijblom, "International Marketing Blunders Revisited—Some Lessons for Managers," *Journal of International Marketing* 4 (1) 1996, 81–91.

[4]Alecia Swasy, *Soap Opera: The Inside Story of Procter & Gamble* (New York: Random House, 1993).

[5]Amit Bose and Khushi Khanna, "The Little Emperor. A Case Study of a New Brand Launch," *Marketing and Research Today,* November 1996, pp. 216–21.

[6]P. S. Raju, "Consumer Behavior in Global Markets: The A-B-C-D Paradigm and Its Application to Eastern Europe and the Third World," *Journal of Consumer Marketing,* 12 (5), 1995, pp. 37–56.

EXHIBIT 4-1
THE A-B-C-D PARADIGM

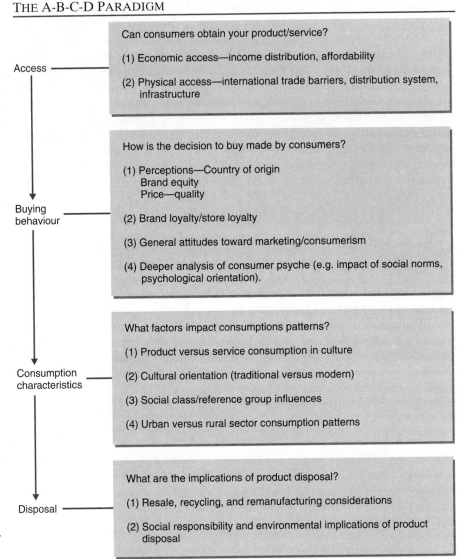

Source: P. S. Raju, "Consumer Behavior in Global Markets: The A-B-C-D Paradigm and Its Applications to Eastern Europe and the Third World," *Journal of Consumer Marketing,* 12, (5), 1995, p. 39. Reprinted with permission.

organizations are also governed internally by their organizational culture. We will look at the different types of organizational cultures that exist. We close the chapter by looking at two very important customer management areas in a global setting, namely, global customer account management and customer relationship management.

DEFINITION OF CULTURE

Culture comes in many guises. Social scientists have not come to any consensus on a definition of culture. The literature offers a host of definitions. The Dutch cultural anthropologist Hofstede, for example, defines culture as "the collective programming of the mind which distinguishes the members of one group or category from those of another."[7] Terpstra and David offer a more business-oriented definition:

---

[7]Geert Hofstede, *Cultures and Organizations: Software of the Mind* (London: McGraw-Hill, 1991), p. 5.

Culture is a learned, shared, compelling, interrelated set of symbols whose meanings provide a set of orientations for members of society. These orientations, taken together, provide solutions to problems that all societies must solve if they are to remain viable.[8]

Despite the wide variety of definitions, some common elements span the different formulations. First of all, culture is *learned* by people.[9] In other words, it is not biologically transmitted via the genes (nurture, not nature). A society's culture is passed on ("cultivated") by various peer groups (family, school, youth organizations, and so forth) from one generation to the next one. Second, culture consists of many different parts that are all *interrelated* with one another. One element (e.g., one's social status) of a person's culture has an impact on another part (e.g., the language that this person uses). So a person's cultural mindset is not a random collection of behaviors. In a sense, culture is a very complex jigsaw puzzle in which all pieces hang together. Finally, culture is *shared* by individuals as members of society. These three facets—cultures being learned, shared, and composed of interrelated parts—spell out the essence of culture.

Cultures may be defined by national borders, especially when countries are isolated by natural barriers. Examples are island nations (e.g., Japan, Ireland, Australia) and peninsulas (e.g., South Korea). However, most cultures cross national boundaries. Also, most nations contain different subgroups (*subcultures*) within their borders. These subgroups could be defined along linguistic (Flemish versus Walloons in Belgium) or religious (Buddhist Sinhalese versus Hindu Tamils in Sri Lanka) lines. Few cultures are homogeneous. Typically, most cultures contain subcultures that often have little in common with one another. Needless to say, the wide variety of cultures and subcultures creates a tremendous challenge for global marketers.

ELEMENTS OF CULTURE

◆ ◆ ◆ ◆ ◆ ◆ ◆ ◆ ◆

Culture consists of many components that interrelate with one another. Knowledge of a culture requires a deep understanding of its different parts. In this section, we describe those elements that are most likely to matter to international marketers: material life, language, social interactions, aesthetics, religion, education, and values.

Material Life

A major component of culture is its material aspect. *Material life* refers primarily to the technologies that are used to produce, distribute, and consume goods and services within a society. Differences in the material environment partly explain differences in the level and type of demand for many consumption goods. For instance, energy consumption is not only much higher in developed countries than in developing nations but also relies on more advanced forms such as nuclear energy. To bridge material environment differences, marketers are often forced to adapt their product offerings. Consider, for instance, the soft drink industry. In many countries outside the United States, store shelf space is heavily restricted, and refrigerators have far less capacity (smaller kitchens) compared to those in the United States. As a result, soft drink bottlers sell one- or one-and-a-half liter bottles rather than two-liter bottles. In markets such as China and India, the road infrastructure is extremely primitive, making distribution of products a total nightmare. In India, Coca-Cola uses large tricycles to distribute cases of Coke along narrow streets.[10]

Technology gaps also affect investment decisions. Poor transportation conditions, unreliable power supply, and distribution infrastructure in many developing countries

---

[8]Vern Terpstra and Kenneth David, *The Cultural Environment of International Business* (Cincinnati, OH: South-Western Publishing Co., 1991), p. 6.

[9]Some biologists have made a compelling case that culture is not a uniquely human domain in the sense that animals (especially primates) can also possess a culture. A good introduction to this perspective is Frans de Waal, *The Ape and the Sushi Master* (London: Penguin Books, 2001).

[10]"Coke Pours into Asia," *Business Week,* October 21, 1996, pp. 22–25.

GLOBAL PERSPECTIVE 4-1

INFILTRATING THE RURAL MARKETPLACE

Having conquered urban markets in Asia, consumer goods behemoths such as Unilever, Procter & Gamble, and Coca-Cola are setting their sights on the millions of potential consumers in rural communities of the region.

Selling shampoo, soap, or detergents to rural consumers is often very demanding, yet the market opportunities offered by these consumers are tremendous. In Indonesia, 135 million people (64 percent of the population) live in areas where many of them can afford inexpensive, fast-moving consumer goods. In India, 75 percent of the population (700 million people) is spread out over 627,000 villages. India's rural market contributes almost 50 percent to Unilever's total sales in the country. The share is even higher for major categories such as detergents and beverages. Fifty percent of consumer durables in India are sold in the rural markets.

Many of these villages are virtually untouched by the mass media. As one India-based advertising executive stated, "Often the nearest thing to brand villagers have experienced is a home-made mud skin care product from a neighboring village." According to the same source, the two biggest barriers are the nearly complete absence of a guaranteed 24-hour power supply and road conditions. To cope with the unreliable power supply, many soft drink makers have tried to develop coolers that can survive up to eight hours of power cuts.

Sources: "Marketing in the Field," *Ad Age Global,* October 2001, p. 8; "Village Leverage," *Far Eastern Economic Review,* August 24, 2000, pp. 50–55; "Unilever's Jewel," *Business Week International,* April 19, 1999, pp. 22–23; "Striving for Success—One Sachet at a Time," *Financial Times,* December 11, 2000, p. 9; and "Rural Consumers Get Closer to Established World Brands," *Ad Age Global,* June 2002, p. 5.

Add to these further hurdles such as high illiteracy rates, low exposure to mass media, and low incomes, and you can imagine that conventional marketing approaches are largely ineffective when reaching out to rural consumers. Instead, multinational corporations need to come up with creative and innovative tools to sell their wares.

To relay marketing messages to villagers, marketers need to resort to unconventional media. To promote its brands in rural India, Hindustan Lever (Unilever's India subsidiary) relies on vans with TV sets and satellite dishes that are set up in village squares. These vans provide local entertainment (e.g., songs from Bollywood movies) along with ads for Lever-branded products. Lever's goal is to establish a physical presence in places where villagers meet frequently such as wells and markets. Lever even uses some form of product placement in local folk performances. Local advertising agencies are asked to write a story around a Lever brand that is then developed into a stage performance in any one of the local dialects. Sampling can also be a very effective promotion tool, especially in places where people have never experienced products such as shampoos or toothpaste.

Besides communication, other concerns are availability and affordability. Unilever uses teams of "motorbike cowboys" and boat salesmen to sell its goods in Vietnam. Soft drink makers Pepsi and Coca-Cola have launched 200 ml bottles priced between 10 and 12 cents in India. A battery-free radio designed by Philips for the rural market enables Indian consumers to save 1,200 rupiahs (about $25) per year. Kodak India has developed a camera pack targeting India's rural consumers. Graphics on the pack visually demonstrate usage instructions.

---

force companies to improvise and look for alternative ways to market and deliver their products. In rural areas of countries such as India, conventional media are incapable of reaching the whole universe of consumers. As is illustrated in Global Perspective 4-1, global marketers in such countries need to come up with innovative ways to access rural consumers. Governments in host nations often demand technology transfers as part of the investment package. Companies that are not keen on sharing their technology are forced to abandon or modify their investment plans. When the Indian government asked Coca-Cola to share its recipe, Coke decided to jump ship and left the Indian marketplace in 1977. The soft drink maker returned to India in 1992.

Language   Language is often described as the most important element that sets human beings apart from animals. Language is used to communicate and to interpret the environment. Two facets of language have a bearing on marketers: (1) the use of language as a communication tool within cultures and (2) the huge diversity of languages across and, often, within national boundaries.

Let us first consider the communication aspect. As a communication medium, language has two parts: the *spoken* and the so-called *silent*. The spoken language consists of the vocal sounds or written symbols that people use to communicate with one another. Silent language refers to the complex of nonverbal communication mechanisms that people use to get a message across. Edward Hall identified five distinctive types of silent languages: space, material possessions, friendship patterns, time, and agreements. *Space* refers to the conversation distance between people: close or remote. The second type, *material possessions,* relates to the role of possessions in people's esteem of one another. *Friendship patterns* cover the notion and treatment of friends. Perceptions of *time* also vary across cultures. Differences exist about the importance of punctuality, the usefulness of "small talk," and so forth. The final type refers to the interpretation of *agreements.* People in some cultures focus on the explicit contract itself. In other cultures, negotiating parties put faith in the spirit of the contract and trust one another.

Not surprisingly, a given gesture often has quite different meanings across cultures. In Japan, scribbling identifying cues on business cards is a major violation of basic business etiquette. On the other hand, foreigners (*gaijin*) are not expected to engage in the bowing rituals used for greeting people of various ranks.[11] Other examples of silent language forms that are harmless in one society and risky in others abound. It is imperative that managers familiarize themselves with the critical aspects of a foreign culture's hidden language. Failure to follow this rule will sooner or later lead to hilarious or embarrassing situations.

The huge diversity of languages poses another headache to multinational companies. Language is often described as the mirror of a culture. Differences exist across and within borders. Not surprising, populous countries contain many languages. In India, Hindi, spoken by 30 percent of the population, is the national language, but there are 14 other official languages.[12] Papua New Guinea, an island nation in the southern Pacific Ocean, has around 715 indigenous languages. Even small countries show a fair amount of language variety. Switzerland with a population of nearly 7.5 million people has four national languages: German (spoken by 63.7 percent of the population), French (20.4 percent), Italian (6.5 percent), and Romansch (0.5 percent).[13]

Even within the same language, meanings and expressions vary a great deal among countries that share the language. A good example is English. English words that sound completely harmless in one English-speaking country often have a silly or sinister meaning in another English-speaking country. Until 15 years ago, Snickers bars were sold under the brand name Marathon in the United Kingdom. Mars felt that the Snickers name was too close to the English idiom for female lingerie (knickers).[14] Cert, a London-based consultant, offers a few rules of thumb about talking to foreigners in English:

1. *Vocabulary.* Go for the simplest words (e.g., use the word rich instead of loaded, affluent, or opulent). Treat colloquial words with care.

2. *Idioms.* Pick and choose idioms carefully (for instance, most non-U.S. speakers would not grasp the meaning of the expression *nickel-and-diming*).

3. *Grammar.* Express one idea in each sentence. Avoid subclauses.

4. *Cultural references.* Avoid culture-specific references (e.g., "Doesn't he look like David Letterman?").

5. *Understanding the foreigner.* This will be a matter of unpicking someone's accent. If you do not understand, make it seem that it is you, not the foreigner, who is slow.

Language blunders easily arise as a result of careless translations of advertising slogans or product labels. Toshiba once had a commercial jingle in China that went

---

[11]"When Fine Words Will Butter No Parsnips," *Financial Times,* May 1, 1992.

[12]These are Bengali, Telugu, Marathi, Tamil, Urdu, Gujarati, Malayalam, Kannada, Oriya, Punjabi, Assamese, Kashmiri, Sindhi, and Sanskrit. Hindustani, a mixture of Hindi and Urdu, is not an official language, though widely spoken.

[13]Note though that only the first three are official languages; http://www.cia.gov/cia/publications/factbook/geos/sz.html, accessed December 30, 2005.

[14]Masterfoods recently launched a new energy bar in the United States under the Snickers Marathon brand name.

"Toshiba, Toshiba." Unfortunately, in Mandarin Chinese, Toshiba sounds a lot like "let's steal it" (tou-chu-ba). The English version of a newspaper ad campaign run by Electricité de France, a French state-owned utility firm, said that the company offered "competitive energetic solutions" and was "willing to accompany your development by following you on all of your sites in Europe and beyond."[15] Certain concepts are unique to a particular language. For example, an expression for the Western concept of romance does not exist in languages such as Chinese, Thai, Malay, and Korean.[16] Exhibit 4-2 shows an example of *Chinglish*.[17] The exhibit is part of a hotel manual that one of the authors found in a hotel in Shanghai.

Mistranslations can convey the image that the company does not care about its customers abroad. Several techniques can be used to achieve good translations of company literature. With **back translation,** a bilingual speaker—whose native tongue is the target language—translates the company document first in the foreign language. Another bilingual translator—whose native tongue is the base language—then translates this version back into the original language. Differences between the versions are then resolved through discussion until consensus is reached on the proper translation.

Firms doing business in multilingual societies need to decide what languages to use for product labels or advertising copy. Multilingual labels are fairly common now, especially in the pan-European market. Advertising copy poses a bigger hurdle. To deal with language issues in advertising copy, advertisers can rely on local advertising agencies, minimize the spoken part of the commercial, or use subtitles. We will revisit these issues in much more detail in Chapter 14.

EXHIBIT 4-2
NOTICE TO GUESTS

1. Show the valid ID card as stated when registering with the Front Office.
2. Please don't make over or put up your guest or your relatives or your friends for the night without registering.
3. Please don't damage and take away, the furniture and equipment in the hotel or something borrowed from the Main Tower and change their usages. If happened, We will claim for damage and loss.
4. Please don't take the things which are subject to burning, explosion, rolling into the Main Tower. Please throw the cigrettend march into the ashtray when smoking in the room. Please don't smoking when lying in the bed.
5. Please don't commit illegal behaviours like gambling, smuggling, whoring, selling drugs. Please don't pick fruit and flower and vomit anywhere, Please don't take the animal and usuall smell things into the hotel.
6. Keep quiet in the hotel, please don't fight and get truck and create a disturbance in the hotel. The security department will handle the person who damage Severely, the order, endanger others' rest, even body safety, according to public security clauses.
7. Guest are advised to deposit their valuables in the Front Office safe. In case of burglary or theft, the hotel haven't responsibility for it.
8. Please don't use dangerous electrical equipment except hairdrier, shaver.
9. The service hour of the hotel is 8:00 am to 10:00 pm the visitor should leave the hotel before 11:00 pm.
10. Please pay attention to and observe all regulations of the hotel. The hotel have access to depriving the quantity of staying of the people who transgress the rules above the neglect the dissuading.

Source: Hotel manual of a guesthouse in Shanghai.

---

[15]"The Case of the Misleading Coffin," *Financial Times,* June 21, 1999, p. 12.

[16]Jocelyn Probert and Hellmut Schütte, "De Beers: Diamonds Are for Asia," INSEAD-EAC, Case Study 599-011-1 (1999).

[17]See http://www.pocopico.com/china/chinglish.php for some other amusing cases of "Chinglish."

$\diamond \diamond$

$\mathcal{G}$LOBAL PERSPECTIVE 4-2

ORACLE CORPORATION : MARKETING BY LANGUAGE

In 2000, Oracle Corporation, the leading California-based software maker, revamped its marketing organization by setting up regional teams by language instead of specific countries. Oracle expected that the move might save up to $100 million each year. A team based in France handles all French-language marketing in France, Belgium, Switzerland, and Canada. A Spanish-language team runs the marketing in Spain and Latin America. Teams for seven other languages—English, Japanese, Korean, Chinese, Portuguese, Dutch, and German—cover Oracle's other markets. Through this overhaul, Oracle not only hopes to save money but also to gain more consistency and control over its marketing messages. Given that Oracle is a high-technology company, localization is less of an issue. Mark Jarvis, Oracle's senior vice president—worldwide marketing, notes, "Our product is identical in every market, and the way we sell it is identical, so why would we want local teams changing the message?"

Oracle also decided to get rid of its 60-plus country-specific Web sites. According to Jarvis, "Sixty-two Websites are a great excuse for high costs—you need 62 Webmasters, and you have 62 opportunities to have the wrong logo, wrong tagline or wrong marketing message. All of that becomes really simple when you have one Website managed at headquarters." First-time visitors to www.oracle.com now need to register a country. They receive local information when they log in afterward. Oracle uses the Web as its key marketing tool because it is cheap, direct, and can have a much higher response rate than more traditional forms of direct marketing. One piece of direct mail that went out to 500 CEOs had a 0.1 percent response rate. Personalized e-mail targeting the same audience had a 76 percent response rate.

Source: "Marketing by Language: Oracle Trims Teams, Sees Big Savings," *Advertising Age International,* July 2000, pp. 4, 38.

In markets such as China, marketers also need to decide whether to keep the original brand or company name or whether to adopt a localized brand identity. Many multinationals in China have localized their brand names by creating equivalent names that sound like their global name with a positive meaning in Chinese. Hewlett Packard, for instance, adopted *Hui-Pu* as its Chinese brand name. *Hui* means "kindness," and *Pu* is "universal." Other companies take a different track and translate their name using characters that do not necessarily have the same sound as the original name. In 2002, Oracle, following a brainstorming session with its Chinese executives, adopted the name *Jia Gu Wen.* The literal translation means the recording of data and information—a nice fit with Oracle's core business. Apparently, the meaning of the phrase stems from a time when tortoise shells were used to record the prophecies from an oracle during the Shang dynasty (16th to 11th century b.c.).[18] Global Perspective 4-2 discusses how language was a key driver behind the overhaul of Oracle's marketing organization.

Social Interactions

The movie *Iron & Silk* neatly illustrates the cultural misunderstandings that arise in cross-cultural interactions. The movie is based on the true-life story of Mark Salzman, a Yale graduate who, after his studies, went to China to teach English in a Chinese village. During his first day of class, his students, out of respect for their teacher, insist on calling him "Mister Salzman." Mark prefers to be addressed on a first-name basis. Ultimately, students and teacher settle on "teacher Mark" as a compromise.

A critical aspect of culture is the social interactions among people. *Social interplay* refers to the manner in which members of society relate to one another. Probably the most crucial expression of social interactions is the concept of kinship. This concept varies dramatically across societies. In most Western countries, the family unit encompasses the **nuclear family,** being the parents and the children. The relevant family unit in many developing countries is the **extended family** which comprises a much wider group of often only remotely related family members. The way families are structured has important ramifications. Family units fulfill many roles, including economic and psychological support. For instance, Sri Lankan banks promote savings

---

[18]"Ancient Symbolism in a New Oracle Logo," *Ad Age Global,* May 2002, p. 12.

programs that allow participants to build up savings to support their parents when they reach retirement. Such saving programs would be unthinkable in the United States. Views on marriage and the role of husband and wife can also be unique to a particular culture. Attitudes toward love and marriage in China are far more materialistic than in most other countries. Marriage is seen as a partnership toward achieving success. Chinese women select prospective husbands based on financial status and career prospects rather than love, which is considered a luxury. Role expectations are very traditional: The man should be provider and protector; the woman should do the cooking, be a good mother, and be virtuous.[19] In countries where extended families are the norm, major purchase decisions are agreed upon by many individuals. Within such communities, members of an extended family will pool their resources to fund the purchase of big-ticket items (e.g., sewing machines).

Countries also vary in terms of the scope of the decision-making authority. A study by Asia Market Intelligence (AMI), a Hong Kong-based research firm, looked at the decision-making influence of husbands and wives on grocery shopping. The study showed that even in Asia's most conservative societies, men are heavily involved in grocery shopping. The reasons for the rising number of men doing the family grocery shopping vary, including the increased number of women entering the workforce and changing attitudes toward gender roles.[20]

Another important aspect of social interactions is the individual's reference groups: the set of people to whom an individual looks for guidance in values and attitudes. As such, reference groups have an enormous impact on people's consumption behavior patterns. The consumer research literature[21] identifies three kinds of reference groups: membership groups to which people belong; anticipatory groups of which one would like to be a part; and dissociative groups with which individuals do not want to be associated. Reference groups are especially influential for consumer products that are socially visible, such as most status goods and luxury items. Knowledge on reference group patterns could provide input in formulating product positioning strategies and devising advertising campaigns. A good example is a campaign that Allied Domecq developed to reposition Kahlúa, a Mexican coffee liqueur brand, in Asia during the Asian recession, as the brand of choice among young Asians. To reach out to its target audience, Allied Domecq sponsored a dance program on MTV Networks Asia called "Party Zone Mixing with Kahlúa." The prime motivation behind the sponsorship was that "young adults throughout Asia look to MTV as a trendsetter and representative of their lifestyle."[22] The "chav" phenomenon in Britain is a good illustration of the importance of dissociative reference groups. Chavs belong to a social underclass of young, white, undereducated, and mostly unemployed individuals. Chavs have adopted the classic Burberry fashion-brand as their clan plaid, though most of what they purchase is counterfeit. Not surprisingly, Burberry is not very pleased with the popularity of its label among chavs.[23]

Aesthetics *Aesthetics* refers to the ideas and perceptions that a culture upholds in terms of beauty and good taste. Cultures differ sharply in terms of their aesthetic preferences, though variations are mostly regional, not national. In the Asia-Pacific region, aesthetic expressions are driven by three principles: (1) complexity and decoration (multiple forms, shapes, and colors), (2) harmony, and (3) nature displays (e.g., mountains, flowers, trees).[24]

---

[19] Probert and Schütte, "De Beers: Diamonds Are for Asia," p. 11.

[20] "As More Women Enter Work Force, More Men Enter the Supermarket," *Asian Wall Street Journal*, March 8, 2001, pp. N1, N7.

[21] James F. Engel, Roger D. Blackwell, and Paul W. Miniard, *Consumer Behavior* (Hinsdale, IL: Dryden, 1986), pp. 318–24.

[22] "Kahlua Gets New Sales Face in Asia," *Advertising Age International*, March 8, 1999, pp. 5–6.

[23] http://www.telegraph.co.uk/news/main.jhtml?xml=/news/2005/01/01/nchav01.xml&sSheet=/news/2005/01/01/ixhome.html.

[24] Bernd H. Schmitt and Yigang Pan, "Managing Corporate and Brand Identities in the Asia-Pacific Region," *California Management Review*, 38 (Summer 1994), pp. 32–48.

EXHIBIT 4-3
THE MEANING OF COLOR

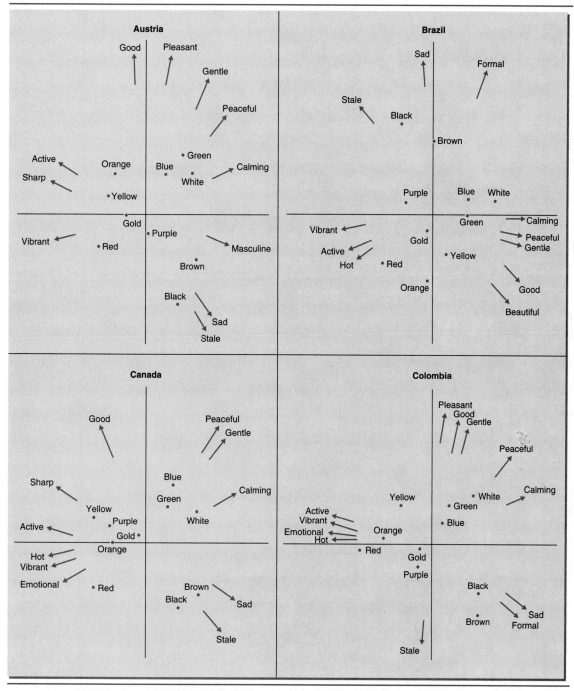

Source: Thomas J. Madden, Kelly Hewett, and Martin S. Roth, "Managing Images in Different Cultures. A Cross-National Study of Color Meanings and Preferences," *Journal of International Marketing,* 8 (4), (2000), pp. 96–97 (Figure 1). Reprinted with permission from the American Marketing Association.

Color also has different meanings and aesthetic appeals. This is illustrated in Exhibit 4-3, which shows color associations in eight different countries. As you can see, three colors—blue, green, and white—appear to convey universal meanings in all eight countries: peaceful, gentle, calming. However, other colors reveal striking cultural differences in the emotions they create. For example, black is seen as "masculine" in Hong Kong and the United States but "formal" in

EXHIBIT 4-3
(*continued*)

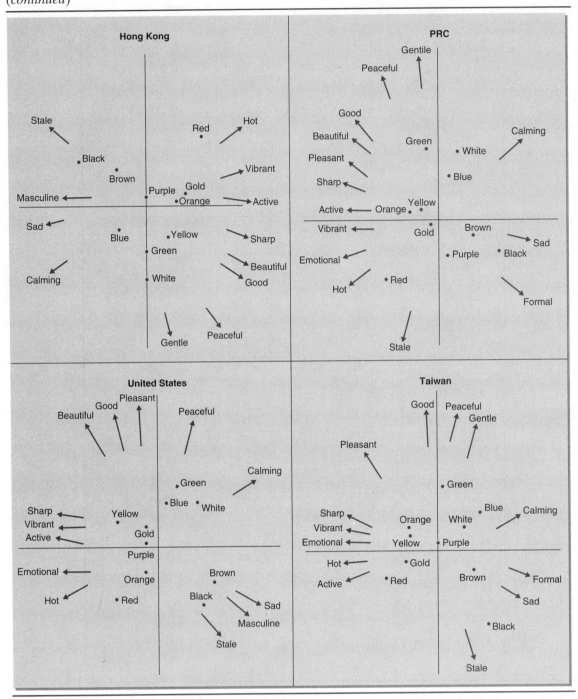

Brazil.[25] In Chinese cultures, red is perceived as a lucky color. Yellow, on the other hand, is perceived as pleasant and associated with authority. In Japan, pastel tones, expressing softness and harmony, are preferred to bright colors.[26] Given that colors may invoke different meanings, it is important to realize how the colors of a particular package, product, or brand are perceived.

[25]Thomas J. Madden, Kelly Hewett, and Martin S. Roth. "Managing Images in Different Cultures: A Cross-National Study of Color Meanings and Preferences," *Journal of International Marketing,* 8 (4), 2000, pp. 90–107.

[26]Bernd H. Schmitt, "Language and Visual Imagery: Issues in Corporate Identity in East Asia," *Journal of World Business* (Winter 1995), pp. 28–36.

Religion refers to a belief in supernatural agents. Religions embrace three distinct elements: explanation (e.g., God seen as a "first cause" behind the creation of the universe), a standardized organization (e.g., priests, churches, rituals), and moral rules of good behavior.[27] Religion plays a vital role in many societies. To appreciate people's buying motives, customs, and practices, awareness and understanding of their religion is often crucial. When religion is an important part of a consumer's life, consumer companies should acknowledge it. In Islamic societies, companies can broaden the appeal of their brands and grow their business by engaging with Muslim consumers. For GlaxoSmithKline (GSK), gaining *halal,* or religiously pure, status for Ribena and Lucozade was an important step to gain clout in Muslim communities.[28] Exhibit 4-4 highlights the various influences of Islam on the marketing function.

Religious taboos often force companies to adapt their marketing mix program. To avoid offending India's religious sensibilities, McDonald's introduced a mutton-based "Maharaj Mac" in India as opposed to its flagship beef-based Big Mac. About three quarters of McDonald's India menu is localized to tantalize Indian customers.[29]

In numerous Asian countries, the ancient Chinese philosophy of *feng shui* (wind-water) plays an important role in the design and placement of corporate buildings and retail spaces. According to feng shui, the proper placement and arrangement of a human-made structure and its interior objects will bring good fortune to its residents and visitors. Good feng shui allows the cosmic energy to flow freely throughout the building and hinders evil spirits from entering it.[30] For instance, Disney decided to shift the angle of the front entrance gate to Hong Kong Disneyland by 12 degrees after consulting a Chinese feng shui master. Other measures included placing cash registers close to corners or along walls, no fourth-floor buttons in elevators (4 is bad luck in Chinese), a ballroom measuring exactly 888 square meters (8 is a number of prosperity), and burning ritual incense whenever a building was finished.[31]

Religion also shapes the holiday calendar in many countries. A country such as Sri Lanka, with several officially recognized religions (Hinduism, Buddhism, Islam), forces a careful examination of one's calendar when meetings are to be scheduled. On the other hand, religious holidays often steer advertising campaigns or may open up untapped market opportunities. In many Western European countries, Saint Nicholas Day (December 6) is the key event for toy companies and candy makers. The holy month of Ramadan (the ninth month of the Muslim calendar) is also becoming an increasingly commercialized event. In major Mideastern cities such as Cairo and Amman, Ramadan has a Christmaslike atmosphere these days.[32]

The role of women in society is sometimes largely driven by the local religion. In Islamic societies, conducting market research that involves women is extremely difficult. For instance, mixing men and women in focus groups is prohibited in Saudi Arabia.

Religious norms also influence advertising campaigns. In Iran, all ads need to be cleared by Islamic censors. This approval process can take up to three months. Iranian authorities frowned on one print ad created for Chiquita because they considered showing only three bananas on a full-page ad a waste of space.[33] Also in Iran, Gillette's local advertising agency had difficulty placing an ad for the Gillette Blue II razor. Islam dictates that its followers refrain from shaving. Ultimately, Gillette's account executive

---

[27] Jared Diamond, "The Religious Success Story," *New York Review of Books,* November 7, 2002, pp. 30–31.

[28] "Muslims Offer a New Mecca for Marketers," *Financial Times,* August 11, 2005, p. 6.

[29] Kishore Dash, "McDonald's in India," Thunderbird, Case Study A07-05-0015 (2005).

[30] Bernd Schmitt and Alex Simonson, *Marketing Aesthetics: The Strategic Management of Brands, Identity, and Image* (New York: The Free Press, 1997), pp. 275–76.

[31] "Disney Bows to Feng Shui," *International Herald Tribune,* April 25, 2005, pp. 1, 6.

[32] "Parts of Mideast Are Split between Ramadan as Time for Prayer and Partying," *Asian Wall Street Journal,* December 5, 2002, pp. A1, A8.

[33] "Multinationals Tread Softly While Advertising in Iran," *Advertising Age International,* November 8, 1993, pp. I–21.

EXHIBIT 4-4

MARKETING IN AN ISLAMIC FRAMEWORK

Elements	*Implications for Marketing*
I. Fundamental Islamic concepts	
A. Unity (Concept of centrality, oneness of God, harmony in life)	Product standardization, mass media techniques, central balance, unity in advertising copy and layout, strong brand loyalties, a smaller evoked size set, loyalty to company, opportunities for brand extension strategies
B. Legitimacy (Fair dealings, reasonable level of profits)	Less formal product warranties, need for institutional advertising and/or advocacy advertising, especially by foreign firms, and a switch from profit-maximizing to a profit-satisfying strategy.
C. Zakaat (2.5 percent per annum compulsory tax binding on all classified as "not poor.")	Use of "excessive" profits, if any, for charitable acts, corporate donation for charity, institutional advertising.
D. Usury (Cannot charge interest on loans. A general interpretation of this law defines "excessive interest" charged on loans as not permissible.)	Avoid direct use of credit as a marketing tool; establish a consumer policy of paying cash for low-value products; for high-value products, offer discounts for cash payments and raise prices of products on an installment basis; sometimes possible to conduct interest transactions between local/foreign firm in other non-Islamic countries; banks in some Islamic countries take equity in financing ventures, sharing resultant profits (and losses).
E. Supremacy of human life (Compared to other forms of life or objects, human life is of supreme importance.)	Pet food and/or products less important; avoid use of statues, busts—interpreted as forms of idolatry; symbols in advertising and/or promotion should reflect high human values; use floral and artwork in advertising as representation of aesthetic values.
F. Community (All Muslims should strive to achieve universal brotherhood—with allegiance to the "One God." One way of expressing community is the required pilgrimage to Mecca for all Muslims at least once in their lifetime, if able to do so.)	Formation of an Islamic Economic Community—development of an "Islamic consumer" served with Islamic-oriented products and services, for example, "kosher" meat packages, gifts exchanged at Muslim festivals, and so forth: development of community services—need for marketing or nonprofit organizations and skills.
G. Equality of people	Participative communication systems; roles and authority structures may be rigidly defined but accessibility at any level relatively easy.
H. Abstinence (During the month of Ramadan, Muslims are required to fast without food or drink from the first streak of dawn to sunset—a reminder to those who are more fortunate to be kind to the less fortunate and as an exercise in self-control.)	Products that are nutritious, cool, and digested easily can be formulated for Sehr and Iftar (beginning and end of the fast).
Consumption of alcohol and pork is forbidden; so is gambling.	Opportunities for developing nonalcoholic items and beverages (for example, soft drinks, ice cream, milk shakes, fruit juices) and nonchance social games, such as Scrabble; food products should use vegetable or beef shortening.
I. Environmentalism (The universe created by God was pure. Consequently, the land, air, and water should be held as sacred elements.)	Anticipate environmental, antipollution acts; opportunities for companies involved in maintaining a clean environment; easier acceptance of pollution-control devices in the community (for example, recent efforts in Turkey have been well received by the local communities).
J. Worship (Five times a day; timing of prayers varies.)	Need to take into account the variability and shift in prayer timings in planning sales calls, work schedules, business hours, customer traffic, and so forth.
II. Islamic culture	
A. Obligation to family and tribal traditions	Importance of respected members in the family or tribe as opinion leaders; word-of-mouth communication, customers' referrals may be critical; social or clan allegiances, affiliations, and associations may be possible surrogates for reference groups; advertising home-oriented products stressing family roles may be highly effective, for example, electronic games.

EXHIBIT 4-4
(continued)

Elements	Implications for Marketing
B. Obligation toward parents is sacred	The image of functional products could be enhanced with advertisements that stress parental advice or approval; even with children's products, there should be less emphasis on children as decision makers.
C. Obligation to extend hospitality to both insiders and outsiders	Product designs that are symbols of hospitality, outwardly open in expression, rate of new product acceptance may be accelerated and eased by appeals based on community.
D. Obligation to conform to codes of sexual conduct and social interaction. These may include the following:	
1. Modest dress for women in public	More colorful clothing and accessories are worn by women at home; so promotion of products for use in private homes could be more intimate—such audiences could be reached effectively through women's magazines; avoid use of immodest exposure and sexual implications in public settings.
2. Separation of male and female audiences (in some cases)	Access to female consumers can often be gained only through women as selling agents—salespersons, catalogs, home demonstrations, and women's speciality shops.
E. Obligations to religious occasions (For example, there are two major religious observances that are celebrated—Eid-ud-Fitr, Eid-ud-Adha.)	Tied to purchase of new shoes, clothing, sweets, and preparation of food items for family reunions, Muslim gatherings. There has been a practice of giving money in place of gifts. Increasingly, however, a shift is taking place to more gift giving; because lunar calendar, dates are not fixed.

Source: Mushtaq Luqmani, Zahir A. Quareshi, and Linda Delene, "Marketing in Islamic Countries: A Viewpoint," *MSU Business Topics,* Summer 1980, pp. 20–21. Reprinted with permission.

was able to convince the advertising manager of one local newspaper by using the argument that shaving sometimes becomes necessary, such as in the case of head injuries resulting from a car accident.[34] In Egypt, Coca-Cola's business was hampered by rumors that its logo read "no Mohammed, no Mecca" when read backward and in Arabic script—a heresy for local Muslims. Coke called on Egypt's Grand Mufti, the country's most senior authority on Sunni Islam, to issue a religious opinion. The Mufti ruled that Coke was *halal.*[35] Rumors also affected Wrigley's sales in Indonesia when an e-mail circulated claiming that the company used pig extract in manufacturing its chewing gum products. Hush Puppies, the U.S.-based shoe brand, lost market share in Malaysia when consumers there discovered that its shoes contained pigskin.[36] Global Perspective 4-3 describes how McDonald's coped with rumors about its food preparation in India.

Education is one of the major vehicles for channeling culture from one generation to the next. Two facets of education that matter to international marketers are the level and the quality of education. The level of education varies considerably among countries. Exhibit 4-5 shows the level of participation in higher education for a range of countries. Most developed countries have compulsory education up to the late teens. In some countries, however, especially Muslim societies, education is largely the preserve of males. As a consequence, males are often far better educated than females in such societies. One powerful indicator of the education level is a country's illiteracy rate. In countries with low literacy levels, marketers need to exercise caution in matters such as product labeling, print ads, and survey research. One baby food company attributed its poor sales in Africa to the product label that was used. The label's picture of a

Education

[34]"Smooth Talk Wins Gillette Ad Space in Iran," *Advertising Age International,* April 27, 1992, p. I–40.

[35]"U.K. Supermarket Sainsbury Travels Mideast's Rocky Road," *Advertising Age International,* July 2000, p. 19.

[36]"Muslim Market Minefield," *Media,* February 8, 2002, pp. 16–17.

GLOBAL PERSPECTIVE 4-3

THE GOLDEN ARCHES IN INDIA: CRISIS MANAGEMENT

McDonald's entered India in October 1996. Out of respect for the local Hindu population, the firm for the first time dropped beef from its menu. To cater to Muslims, it also abandoned pork-based items. Burgers are made from mutton instead. The Big Mac was rechristened the Maharajah Mac—made from chicken and local spices. Vegetarian dishes are prepared in separate areas of the kitchen. All ingredients are sourced from local suppliers.

Despite all of its efforts, McDonald's touched a deep nerve in India within hours of a story breaking in the United States that it had been using oil with a beef extract for cooking its fries. The Indian local media had splashed the story. McDonald's outlets in Mumbai were vandalized by angry mobs. McDonald's India realized that it needed to respond rapidly. Posters

Sources: "Food for Politics," *Far Eastern Economic Review,* October 24, 1996, p. 72; and "McDonald's Averts a Crisis," *Ad Age Global,* July 2001 p. 4.

were made carrying the headline: "100 percent Vegetarian French Fries in McDonald's India." The posters were displayed at all outlets. The company also met with the local press and politicians and offered them samples and information. In addition, McDonald's immediately sent samples to leading laboratories to obtain scientific proof of its nonbeef claims. Two days after the rumor broke, McDonald's held press conferences in Mumbai and New Delhi, with the presence of its fries suppliers again supplying evidence of the absence of animal products in its vegetarian menu items. It ran press ads in mainstream newspapers with similar material. Vigorous response by management of McDonald's India staved off a major crisis. A local joint-venture partner observed, "We had done nothing wrong so we could afford to be bold. We could have been arrogant and said that we don't use beef flavoring in our fries, so why should we be attacked? Instead we kept all lines of communications open and supplied all proof and samples."

baby that local people mistakenly thought meant that the jars contained ground-up babies.[37]

Companies are also concerned about the "quality" of education. Does education meet business needs? Chinese software companies produce less than 1 percent of the world's software, despite the presence of many skilled programmers. One reason for the slow development of China's software industry is cultural. Managers able to supervise large-scale projects are scarce: "Chinese people individually are very, very smart but many, many people together are sometimes stupid."[38]

PISA, a survey sponsored by the Organization for Econonomic Development (OECD), gauges the mathematical skills among 15-year old students.[39] Forty-one countries participated in the 2003 survey. According to the survey's findings, there are huge differences in students mathematical knowledge, even among countries with a similar level of economic development. The highest scorers are mostly students in the Far East–Japan (553), Korea (552), Hong Kong (558). U.S. students (472) score slightly below Russian students (474) but rank far below most of their European counterparts.[40]

Shortages in certain fields often force companies to bid against one another for the scarce talent that is available or to employ expatriates. Many companies try to build up a local presence by hiring local people. However, a shortage of qualified people in the local market usually forces these companies to rely on expatriates until local employees are properly trained.

Value Systems   All cultures have value systems that shape people's norms and standards. These norms influence people's attitudes toward objects and behavioral codes. Value systems tend to be deeply rooted. Core values are intrinsic to a person's identity and inner self. One study of the decision-making process made by executives from the People's Republic of

---

[37]David A. Ricks, *Blunders in International Business* (Cambridge, MA: Blackwell Publishers, 1993).

[38]"China Takes Pivotal Role in High-Tech Production," *International Herald Tribune,* December 5, 2002, p. 2.

[39]PISA stands for Programme for International Student Assessment.

[40]See the project's Web site, http://www.pisa.oecd.org, for further information and additional datasets.

EXHIBIT 4-5
HIGHER EDUCATION ACHIEVEMENT

All Countries

Infrastructure—Education

Percentage of population that has attained at least tertiary education for persons 25–34		2003
1	Canada	53.00
2	Japan	52.00
3	Singapore	49.00
4	Korea	47.00
5	Taiwan	43.20
6	Israel	42.00
7	Finland	40.00
7	Norway	40.00
7	Sweden	40.00
10	Belgium	39.00
10	USA	39.00
12	Spain	38.00
13	Hong Kong	37.40
14	France	37.00
14	Ireland	37.00
16	Australia	36.00
17	Denmark	35.00
18	United Kingdom	33.00
19	New Zealand	32.00
20	Russia	31.00
21	Switzerland	29.00
21	Iceland	29.00
23	Netherlands	28.00
24	Estonia	27.50
25	Greece	24.00
26	Germany	22.00
27	Poland	20.00
28	Slovenia	19.50
29	Luxembourg	19.00
29	Mexico	19.00
31	Thailand	18.00
32	Chile	17.00
32	Hungary	17.00
32	Philippines	17.00
35	Malaysia	16.00
35	Portugal	16.00
37	Argentina	15.00
37	Austria	15.00
39	Colombia	13.49
40	Slovak Republic	13.00
41	Czech Republic	12.00
41	Italy	12.00
43	Turkey	11.00
44	India	9.51
45	Brazil	7.00
46	Indonesia	5.00

Sources: Education at a Glance, OECD Indicators 2005; and National sources, © IMD WORLD COMPETITIVENESS YEARBOOK.

China showed that even after almost four decades of communist philosophy, traditional Chinese values (e.g., saving face, long-term exchange relationships, respect for leaders) heavily influence market entry and product decisions.[41] Exhibit 4-6 is an excerpt of a study commissioned by Dentsu, a Japanese advertising agency, on the beliefs and attitudes of Asian citizens. Note that the data were gathered between between November 1996 and January 1997, prior to the start of the Asian crisis. The figures show that talk about "Asian values" may be a bit premature; there appears to be little common ground among Asian citizens. For instance, 85 percent of Mumbai citizens agree that children should look after aged parents, compared to a mere 15 percent agreement for Tokyo citizens.

---

[41] David K. Tse, Kam-hon Lee, Ilan Vertinsky, and Donald A. Wehrung, "Does Culture Matter? A Cross-Cultural Study of Executives' Choice, Decisiveness, and Risk Adjustment in International Marketing," *Journal of Marketing,* 52 (4) October 1988, pp. 81–95.

EXHIBIT 4-6
DENTSU LIFESTYLE SURVEY

	Beijing	Mumbai	Tokyo	Singapore	Bangkok
Beliefs (% who agree with statement)					
Children should look after aged parents	67%	85%	15%	77%	78%
Parents should not rely on their children	21	11	39	9	8
Cannot say	12	5	46	14	14
Men work, women stay at home	20	37	21	26	24
Concerns (% agree)					
Personal safety	73	38	*	*	*
Economic development	70	62	48	67	87
Cost of living	60	*	56	50	62
Education and culture	46	49	*	39	49
Moral civilization	38	*	*	*	*
Health and welfare	*	48	68	55	49
Pollution	*	*	46	*	39
Employment	*	*	37	*	*
Citizens' rights	*	*	*	35	*
National security	*	50	*	*	*
Image as a nation (% agree)					
Hard working	86	59	65	65	**
Takes good care of family	63	**	**	21	31
Funny	**	53	**	**	**
Polite	41	47	30	29	38
Bad at negotiating	**	**	45	**	**
Loyal to company	**	**	42	**	**
Closed society	**	**	36	**	**
Clean	**	**	**	37	**
Appreciates nature	**	**	**	**	**
What the state must do (% agree)					
Adopt policies according to public opinion	65	56	68	50	67
Grant full social benefits	68	68	65	56	63
Regulate individual rights for greater good	47	67	11	42	51
Promote competition based on ability	33	26	25	26	38
Adopt Western systems	21	38	8	24	36
Have a strong leader push social reform	11	35	5	18	14

*Not among top five concerns.
**Not among top 10 concerns.
Source: Dentsu Institute for Human Studies.

For marketers, a crucial value distinction is a culture's attitude toward change. Societies that resist change are usually less willing to adopt new products or production processes. Terpstra and David suggest several useful guidelines that are helpful to implement innovations in cultures hostile toward changes:

1. Identify roadblocks to change.

2. Determine which cultural hurdles can be met.

3. Test and demonstrate the innovation's effectiveness in the host culture.

4. Seek out those values that can be used to back up the proposed innovation.[42]

---

[42]Terpstra and David, *The Cultural Environment of International Business*, pp. 124–25.

From an international marketer's vantage point, a society's value system matters a great deal. Local attitudes toward foreign cultures will drive the product positioning and design decisions. In many countries, goods with U.S. roots are strongly valued. U.S. companies are able to leverage on such sentiments by using Americana as a selling point. McIlhenny sells Tabasco with the same product label and formulation worldwide, emphasizing its U.S. roots.

CROSS-CULTURAL COMPARISONS

◆ ◆ ◆ ◆ ◆ ◆ ◆ ◆

Cultures differ from one another but usually share certain aspects. Getting a sense of the similarities and dissimilarities between your culture and the host country's culture is useful for scores of reasons. Cultural classifications allow the marketing manager to see how much overlap is possible between the marketing programs to be implemented in different markets. Furthermore, most cultural traits tend to be regional instead of national. For example, Walloons in French-speaking Belgium have much more in common culturewise with the French than with the Flemish of northern Belgium. This section gives you an overview of the most common classification schemes for a culture.

One of the characters in the movie *Chan Is Missing* is a lawyer who describes a confrontation between her client who was involved in a traffic accident and a policeman at the scene of the accident. The client is a recent immigrant from mainland China. The policeman asks the client whether or not he stopped at the stop sign, expecting a yes or no for an answer. The Chinese immigrant instead starts talking about his driving record, how long he has been in the United States, and other matters that he feels are relevant. The policeman, losing his patience, angrily repeats his question. The events described in the movie are a typical example of the culture clash that arises when somebody from a high-context culture (China) is faced with a person from a low-context culture (United States).

High- versus Low-Context Cultures

The notion of cultural complexity refers to the way messages are communicated within a society. The anthropologist Edward Hall makes a distinction between so-called **high-context** and **low-context cultures.**[43] The interpretation of messages in high-context cultures rests heavily on contextual cues. Little is made explicit as part of the message. What is left unsaid is often as important (if not more) as what is said. Examples of contextual cues include the nature of the relationship between the sender and receiver of the message (for instance, in terms of gender, age, balance of power) as well as the time and venue of the communication. Typical examples of high-context societies are Confucian cultures (China, Korea, Japan) and Latin America. Outsiders find high-context cultures often completely mystifying.

Low-context cultures have clear communication modes. What is meant is what is said. The context within which messages are communicated is largely discounted. The United States, Scandinavia, and Germany are examples of low-context cultures. The distinction between high- and low-context cultures matters in many areas of international marketing. For example, in the field of personal selling, many U.S. companies like to rotate salespeople across territories. In high-context societies, where nurturing trust and rapport with the client plays an important role, firms might need to adjust such rotation policies. In the field of international advertising, campaigns that were developed with a high-context culture in mind are likely to be less effective when used in low-context cultures and vice versa.

Recent research in social psychology also reveal key cultural differences between East (high-context) and West (low-context) in how people perceive reality and reasoning.[44] For instance, one study contrasted the eye movements of Chinese and U.S.

[43] Edward T. Hall, *Beyond Culture* (New York: Doubleday, 1977).
[44] "Where East Can Never Meet West," *Financial Times,* October 21, 2005, p. 8.

students scanning pictures of objects placed within surroundings. U.S. students focused on the central object while Chinese students spent more time on the background, putting the object in context. An analysis of crime reports in newspapers found that English-language papers focus on the personality traits of perpetrators while Chinese papers stress the context (e.g., the perpetrators' background). High- and low-context cultures also differ on their view of logic. Westerners have a deep-seated distaste for contradictions. Easterners, however, appreciate them.[45]

Hofstede's Classification Scheme

The Dutch scholar Geert Hofstede developed another highly useful cultural classification scheme.[46] His grid is based on a large-scale research project he conducted among employees of more than 60 IBM subsidiaries worldwide. The first dimension is labeled **power distance.** It refers to the degree of inequality among people that is viewed as being acceptable. Societies that are high in power distance tolerate relatively high social inequalities. Everyone has his rightful place in society; status symbols play a vital role; the ideal boss is a benevolent dictator or a good patriarch. Members of such societies accept wide differences in income and power distribution. Examples of high power distance (PD) countries are Malaysia (PD score = 104), the Philippines (94), Latin American countries such as Mexico (81) and Venezuela (81), Arab countries (80), India (77), and West Africa (77). Low power distance societies tend to be more egalitarian. In Norway, for example, driving fines are linked to income: one drunk Norwegian driver was fined a record 500,000 kroner (around $79,000) after having hit three parked vehicles and punched a policeman.[47] The rich and powerful in low PD societies try to look less powerful; status symbols are frowned upon; the ideal boss is a resourceful democrat. Low power distance countries include the United States (40), Germany (35), Great Britain (35), Scandinavia (e.g., Norway and Sweden scores: 31, Denmark: 18), and Israel (13).

The second dimension is labeled **uncertainty avoidance,** referring to the extent to which people in a given culture feel threatened by uncertainty and rely on mechanisms to reduce it. Societies with strong uncertainty avoidance possess a need for rigid rules and formality that structure life. What is different is threatening. Examples of countries that score high on uncertainty avoidance are Greece (112), Portugal (104), Japan (92), France (86), and Spain (86). Consumers in such countries value naturalness and freshness. The British cosmetics firm Lush is a prime example of a company that has leveraged this desire. Its stores sell cosmetics *au naturel* with the motto "as natural as beauty gets." All products are sold with an expiration date. Lush has been very successful in Japan, a strong uncertainty avoidance country.[48] In weak uncertainty avoidance cultures, people tend to be more easygoing, innovative, and entrepreneurial. What is different is intriguing. Some weak uncertainty avoidance countries are India (40), Malaysia (36), Great Britain (35), Hong Kong (39), and Singapore (8).

The third dimension is called **individualism.** As the label suggests, this criterion describes the degree to which people prefer to act as individuals rather than as group members ("me" versus "we" societies). In societies that are high on individualism, the focus is on people's own interests of a person and her immediate family. In such cultures, a child early on realizes that one day he will need to stand on his own feet. There is little need for loyalty to a group. In **collectivist** societies, the interests of the group take center stage. Members in such societies differentiate between in-group members who are part of its group and all other people. They expect protection from the group and remain loyal to it throughout their life. Individualist countries are the United States (91), Australia (90), and Great Britain (89). Collectivist countries are South Korea (18), Taiwan (17), Indonesia (14), and Venezuela (12).

[45] Richard Nisbett, *The Geography of Thought* (New York: Free Press, 2004).
[46] Geert Hofstede, *Cultures and Organizations* (New York: McGraw-Hill, 1991).
[47] http://news.bbc.co.uk/2/hi/europe/3870967.stm.
[48] www.lush.com.

The fourth distinction, **masculinity,** considers the importance of "male" values such as assertiveness, status, success, competitive drive within society, and achievement versus "female" values such as a focus on people orientation, solidarity, and quality of life. "Masculine" societies are those in which values associated with the role of men prevail. Cultures where people favor values such as solidarity, preserving the environment, and quality of life are more "feminine." Not surprisingly, Japan (95) is a very masculine society. Other high scorers include Austria (79), Italy (70), and Mexico (69). Thailand (34), Chile (28), the Netherlands (14), and Sweden (5) are low-scoring countries on the masculinity trait.

Follow-up research on Hofstede's work in Asia led to a fifth dimension: **long-termism.**[49] This criterion refers to the distinction between societies with a pragmatic, long-term orientation and those with a short-term focus. People in long-term-oriented societies tend to have values that center around the future (e.g., perseverance, thrift). On the other hand, members of short-term-oriented cultures are concerned about values that reflect the past and the present (e.g., respect for tradition). China (118), Hong Kong (96), Japan (80), and South Korea (75) score high on the long-term dimension. However, the United States (29), Great Britain (25), Canada (23), and the Philippines (19) score very low on this criterion.

Exhibit 4-7 (A and B) portrays how different countries score on the various dimensions. One must be cautious when applying these schemes to global buyer

EXHIBIT 4-7A

UNCERTAINTY AVOIDANCE VERSUS POWER DISTANCE

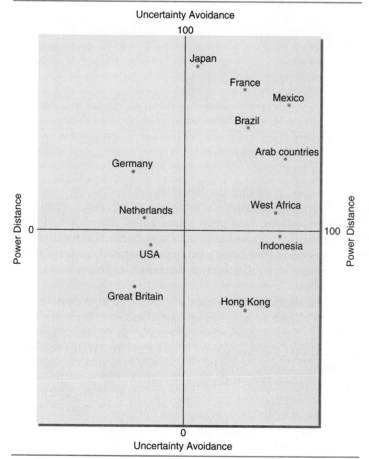

---

[49]Geert Hofstede and Michael H. Bond, "The Confucius Connection: From Cultural Roots to Economic Growth," *Organizational Dynamics,* 16 (4), Spring 1988, pp. 4–21.

EXHIBIT 4-7B
MASCULINITY VERSUS INDIVIDUALISM

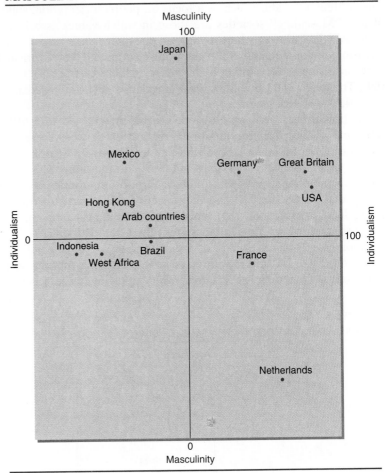

Source: Based on: Geert Hofstede, "Management Scientists are Human," *Management Science,* 40 (1), January 1994, pp. 4–13.

behavior. It is important to bear in mind that the five dimensions and the respective country scores that were derived in Hofstede's work were not determined in a consumption context. In fact, questions have been raised about the ability of these values to make meaningful predictions about consumption patterns.[50] Countries with the same scores can have entirely different buying behaviors. Similarly, countries that have completely different scores on a given cultural dimension could have very similar consumption patterns.

Several researchers have looked at the influence of culture on consumption patterns. Luxury articles are often used as a badge of one's success. They are more appealing to members of masculine cultures than to people in feminine cultures. Indeed, one recent study found that the masculinity of a culture correlates positively with the ownership of expensive (more than $1500) watches ($r = 0.56$) or multiple (>4) watches ($r = 0.53$), sales of jewelry ($r = 0.44$), and the ownership of a suit or dress priced over $750 ($r = 0.68$).[51] Further anecdotal evidence also confirmed these findings. According to a study by Morgan Stanley Dean Witter, Japanese customers (including those traveling overseas) represent 88 percent of the sales of Louis Vuitton, 48 percent of Gucci, and 38 percent of Hermès. One in three Japanese women and one in three

[50]Marieke de Mooij, *Advertising Worldwide* (New York: Prentice-Hall, 1994), p. 159.

[51]Marieke de Mooij and Geert Hofstede, "Convergence and Divergence in Consumer Behavior: Implications for International Retailing," *Journal of Retailing,* 78 (2002), pp. 61–69.

men own a Vuitton product. Many Japanese teenage girls want Louis Vuitton because "everyone has it."[52]

Global Leadership and Organizational Behavior Effectiveness (**Project GLOBE**) is a large-scale research program involving the efforts of a team of 160 scholars. The study explored cultural values and their impact on organizational leadership in 62 cultures.[53] The GLOBE researchers developed a scale of nine cultural dimensions based on a survey of 17,000 middle managers in three industries: banking, food processing, and telecommunications. The first three—uncertainty avoidance, power distance, and collectivism I (societal collectivism)—are the same as Hofstede's constructs described earlier. The remaining six culture dimensions follow:

1. *Collectivism II (in-group collectivism).* The degree to which individuals express pride, loyalty, and cohesiveness in their organizations or families.
2. *Gender egalitarianism.* The degree to which an organization or society minimizes gender role differences and gender discrimination.
3. *Assertiveness.* The extent to which individuals are assertive, confrontational, and aggressive in social relationships.
4. *Future orientation.* The degree to which individuals in societies engage in future-oriented behaviors such as delaying gratification, planning, and investing in the future.
5. *Performance orientation.* The extent to which a society encourages and rewards group members for performance improvement and excellence.
6. *Humane orientation.* The extent to which a culture encourages and rewards people for being fair, altruistic, generous, caring, and kind to others.

Exhibit 4-8 maps a subset of the countries on four of the dimensions. GLOBE has some overlap with the Hofstede scheme that we discussed earlier, but, there are some notable differences. The study and the measurements are far more recent; in fact, the project is still ongoing. The GLOBE scheme includes nine cultural dimensions instead of just four. The project also assigned scores to each country on the nine cultural dimensions from two angles: cultural practices reported in terms of *As Is* and values recorded in terms of *What Should Be.* (Exhibit 4-9 is based on the *As Is* part.)

Our final classification scheme is based on the **World Value Survey (WVS)** conducted by a network of social scientists at leading universities worldwide.[54] This survey assessed people's values and beliefs in about 80 countries, covering 85 percent of the world's population. The first wave of the survey was carried out in the early 1980s; the most recent wave took place in 1999–2001. The WVS scheme differs from the previous ones in two respects: It has been done multiple times and the population covered by the sample is much broader than in other similar studies. The chart in Exhibit 4-9 shows how cultural attitudes in 30 countries stack up against one another. It also shows how these values changed over time by comparing values measured in early waves (1981 or 1990) of the WVS with values recorded for the latest wave (mostly 2001).

The horizontal axis of the grid measures trust, tolerance of outsiders, and the priority given to individual freedom and self-expression. At one end of the spectrum are the survival values related to economic and physical security. At the other end are the individual freedom and self-expression values. The vertical axis shows the importance in each country of religion versus secular values.

---

[52]"Addicted to Japan," *Newsweek International,* October 14, 2002, p. 44.

[53]Robert J. House, Paul J. Hanges, Mansour Javidan, Peter W. Dorfman, and Vipin Gupta, *Culture, Leadership, and Organizations: The GLOBE Study of 62 Societies.* (Thousand Oaks, CA: SAGE Publications, 2004).

[54]See the project's Web site for further background information, http://www.worldvaluessurvey.org/organization/index.html.

EXHIBIT 4-8
PROJECT GLOBE

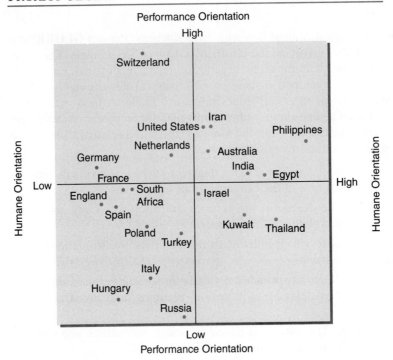

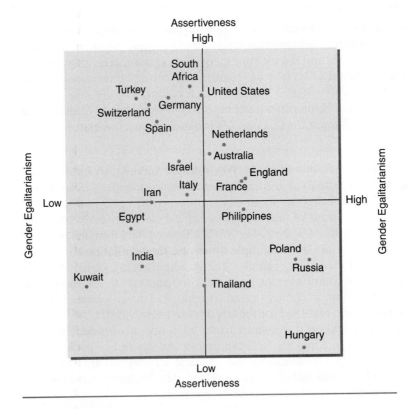

EXHIBIT 4-9
WORLD VALUE SURVEY (WVS)

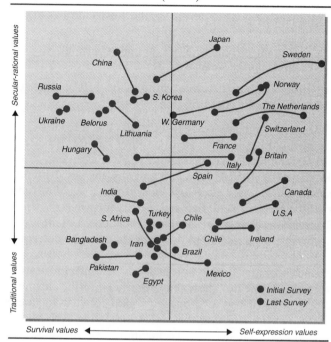

Source: Modernization, Cultural Change, and Democracy, *Ronald Inglehard and Christian Welzel* Image courtesy of *The Atlantic Monthly.* p. 148 in "Mapping America's values," *The Atlantic Monthly,* Jan.-Feb. 2006.

Most developed countries are in the upper right quadrant; developing countries fall in the lower left quadrant. As countries grow wealthier, they move upward (i.e., become more secular) and to the right (i.e., become more individualistic). Interestingly enough, the United States as well as Canada, Ireland, and Mexico occupies the lower-right less crowded quadrant. These are countries that uphold traditional/religious values and individual freedom at the same time.

ADAPTATION TO CULTURES

To function in the global marketplace, you need to become sensitive to cultural biases that influence your thinking, behavior, and decision making. Given the diversity of cultures, cultural mishaps easily arise when global marketers interact with members of a "foreign" culture. Some of these cultural gaffes are relatively harmless and easily forgiven. Unfortunately, many cultural mistakes put the company and its products in an unpleasant situation or even create permanent damage. The globalization efforts of numerous firms have been derailed by cultural mishaps.

Lack of cultural sensitivity takes many forms. Most of us hold cultural stereotypes that distort cultural assessments. Cultural blinders that occur at the subconscious level are difficult to detect. When cultural misassessments do show up, it is usually after the fact. So cultural adaptation is absolutely necessary to make marketing decisions in line with the host culture. Such adaptation is hampered by the tendency to use a **self-reference criterion (SRC),** a term coined by J. A. Lee, a cultural anthropologist. The SRC refers to people's unconscious tendency to resort to their own cultural experience and value systems to interpret a given business situation. Lee outlined a four-step procedure that allows global marketers to identify cross-cultural differences and take the necessary actions to cope with them. The four-step correction mechanism goes as follows:

Step 1: Define the business problem or goal in terms of your own cultural traits, customs, or values.

Step 2: Define the business problem or goal in terms of the host culture's traits, customs, or values.

Step 3: Isolate the SRC influence in the problem and examine it scrupulously to see how it interferes with the business problem.

Step 4: Redefine the business problem, but this time without the SRC influence, and solve for the "optimal" business goal situation.[55]

Even more dangerous than SRC interference is to fall into the trap of **ethnocentrism,** the belief that one's own culture is superior to another culture. Procter & Gamble's experience in Mexico exemplifies cultural adaptation. Ace detergent, which P&G launched in Mexico in the early 1950s, was clobbered by the local brands. Ace, developed for U.S. washing machines, had a low-suds formula. At that time, many Mexicans washed their clothes in the river. High-suds detergents were therefore preferable. Eventually, the formula was changed to have a higher suds content. P&G also adapted the packaging: using smaller sizes and plastic bags (to keep the detergent dry) instead of cardboard.

Toymaker Mattel's experience with the Barbie doll in Japan is a nice illustration of adaptation.[56] Mattel introduced a Barbie doll designed specifically for the Japanese market, called Moba Barbie. Moba's looks were supposedly akin to what Japanese consumers desired, bearing a close resemblance to the major competing doll. Mattel never conquered more than a 5 to 6 percent share of the Japanese doll market. After 8 years of lackluster sales, Mattel decided to re-introduce Barbie with more Western looks. TV commercials also displayed Japanese girls playing with Barbies. Before the new campaign, most Japanese girls mistakenly believed that Moba Barbie was a display doll. As a result of these changes in Mattel's marketing strategy, the sales of Barbie dolls in Japan finally took off.

The lesson offered by the experience of marketing behemoths such as P&G and Mattel is that there is no magic bullet to avoid cultural mishaps. P&G mistakenly believed that what works in the United States would also work across the Rio Grande. Mattel, on the other hand, mistakenly tried to cater to "Japanese" desires. Although Lee's four-step SRC-correction procedure appears flawless, it is often difficult to put into practice.

Still, companies can rely on several techniques to prepare managers for cross-cultural differences.[57] Immersion through prolonged stays in the foreign market often helps. Intensive foreign-language training is one of the more common tools to foster cultural sensitivity. Language skills, however, are not sufficient to become a successful international manager. Other qualities such as humility—a willingness to accept the fact that you will not be as competent as you are in your own environment—also play an important role.[58] Numerous resources exist to familiarize managers with other aspects of the host country's cultural environment. An online resource is the Lonely Planet publisher's Web site (www.lonelyplanet.com). Many providers of cultural training programs (e.g., Berlitz International) offer a cultural orientation for executives. Such programs range from environmental briefings to "cultural assimilator" exercises in which participants are exposed to various simulated settings that could arise during their assignment.

[55] J. A. Lee, "Cultural Analysis in Overseas Operations," *Harvard Business Review,* March–April 1966, pp. 106–14.

[56] "Western Barbie: Mattel Makes Japan Push with Revamped Doll," *Advertising Age,* October 7, 1991.

[57] Howard Tu and Sherry E. Sullivan, "Preparing Yourself for an International Assignment," *Business Horizons,* January–February 1994, pp. 67–70.

[58] "Culture Shock for Executives," *Financial Times,* April 5, 1995, p. 12.

CULTURE AND THE MARKETING MIX ◆ ◆ ◆ ◆ ◆ ◆ ◆ ◆

Culture is a key pillar of the marketplace. To a large extent, the local culture drives the success of international marketing activities. These cultural variables may act as barriers or opportunities. In this section we show how culture and the firm's marketing mix interact. Global Perspective 4-4 shows how Population Services International adapts marketing tools to local Burmese tastes to make condoms acceptable in Myanmar.

Product Policy

Certain products, in particular, food, beverages, and clothing products, are obviously more culture bound than are other products. The changes that General Motors introduced for Buick in China is a good illustration of the role of culture in product design.[59] Whereas U.S. drivers put their children in the back of the car, Chinese companies put their executives there. As a result, the rear seats of Buicks made in China are raised and come with their own air-conditioning and radio controls. They also have more legroom than their U.S. counterparts. To handle China's rough roads, the suspension for the Buick was adjusted. Interestingly enough, the engine size was cut from 3.5 liters to 2.8 to accommodate the rule in China that required cars of more than 3 liters to be limited to government officials of minister level or above.

Products or services can also be banned or restricted due to cultural reasons. In March 2004, the government of Saudi Arabia banned the import and sale of mobile phones with cameras after reports of "misconduct" (photographing women) by owners of such phones.[60]

Cultural values also determine consumers' buying motivations. This is illustrated in Exhibit 4-10, which portrays the buying motives for car purchases in different cultures. As you can see, there are different clusters. In the upper-left quadrant are countries with weak uncertainty avoidance and high femininity. In this cluster, people look for safety and value when buying a car. In contrast, the bottom-right quadrant has clusters of countries that are masculine and have strong uncertainty avoidance. Car buyers in these countries aspire to buy cars that are big and fast.

The implied meanings of brand names also exemplify the role of culture in global marketing. Sometimes the brand name can hurt sales as P&G experienced with its Ariel laundry detergent in Middle Eastern countries such as Egypt. The detergent's name was being tied with Ariel Sharon, Israel's former prime minister. Kit Kat, on the other hand, gained a strong following among Japanese students, especially during exam periods. The name of the chocolate bar, made by Nestlé, closely resembles a Japanese expression, "kitto katsu," used by students to wish each other good luck prior to exams. The phrase roughly translates as "I hope you will win." Often Japanese parents buy Kit Kats as lucky charms for their children during exam days.[61]

Cultural norms sometimes open up new product opportunities. In most Asian countries, white skin is associated with positive values that relate to beauty, class, and an upscale lifestyle. Dark skin is linked with hard labor and toil. In India, the skin whitener market has been growing at an annual rate of around 20 percent. Multinationals such as Unilever, Avon, and Beiersdorf have been able to cash in on this phenomenon by marketing skin whiteners. Indeed, Avon's top-selling product in India is VIP Fairness Cream. The cream that retails for 160 rupees promises a fairer skin in one month.[62] In Vietnam, Unilever customized its brands to reflect local customs. The Vietnamese version of Sunsilk shampoo includes extracts from a seed known as *bo ket,* which Vietnamese women have long used to keep their hair shiny black. Unilever also decided to sell a local fish sauce under its Knorr brand name.

---

[59]"Testing GM's Shock Absorbers," *The Economist,* May 1, 1999, p. 68.

[60]"Saudi Ministries Picture the Future as Embargo on Mobiles Draws in King Fahd," *Financial Times,* November 23, 2004, p. 7.

[61]http://news.bbc.co.uk/2/hi/asia-pacific/4230471.stm.

[62]"Creams for a Lighter Skin Capture the Asian Market," *International Herald Tribune,* April 24, 1998, p. 2.

◆ ◆

𝒢LOBAL PERSPECTIVE 4-4

PREVENTING HIV/AIDS IN MYANMAR

Condoms were seldom used in Myanmar (Burma) just a decade ago. Today they represent one of the country's fastest growing consumer goods, however, more than 40 million were bought in 2005. This compares to only 4.4 million in 1997 (see the following table). This rapid increase reflects higher awareness of HIV/AIDS among the local population. HIV/AIDS rates in Myanmar among high-risk groups are among the highest in the region now: Up to 2.2 percent of adult Burmese have been infected.

The surge in sales of condoms is largely the result of Population Services International (PSI), a nonprofit organization based in Washington, D.C. For the first 16 years after its founding in 1970, PSI concentrated on the area of family planning through social marketing. In the late 1980s, it also entered the areas of malaria and HIV/AIDS prevention. The group, which had a 2005 budget of $297 million, has program offices in almost 70 countries.

PSI launched its social marketing campaign in Myanmar in 1996 despite criticism by prodemocracy groups. PSI supplies about 75 percent of all the condoms used in Myanmar. Heavy subsidies allow them to be sold for one-third of the production cost. Guy Stallworthy, PSI's Myanmar country director, points out, "Price is the number one issue here—you are not going to get a mass market with an expensive product.... Consumers don't have much money but they are discerning and want to buy quality things... if you can somehow make quality affordable, you are bound to be a winner in this country."

Apart from pricing, promotion is a major challenge. When PSI first imported condoms in Myanmar, the brand name was

Sources: "A Golden Opportunity: Preventing HIV/AIDS in Myanmar," http://www.psi.org/resources/pubs/myanmar_profile.pdf, accessed February 22, 2006 and "A Chameleon Enlists in War on Aids," *Financial Times*, February 20, 2006, p. 6.

written in Burmese. However, PSI found that the Burmese associated Burmese-language packaging with inferior quality. In 1998, PSI changed the name to Aphaw ("trusted companion" in English) with usage instructions in Burmese.

CONDOMS DISTRIBUTED IN MYANMAR SINCE THE LAUNCH OF APHAW (IN MILLIONS)

Year	Private Sector	Public Sector	PSI Social Marketing	Total Condom Market
1997	1.4	1.2	1.8	4.4
1998	2.2	2.1	3.3	7.6
1999	2.8	2.0	6.8	11.6
2000	7.0	1.5	7.9	16.4

Source: www.psi.org, accessed February 22, 2006.

PSI built up its own national distribution network, with 28 sales representatives and 50 wholesalers. Aphaw condoms are available in every town and major village. PSI developed its own advertising mascot: a chameleon (a *pothinnyo*) wearing a traditional sun hat. These days, PSI's mascot has an 82 percent recognition among urban Burmese. PSI collaborated with cultural troupes to produce traveling theatrical performances to educated communities about the risks of HIV/AIDS. It also produced soap operas and feature films to stem the spread of HIV/AIDS. In 2005, PSI's mascot made its TV debut when PSI sponsored the broadcast of English Premier League soccer matches on local television. At 0.8 per capita per year, condom use is still minimal compared to that in Thailand or Cambodia. PSI's goal is to raise condom use to 1 per capita per year by 2008.

The sauce is bottled on Phu Quoc, an island where the fish sauce originated. Unilever vowed that it would protect the good name and purity of Phu Quoc fish sauce.[63]

Pricing As you will see in Chapter 13, pricing policies are driven by the interplay of the four C's: customers, company (costs, objectives, strategies), competition, and collaborators (e.g., distributors). Customers' willingness to pay for your product will vary across cultures. Products that are perceived as good value in one culture may have little or no value in other cultures. In Western countries, a high price is often seen as a signal of premium quality for many product categories. However, in emerging markets, charging a high price may be regarded as gouging the customer.

One example of how pricing and culture interact is the practice of odd pricing in which prices end with 9 (or 5) ($19.99 instead of $20). Specific price points like end-9 prices are known to increase unit sales substantially. This sales effect is due to the fact that these "magic prices" signal good value to the customers. In Chinese-speaking

---

[63]"Unilever Has a Taste for Success in Vietnam," *Financial Times*, December 2, 2003, p. 9.

EXHIBIT 4-10
BUYING MOTIVES FOR AUTOMOBILES

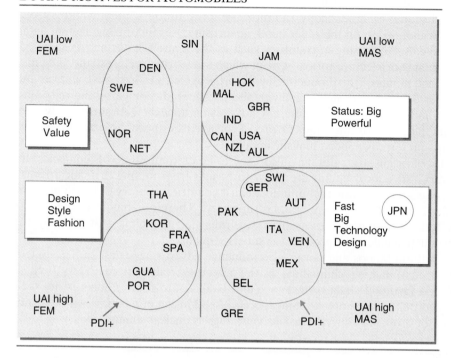

Note: AUL = Australia, AUT = Austria, BEL = Belgium, CAN = Canada, DEN = Denmark, FRA = France, GER = Germany, GBR = Great Britain, GRE = Greece, GUA = Guatemala, HOK = Hong Kong, IND = India, ITA = Italy, JAM = Jamaica, JPN = Japan, KOR = Korea, MAL = Malaysia, MEX = Mexico, NET = the Netherlands, NOR = Norway, NZL = New Zealand, PAK = Pakistan, POR = Portugal, SIN = Singapore, SPA = Spain, SWE = Sweden, SWI = Switzerland, THA = Thailand, USA = the United States, VEN = Venezuela.

Source: Mariek de Mooji, *Global Marketing and Advertising: Understanding Cultural Paradoxes* (Thousand Oaks, CA: SAGE Publications, 1998), p. 147.

cultures such as Hong Kong, however, the price points used often end with 8 instead of 9 because the Chinese word for eight ("ba") has the same sound as the word for wealth.

Distribution

Cultural variables may also dictate distribution strategies. Plagued with lifestyle changes, Avon, the U.S. cosmetics maker, has been forced to fine-tune its direct selling model. In Taiwan and China, for example, Avon is experimenting with alternative distribution modes for selling its products. Some of the alternatives include the use of kiosks, small counters in department stores, the Internet, and selling products on home-shopping TV channels.

Retailers often need to fine-tune their practices when entering foreign markets. Wal-Mart learned this lesson the hard way in Germany where it is still just a secondary player despite almost a 10-year presence. Grocery bagging turned out to be a no-no for German shoppers because they do not like strangers handling their groceries. When clerks followed orders to smile, male customers took that as a come-on.[64]

Cultural hurdles can sometimes be successfully mastered, as Dell Computer has shown in China. When Dell first launched its renowned direct-sales, built-to-order business model in China, many observers were very skeptical. Selling computers direct to corporate customers rather than through distributors was thought to be a recipe for disaster in China where many deals are settled via wining and dining. Nevertheless, Dell's business model has been well accepted in China where Dell's sales have shown strong growth.[65]

Promotion

Of the four marketing mix elements, promotion is the most visible one. People who do not buy your product for whatever reason may still be exposed to your advertising. Culture typically has a major influence on a firm's communication strategy. Advertising

[64]"Wal-Mart: Local Pipsqueak," *BusinessWeek,* April 11, 2005, pp. 25–26.
[65]"Chasing the China Market," *Asiaweek,* June 11, 1999, p. 46.

styles that are effective in certain cultures can be counterproductive in other cultures. In high-context cultures (e.g., Spain, Italy, Japan), communication styles tend to be more indirect and subtle, using less copy and more symbols. In low-context cultures (e.g., Germany, Scandinavia), on the other hand, advertising uses more copy, factual data, and reasoning.[66] Advertising in countries such as the United States and the United Kingdom often uses a lecture-format style in which a celebrity "lectures" the audience about the good points of the product being advertised. Cultures in these countries are low in power distance and high in individualism. One study compared the reactions of Chinese and U.S. subjects to different advertising appeals. Not surprisingly, the study found that Chinese consumers favored a collectivistic appeal, whereas their U.S. counterparts preferred an individualistic appeal.[67]

Country of origin strategies may also need to be customized across countries. In collectivist cultures, local brands are likely to benefit from touting their local roots. However, one study suggests that in individualist countries, country of origin appeals are beneficial only when the local brand is superior.[68] Therefore, buy-local campaigns in highly individualist countries such as Australia and the United States may be counterproductive unless the product has superior quality.

Local cultural taboos and norms also influence advertising styles. In the United States, Gidget, a talking chihuahua, is the advertising mascot for Taco Bell, a Mexican-style fast-food chain owned by Yum! Brands. However, Gidget is not featured in Taco Bell's Singapore ads. Singapore's large Muslim population was the main motivation for dropping Gidget; Muslims view dogs as unclean animals.[69]

◆◆◆◆◆◆◆◆◆ ORGANIZATIONAL CULTURES

So far, we have looked at the importance of national cultures for international marketing operations. At the same time, most companies are also characterized by their **organizational (corporate) culture.** Deshpandé and Webster[70] defined organizational culture as "the pattern of shared values and beliefs that help individuals understand organizational functioning and thus provide them with the norms for behavior in the organization" (p. 4). Shared beliefs relate to leadership styles, organizational attributes, bonding mechanisms within the organization, and overall strategic emphases.[71] As you can see in Exhibit 4-11, organizational culture types can be described along two dimensions. The vertical axis distinguishes between organizations with *organic* (emphasis on flexibility, spontaneity, individuality) and *mechanistic* processes (emphasis on control, stability, order). The horizontal axis describes whether the organizational emphasis is on *internal maintenance* (integration, efficient and smooth operations) or *external positioning* (competitive actions and achievement, differentiation). This scheme leads to four organizational culture types: *clan, adhocracy, hierarchical,* and *market.* Exhibit 4-11 lists for each of these organizational forms the dominant attributes, leadership styles, primary means of bonding, and strategic emphases.

Clan cultures (top left quadrant) stress cohesiveness, participation, and teamwork. They are often headed by a patriarch. The bonding glue is loyalty and tradition. Commitment to such firms runs high. In contrast, *adhocracy cultures* (top right

[66]Marieke de Mooij, *Global Marketing and Advertising: Understanding Cultural Paradoxes* (Thousand Oaks, CA: SAGE Publications, 1998), pp. 157–58.

[67]Yong Zhang and James P. Neelankavil, "The Influence of Culture on Advertising Effectiveness in China and the USA. A Cross-Cultural Study," *European Journal of Marketing,* 31 (1997), pp. 134–49.

[68]Zeynep Gürhan-Canli, and Durairaj Maheswaran, "Cultural Variations in Country of Origin Effects," *Journal of Marketing Research,* 37 (August 2000), pp. 309–17.

[69]"As Taco Bell Enters Singapore, Gidget Avoids the Ad Limelight," *Ad Age International,* January 11, 1999, pp. 13–14.

[70]Rohit Deshpandé and Frederick E. Webster, "Organizational Culture and Marketing: Defining the Research Agenda," *Journal of Marketing,* 53 (1), 1989, pp. 3–15.

[71]Rohit Deshpandé, John U. Farley, and Frederick E. Webster, "Corporate Culture, Customer Orientation, and Innovativeness in Japanese Firms: A Quadrad Analysis," *Journal of Marketing,* 57 (1), 1993, pp. 23–37.

EXHIBIT 4-11
A MODEL OF ORGANIZATIONAL CULTURE TYPES

Organic Processes (flexibility, spontaneity)

TYPE: Clan	TYPE: Adhocracy
DOMINANT ATTRIBUTES: Cohesiveness, participation, teamwork, sense of family	DOMINANT ATTRIBUTES: Entrepreneurship, creativity, adaptability
LEADER STYLE: Mentor, facilitator, parent-figure	LEADER STYLE: Entrepreneur, innovator, risk taker
BONDING: Loyalty, tradition, interpersonal cohesion	BONDING: Entrepreneurship, flexibility, risk
STRATEGIC EMPHASES: Toward developing human resources, commitment, morale	STRATEGIC EMPHASES: Toward innovation, growth, new resources
INTERNAL MAINTENANCE **(smoothing activities, integration)**	**EXTERNAL POSITIONING** **(competition, differentiation)**
TYPE: Hierarchy	TYPE: Market
DOMINANT ATTRIBUTES: Order, rules and regulations, uniformity	DOMINANT ATTRIBUTES: Competititiveness, goal achievement
LEADER STYLE: Coordinator, administrator	LEADER STYLE: Decisive, achievement-oriented
BONDING: Rules, policies, and procedures	BONDING: Goal orientation, production, competition
STRATEGIC EMPHASES: Toward stability, predictability, smooth operations	STRATEGIC EMPHASES: Toward competitive advantage and market superiority

MECHANISTIC PROCESSES (control, order, stability)

Note: Adapted from Cameron and Freeman (1991) and Quinn (1988).
Source: Rohit Deshpandé, John U. Farley, and Frederick E. Webster, "Corporate Culture, Customer Orientation, and Innovativeness in Japanese Firms: A Quadrad Analysis," *Journal of Marketing*, 57, 1, 1993, pp. 23–37.

quadrant) are driven by values such as entrepreneurship, creativity, adaptability, flexibility, and tolerance. Effectiveness in such cultures is viewed in terms of finding new markets and new opportunities for growth. The head of such organizations is usually an entrepreneur or an innovator. Such firms are committed to innovation and new product development. The third form is the *hierarchy culture* (bottom left quadrant), which emphasizes order, rules, and regulations. Such organizations tend to be very formalized and structured. Maintaining a smooth-running operation is very important for such firms. Organizational effectiveness within hierarchical cultures is defined by consistency and achievement of clearly stated goals. Finally, *market culturelike* organizations (bottom right quadrant) value competitiveness, tasks and goal achievement, and productivity. These organizations tend to be production oriented. The major concern is getting the job done.

Most firms have elements of several types of cultures. However, one type of culture typically emerges as the dominant one.[72] Exhibit 4-12 presents the results of a study that contrasts organizations in five different countries. Japanese and French firms are clearly much more hierarchical than are British and U.S. firms. In that respect, Kao, Japan's leading toiletries manufacturer, is a bit unusual. Under the influence of Zen Buddhism, the company tries to foster creativity and open communication by eliminating hierarchical distinctions: executive offices are spartan; departments are not separated by dividing walls, and titles are eliminated.[73]

---

[72]Rohit Desphandé, John U. Farley, and Frederick E. Webster, "Factors Affecting Organizational Performance: A Five-Country Comparison," Working Paper (Cambridge, MA: Marketing Science Institute, 1997).
[73]"Zen and the Art of Profit Making," *Financial Times*, August 29, 2000, p. 10.

EXHIBIT 4-12
ORGANIZATIONAL CULTURE TYPES

	Japan	U.S.	France	England	Germany
Organizational Culture Types					
Hierarchy	99.9	80.3	99.1	76.8	83.2
Market	103.3	112.5	93.7	116.3	89.4
Adhocracy	77.6	105.8	128.3	99.1	131.1
Clan	119.3	101.4	78.9	107.6	96.2

Source: Rohit Desphandé, John U. Farley, and Frederick E. Webster, "Factors Affecting Organizational Performance: A Five-Country Comparison," Working Paper (Cambridge, MA: Marketing Science Institute, 1997).

Anglo-Saxon companies tend to be much more market-type cultures than do German or French firms. Perhaps not surprisingly, Japanese companies are also much more clan-driven than companies in other countries. The same study also found that organizations with a market culture tend to have a better business performance. On the other hand, firms governed by a clan or hierarchy culture are poor business performers. Cross-cultural gaps resulting from a merger are fairly common. DaimlerChrysler, formed by the merger of Daimler and Chrysler, went through a stormy honeymoon period, during which it experienced the cross-cultural clashes stemming from the merger. The old Daimler was bureaucratic and very formal, whereas the old Chrysler was spontaneous. In the end, the German managers moved toward a less formal way of doing business under the influence of their U.S. counterparts.[74]

In the balance of this chapter, we focus on two customer-related areas that are becoming increasingly important to global marketers: global account management and global customer relationship management.

◆◆◆◆◆◆◆◆◆ GLOBAL ACCOUNT MANAGEMENT (GAM)

In business-to-business contexts and in manufacturer-distributor relationships, one major consequence of having a global presence is dealing with global customers. The coordination of the management of such customer accounts across national boundaries is referred to as **global account management (GAM).**

Because of their sheer size, global customer accounts often have major leverage over their suppliers. In their drive to squeeze costs, these customer accounts often strive for global contracts with global prices. Global retailers, such as Carrefour, Wal-Mart, and Royal Ahold, try to gain a cost advantage over their local competitors by negotiating the best terms with their suppliers. At the same time, global customers can also offer tremendous opportunities. Indeed, one survey of global account managers indicated that sales to their global customers had grown on average by 10 to 15 percent per year.[75] Effective global account management could ultimately lead to a win–win situation for both parties.

Global Accounts' Requirements

A recent research project of global customer account practices singled out the following areas that might require a globalized treatment:[76]

- *Single point of contact.* Global customers prefer a single point of contact rather than multiple points. This will improve vendor–supplier relationships.

---

[74]"The DaimlerChrysler Emulsion," *The Economist,* July 29, 2000, pp. 65–66.

[75]David Arnold, Julian Birkinshaw, and Omar Toulan, "Can Selling Be Globalized? The Pitfalls of Global Account Management," *California Management Review* 44, (1), Fall 2001, pp. 8–20.

[76]David B. Montgomery and George S. Yip, "The Challenge of Global Customer Management," *Marketing Management,* Winter 2000, pp. 22–29.

- *Coordination of resources for serving customers.* They also demand better coordination of their suppliers' resources.

- *Uniform prices and terms of trade.* Global customers will also often push for a uniform price, typically meaning the lowest price, unless the supplier can reasonably justify cross-border price gaps. Other nonprice elements in the contract, such as shipping policies, warranties, and volume discounts, could also be vulnerable to single-policy demands.

- *Standardized products and services.* Global customers also often expect that their suppliers are able to deliver standardized products or services unless good reasons for not doing so can be provided.

- *Consistency in service quality and performance.* Coupled to the previous requirement, global accounts request a high degree of consistency in service support quality and performance.

- *Support in countries where the company has no presence.* Finally, global customers also prefer a supplier who is able to service agreements with them in all countries where the customer operates, including the ones where the supplier has no presence.

Managing Global Account Relationships[77]

The first key question that a vendor should ask is which customer accounts should be designated as global accounts. Obviously, one crucial factor involves the client's preferences and organizational setup. Even if a customer desires a global relationship, global account management is not always the appropriate response. One other key criterion is the balance of power between the customer and the company. A major driver here is the degree of internal coordination in each of the parties. If the vendor is less globally integrated than the customer, the vendor might be vulnerable and, hence, have little interest in a global account relationship. The other criterion is the extent of strategic synergies that can flow from a global relationship. If the relationship merely focuses on sales transactions, globalization will most likely imply lower prices and increased pressure for volume discounts. Global account relationships are much more rewarding when they are triggered by strategic synergy rationales. Synergies can be achieved in areas where the two partners can collaborate, such as product innovation, brand building, and market development.

Effective GAM strives to capture the scale and scope benefits of an integrated approach while maintaining the local responsiveness to cope with the account's local needs. The success of a global account relationship depends on the right implementation. The following factors contribute to effective implementation:

- *Clarify the role of the global account management team.* Usually, a global account manager is designated to be dedicated to the global account. Often the manager is based in the country where the customer is headquartered. Typically, the account manager reports to the local country manager and to company headquarters. Global account managers often end up working very closely with their customers; sometimes they or some of their support staff members even have an office at the customer's premises.

- *Make incentive structure realistic.* Having the right incentive mechanisms in place is crucial. This area is also a major headache for companies: If a global account places an order, how should the commission be split between the global account manager and the local unit? Many companies simply pay the commission twice, but that can be an expensive solution.

- *Pick the right global account managers.* Being a successful local or regional salesperson is not always a promise for turning into a good global account manager. Other skills that matter include the ability to coordinate efforts internally, having a long-term perspective, and nurturing the account rather than milking it. Given

[77]This section draws from Arnold, Birkinshaw and Toulan, "Can Selling Be Globalized," pp. 11–19; and David Arnold, Julian Birkinshaw, and Omar Toulan, *"Implementing Global Account Management in Multinational Corporations,"* Working Paper No. 00–103 (Cambridge, MA: Marketing Science Institute, 2000).

that GAM is primarily a matter of internal coordination, good coordination and communication skills are probably most valuable.

- *Create a strong support network.* The strength of the support network is another success factor. Global account managers need support staff, solid customer information (profitability, worldwide sales), communication materials, and so forth. Having solid internal support systems in place is known to be one of the most critical variables in making GAM programs successful.[78]

- *Make sure that the customer relationship operates at more than one level.* Customer relationships should be established at all levels: above and underneath the global account manager, right down to the local field and support team.

- *Make the GAM reconfiguration program flexible and dynamic.* A supplier's GAM program should maintain a fit with the customer's changing needs. The Xerox–BMW relationship is a good example. BMW wanted to make its vehicle ownership manuals personalized and less expensive to make. Most manuals included at least four languages and were quite thick, wasting paper and leading to high printing costs. Xerox cooperated with BMW to offer a new manual with the buyer's name in the buyer's preferred language and other personalized features. The new manual is 80 percent thinner.[79]

◆◆◆◆◆◆◆◆ GLOBAL CUSTOMER RELATIONSHIP MANAGEMENT (CRM)

Customer relationship management (CRM) or **database marketing** is the strategic process of managing interactions between the company and its customers with the objective of maximizing the lifetime value of the customers for the company and satisfying the customers by being customer focused. A successful CRM program creates a formidable competitive edge and can boost profits substantially. MNCs apply CRM programs across national boundaries. DaimlerChrysler successfully introduced a CRM program across Europe.[80] In China, Volkswagen decided to implement a CRM project by building a data warehouse that can store information about millions of dealers and prospective customers. The system would allow VW to track prospective customers from the awareness stage to purchase interest, offering insights into reasons for purchase and nonpurchase. VW spent around $3.75 million to develop the customer database.[81]

Several benefits can be derived from globalizing CRM programs. In some industries (e.g., travel, car rental, credit cards), global customers account for a major share of the business. Furthermore, just as in other areas of global marketing, country units can share ideas and expertise on CRM programs. Typically, customer relationships evolve through distinct phases, each with its unique requirements. The first phase is customer acquisition, which involves prospect evaluation, acquisition management, and recovery of "old" customers (brand switchers, inactive customers). The second phase focuses on retention. The most critical areas here include customer evaluation (lifetime value), consumer complaint management, retention mechanisms (e.g., loyalty programs), up- or cross-selling, and referral management. The final possible phase is the termination of the relationship. This can happen because of customer-related factors (leaving category) or switching to another supplier.

---

[78]See Arnold et al., "Implementing Global Account Management."

[79]Linda H. Shi, et al., "Global Account Management Capability: Insights from Leading Suppliers," *Journal of International Marketing,* 13 (2), (2005), pp. 93–113.

[80]S. Tamer Cavusgil, "Extending the Reach of E-Business," *Marketing Management,* March–April 2002, pp. 24–29.

[81]"Shanghai VW Drives Tailor-Made CRM Plan," *Ad Age Global,* April 2002, p. 12.

Many reasons can motivate the roll out of a CRM program. Otto Versand is the world's largest mail-order company and the second largest Internet retailer (behind Amazon). It decided to introduce CRM for the following reasons:[82]

Motivations

- Decreasing customer loyalty, which puts pressure on the company to improve programs for customer retention and recovery.

- Deteriorating customer response rate in customer acquisition leading to higher acquisition costs. CRM can help here by offering better qualified customer addresses and guidelines on effective acquisition strategies.

- More demanding customers.

- Highly differentiated target segments, which require differentiated marketing campaigns and, in the extreme case, one-on-one marketing.

- Emergence of the Internet, which allows richer communication and interactive marketing.

These motivations overlap to some extent with the reasons why KLM, the Dutch airline, embraced CRM:[83]

- Air travel has become a commodity, putting pressure on margins.

- New entrants (e.g., discount carriers in Europe) have changed the rules of competition.

- Product differentiation has become increasingly tough.

- Competitors in Europe and the United States are investing in CRM.

- Customers are unique; they increasingly expect tailored services.

- Customers are better informed about product offerings and the market (knowledge transparency).

The benefits of effective CRM programs are potentially huge. The key ones include the following:

Gains from CRM

- *Better understanding of customers' expectations and behavior.* This knowledge allows the MNC to develop differentiated strategies. The ultimate goal of CRM is to be able to offer the right product or service to the right customer at the right price and via the proper distribution channel.

- *Ability to measure the customer's value to the company.* Putting value—in terms of current and projected margin contribution—on the customer also facilitates more effective resource allocation. Such insights help the company decide which target customers to nurture, to grow, to protect (against competitive inroads), or to economize on.

- *Lower customer acquisition and retention costs.* In principle, a successful CRM program should enable the MNC to do a better job in acquiring and keeping customers. Obviously, this benefit might not materialize if the major competitors also adopt CRM programs.

- *Ability to interact and communicate with consumers in countries where access to traditional channels is limited.* Access to conventional tools, such as television, press, or radio, might be restricted because of an underdeveloped media infrastructure, government regulations, or high charges. Alternatively, the prospect might be a very particular niche that is difficult to reach with more common tools. A good

---

[82] Norbert Sellin, "Automated Direct Marketing Campaigns at Otto," *Customer Relationship Management: Strategies and Company-wide Implementation,* Conference Summary, Report No. 02–112 (Cambridge, MA: Marketing Science Institute, 2002), pp. 11–12.

[83] Lesley McDermott, "Targeting the Right Customers," *Customer Relationship Management: Strategies and Company-wide Implementation,* Conference Summary, Report No. 02–112 (Cambridge, MA: Marketing Science Institute, 2002), pp. 11–12.

example is Western Union's operations in Asia.[84] Its business model is that people can transfer money overseas without the need for a bank account. This has made the firm very popular among low-paid foreign expatriate workers who often do not have a bank account. Given the niche qualities of this customer group, spending marketing money on mass media would create a considerable waste. Instead, Western Union developed a customer database that facilitates direct mailing campaigns. Under such circumstances, CRM offers a valuable alternative to reach the target customers.

Challenges

Marketing programs can get much mileage out of CRM systems. However, to capture the full benefits of a CRM program in the global marketplace, several challenges have to be met:

- *Customer database.* The success of a CRM program depends to a large degree on the quality of the customer database. Setting up a high-quality customer database can be time consuming and expensive. Access to customer data in some countries can be a major struggle: Creative and inspired thinking is often necessary to come up with innovative ways to gather customer data. Audi's Asia Pacific division used an online campaign in Singapore and South Korea to build its database of prospective customers. To encourage prospects to offer personal data, Audi offered users the chance to win tickets to an Audi driving clinic.[85]

- *Clutter.* One major risk of CRM is that, given all the hype, everybody and his brother jumps on the bandwagon. Indeed, as you saw earlier, this was one reason KLM adopted CRM. As a result, breaking through the clutter can prove to be a major task. When customers start receiving e-mails from every airline they ever flew with, those personalized e-mails most likely get the spam treatment.

- *Cultural and language differences.* Obviously, just as with other endeavors in global marketing, cultural and language differences can prove to be major obstacles, especially when the customer database covers multiple countries. Chinese names, for instance, can be written in multiple ways, creating the risk of duplication.

- *Privacy and other government regulations.* Privacy and personal data protection are highly sensitive issues in many countries. Often, it is difficult—for legal or cultural reasons—to buy a database from third parties. Companies should make themselves familiar with local regulations and laws covering these issues.

- *Local talent.* Qualified staff to run and support CRM projects is often scarce and difficult to find in many countries.

- *Local infrastructure.* CRM is also difficult to run in countries where the direct marketing infrastructure is still underdeveloped.

Guidelines for Successful CRM Implementation

Experience and lessons from implementation of CRM programs have led to the following insights:

- Make the program business driven rather than IT driven. CRM is more than just a data-mining exercise; it goes for beyond technology and having a database in place.

- Monitor and keep track of data protection and privacy laws in those countries where CRM systems are being used or are in the planning stage.

- Remember that the effectiveness of CRM starts with the database. A good database is money in the bank; a bad database is money wasted.

- Make sure that the information and rewards being sent out to customers are relevant, targeted, and personal.

---

[84]"Finance Firm in Loyalty Push to Fend Off Rivals," *Media,* September 6, 2002, p. 10.
[85]"Audi in Web Drive to Collect Data," *Media,* October 18, 2002, p. 18.

SUMMARY

Global marketing does not operate in a bubble. Culture is an intrinsic part of the global marketing environment. Cultural diversity adds an immense richness. "Foreign" cultures may offer a breeding ground for new product ideas, and cultural changes may open up new market opportunities. At the same time, cultural diversity also poses enormous challenges to international marketers and managers in general. Usually, cultural blunders are easily forgiven. Occasionally, however, failure to respect the local culture will create resentment and may even lead to permanent damage of the firm's overseas business operations. Companies such as Coca-Cola learned this lesson the hard way in India. When Coca-Cola reentered India in 1992 after a long absence, it acquired Thums Up, a leading local brand. It subsequently tried to promote its global brand by piggybacking Thums Up's distribution network at the expense of the local brand. Loyal customers of Thums Up were not pleased. In the end, Coke decided to promote Thums Up rather than substitute it with its global brands.[86]

Preventive medicine is more effective than having to lick your wounds afterward. Dictums such as "When in Rome…" are nice catch phrases, but, unfortunately, it is seldom easy to learn what "do as the Romans" exactly means. Sensitivity to the host culture is a nice attribute, but for most people, it remains an ideal rather than an accomplishment. There simply are no tricks of the trade or magic bullets. In fact, an often fatal mistake is to overestimate one's familiarity with the host culture.

This chapter analyzed the meaning of *culture*. We examined several elements of culture in detail. Cultures have differences but also share certain aspects. We examined several frameworks that you can use to analyze and classify different cultures. Once you are aware of the differences and parallels, the next and most formidable task is to become sensitive to the host culture. We described several procedures to foster cultural adjustment. Cross-cultural training is one route toward cultural adaptation; the ideal, however, is to immerse oneself in the foreign culture through intensive language training, prolonged visits, or other means.

The interface between culture and the various marketing mix instruments was studied. Future chapters (Chapters 11 through 16) that look more closely at the global marketing mix will revisit these interactions. In this chapter, we also examined the notion of corporate or organizational culture. As we saw, to some extent corporate cultures are driven by the culture in which the company originated. Finally, we explored two increasingly important areas on the global consumer front, namely, global account management (GAM) and global customer relationship management (CRM).

---

[86]"Hard to Sell to a Billion Consumers," *Financial Times,* April 25, 2002, p. 14.

KEY TERMS

Back translation

Collectivist Culture

Customer relationship management (CRM)

Database marketing

Ethnocentrism

Extended family

Global account management (GAM)

High- (low-) context culture

Individualism (collectivism)

Long-termism (short-termism)

Masculinity (femininity)

Nuclear family

Organizational (corporate) culture

Power distance

Project GLOBE

Self-reference criterion (SRC)

Uncertainty avoidance

World Value Survey (WVS)

REVIEW QUESTIONS

1. How does language complicate the tasks of global marketers?

2. Describe the importance of reference groups in international marketing.

3. What can marketers do to launch new products in countries that tend to resist change?

4. How do high-context cultures differ from low-context ones?

5. What are some possible issues in applying Hofstede's classification scheme in a global marketing context?

DISCUSSION QUESTIONS

1. Focus group research conducted by advertising agencies such as Leo Burnett shows that Asia's youngsters (the proverbial X-generation) mimic U.S. trends but, at the same time, are pretty conservative. Gangsta rap, for instance, is extremely popular in Malaysia. Many of the values that Asian youths hold, however, are quite traditional: family relations, respect

for elders, marriage, and so on. Discuss this seeming contradiction.

2. A recent survey in China of 400 urban children aged 7 to 12 showed that 81.3 percent dreamed of international travel, 61.9 percent wanted space travel, 60.2 percent wanted to be more beautiful, and almost 90 percent wanted to be more intelligent. Given these aspirations, what market opportunities do you see for Western companies that target China's child population?

3. What are some of the possible infrastructural roadblocks (e.g., in terms of transportation, storage) that ice cream manufacturers would face in Southeast Asia?

4. One of the cultural dimensions singled out by Hofstede is the individualism/collectivism distinction. What would this categorization imply in terms of setting up a salesforce for international marketers? For instance, what incentive schemes might work in an individualist culture? collectivist?

5. Countries showing strong uncertainty avoidance such as France, Germany, and Italy have witnessed a rise in the consumption of mineral water since 1970. In fact, according to one study, the correlation between mineral water consumption and the uncertainty avoidance score for 1996 was almost 0.75. What might explain the linkage between uncertainty avoidance and mineral water consumption? What other products might find opportunities in strong uncertainty avoidance countries?

6. The accompanying table compares the economic affluence of different religious groups. Apparently, the world's wealthiest religions are mostly protestant groups (e.g., Lutherans, Episcopalians, Baptists). Do these figures suggest that protestantism leads to more wealth?

Religious Groups	GNP (US$) per capital (1994)
Top 10	
Lutherans (Evangelical)	28,700
Lutheran	28,600
Shinto	26,900
Jehovah's Witnesses	23,300
Episcopalian	23,300
Mormon	22,900
Mennonite	22,800
Baptist	22,700
Seventh-Day Adventists	22,600
Church of God	22,000
Bottom 10	
Animist	804
Sikh	702
Monotheism official	680
Traditional beliefs	644
Voodoo	404
Hindu	392
Jains	368
Hoa-hao	245
Cadoaism	245
Hinduism Official	179

Source: Philip M. Parker, *Religious Cultures of the World. A Statistical Reference* (Westport, CT: Greenwood Press, 1997), p. 5.

7. Certain Muslim countries such as Saudi Arabia do not allow advertisers to show a frontal picture of a woman with her hair. This creates a challenge for companies such as Unilever and Procter & Gamble, which want to advertise hair care products (e.g., shampoo). How would you tackle this challenge?

8. Visit the Culturgrams Web site and download the free sample (www.culturgram.com/culturgram/freedownload.htm). Read the sample. What cultural differences exist between your culture and the one described in the sample? What are the similarities, if any?

9. A survey conducted by the Thailand Marketing Research Society (TMRS) among 1,200 Thai youngsters (13 to 18 years) in the summer of 2002 showed that loss of "Thai identity" was picked as one of the top five most serious issues. At the same time, Thai teenagers are growing more skeptical about advertising and Western brands. What do these findings suggest for Western marketers?

SHORT CASES

CASE 4-1

SELLING BRATZ DOLLS IN ASIA: "HOOKER CHIC" DOES NOT CATCH ON

Bratz is a range of streetwise dolls marketed by MGA Entertainment (www.mgae.com). The dolls have taken the United States and Europe by storm. Global sales in 2004 hit US$2.5 billion compared to Barbie's $3 billion. You need only to stroll in any toy store in the United States or Europe to witness the impact of Bratz. Instead of Barbie's signature pink, the shelves are black and purple, the colors of Bratz. In Europe and the United States, the Barbie look is now passé among teenage girls in spite of an image and lifestyle makeover. Many observers of the industry wonder whether Barbie has any future left.

What made Bratz a runaway success in the United States and Europe is that its dolls resonate far more strongly with today's generation of teenage girls who have grown up with MTV and lifestyle magazines such as *Dolly* and *Seventeen.* Some commentators refer to the Bratz dolls' funky image as "hooker chic." Barbie, however, reflects the bygone era of 1950s Americana.

The success story of Bratz in Europe and the United States has so far not been replicated in Asia. Bratz dolls with their hip looks, heavy make-up, and short skirts caused some

Source: "Asia Balks at Bratz's "Hooker Chic" Image," *Media,* December 16, 2005, p. 16, http://www.mgae.com.

hoopla when they were first launched in the region, but since then reactions have been rather muted. There has been virtually no marketing since their introduction. There are several possible causes behind Bratz's failure to catch on. A range of distributors across different markets, each with inputs at the local level, has made it difficult to coordinate promotional efforts. Barbie reflects a nostalgic image of the United States, but many Asian girls (and their mothers) are not familiar with the Bratz company. MGA may also have misjudged the Asian market. Play patterns and role models for Asian girls differ from those of their U.S. and European peers. Barbie and Hello Kitty dolls still hold strong allure among Asian girls (and even women). One important factor in Asia is the mother, who typically buys the toys. The funky image of Bratz dolls might be far too risqué for mothers in Asia.

DISCUSSION QUESTIONS

1. Examine what cultural factors hindered the takeoff of Bratz in Asia despite the dolls' phenomenal success in the United States and in Europe.

2. Discuss what MGA Entertainment can do to boost the sales of Bratz dolls in Asia.

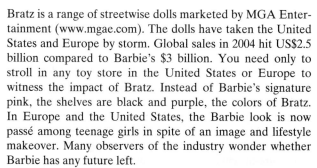

CASE 4-2

SELLING VIDEO GAMES IN GERMANY

Germany has been one of the most challenging markets in Europe for game companies to penetrate. With 38,000,000 households, Germany represents a huge opportunity for the gaming industry. So far, however, the promise has been elusive. For instance, while 24 percent of U.K. households own a Sony PlayStation 2, merely 6 percent of German households have the console. Gerhard Florin, the head of European operations for Electronic Arts (EA), a leading game publisher, noted, "If we could get German game-playing up to the level of the UK, Europe would become EA's largest market, even overtaking the U.S. Germany is not a technological laggard: Internet usage (around 57.1 percent) is among the highest in Europe."

According to industry analysts, sociocultural factors explain the slow adoption of videogames in Germany. One important element is the low birth rate: The average German woman has 1.4 children compared to 1.6 per woman in Britain. German parents are also stricter, steering their children away

from video games toward homework. German children tend to be older when they finally take up the hobby starting at five to six compared to three to four for British children. Germany also has a strong reading culture. Mr. Florin observed, "Germans feel they are supposed to spend their time on their education or career."

Gaming companies are trying hard to change the image of gaming in Germany. Sony is promoting a more family-friendly image. Companies also tailor their games to comply with German decency standards, among the strictest in the world. For instance, games based on World War II leave out Nazi insignia; spurting blood is changed to green, suggesting an alien has been killed rather than a human. Companies also hope that a new generation of handheld game consoles will boost the market. According to a Sony executive, "Most German parents say they don't want kids sitting in front of the TV screen playing games. But they don't mind giving them a handheld console in the back of the car."

DISCUSSION QUESTIONS

1. Discuss what other marketing initiatives gaming companies can take to stimulate their sales in Germany.

Source: "Gunning for players," *Financial Times,* February 1, 2005, p. 9.

FURTHER READING ◆

Baligh, H. Helmy. "Components of Culture: Nature, Interconnections, and Relevance to the Decisions on the Organization Structure." *Management Science* 40, (4), 1994, pp. 14–27.

De Mooij, Marieke, and Geert Hofstede. "Convergence and Divergence in Consumer Behavior: Implications for International Retailing." *Journal of Retailing* 78 (2002), pp. 61–69.

Hall, Edward T. *Beyond Culture.* Garden City, NY: Anchor Press, 1976.

Hofstede, Geert. *Cultures and Organizations: Software of the Mind.* London: McGraw-Hill, 1991.

Hofstede, Geert. *Culture's Consequences: International Differences in Work-Related Values.* Beverly Hills, CA: SAGE Publications, 1980.

Hofstede, Geert, and Michael Bond. "The Confucius Connection: From Cultural Roots to Economic Growth." *Organizational Dynamics,* 1988, pp. 4–21.

House, Robert J., Paul J. Hanges, Mansour Javidan, Peter W. Dorfman, and Vipin Gupta. *Culture, Leadership, and Organizations: The GLOBE Study of 62 Societies.* Thousand Oaks, CA: SAGE Publications, 2004.

Madden, Thomas J., Kelly Hewett, and Martin S. Roth. "Managing Images in Different Cultures: A Cross-National Study of Color Meanings and Preferences." *Journal of International Marketing,* 8 (1), 2000, pp. 90–107.

Nisbett, Richard. *The Geography of Thought: How Asians and Westerners Think . . . and Why.* New York, *The Free Press,* 2004.

Parker, Philip M. *Cross-Cultural Statistical Encyclopedia of the World,* vols 1, 2, 3, and 4. Westport, CT: Greenwood Press, 1997.

Ricks, David A. *Blunders in International Business.* Cambridge, MA: Blackwell Publishers, 1993.

Schwartz, Shalom H., and Lilach Sagiv. "Identifying Culture-Specifics in the Content and Structure of Values." *Journal of Cross-Cultural Psychology,* 26 (1), January 1995, pp. 92–116.

Sebenius, James K. "The Hidden Challenge of Cross-Border Negotiations." *Harvard Business Review,* March 2002, pp. 76–85.

Shi, Linda H., Shaoming Zou, J. Chris White, Regina C. McNally, and S. Tamer Cavusgil. "Global Account Management Capability." *Journal of International Marketing,* 13 (2), 2005, pp. 93–113.

Terpstra, Vern, and Kenneth David. *The Cultural Environment of International Business.* Cincinnati, OH: South-Western Publishing Co., 1991.

Triandis, Harry C. "The Self and Social Behavior in Differing Cultural Contexts." *Psychological Review,* 96 (1), 1989, pp. 506–20.

POLITICAL AND LEGAL ENVIRONMENTS

HAPTER OVERVIEW

1. POLITICAL ENVIRONMENT—INDIVIDUAL GOVERNMENTS

2. POLITICAL ENVIRONMENT—SOCIAL PRESSURES AND POLITICAL RISK

3. TERRORISM AND THE WORLD ECONOMY

4. INTERNATIONAL AGREEMENTS

5. INTERNATIONAL LAW AND LOCAL LEGAL ENVIRONMENT

6. ISSUES TRANSCENDING NATIONAL BOUNDARIES

Business has been considered an integral part of economic forces. Indeed, economics was once called *political economy,* and as such, business could not be conducted devoid of political and legal forces. Although we tend to take political and legal forces for granted most of the time in doing business domestically, they could become central issues in international business and cannot be ignored. It is human nature that we tend to look at other countries' political and legal systems as peculiar because they differ from ours. We might even make some value judgment that our own country's political and legal system is always superior to other countries' and that they should change their system to our way. This ethnocentrism, however, hinders our proper understanding of, and sensitivity to, differences in the system that might have major business implications. By the very nature of their jobs, international marketers cannot afford to be ethnocentric as they interact with a multitude of political and legal systems, including their own at home.

International marketers should be aware that the economic interests of their companies can differ widely from those of the countries in which they do business and sometimes even from those of their own home countries. Various international agreements, treaties, and laws are already in place for them to abide by. Furthermore, there is an increased level of visible distrust of multinational firms around the world, calling for the creation of codes of conduct for them.[1]

---

[1] S. Prakash Sethi, *Setting Global Standards: Guidelines for Creating Codes of Conduct in Multinational Corporations* (Hoboken, NJ: Wiley, 2003).

In this chapter, we examine political and legal forces that affect the company's international marketing activities from the following three perspectives: the political and legal climates of the host country, those of the home country, and the international agreements, treaties, and laws affecting international marketing activities transcending national boundaries. Although political and legal climates are inherently related and inseparable because laws are generally a manifestation of a country's political processes, we will look at political climate first, followed by legal climate.

◆ ◆ ◆ ◆ ◆ ◆ ◆ ◆

POLITICAL ENVIRONMENT—INDIVIDUAL GOVERNMENTS

Government affects almost every aspect of business life in a country. First, national politics affect business environments directly through changes in policies, regulations, and laws. The government in each country determines which industries will receive protection and which will face open competition. The government determines labor regulations and property laws. It determines fiscal and monetary policies, which then affect investment and returns. We summarize those policies and regulations that directly influence the international business environment in a country.

Second, the political stability and mood in a country affect the actions a government will take—actions that may have an important impact on the viability of doing business in the country. A political movement may change prevailing attitudes toward foreign corporations and result in new regulations. An economic shift may influence the government's willingness to endure the hardships of an austerity program. We discuss the strategic importance of understanding political risk in an international business context.

Home Country versus Host Country

Whenever marketing executives do business across national boundaries, they have to face the regulations and laws of both the home and host countries. A **home country** refers to a country in which the parent company is based and from which it operates. A **host country** is a country in which foreign companies are allowed to do business in accordance with its government policies and within its laws. Therefore, international marketing executives should be concerned about the host government's policies and their possible changes in the future, as well as their home government's political climate.

Because companies usually do not operate in countries that have been hostile to their home country, many executives tend to take for granted the political environment of the host country in which they currently do business. Sweeping political upheavals, such as the Cuban crisis in the 1960s, the Iranian Revolution in the 1980s, the breakup of the Soviet Union in the late 1980s, the Persian Gulf War in the 1990s, the Kosovo crisis in Yugoslavia[2] in 1999, the suicide bombings in Indonesia during the last few years, and more recently, the U.S.-led war against Iraq have already made many business executives fully aware of dire political problems in some regions, and many companies have since stayed away from those areas. Despite the fact that those major political upheavals provide the largest single setting for an economic crisis faced by foreign companies, what most foreign companies are concerned about on a daily basis should be a much larger universe of low-key events that may not involve violence or a change in government regime but that do involve a fairly significant change in policy toward foreign companies.[3] In recent years, the end of apartheid in South Africa also signaled foreign companies' cautious yet optimistic attitude toward resuming business relations with this African country.[4] Similarly, Vietnam has begun to attract foreign

---

[2]Now known as *Serbia-Montenegro* as a result of a loose federation of those states established in February 2003.

[3]Stephen J. Kobrin, "Selective Vulnerability and Corporate Management," in Theodore H. Moran, ed., *International Political Risk Assessment: The State of the Art: Landegger Papers in International Business and Public Policy,* (Washington, DC: Georgetown University, 1981), pp. 9–13.

[4]"South Africa: Investment Climate Statement," Tradeport, www.tradeport.org/ts/countries/safrica/climate.html, April 10, 1999, accessed on August 20, 1999.

direct investment to spur its domestic economic growth and shift toward a more market-based economy.[5]

The intertwined nature of home and host government policies is illustrated by the U.S.–China diplomatic relationship having been reestablished in the mid-1970s under the Nixon administration. As a result, the Chinese government finally opened its economy to foreign direct investment, mostly through joint ventures, in the 1980s. The first pioneer foreign companies have stood to gain from the host government policies designed to protect the domestic producers they teamed up with in China. Thus, the U.S.' Chrysler, Germany's Volkswagen, and France's Peugeot, with their respective Chinese partner companies, were such beneficiaries. However, the U.S.–China relationship has since been anything but smooth. The United States, in particular, has been openly critical of China's human rights "violations" since the Tiannanmen Square massacre of 1989 and has tried to make its trade policy with China contingent on measurable improvements in China's human rights policy.

As China entered the World Trade Organization (WTO) in December 2001, the United States also offered extension of permanent normal trade relations to China. The situation is very promising but challenges still lie ahead. The U.S. government needs to do more to help China change its legal and political system to meet the challenges of its accession to the WTO. The wrenching social changes, including increased unemployment in large cities, caused by the opening of China's economy carry the risk of serious political instability. In addition, the current government and Communist Party leadership, which mixed with the politics of WTO implementation, could create systemic instability in China. If the United States, the European Union, and Japan could provide assistance to China in restructuring its financial and legal systems and in developing a public health infrastructure and systems for improved environmental protection, the possibility could be averted. Otherwise, foreign companies operating in or contemplating entry into China may experience undue uncertainties for the foreseeable future.[6]

The emergence of the Internet could also pose problems for Chinese trade relations. Although China seeks to free its markets in response to global pressure, particularly from the United States, the Internet undermines China's general censorship policies. This dilemma was recently shown when China imprisoned a Chinese Internet entrepreneur for exchanging lists of e-mail addresses with a U.S. organization in the hope of growing his Web-based business.[7] Nonetheless, encouraged by reformist leaders, Internet use is growing explosively. In 1997, only 640,000 Chinese were connected. By the end of 2004, China's Internet users totaled 94 million individuals compared to Japan's 67 million. Today e-commerce has become a strong driver of China's market economy by expanding with annual sales rising at 40 percent. According to the China Electronic Commerce Association, in 2004, Beijing, Shanghai, and Guangzhou, the three largest cities in China, generated an e-commerce transaction volume of $8.02 billion, 8.5 billion, and 2.8 billion, respectively.[8] Included in its draft plan for national economic and social development, China is vigorously promoting e-government, which includes systems for taxation management, information, customs management information, financial management information, agricultural management information, and quality supervision management information. E-commerce is on the development agenda, and China is eager to expedite the application of information technology in such key areas as foreign trade, petrochemicals, metallurgy, and machinery.[9]

International marketers must understand the fluid nature of the host country's political climate in relation to home country policies. Some countries are relatively

[5]Sandie Robb, "Investors Eye Favorable Environment," *Foreign Affairs,* 84 (September/October 2005), p. 3.

[6]Andrew Batson, "China Needs Help Meeting Challenges of WTO—Academic," *Dow Jones Newswire,* June 28, 2002.

[7]Craig S. Smith, "China Imprisons Internet Entrepreneur," *Wall Street Journal,* January 21, 1999, p. A13.

[8]"E-Commerce to Grow at Over 50 percent Yearly," *China Daily,* April 19, 2005.

[9]"Report on China's Economic and Social Development Plan," *Xinhua,* March 16, 2005.

stable over time; other countries experience different degrees of political volatility that make it difficult for international marketers to predict and plan ahead. Nonetheless, international executives should know a few crucial political factors that determine the nature of the host country's political climate.

Structure of Government

Ideology.   One way to characterize the nature of government is by its political ideology, ranging from communism and socialism to capitalism. Under strict **communism,** the government owns and manages all businesses and allows no private ownership. As the recent breakup of the Soviet Union shows, the strict government control not only strips its people of private incentives to work but also is an inefficient mechanism to allocate scarce resources across the economy. On the other hand, **capitalism** refers to an economic system in which free enterprise is permitted and encouraged along with private ownership. In a capitalistic society, free-market transactions are considered to produce the most efficient allocation of scarce resources. However, capitalism is not without critics. Even Wall Street financier George Soros has called attention to the threat that the values propagated by global laissez-faire capitalism poses to the very values on which open and democratic societies depend. Without social justice as the guiding principle of civilized life, life becomes a survival of the fittest.[10] For example, capitalism, if unfettered, may result in excessive production and excessive consumption, thereby causing severe air and water pollution in many parts of the world and depleting limited natural resources. Government roles would be limited to those functions that the private sector could not perform efficiently, such as defense, highway construction, pollution control, and other public services. An interesting example can be found in Japan. Although Japanese companies perfected an efficient just-in-time (JIT) delivery system, frequent shipments have caused increased traffic congestion and air pollution in Japan, and thus may not be as efficient in delivering social well-being.[11] Now the Japanese government is trying to regulate the use of JIT production and delivery systems. **Socialism** generally is considered a political system that falls between pure communism and pure capitalism. A socialistic government advocates government ownership and control of some industries considered critical to the nation's welfare.[12]

After the breakup of the Soviet Union, most Central and East European countries converted to capitalistic ideology.[13] Similarly, China is in a transition stage, although some uncertainties still remain. There remain few countries that adhere to the extreme communist doctrine other than North Korea and Cuba. While many countries cherish capitalism and democracy, the extent of government intervention in the economy varies from country to country. (Both capitalistic and socialistic countries in which government planning and ownership play a major role are also referred to as **planned economies**).

Political Parties.   The number of political parties also influences the level of political stability. A one-party regime does not exist outside communist countries. Most countries have a number of large and small political parties representing different views and value systems of their population. In a **single-party-dominant country,** government policies tend to be stable and predictable over time. Although such a government provides consistent policies, these policies do not always guarantee a favorable political environment for foreign companies operating in the country. A dominant party regime may maintain policies, such as high tariff and nontariff barriers, foreign direct investment restrictions, and foreign exchange controls, that reduce the

---

[10]George Soros, *The Crisis of Global Capitalism* (New York: PublicAffairs, 1998).

[11]Kamran Moinzadeh, Ted Klastorin, and Emre Berk, "The Impact of Small Lot Ordering on Traffic Congestion in a Physical Distribution System," *IIE Transactions,* 29 (August 1997), pp. 671–79.

[12]Refers to an excellent classic treatise on capitalism, socialism, and communism by Joseph A. Schumpeter, *Capitalism, Socialism, and Democracy* (New York: Harper & Brothoers, 1947).

[13]Tom Diana, "Steady Economic Progress in Central and Eastern Europe," *Business Credit,* 107 (June 2005), pp. 54–57.

operational flexibility of foreign companies. For example, in Mexico a few political parties have always existed, but one party, the Institutional Revolutionary Party, had been dominant in the past 70 years. However, since 1994, Mexico's ruling party has lost its firm grip on its politics. Although the opening of the Mexican political system may eventually lead to a stronger democracy over time, it is believed that its economy will experience an unknown degree of political instability for the foreseeable future.[14]

The trauma followed by the collapse of one-party-dominant systems can be relatively large, as experienced by the breakup of the former Soviet Union. In the early 1970s, PepsiCo had cultivated ties with Soviet leaders that led to a deal providing the Soviet Union and its East European allies with Pepsi concentrate and state-of-the-art bottling technology in return for the inside track to the huge unexploited soft-drink market within the Soviet Union. However, when it collapsed in 1991, PepsiCo was devastated. Almost overnight, all of the hard-earned skills and nepotism that PepsiCo had developed for operating in a centralized command economy counted for nothing. Making matters worse, PepsiCo was seen to be connected with the discredited former regime. Archrival Coca-Cola almost immediately launched a drive for market share. The results were striking. In Hungary, for example, PepsiCo's market share tumbled from 70 percent to 30 percent almost overnight.[15]

In a **dual-party system,** such as the United States and Britain, the parties are usually not divided by ideology but rather have different constituencies. For example, in the United States, the Democrats tend to identify with working-class people and assume a greater role for the federal government while the Republicans tend to support business interests and prefer a limited role for the federal government. Yet both parties are strong proponents of democracy. In such a dual-party system, the two parties tend to alternate their majority position over a relatively long period. In 1995, the Democrats relinquished control of Congress to the Republican majority after many years. We have since seen some sweeping changes in government policy, ranging from environmental protection to affirmative action, usually in support of business interests.[16]

The other extreme situation is a **multiple-party system** without any clear majority, that is found in Italy and more recently in Japan and Taiwan. The consistency of government policies may be compromised as a result. Because there is no dominant party, different parties with differing policy goals form a coalition government. The major problem with a coalition government is a lack of political stability and continuity, and this portends a high level of uncertainty in the business climate. In Japan, career bureaucrats who are not political appointees used to be in virtual control of government policy development and execution, so the changes in government leadership did not seem to pose any measurable policy change until recently. However, in recent years, owing to Japan's prolonged recession, those nonpolitical elite bureaucrats lost clout, and instead the current prime minister, leading the ruling party, initiated many economic and financial reforms for Japan's resurgence.[17]

Besides the party system, foreign businesses also have to pay attention to the local government structure. Some governments are very weak and have hardly any control at the local level. For example, Indonesia, whose government used to be very centralized and straightforward, now has been steadily releasing power to local communities. This means that foreign businesses now have to deal with the local government and political system in each of Japan's 32 provinces.[18]

It is the role of government to promote a country's interests in the international arena for various reasons and objectives. Some governments actively invest in certain

Government Policies and Regulations

[14]" Mexico: Money, the Machine and the Man," *Economist,* July 7, 2005, p. 30.

[15]Hugh D. Menzies, "PepsiCo's Soviet Travails," *International Business,* November 1995, p. 42.

[16]"Shades of '94—But Cloudier," *CQ Weekly,* August 15, 2005, pp. 2230–38.

[17]"Japan: The Sun Also Rises," *Economist,* October 6, 2005, pp. 3–6.

[18]John McBeth, "Power to The People," *Far Eastern Economic Review,* August 14, 2003, pp. 48–50.

industries that are considered important to national interests. Other governments protect fledgling industries to allow them to gain the experience and size necessary to compete internationally. In general, reasons for wanting to block or restrict trade follow:

1. National security
   - Ability to produce goods necessary to remain independent (e.g., self-sufficiency)
   - Not exporting goods that will help enemies or unfriendly nations
2. Developing new industries
   - Idea of nurturing nascent industries to strength in a protected market
3. Protecting declining industries
   - To maintain domestic employment for political stability

For example, Japan's active industrial policy by the Ministry of International Trade and Industry (MITI) in the 1960s and 1970s is well known for its past success and has also been adopted by newly industrialized countries (NICs), such as Singapore, South Korea, and Malaysia.[19] Governments use a variety of laws, policies, and programs to pursue their economic interests. More recently, the Baltic States of Estonia, Latvia, and Lithuania, controlled by the Soviet regime until the late 1980s, have liberalized their economies significantly by opening up their economies to international trade and foreign direct investment as well as treating foreign companies no differently than domestic companies. As a result of their rapid transition to open market economies, they were formally inducted into the European Union in 2004.[20]

This section focuses on describing those government programs, trade and investment laws, and macroeconomic policies that have an immediate and direct impact on the international business in a country. We discuss laws regulating business behavior—such as antitrust laws and antibribery laws—in a subsequent section on international legal environments. Later sections of this chapter discuss the legal systems that produce and enforce a country's laws.

Incentives and Government Programs. Most countries use government loans, subsidies, or training programs to support export activities and specific domestic industries. These programs are important for host country firms and firms considering production in one country for export to others. In the United States, the International Trade Administration (ITA) has a national network of district offices in every state, offering export promotion assistance to local businesses. Furthermore, in light of federal budget cuts and as a supplement to the ITA's trade promotion efforts, state governments have significantly increased their staff and budgets not only for export assistance, particularly in nurturing small local businesses,[21] but also for attracting foreign direct investment to increase employment in their respective states.[22] Thus, the major objectives of any state government support are (1) job creation and (2) improving the state balance of trade (as in any country).

The state government's export promotion activities are more systematic while its investment attraction activities are characterized by their case-by-case nature. Foreign investment attraction activities generally consist of seminars, various audiovisual and printed promotional materials, and investment missions, among others. Of these,

---

[19]Masaaki Kotabe, "The Roles of Japanese Industrial Policy for Export Success: A Theoretical Perspective," *Columbia Journal of World Business,* 20 (Fall 1985), pp. 59–64; Mark L. Clifford, "Can Malaysia Take That Next Big Step?" *Business Week,* February 26, 1996, pp. 96–106.

[20]"The External Sector: Capital Flows and Foreign Debt," *Country Profile: Estonia,* 2005, pp. 43–45.

[21]Masaaki Kotabe and Michael R. Czinkota, "State Government Promotion of Manufacturing Exports: A Gap Analysis," *Journal of International Business Studies,* 23 (Fourth Quarter 1992), pp. 637–58; and for the most recent comprehensive study, see Timothy J. Wilkinson, Bruce D. Keillor, and Michael d'Amico, "The Relationship between Export Promotion Spending and State Exports in the U.S.," *Journal of Global Marketing,* 18 (3/4), 2005, pp. 95–114.

[22]J. Myles Shaver, "Do Foreign-Owned and U.S.-Owned Establishments Exhibit the Same Location Pattern in U.S. Manufacturing Industries?" *Journal of International Business Studies,* 29 (Third Quarter 1998), pp. 469–92.

investment missions and various tax and other financial incentives appear to play the most important role in investment promotional efforts. Investment missions are generally made by government officials, particularly by the governor of the state, visiting with potential investors. One study has shown that whether or not they participate in foreign investment attraction activities, state governments that are active in export promotion tend to attract more foreign companies' direct investment in their states than those state governments that are not active.[23] For example, export-active states could be more politically favorable and receptive to foreign companies operating there. A well-known example is that to attract a Nissan plant, Tennessee spent $12 million for new roads to the facility and provided a $7 million grant for training plant employees and a $10 million tax break to the Japanese company in 1985.[24] Similarly, Alabama provided a $253 million package of capital investments and tax breaks to lure Mercedes-Benz's sports utility vehicle production facility to the state in the early 1990s.[25] Similarly, to encourage Japanese automakers to produce in Thailand, the Thai government provided cheap labor and an eight-year tax holiday and virtually eliminated excise taxes on domestic pickup sales.[26] Since the mid-1980s, the Chinese government has offered preferential tax rates to attract foreign companies' investment in China. On average, the income tax rate for domestic companies is 33 percent while foreign companies pay half of that. Statistics show that foreign companies get an annual tax break of approximately US$50 billion in China. According to a senior expert from the Ministry of Finance, foreign companies will pay the same rate of corporate income tax as their Chinese competitors beginning in 2007. Reform of the tax system would create a competitive environment for both domestic and foreign investors.[27]

Most governments subsidize certain industries directly. Direct government subsidies are an important international consideration. In Europe, Airbus Industries was established with joint government subsidies from the governments of Britain, France, Germany, and Spain in 1970 to build a European competitor in the jet aircraft industry once dominated by U.S. companies, including Boeing and McDonnell-Douglas-Lockheed. The United States is no exception. When threatened by Japanese competition in the semiconductor industry in the 1980s, the Reagan administration launched a Japanese-style government-industry joint industrial consortium known as Semiconductor Manufacturing Technology (SEMATECH) in 1987, with the federal government subsidizing half of its $200 million operating budget.[28] Thanks to SEMATECH, the U.S. semiconductor industry finally recaptured the leading market share position by 1995, long lost to Japanese in the 1980s.

The point is to recognize how government support for particular industries or for exporting in general will determine which industries are competitive and which are not. International businesses can benefit by planning for and utilizing home country and host country government programs.

Government Procurement.   The ultimate government involvement in trade occurs when the government itself is the customer. It engages in commercial operations through the departments and agencies under its control. The U.S. government accounts for a quarter of the total U.S. consumption, so it has become the largest single consuming entity in the United States. Thus, government procurement policy has an enormous impact on international trade. In the United States, the Buy American Act gives a bidding edge to domestic suppliers, although the U.S. Congress has recently begun to open certain government procurements to goods and services from countries that are

[23]Masaaki Kotabe, "The Promotional Roles of the State Government and Japanese Manufacturing Direct Investment in the United States," *Journal of Business Research,* 27 (June 1993), pp. 131–46.

[24]"Tennessee's Pitch to Japan," *New York Times,* February 27, 1985, pp. D1 and D6.

[25]"Tax Freedom Day Index Would Be Keen Indicator," *Orlando Sentinel,* May 8, 1994, p. D1.

[26]"In a World of Car Builders, Thailand Relies Heavily on a Pickup," *New York Times,* June 16, 2005.

[27]"End of Tax Breaks for Companies in Sight," *China Daily,* May 30, 2005.

[28]Due to the U.S. government's gradual budget cut, SEMATECH became a technology consortium funded solely by member companies in 1998.

parties to various international trade agreements that the United States also belongs to.[29] To win a contract from a U.S. government agency, foreign suppliers' products must contain at least 50 percent of U.S.-made parts or must undercut the closest comparable U.S. product by at least 6 percent.[30] This "buy domestic" policy orientation is not limited to the United States but applies to all other nations. In other words, when a U.S. company tries to sell to any foreign government agency, it should always expect some sort of bidding disadvantage relative to local competitors.

Trade Laws. National trade laws directly influence the environment for international business. Trade controls can be broken into two categories: economic trade controls and political trade controls. Economic trade controls are those trade restraints that are instituted for primarily economic reasons, such as to protect local jobs. Both **tariffs** and **nontariff barriers (NTBs)** work to impede imports that might compete with locally produced goods (see Exhibit 5-1). Tariffs tax imports directly and function as a form of income for the country that levies them. In industrialized countries today, average tariff rates on manufactured and mining products are about 5 to 6 percent. Tariff protection for agricultural commodities is higher than for manufactured products, both in industrial and in developing countries. In industrialized countries, however, the average tariff rate on agriculture is almost double the tariff for manufactured products. Tariffs on labor-intensive products also largely surpass the average for industrial goods. Compared to industrial products as a whole, labor-intensive products are more protected in industrialized countries than in developing countries by an estimated one-third.[31]

Nontariff barriers include a wide variety of quotas, procedural rules for imports, and standards set on import quality that have the effect of limiting imports or making importing more difficult. For example, the biggest problem that equipment manufacturers will encounter if they try to sell in Mexico is that for any equipment that has an electrical connection (a TV, a router, or a server), they need a normas oficiales Mexicanas (NOM), which is a Mexican certification (similar to UL by the FCC in the United States) done by authorized laboratories. This process takes money and time. All importers must certify their products for NOM in Mexico. Each different importer needs to get the NOM even if two companies try to import a model number for which exporting companies, such as HP Compaq and ViewSonic, already have a NOM.[32] For example, to overcome the onerousness of the certification process, ViewSonic has been working with local agencies with extensive experience working with NOM. Political trade controls are trade restraints that are instituted for national interests or for international political reasons. **Embargoes** and **sanctions** are country-based political trade controls. Political trade restraints have become an accepted form of political influence in the international community. They are coercive or retaliatory trade measures often enacted unilaterally with the hope of changing a foreign government or its policies without resorting to military force. Embargoes restrict all trade with a nation for political purposes. The United States maintains an economic embargo on Cuba today in an effort to change the country's political disposition. Sanctions are more narrowly defined trade restrictions, such as the U.S. government's threat in 1999 to impose retaliatory tariffs of 100 percent on hundreds of millions of dollars in European imports to compensate U.S. banana companies for their lost sales to Europe. A trade war waged by the U.S. government could make such seemingly unrelated items as Scottish cashmere sweaters, pecorino cheese (but only the soft kind), German

[29] William T. Woods, "Federal Procurement: International Agreements Result in Waivers of Some U.S. Domestic Source Restrictions," GAO-05-188, *GAO Reports,* January 26, 2005, pp. 1–24.

[30] Robert Fryling, "Buy American Act: Help for United States Manufacturers," *Contract Management Magazine,* 42 (April 2002), pp. 42–43; and "Part 25.001: The Buy American Act," Federal Acquisitions Regulation, http://www.arnet.gov/far/current/html/Subpart%2025_1.html, accessed February 10, 2006.

[31] *Global Economic Prospects and the Developing Countries 2002* (Washington, DC: World Bank, 2002, Chapter 2.

[32] "Latin IT News" latinitnews@mailer.latpro.com posted by Gerard Dada of ITMarketing, September 8, 1999.

EXHIBIT 5-1
TARIFF AND NONTARIFF BARRIERS

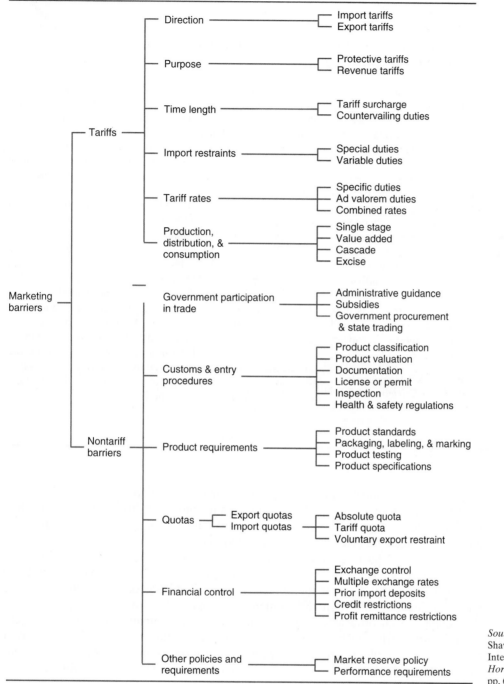

Source: Sak Onkvist and John J. Shaw, "Marketing Barriers in International Trade," *Business Horizons,* 31 (May–June 1988), pp. 66.

coffee makers, and French handbags scarce on U.S. store shelves.[33] Global Perspective 5-1 describes the relationships between the United States and the European Union in terms of government regulations and trade war currently under way.

Export license requirements are product-based trade controls. All U.S. exports officially require a specific export license from the Export Administration of the Department of Commerce. However, most products that are not sensitive to national

---

[33]"Trade Fight Spills Over into Handbags, Coffee Makers," CNN Interactive, www.cnn.com, March 3, 1999.

◆ ◆

$\mathcal{G}$LOBAL PERSPECTIVE 5-1

RELATIONSHIPS BETWEEN THE UNITED STATES AND THE EUROPEAN UNION: GOVERNMENT REGULATIONS AND TRADE WAR

U.S. business has an enormous stake in its trading relationship with the EU, which is its largest trading partner. Together, they account for almost 40 percent of world trade and 60 percent of the world's gross national product. This trade relationship directly supports a total of more than 7 million jobs in the United States and the 15 EU countries.

Over the past 30 years, as a result of a series of treaties agreed to by the member countries of the EU, the EU has won wide and growing powers to regulate business. In every area of economic activity, the EU has used these new powers to push through a determined harmonization program in an effort to unify marketplace standards throughout Europe. Harmonization has made selling to all 350 million western Europeans easier as opposed to selling to each individual country within the EU.

An important factor for U.S. businesses, the EU is now in a much stronger position to punish U.S. companies—and with not only trade sanctions but also domestic European legislation targeted at U.S. companies.

Sources: John Grimley and Anthony Brown, "U.S.-EU Trading Relationships: The Stakes are Mounting," *Financial Executive,* 18 (May 2002), pp. 21–22; and "Transatlantic Tiff," *Economist,* March 6, 2004, pp. 66–67.

The EU is unlike any lawmaking body Americans are familiar with at home. A mixture of different political governance philosophies with a strong bureaucracy supporting the democratic voice of members of the European Parliament and national governments—but without the check on centralization provided by the U.S. Supreme Court—the EU regulatory environment is unique, powerful, and generally the first and last word on regulatory matters.

Trade wars between the United States and Europe are spreading. In 2004, the EU imposed tariffs of $4 billion on the United States—the biggest authorized sanctions in the history of the World Trade Organization (WTO). These latest fines are for so-called foreign sales corporation and extraterritorial income tax breaks for U.S. exporters, which the WTO ruled illegal in 2002. Although the EU had notified the United States of its plans in 2003, the U.S. Congress has done next to nothing to stop the damage. As a result, protectionist sentiment is running higher than ever in the United States. In another case, the WTO ruled that the EU could sue the United States for damages caused by its antidumping laws. In addition, there is a further dispute at the WTO over the U.S. hormone-treated beef, which the EU wants labeled to protect its consumers.

---

security or are in short supply in the country may be sent to another country using only a general license. The application process for more sensitive products, including many high-technology exports, is quite extensive and can include review by numerous government agencies (see Chapter 17 for export control).

International businesses have a number of reasons to be concerned with trade restrictions. First, trade restrictions may completely block a company's ability to export to a country. Even if the company can export its goods, restrictions such as quotas or local modification requirements may make the product so expensive that they eliminate an otherwise lucrative market. Some companies attempt to benefit from import restrictions by establishing production facilities inside the foreign market country. For example, Brazil suddenly raised a tariff on imported cars from 20 percent to 70 percent in late 1994. As a result, foreign auto makers Fiat and Ford, with operating plants in Brazil, enjoyed a definite cost advantage over Chrysler, Toyota, Volvo, and others that exported cars to the country. Naturally, those latecomers decided to begin production in Brazil to avoid its hefty import tariffs. This is one illustration of strategic reasons why firms sometimes have plants in various countries rather than rely solely on exporting from home. In this manner, those companies, domestic or foreign, already manufacturing in the market can access the desired market with little competition from external producers.

However, trade restrictions are not necessarily good, even for companies inside a protected country. Trade restrictions often block companies from purchasing needed inputs at competitive prices. For example, in 1992 the U.S. International Trade Commission levied an import tariff on the flat panel display screens used in laptop computers in response to a complaint that foreign companies were dumping the screens below cost on the U.S. market. Although local producers of computer screens benefited from the protection from competition, U.S. producers of laptop computers, which relied mostly on imported screens, could no longer compete. Many laptop producers were forced to ship their assembly plants overseas to stay in the market.

At a more macro level, if trade laws harm other countries, they are likely to invoke retaliation. For example, wrangling over the U.S. inability to repeal the Byrd Amendment that channeled antidumping duties to U.S. steel companies that filed the antidumping charges against foreign steel producers, the Byrd Amendment literally encourages U.S. steel companies to file antidumping charges against foreign producers for their own interest, and the WTO ruled that the Byrd Amendment violates international trade agreements. Canada is threatening to impose 100 percent duties on U.S.-made bicycles and a few hundred other U.S. products, ranging from fish byproducts to plywood to skis to home exercise equipment. Brazil, Canada, Chile, the European Union, India, Japan, Mexico, and South Korea apparently have drawn the same conclusion and promise to retaliate and target U.S. industries to ensure that Congresspeople feel their constituents' pain.[34] However, trade wars, if left unchecked, usually harm all countries by limiting the ability of competitive firms to export and generate the benefits created by specialization. One thing is clear: Government trade laws have a complex and dynamic impact on the environment for international business.

Trade war can have positive consequences, however, if it leads to freer trade instead of more restricted trade. The Association of Southeast Asian Nations (ASEAN) nations are slashing tariffs among themselves to compete with China. A pact to drop tariffs on goods traded within the 10-nation group to 5 percent or less now makes it possible for Procter & Gamble to export to most of Asia out of its single remaining shampoo factory in Bangkok. Before the pact, P&G had to buy new production gear for separate plants in Thailand, Indonesia, and the Philippines.[35]

Investment Regulations.   International investments have been growing at a much faster pace than international trade. Multinational corporations (MNCs) are making much of these investments. Foreign direct investments are explained in terms of various market imperfections, including government-imposed distortions, but governments also have a significant role in constructing barriers to foreign direct investment and portfolio flows. These barriers can be broadly characterized as ownership and financial controls.

Ownership Controls.   Most countries feel that some assets belong to the public; they have a sense of "national ownership." In a highly nationalistic country, this sentiment could apply to the ownership of any company. In many countries, the natural resources (e.g., the land and mineral wealth) are viewed as part of the national wealth not to be sold to foreigners. For example, Kuwait has a constitutional ban on foreign ownership of its oil reserves. Recently, there was a heated debate as to whether or not state-owned Kuwait Petroleum Corp. (KPC) had the right to sign agreements with foreign oil companies to produce local oil. The government argued that KPC was allowed under existing laws to forge foreign participation accords in return for cash incentives. Its efforts to advance the plan repeatedly came under attack, however, by opposition members of parliament who argued that foreign companies' provision of cash incentives would amount to foreign direct investment and, thus, foreign control.[36] In a similar vein, Russia has decided to revive its ailing auto industry, which is rapidly losing market share to Western and Japanese imports and locally assembled foreign models, through direct state intervention. The Russian government seized control

[34]"U.S. Bike Makers Caught in Trade War with Canada," *Bicycle Retailer & Industry News,* February 1, 2005, pp. 1 and 43.

[35]Michael Shar, "A New Front in the Free-Trade Wars," *Business Week,* June 3, 2002.

[36]Jeanne M. Perdue, "Kuwait Gets Green Light to Invite Majors," *Petroleum Engineer International,* 72 (September 1999), p. 7.

of General Motors' pioneering joint venture with Russia's largest automaker, OAO Avtovas, in early 2006.[37]

The United States has very few restrictions on foreign ownership; however, for reasons of national security, limitations do exist. For example, the Federal Communications Commission limits the control of U.S. media companies to U.S. citizens. This was one of the motivating factors for Rupert Murdoch to relinquish his Australian citizenship for U.S. citizenship to retain control of his media network, Fox Television. Similarly, the U.S. Shipping Act of 1916 limits noncitizen ownership of U.S. shipping lines. The Federal Aviation Act requires airlines to be U.S. citizens (defined as one where 75 percent of the voting rights of the firm are owned and controlled by U.S. citizens) to hold U.S. operating rights. The International Banking Act of 1978 limits interstate banking operations by foreign banks. Consequently, foreign banks cannot purchase or take over U.S. banks with interstate operations.

Financial Controls.   Government-imposed restrictions can serve as strong barriers to foreign direct investments. Some common barriers include restrictions on profit remittances, differential taxation, and interest rates. Restrictions of profit remittances can serve as a disincentive to invest because returns cannot be realized in the parent company's home currency. Although government controls on profit remittance are drawbacks in attracting investment, some governments also use such restrictions as a way to encourage foreign companies to increase exports from the host country. For example, Zimbabwe permits higher profit remittance rates—up to 100 percent—to foreign companies operating in that country that export significantly.[38]

Various multinational companies have been able to exploit legal loopholes to circumvent this problem to some extent. Tactics include currency swaps, parallel loans, countertrade activities, and charging for management services, among others. Also, various countries treat operations of foreign companies differently from those of local companies. Two means through which local companies are supported are lower tax rates and lower interest rates for loans secured from local financial institutions. These differences can put foreign companies at a significant disadvantage relative to domestic companies in that particular market and can act as a deterrent to foreign direct investments.

Macroeconomic Policies.   Companies search internationally for stable growing markets where their profits will not diminish due to exchange loss or inflation. Government policies drive many economic factors such as the cost of capital, levels of economic growth, rates of inflation, and international exchange rates. Governments may directly determine the prime lending rate, or they may print or borrow the funds necessary to increase money supply. Governments may fix their currencies' exchange rates, or they may decide to allow the international currency market to determine their exchange rates. The monetary and exchange policies a government pursues will affect the stability of its currency, which is of critical concern to any company doing business abroad. Mexico kept the peso's exchange rate artificially high despite its increasing trade deficit in the early 1990s. One primary objective for such an exchange rate policy was to make it relatively easy for Mexico to import capital goods, such as machinery, from the United States for economic development. When Mexico's trade deficit rose to well over 8 percent of the country's GNP by 1994, Mexico could no longer hold on to an artificially high value of the peso and let it loose in December 1994. How serious was Mexico's trade deficit? Think, for a moment, that the United States had registered the large trade deficit of $172 billion in 1987, which once ushered in a doomsday prophecy of the decline of U.S. competitiveness, yet the U.S. trade deficit was no more than 3 percent of the country's GNP then! As shown in Chapter 2, the U.S. trade deficit had constantly increased to $666 billion, or about

---

[37]"GM Venture in Russia Hits Snag Following Kremlin Involvement," *Wall Street Journal,* February 18, 2006, p. A7.
[38]Cris Chinaka, "Zimbabwe Announces Measures to Boost Investment," *Reuter Library Report,* April 27, 1993.

6 percent of U.S. GDP by 2004, and it continues to increase. The U.S. trade deficit could not keep growing without a possibility of ominous consequences lurking down the road. Today, the United States is the world's largest debtor with Japan being the largest creditor and China an increasingly important creditor to the United States. A sharp reversal in Japan's and China's appetite for U.S. treasury bonds could send U.S. interest rates soaring.[39] The U.S. government, too, needs to develop policies to reduce the country's trade deficit.

Government fiscal policies also strongly influence macroeconomic conditions. The types of taxes a government employs influence whether a particular type of business is competitive within a country. For example, if a government lowers long-term capital gains taxes or allows accelerated depreciation of corporate capital assets, it will encourage investment in manufacturing facilities. The Japanese government has been known for its probusiness tax abatement and depreciation policies that helped develop the world's leading manufacturing industries in Japan, ranging from steel and shipbuilding in the 1960s and 1970s to machine tools, automobiles, and consumer electronics in the 1970s and 1980s and to semiconductor and semiconductor manufacturing equipment in the 1980s and 1990s.

Although a government can play a role in a thriving economy with accessible capital, a number of other factors determine a country's political environment. Historical considerations, social and political pressures, and the interests of particular constituencies affect the political environment in important ways. For example, during the early 1990s, China was enjoying an unprecedented economic boom. However, companies that tried to take advantage of China's open market policy have met with mixed results.[40] When China joined the WTO in December 2001, it agreed to open its financial industry but only gradually. Foreign companies are not yet permitted to become majority owners. In banking, foreigners' stakes are limited to 15 percent, and foreigners could not conduct local currency business with Chinese citizens in banking until 2006.[41]

India, on the other hand, still has some restrictions on foreign investment. One example is Press Note 18, which requires any investor with previous or existing joint ventures or technology agreements to seek approval from the Foreign Investment Promotion Board (FIPB) for new direct investments in the same or related field. Applicants must prove that the new proposal will not jeopardize the interest of the existing joint venture or technology partner. Press Note 18 is intended to protect the interests of shareholders, public financial institutions, and workers. Although many foreign investors complain about the policy, influential government officials do not want to abandon the guidelines because they consider their domestic industry not strong enough to face direct competition from foreign firms in selected sectors. Under the guidelines, Suzuki, a small Japanese automaker, must include Maruti Udyog, its existing joint venture, in its plans to make new investments for a car assembly plant and a diesel engine plant. According to Suzuki, the governmental regulations have become a tool of the Indian partners to demand unrealistic and opportunistic exit valuations or to create more barriers for foreign competitors.[42]

POLITICAL ENVIRONMENT—SOCIAL PRESSURES AND POLITICAL RISK

◆ ◆ ◆ ◆ ◆ ◆ ◆ ◆

Foreign companies also must consider social factors as part of the political environment of host countries. The political environment in every country is regularly changing. New social pressures can force governments to make new laws or to enforce old

[39]"World Bank Warns Global Recovery Has Peaked," *Wall Street Journal,* April 7, 2005, p. A2.
[40]"To Enter or Not to Enter?" *Country Monitor,* January 28, 2002, p. 5.
[41]"Strings Attached," *Economist,* March 8, 2003, pp. 67–68.
[42]"Can They Let Go?" *Business India Intelligence,* October 16, 2004, pp. 1–2.

policies differently. Policies that supported international investment may change toward isolationism or nationalism. To adequately prepare for international business or investment, the environment in each target country should be analyzed to determine its level of economic and political risk and opportunity.

Social Pressures and Special Interests

Governments respond to pressures from various forces in a country, including the public at large, lobbyists for businesses, the church, nongovernmental organizations (NGOs), and sometimes the personal interests of members of the government. To assess the political stability of a country, it is critical to evaluate the importance of major forces on the government of the country. Many developing countries undertook significant liberalization programs during the 1980s and 1990s.[43] Although these programs have been regularly promoted by the International Monetary Fund (IMF), their success during recent years must be attributed to a larger social acceptance of the potential benefits of necessary austerity measures. For example, one study has shown that the IMF's Structural Adjustment Program helped improve the economic efficiency of both domestic and foreign companies operating in Nigeria in the 1980s.[44] The benefits of liberalization extend beyond the borders of the countries involved. Consider the liberalization in Mexico, where the privatization of the state telephone company (TelMex) led to large investments by Southwestern Bell. Similarly, private companies are moving rapidly to finance other large public projects. An international consortium composed of Mexico's Grupo Hermés, the U.S. AES Corp., and the Japanese firm Nichimen constructed Mexico's first independent power-producing plant in Yucatán state.[45] While liberalization may provide unprecedented opportunities, the forces of special interests or the backlash of public sentiment may also cause governments to limit or entirely curtail certain international business operations.

Feelings of national interest can act as a deterrent to international business. For example, as a manifestation of nationalistic sentiment, Dell China customers regularly complained about the display of Taiwan's flag on the Dell Taiwan Web site. Dell Computer tried to placate these customers in China via various visual interface designs in 2002. During the last Taiwan presidential election in 2005, Chinese customers lodged another massive complaint with Dell over the flag issue. Dell executives came to learn that political events often supercede meticulous business plans. Because Dell Computer sees China as the main revenue growth in Asia, the company finally decided to remove all flags from Dell Asia-Pacific Web sites immediately for fear of a potential boycott of Dell products in China. At the time of this writing, therefore, the site has no flag displays for China, Taiwan, Korea, India, Singapore, Vietnam, and so on, but Dell Japan, retained its own flag display because it is considered a separate business entity from the Asia–Pacific segment (due to maturity of its customer base and purchasing power). Of course, because Dell is dealing with nationalistic sensitivities, it could be only a matter of time before Dell China customers will suddenly realize that the Chinese flag is not being displayed while Dell Japan still has its own flag display. Corporate diplomacy can indeed be very delicate. As one ex-Dell executive confided, "One can never foresee all possibilities, but as marketers, we always need to plan for such contingencies."[46]

Besides such outcries from local customers, large-scale strikes organized by labor unions could equally harm businesses across national boundaries. In June 2002, thousands of passengers across Europe were left stranded as air traffic controllers went

---

[43]Kate Gillespie and Hildy J. Teegen, "Market Liberalization and International Alliance Formation," *Columbia Journal of World Business,* 31 (Winter 1996), pp. 40–54.

[44]Sam C. Okoroafo and Masaaki Kotabe, "The IMF's Structural Adjustment Program and Its Impact on Firm Performance: A Case of Foreign and Domestic Firms in Nigeria," *Management International Review,* 33 (2), 1993, pp. 139–56.

[45]"Mexico's Energy Infrastructure Expanding to Match Growth," *NAFTA Works,* February 1997, pp. 1–2.

[46]This paragraph is based on the authors' personal discourse with Leon Z. Lee, a former executive at Dell Computer in charge of the company's global branding, Web globalization, and intercultural relations, March 10, 2006.

on strike to protest a plan for a continent-wide "single-sky" plan intended to reduce congestion and delays. Ninety percent of Air France's long-haul flights did not take off, and Germany's Lufthansa airlines canceled 130 of its 140 flights to and from France, and British Airways was operating only four of its usual 126 flights into France. Partial strikes in Greece, Hungary, Portugal, Spain, and Italy also halted some flights.[47]

Furthermore, in recent years, the emergence of NGOs as organizational manifestations of broader social movements has dramatically altered the global political-economic landscape. NGOs are relatively informal organizations established by "concerned people" who participate in global value creation and governance. Sometimes NGOs are antigovernment or anti-MNCs that try to address societal and environmental issues that they believe are being unsatisfactorily addressed.[48] The Exxon case presented in Global Perspective 5-2 illustrates the social pressures from NGOs affecting government and corporate policies.

How should a manager evaluate the opportunities and risks a country presents? Obviously, this depends on too many factors to discuss them all. A manager should certainly consider the country's political history as well as the history of similar industries within the country. In the following section, we discuss a number of factors that international managers should consider when determining the economic and political risks associated with a country.

Management of the Political Environment

International managers must manage the political environment in which the international firm operates. This means first and foremost learning to follow the customs of the country in which the firm is operating. Managing the political environment also means knowing which facets of the foreign country must be carefully monitored and which can be manipulated. If managed correctly, the political environment could become a marketing support system rather than an inhibitor for the foreign company.[49]

To make informed decisions, the marketing manager must understand the country's political factors and its national strategies and goals. The political factors in a country include the political stability, the predominant ideology toward business (and foreign business in particular), the roles that institutions have in the country (including the church, government agencies, and the legal system), and the international links to other countries' legal and ideological structures.[50]

To be welcomed in a host country, the foreign firm must offer some tangible benefits that the host government desires. Thus, it is critical that a manager recognize what the host country government's motivations and goals are. Most international business activities offer something to all parties involved. If the host country is actively pursuing job creation goals, then a foreign firm that can offer jobs has leverage for obtaining concessions against other problems. The manager should understand what national policies are being pursued and what policy instruments the government typically uses to promote its interests (see Exhibit 5-2).

It is important to carefully assess the political power structure and mood in a country before making decisions regarding business operations. By evaluating various environmental factors (see Exhibit 5-3), marketing managers can arrive at a more thorough understanding of the likelihood of various problems or opportunities in a country. Managers can also purchase or subscribe to country risk ratings (see Exhibit 5-4), provided by various risk analysis agencies such as the PRS Group's

[47]"Strike Cripples European Air Travel," *CNN News,* June 19, 2002.

[48]Hildy Teegen, Jonathan P. Doh, and Sushil Vachani, "The Importance of Nongovernmental Organizations (NGOs) in Global Governance and Value Creation: An International Business Research Agenda," *Journal of International Business Studies,* 35 (November 2004), pp. 463–83.

[49]Michael G. Harvey, Robert F. Lusch, and Branko Cavarkapa, "A Marketing Mix for the 21st Century," *Journal of Marketing Theory and Practice,* 4 (Fall 1996), pp. 1–15.

[50]James E. Austin, *Managing in Developing Countries: Strategic Analysis and Operating Techniques* (New York: Free Press, 1990).

GLOBAL PERSPECTIVE 5-2

SOCIAL PRESSURES AFFECTING GOVERNMENT AND CORPORATE POLICIES: THE ROLE OF NGOs

The emergence of nongovernmental organizations (NGOs) as organizational manifestations of broader social movements has dramatically altered the global political-economic landscape. NGOs are relatively informal organizations established by "concerned people" who participate in global value creation and governance. Sometimes, NGOs are antigovernment or antimultinational corporations that seek to address societal and environmental issues that they believe are unsatisfactorily addressed. The Exxon case is an example.

Exxon, world's second-largest corporation, is building a 660-mile pipeline from the oil fields of Chad, in the geographic heart of Africa, to the coast of Cameroon. Three feet under ground the pipeline will cut through forests and farmlands as it makes its way to the sea. In addition to local governments, Exxon must confront various NGOs over their environmental concerns. Under pressure from activists, Exxon has been forced to take on the unlikely role of development agency, human-rights promoter, de facto local government, and even environmental watchdog.

Using the Internet and mass media as cudgels, NGOs such as Greenpeace, Human Rights Watch, and Friends of the Earth have grown increasingly adept at singling out multinationals. Oil companies offer particularly ripe targets. Companies like Exxon are big, which NGOs readily translate as "bad." Exxon has highly visible brands, making it vulnerable to boycotts at the pump. The oil company cannot choose where oil deposits are located, meaning that it increasingly operates in countries with unsavory rulers, sensitive environments, and impoverished populations. Its power also tends to dwarf that of its host countries. For example, Exxon's 2001 revenues were $191.6 billion, compared with Chad's GDP of $1.4 billion.

The solution is a complex, four-way agreement between Exxon, the host governments, activists, and the World Bank. In keeping with its mission of alleviating poverty, the World Bank would lend $93 million to the governments of Chad and Cameroon so they could participate as equity investors in the project. By standing between Exxon and its worst critics and

between Exxon and the troublesome host governments, the World Bank could serve as a moral buffer, providing Exxon invaluable political insurance. While reassuring people on its skills and technology, Exxon has helped oversee a $1.5 million initiative in which the oil company has built schools, funded health clinics, dug wells, advised local entrepreneurs, fielded an AIDS-education van, and distributed 32,000 antimalarial mosquito nets. It has also paid for prostitute focus groups, and gorilla habitat studies, even ritual chicken sacrifices.

Between 1993 and 1999, 145 meetings were held involving 250 NGOs and Exxon. The parties agreed to 60 changes in the pipeline's route, and Exxon promised to help create an environmental foundation, two national parks in Cameroon, and an "Indigenous Peoples Plan" for the Pygmies, local minorities in Africa. Exxon will also offer compensation to owners of every mango tree, bean plant, and cotton field on the expected annual yield, local fruit prices, and so forth in the affected area.

To complicate matters for Exxon, the demands of Western NGOs often conflict directly with the wishes of locals. The NGOs want Cameroon's rain forests left untouched; local farmers plead for Exxon to clear them with chain saws. The NGOs want roads routed around villages; villagers sneak out at night to move road markers closer to their homes and stores so that they will receive more compensation to improve their life.

Whether the local Chad government could be trusted with Exxon's oil money remains an unanswered question. Although the World Bank will retain its right to cut off all loans and future aid to Chad, nothing can stop its leader from living high on the hog, paying his army, and saying to heck with the country's other seven million citizens. The last time $25 million was paid to Chad's president, he used $4.5 million to buy weapons.

With the "help" of NGOs, the World Bank, and chicken sacrifice, Exxon is practicing an unfamiliar way of doing business. If the experiment succeeds, observers say, it could rewrite the rule book for how multinationals operate worldwide. The traditional way of doing business to get the oil out of the ground without getting involved in politics human rights, and the environment is not possible anymore.

Source: Jerry Useem, "Exxon's African Adventure," *Fortune,* April 15, 2002, pp. 50–58.

International Country Risk Guide, the Economist Intelligence Unit (EIU), Business Environment Risk Intelligence (BERI), and Business Monitor International (BMI).

Regardless of categories employed in their risk ratings, three general types of risks are involved in operating in a foreign country: risks associated with changes in company ownership, risks associated with changes in company operations, and risks associated with changes in transfers of goods and money. Changes in ownership structure are usually due to dramatic political changes, such as wars or coups d'état. A company

EXHIBIT 5-2

GOVERNMENT POLICY AREAS AND INSTRUMENTS

Policy Instruments	Policy Areas					
	Monetary	Fiscal	Trade	Foreign Investment	Incomes	Sectoral
Legal	• Banking reserve levels	• Tax rates • Subsidies	• Government import controls	• Ownership laws	• Labor laws	• Land tenure laws
Administrative	• Loan guarantee • Credit regulation	• Tax collection	• Import quotas • Tariffs • Exchange rates and controls	• Profit repatriation controls	• Price controls • Wage controls • Investment approvals	• Industry licensing • Domestic content
Direct market operations	• Money creation	• Government purchases	• Government imports	• Government joint ventures	• Government wages	• State-owned enterprises

Source: Adapted from James E. Austin, *Managing in Developing Countries: Strategic Analysis and Operating Techniques* (New York: Free Press, 1990), p. 89. Reprinted with permission.

may face the expropriation or confiscation of its property or the nationalization of its industry. **Expropriation** refers to a foreign government's takeover of company goods, land, or other assets with compensation that tends to fall short of their market value. **Confiscation** is an outright takeover of assets without compensation. **Nationalization** refers to a foreign government's takeover for the purpose of making the industry a government-run industry. In nationalization, companies usually receive some level of compensation for their losses.

To reduce the risk of expropriation or confiscation of corporate assets overseas, many companies use joint ventures with local companies or adopt a domestication policy. Joint ventures with local companies imply shared activities and tend to reduce nationalistic sentiment against the company operating in a foreign country. **Domestication policy** (also known as **phase-out policy**) refers to a company gradually turning over management and operational responsibilities as well as ownership to local companies over time.

However, these risks have been reduced in recent years because many countries have realized the need for international support to receive the loans and investment they need to prosper. Consequently, the number of privatizations of once government-owned industries has increased in the last decade.[51] It is well known that government-owned companies generally do not measure up to the performance standards of private companies.[52]

Other changes in operating regulations can make production unprofitable. For example, local content requirements can force a company to use inputs of higher cost or inferior quality, making its products uncompetitive. Price controls can set limits on the sales price for a company's goods that are too low to recover investments made. Restrictions on the number of foreign employees can force a company to train local citizens in techniques that require years of specialization.

[51] Douglas L. Bartley and Michael S. Minor, "Privatization in Eastern Europe: A Field Report," *Competitiveness Review*, 6 (2), 1996, pp. 31–43; and John Nellis, "Time to Rethink Privatization in Transition Economies," *Finance & Development*, 36 (June 1999), pp. 16–19.

[52] Lien-Ti Bei and Cian-Fong Shang, "Building Marketing Strategies for State-Owned Enterprises against Private Ones Based on the Perspectives of Customer Satisfaction and Service Quality," *Journal of Retailing & Consumer Services*, 13 (January 2006), pp. 1–13.

EXHIBIT 5-3
COUNTRY RISK ASSESSMENT CRITERIA

Index Area	Criteria
Political and economic environment	Stability of the political system
	Degree of control of economic system
	Constitutional guarantees
	Effectiveness of public administration
	Labor relations and social peace
Domestic economic conditions	Population size
	Per capita income
	Economic growth during previous 5 years
	Inflation during previous 2 years
	Accessibility of domestic capital market to foreigners
	Availability of high-quality local labor
	Possibility of giving employment to foreign nationals
	Legal environmental requirements
	Traffic system and communication channels
External economic relations	Restrictions imposed on imports
	Restrictions imposed on exports
	Restrictions imposed on foreign investments in the country
	Legal protection for brands and products
	Restrictions imposed on monetary transfers
	Revaluations of currency during previous 5 years
	Drain on foreign funds through oil or other energy imports
	Restrictions on the exchange of local money into foreign currencies

Source: Adapted from E. Dichtl and H. G. Koglmayr, "Country Risk Ratings," *Management International Review,* 26 (4), 1986, p. 6.

Shifts in regulations on the transfer of goods and money can also dramatically affect the profitability of operating in a country. These changes include exchange rate restrictions or devaluations, input restrictions, and output price fixing. If a country is experiencing a shortage of foreign capital, it can limit the sale of foreign currencies to companies that need to buy some inputs from abroad or repatriate profits back home. Faced with such foreign exchange restrictions, companies have developed creative, if not optimal, means to deal with the foreign exchange restrictions. **Countertrade** is a frequently used method that involves trading products without involving direct monetary payments. For example, to expand its operations in Russia, the Russian subsidiary of PepsiCo needed to import bottling equipment from the United States. However, the Russian government did not allow the company to exchange rubles for dollars, so it exported Russian vodka to the United States to earn enough dollars to import the needed equipment. As a result of the countertrade arrangement, PepsiCo is now considered the most widely available Western consumer product in the Commonwealth of Independent States (formes Soviet states). Firms that use countertrade are also shifting away from short-term marketing motives, such as disposing of surplus, obsolete, or perishable products, to long-term marketing motives, such as establishing relationships with new partners, gaining entry to new or difficult markets, and accessing networks and expertise.[53]

[53] Dorothy Paun and Aviv Shoham, "Marketing Motives in International Countertrade: An Empirical Examination," *Journal of International Marketing,* 4 (3), 1996, pp. 29–47.

EXHIBIT 5-4
EXAMPLES OF COUNTRY RISK RATINGS (SELECTED COUNTRIES RANKED BY
COMPOSITE OVERALL RATING, AS OF MARCH 2005)

Rank	Country	Composite Risk Measure	Economic Risk	Financial Risk	Political Risk
1	Norway	92.0	48.5	47.5	88.0
2	Switzerland	90.0	43.5	47.0	89.5
3	Sweden	88.5	44.5	41.0	91.5
4	Singapore	88.3	47.0	45.0	84.5
5	Finland	87.8	44.5	37.5	93.5
6	Denmark	87.0	43.5	44.0	86.5
7	Canada	86.3	43.5	42.5	86.5
8	Ireland	86.0	41.5	41.0	89.5
9	Austria	85.0	41.0	42.5	86.5
10	Kuwait	84.8	47.5	45.0	77.0
11	Japan	84.5	39.0	47.0	83.0
12	Netherlands	84.5	41.0	41.5	86.5
13	United Arab Emirates	84.0	45.0	43.5	79.5
14	Belgium	83.5	42.5	41.5	83.0
15	Australia	83.0	41.0	36.0	89.0
16	Taiwan	83.0	42.5	46.0	77.5
17	Germany	82.5	41.0	42.0	82.0
18	New Zealand	81.8	41.0	31.5	91.0
19	United Kingdom	81.8	39.0	40.0	84.5
20	Korea, Republic	81.5	43.5	42.5	77.0
21	Saudi Arabia	81.0	47.5	47.5	67.0
22	Chile	80.5	41.0	39.0	81.0
23	Slovenia	80.0	40.0	38.5	81.5
24	Italy	79.5	38.5	42.0	78.5
25	Malaysia	79.0	40.5	41.5	76.0
26	Portugal	79.0	37.5	36.0	84.5
27	Spain	79.0	39.5	38.5	80.0
28	France	78.5	40.0	40.0	77.0
29	Libya	78.0	45.0	47.0	64.0
30	United States	77.3	39.0	33.0	82.5
31	Algeria	76.8	44.5	46.5	62.5
32	China	76.5	38.5	45.5	69.0
33	Russian Federation	76.5	42.5	44.5	66.0
34	Czech Republic	76.0	37.0	39.0	76.0
35	Mexico	75.8	37.5	40.0	74.0
36	Estonia	75.5	39.0	37.5	74.5
37	Hungary	75.5	35.0	35.0	81.0
38	Croatia	75.3	37.0	38.0	75.5
39	Greece	74.5	36.0	36.0	77.0
40	Kazakhstan	74.0	38.0	40.0	70.0
41	Poland	73.8	37.0	36.0	74.5
42	Thailand	73.8	38.0	41.5	68.0
43	South Africa	73.3	36.0	40.0	70.5
44	Costa Rica	73.0	35.0	38.5	72.5
45	Ukraine	73.0	38.5	39.5	68.0
46	Israel	72.8	39.5	39.0	67.0
47	India	71.8	36.0	44.5	63.0
48	Iran	70.5	36.0	44.5	60.5

EXHIBIT 5-4

(continued)

Rank	Country	Composite Risk Measure	Economic Risk	Financial Risk	Political Risk
49	Vietnam	69.8	33.5	39.5	66.5
50	Brazil	69.5	37.0	36.0	66.0
51	Philippines	68.8	36.5	36.0	65.0
52	Argentina	67.8	38.5	31.0	66.0
53	Turkey	67.3	31.0	33.5	70.0
54	Colombia	64.3	34.5	35.0	59.0
54	Cuba	64.3	34.5	35.5	58.5
56	South Korea	63.8	36.0	40.0	51.5
57	Indonesia	63.5	37.0	38.0	52.0
58	Nigeria	58.0	33.5	40.0	42.5
59	Somalia	43.3	28.5	32.5	25.5
60	Iraq	24.0	6.5	9.5	32.0

Note: Lower scores represent higher risk (highest risk = 1, lowest risk = 100)

Source: Compiled from various tables in *Country Reports* (The PRS Group), http://www.prsgroup.com/countryreport/countryreport.html, accessed January 20, 2006.

◆◆◆◆◆◆◆◆ ## TERRORISM AND THE WORLD ECONOMY

Terrorism was once considered a random political risk of relatively insignificant proportions. However, it has gradually escalated in the last decade or so.[54] It culminated on September 11, 2001, in New York City and Washington, D.C., when massive terrorist attacks occurred. No one can ever forget what happened that day in the United States. It stunned Americans and the world not only because of the terror attacks themselves but also because of the vulnerability it revealed. By attacking the World Trade Center and the Pentagon, the symbols of the financial and economic center and the military power in the United States, respectively, terrorists also disrupted the U.S. economy and affected the global market. The cost of the attack is difficult to believe. An IMF study identified the direct loss as totaling about $21.4 billion, or about 0.25 percent of the U.S. GDP.[55] Other studies' estimates are much higher.[56] Short-term lost economic output was estimated as $47 billion and lost stock market wealth at $1.7 trillion.[57] At least 125,000 workers were laid off for 30 days or longer, and according to a Milken Institute study, Metropolitan areas in the United States lost as much as 1.6 million jobs in 2002 because of the attacks.[58] Long-term costs of security spending and antiterrorist activities can also be significant.

The tighter security measures after September 11 affectes international trade tremendously. Security checks cause delays in shipments of goods and raise concerns among businesses that rely on just-in-time delivery. In the United States after the attack, Ford Motor and General Motors experienced periodic parts shortages because of the security check at the Canadian border, which delayed production for hours,

[54]Masaaki Kotabe, "Global Security Risks and International Competitiveness," *Journal of International Management*, 11 (December 2005), pp. 453–56.

[55]International Monetary Fund, "How Has September 11 Influenced the Global Economy," *World Economic Outlook*, (December 2001), p. 16.

[56]Jim Saxton, "The Economic Costs of Terrorism Pose Policy Challenges," Joint Economic Committee Press Release, United States Congress, www.house.gov/jec/, May 1, 2002.

[57]Peter Navarro and Aron Spencer, "September 11, 2001: Assessing the Costs of Terrorism, " *Milken Institute Review*, Fourth Quarter 2001, p. 20.

[58]Ross Devol et. al., "The Impact of September 11 on U.S. Metropolitan Areas," *Milken Institute Research Report*, January 2002.

causing steel makers to slow production and office supply stores in the New York area to run out of ink and paper.

Similarly, the Middle East crisis in which more than hundreds of Israelis killed and thousands wounded has had a large impact on Israel's economy and foreign investment. The Bank of Israel reported that Israel's balance of payments worsened by $1.9 billion in 2001 due to the deteriorating security situation, including a loss of $1.7 billion in tourism revenue. Because international investors are less willing to visit or make fact-finding trips to Israel, Israeli firms find it much more difficult to raise funds abroad. The whole economy shrank in 2001, with GDP falling by 0.6 percent, compared to a 6.4 percent increase in 2000.[59]

The worsened Middle East crisis, the September 11 terrorist attacks on the United States, and subsequently the Iraq war have caused tremendous concern about future oil supply for economic security. Because Arab oil supplies look shakier than ever, U.S. policy makers and oil companies are working on oil pipelines in Africa and other parts of Asia. An oil pipeline currently under construction from Baku through Georgia to the Turkish port of Ceyhan is a vital project for oil security.[60] Reports on terrorism in Moscow, Russia, in October 2002 involving 50 Chechen terrorists who took 700 people hostage in a theater offers more convincing evidence that terrorist activities are clearly on the rise for religious and political reasons. They demanded an end to Russia's military campaign in Chechnya, a runaway state in the Russian Federation.[61] The Chechen revolt could even threaten to cause a disruption to the future oil supply between Baku and Ceyhan.

Even two massive terrorist bombings in Bali, Indonesia, on October 12, 2002, and on October 1, 2005, affected many nationalities ranging from Australia to South Africa and from Ecuador to Sweden. The majority of the dead in the first attack were Australians, who always thought that given their country's relatively geographically isolated location, they were immune to terrorism. Now even Australian firms as well as tourists have to think twice about where to invest and travel.[62] According to the new National Counterterrorism Center, there was a tremendous increase in terrorist attacks in 2004 with 651 significant strikes worldwide. The growing threat today is from the so-called global jihad movement, a mixed group inspired but not directed by Osama bin Laden. This group, in particular, is carrying out most of the terrorist attacks against U.S. and allied interests.[63]

Recently in 2006, the U.S. government, sensitive about Middle-East terrorism, became broiled in a heated dispute over the U.S. port security issues as a result of the proposed purchase of five U.S. major commercial port operations by Dubai Ports World, a United Arab Emirates–owned company and one of the most globally efficient port operators.[64] Clearly, economic efficiency cannot be pursued devoid of international politics.

Terrorist activities and local military skirmishes in various parts of the world disrupt not only international movement of supplies and merchandise but also international financial flow as well as tourism. They threaten the smooth functioning of international marketing activities taken for granted in the past 30 years. International marketers should be aware that global strategy based on coordination of various value-adding activities scattered around the world as envisioned in the 1980s and 1990s may need to be replaced (at least on a case-by-case basis) by more locally and regionally based strategy that requires increased levels of local procurement and local marketing for the sake of political correctness and local sensitivity.[65]

---

[59]"The Cost of Terrorism," *Jerusalem Post*, March 24, 2002, p. 6.

[60]Atul Jain, "Baku-Tbilisi-Ceyhan Oil Pipeline Vital Link for East and West," *Pipeline & Gas Journal*, August 2005, pp. 60–64.

[61]"Terrorism in Russia: The Chechens Strike," *Economist*, October 26, 2002, p. 47.

[62]The Bomber Will Always Get Through," *Economist*, October 8, 2005, pp. 12–13.

[63]Lisa Stein, "The Week," *U.S. News & World Report*, May 9, 2005, pp. 14–18.

[64]"DP World: 'We'll Be Back,'" *Traffic World*, May 29, 2006, p. 48.

[65]Masaaki, Kotabe, "To Kill Two Birds with One Stone: Revisiting the Integration-Responsiveness Framework," in Michael Hitt and Joseph Cheng, ed., *Managing Transnational Firms* (New York: Elsevier, 2002), pp. 59–69.

◆ ◆ ◆ ◆ ◆ ◆ ◆ ◆ INTERNATIONAL AGREEMENTS

International politics has always been characterized by the predominance of strong ideological links centered around and dominated by a relatively small number of large powers. After World War II, those links centered on the two contending superpowers, the United States and the new former Soviet Union. However, the hierarchical structure of world politics recently has been challenged by two processes.

First, the true independence of previously colonial countries has led to a much larger set of nations playing relatively independently on the international stage, entering into contracts and relations with new political and economic partners. Second, the loosening of the tight bipolarity in world politics, combined with the relative decline of the United States as the economic superpower in the free world and the breakup of the Soviet Union that had once led the communist world, has created an increased level of ambiguity in geopolitical stability.[66]

While most nations guard their independence by maintaining the ability to produce critical products domestically, citizens around the world have learned to expect and demand the lifestyle that international trade provides. Thus, domestic politics cannot be isolated from international politics. Political actions in one country will eventually influence the actions of other countries. For example, Mexico's recent decision to devalue its currency caused U.S. exports to Mexico to decrease. If the industries that are harmed by the decrease in sales have enough political force, they could ask the U.S. government to pressure Mexico to invest in strengthening its currency or face trade repercussions.

Nations not only react to each other's actions but also develop relationships that determine their future actions. They form networks for achieving mutual goals, and they develop political and trade histories and dependencies that influence their perceptions of the world. Thus, the international political environment is determined by a dynamic process of the interactions of players, each pursuing its own interests and working together for mutual interests. Coordination is required, for example, to establish and maintain a trade embargo as a viable alternative to military force. Similarly, coordination is required to avoid harmful currency devaluations or the financial insolvency of governments. The level at which governments rely on each other and are affected by each other's actions also leads to regular conflicts and tensions. Indeed, history has shown that war—an ultimate form of international conflicts and tensions—is less likely to occur between the two countries the more they engage in trade with each other.[67]

In the United States, the Congress, not the president, is in charge of international trade negotiations. As a legislative process, any decision making on trade-related issues tends to be slow, and the U.S. government's inaction sometimes becomes a bottleneck to international trade negotiations. As a result, the U.S. government may lose credibility in such negotiations. If the Congress sees the benefit of faster trade negotiations, it can grant **fast-track trade authority** to the president. Doing so gives the president a free hand in directly negotiating trade deals with foreign governments. Although President Bill Clinton did not get a fast-track trade authority, President George W. Bush was granted this authority in 2002.[68] Similarly, Mexico, whose trade volume with the United States and Canada has more than tripled since the implementation of NAFTA in 1994, considered granting president Vicente Fox fast track trade authority to impose a 40 percent tariff on fresh apples imported from the United States. Mexico accused the United States of selling the fruit at an unfair price, hurting domestic growers.[69]

---

[66]Tom Nierop, *Systems and Regions in Global Politics—An Empirical Study of Diplomacy, International Organization and Trade, 1950–1991* (New York: Wiley, 1994).

[67]Edward D. Mansfield, *Power, Trade, and War* (Princeton, NJ: Princeton University Press, 1994).

[68]"Fast-Track Authority: Don't Underestimate Its Clout," *Business Week,* August 12, 2002, p. 35.

[69]Ginger Thompson, "Mexico: Apple Dumping Duties," *New York Times,* August 10, 2002, p. 3.

The roles of the General Agreement on Tariffs and Trade (GATT) and the WTO that succeeded GATT in 1995 were explained in Chapter 2 as part of the economic environment. We limit our discussion to two major international agreements that have shaped and will reshape the political economies of the world.

The **G-7** is an economic policy coordination group made up of political leaders from Canada, England, France, Germany, Italy, Japan, and the United States. The G-7 began during the economic crises of the mid-1970s. The G-7 countries continued to play a major role in world economy. For example, during the G-7 meeting in Washington, D.C. in September 2005, soaring oil prices emerged as the topic dominating the discussion among finance ministers from the G-7 industrialized countries. The Bush administration called for measures that would increase oil supply and stem supply, a disruptions while some in Europe called for measures to reduce consumption. Clearly, a difference mirrored transAtlantic disputes over issues such as global warming. Other issues on the table at the meeting were debt relief for developing countries and the U.S. budget deficit.[70]

Russia joined the G-7 in 1997, and the group consisting of the original G-7 and Russia is known as the **G-8.** Heads of state, senior economic ministers, and heads of central banks typically meet once a year to further economic coordination. G-7 meetings have primarily dealt with financial and macroeconomic issues (such as the Asian and Latin American financial crisis), but since Russia's participation, the G-8 has included some politically sensitive issues such as an effort to make arrangements for the reconstruction of Kosovo—and indeed, of the Balkan states as a whole,—after the Kosovo conflict. Recently, as a result of a remarkable economic and democratic transformation, Russia demonstrated its potential to play a full and meaningful role in addressing the global problems with the seven industrialized nations. The G-8 industrialized nations in a summit meeting in Calgary, Canada, in June 2002, agreed to have Russia become the group's president and host the summit meeting in 2006.[71] In the G-8 Summit held in February 2006, the members' collective concern was about the instability of energy supplies that harm strong global economic growth, and G-8 finance ministers called for increased investments by oil producers in drilling, transport, and refining to ensure stable supply and improved energy efficiency among consumers in a joint quest to curb "high and volatile" oil prices.[72]

The G-7 provides a good example of the role and limitations of multinational agreements and economic groupings in the years to come. The 1990s reflected some of the limitations of coordinated actions, especially at a micro level. Coordinated actions of the federal banks of the G-7 countries in a bid to affect exchange rates have had limited impact on the foreign exchange markets. At best, they have moderated the speed of the movements of exchange rates rather than the extent of the movements. The primary reason is that the volume of foreign exchange traded on the exchanges worldwide far outstrips the combined resources of the federal banks. A recent report of the G-7 finance ministers acknowledged that federal banks can play only a limited role through direct intervention in the markets.

However, a role in which coordinated action is believed to be feasible and effective is ensuring adherence to world accepted political agendas. One example concerns the issue of protection of human rights. The United States has had limited success in ensuring protection of human rights in China. Unilateral measures and bilateral negotiations have resulted in little change of China's human rights record. However, the United States is now determined to use the G-8 forum to coordinate the action of the developed countries in linking China's trade status in all eight countries to its human rights record.

Group of Seven (G-7) and Group of Eight (G-8)

[70]"Oil Likely to Be Focus of G-7 Meeting," *Wall Street Journal,* September 22, 2005, p. A8.

[71]"G-8 : Russia to Lead G-8 , Host Summit in 2006," *Dow Jones Newswire,* June 27, 2002.

[72]"G-8 Calls for Stable Oil Supply, Eyes Solid World Eco Growth," NikkeiNet Interactive, http://www .nni.nikkei.co.jp, February 11, 2006.

Coordinating Committee for Multilateral Controls (COCOM)

COCOM was founded in 1949 to stop the flow of Western technology to the former Soviet Union. Australia, Japan, and the NATO countries (except Iceland) are members. For example, even when U.S. franchises were already operating in the former Soviet Union, it was illegal to export personal computers for them to use! The initial emphasis of COCOM was on all technology products. Subsequently, the focus shifted to various types of dual-purpose hardware and software technology products, that is, products that could be used for civilian as well as military purposes. Two factors, however, exerted pressure on the policies adopted by COCOM. First, technologies that had primarily military applications were increasingly finding more civilian applications. Satellites, computers, and telecommunication technologies were prime examples. Second, the economic liberalization in the newly industrializing and developing countries put further competitive pressures on Western companies to share technologies that were until then privy to the Western world. U.S. firms were particularly adversely affected. Many U.S. companies, including the large telecommunications companies, complained to the government that the restrictions were outdated and that they were losing valuable contracts to competitors from countries without such restrictions.

In 1992, COCOM reevaluated its mission and loosened restrictions on exports of computers, telecommunications equipment, machine tools, and other materials that could assist the newly independent nations of Eastern Europe and the former Soviet republics in their effort to develop market-driven economies. Due to the changed political and economic environment, the COCOM agreement was terminated in 1994 and replaced by the *Wassenaar Arrangement of 1995*. However, the spirit of the committee still lives on. The new group of 28 countries includes not only the original 17 members but also Russia and four other nations of the Warsaw Pact. Unlike COCOM, recommendations by the group to restrict sensitive exports to specified countries are not binding on the members. Two issues of primary importance for being considered within this multilateral system are nuclear technologies and missile (especially ballistic missile) technologies. Today, the United States and some other industrialized countries forbid the export of such generally available technology as software for encoding electronic messages and semiconductor manufacturing equipment. For example, in 2000, the Japanese government imposed an export control on Sony's PlayStation 2 (PS2) electronic game console. PS2's 128-bit central microprocessor developed by Sony and Toshiba has twice the raw number-crunching power of Intel's most advanced Pentium chip used in professional desktop computers. When coupled with a video camera, PS2 could make an ideal missile-guidance system! The biblical prophesy promising peace to those who turn their swords to ploughshares seems very optimistic in today's world of dual-usage technologies, known as *DUTs*. Such provocations led the Japanese government to designate the machine a "general-purpose product related to conventional weapons." Japan's Foreign Exchange and Foreign Trade Control Law requires anyone wishing to take more than 50,000 yen (a little more than $400) worth of such equipment out of Japan to get permission from the Ministry of Economy, Trade and Industry. Violators trying to sneak loads of PS2s abroad could face up to five years in jail.[73] Now think for a moment: Sony's PlayStation 3 (PS3), introduced in late 2006, is several times more powerful than PS2 and is capable of surpassing 250 gigaflops per second, rivaling the best mid-1990s supercomputer.[74]

◆ ◆ ◆ ◆ ◆ ◆ ◆ ◆ **INTERNATIONAL LAW AND LOCAL LEGAL ENVIRONMENT**

International marketing managers should understand two legal environments: the one in each country in which they do business and the more general international one.

---

[73]"War Games," *Economist*, April 22, 2000, p. 60; and Richard Re, "Playstation2 Detonation," *Harvard International Review*, 25 (Fall 2003), pp. 46–50.
[74]"Super Cell," *Forbes*, February 14, 2005, p. 46.

At a macro level, international law and the bodies that evaluate it affect high-level international disputes and influence the form of lower-level arbitration and decisions. Local laws and legal systems directly determine the legal procedures for doing business in a foreign country. Local laws also determine the settlement of most international business conflicts, that is, the country whose laws are used is determined by the jurisdiction for the contract.

International Law

International law, or "the law of nations," can be defined as a body of rules that is binding on states and other international persons in their mutual relations. Most nations and international bodies have voluntarily agreed to subjugate themselves to some level of constraint for the purpose of living in a world in which order, not chaos, is the governing principle. In short, international law represents "gentlemen's agreements" among countries.

Although technically speaking there is no enforceable body of international law,[75] international customs, treaties, and court decisions establish a defined international legal environment. International bodies and policies exist for arbitrating cases that cannot be settled fairly in any given country.

International law comes from three main sources: **customs,** international **treaties,** and national and international **court decisions.** Customs are usages or practices that have become so firmly accepted that they become rules of law. For example, nations have historically claimed sovereignty over the resources in their offshore continental shelves. This historical practice has developed into a consensus that amounts to an international law. Custom-based laws develop slowly.

Treaties and international contracts represent formal agreements among nations or firms that set down rules and obligations to govern their mutual relationships. Treaties and contracts are binding only on those who are members to them, but if a great number of treaties or contracts share similar stipulations, they can take on the character of a custom-based law or a general rule.

National courts often make rulings in cases that apply to international issues. When these rulings offer an unusually useful insight into the settlement of international cases or when they develop into a series of interpretations consistent with other nations' courts, these national rulings may be accepted as international laws. If the issue of conflict is one in which a national court is not acceptable to one or both parties, international courts and tribunals may rule. International tribunals may be turned to for **arbitration** if the parties agree to let the case be tried. The United Nations established the International Court of Justice to settle international conflicts between nations, not between individual parties (such as firms) across national boundaries. However it must be again noted that international court rulings do not establish precedent as they might in the United States but apply only to the case at hand.

Local Legal Systems and Laws

Legal systems and the laws they create differ dramatically in countries around the world. Many legal systems do not follow the common law system followed in the United States. We discuss a number of different legal systems and the types of laws that govern contracts and business in each system. We also discuss the issue of jurisdiction, which determines the critical issue of what courts and what laws are used to decide a legal question. For most business issues, international law is primarily a question of which national laws apply and how to apply them to cases involving international contracts, shipping, or parties.

The laws that govern behavior within a country, as well as the laws that govern the resolution of international contractual disputes, are primarily local or municipal laws.

---

[75]The government of a sovereign nation stipulates its laws with policing authority. Because no supranational (i.e., international) government exists, no supranational laws are binding. Although the United Nations, made up of more than 100 member nations, is the most comprehensive political body, it is not a sovereign state, and therefore does not have enforceable laws that the member nations have to abide by other than voluntarily.

Foreign subsidiaries and expatriate employees live within the legal bounds of their host countries' legal systems. Although U.S. embassy property is considered U.S. territory no matter where it is located, companies and their employees in general must live within the local country laws. The inability of the U.S. government in 1994 to change the Singapore government's caning punishment of Michael Fay, a U.S. teenager charged of vandalism there, illustrates a clear example of the sovereignty of each country's laws.[76] The international marketing manager must be aware of the laws that will govern all business decisions and contracts.

Business Practices and the Legal System. Businesses face a myriad of legal issues every day. Questions relating to such issues as pricing policies and production practices must be clearly answered to avoid legal rapprochement and punishment. Choices relating to legal industry constraints and various regulations on product specifications, promotional activities, and distribution must be understood for a firm to function efficiently and profitably. Legal systems in each country deal with these questions differently. For a brief summary of legal issues facing companies, see Exhibit 5-5.

For example, in many parts of the world, automobiles with engines larger than 2,000 cc displacement face a much stiffer commodity tax than those with smaller engines. Germany has a Rabattgesetz or rebate law stipulating that businesses cannot give special prices to select customers. This law also prevents retailers from discounting more than 3 percent from an advertised price. This makes it extremely difficult for e-commerce retailers, especially auction sites. Other German laws prevent online shops such as Amazon.com from discounting book prices and block sales of prescription drugs and health products online.[77] In some countries, it is illegal to mention a competitor's name in an advertisement. In some countries that follow Islamic law, it is even illegal to borrow money or charge an interest! However, businesses need financial resources to grow; thus, they must learn how to acquire the resources they need within the legal limits established by the country in which they are operating. For example, in Pakistan, importers and exporters of raw materials rely on a technique known as *murabaha* to avoid the ban on interest. In this arrangement, a bank buys goods and sells them to

EXHIBIT 5-5

LEGAL ISSUES FACING THE COMPANY

Type of Decision	Issue
Pricing decisions	Price fixing
	Deceptive pricing
	Trade discount
Packaging decisions	Pollution regulations
	Fair packaging and labeling
Product decisions	Patent protection
	Warranty requirements
	Product safety
Competitive decisions	Barriers to entry
	Anticompetitive collusion
Selling decisions	Bribery
	Stealing trade secrets
Production decisions	Wages and benefits
	Health and safety requirements
Channel decisions	Dealers' rights
	Exclusive territorial distributorships

Source: Adapted from Kottler, Philip and Gary Armstrong, *Principles of Marketing*, 8th ed. (Englewood Cliffs, N.J.: Prentice Hall), 1998.

---

[76]"Singapore's Prime Minister Denounces Western Society," *Wall Street Journal*, August 22, 1994, p. A8.

[77]Neal E. Boudette, "Germany's Primus Online Faces Legal Challenges," *Wall Street Journal*, January 6, 2000, p. A17.

a customer who then pays the bank at a future date and at a markup agreed upon by the bank and its customer. In Indonesia, credit card companies such as Visa and MasterCard receive collateral assets, such jewelry and cattle, which they can sell, from card users instead of charging interest.[78]

In recent years, some countries have started raising legal requirements for environmental protection. As mentioned earlier, Japan's famed just-in-time (JIT) delivery system, such as Toyota and 7-Eleven Japan practice, has been criticized as causing traffic congestion and air pollution. Laws are being considered to reduce the (JIT) practices.[79] **Green marketing** has become fashionable in an increasing number of countries. It is marketers' reaction to governments' and concerned citizens' increased call for reduction of unnecessary packaging materials and increased recycling and recyclability of materials used in the products. Recent developments in the European Union threaten to utilize environmental standards to control internal and external trade in consumer products. Marketers who do not conform may be restricted from participation. Meanwhile, marketers who do meet the requirements enjoy the benefits of improved product development capabilities, although such capabilities may not automatically translate into improved market share.[80]

Regulations on E-Commerce.

Local business laws also affect the use of the Internet. While there are no measurable restrictions for e-commerce in the United States, this is not the case in foreign countries. For example, Germany has strict regulations over providing "digital signatures" to ensure security when making purchases over the Internet.[81] Likewise, France has regulated that the use of "cookies," software or hardware that identifies the user, should be allowed only when consent is granted.[82] Britain has a set of e-commerce laws designed to protect consumers. Interestingly, however, one study shows that almost half of the UK's top 50 retailers are flouting these laws. For example, one Web site failed to contain an appropriate data protection consent form. Another Web site informed users that their personal details would be passed onto other firms unless they sent an e-mail opting out. Both directly violate British laws. With so much business being done over the Internet, it is disconcerting that major retailers are not meeting the letter and the spirit of the laws.[83]

Types of Legal Systems.

Four principal legal "systems" are used in the majority of countries: common law systems, code law systems, and Islamic law systems. **Common law** systems base the interpretation of law on prior court rulings, that is, legal precedents and customs of the time. The majority of the states in the United States follow common law systems (Louisiana is an exception). **Code (written) law** systems rely on statutes and codes for the interpretation of the law. In essence, a code law system has very little "interpretation", the law must be detailed enough to prescribe appropriate and inappropriate actions. The majority of the world's governments rely on some form of code law system. **Islamic law** systems rely on the legal interpretation of the Koran and the words of Mohammed. Unlike common and code law systems, which hold that law

---

[78] Clement M. Henry, ed., "Special Issue: Islamic Banking," *Thunderbird International Business Review*, 41 (July/August and September/October 1999); and Ahmed Al Janahi and David Weir, "How Islamic Banks Deal with Problem Business Situations: Islamic Banking as a Potential Model for Emerging Markets," *Thunderbird International Business Review*, 47 (July/August 2005), pp. 429–45. For broader regulatory issues on Islamic finance, an excellent treatise is found in Mohammed El Qorchi, "Islamic Finance Gears Up: While Gaining Ground, the Industry Faces Unique Regulatory Challenges," *Finance and Development*, 42 (December 2005), pp. 46–49.

[79] Eiji Shiomi, Hiroshi Nomura, Garland Chow, and Katsuhiro Niiro, "Physical Distribution and Freight Transportation in the Tokyo Metropolitan Area," *Logistics and Transportation Review*, 29 (December 1993), pp. 335–43.

[80] William E. Baker and James M. Sinkula, "Environmental Marketing Strategy and Firm Performance: Effects on New Product Performance and Market Share," *Journal of the Academy of Marketing Science*, 33 (Fall 2005), pp. 461–75.

[81] "Germany Moves Digital Signatures to Next Level," *Journal of Internet Law*, February 2002, p. 23.

[82] John Leyden, "Online Data Protection Incites Worry," *Network News*, May 5, 1999, p.4.

[83] "Half of Top 50 UK Retailers Are Breaking Online Trading Laws," *Computer Weekly*, February 13, 2003, p. 18.

EXHIBIT 5-6
THE NUMBER OF
LAWYERS PER 10,000
RESIDENTS

United States	370.4
Britain	175.4
Germany	158.7
France	66.7
Japan	16.9

Source: Compiled from
"Panel Eyes 3-Fold Increase
in Legal Professionals by
2020," *Japan Economic
Newswire,* February 3, 2001.

should be human made and can be improved through time, Islamic legal systems hold that God established a "natural law" that embodies all justice. Finally, **socialist law** developed in the former Soviet Union after the Russian Revolution of 1917 and later assimilated by other communist states, are distinguished from other legal systems by the influence of state ownership of the means of production, the pervasive influence of the Communist Party, and the ties between the legal system and national central planning. Since the breakup of the Soviet Union, socialist laws have mostly faded from world political systems except in countries such as Cuba and North Korea.

Examples of Different Laws.   Legal systems address both criminal and civil law. Criminal law addresses stealing and other illegal activities. **Civil law** addresses the enforcement of contracts and other procedural guidelines. Civil laws regulating business contracts and transactions are usually called **commercial law.** International businesses are generally more concerned with differences in commercial laws across different countries. For example, who is responsible if a shipper delivers goods that are not up to standards and the contract fails to address the issue? What if the ship on which goods are being transported is lost at sea? What if goods arrive so late as to be worthless? What if a government limits foreign participation in a construction project after a foreign company has spent millions of dollars designing the project?

Sometimes the boundary between criminal and civil law is also different across countries. For example, are the officers of a company liable for actions that take place while they are "on duty"? When a chemical tank leak in Bhopal, India, killed more than 3,000 Indian citizens in 1984, it was not immediately clear whether the officers of Union Carbide were criminally liable. Seven years later, in 1991, the Bhopal court finally issued an arrest warrant for the former CEO of Union Carbide, now living in the United States. Union Carbide was subsequently acquired by Dow Chemical in 2001. Also in that year, the same court in Bhopal rejected an attempt by the Indian government to reduce homicide charges to negligence and stepped up demands that the U.S. extradite the former Union Carbide CEO to stand trial. The issue still lingers on to this day.[84]

Cultural Values and Legal Systems.   In Japan, legal confrontations are very rare. As shown in Exhibit 5-6, Japan's population of lawyers is low, which makes it difficult to obtain evidence from legal opponents. Also, rules against class-action suits and contingency-fee arrangements make it difficult to bring suit against a person or company. Japan's system has disadvantages, but it supports the cultural value of building long-term business ties based on trust.

In the United States, there is a strong belief in the use of explicit contracts and a reliance on the legal system to resolve problems in business. In other countries, such as China, a business person who tries to cover all possible problems or contingencies in a contract may be viewed as untrustworthy. Chinese culture values relationships (known as *guanxi*) and therefore relies more heavily on trust and verbal contracts than does U.S. culture.[85] Brazil, however, has a value system that differs from both the U.S.' explicit contractual agreement and China's mutual trust and verbal contract. The Brazilian value system is known as *jeitinho,* in which people believe that they can always find a solution outside the legal contract on a case-by-case basis.[86] If a culture does not respect the value of following through on an obligation, no legal system, whether written or verbal, will afford enough protection to make doing business easy.

---

[84]T.R. Chouhan, "The Unfolding of Bhopal Disaster," *Journal of Loss Prevention in the Process Industries,* 18 (July 2005), pp. 205–8.

[85]Don Y. Lee and Philip L. Dawes, "Guanxi, Trust, and Long-Term Orientation in Chinese Business Markets," *Journal of International Marketing,* 13 (2), 2005, pp. 28–56.

[86]Philip H. Geier, Jr., "Doing Business in Brazil," *Columbia Journal of World Business,* 31 (Summer 1996), pp. 44–53.

Because there is no body of international law in the strictly legalistic sense, the key to evaluating an international contract is by determining which country's laws will apply and where any conflicts will be resolved.

Jurisdiction

Planning Ahead.   By far the easiest way to ensure what laws will apply in a contract is to clearly state the applicable law in the contract. If both a home country producer and a foreign distributor agree that the producer's national laws of contracts will apply to a contract for the sale of goods, then both can operate with a similar understanding of the legal requirements they face. Similarly, to ensure a venue that will interpret these laws in an expected manner, international contracts should stipulate the location of the court or arbitration system that will be relied upon for resolving only conflicts that arise.

If contacts fail to provide for the jurisdiction of the contract, which laws apply is less clear. Courts may apply the laws where the contract is made or the laws where the contract is fulfilled.

Arbitration and Enforcement.   Due to the differences in international legal systems and the difficulty and length of litigating over a conflict, many international contracts rely on a prearranged system of arbitration for settling any conflict. Arbitration can be by a neutral party and both parties agree to accept any rulings.

However if one of the parties does not fulfill its contracted requirements and does not respond to or accept arbitration, the injured party can do little. There is no "international police" to force a foreign company to pay damages.

ISSUES TRANSCENDING NATIONAL BOUNDARIES

◆ ◆ ◆ ◆ ◆ ◆ ◆ ◆

In a bid to establish common product standards for quality management to obviate their misuse to hinder the exchange of goods and services worldwide, the International Standards Organization (ISO) (based in Geneva, Switzerland) has instituted a set of process standards. Firms who conform to these standards are certified and registered with it. This common standard is designated **ISO 9000.** The ISO Technical Committee on Quality Assurance and Quality Management developed the ISO 9000 series between 1979 and 1986 and published it in 1987. The series has been adopted widely by companies in the United States. The adoption of the ISO 9000 standards by member countries of the European Union has spurred companies worldwide to obtain this certification if they intend to trade with the European Union.

ISO 9000 and 14000

Another reason for this is the acknowledgment of the importance of quality by companies worldwide. It must be highlighted that ISO 9000 concerns not only standardized systems and procedures for manufacturing but also for all activities of firms. These activities include management responsibility, quality systems, contract reviews, design control, document control, purchasing, product identification and tracing, (manufacturing) process control, inspection, and testing, control of nonconforming products and necessary corrective actions, handling, storage, packaging and delivering, record keeping, internal quality audits, training, and servicing.

With the growing adoption of the ISO 9000 standards by firms worldwide, an ISO 9000 certification has become an essential marketing tool for firms. Firms that have it will be able to convince prospective buyers of their ability to maintain strict quality requirements. Firms that do not have ISO 9000 certification will increasingly be at a disadvantage relative to other competitors not only in Europe but also in most parts of the world.

Over the past decade, the need to pursue "sustainable development" has been at the center of discussion of environmental issues and economic development. Attainment of sustainable development was articulated as a goal in 1987 by the World Commission on the Environment and Development (World Commission), a body established by the United Nations. The World Commission defined *sustainable development* as development that meets the needs of the present without compromising the ability of future generations to meet their own needs. Sustainable development was the focus of discussion at the United Nations Conference on the Environment and Development held in Rio de Janeiro in 1992, and its attainment was articulated as a goal in the Environmental Side Agreement to the North American Free Trade Agreement (NAFTA). In 1996, the International Standards Organization (ISO) named the attainment of sustainable development as a major goal in its new ISO 14000 Series Environmental Management Standards. The ISO 9000 standards are forerunners to and served as models for the ISO 14000 series.

The **ISO 14000** standards are receiving significant attention from business managers and their legal and economic advise. Business managers view them as a market-driven approach to environmental protection that provides an alternative to "command and control" regulation by government. Businesses view implementation of ISO 14000 as a means to "self-regulate," thereby minimizing their exposure to surveillance and sanctions by the U.S. Environmental Protection Agency and its state-level counterparts. For example, ISO 14000 is already strengthening chemical companies' relations with plant communities by providing third-party audits of a plant's environmental systems. It is an efficient way to show the community that companies are making environmental improvements. Therefore, any person or organization interested in environmental protection or business management should become familiar with the provisions and potential ramifications of ISO 14000.[87]

Intellectual Property Protection

Few topics in international business have attracted as much attention and discussion in recent years as intellectual property rights.[88] For example, according to the Business Software Alliance, a global antipiracy watchdog group, the worldwide software industry was $90 billion in 2004, of which only $59 billion was actually paid for commercially packaged software. This amounts to $31 billion in software piracy in 2004. In percentage terms, Vietnam topped the piracy rate at 92 percent of all software used, followed by Ukraine at 91 percent, China at 90 percent, Zimbabwe at 90 percent, and Indonesia at 87 percent.[89] Piracy rates are much lower in developed countries. The United States boasts the lowest piracy rate of 22 percent; however, in dollar terms, it amounts to almost $7 billion, making it the largest amount in any country in the world.[90]

Now with the convenient online access, it is even more difficult to ensure that copyright rules are not violated in the cyberspace. Recently, "Google's books online" has been under criticism from U.S. publishing organization, which accuse it of breaching copyright laws. Google aims to put 15 million volumes online from four top U.S. libraries—the libraries of Stanford, Michigan, and Harvard Universities and of the New York Public Library by 2015. Critics worry that if the people can read a book online for free, they will not bother purchasing it. A recent court ruling clearly states that even though the copyright of music has lapsed, reproducing and distributing the music is a breach to the copyright law. According to the New York's highest court, Naxos was found to have illegally released classical recordings by Yehudi Menuhim and others because such recordings were still covered by the common law.[91]

---

[87] V. Kanti Prasad and G. M. Naidu, "Perspectives and Preparedness Regarding ISO-9000 International Quality Standards," *Journal of International Marketing*, 2 (2), 1994, pp. 81–98; and Paulette L. Stenzel, "Can the ISO 14 000 Series Environmental Management Standards Provide a Viable Alternative to Government Regulation?" *American Business Law Journal*, 37 (Winter 2000), pp. 237–98.

[88] Clifford J. Shultz III and Bill Saporito, "Protecting Intellectual Property: Strategies and Recommendations to Deter Counterfeiting and Brand Piracy in Global Markets," *Columbia Journal of World Business*, 31 (Spring 1996), pp. 19–27.

[89] "Piracy Pays," *Communications of the ACM*, August 2005, p. 10.

[90] *2004 Global Piracy Study*, Business Software Alliance, http://www.bsa.org/, accessed February 10, 2006.

[91] "Court Secures Classical Copyright," *BBC News*, http://news.bbc.co.uk/2/hi/entertainment/4 415 829.stm, April 6, 2005.

Intellectual property refers to "a broad collection of innovations relating to things such as works of authorship, inventions, trademarks, designs, and trade secrets."[92] Intellectual property rights broadly include patents, trademarks, trade secrets, and copyrights. These ideas typically involve large investments in creative and investigative work to create the product but fairly low costs of manufacturing. As such, they are amenable to being duplicated readily by imitators. Imitation reduces the potential returns that would have accrued to the innovator, thereby limiting its ability to appropriate the large investments made. With increasing movements of goods and services across borders, the potential loss of revenues to innovator firms, most of which reside in industrialized countries, is significant. According to a study by the Organization for Economic Cooperation and Development (OECD) in 1998, the global trade in counterfeit goods as a result of intellectual property infringement was estimated at US$450 billion, representing between 5 to 7 percent of the value of global trade. Apart from hurting legitimate businesses and trade, intellectual property infringement leads to the loss of government tax revenue. More concerning is the counterfeiting of medicines, which threatens public safety and health.[93] From baby powder to electronic chips, China is known as one of the largest markets for pirated products. According to the International Intellectual Property Alliance, some 90 percent of musical recordings sold in China are pirated. By no means the only big exporter of counterfeits, China in fact has started taking a tougher line on protecting intellectual property rights. For example, Japan's Honda won a case against Chongqing Lifan Industry Group selling Honda brand motorbikes,[94] and the U.S. Starbucks won a case against Shanghai Xingbake Cafe Corp. for using the name Xingbake, the Chinese name used by Starbucks.[95] In other regions, the piracy is growing, as witnessed by the 800 percent increase of counterfeit or pirated goods in the EU region from 1998 to 2002. Counterfeiting is not restricted to poor countries, either. Milan, Italy, for example, is a leading producer of counterfeit luxury products, and the U.S. state of Florida is an international haven for fake aircraft parts. Increasingly, all countries of the World Trade Organization (WTO) are required to implement **Trade Related Aspects of Intellectual Property Rights (TRIPS)** to execute intellectual property protection, and companies are joining together to fight against the violations.[96] Revisit Chapter 2 for a discussion of TRIPS.

Patent.   If granted, a patent offers a patent holder a legal monopoly status on the patented technology and/or process for a certain extended period (usually 15 to 21 years, depending on the country). Patent laws in the United States and Japan provide an example of the differences in laws across countries and their implications for corporations.[97] The most significant difference between the two countries is on the principles of **first to file** and **first to invent.** While most countries follow the first-to-file principle, only the United States (and the Philippine) follow the first-to-invent principle. In the majority of countries, the patent is granted to the first person filing an application for the patent. In the United States, however, the patent is granted to the person who first invented the product or technology. Any patent granted prior to the filing of the patent application by the "real" inventor would be reversed to protect the inventor's

[92]Subhash C. Jain, "Intellectual Property Rights and International Business," in Masaaki Kotabe and Preet S. Aukakh, eds., *Emerging Issues in International Business Research* (Northampton, MA: Edward Elgar Publishing, 2002), pp. 37–64.

[93]"Intellectual Property (IP) Crime," *Interpol,* November 12, 2005, http://www.interpol.int/Public/ FinancialCrime/IntellectualProperty/Default.asp,

[94]"Honda Wins China Copyright Ruling," *BBC News,* December 24, 2004,

[95]"Chinese Court Sides with Starbucks In Name Dispute with Chinese Rival," *Wall Street Journal Online,* http://online.wsj.com January 2, 2006.

[96]"Imitating Property Is Theft," May 15, 2003, p. 52; Quality Brands Protection Committee, Chinese Association of Enterprise with Foreign Investment, www.qbpc.org.cn/en/about/about/factsheet, accessed February 10, 2006; and http://news.bbc.co.uk/2/hi/business/4123319.stm.

[97]Masaaki Kotabe, "A Comparative Study of U.S. and Japanese Patent Systems," *Journal of International Business Studies,* 23 (First Quarter 1992), pp. 147–68.

GLOBAL PERSPECTIVE 5-3

TWO WORLDS APART: THE "FIRST-TO-INVENT" PRINCIPLE VERSUS THE "FIRST-TO-FILE" PRINCIPLE

The World Intellectual Property Organization (WIPO) convened a diplomatic conference to discuss the initial draft of patent harmonization treaty in May 2002. Most neutral observers would suggest that U.S. domestic politics is one principal impediment to the conference's success. In the United States, the *first* to *invent* wins the patent, while in the rest of the world a patent is awarded to the *first* to *file* an application. The conference examined the virtue of the U.S. "first-to-invent" principle vis-à-vis the "first-to-file" principle espoused in the rest of the world. The conference's recommendation involved changing the law to award patents to the "first to file" instead of to the "first to invent," which has guided the awarding of U.S. patents since Thomas Jefferson looked at the first ones filed in 1790.

Under current U.S. law, an individual applicant for a patent must prove that he had the idea first, not simply that he won the race to the courthouse. He can assert his priority to the invention at any time; he is entitled to a patent if thereafter he has not "suppressed, abandoned, or concealed" the invention. The U.S. system was established to protect the inventor who lacks the resources to keep up a stream of patent applications merely to invoke their priority. Not surprisingly, the system is championed today by resource-poor universities and independent inventors.

Supporters of the "first-to-file" system, largely lawyers and corporations, argue that it better serves the public because it is simpler and conforms to the systems in the rest of the world. Moreover, it would spur inventors to file for patents earlier and to disclose their inventions sooner, thus speeding the progression from idea to finished product. Many supporters also note that most U.S. companies are equipped to act on a first-to-file basis because they typically apply for patents as soon as inventions are produced. With the adoption of the first-to-file system, this date would also affect patent rights

abroad and thus provide greater security for U.S. patents worldwide.

Many are apprehensive about such a change. The principal objection to the first-to-file system is that it fosters premature, sketchy disclosure in hastily filed applications, letting the courts work things out later. Although unlikely, it leaves open the possibility of someone stealing the profits of an invention from the true inventor by beating him to the courthouse steps. In the end, the Patent Office could be deluged with applications filed for defensive purposes, as is the case in Japan where this phenomenon is called "patent flooding."

Sensitive to these criticisms, the WIPO recommended several other reforms to ensure fairness in implementing the "first-to-file" proposal. These reforms include issuing a provisional patent application at reduced cost while the patent itself is undergoing examination and establishing a grace period for public disclosure without affecting patentability. Most important the commission suggested adopting the rule of "prior-use right," allowing users of inventions to continue their use under certain conditions, even after a patent on the invention is obtained by another party.

The effect of "first to file" versus "first to invent" may be best illustrated by the case of the laser, a discovery generally credited to physicist Charles Townes, who won a Nobel Prize for elucidating the principle of the maser, the theoretical father of the laser. Townes owned the patent on the device. Years later, Gordon Gould, a former graduate student at Columbia University where Townes taught physics, proved by contemporary notebooks and other means that he had developed the idea long before Townes patented it in 1958.

Gould could not have brought his case to the courts in foreign countries that give priority to the first to file. In the United States, however, the court accepted Gould's evidence of priority and awarded him the basic patents to the laser in 1977 and 1979, ruling that Townes and his employer, at the time AT&T Co., had infringed on Gould's idea. Patlex Corp., of which Gould is a director, now collects fees from laser users throughout the world.

Source: Lee Edson, "Patent Wars," *Across the Board,* 30, April 1993, pp. 24–29; and Q. Todd Dickinson, "Harmony and Controversy," *IP Worldwide,* September 2002, pp. 22–24.

---

rights. The difference between the two principles is no small matter. See Global Perspective 5-3 for far-reaching implications.[98]

The marketing implications of this difference for U.S. and foreign companies are significant. To protect any new proprietary technologies, U.S. companies must ensure that their inventions are protected abroad through formal patent applications filed in various countries, especially the major foreign markets and the markets of competitors and potential competitors. Foreign companies operating in the United States must

---

[98]Forty-one nations, including the United States, the European Union, and Japan, reached a basic agreement to draft a treaty for standardizing the patent approval process based on the first-to-file principle in September 2006. If it goes smoothly, the treaty could be adopted as early as 2007. See "Japan, U.S., Others Agree to Craft 1st-to-File Patent Pact, "*NikkeiNet Interactive,* www.nni.nikkei.co.jp, September 26, 2006.

be extremely careful in introducing any technologies that have been invented in the United States. A first-to-file mentality could result in hasty patent applications and significant financial burden in the form of lawsuits that could be filed by competitors that claim to have invented the technology earlier.

In some extreme situations, governments have broken patent law for public health reasons. For example, Brazil's government, after signing an intellectual property protection agreement, announced in August 2001 its plans to break a patent for a drug used to treat AIDS despite the international patent held by Roche, the drug's Swiss-based pharmaceutical company. Federal officials said they were unsuccessful in talks with Roche to lower the prices the country paid for nelfinavir, a drug blocking the HIV virus from replicating itself and infecting new cells.[99] The Brazilian government is not the only one to grab a company's patent rights in the interest of public health. Scared by the anthrax outbreaks in the United States, Canada's health ministry decided that public health came first. It commissioned a generic drug company to make a million doses of ciprofloxacin, a drug used to treat one of the nastier forms of the disease whose patent belongs to German drug giant Bayer.[100]

Copyright.   Copyrights protects original literary, dramatic, musical, artistic, and certain other intellectual works. Copyright protection lasts 50 years in the European Union countries and Japan, compared with 95 years in the United States.[101] The difference in the lengths of period of copyright protection could cause tremendous price differences between countries for those products whose copyrights expired in the EU or Japan but are still effective in the United States. This issue will be discussed in detail in the "Gray Markets" section of Chapter 17.

A computer program is also considered a literary work and is protected by copyright. A **copyright** provides its owner the exclusive right to reproduce and distribute the material or perform or display it publicly, although limited reproduction of copyrighted works by others may be permitted for fair use purposes. In the United States, the use of the copyright notice does not require advance permission of or registration with the Copyright Office. In fact, many countries offer copyright protection without registration while others offer little or no protection for the works of foreign nationals.[102]

The United States passed the **Digital Millennium Copyright Act (DMCA)** in 1998 to address a growing struggle in the cyberspace between industries supplying digital content and those arguing against strict enforcement of copyright on the Internet. The DMCA bans any efforts to bypass software that protects copyrighted digital files. Other countries have passed similar laws. For example, selling "mod" (modification) chips, devices used to play illegally copied games, on a game console is a practice that has turned into a legal landmine for the video game sector. In 2004, Sony filed a lawsuit against David Ball, a British national, in Britain's High Court for selling thousands of Messiah 2 mod chips for Sony's PlayStation 2 games consoles. He also published information explaining how to install the chips in PlayStation 2 consoles. He was found guilty of violating all counts of U.K. copyright law.[103]

Trademark.   A **trademark** is a word, symbol, or device that identifies the source of goods and may serve as an index of quality. It is used primarily to differentiate or distinguish one product or service from another. Trademark laws are used to prevent others from offering a product or service with a confusingly similar mark. In the United States, registration is not mandatory because "prior use" technically determines the

---

[99]"Brazil to Break Patent, Make AIDS Drug," CNN.com, http://www.cnn.com/2001/WORLD/americas/08/23/aids.drug0730/index.html, August 23 2001.

[100]"Patent Problems Pending," *Economist,* October 27, 2001, p. 14.

[101]"Copyright Revisions Have Japan's Majors Jumping into the Vaults," *Billboard,* April 18, 1998, p. 52; and "Companies in U.S. Sing Blues As Europe Reprises 50's Hits," *New York Times,* January 3, 2003, Late Edition, p. A1.

[102]Jain, "Intellectual Property Rights and International Business," pp. 37–64.

[103]"Game Over for Mod Chip Dealer," *Managing Intellectual Property;* September 2004, pp. 113–14.

◆ ◆

𝒢LOBAL PERSPECTIVE 5-4

COULD U.S. FIRMS ALWAYS PROTECT THEIR OWN COPYRIGHT AND TRADEMARK USED BY OTHER FIRMS ABROAD? THE ANSWER IS CLEARLY NO!

Infringement of intellectual property rights is not confined to the United States. Inadequate protection of intellectual property rights in foreign countries could result in copyrights and trademarks illegally used abroad making their way back to the United States. In many industrialized countries, it is possible to stem illegally used copyrights and trademarks from entering the home country. For example, in the United States, the U.S. Customs Service provides protection to copyrights and trademarks.

Prior to receiving U.S. Customs protection, copyrights and trademarks must be registered first with the U.S. Copyright Office and the U.S. Patent and Trademark Office, respectively. Then to obtain U.S. Customs protection, each copyright and trademark must be recorded at the U.S. Customs Service Office. The fee is $190. Although there are no standard application forms, the application requirements for recording a copyright and a trademark are listed in Section 133.1–133.7 of the U.S. Customs regulations. An application should include the following information: (1) a certified status copy and five photocopies of the copyright or trademark registration, (2) the name of its legal owner, (3) the business address of the legal owner, (4) the states or countries in which the business of the legal owner is incorporated or otherwise conducted, (5) a list of the names and addresses of all foreign persons or companies authorized or licensed to use the copyright or trademark to be protected, (6) a list of the names and addresses of authorized manufacturers of goods, and (7) a list of all places in which goods using the copyright or bearing the trademark are legally manufactured. Although it is not necessary to submit a separate application to protect each copyright or trademark, the filing fee of $190 still applies to each and every copyright or trademark being recorded with the Customs Service. Additional information can be obtained by contacting the U.S. Customs Service at the Intellectual Property Rights Branch, Franklin Court, 1301 Constitution Avenue, N.W., Washington, D.C. (202-482-6960).

Unfortunately, the U.S. Patent and Trademark Office has little or no legal recourse when it comes to U.S. copyrights or trademarks used by foreign companies outside the United States. For example, in Brazil, America Online's famous "aol.com" domain is legally owned by StarMedia Network, a small Internet services company in the fast-growing Latin American market. America Online (AOL) sued StarMedia Network, alleging trademark infringement and contested the Brazilian provider's use of the domain name "aol.com.br." However, the Brazilian court ruled in May 1999 that because Brazil's America Online registered the name first, it would not have to surrender the domain name to its U.S. rival. As a result of the Brazilian court's ruling in favor of StarMedia Network, its shares rose 74 percent in its first day of trading. AOL was then forced to market its Brazilian services under "br.aol.com".

Although no other news leaked on a possible out-of-court settlement on StarMedia's "aol.com.br" versus AOL's "br.aol.com," recent news articles suggest that AOL may have eventually purchased the right to use "aol.com.br" for an undisclosed sum of money (which would not be small).

The decision could touch off concerns about international cybersquatting as many Internet dotcom companies begin to launch overseas operations only to find that a country-level version of the domain name has already been registered. For example, the AOL domain had been registered in about 60 countries in addition to Brazil, and not all of these registrations were made by the U.S. company.

Sources: Maxine Lans Retsky, "Curbing Foreign Infringement," *Marketing News,* March 31, 1997, p. 10; "Brazilian ISP Prevails in AOL Lawsuit," a news report provided by LatPro.com ejs@LatPro.com, May 31, 1999; "No Free Ride," *Latin Trade,* May 2001, p. 54; and "AOL Latin America Launches Upgraded Wireless E-Mail in Brazil, Mexico and Argentina," *World IT Report,* February 17, 2002, p. N.

---

rightful owner of a trademark. However, because determining who used the trademark prior to anyone else is difficult and subject to lawsuits, trademark registration is highly recommended. In most foreign countries, registration is mandatory for a trademark to be protected. In this sense, the legal principle that applies to trademarks is similar to the one that applies to patents: the "first-to-use" principle in the United States and the "first-to-file" principle in most other countries. Therefore, if companies are expected to do business overseas, their trademarks should be registered in every country in which protection is desired (see Global Perspective 5-4 for the extent to which U.S. firms could legally protect their own copyright and trademark used by other firms abroad).

Trade Secret. A **trade secret** is another means of protecting intellectual property and fundamentally differs from patent, copyright, and trademark in that protection is sought without registration. Therefore, it is not legally protected. However, it can be protected in the courts if the company can prove that it took all precautions to protect the idea from its competitors and that infringement occurred illegally by way of espionage or hiring employees with crucial working knowledge.

Although patent and copyright laws have been in place in many countries for well over 100 years, laws on trademarks and trade secrets are of relatively recent vintage, having been instituted in the late 19th and beginning of the 20th centuries.[104] Many international treaties help provide intellectual property protection across national boundaries when, in fact, laws are essentially national. Some of the most important treaties are the Paris Convention, Patent Cooperation Treaty, Patent Law Treaty, European Patent Convention, and Berne Convention.

International Treaties for Intellectual Property Protection

Paris Convention. The **Paris Convention** for the Protection of Industrial Property was established in 1883, and the number of signatory countries currently stands at 140. It is designed to provide "domestic" treatment to protect patent and trademark applications filed in other countries. Operationally, the convention establishes rights of priority stipulating that once an application for protection is filed in one member country, the applicant has 12 months to file in any other signatory countries, which should consider such an application as if it were filed on the same date as the original application.[105] It also means that if an applicant does not file for protection in other signatory countries within a grace period of 12 months of original filing in one country, legal protection cannot be provided. In most countries, other than the United States, the "first-to-file" principle is used for intellectual property protection. Lack of filing within a grace period in all other countries in which protection is desired could mean a loss of market opportunities to a competitor who filed for protection of either an identical or a similar type of intellectual property. The two new treaties, explained in the following sections, are additional attempts to make international patent application as easy as a domestic patent application.

Patent Cooperation Treaty. The **Patent Cooperation Treaty (PCT)** was established in 1970, amended in 1979, and modified in 1984. It is open to any signatory member country to the Paris Convention. The PCT makes it possible to seek patent protection for an invention simultaneously in each of a large number of countries by filing an "international" patent application. The patent applicant can file his or her international patent application with his national patent office, which will act as a PCT "receiving" office or with the International Bureau of World Intellectual Property Organization (WIPO) in Geneva. If the applicant is a national or resident of a contracting state that is party to the European Patent Convention, the Harare Protocol on Patents and Industrial Designs (Harare Protocol) or the Eurasian Patent Convention, the international application may also be filed with the European Patent Office (EPO), the African Regional Industrial Property Organization (ARIPO), or the Eurasian Patent Office (EAPO).[106]

Patent Law Treaty. The **Patent Law Treaty (PLT),** adopted in Geneva in June 2000, comes as the result of a WIPO initiative. Its aim is to harmonize the formal requirements set by patent offices for granting patents and to streamline the procedures for obtaining and maintaining a patent. Initially, PLT will apply to all European Union countries, the United States, Japan, Canada, and Australia. Eventually, it will include virtually all countries in the world. While the PLT is concerned only with patent formalities, many of the provisions will prove extremely useful when the PLT comes into force for a large number of states, providing speedier and less costly procedures for years to come.[107]

---

[104]Bruce A. Lehman, "Intellectual Property: America's Competitive Advantage in the 21st Century," *Columbia Journal of World Business,* 31 (Spring 1996), pp. 8–9.

[105]World Intellectual Property Organization, *Paris Convention for the Protection of Industrial Property,* http://www.wipo.int/treaties/en/ip/paris/, accessed February 20, 2006.

[106]World Intellectual Property Organization, *International Protection of Industrial Property–Patent Cooperation Treaty,* http://www.wipo.int/pct/en/treaty/about.htm, accessed February 20, 2006.

[107]Q. Todd Dickinson, "Harmony and Controversy," *IP Worldwide,* September 2002, pp. 22–24.

European Patent Convention.   The **European Patent Convention** is a treaty among 25 European countries (as of January 1, 2003) setting up a common patent office, the European Patent Office, headquartered in Munich, Germany, which examines patent applications designated for any of those countries under a common patent procedure and issues a European patent valid in all of the countries designated. The European Patent Office represents the most efficient way to obtain protection in these countries if a patent applicant desires protection in two or more of the countries. The European Patent Convention is a party to the Paris Convention and thus recognizes the filing date of an application by anyone in any signatory country as its own priority date if an application is filed within 12 months of the original filing date. The European Patent Office receives the application in English, it will be published 18 months after the filing, consistent with the "first-to-file" principle. Once a patent has been approved, registrations in and translations into the language of each designated country will be required. The European Patent Convention does not supersede any signatories' pre-existing national patent system. Patent applicants still should file and obtain separate national patents if they would prefer national treatment (favored over pan-European treatment by individual national courts).[108]

Berne Convention.   The **Berne Convention** for the Protection of Literary and Artistic Works is the oldest and most comprehensive international copyright treaty. It provides reciprocal copyright protection in each of its 15 signatory countries. Similar to the Paris Convention, it establishes the principle of national treatment and provides protection without formal registration. The United States did not join the Berne Convention until 1989.[109]

Although separate laws protect the various types of intellectual property, there appears to be a strong correlation between the levels of intellectual property in various countries. Exhibit 5-7 provides some of the results of a recently published academic study based on survey questionnaires administered to experts/practitioners in the various countries.

A feature that corporations as well as individual managers must deal with is the growing importance of intellectual property as a significant form of competitive advantage. The laws to deal with this issue are neither uniform across countries, nor do they extend across national boundaries (outside of the government pressure). Even if they are similar, the implementation levels vary significantly. Essentially, protection of intellectual property requires registration in all countries in which a firm plans to do business. Managers need to be cognizant of this and take proactive measures to counteract any infringements.

The most recent development in international copyright protection is the WIPO Copyright Treaty, which became effective in March 2002, addressing the copyright protection in the Internet era. This treaty updates and supplements the Berne Convention by protecting the rights of authors of literary and artistic works distributed within the digital environment. The treaty clarifies that the traditional right of reproduction continues to apply in the digital environment and confers a rightholder's right to control on-demand delivery of works to individuals.[110]

Antitrust Laws of the United States

The antitrust laws of the United States[111] need to be highlighted as the U.S. government makes extraterritorial applications of its antitrust laws, affecting both U.S. and foreign

---

[108]Richard Fawcett, "France and the U.K. Spearhead Reform of European Patents," *IP Worldwide,* September 2001, p. 46.

[109]Nancy R. Wesberg, "Canadian Signal Piracy Revisited in Light of United States Ratification of the Free Trade Agreement and the Berne Convention: Is This a Blueprint for Global Intellectual Property Protection?" *Syracuse Journal of International Law & Commerce,* 16 (Fall 1989), pp. 169–205.

[110]Amanda R. Evansburg, Mark J. Fiore, Brooke Welch, Lusan Chua, and Phyllis Eremitaggio, "Recent Accessions to WIPO Treaties," *Intellectual Property & Technology Law Journal,* 16 (August 2004), p. 23.

[111]This section draws from Masaaki Kotabe and Kent W. Wheiler, *Anticompetitive Practices in Japan: Their Impact on the Performance of Foreign Firms* (Westport, CT: Praeger Publishers, 1996).

EXHIBIT 5-7

RATINGS FOR THE LEVEL OF INTELLECTUAL PROPERTY PROTECTION IN
VARIOUS COUNTRIES (MINIMUM = 0, . . . 10 = MAXIMUM)

Country	Patents	Copyrights	Trademarks	Trade Secrets
Argentina	3.8	5.7	7.1	4.4
Brazil	3.3	5.2	3.3	3.3
Canada	8.1	7.7	9.0	7.8
Chile	5.7	5.7	7.6	7.8
China	2.4	2.9	6.2	3.3
Germany	8.6	8.6	9.0	10.0
India	3.3	5.7	3.8	3.3
Israel	7.1	7.1	8.6	8.9
Mexico	3.3	7.6	3.8	3.3
New Zealand	7.1	8.1	9.5	7.8
Philippines	7.1	6.2	7.6	7.8
Singapore	7.1	6.7	8.6	5.6
South Korea	3.3	4.8	3.8	3.3
Thailand	2.4	4.8	6.7	5.6
United States	9.0	8.1	9.0	7.8

Source: Adapted from Belay Seyoum, "The Impact of Intellectual Property Rights on Foreign Direct Investment," *Columbia Journal of World Business,* 31 (Spring 1996), pp. 56.

businesses in both the United States and foreign countries. The U.S. antitrust laws have their foundation in the Sherman Antitrust Act of 1890, the Clayton Act of 1914, the Federal Trade Commission Act of 1914, and the Robinson-Patman Act of 1936. U.S. antitrust laws from the beginning have been concerned with maximizing consumer welfare through the prevention of arrangements that increase market power without concurrently increasing social welfare through reduced costs or increased efficiency.

The Sherman Act specifically forbade every contract, combination, or conspiracy to restrain free and open trade, but it was soon argued that the law was intended to punish only unreasonable restraints. In the *Standard Oil* case of 1911, the courts ruled that an act must be an unreasonable restraint of trade for the Sherman Act to apply. Toward this end, a distinction developed between (1) cases in which a rule of reason should apply and (2) cases considered to be *per se* violations of the law.

The Clayton Act strengthened the U.S. antitrust arsenal by prohibiting trade practices that were not covered by the Sherman Act. It outlawed exclusive dealing and price discrimination. Both are subject to the rule of reason; that is, they are unlawful only if the effect may be to substantially lessen competition. This concept even applies to "any imaginary threat to competition, no matter how shadowy and insubstantial" as being reasonably probable of restraining trade.[112]

Concurrent with the enactment of the Clayton Act, Congress created the Federal Trade Commission (FTC) and empowered it to enjoin unfair methods of competition in commerce. Prior to the FTC, violations of antitrust laws were the jurisdiction of the Antitrust Division of the Justice Department. Since 1914, the organizations have pursued dual enforcement of the antitrust laws with considerable—some argue inefficient—overlap. The Justice Department focuses largely on criminal price-fixing and merger review. The FTC, which does not handle criminal cases, concentrates about 60 percent of its total resources on merger review.

The U.S. antitrust laws were originally aimed at domestic monopolies and cartels, although the act expressly extends coverage to commerce with foreign nations. In the 1940s, the prosecution of Alcoa (*United States vs. Aluminum Company of America,* 148 F. 2 d 416 1945) resulted in a clear extension of U.S. antitrust laws to activities of

---

[112]Robert H. Bork, *The Antitrust Paradox* (New York: Basic Books, 1978), p. 48.

foreign companies, even if those actions occur entirely outside the United States as long as they have a substantial and adverse effect on the foreign or domestic commerce and trade of the United States.

Successful extraterritorial enforcement, however, depends on effective jurisdictional reach. Detecting, proving, and punishing collusion and conspiracy to restrain trade among foreign companies are extremely difficult. From gathering evidence to carrying out retribution, the complexity of nearly every aspect of antitrust litigation is compounded when prosecuting a foreign entity. Issues of foreign sovereignty and diplomacy also complicate extraterritorial antitrust enforcement. If a foreign entity's actions are required by their own government, they are exempt from prosecution under U.S. law. Prior to the 1990s and the demise of the Soviet Union, U.S. trade and economic matters were typically a lower priority to defense and foreign policy concerns. This was particularly true with Japan. In nearly every major trade dispute over steel, textiles, televisions, semiconductors, automobiles, and so on, the Departments of State and Defense opposed and impeded retaliation against Japanese companies for violations of U.S. antitrust laws. A strong alliance with Japan and the strategic geographic military locations the alliance provided were deemed to be of more importance than unrestricted trade. This arrangement helped Japanese companies improve their competitive position.

The extraterritorial application of U.S. antitrust laws has recently been subject to considerably more debate. In 1977, the Antitrust Division of the Justice Department issued its *Antitrust Guidelines for International Operations,* which, consistent with the precedent established in the *Alcoa* case, reaffirmed that U.S. antitrust laws could be applied to an overseas transaction if there were a direct, substantial, and foreseeable effect on the commerce of the United States. The Foreign Trade Antitrust Improvements Act of 1982 again reiterated this jurisdiction. There has been controversy, however, over the degree of U.S. commerce to which jurisdiction extends.

The 1977 Justice *Guidelines* suggested that foreign anticompetitive conduct injuring U.S. commerce raises antitrust concerns when either U.S. consumers or U.S. exporters are harmed. In a 1988 revision of the *Guidelines,* the reference to exporters was omitted. Later, in 1992, U.S. Attorney General William Barr announced that Justice would take enforcement action against conduct occurring overseas if it unfairly restricts U.S. exports, arguing that anticompetitive behavior of foreign companies that inhibits U.S. exports thereby reduces the economies of scale for U.S. producers and indirectly affects U.S. consumers through higher prices than might otherwise be possible.

Critics argue that comity concerns and the difficulties in gathering evidence and building a case around conduct occurring wholly within a foreign country make it unrealistic for the Justice Department to attempt such an extraterritorial application of U.S. laws. Perhaps the gravest concern, however, is that the policy could lead to prosecution of foreign business methods that actually promote U.S. consumer welfare, for it is predominantly believed in the U.S. economic and legal community that antitrust laws should be concerned solely with protecting consumer welfare. U.S. public opinion has also traditionally and strongly supported the government's role as the champion of consumer rights against commercial interests. U.S. antitrust laws have always reflected this grassroots backing. Such a tradition has not existed in Japan, and the development of antitrust laws there has been quite different.

Fully cognizant that many small- and medium-size firms with exportable products were not currently exporting, the U.S. Congress passed the Export Trading Company legislation (ETC Act) in 1982 to encourage those firms to join forces to improve their export performance by exempting them from antitrust laws. Patterned after practices in Germany and Japan, the ETC Act also permits banks to own and operate export trading companies (ETCs) so that the export trading companies will have better access to capital resources, as well as market information through their banks.[113] As a result, the ETC Act assists in the formation of shippers' associations to reduce costs

---

[113]Charles E. Cobb, Jr., and John E. Stiner, "Export Trading Companies: Five Years of Bringing U.S. Exporters Together: The Future of the Export Trading Company Act," *Business America,* 10 (October 12, 1987), pp. 2–9.

and increase efficiency, covers technology licensing agreements with foreign firms, and facilitates contact between producers interested in exporting and organizations offering export trade services. However, those trading companies are not allowed to join forces in their importing businesses; hence, they are called *export trading companies.* In reality, many manufacturing companies import raw materials and in-process components from abroad and export finished products using those imported materials. Japanese trading companies handle both exports and imports and have many manufacturing companies as captive customers for both. In the United States, however, trading companies certified as ETCs under the ETC Act may not fully exploit economies of scale in their operation because they cannot collectively handle manufacturing firms' imports.

Antitrust Laws of the European Union

In addition to antitrust forces in the United States, other countries have organizations that settle antitrust cases. The EU is no exception. While the EU does not apply its antitrust laws extraterritorially outside the region, its laws apply not only to EU-member country companies but also foreign companies as long as their corporate action has antitrust implications within the EU community.

In 2000, the European Commission indicated that it was prepared to block the merger of EMI Group and Time Warner, Inc., unless they came up with concrete proposals to allay concerns that the size of the joint venture will allow it to limit access to its copyrights and raise prices. In September 2000, in an effort to save their proposed music join venture Warner-EMI, which would be by far the largest music publisher, the two companies submitted to the European Commission a new set of antitrust remedies involving sales of music labels and copyrights. They also offered to sell several catalogs of songs to reduce their huge market shares in music publishing.[114] Similarly, Microsoft has faced tough times in Europe although it prevailed in the United States against the government's efforts to unbundle its software code. In 2004, the European regulators forced the company to remove the Media Player software from its Windows operating system. The EU also requested the company to release more of its Windows code to competitors. Furthermore, the EU can levy fines of up to 10 percent, roughly $3.2 billion, of the company's revenue.[115]

To do business in Europe, foreign companies must comply with EU antitrust law, just as European companies must abide by U.S. antitrust law to do business in the United States. In 2001, the EU formally blocked General Electric's $43 billion purchase of Honeywell International, the first time a proposed merger between two U.S. companies has been prevented solely by European regulators. The veto by the EU's 20-member executive commission was widely expected after the U.S. companies failed to allay European fears that the deal would create an unfairly dominant position in markets for jetliner engines and avionics. The deal had already secured regulatory approval from U.S. antitrust authorities but was blocked by EU.[116]

U.S. Foreign Corrupt Practices Act of 1977

Among the many corrupt practices that international marketers face, bribery is considered the most endemic and murky aspect of conducting business abroad. However, special care must be taken to identify and accommodate the differences between international markets and those in the United States. Laws may vary widely from country to country, and these laws may on occasion conflict with one another, although international organizations such as the International Monetary Fund and the OECD have increased global efforts to combat corrupt business practices.[117] Several countries

---

[114]Philip Shishkin and Martin Peers, "EMI Group and Time Warner Submit Concessions to Allay Antitrust Worries," *Wall Street Journal,* September 20, 2000.

[115]"Microsoft Detaches Windows from Media Player in Europe," *Wall Street Journal,* January 25, 2005, p. B3.

[116]Syed Tariq Anwar, "EU's Competition Policy and the GE-Honeywell Merger Fiasco: Transatlantic Divergence and Consumer and Regulatory Issues," *Thunderbird International Business Review,* 47 (September/October 2005), pp. 601–26.

[117]Carolyn Hotchkiss, "The Sleeping Dog Stirs: New Signs of Life in Efforts to End Corruption in International Business," *Journal of Public Policy & Marketing,* 17 (Spring 1998), pp. 108–15.

in the Asia-Pacific Economic Cooperation (APEC) also joined the OECD convention criminalizing foreign commercial bribery in 1997.[118] *Bribery* is a means for one party to get from another party (at the cost of a third party) some special treatment that would otherwise not normally be obtainable. However, what constitutes bribery may also differ, depending on local customs and practices.

To create a level playing field for U.S. companies doing business abroad and to establish a high ethical standard to be followed by foreign countries, the United States passed the **Foreign Corrupt Practices Act (FCPA) of 1977** designed to prohibit the payment of any money or anything of value to a foreign official, foreign political party, or any candidate for foreign political office for purposes of obtaining, retaining, or directing business. For example, in 2005, Monsanto Chemical was fined $1.5 million for violating the FCPA by making illegal cash payment to a senior Indonesian Ministry of Environment official a few years earlier.[119] FCPA sets a high ethical standard for U.S. firms doing business abroad, but it cannot keep foreign firms from engaging in bribery and other anticompetitive acts in foreign countries, potentially giving undue competitive advantage to foreign firms over U.S. firms. However, there is no hard evidence that U.S. firms have suffered competitive loss because of the FCPA.[120]

Although silent on the subject, the FCPA does not prohibit so called facilitating or grease payments, such as small payments to lower-level officials for expediting shipments through customs or placing a transoceanic telephone call, securing required permits, or obtaining adequate police protection—transactions that simply facilitate the proper performance of duties. These small payments are considered comparable to tips left for waiters. While some companies find such payments morally objectionable and operate without paying them, other companies do not prohibit such payments but require that employees seek advice in advance from their corporate legal counsel in cases that could involve facilitating payments.[121]

The FCPA does not prohibit bribery payments to nongovernmental personnel, however. Nor does the United States have laws regulating other forms of payment that approach extortion. What constitutes bribery or extortion also becomes less transparent, and international marketers' ethical dilemma increases (see Global Perspective 5-5). From an ethical point of view, the major questions that must be answered are these:

1. Does such an act involve unfairness to anyone or violate anyone's right?

2. Must such an act be kept secret so that it cannot be reported as a business expense?

3. Is such an act truly necessary to carry on business?

Unless the answers to the first two questions is negative and the one to the third positive, such an act is generally deemed unethical.[122] It is advised that multinational firms maintain good "corporate citizenship" wherever they do business because long-term benefits tend to outweigh the short-term benefit gained from bribes for the reasons just mentioned, for example, corporate contributions to humanitarian and environmental causes, such as the Save the Rain Forest project in Brazil, and moral stands taken on oppressive governments, such as that by two European brewers, Carlsberg and Heineken in pulling out of Burma to protest this Asian country's dictatorship regime.[123]

[118]Madeleine K. Albright, "APEC: Facing the Challenge," *U.S. Department of State Dispatch,* 8 (December 1997), pp. 3–5.

[119]"Bribe Costs Monsanto $1.5 million," *Chemical & Engineering News,* January 17, 2005, p. 28.

[120]Kari Lynn Diersen, "Foreign Corrupt Practices Act," *American Criminal Law Review,* 36 (Summer 1999), pp. 753–71.

[121]Mary Jane Sheffet, "The Foreign Corrupt Practices Act and the Omnibus Trade and Competition Act of 1988: Did They Change Corporate Behavior?" *Journal of Public Policy and Marketing,* 14 (Fall 1995), pp. 290–300.

[122]Richard T. De George, *Business Ethics,* 4th ed. (Englewood Cliffs, NJ: Prentice Hall, 1995), pp. 511–12.

[123]"Brewer Decides to Pull Out of Its Business in Burma," *Wall Street Journal,* July 12, 1996, p. A8A.

*G*LOBAL PERSPECTIVE 5-5

CULTURAL RELATIVISM/ACCOMMODATION—SELLING OUT?

The following is an excerpt from an anonymous source circulating via e-mail on the Global Interact Network Mailing List GINLIST:

Cultural accommodation is an essential element in successful international and cross-cultural relationships. The question faced by the U.S. multinationals is whether to follow the advice, "When in Rome, do as the Romans do." Foreign firms operating in the U.S. are faced with a similar question, "When in America, should you do as the Americans do?" How far does an individual or a company go to accommodate cultural differences before they sell themselves out?... I will attempt to answer this question by looking at issues involving my personal core values, bribery and gift giving, and how these relate to the definitions presented. I will also discuss trust and credibility and how these qualities relate to the subject and present a case for marketplace morality. I will conclude by presenting what I feel is the answer to the question posed above.

The primary issue ... is one of cultural relativism and its place in cross-cultural encounters. Cultural relativism is a philosophical position which states that ethics is a function of culture.... Ethical relativism is the belief that nothing is objectively right or wrong, and that the definition of right or wrong depends on the prevailing view of a particular individual, culture, or historical period.

Cultural or ethical relativists will find themselves in a constant state of conflict within their own society. By definition, it would be impossible to reach an agreement on ethical rights and wrongs for the society. An ethical relativist believes that whatever an individual (any individual) believes to be right or wrong is in fact correct. The only cultural norm would be one of chaos since it would be impossible to hold anyone accountable to a prevailing or arbitrary ethos due to the accepted fact that all is relative and all is correct by definition.

As an example, imagine trying to hold Hitler's Nazi government accountable for their crimes during World War II from this perspective. If ethics is relative and that right and wrong are defined by the prevailing view of a particular individual, culture, or historical period, then Hitler's policies of racial purification were ethically correct. However, according to my ethical beliefs (and those of the world's representatives who presided over the Neurenburg Trials), that conclusion is completely unacceptable. There are some things that are moral and ethical absolutes....

As we adapt to the differences in cultures, each individual and culture must still determine where the line is (which defines) the clear violations of moral absolutes. In pursuing this objective, understanding who we are and what we stand for are essential in identifying the sell-out point. We must come to terms with our core values and how they match up with both the company ethos and that of the host and home countries....

It is interesting to note the Catch 22 that an international company can find itself in on this subject. In reference to China, if the company tries to avoid the appearance of a bribe by not participating in a culture's gift giving custom and just say "thanks," they may be seen as using the "verbal thanks as getting out of their obligation." The international manager must not only understand and respect the cultural subtleties, but know how to find the limits of the ethical behavior. One specific limit put in place by the U.S. Government is the Foreign Corrupt Practices Act (FCPA). This Act was passed in reaction to a "rash of controversial payments to foreign officials by American business in the 1970s." The Act specifically calls for "substantial fines for both corporations and individual corporate officers who engage in the bribery of foreign government officials."

U.S. firms are restricted from bribing; however, many companies in other countries engage in this practice routinely. American firms allege that restricting them from this practice puts them at a serious disadvantage to other nations' firms. In the short term, this may be true. Consider what would happen if every firm bribed. The cost of a project would be driven up so high that the country itself could no longer afford it. The bribe is not free and is always paid either by a higher contract price or through shortcuts in quality and material which may result in serious social costs. Consider a freeway overpass or a bridge not built to adequate safety standards or with poor quality materials. The result could be a collapsed bridge, resulting in loss of both life and property. The bribe also undermines the competitive process so that the purchaser pays more than the competitive price and erodes the trust in the public officials and the firm.

Is there a morality separate from the individual and from the culture?... A multinational corporation doing business in societies with differing moral norms must subscribe to a morality of the marketplace which is based on trust and credibility. Violating such norms would be self defeating. Companies engaging in business practices that result in a loss of trust or credibility will eventually lose their share of the market....

A person who approaches the world from a cultural relativist perspective will change his or her position and standards depending on the prevailing view of the culture or sub-culture that person is in. Trust and credibility can neither be built nor retained from such a position. International or domestic businessmen want to know who they are dealing with. They want to know if they can trust the person and/or company they are about to join together with....

Where is the line drawn that separates accommodation from selling out? In a large part it depends on the individual's value system, since what they're selling out on is really their own core values, trust, and credibility. There are moral absolutes, which, if violated, are always examples of stepping across the line.

Source: An anonymous source, distributed via e-mail on GINLIST, October 11, 1994.

SUMMARY

When doing business across national boundaries, international marketers almost always face what are perceived to be political and legal barriers because government policies and laws can be very different from country to country. In most cases, a foreign company must accept a host country's government policies and laws because they are usually outside its control. Some large multinational firms, if backed by their home country government, can sometimes influence the host country's policies and laws. However, such an extraterritorial interference can have negative consequences in the long run for a short-term gain.

Despite various international agreements brought about by such international organizations as the WTO, G-8, and COCOM, which collectively strive toward freer and more equitable world trade, every nation is sovereign and maintains its special interests, which can occasionally clash with those of the international agreements. Although the world has been moving toward a freer trade and investment environment, the road has not necessarily been smooth. When considering entry or market expansion in foreign countries, companies need to assess country risks. Multinational firms need to be aware of political risks arising from unstable political parties

and government structure, changes in government programs, and social pressures and special interest groups in a host country. Political risks are compounded by economic and financial risks. When disputes arise across national boundaries, they will most likely have to be settled in one country. Therefore, careful planning for establishing the jurisdictional clause in business contracts is needed before entering into the contract.

Although government policies and the laws of a country usually affect business transactions involving that country, increased business activities transcending national boundaries have tested the territoriality of some policies and laws of a country. The United States frequently applies its laws, such as antitrust laws and the Foreign Corrupt Practices Act, outside its political boundary to the extent that U.S. businesses are affected or to the extent that its legal value system can be extended. On the other hand, despite the importance of intellectual property in international business, protection of intellectual property in foreign countries is granted essentially by registration in those countries. International marketing managers should be aware that domestic protection usually cannot be extended beyond their national boundary.

KEY TERMS

Arbitration
Berne Convention
Capitalism
Civil law
COCOM (Coordinating Committee for
    Multilateral Controls)
Code (written) law
Commercial law
Common law
Communism
Confiscation
Copyright
Countertrade
Court decision
Customs
Digital Millennium Copyright Act
    (DMCA)
Domestication (phase-out) policy

Dual-party system
Embargo
European Patent Convention
Export license
Expropriation
Fast-track trade authority
First to file
First to invent
Foreign Corrupt Practices Act (FCPA)
    of 1977
G-7 (Group of 7)
G-8 (Group of 8)
Green marketing
Home country
Host country
International law
Islamic law
ISO 9000

ISO 14000
Multiple-party system
Nationalization
Nontariff barriers (NTBs)
Paris Convention
Patent Cooperation Treaty (PCT)
Patent Law Treaty (PLT)
Planned economies
Sanction
Single-party-dominant country
Socialism
Socialist law
Tariffs
Trade secret
Trademark
Trade Related Aspects of Intellectual
    Property Rights (TRIPS)
Treaty

REVIEW QUESTIONS

1. Describe with examples the role of governments in promoting national interests pertaining to business activities.

2. What different types of trade controls influence international business? What are their intended objectives?

3. How do host country macroeconomic and fiscal policies affect foreign company operations?

4. What factors should international managers consider in determining the economic and political risks associated with a country?

5. International law is derived from three sources. What are these three? Compare and contrast them.

6. Briefly describe the various types of local legal systems. How do differences in these legal systems affect international business?

7. Enumerate some of the legal issues that international business managers need to recognize in host countries.

8. Describe the various types of barriers to international trade and investment.

DISCUSSION QUESTIONS

1. The term *bribery* sounds bad. How about *kickbacks, tips, contingency fees, consultation fees,* and so on? Terms vary, objectives to be accomplished by not-so-easy-to-define payments vary, and to whom such payments are made varies. Personal income levels vary from country to country, and, thus, the level of financial incentive provided by such payments vary. As you learned in Chapter 4, cultural value systems vary; thus, the degree of legalness or social acceptability varies for payments listed earlier. In general, "facilitating" payments—legal or illegal aside—tend to be used more often in countries characterized by high levels of power distance, uncertainty avoidance, and collectivism than in other countries. As debated also in Global Perspective 5-5, could some things be moral and ethical absolutes when it comes to payment of money to someone in the third party to influence and/or facilitate business transactions in your favor? How about the U.S. standard, as stipulated in the Foreign Corrupt Practices Act of 1977? The United States is a country characterized as having low levels of power distance and uncertainty avoidance and a high level of individualism—the opposite of those countries indicated earlier. Discuss how you would like to address this issue.

2. Various foreign companies operating in Russia, especially in the oil and gas exploration business, have faced the vagaries of Russian legislation, which changes frequently, making it difficult to plan activities. Besides being heavily taxed, foreign firms have experienced a change in export duties of crude oil more than a dozen times in the past few years, yet most companies continue to negotiate for making investments worth billions of dollars. Discuss some of the possible reasons for the actions of these companies. Companies take various steps to manage political risk. If you were representing a company negotiating investments in Russia, what steps would you take to manage (and/or reduce) the political risk associated with these investments?

3. The following examples highlight the impact of differences in laws and social norms on various aspects of the marketing program. What are the implications of such differences for using standardized product or advertising strategies (or using standardized advertising themes)?

   a. Pepsi International's humorous global ad campaign fronted by model Cindy Crawford, which includes the use of a Coke can, will not be seen in Germany because German regulations forbid the use of comparative advertising.

   b. Advertising laws in China have restricted Anheuser-Busch's use of its posters featuring young attractive women in Budweiser swimsuits to bars and stores with adult clientele only. Furthermore, when Anheuser-Busch wanted models to wear swimsuits for a beer festival, the mothers of the models used insisted on the girls wearing T-shirts beneath the swimsuits.

   c. An Austin, Texas-based designer of computer games wants to market a game that involves humans fighting against aliens from different planets. One aspect of the game is that if the humans are shot, blood is shown to come out of their bodies. German laws, however, do not permit any depiction of red blood in computer games. The company wants to market this game in Germany, which is a huge market. One suggestion the company is working on is the use of an alternate color to depict human blood. However, it risks the prospect of making the game less realistic: "What would children make out of green liquid coming out of the human figure on being shot?"

4. KFC, a fast-food operator, faced immense resistance from some politically active consumer groups when it opened its operations in India. One group proclaimed that opening KFC outlets in the country would propagate a "junk-food" culture. Others proclaimed that this was "the return of imperialistic powers" and was an attempt to "Westernize the eating habits" of Indians. Overzealous local authorities in the city of Bangalore used a city law restricting the use of MSG (a food additive used in the chicken served by KFC) over a certain amount as a pretext for temporarily closing down the outlet, despite the fact that the authorities did not even have the equipment to measure the MSG content in the proportions stated in the law. In the capital city of New Delhi, a KFC outlet was temporarily closed down because the food inspector found a "house-fly" in the restaurant. While both of these issues were resolved through hectic consultations with these consumer groups and through legal orders issued protecting the interests of the outlets, they reflect how political and social concerns of even a small segment of the population can adversely affect the operations of companies in foreign markets. If you were the country manager of KFC in India, what steps would you have taken to avoid these problems?

5. The entertainment industry has been warring for years to combat computers' copying and transmit music and movies on the Internet. The biggest winner has been consumers who pay very little or nothing to get their favorite movies due largely to the Internet sector's innovations. The entertainment industry is suing individual users in more than 12,000 cases. Recently, the U.S. Supreme Court ruled in favor of copyright holders and against two companies that distribute peer-to-peer (P2P) software, which allows users to share files online with others. Tens of millions of Internet users regularly use P2P to exchange music and, to a lesser extent, films. It appears that with continuous technology introduction, free downloads will

continue to increase. The real challenge for content providers is to use new technology to create value for customers and to make those who fail to use legitimate content feel bad about it. Do you think entertainment companies should craft ways to use innovative technology to realize their wares in ways that will also allow copyrights to be protected? Because the Internet has no virtual borders, what should entertainment companies do to secure their global market, especially in those countries that have weak intellectual property protection?

6. An extension of the antitrust laws into the arena of international trade has taken the form of antidumping laws, which most Western countries have enacted and developing countries are increasingly enacting. On the surface, most of the antidumping laws across the various countries seem to be similar. However, because much of the content of these laws is open to interpretation, their results could vary significantly. The bottom line for the initiation of any antidumping investigation is that if a foreign manufacturer gets an "undue" advantage while selling its products (either through pricing its products higher in other protected markets or through government subsidies) in another country relative to the domestic manufacturer and hurts the domestic industry, the company is resorting to unfair competition and should be penalized for it. While large firms are relatively more aware of the nuances of antidumping laws and have the resources, especially legal ones, to deal with this issue, the smaller firms, that often depend on governmental export assistance in various forms are the most susceptible to it.

One of your friends is planning to start exporting an industrial product to various countries in Europe. To help finance her export endeavor, she plans to utilize concessional export credit provided by the U.S. government to small exporters. This product is highly specialized and caters to an extremely small niche in the market. Europe is a large market for this product. Only two other manufacturers, both based in Europe, make this product. One of these manufacturers is a $100-million company, which manufactures various other products besides the product in question. What would be your advice to your friend in terms of the significance of antidumping laws? What specific steps, if any, would you encourage your friend to take, especially in context of her limited financial resources?

7. Unfortunately, intellectual property law cannot protect the business everywhere. For example, the Chinese market had a flood of cheap imitations of Japanese motorcycles, and Honda Motor finally had to release a line of inexpensive 125cc motorcycles in China in 2002, even though manufacturing motorcycles at such low prices will mean a drastic change in Honda's normal policy of making high-priced, high-quality products. By some estimates, 7 million of 10 million motorcycles produced in China every year are imitations. Do you think all companies should lower their prices to protect themselves from local imitations and fake products? What suggestions would you make to a high-end brand manager if the brand is going to a developing country with less strict government controls on imitation products?

SHORT CASES

CASE 5-1

COCA-COLA IN INDIA

Coca-Cola has had a glorious past selling cola all over the world. In fact, the "Coke" brand is one of the most well-known in the world and carries with it an image of American culture. Coke's experience in the emerging Indian market has always been especially challenging, however, due to the country's protectionist political and legal environment.

Today, the Indian economy is gradually opening its doors to foreign companies in various industrial sectors. When Coke first stepped into the Indian market, it acquired a significant market share and was a popular drink in the market, but was forced to exit India in 1977 when the government at that time demanded that Coca-Cola reduce its stake in its wholly owned Indian subsidiary to 40 percent. Since then, India has revised its attitude toward foreign investment in a major way, and Coca-Cola again entered India in 1994 after staying away from this largely populated and thus attractive market for many years. This time, though, Coca-Cola fully owns its subsidiary and when it returned to the Indian market, it also acquired some local cola and soft drinks brands, including Thums Up, which had a more than 59 percent market share and a great distribution network. Coca-Cola's biggest rival, Pepsi, had already carved its niche in the market with a more than 25 percent market share.

While things went smoothly for a while after Coke's re-entry into India, it soon had run-ins with regional political bodies. Coca-Cola had set up a $12 million plant in Plachimada, a rural town in the southern state of Kerala in India in 2000. In 2004, however, the company had to shut it down, at least temporarily. The anti-Coke "Coca Cola, Quit Plachimada, Quit India" movement began in 2002 when people who were living close to the plant noticed that water in their wells was drying up or becoming polluted, acidic, and therefore not drinkable. Never having faced this water situation before, all fingers pointed toward the newly established Coke plant, which extracted considerable quantities of ground water on a daily basis for its operations. What started off as a small local protest of less than 100 people exploded into nationwide agitation. Soon, social activists and nationalists who were against foreign firms and privatization joined. Before long, the campaign against Coca-Cola had found supporters from all over the world including the United States, Sweden, and France.

The local political body in the area, known as the *Panchayat,* which had initially laid out the red carpet for the Coca-Cola plant, refused to renew the license of Hindustan Coca-Cola Beverages Private Limited in 2003. The state government also chipped in and joined the dispute. Eager to fight back, Coca-Cola approached the High Court in India, which ruled that water, being common property, could not be excessively used by one body. By 2004, the controversy had erupted to such an extent that the Kerala state government ordered the company to stop using the ground water. Shortly thereafter, Coca-Cola was forced to suspend production at the plant.

As a result of this and other incidents in India where researchers found that its beverages contained high levels of pesticides that were potentially harmful to human beings, Coca-Cola lost millions in the Indian market. In September 2003, the Joint Parliamentary Committee in India issued a legal notice to the company's headquarters in Atlanta, Georgia, asking the company to immediately suspend sales in India or it would sue the company for $10 billion for selling dangerous drinks. A similar notice was given to Pepsi. The companies were also expected to recall any already sold products. Coca-Cola overcame this particular setback eventually, but it did not make its survival in the Indian market any easier. Its new product launches in India such as vanilla-flavored Coke and its energy drink Shock proved to be debacles. However, Coca-Cola is not giving up in India this time. It is hanging on with the hope that some day it will be able to win over the world's second largest population. In the summer of 2005, Coke slashed prices of some of its products and invested in heavy marketing in India.

DISCUSSION QUESTIONS

1. What could Coca-Cola do to appease the Indian government and ensure its survival in the market?

2. What effect will this case have on Coca-Cola's operations in India?

3. What lesson does this case have for other multinationals that want to enter the Indian market?

Source: Mark Thomas, "If Water Has Become a Scarce Resource, then the Americans Will Invade Wales and the PM Will Defend Them by Insisting that Wales Could Launch a Water-Borne Chemical Attack," *New Statesman,* February 16, 2004, p. 14; and Terrence H. Witkowski, "Antiglobal Challenges to Marketing in Developing Countries: Exploring the Ideological Divide," *Journal of Public Policy & Marketing,* 24 (Spring 2005), pp. 7–23.

ASE 5-2

CAN I GET A BUD, PLEASE? WHICH BUD—CZECH OR AMERICAN?

The growing power of the European Union (EU) is proving beneficial to European firms, but it is rubbing global trade bodies and many U.S. multinational firms the wrong way. One U.S. firm that is particularly disconcerted is brewer Anheuser-Busch. The reason is the May 5, 2005, protected geographical indication (PGI) status granted to a Czech beer brand, Budweiser Budvar by the EU. The Czech Republic is one of the EU's newest members, having entered in May 2004. Anheuser-Busch claims the Czech product is making its way in international markets using Anheuser-Busch's original beer brand name Budweiser, "Bud," as it is widely known.

The EU has reserved the PGI status for products that can be identified by virtue of their place of origin and the indigenous process of manufacturing these products. A prestigious group of brands enjoys this status, including German beer product Kolsh originating in the north western part of Germany, gruyere cheese from Switzerland and the well-known cognac from France. Another category of products are assigned the title of protected designations of origin (PDO) by the EU Regulation 2081/92. Although the EU believes that this classification is necessary to protect the identity of its region's popular products, the United States and even the World Trade Organization contend that this is just one more political weapon in the hands of the often protectionist EU countries against free trade. Furthermore, compared to the other countries in the EU, the Czech Republic is much smaller in size and bargaining power within the EU. According to Regulation 2081/92, PGI products cannot be made or packaged anywhere except in their own region after which they are named. In the case of Budweiser Budvar beer, for example, it cannot be brewed or packaged anywhere except in its own specific region. If the company should decide in the future to relocate to another region, its status would likely be revoked. For example, when U.K.–based Scottish & Newcastle closed its oldest brewing plant in Newcastle due to a move to rationalize its operations, its brand name Newcastle Brown was revoked because it no longer enjoyed the PGI status.

Budejovicky Budvar (Budvar), which has brewed its beer in the Czech town of Ceske Budejovice (also known as *Budweis*) near Prague since before the beginning of the 20th century, has to be sold in the United States and some other regions outside the EU as CzechVar. Budvar claims that it has been using its brand names, including Budweiser, since times unmemorable, although Anheuser-Busch contends that it has used the same brand names since its establishment in 1876, several years before Budvar came into existence. Budvar

Source: James Curtis, "Provenance or Protectionism?" *Marketing,* May 11, 2005, p. 16; and various other sources.

argues that it has the sole right to the brand name due to the association with the region and that the EU ruling merely brings additional support for this assertion.

The two firms managed to carve out their areas in the early years of their international operation, and remain sellers in those markets, but recently, global competition increased in both technology-intensive industries and the brewing industry; hence, the firms found themselves stepping on each others' toes, thus initiating an intense struggle for market dominance. However, Anheuser-Busch's marketing issues with Budvar go back to 1906 when Budvar first entered the U.S. market and extend to 40 different countries where the two firms and their respective brands, Budvar and Anheuser-Busch's Budweiser, are embroiled in legal battles, making it a truly global marketing crusade for the same brand names: Bud and Budweiser. Although Anheuser-Busch is larger and therefore assumed to be more powerful than the smaller Czech company, it has been losing out to Budvar in many markets. Anheuser-Busch has brought action against Budvar using its trade name Budweiser in different international markets, and the Czechs are winning some of the legal cases, including one some years ago in Switzerland, where Anheuser-Busch was prevented from marketing its products under the Budweiser brand names and most recently Budvar's win in Cambodia. Budvar lost its case against Anheuser-Busch in France a few years ago. A surprising outcome of the legal case occurred in the United Kingdom where the court allowed both firms to market their products with the same brand names.

Industry experts contend that Budvar has a unique global marketing strategy in place to piggyback on the free publicity it gained by its dispute with Anheuser-Busch. The coveted PGI status will be a useful add-on to its marketing strategy because it is believed that consumers will now desire the beer for its authenticity and association with the Czech Republic and therefore perceive more value in purchasing the product. To emphasize its newly found prominence, Budvar is planning to stick blue and gold seals on its beer products its latest twist to its marketing strategy is to promote its beer as a finer quality brew based on provenance, which some believe will take it a long way in sales regardless of whether it wins in the courts or not. This contrasts with Anheuser-Busch's strategy in global markets to promote its Budweiser brands as a more familiar, general brand.

The trademark war between Budvar and Anheuser-Busch has been going on for decades, and because neither company is ready to back down, the battle will probably continue as both firms enter new markets and try to acquire market share.

DISCUSSION QUESTIONS

1. How important is it for Anheuser-Busch to market its products under their original brand names in different countries?

2. If you were asked to be the judge in this case, whom would you side with and why?

3. Because the legal battle between Anheuser Busch and Budvar seems to be never ending, how could the firms possibly settle this matter outside of court?

4. What alternative strategies could both firms adopt in foreign markets in which both of them compete?

FURTHER READING ◆

Anwar, Syed Tariq. "EU's Competition Policy and the GE-Honeywell Merger Fiasco: Transatlantic Divergence and Consumer and Regulatory Issues." *Thunderbird International Business Review,* 47 (September/October 2005), pp. 601–26.

Cragg, Wesley, and William Woof. "The U.S. Foreign Corrupt Practices Act: A Study of Its Effectiveness." *Business & Society Review,* 107 (Spring 2002), pp. 98–144.

Doh, Jonathan P., and Hildy Teegen, ed., *Globalization and NGOs: Transforming Business, Government, and Society.* Westport, CT: Praeger, 2003.

Duina, Francesco G. *Harmonizing Europe: Nation-States within the Common Market.* Albany, NY: State University of New York Press, 1999.

Hoffmann, Stanley. "Clash of Globalizations." *Foreign Affairs,* 81 (July/August 2002), pp. 104–15.

Gillespie, Kate. "Smuggling and the Global Firm." *Journal of International Management,* 9 (3), 2003, pp. 317–33.

Gillespie, Kate, Kishore Krishna, and Susan Jarvis. "Protecting Global Brands: Toward a Global Norm." *Journal of International Marketing,* 10 (Issue 2002), pp. 99–12.

Kotabe, Masaaki. "Special Issue: Global Security Risks and International Competitiveness." *Journal of International Management,* 11 (December 2005).

Naidu, G. M., V. Kanti Prasad, and Arno Kleimenhagen. "Purchasing's Preparedness for ISO 9000 International Quality Standards." *International Journal of Purchasing & Materials Management,* 32 (Fall 1996), pp. 46–53.

Redding, Gordon. "The Thick Description and Comparison of Societal Systems of Capitalism." *Journal of International Business Studies,* 36 (March 2005), pp. 123–55.

Rugman, Alan, John Kirton, and Julie Soloway. *Environmental Regulations and Corporate Strategy: A NAFTA Perspective.* Oxford, England: Oxford University Press, 1999.

Witkowski, Terrence H. "Antiglobal Challenges to Marketing in Developing Countries: Exploring the Ideological Divide," *Journal of Public Policy & Marketing,* 24 (Spring 2005), pp. 7–23.

GLOBAL MARKETING RESEARCH

HAPTER OVERVIEW

1. RESEARCH PROBLEM FORMULATION

2. SECONDARY GLOBAL MARKETING RESEARCH

3. PRIMARY GLOBAL MARKETING RESEARCH

4. MARKET SIZE ASSESSMENT

5. NEW MARKET INFORMATION TECHNOLOGIES

6. MANAGEMENT OF GLOBAL MARKETING RESEARCH

Given the complexity of the global market place, solid marketing research is critical for a host of global marketing decisions. Skipping the research phase in the international marketing decision process can often prove a costly mistake. The following anecdotes illustrate that even marketing behemoths such as Wal-Mart and Procter & Gamble sometimes fail to live up to the "Test, Test, Test" maxim:

• When Wal-Mart first entered the Argentine market, its meat counters featured T-bone steaks, not the rib strips and tail rumps that Argentines prefer. Its jewelry counters were filled with emeralds, sapphires, and diamonds. Argentine women, however, prefer wearing gold and silver. The hardware departments had tools and appliances for 110-volt electric power while the standard throughout Argentina is 220-volt.[1]

• In Japan, Procter & Gamble stumbled into a cultural minefield by showing a Camay commercial that featured a man walking into the bathroom while his spouse was taking a bath. This spot raised eyebrows in Japan where a husband is not supposed to impose on his wife's privacy in the bathroom. A Japanese ad campaign for its all-temperature Cheer laundry detergent brand mistakenly assumed that Japanese housewives wash clothes in different temperatures. Japanese women do their laundry in tap water or leftover bath water.[2]

• In China, Toyota was forced to withdraw an ad showing Chinese stone lions bowing in respect to a Prado Land Cruiser sport-utility vehicle. The ad campaign was intended

---

[1] "Wal-Mart Learns a Hard Lesson," *International Herald Tribune,* December 6, 1999, p. 15.
[2] Alecia Swasy, *Soap Opera: The Inside Story of Procter & Gamble* (New York: Random House, 1993), p. 268.

to reflect Prado's imposing presence when driving in the city, but it struck a historic nerve for some Chinese consumers. Some consumer critics pointed out the close resemblance of the lions with those flanking the Marco Polo bridge, the site near Beijing of the opening battle in Japan's 1937 invasion of China.[3]

Most of such cultural blunders stem from inadequate marketing research. Market research assists the global marketing manager in two ways: (1) to make better decisions that recognize cross-country similarities and differences and (2) to gain support from the local subsidiaries for proposed marketing decisions.[4]

To some degree, the procedures and methods that are followed in conducting global marketing research are close to those used in standard domestic research. Most of the marketing research tricks of the trade available for the domestic market scene (e.g., questionnaire design, focus group research, multivariate techniques such as cluster analysis, conjoint measurement) can be employed fruitfully in the global marketplace. Also, the typical sequence of a multicountry market research process follows the familiar pattern used in domestic marketing research. In particular, these are the steps to be followed to conduct global market research:

1. Define the research problem(s).

2. Develop a research design.

3. Determine information needs.

4. Collect the data (secondary and primary).

5. Analyze the data and interpret the results.

6. Report and present the findings of the study.

A typical example of a multicountry market research project is summarized in Exhibit 6-1. At each of these six steps, special problems may arise when the research

EXHIBIT 6-1
A MULTICOUNTRY MARKETING RESEARCH PROJECT AT ELI LILLY:
ESTIMATING THE MARKET POTENTIAL FOR A PRESCRIPTION WEIGHT
LOSS PRODUCT

- **Research Problem**

  Estimate the dollar potential for a prescription weight loss product in the United Kingdom, Spain, Italy, and Germany.

- **Research Hypothesis**

  Patients would be willing to pay a premium price for the product even without reimbursement by the government.

- **Secondary Data Research**

  – Market share of a similar product (Isomeride).
  – Incidence of overweight and obesity in Europe.*

- **Primary Data Research**

  – Sample size: 350 physicians from the United Kingdom, Italy, Spain and Germany
  – Sampling procedure: random selection from a high prescribers doctor list based on company data
  – Data collected:

  (1) Diary kept by physicians for 2 weeks.
  (2) Questionnaires completed by patients who were judged to be prospects for the product by physician.
  (3) Pricing study done based on 30 additional phone interviews with physicians in the United Kingdom, Italy, and Spain to measure price sensitivity.

*Source: Based on William V. Lawson, "The "Heavy-weights"—Forecasting the Obesity Market in Europe for a New Compound," *Marketing and Research Today,* November 1995, pp. 270–74

---

[3]"Cultural Pitfalls Tarnish Some Ads in China," *Asian Wall Street Journal,* January 19, 2004, p. A8.
[4]Kamran Kashani, "Beware the Pitfalls of Global Marketing," *Harvard Business Review,* September–October 1989, p. 97.

activity takes place in foreign markets. The major challenges that global marketing researchers need to confront follow.

1. Complexity of research design due to environmental differences.
2. Lack and inaccuracy of secondary data.
3. Time and cost requirements to collect primary data.
4. Coordination of multicountry research efforts.
5. Difficulty in establishing comparability across multicountry studies.[5]

In this chapter, you will learn about the major issues that complicate cross-country research. We also suggest ways to cope with these roadblocks. We then describe several techniques that are useful for market demand assessment. During the last two decades, new market information technologies have emerged. We discuss the impact of these technological advances on marketing research. Finally, we consider several issues that concern the management of global market research.

◆ ◆ ◆ ◆ ◆ ◆ ◆ ◆ ◆   RESEARCH PROBLEM FORMULATION

Any research begins with a precise definition of the research problem(s) to be addressed. The cliché of a well-defined problem being a half-solved problem definitely applies in a global setting. Fancy data analysis tools will not compensate for incorrect problem definitions. Once the nature of the research problem becomes clear, it needs to be translated in specific research questions. The scope of market research questions extends to both strategic and tactical marketing decisions. For example, a product-positioning study carried out for BMW in the European market centered around the following three issues:

1. What does the motorist in the country concerned demand of his/her car?
2. What does s/he believe s/he is getting from various brands?
3. What does that imply with regard to positioning the BMW brand across borders?[6]

In an international context, the marketing research problem formulation is hindered by the self-reference criterion, that is, people's habit to fall back on their own cultural norms and values (see Chapter 4). This tendency could lead to incorrect or narrow problem definitions. In a multicountry research process, the self-reference criterion also makes finding a consensus between headquarters and local staff an immensely formidable task. To avoid such mishaps, market researchers must try to view the research problem from the cultural perspective of the foreign players and isolate the influence of the self-reference criterion. At any rate, local subsidiaries should be consulted at every step of the research process if the study will affect their operations, including the first step of the problem definition.

A major difficulty in formulating the research problem is the lack of familiarity with the foreign environment. This can lead to making false assumptions, misdefining research problems, and, ultimately, making misleading conclusions about the foreign markets. To reduce part of the uncertainty, some exploratory research at the early stage of the research process is often very fruitful. A useful vehicle for such preliminary research is an **omnibus survey.**[7] Omnibus surveys are regularly scheduled surveys

---

[5]Susan P. Douglas and C. Samuel Craig, *International Marketing Research,* Englewood Cliffs, NJ: Prentice-Hall, 1983.

[6]Horst Kern, Hans-Christian Wagner, and Roswitha Hassis, "European Aspects of a Global Brand: The BMW Case," *Marketing and Research Today,* February 1990, pp. 47–57.

[7]David A. Aaker, V. Kumar, and George S. Day, *Marketing Research* (New York: John Wiley & Sons, Inc., 1998), p. 237.

conducted by research agencies (e.g., ACNielsen) with questions from different clients. The surveys are administered to a very large sample of consumers, usually a panel created by the agency. The questionnaire contains a plethora of questions on a variety of topics. In most cases, clients are able to incorporate their own proprietary questions. The prime benefit of an omnibus survey is cost because the subscribers to the survey share the expenses. Another selling point is speed; results are quickly available. A major disadvantage is that only a limited amount of company-relevant information is obtainable through an omnibus. Also, the panel is usually not representative of the firm's target market profile.

Still, an omnibus survey is probably the most economical way to gather preliminary information on target markets. An omnibus is particularly suitable when you need to ask a few simple questions across a large sample of respondents. Findings from an omnibus can assist managers and researchers in fine-tuning the research problem(s) to be addressed. An omnibus is also an option to gauge the market potential for your product in the foreign market when you have only a limited budget. Omnibuses conducted on a regular basis can also be useful as a tracking tool to spot changes in consumer attitudes or behaviors. Exhibit 6-2 presents the key features of ACNielsen's China omnibus.

EXHIBIT 6-2
ACNIELSEN'S CHINA OMNIBUS

Geographical Coverage
  (a) Key cities: Guangzhou, Shanghai, Beijing
  (b) 7 other cities: Chengdu, Fuzhou, Hangzhou, Nanjing, Shenyang, Tianjin, Wuhan
Timing
  Four rounds
Sample Size
  500 interviews in each city
Sampling Procedure
  Random probability sampling with face-to-face interviews
Target Respondents
  Individuals aged 9+
Deliverables

  – Self-explanatory charts and computer tables.

  – Demographics (including, gender, age, education, marital data, household size, household purchase decision maker, household head, occupation, nature of work unit, monthly household income) tabulated against proprietary questions.

Examples of Omnibus Questions

  – Do you use X?

  – How often do you use X?

  – What do you like/dislike about X?

  – How much did you pay for X?

  – Have you seen any ad for Y?

Cost
  Total cost depends on:

  (a) Number of questions

  (b) Nature of question: open-ended versus close-ended

  (c) Sample size

  (d) Number of cities

Fee per person is US\$1.00 or less (sample size) with setup cost of US\$2,000 for any project under US\$10,000. For instance, a project covering two cities and a sample size of 1000 subjects will cost US\$3,000.

Source: Based on information provided by ACNielsen China

Once the research issues have been stated, management needs to determine the information needs. Some of the information will be readily available within the company or in publicly available sources. Other information will need to be collected from scratch.

◆ ◆ ◆ ◆ ◆ ◆ ◆ ◆   SECONDARY GLOBAL MARKETING RESEARCH

Assessing the information needs is the next step after the research problem definition. Some pieces of information will already be available. That type of information is referred to as **secondary data.** When the information is not useful, or simply does not exist, the firm will need to collect the data. **Primary data** are data collected specifically for the purpose of the research study. Researchers will first explore secondary data resources because that type of information is usually much cheaper and less time consuming to gather than primary data. Both forms of data collection entail numerous issues in an international marketing setting. We first discuss the major problems concerning secondary data research.

Secondary Data Sources

Market researchers in developed countries have access to a wealth of data that are gathered by government and private agencies. Unfortunately, the equivalents of such databases often are missing outside the developed world. Even when the information is available, it may be difficult to track down. A starting point for data collection is the World Wide Web or a computerized service such as Lexis/Nexis that provides real-time online access to information resources based on user-provided keywords. Exhibit 6-3 shows the wide variety of secondary data resources available to global market researchers. Also, a wealth of international business resources can be accessed via the Internet. One of the most comprehensive resources is the National Trade Data Bank (NTDB), maintained by the U.S. Department of Commerce (http://www.stat-usa.gov).[8] The NTDB includes market research reports, information on export opportunities, how-to-market guides, and so forth. One of the nice features is a search engine that allows users to retrieve any information that is available on the NTDB for a given topic. Another valuable online resource is the Global Resources Directory maintained at the Global Edge site (http://globaledge.msu.edu/ibrd/ibrd.asp) maintained by Michigan State University. This online resource is an extremely well-organized directory that provides linkages to hundreds of on-line international business resources on the Internet.

Obviously, researchers can also tap information resources available within the company. Many companies have their own libraries that provide valuable data sources. Large companies typically compile enormous databanks on their operations. Government publications sometimes offer information on overseas markets. In the United States, the U.S. Department of Commerce offers detailed country reports and industry surveys. Many countries have a network of government-sponsored commercial delegations (e.g., Chambers of Commerce, the Japanese External Trade Organization [JETRO], www.jetro.go.jp). These agencies often provide valuable information to firms that desire to do business in their country despite the fact that the main charter of most of these agencies is to assist domestic companies in the foreign market.

Besides government offices, international agencies such as the World Bank, the Organization for Economic Cooperation and Development (OECD), the International Monetary Fund (IMF), and the United Nations gather a humongous amount of data. Reports published by these organizations are especially useful for demographic and economic information. Given that most of these documents report information across multiple years, their data can be used to examine trends in socioeconomic indicators. Unfortunately, reports published by such international agencies cover only their member states.

---

[8]The National Trade Data Bank information is also available on CD-ROM.

EXHIBIT 6-3
RESOURCES FOR SECONDARY DATA

International Trade

- *Yearbook of International Trade Statistics* (United Nations)
- *US Imports* (U.S. Bureau of the Census)
- *US Exports* (U.S. Bureau of the Census)
- *Exporters' Encyclopaedia* (Dun and Bradstreet)

Country Information (Socioeconomic & Political Conditions)

- *Yearbook of Industrial Statistics* (United Nations)
- *Statistical Yearbook* (United Nations; Updated by *Monthly Bulletin of Statistics*)
- *OECD Economic Survey*
- *The World Competitiveness Yearbook* (IMD)
- *Country Reports* (The Economist Intelligence Unit)
- *Demographic Yearbook* (United Nations)
- *Statistical Yearbook* (United Nations)
- *UNESCO Statistical Yearbook*
- *CIA World Fact Book* (www.cia.gov/cia/publications/factbook)

International Marketing

- Euromonitor publications (www.euromonitor.com): *European Marketing Data and Statistics, International Marketing Data and Statistics, Consumer Europe*, and *European Advertising Marketing and Media Data*
- *Advertising Age* (www.adage.com)
- *FINDEX: The Worldwide Directory of Market Research Reports, Studies & Surveys* (Cambridge Information Group Directories)

Chambers of Commerce

- See http://www.worldchambers.com/chambers.html

Directories of Foreign Firms

- *D & B Europa* (Dun & Bradstreet)
- *Directory of American Firms Operating in Foreign Countries* (World Trade Academy Press)
- *Directory of Foreign Firms Operating in the United States* (World Trade Academy Press)
- *Europe's 15,000 Largest Companies* (E L C Publishing)
- *International Directory of Importers: Europe* (Interdata)
- *Mailing Lists of Worldwide Importing Firms* (Interdata)
- *Moody's International Manual* (Moody's Investors Service)
- *Principal International Businesses; The World Marketing Directory* (Dun & Bradstreet)

Several companies specialize in producing business-related information. Such information is usually far more expensive than government-based data. However, this type of information often has more direct relevance for companies. Two prominent examples are The Economist Intelligence Unit (E.I.U.) and Euromonitor. Among the most useful resources put together by the E.I.U. are the country reports that appear on a quarterly basis. These country reports give a detailed update on the major political and economic trends in the countries covered. Euromonitor has several publications that are extremely useful to global marketers. Two well-known reports are *European Marketing Data and Statistics* and *International Marketing Data and Statistics,* annual volumes covering Europe and the global marketplace outside Europe, respectively. Euromonitor's databases are also accessible online on a subscription basis (www.euromonitor.com).

More recent forms of secondary data sources are syndicated data sets sold by market research companies such as ACNielsen (www.acnielsen.com) and TNS (www .tns-global.com). These firms acquire data sets that cover purchase transactions from retail outlets whose cash registers are equipped with optical scanning equipment. Until about a decade ago, such data sources were only available in the United States. Optical scanners are now well entrenched in most developed countries. GfK, ACNielsen, and TNS, the giants in the syndicated market research data business, all have a global presence now.

As firms move from government publications to syndicated data, the richness of the information increases enormously. At the same time, the cost of collecting and processing data goes up. Just as in a domestic marketing context, firms planning research in the global market place must decide on the value added of additional information and make the appropriate tradeoffs.

Problems with Secondary Data Research

In the global market scene, some of the information sought by market researchers does not exist. When data are missing, the researcher needs to infer the data by using proxy variables or values from previous periods. Even if the data sets are complete, the researcher will usually encounter many problems such as those discussed below in the following sections.

Accuracy of Data. The accuracy of secondary data is often questionable, for various reasons. The definition used for certain indicators often differs across countries. The quality of information can also be compromised by the mechanisms that were used to collect it. Most developed countries use sophisticated procedures to assemble data. Due to the lack of resources and skills, many developing countries rely on rather primitive mechanisms to collect data. The purpose for which the data were collected could affect their accuracy. International trade statistics do not cover cross-border smuggling activities. Such transactions are, in some cases, far more significant than legitimate trade.

Age of Data. The desired information may be available but outdated. Many countries collect economic activity information on a far less frequent basis than the United States does. The frequency of census taking also varies from country to country. In the United States, a census is taken once every decade. In many emerging markets, census taking seldom takes place.

Reliability over Time. Often companies are interested in historical patterns of certain variables to spot underlying trends. Such trends might indicate whether a market opportunity opens up or whether a market is becoming saturated. To study trends, the researcher must know to what degree the data are measured consistently over time. Sudden changes in the definition of economic indicators are not uncommon. Juggling with economic variable measures is especially likely for variables that have political ramifications, such as unemployment and inflation statistics. For instance, government authorities could adjust the basket of goods used to measure inflation to produce more favorable numbers. Market researchers should be aware of such practices and, if necessary, make the appropriate corrections.

Comparability of Data. Cross-country research often demands a comparison of indicators across countries. Different sources on a given item often produce contradictory information. The issue then is how to reconcile these differences. One way to handle contradictory information is to **triangulate,** that is, to obtain information on the same item from at least three different sources and speculate on possible reasons behind these differences.[9] For instance, suppose you want to collect information on the

---

[9]S.C. Williams, "Researching Markets in Japan—A Methodological Case Study," *Journal of International Marketing*, 4 (2), 1996, pp. 87–93.

import penetration of wine as a percentage of total consumption in various European countries. Triangulation might show that some of the figures you collected are based on value while others are based on volume. It might also reveal that some sources include champagne but others do not.

Comparability can also be hindered by the lack of functional or **conceptual equivalence**.[10] **Functional equivalence** refers to the degree to which similar activities or products in different countries fulfill similar functions. Many products perform very different functions in different markets. In the United States, bicycles are primarily used for leisure. In countries such as the Netherlands and China, bicycles are a major means of transportation. Absence of conceptual equivalence is another factor that undermines comparability. **Conceptual equivalence** reflects the degree to which a given concept has the same meaning in different environments. Many concepts have totally different meanings or simply do not exist in certain countries. The concept of "equal rights" for women is unfamiliar in many Muslim societies. Likewise, the notion of "intellectual property" is often hard to grasp in some cultures. Often, what one culture sees as obvious the other does not.

The comparison of money-based indicators (e.g., income figures, consumer expenditures, trade statistics) is hampered by the need to convert such figures into a common currency. The key issues are what currency to use and at what exchange rate (beginning of the year, year-end, or year average). A further complication is that exchange rates do not always reflect the relative buying power between countries. As a result, comparing economic indicators using market exchange rates can be very misleading.

Lumping of Data.   Official data sources often group statistics on certain variables in very broad categories. This compromises the usefulness and the interpretation of such data for international market researchers. Managers should check what is included in certain categories.[11]

Given the hurdles posed by secondary data, it is important to verify the quality of collected information. To assess the quality of data, the researcher should seek answers to the following list:

1. When were the data collected? Over what time frame?
2. How were the data collected?
3. Have the variables been redefined over time?
4. Who collected the data?
5. For what purpose were the data gathered?

Of course, satisfactory answers to each of these questions does not ensure total peace of mind. Researchers and managers should always be on guard regarding the quality of secondary data.

PRIMARY GLOBAL MARKETING RESEARCH   ◆ ◆ ◆ ◆ ◆ ◆ ◆ ◆

Seldom do secondary data prove satisfactory for market research studies. The next step in the research process is to collect primary data specifically for the purpose of the particular research project. Primary data can be collected in several ways: (1) focus groups, (2) survey research, and (3) test markets. In this section, we concentrate on focus group and survey research. Test marketing is discussed in Chapter 11 on global new product development. Global Perspective 6-1 shows the important role of primary market research for multinational companies such as L'Oréal.

---

[10]Michael R. Mullen, "Diagnosing Measurement Equivalence in Cross-National Research," *Journal of International Business Studies,* 26 (3), 1995, pp. 573–96.
[11]S.C. Williams, "Researching Markets in Japan," p. 90.

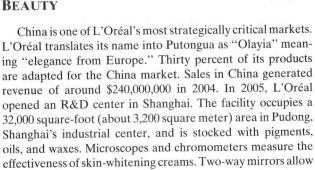

GLOBAL PERSPECTIVE 6-1

GLOBAL MARKET RESEARCH IN THE WORLD OF BEAUTY

Research is an essential weapon in the global cosmetics and grooming market, worth around $231 billion in 2005. L'Oréal, a leading French cosmetics maker, spent €507 million (US$608 million) on research in 2005, more than 3 percent of its sales revenues. The company has a network of 14 research centers spanning the globe. In 2003, the company opened a multimillion dollar R&D lab in Chicago. The Chicago facility boasts being the first lab that focuses on the beauty needs of people of color.

Differences clearly exist in the world of beauty. In Japan, women apply mascara with an average of 100 brush strokes, compared to 50 strokes for European women. South Korean women use no less than 9 to 12 products for their morning grooming routine. In France, L'Oréal researchers created an "atlas for the human hair" based on a study of the hair of test subjects from the Paris region and Chinese cities. Differences between ethnic groups were found in hair growth rates, development of grayness, and hair density.

China is one of L'Oréal's most strategically critical markets. L'Oréal translates its name into Putongua as "Olayia" meaning "elegance from Europe." Thirty percent of its products are adapted for the China market. Sales in China generated revenue of around $240,000,000 in 2004. In 2005, L'Oréal opened an R&D center in Shanghai. The facility occupies a 32,000 square-foot (about 3,200 square meter) area in Pudong, Shanghai's industrial center, and is stocked with pigments, oils, and waxes. Microscopes and chromometers measure the effectiveness of skin-whitening creams. Two-way mirrors allow researchers to observe the way Chinese women apply makeup. The lab also tests the effectiveness of Chinese herbs, roots, and flowers for the skin and hair.

Each year, L'Oréal interviews 35,000 women in China to learn about their tastes. Its researchers discovered a Shanghai woman whose hair is four meters (13 feet) long. The subject is now under contract as a test case to study the impact of aging on hair fiber. L'Oréal researchers also make house calls to get a picture of Chinese women's grooming habits. From these home visits, L'Oréal found out that many Chinese wash themselves and shampoo over a bowl of water to conserve water in places with water supply shortages. Spurred by this finding, L'Oréal developed a new shampoo that allows easy suds rinsing.

Sources: www.loreal.com accessed February 18, 2006; "The World of Beauty: Skin Deep, But So Very Personal," *International Herald Tribune*, February 4–5, 2006, pp. 13–14; "Battle for the Face of China," *Fortune*, December 12, 2005, pp. 156–162.

Focus Groups Before embarking on large-scale quantitative market research projects, most firms conduct exploratory research. One of the most popular tools at this stage is the focus group. A *focus group* is a loosely structured free-flowing discussion among a small group (8 to 12 people) of target customers facilitated by a professional moderator. These groups can be used for many different purposes: to generate information to guide the quantitative research projects, to reveal new product opportunities, to test new product concepts, and so forth.

The rules for designing and running focus groups in a domestic marketing setting also apply to global market research projects.[12] Hiring well-trained moderators is critical in conducting focus groups for international market research. Moderators should be familiar with the local language and social interaction patterns. Cultural sensitivity is an absolute must with these focus groups. For instance, Japanese consumers tend to be much more hesitant to criticize new product ideas than their Western counterparts.[13] Also, many Asian societies such as Japan are highly collective ("Confucian"). Strangers outside the group are excluded. As a result, getting the desired group dynamics for focus groups within such cultures is often very difficult. To stimulate group dynamics, the following steps should be taken:

- Be precise in recruitment to ensure group homogeneity and ease of bonding.
- Hire moderators who are able to develop group dynamics quickly through warm-ups, humor, and role-playing.

---

[12]See, for example, Thomas C. Kinnear and James R. Taylor, *Marketing Research* (New York: McGraw-Hill, Inc., 1996), Chapter 10.

[13]David B. Montgomery, "Understanding the Japanese as Customers, Competitors, and Collaborators," *Japan and the World Economy*, 3 (1), 1991, pp. 61–91.

- Hire moderators who can spot and challenge "consensus"-claimed behaviors and attitudes.[14]

When analyzing and interpreting focus group findings, market researchers should also concentrate on the nonverbal cues (e.g., gestures, voice intonations).[15] Information provided by these nonverbal cues is often as important as the verbal content of the focus groups.

Questionnaires are the most common vehicle for gathering primary data in marketing research. Survey research begins with the design of a questionnaire. The next step is to develop a sampling plan to collect the data. Once these two tasks have been accomplished, the researcher moves to the next phase, the physical collection of responses to the questionnaires. Each stage may lead to major headaches.

Survey Methods for Cross-Cultural Marketing Research

Questionnaire Design. By far the most popular instrument to gather primary data is the questionnaire. Preparing questionnaires for global market research poses tremendous challenges. As in domestic marketing, care should be exercised with the wording and the sequencing of the questions. With multicountry projects, further care is needed to ensure comparability of survey-based results across borders. Measurement issues in cross-country research center around this question: Are the phenomena in countries A and B measured in the same way? Absence of measurement equivalence renders cross-country comparisons meaningless. Earlier we discussed the need for conceptual and functional equivalence of secondary data. The same requirements apply to primary data to avoid cultural biases. Cross-country survey research needs to fulfill two further criteria: **translation** and **scalar equivalence.**

The first aspect deals with the translation of the instrument from one language into another one. Cross-cultural research, even within the same country or parent language (e.g., English, Spanish), demands adequate translations from the master questionnaire into other languages. Careless translations of questionnaires can lead to embarrassing mistakes. Good translations are hard to accomplish. Several methods exist to minimize translation errors. Two procedures often used in practice to avoid sloppy translations are back-translation and parallel translation. **Back translation** is a two-phase process. Suppose a company wants to translate a questionnaire from English into Arabic. In the first step, the master questionnaire is translated into Arabic by a (bilingual) translator whose native language is Arabic, the target language. In the second stage, the Arabic version is translated back into English by another bilingual interpreter whose native language is English, the base language. This version is then compared with the original questionnaire to uncover any bugs or translation errors. The process is repeated until an acceptable degree of convergence is achieved. **Parallel translation** consists of using multiple interpreters who translate the same questionnaire independently. Alternative versions are compared by a committee of translators and differences are reconciled.

Most surveys typically have a battery of questions or "Agree/Disagree" statements with a scale (e.g., 7 point) to record responses. To make the findings of cross-country market research projects meaningful, it is paramount to pursue **scalar equivalence:** scores from subjects of different countries should have the same meaning and interpretation.[16] The standard format of scales used in survey research differs across countries. Keep in mind that high scores in one country are not necessarily high scores elsewhere. Latin Americans, for example, tend to use the high end of the scale. An unenthusiastic respondent may still give your company a 7 or an 8 score. Asians, on the other hand, tend to use the middle of the scale.[17]

---

[14]Chris Robinson, "Asian Culture: The Marketing Consequences," *Journal of the Market Research Society,* 38 (1), 1996, pp. 55–62.

[15]Naresh K. Malhotra, James Agarwal, and Mark Peterson, "Methodological Issues in Cross-Cultural Marketing Research. A State-of-the-Art Review," *International Marketing Review,* 13, (5), 1996, pp. 7–43.

[16]Malhotra et al., "Methodological Issues, p. 15.

[17]Jennifer Mitchell, "Reaching across Borders," *Marketing News,* May 10, 1999, p. 19.

EXHIBIT 6-4
THE FUNNY FACES
SCALE

Very happy

Happy

Not happy
but also
not unhappy

Unhappy

Very unhappy

Source: C. K. Corder, "Problems and Pit-falls in Conducting Marketing Research in Africa," in Betsy Gelb, ed., *Marketing Expansion in a Shrinking World,* Proceedings of American Marketing Association Business Conference (Chicago: AMA, 1978), pp. 86–90.

In some cases, you may also need to adjust the anchors of the scale. One recent study that measured attitudes of Japanese managers adopted scales that included "definitely true," "somewhat true," and "not all true" because pretest of the survey showed that the Japanese respondents had trouble with the concept of "agree/disagree."[18] To make cross-country comparisons meaningful, it is advisable to adjust responses in each country by, for instance, taking deviations from country averages on any given question. By the same token, in some societies people are cued to view "1" as best and the other endpoint of the scale as worst, while in others "1" is considered the worst, regardless of how the scale is designated.

Survey research in developing nations is further compounded by low levels of education. Specially designed visual scales like the Funny Faces scale (see Exhibit 6-4) are sometimes used to cope with illiteracy. In developing countries, market researchers should also try to reduce the verbal content and use visual aids. In countries that are unfamiliar with survey research, it is advisable to avoid lengthy questionnaires or open-ended questions.[19]

Regardless of whether the survey is to be administered in Paris, Texas, or Paris, France, it is absolutely imperative to pretest the questionnaire. Pretesting is the only foolproof way to debug the survey and spot embarrassing and often expensive mistakes. Speed is often critical when collecting data. However, rushing into the field without a thorough pretest of the questionnaire is a highly risky endeavor.

Sampling Plan. To collect data, the researcher has to draw a sample from the target population. A sampling plan basically centers around three issues:

1. Whom should be surveyed? What is our target population (**sampling unit**)?

2. How many people should be surveyed (**sample size**)?

3. How should prospective respondents be chosen from the target population (**sampling procedure**)?[20]

Decisions on each of these issues are determined by balancing costs, desired reliability, and time requirements. In multicountry research, firms also need to decide what countries should be researched. There are two broad approaches. The first approach begins with a large-scale exploratory research project covering many countries. This step might take the form of an omnibus survey. The alternative approach focuses on a few key countries. To choose these countries, a firm might group countries (e.g., along sociocultural indicators) and pick one or two representative members from each cluster. Depending on the findings coming from this first pool of countries, the research process is extended to cover other countries of interest.

The preparation of a sampling plan for multicountry research is often a daunting task. When drawing a sample, the researcher needs a sampling frame, that is, a list of the target population (e.g., a telephone directory). In many countries, such lists simply do not exist or may be very inadequate. The proportion of individuals meeting the criteria of the target population could vary considerably. This forces the researcher to be flexible with the sampling methods employed in different countries.[21]

Computing the desired sample size in cross-country market research often becomes at best guesswork because the necessary pieces of information are missing. Desired sample sizes can also vary across cultures. Typically, heterogeneous cultures (e.g., India) demand larger samples than homogeneous cultures (e.g., South Korea, Thailand).[22]

[18]Jean L. Johnson, Tomoaki Sakano, Joseph A. Cote, and Naoto Onzo, "The Exercise of Interfirm Power and Its Repercussions in U.S.-Japanese Channel Relationships," *Journal of Marketing,* 57 (2), April 1993, pp. 1–10.

[19]Kaynak Erderer, *Marketing in the Third World* (New York: Praeger, 1982) Chapter 4.

[20]See, for example, Naresh K. Malhotra, *Marketing Research. An Applied Orientation* (Englewood-Cliffs, NJ: Prentice-Hall, 1993), Chapter 13.

[21]D.N. Aldridge, "Multi-Country Research," in *Applied Marketing and Social Research,* U. Bradley ed., 2nd ed., (New York: John Wiley, 1987), pp. 364–65.

[22]Malhotra et al., "Methodological Issues," p. 27.

This is due to the fact that diverse cultures typically have much more variance in the traits to be measured than homogeneous ones.

Most researchers prefer some form of probabilistic sampling that enables them to make statistical inferences about the collected data. The absence of sampling frames and various cultural hurdles (e.g., inapproachability of women in Muslim societies) make a nonprobabilistic sampling procedure such as convenience sampling, the only alternative, especially in developing countries.

Contact Method.   After preparing a sampling plan, you need to decide how to contact prospective subjects for the survey. The most common choices are mail, telephone, or person-to-person interviews (e.g., shopping mall intercepts). Several factors explain why some methods prevail in some countries and are barely used elsewhere. Cultural norms often rule out certain data collection methods. Germans tend to show greater resistance to telephone interviewing than other Europeans.[23] By the same token, daytime phone calls will not work in Saudi Arabia because social norms dictate that housewives do not respond to calls from strangers.[24] Cost differentials also make some methods preferable over others. In many emerging markets, the lack of a well-developed marketing research infrastructure is a major hurdle to conduct market research studies. In countries such as Brazil, a significant portion of the mail faces large delays or is never delivered. Lack of decent phone service in many emerging countries creates a challenge for phone surveys. Using the Internet to collect questionnaire data can also be hindered due to the lack of Internet access or low levels of technological literacy. In China, researchers must rely on very basic interviewing techniques because of poor phone coverage (about 7 percent versus 93 percent in the United States) and low response rates with mail surveys.[25] Furthermore, with business-to-business research projects, Chinese managers are often reluctant to discuss issues over the phone and prefer face-to-face interviews instead.[26]

These and other challenges imply that market researchers often need to improvize and settle for the second best alternative. In recent years, marketers increasingly use the Internet as a research tool. For online survey research, three types of online survey methods exist: (1) e-mail surveys, (2) Web site surveys, and (3) panel Web site surveys.[27] E-mail surveys are self-administered questionnaires that are sent as an attachment to e-mails to be completed by the addressee. With random Web site surveys, visitors to a site are asked to fill out a questionnaire. They are directed to the Web page on which the survey is posted. Another variant is the pop-up survey that pops up in a new window while the user is browsing a Web site. These surveys are useful when the target audience is wide. Panel Web site surveys rely on a panel of respondents in which each panel member has an e-mail address. When eligible for a survey, panel members are contacted via e-mail and asked to complete a survey that is accessible only via a password. The different forms have their advantages and disadvantages. Web-based surveys allow a better display of the questionnaire than an e-mail survey. However, e-mail surveys enable better control over who can participate. Exhibit 6-5 summarizes the pros and cons of using online surveys in international marketing research. In many countries, especially those with low Internet penetration, the fact that a sample does not represent the target population is a major hurdle. To remedy this problem, global market research projects should rely on a multimode approach (e.g., Web and phone

[23] Aldridge, "Multi-Country Research," p. 365.

[24] Tuncalp, "The Marketing Research Scene in Saudi Arabia," p. 19.

[25] Cyndee Miller, "China Emerges as Latest Battleground for Marketing Researchers," *Marketing News,* February 14, 1994, pp. 1–2.

[26] Stephen Connell, "Travel Broadens the Mind—The Case for International Research," *International Journal of Market Research,* 44 (Quarter 1), 2002, pp. 97–106.

[27] Jonathan Dodd, "Market Research on the Internet—Threat or Opportunity?" *Marketing and Research Today,* February 1998, pp. 60–66.

EXHIBIT 6-5
PROS AND CONS OF THE INTERNET AS A TOOL FOR GLOBAL
MARKETING RESEARCH

Pros

- Large samples are possible in small amount of time.
- Global access of the Internet.
- Cost—in most cases, online surveys can be done much more cheaply than using other methods—also costs are largely scale independent in the sense that large-scale surveys do not demand far bigger resources than small surveys.
- Anonymity—can be helpful for sensitive topics.
- Data analysis—data can be directly loaded into statistical tools and databases, saving time and resources.
- Short response times.

Cons

- Infrastructure—in many countries, access to the Internet is still fairly limited.
- Sample representativeness—for random Web site surveys and e-mail surveys, representativeness can be a major issue. Likewise, there is also the risk of a self-selection bias.
- Time necessary to download pages (for Web site surveys).
- Technological problems such as incorrect e-mail addresses, poor connections.
- Low response rates—response rates can be fairly low; respondents may quit half-way.
- Multiple responses from same respondent.

Source: Jonathan Dodd, "Market research on the Internet—threat or opportunity?" *Marketing and Research Today* (February 1998), pp. 60–67; Cheryl Harris, "Developing Online Market Research Methods and Tools—Considering Theorizing Interactivity: Models and Cases," *Marketing and Research Today* (November 1997), pp. 267–73; and Janet Ilieva, Steve Baron, and Nigel M. Healey, "Online Surveys in Marketing Research: Pros and Cons," *International Journal of Market Research,* 44 (Quarter 3, 2002), pp. 361–76.

interview).[28] Over time, as technology and Internet access improves, the appeal of online surveys is expected to grow.

Collect the Information. Once the design of your questionnaire and your sampling plan are completed, you need to collect the data in the field. This field will be covered with landmines, some of them fairly visible and others invisible. Primary data collection may be hindered by respondent- and/or interviewer-related biases.

Probably the most severe problem is nonresponse due to a reluctance to talk with strangers, fears about confidentiality, or other cultural biases. In many cultures, the only way to cope with nonresponse is to account for it when determining sample sizes. In China, surveys that are sanctioned by the local authorities lead to a higher response rate.[29]

Courtesy bias refers to a desire to be polite to the other person. This bias is fairly common in Asia and the Middle East.[30] The subject feels obliged to give responses that hopefully will please the interviewer. In some countries, responses may reflect a **social desirability bias** where the subject attempts to reflect a certain social status in his responses. Topics such as income or sex are simply taboo in some regions. There are no panaceas to handle these and other biases. Measures such as careful wording and thorough pretesting of the survey and adequate training of the interviewer should minimize the incidence of such biases. In some cases, it is worthwhile to incorporate questions that measure tendencies such as social desirability. Another option for handling cultural biases is to transform the data first before analyzing them. For instance, one common practice is to convert response ratings or scores to questions into rankings.

House-to-house or shopping mall survey responses could also be scrambled by interviewer-related biases. Availability of skilled interviewers can be a major bottleneck

---

[28] Janet Ilieva, Steve Baron, and Nigel M. Healey, "Online Surveys in Marketing Research: Pros and Cons," *International Journal of Market Research,* 44 (Quarter 3), 2002, pp. 361–76.

[29] Steele, "Marketing Research in China," p. 160.

[30] Kaynak, *Marketing in the Third World,* p. 171.

in cross-country research, especially in emerging markets. Lack of supervision or low salaries will tempt interviewers in some countries to cut corners by filling out surveys themselves or ignoring the sampling procedure. In many cultures, it is advisable to match interviewers to respondents. Disparities in cultural backgrounds could lead to misunderstandings.[31] In some societies (e.g., Latin-America) the local population regard survey takers with suspicion.[32] Obviously, adequate recruiting, training, and supervision of interviewers will lessen interviewer-related biases in survey research. In countries where survey research is still in an early stage and researchers have little expertise, questionnaires should not be overly complex.[33] When developing a survey instrument such as a questionnaire for a global market research project, it is also helpful to have **redundancy:** Ask the same question in different ways and different parts of the questionnaire. That way, the researcher can cross-check the validity of the responses.[34]

In addition to traditional primary data collection methods, companies also rely on less conventional methods such as **ethnographic research.** With this research approach, field-workers (usually cultural anthropologists) embed themselves in the local communities that they are studying. The basic idea is to gather useful information by participating in the everyday life of the people being studied. Part of the data collection exercise often involves videotaping participating consumers in purchase or consumption settings. Techniques such as picture completion or collages are often useful when studying the behavior or feelings of young children.[35] Global Perspective 6-2 describes how Intel uses ethnographic research to gain insights of the role of technology in people's lives.

MARKET SIZE ASSESSMENT

◆ ◆ ◆ ◆ ◆ ◆ ◆ ◆ ◆

When deciding whether to enter a particular country, one of the key drivers is the market potential. In most developed countries, a fairly accurate estimate of the market size for any particular product is easily obtainable. For many frequently purchased consumer goods, information suppliers such as ACNielsen are able to give an up-to-date estimate of category volume and market shares based on scanning technology. Such information, however, does not come cheap. Before investing a substantial amount of money, you might consider less costly ways to estimate market demand. For many industries and developing countries, information on market demand is simply not readily available. Under such circumstances, you need to come up with a market size estimate using "simple" ingredients.

Below we introduce four methods that can be fruitfully employed to assess the size of the market for any given product. All of these procedures can be used when very little data are available and/or the quality of the data is dismal, as is typically the case for many emerging markets. All four methods allow you to make a reasonable guesstimate of the market potential without intensive data collection efforts. Market size estimates thus derived prove useful for country selection at the early stage. Countries that do not appear to be viable opportunities are weeded out. After this preliminary screening stage, richer data regarding market size and other indicators are collected for the countries that remain in the pool.

The first technique, the **analogy method,** starts by picking a country that is at the same stage of economic development as the country of interest and for which the market

Method of Analogy

[31] Aldridge, "Multi-Country Research," p. 371.

[32] Douglas and Craig, *International Marketing Research,* p. 227.

[33] Stafford and Upmeyer, "Product Shortages," p. 40.

[34] Naghi Namakforoosh, "Data Collection Methods Hold Key to Research in Mexico," *Marketing News,* August 29, 1994, p. 28.

[35] C. Samuel Craig and Susan P. Douglas, "Conducting International Marketing Research in the 21st Century," *International Marketing Review,* 18 (1), 2001, pp. 80–90.

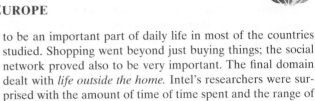

*G*LOBAL PERSPECTIVE 6-2

INTEL'S USE OF ETHNOGRAPHIC RESEARCH IN EUROPE

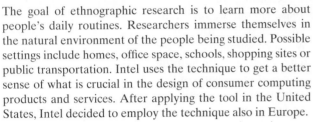

The goal of ethnographic research is to learn more about people's daily routines. Researchers immerse themselves in the natural environment of the people being studied. Possible settings include homes, office space, schools, shopping sites or public transportation. Intel uses the technique to get a better sense of what is crucial in the design of consumer computing products and services. After applying the tool in the United States, Intel decided to employ the technique also in Europe.

The rising penetration of mobile phones and growing popularity of text messaging in Europe provided the incentive for the first application. To learn more about the ramifications of these trends for Intel's business, the firm decided to conduct a series of ethnographic studies. One project was conducted in 1999 in five countries: Italy, the United Kingdom, Germany, France, and Spain. In each country, fieldwork was done in three distinct sites: a small town, a larger population center, and a major urban metropolis. For instance, in France, the team chose Paris, Nantes, and Brittany for the study. Information was gathered by interviewing 100 individuals, taking digital photos, and collecting artifacts (e.g., newspapers, catalogs).

The material offered insights in the "ecology" of the home: how space is used and the ways that activities go on in these spaces. Four important domains of cultural significance emerged. The first one was *togetherness.* Notions of family and community turned out to be very important in European households. The second related to *media experiences.* Intel's researchers were struck by the range of media being consumed and the amount of content being produced. The third domain focused on *consumption habits.* Food shopping was observed

to be an important part of daily life in most of the countries studied. Shopping went beyond just buying things; the social network proved also to be very important. The final domain dealt with *life outside the home.* Intel's researchers were surprised with the amount of time of time spent and the range of activities in public spaces.

One valuable lesson from the project for Intel was that there is no such thing as a single Europe. The research provided feedback that could be used to design or position new products. One example is the way kitchens function in European homes. In northern Italy, the kitchen was seen to be a social hub where information was often consumed. In France, however, the kitchen is solely used to prepare food, not to "consume" entertainment or information content.

Intel also uses ethnographic research in Asia. In a recent study in the region, Intel researchers visited the homes of 100 families in seven countries, asking them questions about their lives and values. One insight was that in some places it is for technology to cross the threshold of people's homes, not simply due to economic reasons but also for religious ones. Values of humility and simplicity could make technology less acceptable in some Hindu homes in India or Muslim homes in Malaysia and Indonesia. Another important finding was Chinese parents' negative attitude toward buying computers for their children: They want their children to learn Mandarin and a PC is seen as a distraction. This insight led Intel to develop a PC aimed at the Chinese home educational market. The PC comes with a touch-sensitive screen that allows users to write in Mandarin. The PC also comes with a physical locking mechanism allowing parents to block Internet access.

Challenges with this kind of research are not minimal. It is important to teach the audience to make sense of and to use the material. The material takes time to digest and to think about. Turning research-based ideas into products is a major challenge. It is often hard to "sell" a study when the fit with the firm's product development plans is not immediately visible.

Sources: Genevieve Bell, "Looking Across the Atlantic: Using Ethnographic Methods to Make Sense of Europe," *Intel Technology Journal,* 3 (2001), pp. 1–10. Downloaded from http://developer.intel.com and http://www.intel.com/labs/about/reallives.htm, December 12, 2002; http://news.bbc.co.uk/2/hi/science/nature/1684773.stm; "For High-Tech Companies, It's No Small World," *International Herald Tribune,* March 7, 2004, p. 2; and "Anthropologists Get to the Bottom of Customers' Needs," *Financial Times,* August 24, 2005, p. 7.

size is known. The method is based on the premise that the relationship between the demand for a product and a particular indicator, for instance, the demand for a related product, is similar in both countries.

Let us illustrate the method with a brief example. Suppose that a consumer electronics company wants to estimate the market size for DVD players in the Ukraine. For the base country, it picks a neighboring Central European country, say Poland, for which it possesses information on the sales of DVD players. It also needs to choose a proxy variable that correlates highly with the demand for DVD players. One reasonable candidate is the number of color televisions in use. So, in this example, we assume that the ratio of DVD player sales to color TV ownership in Ukraine and Poland is roughly equivalent:

$$\frac{\text{DVD Player Demand}_{\text{Ukraine}}}{\text{Color TVs in Use}_{\text{Ukraine}}} = \frac{\text{DVD Player Demand}_{\text{Poland}}}{\text{Color TVs in Use}_{\text{Poland}}}$$

Because the company is interested in the demand for DVD players, it can derive an estimate based on the following relationship:

$$\text{DVD Player Demand}_{\text{Ukraine}} = \frac{\text{Color TVs in Use}_{\text{Ukraine}} \times \text{DVD Player Demand}_{\text{Poland}}}{\text{Color TVs in Use}_{\text{Poland}}}$$

For this specific example, we collected the following bits of information (2001 figures[36]):

	Sales	
	Color TV (000s)	DVD Players (000s)
Poland	14,722.64	69.17
Ukraine	15,626.15	???

Plugging in those numbers gives:

Estimate DVD Player Demand$_{\text{Ukraine}}$ (Annual Retail Sales)

$$= 15{,}626.15 * \frac{69.17}{14{,}722.64} = 73.4$$

The critical part is finding a comparable country and a good surrogate measure (in this case, the number of color television sets in use). In some cases, the analogy exists between different time periods. For example, the stage of economic development in country A 10 years ago is similar to the current state of the economy in country B. In the same fashion as illustrated, we can derive an estimate for the product demand in country B, but this time we would apply the ratio between product demand and the surrogate measure in country A that existed 10 years ago:

$$M_B^{2008} = X_B^{2008} \times (M_A^{1998}/X_A^{1998})$$

where

M = the market size for the product of interest

X = the surrogate measures

This variant is sometimes referred to as the **longitudinal method of analogy.**

Use of either approach produces misleading estimates when the following is true:

1. Consumption patterns are not comparable across countries due to strong cultural disparities.

2. Other factors (competition, trade barriers) cause actual sales to differ from potential sales.

3. Technological advances allow the use of product innovations in a country at an earlier stage of economic development ("leapfrogging").[37]

McDonald's uses a variation of the analogy method[38] to derive market size estimates:

$$\frac{\text{Population of Country X}}{\substack{\text{No. of People per McDonald's} \\ \text{in United States (21,629)}}} \times \frac{\substack{\text{Per Capita Income} \\ \text{of Country X}}}{\substack{\text{Per Capita Income in} \\ \text{United States (\$41,800)}}} = \substack{\text{Potential} \\ \text{Penetration} \\ \text{in Country X}}$$

This method is illustrated in Exhibit 6-6, which contrasts the number of restaurants McDonald's could build with its current (2004) number of outlets for a sample of

---

[36] http://www.euromonitor.com.

[37] Lyn S. Amine and S. Tamer Cavusgil, "Demand Estimation in Developing Country Environment: Difficulties, Techniques and Examples," *Journal of the Market Research Society*, 28(1), pp. 43–65.

[38] "How Many McDonald's Can He Build," *Fortune*, October 17, 1994, p. 104. Population and per capita income based on estimates reported in http://www.cia.gov/cia/publications/factbook/, accessed February 22, 2006.

EXHIBIT 6-6
MARKET POTENTIAL ESTIMATES FOR MCDONALD'S

Country	Current Number of Restaurants (2004)	1996 Number of Restaurants	Market Potential
Japan	3,774	2,004	4,284
Canada	1,362	992	1,190
Germany	1,262	743	2,707
United Kingdom	1,249	737	2,064
France	1,034	540	2,004
Australia	729	608	711
China	639	117	8,958
Brazil	549	214	1,750
Taiwan	346	163	676
Spain	345	121	1,118
South Korea	337	77	1,087
Italy	331	147	1,819
Mexico	304	112	1,175
Sweden	244	129	295
Philippines	242	113	495
Netherlands	227	151	553
Hong Kong	211	125	281
Poland	207	65	542
Argentina	186	88	594
Malaysia	164	129 (1999)	275

Source: "How Many McDonald's Can He Build?" *Fortune,* October 17, 1994, p. 104; *CIA World Factbook 2005:* and http:/www.mcdonalds.com/corp/invest/pub/2004InteractiveFinancialHighlights.html, accessed on February 22, 2006.

countries.[39] As a benchmark, we included the 1996 numbers. Currently, McDonald's has around 31,500 restaurants in 121 countries and territories, out of which about 55 percent are located outside the United States.[40] Interestingly, in several countries, McDonald's appears to have saturated the market. Examples include Canada and Australia. However, in quite a few other countries, the fast-food chain still has a lot of mileage. Not surprisingly, China provides the biggest opportunity.

Trade Audit   An alternative way to derive market size estimates is based on local production and import and export figures for the product of interest. A **trade audit** uses a straightforward logic: Take the local production figures, add imports, and subtract exports:

$$\text{Market Size in Country A} = \text{Local Production} + \text{Imports} - \text{Exports}$$

Strictly speaking, one should also make adjustments for inventory levels. While the procedure is commonsensical, the hard part is finding the input data. For many emerging markets (and even developed countries), such data are missing, inaccurate, outdated, or collected at a very aggregate level in categories that are often far too broad for the company's purposes.

Chain Ratio   The **chain ratio method** starts with a very rough base number as an estimate for
Method   the market size (e.g., the entire population of the country). This base estimate is systematically fine-tuned by applying a string ("chain") of percentages to come up with the most meaningful estimate for total market potential.

To illustrate the procedure, let us look at the potential market size in Japan for Nicorette gum, a nicotine substitute marketed by Pharmacia. Japan's total population is 127 million. In 2002, Japan's smoking rate was around 31 percent.[41] Nicorette's target is adult smokers. The 15–64-year-old age group is about 67.5 percent of Japan's total

---

[39] For a complete listing, see http://www.mcdonalds.com/corp/invest/pub/2004InteractiveFinancialHighlights.html.

[40] http://www.mcdonalds.com/corp/invest/pub/2004InteractiveFinancialHighlights.html.

[41] http://www.jointogether.org/sa/news/summaries/reader/0,1854,554957,00.html.

population.[42] With the chain ratio method, we can then derive a rough estimate for Nicorette's market potential in Japan as follows:

	Japan
Base number	
Total population	127 MM people
Adult population (15–64)	85 MM = 0.675 × 127 MM
Adult smokers	26.5 MM = 0.31 × 85.6 MM

Obviously, given further information, we can refine this market size estimate much further. In this case, Pharmacia learned via surveys that 64 percent of adult smokers would like to quit or cut smoking and, of them, 25 percent would like to quit immediately.[43] So Nicorette's market size potential would be approximately 4.2 million smokers (= 0.25 × 0.64 × 26.5 MM adult smokers).

Statistical techniques such as cross-sectional regression can be used to produce market size estimates. With regression analysis, the variable of interest (in our case, "market size") is related to a set of predictor variables. To apply regression, we first choose a set of indicators that are closely related to demand for the product of interest. We then collect data on these variables and market size figures for a set of countries (the cross-section) where the product has already been introduced. Given these data, we can then fit a regression that will allow you to predict the market size in countries in our consideration pool.[44]

Cross-Sectional Regression Analysis

Again, let us illustrate the procedure with a simple example. Suppose a consumer electronics firm XYZ based in Europe is considering selling DVD players in the Balkan region or the Near East. Five countries are on its short list: Croatia, Greece, Israel, Romania, and Turkey. The company has gathered information on the annual sales figures of DVD players in several (mostly Western) European countries. As predictor variables, the firm chose two indicators: per capita GDP (on a purchasing-power-parity basis) and the number of color TV sets in use. It collected data on these two measures and the (2001) sales of DVD players in 15 European countries.[45] Using these data as inputs, it came up with the following regression model:[46]

$$\text{Annual Unit Sales DVD Players} = -13.3 + 2.43 \times \text{Per Capita Income} + 1.25 \times \text{Number of Color TVs in Use}$$

Based on this regression, we are now able to predict the yearly unit sales of DVD players in the five countries being considered. We plug in the income and number of color TV sets for the respective countries in this equation, with the following results:[47]

Croatia	3,639
Greece	55,403
Israel	36,774
Romania	5,943
Turkey	34,345

---

[42] http://www.cia.gov/cia/publications/factbook/geos/ja.html#People.

[43] "Stubbing Out Japan's Taboo Smoking Habit," *Ad Age Global,* November 2001, p. 23.

[44] For further details, see, for example, David A. Aaker, V. Kumar, and George S. Day, *Marketing Research* (New York: John Wiley & Sons, 1995), Chapter 18.

[45] Our source for the data is http://www.euromonitor.com.

[46] The R^2 equals 0.92; t-statistics are 8.1 and 8.7 for per capita income and number of color TVs, respectively. Note that we transformed the data by taking logarithms first.

[47] GDP per capita figures (2001) are Croatia, $8,300; Greece, $17,900; Israel, $20,000; Romania, $6,800; and Turkey, $6,700. Number of color TV sets in use figures (2001 in thousands) are Croatia, 1,955; Greece, 3,948; Israel, 2,088; and Turkey, 17,262.

Clearly, at least from a unit sales perspective, Greece seems to be the most promising market. Runner-up countries are Israel and Turkey.

When applying regression to determine a market size estimate, you should be careful in interpreting the results. For instance, caution is warranted when the range of one of the predictors for the countries of interest is outside the range of the countries used to calibrate the regression. Having said this, regression is probably one of the most handy tools to estimate market sizes, keeping in mind its constraints.

The methods we just described are not the only procedures you can use. Other, more sophisticated, procedures exist. Finally, some words of advice. Look at the three estimates for the size of the wallpaper market (in terms of number of rolls) in Morocco,[48] based on different market-size estimation techniques:

Chain ratio method	484,000
Method by analogy	1,245,000
Trade audit	90,500

You immediately notice a wide gap among the different methods. Such discrepancies are not uncommon. When using market size estimates, keep the following rules in mind:

1. Whenever feasible, use several different methods that possibly rely on different data inputs.

2. Do not be misled by the numbers. Make sure you know the reasoning behind them.

3. Do not be misled by fancy methods. At some point, increased sophistication will lead to diminishing returns (in terms of accuracy of your estimates), not to mention negative returns. Simple back-of-the-envelope calculations are often a good start.

4. When many assumptions are to be made, do a sensitivity analysis by asking what-if questions. See how sensitive the estimates are to changes in your underlying assumptions.

5. Look for interval estimates with a lower and upper limit rather than for point estimates. The range indicates the precision of the estimates. The limits can later be used for market simulation exercises to see what might happen to the company's bottom line under various scenarios.

◆ ◆ ◆ ◆ ◆ ◆ ◆ ◆ **NEW MARKET INFORMATION TECHNOLOGIES**

These days almost all packaged consumer goods come with a bar code. For each purchase transaction, scanner data are gathered at the cash registers of stores that are equipped with laser scanning technology. The emergence of scanner data coupled with rapid developments in computer hardware (e.g., workstations) and software has led to a revolution in market research. Although most of the early advances in this information revolution took place in the United States, Europe and Japan rapidly followed suit. Scanning technology has spurred several sorts of databases. The major ones include these:[49]

- **Point-of-sale (POS) store scanner data.** Companies such as ACNielsen, GfK, and Information Resources obtain sales movement data from the checkout scanner tapes of retail outlets. These data are processed to provide instant information on weekly

---

[48] Amine and Cavusgil, "Demand Estimation," Table 4.

[49] See, for example, Del I. Hawkins and Donald S. Tull, *Essentials of Marketing Research* (New York: MacMillan, 1994), pp. 115–21.

sales movements and market shares of individual brands, sizes, and product variants. Shifts in sales volume and market shares can be related to changes in the store environment (retail prices, display, and/or feature activity) and competitive moves. In the past, tracking sales was based on store audits or warehouse withdrawal. The advantage of POS scanner data over these traditional ways of data gathering is obvious: far better data quality.[50] The data are collected on a weekly basis instead of bimonthly. Furthermore, they are gathered at a very detailed UPC-level, not just the brand level.

- **Consumer panel data.** Market research companies such as ACNielsen have consumer panels who record their purchases. There are two approaches to collect household level data. Under the first approach, panel members present an ID card when checking out at the cash register. That information is entered each time the household shops. The alternative approach relies on at-home scanning. On returning from each shopping trip, the panel member scans the items bought. The home-scanning method is favored in Japan for two reasons:
  - Japanese supermarket chains are not very cooperative about installing external scanner terminals.
  - Japanese shoppers are highly mobile and shop a lot outside their "designated" panel area.[51]

- **Single-source data.** Such data are continuous data that combine any given household member's TV viewing behavior with purchase transaction (product description, price, promotion, etc.) information. TV viewing behavior is tracked at the panel member's home via Peoplemeters. The TV audience measurement system usually requires cooperation of the panel member. Each time the family member watches a program, he has to push a button to identify himself. More advanced systems involve a camera that records which members of the household are watching TV. Single-source data allow companies to measure, among other things, the effectiveness of their advertising policy.

Household-level scanning data are collected now in most developed countries by research firms such as ACNielsen and GfK. In Europe, ACNielsen set up a partnership with the U.K.-based Safeway supermarket chain that allows companies access to scanning data on all categories from all of the chain's 322 outlets.[52] Companies like Nestlé also put together their own databases. These innovations in marketing decision–support systems have spurred several major developments in the marketing area:

- **Shift from mass to micro marketing.**[53] Better knowledge on shopping and viewing behavior has moved the focus from mass marketing to the individual. New information technologies enable firms to tailor their pricing, product-line, advertising, and promotion strategies to particular neighborhoods or even individuals. Database marketing gives companies an opportunity to enter into direct contact with their customers. Nestlé's strategy for its Buitoni pasta brand offers a good example of the power of database marketing in a pan-European context. In the United Kingdom, Nestlé built up a database of people who had requested a free recipe booklet. The next step was the launch of a Casa Buitoni Club whose members receive a magazine

[50]Gerry Eskin, "POS Scanner Data: The State of the Art, in Europe and the World," *Marketing and Research Today,* May 1994, pp. 107–17.

[51]Hotaka Katahira and Shigeru Yagi, "Marketing Information Technologies in Japan," in *The Marketing Information Revolution,* R.C. Blattberg, R. Glazer, and J.D.C. Little, eds. (Boston, MA: Harvard Business School, 1994).

[52]"IRI vs. Nielsen," *Advertising Age,* October 12, 1992, p. 50.

[53]David J. Curry, *The New Marketing Research Systems. How to Use Strategic Database Information for Better Marketing Decisions* (New York: John Wiley & Sons, 1994).

and opportunities to win a trip for cooking instruction. The goal of the strategy is to build up a long-term commitment to the Buitoni brand.[54] Likewise, in Malaysia, Nestlé built up a database with information on consumption patterns, lifestyle, religion, race, and feelings about specific brands. By building up its database knowledge, Nestlé hopes to do a better job in target marketing and adapting its products to the local market.[55]

- **Continuous monitoring of brand sales/market share movements.** Sales measurement based on scanner data are more accurate and timely than, for instance, data from store audits. In Japan, thousands of new products are launched annually. Accurate tracking information on new brand shares and incumbent brand shares is crucial information for manufacturers and retailers alike.[56]

- **Use of scanning data by manufacturers to support marketing decisions.** Initially, most scanning data were simply used as tracking devices, this has changed. Now scanning data are but increasingly used for tactical decision support. The databases are used to assist in making all types of decisions in inventory management, consumer/trade promotions, pricing, shelf space allocation, and media advertising. Scanning data are also increasingly used for category management.

- **Use of scanning data to provide merchandising support to retailers.** Many manufacturers also employ information distilled from scanning data to help retailers with merchandising programs and build long-term relationships with retailers. Scanning data help manufacturers to show the "hard facts" to their distributors.

Richer market information should help global marketers to improve marketing decisions that have cross-border ramifications. Scanning data from the pan-European region allows marketers to gauge the effectiveness of pan-European advertising campaigns, branding decisions, distribution strategies, and so forth. The information can also be used to monitor competitors' activities. With the emergence of consumer panel data, marketers are able to spot similarities and disparities in cross-border consumer behavior. In short, the consequences of new market research systems are dramatic. Several environmental forces (e.g., single European market, cultural trends) promote the so-called global village with a convergence in tastes and preferences leading to "universal" segments. On the other hand, the new information technologies will ultimately allow marketers to enter into one-on-one relationships with their individual customers.

Despite the promises of scanner databases, their full potential has not yet been exploited in many countries. Many users still simply view scanner data as an instrument to track market shares. Two factors are responsible for this. One reason is the conservatism of the users of the data. Another factor is the attitude of local retailers toward data access. In countries such as the United Kingdom, retailers are reluctant to release their data because they fear that by doing so they might inform their competition. Rivals are not just other retailers but in many cases the manufacturers who compete with the retailer's store brands.

Advances in computer technology have also spurred new data collection techniques such as computer-assisted telephone interviewing (CATI) and computer-assisted personal interviewing (CAPI). Benefits derived from such tools include speed, accuracy, and the ability to steer data collection based on the response. In international marketing research, another material advantage of these techniques is that they can be used to centrally administer and organize data collection from international samples.[57]

---

[54]Stan Rapp and Thomas L. Collins, *Beyond Maxi-Marketing: The New Power of Caring and Sharing* (New York: McGraw-Hill, Inc., 1994).

[55]"Nestlé Builds Database in Asia with Direct Mail," *Ad Age International,* January 1998, p. 34.

[56]Katahira and Yagi, "Marketing Information Technologies in Japan," p. 310.

[57]Craig and Douglas, "Conducting International Marketing Research.", p. 88.

MANAGEMENT OF GLOBAL MARKETING RESEARCH ◆ ◆ ◆ ◆ ◆ ◆ ◆ ◆ ◆

Global marketing research projects cater to the needs of various interest groups: global and regional headquarters and local subsidiaries. Different requirements can lead to tension among the stakeholders. In this section, we center on two highly important issues in managing global marketing research: (1) who should conduct the research project and (2) how to coordinate global marketing research projects.

Even companies with in-house expertise often employ local research agencies to assist with a multicountry research project. The choice of a research agency to run a multicountry research project is made centrally by headquarters or locally by regional headquarters or country affiliates. Reliance on local research firms is an absolute must in countries such as China both to be close to the market and to get around government red tape.[58] Local agencies may also have a network of contacts that give access to secondary datasources. Whatever the motive for using a local research agency, its selection should be based on careful scrutiny and screening of possible candidates. The first step is to see what type of research support services are available to conduct the research project. Each year *Marketing News* (American Marketing Association publication) puts together a directory of international marketing research firms (www.marketingpower.com/ama_custom_honomichl25.php).

Selecting a Research Agency

Several considerations enter the agency selection decision. Agencies that are partners or subsidiaries of global research firms are especially useful when there is a strong need to coordinate multicountry research efforts. The agency's level of expertise is the main ingredient in the screening process: What are the qualifications of its staff and its field-workers? The agency's track record is also a key factor: How long has it been in business? With what type of research problems has it dealt? What experience does the agency have in tackling the current type of research problem(s)? For what clients has it worked? In some cases, it is worthwhile to contact previous or current clients and explore their feelings about the prospective research supplier.

When cross-border coordination is an issue, companies should also examine the willingness of the agency to be flexible and be a good team player. Communication skills should be another important issue. When secrecy is required, it is necessary to examine whether the candidate has any possible conflicts of interest. Has the agency any ties with (potential) competitors? Does it have a good reputation in keeping matters confidential? Again, a background check with previous clients could provide the answer.

Cost is clearly a crucial input in the selection decision. Global research is usually much more expensive than research done in the United States where the infrastructure available to do market research is far more economical than in other parts of the world.[59] However, other costs associated are with global research that are not incurred with domestic research. Items include the cost of multiple translations, multicountry coordination, and long-distance project management.

Budget constraints could force firms to go for a second-tier agency. Quality standards can vary significantly. One golden rule needs to be observed, though: Beware of agencies that promise the world at a bargain price. Inaccurate and misleading information will almost certainly lead to disastrous decisions.

Multicountry research projects demand careful coordination of the research efforts undertaken in the different markets. The benefits of coordination are manifold.[60]

Coordination of Multicountry Research

---

[58] Steele, "Marketing Research in China," p. 158.
[59] Brad Frevert, "Is Global Research Different?" *Marketing Research,* Spring 2000, pp. 49–51.
[60] Aldridge, "Multi-Country Research," p. 361.

Coordination facilitates cross-country comparison of results when such comparisons are crucial. It also can have benefits of timeliness, cost, centralization of communication, and quality control. Coordination brings up two central issues: (1) who should do the coordinating and (2) what should be the degree of coordination. In some cases, coordination is implemented by the research agency that is hired to run the project. When markets differ greatly or when researchers vary from country to country, the company itself will prefer to coordinate the project.[61]

The degree of coordination centers around the conflicting demands of various users of marketing research: global (or regional) headquarters and local subsidiaries. Headquarters favor standardized data collection, sampling procedures, and survey instruments. Local user groups prefer country-customized research designs that recognize the peculiarities of their local environment. This conflict is referred to as the *emic versus etic dilemma*.[62] The **emic** school focuses on the peculiarities of each country. Attitudinal phenomena and values are so unique in each country that they can be tapped only via culture-specific measures. The other school of thought, the **etic** approach, emphasizes universal behavioral and attitudinal traits. To gauge such phenomena requires culturally unbiased measures. For instance, for many goods and services, there appears to be convergence in consumer preferences across cultures. Therefore, consumer preferences could be studied from an etic angle. Buying motivations behind those preferences, however, often differ substantially across cultures. Hence, a cross-country project that looks into buying motivations could demand an emic approach.[63]

In cross-cultural market research, the need for comparability favors the *etic paradigm* with an emphasis on cross-border similarities and parallels. Nevertheless, to make the research study useful and acceptable to local users, companies need to recognize the peculiarities of local cultures. So, ideally, survey instruments that are developed for cross-country market research projects should encompass both approaches, emic *and* etic.[64] There are several approaches to balance these conflicting demands. A pan-European positioning study conducted for BMW accomplished coordination as via the following measures:

1. All relevant parties (users at headquarters and local subsidiaries) were included from the outset in planning the research project.

2. All parties contributed to fund the study.

3. Hypotheses and objectives were deemed to be binding at later stages of the project.

4. Data collection went through two stages. First, responses to a country-specific pool of psychographic statements were collected. The final data collection in the second stage used a mostly standardized survey instrument containing a few statements that were country-customized (based on findings from the first run).[65]

The key lessons of the BMW example are twofold. First, *coordination* means that all parties (i.e., user groups) should be involved. Neglected parties will have little incentive to accept the results of the research project. Second, multicountry research should allow some leeway for country peculiarities. For instance, questionnaires should not be overstandardized but may include some country-specific items. This is especially important for collecting so-called soft data (e.g., lifestyle/attitude statements).

---

[61]"Multi-Country Research: Should You Do Your Own Coordinating?" *Industrial Marketing Digest,* 1985 pp. 79–82.

[62]Douglas and Craig, *International Marketing Research*, pp. 132–37.

[63]Malhotra, et al., "Methodological Issues," p. 12.

[64]Ibid.

[65]Kern, et al., "European Aspects of a Global Brand, pp. 49–50.

SUMMARY

◆ ◆

When you drive to an unknown destination, you probably use a road map, ask for instructions to get there, and carefully examine the road signals. If not, you risk getting lost. By the same token, when you need to make marketing decisions in the global marketplace, market intelligence guides you in these endeavors. Shoddy information invariably leads to shoddy decision making; good information facilitates solid decision making. In this day and age, having timely and adequate market intelligence also provides a competitive advantage. This does not mean that global marketers should do research at any cost. As always, examining the costs and the value added of having more information at each step is important. Usually it is not difficult to figure out the costs of gathering market intelligence. The hard part is the benefit component. Views on the benefits and role of market research sometimes differ between cultures. Global Perspective 6-3 highlights the peculiarities of Japanese firms' approach to marketing research. What can marketers do to boost the payoffs of their global marketing research efforts? As always, there are no simple solutions.

The complexities of the global marketplace are stunning. They pose a continuous challenge to market researchers. Hurdles must be overcome in gathering secondary and primary data. Not all challenges will be met successfully. Mistakes are easily made. One U.S. toiletries manufacturer conducted its market research in (English-speaking) Toronto for a bar soap to be launched in (French-speaking) Québec. The whole venture became a sad soap opera with a tragic ending.[66]

In this chapter, we discussed the intricacies in developing and implementing a market research project in a cross-national setting. We also reviewed several techniques that prove useful to estimate the market size when few or only poor quality data are at your disposal.

To make cross-country comparisons meaningful, companies need to adequately manage and coordinate their market research projects with a global scope. Inputs from local users of the research are desirable for several reasons. When the locals feel that they are treated like stepchildren, it will be hard to "sell" the findings of the research project. As a result, getting locals' support for policies based on the study's conclusions becomes a formidable task. Local feedback also becomes necessary to uncover country-specific peculiarities that cannot be tapped with overstandardized measurement instruments.

---

[66]Sandra Vandermerwe, "Colgate-Palmolive: Cleopatra," Case Study (Lausanne: IMD, 1990).

◆ ◆

𝒢LOBAL PERSPECTIVE 6-3

HOW DOES JAPANESE MARKET RESEARCH DIFFER?

There is a philosophical difference in the role of marketing research between U.S./European and Japanese executives. Marketing researchers in the United States (and to some extent within Europe) believe that various dimensions of consumer attitudes and behaviors can be measured with statistical tools. Japanese marketing researchers, however, believe that those tools are not sufficient enough to gauge the vagrant nature of consumer attitudes. As a result, Japanese marketing researchers rely far less on statistical techniques than their U.S. European counterparts.

Toru Nishikawa, marketing manager at Hitachi, lists five reasons against "scientific" market research in the area of new product development:

1. *Indifference of respondents.* Careless random sampling leads to mistaken judgments because some people are indifferent toward the product in question.

2. *Absence of responsibility.* The consumer is most sincere when spending, not when talking.

3. *Conservative attitudes.* Ordinary consumers are conservative and tend to react negatively to new product ideas.

Sources: Michael R. Czinkota and Masaaki Kotabe, "Product Development the Japanese Way," *Journal of Business Strategy,* 11 (Nov./Dec. 1990), pp. 31–36; and Johny K. Johansson and Ikujiro Nonaka, *Relentless: The Japanese Way of Marketing* (New York: Harper Business, 1996).

4. *Vanity.* It is part of human nature to exaggerate and put on a good appearance.

5. *Insufficient information.* The research results depend on information about product characteristics given to survey participants.

Japanese firms prefer more down-to-earth methods of information gathering. Instead of administering surveys, Japanese market researchers go into the field and observe how consumers use the product. For example, Toyota sent a group of engineers and designers to Southern California to observe how women get into and operate their cars. They found that women with long fingernails have trouble opening the door and handling various knobs on the dashboard. Consequently, Toyota altered some of its automobiles' exterior and interior designs.

Hands-on market research does not negate the importance of conventional marketing research. In fact, scores of Japanese firms assign more people to information gathering and analysis than U.S. firms do. What is unique about Japanese market research is that Japanese research teams include both product engineers and sales and marketing representatives. Engineers gain insights from talking with prospective customers as much as their marketing peers. They can directly incorporate user comments into product specifications.

KEY TERMS ◆

Analogy method
Back translation
Chain ratio method
Conceptual equivalence
Courtesy bias
Emic (etic)
Ethnographic research
Functional equivalence

Longitudinal method of analogy
Omnibus survey
Parallel translation
Primary data
Scalar equivalence
Secondary data
Social desirability bias
Trade audit

Translation equivalence
Triangulate
Redundancy
Sample size
Sampling procedure
Sampling unit

REVIEW QUESTIONS ◆

1. What are the major benefits and limitations of omnibus surveys?

2. What is the notion of triangulation in global market research?

3. Discuss the major issues in running focus group discussions in an international context.

4. Discuss why market size estimates could differ depending on the method being used. How can such differences be reconciled?

5. Contrast the emic versus the etic approach in international marketing research.

DISCUSSION QUESTIONS ◆

1. Chapter 6 suggests two ways to select countries for multi-country market research projects: (1) start with a preliminary research in each one of them or (2) cluster the countries and pick one representative member from each cluster. Under what circumstances would you prefer one option over the other one?

2. Refer to Exhibit 6-6, which presents McDonald's market potential based on the formula given on page 212.

   a. Using the same formula, estimate what McDonald's market potential would be for the following Pacific-Rim countries: India, Indonesia, Malaysia, Myanmar, the Philippines, Singapore, and Thailand.

   b. What factors are missing in the formula that McDonald's uses?

3. In most cases, standard data collection methods are still mail, phone, or personal interviewing. Tokyu Agency, a Japanese ad agency, has started using the Internet to find out how Japanese youngsters spend their money and what their views are on various issues (e.g., environment). What opportunities does the Internet offer as a data-gathering tool in international market research? What are its merits and disadvantages in this regard?

4. Company Euronappy sells disposable diapers in Europe. It would like to expand into the Middle East. After some preliminary market research, it put four countries put on its short list: Bahrain, Kuwait, Saudi Arabia, and the United Arab Emirates (UAE). Given its limited resources, the company can enter only two of these countries. Your assignment is to determine a market size estimate for each country so that Euronappy can decide which one to enter. You decide to run a regression using data from Euronappy's European market. Three variables are presumed to predict the sales of disposable diapers: population size, per capita GDP, and the birth rate. Data were collected on all three variables (source: http://www.cia.gov/cia/publications/factbook/) for the 19 European countries where Euronappy operates. However, the birth rate did not seem to be a factor. The estimated regression model follows:

$$Y = -630.6 + 0.015\,X_1 + 47.15\,X_2$$

Y = Annual Sales of Diapers in Millions of Units

X_1 = Population in Thousands

X_2 = Per Capita Gross Domestic Product (GDP – Purchasing-Power-Parity Basis) in thousands US$

   a. Collect data on the population and per capita GDP for the four countries on the list (Bahrain, Kuwait, Saudi Arabia, and the UAE).

   b. Now use the estimated regression model to predict the yearly sales of disposable diapers for these four countries. Which of these two would you choose?

   c. Suppose that the company is also looking at North Africa, in particular, Egypt, Morocco, and Tunisia. Would you advise it to use the same estimated regression model? Why or why not?

5. Clarion Marketing and Communications, a Connecticut-based marketing research firm, recently launched Global Focus, a technique that allows companies to run focus groups in different countries who interact with each other. The focus groups are held in videoconference centers in the different cities (e.g., one in New York and one in London) with a moderator in each location. Do you see a need for such global focus groups? Why or why not? What are potential benefits and concerns?

6. Imagine that Nokia plans to expand its market in South America. Use the chain ratio method make market size estimates for cellular phones in the following four countries: Argentina, Brazil, Chile, and Peru.

7. When developing a survey instrument for a cross-country study, market researchers often need to construct a scale (e.g., a 7-point disagree/agree scale). What are the major items that they should be concerned about when building such scales?

8. In Singapore, ACNielsen and Taylor Nelson Sofres, two rival market research firms, had a spat about whose panel database is more accurate. ACNielsen uses advanced scanning technology to track purchases of the panel members on the spot in the store. Taylor Nelson Sofres, however, uses the diary method by which panel members keep a diary of their purchase transactions. Their panel size is far larger than ACNielsen's. Discuss what would be more critical here and why, the data collection technology or the sample size?

FURTHER READING ◆

Aldridge, D. N. "Multi-Country Research." In *Applied Marketing and Social Research,* 2nd ed. U. Bradley New York: John Wiley & Sons, 1987.

Amine, S. Lyn, and S. Tamer Cavusgil. "Demand Estimation in a Developing Country Environment: Difficulties, Techniques and Examples." *Journal of the Market Research Society,* 28 (no. 1) pp. 43–65.

Craig, C. Samuel, and Susan P. Douglas. "Conducting International Marketing Research." *International Marketing Review,* 18 (1), (2001), pp. 80–90.

Davis, Tim R. V., and Robert B. Young. "International Marketing Research: A Management Briefing." *Business Horizons,* 45 (2), pp. 31–38.

Eskin, Gerry. "POS Scanner Data: The State of the Art, in Europe and the World." *Marketing and Research Today,* May 1994, pp. 107–17.

Hibbert, Edgar. "Researching International Markets—How Can We Ensure Validity of Results?" *Marketing and Research Today,* November 1993, pp. 222–28.

Johansson, K. Johny, and Ikujiro Nonaka. "Market Research the Japanese Way." *Harvard Business Review,* May–June 1987, pp. 16–22.

Kumar, V. *International Marketing Research.* Upper Saddle River, NJ: Prentice Hall, 2000.

Malhotra, Naresh K., James Agarwal, and Mark Peterson. "Methodological Issues in Cross-Cultural Marketing Research: A State-of-the-Art Review." *International Marketing Review,* 13 (5), 1996, pp. 7–43.

Schroiff, Hans-Willi. "Creating Competitive Intellectual Capital." *Marketing and Research Today,* (November 1998), pp. 148–56.

Steele, Henry C. "Marketing Research in China: The Hong Kong Connection." *Marketing and Research Today,* August, 1990, pp. 155–64.

Tuncalp, Secil. "The Marketing Research Scene in Saudi Arabia." *European Journal of Marketing,* 22 (5) 1988, pp. 15–22.

Williams, S. C. "Researching Markets in Japan—A Methodological Case Study." *Journal of International Marketing,* 4 (no. 2), 1996, pp. 87–93.

GLOBAL SEGMENTATION AND POSITIONING

HAPTER OVERVIEW

1. REASONS FOR INTERNATIONAL MARKET SEGMENTATION

2. INTERNATIONAL MARKET SEGMENTATION APPROACHES

3. SEGMENTATION SCENARIOS

4. BASES FOR COUNTRY SEGMENTATION

5. INTERNATIONAL POSITIONING STRATEGIES

6. GLOBAL, FOREIGN, AND LOCAL CONSUMER CULTURE POSITIONING

Few companies can be all things to all people. Instead of competing across the board, most companies identify and target the most attractive market segments that they can serve effectively. Variation in customer needs is the primary motive for market segmentation. When consumer preferences vary, marketers can design a marketing mix program that is tailored toward the needs of the specific segments that the firm targets. Marketers select one or more segmentation bases (e.g., age) and slice up their prospective customer base according to the chosen criteria. They then develop marketing programs that are in tune with the particular needs of each of the segments that the company wants to serve.

In global marketing, market segmentation becomes especially critical given the sometimes incredibly wide divergence in cross-border consumer needs and preferences. In this chapter, we first focus on the motivations for international market segmentation. Given information on the segmentation criteria you plan to use, you can take several country segmentation approaches. We describe in detail several possible segmentation scenarios. We then consider several bases that marketers might consider for country segmentation. Once the company has chosen its target segments, management needs to determine a competitive positioning strategy for its products. The final sections focus on different international positioning strategies that companies can pursue.

REASONS FOR INTERNATIONAL MARKET SEGMENTATION

♦ ♦ ♦ ♦ ♦ ♦ ♦ ♦

The goal of market segmentation is to break down the market for a product or a service into various groups of consumers who differ in their response to the firm's marketing mix program. That way, the firm can tailor its marketing mix to each individual segment, and, hence, do a better job in satisfying the needs of the target segments. This overall objective also applies in an international marketing context. In that sense, market segmentation is the logical outgrowth of the marketing concept.[1]

The requirements for effective market segmentation in a domestic marketing context also apply in international market segmentation. In particular, segments ideally should be:[2]

1. *Identifiable.* The segments should be easy to define and to measure. This criterion is easily met for "objective" country traits such as socioeconomic variables (e.g., per capita income). However, the size of segments based on values or lifestyle indicators is typically much harder to gauge.

2. *Sizable.* The segments should be large enough to be worth going after. Note that flexible manufacturing technologies enable companies to relax this criterion. In fact, many segments that might be considered too small in a single-country context become attractive once they are lumped together across borders.

3. *Accessible.* The segments should also be easy to reach through promotional and distributional efforts. Differences in the distribution quality (e.g., road conditions, storage facilities) and media infrastructure (e.g., Internet penetration) imply that a given segment could be hard to reach in some countries and easy to target in others.

4. *Stability.* If target markets change their composition or behavior over time, marketing efforts devised for these targets are less likely to succeed.

5. *Responsive.* For market segmentation to be meaningful, it is important that the segments respond differently from each other to differentiated marketing mixes.

6. *Actionable.* Segments are actionable if the marketing mix necessary to address their needs is consistent with the goals and the core competencies of the company.

Let us now consider the major reasons why international marketers implement international market segmentation.

Country Screening

Companies usually do a preliminary screening of countries before identifying attractive market opportunities for their product or service. For preliminary screening, market analysts rely on a few indicators for which information can easily be gathered from secondary data sources. At this stage, the international market analyst might classify countries in two or three piles. Countries that meet all criteria will be grouped in the "Go" pile for further consideration at the next stage. Countries that fail to meet most of the criteria will enter the "No Go" pile. The third set of countries meet some but not all of the criteria. They could become of interest in the future but probably not in the short term.

Companies use different sets of criteria to screen countries depending on the nature of the product. Cultural similarity to the domestic market is one criterion on which companies often rely. Other popular screening criteria include market attractiveness

---

[1] Yoram Wind and Susan P. Douglas, "International Market Segmentation," *European Journal of Marketing,* 6 (1) 1972, pp. 17–25.

[2] Michel Wedel and Wagner A. Kamakura, *Market Segmentation. Conceptual and Methodological Foundations* (Boston: Kluwer Academic Publishers, 1998), Chapters 1 and 2.

in terms of economic prosperity (e.g., per capita GNP), geographic proximity, and the country's economic infrastructure.[3]

Global Marketing Research

Country segmentation also plays a role in global marketing research. Companies increasingly make an effort to design products or services that meet the needs of customers in different countries. Certain features could need to be added or altered, but the core product is largely common across countries. Other aspects of the marketing mix program such as the communication strategy might also be similar. The benefits of a standardization approach often outweigh the possible drawbacks, yet to successfully adopt this approach, companies need to do sufficient market research. Given the sheer number of countries in which many companies operate, doing market research in each one of them is often inefficient. Especially at the early stage, companies are likely to focus on a few select countries. The key question, then, is which countries to choose. One approach is to start grouping prospective markets into clusters of homogeneous countries, and then to choose one prototypical member out of each group. Research efforts will be concentrated on each of the key members, at least initially. Presumably, research findings for the selected key member countries can then be projected to other countries belonging to its cluster. For example, Heineken chose four countries to do market research for Buckler, a nonalcoholic beer: the Netherlands, Spain, the United States, and France. The Dutch brewer wanted to assess the market appeal of Buckler and the feasibility of a pan-European marketing strategy consisting of a roughly common targeting, positioning, and marketing mix strategy across the continent.[4]

Entry Decisions

When a product or service does well in one country, firms often hope to replicate their success story in other countries. The strategic logic is to launch the product in countries that in some regard are highly similar to the country where the product has already been introduced.[5] For example, Cadbury-Schweppes was very confident about launching Schweppes tonic water in Brazil, because the beverage had been well accepted in culturally similar countries such as Mexico.

It is important, though, to realize that a host of factors makes or breaks the success of a new product launch. Tabasco sauce is very popular in many Asian countries such as Japan with a strong taste for spicy dishes. Hence, McLllhenny, the Louisiana-based maker of Tabasco sauce, might view entering Vietnam and India, two of the emerging markets in Asia with a palate for hot food as the logical next step for its expansion strategy in Asia. Other factors, however, such as buying power, import restrictions, or the shoddy state of the distribution and media infrastructure could lessen the appeal of these markets.

Positioning Strategy

Segmentation decisions are also instrumental in setting the company's product positioning strategy. Once the firm has selected the target segments, management needs to develop a positioning strategy to embrace them. Basically, the company must decide how it wants to position its products or services in the mind of the prospective target customers. Environmental changes or shifting consumer preferences often force a firm to rethink its positioning strategy. Cathay Pacific's repositioning strategy in the mid-1990s is a good example. The Hong Kong-based airline carrier realized that its product offerings failed to adequately meet the needs of its Asian clients, who represent 80 percent of its customer base. To better satisfy this target segment, the airline

---

[3]Debanjan Mitra and Peter N. Golder, "Whose Culture Matters? Near-Market Knowledge and Its Impact on Foreign Market Entry Timing," *Journal of Marketing Research,* 39 (August 2002), pp. 350–65.

[4]Sandra Vandermerwe, "Heineken NV: Buckler Nonalcoholic Beer," Case Study (Switzerland. International Institute for Management Development, 1991).

[5]Johny K. Johansson and Reza Moinpour, "Objective and Perceived Similarity for Pacific-Rim Countries," *Columbia Journal of World Business,* Winter 1977, pp. 65–76.

repositioned itself in the fall of 1994 to become the preferred airline among Asian travelers. To that end, Cathay wanted to project an Asian personality with a personal touch. It offered a wide variety of Asian meals and entertainment. Other measures included a new logo (referred to by some people as a shark fin), new colors, repainted exteriors, and redesigned cabins and ticket counters. To communicate these changes to the public, Cathay launched a heavy advertising campaign with the slogan "The Heart of Asia."[6]

Resource Allocation

Market segmentation is also useful in deciding how to allocate the company's scarce marketing resources across different countries. Exhibit 7-1 shows how Nestlé clusters countries using two criteria for Nescafé, its instant coffee brand: per capita coffee consumption and the market share of in-home soluble coffee of overall coffee consumption. Countries where the share of instant coffee is more than 50 percent are classified as *leader* markets; countries where R&G coffee[7] is dominant are *challenger* markets. *Developed markets* are those with an annual per capita consumption of more than 360 cups. Countries below the 360-cups cutoff are developing markets from Nestlé's perspective. A representation such as the one shown in Exhibit 7-1 offers guidance for an MNC in formulating its strategic objectives and allocating resources across groups of countries in a given region or worldwide. For instance, Nestlé's managers could decide to concentrate marketing resources in countries that have a low market share but a high per capita consumption to bolster their firm's market share. Alternatively, resources might be allocated to countries where the firm has a strong competitive position but still fairly low consumption of coffee consumption. At the same time, managers would probably consider cutting resources in markets with low coffee consumption and where Nestlé's market share is weak.

Marketing Mix Policy

In domestic marketing, segmentation and positioning decisions dictate a firm's marketing mix policy. By the same token, country segmentation guides the global marketer's mix decisions. A persistent problem faced by international marketers is how to strike

EXHIBIT 7-1
MARKET CLUSTERING APPROACH FOR
INSTANT COFFEE

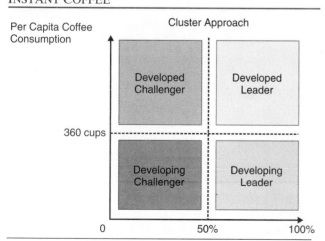

---
[6] John Pies, former Cathay Pacific executive, private communication, 1996.
[7] Roast and ground.

the balance between standardization and customization. International market segmentation could shed some light on this issue. Members falling in the same segment could lend themselves to a standardized marketing mix strategy. The same product design, an identical pricing policy, similar advertising messages and media, and the same distribution channels could be used in these markets. Of course, marketers need to be very careful when contemplating such moves. Segmentation bases and the target customers' responsiveness to any of these marketing mix instruments should have a clear linkage.

Usually, it is very difficult to establish a linkage between market segments and all four elements of the marketing mix. For instance, countries with an underdeveloped phone infrastructure (e.g., Eastern Europe, China, Thailand) are typically prime candidates for mobile phone technologies. However, many of these countries dramatically differ in terms of their price sensitivities given the wide gaps in buying power, so treating them as one group as far as the pricing policy goes could lead to disastrous consequences.

Exhibit 7-2 illustrates how country segmentation can be applied in developing international advertising strategies.[8] The mapping comes from a study that predicted the preference of a country in terms of rational ("think") and emotional ("feel") appeals based on the country's cultural and advertising industry environment (e.g., level of government regulation, per capita ad spending, media characteristics). The "think" strategy uses argumentation and the lecture format to address the target audience. "Feel" appeals are centered around emotions (psychological appeals) often in a dramatic format. The map shows four distinctive clusters. For instance, five

EXHIBIT 7-2
"THINK" AND "FEEL" COUNTRY CLUSTERS

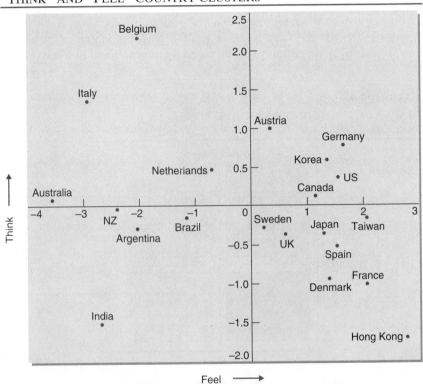

Source: Fred Zandpour and Katrin R. Harich, "Think and Feel Country Clusters: A New Approach to International Advertising Standardization," *International Journal of Advertising,* 15 (1996), pp. 341. Copyright Advertising Association.

[8]Fred Zandpour and Katrin R. Harich, "Think and Feel Country Clusters: A New Approach to International Advertising Standardization," *International Journal of Advertising,* 15 (1996), pp. 325–44.

countries (Austria, Canada, Germany, South Korea, and the United States) fall into the "high feel"/"high think" region.

INTERNATIONAL MARKET SEGMENTATION APPROACHES ◆◆◆◆◆◆◆◆◆

Global marketers approach the segmentation process from different angles. A very common international segmentation procedure classifies prospect countries geographically on a single dimension (e.g., per capita Gross National Product) or on a set of multiple socio-economic, political, and cultural criteria available from secondary data sources (e.g., the World Bank, UNESCO, OECD). This is known as **country-as-segments** or **aggregate segmentation.** In Exhibit 7-3, you can see how the Swiss consumer conglomerate Nestlé geographically segments the Americas. While it treats some countries as stand-alone segments (e.g., Brazil, Canada, the United States), it groups others with neighbouring countries. Exhibit 7-4 presents a list of various general country characteristics that analysts might consider for classifying countries in distinct segments. When numerous country traits exist, the segmentation variables are usually first collapsed into a smaller set of dimensions using data-reduction techniques such as factor analysis. The countries under consideration are then classified into homogeneous groups using statistical algorithms such as cluster analysis (see the Appendix for a brief overview of some of these techniques).

The country-as-segments approach has major flaws. From a global marketer's perspective, the managerial relevance of geographic segments is often questionable. Country boundaries rarely define differences in consumer response to marketing

EXHIBIT 7-3
NESTLÉ'S GEOGRAPHIC SEGMENTATION OF THE AMERICAS

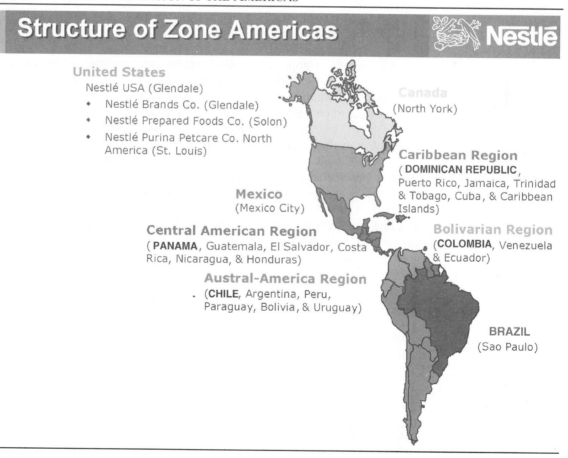

EXHIBIT 7-4
MACRO-LEVEL COUNTRY CHARACTERISTICS

Construct	Items
1. Aggregate production and transportation (mobility)	Number of air passengers/km
	Air cargo (ton/km)
	Number of newspapers
	Population
	Cars per capita
	Gasoline consumption per capita
	Electricity production
2. Health	Life expectancy
	Physicians per capita
	Political stability
3. Trade	Imports/GNP
	Exports/GNP
4. Lifestyle	GDP per capita
	Phones per capita
	Electricity consumption per capita
5. Cosmopolitanism	Foreign visitors per capita
	Tourist expenditures per capita
	Tourist receipts per capita
6. Miscellaneous	Consumer price index
	Newspaper circulation
	Hospital beds
	Education expenditures/Government budget
	Graduate education in population per capita

Source: Kristiaan Helsen, Kamel Jedidi, and Wayne S. DeSarbo, "A New Approach to Country Segmentation Utilizing Multinational Diffusion Patterns," *Journal of Marketing,* 57, (5), October 1993 p. 64. Reprinted with permission from the *journal of Marketing,* published by the American Marketing Association.

strategies. Furthermore, it is seldom clear what variables should be included in deriving the geographic segments.

An alternative approach is **disaggregate international consumer segmentation.** Here the focus is the individual consumer. Just as with domestic marketing, one or more segmentation bases (e.g., lifestyle, demographic, values) are chosen. Consumer segments are then identified in terms of consumer similarities with respect to the chosen bases. The key problem here is that targeting a consumer segment that is geographically dispersed can become a logistical nightmare.

To address the shortcomings of the previous two approaches, **two-stage international segmentation** can offer solace.[9] In the first (aggregate or macro-level) stage, countries are grouped on general segmentation bases. Some bases are independent of the product or service for which the segmentation is being done. They can be observable (e.g., demographic, socioeconomic, cultural) or unobservable (e.g., lifestyle, values, personality) traits. This first step also enables the manager to screen out countries that are unacceptable (e.g., because of high political risk or low buying power) or do not fit the company's objectives. In the second (disaggregate or micro-level) phase, data are gathered on product-specific bases. *Product specific* means that these bases are specifically related to the buying and consumption behavior for the particular product or service of interest. Just as with general segmentation bases, there are two varieties: observable (e.g., user status, loyalty, usage occasion) and unobservable (e.g., attitudes, benefit importance weights, brand images) bases. The particular bases selected depend on the nature of the goal of the segmentation. These disaggregate data then form the ingredients for identifying cross-national segment of consumers within the geographic segment(s) chosen. Two-stage segmentation has several benefits. First, compared to

---

[9]J.-B.E.M. Steenkamp and F. Ter Hofstede, "International Market Segmentation: Issues and Perspectives," *International Journal of Research in Marketing,* September 2002, pp. 185–214.

purely geographic country-level aggregation, the segments will be more responsive to marketing efforts. The segments are also more in tune with a market-orientation perspective as they focus on consumer needs rather than simply macro-level socioeconomic or cultural variables. Second, as opposed to disaggregate consumer segmentation, they will be more accessible.[10]

SEGMENTATION SCENARIOS

When a firm segments foreign markets, different scenarios may arise. A common phenomenon is illustrated in Exhibit 7-5 in which Country X has one universal segment ("A") whereas the other segments are either unique to the country or exist in only two of the three countries. Note also that the size of the different segments varies depending on the country.

One possibility is that you uncover so-called **universal** or **global segments** that transcend national boundaries. They are universal in the sense that customers belonging to such segments have common needs. Note that this segment could also be a universal niche. The standard definition of *niche* is a more narrowly defined group of consumers who seek a very special bundle of benefits. Examples of possible universal segments that are emerging include the MTV generation, international business travelers, the affluent, and technology geeks. How similar customer needs are clearly depends on the product category.[11]

Commonality of consumer needs is high for high-tech consumer durables and travel-related products (e.g., credit cards, airlines). The Nokia 9000 Communicator is an example of a product that is targeted toward a universal segment, in this case the international business traveler. The product combines phone, fax, e-mail, and Internet functions and weighs less than a pound. To roll out the innovation, Nokia used a global campaign with the slogan "Everything. Everywhere."[12] At the other end of the spectrum are food products for which customer needs are usually very localized. Apart from global segments, you may also encounter **regional segments.** Here the similarity in customer needs and preferences exists at the regional level rather than globally. While differences in consumer needs exist among regions, there are similarities within the region.

EXHIBIT 7-5
DIFFERENT SEGMENT SCENARIOS

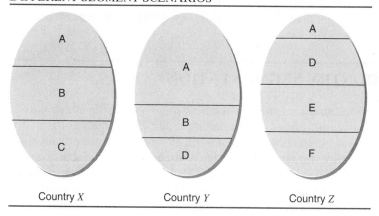

---

[10]Other segmentation approaches allow for cross-border segments with spatial contiguity. One interesting methodology is outlined in F. Ter Hofstede, M. Wedel, and J.-B.E.M. Steenkamp, "Identifying Spatial Segments in International Markets," *Marketing Science,* 21 (Spring 2002), pp. 160–77.

[11]George S. Yip, *Total Global Strategy* (Englewood-Cliffs, NJ: Prentice Hall, 1995), pp. 30–32.

[12]"Nokia Trying to Lighten Business Travelers' Load," *Advertising Age International,* October 1996, pp. I-3, I-4.

With universal or regional segments, the firm still needs to decide the extent to which it wants to differentiate its marketing mix strategy. At one end of the spectrum, management can adopt an undifferentiated marketing strategy that offers a more or less uniform package world- or regionwide. An undifferentiated marketing strategy allows the firm to capitalize on scale economies. To a large extent, this is a strategy that suits high-tech companies. For instance, the corporate advertising director of Microsoft remarked in a forum, "The character of the [Microsoft] product is universal. Technology is an English-based thing, so there's a lot of willingness to embrace Western companies."[13] At the other end of the spectrum are firms that tailor their marketing strategy to local markets. Although consumer needs and preferences may be similar, differentiation of positioning and other marketing mix elements might be necessary to cope with variations in local market conditions. A differentiated strategy allows the company to stay better in tune with the local market and to be more flexible.

Unique (diverse) segments are the norm when gaps in cross-country customer needs and preferences are so substantial that it becomes very hard to derive meaningful cross-border segments. Under such a scenario, marketing mix programs need to be localized to meet local needs. Rather than going after one common cross-border segment, management picks the most attractive target markets in each individual market. A case in point is the Canon AE-1 camera. When Canon launched this camera, it developed three different marketing programs: one for Japan, one for the United States, and one for Europe. In Japan, Canon targeted young replacement buyers. In the United States, it concentrated on upscale, first-time buyers of 35 mm single-lens reflex cameras. In Germany, Canon focused on older and technologically more sophisticated replacement buyers.[14] Jack Daniel's, the Tennessee-based whiskey brand, also pursues diverse target markets. In Australia and New Zealand, the beverage brand pursues young, hip, social drinkers. In China, where a bottle of Jack Daniel's costs $30 or more—double its U.S. price—the target is the 30- to 40-year-old urban professional who earns $1,000 a month working for a joint-venture company.[15]

In most instances, there is a mixture of universal, regional, and country-specific market segments. One final comment to be made here is that markets differ a great deal in terms of their degree of segmentation. Gaps in the degree of segmentation are most visible when contrasting the market structure in a developed country with the one in an emerging market. For most consumer goods, the market structure for a category in the emerging market is often pretty unsophisticated: premium versus economy. Developed countries, on the other hand, have typically many more segments and niches. This is to a large extent due to differences in the degree of market development. Early on in the product life cycle, the market is still relatively undersegmented. As consumers grow more sophisticated and demanding and as the category develops, new segments and niches emerge.

♦ ♦ ♦ ♦ ♦ ♦ ♦ ♦   ## BASES FOR COUNTRY SEGMENTATION

The first step in doing international market segmentation is deciding which criteria to use in the task. Just as in a domestic marketing context, the marketing analyst faces an embarrassment of riches. Literally hundreds of country characteristics could be used as inputs. In a sense, the analyst can pick and choose the variables wanted. However, for the segmentation to be meaningful, the market segments and the response variable(s) the company is interested in should have a linkage. Usually it is not a trivial exercise to figure out a priori which variables will contribute to the segmentation. Instead, the marketing analyst needs to do some experimentation to find the "right"

---

[13]"U.S. Multinationals," *Advertising Age International*, June 1999, p. 41.

[14]Hirotaka Takeuchi and Michael E. Porter, "Three Roles of International Marketing in Global Strategy," in *Competition in Global Industries*, ed. M. E. Porter (Boston, MA: Harvard Business School Press, 1986), pp. 139–40.

[15]"Jack Daniel's Goes Down Smooth in Australia, New Zealand, China," *Ad Age International*, September 1997, pp. i38–i39.

ingredients. Furthermore, information on several segmentation criteria is typically missing, inaccurate, or outdated for some of the countries to be grouped.

We now briefly discuss different types of country variables that are most commonly used for country segmentation purposes. Most of these criteria can be used for the two segmentation approaches discussed earlier. For instance, a socioeconomic variable such as per capita income can be used as a segmentation base to group countries. However, one could also use the income dimension to segment consumers within one country first and then derive regional or global segments (e.g., pan-Asian middle class).

Demographics

Demographic variables are among the most popular segmentation criteria. They are easy to assess (recall the "measurability" requirement for effective market segmentation). Moreover, information on population variables is mostly reasonably accurate and readily available.

Exhibit 7-6 shows the results of a segmentation study that was done by Hakuhodo, one of Japan's biggest ad agencies, of China's so-called pre-elders, the 45- to 54-year-old age group. As you can see, even within this narrowly defined age group striking differences can be found resulting in six types of pre-elders in the study.[16] Note that the study's findings run counter to the stereotypes of middle-aged Chinese being conservative, traditional, and family oriented. In fact, a sizable chunk of people belonging to this age group want to spend money on themselves to get a better lifestyle rather than doting their wealth on their children or grandchildren.

One segment that marketers often overlook is the elderly. Many of them are more prosperous and healthier than ever before. Countries with an aging population clearly offer market opportunities for consumer goods and services that cater to the elderly. Global Perspective 7-1 describes how major global companies are rising to the challenges of the senior citizens segment. To gain a foothold within this target market, it is critical to understand the subtleties of marketing to the over-60 group, especially in youth-obsessed cultures. Gerber's launch of a product similar to baby food called Senior Citizen proved to be a failure because older shoppers have no desire to vividly show their age.[17] Unilever's low-fat Pro-activ margarine spread, however, was a major success. Pro-activ addresses the need for a heart-friendly margarine among aging consumers. The new brand revitalized Unilever's margarine division.

By the same token, countries with high birth rates have similar buying patterns. Examples of goods and services with high potential in such countries include baby food and clothing, toys, prenatal care services, and birth control devices.

Socioeconomic Variables

Satellite photos taken of the European continent at night show a blue curve of light that stretches from Manchester, England, through the Rhineland down to northern Italy. French journalists labeled this area the *blue banana* ("banane bleue"). It has the largest concentration of big cities worldwide, the densest commercial traffic, and the highest production capacity per square kilometer.[18] The region creates tremendous market opportunities for marketers of luxury goods (e.g., LVMH, BMW), high-end services (e.g., resorts, Internet access, mutual funds) and leisure-activity-related goods.

Consumer wealth or a country's level of economic development in general largely drive consumption patterns for many goods and services. Consumers from countries at the same stage of economic development often show similar needs in terms of the per capita amount and types of goods they desire. Not surprisingly, many consumer good marketers view per capita income or a comparable measure as one of the key criteria in grouping international markets. The usual caveats in using per capita income

---

[16]"Hakuhodo Dispels Chinese Stereotypes," *Media*, November 15, 2002, p. 10.

[17]"Over 60 and Overlooked," *The Economist*, August 10, 2002, pp. 51–52.

[18]http://www.msnbc.com/news/844728.asp.

EXHIBIT 7-6
SIX TYPES OF CHINESE PRE-ELDERS

Six Types of Chinese Pre-Elders

Beijing, Shanghai, Guangzhou:
Age 45–54 male/female

Entrepreneurs (5.3%)

• Found largely in Shanghai (43.8%)
• Largely male (78.1%)
• Many with high-school education (50%)
• Many own companies (16.7%)
• Living standard has impoved within the last year (50.0%)
• Living standard has declined within the last year (21.9%)
• Want to work hard to succeed (71.9%)
• Want to be a leader that everyone follows (59.4%)
• Looking for pleasure and enjoyment, want to enjoy life (78.1%)
• Want to look good for the opposite sex (68.6%)
• Frequently try new products (34.4%)
• See word-of-mouth as important source of information (65.6%)

Thrifty Shoppers (7.9%)

• Found largely in Shanghai (52.1%)
• More than half are female (58.3%)
• Many are retired (43.8%)
• Many are junior-high graduates (45.8%)
• Avoid waste and prefer a simple life (68.8%)
• Prefer a settled, stable life (91.7%)
• Want to live as they like (60.4%)
• Compare prices before buying (62.5%)
• See stores where they can receive advice as important (47.9%)
• Will go out of their way to find a store with a wide selection (56.3%)
• Carefully plan most purchases (52.1%)
• Leave TV on all day (41.7%)
• Frequently switch channels to watch multiple programs (50.0%)

Self-Centered (20.4%)

• Found largely in Beijing (41.9%)
• Average in education and income
• Are more likely to own information technology
  - Cable TV (82.3%)
  - Video cassette Player (82.3%)
  - Digital camera (11.3%)
  - Mobile phone (52.4%)
• Seek self-fulfillment (79.0%)
• Looking for pleasure and enjoyment, want to enjoy life (62.1%)
• Few care about what others think of them (8.9%)
• Few will sacrifice for society or friends (6.5%)
• Many are impulse buyers (20.2%)
  - Average scores on other shopping behavior
• Believe that the more information they have the better (61.3%)
  - Average scores on other information behavior

Good Students (18.3%)

• Found largely in Shanghai (45.9%)
• Many are in management (40.0%)
• Many with college education (19.8%)
• See human relationships as important (54.1%)
• Want to help the less fortunate (53.2%)
• Willing to sacrifice for society and friends (45.0%)
• Buy what they like, even if expensive (57.3%)
• Like to try new products (39.6%)
• See mobile phones as indispensable (61.3%)
• See advertising as teaching new lifestyles (43.2%)

Family Oriented (29.6%)

• Found largely in Guangzhou (45.0%)
• More than half are female (58.3%)
• Live with sons or daughters (89.4%)
• Live with grandchildren (7.2%)
• Junior-high or lower education (48.3%)
• Want to live a healthy life (94.4%)
• Would like to be economically affluent (74.4%)
• Family is priority No. 1 (80.6%)
• Know little product information (6.1%)
• Few buy what they like, even if expensive (7.2%)
• Few are active information seekers (6.7 %)
• Very few believe the more information the better (3.3%)

Falling behind (18.6%)

• Relately few in Beijing (25.7%)
• High-school education (51.3%)
• Relatively few see family happiness as No. 1 priority (21.2%)
• Relatively few aspire to an economically affluent life (15.9%)
• Relatively few want to lead a healthy life (32.7%)
• Very few search for stores with wide selections of products (5.3%)
• Home PC ownership is average (55.8%)
• Mobile phone ownership is average (56.6%)

Source: Hakuhudo Inc., Hakuhado Global HABIT. 2002.

GLOBAL PERSPECTIVE 7-1

TAPPING THE GRAY MARKET

In the coming decades, the so-called "gray" market of senior citizens over 60 years of age is expected to rise significantly in most industrialized countries. In many of these countries, the over-60s already account for one-fifth of the population. This proportion is expected to increase to one-third by the year 2050. Also, the gray market's spending power is on the increase. In developed countries, the over-50s own three-quarters of all financial assets. They account for 50 percent of all discretionary spending power, yet in spite of the rising numbers and increasing financial clout, most companies ignore the gray market segment. For instance, companies allocate only 5 percent of their marketing and advertising budget on over-50s. There are several reasons why foreign firms are reluctant to target older consumers. They are often a much tougher sell than young consumers. They tend to be less globalized.

Some companies have been waking up to the opportunities created by these shifting demographics. However, not all initiatives have been quite successful. Gerber, the leading maker of baby food, realized that many elderly buy Gerber baby-food products for their own use. It therefore decided to launch a new line of purees called Senior Citizen designed to address the needs of the elderly for food that copes with

dental or stomach problems. After disappointing sales, Gerber withdrew the product. Not too many aging shoppers like to advertise their demographics, especially in youth-obsessed cultures.

A more successful venture is Unilever's low-fat Pro-activ margarine spread. Pro-activ addresses the need for a heart-friendly margarine among senior citizens. Ad campaigns for the spread feature happy consumers—often over 50—who attest to the fact that the spread lowers their cholesterol. Unilever has rolled out Pro-activ in 20 countries. It rejuvenated Unilever's margarine division.

Japan's Meiji Dairies created a yogurt aimed at the over 40 segment. The yogurt, called LG21, contains a bacterium that kills off another type of bacteria, which is believed to cause stomach ulcers and possibly cancer. Seichi Sato, a manager of Meiji's marketing department, notes that the advantage of the aging consumer segment is that there is virtually no competition.

Nestlé rolled out a new range of functional foods for senior citizens under its baby food division. *Functional foods* have added health ingredients such as fish oil, vitamins, calcium, and Gingko. The product range was first introduced in Germany and then in other markets around the world. Apart from the growth prospects of the gray market segment where competition is weak, many elderly already spend heavily on herbal remedies that can be added to food. Some pharmaceutical companies like Novartis have made efforts to enter the category but abandoned the market as they did not have the right distribution channels for the food sector.

Sources: "Over 60 and Overlooked," *The Economist,* August 10, 2002, pp. 51–2; "Nestle Targets Senior Citizens with Functional Foods," www.adageglobal.com, December 19, 2002; http://www.unilever.com/brands/unileverbrands/spreadscookingproducts/; "As Asians Gray, Marketers Hone New Pitch," *Asian Wall Street Journal,* February 28/March 2, 2003, p. A5.

as an economic development indicator apply when this measure is used for country segmentation:[19]

- *Monetization of transactions within a country.* To compare measures such as per capita GNP across countries, figures based on a local currency need to be translated into a common currency (e.g., the U.S. dollar or the euro). However, official exchange rates seldom reflect a currency's true buying power, so income figures based on GNP or GDP do not really tell how much a household in a given country is able to buy.

- *Gray and black sectors of the economy.* National income figures only record transactions that occur in legitimate sector of a country's economy. Many countries have a sizable *gray* sector consisting of largely untaxed (or undertaxed) exchanges that often involve barter transactions. In cities in the developing world, many professors make ends meet by driving a taxi. In exchange for a dental checkup, a television repairman might fix the dentist's television set. Many societies also thrive on a substantial *black* sector involving transactions that are outright illegal. Examples of such activities include the drug trade, smuggling, racketeering, gambling, and prostitution.

- *Income disparities.* Figures such as the per capita GNP tell only part of the story. Such measures are misleading in countries with wide income inequalities. In Brazil,

[19]Vern Terpstra and Kenneth David, *The Cultural Environment of International Business* (Cincinnati, OH: South-Western Publishing Co., 1991).

the richest 10 percent of the population gets 48 percent of the country's income, while the poorest 10 percent gets a mere 0.7 percent.[20]

To protect against these shortcomings of standard "per capita income" segmentation exercises, marketers could consider other methods to group consumers in terms of their buying power.[21] One alternative is to use the purchasing power parity (PPP) as a criterion. PPP reflects how much a household in each country has to spend (in U.S. dollar equivalents) to buy a standard basket of goods. PPP estimates can be found in the *World Bank Atlas* published annually by the World Bank and in the *CIA World Factbook,* which is also accessible online (http://www.cia.gov/cia/publications/factbook/).

Another alternative for analyzing buying power in a set of countries is via a **socioeconomic strata (SES) analysis.** For instance, Strategy Research Corporation applied an SES analysis to Latin American households using measures such as the number of consumer durables in the household, education level, and so on. Each country was stratified into five socioeconomic segments, each designated with a letter: upper class (A), middle to upper class (B), middle class (C), lower class (D), and poverty level (E). Exhibit 7-7 shows the relative sizes of the various SES segments (D and E are combined) in several Latin American countries.

Other schemes broaden the notion of a country's level of development by going beyond standard of living measures. One popular classification scheme is based on the Human Development Index (HDI), released every year by the United Nations (see http://hdr.undp.org/reports/global/2005/). It covers 175 U.N. member countries, Hong Kong, and Palestine. HDI widens the notion of economic development by looking at a country's achievements in three areas: life expectancy at birth (a long and healthy life), knowledge (e.g., adult literacy), and a decent standard of living (per capita in PPP). The 2005 report classified 57 countries as having achieved a high level of economic development (HDI of 0.80 or above), 88 as medium (HDI of 0.5–0.79), and 36 as low (HDI of less than 0.50). The highest scorers were Norway (HDI of 0.96), Iceland (0.96), and Australia (0.96). At the bottom of the table were Burkina Faso (0.32), Sierra Leone (0.30), and Niger (0.28).[22]

EXHIBIT 7-7

LATIN AMERICAN MARKETS: MANY LATIN HOUSEHOLDS HAVE LOTS OF SPENDING MONEY. (PERCENT DISTRIBUTION OF SELECTED LATIN AMERICAN COUNTRIES BY SES SEGMENTS, 1994)

	Upper Class	Middle-to-Upper Class	Middle Class	Lower Class and Subsistence Level
Argentina	2%	9%	35%	55%
Brazil	3	16	29	53
Chile	2	6	42	50
Colombia	2	8	37	53
Ecuador	2	15	22	61
Mexico	2	12	30	56
Paraguay	3	12	34	51
Peru	3	8	33	56
Uruguay	8	20	36	36
Venezuela	1	4	36	59

Note: Class designations correspond to socioeconomic strata (SES) segments.
Source: Chip Walker, "The Global Middle Class," *American Demographics,* September 1995 40–46. Reprinted with permission. © 1995 American Demographics.

---

[20]"A Continent Falling Apart," *International Herald Tribune,* December 18, 2002, p. 4.

[21]Chip Walker, "The Global Middle Class," *American Demographics,* September 1995, pp. 40–46.

[22]In fact, all bottom-25 countries were African.

EXHIBIT 7-8
EUROPEAN MARKET CLASSIFICATIONS AS OF DECEMBER 31, 1994

Established Markets	Developmental Markets	Underdeveloped Markets
England	Austria	Czech Republic
Finland	Belgium	Denmark
Germany	Ireland	France
Holland	Italy	Hungary
Israel		Portugal
Norway		Spain
Switzerland		

Established = Above-Average Sales/Capita plus Advertising.
Developmental = Average Sales/Capita; may or may not be advertising.
Underdeveloped = Below-Average Sales/Capita; no significant advertising.

Behavior-Based Segmentation

As with domestic marketing, segments can be formed based on behavioral response variables. Behavioral segmentation criteria include degree of brand/supplier loyalty, usage rate (based on per capita consumption), product penetration (that is, the percentage of the target market that uses the product), and benefits sought after. Exhibit 7-8 shows a behavior-based classification of European markets for a personal care company. Note that this particular company divides its markets into three groups: established markets, developmental markets and underdeveloped markets. Two segmentation variables are used: sales per capita and amount of advertising done by the local distributor.

Lifestyle

Marketers can group consumers according to their lifestyles, that is, their attitudes, opinions, and core values. Lifestyle (psychographic) segmentation is especially popular in advertising circles. Many lifestyle segmentation schemes are very general and not related to a specific product category. Others are derived for a specific product field. Distinctions can also be made between whether a given typology was prepared for a specific country or a given region.

A study done in 1997 by Roper Starch Worldwide provides an example of the general lifestyle segmentation approach. The survey covered about 1,000 people in each of 35 countries. Subjects were asked to rank 56 values. Based on the responses, the researchers identified six global values segments:

1. *Strivers (23 percent).* Strivers are slightly more likely to be men than women. They emphasize material things and professional goals. They value wealth, status, power, and ambition. They like products such as personal computers and cellular phones. Strivers are common in Asia (Japan, Philippines) and Russia. Their media habits are limited to newspapers.

2. *Devouts (22 percent).* Devouts include more women than men. They uphold more traditional values such as faith, discipline, respect for elders, and obedience. They are concentrated in the developing nations of Asia, the Middle East, and Africa. Their media habits are very limited. Western products hold very little appeal to them.

3. *Altruists (18 percent).* Altruists are very concerned about social issues and the welfare of society. They tend to be very well educated. Median age is 44 years, and a higher proportion is female. Altruists are primarily found in Russia and Latin America.

4. *Intimates (15 percent).* Intimates are "people" people. They value family, significant others, friends, and colleagues above all else. They can be found in Europe (one out of four) and the United States. They are heavy users of media that allow bonding such as television, movies, and radio.

5. *Fun seekers (12 percent).* Fun seekers, as the label suggests, uphold values such as adventure, pleasure, excitement, and looking good. Not surprisingly, this group—the

MTV generation—is the youngest segment. They frequent bars, restaurants, and clubs and are heavily involved with electronic media. Though strongly represented in developed Asia, this group can be found anywhere else in the world.

6. *Creatives (10 percent).* This segment has a strong interest in education, knowledge, and technology. Members of this group are global trendsetters in terms of owning a PC and surfing the Web. Creatives are primarily located in Western Europe and Latin America. They are the heavy media consumers with a tilt toward newspapers, books, and magazines.[23]

Exhibit 7-9 exemplifies the product-specific approach. It shows a typology that was derived for the pan-European car market. The distribution of the different types varies from country to country. Some of the types (e.g., the "prestige-oriented sporty driver") are more or less uniformly distributed. Other types (e.g., the "understatement" buyer), though, are prominent in some countries but far less visible in other countries.[24]

Lifestyle segmentation has been applied to positioning new brands, repositioning existing ones, identifying new product opportunities, and developing brand personalities.[25] Practitioners and academics alike have raised concerns about the use of lifestyle segmentation:

- Values are too general to relate to consumption patterns or brand choice behavior within a specific product category. As a result, lifestyle segmentation is not very useful as a tool to make predictions about consumers' buying responsiveness. Obviously, this criticism applies only to general value schemes.

- Value-based segmentation schemes are not always "actionable." Remember that one of the requirements for effective segmentation is actionability. Lifestyle groupings do not offer much guidance in terms of what marketing actions should be taken. Also, many typologies have too many different types to be useful for practical purposes.

- Value segments are not stable because values typically change over time.

- Their international applicability is quite limited because lifestyles, even within the same region, often vary from country to country.[26]

EXHIBIT 7-9
TYPOLOGY OF EUROPEAN CAR MARKET

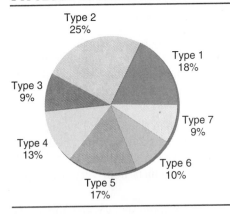

Type 1: The unpretentious car fan

Type 2: The prestige-orientated sporty driver

Type 3: The hedonist

Type 4: The utiltarian thinker

Type 5: The traditionalist

Type 6: The prestige-orientated achiever

Type 7: The understatement buyer

Source: Horst Kern, Hans-Christian Wagner, and Roswitha Hassis, "European Aspects of a Global Brand: The BMW Case," *Marketing and Research Today,* February 1990, p. 54. Permission for using this material which was originally published in *Marketing and Research Today* has been granted by (E.S.O.M.A.R.) the European Society for Opinion and Marketing Research, JJ Viottastraat 29, 1071, JP, Amsterdam, The Netherlands.

[23]Tom Miller, "Global Segments from 'Strivers' to 'Creatives,'" *Marketing News,* July 20, 1998, p. 11; and "Research Finds that Consumers Worldwide Belong to Six Basic Groups that Cross National Lines," *The New York Times,* (June 25, 1998).

[24]Horst Kern, Hans-Christian Wagner, and Roswitha Hassis, "European Aspects of a Global Brand: The BMW case," *Marketing and Research Today,* February 1990, pp. 47–57.

[25]Marieke de Mooij, *Advertising Worldwide,* 2nd ed., (Englewood Cliffs, NJ: Prentice Hall, 1994).

[26]Peter Sampson, "People Are People the World over: The Case for Psychological Market Segmentation," *Marketing and Research Today,* November 1992, pp. 236–44.

Aside from the criteria discussed here, many other country characteristics could form a basis for segmentation. The proper criteria largely depend on the nature of the product and the objectives of the segmentation exercise.

INTERNATIONAL POSITIONING STRATEGIES

Segmenting international markets is only part of the game. Once the multinational company has segmented its foreign markets, the firm needs to decide which target markets to pursue and what positioning strategy to use to appeal to the chosen segments. Some marketing scholars refer to positioning as the fifth P in the marketing mix in addition to product, price, promotion, and place. Developing a positioning theme involves the quest for a unique selling proposition (USP). In the global marketing scene, the positioning question boils down to a battle for the mind of target customers, located not only within a certain country but also in some cases across the globe. The global positioning statement for Budweiser is shown in Exhibit 7-10. The formulation of a positioning strategy, be it local or global, moves along a sequence of steps:

1. Identify a relevant set of competing products or brands. What is the competitive frame?

2. Determine current perceptions held by consumers about the product/brand and the competition.

3. Develop possible positioning themes.

4. Screen the positioning alternatives and select the most appealing one.

5. Develop a marketing mix strategy that will implement the chosen positioning strategy.

6. Over time, monitor the effectiveness of the positioning strategy. If it is not working, determine whether its failure is due to bad execution or an ill-conceived strategy.

Uniform versus Localized Positioning Strategies

Obviously, for global marketers, a key question is the degree to which a uniform positioning strategy can be used. Clearly, one key driver here is the target market decision. Roughly speaking, MNCs have two choices: target a universal segment across countries or pursue different segments in the different markets. When focusing on a uniform segment, management needs to decide whether to use the same positioning worldwide or positioning strategies that are tailored to individual markets. If the firm decides to opt for different segments on a country-by-country basis, the norm is also to customize the positioning appeals. Exhibit 7-11 gives an overview of the different strategic options.

When target customers are very similar worldwide, sharing common core values and showing similar buying patterns, a uniform positioning strategy will probably work. By adopting a common positioning theme, the company can project a shared, consistent

EXHIBIT 7-10
BUDWEISER GLOBAL POSITIONING

Budweiser maintains its leadership positioning in the global beer industry by consistently being a brand that is:

- Refreshingly different from local brands, with its clean, crisp taste and high drinkability
- A premium-quality beer, made using an all-natural process and ingredients
- Global in stature, representing heritage, quality, and U.S. roots
- Well-known as a world-class sponsor of sports and entertainment events
- The world's best-selling beer

Source: www.anheuser-busch.com

EXHIBIT 7-11
GLOBAL POSITIONING AND
SEGMENTATION STRATEGIES

	Universal Segment	Different Segments (case-by-case)
Uniform Positioning Strategy	①	②
Different Positioning Strategies	③	④

brand or corporate image worldwide. The need to have a consistent image is especially urgent for brands that have worldwide exposure and visibility. The "Connecting People" promise made by Nokia is a case in point. A senior Nokia executive made the following observation about the theme: "This is first and foremost an act of consistency and continuity. To communicate our brand values of human technology, individuality, enduring quality and freedom takes planned difference in decided market spheres, but you can always find the same inner feeling, tonality and promise across the globe."[27]

A few years ago, Samsung, a major South Korean consumer electronics manufacturer, announced its intent to obtain the number-one world position in all its main product markets by 2005. To achieve this goal, it positioned its brand as being at the leading edge of digital technology by using an aggressive advertising campaign and developing a whole range of nifty, digital products (e.g., interactive televisions, DVD players, third-generation mobile phones).[28] Having the same positioning theme also enables the firm to use global media. For instance, Samsung sponsored highly visible, global sports events such as the Winter Olympics and the 2002 World Cup Soccer finals. While a uniform positioning goal may be desirable, it is often very difficult to develop a good one that appeals to various markets. Universal themes often run the risk of being bland and not very inspired.

Very rarely do positioning themes "travel." Instead, management usually modifies or localizes them. Appeals that work in one culture do not necessarily work in others. Differences in cultural characteristics, buying power, competitive climate, and the product life cycle stage force firms to tailor their positioning platform. Land Rover, for example, is a brand whose global positioning strategy is difficult to implement.[29] One of the core brand values that Land Rover has cultivated over the years in Europe is "authenticity". This core value is based on Land Rover's heritage of 50 years as a 4 × 4-brand in Europe. The North American market, which Land Rover entered only in the 1980s, presents a different picture. There, Jeep, the DaimlerChrysler 4 × 4-brand, is perceived as the authentic, original four-wheel drive. Hence, Land Rover would have a formidable task creating the same image of authenticity in North America as it did successfully in Europe.

Many firms position a brand that is *mainstream* in its home market as a premium brand in their overseas markets, thereby targeting a narrower segment that is willing to pay a premium for imports. Consider the marketing of the Buick Regal, one of GM's core brands, in China. Buick is just a regular mainstream badge in its home

---

[27]"Fighting to the Finnish," *Ad Age Global*, June 2002, pp. 14–15.

[28]"Koreans Aim to Create a Sharp Image," *Financial Times*, December 28, 2001, p. 14.

[29]Nick Bull and Martin Oxley, "The Search for Focus—Brand Values across Europe," *Marketing and Research Today*, November 1996, pp. 239–47.

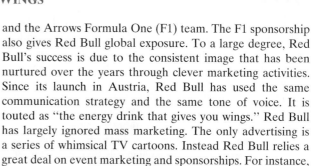

GLOBAL PERSPECTIVE 7-2

SELLING THE ENERGY DRINK THAT GIVES YOU WINGS

Dietrich Mateschitz discovered Red Bull, the infamous energy drink, in Bangkok when he was marketing director for Blendax, a German toothpaste brand. Each time on the way from the airport in Bangkok, he would buy a bottle: "One glass and the jet lag was gone." In fact, he loved the product so much that in 1984 he joined forces with two Thai partners, a father-and-son team, to turn the product into a global brand. They tinkered with the tonic's formula, carbonated it, and translated the Thai words *Krating Daeng* into English: Red Bull. The ingredients are taurine, an amino acid; glucuronolactone, a substance found in the body; and caffeine. The brew went on sale in Austria, Mr. Mateschitz's home country, in 1987. Red Bull was launched in Germany in 1994 and in the United Kingdom in 1993. By 2002, Red Bull had become a global cult drink selling 1.6 billion cans in 62 countries.

Initially, nightclubs and discos were not too keen to take on the product. So Mr. Mateschitz relied instead on traditional retail outlets and petrol stations. Little by little, Red Bull gained a following among extreme sports enthusiasts such as snowboarders and windsurfers because of its alleged potency. Red Bull cultivates the image of being a tonic that makes old-age soft drinks look tame by comparison. According to some critics, its potency is so big that it might in fact be dangerous. The Swedish press linked three deaths to the consumption of Red Bull. In fact, France and Denmark do not allow the brand to be sold.

Red Bull reinforces its edgy image by sponsoring extreme sports (e.g., a mountain bike race down a German salt mine)

and the Arrows Formula One (F1) team. The F1 sponsorship also gives Red Bull global exposure. To a large degree, Red Bull's success is due to the consistent image that has been nurtured over the years through clever marketing activities. Since its launch in Austria, Red Bull has used the same communication strategy and the same tone of voice. It is touted as "the energy drink that gives you wings." Red Bull has largely ignored mass marketing. The only advertising is a series of whimsical TV cartoons. Instead Red Bull relies a great deal on event marketing and sponsorships. For instance, the company sponsors an annual *Flugtag* where contestants build their own flying-machines and leap off a parapet.

In most Western countries, Red Bull is pitched at night-club goers who mix the tonic with alcohol, giving users the energy to party through the night. In several Asian countries, though, a different imaging strategy is needed. For starters, it is sold in a bottle rather than a can to tout a health drink image. In Malaysia, the majority of the population is Muslim. Hence, a bar focus would be unacceptable. Instead, the goal is to project Red Bull as an energy drink that can be consumed on its own. Just as in the West, sports sponsorship is a key activity although the focus is on more traditional motor sports such as motorcycle races and four-wheel drive competitions. Target audiences include students, drivers, and athletes with the main distribution channel being convenience stores. In Thailand, the home of the original Red Bull recipe, a new Red Bull product was created to differentiate between two distinct target markets. The original tonic is promoted as a pick-me-up for taxi drivers and blue-collar workers. Red Bull Extra, the new line extension, targets trendy teens and bar goers. To capture their imagination, the brand uses sponsorships of extreme sports events and concerts.

Sources: "Selling Energy," *The Economist,* May 11, 2002, p. 62; "Red Bull Rethinks Brand Image for Asia," *Media,* October 18, 2002, p. 26; "Extreme Sports and Clubbers Fuel Energetic Rise," *Financial Times,* November 23, 2001, p. 10; and "Red Bull Puts Cash on Lifting Category," *Media,* October 4, 2002, p. 1.

---

market. However, in China, Buick has become a prestigious car with a luxury appeal due to savvy marketing. GM's China Web site touted the Buick as a "sign of respect for successful leaders." Chinese customers are charged as much as $37,000 for a Buick Regal compared to $23,000 for U.S. buyers. As a result, GM earns 15 times more profits on each car sold.[30] Other brands that are mainstream in their home market but perceived as premium in the international marketplace are Heineken, Levi's and Budweiser. This strategy is especially effective in product categories where the local brands already are very well entrenched (such as beer in most countries) and imported brands have a potential to leverage the cachet of being "imported." Local brands usually enjoy a pioneering advantage by the fact of being the first one in the market. Therefore, instead of competing head-on with the local competition, foreign brands (despite the fact that they are a mainstream brand in their home market) are mostly better off by targeting the upscale segment. Although smaller in numbers, this segment is willing to pay a substantial premium price. Global Perspective 7-2 highlights some of the positioning customizations that were made for the energy drink Red Bull.

---

[30] http://www.sfgate.com/cgi-bin/article.cgi?f=/c/a/2005/07/15/BUG0UDO7RE1.DTL.

GLOBAL PERSPECTIVE 7-3
UBS—THE CONCEPT OF "TWO-NESS"

The wealth management group UBS was formed in 1998 by the merger of two major Swiss banks. It has expanded globally, often through acquisitions (e.g., Paine Webber and Warburg in the United States) and now maintains a presence in more than 50 countries. Brands that grow by acquiring existing firms face the task of establishing a clear brand identity both internally (employees) and externally (customers). In February 2004, UBS set out to establish a single consistent brand identity across all markets. This led to the "You and Us" advertising campaign. The campaign has two major targets: the high net worth individual and corporate customers. The focus is the intimacy and strength of UBS's client relationships, backed by the bank's resources. Bernhard Eggli, head of brand management at UBS, noted: "What we found during research is that there's a lot of similarity in terms of the expectations that our client segments have for their preferred financial

services provider, which made it possible for us to move to a single brand. The underlying brand promise works across the globe; the challenge is to find the right execution."

A key task to deliver the universal positioning for the campaign was finding a tagline with global appeal that conveyed UBS's identity. After conducting market research, UBS decided to leave the You and Us tagline in English. "In the attempt to translate the tagline in English, what we have found is that you are losing the simplicity and, to a certain extent, the charm of the tagline," observed Eggli. To underscore the positioning theme, the campaign used images of "two-ness": two chairs, two cups of coffee, two people, and so on. These images symbolized the intimate relationship between the client and the UBS adviser. To cast actors for the campaign, people were chosen in pairs rather than individually. Background images—skyscrapers, offices—were chosen to reinforce the message that a UBS adviser has the support of a large, powerful institution that can mobilize global resources on behalf of the customer.

Sources: http://www.ubs.com/1/e/about/brand.html and http://www.brandchannel.com/features_effect.asp?pf_id=273.

Universal Positioning Appeals

Universal positioning appeals are positioning themes that appeal to consumers anywhere in the world, regardless of an individual's cultural background. Remember that positioning themes can be developed at different levels:

- Specific product features/attributes
- Product benefits (rational or emotional), solutions for problems
- User category
- User application
- Heritage
- Lifestyle

Products that offer universally important benefits or features would meet the criterion of having a universal benefit/feature positioning appeal. In business-to-business markets, where buying behavior is often somewhat less culture bound than for consumer goods, this is often true. Thus, the promise of superior quality performance or productivity for industrial products is one example of a positioning pitch with a universal ring. Benefit- or feature-based positioning can be universal for consumer goods when the core benefit is common worldwide. Superior quality or performance appeals for durables such as television sets (superior picture quality), washing machines (cleaning performance), and so forth. However, for products for which buying motivations are very culture bound (for instance, most food and beverage products), coming up with a universal benefit- or feature-related appeal is a much more difficult task.

A special case in which universal positioning clearly makes sense is the "global citizen" theme often used with corporate image strategies. Here the positioning strategy stresses a global leadership and/or global presence benefit. This strategy is often successfully used in industries where having a global presence is a major plus (e.g., credit cards, banking, insurance, telecommunications). Global Perspective 7-3 discusses Swiss banking firm UBS's universal positioning "You and Us" campaign.

When positioning the product to a specific user category, a uniform approach often succeeds when the user group shares common characteristics. Avon's "Let's Talk" campaign attests to this rule. The campaign, launched in 26 countries in 2000, was designed to reflect Avon's corporate mission of being a "company for women." To project this positioning, the global campaign highlighted Avon's wide product range of beauty products and the company's unique network of 2.8 million sales reps that facilitates one-on-one customer relationships.[31] Likewise, the global positioning used by Kotex, Kimberly-Clark's feminine protection pad brand, turned out to be highly effective in leveraging a common need among the global women segment. Kotex was positioned as the brand "that is designed to fit and feel better for your body, to help you feel better, more like yourself."[32] An example of uniform positioning that is likely to be futile is appeal that centers on the "liberated women" group (e.g., Virginia Slims cigarettes: "You've come a long way, baby"), which is still a very culture-bound phenomenon.

Emotional appeals (e.g., lifestyle positioning) are usually difficult to translate into a universal theme. Values tend to be very culture bound. The trick is to come up with an emotional appeal that has universal characteristics and—at the same time—does not sound dull. One lifestyle survey found that "protecting the family" was seen as a top value in 22 countries, including the United States,[33] so appeals based on family values could be prospective candidates for emotional appeals.

GLOBAL, FOREIGN, AND LOCAL CONSUMER CULTURE POSITIONING[34]

◆ ◆ ◆ ◆ ◆ ◆ ◆ ◆ ◆

Brand managers can position their brand as symbolic of a global consumer culture, a "foreign" culture, or a local culture. The first strategy can be described as **global consumer culture positioning (GCCP).** This strategy tries to project the brand as a symbol of a given global consumer culture. Buying the brand reinforces the consumer's feeling of being part of a global segment. It also fosters the buyer's self-image as being cosmopolitan, modern, and knowledgeable. Examples of brands that successfully use this strategy are Sony ("My First Sony") and Nike ("Just Do It").

At the other extreme is the **local consumer culture positioning (LCCP)** strategy. Despite the fact that the brand may be global, it is portrayed as an intrinsic part of the local culture. It is depicted as being consumed by local people, and, if applicable, manufactured by locals using local supplies or ingredients. Such brands have achieved a **multilocal status.** A good example is Singer, the maker of sewing machines. Singer is German to the Germans, British in the United Kingdom, and American in the United States. In fact, during World War II, German aviators avoided bombing Singer's European factories thinking they were German owned.[35] When Mercedes launched its midprice E-class model in Japan, its ad campaign used Japanese scenery and images. The local imagery was underscored with the tagline: "Mercedes and a beautiful country."[36]

A third strategy is **foreign consumer culture positioning (FCCP).** Here, the goal is to build up a brand mystique around a specific foreign culture, usually one that has highly positive connotations for the product (e.g., Switzerland for watches, Germany for household appliances). In China, U.S. jeans maker Lee targets the children of rich Chinese families and young and upcoming executives. In the past, Lee was perceived as a Chinese company based in the United States (Li is a very common family name in China). At the same time, a market research study showed that the Chinese associate

---

[31]"Avon 'Talks' Globally to Women," *Ad Age Global,* October 2001, p. 43.

[32]"Kotex Wins a Game of Catch-Up," *Ad Age Global,* October 2001, p. 43.

[33]Tom Miller, "Global Segments from 'Strivers' to 'Creatives,'" *Marketing News,* July 20, 1998, p. 11.

[34]Based on Dana L. Alden, Jan-Benedict E.M. Steenkamp, and Rajeev Batra, "Brand Positioning through Advertising in Asia, North America, and Europe: The Role of Global Consumer Culture," *Journal of Marketing,* 63 (January 1999), pp.75–87.

[35]http://www.brandchannel.com/features_effect.asp?pf_id=261.

[36]"Mercedes-Benz Japan Drifts down to Earth alongside Economy," *Ad Age International,* October 1997, p. 36.

jeans with cowboys, the Wild West, freedom, and passion. As a result, the company decided to position Lee jeans as an expensive brand[37] with an American heritage. Lee's U.S. roots are highlighted in print materials with the line "Founded Kansas, USA, 1889."[38] Other U.S. brands such as Nike, Timberland, Cadillac, and Budweiser have been able to position themselves very strongly in their foreign markets as an authentic piece of Americana.

Which positioning strategy is most suitable depends on several factors. One important determinant is obviously the target market. When target consumers share core values, attitudes, and aspirations, using a GCCP strategy could be effective. Another driver is the product category. Products that satisfy universal needs and are used in a similar manner worldwide lend themselves more to a GCCP-type approach. High-tech consumer brands (e.g., Siemens, Nokia, Sony) that symbolize modernism and internationalism would qualify. A third factor is the positioning approach used by the local competition. If every player in the local market is using a GCCP strategy, you might be able to break more easily through the clutter by going for an LCCP strategy (or vice versa). A final factor is the level of economic development. In emerging markets that are still in an early stage of economic development, a GCCP approach might be more beneficial than LCCP. In these markets, a brand with a global image enhances the owner's self-image and status.

Sometimes local brands fight with global brands by using a GCCP or FCCP strategy. For instance, Brand, a local Dutch beer, uses a U.S. setting and English in its advertising. Some brands also use a hybrid approach by combining ingredients of each of the three strategies. McDonald's is portrayed as a global, cosmopolitan fast-food brand (GCCP) but also as an authentic piece of Americana (FCCP). At the same time, in many countries, McDonald's often highlights its local roots, stressing the fact that it provides local jobs, uses local ingredients, and so forth (LCCP). The fast-food chain localizes its menu, selling salmon sandwiches in Norway, McTeriyaki burgers in Japan, McShawarma and McKebab in Israel, Samurai Pork burgers in Thailand, and so forth. According to one story, Japanese Boy Scouts were pleasantly surprised to find a McDonald's restaurant in Chicago.[39] Likewise, many Europeans do not realize that apparel retailer Esprit is a Hong Kong company listed on the Hong Kong stock exchange.

[37]A pair of Lee jeans typically retails for $79, about one-third of the average monthly salary in big Chinese cities.

[38]"Lee Plays Up US Roots to Target China's Elite," *Media,* May 17, 2002, p. 10.

[39]Emiko Ohnuki-Tierney, "McDonald's in Japan," in James L. Watson ed. *Golden Arches East. McDonald's in East Asia* (Stanford, CA: Stanford University Press, 1997), pp. 161–82.

SUMMARY

A common theme in many writings on global marketing is the growing convergence of consumer needs.[40] Colorful phrases have been used to describe this phenomenon such as "global village," "global mall," and "crystallization of the world as a single place," just to mention a few. This phenomenon of increasing globalization is especially visible for many upscale consumer goods and a variety of business-to-business goods and services bought by multinational customers. One director of a global marketing research firm even went so far as to state that "marketers make too much of cultural differences."[41] She supports her claim by two reasons. First, technology has given consumers worldwide the same reference points. People see the same TV ads, share similar life experiences, and are exposed to the same products and services. Second, technology has also given people common aspirations. According to this school of thought, cultures do differ, but the differences do not have any meaningful impact on people's buying behavior.

In the other camp are people like Nicholas Trivisonno, the CEO of ACNielsen, who notes, "There is no global consumer. Each country and the consumer in each country has different attitudes and different behaviors, tastes, spending patterns."[42] The truth of the matter is somewhere between these two extreme opinions. Without proper segmentation of international markets, it is hard to establish whether the "global consumer" segment is myth or reality.

[40]Theodore Levitt, "The Globalization of Markets," *Harvard Business Review,* 61, May–June 1983, pp. 92–102.

[41]Luanne Flikkema, "Global Marketing's Myth: Differences Don't Matter," *Marketing News,* July 20, 1998, p. 4.

[42]"The Global Consumer Myth," *The Financial Times,* April 23, 1991, p. 21.

Global marketers have a continuum of choices to segment their customer base. At one end of the spectrum, the firm could pursue a "universal" segment. Essentially, it offers the same product using a common positioning theme. Most likely there are a few, mostly minor, adaptations of the marketing mix program are needed to recognize cross-border differences. At the other end of the continuum, the firm might consider treating individual countries on a case-by-case basis. In some circumstances, marketers might offer the same product in each country, provided that the positioning is customized. However, the product typically needs to be modified or designed for each country separately. Between these two extremes, there are bound to be many other possibilities.

By the same token, a positioning strategy can take different directions. Going after a uniform segment, a company can adopt a universal positioning strategy or strategies that are custom made. Universal appeals do have benefits. Companies such as UBS, Intel, and Visa have been able to successfully project a uniform, consistent global image. Universal positioning allows the firm to develop a common communication strategy using global or pan-regional media channels. Unfortunately, coming up with a universal appeal that is appealing and not bland is often asking too much.

KEY TERMS

Country-as-segments (aggregate) segmentation

Disaggregate international consumers segmentation

Diverse (unique) segments

Foreign culture consumer positioning (FCCP)

Global culture consumer positioning (GCCP)

Local culture consumer positioning (**LCCP**)

Multilocal status

Regional segments

Socioeconomic strata (SES) analysis

Two-stage international segmentation

Uniform (Localized) positioning

Unique (diverse) segments

Universal positioning appeal

Universal (global) segments

REVIEW QUESTIONS

1. Under what conditions should companies pursue universal market segments?

2. What are the major issues in using per capita GDP or GNP as a country segmentation criterion?

3. Discuss the weaknesses of lifestyle-based segmentation strategies. For what kind of applications would lifestyle segmentation be appropriate?

4. Sometimes local brands use a global consumer culture positioning approach. Explain.

DISCUSSION QUESTIONS

1. Peter Sampson, a managing director of Burke Marketing Research, points out that "lifestyle and value-based segmentations are too general to be of great use in category specific studies... their international application is too limited as lifestyles vary internationally." Do you agree or disagree with his comment?

2. Fiat, the troubled Italian carmaker (www.fiat.com), is looking to sell vehicles in Singapore again after it left the market in 2001. Singapore's auto market is small and very competitive. Fiat sold only 68 cars in Singapore in 1968 and just 5 in 2000 before it pulled out of the market. Fiat's competitors in the small car segment include less expensive Japanese and Korean firms that spend heavily on advertising. Fiat also must overcome the image that its cars are not suitable for local driving conditions. For instance, Fiat failed to offer a "tropicalization pack" for the Punto. Such a pack includes an air conditioning system customized to Singapore's tropical climate. Given Fiat's marketing challenges, what positioning would you prescribe for the car market in Singapore?

3. In a host of emerging markets (e.g., India, Brazil, Thailand), 50 percent and more of the population is under 25. One marketer observes that "teenagers are teenagers everywhere and they tend to emulate U.S. teenagers" (*Advertising Age International,* October 17, 1994, p. I-15). Is there a global teenager segment? Do teenagers in Beijing, for example, really tend to emulate L.A. teenagers? Discuss.

4. *Assignment (advanced).* Select a particular consumption product (e.g., ice cream). Identify at least two variables that you believe might be related to the per capita demand for the chosen product. Collect data on the per capita consumption levels for your chosen product and the selected variables for several countries. Segment the countries using (e.g., cluster analysis; SAS users might consider PROC FASTCLUS). Derive two- and three-cluster solutions. Discuss your findings.

5. Browse through a recent issue of *The Economist*. As some of you may know, it has regional editions. Most of the ads target an international audience (regional or global). Pick four ads and carefully examine each of them. Who is being targeted in each print ad? What sort of positioning is being used?

6. One phenomenon in scores of emerging markets is a rising middle class. In an *Ad Age International* article (October 17, 1994) on the global middle class, one analyst referred to this phenomenon as the *Twinkie-ization* of the world (Twinkie being the brand name of a popular snack in the United States): "It's the little things that are treats and don't cost much and feel like a luxury." What are these "little things"? Do you agree with this statement?

SHORT CASES   ◆ ◆ ◆ ◆ ◆ ◆ ◆

*C*ASE 7-1

CREATIVE TECHNOLOGY—DECLARING WAR ON APPLE IN THE MP3 ARENA

Creative Technology is one of Singapore's most successful companies. Its Sound Blaster soundcards revolutionized PC audio in the 1980s. In 1992, the company was the first Singapore firm to be listed on the Nasdaq. Since that phenomenal success, the company has been searching for the "next big thing." In 2000, it rolled out the world's first hard-disk MP3 player, the Nomad Jukebox, but in late 2001, Apple introduced its first iPod and quickly became the market leader.

In November 2004, Sim Wong Hoo, the founder and CEO of Creative Technology, declared "war" on Apple, confident that his firm's MP3 players would knock the hip iPods down a peg or two. However, it seems safe to say that his company has lost the first rounds. Creative lays claim to second place worldwide but is a distant second. Sales of MP3 players in the first quarter of 2005 were 2 million units, compared to 5.3 million iPods. Creative's share of the worldwide MP3 player market was only 9 percent by the end of 2004.

Source: "Bid to Beat Apple Has Creative Striking Out," *Media,* June 17, 2005, p. 18; http://www.creative.com/products/mp3; "Creative Expands the War against Apple and iPods," www.sfgate.com, accessed January 12, 2006; and "iPod Envy," www.forbes.com, accessed January 12, 2006.

Much of its woes can be attributed to Apple, which launched the iPod Shuffle, followed by iPod Nano, and, most recently, a video-downloadable version of the core iPod product. In the fall of 2005, Creative introduced the Zen Vision:M (http://www.creative.com/products/mp3/zenvisionm/) to compete head-on with Apple's video iPod. Although, the Vision:M has similar features to the high-end, fifth-generation iPod such as a 30-gigabyte hard drive, it claims additional benefits. In particular, Vision:M can play 4 hours' worth of video compared to only 2 hours for iPod. Also, the device supports a variety of audio and video file formats that iPod does not. Despite these superior benefits, iPod still outsells Zen's MP3-players by far. The "war" also seems to have affected Creative's bottom line: The company posted a net loss of $9.3 million for the first quarter of 2006. Creative was a pioneer in the MP3-market. What went wrong? Did Creative lose the war, or can it recuperate and knock iPod from the top? Prepare a brief for Creative's CEO Sim Wong Hoo spelling out a diagnosis of what happened and what he should do for Creative to win the war. Or should he simply concede defeat and shift to another arena?

FURTHER READING   ◆ ◆ ◆ ◆ ◆ ◆ ◆ ◆ ◆ ◆ ◆ ◆ ◆ ◆

Alden, Dana L., Jan-Benedict E.M. Steenkamp, and Rajeev Batra. "Brand Positioning through Advertising in Asia, North America, and Europe: The Role of Global Consumer Culture." *Journal of Marketing,* 63(1), January 1999, pp. 75–87.

Hassan, Salah S., and Lea P. Katsanis. "Identification of Global Consumer Segments." *Journal of International Consumer Marketing,* 3(2), 1991, pp. 11–28.

Helsen, Kristiaan, Kamel Jedidi, and Wayne S. DeSarbo. "A New Approach to Country Segmentation Utilizing Multinational Diffusion Patterns." *Journal of Marketing,* 57 (October 1993), pp. 60–71.

Hinton, Graham, and Jane Hourigan. "The Golden Circles: Marketing in the New Europe." *Journal of European Business,* 1(6) July/August 1990, pp. 5–30.

Johansson, Johny K., and Reza Moinpour. "Objective and Perceived Similarity for Pacific-Rim Countries." *Columbia Journal of World Business.* Winter 1977, pp. 65–76.

Kale, Sudhir, "Grouping Euroconsumers: A Culture-Based Clustering Approach." *Journal of International Marketing,* 3(3), 1995, pp. 35–48.

Kale, Sudhir, and D. Sudharshan. "A Strategic Approach to International Segmentation." *International Marketing Review,* Summer 1987, pp. 60–70.

Sampson, Peter. "People are People the World over: The Case for Psychological Segmentation." *Marketing and Research Today,* November 1992, pp. 236–44.

Steenkamp, Jan-Benedict E., and F. Ter Hofstede. "International Market Segmentation: Issues and Perspectives." *International Journal of Research in Marketing,* 19 (September 2002), pp. 185–213.

Ter Hofstede, Frenkel, Jan-Benedict E. Steenkamp, and Michel Wedel. "International Market Segmentation Based on Consumer-Product Relations." *Journal of Marketing Research,* 36(1), February 1999, pp. 1–17.

Ter Hofstede, F., M. Wedel, and J.-B.E.M. Steenkamp. "Identifying Spatial Segments in International Markets." *Marketing Science,* 21 (Spring 2002), pp. 160–77.

Yavas, Ugur, Bronislaw J. Verhage, and Robert T. Green. "Global Consumer Segmentation versus Local Market Orientation: Empirical Findings." *Management International Review* 32(3), 1992, pp. 265–72.

APPENDIX: SEGMENTATION TOOLS ◆ ◆ ◆ ◆ ◆ ◆ ◆ ◆ ◆ ◆ ◆ ◆ ◆ ◆ ◆ ◆ ◆ ◆

In this appendix, we give an overview of segmentation tools that can be used for a country segmentation. A huge variety of segmentation methodologies has been developed in the marketing literature. Many of these techniques are quite sophisticated. We will give you just the flavor of two of the most popular tools without going through all the technical nitty-gritty.

When only one segmentation variable is used, classifying countries in distinct groups is quite straightforward. You could simply compute the mean (or median) and split countries into two groups based on the value (above or below) of the criterion variable compared to the mean (or median). When more than two groups need to be formed, you can use other quantiles. Things become a bit more complicated when you plan to use multiple country segmentation variables. Typically, the goal of market segmentation is to relate, in some manner, a battery of descriptive variables about the countries to one or more behavioral response variables:

$$\text{Response} = F\,(\text{Descriptor}_1, \text{Descriptor}_2, \text{Descriptor}_3, \ldots)$$

For instance, the response variable might be the per capita consumption of a given product. The descriptor variables could be the stage in the product life cycle, per capita GNP, literacy level, and so on. We now describe two methods that can help you to achieve this goal: cluster analysis and regression.

Cluster Analysis. *Cluster analysis* is an umbrella term that embraces a collection of statistical procedures for dividing objects into groups (*clusters*). The grouping is done in such a manner that members belonging to the same group are very similar to one another but quite distinct from members of other groups.

EXHIBIT 7-12
PRINCIPLES OF CLUSTER ANALYSIS

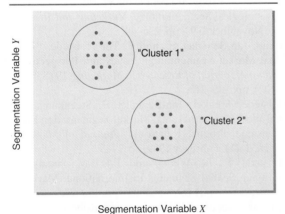

Suppose information was collected for a set of countries on two variables, X and Y. The countries are plotted in Exhibit 7-12. Each dot corresponds to a country. In this case, the clusters are quite obvious. Just by eyeballing the graph, you can distinguish two clear-cut clusters, namely Cluster 1 and Cluster 2. Unfortunately, in real-world applications, clustering is

seldom so easy. Consider Exhibit 7-13, which plots the values of chocolate volume growth rate and market concentration[43] in eight countries. For this example, it is far less obvious how many clusters there are, let alone how they are composed. In addition, most country segmentations involve many more than two criteria.

EXHIBIT 7-13
PLOT OF CONCENTRATION VERSUS CATEGORY GROWTH CHOCOLATE MARKET

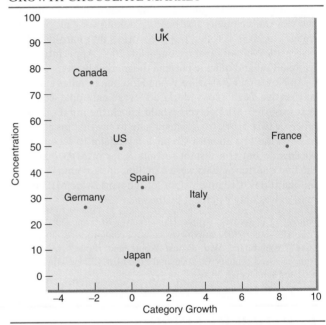

Luckily many statistical algorithms are available to do the job for you. The basic notion is to group countries together that are "similar" in value for the segmentation bases of interest. Similarity measures come under many guises. The most popular way is to use some type of distance measure:

$$\text{Distance}_{\text{country A vs. B}} = (X_{\text{country A}} - X_{\text{country B}})^2 \\ + (Y_{\text{country A}} - Y_{\text{country B}})^2$$

where X and Y are the segmentation variables. These distances[44] would be computed for each pair of countries in the set. The clustering algorithm takes these distances and uses them as inputs to generate the desired number of country groupings. Most "canned" statistical software packages (e.g., SAS, SPPS-X) have at least one procedure that allows you to run a cluster analysis. Exhibit 7-14 provides the two- and three-cluster solutions for the chocolate market example.

Regression. Alternatively, you might consider using regression analysis to classify countries. In regression, you assume that a relationship exists between a response variable, Y, and one or more so-called predictor variables, X_1, X_2, and so on:

---

[43]Measured via the combined market shares of the three largest competitors: Cadbury, Mars, and Nestlé.

[44]Strictly speaking, these are "squared" distances.

$$Y = a + b_1X_1 + b_2X_2 + b_3X_3 + \dots$$

The first term, *a*, is the intercept. It corresponds to the predicted value of *Y* when all *X*s equal 0. The other parameters, the *b*s, are the slope coefficients. For example, b_1 tells you what the predicted change in *Y* will be for a unit change in X_1.

EXHIBIT 7-14
CLUSTER ANALYSIS

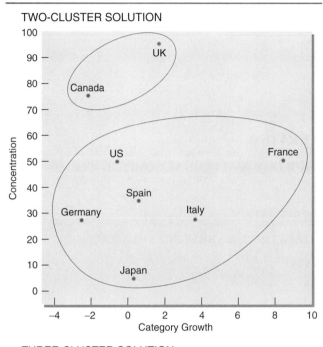

TWO-CLUSTER SOLUTION

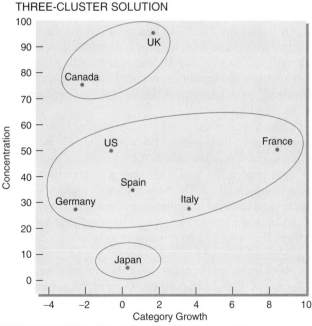

THREE-CLUSTER SOLUTION

In our context, the dependent variable, *Y*, would be a behavioral response variable (e.g., per capita consumption)

and the predictor variables would be a collection of country characteristics that are presumed to be related to the response measure. For given values of the parameters, you can compute the predicted *Y*-values, $\hat{Y}$. Very seldom, these predicted values will match the observed *Y*s. The goal of regression is to find estimates for the intercept, *a*, and the slope coefficients, the *b*s, that provide the "best" fit by minimizing the prediction errors, $\hat{Y} - Y$, between the predicted and observed values of *Y*. The most common regression procedure, ordinary least squares (OLS), minimizes the sum of the squared differences of these prediction errors.

For each of the parameter estimates, the regression analysis also produces a standard error. Dividing the parameter estimate by the standard error yields the *t*-ratio. This ratio tells you whether or not the predictor variable has a "significant" (statistically speaking) relationship with the dependent variable. As a rule of thumb, a *t*-ratio (in absolute value) larger than 2.0 indicates a significant effect of the predictor variable on the response variable. The overall goodness of fit is captured via the R^2 statistic. The higher the R^2 value, the better the ability of your regression model to predict your data.

To illustrate the use of regression analysis as a segmentation tool, let's look at a numerical example. Consider a microwave oven maker that wants to explore market opportunities in the European market. Data were collected for several European countries on the penetration of microwave ovens (as percentage of households owning a microwave). Data were also gathered on three potential segmentation variables: income (per capita GDP), participation of women in the labor force, and per capita consumption of frozen foods.[45] Using these data as inputs, the following results were obtained (*t*-ratios in parentheses):

MICROWAVE OWNERSHIP =
$-76.7 - 0.5$ FROZEN FOOD $+ 2.7$ WOMEN -0.03 PER CAP GDP
$(-2.2)(-1.3)$ (2.9) (-0.04)
$R^2 = 0.52$

Note that the only meaningful segmentation base is apparently the participation of women in the labor force: microwave ownership increases with the proportion of women in the labor force. Because the microwave is a time-saving appliance, this result intuitively makes sense. The other variables appear to have (statistically speaking) not much of an impact on the adoption of microwave ovens. Somewhat surprisingly, high consumption of frozen foods does not lead to an increased ownership of microwave ovens. There is also no relationship with income. Thus, in this case, the European marketing manager could group countries simply on the basis of the degree of participation of women in the labor force.

In addition to these two commonplace tools, many other multivariate statistical procedures can be used to do country segmentation analysis (e.g., latent class analysis, discriminant analysis, Automatic Interaction Detection).

---

[45] The data for this example were collected from *European Marketing Data and Statistics 1992* (London: Euromonitor).

GLOBAL MARKETING STRATEGIES

8

HAPTER OVERVIEW

1. INFORMATION TECHNOLOGY AND GLOBAL COMPETITION

2. GLOBAL STRATEGY

3. GLOBAL MARKETING STRATEGY

4. REGIONALIZATION OF GLOBAL MARKETING STRATEGY

5. COMPETITIVE ANALYSIS

On a political map, country borders are clear as ever, but on a competitive map, financial, trading, and industrial activities across national boundaries have rendered those political borders increasingly irrelevant. Of all the forces chipping away at those boundaries, perhaps the most important is the flow of information that governments previously monopolized, "cooking it up" as they saw fit and redistributing it in forms of their own devising. Their information monopoly on events happening around the world enabled them to fool, mislead, or even control the people, because only the government possessed the facts in detail.[1]

Today people can see for themselves what tastes and preferences are like in other countries. For instance, people in India watching CNN and Star TV now know instantaneously what is happening in the rest of the world. A farmer in a remote village in Rajasthan in India asks the local vendor for Surf (the detergent manufactured by Unilever) because he has seen a commercial on TV. More than 10 million Japanese traveling abroad every year are exposed to larger-size homes and much lower consumer prices abroad than at home. Such information access creates demand that would not have existed before, and it restricts the power of governments to influence consumer choice.

The availability and explosion of information technology such as telecommunications has forever changed the nature of global competition. Geographical boundaries and distance have become less a constraint in designing strategies for the global market. The other side of the coin is that not only firms that compete internationally but also those whose primary market is considered domestic will be affected by competition

---

[1] Kenichi Ohmae, *The Borderless World* (London: Harper Collins, 1990).

from around the world. In this chapter, we explain the nature of global competition and examine various ways to gain competitive advantage for the firm facing global competition.

INFORMATION TECHNOLOGY AND GLOBAL COMPETITION

♦ ♦ ♦ ♦ ♦ ♦ ♦ ♦ ♦

The development of transportation technology, including jet air transportation, cold storage containers, and large ocean carriers, changed the nature of world trade in the 50 years after World War II. Since the 1980s, the explosion of information technology, particularly telecommunications, and more recently electronic commerce (e-commerce) has forever changed the nature of competition around the world. Geographical distance has become increasingly less relevant in designing global strategy.

Since the 1990s the growth of e-commerce on the Internet has exploded, beginning in the United States. In 1995, only 4 percent of Americans used the Internet every day. In March 2005, the figure was 67.8 percent and still growing fast.[2] As mentioned in Chapter 1, the total global e-commerce volume increased over sevenfold from $358 billion in 2000 to $2.58 trillion in 2004. The U.S. share of e-commerce grew from $162 billion to $991 billion; however, in percentage terms relative to the rest of the world, the U.S. share declined from 45 percent to 38 percent of world total,[3] clearly indicating that e-commerce has spread significantly more outside the United States, indicating a further globalization of e-commerce. In the same time period, the number of Internet users in the world rose from 367 million in 2000 to 818 million in 2004.[4]

Electronic Commerce (E-Commerce)

There is no marketing channel other than e-commerce whose revenues are growing at this pace. There is no other way a business can grow unimpeded by the need to build commercial space and hire sales staff. While traditional mass retailers, such as Wal-Mart in the United States, Carrefour in France, and Metro in Germany, will not disappear any time soon, the Internet has fundamentally changed customers' expectations about convenience, speed, comparability, price, and service. Even the traditional mass retailers, such as Wal-Mart, the largest U.S. company with an annual sale close to $300 billion, is trying to generate as much as 30 percent of its total sales over the Internet by 2008.[5] Likewise, Dell Computer rocketed to the top of the personal computer business in the United States by selling directly to consumers online. As commented by Mike George, the chief marketing officer and general manager of its consumer business unit, "If Dell changes prices on its website, its customers' buying patterns change literally within a minute." Many consumers are knowledgeable about their prospective purchase from the Internet before they arrive at a showroom or a retail store.[6] Those new expectations will reverberate throughout the world, affecting every business, domestic or global, in many ways.

Marketing beyond the home country has always been hampered by geographical distance and the lack of sufficient information about foreign markets, although transportation and communications technology has reduced, if not eliminated, many difficulties of doing business across the national boundary. Now as a result of an explosive growth of e-commerce on the Internet, those difficulties are increasingly becoming a thing of the past. In other words, product life cycle is becoming shorter

---

[2]Internet usage statistics for the Americas, The Internet Coaching Library, http://www.internetworldstats.com, accessed December 20, 2005.

[3]IDC, Internet Commerce Market Model, Version 8.3, International Data Corporation, www.idc.com, 2004.

[4]Datamonitor, "Global Internet Software & Services: Industry Profile," www.datamonitor.com, May 2005.

[5]"E-Commerce Retail Sales Jump by 24 %," *Wall Street Journal,* May 23, 2005, p. B2.

[6]"Crowned at Last," *Economist,* April 2, 2005, pp. 3–6.

and shorter. E-commerce breaks every business free of the concept of geographic distance. No longer will geography bind a company's aspirations or the scope of its market. Traditional bookstores used to be constrained to certain geographical areas, probably within a few miles in radius of their physical locations. Now, Amazon.com and BarnesandNoble.com can reach any place on earth whether the consumer is in Amsterdam or Seoul as long as the consumer has access to the Internet. For every early e-commerce mover to eliminate the geographic boundaries of its business, there will be dozens of companies that lose their local monopolies to footloose online businesses.

Although Japan was somewhat slower in adopting personal computers than the United States, the Internet has also taken off in the world's second largest economy. For example, Dell Computer and other U.S. computer manufacturers arguably were the first to market their products directly to Japanese consumers over the Internet. Dell Computer Japan reported that 75 percent of the total number of computers it sold to individual buyers was bought online in Japan. IBM Japan also reported that the number of computers sold over the Internet more than doubled in 2000 from the previous year.[7] Rakuten Ichiba, Japan's largest Internet shopping site with more than 11,000 registered businesses, averages more than 21 million page views a day.[8] Sales grew from $26 million in 2000 to $433 million in 2004, and operating profits reached $146 million in 2004.[9]

Similarly, Canada lagged behind the United States in terms of online business sales in the 1990s. However, it has just about caught up with the United States in terms of e-commerce per capita. According to a report published in 2005, Canadians, on average, spend $506 on e-commerce while Americans spend $591.[10] According to a survey by Sun Microsystems of Canada, 56 percent of business will move online by 2007.[11]

Even the same explosive Internet growth is being experienced in countries that are still catching up technologically to countries such as the United States and Japan. For example, China has already become one of the world's largest Internet markets. According to the China Internet Network Information Center, the Internet community in China increased by more than 150 times over the past seven years, soaring from just 620,000 users in 1997 to 94 million by March 2004. Some large portals in China such as Netease, Sina, Sohu, and Tom, have been making a healthy profit since 2003. Online gaming is fast growing and is one of the three largest money-makers for Internet companies with the other two being e-finance and e-education. Unlike other high Internet usage countries, the majority of gamers play at the Internet Cafes in China rather than at home, and it is estimated that China has 350,000 Internet cafes. China's largest e-game operator, Shanda Interactive Entertainment Limited, grows by operating licensed South Korean online games and has accumulated a huge amount of wealth within a few years. In 2004, the company generated a $373 million online games market, 39.3 percent of China's market share. Now the company is shifting its business focus from the computer platform to the TV platform, including games, music, and literature, through a set-top box to penetrate those 340 million households that already own a television.[12]

---

[7]"Online sales of Home Appliances Skyrocket," *Daily Yomiuri Online,* http://www.yomiuri.co.jp/index-e.htm, January 18, 2001.

[8]"Rakuten Deploys Foundry Networks' Industry-Leading Ethernet Switching to Power Its E-Commerce Site," Foundry Networks Press Release, http://www.foundrynet.com/about/newsevents/releases/pdfs/pr7_01_03.pdf, accessed December 20, 2005.

[9]Rakuten Ichiba, http://www.rakuten.co.jp/info/ir/english/finance/data.html, accessed November 20, 2005.

[10]Chuan-Fong Shih, Jason Dedrick, Kenneth L. Kraemer, "Rule of Law and the International Diffusion of E-Commerce," *Communications of the ACM,* 48 (November 2005), pp. 57–62.

[11]"Canada Warming to Enterprise e-Commerce," *Computing Canada,* June 7, 2002, p. 10.

[12]"Online-Game Developers Eye China Market," *China Daily,* April 25, 2005.

Information that managers have about the state of the firm's operations is almost in real time. Routinely, the chief executive officer of a firm can know the previous day's sales down to a penny and can be alerted to events and trends now instead of in several months, when it may be too late to do anything about them.

In the mid-1990s, Volvo faced a classic supply chain dilemma. For whatever reason—perhaps just capricious consumer tastes—halfway through the year, the company found itself with an excess inventory of green cars. The sales and marketing team responded appropriately by developing an aggressive program of deals, discounts, and rebates to push green vehicles through the distribution channel. The program worked well, and green Volvos began to move out off dealer lots. However, manufacturing planners at the factory, also noted the surge in sales of green cars. Unfortunately, they were unaware of the big push taking place on the sales and marketing side and assumed that customers had suddenly developed a preference for the color green. So they responded by increasing production of green cars. The company soon found itself caught in a feedback loop that resulted in an even larger surplus of green Volvos at end of the year.[13] This story is typical of the kind of disconnect that is far too common in manufacturing companies, especially those that rely on multitier distribution. That inability or failure to share real-time data or knowledge with partners can result in erroneous assumptions and costly errors in decision making. To avoid the problem from happening, companies need to use information technology to link all parts of the organization into a real-time enterprise.

Top retailers such as Wal-Mart and Toys "Я" Us get information from their stores around the world every two hours via telecommunications. Industry analysts say that former leader K-Mart fell behind due to its delay in installing point-of-sale information technology, which would have enabled it to get faster and more accurate information on inventories and shelf movement of products.[14] Such access is now possible because advances in electronic storage and transmission technology allow 26 volumes of *Encyclopaedia Britannica* to be stored on a single chip and transmit that material in a second; these figures are expected to improve by a factor of 10 by the end of the decade.

The combination of information technology, access tools, and telecommunication has squeezed out a huge chunk of organizational slack from corporate operations that were previously inherent due to the slow and circuitous nature of information flow within the firm, with holdups due to human "switches." Ordering and purchasing components, which was once a cumbersome, time-consuming process, is now done by electronic data interchange (EDI), reducing the time involved in such transactions from weeks to days and eliminating a considerable amount of paperwork. Levi-Strauss uses LeviLink, an EDI service for handling all aspects of order and delivery. Customers can even place small orders as needed, say, every week, and goods are delivered within two days. One of Levi-Strauss' customers, Design p.l.c., with a chain of 60 stores, was able to entirely eliminate its warehouses, which were used as a buffer to deal with the long lead times between order and delivery.[15]

Real-Time Management

Sales representatives on field calls who were previously, in effect, tied to the regional or central headquarters due to lack of product information and limited authority, are now able to act independently in the field because laptop computers, faxes, and satellite uplinks enable instant access to data from the company's central database. Changes in prices due to discounts can now be cleared online from the necessary authority. This reduces reaction time for the sales representative and increases productivity. Monitoring problems for the firm are also reduced, as is paperwork.

Online Communication

---

[13]"Does Everyone Have the Same View in Your Supply Chain?," *Frontline Solutions*, 3 (July 2002), pp. 27–30.

[14]Julia King, "OLAP Gains Fans among Data-Hungry Firms," *Computerworld*, 30 (January 8, 1996), pp. 43, 48.

[15]Sidney Hill, Jr., "The Race for Profits," *Manufacturing Systems*, 16 (May 1998), pp. ii–iv + .

Multiple design sites around the world in different time zones can now work sequentially on the same problem. A laboratory in California can close its day at 5 P.M. local time when the design center in Japan is just opening the next day. That center continues work on the design problem and hands it over to London at the end of its day, which continues the work and hands over the cumulated work of Japan and London back to California. Finally, the use of telecommunications improves internal efficiency of the firm in other ways. For instance, when Microsoft came up with an upgrade on one of its applications that required some customer education, a customer, using video conferencing on its global information network, arranged a single presentation for the relevant personnel, dispersed across the world, obviating travel and multiple presentations.

E-Company

The ultimate effect of information networks within the multinational firm is expected to be on the nature of its organizational structure. As information flows faster across the organization and the number of "filtering" points between the source of information (e.g., point-of-sale information or market and industry analysis) and the user of the information (e.g., the brand manager or the chief executive officer) decreases, the nature of the organization chart in the multinational firm changes drastically. An increasing number of multinational firms have begun to use internal Web servers on the Internet to facilitate communications and transactions among employees, suppliers, independent contractors, and distributors.[16]

Many companies today realize the key to this change is e-business. Siemens, for example, is spending €1 billion to turn itself into an e-company. Siemens is expecting to connect the different parts of its far-flung empire into a more coherent whole. In practice, the corporation plans to utilize its information technology to enhance knowledge management and online purchasing, change the company's value chain, and efficiently deal with its customers. Now customers can click on "Buy from Siemens" on the company's home page and place orders. Inevitably, Siemens' demand chain will go smoothly from customers, through Siemens, and then to its suppliers.[17] Similarly, an assembly-line worker in a Procter & Gamble plant knows from his computer that stores have been selling a particular brand of facial cream more briskly than anticipated. Having this information, he can change production scheduling on his own by giving the computer necessary instructions to cut down on some other brands and to increase the production of the brand in question. The foreperson and the section manager of a conventional plant are no longer required.

Faster Product Diffusion

The obvious impact of information technology is the more rapid dispersion of technology and the shorter product life cycles in global markets than ever before. It suggests that the former country-by-country sequential approach to entering markets throughout the world, described in the international product cycle model in Chapter 1, is increasingly untenable.

This trend is already reflected in many product markets. The diffusion lag for color television between the United States on one hand and Japan and Europe on the other was six years. With compact discs, the household penetration rates had come down to one year. For Pentium-based computers, Taiwan, India, Japan, and U.S.-based companies released computers at about the same time in their respective national markets. Thus, a firm selling personal computers would have to launch a new product on a worldwide basis in order not to fall behind in the global sweepstakes.[18] This issue will be discussed further when we discuss new product development in Chapter 11.

---

[16]John A. Quelch and Lisa R. Klein, "The Internet and International Marketing," *Sloan Management Review,* 37 (Spring 1996), pp. 60–75.

[17]"Electronic Glue," *Economist,* May 31, 2001, pp. 77–78.

[18]Shlomo Kalish, Vijay Mahajan, and Eitan Muller, "Waterfall and Sprinker New-Product Strategies in Competitive Global Markets," *International Journal of Research in Marketing,* 12 (July 1995), pp. 105–19.

Another important contributing factor in the globalization of markets is the spread of English as the language of international business. The transformation of the European Union into a monetary union has taken place with the introduction of the euro as its common currency. Global citizenship is no longer just a phrase in the lexicon of futurologists. It has already become every bit as concrete and measurable as changes in gross national product (GNP) and trade flows. In fact, conventional measures of trade flows may have outlived their usefulness, as we discuss later.

Global Citizenship

The global environment thus demands a strategy that encompasses numerous national boundaries and tastes and that integrates a firm's operations across the national borders. This strategy is truly global in nature and has gone beyond the home-country-focused ethnocentric orientation or the multicountry-focused polycentric orientation of many multinational firms in the middle of the 20th century. The firm thus needs to adopt a geocentric orientation that views the entire world as a potential market and integrates firm activities on a global basis.[19]

GLOBAL STRATEGY

◆ ◆ ◆ ◆ ◆ ◆ ◆ ◆

The acid test of a well-managed company is being able to conceive, develop, and implement an effective global strategy. A **global strategy** is to array the competitive advantages arising from location, world-scale economies, or global brand distribution, namely, by building a global presence, defending domestic dominance, and overcoming country-by-country fragmentation. Because of its inherent difficulties, global strategy development presents one of the stiffest challenges for managers today. Companies that operate on a global scale need to integrate their worldwide strategy in contrast to the earlier multinational or multidomestic approach. The earlier strategies would be categorized more truly as multidomestic strategies rather than as global strategies.

We approach the issue of global strategy through various conceptualizations, the first of which is that of a global industry.[20] **Global industry** is defined as *one in which a firm's competitive position in one country is affected by its position in other countries and vice versa.* Therefore, we are talking about not just a collection of domestic industries but also a series of interlinked domestic industries in which rivals compete against one another on a truly worldwide basis. For instance, 25 years after Honda began making cars in its first U.S. Japanese transplant in Marysville, Ohio, the automaker is increasingly relying on the U.S. market. It has boosted its North American production capacity 40 % by 2006. Today, more than half the passenger sedans sold in the United States are import brands, and more than half the vehicles sporting foreign nameplates are made in the United States. Foreign players are the ones reinvigorating the U.S. automobile business and turning the country into the center of a global industry.[21]

Global Industry

Therefore, the first question that faces managers is the extent of globalization of their industry. Assuming that the firm's activities are indeed global or that the firm wishes to grow toward global operations and markets, managers must design and implement a global strategy. This is so because virtually every industry has global or potentially global aspects; some industries have more aspects that are global and more intensely so. Indeed, a case has been made that the globalization of markets has already been achieved, that consumer tastes around the world have converged, and that the global firm attempts, unceasingly, to drive consumer tastes toward convergence.[22] Four major forces determining the globalization potential of industry are presented in Exhibit 8-1.

[19]Shaoming Zou and S. Tamer Cavusgil, *"The GMS: A Broad Conceptualization of Global Marketing Strategy and Its Effect on Firm Performance,"* Journal of Marketing, 66 (October 2002), pp. 40–56.

[20]Michael E. Porter, ed., *Competition in Global Industries* (Boston, MA: Harvard University Press, 1986).

[21]"Autos: A New Industry," *Business Week,* July 15, 2002, p. 98–104.

[22]Theodore Levitt, "The Globalization of Markets," *Harvard Business Review,* 61 (May-June 1983), pp. 92–102.

EXHIBIT 8-1
INDUSTRY GLOBALIZATION DRIVERS

Market Drivers

Market drivers depend on the nature of customer behavior and the structure of channels of distribution. Some common market drivers follow:

- Per capita income converging among industrialized nations
- Emergence of rich consumers in emerging markets such as China and India
- Convergence of lifestyles and tastes (e.g., McDonald's in Moscow and Stolichnaya vodka in the United States)
- Revolution in information and communication technologies (e.g., personal computer, fax machines, and the Internet)
- Increased international travel creating global consumers knowledgeable of products from many countries
- Organizations beginning to behave as global customers
- Growth of global and regional channels (e.g., America's Wal-Mart, France's Carrefour/Promodès, Gremany's Metro, and Japan's 7-Eleven)
- Establishment of world brands (e.g., Coca-Cola, Microsoft, Toyota, and Nestlé)
- Push to develop global advertising (e.g., Saatchi and Saatchi's commercials for British Airways)
- Spread of global and regional media (e.g., CNN, MTV, Star TV in India)

Cost Drivers

Cost drivers depend on the economics of the business. These drivers particularly affect production location decisions, as well as global market participation and global product development decisions. Some of these cost drivers are as follows:

- Push for economies of scale and scope further aided by flexible manufacturing
- Accelerating technological innovations
- Advances in transportation (e.g., FedEx, UPS, DHL, and Yamato Transport)
- Emergence of newly industrializing countries with productive capabilities and low labor costs (e.g., China, India, and many Eastern European countries)
- High product development costs relative to shortened product life cycle

Government Drivers

Rules set by national governments can affect the use of global strategic decision making. Some of these rules/policies include these:

- Reduction of tariff and nontariff barriers
- Creation of trading blocs (e.g., European Union, North American Free Trade Agreement, and MERCOSUR—a common market in South America)
- Establishment of world trading regulations (e.g., World Trade Organization and its various policies)
- Deregulation of many industries
- Privatization in previously state-dominated economies in Latin America
- Shift to open market economies from closed communist systems in China, Eastern Europe, and the former Soviet Union

EXHIBIT 8-1
(*continued*)

Competitive Drivers

Competitive drivers raise the globalization potential of their industry and spur the need for a response on the global strategy levels. The common competitive drivers include the following:

- Increase in world trade
- Rise in countries becoming key competitive battlegrounds (e.g., Japan, Korea, China, India, and Brazil)
- Increased ownership of corporations by foreign investors
- Globalization of financial markets (e.g., listing of corporations on multiple stock exchanges and issuing debt in multiple currencies)
- Rise of new competitors intent on becoming global competitors (e.g., Japanese firms in the 1970s, Korean firms in the 1980s, Taiwanese firms in the 1990s, Chinese and Indian firms in the 2000s, and probably Russian firms in the 2010s)
- Rise of "born global" Internet and other companies
- Growth of global networks making countries interdependent in particular industries (e.g., electronics and aircraft manufacturing)
- Increase in companies becoming geocentric rather than ethnocentric (e.g., Stanley Works, a traditional U.S. company, moved its production offshore; Uniden, a Japanese telecommunications equipment manufacturer has never manufactured in Japan)
- Increased formation of global strategic alliances

Source: Adapted from George S. Yip, *Total Global Strategy II* (Upper Saddle River, N.J.: Prentice Hall, 2003, pp. 10–12.

The implications of a distinction between multidomestic and global strategy are quite profound. In a multidomestic strategy, a firm manages its international activities like a portfolio. Its subsidiaries or other operations around the world each control all important activities necessary to maximize their returns in their area of operation independent of the activities of other subsidiaries in the firm. The subsidiaries enjoy a large degree of autonomy, and the firm's activities in each of its national markets are determined by the competitive conditions in that national market. In contrast, a global strategy integrates the activities of a firm on a worldwide basis to capture the linkages among countries and to treat the entire world as a single, borderless market. This requires more than transferring intangible assets between or among countries.

In effect, the firm that truly operationalizes a global strategy is a geocentrically oriented firm. It considers the whole world as its arena of operation, and its managers maintain equidistance from all markets and develop a system with which to satisfy its needs for both global integration for economies of scale and scope and responsiveness to different market needs and conditions in various parts of the world. (See Chapter 10 for some detailed examples.). In a way, the geocentric firm tries to "kill two birds with one stone."[23] Such a firm tends to centralize some resources at home, some abroad, and distributes others among its many national operations, resulting in a complex configuration of assets and capabilities on a global basis.[24]

This is in contrast to an ethnocentric orientation, where managers operate under the dominant influence of home country practices, or a polycentric orientation, where managers of individual subsidiaries operate independently of each other: The polycentric manager in practice leads to a multidomestic orientation, which prevents integration and optimization on a global basis. Until the early 1980s, Unilever's global operations were a good example of a multidomestic approach. Unilever's various country operations were largely independent of each other, with headquarters restricting itself to data

---

[23]Masaaki Kotabe, "To Kill Two Birds with One Stone: Revisiting the Integration-Responsiveness Framework," in *Managing Transnational Firms,* ed. Michael Hitt and Joseph Cheng, (New York: Elsevier, 2002), pp. 59–69.

[24]Christopher A. Bartlett and Sumantra Ghoshal, *Managing Across Borders* (Boston, MA: Harvard Business School Press, 1989).

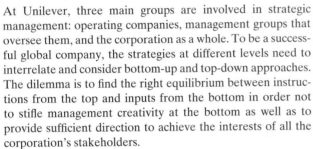

GLOBAL PERSPECTIVE 8-1
GLOBALIZING THE MULTIDOMESTIC CORPORATE CULTURE

At Unilever, three main groups are involved in strategic management: operating companies, management groups that oversee them, and the corporation as a whole. To be a successful global company, the strategies at different levels need to interrelate and consider bottom-up and top-down approaches. The dilemma is to find the right equilibrium between instructions from the top and inputs from the bottom in order not to stifle management creativity at the bottom as well as to provide sufficient direction to achieve the interests of all the corporation's stakeholders.

The company's culture and philosophy influence this equilibrium. Unilever, for example, was formerly highly decentralized with individual operating companies, each with their own identity, linked by a common corporate culture and some common services such as research, finance, and management development. After having experimented with various organizational structures to encourage global strategic management, Unilever adopted a full-time corporate development board member who is on staff with an advisory role, free from major line responsibilities.

Unilever's culture still emphasizes the relative independence of operating companies, where headquarters imposes changes only when there are clear advantages in doing so. Because the problems faced by Unilever did not require an immediate strong reaction, the senior managers could proceed comparatively gradually, having the opportunity to feel a part of the strategy process. The gradual change in strategy orientation fit the company's corporate culture, demanding a gradual dosage rather than a sudden shock, with senior managers being able to feel a greater sense of commitment to the company's strategy.

Sources: F.A. Maljers, "Strategic Planning and Intuition in Unilever," *Long Range Planning,* 23 (2) (1990), pp. 63–68; David Benady, "Unilever in Global Ad Shake-Up," *Marketing Week,* 22 (February 11, 1999), p. 7; and Operations, Unilever Group, http://www.unilever.com/ourcompany/investorcentre/financial_reports/, accessed February 20, 2006.

Unilever undertook its biggest organizational shake-up since 1996 with a review of the way it plans and buys advertising campaigns. The review is designed to increase the efficiency of Unilever's $3.3 billion media expenditure. The review is likely to result in the world's second largest advertiser adopting an integrated approach to promoting its products ranging across detergents, deodorants, and food. The search for cost savings is likely to mean that unilever will buy media globally rather than locally.

Unilever's top decision-making body is its Executive Committee headed by the group's joint chairmen. The other members are the financial director, foods director, home and personal care director, personnel director and the corporate development director. The Executive Committee is responsible for setting global strategy and the overall business performance. Since January 2001, Unilever's operations have been organized into two global divisions: Home and Personal Care (HPC) and Foods headed by divisional directors. Both divisions have an executive board responsible for divisional strategy and for implementation across the world. This structure allows improved focus on Foods and HPC activities at both regional and global levels. It allows for faster decision making and strengthens the company' capacity for innovation by more effectively integrating research into the divisional structure. Reporting to their respective divisional directors are the Foods and HPC business presidents, responsible for the profitability of their regional and global businesses. These businesses remain the driving force behind Unilever, they comprise the operating companies, which provide the key interface with customers and consumers, allowing quick response to the needs of local markets. The growth is based on globally aligned brands backed by deep local consumer understanding, and the company's strong category positions have benefited from improving economies in a number of markets. In these markets, as in other parts of the world, its product portfolio has shifted toward the higher margin personal care sectors.

---

collection and helping out subsidiaries when required. As presented in Global Perspective 8-1, Unilever has started adding some geocentric dimensions to its global strategy.

Competitive Structure

A second aspect of global strategy is the nature of the competitive industry structure. A firm has a competitive advantage when it is able to deliver the same benefits as competitors but at a lower cost or deliver benefits that exceed those of competing products. Thus, a competitive advantage enables the firm to create superior value for its customers and superior profits for itself.[25] Simply stated, *competitive advantage* is a temporary monopoly period that a firm can enjoy over its competitors. To prolong such a monopolistic period, the firm strives to develop a strategy that is difficult for its competitors to imitate.

---

[25]Michael E. Porter, *Competitive Advantage: Techniques for Analyzing Industries and Competitors* (New York: The Free Press, 1980).

The firm that builds its competitive advantage on economies of scale is known as one using a **cost leadership** strategy. Customized flexible manufacturing as a result of computer-aided design and computer-aided manufacturing (CAD/CAM) technology has shown some progress. However, it proved to be more difficult operationally than anticipated, so economies of scale still remain the main feature of market competition. The theory is that the greater the economies of scale are, the greater are the benefits to those firms with a larger market share. As a result, many firms try to jockey for larger market shares than their competitors. Economies of scale come about because larger plants are more efficient to run, and their per unit cost of production is less as overhead costs are allocated across large volumes of production. Additional economies of scale also result from learning effects: The firm learns more efficient methods of production with increasing cumulative experience in production over time. Each of these effects tends to intensify competition. Once a firm achieves a high level of economies of scale, it has strong barriers against new entrants to the market. In the 1970s and early 1980s, many Japanese companies became cost leaders in such industries as automobiles and consumer electronics. However, there is no guarantee that cost leadership will last.

Until flexible manufacturing and customized production becomes fully operational, cost leaders may be vulnerable to firms that use a **product differentiation** strategy to better serve the exact needs of customers. Although one could argue that lower cost will attract customers away from other market segments, some customers are willing to pay a premium price for unique product features that they desire. Uniqueness may come in the form of comfort, product performance, and aesthetics, as well as status symbol and exclusivity. Despite the Japanese juggernaut in the automobile industry (primarily in the North American and Asian markets) in the 1970s and 1980s, BMW of Germany and Volvo of Sweden (currently under Ford's ownership), for example, managed to maintain their competitive strengths in the high-end segments of the automobile market. Indeed, Japanese carmakers have struggled for years to make a dent in the European market, and they are finally seeing a turnaround after releasing a spate of new models that European drivers want to buy—small cars with spacious cabins—but European firms have yet to make, such as Honda's Jazz (known as the Fit in Japan), Toyota's Yaris (known as the Vitz in Japan), and Mazda's Mazda 6 (known as the Atenza in Japan).[26] Due to the surge in gasoline prices in the United States in late 2005, the Japanese carmakers have also decided to introduce those cars in the U.S. market.[27]

Smaller companies may pursue a limited differentiation strategy by keeping a niche in the market. Firms using a **niche** strategy focus exclusively on a highly specialized segment of the market and try to achieve a dominant position in that segment. Again in the automobile industry, Porsche and Saab maintain their competitive strengths in the high-power sports car enthusiast segment. However, particularly in an era of global competition, niche players may be vulnerable to large-scale operators due to sheer economies of scale needed to compete on a global scale.

Competition is not limited to the firms in the same industry. As just discussed, companies may adopt different strategies for different competitive advantage. If firms in an industry collectively have insufficient capacity to fulfill demand, the incentive is high for new market entrants. However, such entrants need to consider the time and investment it takes to develop new or additional capacity, the likelihood of such capacity being developed by existing competitors, and the possibility of changes in customer demand over time. Indirect competition also comes from suppliers and customers, as well as substitute products or services. A conceptual framework that portrays the multidimensional nature of competitive industry structure is presented in Exhibit 8-2.

---

[26]"Japanese Carmakers Make European Dent," *Japan Times Online,* http://www.japantimes.co.jp/, December 31, 2002.

[27]"Nissan Is Expected to Sell New Subcompacts in U.S.," *Wall Street Journal,* September 28, 2005, p. D5.

EXHIBIT 8-2
NATURE OF COMPETITIVE INDUSTRY STRUCTURE

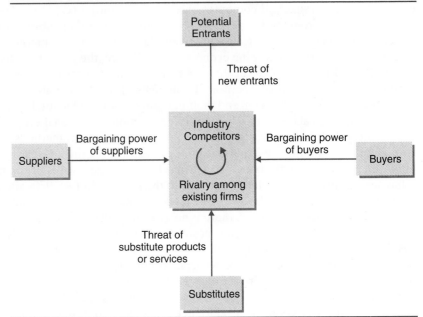

Source: Reprinted with the permission of the Free Press, a division of Simon & Schuster from Michael E. Porter, *Competitive Strategy: Techniques for Analyzing Industries and Competitors,* p. 4. Copyright © 1980 by The Free Press

1. **Industry competitors** determine the rivalry among existing firms.

2. **Potential entrants** may change the rule of competition but can be deterred by entry barriers. For example, Shanghai Jahwa Co., Ltd., whose predecessor was founded in 1898, became the largest cosmetics and personal care products company in China by 1990.[28] Shanghai Jahwa owns such successful brands as Maxam, Liushen, Ruby, and G.LF, among others, and is making gradual inroads into markets outside China. Although not yet known to the Western world, its brands may some day pose a major competitive threat to Clinique, Estée Lauder, Lancôme, Max factor, and other well-known brands and may change the nature of competition in the cosmetics and personal care products industry.

3. The **bargaining power of suppliers** can change the structure of industries. Intel has become a dominant producer of microprocessors for personal computers. Its enormous bargaining power has caused many PC manufacturers to operate on wafer-thin profit margins, making the PC industry extremely competitive.

4. The **bargaining power of buyers** can affect the firm's profitability. It is particularly the case when governments try to get price and delivery concessions from foreign firms. Similarly, Nestlé, whose subsidiaries used to make independent decisions on cocoa purchase, has centralized its procurement decision at its headquarters to take advantage of its consolidated bargaining power over cocoa producers around the world. Given its bargaining power, Nestlé has further completed the trial of a ground-breaking supply chain project that allows suppliers to view its production information and ensure that it can meet fluctuations in demand for its products by removing about 20 percent of excess stock from its supply chain.[29]

5. The **threat of substitute products or services** can restructure the entire industry above and beyond the existing competitive structure. For example, a recent *Economist* article alerts that Playstation 2, the successor to Sony's best-selling Playstation, a

---

[28]Based on the first author's visit to Shanghai Jahwa headquartered in Shanghai, China, August 2002.
[29]Nestlé Links SAP Systems to Allow Suppliers to View Production Data," *Computer Weekly,* October 21, 2003, p. 8.

computer game console introduced in 2000, contains a 128-bit microprocessor having twice the raw number-crunching power of Intel's most advanced Pentium chip and that can play DVD movies, decode digital TV, and surf the Internet for less than $400; it may even challenge the Microsoft-Intel PC standard.[30]

In any given industry, firms jockey among themselves for better competitive position given a set of customers and buyers, the threat of substitutes, and the barriers to entry in that industry. However, Exhibit 8-2 represents the description of a situation without any temporal dimension; there is no indication as to how a firm should act to change the situation to its advantage. For instance, it is not clear how tomorrow's competitor can differ from today's. A new competitor can emerge from a completely different industry given the convergence of industries. Ricoh, a facsimile and copier maker, now has a product that records moving images digitally, which is what camcorders and a movie cameras do using different technologies. This development potentially pits Ricoh as a direct competitor to camcorder and movie camera makers—something not possible 10 or 20 years ago.

Gaining Competitive Advantage

Such a shift in competition is referred to as *creative destruction*. This view of competition assumes continuous change in which the firm's focus is on disrupting the market. In a hypercompetitive environment, a firm competes on the basis of price: quality, timing, and know-how, creating strongholds in the markets it operates in (this is akin to entry barriers) and financial resources to outlast one's competitors.[31] The basic premise of **hypercompetition** is that all firms face a form of aggressive competition that is tougher than oligopolistic or monopolistic competition but is not perfect competition, where the firm is atomistic and cannot influence the market at all. This form of competition is pervasive, not just in fast-moving, high-technology industries such as computers and deregulated industries (airlines) but also in industries that have traditionally been considered more sedate (processed foods). The central thesis of this argument is that no type of competitive advantage can last—it is bound to become eroded.

First-Mover Advantage vs. First-Mover Disadvantage.

For many firms, technology is the key to success in markets where significant advances in product performance are expected. A firm uses its technological leadership for rapid innovation and introduction of new products. The timing of such introductions in the global marketplace is an integral part of the firm's strategy. However, the dispersion of technological expertise means that any technological advantage is temporary, so the firm should not rest on its laurels. The firm needs to move on to its next source of temporary advantage to remain ahead. In the process, firms that are able to continue creating a series of temporary advantages are the ones that survive and thrive. Technology, marketing skills, and other assets that a firm possesses become its weapons to gain advantages in time over its competitors. The firm now attempts to be among the pioneers, or first movers, in the market for the product categories in which it operates.[32] Sony is an excellent example of a company in constant pursuit of first-mover advantage with Trinitron color television, Betamax videorecorder, Walkman, 8 mm videorecorder, and DVD (digital video disc) although not all of its products, such as MiniDisc, succeeded in the market.

Indeed, there could even be some first-mover disadvantages.[33] Citigroup's recent case vividly raises the possibility of first-mover disadvantages. To establish its foothold

---

[30] "War Games," *Economist*, April 22, 2000, p. 60.

[31] Richard D'Aveni, *Hypercompetition: Managing the Dynamics of Strategic Maneuvering* (New York: The Free Press, 1994).

[32] Gerard J. Tellis and Peter N. Golder, "First to Market, First to Fail? Real Causes of Enduring Market Leadership," *Sloan Management Review*, 37 (Winter 1996), pp. 65–75; and Richard Makadok, "Can First-Mover and Early-Mover Advantages Be Sustained in an Industry with Low Barriers to Entry/Imitation?" *Strategic Management Journal*, 19 (July 1998), pp. 683–96.

[33] Marvin B. Lieberman and David B. Montgomery, "First-Mover (Dis)advantages: Retrospective and Link with the Resource-Based View," *Strategic Management Journal*, 19 (December 1998), pp. 1111–125.

in the growing Chinese economy, Citigroup entered into an alliance with Shanghai Pudong Development Bank in China, targeting the country's credit card market. About 10 million cards with revolving credit have been already issued in China. Some experts argued that Chinese credit services would be risky for first-mover companies given that the country has no nationwide credit-rating system and lack of adequate risk management technology.[34]

In general, stable markets favor the first-mover strategy while market and technology turbulence favor the follower strategy. Followers have the benefit of hindsight to determine more preciously the timing, form, and scale of their market entry. It is therefore important for the firm to clearly assess the key success factors and the resulting likelihood of success for achieving the ultimate targeted position in the highly competitive global business environment.[35]

A firm's competitive advantage lies in its capability to effectively anticipate, react to, and lead change continuously and even rhythmically over time. Firms should "probe" into the unknown by making many small steps to explore their environments. These probes could take the form of a number of new product introductions that are "small, fast, and cheap," and can be supplemented by using experts to contemplate the future, making strategic alliances to explore new technologies, and holding meetings where management discusses the future. To compete on the edge, firms need to understand the following:

1. Advantage is temporary. In other words, firms need to have a strong focus on continuously generating new sources of advantages.

2. Strategy is diverse, emergent, and complicated. It is crucial to rely on diverse strategic moves.

3. Reinvention is the goal. It is how firms keep pace with a rapidly changing marketplace.

4. Live in the present, stretch out the past, and reach into the future. Successful firms launch more experimental products and services than others while exploiting previous experiences and trying to extend them to new opportunities.

5. Grow the strategy and drive strategy from the business level. It is important for managers to pay attention to the timing and order in which strategy is grown and agile moves at the business level.

6. To maintain sustainable power in fast-paced, competitive, and unpredictable environments, senior management needs to recognize patterns in firms' development and articulate semicoherent strategic direction.[36]

With these strategic flexibilities in mind, we could think of two primary approaches to gaining competitive advantage. The *competitor-focused* approaches involve comparison with the competitor on costs, prices, technology, market share, profitability, and other related activities. Such an approach can lead to a preoccupation with some activities, and the firm could lose sight of its customers and various constituents. *Customer-focused* approaches to gaining competitive advantage emanate from an analysis of customer benefits to be delivered. In practice, finding the proper links between required customer benefits and the activities and variables controlled by management is needed. In addition evidence suggests that listening too closely to customer requirements can cause a firm to miss the bus on innovations because current customers might not want innovations that require them to change how they operate.[37]

---

[34]"Risks in Credit Card Business," *China Daily,* January 10, 2005.

[35]Dean Shepherd and Mark Shanley, *New Venture Strategy: Timing, Environmental Uncertainty and Performance* (Thousand Oaks, CA: Sage publications, 1998).

[36]Shona L. Brown and Kathleen M. Eisenhardt, *Competing on the Edge* (Boston, MA: Harvard Business Press), 1998.

[37]See, for example, John P. Workman, Jr., "Marketing's Limited Role in New Product Development in One Computer Systems Firm," *Journal of Marketing Research,* 30 (November 1993), pp. 405–21.

Competitor-Focused Approach. Black & Decker, a U.S.-based manufacturer of hand tools, switched to a global strategy using its strengths in the arenas of cost, quality, timing, and know-how. In the 1980s, Black & Decker's position was threatened by a powerful Japanese competitor, Makita. Makita's strategy of producing and marketing globally standardized products worldwide made it a low-cost producer and enabled it to steadily increase its world market share. Within the company, Black & Decker's international fiefdoms combined with nationalist chauvinism to stifle coordination in product development and new product introductions, resulting in lost opportunities.

Then, responding to the increased competitive pressure, Black & Decker moved decisively toward globalization. It embarked on a program to coordinate new product development worldwide to develop core standardized products that could be marketed globally with minimum modification. The streamlining of B&D also offered scale economies and less duplication of effort—and new products could be introduced more quickly. Its increased emphasis on design made it into a global leader in design management. It consolidated its advertising into two agencies worldwide in an attempt to give a more consistent image worldwide. Black & Decker also strengthened the functional organization by giving the functional manager a larger role in coordinating with the country management. Finally, Black & Decker purchased General Electric's small appliance division to achieve world-scale economies in manufacturing, distribution, and marketing. The global strategy initially faced skepticism and resistance from country managers at Black & Decker. The chief executive officer took a visible leadership role and made some management changes to start moving the company toward globalization. These changes in strategy helped Black & Decker increase revenues and profits by as much as 50 percent in the 1990s.[38] To meet further cost competition, Black & Decker's new global restructuring project plans to reduce manufacturing costs by transferring additional power tool production from the United States and England to low-cost facilities in Mexico, China, and a new leased facility in the Czech Republic and by sourcing more manufactured items from third parties where cost advantages are available and quality can be ensured. Its global restructuring plan resulted in a global sales increase of 20 percent to record $5.4 billion and increased earnings of 36 percent to $5.40 per share.[39]

A word of caution is in order. Although a company's financial resources provides durability for its strategy, regulatory and other barriers could prove to be overwhelming even in a very promising market such as China. As presented in Global Perspective 8-2, AOL Time Warner's expansion into China illustrates this difficulty.

Customer-Focused Approach. Estée Lauder is a good corporate example of a corporation that superbly used cost and quality, timing and know-how, strongholds, and financial resources to its advantage. Estée Lauder has grown from a small, female-owned cosmetics business to become one of the world's leading manufacturers and marketers of quality skin care, makeup, fragrance, and hair care products. Its brands include Estée Lauder, Aramis, Clinique, Prescriptives, Origins, M.A.C, La Mer, Bobbi Brown, and Tommy Hilfiger, among others.

How did Estée Lauder accomplish such a feat? The answer lies in its ability to reach consumers in nearly every corner of the world, its internal strengths, and the diversity of its portfolio of brands. Since the beginning of its international operations, the company has always conducted in-depth research to determine the feasibility and compatibility of its products with each particular market, which has led to its high-quality image. Another reason for the company's success lies in its focus on global expansion before its competitors. Estée Lauder's international operations commenced in 1960. Because of its strong visibility in Europe, it served as a springboard to other European markets. Shortly thereafter, the company made its foray with the Estée Lauder brand into

---

[38] Black & Decker, various annual reports.

[39] Black & Decker, Investor Relations, http://www.corporate-ir.net/ireye/ir_site.zhtml?ticker = BDK&script = 2100, accessed December 10, 2005.

GLOBAL PERSPECTIVE 8-2

"ROME" COULD NOT BE BUILT IN A DAY...EVEN BY AOL TIME WARNER IN CHINA

AOL, a Time Warner company, made a foray into China in 2001. It partnered with Lenovo (previously known as Legend), China's largest computer maker, to tackle the world's most promising Internet-service market and became the first foreign broadcaster allowed onto a Chinese cable-TV service. However, AOL realized that it would take years and years to turn a profit. In China, any vendor or operator that wants Internet space needs deep pockets to last at least five years or more before anything happens. It takes so many regulatory hurdles just to get approval to start offering Internet service in China. Furthermore, because China has extensive competition, the margins have come down and Internet service providers cannot become profitable instantly. AOL could not wait. Because of its continued losses in Japan, AOL just closed its Japanese venture. AOL's new portal had many problems. Lenovo is essentially a hardware company with little experience in telecom operations. Thus, this partnership lacked a distribution channel for AOL services. As a result, the business failed to go anywhere, and Lenovo finally pulled out of its legacy relationship with Time Warner in 2004. So far, the only places where Internet service providers make money are in

Source: Ben Dolvens and Alkman Granitsas, "Media—Don't Hold your Breath," *Far Eastern Economic Review,* www.feer.com, May 02, 2002; and "Lenovo Reaches for New Direction," CRN, http://www.crn.com , December 3, 2004.

protected markets such as South Korea or Taiwan or where a firm blows away competition early, as AOL did in the United States. In competitive markets such as Hong Kong, Singapore, and China, price competition for basic services tends to leave everyone unprofitable.

As for television, AOL and other foreign broadcasters still face many regulatory obstacles in China. Although CETV has been granted "landing rights," it can reach only a very small part of Guangdong province, and its competitors include established programmers including Hong Kong's TVB and ATV. Meanwhile, AOL's other channels also have problems. Warner Music faces piracy issues that about 95 percent of all music and movie CDs in China are pirated; Time's two flagship news publications, *Time* and *Fortune,* officially sell fewer than 2,000 copies each in China, although *Fortune China* published through a licensee is helping establish the brand name. As for movies, China promises to double the number of overseas films it allows to be released each year, but that still means only 20 films distributed among all of the world's film studios, a potential not good enough for Time Warner. Each abstacle will take a long time to improve, which means that Time Warner must have the patience and financial resources as well as a strong commitment in the China market, hoping that it will be the first player once China opens its door to foreign media companies.

new markets in the Americas, Europe, and Asia. In the late 1960s, the Aramis and Clinique brands were founded and a manufacturing facility was established in Belgium. In the 1970s, Clinique was introduced overseas, and Estée Lauder began to explore new opportunities in the former Soviet Union. During the 1980s, the company made considerable progress in reaching markets that were still out of reach for many U.S. companies. For example, in 1989 Estée Lauder was the first U.S. cosmetic company to enter the former Soviet Union when it opened a perfumery in Moscow. The same year, it established its first free-standing beauty boutique in Budapest, Hungary. In 1990s the firm moved further into untapped markets such as China. The company is focusing further on China and the rest of Asia. In addition, many opportunities still exist in Europe. The company will continue to look to Latin America for expansion but with caution because of its economic circumstances and political instability there. One more reason for the company' success is its use of financial resources to further strengthen brand value. Since 1989, the firm has opened some of its free-standing stores overseas because it could not find the right channels of distribution to maintain the brand's standards. Estée Lauder has built strong brand equity all over the world with each brand having a single, global image. The company's philosophy of never compromising brand equity has guided it in its selection of the appropriate channels of distribution overseas. In the United States and overseas, it sells products through limited distribution channels to uphold the particular image of each brand.

At the same time, Estée Lauder has successfully responded to the needs of different markets. In Asia, for example, it developed a system of products to whiten the skin. This ability to adapt and create products to specific market needs has contributed greatly to the company's ability to enter new markets. Estée Lauder's global strategies have paid off. In 2001, 61 percent of its net sales came from the Americas; 26 percent from Europe, the Middle East, and Africa; and 13 percent from Asia/Pacific countries. For the past five years, international sales have increased almost 10 percent annually. Estée Lauder currently has manufacturing facilities in the United Sates, Canada, Belgium, Switzerland, and the United Kingdom and research and development laboratories in the United States, Canada, Belgium, and Japan.[40]

Another aspect of global strategy is **interdependency** of modern companies. Recent research has shown that the number of technologies used in a variety of products in numerous industries is rising.[41] Because access to resources limit how many distinctive competencies a firm can gain, firms must draw on outside technologies to be able to build a state-of-the-art product. Because most firms operating globally are limited by a lack of all required technologies, it follows that for firms to make optimal use of outside technologies, a degree of component standardization is required. Such standardization would enable different firms to develop different end products, using, in a large measure, the same components.[42] Research findings indicate that technology intensity—that is, the degree of R&D expenditure a firm incurs as a proportion of sales—is a primary determinant of cross-border firm integration.[43]

Interdependency

The computer industry is a good instance of a case in which firms use components from various sources. HP Compaq, Dell, and Acer all use semiconductor chips from Intel, AMD, or Cyrix, hard drives from Seagate Western Digital, Maxtor, or Hitachi, and software from Microsoft. The final product—in this case, the personal computer—carries some individual idiosyncrasies of Compaq, Dell, or Acer, but at least some of the components are common and, indeed, are portable across the products of the three companies.

In the international context, governments also tend to play a larger role and can, directly or indirectly, affect parts of a firm's strategy. Tariffs and nontariff barriers such as voluntary export restraints and restrictive customs procedures could change cost structures so that a firm could need to change its production and sourcing decisions. It is possible, however, that with the end of the Cold War and the spread of capitalism to previously socialist economies, such factors can decrease in importance. As presented in Chapter 2, the creation of the World Trade Organization in 1995, which launched the Doha Round of trade negotiations in 2001, is an encouraging sign because it leads to increased harmonization of tariff rules and less freedom for national governments to make arbitrary changes in tariff and nontariff barriers and in intellectual property laws.

GLOBAL MARKETING STRATEGY

❖ ❖ ❖ ❖ ❖ ❖ ❖ ❖

Multinational companies increasingly use global marketing and have been highly successful—for example, Nestlé with its common brand name applied to many products in all countries, Coca Cola with its global advertising themes, Xerox with its global leasing policies, and Dell Computer's "sell-direct" strategy. Global marketing is not about standardizing the marketing process on a global basis however. Although every element of the marketing process—product design, product and brand positioning,

[40] Anastasia Xenias, " The Sweet Smell of Success: Estée Lauder Honored at World Trade Week Event," *Export America,* May 2002 (print version) or http://www.trade.gov/exportamerica/.

[41] Aldor Lanctot and K. Scott Swan, "Technology Acquisition Strategy in an Internationally Competitive Environment," *Journal of International Management,* 6 (Autumn 2000), pp. 187–215.

[42] Masaaki Kotabe, Arvind Sahay, and Preet S. Aulakh, "Emerging Roles of Technology Licensing in Development of Global Product Strategy: A Conceptual Framework and Research Propositions," *Journal of Marketing,* 60 (January 1996), pp. 73–88.

[43] Stephen Kobrin, "An Empirical Analysis of the Determinants of Global Integration," *Strategic Management Journal,* 12 (1991), pp. 17–31.

EXHIBIT 8-3
VARIATION IN CONTENT AND COVERAGE
OF GLOBAL MARKETING

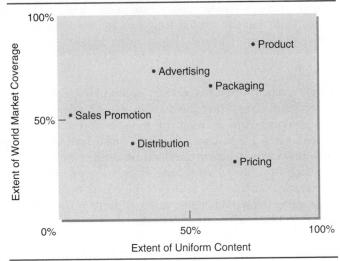

Source: Adapted from George S. Yip, *Total Global Strategy: Managing for Worldwide Competitive Advantage* (Englewood Cliffs, NJ: Prentice Hall, 1992), p. 136

brand name, packaging, pricing, advertising strategy and execution, promotion, and distribution—can be a candidate for standardization, standardization is one part of a global marketing strategy and it can or cannot be used by a company, depending on the mix of the product-market conditions, stage of market development, and the inclinations of the multinational firm's management. For instance, a marketing element can be global without being 100 percent uniform in content or coverage. Exhibit 8-3 illustrates a possible pattern.

Let's take an element from Exhibit 8-3 and look at distribution with a magnitude of less than 50 percent on both coverage of world market and extent of uniform content. If we assume that the firm in question (represented in the diagram) does not have a manufacturing facility in each of the markets it serves, then to the extent that various markets have a uniform content and presumably similar operations, there is a requirement for coordination with manufacturing facilities elsewhere in the firm's global network. Also, when content is not uniform, any change requirements for the nonuniform content of distribution require corresponding changes in the product and/or packaging. Thus, a global marketing strategy requires more intimate linkages with a firm's other functions, such as research and development, manufacturing, and finance.[44]

In other words, a global marketing strategy is but one component of a global strategy. For an analogy, you may think of a just-in-time inventory and manufacturing system that works for a single manufacturing facility to optimize production. Extend this concept now to finance and marketing, and include all subsidiaries of the firm across the world. One can imagine the magnitude and complexity of the task when a manager is attempting to develop and implement a global strategy. One implication is that without a global strategy for R&D, manufacturing, and finance that meshes with the various requirements of its global marketing strategy, a firm cannot best implement that global marketing strategy.

Benefits of Global Marketing

Global marketing strategy can achieve one or more of four major categories of potential globalization benefits: cost reduction, improved quality of products and

---

[44]Masaaki Kotabe, *Global Sourcing Strategy: R & D, Manufacturing, and Marketing Interfaces* (New York: Quorum Books, 1992).

programs, enhanced customer preference, and increased competitive advantage.[45] General Motors and Ford approach global marketing somewhat differently; such a strategic difference suggests that the two U.S. automakers are in search of different benefits of global marketing (see Case Study 8-1).

Cost Reduction.   This results from savings in both workforce and materials. When multiple national marketing functions are consolidated, personnel outlays are reduced by avoiding duplicating activities. Costs are also saved in producing global advertisements and commercials and producing promotional materials and packaging. Savings from standardized packaging include reduction in inventory costs. With typical inventory carrying costs at 20 percent of sales, any reduction in inventory can significantly affect profitability. With the availability of a global span of coverage by various forms of modern communication media, multicountry campaigns capitalizing on countries' common features would also reduce advertising costs considerably. ExxonMobil's "Put a Tiger in Your Tank" campaign and the Tiger in many other forms offer a good example of a campaign that used the same theme across much of the world, taking advantage of the fact that the tiger is almost universally associated with power and grace.[46]

Owning a Web site on the Internet and marketing to consumers is another way to reduce costs of conducting global marketing. It benefits both consumers, who can order to their own specifications everything from cars to swimsuits, and manufacturers by helping avoid inventory buildups. It also allows companies to have direct contact with consumers from different parts of the world, giving them deeper insight into market trends at a fraction of the cost incurred in traditional marketing. Cost savings can also translate into increased program effectiveness by allowing more money and resources into a smaller number of more focused programs. Disney, for example, is trying to break out of its traditional marketing methods with some alternative media. Now the company is launching a multiplayer online game, Virtual Magic Kingdom, intended to drive kids to Disney resorts.[47]

Improved Products and Program Effectiveness.   This could often be the greatest advantage of a global marketing strategy. Good ideas are relatively scarce in the business arena, so a globalization program that overcomes local objections to allow the spread of a good marketing idea can often raise the effectiveness of the program when measured on a worldwide basis. Traditionally, R&D has been concentrated in the headquarters country of a global company. This has sometimes circumscribed a possible synergy from amalgamation of good ideas from around the world.

Procter & Gamble has solved this problem by setting up major R&D facilities in each of its major markets in the Triad—North America, Japan, and Western Europe—and by putting together the pertinent findings from each of the laboratories. As in the saying, "Necessity is the mother of invention," different needs in different parts of the world can lead to different inventions. For example, P&G's Liquid Tide laundry detergent was an innovative product developed in an innovative way by taking advantage of both the company's technical abilities and various market requirements in the key markets around the world. Germans had been extremely concerned about polluting rivers with phosphate, a key whitening ingredient in the traditional detergent. To meet the German customer demand, P&G in Germany developed fatty acid to replace phosphate in the detergent. Similarly, P&G Japan developed surfactant to get off grease effectively in tepid water that Japanese use in washing their clothes. In the United States, P&G in Cincinnati, Ohio, had independently developed "builder" to

[45] George S. Yip, *Total Global Strategy: Managing for Worldwide Competitive Advantage* (Englewood Cliffs, NJ: Prentice-Hall, 1992), pp. 21–23.
[46] If interested in the history of the Esso (ExxonMobil) tiger, probably one of the most recognized mascots in the world in the last 100 years, read "Tiger History," at ExxonMobil's Website http://www 2.exxonmobil.com/Corporate/About/History/Corp_A_H_Tiger.asp, accessed January 20, 2006.
[47] Disney's Virtual Magic Kingdom, http://vmk.disney.go.com/.

keep dirt from settling on clothes. Putting all these three innovations together, the company introduced Liquid Tide and its sister products (e.g., Ariel) around the world.

Three benefits followed from this multiple R&D location strategy. By being able to integrate required product attributes from three separate markets, P&G was able to introduce a much better product than would otherwise be possible and increase its chances of success. Second, its development costs were spread over a much larger market that was more inclined to receive the product favorably because of the incorporation of the product features described. Third, it increased the sources from which product ideas are available to it. Thus, P&G not only had immediate returns but also secured for itself a reliable resource base of future products.

Enhanced Customer Preference. Customer awareness of a product on a worldwide basis increase its value. A global marketing strategy helps build recognition that can enhance customer preferences through reinforcement. With the rise in the availability of information from a variety of sources across the world and in travel across national borders, more and more people are being exposed to messages in different countries. Thus, a uniform marketing message, whether communicated through a brand name, packaging, or advertisement, reinforces the awareness, knowledge, and attitudes of people toward the product or service. Pepsi has a consistent theme in its marketing communication across the world: youthfulness and fun as a part of the experience of drinking Pepsi anywhere in the world.

Increased Competitive Advantage. By focusing resources into a smaller number of programs, global strategies magnify the programs competitive power. Although larger competitors might have the resources to develop different high-quality programs for each country, smaller firms might not. Using a focused global marketing strategy could allow the smaller firm to compete with a larger competitor in a more effective manner. However, the most important benefit of a global strategy could be that the entire organization gets behind a single idea, thus increasing its chances of the success. Avis created a global campaign communicating its idea—"We are number two; therefore we try harder"—not only to its customers but also to its employees. As a result, the entire organization pulled together to deliver on a global promise, not just in marketing but also in all activities that directly or indirectly affected the company's interface with the customer.

Equally if not more important are the benefits of market and competitive intelligence provided by the increased flow of information due to the worldwide coordination of activities. As the global firm meshes the different parts of the organization into the framework of a focused strategy, information flow through the organization improves and enables the strategy to function. A by-product is that the organization as a whole becomes much better informed about itself and about the activities of its competitors in markets across the world. Access to more and timely information enables in the organization to be more prepared and to respond to signals from the marketplace.

Limits to Global Marketing

Although national boundaries have begun losing their significance both as a psychological and a physical barrier to international business, the diversity of local environments, particularly cultural, political, and legal environments, still plays an important role not as a facilitator but as an inhibitor of optimal global marketing strategy development. Indeed, we still debate the very issue raised more than 30 years ago: counteracting forces of "unification versus fragmentation" in developing operational strategies along the value chain. As early as 1969, John Fayerweather wrote emphatically:

> What fundamental effects does [the existence of many national borders] have on the strategy of the multinational firm? Although many effects can be itemized, one central theme recurs; that is, their tendency to push the firm toward adaptation to the diversity of local environments which leads toward fragmentation of operations. But there is a natural tendency in a single firm toward integration and uniformity that is basically at

odds with fragmentation. Thus the central issue ... is the conflict between unification and fragmentation—a close-knit operational strategy with similar foreign units versus a loosely related, highly variegated family of activities.[48]

Many authors have since revisited the same counteracting forces in such terms as "standardization versus adaptation" (1960s), "globalization versus localization" (1970s), "global integration versus local responsiveness" (1980s), and most recently, "scale versus sensitivity" (1990s). Today, we may even add another variant, "online scale versus offline market sensitivity." Basically, the left-side concept (i.e., unification, standardization, globalization, global integration, scale, and online scale) refers to a *supply-side* argument in favor of the benefit of economies of scale and scope while the right-side concept (i.e., fragmentation, adaptation, localization, local responsiveness, sensitivity, and offline market sensitivity) refers to a *demand-side* argument addressing the existence of market differences and the importance of catering to the differing market needs and conditions. Terms have changed, but the quintessence of the strategic dilemma that multinational firms face today has not changed and will probably remain unchanged for years to come.[49]

Now the question is to what extent successful multinational firms can circumvent the impact of local environmental diversity. In some industries, product standardization can result in a product that satisfies customers nowhere. For processed foods, for example, national tastes and consumption patterns differ sufficiently to make standardization counterproductive. In Latin America, a variety of canned spicy peppers, such as jalapeño peppers, is a national staple in Mexico, but is virtually unheard of in Brazil and Chile. Obviously, firms cannot lump together the whole of Latin America into one regional market for condiments.

The Internet is global in nature, and so are Web sites. Being on the Web arguably translates into reaching customers in many corners of the world from day one. However, it does not mean that e-commerce can be developed without any need for local and regional adaptation. To effectively target and reach global consumers online, many companies still need to approach them in their languages, conforming to their cultural value systems.[50] Indeed, one recent study clearly shows that local Web sites in India, China, Japan, and the United States not only reflect cultural values of the country of their origin but also differ significantly from each other on cultural dimensions.[51]

On the other hand, Merck, the world's second largest pharmaceutical company, faces a different kind of problem with global marketing. The company can market the same products around the world for various ailments, but cultural and political differences make it very difficult to approach different markets in a similar way. Merck, which operates internationally as MSD, has to increase public awareness of health care issues in Mexico, Central America, and much of South America by bringing top journalists from these countries together on a regular basis to meet with health care experts ranging from physicians to government officials. The company is trying to change the way it does business in the Pacific Rim. It used to operate through local distributors and licensees without learning the local quirks of pharmaceutical business. Now, the company is creating subsidiaries in nearly all main Asian countries, including Korea, China, the Philippines, Taiwan, Singapore, and Malaysia, to learn what goes on inside those markets. In Eastern Europe, Merck is starting from scratch because its entry had been previously barred under the region's strict communist control. For example, in Hungary, the company devoted its initial investment to establishing

---

[48] John Fayerweather, *International Business Management: Conceptual Framework* (New York: McGraw-Hill, 1969), pp. 133–34.

[49] Kotabe, "To Kill Two Birds with One Stone," (New York: Elsevier), pp. 59–69.

[50] E. James Randall and L. Jean Harrison-Walker, "If You Build It, Will They Come? Barriers to International e-Marketing," *Journal of Marketing Theory & Practice*, 10 (Spring 2002), pp. 12–21.

[51] Nitish Singh, Hongxin Zhao, and Xiaorui Hu, "Analyzing the Cultural Content of Web Sites: A Cross-National Comparison of China, India, Japan, and US," *International Marketing Review*, 22 (2), 2005, pp. 129–45.

resource centers that are affiliated with local hospitals and universities to create a special image for Merck.[52]

Even in supposedly similar cultures, there can be huge differences in what are effective marketing campaigns. The Body Shop found this out when it took a successful ad campaign in Britain and brought it to the United States, assuming it would have the same appeal. The ad showed the naked buttocks of three men and completely misfired in the U.S. market. In the words of Body Shop founder Anita Roddick, "We thought it was funny and witty here, but women in New Hampshire fainted."[53]

However, despite such cultural and political constraints in the markets, Nestlé, for example, has managed to integrate procurement functions to gain bargaining power in purchasing common ingredients such as cocoa and sugar. In other industries, such as computers and telecommunications, consumption patterns are in the process of being established and the associated cultural constraint is getting less prominent. Also, the simultaneous launch of most products in these categories across the world precludes large differences. For these products, governments frequently attempt to exert national control over technological development, the products, or the production process.[54] However, while multinational firms provide the vehicle through which technology, production, and economic activity in general are integrated across borders, *it is the underlying technology and economic activity that are global.* National markets, regardless of how they are organized economically, are no longer enough to support the development of technology in many industries. See Exhibit 8-4 for some generalizations about the degree of product standardization around the world.

EXHIBIT 8-4
DEGREE OF STANDARDIZABILITY OF PRODUCTS IN WORLD MARKETS

Local ← → Universal

Factors Limiting Universality	Culture/ Habits	Design Taste	Language	Size/Package	Technical System	User/ Application	None
Example	• Fish sausage • Root beer • Boxer shorts • Rice cooker	• Furniture • Refrigerator • Processed food	• Word processor • Computer	• Textile • Automotive (seat size) • Soft drinks	• Color TV (PAL system in European voltage)	• Portable radio/cassette player (youths in U.S.) • White-liqueur (young females in Japan)	• Watch • Motorcycle • Petrochemical products • Piano • Money (capital market)

Key functions:

Marketing concept							
Technology							
Product application							
Product concept							

☐ Must modify locally   ☐ Could be shared globally

Source: Reprinted with the permission of The Free Press, a Division of Simon & Schuster Adult Publishing Group, from Kenichi Ohmae, *Triad Power: The Coming Shape of Global Competition,* p. 193. Copyright © 1985 by Kenichi Ohmae and McKinsey & Company, Inc

---

[52]Fannie Weinstein, "Drug Interaction: Merck Establishes Itself, Country by Country, in Emerging Markets," *Profiles,* September 1996, pp. 35–39.

[53]Ernest Beck, "Body Shop Gets a Makeover to Cut Costs," *Wall Street Journal,* January 27, 1999, p. A18.

[54]C. K. Prahalad and Yves L. Doz, *The Multinational Mission* (New York: The Free Press, 1987).

REGIONALIZATION OF GLOBAL MARKETING STRATEGY ◆ ◆ ◆ ◆ ◆ ◆ ◆ ◆

Some firms, such as General Motors, could have difficulty in organizing or could not be willing to organize operations to maximize flexibility and encourage integration across national borders. Beyond various cultural, political, and economic differences across national borders, organizational realities also impair the ability of multinational firms to pursue global marketing strategies. Not surprising, integration has often been opposed by foreign subsidiaries eager to protect their historical relative independence from their parent companies.

In finding a balance between the need for greater integration and the need to exploit existing resources more effectively, many companies have begun to explore the use of regional strategies in Europe, North America, and the Pacific Rim. *Regional strategies* can be defined as the cross-subsidization of market share battles in pursuit of regional production, branding, and distribution advantages.[55] Regional strategies in Europe and North America have been encouraged by the economic, political, and social pressures resulting from the development of regional trading blocs, such as the European Union, North American Free Trade Agreement (NAFTA), and Southern Common Market (MERCOSUR).[56]

Regional trading blocs have had two favorable effects. First, the volatility of foreign exchange rates within a bloc seems to be reduced.[57] Second, with the growing level of macroeconomic integration with regions, the trend is also toward greater harmonization of product and industry standards, pollution and safety standards, and environmental standards, among other things.[58] These regional commonalities further encourage firms to develop marketing strategies on a regional basis.[59] Global marketing strategy cannot be developed without considering competitive and other market forces from different regions around the world. To face those regional forces proactively, three additional strategies need to be considered at the firm level. These are the cross-subsidization of markets, identification of weak market segments, and the lead market concept.[60] See also Global Perspective 8-3 for an example of global competition among Sony PlayStation, Microsoft Xbox, and Nintendo GameCube employing these three strategies on an ongoing basis.

Cross-subsidization of markets refers to multinational firms using profits gained in a market where they have a strong competitive position to beef up their competitive position in a market where they are struggling to gain foothold. For example, Michelin used its strong profit base in Europe to attack the home market of Goodyear in the United States. Goodyear's reducing prices in its home market would have meant that Goodyear would have reduced its own profits from its largest and most profitable market without substantially affecting Michelin's bottom line because Michelin would have exposed only a small portion of its worldwide business by competing with Goodyear in the United States. Goodyear chose to strike back by expanding operations and reducing prices in Europe.

Cross-Subsidization of Markets

---

[55] Allen J. Morrison and Kendall Roth, "The Regional Solution: An Alternative to Globalization," *Transnational Corporations*, 1 (August 1, 1992), pp. 37–55; and Gerald Millet, "Global Marketing and Regionalization—Worlds Apart?" *Pharmaceutical Executive*, 17 (August 1997), pp. 78–81.

[56] Alan M. Rugman, "Regional Strategy and the Demise of Globalization," *Journal of International Management*, 9 (4), 2003, pp. 409–417.

[57] Alan David MacCormack, Lawrence James Newmann, and Donald B. Rosenfield, "The New Dynamics of Global Manufacturing Site Location," *Sloan Management Review*, 35 (Summer 1994), pp. 69–80; and Kotabe, "To Kill Two Birds with One Stone," pp. 59–69.

[58] Edmund W. Beaty, "Standard Regionalization: A Threat to Internetworking?" *Telecommunications*, Americas Edition, 27 (May 1993), pp. 48–51.

[59] Maneesh Chandra, "The Regionalization of Global Strategy," paper presented at 1997 Academy of International Business Annual Meeting, Monterrey, Mexico, October 8–12, 1997.

[60] Gary Hamel and C.K. Prahalad, "Do You Really Have a Global Strategy?" *Harvard Business Review* (July–August 1985), pp. 139–48.

GLOBAL PERSPECTIVE 8-3

SONY, MICROSOFT, AND NINTENDO BATTLING FOR GLOBAL DOMINANCE IN THE VIDEO GAME INDUSTRY

Back in 1995, Sony revolutionized the video game industry when it launched the PlayStation console. The consumer electronics behemoth set a new standard by tapping CD technology in the design of game consoles. Sony was a relative latecomer in the industry whose main rivals Sega and Nintendo had popularized the cartridge for gaming consoles. However, CD technology was perceived as technologically superior to cartridges. CDs could hold up to 650 megabytes of data compared to only 16 megabytes storage capacity for cartridge-based consoles. CDs also yielded higher margins to third-party developers, one of the main reasons why they were attracted to the Sony PlayStation platform. CDs were also a less expensive medium, selling for $35 in retail outlets while Nintendo games were in the $75 price range. When Sony therefore adopted CD technology, the firm created the impression that the PlayStation would become the wave of the future in the videogame industry. Nintendo steadfastly refused to adopt this new technology even when released its 64-bit N64. Nintendo's lack of enthusiasm for the CD-platform was mainly due to the fact that it *owned* the cartridge technology and therefore was reluctant to abandon this platform. Nintendo's slow response in the wake of new technologies proved to be a recipe for disaster.

Five years later in 2000, the second generation of PlayStation, known as PlayStation 2 (PS2), which Sony introduced instantly became dominant in the global gaming market. PS2 is the first video game system to use the digital video disc (DVD) format. The DVD platform allows the PS2 to hold much more information than rival video game systems. Another solid feature of PS2 is that it is able to play most of the original PlayStation games. Due to the blockbuster success of the first generation PS, PS2 penetrated the video game market very easily.

Further, more to position PS2 as a general-purpose entertainment device instead of simply a video game console, PS2 was designed with features of consumer electronics equipment, such as CD and DVD players. PS2 can play back DVD movies and supports both the Dolby Digital and DTS sound platforms. The PS2 can not only play DVD movies but is also a very good DVD player. The emotion engine (central processor) in the PS2 is much faster than any of the MPEG2 decompression chips currently included in stand-alone DVD players. In fact, the picture quality of the PS2's DVD is better than DVD video players in the same price range and in some cases at par with high-end players. In that regard, PS2

Sources: "A Video-Game War That's Just Dandy for Everyone," *Business Week,* March 4, 2002, p. 54; "PlayStation2: Killing the Competition," *Business Week Online,* November 7, 2002; "Games," *Fortune,* December 9, 2002, p. 242; "Strong Players," *Economist,* December 14, 2002, p. 60; Microsoft Gives Xbox Service, Games Big Push," *Asian Wall Street Journal,* September 23, 2002, p. A9; "Nintendo to Launch Snazzier Console," CNN.com, January 23, 2003Q1; "The Complete Home Entertainer?" *Economist,* March 1, 2003, pp. 62–64; "Super Cell," *Forbes,* February 14, 2005, p. 46; and "Xbox 360 to the Rescue," *PC Magazine,* December 6, 2005, p. 97.

became a trendsetter. Now almost all of the consoles have DVD playback capability and Internet access. This means that the gaming console will be a platform from which the consumer can play online games, watch online movies, and play against gamers from all over the world.

With the launch of the second generation PlayStation, Sega dropped out of console development and began concentrating on software development for the major players. However, a new rival entered the industry: Microsoft. Microsoft is nowhere near Sony in the dedicated gaming console market. Microsoft's dominance is in the operating platform (Windows) for the personal home computer. However, Microsoft felt threatened by Sony's foray into the internet via PS2. As such, Microsoft had no choice but to compete with Sony head-on in the gaming market, and Nintendo was caught in the middle. The gaming industry is highly dynamic and constantly changing. As its history indicates, old established players can fall while new dominant players can emerge from nowhere.

The Sony-Microsoft-Nintendo competition is being played out globally, particularly in the Triad regions of North America, Japan, and Europe. The following table shows the launch dates and the sales volumes for Sony PS2, Microsoft Xbox, and Nintendo GameCube.

	Launch Date		
	Sony PlayStation 2	*Microsoft Xbox*	*Nintendo GameCube*
Japan	**March 2000**	February 2002	**September 2001**
United States	October 2000	**November 2001**	November 2001
Europe (U.K.)	November 2000	March 2002	May 2002
Unit sales since launch	40 million	4 million	4 million

Clearly, Sony enjoys the first-mover advantage. Nintendo launched its GameCube in Japan and Microsoft introduced Xbox in the United States six and eight months, respectively, after Sony's PS2. Sony had a strong "timing" advantage because it had a number of crucial months to arouse consumer interest in and build a demand for PS2 during the important holiday season in December 2001 in Japan, North America, and Europe. Microsoft and Nintendo, however, had merely a month or so to build up demand for their products in the two key lead markets of Japan and North America, missing out on the European market. Sony also had the economies of scale in its favor by being able to lower PS2's prices when Xbox and GameCube came on board. The end result is that Sony was pretty much able to dominate the video game console market in the most crucial introductory period. At the end of 2002, Sony enjoyed a more than 80 percent worldwide market share. Microsoft Xbox was in firm second place in the United States. In Europe, it was in second place with Nintendo, but the Xbox is struggling to make any impact in Japan.

The video game market is neither a small market nor just teenagers' market. Sales of games software and hardware exceeded $31 billion globally in 2002. In the United States alone, more money was spent on video games than on movie tickets in 2002. Put another way, the video game industry is larger than Hollywood's movie industry. When PlayStation 1 was launched in 1995, most gamers were indeed teenagers around the world. Today, however, for Sony PS2 and Microsoft Xbox, only about one-third of the users are under the age of 18, and the major market segments are the 22 to 25 year-olds and 25 to 35 year-olds in all the geographical markets. Those two demographic segments represent almost half of all gamers on PS2 and Xbox platforms. PS2 and Xbox have brought mature gamers to the marketplace by offering them compelling storylines and sophisticated graphics while Nintendo's GameCube focuses more on the traditional teenage markets globally.

The good times for the video game industry do not last forever. Analysts concluded that 2002 was the peak of the cycle, and that the market would cool off gradually until the next generation of consoles began appearing in late 2005. A supercharged Microsoft Xbox 360 was introduced with a big fanfare in late November 2005. At the time of this writing, Sony has PlayStation 3 in the works due to be out in late 2006: it is several times more powerful than PS2, rivaling the best mid-1990s supercomputer: A similar project is under way at Nintendo and is expected to be launched in 2006.

The next peak is not expected until 2007, but the industry has two new tricks up its sleeve in the form of online and mobile gaming. Both are dwarfed by console gaming at the moment but could likely become the next generation of gaming instruments.

Sony, Microsoft, and Nintendo are all vying for the market share of the next generation gaming industry. Online gaming got off to a small but promising start in November 2002. At the time of this writing, in the United States, Microsoft had sold 150,000 starter kits for its Xbox Live service within a week of its launch in November 2002. Sony signed up 175,000 subscribers to its rival online service launched in August 2002. While Microsoft is aggressively marketing online gaming, it had only sold around 5 million consoles as of December 2002 compared with sales of more than 40 million PS2s, so its strength poses little danger to Sony yet. On the other hand, Nintendo has been caught in this technological transition from console gaming to online gaming.

This is where the global strategies of these competitors vary. Microsoft is limiting online gaming to broadband users while Sony allows narrowband (modem) users to access its online games with the use of $40 network adaptors that link consoles over the Internet. Of the first 100,000 or so consumer who bought network adapters in August 2002, almost half of the early adopters of online gaming did not have broadband at all. That group would be cut off if they were Xbox players. Japan, in particular, may not yet be ready for a service that requires broadband access. Nevertheless, Microsoft's understanding of computer networking could give it the edge over Sony in online gaming.

Online gaming relies on high-speed, always-on broadband Internet connections, which have taken far longer to spread than the games industry had hoped. Few people sign up for broadband just to play games, so the market for online gaming is limited to those who already have it. The slow spread of broadband means that both firms' online-gaming efforts are really just a warm-up for the next console cycle. Both Sony and Microsoft have a bigger ambition, however: Online consoles could eventually be used to distribute all kinds of entertainment content, including films and music.

Gaming on mobile phones is also taking small but crucial steps forward. The latest handsets have color screens and can download software remotely. Their processing power matches that of the arcade game machines of the 1980s, so classic games such as Pacman run well. Games take roughly a minute to download, but adding one to a handset is almost as easy as downloading a new ringing tone or screen logo. This is where Sony and possibly Nintendo, both based in Japan, have an edge over Microsoft. Japan is home to NTT DoCoMo's i-Mode mobile phone that offers constant Internet access as if it were a desktop or laptop computer. Japanese consumers may not use PCs to the extent that Americans and Europeans use them, but they use their handy Internet mobile phones as their "portable" PCs instead. Sony and Nintendo have a much better feel of consumer needs when it comes to Internet mobile phone use than Microsoft.

Mobile gaming is a very different market from console gaming. Prices of individual games are much lower, but the popularity of mobile phones means that volumes are potentially much higher. Indeed, mobile phones could ultimately become the world's most widespread gaming devices. Nokia, the world's largest cellular handset maker, plans to launch a handset specifically aimed at gamers. Called the N-Gage, it is a direct challenge to Nintendo's handheld console, the Game Boy Advance. Nokia's wireless expertise could prove a crucial advantage as mobile gaming evolves.

No matter how technologically advanced a console may be, it is doomed without enticing game. Thus, game developers play a crucial role in the way Sony, Microsoft, and Nintendo (and others down the road) can compete for gaming customers around the world. In fact, a major reason why Xbox is lagging behind PS2 in Japan is the lack of appealing software games for Japanese gamers: initially, too many Xbox games were rereleases of old PS2 games. Many games popular in the U.S. failed to attract Japanese users because of differences in culture and gaming history (console in Japan versus personal computers in the United States).

Still, the game-developing business is wildly unpredictable. Games for the new 128-bit consoles that deliver complex 3-D graphics are increasingly expensive to develop, and development takes two years and costs $10 million. As the rivalry intensifies, in particular, between Sony and Microsoft, developers may be able to convince hardware companies to help defray the costs of R&D. Again, Sony is not wasting time; it recently bought the troubled U.S. developer Naughty Dog Inc., creator of the popular Crash Bandicoot games. With its huge financial resources, Microsoft is even better positioned than Sony to start buying loyalty. However, it remains too early to predict the outcome of this game war.

Kodak's ongoing rivalry with Fuji in the photographic film market provides another example of the importance of not permitting a global competitor unhindered operation in its home market. Kodak did not have a presence in Japan until the early 1980s. In this omission, Kodak was making the same mistake that many other Western companies have done: avoiding Japan as unattractive on a stand-alone basis while not seeing its strategic importance as the home base of a global competitor and a source of ideas.[61]

Identification of Weak Market Segments

The second strategy that firms should always keep an open eye for is the identification of **weak market segments** not covered by a firm in its home market. Japanese TV makers used small-screen portable TVs to get a foot in the door of the large U.S. market for televisions. RCA and Zenith did not think this segment attractive enough to go after. Another classic example is Honda's entry into the U.S. motorcycle market in the 1960s. Honda offered small, lightweight machines that looked safe and cute, attracting families and an emerging leisure class with an advertising campaign, "You can meet the nicest people on a Honda." Prior to Honda's entry, the U.S. motorcycle market was characterized by the police, military personnel, aficionados, and scofflaws like Hell's Angels and Devil's Disciples. Honda broke away from the existing paradigms about motorcycles and the motorcycle market and successfully differentiated itself by covering niches that did not exist before.[62] Once these Japanese companies were established in a small niche, they had a base to expand on to larger and more profitable product lines. More recently in 1997, Labatt International of Canada took advantage of freer trading relationships under NAFTA and awakened Canadian consumers to things Mexican by importing a Mexican beer, Sol, brewed by Cerveceria Cuauhtemoc Moctezuma, to fill a newly found market segment in Canada. Thus, firms should avoid pegging their competitive advantage entirely on one market segment in their home market.

What directions can this lead to in terms of a global product strategy or a worldwide distribution, pricing, or promotion strategy? We discuss some aspects of a global product strategy for an automobile company. Suppose market data tell the managers that four dozen different models are required if the company desires to design separate cars for each distinct segment of the Triad market, but the company has neither the financial nor the technological resources to make so many product designs. Also, no single global car will solve the problems for the entire world. The United States, Japan, and Europe are different markets, with different mixes of needs and preferences. Japan requires right-hand drive cars with frequent inspections, while many parts of Europe need smaller cars as compared to the United States. The option of leaving out a Triad market would not be a good one. The company needs to be present in all of these three markets with good products.

Use of the "Lead Market" Concept

The solution may be to look at the main requirements of each lead market in turn. A **lead market** is a market where unique local competition is nurturing product and service standards to be adopted by the rest of the world over time. A classic case is facsimile (fax) technology. Siemens in Germany developed a considerable technological advantage in fax technology in the 1970s. However, because of lukewarm reaction from its domestic market, the German company abandoned the fax and concentrated on improving the telex system. In the meantime, sensing a strong demand for this technology, Japanese companies invested continuously in fax technology and introduced a stream of improved and affordable fax machines in Japan and abroad. Backed by the strength of the local markets, the Japanese bandwagon, led by Sharp

---

[61] Yoshi Tsurumi and Hiroki Tsurumi, "Fujifilm-Kodak Duopolistic Competition in Japan and the United States," *Journal of International Business Studies,* 30 (4th Quarter 1999), pp. 813–30.

[62] Richard P. Rumelt, "The Many Faces of Honda," *California Management Review,* 38 (Summer 1996), pp. 103–11; and Richard D. Pascale, "Reflections on Honda," *California Management Review,* 38 (Summer 1996), pp. 112–17.

and Ricoh, spread to the rest of the world, displacing the telex system eventually. In retrospect, Siemens should have introduced fax machines in Japan as the lead market.[63]

Another example is wireless financial services. Although many U.S. banks are globally competitive, banks in Europe and Asia have already surpassed those in the United States when it comes to offering banking services. According to a recent TowerGroup report, more than 90 percent of the estimated 10 million users of wireless financial services are in the Asia-Pacific region and Western Europe. The United States is far behind this trend.[64] There are several reasons, some technological and some cultural. A technological one involves digital phones. Although the push toward smart digital phones that can use the Web and e-mail has started, only one person in five in the United States has digital devices of any kind. Analog phones still account for a majority of cell phones in the United States. Digital caught on earlier in Europe, where 40 percent of people have some sort of wireless digital device. Asia is not far behind. In Scandinavia and Japan, more than half the population has digital devices. In addition, Europe has one generally accepted standard for mobile phones—the Global System for Mobile Communications—that allows for short, two-way messages. The United States has a hodgepodge of competing technologies, making it expensive for financial institutions to reach a broad range of customers. Europe and Japan could serve as lead markets or better learning grounds for U.S. financial institutions to be able to compete in the U.S. market down the road.

As indicated earlier, this is a strategic response to the emergence of lead countries as a market globalization driver. Each country can be a lead country model with a product carefully tailored to meet distinct individual needs. With a short list of lead country models in hand, minor modifications may enable a fair amount of sales in other Triad markets and elsewhere. This will halve the number of basic models required to cover the global markets and, at the same time, cover a major proportion of sales with cars designed for major markets. Additional model types could be developed through adaptation of the lead country models for specific segments. This approach in each of the largest core markets permits development of a pool of supplemental designs that can be adapted to local preferences.

In line with our earlier example of Procter & Gamble, it is not necessary that the design and manufacture of a lead country model be restricted to one R&D and manufacturing facility. Ford has now integrated the design and manufacturing process on a global basis. It has design centers in the United States (Dearborn, Michigan), England, Italy, and Japan, which are connected by a satellite uplink. Designers using fast workstations and massively parallel computers simulate a complete model and the working of the model for various conditions. Separate parts of the car are simulated at different facilities. Thereafter, the complete design for a lead country is integrated in the facility assigned for the purpose. For instance, the complete design for the new Ford Mustang was put together in Dearborn, but it incorporated some significant changes in body design that were made in England based on designs of Jaguar, which Ford had acquired. Similarly, different components of an automobile can be sourced from different parts of the global network of the firm or even from outside the firm. As firms move toward concentrating on developing expertise in a few core competencies,[65] they are increasingly outsourcing many of the components required for the total product system that constitutes the automobile.

This increase in outsourcing raises another question for firms that practice it. How can firms ensure uninterrupted flow of components when the component makers are independent companies? The answer to this question and the set of issues that it raises

[63]Marian Beise and Thomas Cleff, "Assessing the Lead Market Potential of Countries for Innovation Projects," *Journal of International Management,* 10 (October 2004), pp. 453–77.

[64]"Wireless Financial Services: Batteries Running Low," *American Banker,* July 23, 2002, p. 6A; and "Remember Wireless Financial Services? They Never Went Away," *Securities Industry News,* June 16, 2003, p. 38.

[65]C. K. Prahalad and Gary Hamel, "The Core Competence of the Corporation," *Harvard Business Review,* 68 (May–June 1990), pp. 79–91.

takes us into the area of cooperation between firms and strategic alliances, which will be discussed in Chapter 9.

Marketing Strategies for Emerging Markets

As stated earlier in Chapters 1 and 2, one salient aspect of the globalization of markets is the importance of the emerging markets, known as 10 big emerging markets (BEMs) including China, India, Indonesia, Russia, and Brazil. As multinational companies from North America, Western Europe, and Japan search for growth, they have no choice but to compete in those BEMs despite the uncertainty and the difficulty of doing business there. A vast consumer base of hundreds of millions of people—the middle-class market, in particular—is developing rapidly. When marketing managers working in the developed countries hear about the emerging middle-class markets in China or Brazil, they tend to think in terms of the middle class in the United Sates or Western Europe. In the United States, people who earn an annual income of between $35,000 and $75,000 are generally considered middle class.[66] In China and Brazil, people who have the purchasing power equivalent of $20,000 or more constitute only 2 and 9 percent of their respective populations and are considered upper class. In these emerging countries, people with the purchasing power equivalent of $5,000 to $20,000 (and most of them in the $5,000 to $10,000 equivalent bracket) are considered middle class and constitute a little more than 25 percent of the population. Indeed, the vast majority (67 percent of the population) in China and Brazil are in the low-income class with the purchasing power equivalent of less than $5,000. Obviously, the concept of the middle-class market segment differs greatly between developed and emerging countries, and so does what they can afford to purchase.[67]

Consumers in BEMs are increasingly aware of global products and global standards, but they often are unwilling—and sometimes unable—to pay global prices. Even when those consumers appear to want the same products as sold elsewhere, some modification in marketing strategy is necessary to reflect differences in product, pricing, promotion, and distribution. Some unnecessary frills could need to be removed from the product to reduce price yet maintain its functional performance, and packaging could need to be strengthened as the distribution problems, such as poor road conditions and dusty air, in emerging markets hamper smooth handling. Promotion could need to be adapted to address local tastes and preferences. As these emerging markets improve their economic standing in the world economy, they tend to assert their local tastes and preferences over existing global products. Furthermore, access to local distribution channels is often critical to success in emerging markets because it is difficult and expensive for multinational companies from developed countries to understand local customs and a labyrinthine network of a myriad of distributors in the existing channel.

Despite these operational complexities, many European companies, unlike U.S. companies, are actually making BEMs as corporate priority. Consider two retail giants for example. Many of us tend to think that Wal-Mart is one of the most global. However, only 10 percent of its sales are generated outside its core NAFTA market, compared to Carrefour, which generates more than 20 percent of sales outside Europe. What is more, in the all-important emerging markets of China, South America, and the Pacific Rim, Carrefour outpaces Wal-Mart in actual revenue. Carrefour was the first foreign retailer tapping into the attractive Chinese market of a billion-plus consumers in 1997. By 2005, Carrefour has opened 62 stores and is planning to open between 12 and 15 new hypermarkets each year, with one-third of them located in central and western areas of China. Wal-Mart, with more than 5,000 stores worldwide, is catching up with Carrefour with its 46th store in China. In 2004, Carrefour generated a sales revenue of $2 billion, whereas Wal-Mart had a sales revenue of $0.94 billion, or slightly

---

[66]"The Billionaire Next Door," *Forbes,* October 11, 1999, pp. 50–62.
[67]C.K. Prahalad and Kenneth Lieberthal, "The End of Corporate Imperialism," *Harvard Business Review,* 76 (July–August 1998), pp. 69–79.

less than half of Carrefour's revenue.[68] European companies such as Unilever have also broadened the scope of their market by competing for the low-income classes. In Indonesia, Unilever does brisk business by selling inexpensive, small-size products, that are affordable to everyone and available anywhere. For instance, it sells Lifebuoy soap with the motto: "With a price you can afford." Unilever's subsidiary in India, Hindustan Lever, approaches the market as one giant rural market. It uses small, inexpensive packaging, bright signage, and all sorts of local distributors. In fact, Unilever has been so successful and profitable in Indonesia that its biggest rival, P&G, is now trying to follow suit.

Local companies from those emerging markets are also honing their competitive advantage by offering better customer service than foreign multinationals can provide. They can compete with established multinationals from developed countries either by entrenching themselves in their domestic or regional markets or by extending their unique home-grown capabilities abroad. For example, Honda, which sells its scooters, motorcycles, and cars worldwide on the strength of its superior technology, quality, and brand appeal, entered the Indian market. Competing head-on with Honda's strength would be a futile effort for Indian competitors. Instead, Bajaj, an Indian scooter manufacturer, decided to emphasize its line of inexpensive, rugged scooters through an extensive distribution system and a ubiquitous service network of roadside-mechanic stalls. Although Bajaj could not compete with Honda on technology, it has been able to stall Honda's inroads by catering to consumers who looked for low-cost, durable machines. Similarly, Jollibee Foods, a family-owned fast-food company in the Philippines, overcame an onslaught from McDonald's in its home market by not only upgrading service and delivery standards but also developing rival menus customized to local Filipino tastes. In addition to noodle and rice meals made with fish, Jollibee developed a hamburger seasoned with garlic and soy sauce, capturing more than half of the fast-food business in the Philippines. Using similar recipes, this Filipino company has now established dozens of restaurants in neighboring markets and beyond, including Hong Kong, the Middle East, and as far as California.[69]

COMPETITIVE ANALYSIS   ◆ ◆ ◆ ◆ ◆ ◆ ◆ ◆

As we have discussed so far, a firm needs to broaden the sources of competitive advantage relentlessly over time. However, careful assessment of a firm's current competitive position is also required. One particularly useful technique in analyzing a firm's competitive position relative to its competitors is referred to as **SWOT (strengths, weaknesses, opportunities, and threats) analysis.** A SWOT analysis divides the information into two main categories (*internal factors* and *external factors*) and then into positive aspects (*strengths* and *opportunities*) and negative aspects (*weaknesses* and *threats*). The framework for a SWOT analysis is illustrated in Exhibit 8-5. The internal factors viewed as strengths or weaknesses depend on their impact on the firm's positions; that is, they can represent a strength for one firm but a weakness, in relative terms, for another. These include all of the marketing mix (product, price, promotion, and distribution strategy) as well as personnel and finance. The external factors, which, again, can be threats to one firm and opportunities to another, include technological changes, legislation, sociocultural changes, and changes in the marketplace or competitive position.

Based on this SWOT framework, marketing executives can construct alternative strategies. For example, an S*O strategy can be conceived to maximize both the

[68]"Boost for Foreign Retailers," *SPC Asia,* March 2005, p. 4; and "Wal-Mart Aims for 12–15 New China Stores in 2005," *China Daily,* May 18, 2005.

[69]Niraj Dawar and Tony Frost, "Competing with Giants: Survival Strategies for Local Companies in Emerging Markets," *Harvard Business Review,* 77 (March–April 1999), pp. 119–29; and "Fast Food from Asia," *U.S. News & World Report,* February 26, 2001, p. 48.)

EXHIBIT 8-5
SWOT ANALYSIS

SWOT Analysis

External Factors \ Internal Factors	Strengths	Weakness
	Brand Name, Human Resources, Management Know-How, Technology, Advertising, etc.	Price, Lack of Financial Resources, Long Product Development Cycle, Dependence on Independent Distributors, etc.
Opportunities — Growth market Favorable investment Environment, deregulation, stable exchange rate, patent protection, etc.	**S*O Strategy** Develop a strategy to maximize strengths and maximize opportunities	**W*O Strategy** Develop a strategy to minimize weaknesses and maximize opportunities
Threats — New entrants, change in consumer preference, new Environmental protection laws, local content requirement, etc.	**S*T Strategy** Develop a strategy to maximize strengths and minimize threats	**W*T Strategy** Develop a strategy to minimize weaknesses and minimize threats

company's strengths and market opportunities. Similarly, an S*T strategy may be considered to maximize the company's strengths and minimize external threats. Thus, a SWOT analysis helps marketing executives identify a wide range of alternative strategies to think about.

You should note, however, that SWOT is just one aid to categorization; it is not the only technique. One drawback to SWOT is that it tends to persuade companies to compile lists rather than think about what is really important to their business. It also presents the resulting lists uncritically without clear prioritization, so that, for example, weak opportunities may appear to balance strong threats. Furthermore, using the company's strengths against its competitors' weaknesses could work once or twice but not over several dynamic strategic interactions because its approach becomes predictable and competitors begin to learn and outsmart it.

The aim of any SWOT analysis should be to isolate the key issues that will be important to the future of the firm and that subsequent marketing strategy will address.

SUMMARY

Market-oriented firms, facing increased competitiveness in world markets, find it essential to assume a global perspective in designing and implementing their marketing strategies. Cost containment, rising technology costs and the dispersal of technology, a greater number of global competitors in many industries, and the advent of hypercompetition in many markets mean that international business practices need to undergo continuous refinement to keep them aligned with company goals. The explosive growth of e-commerce has added urgency to competitive analysis involving not only established multinational firms but also an increasing number of entrepreneurial start-ups leapfrogging geographical constraints via the Internet.

Strategic planning and the integration of the global activities into one coherent whole needs to be implemented for a firm to maximize its activities and to remain a viable player in international markets. In doing so, the multinational firm needs to mesh in information technology and telecommunications with its global operations make relevant data available to managers in real time. In the end, a global strategy of any kind has to resolve a number of apparent contradictions. Firms have to respond to national needs yet seek to exploit know-how on a worldwide basis while at all times striving to produce and distribute goods and services globally as efficiently as possible.

In recent years, however, as a result of the formation of regional trading blocs, an increasing number of companies have begun to organize their marketing strategies on a regional basis by exploiting emerging regional similarities. Globally minded, proactive firms increasingly exploit their competitive position in some regions by funneling abundant resources and regionally successful marketing programs to other regions where they do not necessarily occupy a strong market position. SWOT analysis helps isolate the key issues that will be important to a firm's competitiveness of and that its subsequent marketing strategy will address.

KEY TERMS

Bargaining power of buyers	Hypercompetition	SWOT (strengths, weaknesses, opportunities, threats) analysis
Bargaining power of suppliers	Industry competitor	Threat of substitute production or services
Cost leadership	Interdependency	Timing and know-how
Cross-subsidization of markets	Lead market	Weak market segments
Global citizenship	Niche	
Global industry	Potential entrant	
Global marketing strategy	Product differentiation	
Global strategy	Regionalization	

REVIEW QUESTIONS

1. How are the developments in information technology impacting firms' global strategies?

2. What are the various factors/forces/drivers that determine the globalization potential of industries? How do global industries differ from multidomestic industries?

3. What do you understand by the term *hypercompetition*? What, according to hypercompetition, are the various arenas of competition?

4. How are the concepts *interdependency* and *standardization* related? What are their implications for global strategy?

5. How is a global marketing strategy distinct from standardization?

6. What are the benefits and limitations of global marketing strategies?

7. How do regional and global strategies differ? What are some advantages and disadvantages of a regional strategy?

DISCUSSION QUESTIONS

1. Food habits have been known to vary considerably across countries and regions. Would you describe the food industry as primarily multidomestic or global in nature? Use the fast-food chain McDonald's as a case example to explain your answer. Note that while there are certain similarities in all of the McDonald's outlets around the world, there are differences, especially in the menu, in various countries. Can the McDonald's example be generalized across the food industry?

2. In the summer of 1995, Procter & Gamble, the U.S. multinational giant, modified its global operational structure. Its new structure included a top-tier management team consisting of four vice presidents, each representing a particular region, namely North America, Europe (to include the Middle East and Africa), Asia (and Pacific Rim), and Latin America. One of the main reasons cited for this organizational change was the elimination of duties and regulations that now allows P&G to distribute its products to foreign consumers more inexpensively and quickly. While acknowledging that more than 50 percent of the company's sales come from North America as do a bulk of its profits, top management mentioned that it took care not to emphasize a particular region over the other. Competing globally with mature brands in saturated markets posed continued challenges, however. In 1999, it launched a belt-tightening initiative called Organization 2005. Since then, a host of marginal and mature brands have been eliminated and a quarter of P&G's brand managers have left the company, yet there is no doubt that most of the company's new products originated in the United States. Few dominant products and brands have originated from its foreign subsidiaries. There are, however, examples of brands, such as Tide, that involved the cross-fertilization of ideas and technologies from its operations around the world.

Based on the facts provided and any popular press information about P&G that you have been exposed to, what would you consider to be P&G's predominant international strategy: global (integrated on a worldwide basis), regional (integrated on a regional level), ethnocentric (predominantly influenced by its operations in North America), or polycentric (primarily independent and autonomous functioning of its international subsidiaries)?

3. Since the early 1980s, researchers in academia and business practitioners have acknowledged the benefits of globalization. However, practitioners have continually indicated the constraints on human management resources in actually implementing global strategies; implementing a global strategy require globally thinking managers. In your opinion, are business schools making progress in developing more global managers? Are corporations doing a good job of training their managers to think globally? What are the deficiencies? What are some of the steps that you would recommend to business schools as well as corporations in order to promote the development of executives who think globally?

4. One of the many advantages of globalization suggested is economies of scale and scope. There is, however, a counterargument to this advantage. Mass customization production techniques could lead to erosion of scale and scope economies with the added advantage of being able to customize products if not for individual customers, then definitely for individual markets. Discuss the strengths and weaknesses of this counterargument.

5. In today's highly competitive business environment, the disruptors rather than the disruptees prolong their competitive advantage. Market disruption takes place much faster online than in the retail world. Today, "to google" is a verb, and the words "Friends Reunited," Britain's most valuable online brand, often appear in newspaper headlines. What we witness is that successful firms are those that reinvent themselves continually and have an open mind about the future. Recently, China's leading Internet search engine, Baidu.com, was listed on America's NASDAQ exchange and became the largest first-day gain since the dotcom bubble with 354 percent stock increase and worth nearly $4 billion. As one of the world's largest Internet markets, China had roughly 94 million Internet users in 2004. Some large portals in China, such as Netease, Sina, Sohu, and Tom, have been making a healthy profit since 2003. Yahoo and Google also have established their presence in China. At the same time, they are facing intense competition from domestic rivals. Should U.S. companies adjust their marketing strategies in China? Should they approach the largest market with regional or global strategies? What are some of the advantages and disadvantages of different marketing strategies?

SHORT CASES

ASE 8-1

GM AND FORD'S PURSUIT OF DIFFERENT BENEFITS FROM GLOBAL MARKETING

GLOBAL MARKETING THOUGHT: 1991–2000

Ford and General Motors approach globalization differently. In its quest for a "world car," Ford developed the so-called Ford 2000 program by creating five new vehicle centers—four in the United States and one in Europe—each responsible for designing and developing a different type of car world-wide. Ford's plan was put to the test when it built a mid-size world car in 1993 known as the Mondeo in Europe and the Ford Contour in North America. Its plan was to manufacture 700,000 cars a year in Europe and North America for nearly a decade with only a "refreshing" after four or five years. Ford executives say they can no longer afford to duplicate efforts and they want to emulate the Japanese, who develop cars that with minor variations can be sold around the world. While the Mondeo/Contour sold 642,000 units in the first two years in Europe, it had disappointing sales in the United States attributed to its comparably higher price relative to the car's predecessors. Successful product development efforts require that the company avoid two problems that can arise from pursuing global design. First, the high cost of designing products or components that are acceptable in many settings could negatively affect efficiency. Second, the product, in this case a "world car," may be low cost but meet the lowest common denominator of taste in all countries.

Alternatively, General Motors took a more regional tack by retaining strong regional operations that develop distinctly different cars for their own area. If a car has a strong crossover potential, engineers and marketers cross the Atlantic to suggest customization. Thus, Cadillac got an Americanized version of the Opel Omega small luxury sedan developed by GM's Opel subsidiary in Germany. GM managers contend that ad hoc efforts provide low cost and flexibility. One senior executive at Ford of Europe countered that "doing two conventional car programs would have cost substantially more than doing one global program. If we did it again, we could do it in $3\frac{1}{2}$ years."

The two automakers' contrasting product development and marketing programs in the 1990s illustrate the traditionally viewed trade-offs of efficiency and effectiveness, global standardization versus customization, market segmentation versus product differentiation, and product orientation versus

Source: "Ford: Alex Trotman's Daring Global Strategy," *Business Week,* April 3, 1995, pp. 94–104; "Ford Be Nimble," *Business Week Online,* http://www.businessweek.com/, September 27, 1999; Larry J. Howell and Jamie C. Hsu, "Globalization within the Auto Industry," *Research Technology Management,* 45 (July/August 2002), pp. 43–49; "Where Are the Hot Cars?" *Business Week,* June 24, 2002, pp. 66–67; "Changing Course," *Country Monitor,* July 29, 2002; and "Small Carmakers Rise in Large China Market," *China Daily,* June 3, 2005.

customer orientation. These debates are framed by the tension between bending demand to the will of supply (i.e., driving the market) versus adjusting to market demand (i.e., driven by the market).

It is difficult to conclude that one strategy is always better than the other. People must be reminded that while the Ford Mondeo/Contour project cost $6 billion and took six years to develop, potential cost savings from the global strategy could also be enormous for years to come. On the other hand, GM's regional strategy could also make sense if regional taste differences remain so large that a Ford-style global strategy could, indeed, end up producing a "blandmobile" that hits the lowest common denominator of taste in different markets.

Which was a winning strategy in the 1990s? Ford's ex-president, Jacques Nasser, wanted to keep the efficiencies generated from central thinking about design and production, but he wanted to reintroduce the market focus in regions across the globe that will give Ford stronger brands and more appealing products. The Ford 2000 was a good idea carried a bit too far. Ford Contour was discontinued from the U.S. market in 2001. Ford is now trying to redefine the Ford 2000 program with a heightened emphasis on the company's brands and to give the various regional and brand units more autonomy.

GLOBAL MARKETING THOUGHT: 2001–PRESENT

The automobile industry today is a growth industry in emerging markets. Only about 12 percent of the earth's 6 billion people enjoy the benefits of vehicle ownership, and industry growth remains positive at about 20 percent per decade with the potential for global annual sales of 65 to 70 million vehicles by 2010. Most of this expansion will occur in emerging markets such as China, India, Russia, and Brazil.

General Motors' strategy in China and other Asian markets is very aggressive. Alliances have been the key to its marketing strategies. For example, GM recently announced plans to take an ownership position in a new company that will be formed from selected assets of Korea's Daewoo Motor. While GM has 100 percent equity ownership of some of its key units—such as Opel and Saab—the company has used an approach that is more akin to a "loose confederation" in joining recently with other partners such as Suzuki, Fuji, and Fiat. GM has a minority equity stake in each of these companies. In addition, GM has major joint ventures in both China and Russia. GM's alliance strategy and its initiatives to develop new markets are key elements in the company's approach to globalization. Alliances afford the opportunity for component and architecture sharing as well as the reduction in R&D costs that will be critical for manufacturers looking ahead to hybrid vehicle technology and, ultimately, hydrogen-based fuel-cell vehicles. By pulling together the talents and resources from its global

R&D network, GM has been able to reduce redundancy, accelerate ongoing development, and jump-start new development. Nevertheless, globalization entails risks from many quarters: economics, political forces, energy, and national differences in social and cultural norms. Consequently, GM is now focusing on the recruitment and empowerment of an international executive team, which will help accelerate the globalization process. For example, GM operates in Australia through a subsidiary Holden, which is closely integrated into GM's' global manufacturing strategies.

Ford's current strategy is to focus on its luxury brands. It now owns Jaguar, Aston Martin, and Volvo and has hired BMW guru Wolfgang Reitzle to run the trio though its new Premier Automotive Group (PAG), which brings together Volvo and Jaguar with the U.S. premium brand Lincoln. Since the mid-1990s, Ford Motor has plowed much of its bountiful profits from sports utility vehicles (SUVs) and trucks into a heady expansion of e-commerce ventures and luxury car brands. As a result, it has paid little attention to the development of mass-market cars and trucks. Ford still does not have the financial resources to implement a regional strategy as GM has done. Ford's global business lost US$5.4 billion in 2001. Consequently, the world's second largest carmaker is restructuring. Five plants were to be closed around the world, while four models, including the Escort, were to be discontinued. In Latin America, a recent automotive trade accord between Brazil and Mexico is fostering integration between Ford's two main industrial bases in Latin America. Meanwhile, the company's operations in Argentina and Brazil, which were becoming an integrated business, are coming apart.

Recently, both GM and Ford reported decreased demand for their vehicles, especially their trucks and SUVs. GM's big Buick sedans, which used to dominate the Chinese car market, are showing sluggish business in China. In the promising growing economy, car demand in China is shifting away from large sedans long favored by government officials to economy models demanded by families. GM faces harsh competition from both homegrown and Korean and Japanese automakers. According to the China Automobile Manufacturers Association, the country experienced a 15.7 percent increase in sales of passenger vehicles in 2005 compared with a year earlier. However, GM's sales volume was down 23 percent during the same time. Today, it is ordinary buyers, not government bureaucrats, who dominate the auto market. Consumers prefer smaller cars, such as the Elantra from Hyundai, Tianjin Xiali, Chery QQ mini-car from China, and Japanese Honda (Fit compact car). A QQ sells for $4,800 to $5,400, compared to GM's lowest priced Santanas that sell for between $10,000 and $12,000. Apparently, compared to Japanese and Korean automakers, GM and Ford are not staying on top of the game, either domestically or internationally.

Although we cannot say that GM's strategy is genuinely better than Ford's, one thing is clear. GM has pursued the benefits of global marketing strategy methodically over time, whereas Ford seems to have been swayed more or less by "fads" of global marketing strategy. The verdict in the first few years in the 21st century seems to be in favor of General Motors over Ford, yet both automakers are struggling in the face of competition from Japanese, Korean, and even Chinese automakers in China.

DISCUSSION QUESTION

1. Discuss what is missing in GM's and Ford's global strategy.

CASE 8-2

P&G: WE'RE ALSO CHINESE

It is common knowledge that having dominated the Triad region of North America, Europe, and Japan for the better half of the last century, multinationals (MNC) firms turned their heads toward emerging economies such as China, India, and other Asian economies, which are no longer just sources of cheap labor for MNC operations but are also large consumer bases. China, with the largest national population in the world, only recently became part of the World Trade Organization and therefore even more attractive to Western multinationals.

However, as MNCs are aware, doing business in China is not simple even though the economy is more open to foreign firms now than it has ever been. Local Chinese firms are growing rapidly and therefore pose a significant threat to foreign firms that are often unable to provide goods at competitive prices the way the local firms can. Today, more MNCs are finding success in the unique Chinese market than they used to, but they have learned the formula to success the hard way.

Take the example of U.S. consumer products giant Proctor & Gamble (P&G) that first set up shop in China in 1998 through a joint venture with a local partner, Hutchison Whampoa. Eventually, P&G bought out the remaining stake in the venture. P&G's brands such as Tide detergent, Crest toothpaste, and Oil of Olay skin care products made their place in homes in more than 75 different countries worldwide and P&G's *modus operandi* included marketing its products as quality goods at profitable prices. When the company started selling its products in China, it soon discovered that its tried and tested global marketing strategy would not work the same way it had in other markets for a variety of reasons.

A developing market like China is characterized by huge disparity in income levels between the wealthy and the not so wealthy. Another glaring feature is the diversity in consumer needs based on whether it is a rural, urban or semiurban area. These differences are further enhanced by the variety of outlets for sale of consumer goods ranging from large-scale foreign stores such as French retailer Carrefour to local Chinese retailers and independent small stores. Therefore, for a

Source: Jacques Penhirin, "Understanding the Chinese Consumer," *McKinsey Quarterly,* 2004 Special Edition, p. 46.

company to succeed in China means offering a wide variety of products at reasonable prices—and succeed P&G did!

After entering the Chinese market, P&G soon figured out that selling its premium priced products would not help it achieve a significant market share let alone grant it the status of market leader as many of its brands had enjoyed in other foreign markets. Therefore, the company planned a detailed marketing strategy specifically for the Chinese market. An important feature of strategic implementation was the three-tiered market system by which P&G divided the Chinese market into three segments. According to Laurent Philippe, head of P&G's Greater China region, "Because we aspire to leadership, we need to compete in more than the premium segment. We need to compete at least in the middle segment as well. In volume terms, you can segment our categories into three price tiers: the top tier is 15 percent of the volume in units, the middle tier is 30 percent, and the bottom tier is 55 percent. The split in value, or revenue, is a little bit different: it is 30 percent in premium, 40 percent in the mid-priced segment, and only 30 percent in the low-end segment. This segmentation, by the way, is not mechanical; it is consumer driven." The main objective behind the company's marketing efforts in China was to promote its global products sold in China as Chinese brands so that consumers could identify with these products. This strategy proved to be important given that P&G's competitors in the market include not only other foreign firms but also indigenous Chinese ones.

So how did the company manage to successfully implement this strategy? In Philippe's words, "You cannot just take a global technology and make it cheaper by simply removing or replacing certain ingredients. The cost gap is too big. So we are now using our research-and-development capabilities to create different value offerings superior to those of the local competitors but at an equal or even lower manufacturing cost. These products are designed from the outset to meet certain cost, and therefore pricing, targets." P&G realized that low-income consumers in China often purchase single use packets of shampoo, detergent, and so on, and it soon began offering some of its products in these sizes. The company is using local resources to achieve its goals. Research and development for the Chinese market is done in Beijing at the Beijing Technical Center. P&G also uses local ingredients desired by consumers. As for publicizing and promoting its products, P&G relies mainly on advertising on television because it is one of the best ways to reach a large number of buyers. In 2004, P&G targeted young consumers by advertising on MTV's popular local shows.

For now, the company seems to have settled comfortably in China. Its skin care brand Oil of Olay was China's biggest selling brand in the year 2004 with a 104 percent increase on the year 2003. Some of P&G's well-known brands such as Crest toothpaste sell more in China than they do in its home country.

DISCUSSION QUESTIONS

1. How does China's entry into the WTO affect multinational firms' outlook toward China and their future investment in the country?

2. What are the drawbacks of P&G's strategy for the Chinese market?

3. What other marketing strategy could P&G have adopted for the Chinese market as an alternative to the tier system one?

FURTHER READING ◆

Bakhtiari, S., and N. Daneshvar. "The Challenges of Globalization and Regionalization for Developing Countries." *Journal of International Marketing & Marketing Research,* 26 (June 2001), pp. 91–98.

Dawar, Niraj, and Tony Frost. "Competing with Giants: Survival Strategies for Local Companies in Emerging Markets," *Harvard Business Review,* 77 (March–April 1999), pp. 119–29.

Ger, Güliz. "Localizing in the Global Village." *California Management Review,* 41 (Summer 1999), pp. 64–83.

Gong, Wen, Zhang Li, and Tiger Li. "Marketing to China's Youth: A Cultural Transformation Perspective." *Business Horizons,* 47 (November/December 2004), pp. 41–50.

Griffith, David A., and Michael G. Harvey. "A Resource Perspective of Global Dynamic Capabilities." *Journal of International Business Studies,* 32 (Third Quarter 2001), pp. 597–606.

Javalgi, Rajshekhar G., Patricia R. Todd, and Robert F. Scherer. "The Dynamics of Global E-Commerce: An Organizational Ecology Perspective." *International Marketing Review,* 22 (4), 2005, pp. 420–35.

Khanna, Tarun, Krishna G. Palepu, Jayant Sinha, Andy Klump, Niraj Kaji, Luis Sanchez, and Max Yacoub. "Strategies That Fit Emerging Markets." *Harvard Business Review,* 83 (June 2005), pp. 63–76.

Leamer, Edward E., and Michael Storper. "The Economic Geography of the Internet Age." *Journal of International Business Studies,* 32 (Fourth Quarter 2001), pp. 641–65.

Lovelock, Christopher H., and George S. Yip. "Developing Global Strategies for Service Businesses." *California Management Review,* 38 (Winter 1996), pp. 64–86.

Luo, Yadong. *Multinational Enterprises in Emerging Markets.* Copenhagen: Copenhagen Business School Press, 2002.

Mascarenhas, Briance, Alok Baveja, and Mamnoon Jamil. "Dynamics of Core Competencies in Leading Multinational Companies." *California Management Review,* 40 (Summer 1998), pp. 117–32.

Melewar, T.C., and Caroline Stead. "The Impact of Information Technology on Global Marketing Strategies." *Journal of General Management,* 27 (Summer 2002), pp. 29–40.

Nakata, Cheryl, and K. Sivakumar. "Instituting the Marketing Concept in a Multinational Setting: The Role of National Culture." *Journal of the Academy of Marketing Science,* 29 (Summer 2001), pp. 255–75.

Townsend, Janell D., Sengun Yeniyurt, Z. Seyda Deligonul, and S. Tamer Cavusgil. "Exploring the Marketing Program Antecedents of Performance in a Global Company." *Journal of International Marketing,* 12 (4), 2004, pp. 1–24.

Zou, Shaoming, and S. Tamer Cavusgil. "The GMS: A Broad Conceptualization of Global Marketing Strategy and Its Effect on Firm Performance." *Journal of Marketing,* 66 (October 2002), pp. 40–56.

GLOBAL MARKET ENTRY STRATEGIES

9

HAPTER OVERVIEW

1. SELECTING THE TARGET MARKET
2. CHOOSING THE MODE OF ENTRY
3. EXPORTING
4. LICENSING
5. FRANCHISING
6. CONTRACT MANUFACTURING (OUTSOURCING)
7. EXPANDING THROUGH JOINT VENTURES
8. ENTERING NEW MARKETS THROUGH WHOLLY OWNED SUBSIDIARIES
9. CREATING STRATEGIC ALLIANCES
10. TIMING OF ENTRY
11. EXIT STRATEGIES

Orange, France Telecom's mobile phone unit, was supposed to offer the marketing savvy and technological expertise.[1] TelecomAsia, at the time a Thai fixed-line phone operator, would leverage its local market knowledge and connections. Together, the two partners expected to conquer Thailand's booming mobile phone market. Alas, the honeymoon was short lived. The joint venture partners split after merely two years. The relationship was troubled by different competing strategic visions. Orange managers wanted to expand the business with a low-price strategy to build up a broad customer base. TelecomAsia managers, however, preferred to push more multimedia options to attract higher-margin subscribers. TelecomAsia agreed to buy Orange's 39 percent stake. Orange left Thailand, and TelecomAsia relaunched its mobile service under a new brand, True. True's president commented: "I learned a lot, I hope they learned too, about how important it is for a local partner to take the lead in the marketing area."

---

[1]"Thailand's Rocky Road," *Far Eastern Economic Review,* September 23, 2004, pp. 39–40.

Making the "right" entry decisions heavily impacts the company's performance in global markets. Granted, other strategic marketing mix decisions also play a big role. A major difference here is that many of these other decisions can easily be corrected, sometimes even overnight (e.g., pricing decisions), while entry decisions are far more difficult to redress.

We can hardly overemphasize the need for a solid market entry strategy. Entry decisions heavily influence the firm's other marketing mix decisions. Several interlocking decisions need to be made. The firm must decide (1) the target product/market, (2) the goals of the target markets, (3) the mode of entry, (4) the time of entry, (5) a marketing mix plan, and (6) a control system to monitor the performance in the entered market.[2] This chapter covers the major decisions that constitute market entry strategies. It starts with the target market selection decision and then considers the different criteria that will impact the entry mode choice. Following that, we will concentrate on the various entry strategy options that multinational corporations (MNCs) might consider. Each of these is described in some detail and evaluated. We will then focus on cross-border strategic alliances. The final two questions that we consider deal with timing-of-entry and divestment decisions.

◆ ◆ ◆ ◆ ◆ ◆ ◆ ◆   ## SELECTING THE TARGET MARKET

A crucial step in developing a global expansion strategy is the selection of potential target markets. Companies adopt many different approaches to pick target markets. A flowchart for one of the more elaborate approaches is given in Exhibit 9-1.

To identify market opportunities for a given product (or service), the international marketer usually begins with a large pool of candidate countries (for example, all central European countries). To narrow down this pool of countries, the company typically does a preliminary screening. The goal of this exercise is to minimize the mistakes of (1) ignoring countries that offer viable opportunities for its product and (2) wasting time on countries that offer no or little potential. Those countries that make the grade are scrutinized further to determine the final set of target countries. The following describes a four-step procedure that a company employs for the initial screening process.

Step 1. *Indicator selection and data collection.* First, the company needs to identify a set of socioeconomic and political indicators it believes are critical. The indicators that a company selects are to a large degree driven by the strategic objectives spelled out in the company's global mission. Colgate-Palmolive views per capita purchasing power as a major driver behind market opportunities.[3] Starbucks looks at economic indicators, the size of the population, and where the company has opportunities to have joint-venture partners.[4] When choosing markets for a particular product, indicators also depend on the nature of the product. P&G chose Malaysia and Singapore as the first markets in Asia (ex-Japan) for the rollout of Febreze, an odor remover for fabrics.[5] Not only were both markets known for "home-proud" consumers but also people there tend to furnish their homes heavily with fabrics. A company might also decide to enter a particular country that is considered as a *trendsetter* in the industry. Kodak, for example, re-entered the digital camera market in Japan precisely for that reason. As the president of Kodak Japan put it, "what happens in Japan eventually happens in the rest of world."[6]

---

[2]Franklin R. Root, *Entry Strategies for International Markets* (New York: Lexington Books, 1994), p. 23.

[3]"Tangney Is Bullish on L. America," *Advertising Age International,* May 17, 1993, pp. I–23.

[4]"Coffee Talk," *Asia Inc,* March 2005, pp. 16–17.

[5]"Grey Showers Febreze over Southeast Asia," *Ad Age Global,* May 2002, p. 18.

[6]"Kodak Sets for Gamble on Re-entry to Japan," *Financial Times,* December 15, 2004, p. 21.

EXHIBIT 9-1
A LOGICAL FLOWCHART OF THE ENTRY DECISION PROCESS

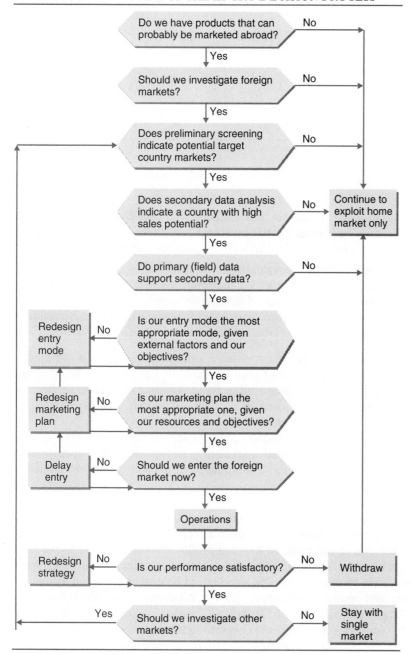

Source: Reprinted with permission from Franklin R. Root, *Entry Strategies for International Markets.* Copyright © 1994 Jossey-Bass Inc., Publishers. First published by Lexington Books. All rights reserved.

Information on these socioeconomic and political country indicators can easily be gathered from publicly available data sources. Typically, countries that do well on one indicator (say, market size) rate poorly on other indicators (say, market growth). Somehow, the company needs to combine its information to establish an overall measure of market attractiveness for these candidate markets.

Step 2. *Determine importance of country indicators.* The second step is to determine the important weights of each of the different country indicators identified in the previous step. One common method is the "constant-sum" allocation technique. This method simply allocates 100 points across the set of indicators according to their importance in achieving the company's goals (e.g., market share), so the more critical the indicator, the higher the number of points it is assigned. The total number of points should add up to 100.

EXHIBIT 9-2
METHOD FOR PRESCREENING MARKET OPPORTUNITIES: EXAMPLE

Country	Per capita Income	Population	Competition	Political Risk	Score
A	50	25	30	40	3400*
B	20	50	40	10	3600
C	60	30	10	70	3650
D	20	20	70	80	3850
Weight	25	40	25	10	

*(25 × 50) + (40 × 25) + (25 × 30) + (10 × 40) = 3400

Step 3. *Rate the countries in the pool on each indicator.* Next, give each country a score on each of the indicators. For instance, you could use a 10-point scale (0 meaning very unfavorable; 100 meaning very favorable). The better the country does on a particular indicator, the higher the score.

Step 4. *Compute overall score for each country.* The final step is to derive an overall score for each prospect country. To that end, the weighted scores that the country obtained on each indicator are simply summed in Step 2. Countries with the highest overall scores are the ones that are most attractive. An example of this four-step procedure is given in Exhibit 9-2.

Sometimes, the company may desire to weed out countries that do not meet a cutoff for criteria that are of paramount importance to it. For instance, Wrigley, the U.S. chewing gum maker, was not interested in Latin America until recently because many of the local governments imposed ownership restrictions.[7] In such cases, the four-step procedure should be done only for the countries that stay in the pool.

Other far more sophisticated methods exist to screen target markets. Kumar and colleagues, for example, developed a screening methodology that incorporates the firm's multiple objectives, resource constraints, and market expansion strategy.[8] One procedure, which is a bit more sophisticated than the method described here, is described in the Appendix.

Over time, companies sometimes must fine-tune their market selection strategy. Grolsch, the Dutch premium beer brewer, once exported to emerging markets such as China and Brazil, but in the wake of flagging profits, Grolsch decided to focus on mature beer markets where buying power is high and the premium segment is growing. Markets that meet those criteria include the United States, the United Kingdom, Canada, Australia, and continental Europe.[9] Exhibit 9-3 shows the market opportunity matrix for the Asia-Pacific division of Henkel, a German conglomerate. The shaded area highlights the countries that look most promising from Henkel's perspective.

◆ ◆ ◆ ◆ ◆ ◆ ◆ ◆ ◆ **CHOOSING THE MODE OF ENTRY**

Decision Criteria for Mode of Entry

Several decision criteria influence the choice of entry mode. Roughly speaking, two classes of decision criteria can be distinguished: internal (firm-specific) criteria and external (environment-specific) criteria. Let us first consider the major external criteria.

---

[7]"Guanxi Spoken Here," *Forbes,* November 8, 1993, pp. 208–10.

[8]V. Kumar, A. Stam, and E.A. Joachimsthaler, "An Interactive Multicriteria Approach to Identifying Potential Foreign Markets," *Journal of International Marketing,* 2 (1), 1994, pp. 29–52; see also Lloyd C. Russow and Sam C. Okoroafo, "On the Way Towards Developing a Global Screening Model," *International Marketing Review,* 13 (1), 1996, pp. 46–64.

[9]"Grolsch Targets Mature Markets," *Financial Times,* February 10, 1999, p. 20.

EXHIBIT 9-3
OPPORTUNITY MATRIX FOR HENKEL IN ASIA PECIFIC

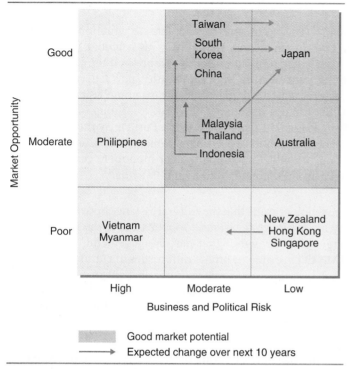

Source: Reprinted from Hellmut Schütte, "Henkel's Strategy for Asia Pacific," *Long Range Planning,* 28 (1), p. 98. Copyright 1995, with kind permission from Elsevier Science Ltd., The Boulevard, Langford Lane, Kidlington OX5 1GB, UK.

Market Size and Growth. In many instances, the key determinant of entry choice decisions is the size of the market. Large markets justify major resource commitments in the form of joint ventures or wholly owned subsidiaries. Market potential can relate to the current size of the market. However, future market potential as measured via the growth rate is often even more critical, especially when the target markets include emerging markets.

Risk. Another major concern when choosing entry modes is the risk factor. The role of risk in global marketing is discussed in Chapter 5. Risk relates to the instability in the political and economic environment that may impact the company's business prospects. Generally speaking, the greater the risk factor, the less eager companies are to make major resource commitments to the country (or region) concerned. Obviously, the level of country risk changes over time. In Bolivia, for example, the recent election of Evo Morales, a left-leaning indigenous former coca farmer, created enormous uncertainty for foreign investors in that country.[10] Many companies opt to start their presence with a liaison office in markets that are high-risk but, at the same time look very appealing because of their size or growth potential. For instance, MetLife, the insurance company, opened a liaison office in Shanghai and Beijing while it was waiting for permission from the Chinese government to start operations. A liaison office functions as a low-cost listening post to gather market intelligence and establish contacts with potential distributors.

Government Regulations. Government requirements are also a major consideration in entry mode choices. In scores of countries, government regulations heavily constrain the set of available options. Trade barriers of all different types restrict the entry choice decision. In the car industry, local content requirements in countries such

---

[10]http://lapaz.usembassy.gov/commercial/2005InvestClimateStat.pdf.

as France and Italy played a major role behind the decision of Japanese carmakers Toyota and Nissan to build up a local manufacturing presence in Europe.

Competitive Environment. The nature of the competitive situation in the local market is another driver. The dominance of Kellogg Co. as a global player in the ready-to-eat cereal market was a key motivation for the creation in the early 1990s of Cereal Partners Worldwide, a joint venture between Nestlé and General Mills. The partnership gained some market share (compared to the combined share of Nestlé and General Mills prior to the linkup) in some of the markets, though mostly at the expense of lesser players such as Quaker Oats and Ralston Purina. By the same token, the acquisition by SABMiller, the London-based beer company, of Colombia-based Bavaria in a $7.8 billion deal brought the company near-monopoly control in four South American countries: Peru, Colombia, Ecuador, and Panama.[11]

Cultural Distance. Some scholars argue that the cultural distance between countries also has an impact on entry mode choice decisions. Opinions about the nature of the relationship differ. Some argue that through higher percentages of equity ownership, multinational enterprises (MNEs) are able to bridge differences in cultural values and institutions. Others note that by relying on joint ventures instead of wholly owned subsidiaries, MNEs are able to lower their risk exposure in culturally distant markets. A comprehensive analysis of a wide range of studies in the literature found no clear-cut evidence in favor of either argument.[12]

Local Infrastructure. The physical infrastructure of a market refers to the country's distribution system, transportation network, and communication system. In general, the poorer the local infrastructure, the more reluctant the company is to commit major resources (monetary or human).

The combination of all of these factors determines the overall market attractiveness of the countries being considered. Markets can be classified in five types of countries based on their respective market attractiveness:[13]

- *Platform* countries that can be used to gather intelligence and establish a network. Examples include Singapore and Hong Kong.
- *Emerging* countries in which the major goal is to build up an initial presence, for instance, via a liaison office. Vietnam and the Philippines are examples.
- *Growth* countries offer early mover advantages that often push companies to build a significant presence to capitalize on future market opportunities as in China and India.
- *Maturing* and *established* countries like South Korea, Taiwan, and Japan, have far fewer growth prospects than the markets of other types. Often local competitors are well entrenched. On the other hand, these markets have a sizable middle class and solid infrastructure. The prime task here is to look for ways to further develop the market via strategic alliances, major investments, or acquisitions of local or smaller foreign players. A case in point is General Electric, the U.S. mega corporation. In the hope of achieving big profits in Europe, GE invested more than $10 billion from 1989 until 1996, half of it for building new plants and half for almost 50 acquisitions despite the fact that Europe is a fairly mature market.[14]

---

[11]"SABMiller to Raise Its Glass to Loyalty," *Financial Times*, July 25, 2005, p. 16.

[12]Laszlo Tihanyi, David A. Griffith, and Craig J. Russell, "The Effect of Cultural Distance on Entry Mode Choice, International Diversification, and MNE Performance: A Meta-Analysis," *Journal of International Business Studies*, 36 (2005), pp. 270–83.

[13]Philippe Lasserre, "Corporate Strategies for the Asia Pacific Region," *Long Range Planning*, 28 (1), 1995, pp. 13–30.

[14]"If Europe's Dead, Why Is GE Investing Billions There?" *Fortune*, September 9, 1996.

EXHIBIT 9-4
ENTRY MODES AND MARKET DEVELOPMENT

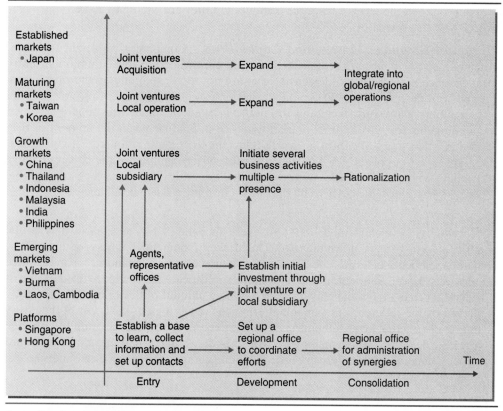

Source: Reprinted from Philippe Lasserre, "Corporate Strategies for the Asia Pacific Region," *Long Range Planning* 28 (1), p.21. Copyright 1995, with kind permission from Elsevier Science Ltd., The Boulevard, Langford Lane, Kidlington OX5 1GB UK.

Different types of countries require different expansion paths although deviations cannot be ruled out (see Exhibit 9-4).

We now give an overview of the key internal criteria.

Company Objectives. Corporate objectives represent a key influence in choosing entry modes. Firms that have limited aspirations typically prefer entry options that entail a minimum amount of commitment (e.g., licensing). Proactive companies with ambitious strategic objectives, on the other hand, usually pick entry modes that give them the flexibility and control they need to achieve their goals. Bridgestone, the Japanese tiremaker, needed a strong foothold in the U.S. market to become a leading firm in the tire industry. To that end, Bridgestone entered into a bidding war with Pirelli to acquire Firestone. More recently, the company set up factories in Central Europe and China and a joint venture in India with Tata, a major truck company, to achieve its goal of a 20 percent market share of the global tire market.[15]

Need for Control. Most MNCs prefer to have a certain amount of control over their foreign operations. Control may be desirable for any element of the marketing mix plan: positioning, pricing, advertising, the way the product is distributed, and so forth. Caterpillar, for instance, prefers to stay in complete control of its overseas operations to protect its proprietary know-how. For that reason, Caterpillar avoids joint ventures.[16] To a large degree, the level of control is strongly correlated with the

---

[15]"The Buck Stops Here," *Forbes,* March 10, 1997, p. 44.
[16]"Engine Makers Take Different Routes," *Financial Times,* July 14, 1998, p. 11.

amount of resource commitment: the smaller the commitment, the lower the control. Most firms therefore face a trade-off between the degree of control over their foreign operations and the level of resource commitment they are willing to make.

Internal Resources, Assets, and Capabilities. Companies with tight resources (human and/or financial) or limited assets are constrained to low-commitment entry modes such as exporting and licensing that are not too demanding on their resources. Even large companies should carefully consider how to allocate their resources among their different markets, including the home market. In some cases, major resource commitments to a given target market could be premature given the amount of risk. On the other hand, if a firm is overly reluctant to commit resources, it could miss major market opportunities. Internal competencies also influence the choice-of-entry strategy. When the firm lacks certain skills that are critical for the success of its global expansion strategy, it can try to fill the gap by forming a strategic alliance.

Flexibility. An entry mode that looks very appealing today necessarily may not be attractive 5 or 10 years down the road. The local environment changes constantly. New market segments emerge. Local customers become more demanding or more price conscious. Local competitors become more sophisticated. To cope with these environmental changes, global players need a certain amount of flexibility. The flexibility offered by the different entry mode alternatives varies a great deal. Given their very nature, contractual arrangements such as joint ventures and licensing tend to provide very little flexibility. When major exit barriers exist, wholly owned subsidiaries are hard to divest and, therefore offer very little flexibility compared to other entry alternatives.

Mode-of-Entry Choice: A Transaction Cost Explanation[17]

Although some of the preceding factors favor high-control entry modes, other criteria suggest a low-control mode. The different entry modes can be classified according to the degree of control they offer the entrant from low-control (e.g., indirect exporting) to high-control modes (e.g., wholly owned subsidiary, majority stake partnerships). To some extent, the appropriate entry-mode decision boils down to the issue of how much control is desirable. Ideally, the entrant would like to have as much control as possible. However, entry modes that offer a large degree of control also entail substantial resource commitments and huge amounts of risk. Therefore, the entrant must make a trade-off between the benefits of increased control and the costs of resource commitment and risk.

One useful framework to resolve this dilemma is the so-called **transaction-cost analysis (TCA)** perspective. A given task can be looked at as a "make-or-buy" decision: The firm either contracts the task to outside agents or partners (low-control mode) or does the job internally (high-control mode). TCA argues that the desirable governance structure (high- versus low-control mode) depends on the comparative transaction costs, that is, the cost of running the operation.

The TCA approach begins with the premise that markets are competitive. Therefore, market pressure minimizes the need for control. Under this utopian scenario, low-control modes are preferable because the competitive pressures force the outside partner to comply with its contractual duties. When the market mechanism fails, high-control entry modes become more desirable. From the TCA angle, market failure typically happens when **transaction-specific assets** become valuable. These are assets that are valuable for only a very narrow range of applications. Examples include brand equity, proprietary technology, and know-how. When these types of assets become very important, the firm might be better off to adopt a high-control entry mode to

[17]Erin Anderson and Hubert Gatignon, "Modes of Foreign Entry: A Transaction Cost Analysis and Propositions," *Journal of International Business Studies,* 11 (Fall 1986) pp. 1–26.

protect the value of these assets against opportunistic behaviors of its managers and uncertainty.[18]

An empirical study of entry decisions made by the 180 largest MNCs over a 15-year period found that MNCs are most likely to enter with wholly owned subsidiaries when one of the following conditions holds:

- The entry involves an R&D-intensive line of business.
- The entry involves an advertising-intensive line of business (high brand equity).
- The MNC has accumulated a substantial amount of experience with foreign entries.

On the other hand, MNCs are most likely to prefer a partnership when one of these is true:

- The entry is in a highly risky country.
- The entry is in a socioculturally distant country.
- There are legal restrictions on foreign ownership of assets.[19]

EXPORTING

♦ ♦ ♦ ♦ ♦ ♦ ♦ ♦

Most companies start their international expansion by exporting. For many small businesses, exporting is very often the sole alternative for selling their goods in foreign markets. A fair number of Fortune 500 companies, such as Boeing and Caterpillar, also generate a major part of their global revenues via export sales.

Chapter 17 discusses in detail export and import management matters. In this chapter we will give you a snapshot overview of exporting as an entry mode. Companies that plan to engage in exporting have a choice between three broad options: indirect, cooperative, and direct exporting. **Indirect exporting** means that the firm uses a middleman based in its home market to do the exporting. With **cooperative exporting**, the firm enters into an agreement with another company (local or foreign) in which the partner uses its distribution network to sell the exporter's goods. **Direct exporting** means that the company sets up its own export organization within the company and relies on a middleman based in a foreign market (e.g., a foreign distributor).

Indirect Exporting. Indirect exporting happens when the firm decides to sell its products in the foreign market through independent intermediaries. An **export merchant** is a trading company that buys the firm's goods outright and then resells them in the foreign market(s). The exporter merchant usually specializes in a particular line of products and/or in a certain geographical region. An **export agent** is a trading company that acts for local manufacturers, usually representing a number of noncompeting manufacturers that seek and negotiate foreign purchases. In return for obtaining an export order, the export agent receives a commission. Unlike the export merchant, the agent does not become the owner of the goods and therefore does not assume the risk of not being able to sell profitably overseas. The use of an **export management company (EMC)** is very popular among small businesses. An EMC is an independent firm that acts as the exclusive export sales department for noncompeting manufacturers. EMCs come in all shapes and sizes. Some act as agents, soliciting orders in foreign markets in the name of the manufacturer. Other EMCs act as distributors on a "buy-sell" basis: The EMC buys from the firm at a set price and resells to the foreign customers at prices set by the EMC. A listing of EMCs is available at http://fita.org/emc.html. Indirect

---

[18]For a good overview of entry-mode choice studies that incorporate the TCA paradigm, see Hongxin Zhao, Yadong Luo, and Taewon Suh, "Transaction Cost Determinants and Ownership-Based Entry Mode Choice: A Meta-Analytical Review," *Journal of International Business Studies,* 35 (2004), pp. 524–44.

[19]Hubert Gatignon and Erin Anderson, "The Multinational Corporation's Degree of Control over Foreign Subsidiaries: An Empirical Test of a Transaction Cost Explanation," *Journal of Law, Economics, and Organization,* 4, (2) Fall 1988, pp. 305–36.

exporting offers several advantages to the exporting company compared to other entry modes. The firm gets instant foreign market expertise because indirect exporters are professionals. They can handle all details involved in processing exporting orders. They also can appraise market opportunities for the manufacturer. Other strengths are their know-how in selecting agents and/or distributors and management of the distribution network. Often very little risk is involved. Generally speaking, no major resource commitments are required. When the intermediary's profits are based on how successfully they export, they are motivated to do a good job.

Indirect exporting has some downsides. The company has little or no control over the way its product is marketed in the foreign country. Lack of adequate sales support, wrong pricing decisions, or poor distribution channels will inevitably lead to poor sales. Ill-fated marketing mix decisions made by the intermediary could also damage the company's corporate or brand image. The middleman may have very limited experience in handling the company's product line. Also, because they are often relatively small, they may have limited resources to handle warehousing or extend credit financing to foreign customers. Intermediaries often focus their efforts on those products that maximize their profits, and as a result, they might not support new product lines or products with low, short-term profit potential.

Given the low commitment required, indirect exporting is often seen as a good beach head strategy for "testing" the international waters: Once the demand for the product takes off, the manufacturer can switch to another, more proactive entry mode. The decision to develop an export business via an independent middleman centers around three basic questions:

1. Does the firm have the time and know-how to enter export markets?
2. Does the firm have money and/or specialized personnel needed to develop an export business?
3. Is the foreign business growing at a satisfactory rate?[20]

If the answer to any of these questions is no, manufacturers should seriously consider relying on specialized export firms.

Cooperative Exporting. Companies that are not willing to commit the resources to set up their own distribution organization but still want to have some control over their foreign operations should consider cooperative exporting. One of the most popular forms of cooperative exporting is **piggyback exporting** through which the company uses the overseas distribution network of another company (local or foreign) to sell its goods in the foreign market. Wrigley, the U.S. chewing gum company, entered India by piggybacking on Parrys, a local confectionery firm. Through this tie-up, Wrigley can plug into Parrys' distribution network, thereby obtaining immediate access to 250,000 retail outlets. The two major attractions that Parrys' network offered to Wrigley was the overlap in product category and the size of the distribution network.

The quality of the distribution network can also play a role. Gillette tied-up with Bangalore-based TTK, an Indian manufacturer of pressure cookers and kitchenware for the distribution of Braun products despite the fact that Gillette has its own distribution network in India. Gillette needed department store outlets for its Braun product range, precisely the distribution channels that TTK uses for the distribution of its merchandise.[21]

Direct Exporting. Under direct exporting, the firm sets up its own exporting department and sells its products via an intermediary located in the foreign market. Once the international sales potential becomes substantial, direct exporting often appears far more appealing than indirect exporting. To some degree, the choice

[20]http://www.powerhomebiz.com/vol7/export.htm.
[21]"India: Distribution Overview," IMI960321, U.S. Department of Commerce, International Trade Administration.

between indirect and direct exporting is a "make-or-buy" decision: Should the company perform the export task, or is it better off delegating the task to outsiders? Compared to the indirect approach, direct exporting has a number of pluses. The exporter has far more control over its international operations. Hence, the sales potential (and profit) is often much more significant than under indirect exporting. It also allows the company to build its own network in the foreign market and get better market feedback.

There is a price to be paid, though. Given that the responsibility for the exporting tasks is now in the hands of the company, the demands on resources, human and financial, are much more intense than with indirect exporting. Besides the marketing mix tasks, these tasks involve choosing target markets, identifying and selecting representatives in the foreign market, and scores of logistical functions (e.g., documentation, insurance, shipping, packaging).

LICENSING

◆ ◆ ◆ ◆ ◆ ◆ ◆ ◆

Companies can also penetrate foreign markets via a licensing strategy. **Licensing** is a contractual transaction in which the firm—the **licensor**—offers some proprietary assets to a foreign company—the **licensee**—in exchange for royalty fees. Examples of assets that can be part of a licensing agreement include trademarks, technology know-how, production processes, and patents. Royalty rates range from one-eighth of 1 percent to 15 percent of sales revenue.[22] For instance, Oriental Land Company owns and operates Tokyo Disneyland under license from Disney. In return for being able to use the Disney name, Oriental Land Company pays royalties to Disney. In high-tech industries, companies often enter **cross-licensing** agreements. Under such agreement, parties mutually share patents without exchange of licensing fees when the patents involved are nearly equal in value. Samsung and Sony, for example, signed a five-year cross-licensing agreement in 2004 covering patents for a range of digital technology products. The agreement took a year to negotiate.[23]

Benefits

For many companies, licensing has proven to be a very profitable means for penetrating foreign markets. In most cases, licensing is not very demanding on the company's resources. Therefore, it is especially appealing to small companies that lack the resources and the wherewithal to invest in foreign facilities. Compared to exporting, another low-commitment entry mode, licensing allows the licensor to navigate around import barriers or get access to markets that are completely closed to imports. For instance, several foreign tobacco companies in China use licensing agreements to avoid the 240 percent import tax levied on imported cigarettes.[24] Local governments may also favor licensing over other entry modes.

Companies that use licensing as part of their global expansion strategy lower their exposure to political or economic instabilities in their foreign markets. The only volatility that the licensor faces are the ups and downs in the royalty income stream. The licensee absorbs other risks.

In high-tech industries, technology licensing has two other appeals. In highly competitive environments, rapid penetration of global markets allows the licensor to define the leading technology standard and to rapidly amortize R&D expenditures.[25] Research in Motion (RIM), the Canadian maker of the BlackBerry device, has entered numerous software licensing agreements with competitors such as Nokia and Palm to establish its software architecture as the platform of choice for wireless communication tools.

[22]"Licensing May Be Quickest Route to Foreign Markets," *Wall Street Journal,* September 14, 1990, p. B-2.
[23]http://www.itworld.com/Man/2687/041214samsungsony/.
[24]"Smoke Signals Point to China Market Opening," *South China Sunday Post,* October 6, 1996, p. 5.
[25]M. Kotabe, A. Sahay, and P.S. Aulakh, "Emerging Role of Technology Licensing in the Development of a Global Product Strategy: Conceptual Framework and Research Propositions," *Journal of Marketing,* 60 (1), January 1996, pp. 73–88.

Caveats   Licensing comes with some caveats, though. Revenues coming from a licensing agreement could be dwarfed by the potential income that other entry modes such as exporting could have generated. Another possible disadvantage is that the licensee may not be fully committed to the licensor's product or technology. Lack of enthusiasm on the licensee's part will greatly limit the licensed product's sales potential. When the licensing agreement involves a trademark, there is the further risk that misguided moves made by the licensee tarnish the trademark covered by the agreement. Other risks include the risk of not getting paid, failure to produce in a timely manner or the desired volume, and loss of control of the marketing of the product.[26]

The biggest danger is the risk of opportunism. A licensing arrangement could nurture a future competitor: Today's comrade in arms often becomes tomorrow's villain. The licensee can leverage the skills it acquires during the licensing period once the agreement expires. Global Perspective 9-1 chronicles the mishaps that Borden went through when its relationship with Meiji Milk, its licensee in Japan, turned sour.

Companies can make several moves to protect themselves against the risks of licensing arrangements.[27] If possible, the company should seek patent or trademark protection abroad. A thorough profitability analysis of a licensing proposal is an absolute must. Such an analysis must identify all costs entailed by the venture, including the opportunity costs that stem from revenues that must be sacrificed. Careful selection of prospective licensees is extremely important. Once a partner has been singled out, the negotiation process starts, which, if successful, will produce a licensing contract. The contract will cover parameters such as the technology package, use conditions (including territorial rights and performance requirements), compensation, and provisions for the settlement of disputes.

◆ ◆

𝒢LOBAL PERSPECTIVE 9-1

THE BORDEN-MEIJI MILK SAGA: THE MELTDOWN OF LADY BORDEN

When Borden, the U.S. multinational food company, entered Japan in 1971, it decided to tie up through a licensing arrangement with Meiji Milk, Japan's leading dairy company. Borden's licensing agreement with Meiji Milk was the envy of many companies. Borden could benefit from Meiji Milk's vast distribution network. Meiji Milk, in turn, was able to acquire the expertise to manufacture various kinds of dairy products. The partnership also developed the premium ice cream market in Japan with its Lady Borden brand.

The venture was not a fairy tale, however. Other brands entered the market, and Lady Borden's market share started to flounder. As a result, Borden wanted to dissolve its partnership with Meiji Milk and market Lady Borden on its own so that

Borden could have more control over the marketing of its products in Japan and could respond more rapidly to the competitive challenges. Meiji Milk retaliated by rolling out two ice cream brands of its own, one of which, Lady Breuges, was in direct competition with Lady Borden. When Borden cut its ties with Meiji Milk, it also lost access to Meiji Milk's distribution channels. The company hoped that brand clout would pull Japanese customers to the Lady Borden brand, but the pull of the Borden brand name did not make up for the loss of Meiji Milk's distribution muscle.

In June 1994, Borden, in a desperate move, licensed its trademarks and formulations for the Lady Borden brand to the confectionery maker Lotte Co. When Borden broke up with Meiji Milk in 1991, its share of Japan's premium ice cream market was around 50 percent. Three years later, when a Japanese newspaper compiled a scorechart of the ice cream market, Meiji had 12 percent while Borden's share was so negligible that it did not make the list.

Sources: "Borden's Breakup with Meiji Milk Shows How a Japanese Partnership Can Curdle," *The Wall Street Journal,* February 21, 1991, pp. B1, B4; and, "Borden's Hopes Melt in Japanese Market," *Advertising Age,* July 18, 1994, p. 38.

---

[26]Sandra Mottner and James P. Johnson, "Motivations and Risks in International Licensing: A Review and Implications for Licensing to Transitional and Emerging Economies," *Journal of World Business,* 35 (2), 2000, pp. 171–87.

[27]Root, *Entry Strategies for International Markets,* Chapter 5.

FRANCHISING

Scores of service industry companies use franchising as a means for capturing opportunities in the global marketplace. For instance, of the 34,277 Yum! restaurants around the world, nearly two-thirds (22,666) are franchised.[28] The internationalization efforts of 10 well-known franchise companies are summarized in Exhibit 9-5. Franchising is to some degree a "cousin" of licensing: It is an arrangement whereby the **franchisor** gives the **franchisee** the right to use the franchisor's trade names, trademarks, business models, and/or know-how in a given territory for a specific time period, normally 10 years.[29] In exchange, the franchisor receives royalty payments and other fees. The package could include the marketing plan, operating manuals, standards, training, and quality monitoring.

To snap up opportunities in foreign markets, the method of choice is often **master franchising.** With this system, the franchisor gives a master franchise to a local entrepreneur, that will, in turn, sell local franchises within its territory. The territory could be a certain region within a country or a group of countries (e.g., Greater China). Usually, the master franchise holder agrees to establish a certain number of outlets over a given time horizon. See Exhibit 9-6 for a list of some of the international franchise resources that are available on the Internet.

Benefits

The benefits of franchising are clear. First and foremost, companies can capitalize on a winning business formula by expanding overseas with a minimum of investment. As with licensing, political risks for the rights owner are very limited. Furthermore, because the franchisees' profits are directly tied to their efforts, franchisees are usually highly motivated. Finally, the franchisor can also capitalize on the local franchisees' knowledge of the local marketplace. They usually have a much better understanding of local customs and laws than the foreign firm.

Caveats

Franchising carries some risks, however. As in the case of licensing, the franchisor's income stream is only a fraction of what it would be if the company held an equity stake in the foreign ventures. Firms with little or no name recognition typically face a major challenge finding interested partners in the foreign market. Finding suitable franchisees or a master franchisee can be a stumbling block in many markets. In many countries, the concept of franchising as a business model is barely understood.[30] A major concern is the lack of control over the franchisees' operations. Dissatisfied with the performance of its franchisees in Mexico and Brazil, Blockbuster Video changed tracks in 1995. It decided to set up joint ventures and equity relations in Mexico and Brazil to replace the franchising arrangements held there, thereby getting more control and oversight.[31] Given the largely intangible nature of many franchising systems, cultural hurdles can also create problems. In fact, a recent study showed that cultural and geographic proximity are the two most popular criteria used by companies for picking international markets in franchising.[32]

---

[28] Yum! Brands, *2005 Annual Report.*

[29] Albert Kong, "How to Evaluate a Franchise," *Economic Bulletin,* October 1998, pp. 18–20.

[30] Colin McCosker, "Trends and Opportunities in Franchising," *Economic Bulletin,* October 1998, pp. 14–17.

[31] "Blockbuster's Fast-Forward," *Advertising Age International,* September 18, 1995, p. I–32.

[32] John F. Preble and Richard C. Hoffman, "Franchising Systems around the Globe: A Status Report," *Journal of Small Business Management,* April 1995, pp. 80–88.

EXHIBIT 9-5
INTERNATIONALIZATION EFFORTS OF TEN WELL KNOWN FRANCHISE COMPANIES

Company	Industry	Year Established	Year of First Franchise	Year of First International Franchise	No. of Operating Units	No. of Countries
General Nutrition Centers	Vitamins retailing	1935	1988	1991	USA:2954 CAN: 18 Row: 227*	27
Mrs. Fields	Cookies	1977	1990	1992	USA: 849 CAN: 11 RoW: 60	12
Uniglobe Travel	Travel agencies	1980	1981	1991	USA: 856 CAN: 192 Row: 87	15
Subway	Sandwiches	1965	1974	1984	USA: 11,452 CAN: 1259 RoW: 693	70+
Computertots	Computer education	1983	1989	1994	USA: 132 CAN: 0 RoW: 92	12
Midas	Automotive services	1956	1956	1968	USA: 1898 CAN: 246 RoW: 561	NA
Mailboxes Etc.	Business support	1980	1981	1988	USA: 2971 CAN: 209 RoW: 377	70+
Sir Speedy	Print & copying services	1968	1968	1984	USA: 1372 CAN: 9 RoW: 49	23
Ponderosa	Steakhouse	1965	1966	1985	USA: 506 CAN: 8 RoW: 40	NA
World Gym Fitness	Fitness	1977	1985	1985	USA: 276 CAN: 3 RoW: 9	NA

Source: www.franchiseintl.com.
*Row = Rest of the World.

◆ ◆ ◆ ◆ ◆ ◆ ◆ ◆ **CONTRACT MANUFACTURING (OUTSOURCING)**

With **contract manufacturing** (also known as **outsourcing**), the international company arranges with a local company to manufacture parts of the product or even the entire product, but keeps the responsibility for marketing the products.

Countless companies have become very successful by specializing in contract manufacturing. Flextronics, headquartered in Singapore, is one of the leading contract manufacturers with fiscal year 2005 revenues of $15.9 billion. The company helps its customers design, build, ship, and service electronics products through its network of facilities in more than 30 countries.[33] Its client list includes companies such as Siemens, HP, Dell, Ericsson, Microsoft, and Alcatel.

---

[33]Contract manufacturing in the electronics industry is often referred to as *electronics manufacturing services (EMS)*.

EXHIBIT 9-6
FRANCHISE RESOURCES
ON THE INTERNET

Australia: www.fac.com.au
Austria: www.franchise.at
Belgium: www.fbf-bff.be
Brazil: http://www.portaldofranchising.com.br/
Britain: www.british-franchise.org
Canada: www.cfa.ca
China: www.ccfa.org.cn
Denmark: www.dk-franchise.dk
Finland: www.franchising.fi
France: www.franchise-fff.com
Germany: www.dfv-franchise.de
Greece: www.franchising.gr
Hong Kong: www.franchise.org.hk
Hungary: www.franchise.hu
Italy: www.infofranchising.it
Malaysia: www.mfa.org.my
Netherlands: www.nfv.nl
New Zealand: www.franchise.org.nz
South Africa: www.fasa.co.za
Spain: www.franquiciadores.com
Switzerland: www.franchiseverband.ch
Taiwan: www.tcfa.org.tw
United States: www.franchise.org

Benefits

Cost savings is the prime motivation behind contract manufacturing. Significant cost savings can be achieved for labor-intensive production processes by sourcing the product in a low-wage country. Typically, the countries of choice have a substantial comparative labor cost advantage. Labor cost savings are not the only factor. Savings can also be achieved via taxation benefits, lower energy costs, raw materials costs, or overhead.

Some of the benefits listed for the previous entry modes also apply here. Subcontracting leads to a small amount of exposure to political and economic risks for the international firm, and it is not very demanding on the company's resources. Contract manufacturing allows access to markets that, because of import barriers, would otherwise be closed.

Caveats

Contract manufacturing does have drawbacks, however. The "nurture-a-future-competitor" concern raised for licensing and franchising also applies here. Consider what happened to Schwinn, the U.S. bicycle company,[34] which once sourced about 80 percent of its bikes from Giant Manufacturing, a Taiwanese company. When Schwinn switched suppliers, Giant, which had until then been a pure contract manufacturer, decided to create high-end bicycles under its own brand name. Giant is now the largest bike maker in the world, selling its bikes in around 50 countries. It has become the second largest brand of high-end bicycles in the United States. Schwinn, meanwhile, filed for bankruptcy and sold its assets. Because of such risk, many companies prefer to make high-value items or products that involve proprietary design features inhouse. Contract manufacturers often make products under their own brand, which usually

---

[34]"Giant Grows, Peddling Its Own Brand," *Asian Wall Street Journal*, January 2, 2003, p. A5.

leads to a conflict of interest with their customers. Acer, a Taiwanese computer maker, wrestled with such issues.[35] In 2000, business from products made for other global computer firms generated $1.8 billion revenue compared with about $1.2 billion revenue from its own brand products. The key concern for many of Acer's clients was that by giving Acer business, they were subsidizing Acer's own brand products, which were often similar but much less expensive. Acer's solution for this predicament was to split up the company. Giant, the Taiwanese bicycle maker mentioned earlier, addressed its customers' concerns by reassuring its clients that the firm would never launch cheap knockoffs of their products.

Contract manufacturing also offers less flexibility to respond to sudden market demand changes. Sony Ericsson Mobile Communications, which relies heavily on contracting for the manufacturing of its cellular phones, lost potential sales when its first color screen model quickly sold out in Europe. Nokia, on the other hand, makes most of its products inhouse. When it faced a last-minute glitch for the roll-out of its first color-screen model, it plugged the gap by increasing the output of an existing model by 50 percent, using its plants in Finland, Germany, and China.[36]

A fixation with low-cost labor can often have painful consequences. Countries that offer low-cost labor typically have very low labor productivity. Some of these countries, such as India and South Korea, also have a long tradition of poor labor relations. Too much reliance on low-cost labor could also create a backlash in the company's home market among its employees and customers. Monitoring quality and production levels is a must, especially during the start-up phase when "teething problems" are not uncommon.

The ideal candidate for foreign subcontractors should meet the following criteria:

- Be flexible and geared toward just-in-time delivery.
- Be able to meet quality standards and implement total quality management (TQM).
- Have solid financial footing.
- Be able to integrate with the company's business.
- Have contingency plans to handle sudden changes in demand.[37]

◆ ◆ ◆ ◆ ◆ ◆ ◆ ◆ **EXPANDING THROUGH JOINT VENTURES**

For many MNCs who want to expand their global operations, joint ventures prove to be the most viable way to enter foreign markets, especially emerging markets. With a joint venture, the MNC agrees to share equity and other resources with other partners to establish a new entity in the target country. The partners typically are local companies, but they can also be local government authorities, other foreign companies, or a mixture of local and foreign players. Depending on the equity stake, three forms of partnerships can be distinguished: majority (more than 50 percent ownership), 50–50, and minority (50 percent or less ownership) ventures. Huge infrastructure or high-tech projects that demand a large amount of expertise and money often involve multiple foreign and local partners. Another distinction is between cooperative and equity joint ventures. A **cooperative joint venture** is an agreement for the partners to collaborate but does not involve any equity investments. For instance, one partner might contribute manufacturing technology whereas the other partner provides access to distribution channels. Cooperative joint ventures are quite common for partnerships between well-heeled MNCs and local players in emerging markets. A good example of the collaborative approach is Cisco's sales strategy in Asia. Instead of investing in its own sales force, Cisco builds up partnerships with hardware vendors (e.g., IBM), consulting

[35]"Reinventing Acer," *Far Eastern Economic Review,* May 24, 2001, pp. 38–43.

[36]"Nokia Defies Odds and Thrives," *Asian Wall Street Journal,* January 6, 2003, pp. A1, A9.

[37]E. P. Hibbert, "Global Make-or-Buy Decisions," *Industrial Marketing Management,* 22 (1993), pp. 67–77.

agencies (e.g., KPMG), or systems integrators (e.g., Singapore-based Datacraft). These partners in essence act as front people for Cisco. They are the ones that sell and install Cisco's routers and switches.[38] An **equity joint venture** goes one step further. It is an arrangement in which the partners agree to raise capital in proportion to the equity stakes agreed upon.

A major advantage of joint ventures compared to lesser forms of resource commitment such as licensing is the return potential. With licensing, for instance, the company receives royalty payments instead of a share of the profits. Joint ventures also entail much more control over the operations than most of the previous entry modes discussed so far. MNCs that like to maximize their degree of control prefer full ownership. However, in many instances, local governments discourage or even forbid wholly owned ventures in certain industries. Under such circumstances, partnerships (joint ventures) are second-best or temporary solutions.

Benefits

Apart from these benefits, the **synergy** argument is another compelling reason for setting up a joint venture. Partnerships are not limited to sharing of capital and risk. Possible contributions by the local partner include land, raw materials, expertise on the local environment (culture, legal, political), access to a distribution network, personal contacts with suppliers, and government officials. Combined with the foreign partner's skills and resources, these inputs offer the key to a successful market entry. The Sony Ericsson partnership offers an excellent example. The tie-up combined Ericsson's technology prowess and strong links to wireless operators with Sony's marketing skills and expertise in consumer electronics. Each partner stood to gain from helping the other grow in regions where it was weak: Japan for Ericsson and Europe for Sony.[39]

For many MNCs, lack of full control is the most significant shortcoming of joint ventures. There are a number of ways for the MNC to gain more leverage. The most obvious way is via a majority equity stake. However, government restrictions often rule this option out. Even when for some reason majority ownership is not a viable alternative, MNCs have other means at their disposal to exercise control over the joint venture. MNCs could deploy expatriates in key line positions, thereby controlling financial, marketing, and other critical operations of the venture. MNCs could offer various types of outside support services to back up their weaker joint ventures in areas such as marketing, quality control, and customer service.[40]

Caveats

As with licensing agreements, the MNC runs the risk that the partner could become a future competitor. Scores of China's most successful domestic companies began as partners of multinationals. A case in point is Eastcom, a state-owned Chinese manufacturer and distributor of telecom equipment. After a 10-year old collaboration with Motorola, the company launched its own digital cell phone, undercutting Motorola's StarTAC model by $120.[41]

Lack of trust and mutual conflicts turn numerous international joint ventures into a marriage from hell. Conflicts could arise over matters such as strategies, resource allocation, transfer pricing, and ownerships of critical assets such as technologies and brand names. In many cases, the seeds for trouble exist from the very beginning of the joint venture. Exhibit 9-7 contrasts the mutually conflicting objectives that the foreign partner and a local Chinese partner could have when setting up a joint venture in China. Cultural strains between partners often spur mistrust and mutual conflict, making a bad situation even worse. Autolatina, a joint venture set up by Ford

---

[38]"Cisco's Asian Gambit," *Fortune,* January 10, 2000, pp. 52–54.

[39]"Sony Ericsson: In Big Bloody Trouble," *Business Week, Asian Edition,* November 4, 2002, pp. 54–55.

[40]Johannes Meier, Javier Perez, and Jonathan R. Woetzel, "Solving the Puzzle: MNCs in China," *The McKinsey Quarterly,* 2 (1995) pp. 20–33.

[41]"The Local Cell-Phone Boys Get Tough," *Business Week,* Asian Edition, September 20, 1999, p. 24.

EXHIBIT 9-7
CONFLICTING OBJECTIVE IN CHINESE JOINT VENTURES

	Foreign Partner	*Chinese Partner*
Planning	Retain business flexibility	Maintain congruency between the venture and the state economic plan
Contracts	Unambiguous, detailed, and enforceable	Ambiguous, brief, and adaptable
Negotiations	Sequential, issue by issue	Holistic and heuristic
Staffing	Maximize productivity; fewest people per given output level	Employ maximum number of local people
Technology	Match technical sophistication to the organization and its environment	Gain access to the most advanced technology as quickly as possible
Profits	Maximize in long term; repatriate over time	Reinvest for future modernization; maintain foreign exchange reserves
Inputs	Minimize unpredictability and poor quality of supplies	Promote domestic sourcing
Process	Stress high quality	Stress high quantity
Outputs	Access and develop domestic market	Export to generate foreign currency
Control	Reduce political and economic controls on decision making	Accept technology and capital but preclude foreign authority infringement on sovereignty and ideology

Source: Reprinted from M. G. Martinsons and C.-S. Tsong, "Successful Joint Ventures in the Heart of the Dragon," *Long Range Planning,* 28 (5), p. 5. Copyright 1995, with kind permission from Elsevier Science Ltd., The Boulevard, Langford Lane, Kidlington OX5 1GB UK.

Motor Co. and Volkswagen AG in Latin America, was dissolved after seven years in spite of the fact that it remained profitable to the very end. Cultural differences between the German and U.S. managers were a major factor. One participating executive noted that "there were good intentions behind Autolatina's formation but they never really overcame the VW-Ford culture shock."[42]

When trouble undermines the joint venture, the partners can try to resolve the conflict via mechanisms built in the agreement. If a mutually acceptable resolution is not achievable, the joint venture is scaled back or dissolved. For instance, a joint venture between Unilever and AKI in South Korea broke up after seven years following disagreements over brand strategies for new products, resource allocation, advertising support, and brand ownership.[43]

Drivers Behind Successful International Joint Ventures

There are no magic ingredients to foster the stability of joint ventures, yet some important lessons can be drawn from past joint venture fairy tales and horror stories.

Pick the Right Partner. Most joint-venture marriages prosper by choosing a suitable partner. That means that the MNC should invest time in identifying proper candidates. A careful screening of the joint venture partner is an absolute necessity. One issue is that it is not easy to sketch a profile of the "ideal" partner. The presence of complementary skills and resources that lead to synergies is one characteristic of successful joint ventures. Prospective partners should also have compatible goals. Exhibit 9-8 lists the attributes that Starbucks requires.

---

[42]"Why Ford, VW's Latin Marriage Succumbed to 7-year Itch," *Advertising Age International,* March 20, 1995, p. I–22.
[43]"How Unilever's South Korean Partnership Fell Apart," *Advertising Age,* August 31, 1992, pp. 3, 39.

EXHIBIT 9-8
STARBUCKS COFFEE'S CRITERIA IN SELECTING
PARTNERS

- Shared values and corporate culture
- Strong multiunit retail/restaurant experience
- Dedicated human resources
- Commitment of customer service
- Quality image
- Creative ability, local knowledge, and brand-building skills
- Strong financial resources

Source: http://www.starbucks.com/
aboutus/international.asp.

Some evidence indicates that partners should be similar in terms of size and resources. Partners with whom the MNC has built up an existing relationship (e.g., distributors, customers, suppliers) also facilitate a strong relationship.[44] The more balanced the contributions by the partners, the more trust and the more harmonious the relationship should be.[45] One issue that latecomers in a market often face is that the "best" partners have already been snapped up. Note, however, that the same issue arises with acquisition strategies. One study on joint venture performance in China offers five guidelines for partner selection.[46] First, integrate partner selection with your strategic goals. Second, obtain as much information as possible about the candidate (e.g., company brochures, business license). Third, visit the site. Fourth, check whether or not the potential partner shares your investment objective. Fifth and finally, do not put too much emphasis on the role of *guanxi* (connections).

Establish Clear Objectives for the Joint Venture from the Very Beginning.[47]
It is important to clearly spell out the objectives of the joint venture from day one. Partners should know what their respective contributions and responsibilities are before signing the contract.[48] They should also know what to expect from the partnership.

Bridge Cultural Gaps.
Many joint venture disputes stem from cultural differences between the local and foreign partners. Much agony and frustration can be avoided when the foreign investor makes an attempt to bridge cultural differences. For instance, when setting up joint ventures in China, having an ethnic Chinese or an "old China hand" as an intermediary often helps a great deal. The problem is that knowledgeable people who share the perspectives of both cultures are often very difficult to find.[49]

Top Managerial Commitment and Respect.
Short of a strong commitment from the parent companies' top management, most international joint ventures are doomed to become a failure. The companies should be willing to assign their best managerial talent to the joint venture. Venture managers should also have complete access to and support from their respective parent companies.[50]

---

[44]Karen J. Hladik, "R&D and International Joint Ventures," in *Cooperative Forms of Transnational Corporation Activity,* P.J. Buckley, ed. (London: Routledge, 1994).

[45]Akmal S. Hyder and Pervez N. Ghauri, "Managing International Joint Venture Relationships," *Industrial Marketing Management,* 29 (2000), pp. 205–18.

[46]Yadong Luo, "Joint Venture Success in China: How Should We Select a Good Partner," *Journal of World Business,* 32 (2), 1998, pp. 145–166.

[47]Dominique Turpin, "Strategic Alliances with Japanese Firms: Myths and Realities," *Long Range Planning,* 26 (4) 1993, pp. 11–16.

[48]Maris G. Martinsons and Choo-sin Tseng, "Successful Joint Ventures in the Heart of the Dragon," *Long Range Planning,* 28 (5), 1995 pp. 45–58.

[49]Martinsons and Tseng, "Successful Joint Ventures in the Heart of the Dragon," p. 56.

[50]Turpin, "Strategic Alliances with Japanese Firms, p. 15.

◆ ◆

𝒢LOBAL PERSPECTIVE 9-2

DUPONT IN CHINA: A COMBINATION OF SMALL STEPS, GOOD PARTNERS, AND FLEXIBLE STRATEGY

DuPont started doing business in China in 1863; after fleeing the communist regime, the company returned in 1984. DuPont avoids costly big-bang entries. Instead, the U.S. multinational has gradually made progress by making small, frequent steps. DuPont has rarely spent more than $50 million at the outset on any of the 18 joint ventures or wholly owned businesses that it has established. All together, DuPont has invested around $700 million in China since its re-entry. Recent initiatives include a 50-50 joint venture with Japan's Asahi Kasei to make plastics, the purchase of a protein plant in Yunmeng, and a joint venture to sell spandex.

As China has become more prosperous, DuPont has transplanted some of its core brands such as Teflon and Lycra. DuPont researchers in Shenzhen worked on getting the right mix of Teflon coating into woks, which usually get a harder beating during food preparation than pots and pans in U.S. kitchens. To boost its corporate image, DuPont paid $1.3 million in January 2002 to sponsor one of China's leading soccer teams for three years. It sells 95 percent of its locally made products to domestic manufacturers. In 2001, 230 million toothbrushes produced in China had DuPont-made bristles, 35 million of the window frames sold contained DuPont-made white pigment, and 500,000 of the pots and pans sold were coated with Teflon.

Sources: "Foreign Direct Investment: Companies Rush In with the Cash," http://www.ft.com, accessed on December 11, 2002; and "Run Silent, Run Deep," *Forbes Global,* June 10, 2002, pp. 28–29.

Incremental Approach Works Best. Rather than being overambitious, an incremental approach toward setting up the international joint venture appears to be much more effective. The partnership starts on a small scale. Gradually, the scope of the joint venture is broadened by adding other responsibilities and activities to the charter. An example of the incremental approach is Dupont's expansion strategy in China as described in Global Perspective 9-2.

A recent study by a team of McKinsey consultants also advises the parents to create a launch team during the launch phase beginning with the signing of a memorandum of understanding and continuing through the first 100 days of operation.[51] The launch team should address the four key joint venture challenges:

1. Build and maintain *strategic alignment* across the separate corporate entities, each of which has its own goals, market pressures, and shareholders.

2. Create a *governance system* that promotes shared decision making and oversight between the parent companies.

3. Manage the *economic interdependencies* between the corporate parents and the joint venture (e.g., compensation of each parent for its contributions).

4. Build the *organization* for the joint venture (e.g., staffing positions, assignment of responsibilities).

◆ ◆ ◆ ◆ ◆ ◆ ◆ ◆ ◆ ENTERING NEW MARKETS THROUGH WHOLLY OWNED SUBSIDIARIES

Multinational companies often prefer to enter new markets with 100 percent ownership. Ownership strategies in foreign markets can essentially take two routes: **acquisitions and mergers,** in which the MNC buys up or merges with existing companies, or **greenfield operations** that are started from scratch. As with the other entry modes, full ownership entry entails certain benefits to the MNC but also carries risks.

---

[51]James Bamford, David Ernst, and David G. Fubini, "Launching a World-Class Joint Venture," *Harvard Business Review,* 82 (February 2004) pp. 90–101.

Wholly owned subsidiaries give MNCs full control of their operations. It is often the ideal solution for companies that do not want to be saddled with all of the risks and anxieties associated with partnerships such as joint venturing. Full ownership means that all of the profits go to the company. Fully owned enterprises allow the investor to manage and control its own processes and tasks in terms of marketing, production, and sourcing decisions. Setting up fully owned subsidiaries also sends a strong commitment signal to the local market. In some markets (China, for example) wholly owned subsidiaries can be created with local companies much faster than joint ventures that may consume years of negotiations before their final take-off.[52] The latter point is especially important when there are substantial advantages of being an early entrant in the target market.

Benefits

Despite the advantages of 100 percent ownership, many MNCs are quite reluctant to choose this particular mode of entry. The risks of full ownership cannot be easily discounted. Complete ownership means that the parent company must carry the full burden of possible losses. Developing a foreign presence without the support of a third party is also very demanding on the firm's resources. Obviously, apart of the market-related risks, substantial political risks (e.g., expropriation) and economic risks (e.g., currency devaluation) must be considered.

Caveats

Companies that enter via a wholly owned enterprise are sometimes perceived as a threat to the host country's cultural and/or economic sovereignty. Shortly after Daewoo's initially successful bid for the multimedia arm of the French group Thomson-CSF in the fall of 1996, the deal sparked controversy among French trade unions and the media. In the end, the French government vetoed the sale of the Thomson group following the negative opinion of the French privatization commission.[53] One way to address hostility to foreign acquisitions in the host country is by "localizing" the firm's presence in the foreign market by hiring local managers, sourcing locally, developing local brands, sponsoring local sports or cultural events, and so forth.[54]

Companies such as Sara Lee have built strong global competitive positions via cleverly planned and finely executed acquisition strategies. MNCs choose acquisition entry to expand globally for a number of reasons. First and foremost, when contrasted with greenfield operations, acquisitions provide a rapid means to get access to the local market. For relative latecomers in an industry, acquisitions are also a viable option to obtain well-established brand names, instant access to distribution outlets, or technology. In recent years, some South Korean *chaebols* have used acquisition entries into foreign markets to gain a foothold in high-tech industries. Highly visible examples include Samsung's acquisition of the U.S. computer maker AST and LG Electronics' takeover of Zenith. LG would have had to invest more than $1 billion to build up a strong global TV brand from scratch.[55] Cadbury Schweppes' $4.2 billion purchase of Adams, Pfizer's candy business, also underscores the advantages of the acquisition entry mode. By acquiring Adams, Cadbury was able to pick up several leading candy and chewing gum brands including Trident, Chiclets, and Certs as well as Halls lozenges. The Adams purchase also bolstered Cadbury's position in the fast-growing candy markets in the United States and Latin America. Global Perspective 9-3 discusses the acquisition of IBM's PC division by Lenovo, the Chinese computer behemoth.

Expansion via acquisitions or mergers carries substantial risks, however. Differences in the corporate culture of the two companies between managers are often

Acquisitions and Mergers

---

[52]Wilfried Vanhonacker, "Entering China: An Unconventional Approach," *Harvard Business Review,* March–April 1997.

[53]http://www.asiatimes.com/96/12/05/05129601.

[54]Vanhonacker, "Entering China.

[55]"Guess Who's Betting on America's High-Tech Losers," *Fortune,* October 28, 1996.

THE LENOVO/IBM DEAL—A WINNING COMBINATION?

The $1.75 billion acquisition of IBM's personal computer business by Lenovo, the Chinese PC maker, marked the dawn of a new era. The cross-border deal gave Lenovo much more than Big Blue's PC business. Lenovo became the first state-controlled Chinese firm to acquire an iconic global brand. "If anyone still harboured any doubts that Chinese corporates were serious players on the global M&A stage those have now totally been dispelled," said Colin Banfield at CSFB.

The talks behind the deal took 18 months. By bringing together China's largest PC maker and IBM's PC division, Lenovo executives hope they can create a formidable force to challenge the dominance of Hewlett-Packard and Dell, the market leaders. Lenovo estimated that it could save $200 million a year by component cost savings. Lenovo would own IBM's Think trademark, and IBM would become Lenovo's "preferred supplier" as part of the deal.

The growth plan spelled out for "new" Lenovo had three key elements: developing the ThinkPad notebook computer franchise; expanding into emerging markets such as India, Brazil, and Russia; and introducing Lenovo-branded PCs for small business owners in the United States and Europe.

Many observers were skeptical about blending the two very diverse corporate cultures. The focus at the "old" Lenovo was on rules. All employees were expected to clock in and clock out. Employees were forbidden to turn up late for meetings. Where Lenovo had rules, IBM had processes: regular meetings, conference calls, and milestones to keep projects on track. To the Chinese, the focus on processes could be as alien as the emphasis on rules for former IBM staff. Another cultural gap stemmed from conversational style differences: Americans like to talk; Chinese like to listen. Still, the enthusiasm is not lacking. The working language for the new Lenovo is English because hardly anyone from the IBM side speaks Chinese. Lenovo shifted its official headquarters from Beijing to Purchase, New York. Steven Ward, formerly head of IBM's PC division, became Lenovo's new CEO but was replaced in December 2005 by William Amelio, who had been incharge of the Asia-Pacific division of Dell, Lenovo's main competitor. With the new CEO, Lenovo hoped to plug a gap in China, its home market. Lenovo had a 32 percent market share in 2005 but was not strong among corporate buyers.

Sources: "IBM Brand Loyalty Holds Key for Lenovo," *Financial Times,* December 9, 2004, p. 16; "Deal Divides Opinion over Future Trends," *Financial Times,* December 9, 2004, p. 16; "Your Rules and My Processes," *Financial Times,* November 10, 2005, p. 10; "Quick-fire Lessons in Globalisation," *Financial Times,* November 11, 2005, p. 8; and http://www.businessweek.com/technology/content/dec2005/tc20051221_376268.htm.

extremely hard to bridge. A well-publicized example of a company that has been plagued with corporate culture disease is Pharmacia & Upjohn, a pharmaceutical company formed in 1995 via the merger of Sweden-based Pharmacia AB and the U.S. drug firm Upjohn. Swedish managers were stunned by the hard-driving, mission-oriented approach of Upjohn executives. Their U.S. counterparts were shocked by European vacation habits.[56]

The assets of the acquisition do not always live up to the expectations of the acquiring company. Outdated plants, tarnished brand names, or an unmotivated workforce are only a few of the many possible disappointments that the acquiring company could face. The local government might also attach certain conditions to the acquisition. Daewoo, for instance, promised the French government to hire 5,000 people when it was bidding for the consumer electronics division of Thomson CSF. A careful screening and assessment of takeover candidates can avoid a lot of heartburn on the part of the acquiring company.

Open hostility toward foreign companies can also complicate acquisition plans. A joint $10.5 billion bid by Cadbury and Nestlé to buy Hershey Foods, the U.S. chocolate maker, was derailed in part of strong opposition against a "foreign takeover" from the local community. Another drawback is that acquisition entry can be a very costly global expansion strategy. Good prospects are usually unwilling to sell themselves. If they are, they do not come cheap. Other foreign or local companies are typically interested, too, and the result is often a painful bidding war. The costs and strains of integrating the acquisition with the company can also be a substantial burden.

---

[56]"A Case of Corporate Culture Shock in the Global Arena," *International Herald Tribune,* April 23, 1997, pp. 1, 11.

Acquisition strategies are not always feasible. Good prospects may already have been nabbed by the company's competitors. In many emerging markets, acceptable acquisition candidates often are simply not available. Overhauling the facilities of possible candidates is sometimes much more costly than building an operation from scratch. In the wake of these downsides, companies often prefer to enter foreign markets through greenfield operations established from scratch. Greenfield operations offer the company more flexibility than acquisitions in areas such as human resources, suppliers, logistics, plant layout, or manufacturing technology. Greenfield investments also avoid the costs of integrating the acquisition into the parent company.[57] Another motivation is the package of goodies (e.g., tax holidays) that host governments sometimes offer to whet the appetite of foreign investors. A major disadvantage, though, of greenfield operations is that they require enormous investments of time and capital.

Greenfield Operations

CREATING STRATEGIC ALLIANCES

A distinctive feature of the activities of global corporations today is that they are using cooperative relationships such as licensing, joint ventures, R&D partnerships, and informal arrangements, all under the rubric of alliances of various forms, on an increasing scale. More formally, a **strategic alliance** can be described as *a coalition of two or more organizations to achieve strategically significant goals that are mutually beneficial.*[58] The business press reports like clockwork the birth of strategic alliances in various industries. Especially eye-catching are those partnerships between firms that have been arch-enemies for ages. A principal reason for the increase in cooperative relationships is that firms today no longer have the capacity of a General Motors of the 1940s, which developed all of its technologies in-house. As a result, firms, especially those operating in technology intensive industries, may not be at the forefront of all required critical technologies.[59]

Strategic alliances come in all shapes. At one extreme, they can be based on a simple licensing agreement between two partners. At the other extreme, they can consist of a thick web of ties. The nature of alliances also varies, depending on the skills brought in by the partners. A first category, very common in high-tech industries, is based on technology swaps. Given the skyrocketing costs of new product development, strategic alliances offer a way for companies to pool their resources and learn from one another. Such alliances must be struck from a position of strength. Bargaining chips could be patents that the company holds. A second type of cross-border alliance involves marketing-based assets and resources such as access to distribution channels or trademarks. A case in point is the partnership established by Coca-Cola and Nestlé to market ready-to-drink coffees and teas under the Nescafé and Nestea brand names. This deal allowed the two partners to combine a well-established brand name with access to a vast proven distribution network. In India, Huggies, Kimberly-Clark's diapers, are manufactured and distributed through an alliance with Hindustan Lever, the local unit of Unilever, whose powerful distribution network covers 400,000 retail outlets. A third category of alliances is situated in the operations and logistics area. In their relentless search for scale economies for operations/logistics activities, companies may decide to join forces by setting up a partnership. Finally, operations-based alliances are driven by a desire to transfer manufacturing know-how. A classic example is the

Types of Strategic Alliances

[57]Jiatao Li, "Foreign Entry and Survival: Effects of Strategic Choices on Performance in International Markets," *Strategic Management Journal,* 16 (1995), pp. 333–51.

[58]Edwin A. Murray, Jr., and John F. Mahon, "Strategic Alliances: Gateway to the New Europe?" *Long Range Planning,* August 1993, pp. 102–11.

[59]Noel Capon and Rashi Glazer, "Marketing and Technology: A Strategic Co-alignment," *Journal of Marketing,* 51 (July 1987), pp. 1–14.

EXHIBIT 9-9
GENERIC MOTIVES FOR STRATEGIC
ALLIANCES

		Business Market Position	
		Leader	Follower
Strategic Importance in Parent's Portfolio	Core	Defend	Catch Up
	Peripheral	Remain	Restructure

Source: Reprinted from P. Lorange, J. Roos, and P. S. Brønn, "Building Successful Strategic Alliances," *Long Range Planning,* 25 (6), 1992, p. 10. Copyright 1992, with kind permission from Elsevier Science Ltd., The Boulevard, Langford Lane, Kidlington OX51GB, UK.

NUMMI joint venture set up by Toyota and General Motors to swap car-manufacturing expertise.

The Logic behind Strategic Alliances

The strategic payoffs of cross-border alliances are alluring, especially in high-tech industries. Lorange and colleagues[60] suggest that there are four generic reasons for forming strategic alliances: defend, catch up, remain, or restructure (see Exhibit 9-9). Their scheme centers around two dimensions: the strategic importance of the business unit to the parent company and the competitive position of the business.

- *Defend.* Companies create alliances for their core businesses to defend their leadership position. Basically, the underlying goal is to sustain the firm's leadership position by learning new skills, getting access to new markets, developing new technologies, or finessing other capabilities that help the company to reinforce its competitive advantage.[61]

- *Catch Up.* Firms may also shape strategic alliances to catch up. This happens when companies create an alliance to shore up a core business in which they do not have a leadership position. Nestlé and General Mills launched Cereal Partners Worldwide to attack the Kelloggs-dominated global cereal market. PepsiCo and General Mills, two of the weaker players in the European snack food business, set up a joint venture for their snack food business to compete more effectively in the European market.

- *Remain.* Firms might also enter a strategic alliance to simply remain in a business. This might occur for business divisions where the firm has established a leadership position but which only play a minor role in the company's business portfolio. That way, the alliance enables the company to get the maximum efficiency out of its position.

- *Restructure.* Lastly, a firm might also view alliances as a vehicle to restructure a business that is not core and in which it has no leadership position. The ultimate intent here is that one partner uses the alliance to rejuvenate the business, thereby turning the business unit in a "presentable bride," so to speak. Usually, one of the other partners in the alliance ends up acquiring the business unit.

Cross-Border Alliances That Succeed

The recipe for a successful strategic alliance will probably never be written. Still, a number of studies done by consulting agencies and academic scholars have uncovered several findings on what distinguishes enduring cross-border alliances from the

---

[60] Peter Lorange, Johan Roos, and Peggy S. Brønn, "Building Successful Strategic Alliances," *Long Range Planning,* 25 (6), 1992, pp. 10–17.

[61] See also David Lei and John W. Slocum, Jr., "Global Strategy, Competence-Building and Strategic Alliances," *California Management Review,* Fall 1992, pp. 81–97.

floundering ones. An analysis of cross-border alliances done by McKinsey[62] made the following recommendations:

- *Alliances between strong and weak partners seldom work.* Building ties with partners that are weak is a recipe for disaster. The weak partner becomes a drag on the competitiveness of the partnership. As David Logan, Hewlett-Packard's corporate development director puts it: "One should go for the best possible partners—leaders in their field, not followers."[63]

- *Autonomy and flexibility.* These are two key ingredients for successful partnerships. Autonomy could mean that the alliance has its own management team and its own board of directors. This speeds up the decision-making process. Autonomy also makes it easier to resolve conflicts that arise. To cope with environmental changes over time, flexibility is essential. Market needs change, new technologies emerge, competitive forces regroup. Being flexible, alliances can more easily adapt to these changes by revising their objectives, the charter of the venture, or other aspects of the alliance.

- *Equal ownership.* In 50–50 ownerships, the partners are equally concerned about the other's success. Both partners should contribute equally to the alliance.[64] Thereby, all partners will be in a win–win situation when the gains are equally distributed. However, 50–50 joint ventures between partners from developed countries and developing countries are more likely to get bogged down in decision-making dead-locks. One recent study of equity joint ventures in China found that partnerships with minority foreign equity holdings run much more smoothly than other equity sharing arrangements. Indeed, 50–50 partnerships ran into numerous internal managerial problems including joint decision making and coordination with local managers. Majority foreign equity ventures had fewer internal problems but encountered many external issues such as lack of local sourcing and high dependence on imported materials.[65] So, in spite of the findings of the McKinsey study, the ownership question—50–50 versus majority stake—remains murky.

We would like to add a few more success factors to these. Stable alliances have the commitment and support of the top of the parents' organization. Strong alliance managers are key to success.[66] Alliances between partners that are related (in terms of products, markets, and/or technologies) or have similar cultures, asset size and venturing experience levels) tend to be much more viable.[67] Furthermore, successful alliances tend to start on a narrow basis and broaden over time. A partnership between Corning, the U.S. glassmaker, and Samsung, the Korean electronics firm, started with one plant making television tubes in South Korea. Over time, the partnership broadened its scope, covering much of East Asia. Finally, a shared vision on the goals and the mutual benefits is the hallmark of viable alliances.

TIMING OF ENTRY   ◆ ◆ ◆ ◆ ◆ ◆ ◆ ◆

Sony used to simply dump its older products in China. By contrast, Samsung, Sony's Korean rival, launched top-of-the-line high-end products such as digital phones, MP3 players, and projection televisions in China. Samsung realized the rise of a consumer

---

[62] Joel Bleeke and David Ernst, "The Way to Win in Cross-Border Alliances," *Harvard Business Review,* November–December 1991, pp. 127–135.

[63] "When Even a Rival Can Be a Best Friend," *Financial Times,* (October 22, 1997), p. 12.

[64] Godfrey Devlin and Mark Bleackley, "Strategic Alliances—Guidelines for Success," *Long Range Planning,* 21(5), 1988, pp. 18–23.

[65] Yigang Pan and Wilfried R. Vanhonacker, "Equity Sharing Arrangements and Joint Venture Operation in the People's Republic of China," Working Paper, February 1994, Hong Kong University of Science & Technology.

[66] Devlin and Bleackley, "Strategic Alliances," pp. 18–23.

[67] Kathryn R. Harrigan, "Strategic Alliances and Partner Assymetries," in *Cooperative Strategies in International Business,* F.J. Contractor and P. Lorange, eds. (Lexington, MA: Lexington Books).

EXHIBIT 9-10
TIMELINE
INTERNATIONAL
EXPANSION OF
STARBUCKS COFFEE

1971	First location in Seattle
1987	Canada (Vancouver, British Columbia)
1996	Hawaii
	Japan
	Singapore
1997	Philippines
1998	Malaysia
	New Zealand
	Taiwan
	Thailand
1999	China
	Kuwait
	Lebanon
	South Korea
2000	Australia
	Bahrain
	Dubai
	Hong Kong
	Qatar
	Saudi Arabia
2001	Austria
	Israel
	Switzerland
2002	Germany
	Indonesia
	Oman
	Spain

Source: www.starbucks.com.

class of young urban Chinese who are eager to buy fashionable electronics. Chinese consumers view Samsung as fun, sporty, and trendy. The brand has the strongest following among Chinese in their 20s and 30s. Sony's brand, however, is seen as lacking "warmth, fun, and involvement." Samsung's hipper image also translated into bigger sales: $1.8 billion sales revenues in 2002 in Greater China compared with $1 billion for Sony. To build up a better brand image, Sony has decided to launch products in China at the same time it does in Japan and other developed countries.[68]

International market entry decisions also cover the timing-of-entry question: When should the firm enter a foreign market? Numerous firms have been burned badly by entering markets too early. Ikea's first foray in Japan in 1974 was a complete fiasco.[69] The Swedish furniture retailer hastily withdrew from Japan after realizing that Japanese consumers were not yet ready for the concept of self-assembly and preferred high quality over low prices. Ikea re-entered Japan in late 2005, but this time offering assembly services and home delivery.

Exhibit 9-10 shows the timeline of Starbucks's international expansion strategy. Note the gap of almost 25 years between the establishment of the first Starbucks store in Seattle and the coffee chain's first international foray in Japan. Since then, the company has expanded very aggressively. Initially, Starbucks concentrated on the Asia-Pacific region, moving on to the Middle East, and then, most recently, to Europe. To date, Starbucks has more than 1,500 outlets in 31 countries outside the United States.

Timing decisions also arise for the global launch of new products or services. Microsoft launched the Xbox videogame console first in its home market (in the fall of 2001), next in Japan (February 2002), and then in Europe (March–April 2002). However, products are not always pioneered in a company's home market. A case in point is the Volkswagen New Beetle, which was first rolled out in the United States and later in Germany. Likewise, Toyota's luxury car marque Lexus was launched in July 2005 in Japan, more than 15 years after its 1989 debut in the United States. Qoo, a Coca-Cola children's fruit drink, was first rolled out in Japan in 1999. It was then introduced rapidly in other Asian markets (Korea, Singapore, China, Thailand, and Taiwan). In January 2003, Coke launched Qoo in its first European market in Germany.[70]

Research on international entry-timing decisions is scarce. One study examined the timing-of-entry decisions of U.S. Fortune 500 firms in China.[71] According to the study's findings, firms tend to enter China earlier:

- The higher the level of international experience.

- The larger the firm size.

- The broader the scope of products and services.

- When competitors have already entered the market.

- The more favorable the risk (political, business) conditions.

- When nonequity modes of entry (e.g., licensing, exporting, nonequity alliances) are chosen.

In general, companies that entered China relatively late often had an advantage over earlier entrants. A main reason is that latecomers faced fewer restrictive business regulations than their predecessors. Companies now have much more flexible ways to set up their joint ventures. In many industries, companies are free now to set up a

---

[68]"Is Sony Cool Enough for China?" *Far Eastern Economic Review,* (December 26, 2002–January 2, 2003), pp. 100–102.

[69]http://www.businessweek.com/magazine/content/05_46/b3959001.htm.

[70]"Coca-Cola's Qoo to Go to Germany," *Advertising Age,* December 16, 2002, p. 12.

[71]Vibah Gaba, Yigang Pan, and Gerardo R. Ungson, "Timing of Entry in International Markets: An Empirical Study of U.S. Fortune 500 Firms in China," *Journal of International Business Studies,* 33 (First Quarter 2002), pp. 39–55.

wholly owned subsidiary instead of partnering with a Chinese company.[72] Still, some early comers such as Yum! (the owner of KFC and Pizza Hut restaurants) and Procter & Gamble have been able to leave their competitors in the dust.

A second study looked at the entry timing pattern for a sample of 19 multinational firms. This study develops the concept of **near-market knowledge** defined as the knowledge (cultural, economic) generated in similar markets in which the MNC already operates. The study's key findings are fourfold:

- Near-market knowledge has an important impact on foreign market entry timing. Near-market knowledge accumulated from successful foreign entries will lead to earlier entry in similar markets.

- Cultural similarity with the home market is not related to foreign market entry timing. Although cultural similarity with the domestic market matters for initial foreign entry forays, it turns out not to be critical for later entries.

- Several economic attractiveness variables matter a great deal. Specifically, countries with wealthier consumers, larger economies, more developed infrastructure, and more easily accessible consumers are likely to be entered earlier.

- Economic factors are more crucial than cultural factors in entry timing decisions.[73]

EXIT STRATEGIES

◆ ◆ ◆ ◆ ◆ ◆ ◆ ◆

So far we have concentrated on international entry strategies. In this section, we will concentrate on their flipside: exit (or divestment) strategies. Exits in global marketing are not uncommon. In 2001, Colgate-Palmolive sold its laundry detergent brands in Mexico to Henkel, its German competitor. Gateway radically overhauled its strategy in 2001 when it decided to discontinue its company-owned operations outside North America.[74] The personal computer maker closed down its manufacturing operations in Ireland and Malaysia. In May 2006 Wal-Mart sold its stores in South Korea, a few months later, in July 2006, the company sold its stores in Germany.

Decisions to exit or divest a foreign market are not taken lightly. Companies may have multiple good reasons to pull out of their foreign markets:

Reasons for Exit

- *Sustained losses.* Key markets are often entered with a long-term perspective. Most companies recognize that an immediate payback of their investments is not realistic and are willing to absorb losses for many years. Still, at some point, the company usually has a limit to how long a period of losses it is willing to sustain.

- *Volatility.* Companies often underestimate the risks of the host country's economic and political environment. Many multinationals have rushed into emerging markets lured by tempting prospects of huge populations with rising incomes. Unfortunately, countries with high growth potential often are very volatile. However, it is easy to ignore or downplay the risks associated with entering such markets, such as those stemming from exchange rate volatility, weak rule of law, political instability, economic risks, and inflation. Numerous multinational companies pulled out of Argentina and Indonesia in the wake of these countries' economic turmoil. As the CEO of Dial joked during an analyst meeting, "I wish we could just close Argentina."[75]

---

[72]"In China, It May Pay to Be Late," *Asian Wall Street Journal,* February 9, 2004, pp. A1, A6.

[73]Debanjan Mitra and Peter N. Golder, "Whose Culture Matters? Near-Market Knowledge and Its Impact on Foreign Market Entry Timing," *Journal of Marketing Research,* 39 (August 2002), pp. 350–65.

[74]http://www.gateway.com/about/news/2001report/01_annual_report.pdf.

[75]"Submerged," *Advertising Age,* March 4, 2002, p. 14.

- *Premature entry.* As we discussed earlier, the entry-timing decision is a crucial matter. Entering a market too early is usually an expensive mistake. Entries can be premature for reasons such as an underdeveloped marketing infrastructure (e.g., in terms of distribution, supplies), low buying power, and lack of strong local partners. Often exiting a market is the only sensible solution instead of hanging on.

- *Ethical reasons.* Companies that operate in countries such as Myanmar (Burma) or Cuba with a questionable human rights record often receive a lot of flak in other markets. The bad publicity engendered by human rights campaigners can tarnish the company's image. Rather than running the risk of ruining its reputation, the company may decide to pull out of the country. Heineken, for instance, pulled out of Myanmar in the wake of protest campaigns against that country's military dictatorship.

- *Intense competition.* Intense rivalry is often another strong reason for exiting a country. Markets that look appealing on paper usually attract many competitors. The outcome is often overcapacity, triggering price wars and loss–loss situations for all players competing against one another. Rather than sustaining losses, the sensible thing to do is to exit the market, especially when rival players have competitive advantages that are difficult to overcome.

- *Resource reallocation.* A key element of marketing strategy formulation is resource allocation. A strategic review of foreign operations often leads to a shake-up of the company's country portfolio, spurring the MNC to reallocate its resources across markets. Of all emerging markets, only China has outgrown the United States in annual economic growth rate over the last three decades. This explains why several European companies such as Unilever, Nestlé, and Reckitt-Benckiser have shifted their focus to North America.[76] Poor results from global operations are often a symptom of overexpansion. For instance, following a review of the results of its global operations in 2002, McDonald's stated that it would concentrate on sales growth in existing restaurants. As a result, the fast-food giant announced that it would (1) close operations in three countries, (2) restructure its business in four other countries, and (3) close 175 restaurants in about 10 other countries.[77]

Risks of Exit   Obviously, exiting a market is a decision that should not be taken lightly. Just as there are barriers to entry, there are exit barriers that could delay or complicate an exit decision. Apart from exit barriers, there are other risks associated with an exit:

- *Fixed costs of exit.* Exiting a country often involves substantial fixed costs. In Europe, several countries have very strict labor laws that make exiting very costly (e.g., offering severance payment packages). It is not uncommon for European governments to cry foul and sue a multinational company when the firm decides to shut down its operations. Long-term contracts that involve commitments such as sourcing raw materials or distributing products often involve major termination penalties.

- *Disposition of assets.* Assets that are highly specialized to the particular business or location for which they are being used also create an exit barrier.[78] The number of prospective buyers may be few, and the price they are willing to pay for these assets will most likely be minimal. Hence, the liquidation value of such assets will be low. Sometimes assets can be sold in markets where the industry is at an earlier stage in the product life cycle.

---

[76]"Western Aggression," *Advertising Age,* March 4, 2002, p. 14.

[77]http://www.mcdonalds.com/corporate/press/financial/2002/11082002/index.html.

[78]Michael E. Porter, *Competitive Strategy: Techniques for Analyzing Industries and Competitors* (New York: The Free Press, 1980).

- *Signal to other markets.* Another concern is that exiting one country or region may send strong negative signals to other countries where the company operates. Exit costs managers jobs; customers risk losing after-sales service support; distributors stand to lose company support and might witness a significant drop in their business. Therefore, an exit in one country could create negative spillovers in other markets by raising red flags about the company's commitment to its foreign markets.

- *Long-term opportunities.* Although exit is sometimes the only sensible thing to do, firms should avoid shortsightedness. Volatility is a way of life in many emerging markets. Four years after the ruble devaluation in August 1998, the Russian economy made a spectacular recovery. The country has become one of the fastest growing markets worldwide for many multinationals, including Procter & Gamble, L'Oréal, and Ikea.[79] Rather than closing shop, it is often better to pay a price in the short term and maintain a presence for the long haul. Exiting a country and re-entering it once the dust settles comes at a price. Rival companies that stayed in the country will have an edge. Distributors and other prospective partners will be reluctant to enter into agreements. Consumers will be leery about buying the firm's products or services, especially when long-term relationships are involved.

Guidelines

Growing through international expansion is not the right formula for all companies. The lure of emerging markets like China, India, or Russia has titillated many marketing managers. Unfortunately, reality does not always live up to hype. Still, companies should handle exit decisions carefully. Here are a few guidelines that managers should consider when pondering an exit decision:

- *Contemplate and assess all options to salvage the foreign business.* Exiting is painful for both the company and other stakeholders. Before making any moves, it is crucial for the company to analyze why results are below expectations and to consider possible alternatives that could save the business. Original targets in terms of market share, return on investment, or payback period may have been too ambitious. Costs could be squeezed, for instance, by sourcing locally rather than importing materials or using local staff instead of expatriates. Repositioning or retargeting the business can offer a solution. Nutrasweet's foray into China provides a good example. When Nutrasweet's consumer division first entered the China market, it targeted the mass market, but sales were far below expectations. Instead of simply exiting China, which was one of the options being contemplated, Nutrasweet decided to lower its sales targets, pursue the diabetics niche market, and position its brand as a medical product.

- *Incremental exit.* Short of a full exit, an intermediate option is an incremental exit strategy. Firms could "mothball" their operations and restart them when demand or cost conditions improve.[80] McDonald's restructured its presence in four countries by transferring ownership to licensees. Dial Corp. revamped its operations in Mexico by licensing its brands instead of selling them directly.

- *Migrate customers.* If exiting proves to be the optimal decision, one delicate matter is how to handle customers who depend on the company for after-sales service support and parts. Obviously, it is important that customers not be "orphaned." One solution is to migrate them to third parties. Gateway, for example, entered into contracts with third-party service providers to offer customer service support to its customers in the affected markets.

---

[79]"To Russia with Love," *Business Week, Asian Edition,* September 16, 2002, pp. 26–27.
[80]David Besanko, David Dranove, and Mark Shanley, *Economics of Strategy* (New York: John Wiley & Sons, 2000), p. 338.

SUMMARY

Companies have a smorgasbord of entry strategy choices to implement their global expansion efforts. Each alternative has its pros and cons (see Exhibit 9-11). There is no one-size-fits-all solution. Many firms use a hodgepodge of entry modes. Starbucks, for instance, uses a combination of company-owned stores, licensing, and joint ventures.

Within the same industry, rivals often adopt different approaches to enter new markets. Cummins Engines, a leading U.S.-based diesel engine maker, uses a strategy based on joint ventures with outside groups, mostly customers but also competitors including Komatsu. Caterpillar, on the other hand, prefers having total control over its new ventures using acquisitions as a route to expand overseas.[81] In the car industry, DaimlerChrysler and Ford like to expand through acquisitions; General Motors prefers to rely on strategic alliances. Rick Wagoner, GM's chief executive, rationalizes the alliance strategy as follows: "Our alliance approach allows us to realize synergies faster than we could in a full buy-out situation. Alliances help us to grow in markets where we are underrepresented."[82] A company's expansion strategies can also vary across regions. Computer Associates' expansion strategy in the United States was to buy up software companies and then integrate their software products with the rest of the firm. In Asia, the software maker has taken a different route. Instead, the firm has expanded by forming joint ventures with local players.[83] In China, for instance, CAI has established

---

[81]"Engine Makers Take Different Routes," *The Financial Times,* July 14, 1998, p. 11.

[82]"Carmakers Take Two Routes to Global Growth," *The Financial Times,* July 11, 2000, p. 29.

[83]"Integrating into Asia," *Far Eastern Economic Review,* March 16, 2000, pp. 55–56.

EXHIBIT 9-11
ADVANTAGES AND DISADVANTAGES OF DIFFERENT MODES OF ENTRY

Entry Mode	Advantages	Disadvantages
Indirect exporting	• Low commitment (in terms of resources) • Low risk	• Lack of control • Lack of contact with foreign market • No learning experience • Potential opportunity cost
Direct exporting	• More control (compared to indirect exporting) • More sales push	• Need to build up export organization • More demanding on resources
Licensing	• Little or no investment • Rapid way to gain entry • Means to bridge import barriers • Low risk	• Lack of control • Potential opportunity cost • Need for quality control • Risk of creating competitor • Limits market development
Franchising	• Little or no investment • Rapid way to gain entry • Managerial motivation	• Need for quality control • Lack of control • Risk of creating competitor
Contract manufacturing	• Little or no investment • Overcome import barriers • Cost savings	• Need for quality control • Risk of bad press (e.g., child labor) • Diversion to gray and/or black markets
Joint venture	• Risk sharing • Less demanding on resources (compared to wholly owned) • Potential of synergies (e.g., access to local distribution network)	• Risk of conflicts with partner(s) • Lack of control • Risk of creating competitor
Acquisition and merger	• Full control • Access to local assets (e.g., plants, distribution network, brand assets) • Less competition	• Costly • High risk • Need to integrate differing national/corporate cultures • Cultural clashes
Greenfield	• Full control • Latest technologies • No risk of cultural conflicts	• Costly • Time consuming • High political & financial risks

six joint ventures, all with industry leaders. A key motivation is that the local government prefers partnerships for the software industry. CAI claims that it is in a much better position to compete with foreign and domestic vendors than if it had followed Microsoft's or Oracle's in-house approaches.[84]

Companies often adopt a phased entry strategy: They start with a minimal-risk strategy; after the perceived risk declines, they switch to a higher commitment mode, such as a wholly owned venture. Caterpillar, Inc., the U.S.-based manufacturer of earth-moving and construction equipment, entered the former Soviet bloc in 1992 via direct exporting to minimize its financial risk exposure. Once sales took off, Caterpillar upped the ante by establishing joint ventures with Russian and U.S. firms.[85]

As this chapter discussed, a broad range of variables impact the entry mode choice. The three major dimensions include the resource commitment the firm is willing to make, the amount of risk (political and market) the firm is willing to take, and the degree of control that is desirable.

To compete more effectively in the global arena, more and more companies use cross-border strategic alliances to build their muscle. Depending on the strategic role and the competitive position of the business unit involved, the goal of the alliance could be to defend, strengthen, sustain, or restructure the Strategic Business Unit (SBU). The benefits that the partners can derive from the synergies of the alliance often downplay the concerns the parent companies might have about the partnership. Still, the formation of an alliance should always be preceded by a meticulous analysis of questions such as these:

- What are the mutual benefits for each partner?
- What learning can take place between firms?
- How can the parties complement each other to create joint capabilities?
- Are the partners equal in strength, or is this the case of the "one-eyed guiding the blind"?[86]

Satisfactory answers to these questions improve the chances of the cross-border alliance becoming a win–win situation for all partners involved.

[84]"Speak Nicely and Carry a Big Check," *Business China,* January 29, 2001, p. 12.

[85]Avraham Shama, "Entry Strategies of U.S. Firms to the Newly Independent States, Baltic States, and Eastern European Countries," *California Management Review,* 37 (3), Spring 1995, pp. 90–109.

[86]Lorange et al., "Building Successful Strategic Alliances," pp. 12–13.

KEY TERMS ✦

Acquisition and merger
Contract manufacturing
Cooperative exporting
Cooperative joint venture
Cross-licensing
Direct exporting
Equity joint venture
Export agent
Export management company (EMC)

Export merchant
Franchisee
Franchisor
Greenfield operation
Indirect exporting
Licensee
Licensing
Licensor
Master franchising

Near-market knowledge
Outsourcing
Piggyback exporting
Strategic alliance
Synergy
Transaction-cost analysis (TCA)
Transaction-specific assets

REVIEW QUESTIONS ✦ ✦ ✦ ✦ ✦ ✦ ✦ ✦ ✦ ✦ ✦ ✦ ✦ ✦ ✦ ✦ ✦ ✦

1. Why do some MNCs prefer to enter certain markets with a liaison office first?

2. What are the possible drawbacks of 50–50 joint ventures?

3. List the respective pros and cons of licensing.

4. What are the respective advantages and disadvantages of greenfield operations over acquisitions?

5. What mechanisms can firms use to protect themselves against ill-fated partnerships?

DISCUSSION QUESTIONS ✦ ✦ ✦ ✦ ✦ ✦ ✦ ✦ ✦ ✦ ✦ ✦ ✦ ✦ ✦ ✦

1. NTT DoCoMo, which dominates Japan's mobile phone market, follows a somewhat unusual international expansion strategy. Its strategy is to take minority stakes rather than full control in a foreign mobile operator. The reason for this is that the company prefers to acquire stakes up to a level that allows it to participate in management but respect the local company's autonomy. DoCoMo claims that it can provide valuable technology expertise in mobile multimedia and 3G to its partners. Assess DoCoMo's expansion strategy.

2. Companies tend to begin their internationalization process in countries that are culturally very close. For instance, U.S-based companies would enter Canada and/or the United Kingdom first before moving into other countries. The so-called psychic distance between the United States and

Canada (or Britain) is small because these countries are supposedly very similar. A recent survey, however, found that only 22 percent of Canadian retailers felt that they were operating successfully in the United States. Explain why culturally close countries are not necessarily easy to manage.

3. *Assignment.* Check some recent issues of *The Wall Street Journal* and/or the *Financial Times.* Look for articles on cross-border strategic alliances. Pick one or two examples and find out more about the alliances you chose via a search on the Internet. Why were the alliances formed? What do the partners contribute to the alliance? What benefits do they anticipate? What concerns/issues were raised?

4. Helmut Maucher, former chairman of Nestlé was quoted as saying, "I don't share the euphoria for alliances and joint ventures. First, very often they're an excuse, and an easy way out when people should do their own homework. Secondly, all joint ventures create additional difficulties—you share power and cultures, and decisions take longer." Comment.

5. Visit the online guide to international franchising set up by the *International Herald Tribune* (www.franchiseintl.com). Note that this guide lists franchises based on industry type. Pick any industry type and two or more competing franchise companies within that industry (e.g., Subway and Blimpie). Contrast their international franchising strategies (in terms of geographic coverage, training provided, services, etc.).

SHORT CASES

CASE 9-1

BENQ'S DEAL OF THE CENTURY?

Like other Taiwanese firms, BenQ has tried to escape the anonymity of contract manufacturing by promoting brands. The consumer electronics company's core products include flat-screen TV sets, notebooks, PC monitors, MP3 players, mobile phones, and other consumer electronics gadgets. Spun off from Acer in 2001, it took the name BenQ ("bringing enjoyment and quality to life"). The US$5.5 billion company wants to do more than churn out hardware with someone else's name on it. At present, 37 percent of BenQ's sales carry the BenQ brand name.

On June 7, 2005, BenQ suddenly became the world's fourth largest cellular phone maker by acquiring the ailing handset division of Siemens AG, the German conglomerate. It looked like the bargain of the century. BenQ was getting the mobile handset business of Siemens for nothing—and the German company was even eating $430 million in costs surrounding the transaction. One Taipei-based brokerage analyst commented, "It's a deal too good to be true for BenQ. They get the whole business and a decent brand for free." BenQ would acquire the rights to the Siemens trademark for 18 months and cobranding rights for 5 years. BenQ would also gain access to Siemens' intellectual property, including its CSM, GPRS, and 3G patents. Furthermore, Siemens agreed to buy 50 million euros' worth of BenQ stock.

As a result of the deal, mobile phones would become one of BenQ's core businesses. Armed with a renowned brand name, new technology, and access to Siemens' customer base in Europe and Latin America, BenQ aspired to become a major player in the mobile phone market. Martin Roll, the author of *Asian Brand Strategy,* commented that "Siemens brand equity will give BenQ a major push in its stride to gain credibility in the European and U.S. markets." Lee Kun-yao, BenQ's chairman, explained the reasoning behind the deal as follows: "In BenQ we come more from the enjoyment side and consumer side of technology. . . Siemens has a very strong heritage in German technologies."

Some skeptics raised major concerns, however. After grabbing the no. 4 slot and 9 percent market share in global handset sales in 2002, the Siemens unit slipped to no. 5 in 2005 with a share of just 5.5 percent. Siemens provided no guarantees to BenQ about the profitability of the handset business. Market leaders Nokia, Motorola, and Samsung, which currently command 60 percent of the worldwide handset market, have been steadily pulling away from their smaller competitors. It is unclear how BenQ plans to turn the Siemens business unit

around. In 2004, it incurred losses of $615 million on sales of $5.8 billion according to Merrill Lynch estimates. Siemens' efforts to squeeze costs were hampered by German trade unions that had resisted relocations to lower-cost sites.

BenQ could use a lift. Vincent Chen, an analyst with CLSA Taipei, said that "Feedback on BenQ's products hasn't been great, and they've been late getting products to market." Kent Chan, an analyst with Citigroup Hong Kong, observed, "The risk is that Siemens could wipe out BenQ profits in 2006." BenQ has little brand name recognition in Europe and the United States. Its handset business was hit hard by a tumble in orders from Motorola, its biggest customers, after BenQ introduced its own brand name. BenQ has tried to make up for some of the Motorola loss with orders from the likes of Nokia and Kyocera, but its handset business is still smarting. BenQ's first quarter 2005 profits tumbled by 90 percent to $9.7 million as its revenues fell 23 percent to $1 billion, compared with a year earlier.

The Siemens deal might solve some of its problems. BenQ planned to start using the Siemens name and then gradually introduce cobranded phones to build up the BenQ name in Europe and the United States. The deal would also help BenQ gain access in new markets such as Latin America. Moreover, BenQ would inherit factories in Brazil and Germany and research facilities that have been working on next-generation products. "This kind of intellectual property is crucial to our success," noted BenQ president Sheaffer Lee.

BenQ and Siemens' combined market share dropped from 13.5 percent in the fourth quarter of 2004 to 9.8 percent in the third quarter of 2005. To reverse the fall, BenQ planned to focus on making handsets for 3G networks. It also sought to differentiate itself by using organic LED displays. Such displays are much brighter than standard LED screens but wear out faster.

Still, BenQ's challenges seem tremendous. Professor Jagdish Sheth, co-author of *The Rule of Three,* said that further consolidation of marginal players would be required for BenQ to succeed. BenQ will also inherit the labor troubles that plagued Siemens when it takes over 3,700 workers in high-cost Germany. BenQ must honor labor contracts through 2006. For BenQ, making this the deal of the century will be a huge task.

DISCUSSION QUESTIONS

1. How do you evaluate BenQ's acquisition deal of the Siemens handset unit? Is it indeed "too good to be true"? What are the pros and cons?

2. Where is BenQ vulnerable?

3. What strategic marketing recommendations would you make to BenQ's going forward?

Sources: "BenQ May Be Getting What It Paid For," *Business Week,* June 20, 2005; "BenQ Must Capitalize on 'Fleeting Platform,' " *Media,* July 29, 2005; "BenQ's Combined Brand in Handset Drive," *Financial Times,* January 18, 2006, p. 18; and www.benq.com.

$\mathcal{C}$ASE 9-2

CAN MCDONALD'S DE-THRONE THE COLONEL IN CHINA?

McDonald's opened its first restaurant in China in Shenzhen in 1990. McDonald's expansion since then has been rapid: it had 750 outlets by the end of 2005 and planned to have 1,000 restaurants by the time of the Beijing Summer Olympics in 2008, for which McDonald's is a sponsor. Contrary to KFC, which is opening outlets in second- and third-tier cities, McDonald's prefers to grow within the large cities. Tim Fenton, McDonald's executive in charge of Asian operation, says, "When you start to get out of the bigger cities you start to fragment your transportation infrastructure."

However, although McDonald's may be the undisputed fast-food brand in the Western world, it is far behind Yum! Brands in China. Yum! operates Pizza Hut (180 restaurants) and, most importantly, KFC, which has more than 1,500 outlets in China and a broader geographic coverage than the Golden Arches. Yum! may have had a first-mover advantage: It was the first fast-food restaurant chain to enter China in 1987 (Pizza Hut was introduced in 1990). The fact that most Chinese consumers prefer chicken over beef also helped Yum! build up a successful business in China. KFC has also a much more localized menu than McDonald's featuring items such as a Dragon Twister, egg tarts, and congee. David Novak, Yum! Brands chief executive, predicts that KFC's China business is on track to become as big as McDonald's in the United States.

Still, McDonald's is not willing to cede China to the Colonel. One way that McDonald's is trying to narrow the gap is by adding drive-through restaurants. KFC was the first Western fast-food chain to open a drive-through in China in 2002. McDonald's opened its first one in November 2005. The three it had by early 2006 were outperforming average volume of existing restaurants by 50 to 80 percent. The chain plans to open 12 to 15 drive-throughs every year for the coming three years. The company hopes to benefit from the rapid growth of car ownership.

McDonald's will also introduce menu changes. The company believes that there are three basic customer tiers: value-conscious diners, less price-sensitive diners loyal to the core menu items of Big Macs and fries, and upper-level consumers who are willing to buy premium items. In China, McDonald's launched nine products priced at US60 cents or less. It will also launch a rice burger, first introduced in Taiwan, targeted at higher spending consumers.

Clearly, McDonald's remains a brand to watch in China in spite of the strides made by Colonel Sanders' KFC army. Fears triggered by bird flu might convince Chinese consumers to enjoy a Big Mac or rice burger instead of the Colonel's fried chicken. Nutritional concerns that have cast a shadow in developed markets are less an issue in China. As Tim Fenton pointed out, "China is obviously the biggest opportunity that we have going right now."

DISCUSSION QUESTIONS

1. Do you agree with the steps McDonald's plans to take to expand its business in China (adding drive-throughs, focusing on big cities, localizing menus)?

2. What other remedies would you prescribe if you were in Tim Fenton's shoes?

Sources: "Can McDonald's Steal Yum!s' China Crown?" *Media,* January 13, 2006, pp. 15; and "McDonald's Drive Towards Big City Sales," *Financial Times,* February 22, 2006: pp. 12.

FURTHER READING

Anderson, Erin, and Hubert Gatignon. "Modes of Foreign Entry: A Transaction Cost Analysis and Propositions." *Journal of International Business Studies,* 11 (Fall 1986), pp. 1–26.

Bamford, James, David Ernst, and David G. Fubini. "Launching a World-Class Joint Venture." *Harvard Business Review,* 82 (February 2004) 2, pp. 90–101.

Bleeke, Joel, and David Ernst. "The Way to Win in Cross-Border Alliances." *Harvard Business Review,* November–December 1991, pp. 127–35.

Cavusgil, S. Tamer. "Measuring the Potential of Emerging Markets: An Indexing Approach." *Business Horizons,* 40 (January–February 1997) 2, pp. 87–91.

Devlin, Godfrey, and Mark Bleackley. "Strategic Alliances–Guidelines for Success." *Long Range Planning,* 21(5), pp. 18–23.

Gaba, Vibha, Yigang Pan, and Gerardo R. Ungson. "Timing of Entry in International Market: An Empirical Study of U.S. Fortune 500 Firms in China." *Journal of International Business Studies,* 33 (1), First Quarter 2002 2, pp. 39–55.

Hyder, Akmal S., and Pervez N. Ghauri. "Managing International Joint Venture Relationships." *Industrial Marketing Management,* 29 (2000) 2, pp. 205–18.

Kumar, V., A. Stam, and E.A. Joachimsthaler. "An Interactive Multicriteria Approach to Identifying Potential Foreign Markets." *Journal of International Marketing,* 2, (1), 1994, pp. 29–52.

Lorange, Peter, Johan Roos, and Peggy S. Brønn. "Building Successful Strategic Alliances." *Long Range Planning,* 25(6), pp. 10–17.

Martinsons, M.G., and C.-S. Tseng. "Successful Joint Ventures in the Heart of the Dragon." *Long Range Planning,* 28(5), pp. 45–58.

Mitra, Debanjan, and Peter N. Golder. "Whose Culture Matters? Near-Market Knowledge and Its Impact on Foreign

Market Entry Timing." *Journal of Marketing Research,* 39 (August 2002) 2, pp. 350–65.

Ostland, Gregory E., and S. Tamer Cavusgil. "Performance Issues in U.S.-China Joint Ventures." *California Management Review,* 38(2), Winter 1996, pp. 106–30.

Preble, John F., and Richard C. Hoffman. "Franchising Systems around the Globe: A Status Report." *Journal of Small Business Management,* April 1995, pp. 80–88.

Root, Franklin R. *Entry Strategies for International Markets.* New York: Lexington Books, 1994.

Shama, Avraham. "Entry Strategies of U.S. Firms to the Newly Independent States, Baltic States, and Eastern European Countries." *California Management Review,* 37(3), Spring 1995, pp. 90–109.

Tihanyi, Laszlo, David A. Griffith, and Craig J. Russell. "The Effect of Cultural Distance on Entry Mode Choice, International Diversification, and MNE Performance: A Meta-Analysis." *Journal of International Business Studies,* 36 (2005), pp. 270–283.

Turpin, Dominique. "Strategic Alliances with Japanese Firms: Myths and Realities." *Long Range Planning,* 28(5), pp. 45–58.

Zhao, Hongxin, Yadong Luo, and Taewon Suh. "Transaction Cost Determinants and Ownership-Based Entry Mode Choice: A Meta-Analytical Review." *Journal of International Business Studies,* 35 (2004), pp. 524–44.

APPENDIX: ALTERNATIVE COUNTRY SCREENING PROCEDURE

When its product has already been launched in some regions, a firm might consider using a variant of the country screening procedure described in this chapter. The alternative method leverages the experience the firm has gathered in its existing markets. It works as follows: Suppose the MNC currently does business in Europe and is now considering an expansion into Asia.

Step 1. *Collect historical data on the European market.*
The MNC should go back to its files and collect the historical data for the European markets on the indicators that it plans to use to assess the market opportunities for the Asian region. Let's refer to these pieces of information as X_{iec}, that is, the score of European country ec on indicator i.

Step 2. *Evaluate the MNC's postentry performance in each of its existing European markets.*
Assess the MNC's postentry performance in each European country by assigning a success score (e.g., on a 10-point scale). If performance is measured on just one indicator, for example, market share achieved five years after entry, it could also simply use that indicator as a performance measure. Let's refer to the performance score for country ec as S_{ec}.

Step 3. *Derive weights for each of the country indicators.*
The next step is to identify importance weights for each country indicator. For this, the MNC could run a cross-sectional regression using the European data gathered in the previous two steps. The dependent variable is the postentry success score (S_{ec}) while the

predictor variables are the country indicators (X_{iec}):

$$S_{ec} = a + w_1 X_{1ec} + w_2 X_{2ec} + \cdots + w_I X_{Iec}$$

where

$$ec = 1, 2, \ldots, EC$$

By running a regression of the success scores, S_{ec}, on the predictor variables, X_{iec} ($i = 1, \ldots, I$), the MNC can derive estimates for the importance weights of the different indicators.

Step 4. *Rate the Asian countries in the pool on each indicator.*
Each of the Asian candidate markets in the pool is given a score on each of the indicators that are considered: X_{iac}.

Step 5. *Predict performance in prospective Asian countries.*
Finally, predict the postentry performance in the prospective Asian markets by using the weights estimated in the previous step and data collected on each of the indicators (the X_{iac}'s) for the Asian countries. For instance, the regression estimates might look like:

$$\text{Performance} = -0.7 + 6.0(\text{Market Size})$$
$$+ 2.9(\text{Growth}) - 1(\text{Competition})$$

By plugging in the ratings (or actual values) for the Asian markets in this equation, the MNC can predict its performance in each of these countries.

DUBLIN BUSINESS SCHOOL LIBRARY

GLOBAL SOURCING STRATEGY

HAPTER OVERVIEW

1. EXTENT AND COMPLEXITY OF GLOBAL SOURCING STRATEGY

2. TRENDS IN GLOBAL SOURCING STRATEGY

3. VALUE CHAIN AND FUNCTIONAL INTERFACES

4. PROCUREMENT: TYPES OF SOURCING STRATEGY

5. LONG-TERM CONSEQUENCES OF GLOBAL SOURCING

6. OUTSOURCING OF SERVICE ACTIVITIES

Global competition suggests a drastically shortened life cycle for most products that no longer permits companies a polycentric, country-by-country approach to international business. If companies that have developed a new product do follow a country-by-country approach to foreign market entry over time, a globally oriented competitor will likely overcome their initial competitive advantages by blanketing the world markets with similar products in a short period of time. Indeed, it is imperative for companies to continuously create and acquire capabilities to help generate a sustainable competitive advantage over their rivals. Increasingly, how to source globally has become a critical strategic decision that is influenced by the capabilities a company needs to compete.

Today we are seeing a gradual power shift in sources of competitive advantage from proprietary technology to manufacturing and marketing competencies and then to design capability. Proprietary technology is essentially a *raw* muscle power to obtain initial competitive advantage, and it is easy to imitate by inventing around, by reverse engineering, or even by industrial espionage. Manufacturing and marketing competencies revolve around the "sweat and tears" of skilled human inputs, which take years to accomplish by continual improvement after improvement and, as a result, are much harder to copy. Now the source of competitive advantage is increasingly determined by product design that meets the fickle and fleeting needs of consumers around the world.

One successful example of a globally oriented strategist is Sony. It developed transistorized solid-state color TVs in Japan in the 1960s and initially marketed them in the United States as the lead market before they were introduced in the rest of the world, including the Japanese market. Mass marketing initially in the United States and then throughout the world in a short time period gave this Japanese company a first-mover advantage as well as economies of scale advantages.

In contrast, EMI is a historic example of the failure to take advantage of global opportunities. This British company developed and began marketing computer-aided tomography (CAT) scanners in 1972, for which its inventors, Godfrey Houndsfield and Allan Cormack, won a Nobel Prize. Despite an enormous demand for CAT scanners in the United States, the largest market for state-of-the-art medical equipment, EMI failed to export them to the United States immediately and in sufficient numbers. Instead, the British company slowly, and probably belatedly, began exporting them to the United States in the mid-1970s, as if to follow the evolutionary pattern suggested by the international product cycle model. Some years later, the British company established a production facility in the United States, only to be slowed by technical problems. By then, EMI was already facing stiff competition from global electronics giants including Philips, Siemens, General Electric, and Toshiba. Indeed, General Electric in a short period of time blanketed the U.S. market and subsequently the rest of the world with its own version of CAT scanners, which were technologically inferior to the British model.[1]

In both cases, technology diffused quickly. Today, quick technological diffusion has virtually become a matter of fact. Without established sourcing plans, distribution, and service networks, it is extremely difficult to exploit both emerging technology and potential markets around the world simultaneously. General Electric's swift global reach could not have been possible without its ability to procure crucial components internally and on a global basis. As a result, the increased pace of new product introduction and reduction in innovational lead time calls for more proactive management of locational and corporate resources on a global basis. In this chapter, we emphasize logistical management of the **interfaces** of R&D, manufacturing, and marketing activities on a global basis, which we call **global sourcing strategy,** and the ability to procure major components of the product inhouse so that companies can proactively standardize either components or products. Global sourcing strategy requires a close coordination among R&D, manufacturing, and marketing activities across national boundaries.[2]

Differing objectives tend to create a tug-of-warlike situation among R&D, manufacturing, and marketing. Excessive product modification and proliferation for the sake of satisfying the ever-changing customer needs will forsake manufacturing efficiency and have negative cost consequences, barring a perfectly flexible computer-aided design (CAD) and computer-aided manufacturing (CAM) facility. CAD/CAM technology has improved tremendously in recent years, but the full benefit of flexible manufacturing is still many years away.[3] Contrarily, excessive product standardization for the sake of lowering manufacturing costs will also be likely to result in unsatisfied or undersatisfied customers. Similarly, innovative product designs and features as desired by customers may indeed be a technological feat but might not be conducive to manufacturing. Therefore, topics such as product design for manufacturability and components/product standardization have become increasingly important strategic issues today. It has become imperative for many companies to develop a sound sourcing strategy to exploit most efficiently R&D, manufacturing, and marketing on a global basis.

---

[1] Fillipo Dell'Osso, "Defending a Dominant Position in a Technology Led Environment," *Business Strategy Review,* Summer 1990, pp. 77–86.

[2] Masaaki Kotabe, *Global Sourcing Strategy: R&D, Manufacturing, and Marketing Interfaces* (Westport, CT: Quorum Books, 1992).

[3] James H. Gilmore and Joseph B. Pine II, "The Four Faces of Mass Customization," *Harvard Business Review,* 75 (January–February 1997), pp. 91–101.

◆ ◆ ◆ ◆ ◆ ◆ ◆ ◆   ## EXTENT AND COMPLEXITY OF GLOBAL SOURCING STRATEGY

Marketing managers should understand and appreciate the important roles that product designers, engineers, production managers, and purchasing managers, among others, play in marketing decision making. Marketing decisions cannot be made in the absence of these people.[4] The overriding theme throughout the chapter is that successful management of the interfaces of R&D, manufacturing, and marketing activities determines a company's competitive strengths and consequently its market performance. Now we will look at logistical implications of this interface management.

Toyota's global operations illustrate one such world-class case. The Japanese carmaker is equipping its operations in the United States, Europe, and Southeast Asia with integrated capabilities for creating and marketing automobiles. The company gives the managers at those operations ample authority to accommodate local circumstances and values without diluting the benefit of integrated global operations. Thus, in the United States, Calty Design Research, a Toyota subsidiary in California, designs the bodies and interiors of new Toyota models, including the Lexus and Solara. Toyota has technical centers in the United States and in Brussels to adapt engine and vehicle specifications to local needs.[5] Toyota operations that make automobiles in Southeast Asia supply each other with key components to foster increased economies of scale and standardization in those components: gasoline engines in Indonesia, steering components in Malaysia, transmissions in the Philippines, and diesel engines in Thailand. Toyota started developing vehicles in Australia and Thailand in 2003. These new bases develop passenger cars and trucks for production and sale only in the Asia-Pacific region. The Australian base is engaged mainly in designing cars, whereas the Thailand facility is responsible for testing them.[6]

Multinational companies such as Toyota not only facilitate the flow of capital among various countries through direct investment abroad but also significantly contribute to the world trade flow of goods and services. Multinational companies combine this production and distribution to supply those local markets hosting their foreign subsidiaries and then export what remains to other foreign markets or back to their parent's home market.

Let us revisit the significance of the foreign production of multinational corporations (MNCs) relative to their exports from their home base. One U.N. official report shows that in 1999, 34 percent of world trade was intrafirm trade between MNCs and their foreign affiliates and between those affiliates, and that an additional 33 percent of world trade was represented by a trading relationship between those MNCs and their trading partners on a long-term contractual agreement popularized by Japanese *keiretsu* (i.e., a quasi-intrafirm relationship). In other words, two-thirds of world trade is managed one way or another by multinational companies.[7] These trade ratios have been fairly stable over time.[8]

As discussed in Chapter 2, two notable changes have occurred in international trade. First, the last 30 years have observed a secular decline in the proportion of

---

[4] David B. Montgomery and Frederick E. Webster, Jr., "Marketing's Interfunctional Interfaces: The MSI Workshop on Management of Corporate Fault Zones," *Journal of Market Focused Management,* 2 (1997), pp. 7–26.

[5] Fumiko Kurosawa and John F. Odgers, "Global Strategy of Design and Development by Japanese Car Makers—From the Perspective of the Resource-Based View," *Association of Japanese Business Studies 1997 Annual Meeting Proceedings,* June 13–15, 1997, pp. 144–46.

[6] "Toyota Design Breaks from Clay and Foam," *Automotive News Europe,* April 4, 2005, p. 38.

[7] Khalil Hamdani, "The Role of Foreign Direct Investment in Export Strategy," presented at 1999 Executive Forum on National Export Strategies, International Trade Centre, the United Nations, September 26–28, 1999.

[8] United Nations Center on Transnational Corporations, *Transnational Corporations in World Development: Trends and Perspectives* (New York: United Nations, 1988); Organisation for Economic Cooperation and Development, *Intra-Firm Trade* (Paris, OECD, 1993); and Stefan H. Robock, "U.S. Multinationals: Intra-Firm Trade, Overseas Sourcing and the U.S. Trade Balance," paper presented at the 1999 Academy of International Business-Southeast Conference, June 4–5, 1999.

EXHIBIT 10-1
HONDA'S WORLDWIDE PRODUCTION AND SOURCE NETWORK

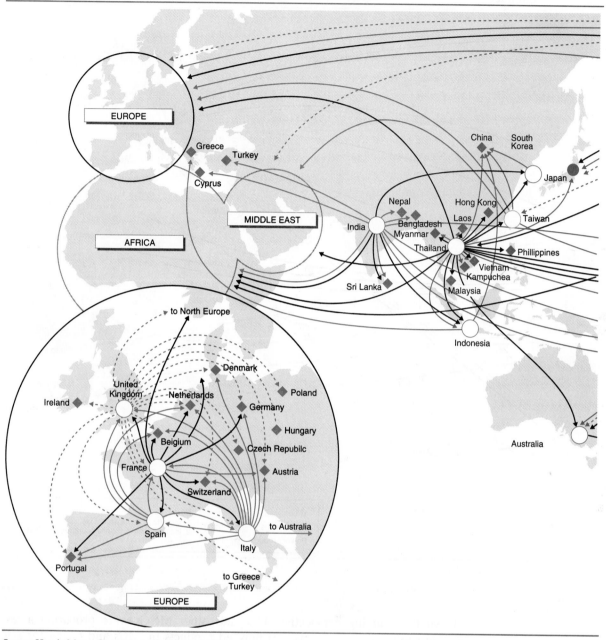

Source: Honda Motor Company Annual Report 1998.

trade between Europe and the United States in the Triad regions and conversely an increase in trade between the United States and Japan, and in particular, between Europe and Japan. This information strongly indicates that European countries and Japan have found each other as increasingly important markets above and beyond their traditional market of the United States. Second, newly industrialized countries (NICs) in Asia (i.e., South Korea, Taiwan, Hong Kong, and Singapore) as well as China have dramatically increased their trading position relative to the rest of the world. These NICs and China have become prosperous marketplaces, but, more significantly, they have become important manufacturing and sourcing locations for many multinational companies.

EXHIBIT 10-1
(continued)

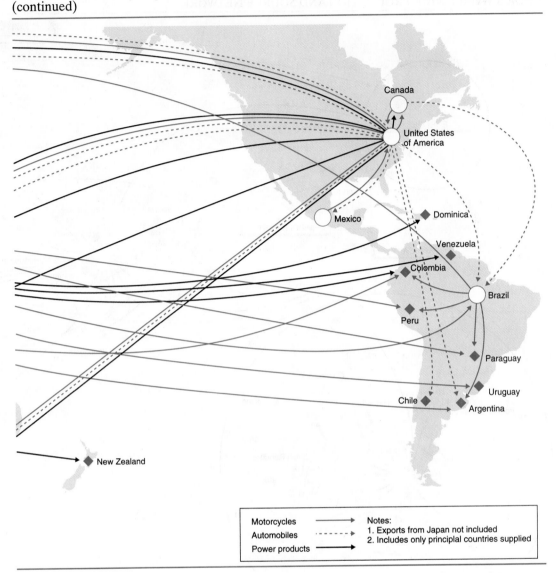

		Notes:
Motorcycles	——→	1. Exports from Japan not included
Automobiles	- - -→	2. Includes only principal countries supplied
Power products	━━▶	

From the sourcing perspective, U.S. and other MNCs were procuring a less expensive supply of components and finished products in NICs and China for sale in the United States and elsewhere. As a result, U.S. bilateral trade with NICs has increased more than 100 times from $1.8 billion in 1970 to $189 billion in 2004, and that with China more than doubled in four years from $95 billion in 1999 to $231 billion in 2004.[9] Trade statistics, however, do not reveal anything other than the amount of bilateral trade flows between countries. It is false to assume that trade is always a business transaction between independent buyers and sellers across national boundaries. It is equally false to assume that a country's trade deficit in a certain industry equates with the decline in the competitiveness of companies in that industry. For example, Honda's production and sourcing network is presented in Exhibit 10-1. Clearly, an increasing segment of international trade of components and finished

[9]"U.S. International Trade in Goods and Services," Annual Revision for 2004 (U.S. Census Bureau, U.S. Department of Commerce), http://www.census.gov/foreign-trade/Press-Release/2004pr/final_revisions/exh13tl.pdf, accessed December 15, 2005.

products is strongly influenced by MNCs' foreign production and sourcing investment activities.

TRENDS IN GLOBAL SOURCING STRATEGY ◆ ◆ ◆ ◆ ◆ ◆ ◆ ◆ ◆

Over the last 30 years or so, gradual yet significant changes have taken place in global sourcing strategy. The cost-saving justification for international procurement in the 1970s and 1980s was gradually supplanted by quality and reliability concerns in the 1990s. Most of the changes have been in the way business executives think of the scope of global sourcing for their companies and exploit various resultant opportunities as a source of competitive advantage. Peter Drucker, the famed management guru and business historian, once said that sourcing and logistics would remain "the darkest continent of business"—the least exploited area of business for competitive advantage. Naturally, many companies that have a limited scope of global sourcing are at a disadvantage over those that exploit it to their fullest extent in a globally competitive marketplace. Five trends in global sourcing are identified.[10] Exhibit 10-2 shows various factors that affect the scope of global sourcing strategy.

EXHIBIT 10-2
FACTORS THAT AFFECT GLOBAL
SOURCING STRATEGY

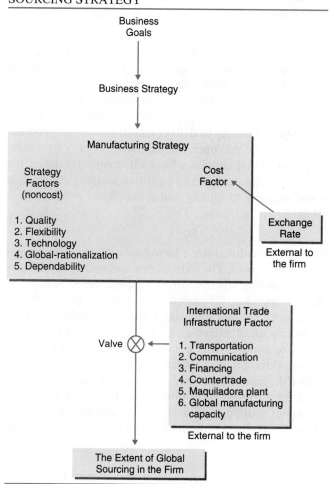

Source: Paul M. Swamidass, "Import Sourcing Dynamics: An Integrative Perspective," *Journal of International Business Studies* (Fourth Quarter 1993), p. 682.

---

[10]This section draws from Paul M. Swamidass, "Import Sourcing Dynamics: An Integrative Perspective," *Journal of International Business Studies,* 24 (Fourth Quarter 1993), pp. 671–91.

Trend 1: The Decline of the Exchange Rate Determinism of Sourcing

Since the mid-1970s, exchange rates have fluctuated rather erratically over time. If a country's currency appreciates, its companies would find it easy to procure components and products from abroad. Contrarily, if the currency depreciates, its companies would find it increasingly difficult to depend on foreign supplies because they have to pay higher prices for every item sourced from abroad. In these scenarios, companies consider the exchange rate determining the extent to which they can engage in foreign sourcing.

However, this exchange rate determinism of sourcing is strictly based on the price factor. Indeed, a recent study shows that exchange rate fluctuations have little impact on the nature of sourcing strategy for crucial components.[11] Foreign sourcing also occurs for noncost reasons such as quality, technology, and so on. First, because it takes time to develop overseas suppliers for noncost purposes, purchasing managers cannot easily drop a foreign supplier when exchange rate changes have an adverse effect on the cost of imported components and products. Second, domestic suppliers are known to increase prices to match rising import prices following exchange rate changes. As a result, switching to a domestic supplier may not ensure cost advantages. Third, many companies are developing long-term relationships with international suppliers whether those suppliers are their subsidiaries or independent contractors. In a long-term supply relationship the parties involved may view exchange rate fluctuations as a temporary problem. Finally, some companies with global operations are able to shift supply locations from one country to another to overcome the adverse effects of exchange rate fluctuations or even developing localized procurement plans to shield their operations completely from exchange rate fluctuations.[12]

Trend 2: New Competitive Environment Caused by Excess Worldwide Capacity

The worldwide growth in the number of manufacturers has added excess production capacity in most industries. The proliferation of manufacturers around the world of less sophisticated, less capital-intensive manufactured products, such as cement, than in more complex, knowledge-intensive products such as computers. Thus, there has been tremendous downward pressure on the prices of many components and products around the world. Although the ability to deliver a high volume of products of satisfactory quality at a reasonable price was once the hallmark of many successful companies, an increasing number of global suppliers have effectively rendered the delivery of volume in an acceptable time no longer a competitive weapon. A strategic shift has occurred from price and quantity to quality and reliability of products as a determinant of competitive strength.[13]

Trend 3: Innovations in and Restructuring of International Trade Infrastructure

Advances in structural elements of international trade have made it easier for companies to employ sourcing for strategic purposes. The innovations and structural changes that have important influences on sourcing strategy are (1) the increased number of purchasing managers experienced in sourcing, (2) improvements in transportation and communication (e.g., fax and Intranet), (3) new financing options, including countertrade (barter that includes all variations of exchange of goods for goods), offering new incentives and opportunities for exports from countries without hard currency, (4) manufacturing facilities diffused throughout the world by globally minded companies, and (5) maquiladora plants (Mexican version of free-trade-zone manufacturing facilities, mostly located close to the U.S.–Mexican border) on the Mexican side of the border providing a unique form of sourcing options to manufacturers operating in the United States. Similarly Hong Kong–based companies may source out of nearby Shenzhen, China.

---

[11]Janet Y. Murray, "A Currency Exchange Rate-Driven vs. Strategy-Driven Analysis of Global Sourcing," *Multinational Business Review,* 4 (Spring 1996), pp. 40–51.

[12]"Manufacturers Reshape Asian Strategies," *Nikkei Weekly,* January 12, 1998, p. 1 and p. 5; and "The World's Most Admired Companies," *Fortune,* October 26, 1998, pp. 206–26.

[13]Martin K. Starr and John E. Ullman, "The Myth of Industrial Supremacy," in *Global Competitiveness,* Martin K. Starr ed. (New York: W. W. Norton and Co., 1988).

During the last 20 years, manufacturers have been under pressure to compete on the basis of improved cost and quality as a growing number of companies adopted just-in-time (JIT) production. JIT production requires close working relationships with component suppliers and places an enormous amount of responsibility on purchasing managers. Furthermore, sourcing directly from foreign suppliers requires greater purchasing know-how and is riskier than other alternatives that use locally based wholesalers and representatives. Locally based representatives are subject to local laws and assume some of the currency risk associated with importing. However, now that purchasing managers are increasingly making long-term commitments to foreign suppliers, direct dealings with suppliers are justified.[14] The finding suggests that purchasing managers are confident about their international know-how and that they may be seeking long-term sourcing arrangements. The key to achieving effective global sourcing is to secure management involvement at both the strategic (top) and the tactical (middle) levels.[15]

Trend 4: Enhanced Role of Purchasing Managers

During the 1980s while U.S. companies continued to locate their operations in various parts of the world, companies from other countries such as Japan, Germany, and Britain expanded the magnitude of their foreign manufacturing operations at a much faster pace. The share of foreign-owned companies in U.S.–based manufacturing activities has increased from 5.2 percent in 1977 to over 20 percent recently. As a global company adds another international plant to its network of existing plants, it creates the need to source components and other semiprocessed goods to and from the new plant to existing plants (see Global Perspective 10-1). Global manufacturing adds enormously to global sourcing activities, either within the same company across national boundaries or between independent suppliers and new plants.

Since the late 1980s, statistical trends have clearly shown that U.S. companies have increased sourcing from abroad regardless of the exchange rate of the U.S. dollar. Their continued sourcing from abroad represents a strategic expansion and rationalization over time. In response to slow productivity growth in the United States relative to other major trading nations in the 1980s, U.S. parent companies' technology had transferred directly to their foreign affiliates for production instead of in the form of equipment and components for local modification in the foreign markets. By the early 1990s, those companies had built an increasingly integrated global manufacturing and delivery structures. Despite the rapid economic and productivity growth at home since the mid-1990s to this day, many companies are increasingly assigning design and other R&D responsibilities to satellite foreign units to design a regional or world product. As a result, foreign affiliates have also developed more independent R&D activities to manufacture products for the U.S. markets in addition to expanding local sales.[16]

For industries such as digital media, global manufacturing is even easier. To curb rising production costs and boost international competitiveness, producers of animated films and video software are increasingly outsourcing part of their production to some Asian countries. According to a Japanese game developer who tied up with a Chinese software firm to outsource part of its work, the cost is only one-fifth that of doing the work in Japan. In *Final Fantasy,* a full-length animated film released in North America in July 2001, some 160 creators from 22 countries cooperated in the three-and-a-half-year production. The production was divided among Tokyo headquarters, a Los Angeles

Trend 5: Trend toward Global Manufacturing

[14]G. Tomas M. Hult, "A Global Learning Organization Structure and Market Information Processing," *Journal of Business Research,* 40 (October 1997), pp. 155–66.

[15]A. Coskin Samli, John M. Browning, and Carolyn Busbia, "The Status of Global Sourcing as a Critical Tool of Strategic Planning: Opportunistic versus Strategic Dichotomy," *Journal of Business Research,* 43 (November 1998), pp. 177–87; and Robert J. Trent and Robert M. Monczka, "Achieving Excellence in Global Sourcing," *Sloan Management Review,* 47 (Fall 2005), pp. 24–32.

[16]Masaaki Kotabe and K. Scott Swan, "Offshore Sourcing: Reaction, Maturation, and Consolidation of U.S. Multinationals," *Journal of International Business Studies,* 25 (First Quarter 1994), pp. 1–27; and Anil K. Gupta and Vijay Govindarajan, "Knowledge Flows within Multinational Corporations," *Strategic Management Journal,* 21 (April 2000), pp. 473–96.

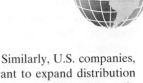

GLOBAL PERSPECTIVE 10-1

TRADE FOLLOWS INVESTMENT

"Trade follows investment in the 1990s.... If you can't invest, you can't trade." As you recall from the Appendix to Chapter 1, the international product cycle argument was used to explain the foreign expansion of many companies in the 1960s to 1980s. It posits that companies tend to engage in exports to similar countries with similar per capita income levels and to invest in foreign production in those "export" markets as they are threatened by local competition there. In other words, trade was generally followed by direct investment. Foreign direct investment was generally considered a *reactive* move for exporters to defend their hard-earned market position in foreign countries by setting up their local operations to better compete with local companies. Then why did the relationship between trade and investment reverse itself in the 1990s? The fundamental reason for such a reversed relationship is that many companies have to act more *proactively* to the ever-increasing tides of global competition. Today, companies do not have the luxury of time to follow the defensive strategic paths described by the international product cycle argument. As mentioned in Chapter 1, we all have to keep in mind what Mark Twain once wrote: "If you stand still, you will get run over." In an era of global competition, companies cannot stay put or satisfied with their current market position domestically as well as internationally. They need to invest and put their production and delivery systems in place in foreign markets much earlier than in the past. If they stood still, they could get "run over" by the onslaught of competitors from many parts of the world.

U.S. Department of Commerce data support that argument. More than 80 percent of all Japanese imports are bought by U.S. affiliates of Japanese multinationals for local production and assembly in the United States. Meanwhile, parts now account for almost half of the value of all Japanese imports, up

from 10 percent in the mid-1980s. Similarly, U.S. companies, such as Motorola and 3M, that want to expand distribution networks in Japan are likely to bring in more U.S.-made components. If there are no U.S. companies abroad, there is not much to pull other U.S. goods into Japan.

It is not only Japanese companies operating in the United States that are sourcing components from Japan; U.S. companies also are procuring components from Japan. Japanese high-tech firms shipped more than $20 billion worth of integrated circuits and other electronic components into the United States. Shipments from Japan-based purchasing offices of U.S. companies made up a hefty chunk of that amount. Companies such as Texas Instruments, Apple Computer, and Digital Equipment now have large purchasing operations in Japan. U.S. companies could no longer rely solely on necessary components either from domestic suppliers or from their in-house production.

A shorter product cycle means that competitive pressure to reduce cost begins immediately after product introduction. Again, there is no luxury of time to watch the international product cycle argument fulfill its prophecy. For example, Russia's economy is a mess, its currency shaky, its government gripped by crisis—a country, it would seem, to avoid at all costs—but the battle for Russia's consumer market has never been fiercer. With the ruble down 75 percent, Russians can no longer afford imported goods, so multinational consumer companies are defending their hard-won market shares by switching from importing to local manufacturing. McDonald's has set up local companies, and its Russian operations have remained profitable despite the currency turmoil. Similarly, Danone, the French food company, has switched from 80 percent of its Russian sales coming from imports to quadrupling its production at one Russian factory while building a new $100 million plant. This local production and delivery have enabled the food giant to lower its costs to keep its prices low for consumers after the ruble crash while solidifying its position in the Russian market for the long haul.

Sources: "The Secret Weapon That Won't Start a Trade War," *Business Week,* March 7, 1994, p. 45; and Carol Matlack, "Betting on a New Label: Made in Russia," *Business Week,* April 12, 1999, p. 122.

subsidiary, and a Hawaiian studio linked by a high-speed Internet network. An Indian company employs some 1,000 animation creators and enables U.S.-based producers to work around the clock by taking advantage of the time difference.[17]

A word of caution should be added to this observation, however. In recent years, exchange rate fluctuations have become increasingly more difficult to predict due to short-term currency speculations sometimes unrelated to economic fundamentals determined by countries' balance of payments positions. Alternatively, as a result, an increasing number of multinational companies have begun to use operational hedging instead of currency hedging (see Chapter 3 for details) by shifting production and

---

[17]"Animation Production Goes Global," *Nikkei Interactive,* http://www.nni.nikkei.co.jp, August 20, 2001.

procurement to, and operating in, a currency area. A **currency area**[18] refers to a group of countries whose currencies tend to fluctuate in tandem, and, therefore, their exchange rates tend to remain relatively stable relative to each other. In other words, those multinational companies procuring materials and components and producing and marketing finished products in a group of countries that constitute a currency area can consider their internal exchange rates as being relatively fixed so that they will not have to worry about exchange rate fluctuations in their sourcing plan. If this trend continues, we will be seeing more regional (i.e., currency area) rather than global procurement and manufacturing operations by manufacturing companies. For example, since the 1997–1998 Asian financial crisis, Japanese companies have increased their regional procurement, manufacturing, and marketing all in a group of Asia-Pacific countries (e.g., Australia, Malaysia, and Singapore) that virtually constitute a currency area.[19]

VALUE CHAIN AND FUNCTIONAL INTERFACES   ◆ ◆ ◆ ◆ ◆ ◆ ◆ ◆ ◆

The design of global sourcing strategy is based on the interplay between a company's competitive advantages and the comparative advantages of various countries. **Competitive advantage** influences the decision regarding what activities and technologies a company should concentrate its investment and managerial resources in relative to those of its competitors in the industry. **Comparative advantage** affects the company's decision on where to source and market, based on the lower cost of labor and other resources in one country relative to another.[20] A company is essentially a collection of activities that are performed to design, procure materials, manufacture, market, deliver, and support its product. This set of interrelated corporate activities is called the **value chain.**

Today, many manufacturing firms increasingly perform only certain activities in the value chain and source components and parts or the final product from suppliers before they market it to their customers. The typical manufacturing firm spends approximately 60 percent of each sales dollar on purchased components, materials, and services from external suppliers.[21] For example, General Motors and Honda struck a deal in which Honda would supply 100,000 Honda-made V-6 engines and transmissions annually to GM for five years.[22] For the Porsche Boxster, the company performs only the tasks of designing, engineering, and marketing activities; the sourcing of components and parts is made from parts suppliers, and Valmet, an engineering firm in Finland performs the final assembly of Boxster.[23] Competing companies constantly strive to create value across various activities in the value chain. Value can be created by performing these activities either at a lower cost or in such a way to offer differentiated products or services or both. Of course, the value that a company creates is ultimately measured by the price buyers are willing to pay for its products. Therefore, the value chain is a useful concept that provides an assessment of the activities that a company performs to design, manufacture, market, deliver, and support its products in the marketplace.

Five continuous and interactive steps are involved in developing a global sourcing strategy along the value chain.

1. Identify the separable links (R&D, manufacturing, and marketing) in the company's value chain.

---

[18]The technical term that economists use is an **optimum currency area.** We simply call it a *currency area* for short. See, for example, James L. Swofford, "Microeconomic Foundations of an Optimal Currency Area," *Review of Financial Economics,* 9(2), 2000, pp.121–28.

[19]"Manufacturers Reshape Asian Strategies," *Nikkei Weekly,* January 12, 1998, pp. 1, 5.

[20]Bruce Kogut, "Designing Global Strategies: Comparative and Competitive Value-Added Chains," *Sloan Management Review,* 26 (Summer 1985), pp. 15–28.

[21]Daniel R. Krause, Mark Pagell, and Sime Curkovic, "Toward a Measure of Competitive Priorities for Purchasing," *Journal of Operations Management,* 19 (2001), pp. 497–512.

[22]"GM and Honda Strike Deal for Engines," *Wall Street Journal,* December 21, 1999, pp. A3, A8.

[23]"Incredible Shrinking Plants," *Economist,* February 23, 2002, pp. 71–73.

2. In the context of those links, determine the location of the company's competitive advantages, considering both economies of scale and scope.

3. Ascertain the level of transaction costs (e.g., cost of negotiation, cost of monitoring activities, and uncertainty resulting from contracts) between links in the value chain, both internal and external, and select the lowest cost mode.

4. Determine the comparative advantages of countries (including the company's home country) relative to each link in the value chain and to the relevant transaction costs.

5. Develop adequate flexibility in corporate decision making and organizational design to permit the company to respond to changes in both its competitive advantages and the comparative advantages of countries.[24]

In this section, we focus on the three most important interrelated activities in the value chain: R&D (i.e., technology development, product design, and engineering), manufacturing, and marketing activities. Management of the interfaces, or linkages, among these value-adding activities is a crucial determinant of a company's competitive advantage. See Exhibit 10-3 for an outline of a basic framework of management of R&D, manufacturing, and marketing interfaces. Undoubtedly, these value-adding activities should be examined as holistically as possible by linking the boundaries of these primary activities. Thus, global sourcing strategy encompasses management of the (1) interfaces among R&D, manufacturing, and marketing on a global basis and (2) logistics identifying which production units will serve which particular markets and how components will be supplied for production. As presented in Global Perspective 10-2, linking R&D and manufacturing with marketing provides enormous direct and indirect benefits to companies operating in a highly competitive environment.

R&D/ Manufacturing Interface

Technology is broadly defined as know-how. It can be classified based on the nature of know-how composed of product technology (the set of ideas embodied in the product) and process technology (the set of ideas involved in the manufacture of the product or the steps necessary to combine new materials to produce a finished product). However, executives tend to focus solely on product-related technology as the driving force of the company's competitiveness. Product technology alone may not provide the company a long-term competitive edge over competition unless it is matched with sufficient manufacturing capabilities.[25]

EXHIBIT 10-3
INTERFACES AMONG R&D, MANUFACTURING, AND MARKETING

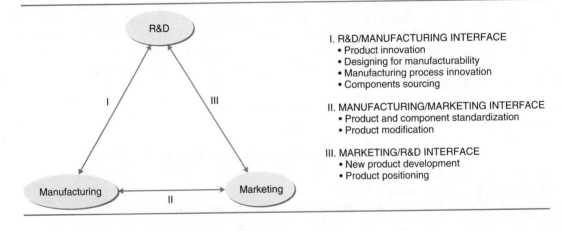

I. R&D/MANUFACTURING INTERFACE
- Product innovation
- Designing for manufacturability
- Manufacturing process innovation
- Components sourcing

II. MANUFACTURING/MARKETING INTERFACE
- Product and component standardization
- Product modification

III. MARKETING/R&D INTERFACE
- New product development
- Product positioning

[24]Richard D. Robinson, ed., *Direct Foreign Investment: Costs and Benefits* (New York: Praeger Publishers, 1987).

[25]Bruce R. Guile and Harvey Brooks, ed., *Technology and Global Industry: Companies and Nations in the World Economy* (Washington, DC: National Academy Press, 1987).

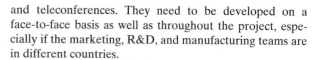

$\mathcal{G}$LOBAL PERSPECTIVE 10-2

POWER OF GOOD LINKAGE MANAGEMENT

In today's world of global competition and high-speed product development, linkage among R&D, manufacturing, and marketing is more vital to successful business than ever before. Delivering a competitive product to the market at the right time with the right specifications and feature benefits, all at a manufacturing cost that allows for profit is one tough assignment. Add to this the global complexity of marketing, R&D, and manufacturing not being colocated in the same place, competing in an environment where world-class product development time is under 50 weeks, and you have a challenge that few companies are dealing with appropriately today.

International marketing executives can no longer have the luxury of time to consider R&D and manufacturing as activities remotely related and remotely relevant to them. They have to deal with all of this complexity and be fully aware that without adequately understanding the linkages necessary among R&D, manufacturing, and marketing, their businesses run a very high risk of failure.

John A. Bermingham, who has served as executive vice president at Sony Corporation of America, president and CEO of AT&T Smart Cards Systems, and most recently as president and CEO of Rolodex Corporation, has a keen appreciation of how important and beneficial it is to manage linkages among R&D, manufacturing, and marketing activities on a global basis. He offers the following advice:

> When marketing determines a product need, the very first thing that marketing managers must do is to bring R&D and manufacturing together to establish a powerful linkage for the duration of the project. Marketing should also include finance, sales, and operations in this project, but the key linkage for the purpose of the product development is among marketing, R&D, and manufacturing.

According to Bermingham, good linkage management has many benefits for these teams:

- A powerful linkage develops the requisite personal/business relationship needed among the three groups that allows for the understanding and empathy for each other's responsibilities. These relationships cannot be fostered via faxes

Source: John A. Bermingham, "Executive Insights: Roles of R&D and Manufacturing in Global Marketing Management," *Journal of International Marketing,* 4 (4), 1996, pp. 75–84.

and teleconferences. They need to be developed on a face-to-face basis as well as throughout the project, especially if the marketing, R&D, and manufacturing teams are in different countries.

- A powerful linkage is necessary to ensure that issues are on top of the table at the beginning of the project and as they develop throughout the project. Marketing must ensure that R&D and manufacturing are aware of the marketing strategy, competitive environment, and global implications. Any situations arising during the project must be discussed openly and positively with mutual understanding and with decisions being made to minimize impairment to the project and with full understanding among the teams.

- A powerful linkage allows for speed. When you consider that world-class product development time is less than 50 weeks—some say it will be less than 40 weeks in the not too distant future—a powerful linkage is imperative. Teams must be working a series parallel effort. Some things have to happen before others, but others can be accomplished simultaneously. Only linkage makes this possible.

- A powerful linkage develops a high sense of urgency. Teams really begin to understand how important speed is in this type of environment when they get beyond understanding their own needs and problems and begin to understand the needs and problems of the other linked teams. Hence, urgency surrounds everything that these linked teams set out to accomplish. They see their linkage to the others and want to meet the needs of the entire team.

- A powerful linkage fosters mutual ownership individually and collectively. It is very important that there be individual ownership in the project, but it is just as important that the teams understand and accept collective ownership in the project. A tight linkage across the teams develops this collective ownership.

- A powerful linkage develops a true team environment that is essential and obligatory for success. Therefore, one of the most important roles for today and for the future for R&D and manufacturing in global marketing management is to ensure that these powerful linkages are established and strengthened.

Consider the automobile industry as an example. R&D is critical today for automakers because manufacturers are under tremendous pressure to provide more innovative products. Customers continue to raise the bar with respect to styling, quality, reliability, and safety. At the same time, manufacturers face difficult technical challenges on the energy and environmental front. They must make continual improvements in vehicle fuel economy and reductions in tailpipe emissions everywhere in the world. Although more improvement can be squeezed out of the conventional internal combustion engine, manufacturers are looking ahead to hybrid vehicle technology and, ultimately, to a hydrogen-based fuel cell vehicle. The development costs and infrastructure changes necessary to take the step to fuel cell technology are staggering, so it makes sense for auto manufacturers to team up and share knowledge to move the industry as a whole ahead faster.

To reduce the R&D costs, General Motors is working with its alliance partners on more than 50 joint-technology development projects ranging from pedestrian protection and 42-volt electrical architecture to all-wheel drive and clean diesel engines. Besides cooperating with other manufacturers, GM has formed research partnerships with suppliers, universities, and governmental agencies. These research alliances cover such areas as advanced internal combustion engine development, fuel cell technology, advanced chassis systems, and electronics and communications systems. They are truly global, involving companies and universities in Canada, Europe, Japan, China, and the Middle East.

By pulling together the talents and resources from this global R&D network, GM has been able to reduce redundancy, accelerate ongoing development, and jump-start new development. Of course, to launch such collaboration successfully requires that the companies involved overcome differences in culture, language, business practices, engineering, and manufacturing approaches.[26] This example suggests that manufacturing processes should also be innovative. To facilitate the transferability of new product innovations to manufacturing, a team of product designers and engineers should strive to design components so that they are conducive to manufacturing without the requirement of undue retooling. Low levels of retooling requirements and interchangeability of components are necessary conditions for efficient sourcing strategy on a global scale. If different equipment and components are used in various manufacturing plants, it is extremely difficult to establish a highly coordinated sourcing plan on a global basis.

| **Manufacturing/Marketing Interface** | A continual conflict exists between manufacturing and marketing divisions. It is to the manufacturing division's advantage if all products and components are standardized to facilitate standardized, low-cost production. The marketing division, however, is more interested in satisfying the diverse needs of customers, requiring broad product lines and frequent product modifications, which add cost to manufacturing. How have successful companies coped with this dilemma? |

Recently, an increasing amount of interest has been shown in the strategic linkages between product policy and manufacturing, long ignored in traditional considerations of global strategy development. With aggressive competition from multinational companies emphasizing corporate product policy and concomitant manufacturing, many companies have realized that product innovations alone cannot sustain their long-term competitive position without an effective product policy linking product and manufacturing process innovations. The strategic issue, then, is how to design a robust product or components with sufficient versatility built in across uses, technology, and situations.[27]

Four different ways of developing a global product policy are generally considered an effective means to streamline manufacturing, thus lowering manufacturing cost, without sacrificing marketing flexibility: (1) core components standardization, (2) product design families, (3) universal product with all features, and (4) universal product with different positioning.[28]

---

[26]Larry J. Howell and Jamie C. Hsu, "Globalization within the Auto Industry," *Research Technology Management,* 45 (July/August 2002), pp. 43–49.

[27]K. Scott Swan, Masaaki Kotabe, and Brent Allred, "Exploring Robust Design Capabilities, Their Role in Creating Global Products, and Their Relationship to Firm Performance," *Journal of Product Innovation Management,* 22 (March 2005), pp. 144–64.

[28]Hirotaka Takeuchi and Michael E. Porter, "Three Roles of International Marketing in Global Strategy," in *Competition in Global Industries,* ed. Michael E. Porter, (Boston, MA: Harvard Business School Press, 1986), pp. 111–46.

THE WORLD AT A GLANCE

CONTENTS

Maps from Goode's World Atlas used with permission, © by Rand McNally, 2000

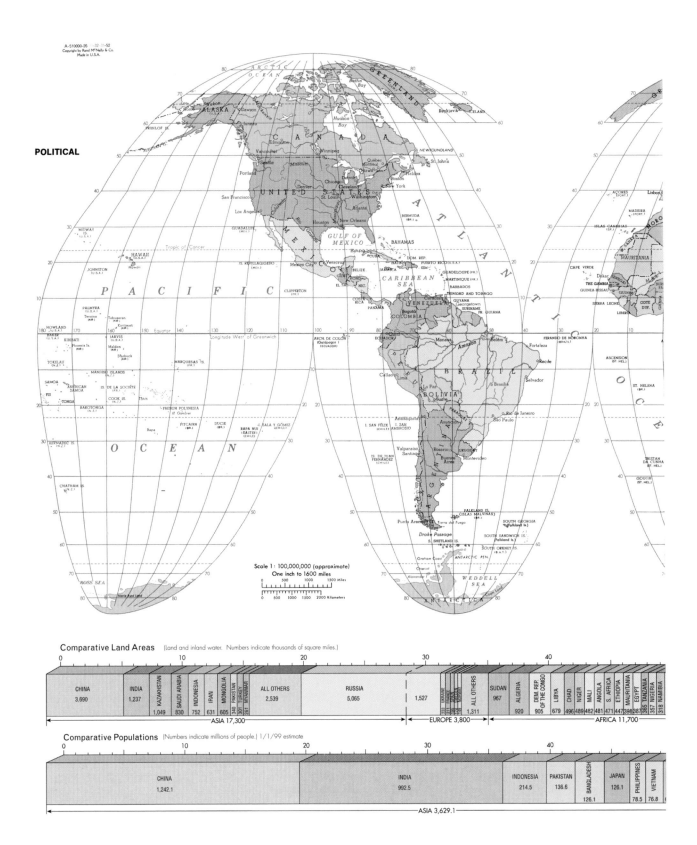

POLITICAL

Scale 1 : 100,000,000 (approximate)
One inch to 1600 miles

0   500   1000   1500 Miles

0   500 1000 1500 2000 Kilometers

Comparative Land Areas (land and inland water. Numbers indicate thousands of square miles.)

CHINA 3,690 | INDIA 1,237 | KAZAKHSTAN 1,049 | SAUDI ARABIA 830 | INDONESIA 752 | IRAN 631 | MONGOLIA 605 | PAKISTAN 340 | TURKEY 301 | MYANMAR 261 | ALL OTHERS 2,539 | RUSSIA 5,065 | 1,527 | UKRAINE / FRANCE / SPAIN / SWEDEN | ALL OTHERS 1,311 | SUDAN 967 | ALGERIA 920 | DEM REP OF THE CONGO 905 | LIBYA 679 | CHAD 496 | NIGER 489 | MALI 482 | ANGOLA 481 | S. AFRICA 471 | ETHIOPIA 447 | MAURITANIA 398 | EGYPT 387 | TANZANIA 365 | NIGERIA 357 | NAMIBIA 318

←————— ASIA 17,300 —————→   ←—EUROPE 3,800—→   AFRICA 11,700

Comparative Populations (Numbers indicate millions of people.) 1/1/99 estimate

CHINA 1,242.1	INDIA 992.5	INDONESIA 214.5	PAKISTAN 136.6	BANGLADESH 126.1	JAPAN 126.1	PHILIPPINES 78.5	VIETNAM 76.8

←————————————— ASIA 3,629.1 —————————————→

A-510000-26   32-11-52
Copyright by Rand McNally & Co.
Made in U.S.A.

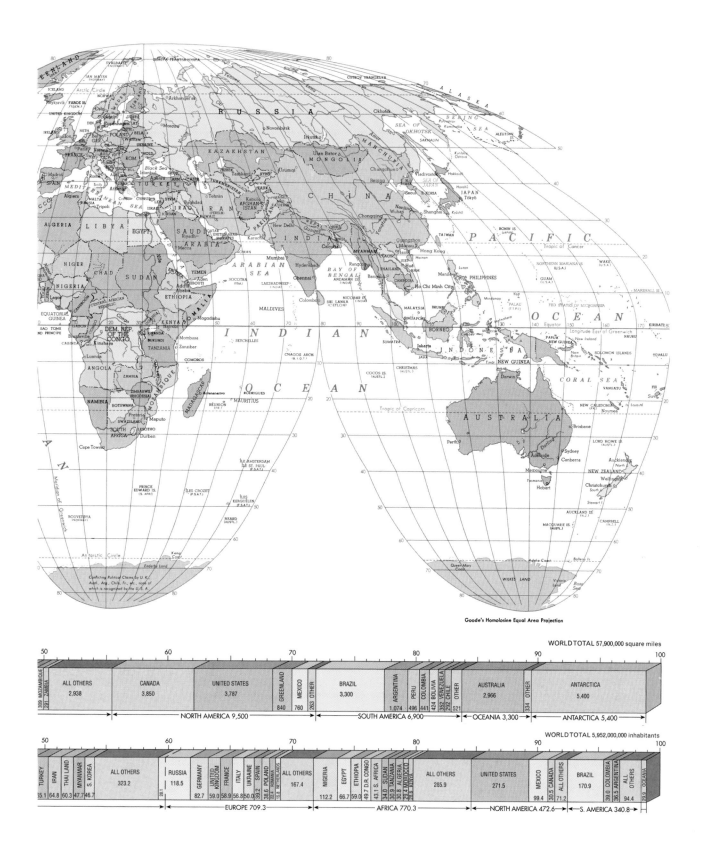

Goode's Homolosine Equal Area Projection

WORLD TOTAL 57,900,000 square miles

	50	60	70	80	90	100

MOZAMBIQUE 309 | ZAMBIA 281 | ALL OTHERS 2,938 | CANADA 3,850 | UNITED STATES 3,787 | GREENLAND 840 | MEXICO 760 | 263 | BRAZIL 3,300 | ARGENTINA 1,074 | PERU 496 | BOLIVIA 424 | VENEZUELA 352 | CHILE 292 | OTHER 521 | AUSTRALIA 2,966 | OTHER 334 | ANTARCTICA 5,400

←——————— NORTH AMERICA 9,500 ———————→ ←——— SOUTH AMERICA 6,900 ———→ ←— OCEANIA 3,300 —→ ←— ANTARCTICA 5,400 —→

WORLD TOTAL 5,952,000,000 inhabitants

	50	60	70	80	90	100

TURKEY 65.1 | IRAN 64.8 | THAILAND 60.3 | MYANMAR 47.7 | S. KOREA 46.7 | ALL OTHERS 323.2 | 28.1 | RUSSIA 118.5 | GERMANY 82.7 | UNITED KINGDOM 59.0 | FRANCE 58.9 | ITALY 56.8 | UKRAINE 50.0 | SPAIN 39.2 | POLAND 38.6 | 22.4 NETHERLANDS 15.6 | ALL OTHERS 167.4 | NIGERIA 112.2 | EGYPT 66.7 | ETHIOPIA 59.0 | D.R. CONGO 49.7 | S. AFRICA 43.1 | SUDAN 34.0 | TANZANIA 30.8 | ALGERIA 30.9 | MOROCCO 29.4 | KENYA 28.5 | ALL OTHERS 285.9 | UNITED STATES 271.5 | MEXICO 99.4 | CANADA 30.5 | ALL OTHERS 71.2 | BRAZIL 170.9 | COLOMBIA 39.0 | ARGENTINA 36.5 | ALL OTHERS 94.4 | OCEANIA 29.9

←——————— EUROPE 709.3 ———————→ ←——— AFRICA 770.3 ———→ ←— NORTH AMERICA 472.6 —→ ←— S. AMERICA 340.8 —→

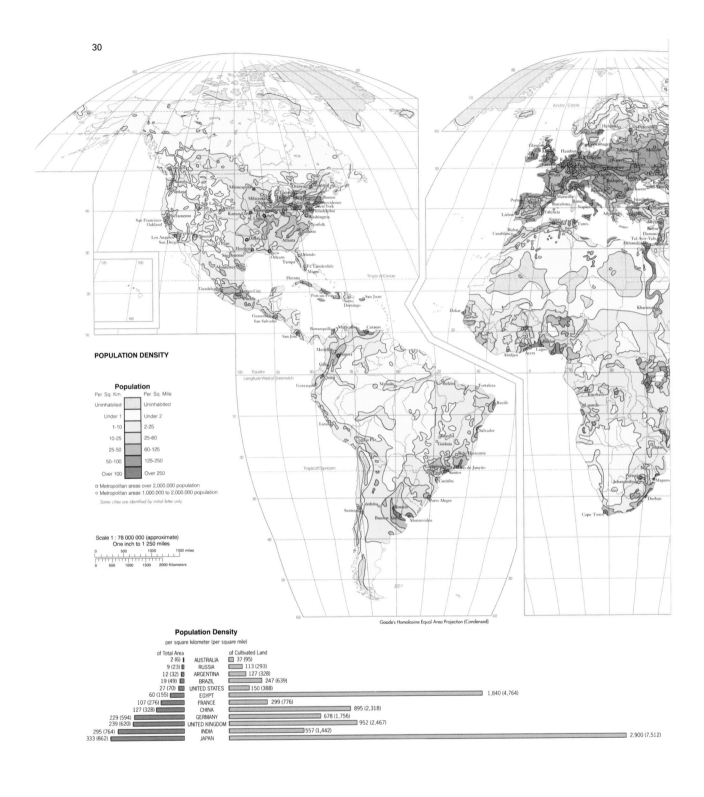

POPULATION DENSITY

Population

Per. Sq. Km.		Per. Sq. Mile
Uninhabited		Uninhabited
Under 1		Under 2
1-10		2-25
10-25		25-60
25-50		60-125
50-100		125-250
Over 100		Over 250

□ Metropolitan areas over 2,000,000 population
○ Metropolitan areas 1,000,000 to 2,000,000 population

Some cities are identified by initial letter only.

Scale 1 : 78 000 000 (approximate)
One inch to 1 250 miles

Goode's Homolosine Equal Area Projection (Condensed)

Population Density

per square kilometer (per square mile)

of Total Area		of Cultivated Land
2 (6)	AUSTRALIA	37 (95)
9 (23)	RUSSIA	113 (293)
12 (32)	ARGENTINA	127 (328)
19 (49)	BRAZIL	247 (639)
27 (70)	UNITED STATES	150 (388)
60 (155)	EGYPT	1,840 (4,764)
107 (276)	FRANCE	299 (776)
127 (328)	CHINA	895 (2,318)
229 (594)	GERMANY	678 (1,756)
239 (620)	UNITED KINGDOM	952 (2,467)
295 (764)	INDIA	557 (1,442)
333 (862)	JAPAN	2,900 (7,512)

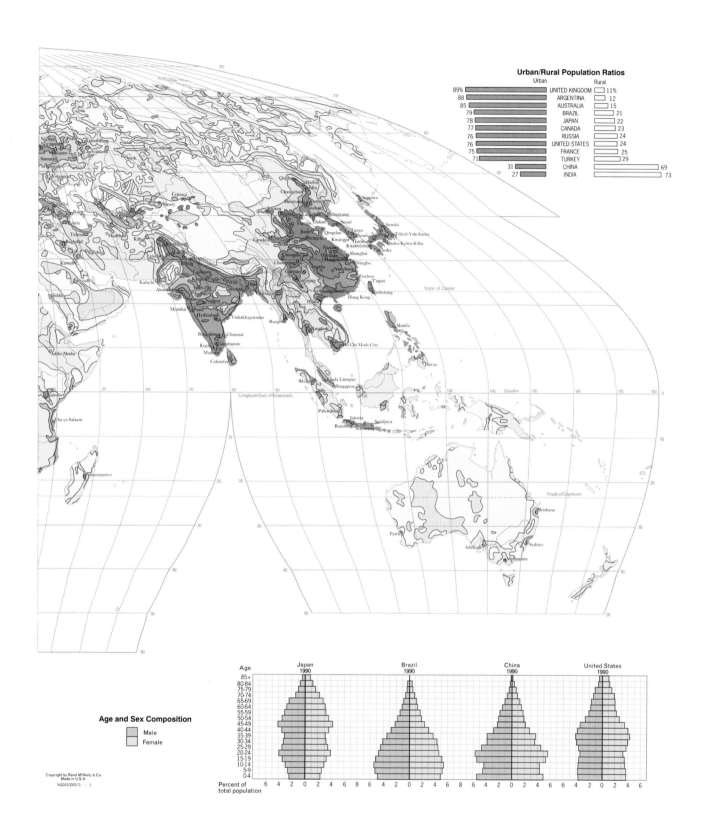

Urban/Rural Population Ratios

Urban		Rural
89%	UNITED KINGDOM	11%
88	ARGENTINA	12
85	AUSTRALIA	15
79	BRAZIL	21
78	JAPAN	22
77	CANADA	23
76	RUSSIA	24
76	UNITED STATES	24
75	FRANCE	25
71	TURKEY	29
31	CHINA	69
27	INDIA	73

Age and Sex Composition

☐ Male
☐ Female

Copyright by Rand McNally & Co.
Made in U.S.A.

NGDS10000-TL· · · ·1

M-5

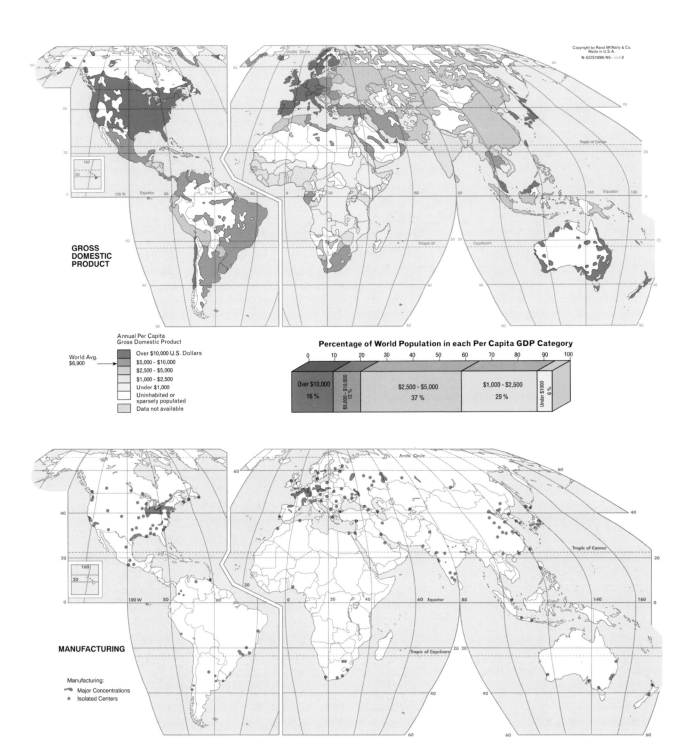

GROSS
DOMESTIC
PRODUCT

**Annual Per Capita
Gross Domestic Product**

World Avg.
$6,900

Over $10,000 U.S. Dollars
$5,000 - $10,000
$2,500 - $5,000
$1,000 - $2,500
Under $1,000
Uninhabited or
sparsely populated
Data not available

Percentage of World Population in each Per Capita GDP Category

| Over $10,000 16% | $5,000 - $10,000 12% | $2,500 - $5,000 37% | $1,000 - $2,500 29% | Under $1000 6% |

MANUFACTURING

Manufacturing:
Major Concentrations
Isolated Centers

Copyright by Rand McNally & Co.
Made in U.S.A.
N-GDS10000-N5- -:/-/-2

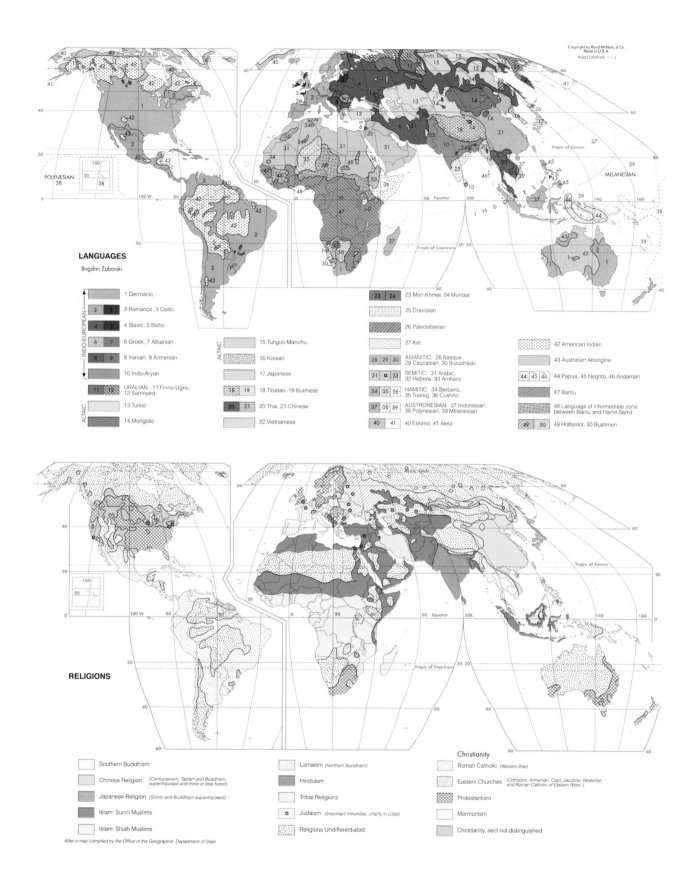

LANGUAGES

Bogdan Zaborski

INDO-EUROPEAN

- 1 Germanic
- 2 Romance, 3 Celtic
- 4 Slavic, 5 Baltic
- 6 Greek, 7 Albanian
- 8 Iranian, 9 Armenian
- 10 Indo-Aryan

URALIAN: 11 Finno-Ugric, 12 Samoyed

ALTAIC

- 13 Turkic
- 14 Mongolic
- 15 Tungus-Manchu
- 16 Korean
- 17 Japanese
- 18 Tibetan, 19 Burmese
- 20 Thai, 21 Chinese
- 22 Vietnamese

- 23 Mon-Khmer, 24 Mundar
- 25 Dravidian
- 26 Paleosiberian
- 27 Ket
- ASIANITIC: 28 Basque, 29 Caucasian, 30 Burushaski
- SEMITIC: 31 Arabic, 32 Hebrew, 33 Amharic
- HAMITIC: 34 Berberic, 35 Tuareg, 36 Cushitic
- AUSTRONESIAN: 37 Indonesian, 38 Polynesian, 39 Melanesian
- 40 Eskimo, 41 Aleut

- 42 American Indian
- 43 Australian Aborigine
- 44 Papua, 45 Negrito, 46 Andaman
- 47 Bantu
- 48 Language of intermediate zone between Bantu and Hamit-Semit
- 49 Hottentot, 50 Bushmen

POLYNESIAN 38

MELANESIAN

RELIGIONS

- Southern Buddhism
- Chinese Religion (Confucianism, Taoism and Buddhism, superimposed and more or less fused)
- Japanese Religion (Shinto and Buddhism superimposed)
- Islam: Sunni Muslims
- Islam: Shiah Muslims
- Lamaism (Northern Buddhism)
- Hinduism
- Tribal Religions
- ✿ Judaism (Important minorities, chiefly in cities)
- Religions Undifferentiated

Christianity
- Roman Catholic (Western Rite)
- Eastern Churches (Orthodox, Armenian, Copt, Jacobite, Nestorian and Roman Catholic of Eastern Rites.)
- Protestantism
- Mormonism
- Christianity, sect not distinguished

After a map compiled by the Office of the Geographer, Department of State

Copyright by Rand McNally & Co.
Made in U.S.A.
N GD510000 V5

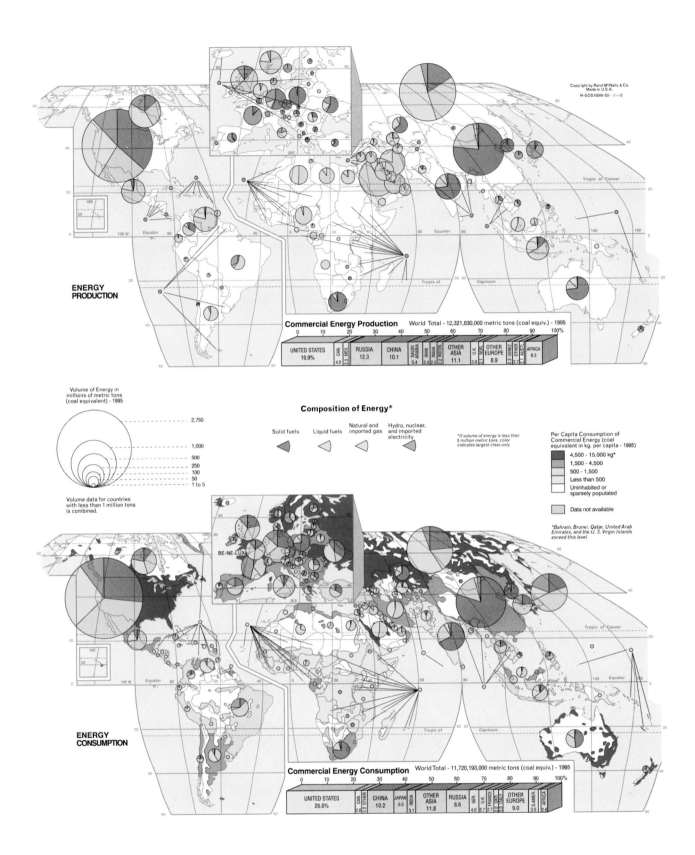

ENERGY
PRODUCTION

Copyright by Rand McNally & Co.
Made in U.S.A.
N-GDS10000-S2- -?-?-?

Commercial Energy Production   World Total - 12,321,830,000 metric tons (coal equiv.) - 1995

0	10	20	30	40	50	60	70	80	90	100%

| UNITED STATES 19.9% | CAN. 4.0 | MEX. 2.3 | RUSSIA 12.3 | CHINA 10.1 | SAUDI ARABIA 5.4 | IRAN 2.6 | INDIA 2.3 | OTHER ASIA 11.1 | U.K. 3.0 | OTHER EUROPE 8.9 | VENEZ. 2.3 | OTHER 2.7 | AUST. | AFRICA 6.3 |

Volume of Energy in
millions of metric tons
(coal equivalent) - 1995

— 2,750
— 1,000
— 500
— 250
— 100
— 50
— 1 to 5

Volume data for countries
with less than 1 million tons
is combined.

Composition of Energy*

Solid fuels   Liquid fuels   Natural and imported gas   Hydro, nuclear, and imported electricity

*If volume of energy is less than
5 million metric tons, color
indicates largest class only.

Per Capita Consumption of
Commercial Energy (coal
equivalent in kg. per capita - 1995)

4,500 - 15,000 kg*
1,500 - 4,500
500 - 1,500
Less than 500
Uninhabited or
sparsely populated

Data not available

*Bahrain, Brunei, Qatar, United Arab
Emirates, and the U. S. Virgin Islands
exceed this level.

BE-NE-LUX

ENERGY
CONSUMPTION

Commercial Energy Consumption   World Total - 11,720,193,000 metric tons (coal equiv.) - 1995

0	10	20	30	40	50	60	70	80	90	100%

| UNITED STATES 26.0% | CAN. 2.8 | OTHER 2.2 | CHINA 10.2 | JAPAN 5.5 | INDIA 3.1 | OTHER ASIA 11.8 | RUSSIA 8.6 | GER. 4.0 | U.K. 2.7 | FRANCE 2.7 | OTHER EUROPE 9.0 | S. AMER. 3.5 | AFRICA 2.6 |

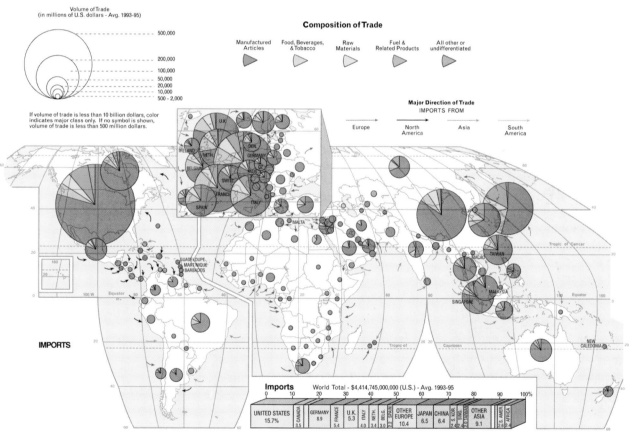

Major Direction of Trade
EXPORTS TO

Europe → North America → Asia → South America

Copyright by Rand McNally & Co.
Made in U.S.A.
N-GDS10000-O3- -:-:-2

EXPORTS

Exports World Total - $4,359,335,000,000 (U.S.) - Avg. 1993-95

0	10	20	30	40	50	60	70	80	90	100%						

| UNITED STATES 12.0% | CANADA 3.9 | GERMANY 10.2 | FRANCE 5.6 | U.K. 4.8 | ITALY 4.5 | NETH. 3.8 | BELG. 3.3 | OTHER EUROPE 12.2 | JAPAN 9.3 | CHINA 6.3 | S. KOR 2.3 | TAIWAN 2.2 | SING. 2 | OTHER ASIA 8.5 | S. AMER. 2.2 | AFRICA 2.2 |

Volume of Trade
(in millions of U.S. dollars - Avg. 1993-95)

	500,000
	200,000
	100,000
	50,000
	20,000
	10,000
	500 - 2,000

If volume of trade is less than 10 billion dollars, color
indicates major class only. If no symbol is shown,
volume of trade is less than 500 million dollars.

Composition of Trade

Manufactured Articles   Food, Beverages, & Tobacco   Raw Materials   Fuel & Related Products   All other or undifferentiated

Major Direction of Trade
IMPORTS FROM

Europe → North America → Asia → South America

IMPORTS

Imports World Total - $4,414,745,000,000 (U.S.) - Avg. 1993-95

0	10	20	30	40	50	60	70	80	90	100%	

| UNITED STATES 15.7% | CANADA 3.5 | GERMANY 8.9 | FRANCE 5.4 | U.K. 5.3 | ITALY 4.0 | NETH. 3.4 | BELG. 3.0 | SPAIN 2.2 | OTHER EUROPE 10.4 | JAPAN 6.5 | CHINA 6.4 | S. KOR 2.42 | SING. 2.5 | TAIWAN 2 | OTHER ASIA 9.1 | S. AMER. 2.6 | AFRICA 2.4 |

M-9

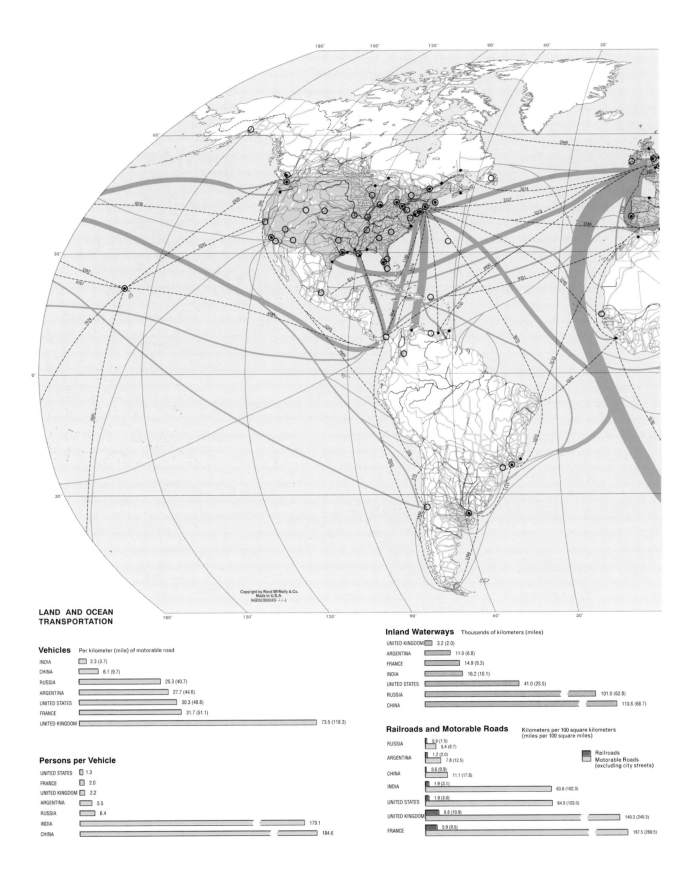

LAND AND OCEAN TRANSPORTATION

Vehicles Per kilometer (mile) of motorable road

INDIA	2.3 (3.7)
CHINA	6.1 (9.7)
RUSSIA	25.3 (40.7)
ARGENTINA	27.7 (44.6)
UNITED STATES	30.3 (48.8)
FRANCE	31.7 (51.1)
UNITED KINGDOM	73.5 (118.3)

Persons per Vehicle

UNITED STATES	1.3
FRANCE	2.0
UNITED KINGDOM	2.2
ARGENTINA	5.5
RUSSIA	6.4
INDIA	179.1
CHINA	184.6

Inland Waterways Thousands of kilometers (miles)

UNITED KINGDOM	3.2 (2.0)
ARGENTINA	11.0 (6.8)
FRANCE	14.9 (9.3)
INDIA	16.2 (10.1)
UNITED STATES	41.0 (25.5)
RUSSIA	101.0 (62.8)
CHINA	110.6 (68.7)

Railroads and Motorable Roads Kilometers per 100 square kilometers (miles per 100 square miles)

Railroads
Motorable Roads (excluding city streets)

	Railroads	Motorable Roads
RUSSIA	0.9 (1.5)	5.4 (8.7)
ARGENTINA	1.2 (2.0)	7.8 (12.5)
CHINA	0.6 (0.9)	11.1 (17.8)
INDIA	1.9 (3.1)	63.6 (102.3)
UNITED STATES	1.9 (3.0)	64.0 (103.0)
UNITED KINGDOM	6.8 (10.9)	149.3 (240.3)
FRANCE	5.9 (9.5)	167.5 (269.5)

Copyright by Rand McNally & Co.
Made in U.S.A.
NGDS1000043

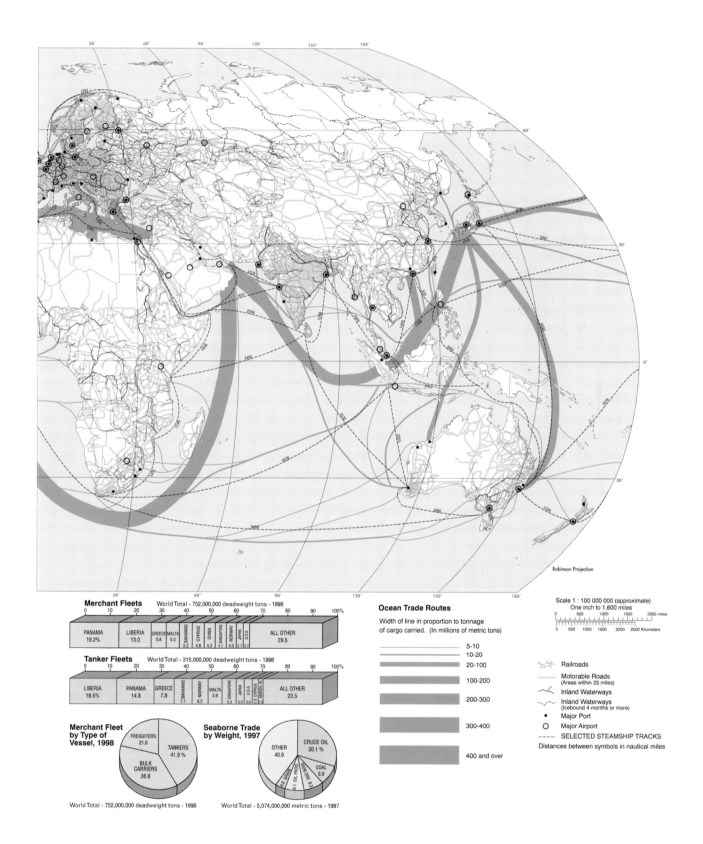

Merchant Fleets World Total - 752,000,000 deadweight tons - 1998

0	10	20	30	40	50	60	70	80	90	100%

| PANAMA 19.2% | LIBERIA 13.0 | GREECE 5.8 | MALTA 5.3 | BAHAMAS 5.2 | CYPRUS 4.8 | CHINA 4.3 | SINGAPORE 4.1 | NORWAY 4.0 | JAPAN 2.7 | U.S.A. 2.2 | ALL OTHER 29.5 |

Tanker Fleets World Total - 315,000,000 deadweight tons - 1998

0	10	20	30	40	50	60	70	80	90	100%

| LIBERIA 18.5% | PANAMA 14.8 | GREECE 7.8 | BAHAMAS 7.1 | NORWAY 6.2 | MALTA 5.9 | SINGAPORE 5.3 | JAPAN 3.3 | U.S.A. 3.3 | CYPRUS 3.0 | MARSHALL IS. 2.2 | ALL OTHER 23.5 |

Merchant Fleet by Type of Vessel, 1998

FREIGHTERS 21.0
TANKERS 41.9 %
BULK CARRIERS 36.8

World Total - 752,000,000 deadweight tons - 1998

Seaborne Trade by Weight, 1997

OTHER 40.6
CRUDE OIL 30.1 %
COAL 8.9
IRON ORE 8.3
OIL PROD. 8.1
GRAIN 4.0

World Total - 5,074,000,000 metric tons - 1997

Ocean Trade Routes

Width of line in proportion to tonnage of cargo carried. (In millions of metric tons)

5-10
10-20
20-100
100-200
200-300
300-400
400 and over

Scale 1 : 100 000 000 (approximate)
One inch to 1,600 miles

| 0 | 500 | 1000 | 1500 | 2000 miles |
| 0 | 500 | 1000 | 1500 | 2000 | 2500 Kilometers |

Railroads

Motorable Roads
(Areas within 25 miles)

Inland Waterways

Inland Waterways
(Icebound 4 months or more)

• Major Port

○ Major Airport

- - - - SELECTED STEAMSHIP TRACKS

Distances between symbols in nautical miles

Robinson Projection

M-11

POPULATION

Note: Size of each country is proportional to population.

Tints indicate rate of natural increase.

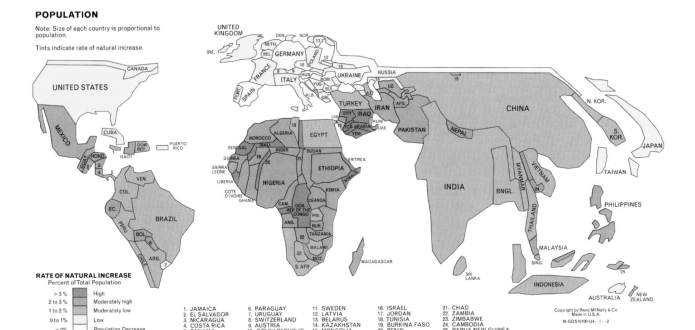

RATE OF NATURAL INCREASE
Percent of Total Population

> 3 %	High
2 to 3 %	Moderately high
1 to 2 %	Moderately low
0 to 1%	Low
< 0%	Population Decrease

1. JAMAICA
2. EL SALVADOR
3. NICARAGUA
4. COSTA RICA
5. PANAMA

6. PARAGUAY
7. URUGUAY
8. SWITZERLAND
9. AUSTRIA
10. CZECH REPUBLIC

11. SWEDEN
12. LATVIA
13. BELARUS
14. KAZAKHSTAN
15. MONGOLIA

16. ISRAEL
17. JORDAN
18. TUNISIA
19. BURKINA FASO
20. BENIN

21. CHAD
22. ZAMBIA
23. ZIMBABWE
24. CAMBODIA
25. PAPUA NEW GUINEA

Copyright by Rand McNally & Co.
Made in U.S.A.
N-GDS10100-U4- -2- -2

Core Components Standardization. Successful global product policy mandates the development of universal products, or products that require no more than a cosmetic change for adaptation to different local needs and use conditions. A few examples illustrate the point. Seiko, a Japanese watchmaker, offers a wide range of designs and models, but they are based on only a handful of different operating mechanisms. Similarly, the best-performing German machine tool-making companies have a narrower range of products, use up to 50 percent fewer parts than their less successful rivals, and make continual, incremental product and design improvements with new developments passed rapidly on to customers.

Product Design Families. A variant of core components standardization involves product design families. It is also possible for companies marketing an extremely wide range of products due to cultural differences in product use patterns around the world, to reap economies of scale benefits. For example, Toyota offers several car models based on a similar family design concept, ranging from Lexus models to Toyota Avalons, Camrys, and Corollas. Many of the Lexus features well received by customers have been adopted into the Toyota lines with just a few minor modifications (mostly downsizing). In the process, Toyota has been able to cut product development costs and meet the needs of different market segments. Similarly, Electrolux, a Swedish appliance manufacturer, has adopted the concept of "design families," offering different products under four different brand names but using the same basic designs. A key to such product design standardization lies in standardizing components, including motors, pumps, and compressors. Thus, two Electrolux subsidiaries, White Consolidated in the United States and Zanussi in Italy, have the main responsibility for components production within the group for worldwide application.

Universal Product with All Features. As just noted, competitive advantage can result from standardization of core components and/or product design families. One variant of components and product standardization is to develop a universal product with all features demanded anywhere in the world. Japan's Canon has done so successfully with its AE-1 and newer model cameras. After extensive market analyses around the world, Canon identified a set of common features customers wanted in a camera, including good picture quality, ease of operation with automatic features, technical sophistication, professional look, and reasonable price. To develop such cameras, the company introduced a few breakthroughs in camera design and manufacturing, such as an electronic integrated circuitry brain to control camera operations, modularized production, and standardization and reduction of parts.

Universal Product with Different Positioning. Alternatively, a universal product can be developed with different market segments in mind. Thus, a universal product can be positioned differently in different markets. This is where marketing promotion plays a major role in accomplishing such a feat. Product and/or components standardization, however, does not necessarily imply either production standardization or a narrow product line. For example, Japanese automobile manufacturers have gradually stretched out their product-line offerings while marketing them with little adaptation in many parts of the world. This strategy requires manufacturing flexibility. The crux of global product or component standardization calls instead for proactive identification of homogeneous segments around the world and is different from the concept of marketing a product originally developed for the home market abroad. A proactive approach to product policy has gained momentum in recent years as it is made possible by intermarket segmentation.[29] In addition to clustering countries and identifying homogeneous segments in different countries, targeting different segments in different countries with the same products is another way to maintain a product policy of standardization.

---

[29]Theodore Levitt, "The Globalization of Markets," *Harvard Business Review,* 61 (May–June 1983), pp. 92–102.

For example, Honda marketed almost identical Accord cars around the world by positioning them differently in the minds of consumers from country to country. Accord has been promoted as a family sedan in Japan, a relatively inexpensive sports car in Germany, and a reliable commuter car in the United States. In recent years, however, Honda has begun developing some regional variations of the Accord. Through a flexible global platform, Honda now offers Accords of different widths, heights, and lengths in the United States, Europe, and Japan. In addition, from the same platform, a minivan, a sport utility vehicle (SUV), and two Acura luxury cars have been developed. From a practical standpoint, the platform is the most expensive and time-consuming component to develop. The global platform allows Honda to reduce the costs of bringing the three distinct Accords to market by 20 percent, resulting in a $1,200 savings per car. Honda clearly adheres to a policy of core component standardization so that at least 50 percent of the components, including the chassis and transmission, are shared across the variations of the Accord.[30]

Marketing/R&D Interface

Both R&D and manufacturing activities are technically outside the marketing manager's responsibility. However, the marketing manager's knowledge of consumers' needs is indispensable in product development. Without a good understanding of the consumers' needs, product designers and engineers are prone to impose their technical specifications on the product rather than fitting them to what consumers want. After all, consumers, not product designers or engineers, have the final say in deciding whether or not to buy the product.

Japanese companies, in particular, excel in management of the marketing/R&D interface.[31] Indeed, their source of competitive advantage often lies in marketing and R&D divisions' willingness to coordinate their respective activities concurrently. In a traditional product development, either a new product was developed and pushed down from the R&D division to the manufacturing and marketing divisions for sales, or a new product idea was pushed up from the marketing division to the R&D division for development. This top-down or bottom-up new product development takes too much time in an era of global competition in which a short product development cycle is crucial to meet constant competitive pressure from new products introduced by rival companies around the world.

R&D and marketing divisions of Japanese companies are always on the lookout for the use of emerging technologies initially in existing products to satisfy customer needs better than their own existing and their competitors' products. This affords them an opportunity to gain experience, debug technological glitches, reduce costs, boost performance, and adapt designs for worldwide customer use. As a result, they have been able to increase the speed of new product introductions, meet the competitive demands of a rapidly changing marketplace, and capture market share.

In other words, *the marketplace becomes a virtual R&D laboratory for Japanese companies to gain production and marketing experience as well as to perfect technology.* This requires close contact with customers, whose inputs help Japanese companies improve their products on an ongoing basis. In the process, they introduce new products one after another. Year after year, Japanese companies unveil not entirely new products that keep getting better in design, reliability, and price. For example, Philips marketed the first practical VCR in 1972, three years before Japanese competitors entered the market. However, Philips took seven years to replace the first generation VCR with the all-new V2000 while the late-coming Japanese manufacturers launched an onslaught of no fewer than three generations of improved VCRs in this five-year period.

---

[30]"Can Honda Build a World Car," *Business Week*, September 8, 1997, pp. 100–8; and "The Also-Rans," *Economist*, February 21, 2004, pp. 61–62.

[31]X. Michael Song and Mark E. Parry, "A Cross-National Comparative Study of New Product Development Processes: Japan and the United States," *Journal of Marketing*, 61 (April 1997), pp. 1–18.

Another example worth noting is the exploitation of the so-called fuzzy logic by Hitachi and others.[32] When fuzzy logic was conceived in the mid-1960s by Lotfi A. Zadeh, a computer science professor at the University of California at Berkeley, nobody other than several Japanese companies paid serious heed to its potential application in ordinary products. The fuzzy logic allows computers to deal with shades of gray or something vague between 0 and 1—no small feat in a world of the binary computers. Today, Hitachi, Matsushita, Mitsubishi, Sony, and Nissan Motors, among others, use fuzzy logic in their products. For example, Hitachi introduced a "fuzzy" train that automatically accelerates and brakes so smoothly that no one reaches for the hanging straps. Matsushita, maker of Panasonics, began marketing a "fuzzy" washing machine with only one start button that automatically judges the size and dirtiness of the load and decides the optimum cycle times, amount of detergent needed, and water level. Sony introduced a palm-size computer capable of recognizing written Japanese with a fuzzy circuit to iron out the inconsistencies in different writing styles. Now fuzzy circuits are put into the autofocus mechanisms of video cameras to get constantly clear pictures. Fuzzy chips have already been incorporated into a wide range of products in Japan yet are virtually unheard of in the rest of the world.[33]

The continual introduction of newer and better designed products also brings a greater likelihood of market success.[34] Ideal products often require a giant leap in technology and product development and naturally are subject to a much higher risk of consumer rejection. The Japanese approach of incrementalism not only allows for continual improvement and a stream of new products but also permits quicker consumer adoption. Consumers are likely to accept improved products more quickly than very different products because the former are more compatible with the existing patterns of product use and lifestyles.

PROCUREMENT: TYPES OF SOURCING STRATEGY ◆ ◆ ◆ ◆ ◆ ◆ ◆ ◆

Sourcing strategy includes a number of basic choices that companies make in deciding how to serve foreign markets. One choice relates to the use of imports, assembly, or production within the country to serve a foreign market. Another decision involves the use of internal or external supplies of components or finished goods.

Sourcing decision making is multifaceted and entails both contractual and locational implications. From a contractual point of view, the sourcing of major components and products by multinational companies takes place in two ways: (1) from the parents or their foreign subsidiaries on an "intrafirm" basis and (2) from independent suppliers on a "contractual" basis. The first type of sourcing is known as **intrafirm sourcing.** The second type of sourcing is commonly referred to as **outsourcing.** Similarly, from a locational point of view, multinational companies can procure components and products either (1) domestically (i.e., *domestic sourcing*) or (2) from abroad (i.e., *offshore sourcing.*) Therefore, as shown in Exhibit 10-4, four possible types of sourcing strategy can be identified.

In developing viable sourcing strategies on a global scale, companies must consider not only the costs of manufacturing and various resources as well as exchange rate fluctuations but also the availability of infrastructure (including transportation, communications, and energy), industrial and cultural environments, ease of working with foreign host governments, and so on. Furthermore, the complex nature of sourcing strategy on a global scale spawns many barriers to its successful execution. In particular,

[32]Larry Armstrong, "Why 'Fuzzy Logic' Beats Black-or-White Thinking," *Business Week,* May 21, 1990, pp. 92–93.
[33]Robert J. Crawford, "Reinterpreting the Japanese Economic Miracle," *Harvard Business Review,* 76 (January–February 1998), pp. 179–84.
[34]Michael R. Czinkota and Masaaki Kotabe, "Product Development the Japanese Way," *Journal of Business Strategy,* 11 (November/December 1990), pp. 31–36.

EXHIBIT 10-4
TYPES OF SOURCING STRATEGY

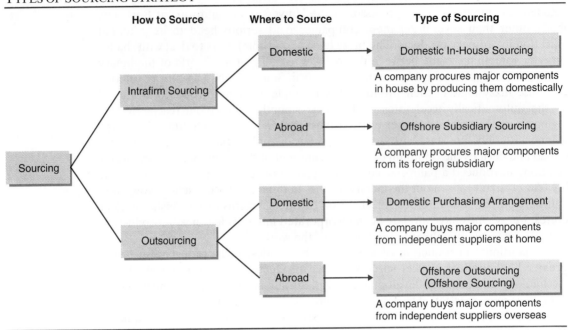

logistics, inventory management, distance, nationalism, and lack of working knowledge about foreign business practices, among others, are major operational problems identified by both U.S. and foreign MNCs engaging in international sourcing.

Many studies have shown, however, that despite, or perhaps as a result of, those operational problems, *where* to source major components seems much less important than *how* to source them. Thus, when examining the relationship between sourcing and competitiveness of multinational companies, it is crucial to distinguish between sourcing on a contractual basis and sourcing on an intrafirm basis, for these two types of sourcing will have a different impact on the firm's long-run competitiveness.

Intrafirm Sourcing   Multinational companies can procure their components in house within their corporate system around the world. They produce major components at their respective home base and/or at their affiliates overseas to be incorporated into their products marketed in various parts of the world. Thus, trade takes place between a parent company and its subsidiaries abroad and between foreign subsidiaries across national boundaries. This is often referred to as *intrafirm sourcing*. If such in-house component procurement takes place at home, it is essentially **domestic in-house sourcing.** If it takes place at a company's foreign subsidiary, it is called **offshore subsidiary sourcing.** Intrafirm sourcing makes trade statistics more complex to interpret because part of the international flow of products and components is taking place between affiliated companies within the same multinational corporate system, which transcends national boundaries. About 30 percent of U.S. exports is attributed to U.S. parent companies transferring products and components to their affiliates overseas, and about 40 percent of U.S. imports is accounted for by foreign affiliates exporting to their U.S. parent companies. For both Japan and Britain, intrafirm transactions account for approximately 30 percent of their total trade flows (exports and imports combined), respectively.[35] Although statistics on intrafirm trade between foreign affiliates are limited to U.S. firms, the share of

---

[35] United Nations Centre on Transnational Corporations, *Transnational Corporations in World Development: Trends and Perspectives* (New York: United Nations, 1988).

exports to other foreign affiliates in intrafirm exports of foreign affiliates rose from 37 percent in 1977 to 60 percent in 1993, and has been stable since then. This also suggests the increased role of foreign affiliates of U.S. multinational firms outside the United States.[36]

Outsourcing (Contract Manufacturing)

In the 1970s, foreign competitors gradually caught up in a productivity race with U.S. companies, which had once commanded a dominant position in international trade. It coincided with U.S. corporate strategic emphasis drifting from manufacturing to finance and marketing. As a result, manufacturing management gradually lost its organizational influence. Production managers' decision-making authority was reduced, such that R&D personnel prepared specifications with which production complied and then marketing personnel imposed delivery, inventory, and quality conditions. In a sense, production managers gradually took on the role of outside suppliers within their own companies.[37]

Production managers' reduced influence in the organization further led to a belief that manufacturing functions could, and should, be transferred easily to independent contract manufacturers, depending on the cost differential between in-house and contracted-out production. A company's reliance on domestic suppliers for major components and/or products[38] is basically a **domestic purchase arrangement.** Furthermore, to lower production costs under competitive pressure, U.S. companies turned increasingly to *outsourcing* of components and finished products from abroad, particularly newly industrialized countries including Singapore, South Korea, Taiwan, Hong Kong, Brazil, and Mexico. Initially, subsidiaries were set up for production purposes (i.e., offshore subsidiary sourcing), but gradually, independent foreign contract manufacturers took over component production for U.S. companies. This latter phenomenon is known by many terms, usually called **offshore outsourcing (offshore sourcing,** for short). For example, Apple, Dell, and Gateway now outsource 100 percent of their laptop computers from Quanta Computer Inc., a Taiwanese company and the world's largest maker of laptop computers. Dell Computer alone accounts for half of Quanta's sales.[39]

In recent years, an increasing number of companies has used the Internet to develop efficient business-to-business (B2B) procurement (outsourcing) systems on a global scale. On February 25, 2000, General Motors, Ford, and DaimlerChrysler made history by jointly forming Covisint (www.covisint.com), which is probably the largest global online B2B procurement system dedicated to the auto industry. The Big Three have been joined by partners Nissan Motor, Renault, Commerce One, Inc., and Oracle Corp. in an effort to provide procurement, supply-chain, and product-development services to the auto industry on a global scale. The auto industry was an early adopter of the B2B procurement business model for a number of marketing-related reasons. First, automakers could develop products with a relatively short life cycle. Second, they would require a fast response time to market. Third, automakers were early adopters of outsourcing, one primary reason for which is the auto industry, their drive for change from a push model to a pull model—their desire to achieve customized make-to-order marketing feasible.[40] However, by 2004, it was clear that Covisint had not been able to build a trust relationship between the participating automakers and

---

[36]*World Investment Report 1996,* pp. 13–14; and *World Investment Report 1998* (New York: United Nations, 1996 and 1998 respectively).

[37]Stephen S. Cohen and John Zysman, "Why Manufacturing Matters: The Myth of the Post-Industrial Economy," *California Management Review,* 29 (Spring 1987), pp. 9–26.

[38]Rodney Ho, "Small Product-Development Firms Show Solid Growth," *Wall Street Journal,* April 22, 1997, p. 32: This article shows that entrepreneurial companies have begun to fill a void of new product development role as large companies trim their internal R&D staffs and expenditures in the United States. Although it makes financial sense, at least in the short term, those outsourcing companies will face the same long-term concern as explained in this chapter.

[39]"Quanta's Quantum Leap," *Business Week,* November 5, 2001, pp. 79–81; and "The Laptop Trail," *Wall Street Journal,* June 9, 2005, pp. B1, B8.

[40]Beverly Beckert, "Engines of Auto Innovation," *Computer-Aided Engineering,* 20 (May 2001), pp. S18–S20.

EXHIBIT 10-5
MAJOR REASONS
FOR OUTSOURCING

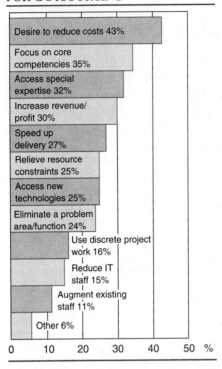

Desire to reduce costs 43%

Focus on core
competencies 35%

Access special
expertise 32%

Increase revenue/
profit 30%

Speed up
delivery 27%

Relieve resource
constraints 25%

Access new
technologies 25%

Eliminate a problem
area/function 24%

Use discrete project
work 16%

Reduce IT
staff 15%

Augment existing
staff 11%

Other 6%

0   10   20   30   40   50   %

Source: Survey results reported in "Outsourcing: Directions and Decisions for 2003," *2003 Outsourcing Trends,* CIO, http://www.cio.com, accessed February 16, 2006.

their suppliers as it had on paper and was eventually sold to Compuware Corp. as a messaging data service and portal.[41] Covisint's failure illustrates how difficult it is to manage outsourcing relationships.[42] The near-term benefits of outsourcing are clear. According to a recent survey (see Exhibit 10-5), cost reduction, focus on core competencies, access to special expertise, improved financial performance, delivery speed, reduction of resource constrains, and access to new technologies are among the most important reasons for outsourcing.

The same logic applies to information technology (IT) sourcing. The number one reason for outsourcing is still to reduce costs. The economic recession in Japan is forcing companies to find a way to cut spending, especially in IT services. For example, Japanese businesses are under increasing cost pressure from new domestic and international competitors, and the new technologies have also opened the door to outsourcing in Japan. Whereas Japanese businesses have traditionally thrived on a very distinct hierarchy, the new workplace is based less on management divisions than on a solid telecommunications infrastructure.[43]

Long-term implications are not so clear, however. Procurement from overseas (i.e., offshore subsidiary sourcing and offshore outsourcing) has received quite a bit of attention, for it not only affects domestic employment and economic structure but sometimes also raises ethical issues (see Global Perspective 10-3). Companies using such a strategy have been described pejoratively as **hollow corporations**.[44] It is occasionally argued that those companies are increasingly adopting a "designer role" in

[41]"Rule of the Road Still Apply to Covisint," *InformationWeek,* February 9, 2004. p. 32.

[42]Martina Gerst and Raluca Bunduchi, "Shaping IT Standardization in the Automotive Industry—The Role of Power in Driving Portal Standardization," *Electronic Markets,* 15 (December 2005), pp. 335–43.

[43]The Outsourcing Institute, http://www.outsourcing.com, accessed December 5, 2002.

[44]"Special Report: The Hollow Corporation," *Business Week,* March 3, 1986, pp. 56–59; and Robert Heller, "The Dangers of Deconstruction," *Management Today,* February 1993, pp. 14, 17.

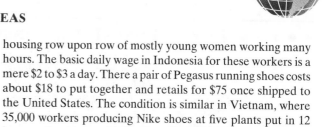

𝒢LOBAL PERSPECTIVE 10-3

OFFSHORE SOURCING AND SWEATSHOPS OVERSEAS

At least 80 people died and another 100 were seriously injured when a garment factory collapsed in Dhaka, Bangladesh, in 2004. The factory made sweaters for European retailers Carrefour and Zara. These people were working in unsafe conditions to produce goods for consumers in the West. It is part of what corporate critics invariably call a "race to the bottom." Multinational companies seek places where labor is cheap and safety, health, and environmental laws are lax.

The rapid globalization linking manufacturing companies, investors, and consumers around the world has touched off some ethical questions in recent years. *Offshore sourcing* is the practice of companies manufacturing or contracting out all or parts of their products abroad. *Outsourcing* makes it possible for those companies to procure products and components much less expensively than manufacturing them in their home country. In many cases, labor cost savings are a strong motive for companies to engage in offshore sourcing. For example, Nike, the leading U.S. footwear company, has subcontractors in Taiwan, South Korea, and Indonesia, which collectively run 12 factories in Indonesia, producing 70 million pairs of Nike sneakers a year. Like other footwear factories everywhere in Asia, work conditions are tough, with mandatory overtime work and constant exhaustion. Although these factories may be modern, they are drab and utilitarian, with vast sheds

housing row upon row of mostly young women working many hours. The basic daily wage in Indonesia for these workers is a mere $2 to $3 a day. There a pair of Pegasus running shoes costs about $18 to put together and retails for $75 once shipped to the United States. The condition is similar in Vietnam, where 35,000 workers producing Nike shoes at five plants put in 12 hours a day to earn $1.60—less than the $2 or so it costs to buy three meals a day.

Although working conditions at these subcontractors' factories have improved over time at Nike's initiation, the company has a long way to go before it lives up to its stated goal of providing a fair working environment for all its workers. In Indonesia, police and factory managers have a not-so-subtle cozy relationship whereby police help keep workers under control. Despite its strong political clout, Nike has not challenged the Indonesian government's control over labor. Nike's code of conduct seems to remain vague, despite its intentions.

The linking of a firm's private interests with the larger public good has been referred to as *corporate citizenship*. Multinational corporations cannot claim ignorance about the workers who produce the products they buy or the conditions in which they work. Large companies have the resources to investigate those with whom they do business. Ethically speaking, they should set standards that their contractors have to meet to continue their contracts. Indeed, in recent years, socially responsible investing (SRI) has increasingly become the practice of making investment decisions on the basis of both financial and social performance. The SRI movement has grown into a $1.185 trillion business, accounting for about 1 in 10 U.S. invested dollars.

Sources: R. Bruce Hutton, Louis D'Antonio, and Tommi Johnsen, "Socially Responsible Investing: Growing Issues and New Opportunities," *Business and Society,* 37 (September 1998), pp. 281–305; "Labor Standards Clash with Global Reality," *New York Times,* April 24, 2001; and "Cops of the Global Village," *Fortune,* June 27, 2005, pp. 158–66.

---

global competition by offering innovations in product design without investing in manufacturing and process technology. Revisit some caveats for contract manufacturing discussed in Chapter 9.

Even Covisint, the global B2B procurement business founded by the Big Three automakers, discussed earlier, was not able to generate results that the companies had initially expected. Typical B2B procurement systems, including Covisint, have tended to rely on auctions that emphasize the lowest bids on a global basis. This Internet-era emphasis on low cost could border on the cost emphasis of the 1960s and 1970s that ignored the importance of quality, technological superiority, delivery, and other noncost aspects of competitive advantage. In fact, for superior product development working jointly with external suppliers, automakers need to emphasize the importance of technical collaborations, such as product design, as well as trust building in supplier-buyer relationships.[45]

This widespread international sourcing practice could have a deleterious impact on companies' ability to maintain their initial competitive advantage based on product

---

[45] Masaaki Kotabe, Xavier Martin, and Hiroshi Domoto, "Gaining from Vertical Relationships: Knowledge Transfer, Relationship Duration, and Supplier Performance Improvement in the U.S. and Japanese Automobile Industries," *Strategic Management Journal,* 24 (March 2003), pp. 293–316.

innovations.[46] Indeed, keeping abreast of emerging technology through continual improvement in manufacturing and process is essential for the company's continued competitiveness.

♦ ♦ ♦ ♦ ♦ ♦ ♦ ♦ ♦ ## LONG-TERM CONSEQUENCES OF GLOBAL SOURCING

Global sourcing strategy requires close coordination of R&D, manufacturing, and marketing activities, among others, on a global basis. In Chapter 8, we discussed the two fundamental forces that have shaped the nature of competition for firms across national boundaries over the years: the firm's desire to integrate and streamline its operations and the diversity of markets. One thing that has changed, however, are the *ability* and *willingness* of these companies to integrate various activities on a global basis in an attempt either to circumvent or to nullify the impact of differences in local markets to the extent possible. It may be *more* correct to say that these companies have been increasingly compelled to take a global view of their businesses due primarily to increased competition particularly among the Triad regions of the United States, Western Europe, and Japan. Remember, "If you stand still, you will get run over...," a contemporary view of competitive urgency that is shared by an increasing number of executives of multinational firms regardless of nationality.

To lower production costs under competitive pressure, many multinational companies have increasingly outsourced components and finished products from China, South Korea, Taiwan, Singapore, Hong Kong, Brazil, and Mexico, among others. Akio Morita, a cofounder of Sony, a highly innovative Japanese electronics company, chided those multinational companies as *hollow corporations* that simply put their well-known brand names on foreign-made products and sold them as if the products were their own.[47] The main characteristics of hollow corporations are illustrated in Global Perspective 10-4.

However, we should not rush to a hasty conclusion that outsourcing certain components and/or finished products from foreign countries will diminish a company's competitiveness. Thanks to the explosive growth of the Internet, outsourcing activities have actually increased and become more efficient. Many multinational companies with plants in various parts of the world are exploiting not only their own competitive advantages (e.g., R&D, manufacturing, and marketing skills) but also the locational advantages (e.g., inexpensive labor cost, certain skills, mineral resources, government subsidy, and tax advantages) of various countries. Thus, it is also plausible to argue that these multinational companies are in a more advantageous competitive position than are domestic-bound companies.

If so, isn't the "hollowing-out" phenomenon indicative of a superior management of both corporate and locational resources on a global basis? Answers to this question hinge on a company's ability and willingness to integrate and coordinate various activities. The real issue is not how far a firm can "hollow out" or outsource its business functions, but how far it should do so for its long-term sustainable competitive advantage. At least one recent study has shown that the effect of outsourcing on corporate profitability would on average stay positive as long as the increase in outsourcing, or the increase in the ratio of industrial purchasing to total sales from 1995 to 1998, did not reach 4.5 percent.[48] There appear to be certain limits to the virtue of outsourcing.

---

[46]Constantinos Markides and Norman Berg, "Manufacturing Offshore Is Bad Business," *Harvard Business Review,* 66 (September–October 1988), pp. 113–20; Masaaki Kotabe, and Michael J. Mol, "Competitive (Dis)advantage of Outsourcing Strategy," in *Sourcing Decision Management,* ed. Alessandro Ancarani and Giovanni Pastore, (Napoli, Italy: Edizioni Scientifiche Italiane, 2005), 115–26.

[47]"Special Report: The Hollow Corporation," pp. 56–59.

[48]Masaaki Kotabe and Michael J. Mol, "A New Paradigm on Outsourcing and the Performance of the Firm," in *Global Corporate Evolution: Looking Inward or Looking Outward?* ed. Michael A. Trick (Pittsburgh, PA: Carnegie Mellon University Press, 2004), 331–39.

$\mathscr{G}$LOBAL PERSPECTIVE 10-4

HOLLOW CORPORATIONS

The following discussion appeared in a now-classic article in the *Business Week* in 1986.

By shifting production overseas or shopping abroad for parts and components, U.S. companies are whittling away at the critical mass essential to a strong industrial base. For example,

- General Electric Co. spent $1.4 billion in 1985 to import products sold in the U.S. under the GE label. Virtually all of its consumer electronics goods are already made in Asia. By the end of summer, the company plans to shut down its last domestic color-TV plant. In appliances, GE now buys its microwave ovens from Japan and began going offshore for room air conditioners as early as 1987.

- Eastman Kodak Co. is counting on foreign-made products to fuel much of its growth. To diversify from the stagnant film business, Kodak is buying video camera recorders and videotape from Japan, along with its midsize copying machines. It also imports floppy disks from a Kodak factory in Britain.

- Honeywell Inc. gets the central processing "brain" for its biggest mainframe computer from a Japanese manufacturer, and two other mainframes that Honeywell sells in the U.S. are imported as finished products from Europe. The Minneapolis company also goes abroad for a host of components used in its factory-automation equipment and commercial air-conditioning systems.

If this trend continues, warns Jack D. Kuehler, senior vice-president of International Business Machines Corp., companies will gradually become less adept at understanding how new technology can be exploited and eventually "lose the ability to design." Adds Robert A. Lutz, chairman of Ford of Europe Inc.: "You're seeing a substantial deindustrialization of the U.S., and I can't imagine any country maintaining its position in the world without an industrial base." Only now U.S. companies are also shifting far more valuable things overseas: fundamental technology, management functions, and even the design and engineering skills that are crucial to innovation.

BACKING AWAY

When Sony Corp. unveiled the first VCRs in 1975, they carried price tags of more than $1,000, and so most U.S. companies dismissed them as too expensive and complex ever to command a major market. Besides, they were already backing away from tape recorders, the source of the technology that went into the VCR. Now, with product simplification and automated production, VCRs are selling—like hotcakes—at less than $300.

Here, too, not one is made in the U.S., although Sony plans to start building a U.S. VCR factory this year. And now it has spun off its VCR technology into the so-called camcorder, a combination video camera recorder that promises to be the last straw for movie cameras and film. Alarmed, Kodak has jumped into the video market—with a camcorder made by Matsushita Electric Industrial Co.

However, as RCA has learned, selling goods made by a foreign competitor can be a rocky partnership. RCA has leveraged its name and distribution resources to grab the biggest share of domestic VCR sales, an estimated 20 percent. Its machines now get stamped with the RCA logo in a Hitachi Ltd. factory. Matsushita used to do that for RCA. But in 1984, with Matsushita gaining market share by undercutting RCA's prices with Panasonic VCRs that were clones of RCA's units, RCA turned to Hitachi. RCA suspects the deal with Hitachi will also prove temporary. "You can only source for a limited time," admits Jack K. Sauter, an RCA group vice-president. But RCA, GE, and Zenith are compelled to endure the situation. Not only do the profits from VCRs help subsidize their manufacturing losses on color TV sets, but also they lack the expertise to produce competitively.

WAITING IN THE WINGS

Of course, not all companies are oblivious to the implications of deindustrialization. A small but growing band is feverishly working to develop the technologies that will be used in the totally automated factory. Caterpillar has launched a major effort to automate production, both in the U.S. and abroad. And Cat is encouraging managers to think long term, planning ten years ahead. "That's a dramatic difference" in philosophy, says Caterpillar's Ranney.

Two decades after this *Business Week* article was published, we still debate the same issue although we have better understanding of the logic about the "boundaries" of the firm. The argument is based on internalization/transaction cost theory (as described in the Appendix to Chapter 1).

Source: "Even American Knowhow Is Headed Abroad," *Business Week,* March 3, 1986, pp. 60–63.

There are two opposing views of the long-term implications of offshore sourcing, especially for strategic inputs, depending on whether the company would differentiate outsourcing activities based on a strategic partnership basis or on an arm's-length transaction basis. Many successful companies have established *strategic partnerships* with their suppliers by developing a dynamic organizational network through increased

Sustainable versus Transitory Core Competencies

use of joint ventures, subcontracting, and licensing activities across international borders.[49] However, if suppliers for strategic inputs are managed based on an arm's-length basis, there could be negative long-term consequences resulting from a company's dependence on independent suppliers and subsequently the inherent difficulty for the company to keep abreast of constantly evolving design and engineering technologies without engaging in those developmental activities. In this case, companies fail to coordinate and integrate their suppliers' design and production as part of their own activities, as would be the case using strategic partnerships. These opposing arguments will be elaborated below.

Benefits of Virtual Network

A network of loosely coupled strategic alliances allows each participant to pursue its particular competencies. Therefore, each network participant can be seen as complementing rather than competing with the other participants for the common goals. Strategic alliances may even be formed by competing companies in the same industry in pursuit of complementary abilities (new technologies or skills) from each other.

The advantage of forming a virtual network is claimed to be its structural flexibility. Such a network of loosely coupled partnerships can accommodate a vast amount of complexity while maximizing the specialized competence of each member and can provide much more effective use of human resources that would otherwise have to be accumulated, allocated, and maintained by a single organization. In other words, a company can concentrate on performing the task at which it is most efficient. This approach is increasingly applied on a global basis, with countries participating in a dynamic network as multinational companies configure and coordinate product development, manufacturing, and sourcing activities around the world.

First, because of the need for rapid internationalization and related diversification, such alliances provide a relatively easy option to access the world markets, thus allowing the firms in the network to create and maintain a sustainable competitive advantage by combining capabilities and technologies in a unique way. Second, reduced investment requirement for each participating company helps improve its return on investment. Thus, for example, Toyota established a joint venture with General Motors so that the Japanese car maker could learn to work with UAW union members while General Motors could learn just-in-time inventory management from Toyota. Today, in the United States, Toyota's Corolla and Tacoma and GM's Pontiac Vibe are all produced by General Motors at its plant in Freemont, California.[50]

Dependence. In contrast with outsourcing based on strategic partnerships, companies that rely on independent external sources of supply of major components tend to forsake part of the most important value-creating activities and come to depend on independent operators for assurance of component quality. Furthermore, those multinational companies tend to promote competition among independent suppliers, ensure continuing availability of materials in the future, and exploit the full benefits of changing market conditions. In addition, in an arm's-length arrangement, competing firms tend to share a common set of suppliers, thus diluting the degree of differentiation of these major components to the buying firms.[51] By attempting to maintain various sources of supply and a high degree of relative bargaining power, those companies also may have restricted the size and scale of their suppliers. Furthermore, individual suppliers are forced to operate in an uncertain business environment that inherently necessitates a shorter planning horizon. The uncertainty about the potential loss of orders to competitors often forces individual suppliers to make operating decisions

[49] Raymond E. Miles and Charles C. Snow, "Organizations: New Concepts for New Forms," *California Management Review,* 28 (Spring 1986), pp. 62–73.

[50] The GM-Toyota joint venture is known as New United Motor Manufacturing, Inc (NUMMI).

[51] Jeffrey H. Dyer, Dong Sung Cho, and Wujin Chu, "Strategic Supplier Segmentation: The Next 'Best Practice' in Supply Chain Management," *California Management Review,* 40 (2) 1998, pp. 57–77.

that will likely increase their own long-term production and materials costs. In the process, this uncertain business environment tends to adversely affect the multinational companies sourcing components and/or finished products from independent suppliers. The rapid decline of IBM in the personal computer market offers the most vivid example of the problems caused by its dependence on independent suppliers for personal computer (PC) production as well as crucial components in the personal computer market. Indeed, in 2005, IBM sold its PC division to Lenovo, a personal computer company from China.[52]

Gradual Loss of Design and Manufacturing Abilities. Those multinational companies that depend heavily on independent suppliers on an arm's-length basis (i.e., without integrating their suppliers into their activities) also tend in the long term to lose sight of emerging technologies and expertise, which could be incorporated into the development of new manufacturing processes as well as new products. Thus, continual sourcing from independent suppliers, as opposed to sourcing based on strategic partnerships, is likely to forebode companies' long-term loss of the ability to manufacture at competitive cost and, as a result, loss of their global competitiveness. However, if technology and expertise developed by an MNC are exploited within its multinational corporate system (i.e., by its foreign affiliates and by the parent company itself), the company can retain its technological base to itself without unduly disseminating them to competitors. The benefit of such internalization is likely to be great, particularly when technology is highly idiosyncratic or specific with limited alternative uses, or when it is novel in the marketplace. For such a technology, the market price mechanism is known to break down as a seller and potential buyers of the technology tend to see its value very differently. Potential buyers, who do not have perfect knowledge of how useful the technology will be, tend to undervalue its true market value. As a result, the seller of the technology is not likely to get a full economic benefit of the technology by selling it in the open market.

In a relationship with a foreign supplier, it is particularly essential that a lead company devise methods to ensure the continued product and service quality. For example, in entering the Chinese industrial tire market recently, Industrial Tires Co. (ITL), Canada's top industrial tire maker, continues to provide technology, patterns, compounds, and trade names, takes care of equipment selection and process and product engineering, and maintains a high-level quality assurance program for Yantai CSI Rubber Company, a manufacturing and marketing partner in China that now is the largest tire manufacturer in the Asia-Pacific region.[53]

In addition, by getting involved in design and production on its own or through strategic partnerships, the MNC can keep abreast of emerging technologies and innovations originating anywhere in the world for potential use in the future. Furthermore, management of the quality of major components is required to retain the goodwill and confidence of consumers in the products, which may be impossible using arm's-length outsourcing. Maintaining the ability to develop major components and finished products in house or via strategic partnerships allows the company to better understand the cost and quality implications of its sourcing relationship even with its suppliers.

OUTSOURCING OF SERVICE ACTIVITIES ◆ ◆ ◆ ◆ ◆ ◆ ◆ ◆ ◆

In 2004, the United States was ranked the largest exporter and importer of services, providing $343.9 billion of services to the rest of the world and receiving $296.1 billion

[52]"Can China's Lenovo Brand in the Land of Dell?" *B to B,* October 10, 2005, pp. 1, 45.

[53]Bruce Meyer, "ITL Building on Global Strategy," *Rubber and Plastics,* July 4, 1994; and Yantai CSI Rubber Co. Ltd. Homepage, http://www.csirubber.com/index.asp, accessed January 10, 2006.

worth of services. Furthermore, according to a recent government estimate, approximately 16 percent of the total value of U.S. exports and imports of services were conducted across national boundaries on an intrafirm basis (i.e., between parent companies and their subsidiaries). Increasingly, U.S. companies have expanded their service procurement activities on a global basis in the same way they procure components and finished products.

As discussed, firms have the ability and opportunity to procure components/finished goods that have proprietary technology on a global basis. This logic also applies equally to service activities. The technological revolution in data processing and telecommunications (transborder data flow, telematics, etc.) either makes the global tradability of some services possible or facilitates the transactions economically. Furthermore, because the production and consumption of some services do not need to take place at the same location or at the same time, global sourcing could be a viable strategy.

Thanks to the development of the Internet and e-commerce, certain service activities are increasingly outsourced from independent service suppliers. The Internet will also accelerate growth in the number of e-workers. This net-savvy and highly flexible corps will be able to perform much or all of their work at home or in small groups close to home, regardless of their locations. International e-workers can also operate in locations far from corporate headquarters. They will be part of the growth in *intellectual outsourcing.* Already such e-workers can write software in India for a phone company in Finland, provide architectural services in Ireland for a building in Spain, and do accounting work in Hong Kong for an insurance company in Vancouver. Globalization of services through the Internet is likely to expand considerably in the future.[54]

Bangalore, India, should particularly be noted. The region is described as the Silicon Valley of that country. Bangalore has rapidly evolved to become the center of offshore programming activities. Many U.S. companies have started outsourcing an increasing portion of software development to companies in Bangalore. According to the National Association of Software and Service Cos., a trade group for India's IT industry, India's revenue from software sales and R&D increased as much as 30 percent to $3 billion during 2004 alone. Established software vendors, including IBM, Microsoft, Oracle, and SAP, already employ Indian talent no longer just to write software code but also to help design and develop commercial offerings that are higher up in the software design food chain. Increasingly, Indian software entrepreneurs want to put their own companies' brand names on products, at home and abroad, by capitalizing on their country's highly educated and low-cost workforce to build and sell software for everything from back-office programs to customer-facing applications.[55] Similarly, China is catching up in this role. Microsoft has four research laboratories located around the globe: Redmond, Washington; Cambridge, UK; Beijing, China and San Francisco, California, with the goal to invent Microsoft's future, by focusing on technologies and technology trends in the next 5–10 year time frame. For example, Microsoft Research (MSR) Asia, founded in 1998 in Beijing, has already produced many research results that have been transferred to Microsoft products, including Office XP, Office System 2003, Windows XP, and Longhorn—the next major release of Windows.[56]

Outsourcing of service activities has been widely quoted in the popular press as a means to reduce costs and improve the corporate focus; that is concentrating on the core activities of the firm. However, outsourcing may also serve (a) as a means of reducing time to implement internal processes, (b) as a means of sharing risk in an increasingly uncertain business environment, (c) to improve customer service, (d) to get access to better expertise not available in-house, (e) for headcount reduction, and

[54]Robert D. Hormats, "High Velocity," *Harvard International Review,* 21 (Summer 1999), pp. 36–41.

[55]"India's Next Step," *InformationWeek,* August 8, 2005, pp. 34–39.

[56]"Labs: Asia," Microsoft Research, http://research.microsoft.com/aboutmsr/labs/asia/, accessed February 20, 2006.

(f) as a means of instilling a sense of competition, especially when departments within firms develop a perceptible level of inertia.[57]

In the case of service companies, the distinction between core and supplementary services is necessary in strategy development. **Core services** are the necessary outputs of an organization that consumers are looking for, while **supplementary services** are either indispensable for the execution of the core service or are available only to improve the overall quality of the core service bundle. Using an example from the health care industry, the core service provides patients with good-quality medical care. The supplementary services could include filing insurance claims, arranging accommodation for family members (especially for overseas patients), handling off-hour emergency calls, and so on. The same phenomenon arises in the computer software industry. When the industry giant Microsoft needed help in supporting new users of Windows operating software, it utilized outsourcing with Boston-based Keane, Inc., to set up a help desk with 350 support personnel.

Core services could gradually partake of a "commodity" and lose their differential advantage vis-à-vis competitors as competition intensifies over time. Subsequently, a service provider could increase its reliance on supplementary services to maintain and/or enhance competitive advantage. "After all, if a firm cannot do a decent job on the core elements, it is eventually going to go out of business."[58] In other words, a service firm exists to provide good-quality core services to its customers; however, in some instances, it simply cannot rely solely on core services to remain competitive. We can expect that core services are usually performed by the service firm itself, regardless of the characteristics of the core service. On the other hand, although supplementary services are provided to augment the core service for competitive advantage, the unique characteristics of supplementary services can influence "how" and "where" they are sourced.[59]

The bottom line is that the quality of the service package that customers experience helps service companies differentiate themselves from the competition. One important category of quality is the variability of the product's or service's attributes: its reliability. As in manufacturing, service companies that choose to differentiate themselves based on reliability must consistently maintain it, or else they will undermine their strategic position by damaging the reputation of their brand name. There is empirical evidence that outsourcing some service activities for the sake of economic efficiency tends to result in less reliable service offerings.[60] The same concern about the advantages and disadvantages of outsourcing in the manufacturing industry appears to apply in the services industry.

---

[57]Maneesh Chandra, "Global Sourcing of Services: A Theory Development and Empirical Investigation," Ph.D. dissertation, The University of Texas at Austin, 1999.

[58]C. H. Lovelock, "Adding Value to Core Products with Supplementary Services," in *Services Marketing, 3rd ed.,* ed. C. H. Lovelock (Englewood Cliffs, NJ: Prentice-Hall, 1996).

[59]Terry Clark, Daniel Rajaratnam, and Timothy Smith, "Toward a Theory of International Services; Marketing Intangibles in a World of Nations," *Journal of International Marketing,* 4(2), 1996, pp. 9–28; and Janet Y. Murray and Masaaki Kotabe, "Sourcing Strategies of U.S. Service Companies: A Modified Transaction-Cost Analysis," *Strategic Management Journal,* 20 (September 1999), pp. 791–809.

[60]C. M. Hsieh, Sergio G. Lazzarini, Jack A. Nickerson, "Outsourcing and the Variability of Product Performance: Data from International Courier Services," *Academy of Management Proceedings,* 2002, pp. G1–G6.

SUMMARY ✦

The scope of global sourcing has expanded over time. Whether or not to procure components or products from abroad was once determined strictly on the basis of price and thus was strongly influenced by the fluctuating exchange rate. The appreciation of the dollar therefore prompted companies to increase offshore sourcing while the depreciation of the dollar encouraged domestic sourcing. Today many companies consider not simply price but also quality, reliability, and technology of components and products to be procured. Those companies design their sourcing decision based on the interplay between their competitive advantages and the comparative advantages of various sourcing locations for long-term gains.

Trade and foreign production managed by multinational corporations are very complex. In growing global competition, sourcing components and finished products around the world within the MNC has increased. The development of global sourcing and marketing strategies across different foreign markets has become a central issue for many MNCs. Traditionally, a polycentric approach to organizing operations on a country-by-country basis allowed each country manager to tailor marketing strategy to the peculiarities of local markets. As such, product adaptations were considered a necessary strategy to better cater to the different needs and wants of customers in various countries. Product adaptation tends to be a reactive rather than a proactive strategic response to the market. A high level of product adaptation could make it difficult for multinational companies to reap economies of scale in production and marketing and to coordinate their networks of activities on a global scale.

Global sourcing strategy requires close coordination of R&D, manufacturing, and marketing activities on a global basis. Managing geographically separated R&D, manufacturing, and marketing activities, those companies face the difficult coordination problems of integrating their operations and adapting them to different legal, political, and cultural environments in different countries. Furthermore, separation of manufacturing activities involves an inherent risk that manufacturing in the value chain will gradually become neglected.

Such neglect can be costly, for continued involvement in manufacturing leads to pioneering product design and innovation over time. An effective global sourcing strategy calls for continual efforts to streamline manufacturing without sacrificing marketing flexibility. Accomplishing this calls for a conscious effort to develop either core components in house or product design families or universal products.

A caveat should be also noted. Although a company's ability to develop core components and products and market them in the world markets on its own is preferred, the enormousness of such a task should be examined in light of rapid changes in both technology and customer needs around the world. Those changes make the product life cycle extremely short, sometimes too short for many multinational companies to pursue product development, manufacturing, and marketing on a global basis without strategic alliance partners. The benefits of maintaining an independent proprietary position should always be weighed against the time cost of delayed market entry.

Although most of our knowledge about sourcing strategy comes from manufacturing industries, a similar logic applies to sourcing of service activities. As a result of the explosive growth of the Internet and e-commerce, supplementary service activities—a type of service that helps improve the delivery of the company's core businesses—are increasingly outsourced from independent suppliers around the world.

KEY TERMS ❖

Comparative advantage	Domestic purchase arrangement	Offshore outsourcing (offshore sourcing)
Competitive advantage	Global sourcing strategy	
Core service	Hollow corporation	Offshore subsidiary sourcing
Currency area (or optimum currency area)	Interface	Outsourcing (contract manufacturing)
	Intrafirm sourcing	Supplementary service
Domestic in-house sourcing		Value chain

REVIEW QUESTIONS ❖

1. Discuss the reasons why trade statistics do not capture the intricacies of global sourcing.

2. Discuss the trends in global sourcing strategy. Why is it necessary for companies to keep up with those trends?

3. Why did U.S. MNCs ignore manufacturing in the 1980s?

4. How do MNCs exploit the value chain on a global basis?

5. What are inherent difficulties in coordinating (a) R&D/manufacturing, (b) manufacturing/marketing, and (c) marketing/R&D interfaces?

6. What are strategic motivations for standardizing either components or products or both?

7. Under what conditions can a company develop its global sourcing strategy without an alliance partner?

DISCUSSION QUESTIONS ❖ ❖ ❖ ❖ ❖ ❖ ❖ ❖ ❖ ❖ ❖ ❖ ❖ ❖ ❖ ❖ ❖

1. Sirena Apparel Group Inc. is a manufacturer and distributor of men's and women's clothing items. Recently, it decided to establish its own manufacturing facility in San Luis Rio Colorado, Mexico. The reason was the intense cost pressures that it faced from foreign imports. The establishment of this manufacturing facility in Mexico would, according to the company, give it the edge in competing effectively with other foreign manufacturers. Sirena is not an isolated example. It is just one of the many companies that have been establishing manufacturing facilities across the border. Would you consider the move by the company as one step toward the hollowing out of the company? Why or why not? Hewlett-Packard is one of the many personal computer manufacturers that has established its own manufacturing facilities abroad, especially in Southeast Asia. Are these companies being hollowed out?

2. There has been considerable emphasis on the declining productivity of U.S. manufacturing firms since the early 1980s when Japanese and Korean manufacturers made their presence felt in the United States. An argument could be made that this emphasis on manufacturing activity may be slightly misplaced, especially given the fact that today only 25 percent of the U.S. GNP comes from manufacturing activities while nearly 70 percent of the GNP is attributable to service activities. Do you agree with this argument? Why or why not?

3. The integration–adaptiveness dichotomy has long plagued international marketers as two opposing forces in the formulation of international strategies. The pressures for integrated strategies include the importance of multinational customers and competitors, high investment intensity, high technology intensity, pressure for reducing costs, universal customer needs, and access to raw materials and energy. The pressures of adaptiveness include differences in customer needs, in markets structure, in distribution channels; availability of substitutes and need to adapt; and host government demands. What implications do these opposing pressures have for the sourcing strategy chosen by the firm? Describe two industries in which a global and integrated sourcing strategy could be more appropriate. Describe two industries in which a local decentralized sourcing strategy could be more appropriate. Which sourcing strategy would be more appropriate for the microprocessor (semiconductor) industry?

4. An important impediment to the implementation of global sourcing strategies is the fluctuation in the foreign exchange rates. You are the executive assistant to the vice president of the international operations of a multibillion-dollar and multinational manufacturer of earth-moving equipment. The company has manufacturing facilities in all three countries in North America, seven countries in Europe, three countries in South America, and six countries in East and Southeast Asia. Approximately 50 percent of the components of each manufacturing facility come from one of the other manufacturing facilities (25 percent from within the same continent and 25 percent from a different continent). The vice president would like you to suggest ways in which the risks of foreign exchange rate fluctuations can be reduced while the benefits of an integrated sourcing strategy can be derived. What are some suggestions you would make?

5. The other side of "outsourcing" is sourcing. Global sourcing from suppliers has become a trend for retailers. Retailers such as Wal-Mart and manufacturers such as P&G and Unilever are the main forces that drive the trend. B2B exchanges, buying alliances, and in-house retailer systems currently allow retailers to source globally, matching them with the right suppliers, increasing supplier-retailer collaboration, and, in the process, consolidating the supply chain. If you are going to persuade a large retailer that global sourcing from international suppliers is good for the company, what benefits would you like to emphasize?

SHORT CASES

CASE 10-1

AMD: GLOBAL SOURCING ON THE WEB

It is a well-accepted fact that the Internet has shrunk the world and changed the way we live as consumers. It is also changing the way businesses manage their operations. An important area in which firms have benefited as a result of the World Wide Web is that of supply chain management, specifically global sourcing. Prior to the penetration of the Internet into every sphere of business, firms used the traditional formula for looking for the best sources and suppliers for components and products. This sourcing process consists of a rigorous search for suppliers followed by innumerable meetings, telephone calls, faxes, mail, and jet-setting around the globe to pin down the appropriate supplier. This entire process takes anywhere between two months to six months on the average. Searching for suppliers on a global basis to lower costs takes even longer at times.

A few smart firms, however, have discovered that sourcing on the Internet instead can be a boon in terms of the time taken to secure a supply deal and the costs of procurement, which the online channel reduces considerably. Semiconductor manufacturer Advanced Micro Devices, better known as AMD, is one multinational company among several in its industry that has learned how to use the Internet to obtain materials and parts such as silicon wafers and certain chemicals for use in semiconductors at competitive prices.

There is increasing pressure to lower costs in a hypercompetitive semiconductor industry, which makes it imperative for these firms to resort to ways to bring down costs via online sourcing practices. The constant updating of technologies requires additional construction of facilities, which is sometimes very expensive due to which a considerable amount of outsourcing takes place in this industry. Therefore, the increasing number of suppliers every year makes it important for semiconductors firms to be on the continuous lookout for supply deals. Striking deals online then proves to be cost and time friendly. Going to the Web for making such deals has proved to be very effective for AMD. AMD's suppliers for semiconductor components include a variety of vendors from all over the world.

As more firms realized the value of online sourcing, there is a growing availability of software and online negotiation services vendors who enable global sourcing online. These firms provide a range of services including market research,

negotiation, and so on. As a result of global sourcing on the Internet, AMD managed to save around 15 to 20 percent of its costs even though it has not yet adopted electronic sourcing in every aspect of its business.

At AMD, the process works in this way. AMD puts out its requirements, and various suppliers from all over the world can place their bid similar to an auction as on popular online auctioneer eBay. Even though the suppliers do not know the exact details of the other bids, they know where their bid stands in comparison with that of rival bidders. For the firm, these online marketplaces also include a database of worldwide suppliers with their transaction histories, products, contract specifics, and the like so that firms can avail themselves of another supplier in case of shortage of components.

AMD is still relatively new to this form of sourcing, but the company believes that in time, it will rely more and more on global sourcing the online way. Some advantages of online sourcing include increasing the visibility of suppliers, lowering overall costs, and reducing the sourcing cycle and time taken to production. This method of procurement has often been used by firms in addition to the traditional mode of sourcing, but now more firms are resorting to searching for, negotiating, and securing supply contracts solely through the online channel, thus abandoning their former ways. According to reports, today probably only between 5 to 10 percent of firms engage in online sourcing. As the cost-cutting benefits of this mode of sourcing become more evident to profit-focused companies, we can expect more firms to select this route. The research group Aberdeen reckons that if more multinational firms were to go online for global sourcing, together they would save more than $1.5 trillion annually while AMR Research firm estimates that such deals reduce the time taken to land a supply contract by two-thirds.

DISCUSSION QUESTIONS

1. How does "trust" become an issue in online sourcing?

2. Do you think offline interaction is better for global sourcing and that online transactions are better for domestic sourcing? Why or why not?

3. Online procurement is creating new terms for management such as Web-based sourcing and procurement. Should these strategies be different from traditional ones for sourcing? How?

4. Should firms entirely give up their traditional sourcing methods? What are the pitfalls of sourcing online only?

Source: Special Report: The Future of e-Business: "Going to the Source, on the Web," *Business Week,* May 13, 2002.

CASE 10-2

INTEL'S FORMULA FOR INDIRECT MATERIALS SOURCING

Intel is the world's largest chip, computer, and networking equipment manufacturer. Intel is also known as a global company that sources its parts from around the world. It uses global procurement for direct and indirect materials. While direct materials include actual parts that Intel sources and uses in its products, indirect materials are essentially ancillary services such as marketing and logistics, facilities, and travel including some goods that Intel, like most other firms, purchases from external suppliers. Even though sourcing of indirect materials often misses most of the attention that direct materials sourcing gets, this expenditure on indirect services adds more than 55 percent to the company's total sourcing costs.

Two years ago, Intel devised a method to reduce the costs of indirect materials sourcing by almost 10 percent. The company experienced pressure to lower costs mainly because in the past several years, Intel had been growing and rapidly globalizing so that it was increasingly obtaining parts from foreign regions. This global practice increased the volume and costs of indirect materials even more than those of direct materials. Until 2002, Intel had been obtaining indirect materials from suppliers based on the geographical region. The indirect materials sourcing process was unconsolidated in that there were personnel in Intel's three major markets (North America, Europe, and Asia) who were responsible for such purchases. However, communication and coordination between personnel in different areas was minimal. Furthermore, Intel's organization structure was highly decentralized, and the company realized that it would need to take proper measures to improve its global sourcing process. Intel did just that and three years later, global sourcing for indirect materials is much more streamlined and organized.

To start, Intel consolidated its indirect materials sourcing operations. It had developed a five-step sourcing process already in use in some other divisions and began applying the process to its sourcing activities. The first step involves organizing sourcing teams based on needs of internal buyers.

The team, which consisted of members from all business units in a particular region, was then responsible for purchasing indirect materials globally after analyzing requirements. Intel also maintained a global database that the sourcing teams could access and utilize to monitor expenditure. Earlier, the company had used several different systems that made it difficult to track overall corporate spending on indirect materials. The second step involves gauging the availability of goods and services through suppliers and in the third step, which is the core of these efforts, the team put together a strategic sourcing plan based on the company's materials requirements, costs, suppliers, and fulfillment of the orders. Most plans so far have been for an average of two years or so. In the last three years, Intel has used this process to source around 95 percent of its indirect materials. The remaining Steps four and five of this process include selecting and negotiating with suppliers and finally managing and evaluating the relationship. The team is responsible for communicating their plans to a companywide global sourcing group.

One area in which Intel has been using this method is for automotive rentals for its employees who travel for business. Car rental and leasing are different for Intel's employees in the United States and Europe, where executives and sales teams rent cars, and in Asia, where cars are leased primarily for employees who have relocated to those areas. Hence, for such ground transportation procurement, Intel has a global sourcing team that operates out of its main office in Ireland but manages and coordinates with teams in the three different areas. These teams then negotiate with various suppliers for the best deal. In this manner, Intel has adopted the sourcing method in almost all areas of indirect materials procurement. Some of the advantages that it has seen are a reduction in costs of procurement, speed, accuracy, and better management and control of inventory.

DISCUSSION QUESTIONS

1. Could Intel possibly take this process online and save additional costs, or would that not be an ideal strategy in this case?

2. How is sourcing for direct materials different from procurement of indirect materials in terms of strategies?

Source: "Intel Goes Global with Indirect Buying Strategy: Leveraging its 5-Step Program Unites Purchasing, Business and Finance Units," *Purchasing,* April 7, 2005, p. 16.

FURTHER READING

Axelsson, Björn, Frank Rozemeijer, and Finn Wynstra, eds. *Developing Sourcing Capabilities: Creating Strategic Change in Purchasing and Supply Management.* Hoboken, NJ: Wiley, 2005.

Kotabe, Masaaki, and Janet Y. Murray. "Global Sourcing Strategy and Sustainable Competitive Advantage." *Industrial Marketing Management,* 33 (January 2004), pp. 7–14.

Krugman, Paul. "Reckonings: Chip of Fools." *New York Times,* April 18, 2001, p. A23.

Quinn, James Brian. "Strategic Outsourcing: Leveraging Knowledge Capabilities." *Sloan Management Review,* 40 (Summer 1999), pp. 9–21.

Samli, A. Coskin, John M. Browning, and Carolyn Busbia. "The Status of Global Sourcing as a Critical Tool of Strategic Planning: Opportunistic versus Strategic Dichotomy." *Journal of Business Research,* 43 (November 1998), pp. 177–87.

Trent, Robert J., and Robert M. Monczka. "Achieving Excellence in Global Sourcing." *Sloan Management Review,* 47 (Fall 2005), pp. 24–32.

Zou, Shaoming, and Matthew B. Myers. "The R&D, Manufacturing and Marketing Competencies and the Firm's Global Marketing Position: An Empirical Study." *Journal of Global Marketing,* 12 (3), 1999, pp. 5–21.

GLOBAL PRODUCT POLICY DECISIONS I: DEVELOPING NEW PRODUCTS FOR GLOBAL MARKETS

CHAPTER OVERVIEW

1. GLOBAL PRODUCT STRATEGIES
2. STANDARDIZATION VERSUS CUSTOMIZATION
3. MULTINATIONAL DIFFUSION
4. DEVELOPMENT OF NEW PRODUCTS FOR GLOBAL MARKETS
5. TRULY GLOBAL INNOVATION

A cornerstone of a global marketing mix program is the set of product policy decisions that multinational corporations (MNCs) constantly need to formulate. The range of product policy questions that need to be tackled is bedazzling: What new products should be developed for what markets? What products should be added to, removed from, or modified for the product line in each of the countries in which the company operates? What brand names should be used? How should the product be packaged, serviced? and so forth. Clearly, product managers in charge of the product line of an MNC have their work cut out for them.

Improper product policy decisions are made easily as the following anecdotes illustrate:

- *Ikea in the United States.*[1] Ikea's foray in the United States was plagued with teething problems. Stores were in poor locations. Ikea stubbornly refused to size its beds and kitchen cabinets to fit U.S. sheets and appliances. Bookshelves were too small to hold a television set. Bath towels were too small and too thin. Customers bought vases to drink from because glasses were too small. Sofas were too hard. Dining tables were too small to fit a turkey for Thanksgiving. Ikea's system of self-service and self-assembly puzzled Americans. Prices were too high. Ikea remedied the situation by adapting the product line, choosing new and bigger store locations, improving service, and slashing prices. Some of the changes that Ikea made in the U.S. have since been introduced in Europe. For instance, U.S.-style softer sofas have become a great hit in Europe.

---

[1] www.brandchannel.com/features_effect.asp?pf_id=256 and www.businessweek.com/magazine/content/05_46/b3959001.htm.

- *Procter & Gamble in Australia.* Rather than manufacturing disposable diapers locally in Australia as Kimberly-Clark did, P&G decided to import them. The size of the Australian and New Zealand markets did not warrant local manufacturing, according to P&G. Unfortunately, by using packaging designed for the Asian region with non-English labeling, P&G alienated its customers in Australia.[2]
- *U.S. carmakers in Japan.* Historically, U.S. car sales in Japan have been pretty dismal. Analysts have blamed import barriers and the fact that most U.S.-made cars were originally sold with the steering wheel on the left-hand side. Other factors are at play, though. Sales of Chrysler's Neon during the first year of introduction in Japan were far below target. Japanese car buyers disliked the Neon's round curves; they preferred boxier designs. The sales of Ford's Taurus in Japan were also lackluster. Part of the problem was that, initially, the Taurus did not fit in Japanese parking spaces. For a car to be registered in Japan, the police need to certify that it will fit in the customer's parking lot (see also Global Perspective 11-1 on Saturn's marketing strategy in Japan).[3]

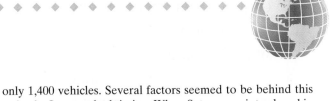

GLOBAL PERSPECTIVE 11-1

SELLING SATURNS IN JAPAN

Saturn, a unit of General Motors Corp., has been phenomenally popular in the United States with its refreshing approach to selling cars. The car's popularity in the U.S. market is due to its unique formula of customer-friendly retailing and no-haggle pricing. In light of its success in the United States, GM figured that Saturn might also do well in fiercely competitive Japan. The car premiered in Japan in April 1997. Saturn's launch strategy in Japan was to take on the local competition by competing as a sedan, an everyday car. It installed right-hand drive steering and added features such as folding side mirrors. Saturn also established its own dealer network, a rather unusual move for car imports. Saturn's goal was to sign up 20 exclusive dealers who would sell only Saturns. It took the firm longer than expected to achieve its target. The car was priced at $14,000, which was competitive with local brands and less expensive than most other imports. Saturn also invested heavily in advertising to build brand recognition. Ads showed scenes of Saturn's headquarters in Tennessee and Japanese salespeople sporting Saturn's casual look.

Despite all of the enthusiasm and GM's gung-ho attitude, sales turned out to be disappointing. In 1998, Saturn sold only 1,400 vehicles. Several factors seemed to be behind this setback. One was bad timing. When Saturn was introduced in Japan, the country was going through a deep economic slump. The launch date happened a few days after the government hiked the sales tax to 5 percent (from 3 percent), a move that weakened the car market overall. Sales of sedans—the only subcategory in which Saturn initially competed—were plunging around the launch time. Some analysts also felt that the Saturn strategy would not appeal to import-car buyers in Japan. The typical foreign-car buyer wants a car to make him or her stand out of the crowd. Successful imports from the United States are quintessentially "American" cars like DaimlerChrysler's Jeep Cherokee and GM's Cadillac Seville. Setting up its own dealership network posed some challenges too. The economic recession meant that few potential dealers were willing to take the risk of selling a relatively unknown car model. Those who were interested had a hard time raising the money. With only 20 dealerships, potential customers also had a hard time locating a dealer outlet.

Sales picked up a bit in 1999 with the launch of a three-door coupe model. In October 1998, Saturn announced that it planned to open 80 new stores over the coming five years. Saturn also set up an Internet showroom (www.saturn.co.jp) to better serve the needs of Internet savvy car-shoppers. However, GM finally pulled the plug after selling only 1,002 Saturn cars in 2001. Still, Saturn appears to have made some impact on the Japanese car market: Toyota adopted Saturn's no-haggle approach toward pricing at some of its dealerships in Japan.

Sources: "Saturn Signs 6 Firms to Sell Cars in Japan," *The Asian Wall Street Journal,* July 9, 1996, p. 6; "In Japan, Saturn Finds the Going Has Been Slow," *The Asian Wall Street Journal,* August 26, 1998, pp. 1, 7; "Saturn in Japan Slows to Crawl," *Advertising Age International,* January 1998, p. 26; "Despite Problems in Japan, GM's Saturn Not Giving Up," *Dow Jones Business News,* April 14, 1999; and "GM's Cruze Gets Lost in Japanese Market," *The Asian Wall Street Journal,* September 16, 2002, pp. A8, A10.

[2] "P&G Puts Nappies to Rest in Australia," *Advertising Age International,* September 19, 1994, I-31.

[3] "Success Continues to Elude U.S. Car Makers in Japan," *The Asian Wall Street Journal,* January 10–11, 1997, pp. 1, 7.

These anecdotes amply show that even seasoned blue-chip companies commit the occasional "blunder" when making product decisions in the global marketplace. In addition to being amusing (at least for outsiders), product blunders sometimes teach valuable lessons. This chapter focuses on new product development strategies for global markets. The first part of this chapter considers the product strategic issues that MNCs face. The second part gives an overview of the new product development process in a global setting. Finally, we examine what it means to be a truly global innovator.

GLOBAL PRODUCT STRATEGIES

◆ ◆ ◆ ◆ ◆ ◆ ◆ ◆ ◆

Companies can pursue three global strategies to penetrate foreign markets.[4] Some firms simply adopt the same product or communication policy used in their home market as an **extension** of their homegrown product/communication strategies to their foreign markets. Other companies prefer to adapt their strategy to the local marketplace. This strategy of **adaptation** enables the firm to cater to the needs and wants of its foreign customers. A third alternative is to adopt an **invention** strategy by which products are designed from scratch for the global marketplace. These three basic strategies can be further classified in five strategic options, as shown in Exhibit 11-1. Let us look at each of these options in greater detail.

At one extreme, a company might choose to market a standardized product using a uniform communications strategy. Early entrants in the global arena often opt for this approach. Small companies with few resources also typically prefer this option. For them, the potential payoffs of customized products and/or advertising campaigns usually do not justify the incremental costs of adaptation. Dual extension might also work when the company targets a "global" segment with similar needs. Blistex's marketing efforts for its namesake product in Europe is a typical example. The product, a lip balm, offers identical needs in each of the various European markets. Except for some minor modifications (e.g., labeling), the same product is sold in each country. In 1995, Blistex ran a uniform European advertising campaign using identical positioning and advertising strategies ("Care-to-Cure") across countries.[5]

Generally speaking, a standardized product policy coupled with a uniform communication strategy offers substantial savings coming from economies of scale. This strategy is basically product driven rather than market driven. The downside is that it is likely to alienate foreign customers, who might switch to a local or another foreign competing brand that is more in tune with their needs. In many industries, modern production processes such as CAD/CAM[6] manufacturing technologies obviate the need for large production batch sizes.

Strategic Option 1: Product and Communication Extension—Dual Extension

Due to differences in the cultural or competitive environment, the same product often is used to offer benefits or functions that dramatically differ from those in the home market. Such gaps between the foreign and home market drive companies to market the same product using customized advertising campaigns. Although it retains the scale economies on the manufacturing side, the firm sacrifices potential savings on the advertising front. Wrigley, the Chicago-based chewing gum company, is a typical practitioner of this approach. It sells most of its brands marketed in the United States in Wrigley's overseas markets, striving for a uniformly superior quality product. To build up the chewing gum category, Wrigley sells its products at a stable and low price.

Strategic Option 2: Product Extension—Communications Adaptation

---

[4]Warren J. Keegan, "Multinational Product Planning: Strategic Alternatives," *Journal of Marketing,* 33 (January 1969), pp. 58–62.

[5]Mark Boersma, Supervisor International Operations, Blistex, Inc., personal communication, 1994.

[6]Computer-aided-design/computer-aided-manufacturing.

EXHIBIT 11-1

GLOBAL EXPANSION STRATEGIES

Strategy	Product Function or Need Satisfied	Conditions of Product Use	Ability to Buy Product	Recommended Product Strategy	Recommended Communications Strategy
1	Same	Same	Yes	Extension	Extension
2	Different	Same	Yes	Extension	Adaptation
3	Same	Different	Yes	Adaptation	Extension
4	Different	Different	Yes	Adaptation	Adaptation
5	Same	—	No	Invention	Invention

Source: Warren J. Keegan, "Multinational Product Planning: Strategic Alternatives." Reprinted from *Journal of Marketing,* (January 1969), pp. 58–62, published by the American Marketing Association.

Given that chewing gum is an impulse item,[7] Wrigley aims for mass distribution. The company sees an opportunity to sell its product at any place where money changes hands. Despite these similarities in Wrigley's product and distribution strategies, there are wide differences in its communications strategy. For example, the benefits that are promoted in Wrigley's advertising campaigns vary from country to country. In the United States, Wrigley has capitalized on smoking regulations by promoting chewing gum as a substitute for smoking. In several European countries, Wrigley's advertising pitches the dental benefits of chewing gum. In the Far East, Wrigley promotes the benefit of facial fitness in its advertising campaigns.[8]

Strategic Option 3: Product Adaptation— Communications Extension

Alternatively, firms might adapt their product but market it using a standardized communications strategy. Local market circumstances often favor the case of product adaptation. Another source behind product adaptation is the company's expansion strategy. Many companies add brands to their product portfolio via acquisitions of local companies. To leverage the existing brand equity enjoyed by the acquired brand, the local brand is usually retained. Although these factors lead to product adaptation, similar core values and buying behaviors among consumers using the product might present an opening for a harmonized communications strategy. Within such a context, clever marketing ideas can be transferred from one country to another country despite the product-related differences. For instance, a Taiwan-produced commercial for P&G's Pantene shampoo was successfully transferred with a few minor changes to Latin America. Likewise, an ad campaign developed in Mexico for Vicks Vaporub was used throughout Latin America.[9]

Strategic Option 4: Product and Communications Adaptation— Dual Adaptation

Differences in *both* the cultural and physical environment across countries call for a dual adaptation strategy. Under such circumstances, adaptation of the company's product and communications strategy is the most viable option for international expansion.

Slim-Fast adapts both product and advertising to comply with varying government regulations for weight-loss products. When Slim-Fast was first launched in Germany, its ads used a local celebrity. In Great Britain, testimonials for diet aids are not allowed to feature celebrities. Instead, the British introduction campaign centered around teachers, an opera singer, a disk jockey, and others. The product is also adapted to the local markets. In the United Kingdom, banana is the most popular flavor but is not available in other countries.[10]

---

[7]*Impulse goods* are products that are bought without any planning.

[8]Doug Barrie, former Group Vice President International, Wrigley Co., personal communication, 1994.

[9]"P&G Sees Success in Policy of Transplanting Ad Ideas," *Advertising Age International,* July 19, 1993, p. I-2.

[10]"Slim-Fast Beefs Up in Europe," *Advertising Age International,* May 17, 1993, p. I-4.

Genuinely global marketers try to figure out how to create products for a global scope rather than just for a single country. Instead of simply adapting existing products or services to the local market conditions, their mindset is to identify global market opportunities. Black & Decker is a company that adopts the product invention approach to global market expansion. It aims to bring out new products that cater to common needs and opportunities around the world. To manage its global product development process, Black & Decker set up a Worldwide Household Board. This steering committee approves global plans, allocates resources, and gives direction and support, among other tasks. One of the product innovations flowing from this global product planning approach is the SnakeLight Flexible Flashlight. The product was first launched in North America and then six months later in Europe, Latin America, and Australia. The product addresses a global need for portable lighting. The SnakeLight proved to be a major hit around the world.[11]

Other companies increasingly adhere to the invention strategy. In the past, Procter & Gamble Europe was a patchwork of country-based operations, each with its own business. These days, P&G seeks to develop products that appeal to the entire European region. Many other companies also recently jumped on the "produce globally, market locally" bandwagon. Not all of these efforts have been successful, though. The Ford Mondeo was part of the Ford 2000 project to put Ford's product development projects on a global basis. The car was among Ford's first efforts toward a world car strategy. Developed in Europe, the car was sold in the United States as the Contour and Mercury Mystique sedans. Although the European version sold pretty well, the U.S. versions were major fiascos.[12] U.S. car buyers considered the models too small and too expensive given their size.[13]

Strategic Option 5: Product Invention

STANDARDIZATION VERSUS CUSTOMIZATION

◆ ◆ ◆ ◆ ◆ ◆ ◆ ◆

Behr, headquartered in Stuttgart, Germany, is one of the leading manufacturers of radiators and air conditioning systems for cars.[14] To adapt its products to satisfy tastes in local markets, the firm relies on a $6 million design lab at its headquarters. By blowing air at the vehicle at different wind speeds and changing the temperature, its lab can simulate driving conditions in any part of the world. Design is also influenced by local preferences: Germans prefer warm legs, Japanese like air being blown at their face, and Americans favor air that is directed over their entire bodies. Working closely with its carmaker customers and based on the lab findings, Behr is able to design air conditioning units that give maximal comfort.

A recurrent theme in global marketing is whether companies should aim for a standardized or country-tailored product strategy. **Standardization** means offering a uniform product on a regional or worldwide basis. Minor alternations are usually made to meet local regulations or market conditions (for instance, voltage adjustments for electrical appliances). However, by and large, these changes lead to only minor cost increases. A standardized product policy capitalizes on the commonalities in customers' needs across countries. The goal is to minimize costs. These cost savings can then be passed through to the company's customers via low prices. With **customization,** on the other hand, management focuses on cross-border differences in the needs and wants of the firm's target customers. Under this strategy, appropriate changes are made to match local market conditions. While standardization has a product-driven orientation—lower costs via mass production—customization is inspired by a market-driven mindset—increase customer satisfaction by adapting products to local needs.

---

[11]Don R. Garber, "How to Manage a Global Product Development Process," *Industrial Marketing Management,* 25 (1996), pp. 483–89.

[12]"The Revolution at Ford," *The Economist,* August 7, 1999, pp. 55–56.

[13]"The World Car Wears New Faces," *The New York Times,* April 10, 1998, p. 1.

[14]"One Size Fits All: Except for Local Preferences," http://www.ft.com, accessed December 26, 2002.

Forces that favor a globalized product strategy include the following:

1. **Common customer needs.** For many product categories, consumer needs are very similar in different countries. The functions for which the product is used can be identical. Likewise, the usage conditions or the benefits sought can be similar. An example of a product that targets a global segment is Pepsi Max, a sugar-free cola that Pepsi rolled out in 1993. Pepsi Max is a one-calorie soda with the "mouth-feel" of a regular cola. The product caters to consumers who shunned traditional diet drinks because of taste.[15] Many product categories also show a gradual but steady convergence in consumer preferences. Growing similarities in consumer preferences have also been observed in the car industry. In the Triad markets (Japan, Europe, and the United States), the preferred car size in terms of length by width has shifted toward a space of 7 to 9 square meters.[16] The size of cars in Europe has not changed much in the last two decades. In the United States, fuel conservation efforts following the 1973 oil crisis spurred a move to more compact cars during the 1970s and 1980s. On the other hand, Japan witnessed an increase in the demand of large cars driven by changes in the tax regime and consumer preferences. People's expectations from a car in the Triad markets are also becoming increasingly alike. Market research done by Nissan showed that car buyers in all three Triad markets rank self-expression, pleasantness of operation, and comfort among their top values. Obviously, the importance of such similarities should not be exaggerated. Despite a convergence of consumer needs in some regards, cultural differences persist and should not be overlooked. A multicountry market research project conducted for BMW underscores the importance of market peculiarities.[17] European motorists have a common desire for reliability, safety, quality, and advanced technology. These are the basic criteria that any decent car should meet. However, beyond these basic requirements, there is a set of other requirements that differ from country to country. In Austria prestige is key: A car is expected to reflect "who" the owner is. Italian car drivers, on the other hand, attach importance to dynamic driving performance, design, and aesthetic qualities.

2. **Global customers.** In business-to-business marketing, the shift toward globalization means that a significant part of the business of many companies comes from MNCs that are essentially global customers. Buying and sourcing decisions are commonly centralized or at least regionalized. As a result, such customers typically require services or products that are harmonized worldwide.

3. **Scale economies.** Scale economies in the manufacturing and distribution of globalized products is in most cases the key driver behind standardization moves. Savings are also often realized because of sourcing efficiencies or lowered R&D expenditures. These savings can be passed through to the company's end-customers via lower prices. Scale economies offer global competitors a tremendous competitive advantage over local or regional competitors. In many industries, however, the "economies of scale" rationale has lost some of its allure. Production procedures such as flexible manufacturing and just-in-time production have shifted the focus from size to timeliness. CAD/CAM techniques allow companies to manufacture customized products in small batch sizes at reduced cost. Although size often leads to lower unit costs, the diseconomies of scale should not be overlooked. Hidden costs associated with size can often be ascribed to bureaucratic bloat and employee dissatisfaction.[18]

---

[15]"Double Entendre: The Life and the Life of Pepsi Max," *Brandweek*, April 18, 1994, p. 40.

[16]Takashi Hisatomi, "Global Marketing by the Nissan Motor Company Limited—A Simultaneous Market Study of Users' Opinions and Attitudes in Europe, USA and Japan," *Marketing and Research Today*, February 1991, pp. 56–61.

[17]Horst Kern, Hans-Christian Wagner, and Roswitha Hassis, "European Aspects of a Global Brand: The BMW Case," *Marketing and Research Today*, February 1990, pp. 47–57.

[18]"Big Is Back: A Survey of Multinationals," *The Economist*, June 24, 1995, p. 4.

4. **Time-to-market.** In scores of industries, being innovative is not enough to be competitive. Companies must also seek ways to shorten the time to bring new product projects to the market. By centralizing research and consolidating new product development efforts on fewer projects, companies are often able to reduce the time-to-market cycle. For example, Procter & Gamble notes that a pan-European launch of liquid laundry detergents was done in 10 percent of the time it took in the early 1980s, when marketing efforts were still very decentralized.[19]

5. **Regional market agreements.** The formation of regional market agreements such as the Single European Market encourages companies to launch regional (e.g., pan-European) products or redesign existing products as pan-regional brands. The legislation leading to the creation of the Single European Market in January 1993 sought to remove most barriers to trade within the European Union. It also provided for the harmonization of technical standards in many industries. These moves favor pan-European product strategies. Mars, for instance, now regards Europe as one giant market. It modified the brand names for several of its products, turning them into pan-European brands. Marathon in the United Kingdom became Snickers, the name used in Continental Europe. The Raider bar in Continental Europe was renamed Twix, the name used in the United Kingdom.[20]

Whether firms should strive for standardized or localized products is a bogus question. The issue should not be phrased as an either-or dilemma. Instead, product managers should look at it in terms of degree of globalization: What elements of my product policy should be tailored to the local market conditions? Which ones can I leave unchanged? At the same time, there are strategic options that allow firms to modify their product while keeping most of the benefits flowing from a uniform product policy. Two of these product design policies are the **modular approach** and the **core-product** or common platform **approach.**[21]

Modular Approach. The first approach consists of developing a range of product parts that can be used worldwide. The parts can be assembled into numerous product configurations. Scale economies flow from the mass production of more-or-less standard product components at a few sites. Vaillant, a French company that is Europe's largest maker of central heating boilers, exemplifies this approach. A wide variation in consumer tastes and building standards within the pan-European market means that Vaillant has to offer hundreds of different boiler models. However, lately, the firm has tried to minimize the costs of customization without narrowing customer offerings. The trick is to develop boilers that meet local requirements but with as many common features (e.g., burners, controls) as is possible.[22]

Core-Product (Common Platform) Approach. As discussed in Chapter 10, the core-product (common platform) approach starts with the design of a mostly uniform core-product or platform. Attachments can be added to the core product to match local market needs. Savings can be achieved by reduced production and purchasing costs. At the same time, companies adopting this approach have the flexibility to modify the product easily. The model design procedures of the French carmaker Renault exemplify this approach. More than 90 percent of Renault's sales revenues comes from the European market. The body, engines, transmissions, and chassis of a given model are the same in the different markets. Minor changes, such as stronger heaters in Nordic countries or better air conditioning for cars sold in Southern Europe are easily

---

[19]Procter & Gamble Annual Report 1993.

[20]Dale Littler and Katrin Schlieper, "The Development of the Eurobrand," *International Marketing Review,* 12(2), 1995, pp. 22–37.

[21]Peter G.P. Walters and Brian Toyne, "Product Modification and Standardization in International Markets: Strategic Options and Facilitating Policies," *Columbia Journal of World Business,* 24 (Winter 1989), pp. 37–44.

[22]"Fired Up to Gather New Ideas," http://www.ft.com, accessed December 9, 2002.

*G*LOBAL PERSPECTIVE 11-2

TWO ILLUSTRATIONS OF THE COMMON PLATFORM APPROACH WITH GLOBAL PRODUCT DESIGN

DEERE

Deere Company is one of the world's largest manufacturers of farm machinery. Deere's tractors worldwide are based on six "families" or platforms on which different elements (e.g., engines, gear boxes) can be fitted to suit needs in local markets. With that system, Deere can easily swap design ideas. For instance, some tractors made in Mannheim, (Germany) Deere's European tractor plant, use a new gear box designed in the United States. Likewise, some of the tractors made in the U.S. plant contain a new axle suspension concept developed in the European site. The platform system allows Deere to meet customers' expectations worldwide while minimizing costs.

Sources: "Difficult Furrow to Plough," *The Financial Times,* March 9, 1999, p. 12; and "Electrolux Sees Future in Fewer, Stronger Brands," *The Financial Times,* February 20, 1999, p. 23.

ELECTROLUX

Electrolux has become the world's largest household appliance maker by owning more than 40 different brands such as Electrolux, Frigidaire, Kelvinator, AEG, and Zanussi. In Europe alone, the firm sells 6,500 different types of oven. In February 1999, the Stockholm-based company announced plans to streamline its brand portfolio and to rationalize its product design process. The company aspires to move its broad product portfolio of 15,000 different product variants toward common product platforms and fewer brands. This move would result in lower purchasing and manufacturing costs. Electrolux plans to have common platforms in refrigerators and ovens with customers able to choose particular features in different markets. Whether Electrolux will succeed is to be seen. When Whirlpool, its global rival, introduced a world washing machine, consumer response was lukewarm.

---

implemented.[23] The common platform approach has emerged as a favored means for many other global carmakers.[24] Jaguar's S-Type marque shared a platform with the Lincoln LS, Ford's other luxury brand. Volkswagen's Golf platform is also used for certain variants of Audi, Seat, and Skoda—some of the other brands that belong to Volkswagen's stable. Swedish Saab, owned by General Motors, uses platforms that were originally developed for Opel, one of GM's other European brands. Global Perspective 11-2 describes how Deere and Electrolux use the core product approach in designing their products.

The balancing act between standardization and adaptation is very tricky. One scholar[25] describes **overstandardization** as one of the five pitfalls that global marketers could commit. Too much standardization stifles initiative and experimentation at the local subsidiary level. However, one should not forget that there is also the risk of **overcustomization.** Part of the appeal of imported brands is often their *foreignness*. By adapting too much to the local market conditions, an import runs the risk of losing its cachet and simply becoming a me-too brand, barely differentiated from the local brands. General Motors apparently made such a mistake in Japan. In 2001, GM rolled out a new subcompact car in Japan, the Chevrolet Cruze, built by Suzuki, GM's affiliate. Seven months after the launch, GM had sold only 6,600 cars. One problem seems to have been that the Cruze was "too Japanese" (except for the price tag!). Despite GM's efforts to give the Cruze an American look, it was very similar to the Suzuki Swift, which is far cheaper (790,000 yen versus a starting price of 1.2 million yen for the Cruze), has the same engine size, and, unlike the Cruze, comes with a stereo system.[26]

---

[23] "Auto Marketers Gas Up for World Car Drive," *Advertising Age International,* January 16, 1995, p. I-16.

[24] "A Platform for Choice," *The Financial Times,* June 28, 2000, p. 23.

[25] Kamran Kashani, "Beware the Pitfalls of Global Marketing," *Harvard Business Review,* September–October 1989.

[26] "GM's Cruze Gets Lost in Japanese Market," *The Asian Wall Street Journal,* September 16, 2002, pp. A8, A10.

MULTINATIONAL DIFFUSION   ◆ ◆ ◆ ◆ ◆ ◆ ◆ ◆ ◆

The speed and pattern of market penetration for a given product innovation usually differs substantially among markets. It is not uncommon for new products that were phenomenally successful in one country or region to be flops in other markets. A good example is Microsoft's Xbox videogame console, which was first released in the United States in November 2001 and subsequently in Japan in February 2002 and Europe in March 2002. Although sales of Xbox were impressive in the United States, they were far below expectations in Japan and Europe. Seven months after the launch of Xbox in Japan, only 274,000 consoles had been shipped.[27] One reason for Xbox's failure to woo Japanese gamers is that Xbox games cater mainly to people who are accustomed to personal computer games, which are far less popular in Japan than in the United States.[28] Obviously, the other reason is that Japan is the home market of two of Xbox's big rivals, Sony and Nintendo.

NTT DoCoMo's iMode offers Internet access via mobile phones. The service has gained a major following, especially among teenagers. KPN Mobile, DoCoMo's European partner, released iMode in the Netherlands, Belgium, and Germany. In the United States, AT&T Wireless rolled out a service called mMode in April 2002. However, neither service has proven so far whether the iMode service model can travel outside Japan.[29] In this section, we introduce several concepts and insights from multinational new product diffusion research. These explain some of the differences in new product performance between different countries.

In general, the adoption of new products is driven by three types of factors: individual differences, personal influences, and product characteristics. Individuals differ in terms of their willingness to try out new products. Early adopters are eager to experiment with new ideas or products. Late adopters take a wait-and-see attitude. Early adopters differ from laggards in terms of socioeconomic traits (income, education, social status), personality, and communication behavior. The influence of prior adopters also plays a prominent role. Word-of-mouth spread by previous adopters often has a much more significant impact on the adoption decision than do nonpersonal factors such as media advertising. For many product categories, peer pressure often determines whether (and when) a person will adopt the innovation. The third set of factors relates to the nature of the product itself. Five product characteristics are key:

1. **Relative advantage.** To what extent does the new product offer more perceived value to potential adopters than existing alternatives?

2. **Compatibility.** Is the product consistent with existing values and attitudes of the individuals in the social system? Are there any switching costs that people might incur if they decide to adopt the innovation?

3. **Complexity.** Is the product easy to understand? Easy to use?

4. **Triability.** Are prospects able to try out the product on a limited basis?

5. **Observability.** How easy is it for possible adopters to observe the results or benefits of the innovation? Can these benefits easily be communicated?[30]

Aside from these variables, several country characteristics can be used to predict new product penetration patterns. Communication leading to the transfer of ideas tends to be easier when it happens between individuals who have a similar cultural mindset. Therefore, the adoption rate for new products in countries with a **homogeneous population** (e.g., Japan, South Korea, Thailand) is usually faster than in countries with

---

[27]"Microsoft Gives Xbox Serves, Games Big Push," *The Asian Wall Street Journal,* September 23, 2002, p. A9.
[28]"Microsoft Shows Slow Reactions," *The Financial Times,* March 12, 2002, p. 20.
[29]"Can Imode's Asian Success Go West?" *The Asian Wall Street Journal,* June 18, 2002, p. T8.
[30]Thomas S. Robertson, *Innovative Behavior and Communication* (New York: Holt, Rinehart and Winston, 1971).

a highly diverse culture. When a new product is launched at different time intervals, there will be **lead countries,** where it is introduced first, and **lag countries** that are entered later. Generally, adoption rates seem to be higher in lag countries than in the lead country. Potential adopters in lag countries have had more time to understand and evaluate the innovation's perceived attributes than their counterparts in the lead country. Also, over time, the product's quality tends to improve and its price usually decreases due to scale economies.[31]

One research study that considered the penetration patterns for consumer durables in Europe identified three more country characteristics that are relevant.[32] The first variable is **cosmopolitanism.** *Cosmopolitans* are people who look beyond their immediate social surroundings while *locals* are oriented more toward their immediate social system. The more cosmopolitan the country's population, the higher is the propensity to innovate. The second country trait is labeled **mobility.** Mobility is the ease with which members of a social system can move around and interact with other members. It is largely determined by the country's infrastructure. Mobility facilitates interpersonal communication and, hence, has a positive impact on the product's penetration in a given market. Finally, the **percentage of women in the labor force** impacts the spread of certain types of innovations. A higher percentage of women participating in the labor force means higher incomes and, hence, more spending power. Time-saving products (such as washing machines, dishwashers) appeal to working women. By the same token, time-consuming durables are less valued in societies where working women form a substantial portion of the labor force.

Another study examined the diffusion of six products in 31 developing and developed countries across the world.[33] A key finding was that developing countries tend to experience a far slower adoption rate than developed countries. Average penetration potential for developing countries was about one-third (0.17 versus 0.52) of that for developed countries. Also, it took developing nations on average 18 percent longer (19.25 versus 16.33 years) to reach peak sales.

A study by Tellis and colleagues[34] looked at the *time-to-takeoff,* that is, the period from the introduction to the takeoff, for 137 new products in 16 European countries. Their key findings were as follows:

1. Sales of most new products display a distinct takeoff at an average six years after the launch (see Exhibit 11-2).

2. Time-to-takeoff varies a great deal across product categories. The mean time-to-takeoff is eight years for white goods (kitchen and laundry appliances) and two years for entertainment and information products.

3. Time-to-takeoff differs dramatically between countries. On average, the interval is almost half as long in Scandinavia (4 years) versus Mediterranean countries (7.4 years).

4. Culture explains some of the variations. The effects of economic factors, however, are small.

5. The probability of takeoff in a target country increases with previous takeoffs in other countries.

[31] Hirokazu Takada and Dipak Jain, "Cross-National Analysis of Diffusion of Consumer Durable Goods in Pacific Rim Countries," *Journal of Marketing,* 55(2), April 1991, pp. 48–54.

[32] Hubert Gatignon, Jehoshua Eliashberg, and Thomas S. Robertson, "Modeling Multinational Diffusion Patterns: An Efficient Methodology," *Marketing Science,* 8(3), Summer 1989, pp. 231–47.

[33] Debabrata Talukdar, K. Sudhir, and Andrew Ainslie, "Investigating New Product Diffusion across Products and Countries," *Marketing Science,* 21 (Winter 2002), pp. 97–144.

[34] Gerard J. Tellis, Stefan Stremersch, and Eden Yin, "The International Takeoff of New Products: The Role of Economics, Culture, and Country Innovativeness," *Marketing Science,* 22 (Spring 2003), pp. 188–208.

EXHIBIT 11-2

TIME-TO-TAKEOFF BY COUNTRY

Country	Categories	Mean Time-to-Takeoff
Denmark	9	3.8
Norway	7	4.0
Sweden	8	4.3
Finland	8	4.6
Ireland	5	4.8
Belgium	9	5.1
Switzerland	3	5.3
Netherlands	7	5.4
Austria	7	5.9
Germany	8	6.4
Italy	10	6.7
Spain	8	7.1
France	9	7.4
United Kingdom	8	8.5
Greece	5	9.0
Portugal	6	9.3
Total	117	6.0

Source: Gerard, J, Tellis, Stefan Stremersch, and Eden Yin, "The International Takeoff of New Products: The Role of Economics, Culture, and Country Innovativeness," *Marketing Science,* 22 (Spring 2003), Table 2A, p. 199.

DEVELOPMENT OF NEW PRODUCTS FOR GLOBAL MARKETS

◆ ◆ ◆ ◆ ◆ ◆ ◆ ◆ ◆

For most companies, new products are the bread and butter of their growth strategy. Unfortunately, developing new products is a time-consuming and costly endeavor with tremendous challenges. The new product development process becomes a major headache especially for MNCs that try to coordinate the process on a regional or sometimes even worldwide basis. The steps to be followed in the global new product development (NPD) process are by and large similar to domestic marketing situations. In this section, we focus on the unique aspects that take place when innovation efforts are implemented on a global scope. Global Perspective 11-3 describes the development of so-called vitamin-fortified beverages that target youngsters in developing nations.

Every new product starts with an idea. Sources for new product ideas are manifold. Companies can tap into any of the so-called 4 *c*'s—*c*ompany, *c*ustomers, *c*ompetition, and *c*ollaborators (e.g., distribution channels, suppliers)—for creative new product ideas. Obviously, many successful new products originally started at the R&D labs. Other internal sources include salespeople, employees, and market researchers. MNCs often capitalize on their global know-how by transplanting new product ideas that were successful in one country to other markets. A good example of this practice is the Dockers line of casual slacks. Levi Strauss Japan introduced this product in Japan in 1985, where it became incredibly successful. As a result, Levi Strauss subsequently decided to launch the line in the United States and Europe as well.[35]

Identifying New Product Ideas

These days many MNCs create organizational structures to foster global (or regional) product development. Unilever set up a network of worldwide innovation centers (ICs) for personal care and food products. Each IC unit consists of marketing, advertising, and technical people and is headed by the company chairman of the country subsidiary where the IC is based. The centers are responsible for developing

---

[35]"The Jeaning of Japan," *Business Tokyo,* February 1991, pp. 62–63.

◆ ◆

$\mathcal{G}$LOBAL PERSPECTIVE 11-3

VITAMIN-FORTIFIED BEVERAGES FOR THE DEVELOPING WORLD

A shortage of essential vitamins and minerals such as vitamin A, iron, and zinc is believed to affect 2 billion children worldwide. The impact of such deficiencies on children's learning capabilities and health is huge. As vitamin pills are costly to distribute, one solution to combat this problem in the developing world is through fortification of foods and drinks with vitamins and minerals. Companies such as Procter & Gamble and Coca-Cola have launched vitamin-loaded beverages aimed at middle- and lower-middle-class families who, although not destitute, can hardly afford the most nutritious diets for their children.

Developing a fortified drink that is affordable, effective, and tasty is a triple challenge. P&G launched Nutridelight, an orange-flavored powdered beverage, in the Philippines in 1999. However, the product never became successful because it was too pricey. P&G rolled out another product, NutriStar, in Venezuela several years later that appeared to be more promising. The powdered drink contains eight vitamins and

five minerals. It promises "taller, stronger, and smarter kids." Flavors include mango and passion fruit. The drink is sold in stores and at local McDonald's restaurants where it has become the drink of choice for about half of the Happy Meals sold.

Coca-Cola tried to develop fortified drinks in the 1970s but did not succeed as the technology was not advanced enough at that time. More recently, it set up Project Mission, whose major goal is to extend relationships with local governments and schools. By becoming a good corporate citizen, Coca-Cola hopes to be able to advance its core brand in the long term. With the aid of pediatricians and health authorities, the soft drink maker experimented with different combinations of vitamins and minerals to come up with a fortified drink that maximizes both taste and effectiveness. Taste tests were run in countries such as South Africa and Botswana.

One result of these efforts is Kapo, which means "the best" in Spanish. The ready-to-drink fruit juice beverage is enriched with vitamins C, B1, and B6. It has been launched in Argentina, Brazil, Chile, Costa Rica, Ecuador, South Africa, Peru, and Turkey. In Peru, Kapo comes in three flavors—bubblegum, orange, and pineapple. Targeting children aged 8 to 12, Kapo is promoted as delicious, fun, and healthy.

Sources: "Coke Launches Kapo Range in Peru," www.adageglobal .com, accessed December 13, 2002; and "New Fortified Drinks May Quench a Need," *The Asian Wall Street Journal,* November 28, 2001, pp. 6, 8.

---

product ideas and research, technology, and marketing expertise. One example of an innovation spurred by a Unilever IC based in Thailand is Asian Delight, a new Asian ice cream brand. The ice cream is mixed with a variety of fruits and vegetables used in desserts throughout the region.[36] Black & Decker sets up business teams to develop global products. Each team is headed by a Product General Manager and has representatives from the various geographic regions. The charter of the teams is to develop new products with "the right degree of commonality and the right amount of local market uniqueness." Project leadership is assigned to that country or region that has a dominant category share position.[37]

Screening   Clearly, not all new product ideas are winners. Once new product ideas have been identified, they need to be screened. The goal here is to weed out ideas with little potential. This filtering process can take the form of a formal scoring model. One example of a scoring model is NewProd, which was based on almost 200 projects from 100 companies.[38] Managers rated each project on about 50 screening criteria and judged in terms of its commercial success. Exhibit 11-3 lists the most important screening dimensions. The model has been validated in North America, Scandinavia, and the Netherlands.[39] In Exhibit 11-3, you can see that the most important success factor

---

[36]"Unilever's Tinkering with Asian Delight Yields Regional Hit," *Advertising Age International,* October 1997, p. 10.

[37]Don R. Graber, "How to Manage a Global Product Development Process," *Industrial Marketing Management,* 25 (1996), pp. 483–89.

[38]Robert G. Cooper, "Selecting New Product Projects: Using the NewProd System," *Journal of Product Innovation Management,* 2(1), March 1985, pp. 34–44.

[39]Robert G. Cooper, "The NewProd System: The Industry Experience," *Journal of Product Innovation Management,* 9(2), June 1992, pp. 113–27.

EXHIBIT 11-3
NEW PROD SCREENING MODEL

Key Dimensions (factor name)	Regression Coefficient (weight of factor)	F-Value	Variables or Items Loading on Factor
Product superiority, quality, and uniqueness	1.744	68.7	Product: • Is superior to competing products • Has unique features for user • Has higher quality than competitors' product(s) • Does unique task for user • Reduces customers' costs • Is innovative—first of its kind
Overall project/resource compatibility	1.138	30.0	A good "fit" between needs of project and company resource base in terms of: • Managerial skills • Marketing research skills • Salesforce/distribution resources • Financial resources • Engineering skills • Production resources
Market need, growth, and size	0.801	12.5	High-need-level customers for product class Large market Fast-growing market
Economic advantage of product to end user	0.722	10.2	Product reduces customers' costs Product is priced lower than competing products
Newness to the firm	−0.354	2.9	Project takes the firm into new areas such as: • New product class to company • New salesforce/distribution • New types of users' needs served • New customers to company • New competitors to company • New product technology to firm • New production process to firm
Technology resource compatibility	0.342	2.5	A good "fit" between needs of project and company resource base in terms of: • R&D resources and skills • Engineering skills and resources
Market competitiveness	−0.301	2.0	Intense price competition in market Highly competitive market Many competitors Many new product intros into market Changing user needs
Product scope	0.225	0.9	Market-driven new product idea Not a custom product (i.e., more mass appeal) A mass market for product (as opposed to one or a few customers)
Constant	0.328		

Source: Robert G. Cooper, "Selecting New Product Projects: Using the NewProd System," *Journal of Product Innovation Management,* 2(1) March 1985, p. 39.

is product advantage (superiority, quality, and uniqueness). Studies that interviewed Chinese[40] and Japanese[41] product managers reinforced the major role of product advantage in screening new product winners from losers. However, the study done in China also showed the following:

1. Competitive activity was negatively correlated with new product success.

2. Being first in the market (pioneer entry) was an important success factor.

3. Product ideas derived from the marketplace were much more likely to be successful than ideas that came from technical work or in-house labs.

Concept Testing

Once the merits of a new product idea have been established in the previous stage, it must be translated into a **product concept.** A product concept is a fairly detailed description, verbally or sometimes visually, of the new product or service. To assess the appeal of the product concept, companies often rely on focus group discussions. Focus groups are a small group of prospective customers typically with one moderator. The focus group members discuss the likes and dislikes of the proposed product and current competing offerings. They also state their willingness to buy the new product if it were to be launched in the market.

A more sophisticated procedure to measure consumer preferences for product concepts is **conjoint analysis** (sometimes also referred to as *tradeoff analysis*). Most products and services can be considered as a bundle of product attributes. The starting premise of conjoint analysis is that people make tradeoffs between the different product attributes when they evaluate alternatives (e.g., brands) from which they must choose. The purpose, then, of conjoint analysis is to gain an understanding of the tradeoffs that consumers make. The outcome of the exercise is a set of "utilities" for each level of each attribute, derived at the individual household or consumer segment level. Summing these utilities for any a specific product concept indicates how attractive that concept is to a particular consumer. The higher this utility score, the more attractive is the concept. This information allows the company to answer questions such as how much their customers are willing to pay extra for additional product features or superior performance. The tool can also be used to examine the degree to which a firm should customize the products it plans to launch in the various target markets.

To illustrate the use of the conjoint analysis for the design of products in an international setting, let us look at a hypothetical example. In what follows, we focus on the use of conjoint analysis in the context of global NPD.[42] Imagine that company XYZ considers selling satellite TV-dishes in two Southeast Asian countries, Thailand and Malaysia.

The first step is to determine the salient attributes for the product (or service). Exploratory market research (e.g., a focus group discussion) or managerial judgment can be used to identify the most critical attributes. At the same time, XYZ also needs to consider the possible levels ("values") that each of the attributes can take. In this example (see Exhibit 11-4), four attributes are considered to be important: (1) the number of channels, (2) the purchase price,[43] (3) the installation cost, and (4) the size of the dish (in terms of inches). Each of the attributes has three possible levels. For instance, the diameter of the dish could be 18, 25, or 30 inches.

EXHIBIT 11-4
SALIENT ATTRIBUTES AND ATTRIBUTE LEVELS FOR SATELLITE DISHES

Product Attributes	Attribute Levels
Number of channels	(1) 30
	(2) 50
	(3) 100
Selling price	(1) $500
	(2) $600
	(3) $700
Installation fee	(1) Free
	(2) $100
	(3) $200
Size of dish	(1) 18″
	(2) 25″
	(3) 30″

---

[40] Mark E. Parry and X. Michael Song, "Identifying New Product Successes in China," *Journal of Product Innovation Management,* 11 (1994), pp. 15–30.

[41] X. Michael Song and Mark E. Parry, "What Separates Japanese New Product Winners from Losers," *Journal of Product Innovation Management,* 13 (1996), pp. 422–39.

[42] Those of you who are interested in the technical background should consult Paul E. Green and Yoram Wind, "New Ways to Measure Consumers' Judgments," *Harvard Business Review,* 53 (July-Aug 1975), pp. 107–17.

[43] In the example, we assume that no intermediaries will be used, so the retail price is the same as the price from the factory.

The next step is to construct product profiles by combining the various attribute levels. Each profile represents a description of a hypothetical product. In most applications, it is unrealistic to consider every possible combination because the number of possibilities rapidly explodes. Instead, we use an experimental design to identify a small but manageable number of product profiles; this number varies from study to study. Obviously, the number of profiles depends on the number of attributes and attribute levels but also on other factors such as the amount of information the study is to collect. In most studies, the number of profiles ranges between 18 and 32. An example of such a profile is given in Exhibit 11-5.

After the profiles have been finalized, the company can go into the field and ask subjects to evaluate each concept. Several prospective target customers in each country will be contacted. For instance, respondents could be asked to rank the product profiles from most to least preferred. In addition, other data (e.g., demographics, lifestyle) that often prove useful for benefit segmentation purposes are collected.

After the preference data have been collected, they are analyzed using a statistical software package (e.g., SAS). The computer program assigns utilities to each attribute level based on the product evaluation judgment data that were gathered. Hypothetical results for our example are shown in Exhibit 11-6. Each country has two segments: a price-sensitive and a quality-sensitive segment. The entries in the columns represent the utilities for the respective attribute levels. For instance, the utility of 100 channels in Thailand would be 5.6 for Segment II compared to 2.5 for Malaysia's performance Segment II. The results can be used to determine which attributes matter most to each of the segments in the different target markets. The relative range of the utilities indicates the attribute importances. In this example, price is most critical for the Thai Segment I (utility range: 0 to −4.6), whereas the number of channels (utility range: 0 to 5.6) matters most for the Thai Segment II. The technical nitty-gritty is less important here, but we would like you to get a flavor of how conjoint analysis can be used to settle product design issues in a global setting. Let us consider the standardization versus customization issue.

EXHIBIT 11-5
EXAMPLE OF A PRODUCT PROFILE

Product Profile 18

(1) Number of channels: 30
(2) Price: $500
(3) Installation fee: $100
(4) Size of dish: 25″

EXHIBIT 11-6
RESULTS OF CONJOINT ANALYSIS FOR SATELLITE DISHES

Attributes	Thailand Segment I	Thailand Segment II	Malaysia Segment I	Malaysia Segment II
Number of channels				
30	0.0	0.0	0.0	0.0
50	1.5	3.4	1.4	1.8
100	3.2	5.6	3.0	2.5
Purchase price				
$500	0.0	0.0	0.0	0.0
$600	−3.2	−1.5	−2.8	−2.5
$700	−4.6	−2.0	−4.8	−3.0
Installation fee				
Free	0.0	0.0	0.0	0.0
$100	−1.5	−0.2	−1.4	−1.0
$200	−1.8	−0.4	−2.1	−1.7
Size of dish (diameter)				
18″	0.0	0.0	0.0	0.0
25″	−0.5	−1.0	−0.4	−2.0
30″	−0.8	−1.5	−1.0	−5.0
Size of segment	12,000	28,000	15,000	16,000

For the sake of simplicity, suppose that currently there is one incumbent competitor, ABC, in the satellite dish industry in Thailand and Malaysia. The ABC brand has the following features:

Number of channels:	30
Selling price:	$500
Installation fee:	Free
Size of dish:	30″

XYZ is looking at two possibilities (1): to sell a standardized product (model XYZST) or (2) to launch a customized product for each of the two markets (models XYZTH and XYZMA). The standardized product (XYZST) has the following profile:

Number of channels:	50
Price:	$600
Installation:	$100
Size of dish:	25″

The customized products would have the following characteristics:

Attribute	Product XYZTH (Thailand)	Product XYZMA (Malaysia)
Number of channels	100	30
Price	$700	$700
Installation	$200	Free
Size of dish	25″	18″

In this example, the selling price for the standardized product is less than the price for the customized product because of scale economies. By computing the overall utility for each alternative, we are able to estimate the market share that each product would have in the two countries. This overall score is simply the sum of the utilities for the attribute levels. See Exhibit 11-7 for the respective utilities for the various product configurations.

Assuming that each customer will pick the alternative that gives the highest overall utility, we can derive market share estimates in the two countries for the two product alternatives. For instance, we find that customers in Segment II in Thailand would prefer the standardized dish over the competing model (0.7 > −1.5). On the other hand, Segment I in Thailand would pick ABC (since −3.7 < −0.8). Hence, the market share for the standardized model (XYZST) in the Thai market would equal 70 percent: the number of households in the quality segment, 28,000 (see bottom row of Exhibit 11-6) divided by the entire market size for satellite dishes in Thailand, 40,000.

EXHIBIT 11-7
UTILITIES FOR RESPECTIVE ALTERNATIVES DERIVED
VIA CONJOINT STUDY

Alternative	Thailand Segment I	Thailand Segment II	Malaysia Segment I	Malaysia Segment II
ABC (competitor)	−0.8	−1.5	−1.0	−5.0
XYZST (standardized)	−3.7*	0.7	−3.2	−3.7
XYZTH (customized for Thailand)	−4.0	2.2	Not offered	Not offered
XYZMA (customized for Malaysia)	Not offered	Not offered	−4.8	−3.0

*1.5 + (−3.2) + (−1.5) + (−0.5) = −3.7

In the same manner, we can compute XYZ's market share for the standardized model in Malaysia and for the customized models in the two countries:

Market Share Standardized Product XYZST in Malaysia = 51.6% (16,000/31,000)

Market Share Customized Product XYZTH in Thailand = 70% (28,000/40,000)

Market Share Customized Product XYZMA in Malaysia = 51.6% (16,000/31,000)

In our example, the market share estimates for the two alternatives (standardized versus customized) are equal. Once we have cost estimates for manufacturing and marketing the different alternatives, we can estimate their expected profits. For instance, let us assume that the variable costs are equal (say, $400 per unit) but the fixed costs (combined across the two markets) differ: $5 million for the standardized product option as opposed to $10 million for the customized product option. Plugging in our market share estimates and these cost estimates, we can assess the profit potential of the various options:

Profits for standardized product approach (combined across the two countries):[44]

(Unit Sales Thailand + Unit Sales Malaysia)(Unit Contribution) − Fixed Costs

or

$$(28{,}000 + 16{,}000) \times (\$600 + \$100 - \$400) - \$5{,}000{,}000 = \$8.2 \text{ million}$$

Profits for the customized product strategy:

$$(28{,}000) \times (\$700 + \$200 - \$400) + (16{,}000) \times (\$700 + \$0 - \$400) - \$10{,}000{,}000$$
$$= \$8.8 \text{ million.}$$

Given the higher profit potential for the second alternative, launching two customized models (model XYZTH in Thailand and model XYZMA in Malaysia) is clearly the winning option here. Obviously, in addition to the economics, other factors need to be considered before settling such issues.

Test Marketing

In many Western countries, test marketing new products before the full-fledged rollout is the norm for most consumer goods industries. Test marketing is essentially a field experiment where the new product is marketed in a select set of cities to assess its sales potential and scores of other performance measures. In a sense, a test market is the dress rehearsal prior to the product launch (assuming that the test market results support a "go" decision). Companies prefer to run a test market before the rollout for several reasons. First, it allows them to make fairly accurate projections of the market share, sales volume, and penetration of the new product. Through surveys or (where available) household scanning panels, firms can also get insights into likely trial, repeat purchase, and usage rates for the product. Second, test marketing allows companies to contrast competing marketing mix strategies to decide which one is most promising in achieving the firm's objectives.

Despite these merits, the use of test markets also has several shortcomings. They are typically time consuming and costly. Apart from the direct costs of running the test markets, there is also the opportunity cost of lost sales that the company would have achieved during the test market period in case of a successful global roll-out. Moreover, test market results can be misleading. It may be difficult to replicate test market conditions with the final roll-out. For instance, certain communication options that were available in the test market cities are not always accessible in all of the final target markets. Finally, there is also a strategic concern: Test markets alert your competitors and thereby allow them to preempt you.

---

[44]The unit contribution in this example is: Selling Price + Installation Fee − Variable Cost.

In light of these drawbacks, MNCs often prefer to skip the test market stage. Instead they use a market simulation or immediately launch the new product. In fact, one survey indicated that pan-European financial institutions conducted test markets less than 20 percent of the time.[45] One alternative to test marketing is the laboratory test market. Prospective customers are contacted and shown commercials for the new item and existing competing brands. After the viewing, they are given a small amount of money and are invited to make a purchase in the product category in a simulated store setting ("lab"). Hopefully, some of the prospects will pick your new product. Those who purchase it take it home and consume it. Those who choose a competing brand are given a sample of the new product. After several weeks, the subjects are contacted again via the phone. They are asked to state their attitude toward the new item in terms of likes and dislikes, satisfaction, and whether they would be willing to buy the product again.

Such procedures, although relatively cheap, still give valuable insights about the likely trial and repeat buying rates, usage, and customer satisfaction for the new product; price sensitivities; and the effectiveness of sampling. The collected data are often used as inputs for a marketing computer simulation model to answer "what-if" questions.

Another route that is often taken is to rely on the sales performance of the product in one country, the lead market, to project sales figures in other countries that are considered for launching. In a sense, an entire country is used as one big test market. One practitioner of this approach is Colgate-Palmolive. For example, it used Thailand as a bellweather for the worldwide introduction of Nouriché, a treatment shampoo.[46] Thailand was chosen as a springboard because of the size and growth potential of its haircare market. BMW used Australia as a global test market for a chain of BMW Lifestyle concept stores selling accessories (e.g., wallets, garments) under the BMW brand name. The concept is a way to keep in touch with BMW customers to build a long-term relationship.[47] Other recent instances of the use of an entire country as a test market are summarized in Exhibit 11-8.

Using a country as a test market for other markets raises several issues. How many countries should be selected? What countries should be used? To what degree can sales experience gleaned from one country be projected to other countries? Generally speaking, cross-cultural and other environmental differences (e.g., the competitive climate) turn cross-country projections into a risky venture. The practice is recommendable only when the new product targets cross-border segments.

Timing of Entry: Waterfall versus Sprinkler Strategies

A key element of a global or regional product launch strategy is the entry timing decision: When should you launch the new product in the target markets? Roughly speaking, there are two broad strategic options: the *waterfall* and the *sprinkler model* (see Exhibit 11-9).[48] The first option is the global phased rollout or **waterfall model,** where new products trickle down in a cascade-like manner.[49] The typical pattern is to introduce the new product first in the company's home market. Next, the innovation is launched in other advanced markets. In the final phase, the multinational firm markets the product in less advanced countries. This whole process of geographic

---

[45] Aliah Mohammed-Salleh and Chris Easingwood, "Why European Financial Institutions Do not Test-Market New Consumer Products," *International Journal of Bank Marketing,* 11(3), 1993, pp. 23–27.

[46] "Colgate Tries Thai for Global Entry," *Advertising Age International,* May 16, 1994, p. I-22.

[47] "In Australia, BMW to Test New Concept in Dealerships: Branded Fashion Sales," *Advertising Age International,* March 8, 1999, p. 2.

[48] Hajo Riesenbeck, and Anthony Freeling, "How Global Are Global Brands?" *The McKinsey Quarterly,* 4 (1991), pp. 3–18.

[49] Kenichi Ohmae, "The Triad World View," *Journal of Business Strategy,* 7 (Spring 1985), pp. 8–19.

EXHIBIT 11-8
EXAMPLES OF TEST MARKET COUNTRIES

Company	Product	Test Market Used	Geographic Coverage
Colgate-Palmolive	Nouriché (shampoo)	Thailand	World
Unilever	Organics (shampoo)	Thailand	World
Toyota	Toyota Soluna	Thailand	Asia
Coca-Cola	Coca-Cola Blak (coffee-flavored cola)	France	World
Honda	Honda City	Thailand	Asia
Miller	Red Dog (beer)	Canada	North America
BMW	Concept stores	Australia	World
Unilever	Dove Cream Shampoo	Taiwan	Asia
Procter & Gamble	Nutristar (Vitamin-packed children's drinks)	Venezuela	Developing world
McDonald's	Golden Arch Hotel	Switzerland	Europe
KFC	Breakfast menu	Singapore	World
Fiat	Palio	Brazil	World
Microsoft	Search-based advertising engine	France, Singapore	World

EXHIBIT 11-9
WATERFALL VERSUS SPRINKLER MODELS

Waterfall Model

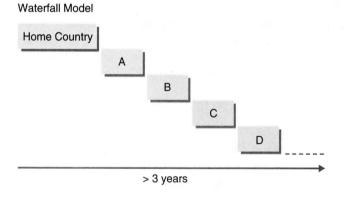

> 3 years

Sprinkler Model

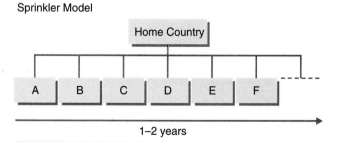

1–2 years

Source: Reprinted by special permission from *The McKinsey Quarterly* (1991). Copyright © 1991 McKinsey & Company. All rights reserved.

EXHIBIT 11-10
ROLL-OUT OF UNILEVER'S DOVE CREAM SHAMPOO
IN ASIA–PACIFIC

Country	Entry Time	Competitive Position	Market Share
Taiwan	March 2000	1	12.7%
South Korea	November 2000	3	8.8%
Hong Kong	January 2001	4	7.3%
Singapore	July 2001	3	9.2%
Japan	September 2001	2	8.2%

Source: Data provided in "Dove Shampoo Cleans Up with New O&M Campaign," *Ad Age Global,* May 2002, p. 17.

expansion may last several decades. The time span between the U.S. launch and the foreign launch was 22 years for McDonald's, 20 years for Coca-Cola, and 35 years for Marlboro.[50] In other cases, the phased rollout can happen much faster (see Exhibit 11-10). The prime motive for the waterfall model is that customization of the product for the foreign market launch can be very time consuming. A phased rollout is also less demanding on the company's resources. Other constraints such as the absence of good local partners can block a global roll-out. On the other hand, staggered rollouts are not always acceptable. In many industries—especially business-to-business markets—consumers worldwide do not want to be left behind. They all want to have access to the latest generation. Furthermore, a phased rollout gives competitors time to catch up.

The second timing decision option is the **sprinkler strategy** of simultaneous worldwide entry. Under this scenario, the global rollout takes place within a very narrow time frame. The growing prominence of universal segments and concerns about competitive pre-emption in the foreign markets are the two major factors behind this expansion approach. A case in point is the recent rollout of Microsoft's Xbox videogame console. Xbox was first released in the United States in mid-November 2001, three days ahead of the launch of Nintendo's Gamecube.[51] Within less than six months, the Xbox was also rolled out in Japan (February 22, 2002) and Europe (March 14, 2002).[52]

The waterfall strategy of sequential entry is preferable over the sprinkler strategy when the following are true:

1. The lifecycle of the product is relatively long.

2. Nonfavorable conditions govern the foreign market, such as:
   - Small foreign markets (compared to the home market).
   - Slow growth.
   - High fixed costs of entry.

3. The foreign market has a weak competitive climate because of such things as:
   - Very weak local competitors.
   - Competitors willing to cooperate.
   - No competitors.[53]

---

[50]Numbers quoted in Riesenbeck et al., "How Global Are Global Brands?"

[51]"Microsoft Unleashes Xbox," http://news.bbc.co.uk, November 15, 2001.

[52]"Xbox Aims to Be Big in Japan," http://news.bbc.co.uk, February 18, 2002.

[53]Shlomo Kalish, Vijay Mahajan, and Eitan Muller, "Waterfall and Sprinkler New-Product Strategies in Competitive Global Markets," *International Journal of Research in Marketing,* 12 (July 1995), pp. 105–19.

TRULY GLOBAL INNOVATION ◆ ◆ ◆ ◆ ◆ ◆ ◆

Scores of companies have research centers that are spread across the world. Unilever, for example, has a network of centers of excellence. However, these centers often concentrate on knowledge and technical expertise that is available in the countries or regions where they are located. Far fewer are those companies that have managed to set up a truly global innovation process that transcends local clusters. Doz and colleagues labeled such companies as **metanational innovators.**[54] Nokia is a company that has excelled as a metanational innovator. It developed its first digital mobile phone from its R&D lab in the United Kingdom, not Finland. After observing consumer trends in Asia, Nokia tapped into design skills in Italy and California to turn the mobile phone into a fashion accessory. Nokia gained experience from Japan in miniaturization and improved user interface. Realizing the potential of mobile telephony to substitute fixed-line communication in China and India, Nokia looked at Asia for skills to lower manufacturing costs.

ProLiant ML150 is a new server developed by Hewlett-Packard[55] that helps companies to manage customer databases and run e-mail systems. The initial idea was born in Singapore. After concept approval in Houston, concept design for the new server was performed in Singapore. Then HP picked a contractor in Taiwan to make the engineering design. Final assembly was made in four countries: Singapore, Australia, China, and India. In the past, design for high-end servers had been performed in the United States. However, by designing the ML150 in Asia, HP could cut costs and make the new product more relevant to its Asian customers, the target market for the new server.

To harvest the benefits of metanational innovation, a company must pursue three things:[56]

1. *Prospecting.* Find valuable new pockets of knowledge from around the world. For this to be effective, companies should keep an open mind on where they can find knowledge. For instance, while many view California as the hotbed for microelectronics innovations, Israel and Singapore are also at the forefront in this area. Geographic proximity of the company's knowledge center to other firms or research institutions in the same industry should *not* be the key driver. Much more advantage can be derived from developing and nurturing relationships with potential pockets of knowledge, regardless of their location.[57]

2. *Assessing.* Decide on the optimal footprint, that is, the number and dispersion of knowledge sources. In terms of the number of knowledge sources, companies must make a tradeoff between improved chances of developing a novel product and increased costs of integration. Often, the footprint evolves as the new product development process unfolds, especially for radical innovations.

3. *Mobilizing.* To harness the benefits of global innovation, companies must find ways to mobilize pockets of knowledge (e.g., technical blueprints, patents, equipment, market knowledge). The optimal strategy for mobilizing knowledge depends on the type (simple versus complex) and nature (technical versus market) of the knowledge involved. This leads to four possible scenarios as shown in Exhibit 11-11.

---

[54] Yves Doz, Jose Santos, and Peter Williamson, *From Global to Metanational: How Companies Win in the Knowledge Economy* (Boston: Harvard Business School Press, 2001) and www.metanational.net.

[55] "H-P Looks Beyond China," *Asian Wall Street Journal,* February 23, 2004, pp. A1, A7.

[56] Jose Santos, Yves Doz, and Peter Williamson, "Is Your Innovation Process Global?" *MIT Sloan Management Review,* 45 (Summer 2004), pp. 31–37.

[57] See also Shankar Ganesan, Alan J. Malter, and Aric Rindfleisch, "Does Distance Still Matter? Geographic Proximity and New Product Development," *Journal of Marketing,* 69 (October 2005), pp. 44–60.

EXHIBIT 11-11
MOBILIZING KNOWLEDGE

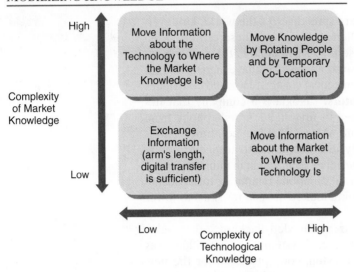

The optimum strategy for transferring knowledge depends
on the complexity of both market knowledge (low versus high)
and technological knowledge (low versus high).

SUMMARY ◆

Global product policy decisions are tremendously important for the success of an MNC's global marketing strategies. This chapter focused on managing the new product development process in a global context. We first gave an overview of the different product strategy options that companies might pursue. Roughly speaking, a multinational company has three options: *extension* of the domestic strategy, *adaptation* of home-grown strategies, and *invention* by designing products that cater to the common needs of global customers. One of the major issues that firms wrestle with is the standardization versus customization issue. By now, you should realize that this issue should not be stated in either-or terms. Instead, it is a matter of degree: To what extent should the firm adapt (or, if you want, standardize) its product strategy? We described the major forces that favor a globalized (or regionalized) product strategy. At the same time, there will always be forces that push the product strategy in the direction of customization.

Ideally, companies strike a neat balance between product standardization and adaptation. We described two product design approaches that enable a firm to capture the benefits of either option: the *modular* and the *core-product* approaches. By adopting these approaches or their variants, firms minimize the risk of overstandardizing their product offerings while still grabbing the scale economies benefits that flow from a uniform product policy. We also demonstrated how firms can use one market research tool—conjoint analysis—to make global product design decisions in practice.

The last part of this chapter highlighted the different stages in the new product development process. By and large, the pattern is similar to the steps followed in developing new products for the home market. However, the firm must address a number of complicating factors: How do we coordinate global NPD efforts across different cultures? What mechanisms and communication channels can we use to stimulate idea exchanges? What alternatives do we have when performing certain steps of the NPD sequence is not possible (e.g., test marketing)? Companies such as Nokia have configured innovation processes that are truly global. In the final section of this chapter, we looked at the characteristics of these so-called metanational innovators.

KEY TERMS ◆

Adaptation	Extension	Mobility	Sprinkler strategy
Conjoint analysis	Homogeneous population	Modular approach	Standardization
Core-product approach	Invention	Overcustomization	Waterfall strategy
Cosmopolitanism	Lead (lag) country	Overstandardization	
Customization	Metanational innovators	Product concept	

REVIEW QUESTIONS

1. Under what conditions is a dual extension strategy advisable? When is product invention more appropriate?

2. Explain the difference between the modular and core-product approaches.

3. Discuss the forces that favor a globalized product design strategy.

4. In what sense is the standardize versus customize question in global product design a bogus issue?

5. MNCs tend to move more and more toward a sprinkler strategy in terms of their global launch timing decisions. What forces lie behind this trend?

6. What are the major dangers in using an entire country as a test market for new products that are to be launched globally (or regionally)?

DISCUSSION QUESTIONS

1. Do you agree/disagree with the following statement recently made by John Dooner, chairman-CEO of McCann-Erickson Worldwide, a global advertising agency (*Advertising Age International,* September 1996, p. I-21): "The old global view was that a centrally developed brand idea could be made relevant in just about any market, depending on how it was adapted. The reality of the new globalism is that a brand viewpoint that starts out being relevant in one market can become relevant in others, because of the nature of converging consumers. Creative ideas literally can come from anywhere, as long as there is a coordinated system for recognizing and disseminating these ideas. Countries that were once thought of as only being on the receiving end of global ideas can now also be the creators and exporters of these ideas."

2. Seagram Co. is well known for its high-end alcohol brands such as Martell and Chivas Regal. In May 2001, Seagram introduced a locally made whiskey branded "30% High" in China. The brand name refers to the brand's 30% alcohol content and the alcohol high that comes with whiskey consumption. The target age group is the 20 to 39 age group who cannot afford Seagram's more expensive brands such as Chivas. Priced at $4.75 per bottle, it is more expensive than baijiu, the spirit made by local manufacturers. More than 100 million cases of baijiu are sold in China's largest cities each year, compared to only 650,000 cases of imported spirits. At the launch, Seagram believed that "30% High" would work because it claimed that there a market for a spirit with a sophisticated but affordable image. What obstacles do you see that Seagram might change with "30% High"? Presuming that "30% High" proves to be successful, can you think of other potential markets where there might be an opportunity for this new brand?

3. A few years ago, Discovery Communications, the parent company of the Discovery Channel, made a decision to create a global TV brand. It now reaches almost 90 million subscribers in 90 countries. The Discovery Channel's programming includes history, nature, science, travel, and technology. In regard to Marshall McLuhan's "global village," do you feel that there is potential for simply offering the U.S. program schedule, or should the Discovery Channel adapt its product to local markets?

4. Ford Motor Company announced its plans for developing a small, mass-marketed vehicle for Europe and the emerging markets in Asia and South America. The new car would be built on a new global platform that would have enough flexibility for regional variations. Mr. Thursfield, a Ford vice-president, stated, "It's got to be sold in Europe, but also needs to be designed for sale in emerging markets. If we're clever we should be using this platform across the globe." Other carmakers such as Toyota are following similar avenues. How do you assess Ford's new initiative? What benefits might this plan deliver? What do you see as the main challenges that Ford might face?

5. Whirlpool's Swedish division developed the VIP microwave oven that uses state-of-the-art technology and has several advanced features. Imagine that Whirlpool would like to introduce this new model in Asia. In its 1995 Annual Report, Whirlpool notes that microwave ovens have become "global products." Would Whirlpool be able to launch the VIP as a truly "global product," or do you believe it probably would need to adapt the product?

6. In the late 1990s McDonald's decided to extend its brand into the hotel sector. Golden Arch Hotels offered high-speed Internet access and an online booking system with special Internet rates. Beds featured distinctive arch-shaped headboards. The target markets encompassed business travelers during weekdays and families and young adults on weekends. McDonald's chose Switzerland as the test market for the Golden Arch Hotel concept. A first branch with 211 rooms ($105 to $118 a night) was opened near Zürich Airport. What is your view about the selection of Switzerland as the first market for the Golden Arch Hotel concept?

7. Many Japanese companies do not follow the typical new product development process (idea generation → screening → . . . → commercialization). Instead, they practice "product churning"; they make a batch of the new product and then see whether or not Japanese consumers buy it. After the product is launched, other entrants often introduce me-too versions. What are the possible benefits of this approach compared to the Western NPD model?

8. What particular challenges do you see for companies introducing product categories that are truly new into foreign markets? Recent examples include TCBY's frozen yogurt, Kellogg's breakfast cereals in China, and Snapple's iced tea in Europe. How might the marketing mix strategies used by the companies involved differ from the strategies used in the more developed markets?

FURTHER READING ◆

Bose, Amit, and Khushi Khanna. "The Little Emperor: A Case Study of a New Brand Launch." *Marketing and Research Today,* November 1996, pp. 216–21.

Czinkota, Michael, and Masaaki Kotabe. "Product Development the Japanese Way." *Journal of Business Strategy,* November/December 1990, pp. 31–36.

Duarte, Deborah, and Nancy Snyder. "Facilitating Global Organizational Learning in New Product Development at Whirlpool Corporation." *Journal of Product Innovation Management,* 14 (1997), pp. 48–55.

Garber, Don. "How to Manage a Global Product Development Process." *Industrial Marketing Management,* 25 (1996), pp. 483–89.

Gatignon, Hubert, Jehoshua Eliashberg, and Thomas S. Robertson. "Modeling Multinational Diffusion Patterns: An Efficient Methodology." *Marketing Science,* 8 (Summer 1989), pp. 231–47.

Gruber, Gerald, Frank Lateur, and Mariana Revesz. "Global Innovation of New Products and Services." MSI Report No. 01-114. Marketing Science Institute: 2001.

Herbig, Paul A., and Fred Palumbo. "A Brief Examination of the Japanese Innovative Process: Part 2." Cambridge; MA: *Marketing Intelligence & Planning,* 12(2), 1994, pp. 38–42.

Kalish, Shlomo, Vijay Mahajan, and Eitan Muller. "Waterfall and Sprinkler New-Product Strategies in Competitive Global Markets." *International Journal of Research in Marketing,* 12 (July 1995), pp. 105–19.

Kleinschmidt, E. J. "A Comparative Analysis of New Product Programmes." *European Journal of Marketing,* 28(7), 1994, pp. 5–29.

Lynn, Michael, and Betsy D. Gelb. "Identifying Innovative National Markets for Technical Consumer Goods." *International Marketing Review,* 13(6), 1996, pp. 43–57.

Nakata, Cheryl, and K. Sivakumar. "National Culture and New Product Development: An Integrative Review." *Journal of Marketing,* 60 (January 1996), pp. 61–72.

Song, X. Michael, and Mark E. Parry. "The Dimensions of Industrial New Product Success and Failure in State Enterprises in the People's Republic of China." *Journal of Product Innovation Management,* 11(2), 1994, pp. 105–18.

Song, X. Michael, and Mark E. Parry. "The Determinants of Japanese New Product Successes." *Journal of Marketing Research,* 34 (February 1997), pp. 64–76.

Song, X. Michael, and Mark E. Parry. "A Cross-National Comparative Study of New Product Development Processes: Japan and the United States." *Journal of Marketing,* 61 (April 1997), pp. 1–18.

Song, X. Michael, C. Anthony Di Benedetto, and Yuzhen Lisa Zhao. "Pioneering Advantages in Manufacturing and Service Industries: Empirical Evidence from Nine Countries." *Strategic Management Journal,* 20 (1999), pp. 811–36.

Takada, Hirokazu, and Dipak Jain. "Cross-National Analysis of Diffusion of Consumer Durable Goods in Pacific Rim Countries." *Journal of Marketing,* 55 (April 1991), pp. 48–54.

Talukdar, Debabrata, K. Sudhir, and Andrew Ainslie. "Investigating New Product Diffusion Across Products and Countries." *Marketing Science,* 21 (Winter 2002), pp. 97–114.

Tellis, Gerard, J., Stefan Stremersch, and Eden Yin. "The International Takeoff of New Products: The Role of Economics, Culture, and Country Innovativeness." *Marketing Science,* 22 (Spring 2003), pp. 188–208.

GLOBAL PRODUCT POLICY DECISIONS II: MARKETING PRODUCTS AND SERVICES

CHAPTER OVERVIEW

1. GLOBAL BRANDING STRATEGIES

2. MANAGEMENT OF MULTINATIONAL PRODUCT LINES

3. PRODUCT PIRACY

4. COUNTRY-OF-ORIGIN (COO) STEREOTYPES

5. GLOBAL MARKETING OF SERVICES

The detergent division of the German company Henkel has long been committed to a strategy of strong local brands. Henkel varies its laundry detergent strategy to address regional variations in laundry practices. Southern Europeans traditionally washed their clothes with lower temperatures than their northern counterparts. They prefer less powerful detergents, often used in combination with bleach. People in the north favor powerful detergents and generally dislike bleach in their laundry. Packaging preferences also differ. People in Northern Europe like compact products, while Southern European consumers favor large boxes. To cope with all of these variations, Henkel customizes its brand portfolio, positioning, and the product formulations. Henkel's flagship brand is Persil. However, Henkel did not own the Persil brand name in France; it offered a similar product under the brand name Le Chat (The Cat). The positioning was also tweaked in different countries. For instance, Persil's whiteness positioning in Germany was replicated for Le Chat in France. In the Netherlands, Persil was positioned as an ecofriendly product. In Italy and Spain, Henkel did not introduce Persil. In Italy, consumers had a strong preference for blue detergents with a stain-fighting capability. This did not fit Persil's core value proposition ("whiteness with care"). Instead, Henkel entered Italy with Dixan, a performance brand. Spain, which is also a performance-oriented market, was entered by acquiring Wipp, a strong local brand.[1]

The challenges that Henkel addressed—global brand and product line management—are the focal issues in this chapter. Companies that brand their products have various options when they sell their goods in multiple countries. More and

---

[1]David Arnold, "Henkel KGaA: Detergents Division," Case Study (Boston: Harvard Business School, 2003).

more companies see global (or at least regional) branding as a must. Nevertheless, quite a few firms still stick to local branding strategies. Between these two extreme alternatives are numerous variations. This chapter considers and assesses different branding approaches. Next, we shift attention to managing an international product line. Multinational product line management entails answering questions such as these: What product assortment should the company launch when it first enters a new market? How should the firm expand its multinational product line over time? What product lines should be added or dropped?

Another concern that global marketers face is the issue of product piracy. In this chapter, we suggest several approaches that can be employed to address counterfeiting. Much research has investigated the impact of country-of-origin effects on consumer attitudes toward a product. We explore the major findings of this research stream and examine different strategies that firms can use to handle negative country-of-origin stereotypes. The balance of this chapter covers the unique problems of marketing services internationally. Services differ from tangible products in many respects. What these differences imply in terms of market opportunities, challenges, and marketing strategies will be discussed in the last section.

◆ ◆ ◆ ◆ ◆ ◆ ◆ ◆ ◆   ## GLOBAL BRANDING STRATEGIES

Sara Lee, a U.S. Fortune 500 company, has 25,000 trademarks registered worldwide, 80 percent of which are in current use.[2] One of the major tasks that international marketers such as Sara Lee face is managing of their company's brand portfolio. For many firms the brands they own are their most valuable assets. A *brand* can be defined as "a name, term, sign, symbol, or combination of them which is intended to identify the goods and services of one seller or group of sellers and to differentiate them from those of competitors."[3] Linked to a brand name is a collection of assets and liabilities, that is, the **brand equity** tied to the brand name. These include brand-name awareness, perceived quality, and any other associations invoked by the brand name in the customer's mind. The concerns that are to be addressed when building up and managing brand equity in a multinational setting include these:

- How do we strike the balance between a global brand that shuns cultural barriers and one that allows for local requirements?
- What aspects of the brand policy can be adapted to global use? Which ones should remain flexible?
- Which brands are destined to become "global" megabrands? Which ones should be kept as "local" brands?
- How do you condense a multitude of local brands (as in the case of Sara Lee) into a smaller, more manageable number of global (or regional) brands?
- How do you execute the changeover from a local to a global brand?
- How do you build up a portfolio of global megabrands?[4]

Suffice it to say, there are no simple answers to these questions. In what follows, we touch on the major issues regarding international branding.

Global Branding   Reflect on your most recent trip overseas and some of the shopping expeditions that you undertook. Several of the brand names that you saw there probably sounded quite familiar: McDonald's, Coca-Cola, Levi Strauss, Canon, and Rolex. On the other hand,

---

[2] Keith Alm, formerly senior vice president for the Pacific Rim, Sara Lee, private communication. 1994.

[3] Philip H. Kotler, *Marketing Management* (Upper Saddle River, NJ: Prentice-Hall, 2000).

[4] Jean-Noel Kapferer, *Strategic Brand Management. New Approaches to Creating and Evaluating Brand Equity* (London: Kogan Page, 1992).

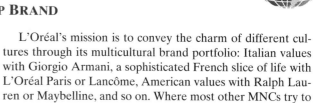

GLOBAL PERSPECTIVE 12-1

MAYBELLINE: CREATION OF A GLOBAL MAKEUP BRAND

In 1996, Maybelline, a U.S. brand specializing in mass-market makeup, generated 90 percent of its revenue in the United States. In that year, L'Oréal, the French cosmetics giant, acquired Maybelline. Since then, L'Oréal has pushed Maybelline into more than 70 countries. Three years after the acquisition, more than half of the brand's sales originate from outside the United States. In China, the brand is sold in more than 2,000 stores. Maybelline is now the leading mass-market makeup brand there. Sales jumped from $350 million in 1996 to $1.1 billion in 2000.

The Maybelline skin care brand is one of the 10 brands on which L'Oréal has founded its global expansion. L'Oréal's motto is to be as strong as the best locals but backed by an international image and strategy. So while Maybelline's formula is adapted to local skin types and weather conditions across the globe, the principal image—sassy, New York urban chic—remains the same.

Sources: "L'Oréal Exports America," *Advertising Age International,* January 11, 1999, p. 9; "L'Oréal: The Beauty of Global Branding," *Business Week,* June 28, 1998, pp. 30–34; www.loreal.com; Alain Evrard, "L'Oréal: Achieving Success in Emerging Asian Markets," in *Brand Warriors,* ed. Fiona Gilmore (London: HarperCollinsBusiness, 1997); and Cosmopolitan Genius," *Forbes Global,* November 27, 2000, pp. 130–136.

L'Oréal's mission is to convey the charm of different cultures through its multicultural brand portfolio: Italian values with Giorgio Armani, a sophisticated French slice of life with L'Oréal Paris or Lancôme, American values with Ralph Lauren or Maybelline, and so on. Where most other MNCs try to homogenize their brands, L'Oréal wants its brands to embody their country heritage.

The launch of Maybelline in India is a fine example of L'Oréal's branding philosophy. When Maybelline was rolled out in India, L'Oréal stressed the brand's American roots and urban chic. The ads featured supermodel Christy Turlington, Maybelline's embodiment since 1992. Print ads appeared in magazines such as *Elle, Cosmopolitan,* and *Femina.* TV spots were aired on satellite channel Star Plus.

One other key success factor is the way L'Oréal's labs collaborate with marketing. Fructis shampoo attests to this partnership. Lab scientists were skeptical when marketers asked for a "natural fruit juice" shampoo aimed at Europe's young eco-friendly teens. However, by adding sugar to shampoo the lab people were able to meet that demand. Fructis, launched in 1996, has been a main contributor to L'Oréal's market share conquest in the European shampoo market.

---

there were most likely some products that carried brand names that you had never heard of before or that were slight (or even drastic) variations of brand names with a more familiar ring. A key strategic issue that appears on international marketers' agenda is whether or not there should be a **global brand.** What conditions favor launching a product with a single brand name worldwide? the same logo? and perhaps even the same slogan? When is it more appropriate to keep brand names local? Between these two extremes are several other options. For instance, some companies use local brand names but at the same time put a corporate banner brand name on their products (e.g., Findus by Nestlé).

Exhibit 12-1 shows two listings of the most valuable brands in the world; one put together by Interbrand and one by BrandZ. For each brand, Interbrand assessed the profit stream likely to be generated by products carrying the brand name.[5] Note that the group is heavily dominated by American brands. This is not surprising because companies based in the United States have had much more experience with brand management than firms from other countries. It also reflects on the strength of the U.S. domestic market as a springboard for companies with global aspirations.[6]

A truly global brand has a consistent identity with consumers across the world. This means it has the same product formulation, the same core benefits and values, the same positioning. Very few brands meet these strict criteria. Even a company like Procter & Gamble has only a few brands in its portfolio that can be described as truly global: Always/Whisper (feminine protection), Pringles (potato chips), and Pantene

---

[5]Some of you may notice that some major brands like Levi's and Lego appear to be missing. The reason is that Interbrand's calculation method relies on publicly available financial data. Privately owned companies such as Levi Strauss and Lego do not offer sufficient financial information.

[6]"Assessing a Name's Worth," *Financial Times,* June 22, 1999, p. 12.

EXHIBIT 12-1
WORLD'S MOST VALUABLE BRANDS (2005)

Interbrand Ranking	BrandZ Ranking	Brand	2005 Brand Value (in $ millions) (Interbrand)	2005 Brand Value (in $ millions) (BrandZ)	Country of Origin
1	3	Coca-Cola	67,525	41,406	USA
2	1	Microsoft	59,941	62,039	USA
3	8	IBM	53,376	36,084	USA
4	2	GE	46,996	55,834	USA
5	15	Intel	35,588	25,136	USA
6	14	Nokia	26,452	26,538	Finland
7	18	Disney	26,441	22,232	USA
8	11	McDonald's	26,014	28,985	USA
9	10	Toyota	24,837	30,201	Japan
10	5	Marlboro	21,189	38,510	USA
11	28	Mercedes	20,006	17,801	Germany
12	9	Citibank	19,967	31,028	USA
13	21	HP	18,866	19,732	USA
14	25	American Express	18,559	18,780	USA
15	27	Gillette	17,534	17,832	USA
16	17	BMW	17,126	23,820	Germany
17	20	Cisco	16,592	20,922	USA
18	24	Louis Vuitton	16,077	19,479	France
19	33	Honda	15,788	14,394	Japan
20	43	Samsung	14,956	12,028	S. Korea
21	26	Dell	13,231	18,303	USA
22	37	Ford	13,159	13,844	USA
23	47	Pepsi	12,399	11,484	USA
24	NA	Nescafé	12,241	NA	Switzerland
25	55	Merrill Lynch	12,018	10,073	USA

Source: "Global Brands," *Business Week,* August 1, 2005, pp. 87–94; and "BrandZ Top 100 Most Valuable Brands," *Financial Times,* April 3, 2006, Special Report Global Brands, p. 2.

(hair care). Four other brands—Ariel/Tide, Safeguard, Oil of Olay, Pampers—are beginning to establish a common positioning.[7]

What is the case for global branding? One advantage of having a global brand name is obvious: economies of scale. First and foremost, the development costs for products launched under the global brand name can be spread over large volumes. This is especially a bonus in high-tech industries (e.g., pharmaceuticals, computing, chemicals, automobiles) for which multibillion-dollar R&D projects are the norm. Scale economies also arise in manufacturing, distribution (warehousing and shipping), and, possibly, promotion of a single-brand product. As we noted in the last chapter, computerized design and manufacturing processes allow companies to harvest the scale benefits of mass production while customizing the product to the needs of the local market. Even then, substantial scale advantages on the distribution and marketing front often strongly favor global branding.

Scale advantage is only one of the reasons for using a global brand name.[8] Part of the task of brand managers is building up brand awareness. By its very nature, a global

---

[7]"Even at P & G, Only 3 Brands Make Truly Global Grade So Far," *Advertising Age International,* January 1998, p. 8.
[8]David A. Aaker, *Managing Brand Equity: Capitalizing on the Value of a Brand Name* (New York: The Free Press, 1991).

brand has much more visibility than a local brand. Prospective customers who travel around can be exposed to the brand both in their home country and in many of the countries they visit. Therefore, it is typically far easier to build up brand awareness for a global brand than for a local brand. A global brand can also capitalize on the extensive media overlap that exists in many regions. Cable TV subscribers in Europe and many Asian countries have access to scores of channels from neighboring countries. Having a global brand that is being advertised on one (or more) of these channels can mean more bang for the buck.

A further benefit is the prestige factor. Simply stated, the fact of being *global* adds to the image of a brand: It signals that the company has the resources to compete globally and the willpower and commitment to support the brand worldwide.[9] Positioning a brand as global can be very effective if the company is able to claim leadership in its home country, especially when there is a favorable match between the product and the country image. After years of an uphill struggle, Marlboro quickly became the leading cigarette brand in Hong Kong when it positioned itself as being the leading brand in the United States. Those global brands that can claim worldwide leadership in their product category have even more clout: Colgate, Intel, Marlboro, Coca-Cola, and Nike, to mention just a few.

In some cases, global brands are also able to leverage the country association for the product: McDonald's is U.S. fast food, L'Oréal is a French cosmetics line, Swatch is a Swiss watch, Nissin Cup is Japanese noodles, and so on. Brown-Forman, the U.S. distiller, pitches Jack Daniel's, its flagship brand, as a U.S. label. In Romania, Brown-Forman set up a company-sponsored event in September 2004 to celebrate the birthday of Jack Daniel. Romanian actors entertained a crowd by dressing up as the Tennessee backwoodsman.[10] A desire to reflect its U.S. roots motivated Disney to change the name for its Paris themepark from Euro Disney to Disneyland Paris.[11] Of course, such positioning loses some of its appeal when the competition has the same heritage. For instance, Marlboro is a U.S. cigarette brand, but so are Camel and Salem.

One important issue here is how consumers value global brands. A 2002 study on this issue identified three key dimensions:[12]

1. **Quality signal.** Consumers perceive global brands as being high in quality. A company's global stature signals whether it excels on quality. Consumers often believe that global brands connote better quality and offer higher prestige.[13]

2. **Global myth.** Consumers look at global brands as cultural ideals. The global brand gives its customer a sense of belonging, of being part of something bigger.

3. **Social responsibility.** Consumers also expect global brands to have a special duty to address social issues, to act as good citizens. The playing field is not level. Global players such as Nike and Shell often face higher hurdles than their local rivals in terms of how they conduct business.[14]

The arguments for global branding listed so far sound very powerful. Note, though, that, like many other aspects of global marketing, the value of a brand, its *brand equity,* usually varies a great deal from country to country. A large-scale brand assessment study done by the advertising agency DDB Needham in Europe illustrates this point:[15]

---

[9]David A. Aaker, *Building Strong Brands* (New York: The Free Press, 1996).

[10]"Drinking to the Dollar," *Forbes Global,* April 18, 2005, pp. 34–38.

[11]"The Kingdom Inside a Republic," *The Economist,* April 13, 1996, pp. 68–69.

[12]Douglas B. Holt, John A. Quelch, and Earl L. Taylor, "How Global Brands Compete," *Harvard Business Review,* 82 (September 2004), pp. 68–75.

[13]Jan-Benedict EM Steenkamp, Rajeev Batra, and Dan L. Alden, "How Perceived Brand Globalness Creates Brand Value," *Journal of International Business Studies,* 34(1), January 2003, pp. 53–65.

[14]"How Model Behavior Brings Market Power," *Financial Times,* August 23, 2004, p. 9.

[15]Jeri Moore, "Building Brands across Markets: Cultural Differences in Brand Relationships within the European Community," in *Brand Equity & Advertising: Advertising's Role in Building Strong Brands,* ed. D.A. Aaker and A.L. Biel (Hillsdale, NJ: Erlbaum Associates, 1993).

brand equity scores for Kodak ranged from 104 in Spain to 130 in the United Kingdom and Italy.[16] Inter country gaps in brand equity may be due to any of the following factors:

1. **History.** By necessity, brands that have been around for a long time tend to have much more familiarity among consumers than latecomers. Usually, early entrants also have a much more solid brand image if they have used a consistent positioning strategy over the years.

2. **Competitive climate.** The battlefield varies from country to country. In some countries, the brand faces only a few competitors. In others, the brand constantly has to break through the clutter and combat scores of competing brands that nibble away at its market share.

3. **Marketing support.** Especially in decentralized organizations, the communications strategy used to back up the brand can vary a great deal. Some country affiliates favor push strategies, using trade promotions and other incentives targeted at distributors. Others might prefer a pull strategy and thus focus on the end consumers. It is not uncommon for the positioning theme used in the advertising messages to vary from country to country.

4. **Cultural receptivity to brands.** Another factor is the cultural reception of brands. Brand receptivity is largely driven by risk aversion. Within Europe, countries such as Spain and Italy are much more receptive to brand names than Germany or France.[17]

5. **Product category penetration.** A final factor is the salience of the product category in which the brand competes. Because of lifestyle differences, a given category can be established much more solidly in some countries than in others. In general, brand equity and product salience go together: The higher the product usage, the more solid is the brand equity.

Local Branding Coca-Cola has four core brands in its brand portfolio (Coke, Sprite, Diet Coke/Coke Light, and Fanta). At the same time, it also owns numerous regional and local brands worldwide. In India, its biggest-selling cola is not Coke but Thums Up, a local brand that Coca-Cola acquired in 1993. In Japan, where carbonated soft drinks are less popular than in most other countries, the ready-to-drink coffee brand Georgia is one of Coca-Cola's best-selling brands. Maytag Corp., the U.S. appliance maker, decided to sell its Chinese appliances using a local name, Rongshida, which comes from its Chinese partner, Hefei Rongshida. The Maytag name was virtually unknown in China. Further, consumer research showed that U.S. appliances are perceived as bulky and big by Chinese consumers. Therefore, rather than selling under the Maytag name, the company preferred to leverage the image of a long-standing Chinese brand, even though it had come to be seen as somewhat dated.[18] Although the advantages of a global brand name are numerous, there are also substantial benefits of using a local brand. Government pressure could be another factor. In China, Coca-Cola promised to help develop China's soft drink industry. To that end, Coca-Cola assisted in developing the Tian Yu Di brand, an umbrella brand for mineral water, tea, and juices.[19]

In some cases, the use of a local brand becomes necessary because the name or a very similar one is already used within the country in another (or even the same) product category. Going back to the example we introduced in this chapter, Henkel owns the Persil trademark in most European countries. However, in the United Kingdom, Unilever, one of its main competitors, owns the brand name due to historical reasons.[20] In the United States, a legal accord prevents Merck KgaA, a German drug

---

[16]The scores were derived via a multiplication formula: Brand Awareness × Brand Liking × Brand Perception.

[17]Moore, "Building Brands across Markets."

[18]"Maytag Name Missing in China Ad Effort," *Ad Age Global,* May 2000, pp. 2, 11.

[19]"Providing the Best Products at Best Price," *China Daily Business Weekly,* September 19/25, 1999, p. 7.

[20]http://www.unilever.co.uk/ourbrands/homecare/persil.asp.

maker, from using the Merck brand name because it is owned by the far larger U.S. Merck. In fact, the latter was once the U.S. unit of the German firm until it was confiscated during World War I and reestablished as a fully independent company. As a solution, the German company uses a twin-name strategy: the Merck brand name outside the U.S. and another name, EMD, for its U.S. activities.[21]

Cultural barriers also often justify local branding. Without localizing the brand name, the name could be difficult to pronounce or have undesirable associations in the local language. Soft drinks such as the Japanese brew Pocari Sweat and the Dutch beverage Sisi would have a hard sell in Anglo-Saxon countries. Associations linked to the brand name often lose their relevance in the foreign market.[22] Brand names like Snuggle, Healthy Choice, Weight Watchers, and I Can't Believe It's Not Butter have little meaning in non-English-speaking foreign markets.

A local linkage can also prove helpful in countries where patriotism and buy-local attitudes matter. Under such circumstances, the local brand name offers a cue that the company cares about local sensitivities. A case in point is the beer industry. Karel Vuursteen, a former chairman of Heineken, said, "There is strong local heritage in the [beer] industry. People identify with their local brewery, which makes beer different from detergents or electronic products."[23] In many emerging markets, once the novelty and curiosity value of Western brands wears off, consumers switch back to local brands. This is partly a matter of affordability. A can of Coca-Cola or a McDonald's Happy Meal is an expensive luxury in developing countries.

When choosing between the local and foreign product, consumers may also prefer the local good because of animosity toward the foreign country.[24] Ariel, P&G's laundry detergent, fell prey to boycott campaigns in the Middle East because of its alleged ties with Ariel Sharon, Israel's former prime minister. Mecca Cola is a new soft drink that a French entrepreneur launched to cash in on anti-American sentiments in Europe and the Middle East. Its bottles bear the none-too subtle slogan "No more drinking stupid, drink with commitment."[25]

If the local brand name stems from an acquisition, keeping the local brand can be preferable to changing it into a global brand name. The brand equity built up over the years for the local brand can often be a tremendous asset. Thus, one motive for sticking with the local brand name is that the potential payoffs from transforming it into a global brand name do not outweigh the equity that would have to be sacrificed. This reasoning lies behind Danone's branding strategy in China. The French food conglomerate expanded in China by acquiring stakes in Chinese companies and continuing to sell their products under the local brand names.[26] For instance, after acquiring a controlling stake in Wahaha, Danone used the Wahaha brand and distribution network to enter the bottled water market. In 2002, Chinese brands accounted for 80 percent of Danone's sales in China.

By now you probably realize that there are no simple answers to the global-versus-local brand dilemma. Companies such as Nestlé, Altria, and Unilever have a portfolio of local, regional, and global brands. The **brand structure** (**brand portfolio**) of a global marketer is the firm's current set of brands across countries, businesses, and product markets.[27] There are basically four main types of branding approaches:

Global or Local Branding?

[21] "Germany's Merck Faces Identity Dilemma," *Asian Wall Street Journal,* May 9, 2001, p. N6.

[22] Rajeev Batra, "The Why, When, and How of Global Branding," in *Brand Equity and the Marketing Mix: Creating Customer Value,* ed. Sanjay Sood. Report No. 95-111 (Marketing Science Institute, September 1995).

[23] "Time for Another Round," *The Financial Times,* June 21, 1999.

[24] Jill Gabrielle Klein, "Us versus Them, or Us versus Everyone? Delineating Consumer Aversion to Foreign Goods," *Journal of International Business Studies,* 33 (2), July 31, 2006, Second Quarter 2002, pp. 345–63.

[25] "Mecca Cola Challenges US Rival," http://news.bbc.co.uk/2/hi/middle_east/2640259.stm.

[26] "China Market Finally Pays Off," *Asian Wall Street Journal,* January 9, 2003, pp. A1, A10.

[27] Susan P. Douglas, C. Samuel Craig, and Edwin J. Nijssen, "Integrating Branding Strategy across Markets: Building International Brand Architecture," *Journal of International Marketing,* 9 (2), 2001, pp. 97–114.

- *Solo branding.* Each brand stands on its own with a product or brand manager running it (e.g., Unilever, Procter & Gamble).
- *Hallmark branding.* The firm tags one brand, usually the corporate one, to all products and services and does not use any subbrands (e.g., most banks).
- *Family (umbrella) branding.* This is a hierarchy of brands that uses the corporate brand as an authority symbol and then has a number of subbrands under the corporate badge (e.g., Sony PlayStation).
- *Extension branding.* The idea is to start with one product and then stretch the brand as far as possible to other categories (e.g., luxury and fashion industries).[28]

A firm's global brand structure is shaped by three factors: firm-based drivers, product-market drivers, and market dynamics.[29]

Firm-Based Drivers. A firm's administrative heritage, in particular its organizational structure, is one key factor to global brand structure. Centralized firms are more likely to have global brands. Decentralized companies whose country managers have a large degree of autonomy have a mish-mash of local and global brands. Another important driver is the company's expansion strategy: Does the firm mainly expand via acquisitions or via organic (that is, internal) growth? Ahold, a Dutch retailer, operates under 25 names worldwide (e.g., Superdiplo in Spain, Stop & Shop and Giant in the United States, and ICA in Sweden).[30] The company started expanding internationally in 1973 by buying established brands. Its policy ever since has been to maintain the local brands governed by the mantra: "Everything the customer sees, we localize. Everything they don't see, we globalize."[31] Each chain has its own positioning, and the store names and logos vary enormously across countries. This local branding strategy is driven by the belief that all retailing is local because shoppers develop a store loyalty to brands they have known for decades. Obviously, the importance of the firm's corporate identity also plays a major role. Finally, product diversity is another important factor. For instance, Unilever's product range is far more diverse than Nokia's.

Product-Market Drivers. The second set of brand portfolio drivers relates to product-market characteristics. Three drivers can be singled out here. The first driver relates to the nature and scope of the target market: How homogeneous are the segments? Are segments global, regional, or localized? The second factor is the degree of cultural embeddedness. Products with strong local preferences (e.g., many foods and beverages) are more likely to succeed as local brands. A final factor is the competitive market structure: Are the key players local, regional, or global competitors?

Market Dynamics. The firm's brand structure is also shaped by the underlying market dynamics. The level of economic integration is the first important driver here. Economic integration typically leads to harmonization of regulations. It also often entails fewer barriers to trade and business transactions within the region. The second factor is the market infrastructure in terms of media and distribution channels (e.g., retailing). Finally, consumer mobility (e.g., travel) also plays an important role. With increased mobility, global brands stand to benefit from enhanced visibility.

Apart from the brand structure, **brand architecture** is another important cornerstone of the firm's international branding strategy. The brand architecture guides the dynamics of the firm's brand portfolio. It spells out how brand names should to be used at each level of the organization. In particular, the brand architecture establishes how new brands will be treated, the extent to which umbrella brands are used to endorse

---

[28]Lars Göran Johansson, "Electrolux Case Study: The Beginning of Branding as We Know It," *Global Branding,* MSI Working Paper Series No. 00-114 (2000), pp. 29–31.

[29]Douglas et al., "Integrating Branding Strategy across Markets," pp. 100–5.

[30]"Ahold Promotes Its Many Brands," *Asian Wall Street Journal,* September 28, 2000, p. 26.

[31]"European Consumers Prefer Familiar Brands for Grocers," *Asian Wall Street Journal,* September 3, 2001, p. N7.

EXHIBIT 12-2
DIMENSIONS OF INTERNATIONAL BRAND ARCHITECTURE

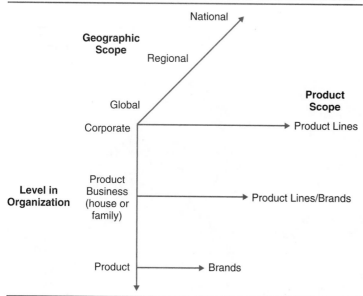

Source: Susan P. Douglas, C. Samuel Craig, and Edwin J. Nijssen, "Integrating Branding Strategy across Markets: Building International Brand Architecture," *Journal of International Marketing 9,* No. 2, 2001, pp. 97–114.

product-level brands, and the degree to which strong brands will be extended to other product categories (brand extensions) and across country borders. Brand architecture has three key dimensions (see Exhibit 12-2): the level in the organization at which the brand is used, the geographic scope of the brand, and the product scope. Electrolux, the leading maker of kitchen, cleaning, and outdoor appliances, settled on the following guidelines:

- Use the Electrolux brand name as the family brand standing for quality, leadership, and trust.

- Reduce the number of brands. Create bigger, stronger ones.

- Converge to worldwide, consistently positioned brands, both geographically and across product lines.

- Leave to the local manager the burden of proving that his local situation should be an exception to the worldwide strategy.[32]

Nestlé provides another example of a company with a well-defined brand architecture. The Swiss food multinational owns nearly 8,000 different brands worldwide. Exhibit 12-3 shows Nestlé's brand architecture; its brands are organized in a branding tree. At the root are 10 worldwide corporate brands—Carnation, Nestlé, and Perrier. The next level consists of 45 strategic brands that are managed at the strategic business unit level. Examples include Kitkat, After Eight, and Smarties. Farther up are the regional strategic brands, which are managed at the regional level. For instance, in the frozen food category, Nestlé markets the Stouffer's brand in America and Asia and the Findus brand in Europe. At the very top of the tree is a multitude of local brands (about 7,000) that are the responsibility of the local subsidiaries.

Although companies often feel driven to build up global brands, there are solid reasons to make an in-depth analysis before converting local brands into regional or global ones. In fact, local brands sometimes can have much more appeal among consumers than their global competing brands. This is especially true when there is not much benefit from being global.

---

[32] Johansson, "Electrolux Case Study," p. 30.

EXHIBIT 12-3
NESTLÉ BRANDING TREE

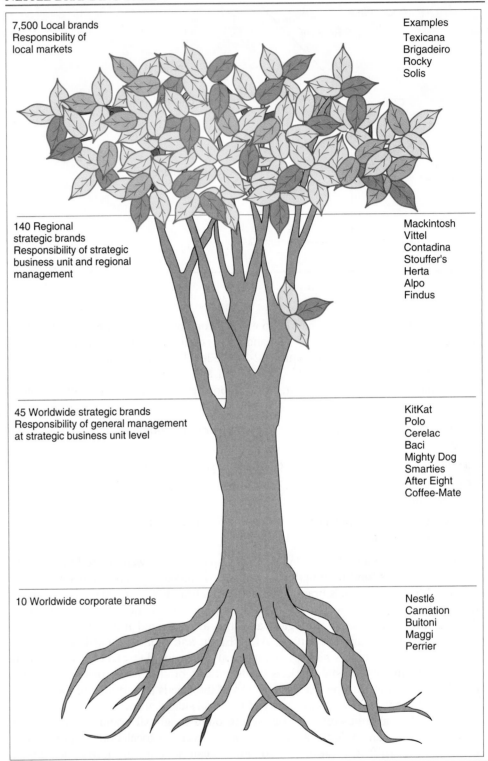

7,500 Local brands
Responsibility of
local markets

Examples
Texicana
Brigadeiro
Rocky
Solis

140 Regional
strategic brands
Responsibility of strategic
business unit and regional
management

Mackintosh
Vittel
Contadina
Stouffer's
Herta
Alpo
Findus

45 Worldwide strategic brands
Responsibility of general management
at strategic business unit level

KitKat
Polo
Cerelac
Baci
Mighty Dog
Smarties
After Eight
Coffee-Mate

10 Worldwide corporate brands

Nestlé
Carnation
Buitoni
Maggi
Perrier

Source: Reprinted with special permission from "*The McKinsey Quarterly,*" 2 (1996). Copyright © 1996 McKinsey & Company. All rights reserved.

David Aaker, an expert on branding, offers the following checklist for analyzing globalization propositions:

1. What is the cost of creating and maintaining awareness and associations for a local brand versus a global one?

2. Are there significant economies of scale in the creation and running of a communication program globally (including advertising, public relations, sponsorships)?

3. Is there value to the association of a global brand or a brand with the source country?

4. What local associations will be generated by the global name? symbol? slogan? imagery?

5. Is it culturally and legally possible to use the brand name, symbol, and slogan across the different countries?

6. What is the value of the awareness and associations that a regional brand could create?[33]

Brand-Name Changeover Strategies

When the case for a transition from a local to a global (or regional) brand name is made, the firm needs to decide how to implement the changeover in practice. Four broad strategic options exist: (1) *fade-in/fade-out,* (2) combine brands via *co-branding* or under one *umbrella brand,* (3) *transparent forewarning,* and (4) *summary axing.*[34]

With **fade-in/fade-out,** the new global brand name is somehow tied with an existing local brand name. After a transition period, the old name is dropped. A typical example is the brand name change that Disney implemented for its Paris theme park. It first shrank the *Euro* part in Euro Disney and added the word *land.* In October 1994, the word *Euro* was dropped altogether, and the theme park is now branded as *Disneyland Paris.*[35]

The second route combines the "old" local brand and the global or regional brand in some manner. One tactic that is sometimes employed is to have the global brand as an umbrella or endorser brand. For example, Pedigree was launched in the late 1980s in France as "Pedigree by Pal." Another possibility is **dual branding (co-branding).** During a transition period, the local and global brand names are kept so that consumers and the trade have sufficient time to absorb the new brand name. When Whirlpool acquired the white goods division of Philips, the company initially employed a dual branding strategy, Philips and Whirlpool. After a transition period, the Philips brand name was dropped. Likewise, Danone used co-branding in South Africa shortly after it bought a stake in the Clover company, South Africa's leading fresh dairy producer. Although Danone is a global brand, at the time the brand name was virtually unknown in South Africa. By using co-branding, Danone was able to leverage the huge brand equity that Clover had in South Africa as well as Clover's strong association with dairy products in the local consumers' mind.[36]

The third approach, **transparent forewarning,** alerts the customers to the brand name change. The forewarning can be done via the communication program, in-store displays, and product packaging. A good example is the transition made by Mars in the pan-European market for Raider, one of its candy products. Mars launched a TV advertising campaign to launch the change saying: "Now Raider becomes Twix, for it is Twix everywhere in the world." The print ad in Exhibit 12-4 is part of a campaign that HSBC, the London-based banking group, undertook when it replaced its local banking brands with the HSBC name.

Far less compelling is the fourth practice, **summary axing,** when the company simply drops the old brand name almost overnight and immediately replaces it with

---

[33] David A. Aaker, *Managing Brand Equity* (New York: The Free Press, 1991).

[34] Trond Riiber Knudsen, Lars Finskud, Richard Törnblom, and Egil Hogna, "Brand Consolidation Makes a Lot of Economic Sense," *The McKinsey Quarterly,* 4 (1997), pp. 189–93.

[35] "The Kingdom inside a Republic," *The Economist,* April 13, 1996, p. 69.

[36] Russell Abratt and Patience Motlana, "Managing Co-Branding Strategies: Global Brands Into Local Markets," *Business Horizons,* September–October 2002, pp. 43–50.

EXHIBIT 12-4
ONE FAMILY, NOW ONE NAME

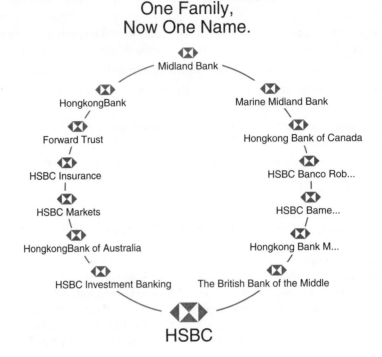

We are uniting our family around the world under one name. HSBC

Why? Because as one of the world's most successful financial services organizations we would like you to understand us better.

You may have met our people already You talk to them every time you are in touch with one of our family members. But you may not yet know just how much we can do for you around the corner and around the world.

With more than 541 billion in capital resources, and 5,500 offices in 79 countries and territories, we are big enough to help and close enough to care.

Talk to us and see. You can be sure of a warm welcome.

---

the global name. This is appropriate only when competitors are rapidly gaining global clout by building up global brands.

To manage the transition effectively, several rules should be respected.[37] First, it is critical to conduct consumer research prior to the brand name changeover to understand consumers' perceptions and gauge their response to any modifications (e.g., packaging, logo, brand name). When the brand name is changed gradually, one of the key concerns is the proper length for the transition period. Coming back to the Philips-Whirlpool example, the two companies had agreed that Whirlpool could use the Philips brand name until 1999. When IBM sold its PC division to Lenovo, part of the deal was that Lenovo would have access to the IBM brand name for five years. For the first 18 months after the sale, the current IBM branding was to remain unchanged. During the next period (18 to 40 months), co-branding (IBM/Lenovo) was to be used. At the final stage (40 to 60 months), the company would switch to the Lenovo brand with an IBM tagline.[38] In principle, the firm should allow sufficient time for the customers to absorb the name change. How long this process will take depends on the product and the strength of the image associated with the old brand name. For some product

---

[37] Marieke de Mooij, *Advertising Worldwide: Concepts, Theories and Practice of International, Multinational and Global Advertising* (Englewood Cliffs, NJ: Prentice-Hall, 1994).

[38] http://www.crn.com/showArticle.jhtml?articleID = 55300503.

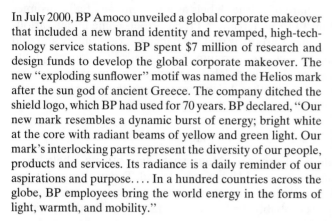

GLOBAL PERSPECTIVE 12-2

BEYOND PETROLEUM: BP AMOCO'S CORPORATE MAKEOVER

In July 2000, BP Amoco unveiled a global corporate makeover that included a new brand identity and revamped, high-technology service stations. BP spent $7 million of research and design funds to develop the global corporate makeover. The new "exploding sunflower" motif was named the Helios mark after the sun god of ancient Greece. The company ditched the shield logo, which BP had used for 70 years. BP declared, "Our new mark resembles a dynamic burst of energy; bright white at the core with radiant beams of yellow and green light. Our mark's interlocking parts represent the diversity of our people, products and services. Its radiance is a daily reminder of our aspirations and purpose. . . . In a hundred countries across the globe, BP employees bring the world energy in the forms of light, warmth, and mobility."

Sources: "BP Amoco Unveils Corporate Makeover," *The Financial Times,* July 25, 2000, p. 26; "Oil Group Hopes Helios Will Bring Sunshine," *The Financial Times,* July 25, 2000, p. 26; "BP's Step Beyond Petroleum," *The Financial Times,* August 9, 2000, p. 19.

Although the revamp happened worldwide, the impetus for the change came from BP's U.S. operations. The U.S. market is home to about one-third of BP's 28,000 retail outlets worldwide. After its merger with Amoco and a major acquisition spree, BP owned four separate brands: BP, Amoco, ARCO, and Castrol. BP Amoco recognized the need for a new, unifying image. However, Arco's service station network on the west coast of the United States was not affected by the rebranding exercise as Arco's existing business has a strong brand identity there.

One reason for the consolidation was the sense to bond BP employees around the world following the merger and acquisitions. However, another key factor was BP's desire to alter the public's perception of BP from a traditional "old economy" British oil company to a global "new economy" energy services group, taking BP into the "Beyond Petroleum" era.

Besides introducing a new logo, BP also upgraded its service stations. New high-tech service stations were rolled out with brightly lit fueling and parking areas. Some stations are solar powered and provide Internet access to customers.

categories, the purchase cycle matters too. Sometimes the phaseout can be completed sooner than scheduled. Whirlpool discovered through its consumer research that the Philips brand name could be dropped far ahead of the originally planned drop date.

It is also important that consumers that are exposed to the changeover messages associate the new brand name with the old one. One of the primary goals of Whirlpool's advertising campaign was to maintain awareness of the Philips brand name while building up association with Whirlpool.[39]

To avoid negative spillovers on the global brand name, companies should also ensure that the local products have acceptable quality before attaching the global brand name to them. Otherwise, the goodwill of the global brand name could be irreparably damaged. As a result, other products launched under the global brand name could be viewed with skepticism by consumers in the foreign market. Part of Whirlpool's geographic expansion in China involved a joint venture that makes air conditioners based on Japanese designs. The air conditioners, sold under a local brand name, Raybo, initially had about half the life expectancy of U.S.-made Whirlpool models. Whirlpool's president declared that his company would not put the Whirlpool name on the product until Raybo's quality problems were fixed.[40]

Finally, companies should monitor the marketplace's response to the brand-name change with marketing research. Such tracking studies enable the firm to ensure that the changeover runs smoothly. These companies also assist firms in determining how long promotional programs that announce the name change should last. Whirlpool tracked brand recognition and buying preference of consumers on a weekly basis during the brand-change period. Global Perspective 12-2 describes the efforts made by British oil company BP to implement a global corporate makeover.

We now consider two other branding practices that companies use, namely, private label branding and umbrella branding.

---

[39]Jan Willem Karel, "Brand Strategy Positions Products Worldwide," *The Journal of Business Strategy,* May/June 1991, pp. 16–19.

[40]"For Whirlpool, Asia Is the New Frontier," *Wall Street Journal,* April 25, 1996, p. B1.

Private Label Branding (Store Brands)

McBride, based near Manchester, England, is not a household name even though European consumers spend nearly $1 billion on goods made by the company. McBride thrives by making household cleaners and personal care goods for European retail chains such as Tesco. These chains sell the goods under their own name.[41] One of the most visible retailing phenomena during the last decade was the spread of **private labels (store brands).** Worldwide, the share of private labels as a percentage of all consumer packaged goods has grown from 14 to 18 percent.[42] Private labels come under various guises. At one extreme are the generic products that are packaged very simply and sold at bottom prices. At the other extreme are premium store brands that deliver quality sometimes superior to national brands. Private labels have made big inroads in several European countries. In Japan and most other Asian countries, on the other hand, store brands are still marginal players. Consumers in this region tend to be extremely brand loyal.[43]

Several factors[44] explain the success of private labels:

1. **Improved quality of private label products.** Many years ago, private labels had a quality stigma: Only bargain hunters would buy a store brand. Today, the quality gap between store brands and their brand-name competitors is gone in most countries. The improved quality image is probably the key success factor behind the spread of store brands. In many product categories, consumers now have the option to buy a good-quality store brand at a lower price than the brand-name alternative.

2. **Development of premium private label brands.** The quality gap has disappeared, and retailers in North America and Europe in collaboration with private label manufacturers have developed private label products that offer premium quality. In some cases, store brand products even have become far more innovative than the competing name brand products.

3. **Shift in balance of power between retailers and manufacturers.** A third factor is the shift in the balance of power from manufacturers to retailers. This reversal has been strong especially in Europe, where large-scale national chains such as Carrefour and Tesco dominate the retailing landscape. Italy is one of the few countries in Europe where private labels have made little progress. It is also a market where government regulations have dampened the development of big chain stores.

4. **Expansion into new product categories.** Private labels used to be limited to a small range of product categories. These days private labels are marketed in an ever-widening range of categories. This spread has helped to make private labels more acceptable among consumers.

5. **Internationalization of retail chains.** Another factor is the growing internationalization of large supermarket chains. In recent years, French hypermarchés such as Carrefour invaded Spain; the German food-store chain Aldi entered the Benelux countries, France, and the United Kingdom; and the Dutch retailer Ahold started to penetrate the U.S. market. Many of these international retailers often like to replicate the private label program they used in the host country.

6. **Economic downturns.** When disposable income drops, consumers usually become more value conscious and tend to switch from national brands to private labels.[45]

As a branding strategy, private labeling is especially attractive to MNCs that face well-entrenched incumbent brands in the markets they plan to enter. Under such circumstances, launching the product as a store brand enables the firm to get the shelf

---

[41] "The Big Brands Go Begging," *Business Week,* March 21, 2005, pp. 24–25.

[42] Nirmalya Kumar and Jan-Benedict Steenkamp, *Private Label Revolution* (Cambridge, MA: Harvard Business School Press, 2006).

[43] "No Global Private Label Quake—Yet," *Advertising Age International,* January 16, 1995, p. I-26.

[44] John A. Quelch and David Harding, "Brands versus Private Labels: Fighting to Win," *Harvard Business Review,* January–February 1996, pp. 99–109.

[45] Stephen J. Hoch and Shumeet Banerji, "When Do Private Labels Succeed?" *Sloan Management Review,* Summer 1993, pp. 57–67.

space access that it would otherwise be denied. In Japan, manufacturers that do not have the resources to set up a distribution channel network have tied up with local retailers to penetrate the market. Agfa-Gevaert, the German/Belgian photographic film maker, agreed to supply a store brand film to Daiei, a major Japanese supermarket chain.[46] Eastman Kodak also decided to offer private label film in Japan. Most of the distribution system is locked up by the local competitors, Fuji and Konica. Kodak hoped to grab a larger share of the Japanese film market by making a private label film for the Japanese Cooperative Union, a group of 2,500 retail stores.[47]

Umbrella branding is a system that uses a single banner brand worldwide, often with a subbrand name, for almost the entire product mix of the company. Often the banner is the company's name: Sony, Kodak, Siemens, Virgin, to name a few. Some companies also use noncompany names. For example, Matsushita, the Japanese consumer electronics maker, employs banner brands including JVC and Panasonic. Umbrella branding is particularly popular among Japanese firms although quite a few non-Japanese companies also opt for this branding system. Researchers have identified several reasons for the appeal of corporate branding in a global marketing context. First and foremost, in many cultures a good corporate image has a strong positive impact on the evaluation of the attributes of the product endorsed by the banner brand. For the customers, the presence of the banner brand's logo on the product means trust, a seal of approval, a guarantee for quality and excellence.[48] The umbrella brand basically serves as a risk-reducing device for the customer.[49] London International Group (LIG), the world's leading condom marketer, mentions this benefit as the reason behind its drive to make the Durex brand the umbrella for its condom business worldwide.[50] Local brand names are now tied with the Durex name. In Germany, for example, the packaging was altered to say "From the house of Durex." One observer described the motives behind this move as follows: "The idea behind it is that anywhere where you go in the world, you will see the Durex name, rather than lots of sub-brands. People want security and safety when they are buying these products."

A second benefit is that umbrella branding facilitates brand building efforts over a range of products. Having a banner brand makes it easier to build up global share of mind and brand integrity.[51] Instead of splitting marketing dollars over scores of different brands, the advertising support focuses on a single umbrella brand. A case in point is Nokia, one of the leading makers of cellular phones. Nokia once had scores of brand names. Today the company pushes the corporate brand name in the global marketplace where the Nokia brand was far less familiar than in Scandinavia. As one company official commented: "We had many brand names but now we believe it is better to stick to one brand."[52]

A final rationale is that a corporate branding system makes it easier to add or drop new products.[53] High-tech companies such as Siemens and Motorola tend to rely very heavily on product innovation to defend their market share. Nurturing a single strong banner brand is far more efficient than creating a distinct brand from scratch for every new product launch.

Umbrella Branding

---

[46]"Japan's Brands Feel the Pinch, too," *Financial Times,* April 28, 1994, p. 9.

[47]"Kodak Pursues a Greater Market Share in Japan with New Private-Label Film," *Wall Street Journal,* March 7, 1995, p. B-4.

[48]Camillo Pagano, "The Management of Global Brands," in *Brand Power,* ed. Paul Stobart (London: Macmillan, 1994).

[49]Cynthia A. Montgomery and Birger Wernerfelt, "Risk Reduction and Umbrella Branding," *Journal of Business,* 65 (1), 1992, pp. 31–50.

[50]"LIG Stretches Durex Identity around World," *Advertising Age International,* March 11, 1996, p. 14.

[51]Gary Hamel and C.K. Prahalad, *Competing for the Future* (Boston, MA: Harvard Business School Press, 1994).

[52]"Scandinavia's Nokia Phones Japan," *Advertising Age International,* December 13, 1993, p. 16.

[53]Hiroshi Tanaka, "Branding in Japan," in *Brand Equity & Advertising: Advertising's Role in Building Strong Brands,* ed. D.A. Aaker and A.L. Biel (Hillsdale, NJ: L. Erlbaum Associates, 1993).

Brand Name Protection

Visitors in Kathmandu who are getting tired of Nepalese cuisine can always try out the local Pizza Hut. Just like Pizza Hut restaurants elsewhere in the world, it serves pizza. However, except for the name and the main menu items, the Kathmandu Pizza Hut has nothing in common with a U.S. Pizza Hut. Brands are vital assets to brand owners. The Coca-Cola trademark is estimated to be worth about $67 billion, nearly 64 percent of the company's market value. Given the strategic importance of brands, protection of the brand name is one of the major tasks faced by the brand owner. The protection challenge entails several questions: How should the brand be protected? Which aspects of the brand? When? Where? For what product classes? Answers to these questions are largely driven by an analysis of the costs and benefits of protecting the brand.[54]

Consider the first issue: how? The most common way to seek protection is by legal registration. The first step is to hire legal counsel in each country where the brand should be protected. Several international agreements in force help this process. The oldest treaty is the Paris Convention for the Protection of Intellectual Property supported by almost 100 countries. The Paris Convention is based on the principle of reciprocity: (1) people of member states have the same rights that the state grants to its own nationals and (2) foreigners have equal access to local courts to combat trademark infringement. In the European Union, the Single Market Act had ramifications for brand protection: Trademark registration in any of the EU member states is now effective for the entire European Union.

One major stumbling block is the difference in opinion held by industrialized and developing countries on intellectual property protection. Developed countries view intellectual property right protection as the reward for innovativeness. Taking the protection away would mean that companies lose their incentive to invest in new product development. Many developing countries, on the other hand, regard intellectual property (IP) as a public good. Easy access to IP spurs economic development and thereby enables the developing country to narrow the gap with the developed world.[55] The two opposing views are summarized in Exhibit 12-5.

What should be protected? Many elements of the brand franchise may require protection. Obviously, a company should register the brand name, but in some countries, it could also consider protecting the translation of the brand name or even the transliteration equivalent, that is, representations in the local language that have the same sound.[56] Other forms of IP that could need protection include slogans, jingles, and visual aspects (e.g., McDonald's Golden Arches)—in short, any distinctive elements that are part of the brand's imagery.

The "when" and "where" issues at first appear trivial: Ideally, a company would like to register the brand's trademarks in as many places and as soon as possible, but there are some constraints. The costs of registration itself are usually quite modest, but legal counsel fees are far more significant. However, the major cost item is often the use cost. In many countries, the company is obliged to "use" the trademarks to enjoy the protection benefits. *Use* means that the company must sell commercially significant volumes of the product under the protected brand name. Most countries, however, give a grace period of several years (usually five) before the brand owner has to use the registered trademarks.

The last concern deals with the scope of the protection: What product classes should be covered? Many companies register their brands in virtually all product categories. A more sensible rule is to register the trademarks in all classes covering goods for which the brand is currently used and related classes.[57] The related classes are product categories that the company could enter in the future via brand extensions using the protected brand name.

---

[54] http://news.bbc.co.uk/2/hi/business/4574400.stm.

[55] Subhash C. Jain, "Problems in International Protection of Intellectual Property Rights," *Journal of International Marketing*, 4 (1), 1996, pp. 9–32.

[56] Garo Partoyan, "Protecting Power Brands," in *Brand Power*, ed. P. Stobart (London: Macmillan, 1994).

[57] Ibid.

EXHIBIT 12-5
DIFFERING VIEWS ON INTELLECTUAL
PROPERTY PROTECTION

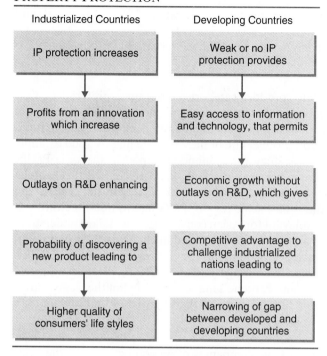

Source: Subhash C. Jain, "Problems in International Property Rights," *Journal of International Marketing,* 4 (1), 1996, pp. 9–32.

MANAGEMENT OF MULTINATIONAL PRODUCT LINES   ◆ ◆ ◆ ◆ ◆ ◆ ◆ ◆

Most companies sell a wide assortment of products. The product assortment is usually described on two dimensions: the width and the length of the product mix.[58] The first dimension—width—refers to the collection of different product lines marketed by the firm. For most companies, these product lines are very related. Heinz has a broad mix of product lines. Besides ketchup, the Heinz flagship product, the company sells baby food, pet food, ice cream, and so forth. All of these product lines, however, are food items. Other companies, especially Japanese and Korean ones, have a much more diverse product mix. Kao, one of Japan's biggest consumer goods manufacturers, has a product mix that covers personal care products, cosmetics, laundry products, and food items. It also sells chemicals, floppy disks, and CD-ROMs. The second dimension—length—refers to the number of different items that the company sells within a given product line. Thus, the product mix for a particular multinational could vary along the width and/or length dimension across the different countries where the firm operates.

When comparing the product mix in the company's host and home markets, there are four possible scenarios. The product mix in the host country could be (1) an extension of the domestic line, (2) a subset of the home market's product line, (3) a mixture of local and nonlocal product lines, or (4) a completely localized product line.

Small firms with a narrow product assortment usually simply extend their domestic product line. Blistex, a tiny U.S. company that makes primarily lip care products, has a very limited range of product lines marketed in all of its foreign markets. On the other hand, larger companies that enter new markets carefully select a subset of their product mix. When Coca-Cola goes into a new market, the focus is obviously first

---

[58]See, for instance, Douglas J. Dalrymple and Leonard J. Parsons, *Marketing Management* (New York: John Wiley & Sons), 1995.

on Coca-Cola. Once the flagship brand is well established, the next introduction is typically Fanta, the flavor line. Fanta is followed by Sprite and Diet Coke. Once the infrastructure is in place, other product lines—including local ones—are added over a period of time.[59] Most MNCs have a product mix that is partly global (or regional) and partly local.

Several drivers impact the composition of a firm's international product line. We briefly discuss the key drivers:

Customer Preferences. In many product categories, consumer preferences vary from country to country. Especially for consumer packaged goods, preferences are still very localized. To cater to distinctive customer needs, marketers may add certain items to the individual country's or region product line or fine-tune the line. A good example is Procter & Gamble's change of strategy for Pantene shampoo in the Asia-Pacific region.[60] Based on consumer research in key markets, P&G revamped the Pantene brand and created new monikers such as Smooth & Sleek, Hydrating Curls, and Vibrant Colors. However, for the Asia-Pacific region, P&G had to fine-tune this new global approach. "Curls" are not relevant for Asian consumers, few Asians understood the meaning of "sheer volume," and few were interested in changing their hair color. Therefore, P&G created new varieties of Pantene for the region: Smooth & Silky, Volume & Fullness, and a Classic Clean range (Balance Clean, Lively Clean, and Anti-Dandruff). Following the revamp, Pantene's market share in Southeast Asia grew from 14 to 16 percent. See Exhibit 12-6 for some of the sandwiches that McDonald's introduced on its menu to cater to local tastes.

Price Spectrum. In emerging markets, companies often compete across the price spectrum by offering premium and budget products. The upscale products target

EXHIBIT 12-6
HOW MCDONALD'S CUSTOMIZED IT'S MENU

Country	Sandwich	Description
France	Croque McDo	A grilled ham and cheese sandwich similar to the traditional croque-monsieur
India	Maharaja Mac	Two grilled chicken patties with smoke-flavored mayonnaise, onions, tomatoes, and cheddar cheese
Japan	Teriyaki burger	A chicken cutlet patty marinated in teriyaki sauce
Middle East	McArabia sandwich	A marinated grilled chicken sandwich in flatbread
New Zealand	Kiwi burger	A hamburger with a fried egg and a slice of pickled beet
Poland	McKielbasa	A kielbasa (Polish sausage) patty topped with ketchup, mustard, and onion
Pakistan	Spicy McChicken	A chicken sandwich with chutney
Thailand	Samurai pork burger	A pork burger flavored with teriyaki sauce
Netherlands	McKroket	A deep fried roll containing beef ragout and potato
Greece	Greek Mac	A pitta bread sandwich with two beef patties and some yogurt
Israel	McShawarma	A Middle-Eastern style sandwich served on flatbread

Source: http://en.wikipedia.org/wiki/McDonald%27s_menu_items#Regional_dishes.

---

[59] www.thecoca-colacompany.com/investors/Divester.html.

[60] "Pantene Shampoo Is Reborn," *Ad Age Global,* May 2002, pp. 18–19.

wealthy consumers. Budget products are offered as entry-level or value products for other consumers. These low-end products often come in smaller sizes, more economical packaging, and/or cheaper formulations. Nestlé, for instance, launched 29 new ice cream brands in China in March 2005. Many of these were low- and mid-range priced value-for-money products selling for as little as 12¢.[61]

Competitive Climate.   Differences in the competitive environment often explain why a company offers certain product lines in some countries but not in others. A telling example is the canned soup industry. In the United States, the wet soup category is basically owned by Campbell Soup: The company has a nearly 70 percent share of it.[62] Given the clout of the Campbell brand name, it is virtually impossible to penetrate the U.S. canned soup market. The picture is quite different in the United Kingdom where Campbell was a relative latecomer. In the United Kingdom, the Heinz soup range owns a 56 percent market share.[63] Coca-Cola's product line strategy in Japan is also driven to a large degree by the local rivalry in the Japanese beverage market. One of the pillars of Coke's marketing strategy in Japan is to improve on its rivals' products. As a result, Coke sells an incredible variety of beverages in Japan that are not available anywhere else (see Exhibit 12-7).

Organizational Structure.   Especially in MNCs that are organized on a country-by-country basis, product lines may evolve to a large degree independently in the different countries. The scope of the country manager's responsibility is increasingly being limited in many MNCs (see Chapter 18). Nevertheless, country managers still have a great deal of decision-making autonomy in many functional areas, including product policy.

EXHIBIT 12-7
COCA-COLA LOCAL BRANDS IN JAPAN

Brand	Launch Year	Product Description
Ambasa	1981	Noncarbonated, lactic soft drink with familiar smooth taste for everyday use.
Calo	1997	"Functional" soft drink with cocoa taste; helps build healthy bones.
Georgia	1975	Authentic, real coffee drink with variety of flavors sourced from around the world.
Ko Cha Ka Den	1992	Line of blended teas.
Lactia	1996	Lactic, noncarbonated soft drink; offers healthy digestion and quick refreshment.
Perfect Water	1997	Mineral-balanced water; helps restore balance to daily life.
Real Gold	1981	Carbonated, herb-mix flavored drink; provides quick energy.
Saryusaisai	1993	Nonsugar Oolong tea drink.
Seiryusabo	1994	Green and barley tea drinks.
Shpla	1996	Citrus-flavored soft drink; helps overcome mental stress and dullness.
Vegitabeta	1991	Peach-flavored soft drink; helps maintain healthy balance.

---

[61]"Nestlé Hits Mainland with Cheap Ice Cream," *Advertising Age,* March 7, 2005, p. 12.
[62]http://www.campbellsoupcompany.com.
[63]http://www.heinz.com/2005annualreport/goodfood_uk.html.

History. Product lines often become part of an MNC's local product mix following geographic expansion efforts. Procter & Gamble, Heinz, and Sara Lee, for example, penetrate new and existing markets via acquisitions. Some of these acquisitions include product lines that are outside the MNC's core business. Rather than divesting these noncore businesses, a company often decides to keep them. As part of its growth strategy in Central Europe, Heinz acquired Kecskemeti Konzervgyar, a Hungarian canned food company. The company makes a broad range of food products, including baby food, ketchup, pickles—staple items for Heinz—but also jams and canned vegetables, items that are not really part of Heinz's core business lines.

Apart from the drivers mentioned earlier, other idiosyncratic reasons can determine a firm's product line outside the home market. A case in point is Danone's cola business in China. When the Chinese government wanted to have a *local* cola to compete with the likes of Coca-Cola and Pepsi, Beijing approached Wahaha, a Chinese company controlled by Danone.[64] As a result, Danone now owns Future Cola, which has become the number 3 cola brand in China, marketed as *the Chinese people's own cola.* China is also the only market where Danone sell soft drinks.

Global marketers need to decide for each market of interest which product lines should be offered and which ones are to be dropped. When markets are entered for the first time, market research can be very helpful for designing the initial product assortment. Market research is less useful for radically new products (e.g., frozen yogurt, electric vehicles) or newly emerging markets. In such situations, the company should consider using a "probing-and-learning" approach. Such a procedure has the following steps:

1. Start with a product line that has a minimum level of product variety.
2. Gradually adjust the amount of product variety over time by adding new items and dropping existing ones.
3. Analyze the incoming actual sales data and other market feedback.
4. Make the appropriate inferences.
5. If necessary, adjust the product line further.[65]

The gist of this procedure is to use the product line as a **listening post** for the new market to see what product items work best.

By and large, add/drop decisions should be driven by profit considerations. In the global marketing arena, it is crucial not to look only at profit ramifications within an individual country. Ideally, the profitability analysis should be done on a regional or even global basis. A good start is to analyze each individual country's product portfolio on a sales turnover basis. Product lines can be categorized as (1) core products, (2) niche items, (3) seasonal products, or (4) filler products.[66] *Core products* are the items that represent the bulk of the subsidiary's sales volume. *Niche products* appeal to small segments of the population, which might grow. *Seasonal products* have most of their sales during limited times of the year. Finally, *filler products* account for only a small portion of the subsidiary's overall sales. These might include "dead-weight" items whose sales were always lackluster or prospective up-and-coming products. From a global perspective, a comparison of the product mix makeup across the various countries provides valuable insights. Such an analysis could provide answers to questions such as these:

- Could some of our "seasonal" products in country A be turned into "core" items in country B?

---

[64] "China Market Finally Pays Off," *Asian Wall Street Journal,* January 9, 2003, pp. A1, A10.

[65] Anirudh Dhebar, "Using Extensive, Dynamic Product Lines for Listening in on Evolving Demand," *European Management Journal,* 13 (2), June 1995, pp. 187–92.

[66] John A. Quelch and David Kenny, "Extend Profits, Not Product Lines," *Harvard Business Review,* September–October 1994, pp. 153–60.

- Given our track record in country A, which ones of our filler products should be considered as up and coming in country B and which ones should be written off as dead-weight products?
- Is there a way to streamline our product assortment in country A by dropping some of the items and consolidating others, given our experience in country B?

PRODUCT PIRACY

◆ ◆ ◆ ◆ ◆ ◆ ◆ ◆

Product piracy is one of the downsides that marketers with popular global brand names face. The World Customs Organization estimated that 7 percent of world merchandise trade (or $512 billion) in 2004 could have been bogus products.[67] Any aspect of the product is vulnerable to piracy, including the brand name, the logo, the design, and the packaging. The impact on the victimized company's profits is twofold. Obviously, it suffers losses stemming from lost sales revenues. The monetary losses due to piracy can be staggering. In China, Procter & Gamble estimates that 15 percent of the soaps and detergent goods carrying P&G brand names are fake, costing $150 million a year in lost sales. Yamaha estimates that five out of six motorbikes and scooters in China bearing its brand name are fake.[68] Rampant piracy in countries such as China is for many companies a reason not to enter these markets. Blockbuster, the world's largest video rental chain, scrapped plans to expand into China due to piracy issues.[69] A new worrisome trend is the increased export of fake products made in China. Counterfeiters also depress the MNC's profits indirectly. In many markets, MNCs often are forced to lower their prices to defend their market share against their counterfeit competitors.

Even more worrisome than the monetary losses is the damage that pirated products could inflict to the brand name. Pirated products tend to be of poor quality. As a result, the piracy scourge often jeopardizes the brand's reputation built over the years. Such risks are especially significant in emerging markets where consumers have only recently been exposed to premium branded products and counterfeits often outnumber the real thing by a large factor.[70] In some categories, counterfeit products can also turn out to be downright dangerous to consumers. The World Health Organization estimates that 5 to 7 percent of medicines sold are copycat—with too few active ingredients, too many impurities, or labels that cover up expiration dates. Dodgy counterfeit aircraft or car parts can have fatal consequences. According to one study, 10 percent of spare car parts sold in the EU were reckoned to be counterfeit. A 2001 American Airlines crash was suspected to have been caused by forged aviation parts.

Several factors lie behind the rise of piracy in countries such as China. The spread of advanced technology (e.g., color copying machines, know-how stolen from multinationals by local partners) is one catalyst. Global supply chains also play a key role. Traders often use the Web and unauthorized distributors to sell fakes around the world. China's weak rule of law and poor enforcement of existing legislation also contributes to the piracy spread. Finally, profits that can be made from piracy are huge. For instance, profit margins on fake Chinese-made car parts such as shock absorbers can reach 80 percent versus 15 percent for the genuine thing.[71]

MNCs have several strategic options at their disposal to combat counterfeiters. The major weapons are as follows:

Strategic Options against Product Piracy

---

[67]"The Global Counterfeit Industry . . . ," *Business Week*, February 7, 2005, p. 48.

[68]"China's Fakes," *Business Week (Asian Edition)*, June 5, 2000, pp. 20–25.

[69]"Blockbuster's China Ambition Ended by Piracy," *Financial Times*, January 31/February 1, 2004, p. 1.

[70]"Business Faces Genuine Problem of Chinese Fakes," *The Financial Times*, April 4, 2000, p. 6.

[71]"China's Fakes" pp. 22–23.

Lobbying Activities. Lobbying a government is one of the most common courses of action that firms use to protect themselves against counterfeiting. Lobbyists pursue different types of objectives. One goal is to toughen legislation and enforcement of existing laws in the foreign market. However, improved protection of intellectual property rights (IPR) is more likely to become reality if a company can draw support from local stakeholders. For instance, Chinese technology developers increasingly favor a tighter IPR system.[72] Another route is to lobby the home government to impose sanctions against countries that tolerate product piracy. Finally, MNCs can also lobby their home government to negotiate for better trademark protection in international treaties such as the WTO or bilateral trade agreements.

Legal Action. Prosecuting counterfeiters is another alternative that companies can employ to fight product piracy. In China, two large foreign brands, Starbucks and Ferrero Rocher, recently won highly publicized IPR court cases. In the case of Starbucks, a Shanghai company, Xingbake Café, was using a logo and a Chinese translation of the name similar to the global coffee giant's. The court ordered Xingbake to pay 500,000 yuan (about US$62,000) in damages to Starbucks. Ferrero Rocher, the Italian chocolate maker, won a ruling (on appeal) in Tianjin against Montresor Foods, a Sino-Belgium joint venture, for copycatting Ferrero's chocolates. Ferrero was awarded 700,000 yuan (about US$87,000) compensation, and the Chinese company was ordered to stop production of the hazelnut chocolates.[73] To sue infringers, companies need to track them down first. In China, for example, foreign firms can hire private agencies to help them with investigations of suspected infringers. Legal action has numerous downsides, though. A positive outcome in court is seldom guaranteed, and the whole process is time consuming and costly. Court action can also generate negative publicity.[74] Microsoft's experience in China illustrates this point. When the company sued Yadu Group, a local humidifier maker, for pirating Microsoft products, the Chinese press had a field day bashing Microsoft for going after a local company. The case was dismissed because of a legal technicality. The only party that gained (apart from the lawyers involved) was the defendant whose brand awareness increased enormously because of the publicity surrounding the case.[75]

Customs. Firms can also ask customs for assistance to seize infringing goods. In countries with huge trade flows, for example, China, customs can monitor only a small proportion of traded goods for IP compliance. Customs officers will most likely attach low priority to items such as Beanie Babies or Hello Kitty dolls. However, courtesy calls can be very effective. IP owners could also pinpoint broader concerns to the customs officials such as risks of fake goods to consumers or to the reputation of the host country.[76]

Product Policy Options. Another set of measures to cope with product piracy covers product policy actions. For instance, software manufacturers often protect their products by putting holograms on the product to discourage counterfeiters, but holograms are only effective when they are hard to copy. Microsoft learned that lesson the hard way when it found out that counterfeiters simply sold MS-DOS 5.0 knockoffs using counterfeit holograms.[77] LVMH, the owner of a wide variety of upscale liquor brands, redesigned its bottles to make it more difficult for copycatters to reuse LVMH

---

[72]Pitman B. Potter and Michel Oksenberg, "A Patchwork of IPR Protections," *The China Business Review* (January–February 1999), pp. 8–11.

[73]http://au.biz.yahoo.com/060112/33/p/guow.html.

[74]"Counter Feats," *The China Business Review*, November/December 1994, pp. 12–15.

[75]"Microsoft-Bashing Is Paying Off for Software Giant's Foes in China," *The Asian Wall Street Journal*, January 3, 2000, pp. 1, 4.

[76]Joseph T. Simone, "Countering Counterfeiters," *The China Business Review*, January–February 1999, pp. 12–19.

[77]"Catching Counterfeits," *Security Management*, December 1994, p. 18.

bottles for their own brews.[78] Yamaha decided to combat China's counterfeiters by launching new motorcycle models at a similar price as the fake products.

Distribution.   Changes in the distribution strategy can offer partial solutions to piracy. When launching Windows XP in China, Microsoft struck a deal with four of China's leading PC makers to bundle the operating system into their computers. Pirated versions of Windows XP were on sale in China for less than $5 shortly after the product was launched in the United States.[79]

Communication Options.   Companies also use their communication strategy to counter rip-offs. Through advertising or public relations campaigns, companies warn their target audience about the consequences of accepting counterfeit merchandise. In Japan, LVMH distributed a million leaflets at three airports. The goal of this campaign was to warn Japanese tourists that the importation of counterfeit products is against the law.[80] Anticounterfeiting advertising campaigns that target end-consumers could also appeal to people's ethical judgments: A "good citizen" does not buy counterfeit goods.[81] The target of warning campaigns is not always the end-customer, however. Converse, the U.S. athletic shoemaker, ran a campaign in trade journals throughout Europe alerting retailers to the legal consequences of selling counterfeits.[82]

COUNTRY-OF-ORIGIN (COO) STEREOTYPES   ◆ ◆ ◆ ◆ ◆ ◆ ◆ ◆

Two of the largest cosmetics companies in the world are Japanese: Kao and Shiseido. While successful in Japan and other Asian countries, Kao and Shiseido have had a difficult time penetrating the European and U.S. markets. Apparently, part of the problem is that they are Japanese. In China, however, Shiseido has built a loyal following. One senior marketing executive of the company observed, "China and Japan are from the same Asian background, so people think Shiseido is a specialist in Asian skin treatment. They may think it is more suitable for them than Western products."[83] One three-nation (Japanese, U.K., U.S.) study conducted jointly by Hakuhodo, one of Japan's largest advertising agencies, and Wolff Olins, a U.K.-based brand consulting agency, that looked into the power of the "made in Japan" label shows why.[84] The least desirable[85] Japanese products in the United States were movies/music (40 percent), luxury goods (36 percent), and animation (35 percent). The most desirable were cars (73 percent), audio equipment (72 percent), and cameras (72 percent).[86] U.S. respondents praised "made in Japan" products for quality, advanced technology, and design. However, they were perceived to be weak in trendiness and status (see Exhibit 12-8).

Consumers can also boycott certain brands for political reasons. In September 2005, Jyllands-Posten published a series of caricatures about the prophet Mohammed. The depictions were seen as blasphemous in the Muslim world and led to a boycott of Danish goods in the Middle East. Some U.S. brands also have suffered an image problem as a result of U.S. foreign policy and military action in recent years.

---

[78]Joël Tiphonnet, former Vice President LVMH Asia Pacific, personal communication, 1997.

[79]"Microsoft Victory in China Software Piracy Battle," *Financial Times,* 1997 December 7, 2001, p. 6.

[80]"Modern Day Pirates a Threat Worldwide," *Advertising Age International,* March 20, 1995, pp. I-3, I-4.

[81]Alexander Nill and Clifford J. Shultz II, "The Scourge of Global Counterfeiting," *Business Horizons,* November–December 1996, pp. 37–42.

[82]"Converse Jumps on Counterfeit Culprits with Ad," *Marketing,* October 21, 1993, p. 11.

[83]"When Chinese Desire Transcends Politics," *Financial Times,* April 1, 2004 p. 9.

[84]http://www.hakuhodo.co.jp/english/news/e/20020605.html.

[85]In terms of purchase intention.

[86]Responses in the United Kingdom were slightly different: the bottom three products were watches (47 percent), movies/music (44 percent), and animation (34 percent); the top three were audio equipment (76 percent), cameras (74 percent), and computers (72 percent).

EXHIBIT 12-8
PRODUCT ATTRIBUTES ASSOCIATED WITH PRODUCTS MADE IN JAPAN

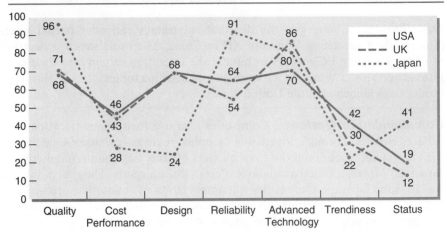

Note: Cf. Japanese responses are to the question, "What product attributes do you think non-Japanese associate with "Made in Japan" products?" © 2002, Hakuhodo Inc. All rights reserved.

EXHIBIT 12-9
PRODUCT-COUNTRY MATCHES AND MISMATCHES: EXAMPLES AND STRATEGIC IMPLICATIONS

		Country Image Dimensions	
		Positive	*Negative*
Dimensions as Product Features	*Important*	I Favorable Match Examples: • Japanese auto • German watch Strategic Implications: • Brand name reflects COO • Packaging includes COO information • Promote brand's COO • Attractive potential manufacturing site	II Unfavorable Match Examples: • Hungarian auto • Mexican watch Strategic Implications: • Emphasize benefits other than COO • Noncountry branding • Joint venture with favorable match partner • Communication campaign to enhance country image
	Not Important	III Favorable Mismatch Example: • Japanese beer Strategic Implications: • Alter importance of product category image dimensions • Promote COO as secondary benefit if compensatory choice process	IV Unfavorable Mismatch Example: • Hungarian beer Strategic Implications: • Ignore COO—such information not relevant

Source: Martin S. Roth and Jean B. Romeo, "Matching Product Category and Country Image Perceptions: A Framework for Managing Country-of-Origin Effects," *Journal of International Business Studies,* Third Quarter 1992, p. 495.

There is ample evidence that for many products, the "made in" label matters a great deal to consumers. Consumers often seem to rely very heavily on country-of-origin cues to evaluate products. Most people prefer a bottle of French champagne over a Chinese-made bottle, despite the huge price gap. Consumers can hold **country-of-origin stereotypes** that influence their product assessments. In some countries, consumers are urged to buy products made by local companies. In Australia, the "Proudly Australian" campaign has proven to be a successful theme for home-grown companies. Dick Smith Foods' peanut butter brand grabbed an 18 percent market share one month after its launch by telling Australian TV audiences that the leading rival brands, Kraft and Eta, are owned by Altria, a foreign company.[87] Research studies of COO effects clearly show that the phenomenon is complex. Some of the key research findings follow:

Country-of-Origin Influences on Consumers

- COO effects are not stable; perceptions change over time.[88] Country images change when consumers become more familiar with the country, the marketing practices behind the product improve over time, or when the product's actual quality improves. A classic example is Japanese-made cars for which COO effects took a 180 degree turn during the last several decades from a very negative to a very positive country image.[89] A similar phenomenon has happened more recently for Korean-made cars.

- In general, consumers prefer domestic products over imports. The number 1 selling car is Renault in France, Toyota in Japan, Volkswagen in Germany, and Fiat in Italy. Not surprising, there is a COO bias against products coming from developing countries. A study conducted in the Philippines found that products made in developing countries are marketable only when they are priced far less than products offered by regional or global competitors.[90] Similarly, a study conducted on rice buying in Ghana found that consumers there preferred foreign sources of rice to domestic alternatives.[91]

- Research also shows that both the country of design and the country of manufacturing/assembly play a role. Foreign companies can target patriotic consumers by becoming a local player in the host market. For instance, they might set up an assembly base in the country. At the same time, they can capitalize on their country image to attract those customers who recognize the country's design image. For instance, Toyota pitched its Camry model as "the best car built in America."[92]

- Demographics make a difference. COO influences are particularly strong among the elderly,[93] less educated, and politically conservative.[94] Consumer expertise also makes a difference: Novices tend to use COO as a cue in evaluating a product under any circumstances; experts rely on COO stereotypes only when product attribute information is ambiguous.[95]

[87] "'Buy Australian' Is the New Battle Cry Down Under," *International Herald Tribune,* August 1, 2001, p. 16.

[88] Van R. Wood, John R. Darling, and Mark Siders, "Consumer Desire to Buy and Use Products in International Markets: How to Capture It, How to Sustain It," *International Marketing Review,* 16 (3), 1999, pp. 231–56.

[89] Akira Nagashima, "A Comparison of Japanese and US Attitudes toward Foreign Products," *Journal of Marketing,* January 1970, pp. 68–74.

[90] John Hulland, Honorio S. Todiño, Jr., and Donald J. Lecraw, "Country-of-Origin Effects on Sellers' Price Premiums in Competitive Philippine Markets," *Journal of International Marketing,* 4 (1), 1996, pp. 57–80.

[91] Fred A. Yamoah, "Role and Impact of Product-Country Image on Rice Marketing: A Developing Country Perspective," *Journal of American Academy of Business,* 7 (September 2005), pp. 265–76.

[92] Glen H. Brodowsky and J. Justin Tan, "Managing Country of Origin: Understanding How Country of Design and Country of Assembly Affect Product Evaluations and Attitudes toward Purchase," in *American Marketing Association Summer Educators' Conference Proceedings,* ed. Steven Brown and D. Sudharshan (Chicago: American Marketing Association, 1999), pp. 307–20.

[93] Terence A. Shimp and Subhash Sharma, "Consumer Ethnocentrism: Construction and Validation of the CETSCALE," *Journal of Marketing Research,* 24 (August 1987), pp. 280–89.

[94] Thomas W. Anderson and William H. Cunningham, "Gauging Foreign Product Promotion," *Journal of Advertising Research,* February 1972, pp. 29–34.

[95] Durairaj Maheswaran, "Country of Origin as a Stereotype: Effects of Consumer Expertise and Attribute Strength on Product Evaluations," *Journal of Consumer Research,* 21, (September 1994), pp. 354–65.

- Cultural orientations play a role. One study contrasted COO influences between members of an individualist (United States) and a collectivist culture (Japan).[96] The study's findings showed that individualists evaluated the home country product more favorably only when it was superior to the competition. Collectivists, however, rated the home country product higher regardless of product superiority.

- Consumers are likely to use the origin of a product as a cue when they are unfamiliar with the brand name carried by the product.[97]

- Finally, COO effects depend on the product category.[98] Japan is strongly linked in consumers' minds with "high-tech" and performance-type attributes but is perceived poorly on attributes such as "design," "hedonism," or "style." So, in Japan's case, a product-country match should occur for cars and consumer electronics but not for cosmetics or designer clothing. As shown in Exhibit 12-9, there are four possible outcomes depending on (1) whether there is a match between the product and country and (2) whether or not the (mis-)match is favorable.[99]

Strategies to Cope with COO Stereotypes

Before exploring strategic options to deal with COO stereotypes, firms should conduct market research to investigate their extent and the impact for their particular product. Such studies would reveal whether the country of origin really matters to consumers and to what degree it hurts or helps the product's evaluation. One useful technique uses a *dollar preference* scale. Participants are asked to indicate how much they are willing to pay for particular brand/country combinations.[100]

Country image stereotypes can either benefit or hurt a company's product. Evidently, when there is a favorable match between the country image and the desired product features, a firm could leverage this match by touting the origin of its product, provided its main competitors do not have the same (or better) origin. The following sections focus on strategies that can be used to counter negative COO stereotypes. The overview is organized along the four marketing mix elements: product policy, pricing, distribution, and communication.

Product Policy. A common practice to cope with COO is to select a brand name that disguises the country-of-origin or even invokes a favorable one.[101] It is probably no coincidence that two of the more successful apparel retailers based in Hong Kong have Italian-sounding names (Giordano and Bossini). Print ads for Finlandia vodka in the U.S. magazines highlight the linkage between the vodka's origin (vodka of Finland) and its ingredients (made from pure glacial spring water, untouched, untainted, and unspoiled). Another branding option to downplay negative COO feelings is to use private label branding. One study that investigated COO influences on prices in the Philippines shows that marketers can overcome negative COO effects by developing brand equity.[102] Sheer innovation and a drive for superior quality usually helps firms to overcome COO biases in the long run.

---

[96] Zeynep Gürhan-Canli and Durairaj Maheswaran, "Cultural Variations in Country of Origin Effects," *Journal of Marketing Research,* 37 (August 2000), pp. 309–17.

[97] Victor V. Cordell, "Effects of Consumer Preferences for Foreign Sourced Products," *Journal of International Business Studies,* Second Quarter 1992, pp. 251–69.

[98] George Balabanis and Adamantios Diamantopoulos, "Domestic Country Bias, Country-of-Origin Effects, and Consumer Ethnocentrism: A Multidimensional Unfolding Approach," *Academy of Marketing Science Journal,* 32 (Winter 2004), pp. 80–95.

[99] Martin S. Roth and Jean B. Romeo, "Matching Product Category and Country Image Perceptions: A Framework for Managing Country-of-Origin Effects," *Journal of International Business Studies,* Third Quarter 1992, pp. 477–97.

[100] Usually the respondents are also given an anchor point (e.g., amount above or below $10,000?). For further details, see Johny K. Johansson and Israel D. Nebenzahl, "Multinational Production: Effect on Brand Value," *Journal of International Business Studies,* Fall 1986, pp. 101–26.

[101] France Leclerc, Bernd H. Schmitt, and Laurette Dubé, "Foreign Branding and Its Effects on Product Perceptions and Attitudes," *Journal of Marketing Research,* 31 (May 1994), pp. 263–70.

[102] Hulland et al., "Country-of-Origin Effects on Sellers' Price Premiums."

Pricing. Selling the product at a relatively low price will attract value-conscious customers who are less concerned about the brand's country of origin. Obviously, this strategy is possible only when the firm enjoys a cost advantage. At the other end of the pricing spectrum, firms could set a premium price to combat COO biases. This is especially effective for product categories in which price plays a role as a signal of quality (e.g., wines, cosmetics, clothing).

Distribution. Alternatively, companies could influence consumer attitudes by using highly respected distribution channels. In the United Kingdom, Hungarian and Chilean wines are becoming increasingly popular. One reason for their success is the fact that they are sold via prestigious supermarket chains in Britain such as Tesco.[103]

Communication. Lastly, the firm's communication strategy can be used to alter consumers' attitudes toward the product. Such strategies could pursue two broad objectives: (1) improve the country image or (2) bolster the brand image. The first goal, changing the country image, is less appealing because it could lead to "free-rider" problems. Efforts carried out by one company to change the country image would also benefit its competitors from the same country of manufacture, even though they do not spend any money on the country-image campaign.

For that reason, country-image campaigns are done mostly by industry associations or government agencies. For instance, in the United States, Chilean wines were promoted with wine tastings and a print advertising campaign with the tag line: "It's not just a wine. It's a country." The $2 to $3 million campaign was sponsored by ProChile, Chile's Ministry of Foreign Affairs' trade group.[104] Seagram UK, on the other hand, developed a strategy to build up the Paul Masson brand image when the California wine was first launched in the United Kingdom.[105]

GLOBAL MARKETING OF SERVICES

◆ ◆ ◆ ◆ ◆ ◆ ◆ ◆

Most of the discussion in this chapter so far has focused on the marketing of so-called tangible goods. However, as countries grow richer, services tend to become the dominant sector of their economy. In most OECD member states, services account for 70 percent of the economy.[106]

In this section, we first focus on the challenges and opportunities that exist in the global service market. We then offer a set of managerial guidelines that might prove fruitful to service marketers who plan to expand overseas.

Compared to marketers of *tangible* goods, *service* marketers face several unique hurdles on the road to international expansion. The major challenges include:

Challenges in Marketing Services Internationally

Protectionism. Trade barriers to service marketers tend to be much more cumbersome than for their physical goods counterparts. Many parts of the world are littered with service trade barriers under many different guises. Most cumbersome are the nontariff trade barriers for which the creative juices of government regulators know no boundaries. In the past, the service sector has been treated rather stepmotherly in trade agreements. The rules of the GATT system, for instance, applied only to visible trade. Its successor, the World Trade Organization (WTO), now expands at least some of the GATT rules to the service sector.[107]

[103] "Non-Traditional Nations Pour into Wine Market," *Advertising Age International,* May 15, 1995, p. I-4.
[104] Ibid.
[105] Paul E. Breach, "Building the Paul Masson Brand," *European Journal of Marketing,* 23 (9), 1989, pp. 27–30.
[106] www.oecd.org, accessed January 23, 2006.
[107] Ibid.

Immediate Face-to-Face contacts with Service Transactions. The human aspect in service delivery is much more critical than for the marketing of tangible goods. Services are *performed,* a feature that has several consequences in the international domain. Most services are difficult to trade internationally and require the service provider's physical presence. Given the intrinsic need for people-to-people contact, cultural barriers in the global marketplace are much more prominent for service marketers than in other industries. Being in tune with the cultural values and norms of the local market is essential to be successful in most service industries. As a result, services are typically standardized far less than are tangible products.[108] At the same time, service companies usually aspire to provide a consistent quality image worldwide. Careful screening and training of personnel to ensure consistent quality is extremely vital for international service firms. To foster the transfer of know-how between branches, many service companies set up communication channels such as regional councils.

The need for direct customer interface also means that service providers often must have a local presence. This is especially the case with support services such as advertising, insurance, accounting, law, and overnight package delivery. In order not to lose MNC customer accounts, many support service companies are often obliged to follow in their clients' footsteps.

Difficulties in Measuring Customer Satisfaction Overseas. Given the human element in services, monitoring consumer satisfaction is an absolute must for successful service marketing. Doing customer satisfaction studies in an international context is often a frustrating job. The hindrances to conducting market research surveys also apply here. In many countries, consumers are not used to sharing their opinions or suggestions. Instead of expressing their true opinions about the service, foreign respondents may simply state what they believe the company wants to hear (the "courtesy" bias).[109]

Opportunities in the Global Service Industries

Despite these challenges, many international service industries offer enormous opportunities to savvy service marketers. The major ones are given here:

Deregulation of Service Industries. While protectionism is still rampant in many service industries, there has been a steady improvement for international service providers in terms of deregulation. As mentioned, some GATT rules that applied only to tangible goods are now extended to the international service trade under the new WTO regime. In scores of countries, government authorities have privatized services such as utilities (e.g., water, electricity), telecommunications, and mail delivery. The underlying thinking is that private firms can run these services more efficiently and have the resources to upgrade the infrastructure. Further more, by shifting these services to the private sector, governments can allocate their resources to other areas (e.g., education, social welfare). Several individual countries are taking steps to lift restrictions targeting foreign service firms. Even sectors that were traditionally off-limits to foreigners are opening up now in scores of countries. India and the Philippines, for example, opened their telephone industry to foreign companies.[110]

---

[108]B. Nicolaud, "Problems and Strategies in the International Marketing of Services," *European Journal of Marketing,* 23 (6), pp. 55–66.

[109]Gaye Kaufman, "Customer Satisfaction Studies Overseas Can Be Frustrating," *Marketing News,* August 29, 1994, p. 34.

[110]"Asia, at Your Service," *The Economist,* February 11, 1995, pp. 53–54.

Increasing Demand for Premium Services. Demand for premium quality services expands with increases in consumers' buying power. International service providers that are able to deliver a premium product often have an edge over their local competitors. There are two major factors behind this competitive advantage. One of the legacies of years of protectionism is that local service firms are typically unprepared for the hard rules of the marketplace. Customer orientation, consumer satisfaction, and service quality are marketing concepts that are especially hard to digest for local service firms that until recently did not face any serious competition. For example, local funeral companies in France invested very little in funeral homes. Prior to the demonopolization of the industry, the funeral business in France was basically a utility: Firms bid for the right to offer funeral services to a municipality at fixed prices. Service Corp. International, a leading U.S. funeral company, planned to gain a foothold in France by selling premium products and upgraded facilities.[111] Despite Malaysia's highly protectionist banking laws, Citibank Malaysia has become one of the country's largest mortgage lenders through a combination of savvy marketing, an assertive sales force, and a strong customer service orientation.[112]

Global service firms can also leverage their "global know-how" base. A major strength for Federal Express, UBS, and AT&T is that they have a worldwide knowledge base into which they can tap instantly.

Increased Value Consciousness. As customers worldwide have more alternatives to choose from and become more sophisticated, they also grow increasingly value conscious. Service companies that compete internationally also have clout on this front versus local service providers because global service firms usually benefit from scale economies. Such savings can be passed through to their customers. McDonald's apparently saved around $2 million by centralizing the purchase of sesame seeds.[113] In Thailand, Makro, a large Dutch retailer, uses computerized inventory controls and bulk selling to undercut its local rivals.[114] Given the size of its business, Toys 'R' Us, the U.S. discount toy retailer, was able to set up its own direct import company in Japan, allowing the firm to deliver merchandise straight from the docks to its warehouses, thereby bypassing distributors' margins.[115]

Global Service Marketing Strategies

To compete in foreign markets, service firms resort to using a plethora of different strategies.

Capitalize on Cultural Forces in the Host Market. To bridge cultural gaps between the home and host market, service companies often customize the product to the local market. Successful service firms grab market share by spotting cultural opportunities and setting up a service product around these cultural forces.

Standardize and Customize. As noted in Chapter 11, one of the major challenges in global product design is striking the right balance between standardization and customization. By their very nature (service delivery at the point of consumption), most services do not need to address that issue. Both standardization and adaptation are possible. The core service product can easily be augmented with localized support service features that cater to local market conditions.[116]

---

[111] "Funereal Prospects," *Forbes,* September 11, 1995, pp. 45–46.

[112] "Citibank Expands Niche in Malaysian Mortgages by Courting Customers," *Asian Wall Street Journal,* November 28, 2002, p. A5.

[113] "Big Mac's Counter Attack," *Economist,* November 13, 1993, pp. 71–72.

[114] "Asia, at Your Service," pp. 53–54.

[115] "Revolution in Toyland," *Financial Times,* April 8, 1994, p. 9.

[116] Christopher H. Lovelock and George S. Yip, "Developing Global Strategies for Service Businesses," *California Management Review,* 38 (2), Winter 1996, pp. 64–86.

Central Role of Information Technologies (IT).   Information technology forms a key pillar of global service strategies. Service firms add value for their customers by employing technology such as computers, intelligent terminals, and state-of-the-art telecommunications. Many service firms have established Internet access to communicate with their customers and suppliers. IT is especially valued in markets that have a fairly underdeveloped infrastructure. Companies should also recognize the potential of realizing scale economies by centralizing their IT functions via "information hubs."[117] A case in point is HSBC, a leading British bank.[118] HSBC relies on 400 low-cost employees in Hyderabad, India, and Guangzhou, China, to industrialize its simple back-room operations on a global scale, freeing up its U.K. backrooms for more complicated tasks.

Add Value by Differentiation.   Services differ from tangible products by the fact that it is usually far easier for services to find differentiation possibilities. As discussed earlier, service firms can appeal to their customers by offering benefits not provided by their competitors and/or lowering costs. In addition to actual monetary expenses, cost items include psychic costs (hassles), time costs (waiting time), and physical efforts.[119] Especially in markets where the service industry is still developing, multinational service firms can add value by providing premium products. AIG allows its customers in China to settle their bills by bank transfer. Local insurance companies require their customers to wait in line to pay the premiums in cash.

Establish Global Service Networks.   Service firms with a global customer base face the challenge of setting up a seamless global service network. One of the key issues is whether the company should set up the network on its own or use outside partners. Given the huge investments required to develop a worldwide network, more and more companies are choosing the latter route. Trends of firms grouping together to establish global networks can be observed in service industries such as airline travel (e.g., the STAR alliance) and advertising.

---

[117]Ibid.
[118]"Bull-terrier Banking," *Forbes Global,* July 24, 2000, pp. 36–38.
[119]"Services Go International," *Marketing News,* March 14, 1994, pp. 14–15.

SUMMARY   ◆

Mission statements in annual reports reflect the aspiration of countless companies to sell their products to consumers worldwide. This push toward global expansion raises many tricky questions on the product policy front. Mastering these global product issues can yield success and, possibly, even worldwide leadership.

Companies need to decide what branding strategies they plan to pursue to develop their overseas business. There is plenty of ammunition to build a case for global brands. At the same time, many arguments in favor of other branding strategies can be made. Developing a global branding strategy involves answering questions such as these:

• Which of the brands in our brand portfolio have the potential to be globalized?

• What is the best route to globalizing our brands? Should we start by acquiring local brands, develop them into regional brands, and, ultimately, if the potential is there, into a "truly" global brand?

• What is the best way to implement the changeover from a local to a global (or regional) brand?

• How do we foster and sustain the consistency of our global brand image?

• What organizational mechanisms should we as a company use to coordinate our branding strategies across markets? Should coordination happen at the regional or global level?

The ultimate reward of mastering these issues successfully is regional, sometimes even worldwide, leadership in the marketplace.

KEY TERMS

◆ ◆

Brand architecture
Brand equity
Brand structure (brand portfolio)
Co-branding
Country-of-origin stereotype

Dual branding
Fade-in/fade-out
Global brand
Listening post
Private label (store brand)

Product piracy
Summary axing
Transparent forewarning
Umbrella branding

REVIEW QUESTIONS

1. For what types of product/service categories would you expect to use global brand names? For which ones would you anticipate using localized names?

2. Why is the market share of private labels much higher in Europe than in Asia?

3. Explain why the strength of a global brand difference can vary enormously from country to country.

4. What factors should MNCs consider when implementing a brand-name facelift in their foreign markets?

5. What strategies can MNCs adopt to cope with product piracy?

6. How does the marketing of global services differ from marketing tangible goods worldwide?

DISCUSSION QUESTIONS

1. Advanced Photo System (APS) is a new digital photography system that was launched in 1996 by several companies in the camera industry. APS cameras have features such as simple loading, adjustable print size, and the ability to download pictures onto computers. The major photo industry companies use quite different branding strategies. Kodak and Nikon use global brand names, Advantix and Nuvis, respectively, for their APS camera and film products. Other competitors, such as Fuji and Canon, use several brand names. Fuji uses Endeavor in the United States, Fotonex in Europe, and Epion in Japan. Why would some competitors (e.g., Kodak) use a global brand name for this product while others (e.g., Fuji, Canon) use several brand names?

2. Under the guidance of Douglas Daft, its new CEO, Coca-Cola is preaching what it calls a "think local, act local" strategy. In the past, "We were looking for similarities, not differences, and we didn't stand for anything in particular for the individual." Decisions ranging from local marketing communications and all the way to charity were made at company headquarters in Atlanta. Now Mr. Daft is trying to rebuild the brand's relevance to different communities around the world. Assess Coca-Cola's move.

3. Dr. Hans-Willi Schroiff, vice president of market research at Henkel, a German company, made the following observation about P&G's multinational marketing strategy: "A strict globalization strategy like P&G's [will not be] successful if 'meaningful' local brands are corpses on the battlefield. It caused severe share losses for P&G here in Europe. Consumers do not switch to the global brand, but to another brand that looks more like 'home' to them." Comment on this statement. Do you agree or disagree (and why)?

4. In September 1999, Unilever announced that it will trim more than 1,000 brands. The company wants to focus on 400 of its current 1,600 brands with a core group of so-called power brands that are known globally or regionwide (e.g., Magnum ice cream, Lipton tea, Vaseline skin cream). These 400 brands

accounted for 90 percent of Unilever's 1998 sales revenues. The brands outside the core group will gradually lose marketing support and will ultimately be sold, withdrawn, or consolidated into larger brands. Discuss Unilever's decision. What do you see as possible advantages? Disadvantages?

5. As noted in the chapter, developing and industrialized countries hold different views about intellectual property protection. Developing countries claim that stringent copyright protection does not enable them to close the gap with the industrialized world. Discuss what rewards developing countries might derive from intellectual property protection.

6. Most luxury watches have a "made in Switzerland" label. What strategies would the maker of a "made in India" watch consider if it wants to target the premium segment in the Western world?

7. Nestlé, the Swiss food conglomerate, has created a Nestlé Seal of Guarantee that it puts on some of its products (e.g., Maggi sauces). It does not use the Seal of Guarantee for many of its other products such as pet food and mineral water. What might be Nestlé's motivations for adding or dropping its Nestlé Seal of Guarantee stamp to the brand-product name?

8. The Rover Mini is a squat, boxy car that was designed in the late 1950s when the Suez Canal crisis prompted gas rationing in Europe (if you are not familiar with the car, check out its Web site: www.mini.co.uk). Rover, now owned by BWM, started exporting the car to Japan in 1985. The Mini sells for between 1.8 million and 2.4 million yen. A Japanese model of the same size costs about half of that, yet the Mini has many takers. Rover rarely does TV ads but relies instead on word of mouth. Despite the price tag and little advertising, Rover sells more Minis in Japan than anywhere else in the world. The car has been far more successful in Japan than most other imported car makes (e.g., GM's Saturn or DaimlerChrysler's Neon). What factors do you think explain the Rover Mini's success in Japan?

◆◆◆◆◆◆◆◆◆ **SHORT CASES**

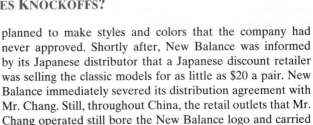

CASE 12-1

WHAT TO DO WHEN YOUR OWN SUPPLIER MAKES KNOCKOFFS?

China's cheap labor and high-quality manufacturing are two major reasons why scores of global brands have decided to source their products from China-based suppliers. Unfortunately, many firms are finding out that they sometimes pay a steep price for doing so. It is not uncommon that the China-based supplier starts selling knockoffs under your brand name. New Balance, the U.S. athletic-shoemaker, learned this the hard way. About 70 percent (35 million pairs a year) of New Balance's global output is made in China. One of the firm's key suppliers was a company headed by Mr. Chang, a Taiwanese businessman, whose factories made shoes for New Balance initially in Taiwan and later in China. In 1995, New Balance made him the official sales and distribution partner for China. After a slow takeoff, sales improved when Mr. Chang convinced New Balance to push lower-price, lower-tech classic-style shoe models for China. In 1998, sales in China were 57,000 pairs. However, New Balance became uneasy when, following a sales conference meeting, Mr. Chang made a pitch to sell 250,000 pairs. The reason for top management's worry was that selling so many classic-style shoes might tarnish its image as a maker of premium quality athletic shoes. Instead of getting a pat on the back, Mr. Chang was told to scale back the sales of classic shoes.

Shortly after the meeting, New Balance learned that Mr. Chang had bought materials to make 460,000 pairs. He also planned to make styles and colors that the company had never approved. Shortly after, New Balance was informed by its Japanese distributor that a Japanese discount retailer was selling the classic models for as little as $20 a pair. New Balance immediately severed its distribution agreement with Mr. Chang. Still, throughout China, the retail outlets that Mr. Chang operated still bore the New Balance logo and carried New Balance shoes. Shoes made by his factories also started showing up in stores in Switzerland, Italy, Spain, and Taiwan.

New Balance then approached China's Administration for Industry and Commerce (AIC), the trademark and intellectual property enforcement agency. This agency raided some of Mr. Chang's warehouses and confiscated 100,000 pairs. Besides New Balance shoes, they also found shoes branded Henkee, whose style and logo had a striking similarity with those of New Balance. However, a court in Shenzhen ruled against New Balance on the basis of a document in which it had guaranteed that Mr. Chang's company could make its shoes until 2003. The company appealed, but a favorable ruling is unlikely. As a result of this whole experience, New Balance cut the number of factories in China to six and monitors them more closely. It also started using more high-tech labels to better keep control of its own production. Still, the whole episode could easily happen again with any other suppliers anywhere in the world.

DISCUSSION QUESTIONS

1. How did New Balance's problem arise?
2. What strategic options can New Balance pursue to protect itself against episodes such as the one described in the case?

Source: "What Happens When Knockoffs Are Made By Your Own Supplier?" *The Asian Wall Street Journal,* December 19, 2002, pp. A1, M8.

CASE 12-2

WILL A MOVE TO THE UNITED STATES TURN THE CURIOUSLY STRONG INTO CURIOUSLY WEAK MINTS?

From the cans with antique typeface to the British-accented voiceovers in TV commercials (see http://www.altoids.com/cinema.do#), Altoids, the "curiously strong" peppermint, has evoked its British heritage since its introduction in the United States in 1918. The mint's original recipe dates back to the reign of King George III. Wrigley paid $1.46 billion in 2004 to buy Altoids and Life Savers from Kraft Foods. As chewing gum sales are slowing, mints are becoming more important for Wrigley. However, in the United States, Altoids' market share has slumped from 24.3 percent in 2003 to 20.6 percent in November 2005.

In late 2005, Wrigley announced plans to shut down the Altoids factory in Bridgend, Wales, and move production to its factory in Chattanooga, Tennessee. Some branding analysts worried that the move might be risky. In the 1970s, the image of Löwenbräu in the United States was damaged after it was

Sources: "Altoids' Brand Dilemma: Keeping English Image," *International Herald Tribune,* October 6, 2005, p. 20; www.altoids.com; and http://www.chicagobusiness.com/cgi-bin/news.pl?id=19051.

bought by Miller Brewing (now SABMiller) and production was transferred from Munich to U.S. breweries. The brand never recovered, even after being taken over in 1999 by a Canadian brewer. Cheryl Swanson, a brand strategy consultant, noted: "They're evoking a British personality, and it's still their heritage." Wrigley was hoping that the shift would not matter to Altoids' consumers. A Wrigley spokesperson declared, "People love the intensity of the product and the quirkiness of the image, so I'm not sure where it's produced is going to matter."

DISCUSSION QUESTIONS

1. Do you feel Wrigley's planned transfer for the production of Altoids is a wise move? Why or why not?

2. Some marketers claim that in an increasingly globalized marketplace, tying the image to a specific region or country is not as valuable as it once was. Do you agree or disagree? For what kind of brands might this brand/country connection still be relevant?

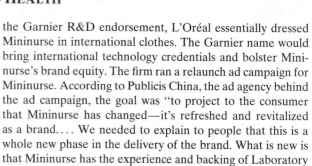

ASE 12-3

L'ORÉAL CHINA: NURSING MININURSE BACK TO HEALTH

When L'Oréal bought Mininurse, a Chinese mass skincare brand, from the Shenzhen firm Raystar Cosmetics in December 2003, the move was seen as a major coup for L'Oréal. Lindsay Owen-Jones, L'Oréal's CEO, commented, "This acquisition is an outstanding opportunity to speed up our growth in the Chinese market. It is a major step forward in L'Oréal's development in a market which is strategically important for the company." Paolo Gasparrini, then-general manager of L'Oréal China, added, "Aimed at women with a natural style, Mininurse complements our brand portfolio perfectly and enables us to move more quickly into the Chinese consumer skincare market." At the time of the deal, which took four years to negotiate, Mininurse was one of China's top three skin care brands with a 5 percent market share. The Chinese cosmetics market is clearly booming. Cosmetic sales in China were $7.25bn in 2004 and projected to be $8.5bn in 2005. Skin care products are now a major rage. They account for 40 percent of the market and are growing rapidly at an annual rate of 20 percent. L'Oréal's sales revenues were $384 million in 2004. The firm markets 17 skin care and hair care brands, all imports except for Mininurse and Yue-Sai, a makeup brand bought shortly after the Mininurse deal.

Mininurse, first launched in 1992, is one of China's best known skin care brands with a 90 percent brand recognition. Recognition was even higher among Mininurse's target group of younger women: 96 percent. The brand had built a solid distribution network of 280,000 outlets. With the deal, L'Oréal got access to the brand, its marketing network, and a manufacturing facility in Hubei province.

Soon after the deal, L'Oréal decided to cobrand Mininurse with Garnier, L'Oréal's global mass-market brand. Through the Garnier R&D endorsement, L'Oréal essentially dressed Mininurse in international clothes. The Garnier name would bring international technology credentials and bolster Mininurse's brand equity. The firm ran a relaunch ad campaign for Mininurse. According to Publicis China, the ad agency behind the ad campaign, the goal was "to project to the consumer that Mininurse has changed—it's refreshed and revitalized as a brand.... We needed to explain to people that this is a whole new phase in the delivery of the brand. What is new is that Mininurse has the experience and backing of Laboratory Garnier." The face for the campaign was Tong Sun Jie, a Chinese actress. It was believed that L'Oréal saw Mininurse as a platform to further develop its mass market Garnier range in China. Until the relaunch, Garnier's presence in China was mainly in the hair care segment.

However, Mininurse has been struggling lately. Market data showed that the brand's market share tumbled from 5.1 percent in October 2003, shortly before the deal, to 3.5 percent two years later (see the following table).

Market Share for Moisturizer Brands in China

Brand	October 2003	October 2005
Da Bao	12.1%	11.0%
Long Li Qi	3.9	5.4
Mininurse	5.1	3.5
Tjoy	2.1	4.1

Sources: ACNielsen. 2006.

DISCUSSION QUESTIONS

1. Was the Mininurse acquisition really worth the wait and the effort for L'Oréal?

2. What might have been the drivers behind Mininurse's market share drop? Was the Mininurse-Garnier cobranding a strategic mistake?

3. What is your prescription to revitalize Mininurse? Should L'Oréal discard the Garnier endorsement? Should the brand be repositioned?

Sources: "New L'Oreal Label Touts Laboratory Garnier Back-Up," *Media,* June 4, 2004, p. 11; http://www.mininursegarnier.com/index/index.asp; http://www.loreal-finance.com/pdf/dwd_pdf.asp?id_page=246&lg=us&doctype=page; http://www.bjreview.com.cn/200408/Business-200408(C).htm; http://www1.cei.gov.cn/ce/doc/cen3/200601191914.htm; http://www.sinomedia.net/eurobiz/v200402/story0402.html; and "Mininurse Problems More than Skin Deep," *Media,* February 10, 2006, p. 17.

FURTHER READING ◆

Aaker, David A., and Erich Joachimsthaler. "The Lure of Global Branding." *Harvard Business Review,* November–December 1999, pp. 137–44.

Abratt, Russell, and Patience Motlana. "Managing Co-Branding Strategies: Global Brands into Local Markets." *Business Horizons,* September–October 2002, pp. 43–50.

Cordell, Victor V. "Effects of Consumer Preferences for Foreign Sourced Products." *Journal of International Business Studies,* Second Quarter 1992, pp. 251–69.

Douglas, Susan P., C. Samuel Craig, and Edwin J. Nijssen. "Integrating Branding Strategy across Markets: Building International Brand Architecture." *Journal of International Marketing,* 9 (2), 2001, pp. 97–114.

Holt, Douglas B., John A. Quelch, and Earl L. Taylor. "How Global Brands Compete." *Harvard Business Review,* 82 (September 2004), pp. 68–75.

Jain, Subhash C. "Problems in International Protection of Intellectual Property Rights." *Journal of International Marketing,* 4 (1), 1996, pp. 9–32.

Leclerc, France, Bernd H. Schmitt, and Laurette Dubé. "Foreign Branding and Its Effects on Product Perceptions and Attitudes." *Journal of Marketing Research,* 31 (May 1994), pp. 263–70.

Lovelock, Christopher H., and George S. Yip. "Developing Global Strategies for Service Businesses." *California Management Review,* 38 (2), Winter 1996, pp. 64–86.

Pagano, Camillo. "The Management of Global Brands." In *Brand Power,* ed. P. Stobart. London: Macmillan, 1994.

Partoyan, Garo. "Protecting Power Brands." In *Brand Power,* ed. P. Stobart. London: Macmillan, 1994.

Roth, Martin S., and Jean B. Romeo. "Matching Product Category and Country Image Perceptions: A Framework for Managing Country-of-Origin Effects." *Journal of International Business Studies,* Third Quarter 1992, pp. 477–97.

Shultz, C., and B. Saporito. "Protecting Intellectual Property: Strategies and Recommendations to Deter Counterfeiting and Brand Piracy in Global Markets." *Columbia Journal of World Business,* Spring 1996, pp. 18–28.

Steenkamp, Jan-Benedict E. M., Rajeev Batra, and Dan L. Alden. "How Perceived Brand Globalness Creates Brand Value." *Journal of International Business Studies,* 34 (1), January 2003, pp. 53–65.

Tanaka, Hiroshi. "Branding in Japan." In *Brand Equity & Advertising: Advertising's Role in Building Strong Brands,* ed. D.A. Aaker and A.L. Biel (Hillsdale, NJ: Erlbaum Associates, 1993).

GLOBAL PRICING

HAPTER OVERVIEW

1. DRIVERS OF FOREIGN MARKET PRICING

2. PRICE ESCALATION

3. PRICING IN INFLATIONARY ENVIRONMENTS

4. GLOBAL PRICING AND CURRENCY FLUCTUATIONS

5. TRANSFER PRICING

6. GLOBAL PRICING AND ANTIDUMPING REGULATION

7. PRICE COORDINATION

8. COUNTERTRADE

Global pricing is one of the most critical and complex issues that global firms face. Price is the only marketing mix instrument that creates revenues, all other elements entail costs. Thus, a company's global pricing policy can make or break its overseas expansion efforts. Furthermore, a firm's pricing policy is inherently a highly cross-functional process based on inputs from the firm's finance, accounting, manufacturing, tax, and legal divisions. Predictably, the interests of one group (e.g., marketing) can clash with the objectives of another group (e.g., finance).

Multinationals also face the challenge of how to coordinate their pricing policy across different countries. A lack of coordination creates a parallel trade or gray market situation (see Chapter 17). With parallel imports, middlemen make a profit by shipping products from low-price countries to higher price markets. These imports will compete with the high-priced equivalent products offered by legitimate distributors. Efforts to trim big price gaps between countries can be hampered by stonewalling attempts of local country managers or distribution channels.

This chapter focuses on global pricing strategies. After presenting an overview of the key drivers of foreign market pricing, we discuss several strategic international pricing issues. The chapter concludes with a discussion of *countertrade*, which is a form of noncash pricing.

◆ ◆ ◆ ◆ ◆ ◆ ◆ ◆   DRIVERS OF FOREIGN MARKET PRICING

Even within the same geographic area such as the pan-European market, wide cross-border price differences are quite common. The launch of the euro was intended to encourage price convergence. Levi jeans were 43 percent cheaper in Brussels than in Paris. However, Pampers diapers cost 56 percent more in Brussels than in Frankfurt. The least expensive shopping basket was in Madrid, where the price was 10 percent less than in Paris, the most expensive euro-area city. Not surprisingly, cross-country price differences become even wider for global brand comparisons around the world. This is illustrated in Exhibit 13-1 for the price of a can of Pringles potato chips. Why these enormous price variations? A hodgepodge of factors governs global pricing decisions. Some of the drivers are related to the following: *Company* (costs, company goals), *Customers* (price sensitivity, segments, consumer preferences), *Competition* (market structure, intensity), and *Channels*. Aside from these, in many countries, multinationals' pricing decisions are often influenced by government policies (price controls, taxes, import duties). We now consider the main drivers that may affect global pricing.

Company Goals   When developing a pricing strategy for its global markets, a firm needs to decide what it wants to accomplish with its strategy. These goals can include maximizing current profits, penetrating the market, projecting a premium image, and so forth. According to one study,[1] the most important pricing objectives of companies doing business in the United States (including foreign-based firms) are to (1) achieve a satisfactory

EXHIBIT 13-1
RETAIL PRICE (INCL. TAXES) OF A 190-GRAM CAN OF PRINGLES SOUR CREAM & ONION CHIPS (NOVEMBER 2005) AROUND THE WORLD

City	US$
Kuala Lumpur (Malaysia)	$1.04
Hong Kong (China)	1.23
Taipei (Taiwan)	1.30
Manila (Philippines)	1.36
Singapore	1.37
Bangkok (Thailand)	1.44
Jakarta (Indonesia)	1.63
Shanghai (China)	1.76
Brussels (Belgium)	1.87
Sydney (Australia)	2.02
Frankfurt (Germany)	2.24
Paris (France)	2.27
Rome (Italy)	2.38
London (UK)	2.43
Tokyo (Japan)	2.48
Seoul (South Korea)	2.50

Source: Asian Wall Street Journal, November 4–6, 2005, p. W6.

---

[1]S. Samiee, "Pricing in Marketing Strategies of U.S. and Foreign-Based Companies," *Journal of Business Research,* 15 (1987), pp. 17–30.

return on investment, (2) maintain market share, and (3) meet a specified profit goal (in that order). Company objectives will vary from market to market, especially for multinationals with a large degree of local autonomy. New Balance, the U.S.-based maker of high-tech running shoes, sells its shoes in France as haute couture items rather than simply athletic shoes (as it does in the United States, for instance). To beef up the premium image, the price is about $130 a pair, almost twice the U.S. price.[2] Company goals are likely to change over time. When a firm initially enters a country, it often sets a relatively low price (compared to other countries) to penetrate the market. Once the firm is well entrenched, it may shift its objectives and bring prices in line with the goals pursued in other countries.

Company Costs

Company costs figure prominently in the pricing decision. Costs set the floor: The company wants to set at least a price that will cover all costs needed to make and sell its products. Cost differentials between countries can lead to wide price gaps. It is important that management considers all relevant costs of manufacturing, marketing, and distributing the product. Company costs consist of two parts: variable costs, which change with sales volume, and fixed costs (e.g., overheads) that do not vary.

Export pricing policies differ depending on the way costs are treated.[3] The most popular practice is **cost-plus pricing.** This approach adds international costs and a markup to the domestic manufacturing cost. At times, a company will offer discounts or rebates to reward its customer. An alternative approach is **dynamic incremental pricing,** a strategy that arrives at a price after removing domestic fixed costs. The premise is that the company will have to bear these costs anyhow, regardless of whether or not the goods are exported. Only variable costs generated by the exporting efforts and a portion of the overhead load (the "incremental" costs) should be recuperated. Examples of exporting-related incremental costs include manufacturing costs, shipping expenses, insurance, and overseas promotional costs. Although the second approach is more appropriate from an economic perspective, there are certain risks. Situations in which the export list price is far below the domestic price could trigger dumping accusations in the export market as discussed later.

When demand is highly price sensitive, the company needs to consider how it can reduce costs from a global perspective. Manufacturing scale economies provide an incentive to standardize product offerings or to consolidate manufacturing facilities. In some markets, logistics costs can be trimmed by centralizing distribution centers or warehouse facilities. By the same token, significant marketing costs may prompt a multinational operating in Europe to develop pan-European advertising campaigns. In many developing countries, high price sensitivity is a big hurdle. Hindustan Lever, Unilever's India subsidiary, spends a large amount of its R&D money on developing new technologies to lower production costs. Companies operating in these countries typically try to source mainly from local suppliers. McDonald's India imports only potatoes, all other ingredients are sourced locally. However, the company has set up a potato research unit to improve the quality of Indian potatoes.[4] Kellogg, on the other hand, entered India with costly packaging (seven-ply cartons, foil pouches, five colors), and expensive advertising. A local competitor, Champion, piggybacked on Kellogg's marketing efforts and conquered the breakfast cereal market with products at one-fifth of Kellogg's price.[5]

---

[2]"The Road to Richesse," *Sales & Marketing Management,* November 1999, pp. 89–96.

[3]S. Tamer Cavusgil, "Unraveling the Mystique of Export Pricing," *Business Horizons,* 31 (May–June 1988), pp. 54–63.

[4]"Hard Sell to a Billion Consumers," *Financial Times,* April 25, 2002, p. 14.

[5]"Slim Pickings for the Global Brand in India," *Financial Times,* October 11, 2000, p. 14.

Customer Demand

Whereas costs set a floor, the consumers' willingness to pay for a company's product set a ceiling to the price. Consumer demand is a function of buying power, tastes, habits, and substitutes, demand conditions that vary from country to country. For instance, Nescafé is fairly expensive in Italy because the Italian demand for instant coffee is very minor.[6]

Buying power is a key consideration in pricing decisions. Countries with low per capita incomes pose a dilemma. Consumers in such countries are far more price sensitive than these in developed markets. Therefore, price premiums are often a major hurdle for most consumers in these markets. Foreign companies targeting the masses in emerging markets such as China or India offer products with lower costs by changing the product formula, packaging, or size. One risk here is brand dilution through which a premium brand loses its cachet when a large number of consumers start using it. Another danger is cannibalization. This occurs when high-income customers switch to the cheaper products in the firm's product line. The marketing of Procter & Gamble's Crest toothpaste in China illustrates how companies can manage these issues. To lure the Chinese middle classes, P&G changed the brand's formulation and packaging to emphasize cavity prevention, a generic benefit. The whitening benefit was reserved for premium Crest products.[7] In Egypt, one of the moves that P&G undertook to revitalize the sales of Ariel, its high suds laundry detergent brand, was to downsize the package size from 200 grams to 150 grams, thereby lowering the cash outlay for ordinary consumers.[8]

Another strategic option is to be a niche player by charging prices in the same range as Western prices and target the upper-end of the foreign market. Companies such as Starbucks and Häagen-Dazs follow this option in their global strategy. Starbucks charges by and large the same price worldwide, whether its coffee is sold in wealthy Western markets or poorer countries such as Thailand or China. A third option is to have a portfolio of products that cater to different income tiers. Hindustan Lever, dominates many consumer goods categories by following this road. One final option—which seldom works—is to sell older versions of the product at a lower price in markets with low buying power. For instance, in India, DaimlerChrysler sold older Mercedes models; United Distillers sold passé brands such as Vat 69. Such a pricing strategy can backfire as it manifests a certain amount of arrogance toward the local population.[9]

Typically, the nature of demand changes over time. In countries that were entered recently, the firm may need to stimulate trial via discounting or a penetration pricing strategy. In more mature markets, the lion's share of customers will be repeat buyers. Once brand loyalty has been established, price will play less a role as a purchase criterion, and the firm may be able to afford the luxury of a premium pricing strategy. Obviously, the success of such a pricing strategy will hinge on the company's ability to differentiate its product from the competition.

Competition

Competition is another key factor in global pricing. Differences in the competitive situation across countries usually lead to cross-border price differentials. The competitive situation varies for a number of reasons. First, the number of competitors typically differs from country to country. In some countries, the firm faces very few competitors (or even enjoys a monopoly position), whereas in others, it has to combat numerous competing brands. Also, the nature of competition differs: global versus local players, private firms versus state-owned companies. Even when local companies are not state owned, they often are viewed as "national champions" and treated accordingly by

---

[6]"Counting Costs of Dual Pricing...," *Financial Times,* July 9, 1990, p. 4.

[7]"The Right Way to Appeal to the Masses," *Financial Times,* September 15, 2004, p. 10.

[8]Mahmoud Aboul-Fath and Loula Zaklama, "Ariel High Suds Detergent in Egypt—A Case Study," *Marketing and Research Today,* May 1992, pp. 130–35.

[9]"Slim Pickings for the Global Brand in India," *Financial Times* (October 11, 2000) p. 14.

their local governments. Such a status entails subsidies or other goodies (e.g., cheap loans) that enable them to undercut their competitors. In some markets, firms must compete with a knockoff version of their own product. The presence of counterfeit products could force the firm to lower its price in such markets. In developing countries, especially in rural areas, the nature of competition can also vary. An Indian villager is not just choosing between a bottle of Coca-Cola and Pepsi but also between buying one soft drink, a disposable razor, or a tube of toothpaste.

The role of competition can be illustrated by considering the pharmaceutical industry. The data in Exhibit 13-2 show the average quarterly volume sales and selling price (charged by manufacturers) for three antidepressants (Prozac, Zoloft, Paxil) marketed in the United States, the United Kingdom, France, Italy, and Germany. The data indicate that Prozac (from Eli Lilly based in the United States) charges a higher price than Paxil (from GlaxoSmithKline in the United Kingdom). However, the reverse is the case in the United Kingdom. An in-depth analysis of this particular industry found that pharmaceutical companies tend to behave much more aggressively toward their competitors in the home market than in foreign markets.[10]

In many markets, legitimate distributors of global brands must compete with smugglers. For instance, industry analysts estimated that 100,000 cars were smuggled into China in 1996 from Japan and South Korea.[11] Smuggling operations put downward pressure on the price of the affected product. The strength of private labels (store brands) is another important driver. In countries where store brands are well entrenched, companies are forced to accept lower margins than elsewhere.

A company's competitive position typically varies across countries. Companies will be price leaders in some countries and price takers in other countries. Heinz policy is to cut prices in markets where it is not the leading brand.[12] Finally, the rules of the game usually differ. Nonprice competition (e.g., advertising, channel coverage) may be preferable in some countries. Elsewhere, price wars are a way of life. Global Perspective 13-1 discusses some of the tactics Microsoft uses to combat the spread of open-source software.

EXHIBIT 13-2

AVERAGE QUARTERLY SALES AND FACTORY SELLING PRICES OF ANTIDEPRESSANTS (1988, Q1–1999, Q1)

Brand	Manufacturer	United States	Germany	Italy	United Kingdom	France
Prozac	Eli Lilly (U.S.)					
Sales		162.13	2.47	3.65	18.88	32.92
Price		1.62	1.48	0.99	1.18	0.84
Zoloft	Pfizer (U.S.)					
Sales		140.05	1.99	1.77	7.30	9.47
Price		1.59	1.00	0.92	1.40	0.70
Paxil	GSK (U.K.)					
Sales		110.46	1.66	4.04	16.70	21.94
Price		1.59	1.48	1.20	1.26	0.65

Source: Based on Table 1 (p. 73) of Pradeep K. Chintagunta and Ramarao Desiraju, "Strategic Pricing and Detailing Behavior in International Markets," *Marketing Science*, 24 (Winter 2005).

---

[10]Pradeep K. Chintagunta and Ramarao Desiraju, "Strategic Pricing and Detailing Behavior in International Markets," *Marketing Science*, 24 (Winter 2005), pp. 67–80.

[11]"Where's the Pot of Gold?" *Business Week (Asian Edition)*, (February 3, 1997), pp. 14–15.

[12]"Counting costs of dual pricing . . .," p. 4.

$\mathcal{G}$LOBAL PERSPECTIVE 13-1

MICROSOFT'S GLOBAL WAR ON OPEN-SOURCE SOFTWARE

Undoubtedly, one of the biggest threats that Microsoft faces in the global market place is the spread of open-source software, which is software whose source code can be copied freely. The best-known example is Linux, which is supported by major computer companies such as IBM, Sun Microsystems, HP, and Dell. To buttress its turf against the inroads posed by free software, Microsoft is waging counterattacks around the globe.

Open-source software could prove especially appealing in the developing world where most people and businesses cannot afford Microsoft's pricey software products. In China, one of Microsoft's hottest prospects, government authorities are wary of the software giant and urge local Chinese companies and institutions to use home-grown Linux-based products. One beneficiary is Red Flag Software Co., which is backed by the son of Jiang Zenmin, the former Chinese president.

Sources: "Asia: Microsoft's Land of Opportunity," *Business Week Online,* http://www.businessweek.com/, November 18, 2002; and "Microsoft Wages Quiet, Global War on Free Software," *Asian Wall Street Journal,* December 10, 2002, p. A7.

In the wake of these threats, Microsoft has launched major lobbying and public relations initiatives. In India, Microsoft announced a $400 million gift of free software and business-development aid. Its Project Shiksha (meaning "education" in Hindi) aims to boost computer literacy to 3.5 million students in government schools around India. The Bill and Melinda Gates Foundation also plans to donate huge amounts of money for anti-AIDS projects. One of India's leading business magazines described all of these good deeds as a "war for India's software soul." Likewise, in South Africa, Microsoft plans to provide software to 32,000 local schools. One critic observed that a large portion of Microsoft's donations goes to countries that have expressed a strong preference for open-source software.

Apart from trying to be a "good citizen," Microsoft has used other tactics. The company plans to pour millions of dollars in China's and India's software industry. Microsoft's research facility in Beijing is now its second largest in the world. It also set up a partnership with Lenovo, China's biggest computer manufacturer.

Distribution Channels

Another driver behind global pricing is the distribution channel. The pressure exercised by channels can take many forms. Variations in trade margins and the length of the channels influence the ex-factory price charged by the company. The balance of power between manufacturers and their distributors is another factor behind pricing practices. Countries such as France and the United Kingdom are characterized by large retailers that are able to order in bulk and to bargain for huge discounts with manufacturers. In the pan-European market, several smaller retailers have formed cross-border co-ops to strengthen their negotiation position with their common suppliers. The power of large-scale retailers in Europe is vividly illustrated by the hurdles that several manufacturers faced in implementing every-day-low-pricing (EDLP). With EDLP, the manufacturer offers consistently lower prices to the retailer (and the ultimate shopper) instead of promotional price discounts and trade promotions. Several German supermarket chains delisted P&G brands such as Ariel, Vizir, and Lenor detergent products and Bess toilet tissue when P&G introduced EDLP in Germany in early 1996.[13] Another example is the personal computer industry. The lower cost markets such as the United States and Germany offer consumers a broad assortment of channel choices: direct marketers, supermarkets (e.g., Aldi in Germany), large specialty retail chains, and so on. However, in Britain, where PC prices are on average 50 percent or more higher than in Germany, the market is dominated by Dixons, a retail chain that, according to Intel, charges "ridiculous margins."[14]

Large cross-country price gaps open up arbitrage opportunities that lead to **parallel imports (gray markets)** from low-price countries to high-price ones. These parallel imports are commonly handled by unauthorized distributors at the expense of legitimate trade channels. To curtail parallel trade, firms can consider narrowing cross-border price disparities. Thus, preemption of cross-border bargain hunting is often a strong motivation behind a company's pricing practices.

---

[13]"Heat's on Value Pricing," *Advertising Age International,* (January 1997), pp. 1–21, 1–22.

[14]"A Byte of the Market," *Financial Times,* (November 22, 1998), p. 7.

Even after the launch of the euro, car prices in the European Union can still vary by up to 50 percent. One of the main reasons for these disparities is the sales tax rate for new cars. These vary from as low as 15 percent in Luxembourg up to 213 percent in Denmark. This taxation gap also has an impact on pretax car prices. In fact, most car makers in Europe subsidize the pretax prices in high-tax countries by charging more in low-tax countries.[15]

Government policies can have a direct or indirect impact on pricing policies. Factors that have a direct impact include sales tax rates (e.g., value-added taxes), tariffs, and price controls. Sometimes government interference is very blatant. The Chinese government sets minimum prices in scores of industries. The goal is to stamp out price wars and protect the Chinese economy against deflation pressures. Firms that ignore the pricing rules are slapped with hefty fines.[16]

An increase in the sales tax rate usually lowers overall demand. However, in some cases, taxes selectively affect imports. For instance, in the late 1980s, the U.S. government introduced a 10 percent luxury tax on the part of a car's price that exceeds $30,000. This tax primarily affected the price of luxury imported cars since few U.S. automakers made luxury cars that sold for more than the $30,000 threshold. Tariffs obviously inflate the retail price of imports. Another concern is price control, which affects either the entire economy (for instance, in high-inflation countries) or selective industries. In many countries, the government bears a substantial part of the health care costs. Prices for reimbursable drugs are negotiated between the government authorities and the pharmaceutical company. Many pharmaceutical companies face the dilemma of accepting lower prices for their drugs or having them registered on a negative list, which contains drugs whose costs the government will not reimburse.[17] Furthermore, several governments heavily encourage the prescription of generics or stimulate parallel imports from low-price countries to put price pressure on drug companies. In the European Union, governments increasingly benchmark their prices against other member states and adjust them if necessary.[18] To sustain higher prices, manufacturers often launch new drugs in high-price markets first so that prices in these countries can be used as reference points.[19]

Aside from direct intervention, government policies can have an indirect impact on pricing decisions. For instance, huge government deficits spur interest rates (cost of capital), currency volatility, and inflation. The interplay of these factors will affect the product cost. Inflation can also impact labor costs in those countries (e.g., Belgium, Brazil) that have a wage indexation system. Such a system adjusts wages for increases in the cost of living.

This section discussed the main factors that drive global pricing decisions. We now highlight the key managerial issues in global pricing.

Government Policies

MANAGING PRICE ESCALATION

◆ ◆ ◆ ◆ ◆ ◆ ◆ ◆

Exporting involves more steps and substantially higher risks than simply selling goods in the home market. To cover the incremental costs (e.g., shipping, insurance, tariffs, margins of various intermediaries), the final foreign retail price is often much higher than the domestic retail price. This phenomenon is known as **price escalation.** It raises two issues that management needs to confront: (1) whether foreign customers will be willing to pay the inflated price for the product and (2) whether this price will make the product less competitive. If the answer is negative, the exporter needs to decide how to cope with price escalation.

---

[15]"Car Price Disparities Highlighted," *Financial Times,* January 7, 1999, p. 2.

[16]"So Much for Competition," *Business Week (Asian edition),* November 30, 1998, pp. 22–23.

[17]Some countries have a "positive" list of drugs from which physicians can prescribe.

[18]Neil Turner, "European Pricing Squeeze," *Pharmaceutical Executive,* October 2002, pp. 84–91.

[19]David Hanlon and David Luery, "The Role of Pricing Research in Assessing the Commercial Potential of New Drugs in Development," *International Journal of Market Research,* 44 (4), 2002, pp. 423–47.

There are two broad approaches to cope with price escalation: (1) find ways to cut the export price or (2) position the product as a (super) premium brand. Several options exist to lower the export price:[20]

1. **Rearrange the distribution channel.** Channels are often largely responsible for price escalation, either due to the length of the channel (number of layers between manufacturer and end-user) or because of exorbitant margins. In some circumstances, it is possible to shorten the channel. Alternatively, firms could look into channel arrangements that provide cost efficiencies. In recent years, several U.S. companies have decided to penetrate the Japanese consumer market through direct marketing (e.g., catalog sales, telemarketing, selling through the Internet). This allows them to bypass the notorious Japanese distribution infrastructure and become more price-competitive.

2. **Eliminate costly features (or make them optional).** Several exporters have addressed the price escalation issue by offering no-frills versions of their product. Rather than having to purchase the entire bundle, customers can buy the core product and then decide whether they want to pay extra for optional features.

3. **Downsize the product.** Another route to dampen sticker shock is by downsizing the product by offering a smaller version of the product or a lesser count.[21] This option is desirable only when consumers are not aware of cross-border volume differences. To that end, manufacturers can decide to go for a local branding strategy.

4. **Assemble or manufacture the product in foreign markets.** A more extreme option is to assemble or even manufacture the entire product in foreign markets (not necessarily the export market). Closer proximity to the export market lowers transportation costs. To lessen import duties for goods sold within European Union markets, numerous firms have decided to set up assembly operations in EU member states.

5. **Adapt the product to escape tariffs or tax levies.** Finally, a company could also modify its export product to bring it into a different tariff or tax bracket. When the United States levied a new 10 percent tax on luxury cars priced over $30,000, Land Rover increased the maximum weight of its Range Rover models sold in the United States to 6,019 pounds. As a result, they were classified as trucks (not subject to the 10 percent luxury tax) rather than luxury cars.

These measures represent different ways to counter price escalation. Alternatively, an exporter could exploit the price escalation situation and go for a premium positioning strategy. LEGO, the Danish toymaker, sells building block sets in India that are priced between $6 and $223, far more than most other toys that Indian parents can purchase. To justify the premium price, LEGO uses a marketing strategy that targets middle-class parents and stresses the educational value of LEGO toys.[22] Of course, for this strategy to work, other elements of the export marketing mix should be in tandem with the premium positioning. In Europe and Japan, Levi Strauss sells its jeans mainly in upscale boutiques rather than in department stores.[23]

◆ ◆ ◆ ◆ ◆ ◆ ◆ ◆   PRICING IN INFLATIONARY ENVIRONMENTS

When McDonald's opened its doors in Moscow in January 1990, a Big Mac meal (including fries and a soft drink) cost 6 rubles. Three years later, the same meal cost 1,100 rubles.[24] Rampant inflation is a major obstacle to doing business in many countries.

---

[20]Cavusgil, "Unraveling the Mystique of Export Pricing," 56.

[21]Loyal Coca-Cola cross-border travelers may have noticed can size differences of their favorite tipple. For instance, for Diet Coke, can sizes range from 325 mL (e.g., Malaysia, Thailand) up to 355 mL (United States). See http://xoomer.virgilio.it/davide.andreani/Cokesize.htm for a complete listing of Coke can sizes around the world.

[22]"LEGO Building Its Way to China," *Advertising Age International*, March 20, 1995, p. 1–29.

[23]"The Levi Straddle," *Forbes*, January 17, 1994, p. 44.

[24]"Inflation Bites Russians, Who Still Bite into Big Mac," *Advertising Age International*, March 15, 1993, pp. I-3, I-23.

Moreover, high inflation rates are usually coupled with highly volatile exchange rate movements. In such environments, price setting and stringent cost control become extremely crucial. Not surprisingly, in such markets, companies' financial divisions are often far more important than other departments.[25]

There are several alternative ways to safeguard against inflation.

1. **Modify components, ingredients, parts and/or packaging materials.** Some ingredients are subject to lower inflation rates than others. This might justify a change in the ingredient mix. Of course, before implementing such a move, the firm should consider all of its consequences (e.g., consumer response, impact on shelf life of the product).

2. **Source materials from low-cost suppliers.** Supply management plays a central role in high-inflation environments. A first step is to screen suppliers and determine which ones are most cost efficient without cutting corners. If feasible, materials could be imported from low-inflation countries. Note, however, that high inflation rates are coupled with a weakening currency. This pushes up the price of imports.

3. **Shorten credit terms.** In some cases, profits can be realized by juggling the terms of payment. For instance, a firm that is able to collect cash from its customers within 15 days but has one month to pay its suppliers can invest its money during the 15-day grace period. Thus, firms strive to push up the lead time in paying their suppliers. At the same time, they also try to shorten the time to collect from their clients.[26]

4. **Include escalator clauses in long-term contracts.** Many business-to-business marketing situations involve long-term contracts (e.g., leasing arrangements). To hedge their position against inflation, the parties include escalator clauses that provide the necessary protection.

5. **Quote prices in a stable currency.** To handle high inflation, companies often quote prices in a stable currency such as the U. S. dollar or the euro.

6. **Pursue rapid inventory turnovers.** High inflation also mandates rapid inventory turnarounds. As a result, information technologies (e.g., scanning techniques, computerized inventory tracking) that facilitate rapid inventory turnovers or even just-in-time delivery yield a competitive advantage.

7. **Draw lessons from other countries.** Operations in countries with a long history of inflation offer valuable lessons for ventures in other high-inflation countries. Cross-fertilization by drawing from experience in other high inflation markets often helps. Some companies—McDonald's[27] and Otis Elevator International,[28] for example—have relied on expatriate managers from Latin America to cope with inflation in the former Soviet Union. One of the lessons drawn from Brazil was that McDonald's negotiates a separate inflation rate with each supplier. These rates are then used for monthly realignments instead of the government's published inflation figures.

To combat hyperinflation, governments occasionally impose price controls (usually coupled with a wage freeze). For instance, Brazil went through five price freezes over a six-year interval. Such temporary price caps could be selective, targeting certain products, but, in extreme circumstances, apply across the board to all consumer goods. Price freezes have proven to be very ineffective to dampen inflation, as witnessed by the experience of Brazil. Often, expectations of an imminent price freeze start in the rumor mill and spur companies to implement substantial price increases, thereby setting off a vicious cycle. One consequence of price controls is that goods are diverted to the black market or smuggled overseas, leading to shortages in the regular market.

---

[25]"A Rollercoaster Out of Control," *Financial Times,* February 22, 1993.
[26]Ibid.
[27]"Inflation Lessons over a Big Mac," *Financial Times,* February 22, 1993.
[28]"Russians Up and Down," *Financial Times,* October 18, 1993, p. 12.

Companies faced with price controls can consider several action courses.

1. **Adapt the product line.** To reduce exposure to a government-imposed price freeze, companies diversify into product lines that are relatively free of price controls.[29] Of course, before embarking on such a changeover, the firm must examine the long-term ramifications. Modifying the product line could imply loss of economies of scale, an increase in overheads, and adverse reactions from the company's customer base.

2. **Shift target segments or markets.** A more drastic move is to shift the firm's target segment. For instance, price controls often apply to consumer food products but not to animal-related products. So, a maker of corn-based consumer products might consider a shift from breakfast cereals to chicken-feed products. Again, such action should be preceded by a thorough analysis of its strategic implications. Alternatively, a firm might consider using its operations in the high-inflation country as an export base for countries that are not subject to price controls.

3. **Launch new products or variants of existing products.** If price controls are selective, a company can navigate around them by systematically launching new products or modifying existing ones. Faced with price controls in Zimbabwe, bakers added raisins to their dough and called it raisin bread, thereby, at least momentarily, escaping the price control for bread.[30] Also, the firm should consider the overall picture by answering questions such as these: Will there be a demand for these products? What are the implications in terms of manufacturing economies? inventory management? How will the trade react? Furthermore, if these products are not yet available elsewhere, this option is a long-term solution.

4. **Negotiate with the government.** In some cases, firms are able to negotiate for permission to adjust their prices. Lobbying can be done individually but is more likely to be successful on an industrywide basis.

5. **Predict incidence of price controls.** Some countries have a history of price freeze programs. Given historical information on the occurrence of price controls and other economic variables, firms can construct econometric models to forecast the likelihood of price controls. Managers can use that information to determine whether price adjustments are warranted, given the likelihood of an imminent price freeze.[31]

A drastic action is simply to leave the country. Many consumer goods companies chose this option when they exited their South American markets during the 1980s. However, companies that hang on and learn to manage a high-inflation environment will be able carry their expertise to other countries. Furthermore, they will enjoy a competitive advantage (due to entry barriers such as brand loyalty, channel, and supplier ties) versus companies that reenter these markets once inflation has been controlled.

◆ ◆ ◆ ◆ ◆ ◆ ◆ ◆ GLOBAL PRICING AND CURRENCY MOVEMENTS

In May 1992, two of the most expensive car markets in the European Union were Spain and Italy. One year later, they were the two lowest priced markets.[32] Currency volatility within the European Union was mostly responsible for these car price reversals. With a few exceptions (e.g., some Caribbean islands, Ecuador), most countries have their own currency. Exchange rates reflect how much one currency is worth in terms of another currency. Due to the interplay of a variety of economic and political factors,

[29] Venkatakrishna V. Bellur, Radharao Chaganti, Rajeswararao Chaganti, and Saraswati P. Singh, "Strategic Adaptations to Price Controls: The Case of the Indian Drug Industry," *Journal of the Academy of Marketing Science*, 13 (1), Winter 1985, pp. 143–59.

[30] "The Zimbabwean Model," *Economist*, November 30, 2002, p. 72.

[31] James K. Weekly, "Pricing in Foreign Markets: Pitfalls and Opportunities," *Industrial Marketing Management*, 21 (1992), pp. 173–79.

[32] "Fluctuating Exchange Rates Main Factor in European Car Price Comparisons," *Financial Times*, July 5, 1993.

EXHIBIT 13-3

EXPORTER STRATEGIES UNDER VARYING CURRENCY CONDITIONS

When Domestic Currency is WEAK...	*When Domestic Currency is STRONG...*
• Stress price benefits	• Engage in nonprice competition by improving quality, delivery, and aftersale service
• Costly features expand product line and add more	• Improve productivity and engage in vigorous cost reduction
• Shift sourcing and manufacturing to domestic market	• Shift sourcing and manufacturing overseas.
• Exploit export opportunities in all markets	• Give priority to exports to relatively strong-currency countries
• Conduct conventional cash-for-goods trade	• Deal in countertrade with weak-currency countries
• Use full-costing approach but use marginal-cost pricing to penetrate new/competitive markets	• Trim profit margins and use marginal-cost pricing
• Speed repatriation of foreign-earned income and collections	• Keep the foreign-earned income in host country, slow collections
• Minimize expenditures in local, host-country currency	• Maximize expenditure in local, host-country currency
• Buy needed services (advertising, insurance, transportation, etc.) in domestic market	• Buy needed services abroad and pay for them in local currency
• Minimize local borrowing	• Borrow money needed for expansion in local market
• Bill foreign customers in domestic currency	• Bill foreign customers in their own currency

Source: S. Tamer Cavusgil, "Unraveling the Mystique of Export Pricing," reprinted from *Business Horizons* (May–June 1988). Copyright 1988 by the Foundation for the School of Business at Indiana University. Used with permission.

exchange rates continuously float up- or downward. Even membership to a monetary union does not guarantee exchange rate stability. For instance, in September 1992, the Italian lira and the pound sterling were forced to withdraw from the European Monetary System. At the same time, the bands within which the remaining currencies could move without intervention were broadened. In early 1994, the CFA, the currency unit shared by several former French African colonies, was devalued by 50 percent. Given the sometimes dramatic exchange rate movements, setting prices in a floating exchange rate world poses a tremendous challenge.[33] Exhibit 13-3 lists several exporter strategies under varying currency regimes.

Currency Gain/Loss Pass Through

Two major managerial pricing issues result from currency movements: (1) how much an exchange rate gain (loss) should be passed through to our customers and (2) in what currency should a company quote its prices. Let us first address the **pass-through issue.** Consider the predicament of U.S. companies exporting to Japan. In principle, a weakening of the U.S. dollar versus the Japanese yen will strengthen the competitive position of U.S.-based exporters in Japan. A weak dollar allows U.S.-based firms to lower the yen price of U.S. goods exported to Japan. This enables U.S. exporters to steal market share from the local Japanese competitors without sacrificing profits. By the same token, a stronger U.S. dollar will undermine the competitive position of U.S. exporters. When the dollar appreciates versus the yen, the mirror picture of the previous situation occurs: The retail price in yen of U.S. exports goes up. As a result, U.S. exporters might lose market share if they leave their ex-factory prices unchanged.

---

[33]Llewlyn Clague and Rena Grossfield, "Export Pricing in a Floating Rate World," *Columbia Journal of World Business,* Winter 1974, pp. 17–22.

To maintain their competitive edge, they may be forced to lower their ex-factory dollar prices. Of course, the ultimate impact on the exporter's competitive position will also depend on the impact of currency movement on the exporter's costs and the nature of the competition in the Japanese market. The benefits of a weaker dollar could be washed out when many parts are imported from Japan because the weaker dollar will make these parts more expensive. When most of the competitors are U.S.-based manufacturers, changes in the dollar's exchange rate might not matter.

Let us illustrate these points with a numerical example. Consider the situation in Exhibit 13-4, which looks at the dilemmas that a hypothetical U.S.-based exporter to Japan faces when the exchange rate between the U.S. dollar and the Japanese yen changes. The example assumes a simple linear demand schedule:

$$\text{Demand (in units) in Japanese Export Market} = 2{,}000 - 50 \times \text{Yen Price}$$

We also make an admittedly dubious assumption: Our exporter does not face any costs (in other words, total revenues equal total profits). Initially, one U.S. dollar equals 100 yen, and the firm's total export revenue is $55.5 million. Suppose now that the U.S. dollar has strengthened by 30 percent versus the Japanese yen, moving from an exchange rate of 100 yen to 1 US$ to a 130-to-1 exchange rate (row 2 in Panel A, Exhibit 13-4). If the U.S. dollar-factory price remains the same (i.e., $30,000), Japanese consumers face a 30 percent price increase. Total demand decreases (from 1,850 units to 1,805 units), and revenue in U.S. dollars goes down by $1.35 m. Our American exporter faces the problem of whether or not to pass through exchange rate losses, and if so, how much of the loss to absorb. If the exporter does not lower the U.S. dollar ex-factory price, it is likely to lose market share to its Japanese (and/or European) competitors in Japan. Thus, to sustain its competitive position, the U.S.-based manufacturer would be forced to lower its ex-factory price. In this situation, U.S. exporters face the tradeoff between sacrificing short-term profits (maintaining price) and sustaining long-term market share in export markets (cutting ex-factory price). For example, in the extreme case, the U.S. firm might consider sustaining the yen-based retail price (i.e., 3 million yen). In that case, revenues in U.S. dollars would go down by $11.45 million.

EXHIBIT 13-4
A NUMERICAL ILLUSTRATION OF PASS THROUGH AND LOCAL CURRENCY STABILITY

Demand in Japan (Units) = 2000 − 50 × Price (in Yen)
Costs = $0.0

Panel A: 100% Pass Through

Exchange Rate	Unit Price in US$	Unit Price in Yen*	Units Sold	US$ Revenue*
100 yen = $1	$30,000	3.0	1,850	$55.50
130 yen = $1	30,000	3.9	1,805	54.15
70 yen = $1	30,000	2.1	1,895	56.85

Panel B: Local Currency Price Stability (in millions except units sold)

Exchange Rate	Unit Price in US$	Unit Price in Yen*	Units Sold	US$ Revenue*	Revenue Gain(Loss) vs. 100% PT*
100 yen = $1	$30,000	3.0	1,850	$55.50	$0.00
130 yen = $1	23,077	3.0	1,850	42.69	(11.45)
70 yen = $1	42,857	3.0	1,850	79.28	22.45

*In millions.

Generally speaking, the appropriate action to take depends on four factors: (1) customers' price sensitivity, (2) size of the export market, (3) impact of the dollar appreciation on the firm's cost structure, (4) amount of competition in the export market, and (5) firm's strategic orientation. The higher the consumers' price sensitivity in the export market, the stronger the case for lowering the ex-factory price. One route to lower price sensitivity is by investing in brand equity. High brand equity provides a buffer to global price competition. With vast markets such as the United States, firms are usually more inclined to absorb currency losses than with smaller countries. A decline in costs resulting from the strengthening of the U.S. dollar (e.g., when many parts are imported from Japan) broadens the price-adjustment latitude. The more intense the competition in the export market, the stronger the pressure to cut prices. The fifth factor is the firm's strategic orientation. Firms could be market share oriented or focus on short-term profits. Naturally, market share-oriented firms would tend to pass through less of the cost increase than their financial performance-oriented counterparts.[34] The bottom row of Exhibit 13-4 shows what happens when the U.S. dollar weakens by 30 percent. That case is the mirror picture of the previous scenario.

U.S. exporters might lower their markups much higher in price-conscious export markets than in price-insensitive markets. Such destination-specific adjustment of markups in response to exchange rate movements is referred to as **pricing-to-market (PTM).** PTM behaviors differ across source countries. One study of export pricing adjustments in the U.S. automobile market contrasted pricing decisions of Japanese and German exporters over periods in which both the Japanese yen and the German mark depreciated against the U.S. dollar.[35] The results of the study showed that there was much more pass-through (and less PTM) by German exporters than by their Japanese rivals (see Exhibit 13-5).

Playing the PTM game carries certain risks. Frequent adjustments of prices in response to currency movements will distress local channels and customers. When local currency prices move up, foreign customers could express their disapproval by switching to other brands. On the other hand, when prices go down, it is often difficult to raise prices in the future. Therefore, the preferred strategy often is to adjust markups in such a way that local currency prices remain fairly stable. This special form of PTM has been referred to as **local-currency price stability (LCPS)** where mark-ups are adjusted

EXHIBIT 13-5
RETAIL PRICE CHANGES DURING DOLLAR APPRECIATIONS: JAPANESE AND GERMAN EXPORTS TO THE U.S. MARKET

Model	Real Dollar Appreciation	Real Retail Price Change in U.S. Market
Honda Civic 2-Dr. Sedan	39%	−7%
Datsun 200 SX 2-Dr.	39	−10
Toyota Cressida 4-Dr.	39	6
BMW 320i 2-Dr.	42	−8
BMW 733i 4-Dr.	42	−17
Mercedes 300 TD Sta. Wgn.	42	−39

Note: The dollar appreciation measures the movement of the U.S. producer price index relative to the Japanese and German producer price indices converted into dollars by the nominal exchange rate. The real retail price change measures the movement of the dollar retail price of specific auto models relative to the retail unit value of all domestically produced cars.

Source: Reprinted from Joseph A. Gagnon and Michael M. Knetter, "Markup Adjustment and Exchange Rate Fluctuations: Evidence from Panel Data on Automobile Exports," *Journal of International Money and Finance* 14 (2), p. 304. Copyright 1995, with kind permission from Elsevier Science Ltd, Langford Lane, Kidlington OX5 IGB, UK.

[34] Terry Clark, Masaaki Kotabe, and Dan Rajaratnam, "Exchange Rate Pass-Through and International Pricing Strategy: A Conceptual Framework and Research Propositions," *Journal of International Business Studies,* 30 (Second Quarter 1999), pp. 249–68.

[35] Joseph A. Gagnon and Michael M. Knetter, "Markup Adjustment and Exchange Rate Fluctuations: Evidence from Panel Data on Automobile Exports," *Journal of International Money and Finance,* 14 (2), 1995, pp. 289–310.

to stabilize prices in the buyer's currency.[36] A case in point is Heineken's pricing policy in the United States. In the three-year period since January 2002, the U.S. dollar lost about one-third of its value against the euro. However, the U.S. wholesale price of Heineken and Amstel Light were increased just twice during the same period, each time by a tiny 2.5 percent. U.S. beer drinkers' gain was Heineken's pain. According to analysts, Heineken's annual operating profit from the United States must have fallen from €357 m to €119 m between 2002 and 2006.[37] Panel B of Exhibit 13-4 reports the revenue losses or gains of an exporter who maintains LCPS. To pass through exchange rate gains from U.S. dollar devaluations, U.S.-based exporters could resort to temporary price promotions or other incentives (e.g., trade deals) rather than a permanent cut of the local currency regular price.

Currency Quotation

Another pricing concern "a" rising from floating exchange rates centers on the currency unit to be used in international business transactions. Sellers and buyers usually prefer a quote in their domestic currency. That way, the other party bears currency risks. The decision largely depends on the balance of power between the supplier and the customer. Whoever yields must cover currency exposure risk through hedging transactions on the forward exchange market. A survey of currency choice practices of Swedish, Finnish, and U.S. firms found that firms using foreign currencies have higher export volumes and transaction values than exporters using their home currency. However, profit margins suffer.[38] Some firms decide to use a common currency for all of their business transactions, world- or regionwide. In the wake of the euro, companies such as DaimlerChrysler and Siemens are switching to a euro regime for both their internal (e.g., transfer pricing) and external (suppliers and distributors) transactions.

◆ ◆ ◆ ◆ ◆ ◆ ◆ ◆ TRANSFER PRICING

Determinants of Transfer Prices

Most large multinational corporations (MNCs) have a network of subsidiaries spread across the globe. Sales transactions between related entities of the same company can be quite substantial, involving trade of raw materials, components, finished goods, and services. **Transfer prices** are prices charged for such transactions. Transfer pricing decisions in an international context need to balance the interests of a broad range of stakeholders: (1) parent company, (2) local country managers, (3) host government(s), (4) domestic government, and (5) joint venture partner(s) when the transaction involves a partnership. Not surprising, reconciling the conflicting interests of these various parties can be a mind-boggling juggling act.

A number of studies have examined the key drivers behind transfer pricing decisions. One survey of U.S.-based multinationals found that transfer pricing policies were primarily influenced by the following factors (in order of importance):

1. Market conditions in the foreign country
2. Competition in the foreign country
3. Reasonable profit for foreign affiliate
4. U.S. federal income taxes
5. Economic conditions in the foreign country
6. Import restrictions

---

[36] Michael M. Knetter, "International Comparisons of Pricing-to-Market Behavior," *American Economic Review,* 83 (3), pp. 473–86.

[37] "Taking the Hit: European Exporters Find the Dollar's Weakness is Hard to Counter," *Financial Times,* May 3, 2005, p. 11.

[38] Saeed Samiee and Patrik Anckar, "Currency Choice in Industrial Pricing: A Cross-National Evaluation," *Journal of Marketing,* 62 (July 1998), pp. 112–27.

7. Customs duties

8. Price controls

9. Taxation in the foreign country

10. Exchange controls.[39]

Other surveys have different rankings.[40] However, a recurring theme appears to be the importance of market conditions (especially the competitive situation), taxation regimes, and various market imperfections (e.g., currency control, custom duties, price freeze). Generally speaking, MNCs should consider the following criteria when making transfer pricing decisions:[41]

- **Tax regimes.** Ideally, firms would like to boost their profits in low-tax countries and dampen them in high-tax countries. To shift profits from high-tax to low-tax markets, companies set transfer prices as high as possible for goods entering high-tax countries and vice versa for low-tax countries. However, manipulating transfer prices to exploit corporate tax rate differentials will undoubtedly alert the tax authorities in the high-tax rate country and can lead to a tax audit. Most governments impose rules on transfer pricing to ensure a fair division of profits between businesses under common control. We revisit the taxation issue shortly.

- **Local market conditions.** Another key influence is the local market condition. Examples of market-related factors include the market share of the affiliate, the growth rate of the market, and the nature of local competition (e.g., nonprice- versus price-based). To expand market share in a new market, multinationals can initially underprice intracompany shipments to a start-up subsidiary.[42]

- **Market imperfections.** Market imperfections in the host country, such as price freezes and profit repatriation restrictions, hinder the multinational's ability to move earnings out of the country. Under such circumstances, transfer prices can be used as a mechanism to get around these obstacles. Also, high import duties might prompt a firm to lower transfer prices charged to subsidiaries located in that particular country.

- **Joint venture partner.** When the entity concerned is part of a joint venture, the parent company should also factor in the interests of the local joint venture partner. Numerous joint venture partnerships have hit the rocks because of disagreements over transfer pricing decisions.

- **Morale of local country managers.** Finally, firms should also be concerned about the morale of their local country managers. Especially when performance evaluation is primarily based on local profits, transfer price manipulations can distress country managers whose subsidiary's profits are artificially deflated.

Setting Transfer Prices

Two broad transfer pricing strategies are market-based transfer pricing and nonmarket-based pricing. The first perspective uses the market mechanism as a cue for setting transfer prices. Such prices are usually referred to as **arm's-length prices.** Basically, the company charges the price that any buyer outside the MNC would pay as if the transaction had occurred between two unrelated companies (at "arm's length"). Tax authorities typically prefer this method over other transfer pricing approaches. Because an objective yardstick is used—the *market price*—transfer prices based on this approach are easy to justify to third parties (e.g., tax authorities). The major problem with arm's-length transfer pricing is that an appropriate benchmark is often lacking due to the absence of competition. This is especially the case for intangible services. Many

[39] Jane Burns, "Transfer Pricing Decisions in U.S. Multinational Corporations," *Journal of International Business Studies,* 11, (2), Fall 1980, pp. 23–39.

[40] See, for example, Seung H. Kim and Stephen W. Miller, "Constituents of the International Transfer Pricing Decision," *Columbia Journal of World Business,* Spring 1979, p. 71.

[41] S. Tamer Cavusgil, "Pricing for Global Markets," *Columbia Journal of World Business,* Winter 1996, pp. 66–78.

[42] Mohammad F. Al-Eryani, Pervaiz Alam, and Syed H. Akhter, "Transfer Pricing Determinants of U.S. Multinationals," *Journal of International Business Studies,* 21 (Third Quarter 1990), pp. 409–25.

services are available only within the multinational. A high-stakes dispute between the U.S. Internal Revenue Service and GlaxoSmithKline PLC, the British pharmaceuticals company, illustrates the issue of valuing intangibles vividly.[43] According to the IRS, Glaxo's U.S. subsidiary overpaid its European parent for the royalties associated with scores of drugs, including its blockbuster, Zantac. Glaxo allegedly had overvalued the drugs' R&D costs in Britain and undervalued the value of marketing activities in the United States, thereby, artificially cutting the U.S. subsidiary's profits and tax liabilities. Glaxo vehemently denied this charge. The case centered around the issue of where value is created and where credit is due: on the marketing or on the R&D front?

Nonmarket-based pricing covers various policies that deviate from market-based pricing, the most prominent ones being cost-based pricing and **negotiated pricing. Cost-based pricing** simply adds a markup to the cost of the goods. Issues revolve around getting a consensus on a "fair" profit split and allocation of corporate over-head. Furthermore, tax authorities often do not accept cost-based pricing procedures. Another form of nonmarket-based pricing is negotiated transfer prices. With it, con-flicts between country affiliates are resolved through the negotiation of transfer prices. This process may lead to better cooperation among corporate divisions.[44]

One study showed that compliance with financial reporting norms and fiscal, custom, and antidumping rules prompt companies to use market-based transfer pric-ing.[45] Government-imposed market constraints (e.g., import restrictions, price controls, exchange controls) favor nonmarket-based transfer pricing methods. The answer to the question of which procedure works best is that there is no "universally optimal" system.[46] In fact, most firms use a mixture of market-based and nonmarket-pricing procedures.

Minimizing the Risk of Transfer Pricing Tax Audits[47]

Cross-country tax rate differentials encourage many MNCs to set transfer prices that shift profits from high-tax to low-tax countries to minimize their overall tax burden. This practice is sometimes referred to as *international tax arbitrage*. At the same time, MNCs need to comply with the tax codes of their home country and the host countries involved. Noncompliance can risk accusations of tax evasion and lead to tax audits. In January 2004, the U.S. government presented GlaxoSmithKline, the pharmaceuticals company, a $5.2 billion bill for extra taxes and interest following an investigation of the firm's transfer pricing policies (discussed earlier). According to one estimate, the total tax loss in the United States due to "creative" transfer pricing was $53 billion in 2001.[48] Therefore, the issue that MNCs face can be stated as follows: how do we as a company draw the line between setting transfer prices that maximize corporate profits and complying with tax regulations?

To avoid walking on thin ice, experts suggest setting transfer prices that are as close as possible to the Basic Arm's-Length Standard (BALS). This criterion is now accepted by tax authorities worldwide as the international standard for assessing transfer prices. In practice, there are three methods to calculate a BALS price: comparable/uncontrollable price, resale price, and cost-plus price. The comparable/uncontrollable method states that the parent company should compare the transfer price of its "controlled" subsidiary to the selling price charged by an independent seller to an independent buyer of similar goods or services. The problem is that such "comparable products" often do not exist. The resale price method determines the

[43] "Glaxo Faces Allegations of Tax Underpayment in U.S.," *Asian Wall Street Journal* (December 8, 2002), p. A7.

[44] R. Ackelsberg and G. Yukl, "Negotiated Transfer Pricing and Conflict Resolution in Organization," *Decision Sciences*, July 1979, pp. 387–98.

[45] M. F. Al-Eryani et al., "Transfer Pricing Determinants," p. 422.

[46] Jeffrey S. Arpan, "International Intracorporate Pricing: Non-American Systems and Views," *Journal of International Business Studies*, Spring 1972, p. 18.

[47] This section is based on John P. Fraedrich and Connie Rae Bateman, "Transfer Pricing by Multinational Marketers: Risky Business," *Business Horizons*, January–February 1996, pp. 17–22.

[48] "A Big Squeeze for Governments: How Transfer Pricing Threatens Global Tax Revenues," *Financial Times*, July 22, 2004, p. 11.

BALS by subtracting the gross margin percentage used by comparable independent buyers from the final third-party sales price. Finally, the cost-plus method fixes the BALS by adding the gross profit markup percentage earned by comparable companies performing similar functions to the production costs of the controlled manufacturer or seller. Note that this rule differs somewhat from the cost method discussed earlier because, strictly speaking, the latter method does not rely on markups set by third parties. The Organization for Economic Co-operation and Development (OECD) has drawn up guidelines on transfer pricing that cover complex taxation issues. The OECD presented the latest version of these rules in *Transfer Pricing Guidelines for Multinational Enterprises and for Tax Administrations.*[49]

Exhibit 13-6 gives a flowchart that can be used to devise transfer pricing strategies that minimize the risk of tax audits. Decisions center around the following five questions:

1. Do comparable/uncontrolled transactions exist?
2. Is the most value added by the parent or the subsidiary?
3. Are combined profits of parent and subsidiary shared in proportion to contributions?
4. Does the transfer price meet the benchmark set by the tax authorities?
5. Does the MNC have the information to justify the transfer prices used?

EXHIBIT 13-6
DECISION-MAKING MODEL FOR ASSESSING RISK OF TP STRATEGY

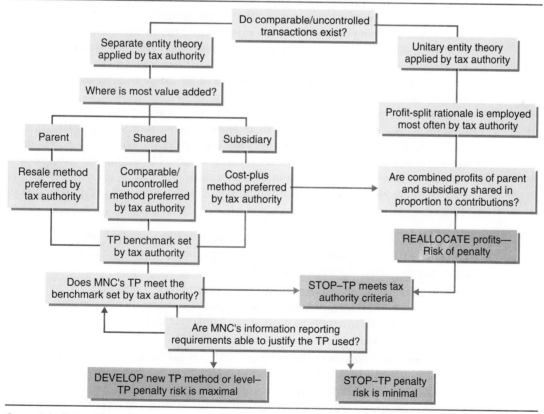

Source: John P. Fraedrich and Connie Rae Bateman, "Transfer Pricing by Multinational Marketers: Risky Business." Reprinted from *Business Horizon,* January–February 1996. Copyright 1996 by the Foundation for the School of Business at Indiana University. Used with permission.

---

[49] A hard copy of this document is available via http://www.oecdbookshop.org/oecd/display.asp?sf1=identifiers&st1=232001041P1. The most recent version came out in early 2006 and also includes an electronic version.

♦ ♦ ♦ ♦ ♦ ♦ ♦ ♦   ## GLOBAL PRICING AND ANTIDUMPING REGULATION

A potential minefield for global pricing policies involves the antidumping laws that most governments use to counter dumping practices. *Dumping* occurs when a company sells imports at an unfair price. To protect local producers against the encroachment of low-priced imports, governments may levy countervailing duties or fines. Thus, it is important for exporters to realize that pricing policies, such as penetration pricing, may trigger antidumping actions. The number of antidumping initiatives has been staggering in recent years. Most of it takes place in the United States and the European Union. However, antidumping cases are increasingly being initiated in Japan, India, and other developing countries. Economists often refer to this trend as a *rise in protectionism.*[50]

Several possible reasons can explain the growing popularity of antidumping litigation. The removal of traditional trade barriers (tariffs, quotas) has encouraged several countries to switch to nontariff barriers such as antidumping to protect their local industries. A World Bank study showed that the impact of dumping duties in the U.S. manufactured goods sector has boosted average tariffs from a nominal 6 percent rate to 23 percent.[51] There is also a huge imbalance between plaintiffs (local producer[s]) and defendants (importer[s]) in antidumping cases. Plaintiffs typically face no penalties for frivolous complaints. Moreover, plaintiffs clearly have a home advantage (local legislation, local judge).[52] Antidumping action is often utilized as a tactical tool to foster voluntary export restraints (VER). Foreign competitors, faced with the prospect of antidumping action, may decide to fall back on VERs as the lesser of two evils.[53] Finally, the concept of a "fair" price is usually murky. The U.S. trade law states that **dumping** occurs when imports are sold below the home-country price (price discrimination) or when the import price is less than the "constructed value" or average cost of production ("pricing below cost"). Either concept can be very vague. In some situations, the imported good is not sold in the home country so that no basis of comparison exists (absence of domestic price).

Antidumping actions will persist in the future. Multinationals need to consider antidumping laws when determining their global pricing policy. Aggressive pricing could trigger antidumping measures and, thus, jeopardize the company's competitive position. Global companies should also monitor changes in antidumping legislation and closely track antidumping cases in their particular industry.

To minimize risk exposure to antidumping actions, exporters can pursue any of the following marketing strategies:

- **Trading up.** Move away from low-value to high-value products via product differentiation. Most Japanese carmakers have stretched their product line up to tap into the upper-tier segments of their export markets.

- **Service enhancement.** Exporters can also differentiate their product by adding support services to the core product. Both moves—trading up and service enhancement—are basically attempts to move away from price competition, thereby making the exporter less vulnerable to dumping accusations.

- **Distribution and communication.** Other initiatives on the distribution and communication front of the marketing mix include (1) the establishment of communication channels with local competitors, (2) entering into cooperative agreements with them (e.g., strategic alliances), or (3) reallocation of the firm's marketing efforts from

[50]Jagdish Bhagwati, *Protectionism* (Cambridge, MA: The MIT Press, 1988), Chapter 3.

[51]"Negotiators Down in the Dumps over US Draft," *Financial Times,* November 25, 1993, p. 6.

[52]Bhagwati, *Protectionism,* pp. 48–49.

[53]James E. Anderson, "Domino Dumping, I: Competitive Exporters," *American Economic Review,* 82 (1), March 1992, pp. 65–83.

vulnerable products (that is, those most likely to be subjected to dumping scrutiny) to less sensitive products.[54]

PRICE COORDINATION ◆ ◆ ◆ ◆ ◆ ◆ ◆ ◆

When developing a global pricing strategy, one of the thorniest issues is how much coordination should exist between prices charged in different countries. This issue is especially critical for global (or regional) brands that are marketed with no or very few cross-border variations. Economics dictates that firms should price discriminate between markets to maximize overall profits. So, if (marginal) costs are roughly equivalent, multinationals would charge relatively low prices in highly price sensitive countries and high prices in insensitive markets. Unfortunately, reality is not that simple. In most cases, markets cannot be perfectly separated. Huge cross-country price differentials encourage gray markets created when unauthorized distributors ship goods from low-price to high-price countries. Thus, some coordination is usually be necessary. In deciding how much coordination, several considerations matter:

1. **Nature of customers.** When information on prices travels fast across borders, it is fairly hard to sustain wide price gaps. Under such conditions, firms need to make a convincing case to their customers to justify price disparities. With global customers (e.g., multinational clients in business-to-business transactions), price coordination definitely becomes a must. General Motors applies "global enterprise pricing" to many of the components it purchases. Under this system, suppliers are asked to charge the same universal price worldwide.[55] In Europe, Microsoft sets prices that differ by no more than 5 percent between countries due to pressure from bargain-hunting multinational customers.[56]

2. **Amount of product differentiation.** The amount of coordination also depends on how well differentiated the product is across borders. Obviously, the less differentiation, the larger the need for some level of price coordination. In Europe, the spin speed of washing machines varies, making comparison shopping less easy. In cold, wet countries (e.g., Britain) the average spin speed is 1200 rpm, twice as fast as the 600 rpm speed of washers in Spain. Henkel, the German conglomerate, adjusts the formula for its Persil laundry detergent brand to suit local market conditions. Stains in Southern Europe differ from stains in Scandinavia because of different food habits.[57]

3. **Nature of channels.** In a sense, distribution channels can be viewed as intermediate customers, so the same logic applies here: Price coordination becomes critical when price information is transparent and/or the firm deals with cross-border distribution channels. Pricing discipline becomes mandatory when manufacturers have little control over their distributors.

4. **Nature of competition.** In many industries, firms compete with the same rivals in a given region if not worldwide. Global competition demands a cohesive strategic approach for the entire marketing mix strategy, including pricing. From that angle, competition pushes companies toward centralized pricing policies. On the other hand, price changes made by competitors in the local market often require a rapid response. Should the subsidiary match a given price cut? If so, to what extent? Local subsidiaries often have much better information about the local market conditions to answer such questions than corporate or regional headquarters. Thus,

---

[54]Michel M. Kostecki, "Marketing Strategies between Dumping and Anti-dumping Action," *European Journal of Marketing,* 25 (12), 1991, pp. 7–19.

[55]"GM Powertrain Suppliers Will See Global Pricing," *Purchasing,* February 12, 1998.

[56]"European Software-Pricing Formulas, Long Abstruse, Develop a Rationale," *Wall Street Journal,* June 11, 1993.

[57]"A Shopping Contest for the Euro," *Financial Times,* January 5/6, 2002, p. 7.

the need for alertness and speedy response to competitive pricing moves encourages a decentralized approach toward pricing decisions.

5. **Market integration.** When markets integrate, barriers to cross-border movement of goods come down. Given the freedom to move goods from one member state to another, the pan-European market offers little latitude for perfect price discrimination.[58] Many of the transaction costs plaguing parallel imports that once existed have now disappeared. In fact, the European Commission imposes heavy penalties against companies that try to limit gray market transactions. The Commission fined Volkswagen almost $110 million when it found VW guilty of competition abuses. VW had ordered its Italian dealers not to sell cars to citizens from outside Italy. Austrian and German shoppers tried to buy VW cars in Italy where they were 30 percent cheaper.[59]

   Several multinationals doing business in the European Union harmonize their prices to narrow price gaps between different member states. Mars and Levi Strauss reduced their pan-European price gaps to no more than 10 percent.[60]

6. **Internal organization.** The organization setup is another important influence. Highly decentralized companies pose a hurdle to price coordination efforts. Many companies leave the pricing decision to their local subsidiaries. Moves to take away some of the pricing authority from country affiliates will undoubtedly spark opposition and lead to bruised egos. As with other centralization decisions, it is important that performance evaluation systems be fine-tuned if necessary.

7. **Government regulation.** Government regulation of prices puts pressure on firms to harmonize their prices. A good example is the pharmaceutical industry as discussed earlier. In many countries, multinationals need to negotiate the price for new drugs with the local authorities. Governments in the European Union increasingly use prices set in other EU member states as a cue for their negotiating position. This trend has prompted several pharmaceutical companies, such as Glaxo, to negotiate a common EU price for new drugs.

Global-Pricing Contracts (GPCs)[61]

Increasingly, purchasers demand **global-pricing contracts (GPCs)** from their suppliers. There are several reasons behind the shift toward GPCs: centralized buying, information technology that provides improved price monitoring, and standardization of products or services. GPCs, however, can also benefit suppliers: Global customers can become showcase accounts; a GPC can offer the opening to nurture a lasting customer relationship; small suppliers can use GPCs as a differentiation tool to get access to new accounts.

However, before engaging in a GPC with a purchaser it is important do your homework. Exhibit 13-7 offers a checklist of the things to do before signing the contract. To achieve successful GPC implementation, Narayandas and colleagues provide the following guidelines:

1. Select customers who want more than just the lowest price.

2. Align the supplier's organization with the customer's. Ideally, the supplier's account management organization should mirror the client's procurement setup.

3. Hire global account managers who can handle diversity. Get team members who can handle intelligence gathering, problem spotting, and contract compliance monitoring in addition to sales.

4. Reward those global account managers and local sales representatives who make the relationship work.

---

[58]Wolfgang Gaul and Ulrich Lutz, "Pricing in International Marketing and Western European Economic Integration," *Management International Review*, 34 (2), 1994, pp. 101–24.

[59]"On the Road to Price Convergence," *Financial Times*, November 12, 1998, p. 29.

[60]"Counting Costs of Dual Pricing in the Run-Up to 1992," *Financial Times*, July 9, 1990, p. 4.

[61]This section benefited from Das Narayandas, John Quelch, and Gordon Swartz. "Prepare Your Company For Global Pricing," *Sloan Management Review*, Fall 2000, pp. 61–70.

EXHIBIT 13-7
CHECKLIST BEFORE SIGNING A GPC

1. Have a clear plan and avoid reactive strategy making.

2. Scrutinize customers' strategies in individual markets and quantify the variances in the service-level needs across country markets.

3. Customize only what lends itself to economies of scale (not just the basic product, but also services such as logistics or credit management).

4. Decide whether your size relative to the customer's increases or reduces risks.

5. Be careful not to share detailed cost information.

6. Anticipate how you will cope if a customer's business volumes change suddenly.

7. Make a plan for increased transparency that standardization gives your business practices.

8. Identify your competitors and collaborators in country markets.

9. Decide if your local customers are really more important than global ones.

10. Be wary of contracts demanding that you stay away from the customer's competitors.

11. Find out if GPC compliance from the customer's local units is essential to the customer's strategy.

12. Gather information on the profit-and-loss responsibility of the customer's local units.

13. Find out if the customer charges its own customers different prices and use that for negotiating leverage.

14. Go to the negotiating table only when you have more information than the customer on country-by-country variance in volumes, prices, service levels, costs-to-serve, legal and other environmental factors.

Source: Das Narayandas, John Quelch, and Gorden Swartz, "Prepare Your Company for Global Pricing," *Sloan Management Review* (Fall 2000): p. 64.

5. Allow for some price flexibility.

6. Build information systems to monitor the key variables (e.g., cost variations, competitive situation).[62]

Given the pressure toward increased globalization, some degree of price coordination becomes absolutely necessary. In some cases, firms set a uniform pricing formula that all affiliates apply. Elsewhere, coordination is limited to general rules that indicate only the desired pricing positioning (e.g., premium positioning, middle-of-the road positioning).

Aligning Pan-Regional Prices

Simon and Kucher[63] propose a three-step procedure to align prices in regional markets with arbitrage opportunities. Pressure to narrow down price gaps could lead to two scenarios (see Exhibit 13-8). The scenario (panel (A) in Exhibit 13-8), all prices sink to the lowest price. Calculations by Lehman Brothers, an investment bank, have shown that, if all car prices in the euro area fell to the lowest levels, the revenues of the French car makers, Peugeot and Renault, would drop by 12 percent and 9 percent respectively.[64] At the other extreme, companies may try to sustain cross-border price gaps. Under the desired scenario ((B) in Exhibit 13-8) the company tries to find the middle ground by raising prices in low-price countries and cutting them in high-price countries. To pursue this scenario, firms should set a **pricing corridor** within the region.

The procedure works as follows.

Step 1. *Determine optimal price for each country.* Find out what price schedules will maximize overall profits. Given information on the demand schedule and the

---

[62] Das Narayandas, John Quelch, and Gorden Swartz, "Prepare your Company for Global Pricing," *Sloan Management Review,* Fall 2000, p. 64.

[63] Hermann Simon and Eckhard Kucher, "The European Pricing Time Bomb—And How to Cope with It," *Marketing and Research Today,* February 1993, pp. 25–36.

[64] "Faster Forward," *Economist,* November 28, 1998, pp. 83–84.

EXHIBIT 13-8
PAN-EUROPEAN PRICE COORDINATION

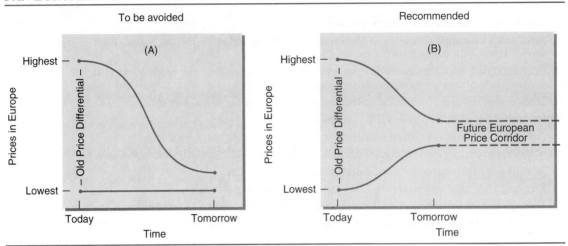

Courtesy Professor Hermann Simon

costs incurred in each market, managers are able to figure out the desirable prices in the respective markets.

Step 2. *Find out whether parallel imports ("gray markets") are likely to occur at these prices.* Parallel imports arise when unauthorized distributors purchase the product (sometimes repackaged) in the low-price market and then ship it to high-price markets. The goal of Step 2 is not to pre-empt parallel imports but to boost profits to the best possible degree. Given the "optimal" prices derived in the first step, the manager needs to determine to what extent the proposed price schedule will foster parallel imports. Parallel imports become harmful when they damage authorized distributors. They could also hurt the morale of the local salesforce or country managers. Information is needed on the arbitrage costs of parallel importers. For instance, in the European drug industry, parallel importers target drugs with more than 20 percent price differentials. Conceivably, firms could decide to abandon (or not enter) small, low-price markets, thereby avoiding pricing pressure on high-price markets. MNCs should also consider the pros and cons of nonpricing solutions to cope with parallel imports. Possible strategies include product differentiation, intelligence systems to measure exposure to gray markets, and creating negative perceptions in the mind of the end-user about parallel imports.[65]

Step 3. *Set a pricing corridor.* If the "optimal" prices derived in Step 1 are not sustainable, firms need to narrow the gap between prices for high-price and low-price markets. Charging the same price across the board is not desirable. Such a solution would sacrifice company profits. Instead, the firm should set a pricing corridor. The corridor is formed by systematically exploring the profit impact from lowering prices in high-price countries and raising prices in low-price countries, as shown in panel (B) of Exhibit 13-8. The narrower the price gap, the more profits the firm has to sacrifice. At some point, there will be a desirable tradeoff between the size of the gray market and the amount of profits sacrificed.

Of course, this method is not foolproof. Competitive reactions (e.g., price wars) need to be factored in. Also, government regulations may restrict pricing flexibility. Still, the procedure is a good start when pricing alignment becomes desirable.

---

[65] Peggy A. Chaudhry and Michael G. Walsh, "Managing the Gray Market in the European Union: The Case of the Pharmaceutical Industry," *Journal of International Marketing*, 3(3), 1995, pp. 11–33.

Global marketers can choose from four alternatives to promote price coordination within their organization, namely:

1. **Economic measures.** Corporate headquarters is able to influence pricing decisions at the local level via the transfer prices set for the goods that are sold to or purchased from local affiliates. Another option is *rationing;* that is, headquarters sets upper limits on the number of units that can be shipped to each country. To sustain price differences, luxury marketers (e.g., Louis Vuitton) set purchase limits for customers shopping at their European boutiques. Louis Vuitton products bought in Europe or Hawaii are often resold in Japan by discount stores as "loss leaders."

2. **Centralization.** In the extreme case, pricing decisions are made at corporate or regional headquarters level. Centralized price decision making is fairly uncommon because of its numerous shortcomings. It sacrifices the flexibility that firms often need to respond rapidly to local competitive conditions.

3. **Formalization.** Far more common than the previous approach is formalization by which headquarters establishes a set of pricing rules with which country managers should comply. Within these norms, country managers have a certain level of flexibility in determining their ultimate prices. One possibility is to set prices within specified boundaries; prices outside these bounds would need the approval from the global or regional headquarters.

4. **Informal coordination.** Finally, firms can use various forms of informal price coordination. The emphasis here is on information and persuasion rather than prescription and dictates. Examples of informal price coordination tactics include discussion groups and "best-practice" gatherings.[66]

Which one of these four approaches is most effective is contingent on the complexity of the environment in which the firm is doing business. When the environment is fairly stable and the various markets are highly similar, centralization is usually preferable over the other options. However, highly complex environments require a more decentralized approach.

Implementing Price Coordination

COUNTERTRADE

◆ ◆ ◆ ◆ ◆ ◆ ◆ ◆

Countertrade is an umbrella term used to describe unconventional trade-financing transactions that involve some form of noncash compensation. During the last decade, companies have increasingly been forced to rely on countertrade. Estimates on its overall magnitude vary, but the consensus estimate is that it covers 10 to 15 percent of world trade.[67] A Google search on countertrade generates around 325,000 hits. One of the most publicized deals was PepsiCo's $3 billion arrangement with the former Soviet Union to swap Pepsi for profits in Stolichnaya vodka and ocean freighters and tankers.[68] Given the growth of countertrade, global marketers should be aware of its nuts and bolts.

Countertrade comes in six guises: barter, clearing arrangements, switch trading, buyback, counterpurchase, and offset. Exhibit 13-9 classifies these different forms of countertrade.

The main distinction is whether or not the transaction involves monetary compensation. Let's look at each form in more detail:[69]

Forms of Countertrade

---

[66]Gert Assmus and Carsten Wiese, "How to Address the Gray Market Threat Using Price Coordination," *Sloan Management Review,* Spring 1995, pp. 31–41.

[67]Jean-François Hennart and Erin Anderson, "Countertrade and the Minimization of Transaction Costs," working paper no. 92-012 R, (Philadelphia: The Wharton School, University of Pennsylvania)

[68]"Worldwide Money Crunch Fuels More International Barter," *Marketing News,* March 2, 1992, p. 5.

[69]Costas G. Alexandrides and Barbara L. Bowers, *Countertrade. Practices, Strategies, and Tactics* (New York: John Wiley, 1987), Chapter 1.

EXHIBIT 13-9
CLASSIFICATION OF FORMS OF COUNTERTRADE

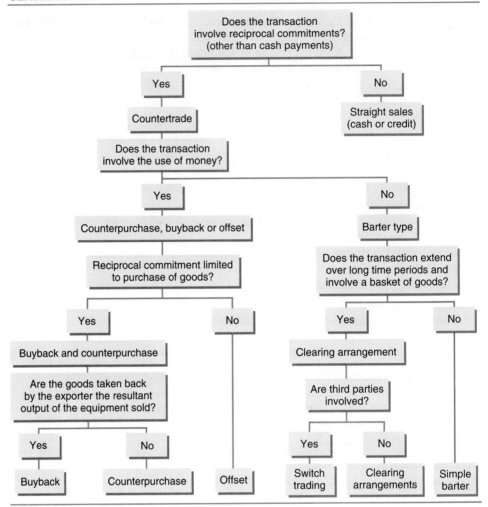

Source: Jean-François Hennart, "Some Empirical Dimensions of Countertrade," *Journal of International Business Studies* Second Quarter 1990, p. 245.

- **Simple barter.** A swap of one product for another product without the use of any money is *simple barter.* Usually, no third party is involved to carry out the transaction. Although one of the oldest forms of countertrade, it is very seldom used today. China's Farm Chemical Sales Promotion Group and the Moroccan government arranged a barter agreement in which $260 million worth of plant-protection chemicals were swapped for the equivalent value of Moroccan phosphate products.[70]

- **Clearing Arrangement.** Under this countertrade form, two governments agree to import a specified set value of goods from each other over a given period. Each party sets up an account that is debited whenever goods are traded. Imbalances at the end of the contract period are cleared through payment in hard currency or goods. One clearing agreement between Indonesia and Iran specified that Indonesia would supply paper, rubber, and galvanized sheets in exchange for 30,000 barrels per day of Iranian crude oil.[71]

- **Switch trading.** This is a variant of clearing arrangements involving a third party. In such deals, rights to the surplus credits are sold to specialized traders **(switch traders)**

---

[70] Aspy P. Palia and Oded Shenkar, "Countertrade Practices in China," *Industrial Marketing Management,* 20 (1991), pp. 57–65.

[71] Aspy P. Palia, "Countertrade Practices in Indonesia," *Industrial Marketing Management,* 21 (1992), pp. 273–79.

at a discount. The third party then uses the credits to buy goods from the deficit country.

None of these preceding types entails cash payment flows. The remaining forms involve some use of money. They lead to two parallel agreements: (1) the original sales agreement between the foreign customer and supplier and (2) a second contract by which the supplier commits to purchasing goods in the customer's country.

- **Buyback (compensation).** Buyback arrangements typically occur with the sale of technology, turn-key plants, or machinery equipment. In such transactions, the seller provides the equipment and agrees to be paid (partially or fully) by the products resulting from using the equipment. Such arrangements are much more mutually beneficial than the other forms of countertrade. A typical example of a buyback contract is the agreement that was settled between PALMCO Holdings, Malaysia's largest palm oil refiner, and Japan's Kao Corporation. The contract set up a $70 million joint venture to produce palm oil by-products in Malaysia. Kao was to be compensated by 60 percent of the output, which it could use as inputs for producing detergents, cosmetics, and toiletries.[72]

- **Counterpurchase.** Counterpurchase is the most popular form of countertrade. Similar to buyback arrangements, two parallel contracts are set up. Each party agrees to buy a specified amount of goods from the other for hard currency over a set period. Contrary to buybacks, the products are unrelated. Typically, the importer provides a shopping list from which the exporter can choose. In October 1992, PepsiCo set up a joint venture in the Ukraine with three local partners. Under the agreement, the partnership was to market Ukrainian-built ships. Proceeds from the ship sales were to be used to buy soft-drink equipment, to build bottling plants, and to open Pizza Hut restaurants in Ukraine.[73]

- **Offset.** Offset is a variation of counterpurchase: The seller agrees to *offset* the purchase price by sourcing from the importer's country or transferring technology to the other party's country. Offset is very common with defense contracts. An offset contract concluded between Indonesia to buy F-16 aircraft from General Dynamics stipulated that some of the parts would be supplied by PT Nusantara, an Indonesian manufacturer.

Companies engage in countertrade for various motives. The most commonly cited benefits follow.

- **Gain access to new or difficult markets.** Countertrade in many ways is a "necessary evil." It can be very costly and risky. Nevertheless, being prepared to accept countertrade deals enables many companies to have a competitive edge that allows them to penetrate markets with a lack of hard currency cash. Many exporters accept countertrade arrangements because their rivals offer it. A U.K. survey found that 80 percent of the exporters' competitors were also involved in countertrade.[74]

- **Overcome exchange rate controls or lack of hard currency.** Shortages of hard currency often leads to exchange controls. To navigate around government-imposed currency restrictions, firms use countertrade.

- **Overcome low country creditworthiness.** This benefit applies to trade with parties located in countries with low credit ratings. Under such conditions, the other party faces high interest rates or difficult access to credit financing. Countertrade allows both parties to overcome such hurdles.

Motives Behind Countertrade

---

[72] Ibid., pp. 125–32.

[73] "PepsiCo to Finance Ukraine Expansion with Ship Exports," *Financial Times*, October 23, 1992.

[74] David Shipley and Bill Neale, "Industrial Barter and Countertrade," *Industrial Marketing Management*, 16 (1987), pp. 1–8.

- **Increase sales volume.** Firms with a substantial amount of overhead face much pressure to increase sales. Despite the risks and costs of countertrade, such deals provide a viable opportunity to utilize full capacity. Also, companies often engage in countertrade to dispose of surplus or obsolete products.
- **Generate long-term customer goodwill.** A final payoff is that willingness to accept countertrade deals fosters long-term customer goodwill. Once the credit and/or currency situation in the client's country improves, sellers will be able to capitalize on the customer goodwill cemented over the years.

Among these marketing objectives, a survey of industrial firms in 23 countries showed that the most important ones are (1) sales increase (mean response of 3.91 on a 5-point scale), (2) increased competitiveness (3.90), and (3) entry to new markets (3.54).[75] A study of U.S. companies countertrading with Latin America found that the main reasons included these (ranked in order of importance):

1. To address customers' inadequate reserves of foreign currency
2. To engage in business the only way it could be done
3. To meet customer demand
4. To gain a competitive advantage
5. To facilitate transactions with government and expanding business contacts
6. To achieve growth
7. Better capacity utilization
8. To expand distribution channels in significant markets
9. To release blocked funds
10. To avoid the impact of protectionist regulations.[76]

Note that several of these motives have a long-term orientation (e.g., gain entry to new markets, generate goodwill) while some have a short-term orientation (e.g., use excess production capacity). Firms that are driven by long-term benefits tend to be much more proactive in soliciting countertrade business and pursuing countertrade transactions than short-term oriented firms.[77] Whatever the motive for entering a countertrade agreement, it is important to realize the drawbacks of such arrangements.

Shortcomings of Countertrade

Not every exporter is willing to jump on the countertrade bandwagon. In many cases, the risks and costs of a countertrade deal far outweigh its potential advantages. Some of the shortcomings that have been identified by exporters include these:

- **No "in-house" use for goods offered by customers.** Exporters often face the problem of what to do with the goods they are offered. Goods that cannot be used in house need to be resold. Getting rid of the goods can be a major headache, especially when the quality of the merchandise is poor or when there is an oversupply. Some firms rely on specialist brokers to sell their goods.
- **Timely and costly negotiations.** Arranging a countertrade deal requires a time-consuming and complex bargaining process. A prospective customer with a long track record usually has a tremendous edge over an exporter with little negotiation skills. Parties will haggle over the goods to be traded, their respective valuation, the mixture cash/merchandise, the time horizon, and so on.

---

[75]Dorothy A. Paun, "An International Profile of Countertrading Firms," *Industrial Marketing Management*, 26 (1), 1997, pp. 41–50.

[76]John P. Angelidis, Faramarz Parsa, and Nabil A. Ibrahim, "Countertrading with Latin America: A Comparative Analysis of Attitudes of United States Firms," *International Journal of Management*, 21 (December 2004) pp. 435–44.

[77]Dorothy A. Paun and Aviv Shoham, "Marketing Motives in International Countertrade: An Empirical Examination," *Journal of International Marketing*, 4 (3), 1996, pp. 29–47.

- **Uncertainty and lack of information on future prices.** When part of the traded goods involve commodities, firms run the risk that their price will sink before the goods can be sold. Apart from price uncertainty, there is uncertainty about the quality of the goods.

- **Transaction costs.** Costs flowing from countertrade quickly add up: cost of finding buyers for the goods (if there is no in-house use), commissions to middlemen (if any), insurance costs to cover risk of faulty or nondelivery, and hedging costs to protect against sinking commodity prices.[78]

The study of countertrading with Latin America cited earlier found that the most serious problems (ranked in order of importance) were as follows:

1. Time-consuming negotiations
2. Complicated negotiations
3. Product mismatch
4. Cost increases
5. Inferior quality of goods
6. Difficulty in selling the received products
7. Profitability reduction
8. Price-setting problems
9. Involvement of third parties
10. Loss of purchasing flexibility[79]

Given the potential risks and costs an exporter could run, one of the key questions is whether to handle deals in-house or to use specialist middlemen. This decision will basically be driven by a tradeoff of the benefits of using outsiders (reduction of risks and transaction costs) with the costs to be incurred (mainly commission).

Countertrade has probably reached its peak. In fact, some former east bloc countries are trying to avoid such trade to signal their commitment to free markets.[80] Still, countertrade will survive because many countries remain strapped for hard-currency cash.[81] Finally, here are a few words of advice:

1. Always evaluate the pros and cons of countertrade against other options.
2. Minimize the ratio of compensation goods to cash.
3. Strive for goods that can be used in house.
4. Assess the relative merits of relying on middlemen versus in-house staff.
5. Check whether the goods are subject to any import restrictions.
6. Assess the quality of the goods.[82]

---

[78]Shipley and Neale, "Industrial Barter and Countertrade," pp. 5–6.

[79]John P. Angelidis et al., "Countertrading with Latin America."

[80]"A Necessary Evil," *Economist,* November 25, 1989, p. 79.

[81]"Worldwide Money Crunch Fuels More International Barter," *Marketing News,* March 2, 1992, p. 5.

[82]Based on Shipley and Neale, "Industrial Barter and Countertrade,"; and J. R. Carter and J. Gagne, "The Dos and Don'ts of International Countertrade," *Sloan Management Review,* Spring 1988.

SUMMARY   ◆

Two types of mistakes can be made when setting the price in foreign markets: pricing the product too high or pricing it too low. When the price is set too high, customers will stay away from the firm's products. As a result, profits will be far less than they could have been. In India, Procter & Gamble's Ariel detergent brand initially created huge losses, partly because P&G charged a retail price far higher than Unilever did for its Surf Ultra.[83] Setting prices too low might also generate numerous pains. Local governments could cry foul and accuse the firm of dumping. Local customers might view the low price

---

[83]"Ariel Share Gain Puts P&G India through the Wringer," *Advertising Age International,* November 8, 1993, pp. I–3, I–22.

as a signal of low quality and avoid the product. Local competitors may interpret the low price as an aggressive move to grab market share and start a price war, or they could see it as an opportunity to launch a knockoff version of the company's product. And when the price is far lower than in other markets, distributors (local and nonlocal) could spot an arbitrage opportunity and ship the product from the low-price to the high-price markets, thereby creating a gray market situation. Making pricing decisions is one of the most formidable tasks that international marketers face. Many different elements influence global pricing decisions: customers, competition, channels, and company. Marketers also need to factor in the impact (direct or indirect) of local government decisions.

In this chapter, we covered the major global pricing issues that matter to marketers: export price escalation, inflation, currency movements, antidumping regulations, and price coordination. Even though pricing is typically a highly decentralized marketing decision, cross-border price coordination becomes increasingly a prime concern. We introduced several approaches through which international marketers can implement price coordination. Especially in industrial markets, firms increasingly become aware of the long-term rewards of countertrade as a way of doing business in the global arena. In many cases, countertrade is the sole means for gaining access to new markets. Companies that decide to engage in countertrade should consider the numerous road bumps that these transactions involve.

KEY TERMS ◆

Arm's-length price
Cast-based pricing
Cost-plus pricing
Countertrade
Dumping
Dynamic incremental pricing

Global-pricing contract (GPC)
Local-currency price stability
Negotiated pricing
Parallel imports (gray markets)
Pass-through
Pricing corridor

Price escalation
Pricing to market (PTM)
Switch trader
Transfer price

REVIEW QUESTIONS ◆

1. What mechanisms can exporters use to curtail the risks of price escalation in foreign markets?

2. How does competition in the foreign market affect a company's global pricing decisions?

3. A study quoted in Chapter 13 reports that there was much more pass through by German carmakers than their Japanese counterparts in the U.S. carmarket when both currencies depreciated against the U.S. dollar. What might explain these different responses?

4. Should MNCs always try to minimize their transfer in high-tax countries? Why or why not?

5. What measures should exporters consider in hedging themselves against antidumping accusations?

6. Explain why countertrade is often viewed as a necessary evil.

DISCUSSION QUESTIONS ◆

1. Many multinational corporations that consider entering emerging markets face the issue that the regular price they charge for their goods (that is, the retail price in developed markets) could be far beyond the buying power of most local consumers. What strategic options do these companies have to penetrate these markets?

2. Company XYZ sells a body-weight control drug in countries A and B. The demand schedules in the two countries follow:

Country A: Sales in A = $100 - 10 \times$ Price in A

Country B: Sales in B = $100 - 6.67 \times$ Price in B

The marginal costs are 4 in both countries. There are no fixed costs.

a. What prices should XYZ set in A and B if it optimizes the price in A and B individually? What would be total profits?

b. Suppose that due to parallel imports, prices in the high-price countries drop to the level of the low-price country? What would be total profits under that scenario?

c. Suppose now that the two countries are treated as one large market: What would be the optimal price then? What would be total profits?

d. Set a pricing corridor between A and B by completing the following table:

Price Corridor (%)	Price in A	Price in B	Sales Revenue in A	Sales Revenue in B	Profits in A	Profits in B	Total Profit	Profit Sacrifice (%)
0								
5								
10								
20								
25								

3. Countertrade accounts for a substantial proportion of international trade. Do you foresee that the share of countertrade will increase or decline? Why?

4. How will a weakening of the euro versus the Japanese yen affect German carmakers such as BMW and Volkswagen in Japan? What measures do you suggest German carmakers might consider taking to cope with a weaker euro?

5. A major bone of contention in recent years has been the prices charged for AIDS drugs in the developing world by Western pharmaceutical giants such as Merck and Glaxo-SmithKline. Merck and others have now agreed to provide AIDS drugs in developing nations such as South Africa at a price that is roughly equivalent to the manufacturing costs. What potential hurdles do you see with this new pricing scheme?

6. How can local competitors use antidumping procedures as a competitive tool against foreign competitors?

7. In Russia, Procter & Gamble markets Tide, its U.S. premium laundry detergent brand, as an economy brand with the slogan "Tide is a guarantee of clean clothes." Except for the brand name and the product category, all aspects of the products (formula, price, positioning) differ for the U.S. and the Russian products. What might be the rationale behind this strategy? Was this strategy a good idea?

♦ ♦ ♦ ♦ ♦ ♦ ♦ ♦   **SHORT CASES**

ASE 13-1

WHISTLE-BLOWERS RAISE SOME SERIOUS QUESTIONS ABOUT SWATCH'S TRANSFER PRICING POLICIES

Swatch Group is one of the world's leading watch makers. The group owns a stable of 17 watch brands, including Breguet and Omega. As do many other multinational companies, Swatch devotes considerable energy to devising tax arrangements that minimize its overall tax burden. In general, such practices (sometimes referred to as *international tax arbitrage*) are perfectly legal. However, in the summer of 2004, two whistle-blowers who had left the company asked U.S. tax authorities to take a closer look at Swatch's tax policies. They had built up their case with a stash of internal e-mails and company documents.

They raised concern about the activities of Swatch Group (Asia), a subsidiary based in Hong Kong and registered in the tax haven of the British Virgin Islands. Invoices indicated that goods shipped through this subsidiary received a major markup before being sent to other units of Swatch. For instance, Omega watches were given a 40 percent markup if they went out to Singapore and a 50 percent markup when bound for Japan. One company e-mail stated: "Externally for tax reasons we credit only 60 percent. That means that we have an internal credit note and different external credit note.... The advantage of this procedure is that we have absolutely no negative impact on the internal [reporting] figures in Japan."

Tax lawyers interviewed about the matter said that to justify the markup differences as they pass through the sub-

Source: "A Swiss Movement on Tax Bills," *Financial Times,* August 13, 2004, p. 18; and "Swatch Group Defends Its Pricing Policy," *Financial Times,* August 13, 2004, p. 18.

sidiary, the intermediary has to be adding value to the product or incurring some risk by its role in the transaction. If not, the tax rate of the jurisdiction of origin should apply. Also, the values attributed to goods internally should be close to their market prices at the destination.

The e-mails signalled that Swatch staff had concerns about its transfer-pricing practices and how they might appear to tax authorities. One e-mail from a finance department official stated: "We have to be very cautious when the source is Swatch Group internal. I have not the intention to endanger the whole system." Mr. Rentsch, the group's general counsel, denied any wrongdoing. According to him, the two whistle-blowers were disgruntled former employees who "were trying to build up something against the company." Still, the company was concerned about the allegations and decided to set up an internal investigation. In comments to the press, Swatch pointed out that transfer pricing is a very complex issue that depends on a large number of variables including exchange rates, working conditions in different countries, and differing distribution structures. Also, as a policy matter, Swatch tries to avoid major price gaps between markets to minimize the risk of gray markets where local traders sidestep authorized distributors.

DISCUSSION QUESTIONS

1. Explain why transfer pricing is so complicated especially for a company like Swatch.

2. What measures could Swatch implement to avoid similar predicaments in the future?

FURTHER READING   ♦ ♦ ♦ ♦ ♦ ♦ ♦ ♦ ♦ ♦ ♦ ♦ ♦ ♦ ♦ ♦

Adler, Ralph A. "Transfer Pricing for World-Class Manufacturing." *Long Range Planning,* 29 (1), pp. 69–75.

Assmus, Gert, and Carsten Wiese. "How to Address the Gray Market Threat Using Price Coordination." *Sloan Management Review,* Spring 1995, pp. 31–41.

Carter, Joseph R., and James Gagne. "The Dos and Don'ts of International Countertrade." *Sloan Management Review,* 29, (3), Spring 1988, pp. 31–37.

Cavusgil, S. Tamer. "Pricing for Global Markets." *The Columbia Journal of World Business,* Winter 1996, pp. 66–78.

Cavusgil, S. Tamer. "Unraveling the Mystique of Export Pricing." *Business Horizons,* 31 (May–June 1988), pp. 54–63.

Chintagunta, Pradeep K., and Ramarao Desiraju. "Strategic Pricing and Detailing Behavior in International Markets." *Marketing Science,* 24 (Winter 2005) pp. 67–80.

Fraedrich, John P., and Connie Rae Bateman. "Transfer Pricing by Multinational Marketers: Risky Business." *Business Horizons,* January–February 1996, pp. 17–22.

Kostecki, Michel M. "Marketing Strategies between Dumping and Anti-Dumping Action," *European Journal of Marketing,* 25 (12), 1991, pp. 7–19.

Narayandas, Das, John Quelch, and Gordon Swartz. "Prepare Your Company for Global Pricing." *Sloan Management Review,* Fall 2000, pp. 61–70.

Paun, Dorothy. "An International Profile of Countertrading Firms." *Industrial Marketing Management,* 26 (1997), pp. 41–50.

Paun, Dorothy, and Aviv Shoham. "Marketing Motives in International Countertrade: An Empirical Examination." *Journal of International Marketing,* 4 (3), 1996, pp. 29–47.

Rabino, Samuel, and Kirit Shah. "Countertrade and Penetration of LDC's Markets." *Columbia Journal of World Business,* Winter 1987, pp. 31–38.

Samiee, Saeed. "Pricing in Marketing Strategies of U.S.- and Foreign-Based Companies." *Journal of Business Research,* 15 (1987), pp. 17–30.

Shipley, David, and Bill Neale. "Industrial Barter and Countertrade." *Industrial Marketing Management,* 16 (1987), pp. 1–8.

Simon, Hermann, and Eckhard Kucher. "The European Pricing Time Bomb—and How to Cope with It." *Marketing and Research Today,* February 1993, pp. 25–36.

Sims, Clive, Adam Phillips, and Trevor Richards, "Developing a Global Pricing Strategy." *Marketing and Research Today,* March 1992, pp. 3–14.

Weekly, James K. "Pricing in Foreign Markets: Pitfalls and Opportunities." *Industrial Marketing Management,* 21 (1992), pp. 173–79.

COMMUNICATING WITH THE WORLD CONSUMER

14

$\mathcal{C}$HAPTER OVERVIEW

1. GLOBAL ADVERTISING AND CULTURE

2. GLOBAL ADVERTISING BUDGET

3. CREATIVE STRATEGY

4. GLOBAL MEDIA DECISIONS

5. ADVERTISING REGULATIONS

6. CHOICE OF AN ADVERTISING AGENCY

7. COORDINATION OF INTERNATIONAL ADVERTISING

8. OTHER FORMS OF COMMUNICATION

9. GLOBALLY INTEGRATED MARKETING COMMUNICATIONS (GIMC)

To promote its Temptations range of chocolates in India, the British chocolate maker Cadbury put out a print ad that was timed to coincide with India's Independence Day.[1] The ad showed a map of India with the words "Too good to share" printed across the states of Jammu and Kashmir. The reference to Kashmir, which is at the center of a longstanding dispute between India and Pakistan, did not please Hindu nationalists. Cadbury was forced to issue a statement apologizing for the advertisement. One of Procter & Gamble's biggest advertising blunders happened in Japan when the firm introduced its disposable diapers Pampers brand. Around that time, P&G aired a TV commercial in the United States showing an animated stork delivering Pampers diapers at home. P&G's U.S. managers in Japan figured that this could be an excellent piece of advertising they could transplant into the Japanese market to back up the launch of Pampers. The copy was dubbed in Japanese, and the Japanese package replaced the U.S. one. Unfortunately, this cute commercial failed to seduce Japanese mothers. After some consumer research, P&G discovered that Japanese consumers were confused about why a bird was delivering disposable diapers. Contrary to Western folklore,

---

[1] "Anger over Kashmir Chocolate Ad," http://news.bbc.co.uk, August 21, 2002.

storks in Japan are not supposed to deliver babies. Instead, babies allegedly arrive in giant peaches that float on the river to deserving parents.[2] These days, P&G uses a more relevant advertising model to promote Pampers to Japanese consumers: the testimonial of a nurse who also happens to be a mother—the "expert mom."[3] As both the Cadbury and P&G cases illustrate, international advertising can prove to be very tricky.

The first part of this chapter focuses on global advertising. We first cover the cultural challenges that advertisers face. We then examine the major international advertising planning decisions that marketers need to address. In particular, we consider budgeting and resource allocation issues, message strategy, and media decisions. One hurdle that advertisers face is the maze of advertising regulations across the world. We highlight the different types of regulations and discuss several mechanisms to cope with them. Next we address another important global advertising concern: advertising agency selection for foreign markets. Coordination of multicountry communication efforts becomes paramount for regional or global campaigns. We discuss several approaches that companies can use to coordinate multicountry advertising campaigns. The second part of this chapter explores other forms of communication tools that global marketers utilize.

GLOBAL ADVERTISING AND CULTURE   ◆ ◆ ◆ ◆ ◆ ◆ ◆ ◆

Advertising is to some extent a cultural phenomenon. As the P&G example in the introduction demonstrated, when advertising appeals are not in sync with the local culture, the ad campaign will falter. In the worst-case scenario, the ad might even stymie the advertised product's sales. Effective ad campaigns do a great job in leveraging local cultural phenomena. A recent TV ad that was developed for Unilever's Vaseline brand in India is an excellent example.[4] The commercial shows the distress of a woman buying shoes. As the woman prepares to try out a shoe, the salesman spots cracks in her feet and tells her that the shoe is not within her budget. An onscreen message then asks: "Why should someone peep in your life because of cracks in the skin of your feet?" An image of Vaseline cream follows, with the promise that it will soften hard skin and get rid of cracks. The ad cleverly plays on Indian women's embarrassment of having cracked feet and not being able to afford servants. Global Perspective 14-1 gives another nice example. Because most advertising has a major verbal component, we first look at the language barriers.

Language is one of the most formidable barriers that international advertisers must surmount. Numerous promotional efforts have misfired because of language-related mishaps. Apart from translation, another challenge is the proper interpretation of ideas. The IBM global slogan "Solutions for a Small Planet" became "small world" in Argentina as "planet" failed to convey the desired concept there.[5] Given the bewildering variety of languages, advertising copy translation mistakes are easily made. Three different types of translation error are: simple carelessness, multiple-meaning words, and idioms.[6] Some typical instances of translation blunders that can be ascribed to pure carelessness are the following examples:

Language Barriers

---

[2]The story goes as follows. A long time ago—in the 14th century—an old man and his wife had been childless. They were very sad. When the old lady went to a nearby river to do the laundry, she saw a huge "momo" (peach) floating on the river. She brought it back home. And lo and behold, the peach suddenly broke into two halves and a baby came out from inside. They named this baby "Momotaro," meaning a boy from a peach.

[3]"Even at P&G, Only 3 Brands Make Truly Global Grade So Far," *Advertising Age International,* January 1998, p. 8.

[4]"Vaseline Plays on Indian Women's Embarrassment of Not Having a Servant," http://www.adageglobal.com, accessed December 24, 2002.

[5]David A. Aaker and Erich Joachimsthaler, "The Lure of Global Branding," *Harvard Business Review* (November–December 1999), p. 144.

[6]David A. Ricks, *Blunders in International Business* (Cambridge, MA: Blackwell Publishers, 1993).

GLOBAL PERSPECTIVE 14-1

DUNKIN' DONUTS 'LONGEST LOVE MESSAGE TO MOMS' CAMPAIGN IN THAILAND

Dunkin' Donuts entered Thailand in 1981 and now operates almost 130 outlets serving more than 300,000 customers a week. In fact, Thailand is home to the chain's largest shop in the world with a seating capacity of 130. Dunkin' Donuts portrays itself as a company that cares for society and honors the family. Contrary to Western countries, a Thai Dunkin' Donuts restaurant tends to be a meeting place where people come with their family and friends to relax and socialize.

In the summer of 1999, Dunkin' Donuts ran a five-week promotional campaign centered around the birthday of Thailand's queen (August 12), which coincides with national mother's day. The goal of the promotion was twofold. One objective was to increase the chain's market share by 2 percent. The second goal was to increase brand loyalty among its target consumers, teenagers and young adults. The cornerstone of the "Longest Love Message to Moms" campaign was an invitation to Thais to come to the stores and pen a love note to their

Source: "Thais Sweet on Mom, 'Love' Campaign," *Marketing News,* September 11, 2000, pp. 6–7.

mothers on a special banner. Customers could also participate in a contest in which they could win cash and product prizes. The grand prize was a company-sponsored lunch hosted by the winner and his or her mother for underprivileged children in Bangkok.

The campaign received a lot of publicity. A mile-long banner marked with 50,000 plus love-to-mom messages was carried around by more than 400 Dunkin Donuts store employees in the national parade for the queen's birthday. The promotion did an excellent job in billing Dunkin' Donuts as a company that, although foreign, cares about the local culture, Thai people, and Thailand's royal family. Overall, the company spent only $14,000 on the promotion. Did the chain achieve its objectives? You bet. Sales increased by $373,000 over normal sales volume during the promotion period. Dunkin' Donuts' market share in the doughnut category rose from 67 percent (May 1999) to 71 percent (September 1999), twice the 2 percent share increase target. An ACNielsen survey also found that Dunkin' Donuts was perceived as a "caring corporate citizen, dedicated to the Thailand market and its people."

Original slogan: "It takes a tough man to make a tender chicken."

Translation: "It takes a sexually excited man to make a chick affectionate."

Original slogan: "Body by Fisher."

Translation: "Corpse by Fisher."

Original slogan: "When I used this shirt, I felt good."

Translation: "Until I used this shirt, I felt good."

The second group of translation mishaps relates to words that have multiple meanings. Consider a campaign ran by the Parker Pen Company in Latin America. When entering Latin America, Parker used a literal translation of a slogan the company was using in the United States: "Avoid embarrassment—use Parker Pens." However, the Spanish word for *embarrassment* has also the meaning of pregnancy. As a result, Parker was unconsciously advertising its products as a contraceptive.[7]

The third class of language-related advertising blunders stems from idioms or local slang. Idioms or expressions that use slang from one country may inadvertently lead to embarrassing meanings in another country. One U.S. advertiser ran a campaign in Britain that used the same slogan as the one that was used back home: "You can use no finer napkin at your dinner table." Unfortunately, in Britain, the word *napkin* is slang for diapers.[8] See Exhibit 14-1 for the different words that Goodyear has used for *tires* in Spanish.

So what are the solutions for overcoming language barriers? One obvious cure is to involve local advertising agencies or translators in the development of promotional campaigns. Their feedback and suggestions are often highly useful.

Another tactic is simply not to translate the slogan into the local language but to use the English slogan worldwide. The Swiss luxury watch maker TAG Heuer used the

---

[7] Ibid.
[8] Ibid.

EXHIBIT 14-1

FIVE DIFFERENT WAYS OF SAYING *TIRES* IN SPANISH

Spanish Word for Tires	Countries Using Each World
Cauchos	Venezuela
Cubiertas	Argentina
Gomas	Puerto Rico
Llantas	Mexico, Peru, Guatemala, Colombia, and elsewhere in Central America
Neumaticos	Chile

Source: D.A. Hanni, J.K. Ryans, Jr. and I.R. Vernon, "Coordinating International Advertising—The Goodyear Case Revisited for Latin America." This article originally appeared in *Journal of International Marketing,* 3(2), 1995, published by Michigan State University Press, p. 84.

tag line "Don't crack under pressure" without translating it in each of its markets, even Japan, where over 60 percent of the audience had no clue of the slogan's meaning.[9] Other examples of universally used slogans that were left untranslated are "You and us: UBS," "Coke is it," and "United Colors of Benetton." For TV commercials, the ad can add subtitles in the local language. This is exactly what the U.S. Meat Export Federation (USMEF) did with the "aisareru" beef or "desire beef" campaign in Japan.[10] USMEF launched the campaign in March 2002 to deliver messages of safety, taste, and nutrition to the Japanese consumers, who had become leery about eating beef when the disease BSE was found six months earlier. The TV commercials featured three U.S. women, working in the U.S. beef industry, who share the concerns of their Japanese counterparts about the safety of the food that they serve to their families.

For radio or TV commercials, voice-overs that use the local slang often become necessary. However, this rule cannot be generalized. For instance, Egyptian consumers prefer colloquial Egyptian Arabic in their advertising, but use of local slang is less advisable for Arabs in the Gulf area.[11] Finally, meticulous copy research and testing should enable advertisers to pick up translation glitches.

Other Cultural Barriers

Many of the trickiest promotional issues occur in the domain of religion. In Saudi Arabia, for example, only veiled women can be shown in TV commercials except from the back. As you can imagine, such restrictions lead to horrendous problems for hair care advertisers. Procter & Gamble navigated around that constraint by creating a spot for Pert Plus shampoo that showed the face of a veiled woman and the hair of another woman from the back. In Brazil, Pirelli, the Italian tire maker, used an ad with a Christlike depiction of Ronaldo, the Brazilian soccer star. The ad shows Ronaldo with his arms spread and a tire tread on the sole of his foot, standing in place of the "Christ the Redeemer" statue. The ad drew heavy criticism from the Brazilian church authorities and the Vatican. In another example, after protests from local bishops, Volkswagen withdrew a billboard campaign in France of an ad for the Golf relaunch with a modern version of the Last Supper.[12]

As the Cadbury Kashmir gaffe described at the beginning of this chapter shows, political sensitivities are also crucial. Canon came under fire in the Chinese media for a promotional CD-Rom that mistakenly referred to Taiwan and Hong Kong as countries, a major affront to China's one-country policy.[13] For similar reasons, Toyota ran into trouble in China with a print ad campaign for the Land Cruiser. One of the ads showed stone lions saluting a passing Land Cruiser. Stone lions are a symbol of power

---

[9]"TAG Heuer: All Time Greats?" *Director,* April 1994, pp. 45–48.

[10]http://animalrangeextension.montana.edu/Articles/Beef/Q&A2002/Promote.htm.

[11]"Peace Process Forges New Middle East Future," *Advertising Age International,* April 1996, p. I–13.

[12]"Brazilian Ad Irks Church," *Advertising Age International,* April 13, 1998, p. I–11.

[13]"China's Paper Tigers Swift to Bite," *Financial Times,* (August 23, 2000), p. 9. Part of the animosity stemmed also from the fact that Canon is a Japanese company. Many Chinese still feel very ambivalent toward Japan.

and authority in China. The campaign caused outrage among the Chinese media and public as it was seen as a display of Japanese imperialism.[14]

As with language barriers, advertisers can escape falling into cultural traps by getting input from local staff, distributors, or ad agency people. One framework that helps in studying the influence of culture on global advertising is the Hofstede cultural grid discussed in Chapter 4. As you may recall, the model classifies national cultures based on their value systems. Five dimensions were derived: power distance, uncertainty avoidance, individualism, masculinity, and long-termism.[15] This model can then be used to assess the effectiveness of advertising campaigns.[16] Ideally, advertising campaigns should be in tune with the cultural value systems of the target audience.

Exhibit 14-2 shows how the Hofstede grid can be handled to assess the suitability of comparative advertising campaigns where one brand is contrasted with a competing brand (identified or unidentified).[17] The upper left-hand quadrant is the combination of collectivism/feminine values. In group-oriented cultures, comparison with the competition is not acceptable because the other party risks losing face. In feminine cultures, comparative advertising is too aggressive. Moving to the right, we have a mixture of

EXHIBIT 14-2
COMPARATIVE ADVERTISING*

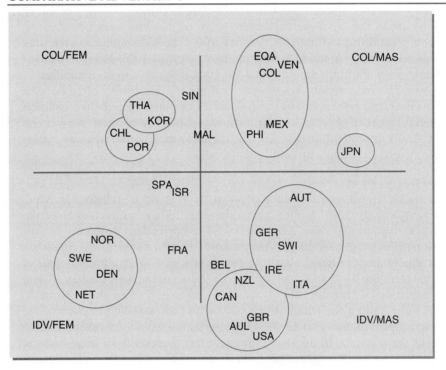

Note: AUL = Australia, AUT = Austria, BEL = Belgium, CAN = Canada, CHL = Chile, COL = Colombia, DEN = Denmark, EQA = Equador, FRA = France, GER = Germany, GBR = Great Britain, IRE = Ireland, ISR = Israel, ITA = Italy, JPN = Japan, KOR = Korea, MAL = Malaysia, MEX = Mexico, NET = the Netherlands, NOR = Norway, NZL = New Zealand, PHI = Philippines, POR = Portugal, SIN = Singapore, SPA = Spain, SWE = Sweden, SWI = Switzerland, THA = Thailand, USA = the United States, VEN = Venezuela. COL = Collectivism, IDV = Individualism, MAS = Masculine, FEM = feminine.
Source: Marieke de Mooij, *Global Marketing and Advertising* (Thousand Oaks, CA: SAGE Publications, 1998).

[14]"Toyota Looks for Road to Recovery in China," *Media,* March 12, 2004, p. 19.

[15]Geert Hofstede, "Management's Scientists Are Human," *Management Science,* 40(1), January 1994, pp. 4–13.

[16]"Individualism Is Major Element in Effective Global Advertising," *Advertising Age International,* February 12, 1996, p. 1-8.

[17]Marieke de Mooij, *Global Marketing and Advertising* (Thousand Oaks, CA: SAGE Publications, 1998), pp. 252–54.

collectivism and masculinity. Overt comparative advertising that focuses on competing brands is again limited because of the "losing face" issue. However, advertisers are able to make comparisons with another product from the same company to show how much better the new product is than the old one. The third quadrant has cultures that combine individualism with feminine values. Here, comparative advertising works as long as it is done in a subtle, nonaggressive manner. A good example is the tagline used by Carlsberg, the Danish beer brewer: "Probably the best beer in the world." The fourth quadrant—masculinity combined with individualism—embraces cultures where comparative advertising is likely to be most effective.

Although such cultural schemes can be useful, it is important to remember that value systems change over time; otherwise, you risk falling into the trap of cultural stereotypes. For instance, Japan has become much more family oriented during the 1990s. This shift from materialism and status toward family values in Japan has spurred commercials that center around family life.[18]

GLOBAL ADVERTISING BUDGET

◆ ◆ ◆ ◆ ◆ ◆ ◆ ◆

One of the delicate decisions that marketers face when planning their communication strategy centers around the "money" issue. As an illustration, Exhibit 14-3 contrasts the spending levels of two global rivals, P&G and Unilever, in several countries around the globe. Glancing at the figures, it seems that P&G concentrates on China, North America, and Latin America (except for Brazil and Argentina), the Middle East, and the former Eastern Bloc countries. Unilever appears to focus on Southeast Asia, Australia/New Zealand, and most of Western Europe. The key spending questions for global marketers are: How much should we spend? What budgeting rule shall we use? How should we allocate our resources across our different markets? Let us first look at the budgeting question. Companies rely on different kinds of advertising budgeting rules,[19] notably percentage of sales, competitive parity, and objective-and-task.

The rule based on **percentage of sales** method simply sets the overall advertising budget as a percentage of sales revenue. The base is either past or expected sales revenues. The obvious appeal of this decision rule is its simplicity. One nagging question, though, is what percentage to choose. The largest downside of this rule is that sales revenue (past or projected) drives advertising spending, whereas the purpose of advertising is to impact sales. The method is clearly not a sound strategy for recently entered markets, especially if the percentage base is historical sales revenues.[20]

Percentage of Sales Method

The principle of the **competitive parity** rule is extremely simple: Use competitors' advertising spending as a benchmark. For instance, a company could simply match its rivals' spending amounts. The rationale for this approach is that the competitors' collective wisdom signals the "optimal" spending amount. The rule also allows the company to sustain a minimum "share of voice" (brand advertising as a share of total industry advertising) without rocking the boat. Advertising scholars have pointed out several shortcomings of competitive parity as a budgeting norm. Obviously, the industry's spending habits could well be questionable. Also, marketers that recently entered a new market probably should spend far more relative to the incumbent brands to break through the clutter.

Competitive Parity Method

[18]"It's All in the Family for Japan Ads," *Advertising Age International,* July 19, 1993, pp. I-3, I-22.

[19]See, for instance, Rajeev Batra, John G. Myers, and David A. Aaker, *Advertising Management,* 5 ed. (Englewood Cliffs, NJ: Prentice-Hall, 1996).

[20]N.E. Synodinos, C.F. Keown, and L.W. Jacobs, "Transnational Advertising Practices: A Survey of Leading Brand Advertisers in Fifteen Countries," *Journal of Advertising Research,* April/May 1989, pp. 43–50.

EXHIBIT 14-3
COMPARISON OF AD SPENDING BY PROCTER & GAMBLE
AND UNILEVER (2004)

Country	Procter & Gamble	Unilever	Spending Ratio: Column (2) Column (3)
Asia			
China	$1,195.8	$132.9	9.00
India	201.4	474.8	0.42
Malaysia	28.2	15.8	1.78
Philippines	27.5	17.8	1.54
Taiwan	66.9	25.7	2.60
Thailand	41.9	94.3	0.44
Vietnam	10.2	29.0	0.35
Europe			
Belgium	106.5	78.1	1.36
Bulgaria	19.2	7.2	2.67
Croatia	20.1	7.3	2.75
Czech Republic	30.1	17.4	1.73
Finland	10.2	14.3	0.71
Germany	435.5	245.6	1.77
Greece	40.4	29.8	1.36
Hungary	60.8	72.9	0.83
Ireland	23.8	17.7	1.34
Italy	111.9	105.3	1.06
Netherlands	147.7	161.7	0.91
Poland	109.3	70.1	1.56
Russia	155.4	49.3	3.15
Spain	125.9	71.0	1.77
Sweden	53.9	59.0	0.91
Switzerland	45.2	25.9	1.75
United Kingdom	516.8	431.4	1.20
Americas			
Argentina	13.6	26.2	0.52
Chile	7.3	9.8	0.74
Mexico	74.2	44.3	1.67
Peru	8.9	2.0	4.45
United States	3,572.0	603.0	5.92
Venezuela	14.9	6.1	2.44
Africa & Middle East			
South Africa	33.9	48.1	0.70
Turkey	76.2	68.3	1.11

Note: Figures are in millions of U.S. dollars.

Source: Figures reported in database available in 19th Annual Global Marketing, *Advertising Age,* November 14, 2005.

Objective-and-Task Method

The most popular budgeting rule is the so-called **objective-and-task method.** Conceptually, this is also the most appealing budgeting rule. It treats promotional efforts as a means to achieve the advertiser's stated objectives.[21] The concept of this budgeting rule is very straightforward. The first step is to spell out the goals of the communication strategy. The next step is to determine the tasks that are needed to achieve the desired objectives. The planned budget is then the overall cost that will be required to complete these tasks. The objective-and-task method necessitates a solid understanding of the

---

[21] Ibid.

relationship between advertising spending and the stated objectives (e.g., market share, brand awareness). One way to assess these linkages is to use field experiments. With experimentation, the advertiser systematically manipulates the spending amount in different areas within the country to measure the impact of advertising on the key objectives of the campaign (e.g., brand awareness, sales volume, market share).

The budgeting process involves the allocation of resources across the different countries in which the firm operates. As an illustration, Exhibit 14-4 shows the advertising spending amounts for Procter & Gamble in various markets. To put these figures in perspective, we also include a column that shows the per capita spending amount for each country. The amounts range from $0.12 in Vietnam up to $12.10 in the United States.

Resource Allocation

At one extreme are companies such as Microsoft and FedEx where each country subsidiary independently determines how much should be spent within its market and then requests the desired resources from headquarters. This is known as **bottom-up budgeting. Top-down budgeting** is the opposite approach. Headquarters sets the overall budget and then splits the pie among its different affiliates. EDS, a U.S.-based information technology consulting company, allocates advertising budgets proportionally to the revenue contribution of the different regions for a major global ad campaign.[22] Motorola also centralizes budget decisions. The company puts its budget together centrally and then allocates it depending on regional and local needs. Other companies that centralize budgeting decisions include Sun Microsystems, Bausch & Lomb, and

EXHIBIT 14-4

PER CAPITA AD SPENDING BY PROCTER & GAMBLE

Country	Advertising Spending*	Advertising Spending per Capita
United States	$3,572.0	$12.08
Belgium	106.5	10.27
United Kingdom	516.8	8.55
Argentina	13.6	6.34
Canada	174.5	5.32
Germany	$435.5	5.28
France	282.1	4.65
New Zealand	16.5	4.10
Japan	507.4	3.98
Spain	125.9	3.12
Czech Republic	30.1	2.95
Taiwan	66.9	2.92
Italy	111.9	1.92
Malaysia	28.2	1.73
Russia	155.4	1.08
China	1,195.8	0.92
South Africa	33.9	0.76
Mexico	74.2	0.70
Thailand	41.9	0.64
Philippines	27.5	0.31
India	201.4	0.19
Vietnam	10.2	0.12

Source: Ad spending based on figures reported in database available in 19th Annual Global Marketing, *Advertising Age,* November 14, 2005. Population figures based on http://www.cia.gov/cia/publications/factbook/.
Note: *Figures are U.S. dollars in millions.

[22]"EDS in Global Push to Boost Understanding of Who It Really Is," *Media,* October 1, 1999, p. 30.

Delta Airlines.[23] A third approach, which becomes increasingly more common, takes a regional angle. Each region decides the amount of resources that it needs to achieve its planned objectives and then proposes its budget to headquarters. A survey conducted by *Advertising Age International* in 1995 found that the most favored approaches are bottom-up (28 percent of respondents) and region-up budgeting (28 percent).[24] Only 20 percent of the responses indicated that the headquarters office has direct control over funding decisions. The survey also indicated substantial cross-industry differences in resource allocation practices.

♦ ♦ ♦ ♦ ♦ ♦ ♦ ♦ CREATIVE STRATEGY

The Standardization versus Adaptation Debate

One of the thorniest issues that marketers face when developing a communication strategy is the choice of a proper advertising theme. Companies that sell the same product in multiple markets need to establish the degree to which their advertising campaign should be standardized. *Standardization* simply means that one or more elements of the communication campaign are kept the same. The major elements of a campaign are the message (strategy, selling proposition, platform) and the execution.

The issue of standardize-versus-adapt has sparked a fierce debate in advertising circles. A truly global campaign is uniform in message and often also in execution (at least, in terms of visuals). When necessary, minor changes might need to be made in the execution to comply with local regulations or to make the ad more appealing to local audiences (voice-overs, local actors). Typically, global campaigns heavily rely on global or panregional media channels. "Truly" global campaigns are still quite uncommon.

Merits of Standardization

Ricoh is one of Xerox's biggest rivals; in the United States, for instance, Ricoh's market share was 14.5 percent in 2001, slightly below Xerox's 14.9 percent.[25] In recent years the Japanese office machine company has grown by buying up competing brands such as Lanier and Savin. Still, despite its rise, only 15 percent of the consumers outside Japan recognize its name. As price competition intensifies in Ricoh's core businesses, the company aspires to move into higher-margin products such as networked office equipment systems. To grab the attention of senior executives, Ricoh kicked off a global advertising campaign in 2002. The ads showed communicators in unlikely places. For instance, one ad featured an African chieftain who uses clicks and whistles to communicate with his tribe. The message tried to make people wonder whether their business communications are as effective as they can be. See Global Perspective 14-2 for another example of a global campaign. What makes the case of standardization so compelling in the eyes of many marketers? A variety of reasons have been offered to defend global, if not panregional, advertising campaigns. The major ones are listed here.

Scale Economies. Of the factors encouraging companies to standardize their advertising campaigns, the most appealing one is the positive impact on the advertiser's bottom line. The savings coming from the economies of scale of a single campaign (as opposed to multiple country-level ones) can be quite eye catching. Levi Strauss reportedly saved around $2.2 million by shooting a single TV ad to cover six European markets.[26] Several factors lie behind such savings. Producing a single commercial is often far cheaper than making several different ones for each individual market. Savings are also realized because firms can assign fewer executives to develop the campaign at the global or panregional level.

---

[23]"U.S. Multinationals," *Advertising Age International,* June 1999, pp. 39–40.

[24]"Ad Decision-Makers Favor Regional Angle," *Advertising Age International,* May 15, 1995, pp. I-3, I-16.

[25]"Ricoh Wants World to Know Its Name," *Asian Wall Street Journal,* November 18, 2002, p. A8.

[26]"A Universal Message," *Financial Times,* May 27, 1993.

◆ ◆

$\mathcal{G}$LOBAL PERSPECTIVE 14-2

NISSAN'S GLOBAL "SHIFT" ADVERTISING CAMPAIGN

In the past, Nissan Motor's advertising messages varied enormously across markets. In Europe, it had no tagline. In the United States, the tagline was "Driven" and in Japan it used the slogan "Bringing more to your life every day." To beef up its global brand image, Nissan kicked off its global "Shift" campaign in 2002. In the United States, where the campaign coincided with the launch of the Nissan 350Z sports car, the tagline varied, including "Shift passion," "Shift joy," and "Shift forward." One TV ad in the U.S. shows a baby trying to make its first steps with the tagline "Shift achievement."

Source: "Nissan Shifts Focus to Unified Strategy for Its Global Campaign," *Asian Wall Street Journal,* October 10, 2002, p. A7.

In Europe, the slogan is "Shift expectations." In Japan, the tagline is "Shift the future."

The "Shift" campaign was born from a cooperative process between Nissan managers from advertising and marketing divisions worldwide. Brainstorming over a 10-month period spawned hundreds of candidates for a global tagline. One major obstacle was that many of the most common words (e.g., "power," "exciting") were already pre-empted by copyright somewhere. In the end, "Shift" was the winning idea. The "Shift" slogan appeared to best convey the sense of change message that Nissan hoped to get across. Moreover, it could easily be understood in non-English-speaking countries. To give local subsidiaries some amount of control, Nissan allowed local variations for the second half of the tagline.

Consistent Image. For many companies that sell the same product in multiple markets, having a consistent brand image is extremely important. Consistency was one of the prime motives behind the pan-European campaign that Blistex, a U.S.-based lip care manufacturer, started to run in 1995. Prior to the campaign, its advertising theme varied from country to country, often highlighting only one item of Blistex's product line. The entire product range consists of three items, each one for a different need. In many of its markets, brand awareness was dismally low. The objectives for the pan-European campaign were (1) to increase brand awareness and (2) to have the same positioning theme by communicating the so-called care-to-cure concept behind Blistex's product line.[27] Campbell's pan-European advertising strategy for the Delacre cookie brand was also driven by a desire to establish a single brand identity across Europe. The brand's platform is that Delacre is a premium cookie brand with the finest ingredients based on French know-how. The same campaign was aired in English reaching 30 million people in more than 20 countries.[28] Message consistency matters a great deal in markets with extensive media overlap or for goods that are sold to global target customers who travel the globe.

Global Consumer Segments. Cross-cultural similarities are a major catalyst behind efforts toward a standardized advertising approach. The "global village" argument often pops up in discussions on the merits of global or panregional advertising campaigns. The argument of cultural binding especially has clout with respect to product categories that appeal to the elites or youngsters as observed by David Newkirk, a consultant with Booz Allen & Hamilton: "The young and the rich have very similar tastes the world over, and that's what's driving the convergences in advertising and media."[29] Bausch & Lomb's first pan-Asian campaign for Ray-Ban sunglasses is a good example.[30] The campaign targeted Asia's Generation X young—16-to-25-year-old—and trendy people with buying power. A Bausch & Lomb senior executive stated, "We are trying to talk to Asian youth in a language that they understand and relate to across the region. It's a language of music and fast-paced images." The campaign was built around

---

[27] Mark Boersma, Blistex, personal communication. 1994.

[28] "Rebuilding in a Crumbling Sector," *Marketing,* February 18, 1993, pp. 28–29.

[29] "A Universal Message," *Financial Times,* May 27, 1993.

[30] The eyewear division (including Ray-Ban) of Bausch & Lomb was sold in 1999 to Luxottica.

a series of questions that youngsters ask. Each one of the spots ended with the tag line: "Whatever you're looking for. Ray-Ban, the new look."[31]

Creative Talent.   Creative talent among ad agencies is a scarce supply. It is not uncommon that the most talented people within the agency are assigned to large accounts, leaving small accounts with junior executives. The talent issue matters especially in countries that are plagued with a shortage of highly skilled advertising staff. By running a global campaign, small markets can benefit from having the same high-quality, creative ads as larger ones have.

Cross-Fertilization.   More and more companies try to take advantage of their global scope by fostering cross-fertilization. In the domain of advertising, cross-fertilization means that marketers encourage their affiliates to adopt, or at least consider, advertising ideas that have proven successful in other markets. This process of exploiting "good" ideas does not even need to be restricted to "global" brands. Nestlé used the idea of a serialized "soap-mercial" for the Nescafé brand in the United Kingdom for its Tasters Choice coffee brand in the United States. The campaigns, chronicling a relationship between two neighbors that centers around coffee, were phenomenally successful in both markets. Likewise, when Procter & Gamble introduced Pantene shampoo in Latin America, it used a spot that was originally produced in Taiwan. Only a few minor changes were made to allow for local cultural differences.[32] Coming up with a good idea typically takes a long time. Once the marketer has hit on a creative idea, it makes common sense to try to leverage it by considering how it can be transplanted to other countries.[33]

In addition to these reasons, there are other considerations that might justify standardized multinational advertising. A survey conducted among ad agency executives found that the single brand image factor was singled out as the most important driver for standardizing multinational advertising. Two other critical factors are time pressure and corporate organizational setup.[34] Obviously, developing a single campaign is less time consuming than creating several. The firm's organizational setup also plays a major role, in particular the locus of control. In general, if the MNC's control is highly centralized, it is highly likely that its theme development is standardized. Advertising is usually localized in decentralized organizations. Also, local advertising for many small companies is typically the responsibility of local distributors or franchisees. The shift toward regional organizational structures is definitely one of the major drivers behind the growing popularity of regional campaigns.

Barriers to Standardization   Faced with the preceding arguments for standardization, advocates of adaptation easily can bring forward an equally compelling list to build up the case for adaptation. The four major barriers to standardization relate to (1) cultural differences, (2) advertising regulations, (3) differences in the degree of market development, and (4) the "not-invented-here" (NIH) syndrome.

Cultural Differences.   Notwithstanding the "global village" headlines, cultural differences still persist for many product categories. Cultural gaps between countries may exist in terms of lifestyles, benefits sought, usage contexts, and so forth. A case in point is the use of references to sex in ad campaigns. While references to sex are not unusual in many Western ads, sex is rarely used in Asia to promote products due to both regulations and market acceptance. The U.S. version of an ad for personal care brand Herbal Essences, full of sexual innuendo, was also used in Australia. However,

---

[31]"Ray-Ban Ogles 16–25 Group in Southeast Asia Blitz," *Advertising Age International,* June 1996, p. I-30.

[32]"P&G Sees Success in Policy of Transplanting Ad Ideas," *Advertising Age International,* July 19, 1993, p. I-2.

[33]T. Duncan and J. Ramaprasad, "Standardizing Multinational Advertising: The Influencing Factors," *Journal of Advertising,* 24(3), Fall 1995, pp. 55–68.

[34]Ibid.

the ad was reshot for Thailand, showing girls having a fun time rather than an erotic experience. Unless it is done in a funny manner, sex is not used in Thai advertising, for it runs counter to Buddhist values and Thai culture.[35]

Cultural gaps may even prevail for goods that cater to global segments. A case in point involves luxury goods that target global elites. The user benefits of cognac are by and large the same worldwide. The usage context, however, varies a lot: in the United States, cognac is consumed as a stand-alone drink; in Europe, often as an after-dinner drink; and in China with a glass of water during dinner. As a result, Hennessy cognac, adapts its appeals according to local customs while promoting the same brand image.[36] Even in industrial marketing, advertisers occasionally need to make allowances for cultural differences. A print ad originally created for Siemens in Germany to convey "energy" was deemed unsuitable for the Hong Kong market (see Exhibit 14-5). The German ad showed a crowd of enthusiastic youngsters at a pop concert. Audiences at Canto-pop concerts tend to be much more subdued than their Western counterparts. Instead of using the German print ad, Siemens Hong Kong came up with an ad that showed a fireworks display with a view of the Hong Kong skyline.[37]

Advertising Regulations.   Local advertising regulations pose another barrier for standardization. They usually affect the execution of the commercial. The Ray-Ban example cited earlier used the same theme across Asia, but the execution sometimes differed due to local rules. In Malaysia, for instance, foreign-made commercials or ads featuring Caucasians are not allowed. Hence, Ray-Ban was forced to shoot local commercials for Malaysian TV.[38] Later in this chapter, we cover the regulations hurdle in more detail.

Market Maturity.   Differences in the degree of market maturity also rule out a standardized strategy. Gaps in cross-market maturity levels mandate different advertising approaches. When Snapple, the U.S.-based "New Age" beverage, first entered the European market, its biggest challenge was to overcome initial skepticism among consumers about the concept of iced tea. Typically, in markets that were entered very recently, one of the main objectives is to create brand awareness. Products that are relatively new to the entered market also demand education of the customers on what benefits the product or service can deliver and how to use it. As brand awareness builds up, other advertising goals gain prominence.

"Not-Invented-Here" (NIH) Syndrome.   Finally, efforts to implement a standardized campaign often must cope with the NIH syndrome. Local subsidiaries and/or local advertising agencies could stonewall attempts at standardization. Local offices generally have difficulty accepting creative materials from other countries. Later in this chapter we suggest some guidelines that can be used to overcome NIH attitudes.

Marketers adopt several approaches to create multinational ads. At one extreme, the entire process could be left to the local subsidiary or distributor with only a minimum of guidance from headquarters. At the other extreme, global or regional headquarters makes all the decisions, including all the nitty-gritty surrounding the development of ad campaigns. The direction the MNC takes depends on the locus of control and corporate headquarters' familiarity with the foreign market. MNCs that fail to adopt a learning orientation about their foreign markets risk being challenged by the local subsidiaries when they attempt to impose a standardized campaign.[39] In any event,

Approaches to Creating Advertising Copy

---

[35]"Pushing the Sex Envelope," *Media*, September 20, 2002, pp. 16–17.

[36]"Cachet and Carry," *Advertising Age International*, February 12, 1996, p. I-18.

[37]Monika Sturm, Senior Communications Manager, Siemens Hong Kong Ltd., personal communication. 1996.

[38]"Ray-Ban Ogles 16–25 Group."

[39]Michel Laroche, V.H. Kirpalani, Frank Pons, and Lianxi Zhou, "A Model of Advertising Standardization in Multinational Corporations," *Journal of International Business Studies,* 32 (2), Second Quarter 2001, pp. 249–66.

EXHIBIT 14-5
ADAPTATION OF SIEMENS PRINT AD

SIEMENS

For the power of Hong Kong

Simply meeting today's demand for energy is not enough. The challenge is to go beyond. To increase efficiency. To conserve resources. And to offer cost effective, renewable energy solutions. At Siemens, we're going beyond. By developing power generation and transmission systems that actually make resources last longer. Perhaps that's why Siemens can take pride in developing some of the most energy efficient power plants in the world. It's an achievement matched only by our ability to draw from a broad base of energy solutions to meet the energy needs of today - and generations to come.

Siemens power engineering saves resources for tomorrow.

For information please call Siemens Ltd., Tel: 2583 3308

Turnkey gasturbine plant for Yangpu on Hainan Island

SIEMENS

For the power of a new generation.

Simply meeting today's demand for energy is not enough. The challenge is to go beyond. To increase efficiency. To conserve resources. And to offer cost effective, renewable energy solutions. At Siemens, we're going beyond. By developing power generation and transmission systems that actually make resources last longer. Perhaps that's why Siemens can take pride in developing some of the most energy efficient power plants in the world. It's an achievement matched only by our ability to draw from a broad base of energy solutions to meet the energy needs of today – and generation to come.

Siemens power engineering saves resources for tommorow.

Gas turbines: resource-conserving and state-of-the-art.

| Print ad used in Hong Kong | Print ad used in Germany |

Source: Siemen's, Hong Kong. Reproduced with permission.

most MNCs adopt an approach that falls somewhere between a purely standardized and purely localized campaign. Let us look at the main approaches.

"Laissez Faire." With the "laisser faire" approach, every country subsidiary follows its own course developing its own ads based on what it thinks works best in its market. There is no centralized decision-making.

Export Advertising. With **export advertising,** the creative strategy is developed by an ad agency from the head office and then exported without local office inputs. A universal copy is developed for all markets. The same positioning theme is used worldwide. Visuals and most of the other aspects of the execution are also the same. Minor allowances are made for local sensitivities, but by and large, the same copy is used in each of the company's markets. Obviously, export advertising delivers all of the benefits of standardized campaigns: (1) the same brand image and identity worldwide, (2) no confusion among customers, (3) substantial savings, and (4) strict control over

EXHIBIT 14-6

EXAMPLES OF UNIVERSAL APPEALS

Superior quality. Clearly, the promise of superior quality is a theme that makes any customer tick. A classic example here is the "Ultimate Driving Machine" slogan that BMW uses in many of its markets.

New product/service. A global rollout of a new product or service is often coupled with a global campaign announcing the launch. One example is the marketing hype surrounding the launch of Windows 2000 by Microsoft.

Country of origin. Brands in a product category with a strong country stereotype often leverage their roots by touting the "Made in" cachet. This positioning strategy is especially popular among fashion and luxury goods marketers.

Heroes and Celebrities. Tying the product with heroes or celebrities is another form of universal positioning. A recurring issue on this front is whether advertisers should use "local" or "global" heroes. When sports heroes are used, most advertisers will select local, or at least regional, celebrities. Reebok International's advertising strategy in the Asian region heavily relies on Asian athletes such as tennis player Michael Chang, Indian cricketer Mohammed Azharuddin, or New Zealand rugby player Jonah Lomu.* With movie personalities, the approach usually differs. Swiss watchmaker SMH International promoted its Omega brand with a TV commercial featuring the actor Pierce Brosnan after the release of the James Bond movie *Golden Eye.*

Lifestyle. The mystique of many global upscale brands is often promoted by lifestyle ads that reflect a lifestyle shared by target customers, regardless of where they live. As one media buyer commented: "It's not just a question of money. It's being able to afford it and having the lifestyle that lets you say, 'I need a pen worth $300.' "**

Global presence. Many marketers try to enhance the image of their brands via a "global presence" approach—telling the target audience that their product is sold across the globe. Obviously, such a positioning approach can be adopted anywhere. The "global scope" pitch is often used by companies that sell their product or service to customers for whom this attribute is crucial. The concept is also used by other types of advertisers, though. Warner-Lambert created commercials for its Chiclets chewing gum brand that tried to project the cross-cultural appeal of the brand. One spot showed a young man in a desert shack rattling a Chiclets box. The sound of Chiclets triggers the arrival of a cosmopolitan group of eager customers.***

Market leadership. Regardless of the country, being the leading brand worldwide or within the region is a powerful message to most consumers. For products that possess a strong country image, a brand can send a strong signal by making the claim that it is the most preferred brand in its home country.

Corporate image. Finally, corporate communication ads that aspire to foster a certain corporate image also often lend themselves to a uniform approach.

*"Reebok Sets Strategy to Get Sales on Track in Fast-growing Asia." p. 12.
***"Cachet and Carry," p. I–15.
****"Chiclets Tries New Language," *Advertising Age International,* April 19, 1993, pp. I–1, I–21.

the planning and execution of the global communication strategy.[40] On the creative strategy front, a centralized message demands a universal positioning theme that travels worldwide. Exhibit 14-6 offers several examples of universal appeals. Export advertising is very common for corporate ad campaigns that aim to create awareness, reposition the company, or reinforce an existing company image.

Prototype Standardization. With **prototype standardization,** advertising guidelines are given to the local affiliates concerning the execution of the advertising. These guidelines are conveyed via the company's Web site, manuals, or audiovisual materials. Mercedes uses a handbook to communicate its advertising guidelines to the local subsidiaries and sales agents. Instructions are given on the format, visual treatment, print to be employed for headlines, and so on.[41] Likewise, the Swiss watchmaker TAG Heuer has a series of guidebooks covering all of the nuts and bolts of its communication

---

[40]M.G. Harvey, "Point of View: A Model to Determine Standardization of the Advertising Process in International Markets," *Journal of Advertising Research,* July/August 1993, pp. 57–64.

[41]Rein Rÿkens. European Advertising Strategies, (London: Castells 1992).

approach, including rules on business card design.[42] Wrigley, the Chicago-based candy maker, produced a videotape for its international advertising program. The tape offers guidelines on ad execution, including minutiae such as how the talent should put the gum in his or her mouth, the background of the closing shot, tips on handling the gum before shooting the commercial, and so forth. It shows examples of clips that follow and do not follow the guidelines. The tape also explains under what circumstances deviations from the norms are acceptable.

Regional Approach. According to the regional approach, every region produces its own interpretation and execution of the campaign. In that sense, this approach is a compromise between centralized and laissez faire decision making. One company that adopted the regional approach is Nokia.[43] Strategic decision making for the Nokia brand are made centrally by a "brand forum." Regional affiliates decide on the execution of marketing communications.

Pattern Standardization. With **pattern standardization,** headquarters spells out guidelines on the positioning theme (platform) and the brand identity to be used in the ad and maps out worldwide brand values. Responsibility for the execution, however, is left to the local markets. That way, brand consistency is sustained without sacrificing the relevance of the ad campaign to local consumers. Smirnoff's "pure thrill" campaign exemplifies this approach. All of its global advertising showed distorted images becoming clear when viewed through the Smirnoff bottle. However, the specific scenes that were used varied across countries as consumers hold different perceptions about what is "thrilling."[44] Seagram's took a **modular approach** for a campaign it ran for its spirits brand Chivas Regal. After doing a copy test in seven countries, Seagram's picked a campaign that consisted of a series of 24 ads, each using the slogan "There will always be a Chivas Regal." Marketing executives in each country, however, were able to pick the specific ads from the series for their market. As with pattern standardization instructions on proper positioning themes and concepts are shared with the local agencies and affiliates through manuals, videotapes, or other communication tools.

◆ ◆ ◆ ◆ ◆ ◆ ◆ ◆   **GLOBAL MEDIA DECISIONS**

Another decision that international marketers must make is the choice of the media in each of the country where the company is doing business. In some countries, media decisions are much more critical than the creative aspects of the campaign. In Japan, for instance, media buying is crucial in view of the scarce supply of advertising space. Given the choice between an ad agency that possesses good creative skills and one that has enormous media-buying clout, most advertisers in Japan would pick the latter.[45]

International media planners must surmount a wide range of issues. The media landscape varies dramatically across countries or even between regions within a country. Differences in the media infrastructure exist in terms of media availability, accessibility, costs, and habits.

Media Infrastructure Most Western countries offer an incredible abundance of media choices. New media channels emerge continuously. Given this embarrassment of riches, the marketer's task is to decide how to allocate its promotional dollars to get the biggest bang for the buck. In other countries, though, the range of media channels is extremely limited.

[42]"TAG Heuer: All time Greats?" pp. 45–48.
[43]"Fight to the Finnish," *Ad Age Global,* (June 2002), pp. 14–15.
[44]D. A. Aaker and E. Joachimsthaler, "The Lure of Global Branding," *Harvard Business Review* November–December 1999, p. 144.
[45]"The Enigma of Japanese Advertising," *Economist,* August 14, 1993, pp. 59–60.

Many of the media vehicles that exist in the marketer's home country are simply not available in the foreign market. Government controls heavily restrict the access to mass media options such as television in a host of countries. In Germany, for instance, TV advertising is allowed only during limited times of the day.

The media infrastructure differs dramatically from country to country, even within the same region. Whereas TV viewers in the West can surf an abundance of 25 or more TV channels, their Asian counterparts have access, on the average, to a measly choice of two to three channels. The standard media vehicles such as radio, cinema, and TV are well established in most countries. New media such as cable, the internet, mobile phones, satellite TV, and pay TV are steadily growing. Given the media available, advertisers are forced to adapt their media schedule to the parameters set by the local environment. Exhibit 14-7 contrasts media allocation patterns in various countries.

One of the major limitations in many markets is media availability. The lack of standard media options challenges marketers to use their imagination by coming up with "creative" options. Intel, the U.S. computer chip maker, built up brand awareness in China by distributing bike reflectors in Shanghai and Beijing with the words "Intel Inside Pentium Processor." Advertisers in Bangkok have taken advantage of the city's notorious traffic jams by using media strategies that reach commuters. Some of the selected media vehicles include outdoor advertising, traffic reports on radio stations, and three-wheeled taxis (*tuk-tuks*).[46]

Media Limitations

Marketers must also consider media costs. For all types of reasons, media costs differ enormously between countries. Exhibit 14-8 compares the advertising rates in 10 different countries for major media vehicles. In general, high cost per thousand (CPMs) are found in areas that have a high per capita GNP. For instance, advertising rates in China are far below the rates in Western markets though they are rapidly catching up.[47] The amount of competition within the media market is another important factor. In China, advertising rates differ greatly across regions. Also, different TV advertising rates are charged to local firms, foreign companies, and joint ventures, although the

EXHIBIT 14-7
AD SPENDING (2002) BY MEDIUM*

Country	Television	Newspapers	Magazines	Radio	Outdoor	Total Amount (in $billions)
Australia**	33.6%	43.2%	10.8%	7.7%	4.0%	$5.0
Brazil	48.4	35.4	11.4	3.1	1.7	6.4
Canada	39.0	39.0	5.0	13.0	4.0	5.5
China***	67.0	23.0		1.0	9.0	5.5
France**	34.5	24.1	23.1	6.5	11.1	11.1
Germany	24.3	43.5	23.5	3.8	3.9	17.5
Italy	52.0	22.0	16.0	5.0	5.0	7.4
Japan	46.1	27.3	9.6	4.6	12.4	41.6
South Korea	28.0	47.0	4.0	2.0	n/a	6.1
Spain**	41.4	32.5	11.6	9.1	4.5	5.4
U.K.	29.8	40.3	17.5	4.6	6.3	15.3
U.S.A.	38.0	32.9	11.2	14.2	3.7	133.6

Various sources.

*Percentages do not always sum to 100% because in some countries other media are also important (e.g., cinema advertising).

**Figures are year 2000 estimates.

***For China, the 23% is all print (newspapers + magazines) advertising.

---

[46]"Bangkok Is Bumper to Bumper with Ads," *Advertising Age International,* February 20, 1996, p. I-4.

[47]One exception to the per-capita GNP rule is Brazil. Prime TV advertising rates are far higher than in many European countries (see Exhibit 14-8).

EXHIBIT 14-8
ADVERTISING RATES IN 10 LEADING AD MARKETS

Country	Top Circulation Magazine (color full page ad—in US$)	Top Circulation Women's Magazine (color full page ad—in US$)	Top Circulation Newspaper (color full page ad—in US$)	Top News Program (:30 ad—in US$)	Top TV Adult Program (:30 ad—in US$)
United States	$281,750	$296,000	$110,300	$84,100	$288,000
Japan	12,030	20,301	424,436	n/a	n/a
Germany	44,368	37,206	266,520	34,469	82,888
United Kingdom	39,043	23,021	64,493	49,913	118,367
France	42,330	34,880	106,100	36,785	70,400
Italy	55,800	53,730	126,360	54,900	137,700
Brazil	46,500	22,000	92,170	76,130	70,860
South Korea	5,652	6,028	58,600	17,925	17,973
Canada	20,712	26,200	35,046	6,503	42,522
China	15,917	8,215	n/a	2,717	19,565

Source: Based on "Top 10 Global Ad Markets," *Ad Age Global* (April 2002) pp. 18–23.

gap is narrowing.[48] In the United Kingdom, TV ad rates are relatively low because it is a mature market and has many competing channels.[49]

A major obstacle in many emerging markets is the overall quality of the local media. In China, for instance, no reliable statistics for many print media are available on circulation figures or readership profiles. Print quality of many newspapers and magazines is appalling. Newspapers may demand full payment in advance when the order is booked and ask for additional money later on. There are no guarantees that newspapers will run an ad or that TV broadcasters will show a spot on the agreed date.

Recent Developments in the Global Media Landscape

To illustrate the rapid changes in the media landscape, we would like to pinpoint some major trends:

- *Growth of commercialization and deregulation of mass media.* One undeniable shift in scores of countries is the growing commercialization of the mass media, especially the broadcast media. In Belgium, for example, until the late 1970s, commercial TV was basically nonexistent. Advertisers who wanted to use TV as a medium either had to rely on cinema as a substitute or TV channels in neighboring countries. Following the introduction of several commercial TV stations, the situation is totally different now. Similar moves toward commercialization and lifting government restrictions on the local media can be observed in many other countries.

- *Shift from radio and print to TV advertising.* The rise of commercial TV has turned it into the medium of choice for advertisers worldwide.[50] Some advertisers who traditionally focused mostly on print media are increasingly shifting their advertising dollars to television. Television also offers novel ways of reaching target customers. TVSN (Television Shopping Network) is a 24-hour shopping network that is viewed by satellite and cable TV viewers in Japan, Korea, Taiwan, Hong Kong, and the Philippines. Merchandise can be ordered via a toll-free number, paid for with a credit card, and delivered by courier.[51] Global marketers also recognize the power

---

[48]"China TV Stations Narrow Pricing Gap," *Media,* March 15, 1996, p. 4.

[49]"TV Is Advertisers' Big Pick in Europe," *Advertising Age International,* June 21, 1993, p. I-19.

[50]John M. Eger, "Global Television: An Executive Overview," *Columbia Journal of World Business,* Fall 1987, pp. 5–10.

[51]"As Advertised on TV," *Asiaweek,* July 12, 1996, p. 48.

of infomercials as a selling tool. In Japan, for instance, infomercial marketers now have access to more than half of Japan's population. The head of one infomercial marketing firm underscores the opportunities available in international markets as follows: "Down the road we'll be able to put a product simultaneously into the homes of 300 to 500 million people around the globe. Now that's powerful."[52]

- *Rise of global and regional media.* One of the most dramatic developments in the media world has been the proliferation of regional and global media. Several factors explain the appeal of global or regional media to international advertisers. In some countries, it is very difficult to get access to the local media. By using international media, advertisers get a chance to target customers who would otherwise be hard to reach. International media also facilitate the launch of global or panregional ad campaigns. Another major asset is that most international media have well-defined background information on their audience reach and profile. In contrast to most local media, international media tend to have a very well-defined audience. The major barrier to advertising on global media has been the cultural issue. Satellite TV broadcasters, for instance, initially planned to broadcast the same ads and programs globally. Because of that, viewership for many of the satellite channels was extremely low. As a result, very few advertisers were interested in airing spots on satellite TV. Lately, however, more and more satellite networks have started to customize the content of their programs. NBC Super Channel even broadcasts many of its programs in Europe with subtitles or local voice-overs to overcome the language barrier. Likewise, cable TV channels such as MTV and ESPN customize their content to different countries or regions. A push toward localization also exists among many publishing houses of international magazine titles. In Japanese bookstores, magazine racks offer Japanese editions of titles such as *GQ, National Geographic,* and *Cosmopolitan.*

- *Growing spread of interactive marketing.* More and more advertisers worldwide are experimenting with multimedia tools that allow interactive advertising.[53] The idea is that when viewers interact with the ad, it will be easier to get the message across. By coming up with innovative approaches, marketers hope to be able to break through the advertising clutter and grab the viewer's attention. However, interactive marketing can be hindered by viewer apathy and sheer laziness. Obviously, the most visible form is the Internet, though clearly interest in the Internet as an advertising vehicle is still very minimal (see Chapter 19).[54] Other tactics exist, however. To promote the Xbox videogame player in Europe, Microsoft gave away two million DVDs with an interactive commercial.[55] At various points, viewers can click on text or icons to get information about the Xbox or upcoming videogames. Targeting 16- to 34-year-old males, the DVDs were distributed by adding them to videogame magazines and holiday catalogs.

- *Increased popularity of text messaging.* The spread of mobile phone service globally has spurred a new phenomenon: text messaging or SMS (short messaging service) ads. With SMS, mobile phone users use their cell phone to transmit text messages. In 2002, mobile phone users were estimated to send 400 billion text messages worldwide. SMS is particularly popular in Asia, where mobile phone penetration is higher than that of fixed-line phones in many parts of the continent. Global Perspective 14-3 describes how firms leverage text messaging to come up with creative communication campaigns.

---

[52]"Infomercial Audience Crosses over Cultures," *Advertising Age International,* January 15, 1996, p. I-8.

[53]"Scoping out Europe's Interactive Activity," *Advertising Age International,* January 16, 1995, p. I-12.

[54]John A. Quelch and Lisa R. Klein, "The Internet and International Marketing," *Sloan Management Review,* Spring 1996, pp. 60–75.

[55]"Microsoft, Others Target Teenagers Via Interactive DVDs," *Asian Wall Street Journal,* December 30, 2002, p. A5.

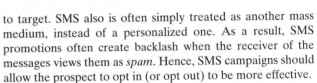

GLOBAL PERSPECTIVE 14-3

SMS ADVERTISING IS HOT

Short messaging service (SMS) lets mobile phone subscribers send text messages quickly and cheaply. In 2002, mobile phone users were estimated to send 400 billion text messages globally, up from 250 billion in the previous year. SMS has a wide following in Asia. In China alone, cell phone users transmitted 60 billion messages in 2002. The rise of SMS, especially among tech-savvy youth, has turned it into a communication channel that marketers cannot ignore. The most successful uses of SMS marketing is for digital coupons and event-based messages. The latter often involve other media.

SMS has several appeals for marketers. First, costs can be fairly low. The costs of a campaign range from a few cents to 50 cents per customer, depending on a wide range of factors, such as involvement of an ad agency, third-party costs (e.g., telecom carriers), cost of the software being used, and the complexity of the campaign. SMS enables personalized, one-on-one marketing. As such, SMS is an excellent vehicle to communicate brand values. Response to SMS campaigns can also be tracked very easily. There are a few obstacles however. One major hurdle is often the telecom carrier. Carriers can be reluctant to give away phone numbers, even though they often stand to benefit from such campaigns with the revenues being generated each time consumers respond. In countries like the Philippines, where prepaid phone cards are prominent, mobile phone users are difficult to profile and, hence, difficult

to target. SMS also is often simply treated as another mass medium, instead of a personalized one. As a result, SMS promotions often create backlash when the receiver of the messages views them as *spam*. Hence, SMS campaigns should allow the prospect to opt in (or opt out) to be more effective.

Still, in spite of these obstacles, several companies have been very creative and successful in using SMS as an advertising medium. In July 2002, Coca-Cola ran a 40-day contest in China in which cell phone users were invited to guess the next day's temperature in Beijing. Contestants could win a Siemens phone or a one-year supply of Coke. Those who did not win could download Coke's jingle as a free ring tone. The response was huge: 4 million messages were exchanged; nearly 50,000 contestants downloaded the jingle. Singapore's Navy ran an SMS recruiting drive targeting 16- to 20-year-old students. As part of the campaign, students could play a battleship game against their friends on a computer. The campaign had a 14 percent response rate.

Kellogg's India extended an advertising campaign for Kellogg's Corn Flakes with an SMS campaign whose goal was to communicate the benefits of iron shakti, the main ingredient of Corn Flakes. The campaign used a contest that targeted adults 25 and up. Participants had to answer questions based around Corn Flakes' product features and send in their answers through SMS.

The next advance will be the jump from SMS to MMS—multimedia messaging services. The advent of MMS will add a whole new layer by allowing advertisers to incorporate audio and video images with traditional text messages.

Source: "Text Messaging Ads on Fast Track in Asia," *Advertising Age,* December 2, 2002, p. 12; "U.S. Lags Behind," *Advertising Age,* December 2, 2002, p. 12; and "Kellogg's Adopts SMS for Corn Flakes Boost," *Media,* February 13, 2004, p. 14.

- *Improved monitoring.* Some years ago, Speedo, a Kenyan pen maker, tried to boost its sales in Kenya during the Christmas season with a massive advertising campaign. The results were discouraging. Follow-up on the campaign quickly pointed out the reason: None of the scheduled TV spots was ever broadcast.[56] Obviously, having an infrastructure in place that allows advertisers to monitor broadcast and print media is highly desirable to avoid this and related problems. Moreover, advertisers can track how much, when, and in what media their competitors advertise. Fortunately, in more and more countries, watchdog agencies provide the wherewithal for monitoring the media landscape.

- *Improved TV viewership measurement.* To plan a TV ad campaign, high-quality viewership data are an absolute must for marketers. In many markets, measurement of TV viewership relied on diary data collected by a local market research agency from household panel members. Not surprising, the value of such data was highly questionable. The advent of new technologies has led to monitoring devices that allow far more precise data collection than in the past. The most advanced tool is the so-called people meter, a device hooked up to the TV set of a household panel member that automatically registers viewing behavior.

---

[56]"Watchdog Agency Monitors Ad Space in Kenya's Media," *Advertising Age International,* June 19, 1995, p. I-11.

ADVERTISING REGULATIONS

◆ ◆ ◆ ◆ ◆ ◆ ◆ ◆

The Malaysian government banned a Toyota ad that featured Brad Pitt, the Hollywood actor, as celebrity endorser. According to Malaysia's then Deputy Information minister, "Western faces in advertisements could create an inferiority complex among Asians... [the advertisement] was a humiliation against Asians.... Why do we need to use [Western] faces in our advertisements? Are our own people not handsome?"[57] Exhibit 14-9 lists some of the other strict rules and regulations that advertisers should comply with in Malaysia. While some of the rules make sense given Malaysia's Muslim background, others border on absurdity. No wonder Malaysian TV commercials have difficulty winning awards in international advertising contests.

A major roadblock that global advertisers face is the bewildering set of advertising regulations advertisers need to cope with in foreign markets. Advertising regulations are usually imposed by the local government bodies. In many countries, the local advertising industry is also governed by some form of self-regulation, which can take various forms.[58] One possibility is that local advertisers, advertising agencies, and broadcast media jointly agree on a set of rules. Alternatively, the local advertising industry and government representatives decide on a code of advertising ethics. Several factors lie behind self-regulation of the advertising industry, including protection of consumers against misleading or offensive advertising, protection of legitimate advertisers against false claims, and accusations made by competitors. Another forceful reason to set up self-regulatory bodies is to preempt more stringent government-imposed regulation or control of the advertising industry. This section summarizes the major types of advertising regulations and offers some recent examples of each.

Advertising "Vice Products" and Pharmaceuticals.

Tough restrictions, if not outright bans, apply to the advertising pharmaceuticals and so-called vice products in many countries. Japan, for example, prohibits the use of the word "safe" or "safety" or any derivatives when promoting over-the-counter drugs (e.g., pain relievers, cold medicines).[59] Despite the opposition of advertising agencies, advertisers, and media channels, rules on the advertising of tobacco and liquor products are becoming increasingly more severe.

Comparative Advertising.

Another area of contention is comparative advertising in which advertisers disparage the competing brand. While such advertising practices are commonplace in the United States, other countries heavily constrain or even prohibit them. For example, until recently, advertisers in South Africa were forbidden to name competitors, show rival brands, or make comparisons that allude to the competing brand.[60] In China, advertisers are not allowed to compare their products with their competitors' or to include superlative terms such as "best." Anheuser-Busch, however, was able to air a commercial with Budweiser's slogan that it was "America's favorite beer" after it supported the claim with statistical evidence.[61] In Japan, although comparative advertising is not illegal, it is a cultural taboo. It is seen as immodest and underhanded. Often the Japanese side with the competitor![62]

Content of Advertising Messages.

The content of advertising messages could be subject to certain rules or guidelines. Dorf Industries, an Australian plumbing fixtures marketer, ran a campaign that featured a spurned lover getting even with her boyfriend by turning on all taps. The slighted girlfriend leaves the house that is filling

[57]"Malaysia Bans Toyota Ad," http://www.asiamarketresearch.com, accessed December 20, 2002.

[58]Marieke de Mooij, *Advertising Worldwide,* 2nd ed. (Englewood Cliffs, NJ: Prentice-Hall, 1994).

[59]John Mackay, McCann-Erickson Japan, private communication.

[60]"Comparative Ads Mulled," *Advertising Age International,* March 15, 1993, p. 16.

[61]"China's Rules Make a Hard Sell," *International Herald Tribune,* August 18, 2000, p. 13.

[62]John Mackay.

EXHIBIT 14-9
MALAYSIA'S ADVERTISING CODE OF ETHICS (*KOD ETHIKA PENGIKLANAN*)
—EXTRACTS

Rules and regulations:

- Advertisements must not project and promote an excessively aspirational lifestyle.
- Adaptation or projection of foreign culture which is not acceptable to a cross-section of the major communities of the Malaysian society either in the form of words, slogans, clothing, activity or behavior is not allowed.
- The use of man or woman as principal agent by highlighting characteristics which appeal to the opposite sex as the main ingredient in the selling of products should not be allowed.
- The body of the female model should be covered until the neckline, which should not be too low. The length of a skirt worn should be below the knees. Arms may be exposed up to the edge of the shoulder but armpits cannot be exposed. Costumes, although complying with the above, must not be too revealing or suggestive. Women in swimming costumes or shorts and men in swimming trunks or shorts will only be allowed in scenes involving organized sporting or outdoor activities provided that they are generally decently dressed on groups and only in long shots. A "long shot" is technically described as a shot with full frame.
- Scenes involving models (including silhouettes) undressing or acts which could bring undesirable thoughts will not be allowed.
- Strong emphasis on the speciality of the country of origin of an imported product is not allowed. Any reference should only state the name of the foreign country. Words should not be used to suggest superior quality or promise a greater benefit.
- All scenes of shots must be done in Malaysia. If foreign footage is deemed necessary, only 20% of the total commercial footage is allowed and prior approval from this Ministry must be obtained. However, foreign footage for advertisements on tourism to ASEAN* countries can be approved up to 100%.
- Musicals and other sounds must be done in Malaysia.
- Promos of foreign programs/events that are not telecast in this country are not allowed.
- All advertisements on food and drinks must show the necessity of a balanced diet.

Unacceptable products, services, and scenes:

- Liquor and alcoholic beverages.
- Blue denims—jeans made from other material can be advertised provided the jeans are clean and neat.
- Promotions of any contest, except in sponsored programs.
- Application of a product to certain parts of the body such as armpits.
- Clothes with imprinted words or symbols which could convey undesired messages or impressions.
- Scenes of amorous, intimate, or suggestive nature.
- Disco scenes.
- Feminine napkins.
- The use of the word 1 (one) either in numeric or in words.
- Kissing between adults.

Source: "The Malaysian Advertising Code of Ethics for TV and Radio," http://www.asianmarketresearch.com, accessed May 16, 2002.

up with water. The spots were aired during an Australian drought. The campaign was banned by the Advertising Standards Council for its "wanton and irresponsible waste of water."[63] Also in Australia, Toyota was forced to withdraw a series of spots advertising the Celica model because of their content. One of the spots was a "Jaws" spoof in which sharklike Celicas speed down a jetty. The ad violated the Advertising

---

[63]"Aussie Ad Probe Comes to a Boil over Dorf Ads," *Advertising Age International,* February 20, 1995, I-6.

Standards Council's guidelines on "dangerous behavior or illegal or unsafe road usage practices."[64]

In Vietnam, the Ministry of Trade, The Ministry of Culture and Information, the Customs Department, and any single TV station or newspaper can censor ads. Ho Chi Minh City authorities nixed a pan-Asian campaign that San Miguel, the Philippine beer brewer, planned to run in Vietnam. The campaign, showing a Western businessman who offered a San Miguel to an Asian colleague, used the slogan "San Miguel: A Sign of Friendship." The ad was banned because the local authorities claimed that beer couldn't be a sign of friendship.[65]

Ads may also be banned or taken off the air because they are offensive or indecent. For example, ads that show skin or revealing lingerie are banned from TV advertising in Singapore.[66] Many countries also have regulations against sexist advertising or ads with exaggerated ("puffery") claims.

Advertising Targeting Children. Another area that tends to be heavily regulated is advertising targeted to children. Some markets (e.g., Québec) simply prohibit TV stations from airing ads to children.[67] In Europe, rules to curb advertising to children are widespread. Greece bans all TV advertising of toys between 7 A.M. and 10 P.M.[68] In Finland, children cannot speak or sing the name of a product in commercials. In Turkey, children are allowed to watch TV ads only with "parental guidance." Italy bans commercials in cartoon programs that target children. China poses a series of rules that advertisers to children need to respect. Contrary to regulations in Western countries, most of the standards center around cultural values: respect for elders and discipline. For instance, one of the rules bans ads that "show acts that children should not be doing alone."[69]

Scores of other advertising regulations usually litter the marketing landscape. Some countries allow advertising only in the local language or commercials that were produced with local talent. A number of countries view advertising as an easy source to raise money; ad spending is taxed in Italy and Colombia, for example.

Although many ad regulations often sound annoying or frivolous, having a clear set of advertising rules and restrictions is a boon for consumers and advertisers alike. If there are no restrictions, the law of the jungle applies. In China, most of the advertising malpractice cases in the past involved ads for drugs, medical services, and food. It was not unusual to have some soaps claim to help people lose weight and some tonics promise to make users smarter.[70]

How should marketers cope with advertising regulations? The following are possible actions.

1. *Keep track of regulations and pending legislation.* Monitoring legislation and gathering intelligence on possible changes in advertising regulations are crucial. Remember that advertising regulations change continuously. In many countries, the prevailing mood favors liberalization with the important exception of tobacco and alcohol advertising. European Union member states are also trying to bring their rules in line with EU regulations. Many companies have in-house legal counsels to assist them in handling pending advertising legislation.

2. *Screen the campaign early.* Given the huge budgets at stake, it is important to get feedback and screen advertisements as early as possible to avoid costly mistakes. In China, TV commercials must be submitted to each regional office of the State

[64]"ASC Slams Brakes on Australian Toyota Ads," *Advertising Age International,* May 16, 1994, p. I-6.

[65]"Get My Censor Sensor," *Far Eastern Economic Review,* June 6, 1996, p. 61.

[66]"Sensitive Sensors," *Advertising Age International,* November 23, 1992, p. I-13.

[67]"Group Wants Children's Ads in Quebec," *Advertising Age International,* April 1996, p. I-10.

[68]"Kid Gloves," *Economist,* January 6, 2001, p. 53.

[69]Louisa Ha, "Concerns about Advertising Practices in a Developing Country: An Examination of China's New Advertising Regulations," *International Journal of Advertising,* 15 (1996), pp. 91–102.

[70]"China's Rules Make a Hard Sell."

Administration for Industry and Commerce prior to airing. To be on the safe side, many companies submit their storyboards and scripts before producing the commercial.

3. *Lobbying activities.* A more drastic action is to lobby local governments or international legislative bodies such as the European Parliament. Lobbying activities are usually sponsored jointly by advertisers, advertising agencies, and the media. As usual, too much lobbying carries the risk of generating bad publicity, especially when the issues at hand are highly controversial.

4. *Challenge regulations in court.* Advertisers can consider fighting advertising legislation in court. In Chile, outdoor board companies, advertisers, and sign painters filed suit in civil court when the Chilean government issued new regulations that required outdoor boards to be placed several blocks from the road.[71] In EU member states, advertisers have sometimes been able to overturn local laws by appealing to the European Commission or the European Court of Justice. For instance, a host of retailers (including Amazon.com), ad agencies, and media in France filed a complaint with the European Commission in an attempt to overturn a 40-year old French law that bans TV advertising by retailers. They argued that the law ran counter to EU rules.[72]

5. *Adapt marketing mix strategy.* Tobacco marketers have been extremely creative in handling advertising regulations. A widely popular mechanism is to use the brand extension path to cope with tobacco ad bans. For instance, the Swedish Tobacco Co., whose brands have captured more than 80 percent of the Swedish cigarette market, started promoting sunglasses and cigarette lighters under the Blend name, its best-selling cigarette brand, to cope with a complete tobacco ad ban in Sweden.[73] In the United Kingdom, Hamlet, the leading cigar brand, shifted to other media vehicles following the ban on all TV tobacco advertising in October 1992. Hamlet started using outdoor boards for the first time, installing them at 2,250 sites. It ran a sales promotion campaign at a horse race where losing bettors got a free Hamlet cigar. It also developed a videotape with about 20 of its celebrated commercials that was made available for purchase or rent.[74] South Korea is the only country where Virginia Slims is pitched as the successful man's cigarette. Why? Because Korean law forbids advertising cigarettes to women and young adults.[75]

◆◆◆◆◆◆◆◆ CHOICE OF AN ADVERTISING AGENCY

Although some companies (e.g., Benetton, Diesel, Avon, and Hugo Boss) develop their advertising campaigns in house, most firms heavily rely on the expertise of an advertising agency. In selecting an agency, the international marketer has several options:

1. Work with the agency that handles the advertising in the firm's home market.

2. Pick a purely local agency in the foreign market.

3. Choose the local office of a large international agency.

4. Select an international network of ad agencies that spans the globe or the region.

---

[71]"Chilean Fight for Outdoor Ads," *Advertising Age International,* April 27, 1992, p. I-8.

[72]"Retailers Fight French Law That Bans Advertising on TV," *Asian Wall Street Journal,* February 22, 2001, p. N7.

[73]"Swedish Marketers Skirt Tobacco Ad Ban," *Advertising Age International,* June 20, 1994, p. I-2.

[74]"Hamlet Shifts to Other Media Since TV Spots Are Banned," *Advertising Age International,* April 27, 1992, p. I-8.

[75]"Real Men May Not Eat Quiche . . . But in Korea They Puff Virginia Slims," *Asian Wall Street Journal,* December 27/28, 1996, pp. 1, 7.

When screening ad agencies, the following set of criteria can be used.

- *Market coverage.* Does the agency cover all relevant markets? What is its geographic scope?

- *Quality of coverage.* What are the agency's core skills? Does the level of these skills meet the standards set by the company? Is there a match between the agency's core skills and the market requirements? For instance, in Japan where media space is scarce, media-buying skills are far more critical than creative development.

- *Expertise with developing a central international campaign.* When the intent of the marketer is to develop a global or panregional advertising campaign, expertise in handling a central campaign becomes essential. One survey suggests, however, that the agency's lack of international expertise and coordination ability is still a problem for many companies.[76]

- *Creative reputation.* The agency's creative reputation is often the most important criterion for many advertisers when choosing an ad agency.

- *Scope and quality of support services.* Most agencies are not hired only for their creative skills and media buying. They are also expected to deliver a range of support services such as marketing research and developing other forms of communication (e.g., sales promotions, public relations, event sponsorships).

- *Desirable image ("global" versus "local").* The image—global or local—that the company wants to project through its communication efforts also matters a great deal. Companies that aspire to develop a "local" image often assign their account to local ad agencies. One risk of relying on local agencies, however, is that their creative spark may lead to off-message, provocative advertising. Coke's senior executives were not amused with an Italian campaign that featured nude bathers on the beach. A Singapore ad made for McDonald's to promote its new Szechuan burger featured a brothel-like "mama-san," not exactly in tune with McDonald's core family values.[77]

- *Size of the agency.* Generally speaking, large agencies have more power than small agencies. This is especially critical for media buying when a healthy relationship between the media outlet and the ad agency is very critical.

- *Conflicting accounts.* Does the agency already work on an account of one of the company's competitors? The risk of conflicting accounts is a major concern to many advertisers. There are two kinds of risks here. First is the confidentiality issue: Marketers share much proprietary data with their advertising agency. Second is the fear that the ad agency might assign superior creative talent to the competing brand's account.

Note that sometimes these criteria may conflict. A characteristic of the Japanese agency industry is that the large agencies service competing brands. Hence, companies that approach a large Japanese ad agency such as Dentsu or Hakuhodo may need to accept the fact that the agency also handles the accounts of competing brands.

Coordination of International Advertising   ◆ ◆ ◆ ◆ ◆ ◆ ◆ ◆

Global or panregional advertising approaches require a great deal of coordination across and communication among the various subsidiaries. In this section, we discuss a number of mechanisms that can be used to facilitate this process.

---

[76]"Clients and Agencies Split over Ad Superstars," *Ad Age Global,* May 2001, p. 16.
[77]"A Little Local Difficulty," *Ad Age Global,* (February 2002), p. 4.

Monetary Incentives (Cooperative Advertising)

Small companies often assign the advertising responsibility to their local distributors. In such a setup, the marketer could face two issues. First, relative advertising efforts may vary a great deal across different distributors. Second, the message that is conveyed in each of the different markets where the product is sold lacks consistency. To address these concerns, marketers often provide monetary incentives to their respective distributors to get some level of coordination. Most often, the incentive takes the form of cooperative advertising when the firm contributes to the local distributor's advertising spending activities.

Blistex, a U.S. maker of lip care products, set up a cooperative advertising system to implement a pan-European advertising campaign. One campaign objective was to get all distributors to advertise Blistex. The second priority was to use a common advertising theme across all European markets. To achieve these goals, Blistex set up an advertising fund from which each distributor could withdraw money up to a certain amount to fund its advertising activities.[78]

Advertising Manuals

The use of an **advertising manual (brand book)** or DVD to guide international advertising efforts is fairly common. Mercedes-Benz puts together a handbook that spells out its advertising guidelines for its European subsidiaries and sales agents. Likewise, Seiko, the Japanese watchmaker, guides its local affiliates and advertising agencies via an advertising manual.[79]

Lead-Country Concept

With this approach the initial campaign is prepared by the lead country's subsidiary. The details of the campaign are summarized in a "bundle" that is sent to the various subsidiaries.[80] Dupont's handling of its Lycra brand advertising is an interesting example.[81] The product is used in a wide variety of applications (e.g., swimsuits, running shorts). Its brand identity is communicated via the global tagline "Nothing moves like Lycra." However, each application also needs its own positioning. Responsibility for coming up with application-specific positioning themes is delegated to country managers in the country where the application is most prominent. For instance, the Brazilian country manager was in charge of swimsuit positioning as Brazil is the lead market for this particular use of Lycra.

Global or Pan Regional Meetings

Numerous multinationals rely on global or panregional meetings to coordinate their international advertising. These meetings can be very informal. To create a new communication campaign for the Latin-American region, Goodyear, the U.S. tire maker, set up an informal two-day working conference in Miami. Participants included the marketing executives from each country, regional senior executives, and several key creative staff people from Leo Burnett's Latin American offices, the ad agency in charge of the account.[82] The different steps behind the development of Goodyear's 1992 Latin American ad campaign are presented in Exhibit 14-10. Note that the entire process took about six months.

Robert Jordan offers six guidelines to implement a global or panregional advertising approach:

1. Top management must be dedicated to going global.

2. A third party (e.g., the ad agency) can help sell to key managers the benefits of a global advertising approach.

---

[78] Mark Boersma.

[79] Rijkens, *European Advertising Strategies.*

[80] Ibid.

[81] Aaker and Joachimsthaler, (see Footnotes) p. 143.

[82] D.A. Hanni, J.K. Ryans, Jr., and I.R. Vernon, "Coordinating International Advertising—The Goodyear Case Revisited for Latin America," *Journal of International Marketing,* 3 (2), 1995, pp. 83–98.

EXHIBIT 14-10

Other Forms of Communication • 463

FRAMEWORK FOR PANREGIONAL AD CAMPAIGN
DEVELOPMENT AT GOODYEAR

1. Preliminary Orientation

September 1992

Subsidiary strategic information input on business and
communications strategy on country-by-country basis.

Home Office Review

2. Regional Communications Strategy Definition

Strategy Definition Meeting

October 1992

Outputs: Regional positioning objective, communication
objectives, and creative assignment for advertising agency.

3. Advertising creative Review

Creative Review Meeting

November 12, 1992

Outputs: Six creative concepts (story boards). Research questions
regarding real consumer concerns to guide research.

4. Qualitative Research Store

Qualitative Research

November-December 1992

Consistent research results across five countries on purchase
intentions and consumer perceptions of safety.

5. Research Review

Research Review Meeting

January 15, 1993

Sharply defined "consumer proposition" identified and agreed
upon with new creative assignment for agency.

6. Final Creative Review

Final Creative Review Meeting

March 12, 1993

Campaign Adoption

7. Budget Approval—Home Office
8. Campaign Execution—Media Buys Local Countries

Source: D.A. Hanni, J.K. Ryans, Jr. and I.R. Vernon,
"Coordinating International Advertising—The Goodyear Case
Revisited for Latin America."

This article originally appeared in *Journal of International
Marketing,* 3(2), 1995, published by Michigan Sate University
Press.

3. A global brief based on cross-border consumer research can help persuade managers to think in terms of global consumers.

4. Find product champions and give them a charter for the success of the global marketing program.

5. Convince local staff that they have an opportunity in developing a global campaign.

6. To get local managers on the global marketing team, have them do the job themselves.[83]

OTHER FORMS OF COMMUNICATION ◆ ◆ ◆ ◆ ◆ ◆ ◆ ◆

For most companies, media advertising is only one part of the communication package. While advertising is the most visible form, other communication tools play a vital role in a company's global marketing mix strategy. In this section, we review four key

---

[83] R.O. Jordan, "Going Global: How to Join the Second Major Revolution in Marketing: Commentary," *Journal of Consumer Marketing,* 5(1), Winter 1988, pp. 39–44.

tools: sales promotions, sponsorships, direct marketing, and trade shows. Managing a salesforce, which can be regarded as both a promotion and a distribution tool, is discussed in Chapter 15.

Sales Promotions

Sales promotions refer to a collection of short-term incentive tools that lead to quicker and/or larger sales of a particular product by consumers or the trade.[84] There are basically two kinds of promotions: consumer promotions that target end users (e.g., coupons, sweepstakes, rebates) and trade promotions that are aimed at distributors (e.g., volume discounts, advertising allowances). For the majority of MNCs, the sales promotion policy is a local affair. Several rationales explain the local character of promotions:[85]

- *Economic development.* Low incomes and poor literacy in developing countries make some promotional techniques unattractive but, at the same time, render other tools more appealing.[86]

- *Market maturity.* Product categories have a great deal of variation in terms of market maturity. In countries where the product is still in an early stage of the product life cycle, trial-inducing tools such as samples, coupons, and cross-promotions are appropriate. In more established markets, one of the prime goals of promotions is to encourage repeat purchase. Incentives such as bonus packs, in-pack coupons, and trade promotions that stimulate brand loyalty tend to be favored.

- *Cultural perceptions.* Cultural perceptions of promotions differ widely across countries. Some types of promotions (e.g., sweepstakes) can have a negative image in certain countries. According to one study, Taiwanese consumers have less-favorable attitudes toward sweepstakes than consumers do in Thailand or Malaysia. Taiwanese are not concerned about losing face when using coupons. Malaysians, on the other hand, favor sweepstakes over coupons.[87] Shoppers in Europe redeem far fewer coupons than their counterparts in the United States.[88]

- *Trade structure.* One major issue that companies face is how to allocate their promotional dollars among consumer promotions, which are directly aimed at the end user ("pull"), and trade promotions which target the middlemen ("push"). Because of differences in the local trade structure, the balance of power between manufacturers and trade is tilted in favor of the trade in certain countries. When Procter & Gamble attempted to cut back on trade promotions by introducing every-day-low pricing in Germany, several major German retailers retaliated by delisting P&G brands.[89] Differences in distributors' inventory space and/or costs also play a role in determining which types of promotions are effective.

- *Government regulations.* When C&A, a Brussels-based clothing retailer, offered a 20 percent discount to German customers paying with a credit card instead of cash, it was threatened with huge fines by a German court.[90] C&A's scheme was apparently in violation of a 70-year-old German law regulating sales and special offers.[91] By the same token, Land's End, the U.S. mail order retailer, was forced to withdraw a lifetime guarantee offer in Germany. According to Germany's supreme court, the

---

[84] Philip Kotler, *Marketing Management* (Upper Saddle River, NJ: Prentice-Hall, 2000).

[85] K. Kashani and J.A. Quelch, "Can Sales Promotions Go Global?" *Business Horizons,* 33 (3), May–June 1990, pp. 37–43.

[86] J.S. Hill and U.O. Boya, "Consumer Goods Promotions in Developing Countries," *International Journal of Advertising,* 6 (1987), pp. 249–64.

[87] Lenard C. Huff and Dana L. Alden, "An Investigation of Consumer Response to Sales Promotions in Developing Markets: A Three-Country Analysis," *Journal of Advertising Research,* May–June 1998, pp. 47–56.

[88] "Coupon FSIs Dropped," *Advertising Age International,* October 11, 1993, p. I-8.

[89] "Heat's on Value Pricing," *Advertising Age International,* January 1997, pp. I-21, I-22.

[90] The purpose of this somewhat unusual promotion was to cut cash register lines during the euro introduction period.

[91] "Defiant C&A Reignites Debate on German Shopping Laws," *Financial Times,* January 9, 2002, p. 2.

EXHIBIT 14-11

WHICH TECHNIQUES ARE ALLOWED IN EUROPE

Key: Y = permitted X = not permitted ? = may be permitted

Promotion Technique	UK	NL	B	SP	IR	IT	F	G	DK
On-pack promotions	Y	Y	?	Y	Y	Y	?	Y	Y
Banded offers	Y	?	?	Y	Y	Y	?	Y	Y
In-pack premiums	Y	?	?	Y	Y	Y	?	Y	?
Multipurchase offers	Y	?	?	Y	Y	Y	?	Y	Y
Extra product	Y	Y	Y	Y	Y	Y	?	?	Y
Free product	Y	?	Y	Y	Y	Y	Y	X	?
Reusable/other use packs	Y	Y	Y	Y	Y	Y	Y	Y	Y
Free mail-ins	Y	Y	?	Y	Y	Y	?	Y	Y
With purchase premiums	Y	?	Y	Y	Y	Y	?	?	?
Cross-product offers	Y	Y	X	Y	Y	Y	?	Y	Y
Collector devices	Y	Y	Y	Y	Y	Y	Y	Y	Y
Competitions	Y	?	?	Y	Y	?	Y	Y	?
Self-liquidating premiums	Y	Y	Y	Y	Y	Y	Y	Y	Y
Free draws	Y	X	?	Y	Y	Y	Y	Y	Y
Share outs	Y	Y	?	Y	Y	?	?	Y	?
Sweepstake/lottery	?	X	?	Y	X	?	?	Y	X
Money off vouchers	Y	Y	Y	Y	Y	Y	Y	?	Y
Money off next purchase	Y	Y	Y	Y	Y	Y	Y	?	Y
Cash backs	Y	Y	Y	Y	Y	X	Y	X	Y
In-store demos	Y	Y	Y	Y	Y	Y	Y	Y	Y

Source: The Institute of Sales Promotion, www.isp.org.uk 2006.

offer violated the 1932 German Free Gift Act and was anticompetitive.[92] Probably the most critical factor in designing a promotional package is local law. Certain practices can be severely restricted or simply forbidden. In Germany, for instance, coupon values cannot be more than 1 percent of the product's value. Norway bans vouchers, stamps, and coupons.[93] See Exhibit 14-11 for promotion techniques that are allowed in nine European countries. Germany appears to be one of the most restrictive environments for promotion campaigns. The United Kingdom, on the other hand, seems to be very liberal.

Kashani and Quelch suggest that multinational companies appoint an international sales promotion coordinator. The manager's agenda would involve tasks such as these:

- Promote the transfer of successful promotional ideas across units.
- Transplant ideas on how to constrain harmful trade promotional practices.
- Gather performance data and develop monitoring systems to evaluate the efficiency and effectiveness of promotions.
- Coordinate relations with the company's sales promotion agencies worldwide.[94]

Direct Marketing

Direct marketing includes various forms of interactive marketing that enables the company to obtain direct access to the end consumer and establish a one-to-one relationship. The most prominent forms of direct marketing are direct mail, telemarketing, and door-to-door, Internet, and catalog selling. In a sense, direct marketing is both a

---

[92]"Lands' End to File Brussels Complaint," *Financial Times*, January 11, 2000, p. 2.

[93]"Coupon FSIs Dropped."

[94]Kashani and Quelch, "Can Sales Promotions Go Global?"

promotional tool and a distribution tool. For companies such as Avon, Amazon.com, Dell, E-Trade, and Amway, direct marketing goes even beyond just being a marketing mix instrument: It is basically a business model.

Direct marketing is growing rapidly internationally. Many celebrated firms have been able to successfully transplant their direct marketing model to other markets. About one year after Dell entered China, it was able to become one of the leading PC brands there despite skepticism that its practice of direct selling would not work in a country where sales ability centers around connections.[95]

Some firms have been able to successfully implement global direct marketing campaigns although it is still rare. A good illustration was a campaign run by Unisys, a U.S.-based information technology company. Its "Customer Connection" program was a million-dollar-plus, multilingual program that combined direct mail and telemarketing worldwide. Every quarter, Unisys sent out direct mail to key decision makers in 23 countries. The mailing described product and technology offerings in seven languages and came with a personalized letter signed by a Unisys region or country manager. Native-speaking telemarketers then followed up to ask if the client manager recalled the mailing, had any queries, and would like to remain on the mailing list. Follow-up surveys showed that 70 percent of the contacted executives responded positively to the program.[96]

As with other promotion tools, direct marketing can also encounter hurdles in foreign markets. A notorious case was the Chinese government's complete ban on direct selling in the spring of 1998.[97] Well-established selling companies such as Avon, Amway, and Mary Kay basically had to shut down their operations. As a result, these companies had to rethink their way of doing business in China. Avon struck a deal with Watson's, a Hong Kong-based drugstore chain, to set up small counters in its stores.[98]

Event Sponsorships

Sponsorship is one of the fastest growing promotion tools. Worldwide, companies spent around $30 billion on sponsorships in 2004.[99] Given the global appeal of sports, more and more MNCs are using sports sponsorships as their weapon of choice in their global battle for market share. Adidas, the German sportswear maker, paid a hefty $80 million to $100 million in cash and services for sponsorship of the Beijing Summer Olympics. As part of the deal, Adidas will outfit Chinese athletes at the medal ceremonies even if the athletes compete in garb from other companies. Other multinationals that are shelling out huge sponsorship money include Volkswagen and Johnson & Johnson. These companies see the Olympics as key to shore up their competitive position in China.[100] Sponsorship also stretches to other types of events, such as concert tours, charity, and art exhibitions.

Ideally, the sponsored event should reinforce the brand image that the company is trying to promote. Red Bull, one of the dominant energy drink brands, is a case in point. From its very launch, Red Bull has promoted a daring macho image by sponsoring extreme sports events ranging from wind surfing to hang gliding.[101] In 2004, Red Bull acquired the Jaguar Formula One racing team. With this sponsorship Red Bull is able to reinforce its image as the brew that gives "Wings to Body and Mind." Formula One can also help the company get more visibility in the United States, the Middle East, and Central America, where it is less established.[102]

---

[95] "Chasing the China Market," *Asiaweek,* June 11, 1999, p. 46.

[96] "Unisys Cuts Clear Path to int'l Recovery," *Marketing News,* September 27, 1999, pp. 4–6.

[97] The direct marketing ban was lifted in 2005.

[98] "Avon Scrambles to Reinvent Itself in China after Beijing's Ban on Direct Selling," *Far Eastern Economic Review,* October 22, 1998, pp. 64–66.

[99] http://www.brandweek.com/bw/research/article_display.jsp?vnu_content_id=1001010356. Jan 3, 2006.

[100] http://www2.chinadaily.com.cn/english/doc/2006-01/28/content_516253.htm.

[101] "Extreme Sports and Clubbers Fuel Energetic Rise," *Financial Times,* November 23, 2001, p. 10.

[102] "Red Bull Charges into Ailing Jaguar," *Financial Times,* April 22, 2004, p. 16.

Event sponsorship carries three major risks. First, the organizers of the event could sell too many sponsorships, leading to clutter. Second, the event may be plagued by controversy or scandal. Following the 1998 drug-plagued Tour de France, Coca-Cola drastically scaled down its sponsorship activities for that cycling event.[103] The third risk is known as *ambush marketing* by which a company seeks to associate with an event (e.g., the Olympics) without any payments to the event organizer. The culprit thus steals the limelight from its competitor who sponsors the event. By associating with the event, the ambushing company misleads the public by creating the impression that it is a legitimate sponsor. Although Coca-Cola was the official sponsor of the 2002 World Cup Soccer, Pepsi managed to sign up some of the biggest soccer celebrities, including England's David Beckham. Likewise, Nike was Brazil's sponsor even though Adidas was the official tournament sponsor. In fact, research done after the 1998 World Cup Soccer found that Nike had better recall among TV viewers than Adidas, the official sponsor.[104] Apart from these risks, there is the issue of response measurement. In general, measuring the effectiveness of a particular sponsorship activity is extremely hard. Some firms have come up with very creative procedures to do just that. In Asia, Reebok[105] tested a campaign on Star TV's Channel V music channel in which the veejays wear Reebok shoes. To gauge the impact of the campaign, TV viewers were directed to Reebok's Web site on the Internet. At the site, the viewer was able to download a coupon that could be used for the next shoe purchase.[106]

Trade Shows

Trade shows (trade fairs) are vital parts of the communication package for many international business-to-business marketers. There were more than 16,000 trade shows outside North America in 1999. Trade shows have a direct sales effect—the sales coming from visitors to the trade show booth—and indirect impacts on the exhibitor's sales.[107] Indirect sales effects stem from the fact that visitors become more aware of and interested in the participating company's products. Trade fairs are often promoted in trade journals and by government agencies such as the U.S. Department of Commerce, which provides detailed information on international trade fairs.

There are some notable differences between overseas trade shows and North American ones.[108] Foreign fairs are usually much larger than the more regional, niche-oriented shows in the United States, and, therefore, international shows attract a much wider variety of buyers. Hospitality is another notable difference between trade show affairs in the United States and in foreign markets. For instance, even the smallest booths at German shows offer visitors a chair and a glass of orange juice. Larger booths have kitchens and serve full meals. Empty booths have a coffee table and water cooler. In the United States, trade show events tend to be pure business.

When attending an international trade show, the following guidelines could be useful:

- Decide on what trade shows to attend at least a year in advance. Prepare translations of product materials, price lists, and selling aids.

- Bring plenty of literature. Bring someone who knows the language or provide a translator.

- Send out, ahead of time, direct mail pieces to potential attendees.

- Find out the best possible space, for instance, in terms of traffic.

---

[103]"Sponsors Rethink the Tour," *Ad Age Global,* March 2001, p. 48.

[104]"Sponsors' Asian Gamble," *Ad Age Global,* March 2002, pp. 24–25.

[105]Reebok was acquired by Adidas in 2005.

[106]"Reebok Sets Strategy to Get Sales on Track in Fast-Growing Asia," *Asian Wall Street Journal,* May 31–June 1, 1996, p. 12.

[107]S. Gopalakrishna, G.L. Lilien, J.D. Williams, and I.K. Sequeira, "Do Trade Shows Pay Off?" *Journal of Marketing,* 59 (July 1995), pp. 75–83.

[108]"Trading Plätze," *Marketing News,* July 19, 1999, p. 11.

- Plan the best way to display your products and to tell your story.[109]
- Do your homework on potential buyers from other countries.[110]
- Assess the impact of trade show participation on the company's bottom line.[111] Performance benchmarks may need to be adjusted when evaluating trade show effectiveness in different countries since attendees might behave differently.[112]

On-line information resources on trade show events are plentiful (e.g., www.tsnn .com and www.fita.org/tshows.html). A recent phenomenon is the emergence of virtual trade shows, which allow buyers to walk a "show floor," view products, and request information without physically being there.[113] Unisfair is one company that hosts online expos. Its Web site also offers several showcases of such events (see

* *

*G*LOBAL PERSPECTIVE 14-4

SIEMENS EXIDER—A TRADE SHOW ON WHEELS: "SIEMENS IS REALLY COOL!"

Siemens AG is a German conglomerate founded more than 150 years ago. The company sells primarily to other businesses. Like many other firms, the company tried the entire range of traditional advertising campaigns and promotional techniques but had limited success. Especially in North America, Siemens has always had to face an uphill task of fighting low brand awareness. So, what to do? In March 2002, Siemens announced a mobile trade show on rails using a train, Exider, 1,000 feet (300 meters) long with 14 railroad cars. The activity had elements of a multimedia blitz and a traditional trade show. Some cars held Siemens products; others were fitted with video monitors or interactive screens showcasing Siemens products at work. Each wagon was staffed with Siemens experts on hand to explain the technology. The head of the Siemens division behind the project explained, "With the Exider, we want to take our show out to the customers and join them on a trip

through the world of modern industrial automation, drive, switching and installation technology."

The train journey started in Spain. Siemens' market share rose 3 percentage points after Exider passed through. Other destinations included Britain, China, Singapore, and ultimately the United States. Invitations to visit the train went out to anyone Siemens deemed to be a potential customer. Siemens hoped that people taking the tour would ask questions, pick up brochures, attend technical seminars, and exchange business cards with a Siemens salesperson. For Siemens, the train was a vehicle to bring its technology close to customers, even those in remote areas. A vice president of Polo Ralph Lauren visited the train "to see what other things I might buy from them." Customers on the train were overheard saying that they had never realized that Siemens had such a broad portfolio of solutions in so many industry segments. Some customers looking at a display in one of the coaches said, "Oh? This is really cool!" Stephen Greyser, a Harvard Business School professor, said, "Anyone who steps inside that train becomes a willing collaborator in the process of learning more about what Siemens is and does." Likewise, Michael Watras, a brand consultant, noted, "It's out-of-the-box thinking that positions the brand as cutting-edge."

Sources: "Siemens Makes Tracks toward Higher Profile," *International Herald Tribune,* (March 27–28, 2004), p. 11; http://www2 .automation.siemens.com/mes/simatic_it/html_76/download/adbv20- 0203215e.pdf; and http://www.frost.com/prod/servlet/market-in- sight-top.pag?docid=19829104&ctxixpLink=FcmCtx3&ctxixpLabel= FcmCtx4. March 15, 2002.

---

[109]B. O'Hara, F. Palumbo, and P. Herbig, "Industrial Trade Shows Abroad," *Industrial Marketing Management,* 22 (1993), pp. 233–37.

[110]"Trading Plätze."

[111]See S. Gopalakrishna and G.L. Lilien, "A Three-Stage Model of Industrial Trade Show Performance," *Marketing Science,* 14 (1), Winter 1995, pp. 22–42 for a formal mathematical model to assess trade show effectiveness.

[112]Marnik G. Dekimpe, Pierre François, Srinath Gopalakrishna, Gary L. Lilien, and Christophe Van den Bulte, "Generalizing about Trade Show Effectiveness: A Cross-National Comparison," *Journal of Marketing,* 61 (October 1997), pp. 55–64.

[113]"All Trade Shows, All the Time," *Marketing News,* July 19, 1999, p. 11.

http://www.unisfair.com/Showcase.asp). See Global Perspective 14-4 discusses a non-traditional approach that Siemens took to promote its products through a mobile trade show.

GLOBALLY INTEGRATED MARKETING COMMUNICATIONS (GIMC)

◆ ◆ ◆ ◆ ◆ ◆ ◆ ◆

In a recent pan-European campaign to promote Sony Ericsson's new T300 mobile phone, hundreds of drooling dogs were walked several times a day during a six-week period in major European cities.[114] The dogs, as well as their walkers, were wearing specially designed branded clothing. The walking activity was part of an integrated campaign centering around the "drooling" theme. Other elements included TV, the Web (www.drool-uk.com), posters, viral e-mail, radio, and sponsorships. According to one of Sony Ericsson's European marketing managers: "The drool campaign is about creating lust for THE BAR (the handset's nickname).... The entire drool campaign has a real edge to it—something that the target audience (16- to 24-year-olds) all over Europe will relate to."

For most companies, media advertising is only one element of their global communications efforts. As we saw in the previous section, marketers use many other tools. In recent years, advertising agencies and their clients have recognized the value of an **integrated marketing communications (IMC)** program—not just for domestic markets but globally. The "drool" campaign is just one example of the push toward IMC. The goal of IMC is to coordinate the different communication vehicles—mass advertising, sponsorships, sales promotions, packaging, point-of-purchase displays, and so forth—to convey one and the same idea to prospective customers with a unified voice.[115] Instead of having the different promotional mix elements send out a mish-mash of messages with a variety of visual imagery, each and every one of them centers around that single key idea. By having consistency, integration, and cohesiveness, marketers will be able to maximize the impact of your communication tools.

A five-nation survey of ad agencies found that the use of IMC varies a lot. The percentage of client budgets devoted to IMC activities was low in India (15 percent) and Australia (22 percent). The percentage was far higher in New Zealand (40 percent) and the United Kingdom (42 percent).[116] A **globally integrated marketing communications (GIMC)** program goes one step further. GIMC is a system of active promotional management that strategically coordinates global communications in all of its component parts both horizontally (country-level) and vertically (promotion tools).[117]

To run a GIMC program effectively places demands on both the advertiser's organization and the advertising agencies involved. Companies that want to pursue a GIMC for some or all of their brands should have the mechanisms in place to coordinate their promotional activities vertically (across tools) and horizontally (across countries). By the same token, ad agencies should be willing to integrate and coordinate the various communication disciplines across countries. GIMC also requires frequent communication both internally and between ad agency branches worldwide.[118]

---

[114]"Packs of Dogs Provide 'Ad Space' for Euro Launch of Sony T300 Handset," http://www.adageglobal.com, accessed December 16, 2002.

[115]"Integrated Marketing Communications: Maybe Definition Is in the Point of View," *Marketing News,* January 18, 1993.

[116]Philip J. Kitchen and Don E. Schultz, "A Multi-Country Comparison of the Drive for IMC," *Journal of Advertising Research,* January–February 1999, pp. 21–38.

[117]Andreas F. Grein and Stephen J. Gould, "Globally Integrated Marketing Communications," *Journal of Marketing Communications,* 2 (3), 1996, pp. 141–58.

[118]Stephen J. Gould, Dawn B. Lerman, and Andreas F. Grein, "Agency Perceptions and Practices on Global IMC," *Journal of Advertising Research,* January–February 1999, pp. 7–20.

SUMMARY ◆

Global advertising is for many marketers one of the most daunting challenges they face. A multitude of decisions need to be carried out on the front of international advertising. This chapter gave you an overview of the major decisions: creating advertising campaigns, setting and allocating the budget, selecting media vehicles to carry the campaign, choosing advertising agencies, and coordinating cross-country advertising programs. The development of a global advertising plan involves many players—headquarters, regional and/or local offices, advertising agencies—which typically makes the entire process frustrating. However, the potential rewards—in the form of increased market share and an improved profit picture—of a brilliant and well-executed international advertising strategy are tantalizing.

One of the front-burner issues that scores of international advertisers face is to what degree they should push for pan-regional or even global advertising campaigns. The arguments for standardizing campaigns are pretty compelling: (1) cost savings, (2) a coherent brand image, (3) similarity of target groups, and (4) transplanting of creative ideas. By now, you should also be quite familiar with the counterarguments:

(1) cultural barriers, (2) countries being at different stages of market development, (3) role of advertising regulations, and (4) variations in the media environment. Most global marketers balance between the two extremes by adopting a compromise solution. [119]

Overall, there seems to be a definite move toward more pan-regional (or even globalized) campaigns. Numerous explanations have been put forward to explain this shift: the "global" village rationale, the mushrooming of global and pan-regional media vehicles, restructuring of marketing divisions and brand systems along global or pan-regional lines. Another important development is the emergence of new media outlets, including the Internet. Although it is hard to gaze into a crystal ball and come up with concrete predictions, it is clear that international advertisers will face a drastically different environment 10 years from now.

_____

[119]Ali Kanso and Richard Alan Nelson, "Advertising Localization Overshadows Standardization," *Journal of Advertising Research,* (January–February 2002), pp. 79–80.

KEY TERMS ◆

Advertising manual (brand book)
Bottom-up advertising
Competitive parity
Export advertising
Globally integrated marketing
    communications (GIMC)

Integrated Marketing Communication
    (IMC)
Modular approach
Objective-and-task method
Pattern standardization
Percentage of sales

Prototype standardization
Percentage of sales
Top-down advertising

REVIEW QUESTIONS ◆

1. Most luxury products appeal to global segments. Does that mean that global advertising campaigns are most appropriate for such products?

2. Discuss the major challenges that international advertisers face.

3. Describe the steps that international advertisers should consider to cope with advertising regulations in their foreign markets.

4. What factors entice international advertisers to localize their advertising campaigns in foreign markets?

5. What are the major reasons for standardizing an international advertising program?

6. What will be the impact of satellite TV on international advertising?

7. What do you see as the major drawbacks of the Internet as a communication tool from the perspective of an international advertiser?

8. What mechanisms should MNCs contemplate to coordinate their advertising efforts across different countries?

DISCUSSION QUESTIONS ◆ ◆ ◆ ◆ ◆ ◆ ◆ ◆ ◆ ◆ ◆ ◆ ◆ ◆ ◆ ◆ ◆ ◆

1. Poland recently imposed a ban on advertising alcoholic drinks. How do you think brewers such as United Distillers and Seagram should adjust their marketing mix strategy to cope with this ban?

2. One of the hottest topics in advertising is whether it is ethical to advertise to children. On side of the debate are the moralists who claim that children up to the age of 10

cannot distinguish advertising from programming. By this logic, the state should intervene and protect children from advertising. Some researchers disagree, however. One British study showed that the idea that children under the age of 12 fail to understand the purpose of advertising is just plain wrong. Lego, the Danish toy group, favors industry self-regulation. The company claims that Lego's toys are designed to educate and entertain. Advertising allows the firm to explain the virtues of its toys. Some people argue that advertising bans and regulations are often matters of vested interests dressed up as moral causes. Sweden's restrictions on toy advertising could explain why Swedish toys are at least 30 percent more expensive than elsewhere in Europe. Likewise, some claim that the real purpose of Greece's ban on TV toy advertising was to protect the local toy industry from cheap Asian imports that have to advertise their way into the marketplace. What is your viewpoint in this debate? Is self-regulation the ultimate solution here as Lego claims?

3. The allocation of promotional dollars between "pull" (consumer promotions + media advertising) and "push" (trade promotions targeting distributors) varies drastically for many advertisers across countries. What are the factors behind these variations?

4. In emerging markets such as India, consumers shop far more frequently than in most Western countries, often on a daily basis. As a result, consumers there have many more chances to switch brands. What does this buying behavior imply in terms of the communication approaches that a foreign firm such as Unilever or Colgate uses to foster repeat purchase and brand loyalty?

5. For a particular brand, select at least three different print ads from different countries that came out during the same period. What do the ads have in common? How do they differ? Speculate about the reasons for the commonalities and differences.

◆◆◆◆◆◆◆◆ **SHORT CASES**

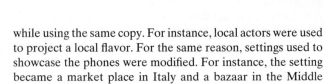

CASE 14-1

NOKIA: 1,001 REASONS TO GO GLOBAL?

In the fall of 2004, Nokia, the world's largest mobile phone maker, rolled out its first truly global corporate advertising campaign on television, in print, and on line with the slogan "1,001 reasons to have a Nokia imaging phone." The purpose of the campaign was to create a stronger, more consistent brand identity. It was a landmark for Nokia, which in the past had created different images and messages for its different markets.

The ad agency Grey Worldwide created the ads for Europe, the Middle East, and Africa. Bates Advertising in Singapore, part of the WPP Group, was responsible for the Asia-Pacific area. The two agencies collaborated to come up with one single campaign.

The ad does not actually spell out 1,001 reasons for having a Nokia imaging phone; it just says that there are that many. Some of the ads and commercials use the face of a cherubic baby to suggest using a Nokia phone to store favorite pictures. Nokia localized some aspects in the execution of the campaign

Source: "Advertising: One World, One Message: Nokia Goes Global with Ads," *Asian Wall Street Journal,* September 27, 2004, p. A6; and http://www.nokia.be/UK/Phones/Imaging/downloads.html.

while using the same copy. For instance, local actors were used to project a local flavor. For the same reason, settings used to showcase the phones were modified. For instance, the setting became a market place in Italy and a bazaar in the Middle East.

Nokia argues that the case for a global ad campaign is strong these days. Because most countries now use the same mobile phone technology (GSM), new products can now be rolled out globally simultaneously.

DISCUSSION QUESTIONS

1. What are the benefits of a global advertising campaign such as the Nokia 1,001 reasons described in the case?

2. What are the risks of such a campaign? Do you think Nokia is on the right track?

3. How do you assess the campaign (message strategy, slogan, visuals)? Overall, do you judge Nokia's approach to have been successful or a failure?

4. Do you believe global advertising campaigns will become more prominent in the future? For which products or services?

CASE 14-2

P&G CHINA—A LEGAL CLOUD OVER SK-II

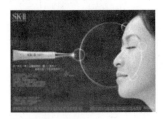

SK-II is a ultra-premium skincare range that originated from Procter & Gamble's Japan division. According to P&G's product literature, the SK-II product combines the magic of nature with the advances of science. A Japanese monk visiting a sake brewery noticed that brewery workers had very soft and youthful hands. Even an elderly wrinkled man had the silky

Source: http://www.sk2.co.uk/our_legend1.htm; "P&G Accepts Fine For 'Bogus' Advertising, *China Daily,* April 11, 2005; "Famous Brands Lose Face," www.en.ce.cn, accessed October 7, 2005; and "P&G Acts Fast to Calm Legal Cloud over SK-II," *Media,* April 8, 2005.

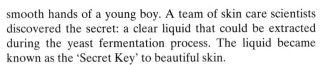

smooth hands of a young boy. A team of skin care scientists discovered the secret: a clear liquid that could be extracted during the yeast fermentation process. The liquid became known as the 'Secret Key' to beautiful skin.

De-Wrinkle Active, the latest launch in China from P&G's SK-II skin care line, attracted unwelcome publicity in early March 2005 when Lu Ping, a woman from Jiangxi province, filed a lawsuit against P&G, China's biggest advertiser, the company that distributed it, and even Carina Lau, the celebrity who endorsed SK-II in P&G's advertising. The plaintiff said she had spent Rmb. 840 (US$100) on a 25-gram bottle of SKII antiaging De-Wrinkle Essence in the hope that "the concentrated treatment would work to help iron out 47 percent of deep lines and wrinkles after 28 consecutive days of usage," as the product's promotional materials had promised.

Unfortunately for Mrs. Lu, the "miracle cure" failed to removed her wrinkles. Instead, it triggered an allergic reaction that left her in pain. Lu alleged that she was misled by the brand's advertising. A local industrial watchdog group claimed

that P&G's statistics for SK-II's claims came from a lab experiment on 300 Japanese women and lacked authoritative proof. After a 20-day investigation into SK-II. The Nanchang Commercial and Industrial Bureau fined P&G with a penalty of Rmb. 200,000 (US$24,000) for making false advertising claims.

Initially, P&G considered Lu's case a spiteful act to draw media attention. It insisted that all of its cosmetic products had undergone stringent tests and were well received in Japan and the United States. On March 25, the firm softened its tone and admitted that its advertising had been misleading. In April, P&G paid the fine and apologized to consumers. Lu, on the other hand, lost her case because of insufficient evidence. She said she would appeal the verdict. Sales of SK-II brand slipped by nearly 30 percent. P&G planned to launch a new SK-II campaign in September 2005.

The SK-II case underlines an emerging trend in China, consumer activism, which has become a major force in Chinese society today.

DISCUSSION QUESTIONS

1. What lessons does P&G's mishap with SK-II in China have for advertisers in China?

2. Did P&G handle the SK-II case correctly? What would you recommend to P&G China in marketing its SK-II product line?

FURTHER READING ◆◆◆◆◆◆◆◆◆◆◆◆◆◆◆◆◆◆◆◆◆◆◆◆◆◆

Al-Makaty, Safran S., G. Norman van Tubergen, S. Scott Whitlow, and Douglas A. Boyd. "Attitudes toward Advertising in Islam." *Journal of Advertising Research,* May/June 1996, pp. 16–26.

Davison, Andrew, and Erik Grab. "The Contributions of Advertising Testing to the Development of Effective International Advertising: The KitKat Case Study." *Marketing and Research Today,* February 1993, pp. 15–24.

De Mooij, Marieke. *Advertising Worldwide,* 2nd ed., (Englewood Cliffs, NJ: Prentice-Hall, 1994).

Domzal, Teresa J., and Jerome B. Kernan. "Mirror, Mirror: Some Postmodern Reflections on Global Advertising." *Journal of Advertising,* 22, (4), December 1993, pp. 1–20.

Duncan, Tom, and Jyotika Ramaprasad. "Standardizing Multinational Advertising: The Influencing Factors." *Journal of Advertising,* 24 (3), Fall 1995, pp. 55–68.

Hanni, D.A., J.K. Ryans, Jr., and I.R. Vernon. "Coordinating International Advertising—The Goodyear Case Revisited for Latin America." *Journal of International Marketing,* 3 (2), 1995, pp. 83–98.

Harvey, M.G. "Point of View: A Model to Determine Standardization of the Advertising Process in International Markets." *Journal of Advertising Research,* July/August 1993, pp. 57–64.

Hill, John S., and Unal O. Boya. "Consumer Goods Promotions in Developing Countries." *International Journal of Advertising,* 6 (1987), pp. 249–64.

James, W.L., and J.S. Hill. "International Advertising Messages: To Adapt or not to Adapt (That Is the Question)". *Journal of Advertising Research,* June/July 1991, pp. 65–71.

Johansson, Johny K. "The Sense of "Nonsense: Japanese TV Advertising." *Journal of Advertising,* 23 (1), March 1994, pp. 17–26.

Kashani, Kamran, and John A. Quelch. "Can Sales Promotions Go Global?" *Business Horizons,* 33 (3), May–June 1990, pp. 37–43.

Kaynak, Erderer. *The Management of International Advertising.* New York: Quorum Books, 1989.

Laroche, Michel, V.H. Kirpalani, Frank Pons, and Lianxi Zhou. "A Model of Advertising Standardization in Multinational Corporations," *Journal of International Business Studies,* 32 (2), Second Quarter 2001, pp. 249–66.

McCullough, Wayne R. "Global Advertising Which Acts Locally: The IBM Subtitles Campaign." *Journal of Advertising Research,* May/June 1996, pp. 11–15.

Maynard, Michael L., and Charles R. Taylor. "A Comparative Analysis of Japanese and U.S. Attitudes toward Direct Marketing." *Journal of Direct Marketing,* 10 (Winter 1996), pp. 34–44.

Mehta, Raj, Rajdeep Grewal, and Eugene Sivadas. "International Direct Marketing on the Internet: Do Internet Users Form a Global Segment?" *Journal of Direct Marketing,* 10 (Winter 1996), pp. 45–58.

O'Hara, B., F. Palumbo, and P. Herbig. "Industrial trade shows abroad." *Industrial Marketing Management,* 22 (1993), pp. 233–37.

Quelch, John A., and Lisa R. Klein. "The Internet and International Marketing." *Sloan Management Review,* Spring 1996, pp. 60–75.

Rijkens, Rein. *European Advertising Strategies.* London: Cassell, 1992.

SALES MANAGEMENT

15

HAPTER OVERVIEW

1. MARKET ENTRY OPTIONS AND SALESFORCE STRATEGY

2. CULTURAL CONSIDERATIONS

3. CULTURAL GENERALIZATION

4. IMPACT OF CULTURE ON SALES MANAGEMENT AND PERSONAL SELLING PROCESS

5. CROSS-CULTURAL NEGOTIATIONS

6. EXPATRIATES

Think of two major markets in Asia, Japan and China. Japan is a well-established developed country similar to the United States. One might assume that foreign firms can sell products there pretty much the same way as they do in the United States. Such an assumption may prove to be very wrong! For example, U.S. automakers still have great difficulty making inroads into the Japanese market, although Japan does not impose any tariffs or quotas on foreign cars and although BMW, Mercedes-Benz, and Volkswagen have become familiar names in Japan. One major, yet little known, reason is in the way cars are sold in Japan. Unlike the United States where customers visit car dealers, a majority of cars are sold by door-to-door salespeople in Japan, much the same way Avon representatives sell personal care and beauty products. Now the situation is gradually changing, however, and Japanese dealers are diversifying. They are investing more money in significantly larger U.S.-style dealership operations and less in door-to-door sales and small one-car showrooms. The reason for this shift in sales strategies is that Japanese consumers increasingly dislike at-home sales call, especially women, who today play a major role in new car purchasing decisions. However, traditional door-to-door sales remain effective and will not disappear any time soon.[1]

---

[1] Alexandra Harney, "Death of the Salesman Spells Boost for Japan," *Financial Times,* January 5, 1999, p. 6; and Masataka Morita and Kiyohiko G. Nishimura, "Information Technology and Automobile Distribution: A Comparative Study of Japan and the United States," a working paper (University of Tokyo, August 25, 2000).

China, on the other hand, is an emerging economic and political giant. Foreign and local companies are fighting an increasingly fierce battle for a slice of the potentially lucrative Chinese market with its 1.3 billion potential consumers. However, it is not easy for foreign enterprises to establish a presence in the unfamiliar, rapidly changing market, where old and new social systems coexist. The truth is that selling products is far more difficult in China than manufacturing them there. Business morals and practices have yet to develop sufficiently in the distribution sector. It is quite common for sales agents to channel products into the black market or for manufacturers' salespeople to discount prices for agents in exchange for secret rebates. Faced with China's labyrinthine sales channels, which even local manufacturers find difficult to manage, foreign businesses are often at a loss as to how to maneuver in them. In such a market, the local salesforce is crucial in penetrating the market. (See Global Perspective 15-1.) All these examples vividly illustrate the importance of international sales management.

We can think of many different types of salespeople from entry-level laborers who stand behind the counter at an ice cream store to industrial experts who work entirely within the offices of a corporate client. Some salespeople sell products, and others sell services. Some are focused on the immediate sale; some take overall responsibility for all aspects of a customer's business literally on a global basis. Salespeople take orders, deliver products, educate buyers, build relationships with clients, and provide technical knowledge.

In all cases, the salesperson is the front line for the company. The customer sees only the salesperson and the product. Through the salesperson, the customer develops an opinion of the company, and the success or failure of the company rests largely on the ability of the salesforce. We cannot overstate the importance of making good decisions when those decisions affect the quality and ability of the company's salesforce. This chapter investigates how the processes of sales management and personal selling are changed when taken overseas into another culture.

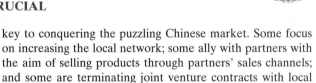

 **LOBAL PERSPECTIVE 15-1**

FOREIGN BUSINESS IN CHINA: SALESFORCE IS CRUCIAL

The world's top soy sauce producer, Kikkoman Corp. of Japan, opened a plant in Kunshan, Jiangsu Province, near Shanghai in May 2002 to produce high-end soy sauce. The leader of the company places high hopes on the Chinese operation because potential consumers of soy sauce in China, albeit a mere 1 percent of the country's population, total as many as 13 million, equal to the population of Tokyo. The company, which makes and sells soy sauce in the United States and Europe, does not engage in marketing in China, leaving sales activities to a local joint venture with Ton Yi Industrial Corp., Taiwan's leading food processor, which has significant experience in China and has its own sales network there. "We have realized that bill collection and other sales-related jobs in China are beyond our ability," said the president of Kikkoman.

Many foreign companies are repeating the process of trial and error in their attempts to take control of distribution, a key to conquering the puzzling Chinese market. Some focus on increasing the local network; some ally with partners with the aim of selling products through partners' sales channels; and some are terminating joint venture contracts with local state-run firms with weak marketing muscle in an attempt to build up sales networks of their own.

Under the circumstances, foreign manufacturers, which fear getting bogged down in the local distribution system, are being forced to take an approach in which they sell a small amount of expensive products to China's new rich through foreign sales agents, who may be inferior in marketing ability but reliable in regard to paying for the goods they purchase. Currently, Kikkoman sells its soy sauce at five or six times the price of the Chinese local product. According to its chairman and CEO, it will be another 10 years before increased purchasing power allows Chinese consumers to trade up to Kikkoman. To grow businesses in China, only those who have a strong sales network, such as the Kikkoman–Ton Yi joint venture, are more likely to control and market to the mass consumers in China.

Sources: "China Market Huge but Hard to Crack," *Nikkei Weekly,* http://www.nni.nikkei.co.jp accessed July 1, 2002; and "Kikkoman to Diversify Ops Abroad," *Nikkei Weekly,* June 20, 2005.

EXHIBIT 15-1
INTERNATIONAL SALES STRATEGY
AND INTERCULTURAL CONSIDERATIONS

International Sales Strategy Issues	Intercultural Issues within the Foreign Country
Global/International vs. local account management	Motivation
Salesforce skill availability	Cultural sensitivity
Country image	Ethical standards
Expatriate recruiting	Fairness
Centralized training	Relationship building
Home to host communications	Selling style differences

So what is international about sales management and personal selling? First, we can break international sales management issues into two categories that provide a clarification of the use of the term *international:* (1) *international strategy considerations:* issues that analyze more than one country's assets, strengths, and situations, or that deal directly with cross-border coordination and (2) *intercultural considerations:* issues that focus on the culture of the foreign country and its impact on operations within that country.

Although these two categories are not mutually exclusive, they help to clarify what makes international sales management considerations different from domestic sales management. A list of examples appears in Exhibit 15-1.

In this chapter, we highlight issues related to the choice of market entry method and the sales management step to setting salesforce objectives. In relating foreign entry choices to sales management, we provide a framework for thinking about the effects of various salesforce management issues. Subsequently, we ask the student to carefully consider the cultural generalizations that influence international decisions and interactions. Poor generalizations will produce flawed sales management. Good tools for generalizing about cultures can help the international manager make decisions that accurately take into account cultural differences.

We discuss how cultural differences, in general, affect issues central to sales management. We consider cultural impacts on recruiting, training, supervising, and evaluating salespeople, as well as on the personal sales process. We also examine a special form of cross-cultural interactions: international negotiations.

Finally, we discuss the complex issues involved when a company sends its employees overseas. The successful use of expatriates gives a company significant advantages but requires careful selection, training, supervision, and evaluation.

MARKET ENTRY OPTIONS AND SALESFORCE STRATEGY ◆ ◆ ◆ ◆ ◆ ◆ ◆ ◆

In the salesforce management "process," we start with setting objectives and strategy. These steps include determining the goals and purposes of the salesforce and the structure that will best meet those goals. To a large extent, these initial steps determine the requirements for the subsequent steps in the process: recruiting, training, supervising, and evaluating.

The question of *how to enter the market* is central to marketing. As a company decides what form its market entry will take, it is making a decision that limits and defines key underlying aspects of its future salesforce management. For example, if a company decides to sell its products in the United States through a large, integrated distributor, it may only need a small, highly mobile salesforce.

In international sales, the form of entry has even greater implications in international sales. The form of entry determines how large the salesforce needs to be and influences how much training it will require. It also influences whether the salesforce comprises predominantly local foreign citizens or primarily expatriates. This composition then influences the compensation scale required. Clearly, the form of entry directly influences many of the *downstream* salesforce management options. This section reviews various options for entering a foreign market and summarizes the principal implications and questions each option raises.

The entry method we have been referring to is also termed the *level of integration* in the market. Forward integration suggests greater ownership and control of the distribution channel. For example, a company might begin its foreign sales by exporting through a merchant distributor that takes title to the product and performs all necessary foreign sales functions. Later, the company might integrate forward into the distribution channel by hiring its own commissioned sales agents in the foreign country. Still greater forward integration might consist of the company purchasing a sales subsidiary and establishing product warehouses abroad.[2]

Determining the best level of integration is an issue more appropriate for a chapter on international strategy than sales management. However, in determining the entry form, the company must consider the subsequent influences it will have on its sales management options. In general, greater forward integration is preferred when (1) the operation is large enough to spread out the overhead costs of owning and maintaining infrastructure and training and supervising employees or (2) an inability to enforce contractual obligations on outside intermediaries or some other need for greater control of the sales process requires a strong presence in the host country. Additionally, (3) sales of a service usually require a presence in the country earlier than would otherwise be considered.

A number of typical entry approaches and the sales management concerns each raises are presented in Exhibit 15-2.

Selling through an export management company or an export trading company is considered a low-involvement approach to international sales. **Export management companies (ETCs),** in general, serve the needs of their clients in entering a market or sourcing goods from a market. They are characterized by their "service" nature and efforts to interact with and meet the needs of the exporter client. Many EMCs have specific expertise in selecting markets abroad and finding customers due to their language capabilities, previous business experience in the country, or a network of their business contacts. The EMC works with an exporter in one of two ways. First, the EMC can act as an agent distributor performing marketing services for the exporter client, responsible primarily for developing foreign business and sales strategies and establishing contact abroad. For this prospecting role, the EMC earns its income from a commission on the products it sells on the exporter's behalf. Second, the EMC can act as a merchant distributor who purchases products from the domestic exporter, takes title, sells the product in its own name, and consequently assumes all trading risks. The domestic exporter selling directly to the merchant EMC receives its money without having to deal with the complexities and trading risks in the international market. On the other hand, the exporter is less likely to build its own international experience. Many inexperienced exporters use EMCs services mainly to test the international arena with some desire to become direct participants once a foreign customer base has been established. This can cause conflict between the interests of the EMC and those of the client exporter.

Export trading companies (ETCs) are usually large conglomerates that import, export, countertrade, invest, and manufacture in the global arena. The ETC can purchase products, act as a distributor abroad, or offer services. Mitsubishi, Mitsui, Sumitomo, and Marubeni, among others, are major ETCs, known in Japan as

---

[2]Saul Kline, Gary L. Frazier, and Victor J. Roth, "A Transaction Cost Analysis Model of Channel Integration in International Markets," *Journal of Marketing Research,* 27 (May 1990), pp. 196–208.

EXHIBIT 15-2
DEGREE OF INVOLVEMENT AND SALES MANAGEMENT ISSUES

Degree of Involvement	Examples	Description	Sales Management Concerns
Limited foreign involvement and visibility	Export management companies (EMC), export trading companies (ETC), direct exporting, licensing	• Concerned with contract for sales from the U.S. • No salesforce or representatives abroad • Little or no control over foreign marketing process	• Goals of the company may not take precedence • Low foreign image and stability • Impossibility of training salesforce
Local management and salesforce	Piggybacking, selling through chains	• Little attempt to make foreign sales imitate U.S. sales culture • May "borrow" a salesforce or sell via direct contracts from abroad with multidistributor outlets	• Ineffective customs (lack of influence) • Low product knowledge • Control (trust, commitment) • Poor communications
Expatriate management and local salesforce (mixed)	Selling through chains with locals, direct selling with locals	• Expatriates oversee sales regions, lead training	• Perceptions of equality and fairness • Cultural interactions
Heavy to complete expatriate salesforce	Traveling global salesforce, high technology experts	• Client-by-client sales by expatriate salesforce	• Lack of local understanding of insiders and market workings • High cost • Difficulty in recruiting expatriates • Country limits on expatriates or rules, such as taxes, which vary depending on foreign presence

sogoshosha (general trading companies).[3] ETCs utilize their vast size to benefit from economies of scale in shipping and distribution. In the United States, the Export Trading Company Act of 1982 exempted ETCs from antitrust laws.[4] The intent was to improve the export performance of small and medium-size companies by allowing them joint participation with banks through an ETC. ETCs offer the exporting company a stable, known distributor, but they do not give the exporting company much control over or knowledge about the international sales process.

Licensing also represents a low-involvement approach to foreign sales. The company licenses its product or technology abroad and allows the contracting foreign company to coordinate the production and foreign distribution of the product.

Limited involvement approaches to international market entry simplify sales management greatly by reducing it to a predominantly domestic activity. There is little need to recruit, train, supervise, or evaluate a foreign or expatriate salesforce. However, companies that follow a limited involvement approach sacrifice the benefits that hiring and training their own salesforce can provide. These benefits include the ability to

---

[3]Lyn S. Amine, S. Tamer Cavusgil, Robert I. Weinstein, "Japanese Sogo Shosha and the U.S. Export Trading Companies," *Journal of the Academy of Marketing Science,* 14 (Fall 1986), pp. 21–32.
[4]Daniel C. Bello and Nicholas C. Williamson, "The American Export Trading Company: Designing a New International Marketing Institution," *Journal of Marketing,* 49 (Fall 1985), pp. 60–69.

motivate and monitor the salesforce and to train them to better serve the customer, the customer loyalty that a dedicated salesforce can generate, and the perception of permanence and commitment that a dedicated salesforce conveys. Many foreign companies look for such an indication of stability and commitment when selecting suppliers.

Mid-level involvement approaches to foreign sales are those in which the company controls some portion of the distribution process. Thus, the company must employ some management or salesforce abroad. This workforce may be either predominantly host country employees, or it may include a large share of expatriates. In either case, the company deals face to face with the foreign culture, and intercultural communication becomes a significant issue. Training can help reduce misunderstandings and miscommunications and can provide both sides with tools to understand the perspectives of the others. For example, training helps the local salespeople better understand the company's policies by reviewing its history and goals. Training also helps the expatriates understand the local market by reviewing the norms of business within their industry and country.

The choice of whether to rely on expatriate involvement is not an easy one. Without expatriate involvement, the company could decide that it is difficult to control the sales process, even though it owns part of the process. With expatriate involvement, local nationals could envy the expatriates' higher levels of pay or resent the limitations on their career opportunities with the company.

High involvement approaches are those in which the company substantially controls the foreign distribution channels. The company could own warehouses to store products and outlets where the products are sold, and it could manage a large, dedicated salesforce abroad. Typically, if a domestic company is highly involved in a foreign market, at least some of that presence will be expatriates. For some companies, only the top officer abroad is an expatriate. For others, the expatriate presence is much stronger.

The benefits of controlling distribution include the ability to recruit, train, and supervise a foreign salesforce that can best represent the company abroad. However, controlling distribution requires that the sales volume be large enough to justify the costs, and it also requires enough experience to avoid costly errors.

Role of Foreign Governments

At the time the company is considering its entry strategy, it should consider foreign government rules and practices. Many host country governments design regulations to protect local firms from international competition and ensure that local citizens benefit from experience in management positions at international companies. Thus, governments limit the number of international companies they allow to sell in the market, and they require that foreign companies fill a large number of positions with local citizens. Even the United States follows such practices. The U.S. Immigration and Naturalization Service does not let foreign managers enter the United States to work when it believes that there are U.S. citizens capable of performing the same jobs. Foreign countries also often dictate who can enter, for how long, and for what jobs. These requirements can determine which entry strategy makes sense for a company.

A second issue in deciding the entry approach is the role expected of companies as "corporate citizens" in the country. If a company sets up a complete sales and distribution subsidiary, it may be expected to build local infrastructure, support local politicians, or take part in local training initiatives. Such considerations will weigh in on the choice of the sales approach.

◆ ◆ ◆ ◆ ◆ ◆ ◆ ◆   ## CULTURAL CONSIDERATIONS

Personal Selling

At the level of **personal selling,** there is little true *international* selling. The sales task tends to take place on a national basis. Generally, salespeople perform the majority of their sales within one country, probably even within one region or area of a country. A salesperson selling big-ticket items, such as airplanes or dam construction, could sell to many countries, but even then, each sale is a sale within one country, and the entire sales process takes place in one country. Furthermore, despite growing "international sales," salespeople typically work in only one region. Even in the European Union (EU), for example, where close borders and similar economies could encourage salespeople to work over larger areas, personal selling activities still remain bound mostly to a country or a region. Thus, an analysis of *international* personal selling is a study of how differences in culture impact the forms, rules, and norms for personal selling within each country.[5]

Personal selling is predominantly a personal activity. It requires that the salesperson understand the customer's needs and wants. The salesperson must understand local customs well enough to be accepted and be able to form relationships with the customers. Do customers require a close, supportive relationship where the salesperson regularly checks up on them and knows the names of relatives? Does the customer expect some favors to "lubricate the process"? Each culture has different norms for the process of selling and buying.[6]

Throughout this chapter, we refer to the need to adapt sales and management techniques to the local culture to be successful.[7] It would be wonderful if a diagram were available that could help managers plot the appropriate solutions for each country. Although such a diagram is too much to hope for, we can look at some common generalizations and categorizations of cultural traits and consider how they could affect our sales approach. We must take care, however, not to imply that any culture can be described accurately in a few words or categories.

CULTURAL GENERALIZATION

◆ ◆ ◆ ◆ ◆ ◆ ◆ ◆

As an example of a cultural generalization with both helpful insights and misleading oversights, consider the foreign view of Germans. Germans are typically viewed as scientifically exacting and industrious people. We could therefore approach sales in Germany by building a small core of technically trained, independent sales agents. If we think Germans look at work the same way Americans do, however, we will be misguided! The typical German manufacturing workweek is only 30 hours. Also, Germans jealously guard their free time and show little interest in working more to earn more.[8]

We must also be careful not to group people from what may appear to us as very similar cultures but who consider themselves, and react to situations, in a very distinct manner. Consider, for example, South Korea and Japan. We may think that Koreans would be accustomed to the same bottom-up, consensual decision-making approach for which the Japanese are known. Korean workers, however, tend to work within a top-down, authoritarian leadership structure[9] and require a higher level of definition in their job structure to avoid suffering from role conflict. A Korean salesperson might

---

[5]See, for example, Joel Herche and Michel J. Swenson, "Personal Selling Constructs and Measures: Emic versus Etic Approaches to Cross-National Research," *European Journal of Marketing,* 30 (7), 1996, pp. 83–97; Ravi Sohi, "Global Selling and Sales Management-Cross Cultural Issues-National Character," *Journal of Personal Selling & Sales Management,* 19 (Winter 1999), pp. 80–81; and Nina Reynolds and A. Simintiras, "Toward an Understanding of the Role of Cross-Cultural Equivalence in International Personal Selling," *Journal of Marketing Management,* 16 (November 2000), pp. 829–51.

[6]Bruce Money, Mary C. Gilly, and John L. Graham, "Explorations of National Culture and Word-of-Mouth Referral Behavior in the Purchase of Industrial Services in the United States and Japan," *Journal of Marketing,* 62 (October 1998), pp. 76–87.

[7]Chanthika Pornpitakpan, "The Effects of Cultural Adaptation on Business Relationships: Americans Selling to Japanese and Thais," *Journal of International Business Studies* 30 (Second Quarter 1999), pp. 317–38.

[8]Daniel Benjamin and Tony Horwitz, "German View: You Americans Work Too Hard—And For What?" *Wall Street Journal,* July 14, 1994, p. B1.

[9]Hak Chong Lee, "Managerial Characteristics of Korean Firms," in *Korean Managerial Dynamics,* ed. K. H. Chung and H. C. Lee (New York: Praeger, 1989), pp. 147–62.

accept as normal a short-term position with few prospects for long-term progress, whereas a Japanese salesperson would not dream of it.[10]

Another example is the differences in the orientation of salespeople in Australia and New Zealand. Most of us tend to think that their cultures are very similar. However, salespeople in New Zealand tend to be more committed to, and generally more satisfied with, their work than their Australian counterparts. Additionally, there are differences in preferences toward compensation (Australians preferring greater security in the form of larger salary) and special incentives (New Zealanders having a much higher preference for travel with other winners and supervisory staff).[11] In a way, salespeople in New Zealand share more similarities in their value system with their Japanese counterparts than their Australian neighbors.

These and other observations suggest that cultural generalizations may be risky even among seemingly similar countries, particularly at the operational level. As explained in Chapter 4, one of the most widely used tools for categorizing cultures for managerial purposes is Hofstede's scale of five cultural dimensions (i.e., power distance, uncertainty avoidance, individualism/collectivism, masculinity/femininity, long-term/short-term orientation). Hofstede's scale uses many questions to determine where countries, not individual people, stand on each dimension.

Corporate (Organizational) Culture

As also explained in Chapter 4, companies also have their own distinct **corporate (organizational) cultures.** The culture at a company helps determine the norms of behavior and the mood at the workplace. This corporate culture acts in conjunction with national or country culture to set the values and beliefs that employees carry in the workplace.

The differences between the cultures of any two companies have been found to be determined significantly by the *practices* of those already in the company, especially the founders. By contrast, the differences between the cultures of companies in two countries are based more in the ingrained cultural *values* of the employees.[12] Values are learned earlier in life and are much more difficult to change than practices. Consider an example of the difference in trying to modify each. We could expect to initiate novel work practices without strong negative reactions from the employees. For example, we could ask salespeople to report to a group instead of to a boss in an effort to instill a sense of group responsibility. However, if we attempt to change procedures that are strongly rooted in the values of a country's culture, we could be asking for a negative response. Consider the troubles we could encounter if we attempted to integrate men and women in the salesforce in Saudi Arabia. At the very least, we would not bring out the best the salesforce has to offer.

Thus, although corporate cultures determine much about the working environment and even the success of an organization, the practices that characterize them are fairly malleable. Country cultures and, more specifically, the values people build at an early age in life, also greatly influence which management practices will succeed. However, cultural values are fairly fixed—do not underestimate the importance of cultural values and people's unwillingness to change them.[13]

---

[10] Alan J. Dubinsky, Ronald E. Michaels, Masaaki Kotabe, Chae Un Lim, and Hee-Cheol Moon, "Influence of Role Stress on Industrial Salespeople's Work Outcomes in the United States, Japan, and Korea," *Journal of International Business Studies,* 23 (First Quarter 1992), pp. 77–99.

[11] William H. Murphy, "Hofstede's National Culture as a Guide for Sales Practices across Countries: The Case of a MNC's Sales Practices in Australia and New Zealand," *Australian Journal of Management,* 24 (June 1999), pp. 37–58.

[12] Geert Hofstede, Bram Neuijen, Denise Daval Ohayv, and Geert Sanders, "Measuring Organizational Cultures: A Qualitative and Quantitative Study Across Twenty Cases," *Administrative Science Quarterly,* 35 (1990), pp. 286–316.

[13] Ibid.

In the last 20 years, influenced by Japan's vertical *keiretsu* (a closely knit group affiliation among the principal company, upstream suppliers of components and other materials, and downstream retailers for its finished products along the value chain), an increasing number of companies, such as Bose, Compaq, and Motorola, have begun to station their engineering personnel in their independent parts suppliers for more effective product development and to station their sales personnel work in the retailer's offices. The principal companies can track demand at store levels directly and place orders on a just-in-time basis. Both up-stream and down-stream involvements by the principal companies along the value chain can manage information flow from the retailers and customers more effectively and step up the pace of new product development.[14]

Relationship Marketing

This type of buyer–seller relationship is a win–win situation because both sides gain from the deal (albeit in different ways). Thus, they start out with the intention of producing a mutually beneficial arrangement. An increasing number of organizations have, indeed, come to see the relationship as one of interdependence; the two sides adopt a peer-to-peer relationship.

Indeed, the relationship between a seller and a buyer seldom ends when the sale is made. In an increasing proportion of transactions, the relationship actually intensifies subsequent to the sale. This becomes the critical factor in the buyer's choice of the seller the next time around. How good the seller-buyer relationship is depends on how well the seller manages it.[15] Again, many companies are finding that adoption of the personal computer technology in maintaining product, pricing, and technical data for effective customer relationships is crucial for their success.

It has been almost a decade since management consultancy Bain & Co. carried out its groundbreaking research into the key differences between customer acquisition and customer retention.[16] By considering the real costs and long-term returns, it found that most companies often understated acquisition costs, while cross-selling to an existing customer cost one-sixth of the price of making a sale to a prospect. Bain introduced one of the most famous equations in marketing: a 5-percent increase in customer retention would increase the value of each customer by between 25 and 100 percent. The potential implied in that finding led directly to customer relationship marketing.[17]

Good customer relationships are important by any means in any market. However, they tend to be more conspicuous in high-context cultures, such as Asian and Latin American countries. As discussed in Chapter 4, people in high-context culture countries tend to prefer group-oriented decision-making processes, unlike low-context culture countries, such as the United States and Western and Northern European countries, where decision-making processes are individualistic. In many firms, salespeople are also the primary source of information exchange within a customer-seller relationship and thus play a critical role in the formation and sustainability of customer relationships. To the extent that customer relationship marketing is important, the personal traits of sales managers need to be carefully examined, particularly when they engage in "selling" to corporate clients in other countries.

One popular tool for characterizing people that addresses their cognitive styles is the **Myers–Briggs Type Indicator (MBTI).** The MBTI is based on the following four personal dimensions: (1) extrovert versus introvert, (2) sensing versus intuitive, (3) thinking versus feeling, and (4) judging versus perceiving (see Exhibit 15-3).

Myers–Briggs Type Indicator

---

[14]Michiel R. Leenders and David L. Blenkhorn, *Reverse Marketing: The New Buyer-Supplier Relationship* (New York: Free Press, 1988).

[15]Gila E. Fruchter and Simon P. Sigué, "Transactions vs. Relationships: What Should the Company Emphasize?" *Journal of Service Research,* 8 (August 2005), pp. 18–36.

[16]Frederick Reichheld, *The Loyalty Effect* (Boston, MA: Harvard Business School Press, 1996).

[17]David Reed, "Great Expectations," *Marketing Week,* April 29, 1999, pp. 57–58.

EXHIBIT 15-3
MYERS–BRIGGS TYPE INDICATOR
OF PERSONAL CHARACTERISTICS

Personal Dimension	*Description*
Extrovert vs. Introvert	An extrovert tends to rely on the environment for guidance, be action-oriented, sociable, and communicate with ease and frankness
	An introvert tends to show a greater concern with concepts and ideas than with external events, relative detachment, and enjoyment of solitude and privacy over companionship.
Sensing vs. Intuitive	A sensing person tends to focus on immediate experience, become more realistic and practical, and develop skills such as acute powers of observation and memory for details.
	An intuitive person tends to value possibility and meaning more than immediate experience, and become more imaginative, theoretical, abstract, and future oriented.
Thinking vs. Feeling	A thinking person tends to be concerned with logical and impersonal decision making and principles of justice and fairness, and is strong in analytical ability and objectivity.
	A feeling person tends to make decisions by weighing relative values and merits of issues, be attuned to personal and group values, and be concerned with human, rather than technical, aspects of a problem.
Judging vs. Perceiving	A judging person tends to make relatively quick decisions, be well planned and organized, and seek closure.
	A perceiving person tends to be open to new information, not move for closure to make quick decisions, and stay adaptable and open to new events or change.

Source: Neil R. Abramson, Henry W. Lane, Hirohisa Nagai, and Haruo Takagi, "A Comparison of Canadian and Japanese Cognitive Styles: Implications for Management Interactions," *Journal of International Business Studies,* 24, Third Quarter 1993, pp. 575–87.

   Using this scale, Abramson, Lane, Nagai, and Takagi[18] found significant cognitive distinctions between Canadian and Japanese MBA students. The English-speaking Canadian students preferred intuition, judgment, and thinking, whereas the Japanese students preferred sensing, perceiving, and thinking but were more feeling oriented than the Canadian students. In summary, the English-speaking Canadians displayed a logical and impersonal, or objective, style that subordinates the human element. The Japanese displayed a more feeling style, which emphasized the human element in problem solving, such as being sympathetic and building trust in human relations. English-speaking Canadians have a tendency to seek fast decisions and rush to closure on data collection. The Japanese were found to resist quick decision making because of their preference for obtaining large amounts of information. A recent study also shows that French-speaking Canadians in Quebec, unlike the English-speaking Canadians, are indeed a bit more similar to Japanese in terms of their emphasis on trust building.[19]

---

[18]Neil R. Abramson, Henry W. Lane, Hirohisa Nagai, and Haruo Takagi, "A Comparison of Canadian and Japanese Cognitive Styles: Implications for Management Interactions," *Journal of International Business Studies,* 24 (Third Quarter 1993), pp. 575–87.

[19]Joseph P. Cannon, Patricia M. Doney, and Michael R. Mullen, "A Cross-Cultural Examination of the Effects of Trust and Supplier Performance on Long-Term–Buyer-Supplier Relationships," *Enhancing Knowledge Development in Marketing,* 1999 American Marketing Association Educators' Proceedings, Summer 1999, p. 101.

Indeed, Japanese salespeople, who emphasize trust building, use more word-of-mouth referrals in consummating sales than American counterparts.[20]

Such differences in style must be taken into consideration whenever two cultures interact. In international sales, cross-cultural interaction takes place between the home office and the subsidiary, between expatriate managers and the salesforce, or between an expatriate salesperson and the customer. If the cultural norms and cognitive styles of both sides are more clearly understood, it will help reduce misconceptions and miscommunications.

IMPACT OF CULTURE ON SALES MANAGEMENT AND PERSONAL SELLING PROCESS

♦ ♦ ♦ ♦ ♦ ♦ ♦ ♦

In general, the human resource practices of multinational corporations (MNCs) closely follow the local practices of the country in which they operate.[21] These human resource practices include time off, benefits, gender composition, training, executive bonuses, and participation of employees in management. However, human resource practices also depend on the strategy desired, the culture of the company, and even the country from which the company originated.

Thus, although we can say that the sales management process should adapt to the local environment,[22] we acknowledge the difficult give-and-take involved in adapting a company's culture and procedures with the sales and management practices of a foreign country.

> When host-country standards seem substandard from the perspective of the home country (manager), the manager faces a dilemma. Should the MNC implement home country standards and so seem to lack respect for the cultural diversity and national integrity of the host (country)? Or, should the MNC implement seemingly less optimal host country standards?[23]

One recent study suggests that international differences in the effectiveness of different sales management should be incorporated into the design of control systems, should involve local personnel in the decision, and should allow local countries' flexibility in the implementation of control strategy. The transfer of sales management practices across different countries without careful attention to local differences is very risky.[24] One good exemplary hiring policy is presented in Global Perspective 15-2.

The process of salesforce management provides a framework for a closer look at the challenges involved in adapting management practices to a new culture. Salesforce management consists of the following six steps:

1. Setting salesforce objectives

2. Designing salesforce strategy

3. Recruiting and selecting salespeople

4. Training salespeople

---

[20]R. Bruce Money, Mary C. Gilly, and John L. Graham, "Explorations of National Culture and Word-of-Mouth Referral Behavior in the Purchase of Industrial Services in the United Sates and Japan,"*Journal of Marketing,* 62 (October 1998), pp. 76–87.

[21]Philip M. Rosenzweig, and Ritin Nohria. "Influences on Human Resource Management Practices in Multinational Corporations," *Journal of International Business Studies,* 25 (Second Quarter 1994), pp. 229–51.

[22]A recent study proves that when management practices are adapted to the national culture of a country in which the company operates, its financial performance tends to improve. See Karen L. Newman and Stanley D. Nollen, "Culture and Congruence: The Fit between Management Practices and National Culture," *Journal of International Business Studies,* 27 (Fourth Quarter 1996), pp. 753–79.

[23]Thomas Donaldson, "Multinational Decision-Making: Reconciling International Norma," *Journal of Business Ethics,* 4 (1985), pp. 357–66.

[24]Nigel F. Piercy, George S. Low, and David W. Cravens, "Consequences of Sales Management's Behavior- and Compensation-Based Control Strategies in Developing Countries," *Journal of International Marketing,* 12 (3), 2004, pp. 30–57.

◆ ◆

𝒢LOBAL PERSPECTIVE 15-2

TGI FRIDAYS, INC

In setting up overseas, the restaurant chain TGI Fridays, a U.S. bar and grill concept, follows a key series of guidelines:

- Choose a local development partner to guide it through government obstacles, local hiring practices, and on-site business hurdles.

- Concentrate on hiring fun employees who "fit" the company's image: those willing to sing "Happy Birthday" to a customer, for example.

- Entrust the entire operation to the overseas management after business practices and philosophy have been completely transferred.

- In seeking new overseas managers, look for foreign nationals on assignment or pursuing studies in the United States and offer them an opportunity to return home, bringing back with them the knowledge they have acquired about U.S. culture, business, and service standards. Just as important, however, they are experts in the traditions, ethics, and ways of life of the customers the company wants to serve in foreign markets.

An example of these guidelines put into practice is TGI Friday's expansion into England. Its success can be attributed

Sources: Mark Hamstra, "Operators Bullish about Opportunities in Overseas Markets, Despite Turmoil," *Nation's Restaurant News,* October 5, 1998, p.86; and Conrad Lashley, "Empowerment through Involvement: A Case Study of TGI Fridays Restaurants," *Personnel Review,* 29 (5/6, 2000), pp. 791–815.

to the chain's strong local partner, Whitbread PLC, successfully operating under license from the parent company in the United States.

The company's own research showed that 25 percent of customers return to the restaurant at least once per month. During weekdays, the typical customer is female in her 30s in a professional, managerial, or white collar occupation. However, the typical customer profile changes throughout the day: business lunches, families in the afternoon and early evening, and couples and young adults in the later evening. On the weekend, customers typically include large numbers of families. Some significant differences for customer profiles in London and in the other areas exist.

In these circumstances, employee performance, particularly of front-line staff, has a crucial role to play. The success of the service depends on the worker's ability to construct particular kinds of interactions. "Dub-Dubs," as the waiting staff are called, advise customers on the menu and how best to structure their meal. They must also identify the customer's service requirements and deliver what is needed. In some cases, having a good laugh with the customers is needed. At other times, Dub-Dubs have to entertain restive children. Employee performance requires more than the traditional acts of greeting, seating, and serving customers. Employees must be able to provide both the behaviors and the emotional displays to match customer wants and feelings. In other words, the ability to "connect with others" is a crucial ingredient for high employee performance.

5. Supervising salespeople

6. Evaluating salespeople

Salesforce Objectives

Setting salesforce objectives depends on having already determined the larger, strategic objectives of the company. A company can have the strategic objective of adding value by providing the customer more understanding of a product's use, or the company could want to enter the market as the low-cost provider. Once such strategic objectives are decided upon, the company can evaluate what roles the salesforce will play in reaching these goals. These roles are the salesforce objectives. They explicitly state *what* the salesforce will be asked to do, whether it is solving customer complaints or pushing for publicity of the product.

Salesforce objectives will then influence much of the rest of the sales management process. If a salesforce objective is to expand market share, then the salesforce will be designed, recruited, trained, supervised, and evaluated using that objective as a guideline. Salesforce objectives will guide how much salesforce time and effort will be required for digging up leads versus working with existing customers, or how much effort will be placed on new products versus older products, or how much effort will be spent on customer satisfaction compared to sales volume.

Setting salesforce objectives will require a very similar approach internationally as it does domestically. In fact, many "international" salesforce issues are really local issues in a foreign country. However, setting the best international salesforce objectives depends not only on the company goals, but also on an analysis of the culture and values of the country it is entering. The company could use a standardized approach for all countries, or it might customize its salesforce management approach from the ground up for each country. Most companies will probably customize some aspects of each country's salesforce objectives but will follow previously held beliefs about the purpose of the salesforce to decide most objectives. Once the objectives are known, the company can begin designing the structure of the proposed salesforce.

With the salesforce's objectives set, the company can concentrate on the strategies needed to achieve those objectives. Salesforce strategy addresses the structure, size, and compensation of the salesforce.

Salesforce Strategy

The structure determines the physical positioning and responsibilities of each salesperson. A company selling one product to a dispersed client base might consider a *territorial salesforce* with each salesperson responsible for a particular area and reporting up the line to regional sales managers. Another company, with numerous, unrelated, complex products, could consider a *product salesforce* structure in which each salesperson sells only one product or product line, even when selling to a single customer. A third company, which requires close contact with its customers to keep up with customer needs and build tight relationships, could employ a *customer salesforce* structure in which account managers are responsible for particular clients. Each of these approaches has advantages and disadvantages. Choosing the most appropriate international salesforce strategy requires analyzing many of the same considerations as it does domestically. However, additional considerations arise concerning the lack of capable local salespeople, the cultural expectations of clients, and the dramatically increased costs of maintaining expatriate personnel abroad.

The size of the salesforce depends on the sales structure. The company often calculates how many salespeople are needed by determining how many visits or calls each type of customer should receive and how many salespeople will be needed to make the necessary number of visits. In a foreign culture, customers' distinct expectations could modify the calculations. Although a client in the United States might be satisfied with buying large quantities of a product and hearing from the salesperson every six months, the foreign client could expect a salesperson to be in regular contact and could want to buy smaller quantities more regularly. Such considerations impact the salesforce size. For example, Wal-Mart, the world's largest company, has recognized that the key to its growth lies in rapidly growing China. Unlike Western consumers, Chinese customers tend to buy in smaller quantities and are accustomed to going to supermarket every one or two days. Thus, Wal-Mart supercenters have to devote more floor space and sales associates to food than to other departments. Furthermore, because Chinese customers need to "feel" the merchandise (put their hands on it) before making the purchase, salesforce assignment needs to be carefully examined to cater to Chinese consumers' characteristics. When Wal-Mart opened its supercenter in Chongqing, a metropolis of 31 million in southwest China, it had to open 75 checkout lanes and embraced roughly 120,000 visitors in one single day.[25]

Salesforce compensation is the chief form of motivation for salespeople. However, companies do not pay salesforces equally in all countries. The purchasing power of the "same" quantity of money may not be the same. More important, pay expectations, or the "going rate," varies dramatically from country to country. The company must carefully consider the social perceptions of its compensation scale. A commission-based compensation could not motivate salespeople in some other countries. A salary scale with large rewards for success could be viewed as unfair. The company must evaluate the impact that compensation system will have on the employees and then consider what impact the system will also have on the final customer. The pay system must

---

[25]"The Great Wal-Mart of China," *Fortune,* July 25, 2005, pp. 104–16.

motivate salespeople to leave customers with the appropriate, desired perceptions of the company.

Recruitment and Selection

To successfully recruit and select salespeople, the company must understand what it wants in its salespeople and know how to find and attract people with the necessary skills. The first decision is whether the company will recruit from the local, foreign labor force for the jobs it is creating or whether it will fill them by sending domestic employees overseas. The company could find a strong cultural bias against salespeople in the local market and find it difficult to recruit the necessary talent. Even if it can recruit "talented" people, the company may not clearly know what skills and character traits will work the best in the unfamiliar culture. If the company tries to recruit employees at home, it may have a tough time convincing salespeople or managers with the necessary skills to take the time off from the "fast track" at home.

Complicating the search for talent is the fact that the desired skills and characteristics are not as clear as it first appears. Employers could base their expectations for salespeople on their domestic standards. For example, the employer could look for candidates with an outgoing attitude. However, in some cultures, a quieter, more patient approach will truly maximize sales. The skills required for success as a salesperson depend on the culture in which the sales take place.

Finally, the employer must consider the strong influences of tribal, religious, or other group relations within a country. A Hindu might not want to make purchases from a Muslim. English companies could do better to hire Irish salespeople to make sales in Ireland. History could give one group a distinct advantage, especially where they have become accepted as a strong business force. For example, the Parsees in India manage an unusually large portion of the nation's business, and Chinese salespeople, the descendants of the Chinese merchant clan, are prominent throughout Asia.[26] A wise sales manager will look for and recruit a salesforce that takes advantage of each country's natural distinctions.

One way for the company to accelerate the difficult process of building a salesforce from scratch is to establish a joint venture with or acquire a local company that already has a functional salesforce. For example, when Merck wanted to expand its pharmaceutical business in Japan, it acquired Banyu Pharmaceutical instead of building its subsidiary and distribution channel from scratch. Merck had immediate access to Banyu's field salesforce of more than 1,000. In Japan, where personal relationships probably weigh more in importance than the quality of products per se, personal selling is all the more critical in relationship-building and -maintaining purposes. Similarly, when Wal-Mart wanted to expand into Europe, its first move was to buy out Wertkauf, a German national chain store, to have instant distribution channel members working for it and supply channels already established, as well as a beachhead for the rest of Europe.[27]

Training

Most sales training takes place in the country where staff reside. The company determines how much technical, product knowledge, company history and culture, or other training its local salesforce requires. However, this country-by-country approach usually fails to develop a globally consistent sales and marketing strategy for MNCs. Therefore, an increasing number of globally oriented companies are now developing a globally consistent sales and marketing program to serve customers and foster long-term partnerships that would engage customers and meet their specific local needs and preferences. For example, BSC, a U.S. manufacturer of medical devices, selected AchieveGlobal, in Tampa, Florida, to train its international sales and marketing staff.

---

[26] See an excellent treatise, Min Chen, *Asian Management Systems: Chinese, Japanese and Korean Styles of Business* (London: Routledge, 1995), pp. 69–83.

[27] John Fernie and Stephen J. Arnold, "Wal-Mart in Europe: Prospects for Germany, the UK and France," *International Journal of Retail & Distribution Management*, 30 (2/3), 2002, pp. 92–102.

The two companies have developed a comprehensive training program, consisting of a three-day sales program for all employees and a two-day coaching seminar for sales managers. The sales training program incorporates product knowledge orientation with needs-satisfaction selling, extensive role-playing, and case studies. The session for managers shows them effective ways to coach their teams without handholding. Both companies ensure that BSC's entire sales and marketing staff is trained in the language of their specific country and that the program can be adapted to meet each local culture. This means not only translating the program's language into the local vernacular but also making sure the whole approach meets each country's specific needs. As a result, those sales managers are transferred to local markets with more consistent sales and marketing programs internationally.[28]

An additional consideration with regard to international sales training is adapting the training to the needs of the local market. For example, Carrefour, the French retail giant, has created the Carrefour China Institute to train its staff in China to engender the "Carrefour Spirit." Before opening stores in China, the company conducted in-depth research for store location, understanding the local culture and traditions, and local consumer purchasing behaviors. Inevitably, Carrefour's concepts of "localization management" and "low price and high quality" have worked in the Chinese world. The company was rewarded with $1.9 billion revenue in 2004.[29] The training that the salesforce receives must reflect cultural differences in purchasing patterns, values, and perspective of the selling process.

Although international companies often benefit in the local market by offering their employees better training than local competitors, they face the problem of protecting their investment in their employees. National companies often "raided" companies with well-trained salesforces for employees. To protect their investments, the MNCs must offer higher compensation and better promotion opportunities than their competitors.

Supervision

Supervising the salesforce means directing and motivating the salesforce to fulfill the company's objectives and providing the resources that allow them to do so. The company can set norms concerning how often a salesperson should call each category of customer and how much of his time the salesperson should spend with each of various activities. The company can motivate the salesperson by establishing a supportive, opportunity-filled organizational climate or by establishing sales quotas or positive incentives for sales. The company often provides the salesperson tools, such as laptop computers or research facilities, to provide better chances to achieve his goals. International sales management addresses how each of these supervising approaches will be received by the salesforce and what the cultural implications are. For example, cultures that value group identity over individuality will probably not respond well to a sales contest as a motivator.

Motivation and Compensation.   Financial compensation is one of the key motivators for employees in all cultures. However, successful sales programs use a wide variety of motivators. The sales manager will want to adapt the incentive structure to best meet local desires and regulations. The use of commissions in motivating salespeople is not publicly acceptable in many countries. Commissions reinforce the negative image of the salesperson benefiting from the sale with no regard for the purchaser's well-being. Salary increases can substitute for commissions to motivate salespeople to consistently perform highly. However, under certain circumstances, large salary discrepancies between employees are also not acceptable. Strong unions can tie a company's hands in setting salaries, or the "collectivist" culture of a country such as

---

[28]Slade Sohmer, "Emerging as a Global Sales Success," *Sales & Marketing Management*, 152 (May 2000), pp. 124–25.

[29]"Carrefour China: A Local Market," *China Business*, April 28, 2005.

Japan cannot accept that one person should earn substantially more than another in the same position. Koreans, for example, are used to working under conditions in which compensation is not directly contingent on performance but rather on seniority. When financial rewards are not acceptable, the company must rely more heavily on nonfinancial rewards, such as recognition, titles, and perquisites for motivation.

Foreign travel is another reward employed by international companies. For example, Electrolux rewards winning sales teams in Asia with international trips. When necessary, companies can combine an international trip with training and justify it as an investment in top salespeople.

Management Style. *Management style* refers to the approach the manager takes in supervising employees. The manager can define the employee's roles explicitly and require a standardized sales pitch or set broad, general goals that allow each salesperson to develop her own skills. A number of studies have found that the best management approach varies by culture and country. For example, Dubinsky et al.[30] found that role ambiguity, role conflict, job satisfaction, and organizational commitment were just as relevant to salespeople in Japan and Korea as in the United States and that role conflict and ambiguity have deleterious effects on salespersons in any of the countries. However, specific remedies for role ambiguity, such as greater job formalization (or more hierarchical power, defined rules, and supervision), have a distinct effect on the salespeople in different countries.

One fair generalization is that greater formalization invokes negative responses from the salesforce in countries in which the power distance is low and the individualism is high (as in the United States). Greater formalization also invokes positive responses from the salesforce in countries in which the power distance is high and the individualism is low (as in India).[31]

Ethical Perceptions. Culture, or nationality, also influences salespeople's beliefs about the ethics of common selling practices and the need for company policies to guide those practices. Why is this important? Salespeople need to stay within the law, of course, but more important to maintain the respect of customers, salespeople must know what is ethically acceptable in a culture. For example, in the United States, giving a bribe is tantamount to admitting that your product cannot compete without help. However, in many cultures, receiving a bribe is seen as a privilege of having attained a position of influence. An understanding of the ethical norms in a culture will help the company maintain a clean image and will help the company create policies that keep salespeople out of the tense and frustrating situations where they feel they are compromising their ethical standards.

As an example of differences in ethical perceptions, consider the results of a study by Dubinsky et al.[32] The study presented salespeople in Korea, Japan, and the United States with written examples of "questionable" sales situations. Examples of the situations used follow:

- Having different prices for buyers for which you are the sole supplier
- Attempting to circumvent the purchasing department and reach other departments directly when it will help sales
- Giving preferential treatment to customers whom management prefers or who are also good suppliers

---

[30] Dubinsky et al., "Influence of Role Stress on Industrial Salespeople's Work Outcomes, pp. 77–99.

[31] Sanjeev Agarwal, "Influence of Formalization on Role Stress, Organizational Commitment, and Work Alienation of Salespersons: A Cross-National Comparative Study," *Journal of International Business Studies,* 24 (Fourth Quarter 1993), pp. 715–40.

[32] Alan J. Dubinsky, Marvin A. Jolson, Masaaki Kotabe, and Chae Un Lim, "A Cross-National Investigation of Industrial Salespeople's Ethical Perceptions," *Journal of International Business Studies,* 22 (Fourth Quarter 1991), pp. 651–70.

The salespeople were asked to rate the extent to which it was unethical to take part in the suggested activity. The results indicated that in general, U.S. salespeople felt that the situations posed fewer ethical problems than did salespeople from Japan and Korea. Another interesting finding of the study—the assumption that Japanese "gift-giving" would extend into the sales realm—was found to be untrue. In fact, Japanese salespeople felt giving free gifts to a purchaser was more an ethical problem than did U.S. salespeople. For Koreans, however, gift-giving was less an issue.

Paradoxically, U.S. salespeople indicated that they wanted their companies to have more policies explicitly addressing these ethical questions. Why? Apparently, salespeople in the United States feel more comfortable when the ethical guidelines are explicitly stated, whereas in other countries (Korea and Japan here), the cultural exchange of living in a more community-oriented society provides the necessary guidelines.

Evaluation

Evaluating salespeople includes requiring them to justify their efforts and provide the company information about their successes, failures, expenses, and time. Evaluations are important to motivate the salesforce, to correct problems, and to reward and promote those who best help the company achieve its goals. Two types of evaluations are common: *quantitative* and *qualitative*. Examples of quantitative evaluations are comparisons of sales, of sales percents, or increases in sales. Examples of qualitative evaluations include tests of the knowledge and manner of the salesperson. Because net profit is often the company's primary objective, evaluations should serve to promote long-term net profits. In some foreign cultures, however, evaluations could be seen as an unnecessary waste of time, or they may invade the sense of privacy of salespeople.

Evaluations help management keep up on sales progress and help employees receive feedback and set goals. International salesforce evaluations must consider the culture's built-in ability to provide feedback to employees. For example, in Japan the "collectivist" nature of the culture may provide the salesperson with much more sense of performance feedback than the "individualistic" culture in the U.S. would. Thus, it makes sense that U.S. sales managers use more regular, short-term performance evaluations than Japanese sales managers in order to provide their salesforce more feedback.[33]

Evaluations in international sales management can provide useful information for making international comparisons. Such comparisons can help management identify countries where sales are below average and refine the training, compensation, or salesforce strategy as necessary to improve performance.

CROSS-CULTURAL NEGOTIATIONS

◆ ◆ ◆ ◆ ◆ ◆ ◆ ◆

Conducting successful cross-cultural negotiations is a key ingredient for many international business transactions. International bargaining issues range from establishing the nuts and bolts of supplier agreements to setting up strategic alliances. Negotiation periods can run from a few hours to several months, if not years, of bargaining. Bargaining taps into many resources, skills and expertise. Scores of books have been devoted to negotiation "dos and don'ts."[34] Cross-cultural negotiations are further complicated by divergent cultural backgrounds of the participants in the negotiation process.[35] In this section, we discuss the cultural aspects of international negotiations and bargaining.

[33] Susumu, Ueno and Uma Sekaran, "The Influence of Culture on Budget Control Practices in the U.S. and Japan: An Empirical Study," *Journal of International Business Studies,* 23 (Fourth Quarter 1992), pp. 659–74.

[34] See, for example, Mel Berger, *Cross Cultural Team Building: Guidelines for More Effective Communication and Negotiation* (New York: McGraw-Hill, 1996).

[35] For those interested in learning more about the complexities of cross-cultural negotiations, see a recent special issue on this topic, edited by Yahir H. Zoubir and Roger Volkema, *Thunderbird International Business Review,* 44 (November/December 2002).

Stages of Negotiation Process

Roughly speaking, four stages are encountered in most negotiation processes:[36] (1) nontask soundings, (2) task-related information exchange, (3) persuasion, and (4) concessions and agreement. Nontask soundings include all activities that are used to establish rapport among the parties involved. Developing rapport is a process that depends on subtle cues.[37] The second stage relates to all task-related exchanges of information. Once the information exchange stage has been completed, the negotiation parties typically move to the persuasion phase of the bargaining process. Persuasion is a give-and-take deal. The final step involves concession making intended to result in a consensus. Not surprising, negotiation practices vary enormously across cultures. Japanese negotiators devote much more time to nurturing rapport than U.S. negotiators. For Americans, the persuasion stage is the most critical part of the negotiation process. Japanese bargainers prefer to spend most of their time on the first two stages so that little effort is needed for the persuasion phase. Japanese and U.S. negotiators also differ in the way they make concessions. Americans tend to make concessions during the course of the negotiation process, whereas Japanese prefer to defer this stage to the end of the bargaining.[38] See Exhibit 15-4 for negotiation styles in five other countries.

Cross-Cultural Negotiation Strategies[39]

Exhibit 15-5 represents a framework of culturally responsive negotiation strategies driven by the level of cultural familiarity that the negotiating parties possess about one another's cultures. Cultural familiarity is a measure of a party's current knowledge of his counterpart's culture and ability to use that knowledge competently. Depending on the particular situation, eight possible negotiation strategies can be selected. Let us briefly consider each one of them.

Employ an Agent or Adviser. Outside agents, such as technical experts or financial advisers, can be used when cultural familiarity is extremely low. These agents can be used to provide information and to advise on action plans.

Involve a Mediator. Whereas the previous strategy can be used unilaterally, both parties can also jointly decide to engage a mutually acceptable third party as a mediator. Successful mediation depends on maintaining the respect and trust of both parties.

Induce the Counterpart to Follow One's Own Negotiation Script. Effective negotiators proceed along a *negotiation script:* the rules, conduct, ends targeted, means toward those ends, and so forth. When the counterpart's familiarity with your culture is high, it could be feasible to induce the other party to follow your negotiation script. This strategy is especially useful when cultural knowledge is asymmetrical: The other party is knowledgeable about your culture, but you are not familiar with hers. Inducement could be via verbal persuasion or subtle cues.

Adapt the Counterpart's Negotiation Script. With moderate levels of familiarity about the counterpart's cultural mindset, it becomes possible to adapt to his negotiation script. Adaptation involves a deliberate decision to adjust some common negotiation rules.

[36]John L. Graham and Yoshihiro Sano, "Across the Negotiating Table from the Japanese," *International Marketing Review,* 3 (Autumn 1986), pp. 58–71.

[37]Kathleen K. Reardon and Robert E. Spekman, "Starting Out Right: Negotiation Lessons for Domestic and Cross-Cultural Business Alliances," *Business Horizons,* January–February 1994, pp. 71–79.

[38]John L, Graham, "Negotiating with the Japanese (Part 1)," *East Asian Executive Reports,* November 15, 1988, pp. 8, 19–21.

[39]Stephen E. Weiss, "Negotiating with "Romans—Part 1," *Sloan Management Review,* Winter 1994, pp. 51–61; Stephen E. Weiss, "Negotiating with "Romans"—Part 2," *Sloan Management Review,* Spring 1994, pp. 85–99.

EXHIBIT 15-4
NEGOTIATION STYLES AND GUIDELINES IN FIVE COUNTRIES

	France	Poland	Turkey	Russia	Spain
Language	– Younger people: English acceptable – Older people: French–if necessary, agree at early stage to use an interpreter	– English or German – Do not overestimate fluency – Be willing to use an interpreter	– Be careful with terminology; allow extra time for language problems – Be clear and succinct – Avoid being negative	– Do not expect partner to speak English (especially outside big cities); find good interpreter	– Do not assume command of English – Consider using interpreter – Documents and business cards should be in Spanish, not just English
Sequence	– General principles → rough outline → details	– Goal-directed – Little small talk – Prepare for lengthy delays	– Small talk matters a lot – Wait to talk business until host brings it up	– Negotiations can be protracted – Starting times not always respected – Frequent interruptions	
Communication style	– Abstract and elaborate – Relish in logic, battle of wits – Straightness = blunt, rude – Avoid bluntness	– Unemotional – Lack of flexibility of Polish counterparts	– Be flexible to manage delays; factor in unexpected – Avoid bluntness – Stick to main message; avoid weakening arguments with minor points – Listen first, then ask questions; don't put words into counterpart's mouth	– Personal relationships play vital role – Russian partners can be "slow"	– Personal relationships play vital role; regard personal invitations as a partnership investment – Be prepared for delays – Interruptions common – Several people may talk at once – Discussions can be lively – Spanish people rely on quick thinking, spontaneity – Negotiations can be lengthy
Contract	– Very formal, flowery – Fairly brief	– Technical – Very detailed		– Avoid any changes to contracts; if necessary you will need to make a strong case	

EXHIBIT 15-4
(continued)

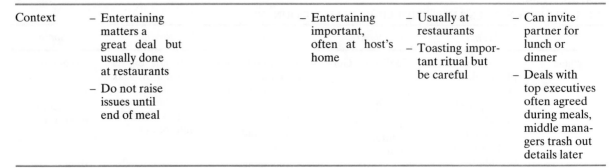

Context	– Entertaining matters a great deal but usually done at restaurants – Do not raise issues until end of meal	– Entertaining important, often at host's home	– Usually at restaurants – Toasting important ritual but be careful	– Can invite partner for lunch or dinner – Deals with top executives often agreed during meals, middle managers trash out details later

Source: "Enjoy a Battle of Wits and a Good Lunch," *Financial Times,* September 11, 2000, p. 9; Poland: "Crossing Cultural Barriers," *Financial Times* (September 25, 2000), p. 11; Turkey: "Contacts that Make or Break Turkish Ventures," *Financial Times,* November 6, 2000, p. 14; Russia: "A Market Emerging from a Country in Turmoil," *Financial Times,* February 19, 2001, p. 7; and Spain: "Formality, Feasting and Patience," *Financial Times,* October 9, 2000, p. 12.

EXHIBIT 15-5
CULTURALLY RESPONSIVE STRATEGIES
AND THEIR FEASIBILITY

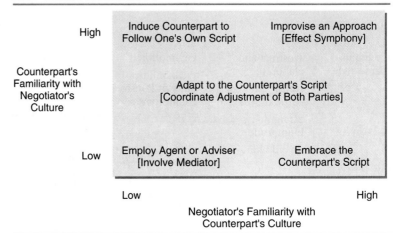

Source: Reprinted with permission from Stephen E. Weiss, "Negotiating with 'Romans'—Part 1," *Sloan Management Review,* Winter 1994, pp. 51–61. Copyright 1994 by Sloan Management Review Association. All rights reserved.

Coordinate Adjustment of Both Parties. When the circumstances lend themselves, both parties can jointly decide to arrive to a common negotiation approach that blends both cultures. Occasionally, they propose to adopt the negotiation script of a third culture.

Embrace the Counterpart's Script. With this strategy, the negotiator volunteers to adopt the counterpart's negotiation approach. This demands a tremendous effort from the negotiator. It can be effective only when the negotiator possesses a great deal of familiarity about the other party's cultural background.

Improvize an Approach. This strategy constricts a negotiation script over the course of negotiating. This approach is advisable when both parties feel very comfortable with their counterpart's culture. It can be effective when bargaining with members from a high-context culture in which mutual bonding and other contextual cues are at least as important (nontask-related aspects) as the immediate negotiation concerns.

Effect Symphony. The final strategy capitalizes on both parties' high cultural familiarity by creating an entirely new script or by following some other approach atypical to their respective cultures. For instance, the coordination could select parts from both cultures.

The choice of a particular strategy partly depends on how familiar the negotiators are with the other party's culture. To pick a particular strategy, consider the following steps:

1. *Reflect on your culture's negotiation practices.* What negotiation model do you use? What is the role of the individual negotiator? What is the meaning of a satisfactory agreement?

2. *Learn the negotiation script common in the counterpart's culture.* This involves reflecting on questions such as these: Who are the players? Who decides what? What are the informal influences that can make or break a deal?[40] Answers to these questions will help the negotiator to anticipate and interpret the other party's negotiating behaviors. Expectations about the process and the outcome of the bargaining will differ. People can view the process as win–win or win–lose. The approach to building an agreement can focus first on either general principles or specifics. The level of detail required can vary. Perspectives on the implementation of an agreement can also differ. In some cultures, renegotiation is frowned upon. In other cultures, an agreement is seen as a starting point of an evolving relationship.[41]

3. *Consider the relationship and contextual clues.* Different contexts necessitate different negotiating strategies. What circumstances define the interaction between the negotiation parties? Contextual clues include considerations such as the life of the relationship, gender of the parties involved, and balance of power.

4. *Predict or influence the counterpart's approach.* Prediction could be based on indicators such as the counterpart's prenegotiation behavior or track record. In some cases, it is desirable to influence the other party's negotiation strategy via direct means (e.g., explicit request for a negotiation protocol) or through more subtle means (e.g., disclosing one's familiarity with the counterpart's culture).

5. *Choose a strategy.* The chosen strategy should be compatible with the cultures involved, conducive to a coherent pattern of interaction, in line with the relationship and bargaining context, and ideally acceptable to both parties.

EXPATRIATES

◆ ◆ ◆ ◆ ◆ ◆ ◆ ◆

Most companies with a salesforce abroad will, at the very least, send a few expatriates abroad as operations begin in a new country. **Expatriates** are home country personnel sent overseas to manage local operations in the foreign market. The general trend among U.S. multinationals since the 1990s has been a decreasing use of expatriate managers overseas and an increasing reliance on local foreign talent.[42] This trend reflects the increasingly international perspective of MNCs, increasing competence of foreign managers, and the relatively increasing competitive disadvantage of the cost of maintaining home country personnel abroad. Despite the relative decline, more employees than ever are involved in international assignments due to the increase in international sales and production. Expatriates have a number of advantages over foreign nationals for companies that sell their products internationally. In general, a successful expatriation starts with a selection of good candidates who are willing to try

---

[40]James K, Sebenius, "The Hidden Challenge of Cross-Border Negotiations," *Harvard Business Review,* March 2002, pp. 76–85.

[41]Ibid. p. 84.

[42]Gunter K. Stahl, Edwin L. Miller, and Rosalie L. Tung, "Toward the Boundaryless Career: A Closer Look at the Expatriate Career Concept and the Perceived Implications of an International Assignment," *Journal of World Business,* 37 (Autumn 2002), pp. 216–27.

new things and persist in exhibiting an open-minded and flexible personality to accept the host country's norms. Therefore, firms should select expatriates whose personal values are in line with those of the host countries so that expatriates would have more social interaction with host nationals. For example, when U.S. expatriates possess collective norms that are similar to those of Asian and Latin American cultures, they would have more social interaction with the locals and are more attitudinally attached to the host culture.[43]

Advantages of Expatriates

Jack Welch, the former CEO of General Electric, stated in a speech to GE employees:

> The Jack Welch of the future cannot be me. I spent my entire career in the United States. The next head of General Electric will be somebody who spent time in Bombay (Mumbai), in Hong Kong, in Buenos Aires. We have to send our best and brightest overseas and make sure they have the training that will allow them to be the global leaders who will make GE flourish in the future.[44]

His statement clearly summarizes the importance of expatriates and their international experiences for improved communications between the company's headquarters and its foreign subsidiaries and affiliates and the development of talent within the company.

Better Communication. Expatriates understand the home office, its politics, and its priorities. They are intimately familiar with the products being sold and with previously successful sales techniques. Expatriates can rely on personal relationships with home office management, which increases trust on both sides of the border and can give the expatriate the ability to achieve things that a third-country national or a host country national could not achieve. With an expatriate abroad, communications with the home country will be easier and more precise owing to the groundwork of cultural and corporate understanding. The expatriate will also give the home office the sense that it has someone in place who it is sure understands the company's intent and expectations.

Development of Talent. Sending employees abroad provides the company another advantage that hiring foreign locals may not provide: The company develops future managers and executives who can later use their international perspective in management. For example, the leaders of General Motors, Avon, Campbell Soup, Ford, Gillette, Tupperware, Goodyear, General Mills, Case, and Outboard Marine all have significant overseas experience in their careers.[45] According to research by Gregersen, Morrison, and Black, senior executives of multinationals who have had international assignments indicated that those jobs provided their single most influential leadership experience.[46] Thus, by sending their most promising rising stars overseas, companies are sowing the seeds to harvest the next generation of executives.

Difficulties of Sending Expatriates Abroad

Although the benefits of sending expatriates abroad are clear, difficulties can also arise for various reasons ranging from organizational to personal ones and even to security risk. Some of the major difficulties are as follows.

[43]Sunkyu Jun and James W. Gentry, "An Exploratory Investigation of the Relative Importance of Cultural Similarity and Personal Fit in the Selection and Performance of Expatriates," *Journal of World Business,* 40 (February 2005), pp. 1–8.

[44]Mansour Javidan and Robert J. House, "Leadership and Cultures around the World: Findings from GLOBE," *Journal of World Business,* 37 (Spring 2002), pp. 3–10.

[45]Mason A. Carpenter and Gerard Sanders, "International Assignment Experience at the Top Can Make a Bottom-Line Difference," *Human Resource Management,* 39 (Summer/Fall 2000), pp. 277–85.

[46]Hal B. Gregersen, Allen J. Morrison, and J. Stewart Black, "Developing Leaders for the Global Frontier," *Sloan Management Review,* 40 (Fall 1998), pp. 21–32.

Cross-Cultural Training. As with so many other complex situations in life, a little shared understanding goes a long way. In the case of the expatriate, training can significantly help in understanding the cultural differences of the foreign country. U.S. companies used to overlook such "cultural sensitivity training"; expatriates were expected to "pick it up as they go." Cultural misunderstandings can have a large impact, however. GMAC's Global Relocation Services' 2003/2004 survey reported that about 7 percent of expatriate assignments failed prematurely.[47] As a result, **cross-cultural training** has been on the rise in recent years as more globally oriented companies moving fast-track executives overseas want to curb the cost of failed expatriate stints.

Also according to the GMAC survey, 31 percent of respondents cited an increase in the expatriate population during 2003 and 39 percent in 2004. It also reported that 17 percent of all expatriates were new hires and 21 percent of expatriates had previous international experience. Companies are becoming more flexible about the length of international assignments and are moving away from long-term assignments to a variety of short-term alternatives. The survey also found that more companies have embraced a global perception of their entire workforce, therefore utilizing their human resources more effectively and have chosen to outsource their relocation programs to achieve higher levels of financial return, expatriate performance, and satisfaction. Most companies (60 percent) provide formal cross-cultural preparation of at least one day, and some provide training for the entire family. Most participants (73 percent) indicated that these formal programs had a high value.[48] On average, a cross-cultural training program costs $3,000 to $6,000 per expatriate to be. Although cultural orientation and foreign language training are two of the most important parts of the cross-cultural training program, companies need cultural orientation (including history and background of country) more than foreign language training.[49]

Once the expatriate is abroad, it becomes more difficult to provide training, but doing so is even more important. The expatriates are not in constant contact with colleagues and could not be picking up the newest technology in their company's field. They could be missing out on important policy or procedural changes that the company is undertaking. Ongoing training, whether in a foreign or the home country, can make a huge difference in the success of an overseas assignment.

It is advised that the more different the culture into which people are venturing, the more specific and rigorous the training needs to be and the more the training needs to incorporate experiential tactics such as simulations and role-plays aimed at specific differences.[50]

However, expatriates must recognize that within an average two- to four-year assignment abroad, they will never internalize enough of the local culture to overcome all social and communication concerns. Even with appropriate training, the expatriates are the product of their home culture. They will eat with a fork when a hand is more polite, shake on a deal and thereby show their lack of faith, or require that a contract with all possible legal contingencies spelled out be signed in triplicate when honor and trust dictate that the deal go through on a shared local drink. These could appear to be small social problems, but such social problems can keep the expatriate out

---

[47]"Global Relocation Trends 2003/2004 Survey Report," GMAC Relocation Services, http://www
.gmacglobalrelocation.com/ accessed May 2004.

[48]Ibid.

[49]Maali H. Ashamalla, "International Human Resource Management Practices: The Challenge of Expatriation," *Competitiveness Review,* 8(2), 1998, pp. 54–65.

[50]J. Stewart Black, Mark Mendenhall, and Gary Oddou, "Toward a Comprehensive Model of International Adjustment. An Integration of Multiple Theoretical Perspectives," *Academy of Management Review,* 16 (April 1991), pp. 291–317.

of important deals. As Black and Porter[51] noted in their article title, "a successful manager in Los Angeles may not succeed in Hong Kong." The expatriate could find after some time that the best place to make sales is not at the client's offices but at the bar watching soccer with other executives.

Motivation. Motivating expatriates to accept and succeed at positions abroad requires a combination of carefully planned policies and incentives. Appropriate policies help make the prospect of going overseas attractive before, during, and after it takes place. Expatriates often express dissatisfaction that their stints abroad hinder their career progress. Companies should set up and publicize career paths that reward and use skills that expatriates acquire overseas. Additionally, while expatriates are overseas, regular communication with the home office will help allay fears that "out of sight, out of mind" will hinder their career progress.[52] Intranet Web sites for expatriates will help facilitate such communication.

A recent study also shows that employees who choose an expatriate assignment place a high intrinsic value on the overseas experience per se, especially on the opportunities it brings for personality development and enrichment of their personal lives. They also believe that their overseas assignment will help improve their professional and management skills and enhance their careers, although not necessarily within their current company.[53]

Compensation. The average cost of maintaining a home country executive can cost three to five times what it costs to maintain an employee at home.[54] Compensation packages include various premiums including overseas premiums, housing allowances, cost-of-living allowances, tax equalizations, repatriation allowances, all-expense-paid vacations, and performance-based bonuses. Most compensation premiums are paid as a percentage of base salary. Despite this, according to GMAC's Global Relocation Trends 2003/2004 Survey, 54 percent of expatriates were sometimes dissatisfied with their expatriation salaries and benefits and with their international compensation packages in general.[55] How much should overseas assignments pay?

One approach has been to pay expatriates a premium for their willingness to live in adverse conditions. Such special "hardship packages" can cause problems, however. Overseas employees could notice the discrepancy in remuneration among expatriates, local nationals, and third-country nationals.[56] An expatriate sales manager in Japan could be motivated by an incentive system through which she would earn a higher salary for stellar performance. However, such an individual approach would not sit well with Japanese colleagues who subscribe to a collective approach that does not favor standing out of others of similar seniority. Furthermore, expatriates who receive a generous compensation package while abroad could lose motivation on returning home to their previous salary scale.[57] A more recent approach has been to consider the overseas assignment a necessary step for progress within the company. In other words, it is viewed more as a learning experience than as a hardship.

---

[51]J. Stewart Black and Lyman W. Porter, "Managerial Behaviors and Job Performance: A Successful Manager in Los Angeles May Not Succeed in Hong Kong," *Journal of International Business Studies,* 22 (First Quarter 1991), pp. 99–113.

[52]Thomas F. O'Boyle, "Little Benefit to Careers Seen in Foreign Stints," *Wall Street Journal,* December 11, 1989, pp. B1, B4.

[53]Gunter K. Stahl, Edwin L. Miller, and Rosalie L. Tung, "Toward the Boundaryless Career: A Closer Look at the Expatriate Career Concept and the Perceived Implications of an International Assignment," *Journal of World Business,* 37 (Autumn 2002), pp. 216–27.

[54]Eric Krell, "Evaluating Returns on Expatriates," *HR Magazine,* 50 (March 2005), pp. 60–65.

[55]"Global Relocation Trends 2003/2004 Survey Report."

[56]So Min Toh and Angelo S. DeNisi, "A Local Perspective to Expatriate Success," *Academy of Management Executive,* 19 (1), 2005, 132–47.

[57]Michael Harvey, "Empirical Evidence of Recurring International Compensation Problems," *Journal of International Business Studies,* 24 (Fourth Quarter 1993), pp. 785–99.

The company must also consider the impact of the family life cycle on compensation. Expatriates with spouses and children encounter higher needs abroad, including the loss of a spouse's income and the cost of enrolling children in private schools. A program must be flexible enough to adjust to the varying needs of different employees.

Family Discord. The typical candidate for an international assignment is married, has school-age children, and is expected to stay overseas for three years. In this age of two-career families, an international assignment means that a spouse could have to suspend a stateside career. Thus, many employees are reluctant to move abroad. Others who accept transfers grow frustrated as they find that their spouses cannot get jobs or even work permits abroad. Schools where English is spoken must be found, or children must learn the local language. Concerns about the safety and happiness of family members can keep the candidate from accepting an overseas position. Given such complexities, it is clear why it can be difficult to motivate typical candidates to accept an overseas stint.[58]

Unsuccessful family adjustment is the single most important reason for expatriate dissatisfaction compelling an early return home. Expatriates as well as their family members are in crisis because of culture shock and stress. As a result, marriages break up and some people become alcoholic.

Thus, international companies try to cut costs by reducing the problems that can hurt expatriates' job satisfaction and performance. For example, AT&T has begun putting prospective expatriates through management interviews, a written test, and a self-assessment checklist of "cultural adaptability" (see Global Perspective 15-3) as well as interviews with a psychologist. To help spouses find jobs abroad, Philip Morris Company hired an outplacement firm to provide career counseling and job leads.[59]

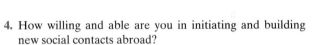

GLOBAL PERSPECTIVE 15-3

SCREENING CANDIDATES FOR EXPATRIATION

An increasing number of companies are screening prospective expatriates and their spouses for cross-cultural adaptability. The following are some of the questions asked at AT&T:

1. Would your spouse's career be put on hold to accompany you on an international assignment? If so, how would this affect your spouse and your relationship with each other?

2. Would you enjoy the challenge of making your own way in new environments?

3. How would you feel about the need for networking and being your own advocate to secure a job upon return from your foreign assignment?

4. How willing and able are you in initiating and building new social contacts abroad?

5. Could you live without television?

6. How important is it for you to spend a significant amount of time with people of your own ethnic, racial, religious, and national background?

7. Have you ever been genuinely interested in learning about other peoples and cultures?

8. Do you like vacationing in foreign countries?

9. Do you enjoy ethnic and foreign cuisine?

10. How tolerant are you of having to wait for repairs?

Source: Gilbert Fuchsberg, "As Costs of Overseas Assignments Climb, Firms Select Expatriates More Carefully," *Wall Street Journal,* January 9, 1992, p. B1.

---

[58]Maali H. Ashamalla, "International Human Resource Management Practices: The Challenge of Expatriation," *Competitiveness Review,* 8 (2), 1998, pp. 54–65.

[59]Carla Joinson, "Relocation Counseling Meets Employees' Changing Needs," *HRMagazine,* 43 (February 1998), pp. 63–70.

Security Risk. Since the September 11, 2001, terrorist attacks in the United States, security risk has become a serious issue. Clearly, these terrorist attacks, among others, have had an impact on human resource management. Particularly, expatriate executives from U.S. companies and their families are not as eager to take international assignments, especially in countries viewed as security risks. Perceived or real security risk concern requires more development, training, and recruiting of local executives, which in the long run should be beneficial to all.

Despite such an anxiety factor causing some dent in the globalization movement, the forces of market and financial globalization are unlikely to be reversed. In fact, more executives have been trained to believe that international experience is critical to their long-term career success. Because of the increased number of international MBA students in many business schools around the world, they are increasingly being placed in countries in which they fit right in culturally, religiously, and racially. These "indigenized" managers increase the frequency of international travel, cross-border migration, and lower communication costs across national boundaries.[60]

The Return of the Expatriate—Repatriation

Repatriation is the return of the expatriate employee from overseas. Although companies are making efforts to prevent this, many returning expatriates have difficulty finding good job assignments when their foreign positions end. The postreturn concern that an overseas assignment can damage a career back home can discourage employees from taking a foreign position. GMAC Relocation Services' 2001 survey reported a deplorable picture: of companies surveyed, 66 percent indicated that they offered no postexpatriate employment guarantees; and worse yet, 49 percent did not even know the attrition rates of repatriates. Repatriated managers in U.S. firms leave their companies at twice the rate of domestic managers without international experience. The survey also indicates that 13 percent of repatriate managers leave their companies within one year after returning from overseas assignments and another 10 percent within two years.[61] In the past two decades, U.S. companies have failed to make any measurable improvement in their repatriation policies.

Repatriation is distinct from other forms of relocation. After an average absence of 3.5 years, expatriates themselves have changed, adopting certain values, attitudes, and habits of their host countries—and the United States has changed, politically, economically, and technologically. The results of poorly handling repatriates are poor employee performance and high employee turnover—both very costly to the organization.

Expatriates face a long list of difficulties upon returning home. Their standard of living often declines, and they often face a lack of appreciation for the knowledge they gained overseas. Without a clear use for their skills, returned expatriates often suffer from a lack of direction and purpose. New stateside assignments often do not give the repatriated employee the same responsibility, freedom, or respect that was enjoyed overseas. It is difficult to adjust to being just another middle manager at home, and poor communications with the home office while abroad leave the returnee cut off from the internal happenings and politics of the company, limiting opportunities for career growth.[62]

GMAC Relocation Services' 2001 survey also reported a number of effective ways to reduce attrition rates. These include providing (1) chances to use international experience, (2) a choice of positions upon return, (3) recognition, and (4) repatriation career support. Pretrip training should state the details for the candidate, including future training expected, help the company will provide, and, importantly, the career

---

[60]Sevgin Eroglu, "Does Globalization Have Staying Power?" *Marketing Management,* 11 (March/April 2002), pp. 18–23.

[61]"Global Relocation Trends 2003/2004 Survey Report."

[62]Aaron W. Andreason and Kevin D. Kinneer, "Bringing Them Home Again," *Industrial Management,* 46 (November/December 2004), pp. 13–19.

path that the move will help. The effort and cost of such comprehensive planning sends a strong signal of the importance of foreign assignments to expatriate candidates.

Expatriates are important whenever communication with the home country office is at a premium. Communication is facilitated among managers of the same nationality. Thus, the company is better off with a stronger expatriate base abroad when the overseas situation puts pressure on communications with the home office. Thus, expatriates are especially important in complex operating environments, when elevated political risk requires constant monitoring, or when a high cultural distance separates the home and host countries. On the other hand, in very competitive environments, local nationals could provide important links to the local business community and perhaps play a key strategic role in gaining business.

Generalizations about When Using Expatriates Is Positive/ Negative

SUMMARY ✦

No matter how global a company becomes, its salesforce remains its front line. On the other hand, actual sales activities are truly local activities, far detached from decision making at headquarters. Particularly in Latin European, Latin American, and Asian countries, salespeople's ability to build trust with prospective customers prior to sales is extremely important. An effective salesforce management is most elusive yet crucial to developing a coherent international marketing and distribution strategy.

Because sales activities are local activities, they tend to be strongly affected by cultural differences (e.g., shopping habit, negotiation style) around the world, making it difficult, if not impossible, for the international marketing manager to integrate overseas sales operations. Many companies rely on merchant distributors at home or sales agents in the foreign market who have more intimate knowledge of the marketplace. As sales increase, these companies begin to increase their commitment to developing their own distribution and salesforce in the foreign market.

The development of an effective sales organization requires salesforce objectives and a salesforce strategy adapted to local differences and calls for careful recruiting, training, supervising, motivating, and compensating local salespeople. We

also provided some background on a very complex form of cultural interface: cross-cultural negotiations. Several strategies are introduced to assist you in international bargaining situations.

Furthermore, an increasing number of expatriate managers are sent to overseas posts to directly manage the company's local salesforce. Expatriate managers function as a bridge between headquarters and local operations and must be culturally adaptive and versatile. Although international assignments have increasingly become a necessary requirement for fast-track managers, cultural adaptability is not always an inborn qualification of many expatriate managers. Cross-cultural training is crucial because failed expatriate assignments cost the company dearly in terms of lower business performance and dejected employee morale. Use of expatriate managers with personal profiles that fit in well with local cultures is also on the increase for reasons of political correctness. Companies recently have also begun to develop a repatriation program to ease returned expatriates back into their stateside positions. Such a well-organized repatriation program is important to encourage managers to take up expatriate assignments.

KEY TERMS ✦

Corporate (organizational) culture
Cross-cultural training
Expatriate
Export management company (EMC)

Export trading company (ETC)
Myers–Briggs Type Indicator (MBTI)
Negotiation script
Personal selling

Repatriation
Sogoshosha (general trading company)

REVIEW QUESTIONS ✦

1. In what ways does international sales management differ from domestic sales management?

2. Discuss why mode of entry and sales management are closely related.

3. For what type of business does a company employ a traveling global salesforce?

4. How could a foreign government affect a company's salesforce management?

5. Why is it generally considered difficult to adopt a U.S.-style commission-based salesforce management in such countries as Japan and Mexico?

6. Discuss why expatriate managers are important to a parent company despite the enormous cost of sending them overseas.

7. Suppose you are developing a cultural training program for employees to be sent to overseas posts. What courses would you include in your two-week program? Why?

DISCUSSION QUESTIONS ◆

1. One feature in international selling that is becoming more common is the idea of piggybacking (i.e., tying up with existing sales channels to distribute and sell your products). Examples include Dunkin Donuts (as the name suggests, the confectionery chain) combining with Baskin-Robbins (the ice cream chain) units to sell in Canada, Mexico, and Indonesia. According to business proponents of piggybacking, it allows a significant reduction in costs and risks by sharing resources such as dining space, staff, and so on, leading to better profitability. However, the concern is that a foreign partner often chosen as the piggybacking partner (unlike the example just stated) could devote less attention to the foreign product. If the piggybacking is with a unit in the same business, considerable cannibalization can also take place. Discuss the conditions under which a piggyback strategy would be appropriate and under which conditions it would not be appropriate.

2. Many U.S. companies such as Home Depot, Intel, Kodak, Nike, and Whirlpool have set up sales offices in China. One thing sales managers must be aware of is that the differences in sales styles between the United States and China are vast. For example, relationship building is very important in sales and in hiring sales people in China. Furthermore, companies need to figure out what part of the country and what market segments they are to enter. Generally speaking, Chinese consumers are more price conscious than Japanese and Korean consumers. However, Chinese youth are less likely to follow the traditional values of collectivism, restraint, and harmony, but exhibit strong tendencies of individualism and self-reliance. They worship more Western brands in comparison to domestic brands. If U.S.-based companies were to set up sales offices in China, what would be their challenges and opportunities? Given the differences in sales styles between the United States and China, what should the company do to enhance its sales management?

3. Domino's Pizza International, the pizza chain based in Ann Arbor, Michigan, is known worldwide for its delivery service. Its policy of giving away its pizza free if not delivered within half an hour was a legendary service theme, and it earned the company a unique position in the consumer's mind. However, the company's foray into Poland in 1994 proved how modifications to positioning strategies can become essential in certain international markets. In 1994, the company wanted to open franchises in Poland. It was keen on opening delivery units as it has in most other countries. However, the lack of reliable and appropriate infrastructure in terms of telephone service in Poland posed a problem. Its delivery concept would not ride very far if potential customers could not phone in their orders. So, in stark contrast to its policy in other countries, Domino opened a sit-in restaurant in Poland, followed by another one several months later. Only after some time did it open its standard delivery unit. While this was one way of tiding over the selling constraints peculiar to this market, there was the risk that it was deviating from its most salient positioning theme. Do you think the strategy adopted by Domino's was a wise one? If so, give reasons. If not, provide an alternate strategy, giving your justification for the same.

4. Many firms in the past followed an incremental approach to the sales channels used in international markets. Typically, these companies started by selling in foreign markets through sales agents or distributors. This was followed by opening liaison offices to assist and monitor the activities of the appointed distributors. With subsequent growth in business, the company would set up its own sales subsidiary to manage sales and customer service. This incremental strategy has worked quite effectively for many companies in the past. In your opinion, would the current emphasis being placed on globalization have any bearing on the effectiveness of this incremental strategy? If so, what would this effect be, and why?

SHORT CASES

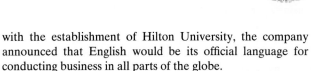

ASE 15-1

HILTON UNIVERSITY—FOR EMPLOYEES ONLY!

Product-based multinational firms with worldwide operations and therefore a diverse workforce face a major task training employees in different regions to maintain a uniform organizational culture throughout the global company. For multinational service firms, maintaining an educated, well-trained workforce is even more challenging. That is why many service firms have made it a priority to establish training programs. Consider the hospitality industry as an example. In the pre-World Wide Web era, these training programs were face-to-face activities carried out in various foreign locations. The downside of this form of classroom instruction was cost, time, and the wide disparity of teaching methods in different places. Today, however, more and more global service firms are taking their classrooms online. This form of training not only lowers overall costs but also attempts to transfer the image of corporate culture.

Premier hotel group Hilton International launched its Hilton University in 2002, solely for training and educating its global employees. Prior to this initiative, employee training was conducted on every Hilton hotel's premises in more than 65 countries. Needless to say, the costs of training, time taken, and the training programs differed to a certain extent based on location. Also, the company does not own all of Hilton's hotels. Some hotels are managed by outsiders. The company felt the need to consolidate employee training and introduced online training. Another reason for establishing Hilton University was that corporate headquarters felt the need to monitor and control training programs, mainly the content of the training program and its effect on employee skills.

Hilton University conducts several different online training programs. Its employees worldwide are expected to get training for at least 40 hours in a year. One of the business's primary needs is the ability of its hotel staff to effectively communicate with its customers. Given that many of its hotels are located in non-English speaking countries, the English training program has become one of the most important. Hilton's main clientele are of high-income, educated travelers who are willing to pay a premium for good service and comfort. A large number of its patrons are also from its home country (United States). Hence, a majority of its customers are English speaking and

Source: John Guthrie, "Hilton International: Creating a Global Service Culture," *Chief Learning Officer*, 4, (January 2005), pp. 54–56.

with the establishment of Hilton University, the company announced that English would be its official language for conducting business in all parts of the globe.

Theoretically, the establishment of the online university seemed useful. In reality, however, less than 10 percent of Hilton's foreign staff was fluent in English and since most of the courses were in English, this posed a major problem. Most of these courses were thus not comprehensible to the majority of its employees. A possible solution to this problem was to introduce courses in different languages. In addition to the complexity of this task, the company was unable to provide similar learning opportunities to its non-English speaking staff.

In response to this need to have all its employees well versed in the English language, Hilton University started an English course. Another reason for the introduction of this course was that the company wanted to create an organization culture of shared beliefs about the company and for employees to be able to share knowledge, information, and ideas.

The results of the English training program were good. On an average, more than 75 percent of Hilton's foreign employees commended the program and claimed that it had given them the necessary language skills to be able to confidently perform their jobs. As mentioned earlier, Hilton had set a target of 40 hours per employee, but the number of hours actually clocked in by employees exceeded the target by 10 hours on an average.

Boosted by the success of its online programs, Hilton University has introduced several others that the company expects to increase employee productivity and improve service at its hotels all over the world. This initiative by the company has also raised its image in the eyes of employees, and positioned the company much closer to its objective of maintaining a global service-oriented organization culture.

DISCUSSION QUESTIONS

1. Should the sales force of service multinationals have a global service strategy like Hilton does, or should it be more locally oriented to serve the needs of regional customers? Why?

2. How is sales force training in manufacturing firms different from that in service firms?

3. What are the pros and cons of online training versus face-to-face classroom based training?

$\mathscr{C}$ASE 15-2

PROGEON CALL CENTER SERVICES

Western firms have been outsourcing manufacturing operations to low-cost countries for more than five decades now. Business Process Outsourcing, or BPO as it is commonly known, is a relatively new practice and highly controversial at best. The volume of this form of outsourcing has grown exponentially in the last few years. BPO has been mainly used by firms in emerging economies that can provide low-cost services. Its use has led to the establishment of call centers in countries such as India, where a significant part of the population is able to communicate in English. A *call center* is any organization or a part of an organization that handles incoming and outgoing consumer telephone calls. The way a foreign call center works is that calls to a company such as Cisco from customers in the United States, for example, are routed to call centers such as Progeon in Bangalore, India. Progeon's employees answer these calls and address their purposes. Sometimes, Progeon's staff is also required to make calls to its client's customers overseas. This enables Western firms to provide services round the clock to their customers and avail itself of such services at lower costs. Thus, call center employees indirectly make up a part of the foreign sales force of Western firms. Until some years ago, Western multinationals operated their own call centers in their home countries. Recently, these operations have shifted to emerging countries.

The Indian information systems company Infosys, one of the fastest growing companies in Asia, set up a subsidiary in April 2002 to respond to this growth in demand for services. The unit, known as Progeon, is jointly owned by Infosys, which owns around 80 percent of the company and by one of Citigroup's finance companies. Since its establishment, Progeon has nabbed BPO contracts with Western firms such as Cisco and British Telecom. Today, the company has more than 20 such large contracts. Progeon provides services related to insurance, banking, finance, and telecom to its customers. These services are grouped into voice jobs and data jobs. Voice jobs are housed in a call center. Most of the firm's clients also have information–technology, related contracts with one of its parent companies, Infosys.

Progeon's call center operations cater to customers of its Western client firms.

Source: Charlotte Huff, "Accent on Training," *Workforce Management,* 84, March 2005, p. 54.

Often when Western customers dial a phone number to reach a company such as Cisco, they are unaware that their call has been routed overseas. A major part of the task for call center employees all over India then is to perfect an American or British accent, depending on where their corporate client is based. While most call center employees are hired subject to their ability to speak and write English their language very often is heavily accented. This is true in case of India, which has more than 15 different main languages and 100 dialects. Therefore, training call center personnel is important before allowing them to get on the job. Most call centers have rigorous training programs that last around a month for new employees before putting them on the job. These programs include training through singing, skits, conversation simulations, and so forth, all with the required accent. Quick learners among new employees are often given awards to motivate them.

Progeon developed its own version of the new sales force training program, for which it won the Optimas Award given by *Workforce Management* magazine in 2005. Whereas call center employees in other firms are also accent and language trained, Progeon's new recruits are taught about the industry in which their client firm operates in addition to accent training. They also are educated about the firm's history, common usage terms, recent news, and strategies so that they are well versed with the firm's operations. New recruits are made to perfect their accents based on instructions and a thorough analysis of their recorded voices. Recently hired employees are given a course on variation in social behavior in different cultures. As a result, the company has considerably improved the overall quality of its staff. Progeon has significantly reduced employee turnover and enabled the company to gain an upper hand over its rivals. In a country where call centers have sprung up in nearly every corner of major cities, Progeon has managed to differentiate itself.

DISCUSSION QUESTIONS

1. What are some of the problems that Progeon's well-trained staff could still face given that their clients are from culturally distant countries?

2. What are the drawbacks of BPO through call centers in far-off locations for multinational firms?

FURTHER READING

Blodgett, Jeffrey G., Long-Chuan Lu, Gregory M. Rose, and Scott J. Vitell. "Ethical Sensitivity to Stakeholder Interests: A Cross-Cultural Comparison." *Academy of Marketing Science,* 29 (2), 2001, pp. 190–202.

DeCarlo, Thomas E., Raymond C. Rody, and James E. DeCarlo. "A Cross National Example of Supervisory Management Practices in the Sales Force." *Journal of Personal Selling & Sales Management,* 19 (Winter 1999), pp. 1–14.

Elahee, Mohammad N., Susan L. Kirby, and Ercan Nacif. "National Culture, Trust, and Perceptions about Ethical Behavior in Intra and Cross-Cultural Negotiations: An Analysis of NAFTA Countries." *Thunderbird International Business Review,* 44 (November/December 2002), pp. 799–818.

Engle, Robert L. "Global Marketing Management Scorecard: A Tale of Two Multinational Companies." *Problems & Perspectives in Management,* 3 (2005), pp. 128–136.

Evans, Jody, and Felix T. Mavondo. "Psychic Distance and Organizational Performance: An Empirical Examination of International Retailing Operations." *Journal of International Business Studies,* 33 (3), 2002, pp. 515–32.

Gorchels, Linda, Thani Jambulingam, and Timothy W. Aurand. "International Marketing Managers: A Comparison of Japanese, German, and U.S. Perceptions." *Journal of International Marketing,* 7 (1), 1999, pp. 97–105.

Honeycutt, Earl D., Jr., and John B. Ford. "Selecting and Training the International Sales Force." *Industrial Marketing Management,* 28 (November 1999), pp. 627–35.

Jantan, M. Asri, and Earl Honeycutt, Jr. "Sales Training Practices in Malaysia." *Multinational Business Review,* 10 (Spring 2002), pp. 72–78.

Lenartowicz, Tomasz, and Kendall Roth. "Does Subculture within a Country Matter? A Cross-Cultural Study of Motivational Domains and Business Performance in Brazil." *Journal of International Business Studies,* 32 (2), 2001, pp. 305–25.

Neale, Margaret E. *Business Week's Guide to Cross-Cultural Negotiating. Maximizing Profitability in Intra- and Inter-Cultural Negotiations.* New York: McGraw-Hill, 1995.

Palich, Leslie E., Gary R. Carini, and Linda P. Livingstone. "Comparing American and Chinese Negotiating Styles: The Influence of Logic Paradigms." *Thunderbird International Business Review,* 44 (November/December 2002), pp. 777–98.

Piercy, Nigel F., George S. Low, and David W. Cravens. "Consequences of Sales Management's Behavior- and Compensation-Based Control Strategies in Developing Countries." *Journal of International Marketing,* 12 (3), 2004, pp. 30–57.

Sebenius, James K. "The Hidden Challenge of Cross-Border Negotiations." *Harvard Business Review,* 80 (March 2002), pp. 76–85.

Ulijn, Jan, and Dean Tjosvold. "Innovation in International Negotiation: Content and Style." *International Negotiation,* 9 (2), 2004, pp. 195–199.

Zoubir, Yahir H., and Roger Volkema. "Special Issue: Cross-Cultural Negotiations." *Thunderbird International Business Review,* 44 (November/December 2002).

GLOBAL LOGISTICS
AND DISTRIBUTION

16

HAPTER OVERVIEW

1. DEFINITION OF GLOBAL LOGISTICS

2. MANAGEMENT OF GLOBAL LOGISTICS

3. FREE TRADE ZONES

4. MAQUILADORA OPERATION

5. GLOBAL RETAILING

Global logistics and distribution have played a critical role in the growth and development of world trade and in the integration of manufacturing on a worldwide scale. In fact, the level of world trade in goods and, to some extent, services, depends to a significant degree on the availability of economical and reliable international transportation services. Decreases in transportation costs and increases in performance reliability expand the scope of manufacturing operations and increase the associated level of international trade and competition.[1] The use of appropriate distribution channels in international markets increases the chances of success dramatically. Coca-Cola's success relies largely on its global distribution arm, Coca-Cola Enterprises, the world's largest bottler group. It helps Coca-Cola market, produce, and distribute bottled and canned products all over the world. The group also purchases and distributes certain noncarbonated beverages such as isotonies, teas, and juice drinks in finished form from the Coca-Cola company. The amount of bottles and cans distributed by the company represents up to 21 percent of Coca-Cola's volume worldwide.[2]

The concept of business logistics is relatively new. John F. Magee is generally credited with publishing the first article on logistics theory in 1960.[3] As far back as 1954, Peter Drucker had said that logistics would remain "the dark continent of

---

[1] John H. Dunning, "Reappraising the Eclectic Paradigm in an Age of Alliance Capitalism," *Journal of International Business Studies,* 26 (Third Quarter 1995), pp. 461–91.

[2] Coca-Cola Enterprises, http://www.cokecce.com, accessed December 22, 2005.

[3] John F. Magee, "The Logistics of Distribution," *Harvard Business Review,* 38 (July 1960), pp. 89–101.

business"[4]—the least well understood area of business—and his prediction proved true until well into the 1980s. It is not too difficult to demonstrate the importance of the physical handling, moving, storing, and retrieving of material. In almost every product, more than 50 percent of product cost is material related while less than 10 percent is labor. Over the years, however, this fact has not received much attention. In 2004, the total logistics cost represented about 9 percent of the GDP, or $1 trillion, in the United States. Among them, transportation costs alone accounted for $644 billion in 2004 compared to $604 billion a year earlier.[5]

Since the 1990s, a variety of issues has been driving the increased emphasis on logistics and distribution management. It was epitomized in 1998 by General Motors' lawsuit against Volkswagen over the defection of José Ignacio Lopez, the former vice president of purchasing at General Motors and one of the most renowned logistics managers in the automobile industry.[6] His expertise is said to have saved General Motors several billion dollars from its purchasing and logistic operations, which would directly affect the company's bottom line. The importance of distribution channels is further evidenced by the recent mergers in the auto industry, in which giant multinationals are gobbling up smaller manufacturers with strong brand names but inadequate global distribution, such as Ford's acquisition of Volvo.[7]

As firms start operating on a global basis, logistics managers need to manage the shipping of raw materials, components, and supplies among various manufacturing sites at the most economical and reliable rates. Simultaneously, these firms need to ship finished goods to customers in markets around the world at the desired place and time. The development of intermodal transportation and electronic tracking technology has caused a quantum jump in the efficiency of the logistic methods employed by firms. **Intermodal transportation** refers to the seamless transfer of goods from one mode of transport (e.g., aircraft or ship) to another (e.g., truck) and vice versa without the hassle of unpacking and repackaging the goods to suit the dimensions of the mode of transport being used. *Tracking technology* refers to the means for keeping continuous tabs on the exact location of the goods being shipped in the logistic chain—this enables quick reaction to any disruption in the shipments because (1) the shipper knows exactly where the goods are in real time and (2) the alternative means can be quickly mobilized.

DEFINITION OF GLOBAL LOGISTICS ◆ ◆ ◆ ◆ ◆ ◆ ◆ ◆

Global logistics is defined as the design and management of a system that directs and controls the flows of materials into, through, and out of the firm across national boundaries to achieve its corporate objectives at a minimum total cost. As shown in Exhibit 16-1, global logistics encompasses the entire range of operations concerned with products or components movement, including both exports and imports simultaneously. Global logistics, like domestic logistics, encompasses materials management and physical distribution.[8]

Materials management refers to the inflow of raw materials, parts, and supplies in and through the firm. This topic was explored earlier in Chapter 10 in the context of global sourcing strategy, or management of R&D, manufacturing, and marketing interfaces. **Physical distribution** refers to the movement of the firm's finished products to its customers consisting of transportation, warehousing, inventory, customer

---

[4]Peter F. Drucker, *The Practice of Management* (New York: Harper & Brothers, 1954).

[5]William Hoffman, "End of an Era?" *Traffic World,* July 4, 2005, pp. 9–13.

[6]"No Ordinary Car Thief," *U.S. News & World Report,* June 5, 2000, p. 52.

[7]Alzira Salama, Wayne Holland, and Gerald Vinten, "Challenges and Opportunities in Mergers and Acquisitions: Three International Case Studies—Deutsche Bank–Bankers Trust; British Petroleum–Amoco; Ford–Volvo," *Journal of European Industrial Training,* 27 (6), 2003, pp. 313–21.

[8]Donald J. Bowersox, David J. Closs, and M. Bixby Cooper, *Supply Chain Logistics Management* (Boston: McGraw-Hill, 2002).

EXHIBIT 16-1
GLOBAL LOGISTICS

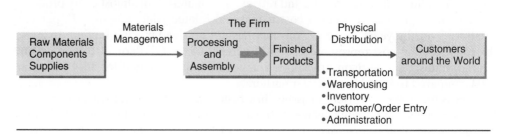

service/order entry, and administration. In this chapter, we focus on physical distribution management.

Although the functions of physical distribution are universal, they are affected differently by the tradition, culture, economic infrastructure, laws, and topography, among others, in each country and each region. In general, in geographically large countries such as the United States where products are transported over a long distance, firms tend to incur relatively more transportation and inventory costs than do firms in smaller countries. On the other hand, in geographically concentrated countries, such as Japan and Britain, firms tend to incur relatively more warehousing, customer service/order entry, and general administrative costs than in geographically larger countries. This is so primarily because a wide variety of products with different features have to be stored to meet the varied needs of customers in concentrated areas. The results of a recent survey of physical distribution costs in various European countries relative to the United States are presented in Global Perspective 16-1. Although it is possible to attribute all cost differences to topography, customs, laws of the country, and other factors, the cost differences could also reflect how efficiently or inefficiently physical distribution is managed in various countries and regions.

*G*LOBAL PERSPECTIVE 16-1

REGIONAL VARIATIONS IN PHYSICAL DISTRIBUTION COSTS IN EUROPE AND ROOM FOR IMPROVEMENT

Physical distribution costs consist of transportation, warehousing, inventory, customer service/order entry, and administration. Let's compare these components of distribution costs in the United States and the European Union. The following table shows cost comparisons as a percentage of revenue.

The largest disparity was in warehousing, where European costs measured 3.03 percent, almost one-third of total distribution costs, compared to 1.98 percent in the United States. These expenses include the cost of both plant and field warehouses including labor, space, direct materials, and so on. Similarly, a large difference exists in customer service/order entry—the cost of people, space, and materials needed to take orders and handle inquiries—0.83 percent in Europe, compared to 0.49 percent in the United States.

	European Union	The United States
Transportation	2.79%	3.23%
Warehousing	3.03	1.98
Inventory	1.73	1.93
Customer service/ order entry	0.83	0.49
Administration	0.79	0.44
Total	9.17	8.07

European governments have begun to privatize transportation services. Since January 1, 1993, the European Union (EU) has been able to offer opportunities to reduce logistics costs and boost efficiency. Both Europeans and foreign manufacturers, including those in North America, are finding that political changes in Europe have created opportunities for greater efficiency and lower costs in their logistics.

However, many political, legal, and technical issues must be settled before Europe truly is unified. Across the region, borders have all but disappeared with the advent of high-speed passenger trains, highways without customs posts and now a single currency. Europe's state-owned phone monopolies, electric utilities, airlines, and other national franchises have all been pried open to competition. However, rail freight remains a bastion of Europe's old ways, a patchwork of protected, antiquated national networks. No two European countries use the same signaling systems or electric current for their trains. For example, Trains in Britain and France run on the left side of dual-track lines while those in the rest of Europe run on the right. Because Britain and France use two different gauges of track, trains crossing their shared border along the Channel Tunnel must stop to let each car be lifted so that its wheels can be changed.

As a result, European industry has taken to the highways for transportation. Railways' share of goods transport with the EU has fallen to about 14 percent from 32 percent in 1970. In the United States, railways account for 41 percent of freight traffic. The downside to the increase in truck traffic is increased traffic congestion, which hampers efficient transportation despite the unified European economy. The most conservative estimate of the cost of traffic jams is a little over 2 percent of Europe's GDP at minimum; it could be as high as 6 percent.

Furthermore, with the expansion of the EU in May 2004, traditional distribution hubs in western and central Europe faced tougher competition. In the process of integrating the candidate countries into all of the EU systems and practices, the EU must restrict access to road and rail networks in some countries for two to three years. Meanwhile, European governments and the EU have developed programs and

Sources: "Logistics Strategies for a New Europe," *Traffic Management,* 33 (August, 1994) p. 49A; "In the Unified Europe, Shipping Freight by Rail is a Journey into the Past," *Wall Street Journal,* March 29, 1999, pp. A1, A8; "European Transport Policy," *Logistics & Transport Focus,* 4 (July/August 2002), pp. 40–41; and "Distribution Hubs Face Competition," *Logistics and Transport Focus,* May 2004, p. 6.

initiatives to reduce road congestion and encourage companies to transport goods via methods other than by truck to ensure the important infrastructure development.

Thus, logistics managers must plan how to respond to changes such as these that are reshaping European logistics strategies as they occur:

CUSTOMS PROCEDURES

For the most part, customs check points as a shipment crosses each nation's border have been eliminated. Duties and trade statistics now are a matter strictly between the originating and destination countries, and intermediate countries no longer are involved. Consequently, transit times and paperwork between EU countries, particularly for truck traffic, are steadily being reduced.

HARMONIZED PRODUCT STANDARDS

Prior to unification, each European country had its own manufacturing, packaging, labeling, and safety standards for almost every item sold within its borders. Under the European Union, pan-European harmonized standards are being developed and replacing most of those country-by-country regulations. As a result, companies can design and manufacture a single version of a product for sale in all parts of the EU rather than making different versions of the same item for each member country. Product harmonization will allow shippers to redesign both their distribution patterns and facilities as well as their customer service strategies.

TRANSPORTATION DEREGULATION

The European Commission is deregulating transportation in Europe to open markets in member states to competition and to eliminate conflicting regulations that impede the flow of traffic between EU countries. The deregulation promises to promote the development of efficient, cost-effective services in all modes.

TRANSPORTATION INFRASTRUCTURE

As in Japan and the United States, growing demand for just-in-time deliveries is increasing traffic and exacerbates transportation bottlenecks (particularly in inter-regional trucking). The European Commission and individual governments are actively encouraging private development of rail and water alternatives.

MANAGEMENT OF GLOBAL LOGISTICS ◆ ◆ ◆ ◆ ◆ ◆ ◆ ◆

Logistics management is inextricably tied with international trade, multinational manufacturing, and sourcing of raw materials, components, and supplies. Global logistics has become considerably more complex, more costly, and, as a result, more important for the success of a firm. A variety of factors contributes to the increased complexity and cost of global logistics as compared to domestic logistics.

- *Distance.* The first fundamental difference is distance. Global logistics frequently require the transportation of parts, supplies, and finished goods over much longer distances than is the norm domestically. A longer distance generally suggests higher direct costs of transportation and insurance for damages, deterioration, and pilferage in transit and higher indirect costs of warehousing and inventory.

- *Exchange rate fluctuation.* The second difference pertains to currency variations in international logistics. The corporation must adjust its planning to incorporate the existence of currencies and changes in exchange rates. For example, in the mid-1990s when the Japanese yen appreciated faster than the U.S. dollar against key European currencies, Honda found it much more economical to ship its Accord models to Europe from its U.S. plant in Marysville, Ohio, rather than from its plants in Japan.

- *Foreign intermediaries.* Additional intermediaries participate in the global logistics process because of the need to negotiate border regulations of countries and deal with local government officials and distributors. Although home country export agents, brokers, and export merchants work as intermediaries providing an exporting service for manufacturing firms, those home-based intermediaries do not necessarily have sufficient knowledge about the foreign countries' market conditions or sufficient connections with local government officials and distributors. In Asian countries such as Japan, Korea, and China, personal "connections" of who knows whom frequently seem to outweigh the Western economic principle of profit maximization or cost minimization in conducting business.[9] Therefore, working with local distributors has proved very important in building initial connections with the local business community as well as local government regulators.

- *Regulation.* A bulk of international trade is handled by ocean shipping. Because the United States is the the world's largest single trading country in both exports and imports and most of its trading partners are located across the Pacific and the Atlantic Oceans, U.S. regulations on ocean transport services directly affect foreign exporters to the United States (as well as U.S. importers of foreign goods) in terms of shipping costs and delivery time. The U.S. Merchant Marine Act of 1920 (also known as the *Jones Act*) forbids foreign-owned freighters from transporting passengers and merchandise from one domestic port to another by restricting foreign access to the domestic shipping market. The act requires passengers and merchandise being transported by ship in the United States to travel on U.S.-built, U.S.-owned, and U.S.-staffed vessels while allowing unilateral retaliatory action against restrictions imposed by other countries. In March 2003, more than 50 nations, including Australia, Canada, China, the European Union, and Japan, filed a joint statement with the World Trade Organization calling for the liberalization of international marine transport services during the WTO's new round of multilateral trade negotiations.[10] Until resolved by the WTO, the barriers imposed by this act continue to add to the costs of logistics in and around the United States.

- *Security.* Security was not an acutely serious concern until September 11, 2001, when the blatant terrorist attacks in the United States awakened the world to the importance of domestic and international security measures. Transportation costs for exporters have increased because of the extra security measures that shipping lines and terminal operators face.[11] However, if the government-imposed user fees or carrier surcharges are too high or come without sufficient advance notice, some exporters could even lose their overseas markets due to increased shipping costs and insurance premiums (refer to "Terrorism and the World Economy" in Chapter 5).

Modes of Transportation

The global logistics manager must understand the specific properties of the different modes of transport in order to use them optimally. The three most important factors in determining an optimal mode of transportation are the value-to-volume ratio,

---

[9]See, for example, Jean L. Johnson, Tomoaki Sakano, and Naoto Onzo, "Behavioral Relations in Across-Culture Distribution Systems: Influence, Control, and Conflict in U.S.–Japanese Marketing Channels," *Journal of International Business Studies,* 21 (Fourth Quarter 1990), 639–55; and Chris Rowley, John Benson, and Malcolm Warner, "Towards an Asian Model of Human Resource Management: A Comparative Analysis of China, Japan and South Korea," *International Journal of Human Resource Management,* 15 (June/August 2004), pp. 917–33.

[10]"Japan Joins Call for Opening Marine Services Market In WTO Talks," *NikkeiNet Interactive,* http://www.nni.nikkei.co.jp/, accessed March 4, 2003.

[11]Robert Spich and Robert Grosse, "How Does Homeland Security Affect U.S. Firms' International Competitiveness?" *Journal of International Management,* 11 (December 2005), pp. 457–78.

perishability of the product, and cost of transportation. The **value-to-volume ratio** is determined by how much value is added to the materials used in the product. **Perishability** of the product refers to the quality degradation over time and/or product obsolescence along the product life cycle. The **cost of transportation** should be considered in light of the value-to-volume and perishability of the product.

Ocean Shipping. **Ocean shipping** offers three options. **Liner service** offers regularly scheduled passage on established routes; **bulk shipping** normally provides contractual service for prespecified periods of time; and *irregular runs.* Container ships carry standardized containers that greatly facilitate the loading and unloading of cargo and intermodal transfer of cargo. Ocean shipping is used extensively for the transport of heavy, bulky, or nonperishable products, including crude oil, steel, and automobiles. Over the years, shipping rates have been falling as a result of a price war among shipping lines. For example, an average rate for shipping a 20-foot container from Asia to the United States fell from $4,000 in 1992 to as low as $1,900 in 2004.[12] Although most manufacturers rely on existing international ocean carriers, some large exporting companies, such as Honda and Hyundai, have their own fleets of cargo ships. For example, Honda, a Japanese automobile manufacturer, owns its own fleet of cargo ships not only to export its Japanese-made cars to North America on its eastbound journey but also to ship U.S.-grown soybeans back to Japan on its westbound journey. This strategy is designed to increase the vessels' capacity utilization.[13] Indeed, Honda even owns a number of highly successful specialty tofu restaurants in Tokyo frequented by young trendsetters in Japan.[14]

Air Freight. Shipping goods by air **(airfreight)** has grown rapidly over the last 30 years. Although the total volume of international trade using air shipping remains quite small—still less than 2 percent of international trade in goods—it represents more than 20 percent of the value of goods shipped in international commerce. High-value goods are more likely to be shipped by air, especially if they have a high value-to-volume ratio. Typical examples are semiconductor chips, LCD screens, and diamonds. Perishable products such as produce and flowers also tend to be airfreighted. Changes in aircraft design have now enabled air transshipment of relatively bulky products. Three decades ago, a large propeller aircraft could hold only 10 tons of cargo. Today's jumbo cargo jets carry more than 30 tons, and medium- to long-haul transport planes (e.g., the C-130 and the AN-32) can carry more than 80 tons of cargo. These supersize transport planes have facilitated the growth of global courier services, such as FedEx, UPS, and DHL. Of all world regions, the entire Asia–Pacific area is the most popular air freight market today with double-digit, year-after-year growth. Asia has become the world's factory floor to outsource the manufacture of goods and services. The top five commodities moving from the Asia Pacific area to the United States include office machines and computers, apparel, telecom equipment, electrical machinery, and miscellaneous manufactured products. The west-bound (from the United States to Asia/Pacific) commodities mainly include documents and small packages, electrical machinery, and fruits and vegetables. In the next 20 years, west-bound and east-bound air cargo traffic will grow at roughly the same pace, an estimated 7 percent.[15]

Intermodal Transportation. More than one mode of transportation for distribution is usually employed. Naturally, when shipments travel across the ocean, surface or air shipping is the initial transportation mode crossing national borders. Once on land, they can be shipped by truck, barge, railroad, or air. Even if countries are contiguous,

---

[12]Bridget McRea, "Ocean Outlook: Rough Seas Ahead," *Logistics Management,* 44 (February 2005), pp. 51–54.

[13]"Confidential," *Automotive News Europe,* May 2, 2005, p. 11.

[14]The first author's personal knowledge.

[15]Roger Morton, "Something in the Air," *Logistics Today,* 46 (July 2005), pp. 23–26.

such as Canada, the United States, and Mexico, for example, various domestic regulations prohibit the use of the same trucks between and across the national boundaries. When different modes of transportation are involved or even when shipments are transferred from one truck to another at the national border, it is important to make sure that cargo space is utilized at full load so that the per unit transportation cost is minimized.

Managing shipments so that they arrive in time at the desired destination is critical in modern-day logistics management. Due to low transit times, greater ease of unloading and distribution, and higher predictability, many firms use airfreight, either on a regular basis or as a backup to fill in when the regular shipment by an ocean vessel is delayed. For footwear firms Reebok and Nike and fashion firm Pierre Cardin, the use of airfreight is becoming almost a required way of doing business as firms jostle to get their products first into the U.S. market from their production centers in Asia and Europe. The customer in a retail store often buys a product that could have been airfreighted from the opposite end of the world the previous day or even the same day. Thus, the face of retailing is also changing as a result of advances in global logistics.

Distance between the transacting parties increases transportation costs and requires longer-term commitment to forecasts and longer lead times. Differing legal environments, liability regimes, and pricing regulations affect transportation costs and distribution costs in a way not seen in the domestic market. Trade barriers, customs problems, and paperwork tend to slow the cycle times in logistics across national boundaries. Although this is true, the recent formation of regional trading blocs, such as the European Union, the North American Free Trade Agreement, and the MERCOSUR (The Southern Cone Free Trade Area), is also encouraging the integration and consolidation of logistics in the region for improved economic efficiency and competition.

Warehousing and Inventory Management

A firm's international strategy for logistics management depends, in part, on the government policy and on the infrastructure and logistic services environment. The traditional logistics strategy involves anticipatory demand management based on forecasting and inventory speculation.[16] With this strategy, a multinational firm estimates the requirements for supplies as well as the demand from its customers and then attempts to manage the flow of raw materials and components in its worldwide manufacturing system and the flow of finished products to its customers to minimize holding inventory without jeopardizing manufacturing runs and without losing sales due to stockouts.

In the past, the mechanics and reliability of transportation and tracking of the flow of goods was a major problem. With the increasing use of information technology, electronic data interchange, and intermodal transportation, the production, scheduling, and delivery of goods across national borders is also becoming a matter of just-in-time delivery, although some structural problems still remain. For instance, current restrictions on U.S.–Canada air freight services and U.S.-Mexico cross-border trucking restrain the speed of goods flow, add to the lead times, and are examples of government restrictions that need changing to facilitate faster movement of goods across borders.

Despite those restrictions, forward-looking multinational companies can still employ nearly just-in-time inventory management. For example, Sony's assembly plant in Nuevo Laredo, Mexico, just across the Texas border, imports components from its U.S. sister plants in the United States. While cross-border transportation across the U.S.–Mexico international bridges experiences traffic congestion and occasionally causes delays in shipment, Sony has been able to manage just-in-time inventory management with a minimum of safety stock in its warehouse.

---

[16]Louis P. Bucklin, "Postponement, Speculation and the Structure of Distribution Channels," *Journal of Marketing Research,* 2 (February 1965), pp. 26–31.

Hedging against Inflation and Exchange Rate Fluctuations. Multinational corporations can also use inventory as a strategic tool to deal with currency fluctuations and to hedge against inflation. By increasing inventories before imminent depreciation of a currency instead of holding cash, a firm can reduce its exposure to currency depreciation losses. High inventories also provide a hedge against inflation because the value of the goods/parts held in inventory remains the same compared to the buying power of a local currency, which falls with a devaluation. In such cases, the international logistics manager must coordinate operations with that of the rest of the firm so that the cost of maintaining an increased level of inventories is more than offset by the gains from hedging against inflation and currency fluctuations. Many countries, for instance, charge a property tax on stored goods. If the increase in the cost of carrying the increased inventory along with the taxes exceeds the saving from hedging, increased inventory may not be a good idea.

Benefiting from Tax Differences. Costs can be written off before taxes in creative ways so that internal transit arrangements can actually make a profit. This implies that what and how much a firm transfers within its global manufacturing system is a function of the tax systems in various countries to and from which the transfers are being made. When the transfer of a component A from country B to country C is tax deductible in country B (as an export) and gets credit in country C for being part of a locally assembled good D, the transfer makes a profit for the multinational firm. Access to and use of such knowledge is the forte of logistics firms that sell these services to the multinational firm interested in optimizing its global logistics.

Logistical Integration and Rationalization. **Logistical integration** refers to coordinating production and distribution across geographic boundaries, a radical departure from the traditional country-by-country–based structure consisting of separate sales, production, warehousing, and distribution organizations in each country. **Rationalization,** on the other hand, refers to reducing resources to achieve more efficient and cost-effective operations. Although conceptually separate, most companies' strategies include both aspects of the logistics strategy.

For example, DuPont expects to save millions annually by centralizing logistics management and consolidating its logistics spending to get better pricing and service from its providers. The company currently uses a wide range of freight carriers, logistics providers, and freight forwarders to handle its shipments. By centralizing its logistical activities, DuPont can optimize its shipments and combine small shipments into larger ones (integration). The company has replaced the disconnected legacy mainframe logistics system used by 70 percent of its individual strategic business units, subsidiaries, joint ventures, and affiliates with Global Logistics Technologies Inc.'s G3 Web-based transportation and logistics management software (rationalization). Since 2001, the company has been able to manage almost all of its operations using the software, including shipments for U.S. domestic, Europe domestic, and some intra-Asia areas. DuPont's logistic management has not only enhanced its product delivery time but also ensured security of shipments, a significant factor because more than 40 percent of what the company ships is classified as a hazardous material. Furthermore, the company has benefited from shortened inventory through improved visibility and standardization of data.[17]

As presented in Global Perspective 16-1, dramatic economic integration is taking place in the enlarged European Union. However, a word of caution is in order. Remember that although the laws of the European Union point toward further economic integration, there still are and will continue to be political, cultural, and legal differences among countries as well. Similarly, the North American Free Trade Agreement is not free of arcane regulations, either (see Global Perspective 16-2).

---

[17]"DuPont Streamlines Logistics and IT Costs with Centralized, Web-Based System," *Manufacturing Systems,* April 2004, p. 52.

◆ ◆

*G*LOBAL PERSPECTIVE 16-2
CABOTAGE RULES IN THE NORTH AMERICAN FREE TRADE AGREEMENT

Cabotage refers to the right of a trucker to carry goods in an assigned territory. Traditionally, countries have restricted cabotage rights of foreign truckers. If a U.S. trucking company has a scheduled load to the United States from Toronto, the truck may carry the load, but the driver must be Canadian. Similarly, a U.S. trucker, after delivering goods in Toronto, cannot pick up another load and deliver it in Ottawa, a violation of current cabotage rules. Even under the North American Free Trade Agreement (NAFTA), Canada, the United States, and Mexico have varying degrees of and sometimes confusing regulations on cabotage rights. In theory, the NAFTA should have worked out truly free mobility of goods by allowing the cabotage rights of truckers from Canada, the United States, and Mexico. The reality is still far from it, although it is improving.

The U.S. government refused to allow Mexican truckers to have full access to the United States until recently. Safety concerns were cited in keeping Mexican trucks from operating throughout the country, although those fears may not be supported by facts. Similarly, the Mexican trucking association, Camara Nacional del Autotransporte de Carga, continues to oppose opening up cabotage to allow point-to-point coverage in Mexico by U.S. trucking companies.

Sources: "U.S. Transportation Department Implements NAFTA Provisions for Mexican Trucks, Buses," FDCH Regulatory Intelligence Database, November 27, 2002; "DOT Eyes Truck Inspection Harmony for All of North America," *Occupational Health & Safety,* December 2002, p. 10; and John C. Taylor, Douglas R. Robideaux, and George C. Jackson, "U.S.–Canada Transportation and Logistics: Border Impacts and Costs, Causes, and Possible Solutions," *Transportation Journal,* 43 (Fall 2004), pp. 5–21.

In March 2002, President George W. Bush finally modified the moratorium on granting operating authority to Mexican motor carriers. This action means that the United States has fulfilled its obligations under the North American Free Trade Agreement and that Mexican truck and regular-route bus service into the U.S. interior can begin. As a practical matter, this service will begin only after the U.S. Department of Transportation's Federal Motor Carrier Safety Administration (FMCSA) reviews Mexican carrier applications and grants provisional operating authority to qualified Mexican truck and bus companies seeking this authority.

The United States does not have a coherent cabotage regulation with Canada. The U.S. Immigration and Naturalization Service is going after Canadian drivers who have "violated" cabotage rules by moving trailers within the United States even though U.S. Customs permits such movements. A number of Canadian drivers have had their trucks seized, been fined, and kicked out of the United States. Under an agreement engineered by the Canadian and U.S. trucking associations, Canadian officials have been allowing U.S. drivers to perform cabotage movements in Canada. Now the Canadian government is thinking about retaliating against the United States by mounting a crackdown on U.S. truck drivers entering Canada to parallel the aggressive treatment Canadian drivers are facing from the U.S. Immigration and Naturalization Service.

Despite these arcane regulations still in place in the NAFTA countries, the U.S. Department of Commerce hopes to establish conformity among Canada, Mexico, and the United States in cargo securement regulations in compliance with the North American Cargo Securement Standard Model Regulations.

Consequently, despite the promised benefit of logistics integration and rationalization, international marketers as well as corporate planners must have specialized local knowledge to ensure smooth operations. Customer service strategies particularly need to be differentiated, depending on the expectations of local consumers. For example, German buyers of personal computers may be willing to accept Dell Computer's mail-order service or its Web site ordering service, but French and Spanish customers might assume that a delivery person will deliver and install the products for them.

E-Commerce and Logistics.   Another profound change in the last decade is the proliferation of the Internet and electronic commerce (*e-commerce*). The Internet opened the gates for companies to sell direct-to-consumers easily across national boundaries. We stated in Chapter 1 that manufacturers that traditionally sell through the retail channel *can* benefit the most from e-commerce. Furthermore, customer information no longer is held hostage by the retail channel.

We emphasize "can" because *logistics cannot go easily as global as e-commerce in reality.* This revolutionary way of marketing products around the world is epitomized by Dell Computer, which put pressure on the industry's traditional players with a simple concept: Sell personal computers directly on the Internet to customers with no complicated channels. Michael Dell successfully introduced a new way for PC companies to compete: not by technology alone but by emphasizing customers' needs with an ability to satisfy and serve them quickly and efficiently and above and beyond the traditional national boundary. Now, major PC companies are compressing the supply chain via such concepts as "build to order" rather than "build to forecast." However, order taking can take place globally, but shipping PCs needs to be rather local or regional for various reasons.

You may ask why most e-businesses do not ship overseas if the Web makes any company instantly global. Also, why do more companies not make their Internet-powered supply chains globally accessible? The answer is that it remains very difficult to manage the complex logistics, financial, linguistic, and regulatory requirements of global trade. E-businesses operating from one central location could not also address logistical problems associated with local competition and exchange rate fluctuations. For example, in Australia, OzBooks.com sells 1.2 million books and Dymocks, Australia's largest bookseller, offers just over 100,000 books online. These Australian companies are no comparison in size to Amazon.com with some 5 million books available online. These smaller Australian online booksellers have a competitive advantage over Amazon .com, however: They have a comprehensive offering of books published in Australia while Amazon.com does not. Furthermore, competing on price for international sales without local distribution is tricky because exchange rates fluctuate. When the Australian dollar depreciated during the Asian financial crisis, buying from Amazon.com and other U.S. Web retailers became more expensive in Australia. Australian consumers log on to local alternatives such as OzBooks.com instead. As a result, leading e-commerce sites now offer regional Web sites to handle sales in various parts of the world. For example, Amazon.com now has eight regional Web sites around the world to cater to these regional and local differences.

Another example is Compaq Computer in Latin America. The company has been extremely successful in selling computers over the Internet throughout Latin America since October 1999. The company guarantees delivery within 72 hours of placing orders online. Latin Americans shopping online can buy the computers in local currency and do not have to bring the computers through customs. This requires local assembly of Compaq computers. Compaq has assembly plants in Mexico, Ecuador, Argentina, Brazil, Venezuela, Chile, Puerto Rico, Colombia, and Peru.[18]

The Web may have dispensed with physical stores, but local adaptation of product offerings and setting up local distribution centers remain as crucial as ever. The local competition has forced Amazon.com and other U.S. e-commerce companies to reassess what it means to operate globally on the Internet.

Third-Party Logistic (3PL) Management

Good logistics can make all the difference in a company's ability to serve its customers. The crucial factor is not just what the company makes or how the product is made. It is also how quickly the company can get the parts together or shift finished products from its factories to markets. Despite the immense competitive advantage that logistics can generate for the organization, manufacturers often find that logistics operations are usually faster and less expensive if they are outsourced and organized by specialists and professionals who have competence in integrated logistics management and the ability to service multiple clients and products. According to management consultants at McKinsey who track the logistics outsourcing industry, U.S. companies currently spend around $50 billion a year on **third-party logistics (3PL) services.** This 3PL market is growing at 9 percent a year in the United States. The European 3PL market was worth around $147 billion in 2001 and is growing at a similar rate as in the United States.[19] The largest 3PL sector is the value-added warehousing and distribution industry. Survey statistics show two important factors: (1) the 3PL industry has a tremendous untapped

---

[18]"IT Watch," *Business Latin America,* September 13, 1999, p. 7; and "Latin American PC Market Continues to Grow," *World IT Report,* February 19, 2002, p. N.

[19]Bernard L. Bot and Carl-Stefan Neumann, "Growing Pains for Logistics Outsourcers," *McKinsey Quarterly,* 2 (2003).

opportunity for growth with Fortune 500 companies and (2) mid-size companies are making the best use of savings and service advantages that outsourcing can offer.[20]

To stay competitive, Ford has established a contract with TPG, a Dutch logistics company, to service its Toronto factory. This plant produces 1,500 Windstar minivans a day. To keep it running virtually round the clock, TPG organizes 800 deliveries a day from 300 different parts manufacturers. Its software must be tied into Ford's computerized production system. Shipments must arrive at 12 different points along the assembly lines without ever being more than 10 minutes late. Parts must be loaded into trucks in a prearranged sequence to speed unloading at the assembly line. This upstream procurement capability is extremely important when it comes to addressing the ever-changing needs of consumers in the downstream marketing activities. Another example is an arrangement between Maxtor, a maker of computer disk drives, and Excel, the world's leading logistics firm. Excel, formed from the merger of a shipping line and a trucking company, now owns no ships or trucks but focuses instead on logistics contracts. The Maxtor deal requires it to shift computer drives from factories in Asia to companies such as Dell, Compaq, and HP in Asia and the United States, all within 48 hours.[21]

Multinational companies also benefit from 3PL arrangements, particularly in culturally and/or geographically diverse markets, such as India and China. For example, in India, Whirlpool Corporation, a leading U.S. manufacturer of major household appliances, works with Quality Express whose national delivery network serves more than 10,000 retailers and 50,000 construction sites scattered all over India. The result was ERX Logistics, a joint venture that provides Whirlpool full logistics service for its finished products from warehousing to final delivery. Whirlpool has been able to lower its minimum order quantity from about one-third of a truckload to five or six pieces.[22]

Logistical Revolution with the Internet. The trend toward third-party logistics is a result of the Internet and the Intranet (a specialized secure Internet channel established between the companies) as well as concentrating on core competencies (see Global Perspective 16-3). The Internet and the Intranet facilitate on-time inventory and distribution coordination without constraint of geographical boundaries. *Core competencies* refer to the mix of skills and resources that a firm possesses that enable it to produce one set of goods and/or services in a much more effective manner than another firm. Also, competent logistics firms can save money for a multinational firm shipping components between its facilities in different countries because shipping costs paid internally can vary according to the fluctuation of foreign currencies.

We illustrate how some major companies take advantage of the Internet and the Intranet for streamlining their logistics. At Dell Computer, the international logistics manager makes certain that the third-party logistics provider has state-of-the-art logistics and keeps it involved in Dell's strategic planning. Dell buys monitors finished and packaged, ready to deliver directly to the customer the world over. It does not add any value to the monitor itself, so Dell tries to avoid handling the monitor, preferring instead to have the logistic provider warehouse it and move it to Dell when the information system link with Dell drops an order into the warehouse computer. This saves Dell inventorying costs and gives it more operational flexibility.[23]

Pharmaceutical giant Eli Lilly has gradually outsourced more of its global logistic to Swiss-based Danzas AEI Intercontinental. This e-logistics company's famed ''MarketLink'' system manages seamless logistic services driven by the real-time flow of data between the company and its customers. Danzas AEI was recently put in charge of handling customs and delivering Eli Lilly's airborne and ocean imports. Based in the

[20]''1999 Annual Report—Third-Party Logistics: No End to the Good News,'' *Logistics Management and Distribution Report,* 38 (July 1999), pp. 73–74.

[21]''A Moving Story,'' *Economist,* December 7, 2002, pp. 65–66.

[22]''India: Logistics Gives the Competitive Edge,'' *Businessline,* November 5, 2001.

[23]Silvia Ascarelli, ''Dell Finds U.S. Strategy Works in Europe,'' *Wall Street Journal,* February 3, 1997, p. A8.

$\mathcal{G}$LOBAL PERSPECTIVE 16-3

LOGISTICAL REVOLUTION WITH THE INTERNET

It is commonplace for even seasoned managers of domestic logistics to grossly underestimate the complexity of international trade logistics (ITL). Procuring global transportation and related services involves far more players, handoffs, and documentation than for strictly domestic shipments and almost always involves longer order-to-delivery times. Estimating the arrival times of international shipments is often more voodoo than science.

Once a shipment began moving, it often would go into a veritable black hole, disappearing for weeks. Even the best-laid plans could be disrupted. For instance, a ship from Asia could hit rough weather, delaying its arrival on the west coast of the United States for two days. In response, the west coast trucks awaiting that shipment either left empty or sat idly for the two days. Such inefficiencies are rampant in global logistics.

The Internet has completely changed ITL, however. Today vendors such as Vastera can aggregate large numbers of international shipments. In doing so, they can develop and maintain huge databases covering country-specific regulations. Literally millions of combinations of carriers, seaports, and so forth are possible for moving a shipment. Consequently, ITL vendors also tap rate and route information on thousands of carriers operating in dozens of countries. Searching this vast space both lowers freight bills and shortens delivery times. Ford

Motor Company, for instance, outsourced much of this work to Vastera even though it had a dedicated staff of 150 ITL specialists. The expected cost saving is $51.4 billion. DuPont de Nemours, on the other hand, picked G-Log (Global Logistics Technologies) to manage its ITL.

A bugaboo in ITL is the great uncertainty in shipment arrival times. Materials managers have had little choice but to hedge by increasing safety stocks. Inventory costs consequently are typically high for foreign sourced parts. Remediating the uncertain delivery problem involves closely tracking international shipments every step of the way. This is easier said than done. Nevertheless, vendors such as Descartes Systems Group (including its Centricity subsidiary) offer such tracking. Such vendors are working hard to get close to the ideal "end-to-end tracking," which means both a global logistics infrastructure network and electronic visibility in every facility and carrier along the way.

In every sense, logistics companies are expanding their services and reach. For instance, Grimaldi Lines, once a traditional ocean carrier, now moves Fiat vehicles from the assembly plant right to the dealers in multiple countries. To do so, Grimaldi acquired or built trucking firms and distribution centers in several countries. Despite obvious shortcomings, global logistics should markedly improve. Web-based companies and technologically innovative carriers such as UPS Logistics, Ryder, and others continue to lead the way.

Source: Martin Piszczalski, "Global Logistics Issues," *Automotive Design & Production,* January 2002, p. 16.

---

pharmaceutical hub of Basel, Switzerland, Danzas AEI has increasingly specialized in pharmaceutical products, working also with SmithKline Beecham and Hoffman-La Roche.[24]

As the market for third-party logistics has increased substantially since the 1990s, many traditional shippers, such as UPS, Federal Express, DPWN, and TNT, have developed large business units solely devoted to integrated logistics. Many logistic companies are now moving to provide tailored logistic solutions in international markets for their clients. One major player is UPS Logistics Group, a subsidiary of United Parcel Service, founded in 1995. UPS Logistics offers a full spectrum of supply chain services and logistics expertise throughout the world. Now its operations in North America, Europe, Asia, and Latin America include more than 500 distribution facilities and strategic stocking locations. The subsidiary is composed of industrial engineers, software systems integrators and developers, facility designers, operations managers, high-tech repair technicians, logisticians, and transportation, financial, e-commerce, and international trade experts.[25]

Even online companies, such as Amazon.com, rely increasingly on 3PL services in foreign markets. Amazon.com launched its Canadian Web site (www.amazon.ca) in July 2002, but Canada Post Corp. handles its logistics. In 2001, more than 250,000 Canadians ordered products from Amazon's U.S. site; the country represents Amazon's

---

[24]Robert Koenig, "Danzas Expands Pharmaceutical Logistics Business with Eli Lilly," *Journal of Commerce,* December 7, 1998, p.14A; and "Danzas AEI Intercontinental," *Journal of Commerce,* November 25, 2002, p. 32.

[25]UPS Logistics Group, http://www.upslogistics.com, accessed January 20, 2006.

largest export market. Now Amazon.ca features bilingual Canadian content and 1.5 million items, and Canada Post handles domestic deliveries. Canada Post's subsidiary, Assured Logistics, handles supply chain services such as warehousing, inventory management, and online fulfilment. This has proved to be mutually beneficial arrangement. Canada Post is establishing itself as a competent player in the online world, and as a result, its business is picking up with about 300 Canadian companies now using its online logistical services. On the other hand, Amazon spent US$200 million a year on technology to keep its U.S. operation running but does not incur that cost in its Canadian operation through Amazon.ca. Furthermore, this arrangement permits Amazon to better cater to the local market needs in Canada.[26]

Some distribution companies even find that the best way to be successful is to create a distribution alliance and pool their logistics resources. An example is the global distribution alliance between three international electronics distribution companies: the U.S. company Pioneer-Standard, the British company Eurodis, and Taiwan's World Peace Industrial. The alliance's ability to cover almost the entire globe has enabled it to obtain worldwide exclusive distribution contracts from electronics manufacturers such as Philips Semiconductors.[27] Similarly, six European logistics companies have joined forces to launch Eunique Logistics, a new pan-European alliance that provides customers a single point of contact for a range of distribution and logistics services throughout Europe.[28]

◆ ◆ ◆ ◆ ◆ ◆ ◆ ◆   FREE TRADE ZONES

A **free trade zone (FTZ)** is an area located within a nation (say, the United States) but is considered outside the custom's territory of the nation. Many countries have similar programs. In the United States, a free trade zone is officially called a *foreign trade zone*. FTZs are licensed by the Foreign Trade Zone Board and operated under the supervision of the Customs Service. The level of demand for FTZ procedures has followed the overall growth in global trade and investment. Presently, some 700 FTZs are in operation and, as part of their activity, about 540 manufacturing plants are operating with subzone status. Subzones are adjuncts to the main zones when the main site cannot serve the needed purpose and are usually found at manufacturing plants. Across the United States, about 335,000 jobs are directly related to activity in FTZs, Companies operating in them are saving money, improving cash flow, and increasing logistical efficiency.[29] Legally, goods in the zone remain in international commerce as long as they are held within the zone or are exported. In other words, those goods (including materials, components, and finished products) shipped into an FTZ in the United States from abroad are legally considered not having landed in the customs territory of the United States and thus are not subject to U.S. import tariffs, duties, or taxes as long as they are not sold outside the FTZ in the United States. An FTZ provides many cash flow and operating advantages to zone users (see Exhibit 16-2). Even when these goods enter the United States, customs duties can be levied on the lesser of the value of the finished product or its imported components.

Operationally, an FTZ provides an opportunity for every business engaged in international commerce to take advantage of a variety of efficiencies and economies in the manufacture and marketing of their products. Merchandise within the zone can be unpacked and repacked; sorted and relabeled; inspected and tested; repaired or discarded; reprocessed, fabricated, assembled, or otherwise manipulated. It can be combined with other imported or domestic materials, stored or exhibited, transported

[26]"Amazon Lands in Canada, Outsources Logistics," *Computing Canada,* July 5, 2002, p. 6.

[27]"Arrow Hooks US Components Division," *Electronics Weekly,* January 22, 2003, p. 3.

[28]"New European Alliance," *Logistics and Transport Focus,* June 2002, p. 13.

[29]"US Foreign–Trade Zones Boost Employment, Exports," *Journal of Commerce,* September 5, 2005, p. 24.

EXHIBIT 16-2
BENEFITS OF USING A FREE TRADE ZONE (FTZ)

1. *Duty deferral and elimination.* Duty will be deferred until products are sold in the United States. If products are exported elsewhere, no import tariff will be imposed.

2. *Lower-tariff rates.* Tariff rates are almost always lower for materials and components than for finished products. If materials and components are shipped to an FTZ for further processing and finished products are sold in the United States, a U.S. import tariff will be assessed on the value of the materials and components rather than on the value of the finished products.

3. *Lower tariff incidence.* Imported materials and components that through storage or processing undergo a loss or shrinkage may benefit from FTZ status because the tariff is assessed only on the value of materials and components that actually found their way into the product.

4. *Exchange rate hedging.* Currency fluctuations can be hedged against by requesting customs assessment at any time.

5. *Import quota not applicable.* Import quotas are not generally applicable to goods stored in an FTZ.

6. *"Made in U.S.A." designation.* If foreign components are substantially transformed within an FTZ located in the United States, the finished product may be designated as "Made in U.S.A."

---

in bond to another FTZ; sold, or exported. Foreign goods can be modified within the zone to meet U.S. import standards and processed using U.S. labor.

Aging imported wine is an interesting way to take advantage of an FTZ. A U.S. wine importer purchases what is essentially newly fermented grape juice from French vineyards and ships it to an FTZ in the United States for aging. After several years, the now-aged French wine can be shipped throughout the United States when an appropriate U.S. import tariff will be assessed on the original value of the grape juice instead of on the market value of the aged wine. If tariff rates are sufficiently high, the cost savings from using an FTZ can be enormous.

Another effective use of an FTZ is illustrated by companies such as Ford and Dell Computer. These companies rely heavily on imported components such as auto parts and computer chips, respectively. In such a case, the companies can have part of their manufacturing facilities designated as subzones of an FTZ. This way, they can use their facilities as they ordinarily do yet enjoy all of the benefits accruing from an FTZ.

At the macro level, all parties to the arrangement benefit from the operation of trade zones. The government maintaining the trade zone achieves increased investment and employment. The firm using the trade zone obtains a beachhead in the foreign market without incurring all costs normally associated with such an activity. As a result, goods can be reassembled, and large shipments can be broken down into smaller units. Duties could be due only on the imported materials and the component parts rather than on the labor that is used to finish the product.

In addition to free trade zones, various governments have also established export processing zones and special economic areas. Japan, which has had a large trade surplus over the years, has developed a unique trade zone program specifically designed to increase imports rather than exports (see Global Perspective 16-4). The common dimensions of all of these zones are that special rules apply to them, when compared with other regions of the country, and that the purpose of these rules is the desire of governments to stimulate the economy, especially the export side of international trade. Export-processing zones usually provide tax- and duty-free treatment of production facilities whose output is destined for foreign markets. The maquiladoras of Mexico are one example.[30]

---

[30]Lance Eliot Brouthers, John P. McCray, and Timothy J. Wilkinson, "Maquiladoras: Entrepreneurial Experimentation to Global Competitiveness," *Business Horizon,* 42 (March/April 1999), pp. 37–44.

◆ ◆

𝒢LOBAL PERSPECTIVE 16-4

JAPAN'S FOREIGN ACCESS ZONE TO INCREASE IMPORTS AND INWARD DIRECT INVESTMENT RATHER THAN EXPORTS

Japan has made some of its major trading partner countries turn protectionistic because it has run a huge trade surplus over the years. To increase imports into Japan rather than encourage exports from Japan, the Japanese government announced a Basic Plan for the Expansion of Imports in 1993. It is a $20 billion program that created a national network of 31 import promotion areas scattered across the country or, as the Japanese call them, "foreign access zones," where importers and foreign investors get special tax breaks and other advantages. The foreign access zones provide a major opportunity for U.S. and other foreign businesses setting up beachhead in Japan.

Operations based in the access zones also get around most, if not all, of the existing impediments to foreign investment in Japan. The zones provide inexpensive warehousing and storage, free or low-cost translation and marketing assistance, access to less expensive regional labor, and, most important,

Sources: Ronald A. Morse and Alan Kitchin, "Japan: A Place in the Sun," *Director*; 51 (September 1997), pp. 77–80; "Measures to Promote Imports," the Ministry of Economic, Trade, and Industry's Web site, http://www.meti.go.jp/english/report/data/cFDI071e.html, accessed January 10, 2006; and "Kitakyushu: Transportation and Distribution," http://www.city.Kitakyushu.jp//page/english/02transport/index .html, accessed August 3, 2006.

local marketing opportunities that bypass the large trading companies and their traditional keiretsu distribution channels.

Kyushu, Japan's southernmost island, has been one such testing ground for this open approach. It has been promoted as the "crossroads of Asia" (it is closer to Shanghai and Seoul than it is to Tokyo). Also known as "Silicon Island," Kyushu hosts a clutch of U.S. high-tech manufacturers (including Texas Instruments, which employs 1,000 people at its Hiji plant). The island's two main cities, Fukuoka and Kitakyushu, have fully espoused the Japanese government's foreign access zone concept. Across Kyushu, cities and prefectures are competing with one another to offer the best incentives to incoming business.

In late 1990s, Kitakyushu raised its cash incentives for building new factories and software houses from $1.8 million to $4.5 million. Other incentives include discounted office space in a newly constructed Asian trade center, a land leasing program at 8 percent of evaluated cost, and joint venture opportunities with local companies boasting private electricity supplies.

Kitakyushu's port, Hibikinada, is being deepened, and a new $1.5 billion international airport is being constructed on reclaimed land nearby. Kyushu is committed to a future role as an Asian production base, but for the moment, it is more likely to be used as an entry point for the Japanese market.

For the logistician, the decision of whether to use such zones is framed by the overall benefit for the logistics system. Clearly, transport and retransport are often required, warehousing facilities need to be constructed, and material handling frequency increases. However, the costs could well be balanced by the preferential government treatment or by lower labor costs.

◆ ◆ ◆ ◆ ◆ ◆ ◆ ◆ ◆   ## MAQUILADORA OPERATION

The maquiladora industry, also known as the *in-bond* or *twin-plant program,* is essentially a special Mexican version of a free trade zone. Mexico allows duty-free imports of machinery and equipment for manufacturing as well as components for further processing and assembly, as long as at least 80 percent of the plant's output is exported. Mexico permits 100 percent foreign ownership of the maquiladora plants in designated maquiladora zones.

Mexico's Border Industrialization Program developed in 1965 set the basis for **maquiladora operations** in Mexico. It was originally intended to attract foreign manufacturing investment and increase job opportunities in areas of Mexico suffering from chronic high unemployment. Most of them are located along the U.S.–Mexican border, such as Tijuana across from San Diego, Ciudad Juarez across from El Paso, and Nuevo Laredo across from Laredo. Over the years, however, Mexico has expanded the maquiladora programs to major industrialized cities such as Monterrey, Mexico City, and Guadalajara, where more skilled workers can be found. This duty-free export assembly program has helped transform Mexico, once a closed economy, into the world's ninth largest exporter.[31] Automobile and electronics product assembly makes up the bulk of maquiladora industries.

The competitive pressures of the world economy forced many large manufacturing companies to abandon their assembly plants in the United States and move to Mexican maquiladoras. Furthermore, to meet local content requirements imposed by NAFTA, foreign firms also had expanded their manufacturing operations in maquiladoras. Particularly, Asian companies, such as Panasonic, Sanyo, Sony, Samsung, and Daewoo, have invited some of their traditional components suppliers to join them in maquiladoras to increase local procurement.

Mexico had long been an attractive location for labor-intensive assembly because its hourly labor cost declined in dollar terms from $2.96 in 1980 to $1.20 in 1990 and to about $0.50 in 1999. This decline resulted from a series of peso depreciations beginning in 1976, including the devastating depreciation that shook the Mexican economy in late 1994 and 1995. However, since 1999, the Mexican economy has grown rapidly, and the Mexican peso has started appreciating against the U.S. dollar, driving up the costs of maquiladora operations over time. In addition, rising wages are also making maquiladora operations less attractive. Furthermore, as part of the NAFTA agreement, which took effect in 1994, maquiladoras have also been stripped of many of the tax and tariff exemptions.[32] By 2002, the average labor cost in Mexico had risen to $2.45 per hour, losing cost competitiveness to China, where the average labor cost was $0.68 in the interior region and $0.88 in the eastern coastal region. As recently as 2000, 90 percent of all maquiladora inputs in Mexico came from the United States, 9 percent came from Asia, and China contributed only 1 percent of the total. By 2003, however, the U.S. share of maquiladora inputs had declined to 69 percent, while Asia's share had increased to 28 percent, including 8 percent from China. In other words, instead of manufacturing materials in Mexico's maquiladoras, U.S.-based suppliers (both domestic and foreign companies operating in the United States) are increasingly having their materials partially or completely manufactured in Asia to take advantage of cheaper labor and then sending them to Mexican maquiladoras for final assembly for eventual export to the United States.[33] Although maquiladora exports continued to grow from $14 billion in 1990 to nearly $105 in 2005, the role of maquiladoras as a cheap manufacturing location is ending. As a result, the only companies that are still operating successfully on the U.S.–Mexican border are high-tech plants. Mexico should become more capital intensive with efforts toward more value-added production by

---

[31]*World Trade Report 2005: Exploring the Link between Trade, Standards, and the WTO* (Geneva, World Trade Organization, 2005).

[32]The dramatic growth of maquiladoras in Mexico is not entirely attributed to Mexico's Border Industrialization Program and inexpensive labor cost. Special U.S. tariff provisions have also encouraged U.S.-based companies to export U.S.-made components and other in-process materials to foreign countries for further processing and/or assembly and subsequently to reimport finished products into the United States. U.S. imports under these tariff provisions are officially called **Tariff 9802 tariff provisions U.S. imports under Items 9802.00.60 and 9802.00.80 of the U.S. Harmonized Tariff Schedule** (the 9802 tariff provisions for short).

The 9802 tariff provisions permit U.S.-based companies to import duty free their materials previously sent abroad for further processing or assembly (i.e., tariffs are assessed only on the foreign value-added portion of the imported products). More specifically, item 9802.00.60 applies to the reimportation for further processing into the United States of any metal initially processed or manufactured in the United States that was shipped abroad for processing. Item 9802.00.80 permits reimportation for sale in the United States of finished products assembled abroad in whole or in part made up of U.S.-made components. Therefore, the higher the U.S. import tariff rates, the more beneficial it is for U.S.-based companies to be able to declare U.S. imports under the 9802 tariff provisions. Consequently, many U.S.-based companies have taken full advantage of both the 9802 tariff provisions of the United States and the maquiladora laws of Mexico in pursuit of cost competitiveness.

Under the provisions of NAFTA, however, U.S. import tariffs on products originating from Canada and Mexico continue to be reduced over the next decade or so. As a result, the tariff advantage for products reimported from Mexico into the United States under the 9802 tariff provisions will eventually diminish over time. However, because many items still have 5-, 10-, and sometimes 15-year phase-in periods before elimination of tariffs, the 9802 tariff provisions will remain useful even within the NAFTA for the foreseeable future. Keep in mind that these tariff provisions still benefit U.S.-based companies manufacturing *outside the NAFTA region* as long as U.S.-made materials and components are used in production.

[33]"No Rest for the Weary," *Journal of Commerce*, February 21, 2005, pp. 20–22.

attracting and retaining high-tech plants tailored to high-end customers by offering just-in-timely delivery.[34]

♦ ♦ ♦ ♦ ♦ ♦ ♦ ♦ ♦   GLOBAL RETAILING

The face of distribution that consumers interact with is the retail store at which they shop. In developed parts of the world, retailing employs between 7 percent and 12 percent of the workforce and wields enormous power over manufacturers and consumers. Retailers have grown into some of the world's largest companies, rivaling or exceeding manufacturers in terms of global reach. Wal-Mart, a U.S. discount chain, has become the largest company in the United States and the world's largest retailer with annual revenues of about $312 billion in 2004. As of June 30, 2006, the company had 1,156 Wal-Mart stores, 2,074 supercenters, 566 SAM'S Clubs, and 104 Neighborhood Markets in the United States. Internationally, the company operated units in Argentina (12), Brazil (293), Canada (278), Costa Rica (130), China (60), Germany (85), Guatemala (119), Honduras (37), Japan (394), Mexico (807), Nicaragua (35), Puerto Rico (54), El Salvador (59), South Korea (16) and the United Kingdom (322). Despite its aggressive foreign expansion, however, Wal-Mart experienced difficulties in its recent entry into China and has low market shares in South Korea, Argentina, and Germany as well as declining sales in Japan.

Wal-Mart is Procter & Gamble's single largest customer, buying as much as the household product giant sells to Japan. Wal-Mart is extremely successful in the NAFTA region, but not necessarily the most global retailer. Actually, only 10 percent of its sales are generated outside its core NAFTA market, compared to Carrefour, which generates more than 20 percent of sales outside Europe. Wal-Mart's success lies in low tariffs in the NAFTA zone, cheap labor and low-cost logistics, with savings passed on to consumers.[35] In other foreign markets, however, Wal-Mart's performance has been lackluster, primarily due to its unwillingness to adapt to local market conditions (see, for example, the case study on Wal-Mart operations in Brazil, included in the textbook.)

Retailing involves very locally entrenched activities, including stocking an assortment of products that local consumers prefer, catering to local shopping patterns (e.g., shopping frequency, time of shopping, and traffic jam), and seasonal promotion as well as meeting local competition on a daily basis. International retailers that are willing to adapt their strategy to local ways of doing things while taking advantage of their managerial and information technology capabilities seem to be more successful than those that try to extend their ways of doing things abroad. In general, European retailers tend to be more willing to customize their marketing and procurement strategies to various local market peculiarities than are U.S. or Japanese retailers.[36] Wal-Mart, which tended to extend its U.S.-based procurement and product assortment strategies in its earlier foreign expansion, resulting in a huge market adjustment problem, is now moving slowly to convert the stores it has acquired in Europe into retailers unlike anything that Americans would recognize as Wal-Marts.[37]

Wal-Mart also began its entry into the difficult Japanese retail market in mid-2002. It increased its equity stake in Seiyu, Japan's fourth-largest supermarket group, paving the way for a low-cost strategy in Japan. However, Wal-Mart is expected to have an upward battle in Japan as quality-conscious Japanese consumers associate its emphasis on "Everyday Low Price" with poor quality, or "yasu-karou, waru-karou," which is a Japanese phrase used to express the feeling that "you get what you pay for" or conversely, the more you pay, the better quality you must be getting. Organic food is

[34]"NAFTA Helps Mexico Compete Globally," *Expansion Management,* October 2005, p. 20.

[35]"How Nafta Helped Wal-Mart Reshape the Mexican Market," *Wall Street Journal,* August 31, 2001, p. A1.

[36]Brenda Sternquist, *International Retailing* (New York: Fairchild Publications, 1998).

[37]Earnest Beck and Emily Nelson, "As Wal-Mart Invades Europe, Rivals Rush to Match Its Formula," *Wall Street Journal Interactive Edition,* http://interactive.wsj.com/, accessed October 6, 1999.

one example. Japanese consumers tend to be less tolerant of skin blemishes and lack of size and shape uniformity in organic produce.[38] Consequently, Wal-Mart in Japan suffered continued declining sales and increasing losses in 2005.[39]

On the other hand, Carrefour, as a typical European retailer willing to be more accommodating to local needs and culture, approaches foreign markets differently. With some 10 years of experience in the Chinese market and a good understanding of the Chinese consumer, the French retailer understands that Chinese consumers are eager to learn about Western products and has incorporated numerous signs providing detailed product information in its supermarkets in China. For example, in the bakery department, Carrefour provides detailed explanation regarding the different flours used and their associated benefits. To promote French wine to consumers, Carrefour had a French wine specialist provide advice and offer wine tasting to passing shoppers. The company was greatly rewarded with a revenue of $1.9 billion in 2004, and it was a clear market leader in Shanghai and other primary and secondary cities (see Exhibit 16-3 for Carrefour's SWOT analysis of its China and global operations). After all, it is crucial for retailers to understand that there is no such thing as a homogenous consumer market. For example, each Asia-Pacific market is different and presents a different level of opportunity. Because each consumer has his or her own purchasing habits, there is no one winning Asian retail formula for both retailers and suppliers.[40]

At the heart of this retailing revolution is the fundamental change in the way goods and services reach the consumer. Previously, the manufacturer or the wholesaler controlled the distribution chain across the world. The retailer's main competitive advantage lay in the merchandising skills of choosing the assortment of goods to sell in the store. The retailer's second advantage—closeness to the customer—was used to beat the rival retailer across the street. The manufacturer decided what goods were available and, in most countries, at what price they could be sold to the public.	**"Push" versus "Pull"**

That distribution system of earlier times has been turned upside down. The traditional supply chain powered by the manufacturing *push* is becoming a demand chain driven by consumer *pull,* especially in the developed countries where the supply and variety of goods is far above base-level requirements of goods and services. In most industrialized countries, resale price maintenance—which allows the supplier to fix the price at which goods can be sold to the final customer—has either been abolished or bypassed. The shift in power in the distribution channel is fundamentally a product of the application of information technology to store management.

Many multinational companies from industrialized countries are now entering markets and developing their distribution channels in developing countries. A study by New York University's Tish Robinson showed that companies from Western countries seem to have difficulty competing with Japanese companies in fast-growing Southeast Asian markets and attributed this to different styles in managing distribution channels. In just three decades, for example, the consumer electronics distribution systems in Malaysia and Thailand have come to be characterized by a striking presence of exclusive dealerships with Japanese multinational manufacturers such as Matsushita, Sanyo, and Hitachi.

For example, Matsushita (the maker of Panasonic, National, and Technics brand names) practices a push strategy with 220 exclusive dealerships in Malaysia and 120 in Thailand. In Malaysia, these exclusive dealerships represent 65 percent of total

[38]Hatakeyama Noboru, "Highly Demanding Japanese Consumers," *Japan Spotlight Bimonthly,* 23 (September/October 2004), pp. 2–5; and "Wal-Mart to Make Seiyu a Group Company," *NikkeiNet Interactive,* http://www.nni.nikkei.co.jp/, accessed November 2, 2005.

[39]"Wal-Mart's Japan Unit Posts Wider Loss in 2005," *Wall Street Journal,* http://online.wsj.com/, accessed February 17, 2006.

[40]"Carrefour 2005," retail analysis, iReport series, http://www.igd.com/analysis/, accessed February 20, 2006. See also Masaaki Kotabe and Crystal Jiang, Three Dimensional: The Markets of Japan, Korea and China Are Far from Homogeneous, *Marketing Management,* 15(2), 2006, 39–43.

EXHIBIT 16-3
SWOT ANALYSIS OF CARREFOUR'S OPERATIONS IN CHINA
AND WORLDWIDE

Strengths (in the Chinese market)

- 10 years of experience in China
- Good understanding of the Chinese consumer
- Clear leader in the Shanghai market
- First mover advantage in many of the primary and secondary cities
- Chinese managers trained in its own in-house training center
- Corner on the expatriate and high-end market in primary cities
- Good competition on price, putting pressure on both international and domestic retailers
- Dia format expansion plans to enable Carrefour to compete in growing convenience market

Weakness (in the Chinese market)

- Tailored hypermarkets to the upper end of the market, which could be a problem when penetrating less affluent cities
- Received negative media coverage regarding its relationship with the government, local supplier management, and store opening strategy impact on local retailers

Opportunities (in the global market)

- Dominant "enlarged home market" position
- Unrivalled international presence and experience of emerging markets
- Multiformat strategy
- Global vision and organization
- World-class merchandising
- Customer knowledge

Threats (in the global market)

- Key gaps in international presence (i.e., United States, United Kingdom, and Germany)
- Relatively small turnover in comparison with Wal-Mart
- Slow pace of expansion in some emerging markets
- Lack of scale in Central European markets

Source: "Carrefour 2005," Retail Analysis, iReport series, http://www.igd.com/analysis/, accessed February 20, 2006.

Matsushita sales, although the numbers represent only 30 percent of the retailers selling Matsushita products. On the other hand, General Electric and Philips use a pull strategy, relying on the multivendor distribution system without firm control of the distribution channel as practiced in Western countries. Competitors from the United States and Europe are feeling locked out of Japanese companies' tightly controlled distribution channels in Southeast Asia.[41] This information suggests that a push strategy is more effective than a pull strategy in emerging markets.

On-Time Retail Information Management

Computer systems can now tell a retailer instantly what it is selling in hundreds of stores across the world, how much money it is making on each sale, and increasingly, who its customers are. This information technology has had two consequences.

---

[41] Patricia Robinson, "The Role of Historical and Institutional Context in Transferring Distribution Practices Abroad: Matsushita's Monopolization of Market Share in Malaysia," *The American Marketing Association and the Japan Marketing Association Conference on the Japanese Distribution Strategy,* November 22–24, 1998.

Reduced Inventory. First, a well-managed retailer no longer must keep large amounts of inventory; the stock burden has been passed upstream to the manufacturer. In addition, the retailer has a lower chance of running out of items. For example, the moment a 7-Eleven customer in Japan buys a soft drink or a can of beer, the information goes directly to the bottler or the brewery and immediately goes into the production schedule and the delivery schedule, actually specifying the hour at which the new supply must be delivered and to which of the 4,300 stores. In effect, therefore, Ito-Yokado Co. controls the product mix, the manufacturing schedule, and the delivery schedule of major suppliers such as Coca-Cola or Kirin Breweries. The British retailer Sainsbury's supply chain is geared to provide inputs on demand from the stores with a scheduled truck service to its 350 stores. The stores' ordering cycle is also set to match the loading and arrival of the trucks, which run almost according to a bus schedule.

Further attempts to reduce inventory can also be made jointly by retail chains for their mutual benefit. For example, in February 2000, Sears, Roebuck & Co. and Carrefour, joining the rush to the business-to-business electronic commerce arena, announced a joint venture to form an online purchasing site where the retailers would buy about $80 billion in combined purchases. The venture, GlobalNetXchange (GNX), created the industry's largest supply exchange on the Internet. GNX is an e-business solution and service provider for the global retail industry. Now suppliers can monitor retailers' sales, reduce inventory levels to a minimum, and better plan manufacturing of products on a hosted platform. It makes money by charging fees to suppliers or retailers using the exchange and is set up as a separate entity with its own management, employees, and financing.[42]

Market Information at the Retail Level. Second, the retailer is the one that has real-time knowledge of what items are selling and how fast. It uses this knowledge to extract better terms from the manufacturers. This trend in the transfer of power to the retailer in the developed countries has coincided with the lowering of trade barriers around the world and the spread of free-market economies in Asia and Latin America. As a result, retailers such as the U.S. Toys "Я" Us, Tower Records, and Wal-Mart; Britain's Mark & Spencer and J. Sainsbury; Holland's Mark; Sweden's IKEA; France's Carrefour; and Japan's 7-Eleven Stores are being transformed into global businesses.

A firm can use its strong logistics ability as an offensive weapon to help it gain competitive advantage in the marketplace by improving customer service and consumer choice and by lowering the cost of global sourcing and finished goods distribution.[43] These capabilities become increasingly important as the level of global integration increases and as competitors move to supplement low-cost manufacturing strategies in distant markets with effective logistic management strategies. This point is well illustrated by Ito-Yokado's takeover in 1991 of the Southland Corporation, which had introduced 7-Eleven's convenience store concept in the United States and subsequently around the world. Ito-Yokado of Japan licensed the 7–Eleven store concept from Southland in the 1970s and developed just-in-time inventory management and revolutionized its physical distribution system in Japan. The key to Ito-Yokado's success with 7–Eleven Japan has been the use of its inventory and physical distribution management systems to accomplish lower on-hand inventory, faster inventory turnover, and most important, accurate information on customer buying habits. Ito-Yokado's 7–Eleven Japan now implements its just-in-time physical distribution system in 7–Eleven stores in the United States.[44]

Thus, distribution is increasingly becoming concentrated; manufacturing, by contrast, is splintering. Thirty-five years ago, the Big Three automakers shared the U.S. auto market. Today the market is split among 10: Detroit's Big Three, five Japanese

[42] "Leading Trading Exchanges Link Together," *Food Logistics,* June 2005, p. 8.

[43] Roy D. Shapiro, "Get Leverage from Logistics," *Harvard Business Review,* 62 (May–June 1984), pp. 119–26.

[44] Masaaki Kotabe, "The Return of 7-Eleven . . . from Japan: The Vanguard Program," *Columbia Journal of World Business,* 30 (Winter 1995), pp. 70–81.

carmakers, and two German carmakers. Thirty-five years ago, 85 percent of all retail car sales occurred at single-site dealerships; even three dealership chains were uncommon. Today, a fairly small number of large chain dealers account for 40 percent of the retail sales of cars.

Given the increased bargaining power of distributors, monitoring their performance has become an important management issue for many multinational companies. Although information technology has improved immensely, monitoring channel members' performance still remains humanistic. In general, if companies are less experienced in international operations, they tend to invest more resources in monitoring their channel members' activities.[45] As they gain in experience, they may increasingly build trust relationships with their channel members and depend more on formal performance-based control.[46]

Retailing Differences across the World

The density of retail and wholesale establishments in different countries varies greatly. As a general rule, industrialized countries tend to have a lower distribution outlet density than do emerging markets. Part of the reason for this difference stems from the need in emerging markets to purchase in very small lots and more frequently because of low income and the lack of facilities in homes to keep and preserve purchased items. At the same time, the advanced facilities available in the developed world allow a much higher square footage of retail space per resident, due to the large size of the retail outlets.

Japan's retail industry has a number of features that distinguish it from retailing in Western countries. The major ones are a history of tight regulation (albeit being increasingly deregulated), less use of cars for shopping, and the importance of department stores in the lives of most people. For more than 40 years until recently, the Large-Scale Retail Store Law[47] in Japan helped to protect and maintain small retail stores (in 1994, 12 retail stores per 1,000 residents in Japan versus 6 retail stores per 1,000 residents in the United States) and, partly in consequence, a multilayered distribution system. Consequently, Japan has experienced relatively poor proliferation of megastores and large-scale shopping centers. Because Japan's urban areas are crowded, roads are congested, and parking is expensive or does not exist, many people use public transport to shop. Consequently, shopping is usually within a rather small radius of the home or workplace and products, especially food, generally are bought in small quantities. Shopping, therefore, is more frequent. This situation is further encouraged by Japanese cooking's requirement for fresh ingredients. Retail stores that not only stay open 24 hours a day throughout the week but also practice just-in-time delivery of fresh perishable foods, such as 7-Eleven and Lawson, are extremely popular in Japan. Discount stores have also gained in popularity among recession-weary, now price-conscious Japanese consumers. Similarly, department stores are crucial in everyday Japanese life. The variety of goods and services offered by the average department store ranges well beyond that in most retail outlets abroad. Large department stores stock everything from fresh food and prepared dishes to discount and boutique clothing, and household and garden goods. Many have children's playgrounds and pet centers, some with displays resembling a miniature zoo. Museum-level art and craft exhibitions often are housed on upper floors, and both family and exquisite restaurants usually on the top floor. It is a very different—and often difficult—market for foreign retailers to enter. See Global Perspective 16-5 for information on international retailers entering the Japanese market.

---

[45] Esra F. Gencturk and Preet S. Aulakh, "The Use of Process and Output Controls in Foreign Markets," *Journal of International Business Studies,* 26 (Fourth Quarter, 1995), pp. 755–86.

[46] Preet S. Aulakh, Masaaki Kotabe, and Arvind Sahay, "Trust and Performance in Cross Border Marketing Partnerships: A Behavioral Approach," *Journal of International Business Studies,* 27 (Special Issue 1996), pp. 1005–32.

[47] Jack G. Kaikati, "The Large-Scale Retail Store Law: One of the Thorny Issues in the Kodak-Fuji Case," *The American Marketing Association and the Japan Marketing Association Conference on the Japanese Distribution Strategy,* November 22–24, 1998.

◆ ◆

𝒢LOBAL PERSPECTIVE 16-5
FOREIGN RETAILERS AND DIRECT MARKETERS ENTERING JAPAN EN MASSE

In Japan, until early 1990s, the Large-Scale Retail Store Law gave small retailers and wholesalers disproportionate influence over the Japanese market by requiring firms planning to open a large store to submit their business plan to the local business regulation council, the local chamber of commerce (made up of those small retailers and wholesalers to be affected), and the Ministry of Economy, Trade and Industry (METI). As a result of this "catch-22" requirement, the process would take between one year and 18 months and was seen by foreign retailers as an almost insurmountable entry barrier.

Under U.S. government pressure, the Large-Scale Retail Store Law was relaxed in 1992 and in 1994. Under the amendments, the task of examining applications for new stores was transferred from the local business regulation council to the Large-Scale Retail Store Council, a government advisory board under the METI. Consequently, the maximum time required for various applications and approvals is now set at 12 months. These two revisions of the Large-Scale Retail Store Law have contributed to the increase in the number of applications requesting approval to establish a large retail store. According to the Japan Council of Shopping Centers estimate, shopping centers have opened at the rate of more than 100 per year since 1992.

Toys "Я" Us exploited this opportunity and was ultimately successful in cracking the Japanese market. It boasted a total of 37 stores in 1996 and planned to open an average of 10 more per year across the country. Following the success of Toys "Я" Us, other foreign-based retailers have begun to crack the Japanese market. Nearly a dozen other such foreign retailers have opened their stores in Japan. Foreign firms face more difficulties when opening a general merchandise store than one for a niche product because the large Japanese general merchandise stores, such as Daiei and Ito-Yokado, are well entrenched and dominate the market. Despite such difficulties, Wal-Mart (U.S.) with a partial acquisition of Japan's struggling Seiyu, Carrefour (France), and Metro (Germany) entered the Japanese market. (As attested by Carrefour's early departure, whether they can take root there is too early to tell, however.)

On the other hand, foreign niche retailers, including Toys "Я" Us, which face few competitors, have been fairly successful. For example, U.S.-based Tower Records and U.K.-based HMV and Virgin Megastores have opened comparably large stores, selling both imported and domestic music tapes and CDs at competitive prices. Specialty retailers of outdoor goods

and clothes are other retailers to pour into the Japanese market in the last ten years. Among them, U.S.-based L.L. Bean and Eddie Bauer are the market leaders.

While Toys "Я" Us and Tower Records have a wholly owned subsidiary in Japan, L.L. Bean and Eddie Bauer teamed up with a well-known Japanese company. L.L. Bean Japan is a Japanese franchise 70 percent owned by Japan's largest retailing group, Seibu, and 30 percent by Matsushita Electric, a maker of Panasonic, Technics, JVC, and Quasar brands. Eddie Bauer Japan is a joint venture of Otto-Sumitomo, a Sumitomo Group mail-order retailer, and Eddie Bauer USA. In general, forming a joint venture or a franchise allows new entrants to start faster, although they could lose control of the company's operation in Japan. Future would-be entrants should bear in mind that Japan is not an easy place to do business because, in addition to regulations, land and labor costs are extremely high.

On the other hand, direct marketing—another form of retailing—has blossomed into a $20-billion industry despite Japan's continued recession. Ten percent of this market belongs to foreign companies including Lands' End, an outdoor clothing maker, and Intimate Brands, which distributes Victoria's Secret catalogs. "For those companies and individuals who say that Japan is a closed market, I really can't think of an example of an easier market entry than catalog sales," says Cynthia Miyashita, president of mail-order consultant Hemisphere Marketing Inc. in Japan. In high-context cultures like Japan, however, less direct, low-key approaches in which a mood or image is built in an attempt to build a relationship with the audience is considered more appropriate in approaching prospect customers than in low-context cultures such as the United States.

Foreign mail-order companies sidestep Japan's notoriously complex regulations, multilevel distribution networks, and even import duties. A few cases in point follow:

- Japan's post offices are not equipped to impose taxes on the hundreds of thousands of mail-order goods that flood the postal system, making direct marketing products virtually duty free. Local competitors who import products in bulk have to pay duties, forcing up their prices.

- Many products, such as vitamins and cosmetics, are subject to strict testing regulations in Japan, but those rules do not apply if the products are sold through mail order for personal consumption. That gives direct-mail customers in Japan access to a wide array of otherwise unavailable products.

- Mail costs in the United States are so low that it is more economical to send a package from New York to Tokyo than from Tokyo to Osaka, which reduces overhead costs for direct-mail products.

- Although Japanese companies are not allowed to mail goods from foreign post offices for sale at home, foreign companies face no such restrictions.

Sources: Joji Sakurai, "Firms Challenge Image of Japan's Closed Markets," *Marketing News,* July 20, 1998, p. 2; Jack G. Kaikati, "The Large-Scale Retail Store Law: One of the Thorny Issues in the Kodak-Fuji Case," in *Japanese Distribution Strategy,* ed. Michael R. Czinkota and Masaaki Kotabe (London: Business Press, 2000), pp. 154–63; and "Attitudes toward Direct Marketing and Its Regulation: A Comparison of the United States and Japan," *Journal of Public Policy & Marketing,* 19 (Fall 2000), pp. 228–37; and "Wal-Mart to Make Seiyu a Group Company," *NikkeiNet Interactive,* http://www.nni.nikkei.co.jp/, accessed November 2, 2005.

In Germany, store hours are limited. Stores do not open on Sundays and generally close on weekdays by 6 P.M. They can be open one Saturday in a month until 2:30 P.M. In a German government-commissioned report, the IFO Economic Research Institute recommended that stores be allowed to remain open from 6 A.M. to 10 P.M. on weekdays and until 6 P.M. on Saturdays; however, stores are still expected to be closed on Sundays.[48] Hence, although these laws are now being reviewed, the proposed changes contrast with the situation in the United States, where retail stores may remain open seven days a week, 24 hours a day. Keeping stores open in this manner requires very strong logistics management on the part of retailers and the manufacturing firms supplying the retailers. The sending organization, the receiving organization, and the logistics provider (if applicable) have to work very closely together.

In China, basket shopping is still considered the norm for most consumers, and they spend on average $5 per visit. Retailers adjust their store layouts to cope with a large number of basket shoppers. Wal-Mart, for instance, has set up basket-only checkouts in its supercenters to enable faster checkout. Because low price is the most competitive advantage, retailers spread a strong price message throughout most of the stores in both Chinese and English that promote both everyday low prices and promotional items throughout food and nonfood departments. As a result, high volumes of goods are heavily merchandised by large promotions in bins and in bulk floor stacks. In general, a store flyer is a major marketing tool and is designed to drive foot traffic by presenting discounts for household commodities. Recent research analysts summarized the following key differences between hypermarkets in China with those in the West. In China:

- The majority of hypermarkets are located on two floors, normally with nonfood items located on the upper floor and food on the lower.
- Many hypermarkets are located inside shopping centers in the heart of the city.
- They have high staffing levels due to the presence of suppliers' staff working as in-store "merchandisers."
- Retailers provide courtesy buses to bring customers from residential areas into the center city because China has a low car ownership.[49]

E-Commerce and Retailing. Despite these cultural differences and regulations in retailing, countries such as Japan and Germany are warming up to the e-commerce revolution that the United States has already experienced. In Japan, for example, Rakuten Ichiba Internet Mall (http://www.rakuten.co.jp) has achieved stellar growth since its launch with a mere $500,000 in capital and 13 stores in May 1997. By the end of 2004 it had more than 11,000 stores and generated a total sales revenue of $433 million with operating profits of $146 million.[50] In Germany, SAP dominates the market for so-called enterprise software (i.e., enterprise resource planning and customer relationship software). Some 27,000 of the world's largest organizations now automate everything from accounting and manufacturing to customer and supplier relations using SAP software, making it by far the leading source of large corporate programs with a record revenue of $9.5 billion and profits of more than $1.6 billion in 2004.[51]

E-commerce is not limited to developed countries. China is already the fastest growing Internet market in Asia. Its number of online users reached 111 million by July 2006, second only to the United States with 204 million. As a result of the unfortunate outbreak of the severe acute respiratory syndrome (SARS) in China in

[48]Marco Grühnhagen, Robert A. Mittelstaedt, and Ronald D. Hampton, "The Effect of the Relaxation of 'Blue Laws' on the Structure of the Retailing Industry in the Federal Republic of Germany," paper presented at 1997 AMA Summer Educators' Conference, August 2–5, 1997.

[49]"Retailing in China," Retail Analysis, iReports, www.igd.com/analysis, accessed January 10, 2006.

[50]Rakuten Ichiba, http://www.rakuten.co.jp/info/ir/english/finance/data.html, accessed November 20, 2005.

[51]"SAP: A Sea Change in Software," *Business Week,* July 11, 2005, pp. 46–47.

2003, the Chinese government began to take advantage of the Internet to encourage business transactions without unnecessary human contacts, This government effort further helped build the Internet market in China.[52] In Brazil, the number of people using the Internet grew rapidly from 14 million in 2002 to 26 million in 2006, making it Latin America's most wired nation, and accounting for more than 40 percent of the region's Internet user.[53] A similar growth in entrepreneurial e-commerce operators is expected with the growing Internet access.

As explained earlier in this chapter, despite the rapid increase in Internet users and e-commerce participants around the world, the need for the local or regional distribution of products remains as important as it was before the Internet revolution.

---

[52]"China Has World's 2nd Largest Number of Netizens," *XINHUA,* January 16, 2003; and "China Takes Steps to Ensure SARS Does not Hinder Construction Plans," *XINHUA,* May 23, 2003.

[53]Computed from Internet user statistics available at ClickZ Network, http://www.clickz.com/, accessed August 2, 2006.

SUMMARY ◆

Logistics and distribution have traditionally been local issues related to getting goods to the final customer in a local market. However, while the intent of serving the customer remains, retailers have been transformed into global organizations that buy and sell products from and to many parts of the world. At the same time, with the increase in the globalization of manufacturing, many firms are optimizing their worldwide production by sourcing components and raw materials from around the world. Both of these trends have increased the importance of global logistic management for firms.

The relevance of global logistics is likely to increase in the coming years because international distribution often accounts for between 10 percent and 25 percent of the total cost to obtain an international order. The international logistics manager must deal with multiple issues, including transport, warehousing, inventorying, and the connection of these activities to the firm's corporate strategy. Inflation, currency exchange, and tax rates that differ across national boundaries, complicate these logistics issues but international logistics managers can exploit those differences to their advantage, which are not available to domestic firms.

Logistics management is closely linked to manufacturing activities, even though logistics management is increasingly being outsourced to third-party logistics specialists. Many companies, particularly those in the European Union, are trying to develop a consolidated production location so that they can reduce the number of distribution centers and market their products from one or a few locations throughout Europe. Firms including Federal Express, Airborne Express, and TNT have evolved from document shippers to providers of complete logistics functions; indeed, all of these firms now have a business logistics division whose function is to handle the outsourced logistics functions of corporate clients.

Various governments, including the United States, have developed free trade zones, export-processing zones, and other special economic zones designed chiefly to increase domestic employment and exports from the zone. Various tax and other cost benefits available in the zones attract both domestic and foreign firms to set up warehousing and manufacturing operations. Many U.S.-based multinational firms, both domestic and foreign, take advantage of U.S. tariff provisions 9802.00.60 and 9802.00.80 as well as many of Mexico's maquiladoras (a special Mexican version of free trade zones). Historically, the cost advantage accruing from the use of a combination of U.S. tariff provisions and Mexico's maquiladoras has benefited many large multinational firms that could easily relocate labor-intensive assembly or processing operations there. As a result of NAFTA, however, maquiladoras have begun to attract increasingly high-tech industries as well.

Retailing has long been considered a fairly localized activity subject to different customer needs and different national laws regulating domestic commerce. Nevertheless, significant change is taking place in the retail sector. Information technology makes it increasingly possible for large retailers to know what they are selling in hundreds of stores around the world. Given this intimate knowledge of customers around the world, those retailers have begun to overtake the channel leadership role from manufacturers. The United States' Wal-Mart and Toys "Я" Us, Japan's 7-Eleven, and Britain's Mark & Spencer are some of the major global retailers changing the logistics of inventory and retail management on a global basis.

Finally, e-commerce is increasingly dispensing with physical stores. However, local adaptation of product offerings and setting-up of local distribution centers remain as important as it was before the Internet revolution. Furthermore, complex international shipping requirements and exchange rate fluctuations hamper smooth distribution of products around the world.

KEY TERMS ❖

Airfreight

Bulk shipping

Cost of transportation

Free trade zone (FTZ)

Global logistics

Intermodal transportation

Liner service

Logistical integration

Maquiladora operation

Materials management

Ocean shipping

Perishability

Physical distribution

Rationalization

Third-party logistics (3PL) services

9802 Tariff Provisions (U.S. imports under Items 9802.00.60 and 9802.00.80 of the U.S. Harmonized Tariff Schedule)

Value-to-volume ratio

REVIEW QUESTIONS ❖

1. Define the term *global logistics*. Enumerate and describe the various operations encompassed by it.

2. What factors contribute to the increased complexity and cost of global logistics as compared to domestic logistics?

3. What role do third-party logistics companies play in international trade? What are the advantages of using these companies over internalizing the logistics activities?

4. Describe the role of free trade zones (FTZs) in global logistics.

5. What are the reasons for the dramatic increase in cross-border trade between the United States and Mexico?

6. How is information technology affecting global retailing?

7. The United States and Japan have similar income and purchasing-power levels, yet, the retail structures in the two countries have significant differences. Describe some reasons for these differences.

DISCUSSION QUESTIONS ❖ ❖ ❖ ❖ ❖ ❖ ❖ ❖ ❖ ❖ ❖ ❖ ❖ ❖ ❖ ❖ ❖ ❖ ❖

1. Some economists have brought attention to the importance of the role of geography in international trade. One example of this is the dramatic rise in trade between the United States and Mexico. This increase is attributed primarily to wage differences between the two countries and their proximity in sharing a border over 2,000 miles in length. Geographic proximity allows for the relative inexpensive movement of goods by train from the heart of Mexico to any corner of the United States within three to four days. On the other hand, advocates of globalization claim that the role of geography in international trade is limited and is being reduced constantly. They contend that direct transportation costs as a percentage of the total value of the goods for most goods is low and is declining. Furthermore, the coordination of managerial resources and information rather than actual transportation costs is the key to savings through global logistics. This reduces the role of geography in international trade to a minimal level. Comment on the two views.

2. Beginning in 2000 with the announcement by the Big Three U.S. automakers of plans for a single online supplier exchange Newco, major manufacturers in at least half a dozen industries have followed suit. In the wake of the Big Three's announcement, other corporations have come together on customer-facing and supplier-facing initiatives to create online joint ventures. Among the most prominent are liaisons between DuPont, Cargill, and Cenex Harvest States Cooperative; Sears and Carrefour; and Kraft, H. J. Heinz Co., and Grocery Manufacturers of America with other major food companies. This represents an enormous shift in online business strategy and raises major challenges for marketers and market makers. The question is whether these e-marketplaces will be the type founded by consortia of manufacturers, by independent third-party companies, or by a combination of both? At least in the auto industry, there is no question that both material management (supply chains) and distributions (dealerships) are more concentrated while manufacturing is splintering. What does this implicate for other manufacturing industries? What does this mean in terms of international marketing strategies?

3. The world is moving closer to an era of free trade and global economic interdependence. The worldwide reduction in tariff and nontariff barriers and the increasing levels of world trade are testimony to this fact. These reductions in trade barriers will in the very near future make free trade zones an anachronistic concept. Hence, if you were making an investment decision on behalf of your company to establish a manufacturing facility in a developing country, placing too much emphasis on investing in free trade zones can be a short-term workable proposition but a long-term mistake. Do you agree or disagree with this statement? Give reasons for your answer.

4. As discussed in the text, with the expansion of the European Union in May 2004, traditional distribution hubs in western and central Europe faced tougher competition. For instance, despite integration of all candidate countries into the EU's systems and practices, it would take two to three years for those countries to open their road and rail networks under the transition arrangements. Even though individual governments and the EU have developed programs and initiatives to reduce road congestion and advised the use of other transport networks as alternatives to roads, companies that operate in Bulgaria, the Czech Republic, Estonia, Hungary, Latvia, Poland, and Slovakia are still concerned about the costs and benefits of transporting goods from roads and the viability of alternative modes of transport. What opportunities and threats does the new EU body offer to transporters, freight forwarders, and exporters?

5. Reduced trade barriers and saturation of domestic markets are two market forces that encouraged large retail chains to move overseas. Large retail chains in the United States, Japan, and Europe are aggressively making forays into international markets, although there is a significant regional bias in these efforts. U.S. retail chains such as Wal-Mart have primarily focused on Canada and have now turned their focus to Mexico. Japanese retail chains such as JUSCO and Daimaru have made significant inroads into Southeast Asia, and Western European chains such as Julius Meinl (Austria), Promodes (France), Ahold (The Netherlands), and TESCO (United Kingdom) are diversifying into Eastern Europe and other European countries. Industry analysts point out that this internationalization of retail business is significantly altering the nature of competition. Significant rationalization through acquisitions of retail businesses is taking place. The verdict on the expected effects of this rationalization and increased competition on specialty chains is still unclear. What would you predict the retail business to look like in 10 years? What would be the role of specialty stores and specialty chains?

6. The concept of "one-stop-shopping" for global logistics is quickly catching on. There are now more than 30 large logistic companies, called *megacarriers,* that can provide truly global and integrated logistic services. What are the opportunities and threats that these trends offer to small and large transporters, freight forwarders, and shippers (exporters)?

◆ ◆ ◆ ◆ ◆ ◆ ◆ ◆ SHORT CASES

*C*ASE 16-1

DELL: SURVIVING A LOGISTICAL NIGHTMARE

Well-known U.S.-based computer maker Dell seems to have perfected the art of making just-in-time (JIT) computers and supplying them to its consumers. The company is known to keep costs under control by directly reaching the consumer without the additional expense of intermediaries. Dell owns no warehouses but manages to assemble more than 75,000 computers a day and its build-to-order business model is a case study in itself. Add to that an effective after-sales service, and Dell has itself a competitive advantage that has been almost unbeatable. Maintaining this position takes work, however, especially for a company that sources its computer parts from numerous suppliers all over the world.

Companies such as Dell usually ship computer parts to various U.S. and international ports from their suppliers. What happens, however, when dock worker unions on the west coast of the United States go on strike for days at a stretch? Most companies would lose millions in such an unexpected disruption in the supply chain, but not Dell! Dell faced this situation in the recent past. While many U.S. firms faced adversity, Dell managed to get by with the fewest scratches. This is how.

When the strike prevented parts sourced internationally from reaching Dell's plants in the United States, the company faced the probability that as the strike continued, its U.S. factories would run out of parts. Dell would soon be unable to put together its computers without the necessary parts, and the company would then be left idling like so many others.

However, unlike a hurricane or a tsunami that is difficult to predict, most U.S. firms were aware of the impending dock workers strike a few months in advance. Dell started preparing for it by having a plan in place in case its supply chain was disrupted. One important move was up-to-the-hour communication with the concerned parties, such as its international suppliers most of which were in Asia, the port authorities, and the sea transport companies that it relied on to ship the products.

When the dock workers formally announced the strike, Dell put its plan in action. The measures Dell took were no different from those taken by other firms. Obviously, most firms use sea transport for shipping their parts and products from overseas because it is the least expensive form of

transport. However, when that route was temporarily eliminated due to the strike, most firms sought the expensive but fastest air transport. Thus, most U.S. firms started booking airlines to transport their much needed parts from abroad. Consequently, they incurred high costs by flying in parts and had to compete with other firms for flights with UPS, FedEx, and other major airlines. Dell had already accounted for the use of air travel well in advance and, as a result, was able to charter planes to ship its foreign parts to the U.S. at almost half the cost of other companies. Furthermore, up-to-the-minute communication with its suppliers ensured that parts were always ready and waiting to be shipped to the United States so the aircraft did not have to wait in the hangars until the parts were there.

When the strike was over, the tens of ships arrived with Dell-destined parts. The company had planned for this as well. It calculated the unloading cycle so that company associates could collect the company's containers as they arrived rather than waiting to sort through the backed-up loads. During the week and a half of the strike, Dell was on time to deliver every single computer. Consumers thus had no reason to even consider that the company was in the middle of a logistical crisis.

Firms with global operations are able to reap the benefits of low cost sourcing, but what comes with the territory is a constant threat to operations and having contigency plans in place plays an important role in successfully combating such hard times. The dock workers strike and the terrorist attacks on the United States in 2001 brought home to some global firms the need either to maintain warehouses and spare inventory or to keep their suppliers close by or be prepared to make contingency plans the way Dell did.

DISCUSSION QUESTIONS

1. Would it be a good strategy for Dell to own some warehouses in case of unforeseen events? How would that affect its business model?

2. What were the important elements of Dell's contingency plan that made it successful?

3. Dell spent a considerable amount of time and money in advance planning in case of a disruption in its supply chain. What should the company do to avoid the additional expenditure in case of future disruptions?

Source: Bill Breen and Michael Aneiro, "Living in Dell Time," *Fast Company Magazine*, November 2004, pp. 86–96.

CASE 16-2

FRENCH RETAILER CARREFOUR: LOSES IN JAPAN BUT WINS IN CHINA?

For Western firms in general and, more recently, global retailers in particular, succeeding in the Japanese market has always been challenging. International business history abounds with stories of their struggles. Noted examples of global retailers that have faced difficulties in Japan include Wal-Mart's affiliate Seiyu and Germany's Metro Group, and the U.K.'s Boots and French Sephora exited Japan just two years after entering it, which made the retail industry sit up and take notice. The latest casualty of the hard-to-please Japanese market is France's Carrefour, the largest retailer in Europe and the second largest in the world (after the U.S.-based giant Wal-Mart) with worldwide sales of over 72.6 billion euros (2005). Carrefour operates around 11,000 stores in more than 30 different countries. More than 50 percent of its sales come from its home country France, 37 percent from operations in other European countries, 6.5 percent from Latin America, and 7 percent in Asian economies.

At the beginning, Western retailers started eyeing the Japanese market in the 1990s when the Japanese government finally revoked its Large-Scale Stores Law that prevented foreign entry by retailers and when real estate prices in Japan started falling. At the dawn of the 21st century, several global retailers set up shop in Japan. These firms include Boots, Sephora, Wal-Mart, and finally U.K.'s Tesco in 2003. Carrefour made its entry into Japan in 2000 and initially opened four stores in Tokyo, Osaka, Saitama, and Hyogo, followed by four more in Kansai. At the time of its entry, it planned to have a total of around 15 stores by the end of 2003. It was not only unable to reach that number but also by the beginning of 2005, the company had started denying rumors that it was going to quit Japan only to exit the Japanese market a few months later. Industry experts claim that the low-price focus of firms like Carrefour and Wal-Mart do not meet the expectations of discerning Japanese consumers who prefer better quality over lower price. The establishment of specialized retailers and changes in the consumption patterns also has exacerbated the situation for foreign retailers.

Carrefour, which engages in all types of retailing with a focus on food retailing at competitive, low prices, operates stores in three main forms in foreign markets: hypermarkets, supermarkets, and hard discounters. Hypermarkets are the largest in terms of floor area and stock; hard discounters are the smallest of the three. When Carrefour's first few stores opened in Japan, the large floor spaces were filled with piles of products that did not allow consumers to easily find an item they needed. Furthermore, according to some, Japanese consumers saw Carrefour as a French retailer and expected to see more French style clothing and products. Tapping into this perception of its stores, Carrefour revamped them in Japan and brought in more French-made products but even then, it failed to carve a niche for itself in the mature Japanese market. On the supply side, Carrefour originally planned to source its products directly from manufacturers but with inadequate purchase orders, it was unable to secure purchase contracts directly from producers. Thus, it was forced to approach wholesalers for products. However, it was unable to break through the tightly knit network between local suppliers and the home-grown Japanese supermarkets and therefore could not offer a wide range of products to its Japanese clients. Finally, four years after its entry into the market, motivated by a drop in worldwide revenues and unprofitable stores in Japan, Carrefour decided to sell off all of its stores in Japan, ultimately to Japan's largest retailer, Aeon Co. Ltd.

On the other hand, Carrefour's experience in Mainland China has been very different, and it is now one of the top five retailers in the country. Carrefour entered China in 1995 with a store in Beijing and by 2000, it had more than 25 stores in 15 major cities in Mainland China. In 2004, it added 12 stores, and its Chinese operations brought in revenues of almost $2 billion. The company invested a great deal in identifying Chinese consumers' tastes and preferences so that it could meet their needs. In China, Carrefour's formula of low prices, huge stores, and a high degree of localization seemed to have worked so well that it is in global management books as Carrefour's Chinese success story. Moreover, Carrefour has decentralized store operation in China and established the Carrefour China Institute for employee training.

The company's success in China, despite periodical run-ins with protective Chinese regulatory authorities, has come as both a surprise and an important lesson to global firms. China, like Japan, has not been an easy market for foreign firms to conduct business in, given its varying cultures within the same country, the stark differences between lifestyles in urban cities and in provinces, and its political structure. With China's entry into the World Trade Organization (WTO) and spurred by its accomplishments in China, Carrefour's ambitious plans for the Chinese market include opening a store a month and investing more than $750 million in its stores. The company still has something to smile about!

DISCUSSION QUESTIONS

1. Do you think it was the right decision for Carrefour to leave Japan? Could it instead have adopted other strategies that could have led to a different outcome?

2. What are implications of the pullout from Japan by Carrefour, the second largest retailer in the world, for other global retailers such as Wal-Mart, which is struggling to survive?

3. Why did Carrefour exit Japan but succeed in China?

Sources: "Carrefour at the Crossroads," *Economist,* October 22, 2005, p. 71; and various other sources.

CASE 16-3

WHICH DISTRIBUTOR TO CHOOSE IN COSTA RICA?

Not long ago, TransMotors (a disguised name), a U.S. export management company that had a joint venture in China manufacturing motorcycles, began to search for new distributors in Central America. TransMotors had previously been highly successful locating distributors for its line of basic transportation motorcycles in South America and Africa. Using Honda technology, the Chinese motorcycles proved to be of high quality and reliability. Most important, they sold for less than one-third of the cost of the competing Japanese models.

The first stop in Central America was Costa Rica, the most prosperous country in the region. A growing economy and political stability provided optimal market conditions for successful sales: a rising middle-class that could now afford a dependable motorcycle for its transportation needs. Such a formula had worked very well in Colombia, Ethiopia, Venezuela, Burkina Faso, Argentina, South Africa, Brazil, Nigeria, Peru, and Cameroon. For TransMotors, like most others seeking to gain entry into high-growth, emerging markets, the key to success was selecting and recruiting the right distributors for its products.

Full of pride because of success in these and others markets, Robert Grosse, the executive in charge of developing the entry strategy for TransMotors, believed himself invincible when it came to identifying who would be the best representative for his company's products. He identified two possible distributors in Costa Rica.

Harvey Arbelaez, the first candidate for the Costa Rican distributor, was a young upstart entrepreneur who had cut his teeth in the agriculture business by importing farm implements and fertilizers. Arbelaez had built a nice network that covered the entire market in Costa Rica and was interested in the Chinese motorcycles because he believed they would complement his existing product lines.

Jaime Alonso Gomez, the other candidate, appeared to be the better fit. Gomez was one of the richest individuals in the country having made his fortune as the exclusive distributor of Honda cars, Scania trucks, and Komatsu heavy equipment. He had sold some Honda motorcycles in the past and was interested in getting back into the low-end transportation business. To the U.S. executive, this appeared to be the logical choice.

When it came time to travel to San Jose to interview the two prospects, Grosse had as his goal the sale of 250 motorcycles a year for each of the first three years. According to his research, the annual sale of motorcycles for the entire country was approximately 2,700 units and growing nicely at a rate of 10 percent per year. The sale of 250 units annually would establish a foundation that could be leveraged down the road to build market share ultimately to 20 to 25 percent.

The first stop on the trip was at Arbelaez's office. On a personal level, the two did not hit it off, although it was clear to Grosse that Arbelaez was wildly enthusiastic about the opportunity to offer the Chinese motorcycles throughout his network. Any positive feelings on the U.S. executive's part soon evaporated, however, when the young man showed projections that the annual sale would be no more than 100 units for the first several years. Arbelaez said it would take a long while for the marketplace to adjust to a Chinese-branded product, but once it did, the potential would be tremendous. At this point, Grosse ended the conversation and told his counterpart, "I will take your plan under advisement." He immediately went to the sparkling offices of the Honda/Scania/Komatsu distributor, Jaime Alonso Gomez.

Within an hour of their meeting, Grosse and Gomez agreed that Gomez would become the exclusive distributor for the Chinese motorcycles. It was clear that his operation had the sales staff, service capability, financial resources, and knowledge of distribution to handle the motorcycles. If that wasn't enough, the first order was to be 1,000 units—four times what Grosse thought it would be! Dinner that night was a celebration of the new relationship at San Jose's most prestigious private club. All that was needed was an exclusive distribution agreement giving the Costa Rican sole rights for the Chinese motorcycles for five years. Then, once the agreement was in place, a revolving letter of credit would be opened to begin shipping the motorcycles in 125 unit increments over the first year.

After the exclusive agreement was consularized and notarized, the first 125 units were shipped from China to Costa Rica without incident. The letter of credit went smoothly, and communication between the two firms was regular and efficient. However, everything changed when it came time to ship the next 125 units. To re-initiate the revolving letter of credit, a document was required from the distributor to the confirming bank. For more than a month, the U.S. firm called, e-mailed, and faxed its exclusive distributor. The only individuals that TransMotors could reach were administrative assistants who generated the same, pat answers. "He's away on a trip . . . in a meeting . . . away from his desk." With the second lot of motorcycles languishing at the dock in Shanghai and another 700 units ready for production, pressure was building.

Unannounced, Grosse grabbed a plane and flew to San Jose to see what was going on. He took a taxi at the airport and went right to his new distributor's office. Not surprising, his new distributor was "in meetings all day and unavailable." Nor were any of the motorcycles or promotional material anywhere to be found on the showroom floor.

Distraught, Grosse took a cab to his hotel. During the 30-minute trip, he was startled to see so many small motorcycles on the streets of San Jose, something that had not been the case during his visit a few months earlier. Many of them were the models of one of his leading competitors from Taiwan.

Source: This case was provided by Professor Timothy J. Wilkinson of the University of Akron based on Andrew R. Thomas and Timothy J. Wilkinson, "It's the Distribution, Stupid!" Business Horizons, 48 (2005), pp. 125–34.

Grosse swallowed his pride and called Harvey Arbelaez, the young entrepreneur whom he had rejected earlier as the exclusive distributor. Half expecting him to hang up, Grosse was shocked when the young man agreed to join him for dinner to discuss what was happening with the motorcycles. Not gloating too much, the young Costa Rican showed pictures of TransMotors' motorcycles still sitting in a bonded warehouse at the port. He also showed photos of a brand new motorcycle distribution company located in the heart of San Jose that was importing small motorcycles from Taiwan. Newspaper articles stated that sales of the Taiwanese products, which were without competition, could exceed 500 units that year. In scanning the articles, Grosse recognized the last name of the distributor. The name was Gomez the brother of TransMotor's exclusive distributor.

DISCUSSION QUESTIONS

1. What mistakes did Robert Grosse make in selecting a distributor?

2. What steps should Robert Grosse have taken that could have helped him do a better job in distributor selection?

FURTHER READING ✦

Barnes, Paul and Richard Oloruntoba. "Assurance of Security in Maritime Supply Chains: Conceptual Issues of Vulnerability and Crisis Management." *Journal of International Management,* 11 (December 2005), pp. 519–40.

Bowersox, Donald J., David J. Closs, and M. Bixby Cooper. *Supply Chain Logistics Management.* New York: McGraw-Hill, 2002.

Colla, Enrico, and Marc Dupuis. "Research and Managerial Issues on Global Retail Competition: Carrefour/Wal-Mart." *International Journal of Retail & Distribution Management,* 30 (2/3), 2002, pp. 103–11.

McGurr, Paul T. "The Largest Retail Firms: A Comparison of Asia-, Europe- and U.S.-based Retailers." *International Journal of Retail & Distribution Management,* 30 (2/3), 2002, pp. 145–47.

Dowlatshahi, Shad. "The Role of Purchasing and TQM in the Maquiladora Industry." *Production and Inventory Management Journal,* 39 (Fourth Quarter 1998), pp. 42–49.

"Global Department Stores." DATAMONITOR, www.datamonitor.com. Reference Code: 0199–2037, May 2004.

Grieger, Martin. "Electronic Marketplaces: A Literature Review and a Call for Supply Chain Management Research." *European Journal of Operational Research,* 144, January 16, 2003, pp. 280–94.

Hanks, George F., and Lucinda Van Alst. "Foreign Trade Zones." *Management Accounting,* 80 (January 1999), pp. 20–23.

Harryman, Roy. "Foreign Trade Zones Give Companies A Competitive Edge." *Expansion Management,* 20 (June 2005), pp. 25–28.

Hult, G. Tomas M., David J. Ketchen, Jr. and Ernest L. Nichols, Jr. "An Examination of Cultural Competitiveness and Order Fulfillment Cycle Time within Supply Chains." *Academy of Management Journal,* 45 (June 2002), pp. 577–86.

Johnson, Jean L., John B. Cullen, and Tomoaki Sakano. "Opportunistic Tendencies in IJVs with the Japanese: The Effects of Culture, Shared Decision Making, and Relationship Age." *International Executive,* 38(1), 1996, pp. 79–94.

Lieb, Robert, and Brooks A. Bentz. "*The Use of Third-Party Logistics Services by Large American Manufacturers: The 2004 Survey.*" *Transportation Journal,* 44 (Spring 2005), pp. 5–15.

Mathur, Lynette Knowles, and Ike Mathur. "The Effectiveness of the Foreign-Trade Zone as an Export Promotion Program: Policy Issues and Alternatives." *Journal of Macromarketing,* 17 (Fall 1997), pp. 20–31.

EXPORT AND IMPORT MANAGEMENT

CHAPTER OVERVIEW

1. ORGANIZING FOR EXPORTS

2. INDIRECT EXPORTING

3. DIRECT EXPORTING

4. MECHANICS OF EXPORTING

5. ROLE OF THE GOVERNMENT IN PROMOTING EXPORTS

6. IMPORT—THE OTHER SIDE OF THE COIN

7. MECHANICS OF IMPORTING

8. GRAY MARKETS

Exporting is the most popular way for many companies to become international. The main reasons for this are that exporting (1) requires minimum resources while allowing high flexibility and (2) offers substantial financial, marketing, technological, and other benefits to the firm. Because exporting is usually the first mode of foreign entry used by many companies, exporting early tends to give them first-mover advantage.[1] However, exporting requires experiential knowledge. Exporters must acquire foreign market knowledge (i.e., clients, market needs, and competitors) and institutional knowledge (i.e., government, institutional framework, rules, norms, and values) as well as develop operational knowledge (i.e., capabilities and resources to engage in international operations).[2] Selling to a foreign market involves numerous high risks arising from the lack of knowledge of and unfamiliarity with foreign environments, which can be heterogeneous, sophisticated, and turbulent. Furthermore, conducting market research across national boundaries is more difficult, complex, and subjective than for its domestic counterpart.

[1] Yigang Pan, Shaomin Li, and David K. Tse, "The Impact of Order and Mode of Market Entry on Profitability and Market Share," *Journal of International Business Studies,* 30 (First Quarter 1999), pp. 81–104.

[2] Kent Eriksson, Jan Johanson, Anders Majkgård, and D. Deo Sharma, "Effect of Variation on Knowledge Accumulation in the Internationalization Process," *International Studies of Management and Organization,* 30 (2000), pp. 26–44.

For successful development of export activities, systematic collection of information is critical. Market information can be well documented and come from public and private data sources, but it can also be so tacit that only seasoned marketing managers with international vision and experience could have a "gut feel" in understanding it.[3] Market information helps managers to assess the attractiveness of foreign markets and decide whether to engage in exporting. After a firm has decided to start exporting, it requires information on how to handle the mechanics of it, including how to enter overseas markets and what adaptations to make to the marketing mix elements.[4] A recent study that compared export leaders—defined as companies that distribute products or services to six or more countries—to export laggards shows that the more companies export, the more they spend in information technology. According to the same study, much of the investment the leading export companies make in IT is for e-business from Web-based commerce and supply chain networks to electronic marketplaces. This focus seems to be paying off.[5]

As presented in Chapter 2, the nature of international exports and imports has also improved since the beginning of this new century. Global output and trade grew more strongly in 2004 than in the previous three years. Global gross domestic product (GDP) growth amounted to 4 percent in 2004, providing a solid basis for strong trade growth. World merchandise exports increased by 21 percent in 2004, amounting to $8.88 trillion. This compares with growth in commercial services trade of 16 percent in 2004, reaching $2.1 trillion. These trade growth rates were the best performance since 2000 and the third highest rate over the last decade. Trade growth has outstripped GDP growth by a significant margin. As this pattern continues, trade becomes an ever more crucial component of global economic activity. The most dynamic trading nations in 2004 were in Asia, South, and Central America, and the Commonwealth of Independent States (CIS).[6] Africa's trade grew strongly in 2004, buoyed in part by firmer commodity prices, particularly for oil and metals. Oil prices also had a strong influence on trade growth in the Middle East. North America's exports gained further momentum in 2004 compared to previous years, but growth was below the global average. Similarly, improved merchandise trade growth in Europe in 2004 was also very important for world trade growth, but Europe's trade and output growth remained well below the global average. In current price terms, both merchandise and services trade grew for the third successive year, amounting to the strongest rise since 2000.[7]

Although the United States is still relatively more insulated from the global economy than other nations (See Chapter 2), exports of goods and services combined represented about 10 percent of the U.S. GDP as of 2004, yet account for more than 25 percent of U.S. economic growth in the past decade. Roughly 10 percent of all U.S. jobs (approximately 12 million) rely on exports. In general, one in five factory jobs depends on international trade in the United States. Between 1990 and 2000, export-related jobs grew by 56 percent, an increase that is three times faster than the rate of job growth in the rest of the economy. These facts demonstrate that export is an important source of U.S. economic growth and job creation. Furthermore, jobs that depend on trade pay between 13 to 18 percent more than the average wage, indicating that these employees generally earn more than the others. [8]

---

[3]Gary A. Knight and Peter W. Liesch, "Information Internalization in Internationalizing the Firm," *Journal of Business Research,* 55 (December 2002), pp. 981–95.

[4]Leonidas C. Leonidou and Athena S. Adams-Florou, "Types and Sources of Export Information: Insights from Small Business," *International Small Business Journal,* 17 (April–June 1999), pp. 30–48.

[5]Mary E. Thyfault, "Heavy Exporters Spend Big on Leading-Edge IT," *InformationWeek,* (April 23, 2001), p. 54.

[6]Republics in the former Soviet Union.

[7]*World Trade Report 2005: Exploring the Link between Trade, Standards, and the WTO* (Geneva: World Trade Organization, 2005).

[8]National Council on Economic Education, http://www.econedlink.org/lessons/index.cfm?lesson=EM208; Trade Resource Center, http://trade.businessroundtable.org/trade_2005/wto/us_economy.html; and Trade Resource Center, http://trade.businessroundtable.org/trade_basics/trade_jobs.html, accessed October 1, 2006.

This chapter primarily considers the export function; it attempts to explain the import function as the counterpart of the export function because for every export transaction there is, by definition, an import transaction as well. Aside from some differences between the procedure and rationale for exports and imports, both are largely the same the world over.

◆ ◆ ◆ ◆ ◆ ◆ ◆ ◆ ORGANIZING FOR EXPORTS

Research for Exports

The first step for a firm exporting for the first time, is to use available secondary data to research potential markets. Increasingly, international marketing information is available in the form of electronic databases ranging from the latest news on product developments to new material in the academic and trade press. Well over 6,000 databases are available worldwide, with almost 5,000 available online. The United States is the largest participant in this database growth, producing and consuming more than 50 percent of these database services. When entering a culturally and linguistically different part of the world, managers need to understand a completely new way of commercial thinking that is based on a different culture and works on a different set of premises. Often, seasoned managers' flexibility and adaptability acquired through experience and learning prove to be important in building export contracts.[9] It is also to be noted that export research for markets such as China and the CIS still must be done largely in the field because very little prior data exist for them, and when they are available, they are often not reliable.[10] See Global Perspective 17-1 for how complex the task of exporting is relative to domestic sales.

The identification of an appropriate overseas market and an appropriate segment involves grouping by the following criteria:

1. Socioeconomic characteristics (e.g., demographic, economic, geographic, and climatic characteristics)

2. Political and legal characteristics

3. Consumer variables (e.g., lifestyle, preferences, culture, taste, purchase behavior, and purchase frequency)

4. Financial conditions

On the basis of these criteria, an exporter can form an idea of the market segments in a foreign market.[11] First, regions within countries across the world are grouped by macroeconomic variables indicating the levels of industrial development, availability of skilled labor, and purchasing power. For example, from an exporter's point of view, the Mumbai–Thane–Pune area in Western India has more in common with the Monterrey area and the Mexico City area in Mexico, California, and the Shanghai–Wuxi area in China than with other areas in India. All three areas already have a well-developed industrial base and purchasing power that is equal to that of the middle class in developed nations. Such economically homogeneous groups across the world are a result of the globalization of markets. These apparently similar markets can, however, differ along political and legal dimensions. An exporter or importer that violates terms has legal recourse in India, and the court of adjudication is in India. Legal recourse is still largely wishful thinking in China. By addressing consumer and macroeconomic variables, the exporter can successfully segment the international market into homogenous segments where similar elements of the marketing mix can be applied.

---

[9] Amal R. Karunaratna, Lester W. Johnson, and C.P. Rao, "The Exporter–Import Agent Contract and the Influence of Cultural Dimensions," *Journal of Marketing Management,* 17 (February 2001), pp. 137–58.

[10] Peter G. P. Walters and Saeed Samiee, "Marketing Strategy in Emerging Markets: The Case of China," *Journal of International Marketing,* 11 (1), 2003, pp. 97–106.

[11] For a comprehensive review of the export development process, see Leonidas C. Leonidou and Constantine S. Katsikeas, "The Export Development Process: An Integrative Review of Empirical Models," *Journal of International Business Studies,* 27 (Third Quarter 1996), pp. 517–51.

♦ ♦

𝒢LOBAL PERSPECTIVE 17-1

THE COMPLEXITIES OF EXPORTING VERSUS DOMESTIC SALES

Major differences exist in processing domestic and export sales, but the two most important may be the complexity and the number of people involved in exporting products. These differences are also major contributors to new and better paying jobs for the domestic labor market.

PROCESS FOR DOMESTIC SALES

The order is entered or given to a salesperson via e-mail, fax, Internet, or phone. If the product is in stock, the salesperson sends the request to the shipping department where the order is filled and then boxed, crated, or skidded. The box(es) is marked, labeled, and put on a truck for delivery the next day or as soon as possible.

THE PROCESS FOR EXPORT SALES

An order entry person (often bilingual) enters the order that is received via e-mail, fax, Internet, or phone. An export compliance officer reviews all foreign inquiries, requests, and purchase orders. The officer also monitors Export Administration Regulations, tariffs, harmonized codes, export licenses, boycotts, languages, checklists for denied parties, and shipper's security endorsement, and engineering reviews for compliance and product certifications. These tasks are usually outsourced to labs. Companies can use separate production lines designated specifically for export because of major differences in technical specifications, certifications, and designs. Different sources of outside suppliers can also be needed for exported goods. Drawings, designs, and instructions need to be translated and printed in several foreign languages. The export shipping department is experienced in export

Source: Richard Gref, "Are Export Sales Really Good for the U.S. Economy?" *Business Credit,* (September 2000), p. 52.

packing, containerizing, and creating detailed packing lists. The department also references metric weights and measurements while providing export labeling and routing that identifies INCOTERMS, FOB, FAS, CIF, or CFR.

A freight forwarder is an export documentation specialist who handles export declarations, certificates of compliance, consular, origin, Chambers of Commerce signatures, export insurance, and airway and ocean bills of lading. In terms of transportation, trucks and railroad cars are used to deliver export containers to domestic ports to meet shipping schedules. The banking sector handles foreign open account payments, wire transfers, letters of credit, drafts, and financing (short, medium, and long term). Factoring houses, forfeiting agencies, and insurance agencies (public and private) augment this process as well. U.S. government employees including U.S. Customs officers, Export Administration personnel (at the Bureau of Industry and Security) and Ex-Im Bank, Small Business Administration, World Bank and USAID representatives, also may contribute to the export sales process. Other government agencies represented in this process include the Department of Commerce, Department of Treasury, and Export Assistance. Monitoring export sales (analysis and statistics) is completed by the Departments of State and Defense as well as the Nuclear Energy Commission and the Central Intelligence Agency. Other service providers include international telecommunications and foreign travel service agents as well as international newspapers, magazines, and publications and international credit reporting agencies such as FCIB. Finally, attorneys, accounting firms, tax experts, and consultants specializing in international markets provide their services.

The next time someone asks whether export sales are really easy to handle, you may want to share a copy of this article.

Data for grouping along macroeconomic criteria are available from international agencies such as the World Bank, which publishes the *World Development Report.* In addition, the United Nations produces a series of statistical abstracts on a yearly basis covering economic, demographic, political, and social characteristics that are very useful for grouping analysis. The International Monetary Fund publishes data on international trade and finance quarterly and annually. Both the Organization for Economic Cooperation and Development (OECD, a group of advanced nations) and the European Union (EU) publish a variety of statistical reports and studies on their member countries.

As discussed in Chapter 7, the grouping of countries and regions among countries enables a firm to link various geographical areas into one homogeneous market segment that the firm can cater to in meeting its export objectives. The next task is to develop a product strategy for the selected export markets. The export market clusters obtained by clustering regions within different nations would fall into various levels. At the country level would be countries with the same characteristics as the U.S. market. At a regional level within nations, there would be geographical and psychographic segments

Export Market Segments

in many different countries to which the firm can export the same core product it sells in domestic markets without any significant changes. Doing so is a form of market diversification in which the firm is selling a standardized, uniform product across countries and regions.[12] Mercedes-Benz automobiles and Rolex watches sell to the same consumer segment worldwide. Another standardized product that sells worldwide is the soft drink. The Coca-Cola Company markets essentially one Coke worldwide.

Products that can be standardized could satisfy basic needs that do not vary with climate, economic conditions, or culture. A standardized product is the easiest to sell abroad logistically because the firm incurs no additional manufacturing costs and is able to use the same promotional messages across different regions in different countries across the world. If those different regions have comparable logistics and infrastructural facilities, the distribution requirements and expenses would also be similar.

Where it is not possible to sell standardized products, the firm could need to adapt its products for the overseas marketplace. In such instances, either the firm's product does not meet customer requirements or it does not satisfy the administrative requirements of foreign countries. Such markets can require modification of the product if it is to succeed in the foreign market.[13] Brand names, for example, frequently need to be changed before a product can be sold because the brand name could mean something detrimental to the product's prospects. For example, Ford recently released its new European Ka model in Japan. *Ka* means "mosquito" in Japanese, a less than popular disease-carrying pest. Analysts called the Ka dead on arrival.[14] Beauty-products giant Estée Lauder found out that its perfume Country Mist would not sell in Germany because *mist* means manure in German slang. Sometimes, a new product has to be developed from a manufacturing viewpoint because the product is not salable as it is in the export market. For example, room air conditioner units being exported to Egypt have to have special filters and coolers and must be sturdy enough to handle the dust and heat of Egyptian summer.

◆ ◆ ◆ ◆ ◆ ◆ ◆ ◆ INDIRECT EXPORTING

Indirect exporting involves the use of independent intermediaries or agents to market the firm's products overseas. These agents, known as *export representatives,* assume responsibility for marketing the firm's products through their network of foreign distributors and their own salesforce. It is not uncommon for a U.S. producer who is new to exporting to begin export operation by selling through an export representative. Many Japanese firms have also relied on the giant general trading companies known as *sogoshosha.* Use of agents is not uncommon when it is not cost effective for an exporter to set up its own export department. Such firms can initiate export operations through export representatives who know the market and have experience in selling to them. There are several types of export representatives in the United States. The most common are the combination export manager (CEM), export merchant, export broker, export commission house, trading company, and piggyback exporter.

The **combination export manager (CEM)** acts as the export department to a small exporter or a large producer with small overseas sales. CEMs often use the letterhead of the company they represent and have extensive experience in selling abroad and in the mechanics of export shipments. CEMs operate on a commission basis and are usually most effective when they deal with clients who have businesses in related lines. Because credit plays an increasingly important role in export sales, CEMs have found it increasingly difficult to consummate export sales on behalf of clients without their

---

[12]Lloyd C. Russow, "Market Diversification: 'Going International'," *Review of Business,* 17 (Spring 1996), pp. 32–34.

[13]Roger J. Calantone, S. Tamer Cavusgil, Jeffrey B. Schmidt, and Geon-Cheol Shin, "Internationalization and the Dynamics of Product Adaptation—An Empirical Investigation," *Journal of Product Innovation Management,* 21 (May 2004), pp. 185–98.

[14]Keith Naughton, "Tora, Tora, Taurus," *Business Week,* (April 12, 1999), p.6.

credit support. As more and more firms begin exporting on a regular basis, CEMs are becoming a vanishing breed. A list of them can be found in the *American Register of Exporters and Importers* and in the telephone yellow pages.

Export merchants, in contrast to the CEM, buy and sell on their own accounts and assume all responsibilities of exporting a product. In this situation, the manufacturers do not control the sales activities of their products in export markets and depend entirely on the export merchant for all export activities. This loss of control over the export marketing effort is a major drawback to using export merchants. The **export broker,** as the name implies, is someone who brings together an overseas buyer and a domestic manufacturer for the purpose of an export sale and earns a commission for establishing a contact that results in a sale.

Foreign buyers of U.S. goods sometimes contract for the services of a U.S. representative to act on their behalf. This resident representative is usually an **export commission house** that places orders only on behalf of its foreign client with U.S. manufacturers and acts as a finder for its client to get the best buy. A **trading company** is a large, foreign organization engaged in exporting and importing. It buys on its own account in one country and exports the goods to another country. Most of the well-known trading companies are Japanese or Western European in origin. Japanese trading companies, known as *sogoshosha,* such as Mitsui, Mitsubishi, and Sumitomo operate worldwide and handle a significant proportion of Japanese foreign trade. United Africa Company, a subsidiary of Unilever, operates extensively in Africa. Another European trading company is Jardine Matheson in Hong Kong, a major trading force in Southeast Asia. See Exhibit 17-1 for the major types of trading companies.

Piggyback exporting refers to the practice by which carrier firms that have established export departments assume, under a cooperative agreement, the responsibility of exporting the products of other companies. The carrier buys the rider's products and markets them independently. The rider plays a peripheral role in the export marketing overseas. Piggybacking can be an option to enter an export market but is normally

EXHIBIT 17-1
MAJOR TYPES OF TRADING COMPANIES AND THEIR COUNTRIES OF ORIGIN

Type	Rationale for Grouping	Some Examples by Country of Origin
General trading company	Historical involvement in generalized imports/exports	C. Itoh (Japan), East Asiatic (Denmark), SCOA (France), Jardine Matheson (Hong Kong)
Export trading company	Specific mission to promote growth of exporters	Hyundai (Korea), Interbras (Brazil), Sears World Trade (US)
Federated export marketing group	Loose collaboration among exporting companies supervised by a third party and usually market specific	Fedec (UK), SBI Group (Norway), IEB Project Group (Morocco)
Trading arm of MNCs	Specific international trading operations in parent company operations	General Motors (US), IBM (US)
Bank-based or affiliated trading group	A bank at the center of a group extends commercial activities	Mitsubishi (Japan), Cobec (Brazil)
Commodity trading company	Long-standing export trading in a specific market	Metallgesellschaft (Germany), Louis Dreyfus (France)

Source: Adapted from Lyn Amine, "Toward a Conceptualization of Export Trading Companies in World Markets," in *Advances in International Marketing,* vol. 2, S. Tamer Cavusgil, ed. (Greenwich, CT: JAI Press, 1987), pp. 199–208.

avoided by firms who wish to be in exports over the long haul because of the loss of control over the foreign marketing operations.

♦ ♦ ♦ ♦ ♦ ♦ ♦ ♦   DIRECT EXPORTING

Direct exporting occurs when a manufacturer or exporter sells directly to an importer or buyer located in a foreign market. It requires export managers' full commitment in both their attitudes and behavior for export success.[15] Direct exporting can manifest itself in various organizational forms, depending on the scale of operations and the number of years that a firm has been engaged in exporting. In its most simple form, a firm has an export sales manager with some clerical help responsible for the actual selling and directing of activities associated with the export sales. Most of the other export marketing activities (advertising, logistics, and credit, for example) are performed by a regular department of the firm that also handles international trade transactions.

As export activities grow in scale and complexity, most firms create a separate **export department** that is largely self-contained and operates independently of domestic operations. An export department can be structured internally on the basis of function, geography, product, customer, or some other combination. Some firms prefer to have an **export sales subsidiary** instead of an export department to keep export operations separate from the rest of the firm. In terms of internal operations and specific operations performed, an export sales subsidiary differs very little from an export department. The major difference is that the subsidiary, being a separate legal entity, must purchase the products it sells in the overseas markets from its parent manufacturer. This means that the parent has to develop and administer a system of transfer pricing. A subsidiary has the advantage of being an independent profit center and is therefore easier to evaluate; it can also offer tax advantages, ease of financing, and increased proximity to the customer.

Instead of a foreign sales subsidiary, a firm also has the option of establishing a **foreign sales branch.** Unlike a subsidiary, a branch is not a separate legal entity. A foreign sales branch handles all of sales, distribution, and promotional work throughout a designated market area and sells primarily to wholesalers and dealers. Where it is used, a sales branch is the initial link in the marketing channel in the foreign market. Often the branch has a storage and warehousing facility available so it can maintain an inventory of products, replacement parts, and maintenance supplies.

EXHIBIT 17-2
COMPARISON OF DIRECT AND INDIRECT EXPORTING

Indirect Exporting	*Direct Exporting*
• Set-up costs tend to be low	• Set-up costs tend to be high
• Does not help exporter to gain good knowledge of export markets	• Leads to better knowledge of export markets and international expertise due to direct contact
• Credit risk lies mostly with the intermediary	• Credit risks are higher especially in the early years
• It is not in the interest of the intermediary doing the exporting to develop customer loyalty	• Customer loyalty can be developed for the exporter's brands more easily

[15]Rodney L. Stump, Gerard A. Athaide, and Catherine N. Axinn, "The Contingent Effect of the Dimensions of Export Commitment on Exporting Financial Performance: An Empirical Examination," *Journal of Global Marketing,* 12 (1), 1998, pp. 7–25; and David L. Dean and Bulent Menguc, "Revisiting Firm Characteristics, Strategy, and Export Performance Relationship," *Industrial Marketing Management,* 29 (September 2000), pp. 461–77.

Indirect exporting and direct exporting are compared in Exhibit 17-2. Both have advantages and disadvantages, although over the long-term, that is, for a firm desiring a permanent presence in international markets, direct exports tend to be more useful.

MECHANICS OF EXPORTING ◆ ◆ ◆ ◆ ◆ ◆ ◆ ◆

To the uninitiated, the mechanics of exporting can seem to be cumbersome and full of meaningless, irrelevant paperwork. In the United States, the Shipper's Export Declaration (Form 7525-V), which is one of the many forms required to be filed by a prospective exporter (see Exhibit 17-3), provides a glimpse at the details that the government requires of exporters. However, it is precisely a summarized, collated, and edited version of such data that was the basis of at least some of the secondary data that prospective exporters use in their research when exploring foreign markets. These data are also used to compile trade statistics, which are barometers of the health of a country's economy, its stock market, and foreign exchange rates.

Automated Export System (AES) on the Internet

The paperwork involved in export declaration forms can be time consuming no matter how useful information provided on the forms can be. To expedite the exporting process, the U.S. Commerce Department's Census Bureau launched a new system, the **Automated Export System (AES),** on October 1, 1999. AES enables exporters to file export information at no cost over the Internet; it is part of an effort to make government more efficient and boost U.S. exports.[16]

AES is a joint venture between the U.S. Customs Service, the Foreign Trade Division of the Bureau of the Census (Commerce), the Bureau of Industry and Security (Commerce), the Office of Defense Trade Controls (State), other federal agencies, and the export trade community. It was designed to improve trade statistics, reduce duplicate reporting to multiple agencies, improve customer service, and to ensure compliance with and enforcement of laws relating to exporting. It is the central point through which export shipment data required by multiple agencies are filed electronically on the Internet to Customs, using electronic data interchange (EDI). AES is a completely voluntary system that provides an alternative to filing the paper Shipper's Export Declarations. AES export information is collected electronically and edited immediately, and errors are detected and corrected at the time of filing. AES is a nationwide system operational at all ports and for all methods of transportation.

This Internet-based system will allow exporters, freight forwarders, and consolidators to file shippers' export declaration information in an automated, cost-free way. AES has the goal of paperless reporting of export information.[17] The new system will reduce the paperwork burden on the trade community, make document storage and handling less costly, improve the quality of export statistics, and facilitate exporting in general. Before AES, the export system was paper bound, expensive, labor intensive, and error prone.

Legality of Exports

Exporting starts with the search for a buyer abroad. It includes the research to locate a potential market, a buyer, and information concerning the process of closing a sale. We covered the process of getting an order earlier in this chapter. Once an export contract has been signed, the wheels are set in motion for the process that results in the export contract. The *first* stage has to do with the legality of the transaction. The exporter must determine that the goods can be imported by the importing party; importing country licensing law can halt a transaction unless it is studied in advance.

[16]"Two Major Export Compliance Changes Coming in Early 2006," *Managing Exports & Imports,* (October 2005), pp. 1-13.

[17]David Biederman, "AES a Must for Dual-Use Goods," *Traffic World,* (January 3, 2000), p. 30.

EXHIBIT 17-3

FORM 7525-V: INFORMATION TO BE REPORTED ON THE SHIPPER's
EXPORT DECLARATION

U.S. DEPARTMENT OF COMMERCE – Economics and Statistics Administration – U.S. CENSUS BUREAU – BUREAU OF EXPORT ADMINISTRATION

FORM **7525-V** (7-18-2003)   **SHIPPER'S EXPORT DECLARATION**   OMB No. 0607-0152

1a. U.S. PRINCIPAL PARTY IN INTEREST (USPPI)(Complete name and address)

ZIP CODE

2. DATE OF EXPORTATION

3. TRANSPORTATION REFERENCE NO.

b. USPPI'S EIN (IRS) OR ID NO.

c. PARTIES TO TRANSACTION
☐ Related ☐ Non-related

4a. ULTIMATE CONSIGNEE *(Complete name and address)*

b. INTERMEDIATE CONSIGNEE *(Complete name and address)*

5a. FORWARDING AGENT *(Complete name and address)*

5b. FORWARDING AGENT'S EIN (IRS) NO.

6. POINT (STATE) OF ORIGIN OR FTZ NO.

7. COUNTRY OF ULTIMATE DESTINATION

8. LOADING PIER *(Vessel only)*

9. METHOD OF TRANSPORTATION *(Specify)*

14. CARRIER IDENTIFICATION CODE

15. SHIPMENT REFERENCE NO.

10. EXPORTING CARRIER

11. PORT OF EXPORT

16. ENTRY NUMBER

17. HAZARDOUS MATERIALS ☐ Yes ☐ No

12. PORT OF UNLOADING *(Vessel and air only)*

13. CONTAINERIZED *(Vessel only)* ☐ Yes ☐ No

18. IN BOND CODE

19. ROUTED EXPORT TRANSACTION ☐ Yes ☐ No

20. SCHEDULE B DESCRIPTION OF COMMODITIES *(Use columns 22–24)*

D/F or M (21)	SCHEDULE B NUMBER (22)	QUANTITY – SCHEDULE B UNIT(S) (23)	SHIPPING WEIGHT (Kilograms) (24)	VIN/PRODUCT NUMBER/ VEHICLE TITLE NUMBER (25)	VALUE (U.S. dollars, omit cents) (Selling price or cost if not sold) (26)

27. LICENSE NO./LICENSE EXCEPTION SYMBOL/AUTHORIZATION

28. ECCN *(When required)*

29. Duly authorized officer or employee

The USPPI authorizes the forwarder named above to act as forwarding agent for export control and customs purposes.

30. I certify that all statements made and all information contained herein are true and correct and that I have read and understand the instructions for preparation of this document, set forth in the "**Correct Way to Fill Out the Shipper's Export Declaration.**" I understand that civil and criminal penalties, including forfeiture and sale, may be imposed for making false or fraudulent statements herein, failing to provide the requested information or for violation of U.S. laws on exportation (13 U.S.C. Sec. 305; 22 U.S.C. Sec. 401; 18 U.S.C. Sec. 1001; 50 U.S.C. App. 2410).

Signature

Confidential – Shipper's Export Declarations (or any successor document) wherever located, shall be exempt from public disclosure unless the Secretary determines that such exemption would be contrary to the national interest (Title 13, Chapter 9, Section 301 (g)).

Title

Export shipments are subject to inspection by U.S. Customs Service and/or Office of Export Enforcement.

Date

31. AUTHENTICATION *(When required)*

Telephone No. (Include Area Code)

E-mail address

Clear fields 1 to 19

Clear Fields 20 to 26

Clear Fields 27 to 31

Clear all fields

This form may be printed by private parties provided it conforms to the official form. For sale by the Superintendent of Documents, Government Printing Office, Washington, DC 20402, and local Customs District Directors. The "**Correct Way to Fill Out the Shipper's Export Declaration**" is available from the U.S. Census Bureau, Washington, DC 20233.

Source: U.S. Census Bureau, Foreign Trade Statistics, http://www.census.gov/foreign-trade/regulations/forms/, accessed October 2, 2006.

Standard specifications for products and services are especially important in Europe and Japan as far as U.S. exporters are concerned. As far as export transactions to third-world countries are concerned, the convertibility of the importing country's currency must be determined even in this day of liberalization. If the country's currency is not convertible, the importing party must have permission to remit hard currency. Finally, the exporter must ensure that there are no export restrictions on the goods proposed to be exported from the United States. Security concerns on encryption technology, for example, permit the exports of encryption technology that incorporates no more than 40 bits. All exports from the United States (except those to Canada and U.S. territories) require an **export license,** which can be a general export license or a validated export license. A **general license** permits exportation within certain limits without requiring that an application be filed or that a license be issued. A **validated license** permits exportation within specific limitations; it is issued only on formal application. Most goods can move from the United States to the free world countries under a general license. A validated license is required to export certain strategic goods regardless of their destination. For most goods, the license is granted by the U.S. Department of Commerce's Bureau of Industry and Security. For certain specific products, however, the license is granted by other U.S. government agencies (see Exhibit 17-4).

As onerous as export validation procedure appears, large companies are proactively dealing with it. For example, Philips, with $4 billion in annual exports to over 150 countries from some 260 U.S. locations, has automated its export process to a significant degree by implementing its PROTECT system, which is basically a database that permits export managers to simulate their export transaction before it is approved. The PROTECT database includes (1) all Philips products that fall under any type of export control, (2) a full listing of proscribed or sensitive countries and customers, (3) all export control laws and regulations, and (4) concrete instruction on how to act in specific export control matters. In general, the Philips export management system clearly identifies who are its customers, how it takes orders, and who is responsible for exports to ensure that export activities follow the company's export compliance guidelines and procedures.[18]

The second pillar of an export transaction involves the logistics of the export transaction, which includes (1) the terms of the sale, including payment mode and schedule, dispute settlement mechanism, and service requirements (if applicable); (2) monitoring the transportation and delivery of the goods to the assigned party—the assignee in the bill of lading and obtaining proof of delivery—the **customs receipt**; and (3) shipping and obtaining the bill of lading.

When a company has a firm order for exports, it must execute the order by delivering the product or service promised to the overseas customer. A **bill of lading** is a contract between the exporter and the shipping company indicating that the shipping company has accepted responsibility for the goods and will provide transportation in return for payment. The bill of ownership can also be used as a receipt and to prove ownership of the merchandise, depending on the type of bill of lading. A **straight**

Export Transactions

EXHIBIT 17-4
U.S. GOVERNMENT DEPARTMENTS AND AGENCIES WITH EXPORT CONTROL RESPONSIBILITIES

Commodity	*Licensing Authority*
Defense services and defense articles	Department of State
Nuclear material and equipment	Nuclear Regulatory Commission
Nuclear technology and technical data for nuclear power, natural gas and electric power	Department of Energy
Endangered fish and wildlife	Department of the Interior
Medical devices, drugs	Food and Drug Administration
Controlled substance and related chemicals	Drug Enforcement Administration
Patent filing data	Patent and Trademark Office
Toxic waste	Environment Protection Agency

Source: Bureau of Industry and Security, U.S. Department of Commerce, http://www.bis.doc.gov/reslinks.htm, accessed August 4, 2006.

[18]"AAEI Conference Highlights: How Microsoft, Philips Meet New Post-9/11 Compliance Requirements," *Managing Exports*, (August 2004), pp. 1–4.

bill of lading is not negotiable and is usually used in prepaid transactions. The goods are delivered to a specific individual or company. A **shipper's order bill of lading** is negotiable; it can be bought, sold, or traded while the goods are still in transit, (i.e., title of the goods can change hands). The customer usually needs the original or a copy of the bill of lading to take possession of the goods (depending on the terms of the export contract).

A **commercial invoice** is a bill for the goods stating basic information about the transaction, including a description of the merchandise, total cost of the goods sold, addresses of the buyer and the seller, and delivery and payment terms. The buyer needs the invoice to prove ownership and to arrange payment terms. Some governments also use commercial invoices to assess customs duties. Other export documentation that can be required includes export licenses, certificates of origin, inspection certification, dock and/or warehouse receipts, destination control certificates (to inform shippers and other foreign parties that the goods can be shipped only to a particular country), shippers' export declaration (Form 7525-V provided in Exhibit 17-3 used to compile export trade statistics), and export packaging lists. To ensure that all required documentation is accurately completed and to minimize potential problems, firms entering the international market for the first time with an export order should consider using **freight forwarders** who are shipping agents and specialists in handling export documentation.

Terms of Shipment and Sale

The responsibilities of the exporter, the importer, and the logistic provider should be spelled out in the export contract in terms of what is and what is not included in the price quotation and who owns title to the goods while in transit. **INCOTERMS 2000,** which went into effect on January 1, 2000 and is an acronym for International Commercial Terms, are the internationally accepted standard definitions for the terms of sale by the International Chamber of Commerce.[19] The commonly used terms of shipment are summarized in Exhibit 17-5.

The terms of shipment used in the export transaction and their acceptance by the parties involved are important to prevent subsequent disputes. These terms of shipment also have significant implications on costing and pricing. The exporter should therefore learn what terms of shipment importers prefer in a particular market and what the specific transaction requires. A CIF quote by an exporter clearly shows the importer the cost to get the product to a port in a desired country. An inexperienced importer may be discouraged by an EXW quote because the importer may not know how much the EXW quote translates in terms of landed cost at home.

Payment Terms

The financing and payments of an export transaction constitute the third set of things to do with regard to an export transaction. For example, is export credit available from an Export–Import Bank (discussed later in the chapter) or a local agency supporting exports? What payment terms have been agreed on? Customary payment terms for noncapital goods transactions include advance payment, confirmed irrevocable letter of credit, unconfirmed irrevocable letter of credit, documents against payment (D/P), documents against acceptance (D/A), open account, and consignment basis payments. These terms are explained in Exhibit 17-6. The terms of payment between the exporter and the importer are a matter of negotiation and depend on a variety of factors including the buyer's credit standing, the amount of the sale transaction, the availability of foreign exchange in the buyer's country, the exchange control laws in the buyer's country, the risks associated with the type of merchandise to be shipped, the usual practice in the trade, and market conditions (i.e., a buyer's market or a seller's market and payment terms offered by competitors).

---

[19]http://www.ltdmgmt.com/incoterms.htm, accessed August 4, 2006.

EXHIBIT 17-5
TERMS OF SHIPMENT

Ex-works (EXW) at the point of origin	The exporter agrees to deliver the goods at the disposal of the buyer to the specified place on the specified date or within a fixed period. All other charges are borne by the buyer.
Free alongside ship (FAS) at a named port of export	Title and risk pass to the buyer, including payment of all transportation and insurance cost, once delivered alongside ship by the seller. Used for sea or inland waterway transportation. The export clearance obligation rests with the seller.
Free on board (FOB) at a named port of export	The exporter undertakes to load the goods on the vessel to be used for ocean transportation, and the price the exporter quoted reflects this cost.
Free carrier (FCA) at a named place	Pricing conditions that are very similar to those of FOB; mainly quoted for air transport and multimodal transport.
Cost and freight (CFR) to a named overseas port of disembarkation	The exporter quotes a price for the goods, including the cost of transportation, to a named overseas port of disembarkation. The cost of insurance and the choice of the insurer are left to the importer.
Carriage paid to (CPT) at named place of destination	Pricing conditions are very similar to those of CFR; mainly quoted for air transport and multimodal transport.
Cost, insurance, and freight (CIF) to a named overseas port of disembarkation	The exporter quotes a price including insurance and all transportation and miscellaneous charges to the port of disembarkation from the ship, influenced by port charges (unloading, wharfage, storage, heavy lift, demurrage), documentation charges (certification of invoice, certification of origin, weight certificate) and other miscellaneous charges (fees of freight forwarder, insurance premiums)
Carriage and insurance paid to (CIP) at named place of destination	Pricing conditions are very similar to those of CIF; mainly quoted for air transport and multimodal transport.
Delivery duty paid (DDP) to an overseas buyer's premises	The exporter delivers the goods with import duties paid, including inland transportation from the docks to the importer's premises

When negotiating payment terms with an importer, an exporter must consider the risks associated with the importer and the importer's country including credit risk, foreign exchange risks, transfer risks, and the political risks of the importer's country. **Credit risk** is the risk that the importer will not pay or will fail to pay on the agreed terms. **Foreign exchange risk** exists when the sale is in the importer's currency and that currency can depreciate in terms of the home currency, leaving the exporter with less in the home currency.[20] **Transfer risk** refers to the chances that payment will not be made due to the importer's inability to obtain foreign currency (usually U.S. dollars) and transfer it to the exporter. **Political risk** refers to the risk associated with war, confiscation of the importer's business, and other unexpected political events.

If an exporter sells for cash, there is virtually no risk. The possible nominal risk is associated with the timing of the order as compared to the receipt of payment. A sale on a **confirmed irrevocable letter of credit** has slightly more risk. The confirmation places a home bank or other known bank acceptable to the seller; the payment risk assumed by the exporter devolves almost completely to this bank. If the sale is in a foreign currency, the exporter is still exposed to the risk of depreciation of the foreign currency relative to the dollar. An **unconfirmed irrevocable letter of credit** exposes the exporter to the creditworthiness of the buyer's bank in the foreign country because the exporter's home bank is no longer guaranteeing payment. The exporter thus faces the additional risk of a change in the value of the foreign currency (if the sale is not in the exporter's home currency), the risk that the payment cannot be transferred to the

---

[20] A recent study shows that exporters who accept foreign currency as a medium of payment tend to sell a higher volume and have more satisfied customers (i.e., importers) but tend to have lower profit margins than those exporters who accept domestic currency. This probably is due to foreign exchange rate risk. For details, see Saeed Samiee and Patrik Anckar, "Currency Choice in Industrial Pricing: A Cross-National Evaluation," *Journal of Marketing,* 62 (July 1998), pp. 112–27.

EXHIBIT 17-6

TERMS OF PAYMENT IN AN EXPORT TRANSACTION

Advance payment	An importer pays exporter first; an exporter sends goods afterward.
Confirmed irrevocable letter of credit	A letter of credit issued by the importer's bank and confirmed by a bank usually in the exporter's country. The obligation of the second bank is added to the obligation of the issuing bank to honor drafts presented in accordance with the terms of credit.
Unconfirmed irrevocable letter of credit	A letter of credit issued by the importer's bank. The issuing bank still has an obligation to pay.
Documents against payment (D/P)	An importer pays bills and obtains documents and then goods. Therefore, the exporter retains control of the goods until payment.
Documents against acceptance (D/A)	An importer accepts bills to be paid on due date and obtains documents and then goods. Therefore, the exporter gains a potentially negotiable financial instrument in the form of a document pledging payment within a certain time period.
Open account	No draft drawn. Transaction payable when specified on invoice.
Consignment	A shipment that is held by the importer until the merchandise has been sold, at which time payment is made to the exporter.

Source: Lakshman Y. Wickremeratne, *ICC Guide to Collection Operations: For the ICC Uniform Rules for Collections* (URC 522) (Paris: International Chamber of Commerce, 1996), pp 22–26; and "Documentary Collections DC Payment Terms Offer Intermediate Level of Risk for International Collections," *Managing Exports,* (December 2002), pp. 4–5.

exporter's home bank, and the risk that the political conditions in the buyer's country will change to the exporter's detriment.

A **document against payment (D/P)** and a **document against acceptance (D/A)** are an importer's IOUs, or promises to pay. These payment terms (D/P and D/A) are much less expensive and easier for both exporters and importers to use than securing letters of credit. D/P and D/A are employed widely around the world but are historically underutilized by U.S. exporters.[21] Exports on a D/P are paid for by an importer when it accepts an exporter's export documents. Exports on a D/A are paid for by an importer on the due date of bill. Relative to a sale on a letter of credit, D/P basis increases the payment risk in an export transaction because no financial institution such as a bank has assumed the risk of payment. A D/A further escalates the risk because the buyer, by "accepting the bill," will receive the title documents and can pick up the goods without payment. Finally, an **open account** sale has no evidence of debt (promissory note, draft, etc.) and the payment may be unenforceable. Usually conducted only on the basis of an invoice, an open account transaction is recommended only after the exporter and the importer have established trust in their relationship.

Currency Hedging

The fourth task of an exporter is to arrange a foreign exchange cover transaction with the banker or through the firm's treasury in case there is a foreign exchange risk in the export transaction. Such arrangements include reversing the forward currency transaction, if required, and hedging the foreign exchange risk using derivative instruments in the foreign exchange markets, for example, currency options and futures. In general, customer-oriented exporters tend to use invoicing in foreign currency. Thus, currency hedging becomes all the more important to customer-oriented exporters.[22] When the exporter is receiving some currency other than its domestic currency, covering a trade transaction through forward sales, currency options, and currency futures enables the exporter to lock in the domestic currency value of the export transaction up to a year in the future, thus ensuring more certain cash flows and forecasting. Due care needs to be exercised in the use of currency hedging because

---

[21]"Documentary Collections DC Payment Terms Offer Intermediate Level of Risk for International Collections," *Managing Exports,* (December 2002), pp. 4–5.

[22]Patrik Anckar and Saeed Samiee, "Customer-Oriented Invoicing in Exporting," *Industrial Marketing Management,* 29 (November 2000), pp. 507–20.

an unwary or uninformed firm can lose large amounts of money (see Chapter 3 for details).

ROLE OF THE GOVERNMENT IN PROMOTING EXPORTS[23]   ◆ ◆ ◆ ◆ ◆ ◆ ◆ ◆

Government export promotion activities generally comprise (1) export service programs (e.g., seminars for potential exporters, export counseling, how-to-export handbooks, and export financing) and (2) market development programs (e.g., dissemination of sales leads to local firms, participation in foreign trade shows, preparation of market analysis, and export news letters).[24] In addition, program efforts can be differentiated as to whether the intent is to provide informational or experiential knowledge. Informational knowledge typically is provided through "how-to" export assistance, workshops, and seminars; experiential knowledge is imparted through the arrangement of foreign buyers' or trade missions, trade and catalog shows, or participation in international market research.

As stated at the beginning of this chapter, export is an important source of economic growth and job creation. Furthermore, jobs that depend on trade pay between 13 to 18 percent more than the average wage. Therefore, government efforts to promote exports seem to make sense. Although exports may be considered a major engine of economic growth in the U.S. economy, many U.S. firms do not export. Many firms, particularly small- to medium-size ones, appear to have developed a fear of international market activities. Their management tends to see only the risks—informational gaps, unfamiliar conditions in markets, complicated domestic and foreign trade regulations, absence of trained middle managers for exporting, and lack of financial resources—rather than the opportunities that the international market can present. These very same firms, however, may well have unique competitive advantages to offer that may be highly useful in performing successfully in the international market.

For example, small- and medium-size firms can offer their customers short response times. If some special situation should arise, there is no need to wait for the "home office" to respond. Responses can be immediate, direct, and predictable to the customer, therefore providing precisely those competitive ingredients that increase stability in a business relationship and reduce risk and costs. These firms also can often customize their operations more easily. Procedures can be adapted more easily to the special needs of the customer or to local requirements. One could argue that in a world turning away from mass marketing and toward niche marketing, these capabilities may well make smaller firms the export champions of the future.

Through the **Export Enhancement Act of 1992,** the U.S. government announced the National Export Strategy, a strategic, coordinated effort to stimulate exports.[25] In pursuit of this objective, the International Trade Administration of the U.S. Department of Commerce has devoted a substantial amount of the tax dollars allocated to it to help U.S. firms export their goods and services. For instance, the Japan Export Information Center (JEIC), established in April 1991, is the primary contact point within the Department of Commerce for U.S. exporters seeking business counseling and commercial information necessary to succeed in the Japanese market. The JEIC's principal function is to provide guidance on doing business in Japan and information on market entry alternatives, market data and research, product standards and testing requirements, intellectual property protection, tariffs, and nontariff barriers. The Japanese External Trade Organization (JETRO), affiliated with Japan's Ministry of Economy, Trade and Industry has also in recent years switched from promoting

[23]This section draws from Esra F. Gencturk and Masaaki Kotabe, "The Effect of Export Assistance Program Usage on Export Performance: A Contingency Explanation," *Journal of International Marketing,* 9 (2), 2001, pp. 51–72.

[24]William C. Lesch, Abdolreza Eshghi, and Golpira S. Eshghi, "A Review of Export Promotion Programs in the Ten Largest Industrial States," in *International Perspectives on Trade Promotion and Assistance,* ed. S. Tamer Cavusgil and Michael R. Czinkota (New York: Quorum Books, 1990), pp. 25–37.

[25]Richard T. Hise, "Globe Trotting," *Marketing Management,* 6 (Fall 1997), pp. 50–58.

Japanese exports to helping U.S. and other foreign companies export and invest in Japan. The new emphasis on import promotion is part of the Japanese government's broader strategy to pull more foreign business into Japan, particularly from small to mid-size companies. These efforts are also an attempt to chip away at Japan's trade surplus with the United States and hopefully encourage a greater balance of trade for the future.[26]

In the United States, the Department of Commerce (DOC) also has industry specialists and country specialists in Washington, D.C. The industry specialists are available to give exporters information on the current state of the exporter's products overseas; comment on marketing and sales strategies; inform on trade missions, trade shows, and other events; and give other counsel. The country specialists are available to give information on the target country, any current trade issues with the United States, customs and tariff information, insight on the business climate and culture, and any other information on a country required by the exporter. For example, Purafil, a company based in Doraville, Georgia that produces a dry chemical filtration system, benefited handsomely by participating in a DOC-sponsored trade mission to the Middle East for the first time. As part of the trade mission, the DOC provided a venue for Purafil and other companies to network and establish business relationships with prospective clients. One area in which the DOC is particularly helpful is in establishing credibility for the company marketing overseas. As a result, Purafil has been able to increase exports to 60 percent of all its revenues.[27]

Similarly, the DOC's Commercial Service has developed BuyUSA.com, an e-marketplace with a worldwide network of offices and expertise. The service offers online access to U.S. trade specialists who can assist buyers and sellers with exporting issues. For example, J.D. Streett & Company, a small auto lubricant and antifreeze manufacturer based in Maryland Heights, Missouri, spent some $400 to list its products on BuyUSA.com, resulting in major sales to Vietnam in 60 days.[28] Clearly, the government helps exporters find business leads in foreign markets.

Some governments even proactively engage in attracting inward foreign direct investment in the hope that their countries could increase exports. For example, Argentina, home to one of Latin America's most educated workforces and modern telecommunications, has the potential to become one of the region's leading software exporters. Hoping to lure software makers, the Argentine government enacted a law in 2005 offering technology companies tax benefits. The law has helped draw commitments of new investments of $60 million over the next three years from Intel and Microsoft to develop software in Argentina. Software company executives have lauded Argentina as a potential software-producing leader.[29]

Export–Import Bank

The **Export-Import Bank (Ex-Im Bank)** is an independent U.S. government agency that plays a crucial role in promoting exports by helping finance the sale of U.S. exports primarily to emerging markets throughout the world by providing loans, guarantees, and insurance. In fiscal year 2005, Ex-Im Bank of the United States supported 3,128 export sales amounting to $18 billion through $14 billion worth of loans, guarantees, and insurance.[30] Ex-Im Bank is not an aid or development agency but a government-held corporation managed by a board of directors consisting of a chairman, vice chairman, and three additional board members. Members serve for staggered terms and are chosen and serve at the discretion of the president of the United States.

Ex-Im Bank is designed to supplement, but not compete with, private capital. Ex-Im Bank has historically filled gaps created when the private sector is reluctant to engage in

---

[26]Rosalind McLymont, "In an About Face, Japanese Group Provides Help to Foreign Exporters," *Journal of Commerce,* April 19, 1999, p. 5A.

[27]"Clearing the Air," *Export America,* 3 (September 2002), pp. 6–7.

[28]"Speeding to New Global Markets," *Export America,* 3 (March 2002), p. 9.

[29]Reuters, "Argentina Has Potential to Be Software Leader," November 25, 2005.

[30]The Annual Report of the Export Import Bank of USA, http://www.exim.gov, accessed October 2, 2006.

export financing. Ex-Im Bank (1) provides guarantees of *working capital loans* for U.S. exporters, (2) guarantees the *repayment of loans* or makes loans to foreign purchasers of U.S. goods and services, and (3) provides *credit insurance* against nonpayment by foreign buyers for political or commercial risk. To carry out the U.S. government's strategy for continuing export growth, the Ex-Im Bank is focusing on critical areas such as emphasizing exports to developing countries, aggressively countering the trade subsidies of other governments, stimulating small business transactions, promoting the export of environmentally beneficial goods and services, and expanding project finance capabilities.

The Ex-Im Bank also helps large U.S. companies to win contracts for major infrastructure projects, especially in the emerging markets. It recently approved two long-term loan guarantees totaling $57 million to support the export by Siemens Transportation Systems Inc., Sacramento, CA, of $62 million of equipment for light rail mass transportation systems in two Venezuelan cities.[31]

The Ex-Im Bank is also combating the "trade-distorting" loans of foreign governments through the aggressive use of its Tied Aid Capital Projects Fund. The idea is that the Ex-Im Bank is willing, on a case-by-case basis, to match foreign tied-aid offers that are commercially viable and pending to be able to preemptively counter a foreign tied-aid offer. For instance, if a highway project in China gets a bid from a European or Japanese consortium of firms that offer to give concessional aid for the project but stipulate that in return for the aid the Chinese should buy machinery and materials from suppliers to be specified by the Europeans (or the Japanese), a U.S. firm bidding for the same project can depend on being able to provide concessional financing through the resources of the Ex-Im Bank. In addition, the U.S. government is no longer shy about openly representing U.S. firms and about being powerful advocates on behalf of U.S. businesses. Cabinet secretaries in the U.S. government have led groups of top business executives to many emerging markets. Accompanying administration officials on foreign missions give business executives a chance to get acquainted with decision makers in foreign governments, which award many infrastructure projects. The U.S. government lobbied hard to obtain airplane orders for Boeing from Singapore Airlines, Cathay Pacific, and Saudia, all of which were being lobbied by the French government to buy from the Airbus–European consortium.

Critics may cavil at this active role of the U.S. government in promoting exports; however, if U.S. firms are to retain their position in existing markets and if they are to gain access to new markets, they must have the same facilities that are available to firms from other nations. For this reason, the policy of advocacy on behalf of U.S. firms fighting to enter new markets or to retain existing markets is a cornerstone of the national export policy.[32]

Tariff Concessions

Other areas in which the government plays a role in promoting exports include the establishment and maintenance of foreign trade zones (FTZs) and the Export Trading Company Act of 1982.

Foreign Trade Zone. As discussed in detail in Chapter 16, **foreign trade zones (free trade zone)** enable businesses to store, process, assemble, and display goods from abroad without paying a tariff. Once these goods leave the zone and enter the United States, they are charged a tariff but not on the cost of assembly or profits. If the product is re-exported, no duties or tariffs apply. Thus, a U.S. firm can assemble foreign parts for a camera in a Florida FTZ and ship the finished cameras to Latin America without paying duty.

---

[31] Press releases from Export-Import Bank's Web site, www.exim.gov, accessed February 20, 2002.
[32] "Ex-Im Bank Head Says U.S. Companies Need More Aid to Compete Overseas," *Wall Street Journal Interactive Edition,* (May 15, 2000).

American Export Trading Company. The **Export Trading Company Act of 1982** encourages businesses to join together and form export trading companies. The act provides antitrust protection for joint exporting and permits banking institutions to own interests in these exporting ventures. This act makes it practical for small- and medium-size exporting firms to pool resources without the fear of antitrust persecution and inadequate capitalization. A bank may hold up to 100 percent stock in an export trading company and is exempted from the collateral requirements contained in the Federal Reserve Act for loans to its export trading company.[33]

Export Regulations

Although the U.S. government has become earnest in promoting exports, it also takes a hand in regulating exports. The Foreign Corrupt Practices Act of 1977 (as amended in 1986) imposes jail terms and fines for overseas payoffs that seek to influence overseas government decisions, although payments to expedite events that are supposed to take place under local laws are no longer illegal. Many U.S. exporters, especially exporters of big-ticket items, believe that the Foreign Corrupt Practices Act provides an unfair advantage to exporters from Europe and Japan that have been able to make such payments and get tax write-offs for the payments under export expenses. In 1996, under newly agreed provisions of WTO, firms from other countries were no longer allowed to make such payments without incurring penalties, thus leveling the playing field somewhat for U.S. exporters. Under the Wassenaar Arrangement of 1995 (see Chapter 5), domestic laws also exist that restrict exports of security-sensitive technology such as sophisticated machine tools and encryption technology for computer software and hardware (see Global Perspective 17-2).

Antitrust laws prevent U.S. firms from bidding jointly on major foreign projects. Human rights legislation and nuclear nonproliferation policies require that every year the federal government recertify the Normal Trade Relations (NTR)[34] status of major foreign trade partners (e.g., China). These are examples of the U.S. exporting its own rules to other nations under the aegis of the WTO. To the extent that such actions result in the same rules for all nations engaging in international trade, such behavior benefits trade; however, such behavior can also be perceived as an infringement of national sovereignty by many nations.

Sometimes the actions of a foreign government can affect exports. These actions relate to tariffs and local laws relating to product standards and classification. For example, computer networking equipment exported from the United States to the European Union is charged a 3.9 percent tariff. A 1996 EU ruling decided that computer networking equipment (e.g., adapters, routers, and switches) do not crunch data but transport them and so should be classified as telecommunication equipment. Telecommunication equipment, however, carries a higher tariff rate of 7.5 percent, increasing the landed price of these products in Europe.[35] Such actions by foreign governments are usually attempts to provide protection to local industry.

Finally, a government could tax exports with the purpose of satisfying domestic demand first or of taking advantage of higher world prices. For example, in 1998, two typhoons damaged trees in the northern Philippines, stripping away mature coconuts. Coconut oil shipments during the fourth quarter of 1998 were 60 percent below their normal level. The coconut oil market continued to face production declines and the threat of higher prices. Indonesia, the second largest producer, continued to impose high export duties on coconut oil.[36] The goal of such measures is to curb exports and try to keep a lid on internal food industry costs as coconut oil prices soared.

---

[33] William W. Nye, "An Economic Profile of Export Trading Companies," *Antitrust Bulletin,* 38 (Summer 1993), pp. 309–25.

[34] See Chapter 2 for details.

[35] "Europe's Computer Networking Tariffs May Lead to U.S. Complaint to WTO," *Wall Street Journal,* (May 1, 1996), p. B7.

[36] Jim Papanikolaw, "Coconut Oil Market Tightens Because of Bad Weather in 1998," *Chemical Market Reporter,* (January 25, 1999), p. 8.

$\mathcal{G}$LOBAL PERSPECTIVE 17-2

EXPORT CONTROL IN THE UNITED STATES: THE BALANCING ACT BETWEEN FREE TRADE AND TIGHT SECURITY

Control of high-tech exports has been regulated under a continuing executive order since 1994 when the Export Administration Act (EAA) of 1979 expired. In the past several years, the technology industry has argued that the current export control regime is outmoded. Current export control rules use a performance rating called *millions of theoretical operations per second (MTOPS)* to determine which microprocessors and computers must apply for export licenses to certain countries. Computing power has become so prolific, however, that it is nearly impossible to regulate by using performance-based controls such as MTOPS.

Indeed, the federal government has had to race with the market over the past several years to keep export control regulations from barring the export of readily available, mass-market computers. For example, as recently as 1999, microprocessors with an MTOPS rating of 1,200 and computers with a rating of 2,000 were subject to controls. Those limits have been raised repeatedly over the past few years. The limits on chips apply to export to certain countries such as China and the former Soviet countries. The limits on computers apply to so-called Tier III countries, which include China, Russia, Israel, Pakistan, and India.

In 2001, key senators introduced the Export Administration Act of 2001, aimed at balancing competing priorities: free trade and tight security. The bill attempted a narrower, more surgical application of controls on dual-use items—commercial exports in aerospace, computers, encryption, and machine tools—that could be diverted to military use by overseas companies or countries. The bill would stiffen fines and prison terms for violators, both individual and corporate, in an attempt to bolster control of advanced technologies that are less widely dispersed. The bill also contained a provision that would eliminate the requirement that computer export controls be based on MTOPS levels. The House of Representatives was unable, however, to pass a similar bill.

The failure of Congress to enact a new EAA requires the president to continue to use his authority under the International Economic Emergency Powers Act (IEEPA) to regulate export controls. The Department of Commerce is currently working to establish a new metric to replace the MTOPS standard for high-performance computers. Meanwhile, the Bush Administration raised the MTOPS limit on computers from 85,000 to 190,000 MTOPS in March 2002. This rating would allow for the export of multiprocessor servers with up to 32 Intel Itanium CPUs.

Since the September 11th terrorist attacks, U.S. companies have had to adjust to new export control challenges because license applications take longer, are rejected more often, and require more backup information. Microsoft, for instance, has outsourced certain export functions through partnering to achieve export efficiency in all processes. Furthermore, the company has implemented the SAP GTS system to conduct country screening process. Currently, Microsoft is proactively partnering with the U.S. government to secure global supply chains by participating in the C-TPAT (customers-trade partnership against terrorism) program. Evidently, Microsoft is not the only company that must adjust to the post 9/11 export paradigm shift.

Sources: Tam Harbert, "One Step Forward on Export Control," *Electronic Business,* (March 2002), p. 36; "AAEI Conference Highlights: How Microsoft, Philips Meet New Post-9/11 Compliance Requirements," *Managing Exports & Imports,* (August 2004), pp. 1–4; and "OEE 2005 Enforcement Actions and Fines Expected to Easily Surpass 2005," *Managing Exports & Imports,* (May 2005), p. 8.

MANAGING IMPORTS—THE OTHER SIDE OF THE COIN ◆ ◆ ◆ ◆ ◆ ◆ ◆ ◆

So far the chapter has been devoted exclusively to exports, and we now turn to imports. For organizations in the United States, importing is considerably easier than for most firms in the rest of the world. One of the primary reasons for this is the fact that unlike importers in most of the rest of the world, U.S. importers can pay the seller abroad in their own currency—the U.S. dollar—because the U.S. dollar is an internationally accepted denomination of exchange. Thus, unlike importers in Brazil or Indonesia who must find U.S. dollars (or other hard currencies) to pay for imports, an importer in the United States can manage by shelling out U.S. dollars. About 60 percent of the world's trade is still denominated in U.S. dollars; exporters want dollars in return for the goods or services sold.

However, denomination of trade in dollars is changing, especially in Europe, where the euro has emerged as the currency in which trade is denominated. Most of the time, therefore, a U.S. importer does not have to bother to hedge foreign exchange transactions or try to accumulate foreign currency to pay for imports. On occasion, a U.S. importer does not even need a letter of credit. This same advantage has become available to the European Union (EU) member countries. EU member countries are now able to pay in euro for their imports from other member countries. Similarly, in Asia, where the Japanese yen is emerging as the currency in which trade is denominated. Japan benefits from this on a more limited geographical basis. Japan is now able to pay in Japanese yen for much of its imports from Southeast Asia.

This is not to suggest that a firm can import anything for sale in the United States. There are restrictions on trade with countries including Iran, Libya, Iraq, and Cuba. Iran and Libya are thought to be supporters of state-sponsored terrorism. The United States is at war with Iraq (at the time of this writing), and Cuba has been a pariah for the United States since 1959. The same restrictions exist with respect to North Korea since the Korean War that ended in 1953. Production and marketing considerations also limit what can be imported and sold profitably in the United States. For soaps and cosmetics, for example, the demand for imports is minimal. However, the United States is a surplus producer of many categories of goods including aircraft, defense equipment, medical electronics, computer software, and agricultural goods.

Importing any good is thus predicated on the existence of a situation in which the domestic production of the good in question is not sufficient to satisfy demand. For example, annual sales of cut flowers in the United States is nearly $10 billion, but domestic production meets only about 30 percent of the demand, with Americans purchasing flowers not just for special occasions but also for sending messages, as a token of friendship, as a get-well wish, or just to convey "have a nice day" to someone. Imports of cut flowers are primarily from Colombia, Mexico, Costa Rica, Ecuador, Peru, and Kenya.[37] The imported flowers must satisfy the selective U.S. consumer and must comply with the U.S. Plant Protection Quarantine Inspection Program and antidumping regulations. Because the product is highly perishable, air transportation and rapid transit through customs must be ensured. Thus, the importer of flowers has to go through many hoops to locate a reliable seller and arrange the logistics. Importer behavior will, of course, depend on the category of goods being purchased abroad.

However, importer buyer behavior is a relatively under-researched area in the field of international trade, partly because most nations are more interested in maximizing exports rather than imports and restricting imports is relatively simple as compared to being a successful exporter. The most important of the organizational buying models is the BuyGrid model.[38] Besides elaborating on how the purchasing process evolves and highlighting the role of buyers' search in choice decisions, this framework was the first to categorize buy decisions as (1) straight buys, (2) modified rebuy, and (3) new tasks.

Although this framework was developed primarily for domestic purchases, it is applicable to import decisions as well. Applying the framework for an import decision and taking into account the increased uncertainty in international markets would translate into a procedure presented in Exhibit 17-7. This sequence of actions in an import situation appears logical, as it does for exports, but many international supplier relationships start with an "unsolicited export order," in which importers place an order with a selected foreign vendor without any systematic vendor search and evaluation. The lack of a systematic approach to vendor identification and evaluation can stem from a difficulty in accessing all relevant information and from the idea of bounded rationality—the notion that due to limited cognitive abilities, humans tend to satisfice, not optimize. Thus, given the information available, which cannot be complete, managers will not be able to make the best decision.[39]

---

[37] "Say it with Flowers," *New Statesman*, (February 16, 2004), pp. 22–23.

[38] Patrick J. Robinson, Charles W. Faris, and Yoram Wind, *Industrial Buying and Creative Marketing* (Boston: Allyn and Bacon, 1967).

[39] Neng Liang and Rodney L. Stump, "Judgmental Heuristics in Overseas Vendor Search and Evaluation: A Proposed Model of Importer Buyer Behavior," *International Executive*, 38 (November/December 1996), pp. 779–806.

EXHIBIT 17-7
MODEL OF IMPORTER BUYER BEHAVIOR

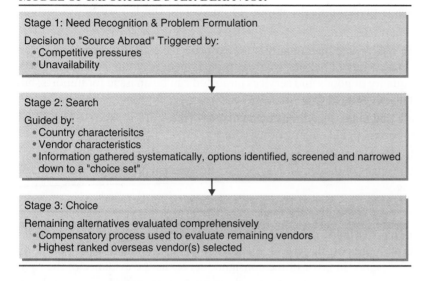

Stage 1: Need Recognition & Problem Formulation

Decision to "Source Abroad" Triggered by:
 • Competitive pressures
 • Unavailability

Stage 2: Search

Guided by:
 • Country characterisitcs
 • Vendor characteristics
 • Information gathered systematically, options identified, screened and narrowed down to a "choice set"

Stage 3: Choice

Remaining alternatives evaluated comprehensively
 • Compensatory process used to evaluate remaining vendors
 • Highest ranked overseas vendor(s) selected

Source: Neng Liang and Rodney L. Stump, "Judgmental Heuristics in Overseas Vendor Search and Evaluation: A Proposed Model of Importer Buyer Behavior," *International Executive,* Copyright (November 1996), pp. 779–806. Reprinted by permission of John Wiley & Sons, Inc.

MECHANICS OF IMPORTING ◆ ◆ ◆ ◆ ◆ ◆ ◆ ◆ ◆

An import transaction is like looking at an export transaction from the other end of the transaction. Instead of an exporter looking for a prospective buyer, an importer looks for an overseas firm that can supply it the raw materials, components, or finished products that it needs for its business. Once an importer locates a suitable overseas exporter, it negotiates with the exporter the terms of the sale including, but not restricted to, the following:

• Finding a bank that either has branches in the exporter's country or has correspondent bank located in the exporter's country and establishing a line of credit with the bank if this has not already been done.

• Establishing a letter of credit with a bank stating the terms of payment and how payment is to be made. This includes terms of clearing the goods from the docks/customs warehouse (sometimes with title for goods going temporarily to the bank), insurance coverage, terms of transfer of title, and so on.

• Deciding on the mode of transfer of goods from exporter to importer and transfer of funds from importer to exporter. Transportation partly provides proof of delivery to the exporter's bank or the exporter. The exporter (or its bank) presents the proof of delivery to the importer's bank (branch in importer's own country/correspondent bank). The importer's bank transfers funds to the exporter's bank and simultaneously debits the importer's account or presents a demand draft to the importer.

• Checking compliance with national laws of the importing country and the exporting country. Import restrictions into the U.S. include quotas on automobiles, textiles, and steel and quarantine checks on food products as well as a ban on imports from Cuba, North Korea, and Iran.

• Making allowances for foreign exchange fluctuations by making covering transactions through the bank so that the dollar liability for the importer either remains fixed or decreases.

• Fixing liability for payment of import duties and demurrage and warehousing in case the goods are delayed due to congestion at ports. These payments are normally the responsibility of the importer.

An examination of these mechanics of an import transaction reveals that the transaction is materially the same as an export transaction. The differences that are of interest to managers involved in the import of goods into the United States include these:

- A difference in risk profile, meaning that an exporter faces the risk of receiving no payment due to a variety of factors, whereas nonpayment is not an issue in imports. However, the quality of goods and services imported can be an issue for imports, but this is not usually an issue in exports.
- The facility of being able to pay in its own currency (most of the time), which is not available to importers in almost any other country.
- Everything else being equal, the ease for a U.S. firm to import rather than to export because of the primacy of the U.S. dollar despite the gradual depreciation of the U.S. dollar over time.

Import Documents and Delivery

When a shipment reaches the United States, the consignee (normally the importer) files entry documents with the port director at the port of entry. The bill of lading properly endorsed by the consignor in favor of the consignee serves as the evidence of the right to make entry. The entry documents also include an entry manifest, Customs Form 7533, Customs Form 3461, packing lists if appropriate, and the commercial invoice. The entry should be accompanied by evidence that a bond is posted with customs to cover any potential duties, taxes, and penalties that may accrue. A **bond** is a guarantee by someone that the duties and any potential penalties will be paid to the customs of the importing country. In the event that a custom broker is employed for the purpose of making entry, the broker can permit the use of the bond to provide the required coverage.

Entry can be for immediate delivery, for ordinary delivery, or for a warehouse, or can be unentered for a period of time. Merchandise arriving from Canada and Mexico, trade fair goods, perishable goods, and shipments assigned to the U.S. government almost always utilize the **Special Permit for Immediate Delivery** on Customs Form 3461 prior to the arrival of the goods to enable fast release after arrival. An entry summary then must be filed within 10 days of the release of the goods. Imported goods coming in under ordinary delivery use normal channels including Form 7533. Under warehousing, goods are placed in a custom-bonded warehouse if the entry of the imported goods is desired to be delayed. The goods can remain in a bonded warehouse for a period of five years. At any time during the period, warehoused goods may be re-exported without payment of duty or may be withdrawn for consumption upon the payment of duty. If the importer fails to enter the goods at the port of entry or the port of destination within five working days after arrival, they may be placed in the general warehouse at the risk and expense of the importer.

Import Duties

Import duties that have to be paid are either ad valorem, specific, or compound. An **ad valorem duty,** which is the one most frequently applied, is a percentage of the value of the merchandise, such as 5 percent ad valorem. Thus, an auto shipment worth $100 million that has an ad valorem rate of 3.9 percent will pay $3.9 million as customs duty. A **specific duty** rate is a specified amount per unit of weight or other quantity, such as 5.1 cents per dozen, 20 cents per barrel, or 90 cents per ton. A **compound duty** rate is a combination of an ad valorem rate and a specific rate, such as 0.7 cents per kilogram plus 10 percent as valorem. Average import duty rates in Japan (3.4 percent), the United States (5.2 percent), and the European Union (7.7 percent) are relatively low compared to those in many other countries (e.g., Mexico with 18.0 percent),[40] but used to be much higher. After the Uruguay Round, the major global

---

[40]"Trends in Market Openness," *OECD Economic Outlook,* 65 (June 1999), pp. 207–21.

trade negotiations from 1986 to 1994, developed countries—the most important buyers of developing countries' exports—were opening their markets further. Their import duties for industrial products fell from 6.3 percent on average before the Uruguay Round to 3.8 percent afterward. Also due to the Uruguay Round, significantly more products exported to developed countries enjoy zero import duties. The entry of imported merchandise into a foreign country is complete after customs clears the goods from the port of entry or the port of destination.

Antidumping import duties are assessed on imported merchandise sold to importers in a foreign country at a price that is less than the fair market value. The *fair market value of merchandise* is defined under articles of the World Trade Organization as the price at which the good is normally sold in the manufacturer's home market. In the United States, countervailing duties are assessed for some imported goods to counter the effects of subsidies provided by foreign governments because without the **countervailing duty,** the price of these imported goods in the U.S. market would be artificially low, causing economic injury to U.S. manufacturers.

The U.S. importer could even avoid payment of import duties by applying for a duty-drawback refund under Temporary Importation under Bond (TIB) in the United States. A **duty drawback** is a refund of up to 99 percent of all ordinary customs duties. It can be a direct identification drawback or a substitution drawback. A *direct identification drawback* provides a refund of duties paid on imported merchandise that is partially or totally used within five years of the date of import in the manufacture of an article that is exported. A *substitution drawback* provides a refund of duties paid on designated imported merchandise upon exportation of articles manufactured or produced with the use of substituted domestic or imported merchandise that is of the same quality as the designated import merchandise.[41] All countries have procedures allowing for the temporary importation of goods across their borders.[42]

As explained in Chapter 16, importing firms can also utilize foreign trade zones profitably. They can set up facilities in an FTZ to import finished goods, component parts, or raw materials for the eventual domestic consumption or import of merchandise that is frequently delayed by customs quota delays or import merchandise that must be processed, generating significant amounts of scrap. An important feature of foreign trade zones for foreign merchants entering the U.S. market is that the goods may be brought to the threshold of the market, making immediate delivery certain and avoiding the possible cancellation of orders due to shipping delays.

GRAY MARKETS

◆ ◆ ◆ ◆ ◆ ◆ ◆ ◆

Gray market channels refer to the legal export/import transaction involving genuine products into a country by intermediaries other than the authorized distributors. From the importer's side, it is also known as a **parallel import.** Distributors, wholesalers, and retailers in a foreign market obtain the exporter's product from some other business entity. Thus, the exporter's legitimate distributor(s) and dealers face competition from others who sell the exporter's products at reduced prices in that foreign market. High-priced branded consumer goods (cameras, jewelry, perfumes, watches, and so on) whose production lies principally in one country are particularly prone to gray market imports. Brand reputation is a critical element in gray market goods exports, and the distribution is typically through exclusive wholesalers and distributors.[43]

---

[41]Michael V. Cerny, "More Firms Establish Drawback Programs as $1.5B Goes Unclaimed," *Managing Exports,* (October 2002), pp. 1–6.

[42]Lara L. Sowinski, "Going Global in a Flash," *World Trade,* 18 (August 2005), pp. 28–32.

[43]This section draws from Dale F. Duhan and Mary Jane Sheffet, "Gray Markets and the Legal Status of Parallel Importation," *Journal of Marketing,* 52 (July 1988), pp. 75–83; Tunga Kiyak, "International Gray Markets: A Systematic Analysis and Research Propositions," paper presented at 1997 AMA Summer Educators' Conference, August 2–5, 1997; and Michael R. Mullen, C. M. Sashi, and Patricia M. Doney, "Gray Markets: Threats or Opportunity? The Case of Herman Miler vs. Asal GMBH," in *Reviving Traditions in Research on International Market,* ed. Tiger Li and Tamer S. Cavusgil, (Greenwich, CT. : JAI Press, 2003).

In the information technology sector alone, gray market sales exceed $20 billion globally. A study of manufacturers of health and beauty aids determined that gray market sales amounted to 20 percent of authorized sales in some markets and as much as 50 percent of authorized sales in others. The gray market problem is so serious that multinational companies such as Motorola, HP, DuPont, and 3M devote full-time managers and staff to dealing with gray market issues.[44] Gray market is pervasive across all industries. For example, if purchased on the gray market, a $92,000 brand-new Mercedes-Benz SL55 AMG Convertible, which meets all U.S. safety and pollution control requirements, can be purchased for 20 percent less than the price ($114,580) charged by the local authorized dealer. Similarly, in the luxury boat market, many foreign dealers of U.S. manufacturers are seriously affected by gray market activity. To avoid higher prices abroad, foreign retailers too often come to the United States and purchase their boat from a U.S. dealer, and then arrange their own transportation, circumventing the licensed dealer in their own home country.[45] Although gray market products look similar to their domestic counterparts, they could not be identical and not carry full warranties. Nevertheless, the volume of gray market activities is significant. Three conditions are necessary for gray markets to develop. First, the products must be available in other markets. In today's global markets, this condition is readily met. Second, trade barriers such as tariffs, transportation costs, and legal restrictions must be low enough for parallel importers to move the products from one market to another. Again, under the WTO principles, trade barriers have been reduced so low that parallel importation has become feasible. Third, price differentials among various markets must be great enough to provide the basic motivation for gray marketers. Such price differences arise for various reasons, including currency exchange rate fluctuations, differences in demand, legal differences, opportunistic behavior, segmentation strategies employed by international marketing managers, and more recently, the World Wide Web's information transparency.

- **Currency fluctuations.** The fluctuating currency exchange rates among countries often produce large differences in prices for products across national boundaries. Gray marketers can take advantage of changes in exchange rates by purchasing products in markets with weak currencies and selling them in markets with strong currencies.

- **Differences in market demand.** Similarly, price differences can be caused by differences in market demand for a product in various markets. If the authorized channels of distribution cannot adjust the market supply to meet the market demand, a large enough price difference could develop for unauthorized dealers to engage in arbitrage process, that is, buying the product inexpensively in countries with weak demand and selling it profitably in countries with strong demand.

- **Legal differences.** Different prices across different markets due to different legal systems similarly motivate gray marketing activities. For example, as explained in Chapter 5, copyright protection lasts only 50 years in the European Union and Japan compared with 95 years in the United States. In other words, even if the music recordings were originally made and released in the United States, the recordings made in the early- to mid-1950s by such figures as Elvis Presley and Ella Fitzgerald are entering the public domain in Europe, opening the way for any European recording company to release albums that had been owned exclusively by particular labels. Although the distribution of such albums would be usually limited to Europe, CD-store chains and specialty outlets in the United States routinely stock cheaper foreign imports via gray markets.[46]

---

[44]Kersi D. Antia, Mark Bergen, and Shantanu Dutta, "Competing with Gray Markets," *Sloan Management Review,* 46 (Fall 2004), pp. 63–69.

[45]Frank Reynolds, "Senior Management Apathy Could Sink U.S. Pleasure Boat Exports," *Journal of Commerce,* (March 24, 1999), p. 9A.

[46]"Companies in U.S. Sing Blues as Europe Reprises 50's Hits," *New York Times,* January 3, 2003, Late Edition, p. A1.

- **Opportunistic behavior.** Opportunistic behavior by distributors tends to occur when the distributor's gross margin is disproportionately large relative to the marketing task performed and is particularly attractive if the transaction occurs outside the distributor's assigned territory. For example, if the sale takes place in a neighboring foreign country (i.e., outside the territory), the opportunistic distributor could lower the selling price in that market because the sale is not made at the expense of the distributor's own full markup sales in its domestic market. In other words, this opportunistic behavior typifies the attitude, "Somebody else's problem is not my problem."

- **Segmentation strategy.** Although currency exchange rates and differences in market demand could be beyond the control of international marketing managers, segmentation strategy can result in (1) planned price discrimination and (2) planned product differentiation among various markets. Even for an identical product, different pricing strategy can be adopted for various reasons, including differences in product life cycle stage, customer purchase behavior, and price elasticity across different markets. Different prices across different markets motivate gray marketers to exploit the price differences among the markets.

- **The World Wide Web.** As an information medium, the World Wide Web raises a customer's awareness of special offers that were initially designed to be limited to specific regions, countries, or classes of customers. Web-based gray marketers can also advertise merely by using the product's brand name or model number on their Web sites and waiting for search engines to direct consumers there. The Internet greatly stimulates gray market activity by presenting different price quotations from multiple merchants. Gray marketers can pay for presence on shopping bots, such as mysimon.com, cnet.com, shopping.yahoo.com, or bottomdollar.com. One example of the Web's potential as a distribution medium for gray market goods is www.yesmoke.com, a site that sells popular tobacco brands produced overseas at half the U.S. price. What happens is that online businesses do not pay either state or city cigarette taxes, which can be as high as $3 per pack. No wonder online tobacco sales grew from $750 million in 2001 to around $5 billion in 2005.[47]

Alternatively, the product can be modified to address the specific needs of different markets. Contradictory to common sense, adaptation of individual products for a specific market also leads to substantially more gray marketing. This occurs for two reasons. First, when, for example, a stripped version of the product is marketed in Europe and an enhanced version is marketed in the United States, some U.S. consumers, who may not be willing to pay for the enhanced model with too many refinements, import the simpler, less expensive version from an unauthorized distributor through a gray marketing channel. Second, some consumers simply want to purchase the product models that are not available in their domestic markets to differentiate themselves from the rest of the consumers. This is increasingly likely as markets around the world become more homogeneous.[48]

Gray marketing activity can also bring about some beneficial effect to manufacturers. Parallel channels foster intrabrand competition that can force authorized channels to do a better job serving their local customers and lead to improved customer satisfaction. It is conceivable that manufacturers can add gray marketers to the authorized channel or even acquire them, provided that such actions do not lead to increased conflict with existing authorized distributors. In industries with high fixed

---

[47]Barry Berman, "Strategies to Combat the Sale of Gray Market Goods," *Business Horizons,* 47 (July/August 2004), pp. 51–60; and Sarah Lysecki, "Grey Market Alive but Slowing," *Computer Dealer News,* (April 16, 2004), p. 8.

[48]Matthew B. Myers, "Incidents of Gray Market Activity among U.S. Exporters: Occurrences, Characteristics, and Consequences," *Journal of International Business Studies,* 30 (First Quarter 1999), pp. 10–126.

◆ ◆

𝒢LOBAL PERSPECTIVE 17-3

SMUGGLING AND BLACK MARKETS: AN ETHICAL DILEMMA FOR MULTINATIONAL COMPANIES SELLING LAWFUL PRODUCTS

Conventional wisdom has it that trade liberalization (i.e., adopting freer trade policy) in many emerging markets would reduce smuggling and black market phenomena because it reduces unnecessary and artificial price differences across countries. Economists call this tendency the *law of one price*. However, in a seminal work on smuggling in 1996, Kate Gillespie and Brad McBride found quite the opposite: These countries are likely to see the resurgence of organized smuggling and black market distribution as a result of trade liberalization. A number of reasons may be considered. First, liberalization is rarely complete, and smugglers could still take advantage of evading income, sales, and other taxes as well as tariffs. Second, as the reduced price differences (thanks indeed to trade liberalization) make it difficult for casual smugglers to make enough money, smugglers need to be larger and better organized in pursuit of "economies of scale" in their operations. As a result, smuggling shifts to organized crime and takes on a more sinister aspect. Third, evidence indicates that both the evolution of smuggling into organized crime and the use of smuggling as a way to launder money for international drug cartels and possibly terrorist organizations are increasing.

Smuggling is an illegal importation of either legal products (e.g., TVs, computers, music CDs) or illegal products (e.g., narcotics and child pornographic material). We focus only on smuggling of legal products here. What does smuggling have to do with multinational companies that engage in the business of selling legal products internationally? Nothing directly.

In June 2000, U.S. Customs estimated the global volume of money laundering, much of which is related to the illicit trade in narcotics, to total more than $600 billion a year or between 2 and 5 percent of the world's GDP. The problem is that money is *fungible* (simply stated, money is money wherever it comes from). U.S. exports are often purchased with narcotics dollars. Those exports include otherwise lawful goods including household appliances, consumer electronics, liquor,

cigarettes, used auto parts, and footwear. The connection between money laundering and smuggled consumer products has been a major concern of U.S. Customs for several years, particularly after the government cracked down on money laundering through U.S. banks.

This is how the system works. A drug cartel in a Latin American country exports narcotics to the United States where they are sold for U.S. dollars. The cartel in this Latin American country contacts a third party—a peso broker—who agrees to exchange pesos for the U.S. dollars that the cartel controls in the United States. The peso broker uses contacts in the United States to place the drug dollars purchased from the cartel into the U.S. banking system. Latin American importers then place orders for items and make payments through the peso broker who uses contacts in the U.S. to purchase the requested items from U.S. manufacturers and distributors. The peso broker pays for these goods with cash or drafts drawn on U.S. bank accounts. The purchased goods are shipped to some Caribbean or South American destinations, sometimes via Europe or Asia, and are then smuggled into this Latin American country. The Latin American importer avoids paying high tariffs, and the peso broker profits by charging both the cartel and the importers for services rendered.

The U.S. multinational companies that sell these products have routinely denied having any idea that they were involved in money laundering. Beginning in June 2000, however, a group of corporate executives began a series of meetings at the Justice Department. The companies included Hewlett-Packard, Ford Motor, Whirlpool, General Motors, Sony, Westinghouse, and General Electric (GE). With the exception of GE, the companies called to participate had products appearing in the black market in a Latin American country. GE was invited as the example of a good corporate citizen that was successfully cleaning up the smuggling of its goods into South America. However, GE's shutting down smuggling came at a fairly steep price to the company and to the benefit of those competitors that kept their eyes closed on the fact. Between 1995 and 2000, General Electric estimated that its good corporate citizenship policy cost the company about 20 percent of its sales to South America.

Sources: Kate Gillespie and J. Brad McBride, "Smuggling in Emerging Markets: Global Implications," *Columbia Journal of World Business,* 31 (Winter 1996), pp. 40–54; and Kate Gillespie, "Smuggling and the Global Firm," *Journal of International Management,* 9 (3), 2003.

---

costs where capacity utilization and economies of scale are important, manufacturers may require the incremental sales generated by parallel channels to sustain high production volumes.[49]

A key question for the manufacturer of branded products is whether a gray market will cause a global strategy to become less desirable. Closer control and monitoring of international marketing efforts can certainly reduce the threat of gray market

---

[49]Mullen, et al., "Gray Markets: Threats or Opportunity?" pp. 77–105.

EXHIBIT 17-8
HOW TO COMBAT GRAY MARKET ACTIVITY

A. Reactive Strategies to Combat Gray Market Activity

Type of Strategy	Implemented by	Cost of Implementation	Difficulty of Implementation	Does It Curtail Gray Market Activity at Source?	What Relief Does It Provide Authorized Dealers?	Long-Term Effectiveness	Legal Risks to Manufacturers or Dealers	Company Examples
Strategic confrontation	Dealer with manufacturer support	Moderate	Requires planning	No	Relief in the medium term	Effective	Low	Creative merchandising by Caterpillar and auto dealers
Participation	Dealer	Low	Not difficult	No	Immediate relief	Potentially damaging reputation of manufacturer	Low	Dealers wishing to remain anonymous
Price cutting	Manufacturer and dealer jointly	Costly	Not difficult	No, if price cutting is temporary	Immediate relief	Effective	Moderate to high	Dealers and manufacturers remain anonymous
Supply interference	Either party	Moderate at the wholesale level; high at the retail level	Moderately difficult	No	Immediate relief or slightly delayed	Somewhat effective if at wholesale level; not effective at retail level	Moderate at wholesale level; low at retail	IBM; Hewlett-Packard; Lotus Corp.; Swatch Watch USA; Charles of the Ritz Group, Ltd.; Leitz, Inc.; NEC Electronics
Promotion of gray market product limitations	Jointly, with manufacturer leadership	Moderate	Not difficult	No	Slightly delayed	Somewhat effective	Low	Komatsu, Seiko, Rolex, Mercedes-Benz IBM
Collaboration	Dealer	Low	Requires careful negotiations	No	Immediate relief	Somewhat effective	Very high	Dealers wishing to remain anonymous
Acquisition	Dealer	Very costly	Difficult	No	Immediate relief	Effective if other gray market brokers don't creep in	Moderate to high	No publicized cases

(*continued*)

EXHIBIT 17-8 (continued)

B. Proactive Strategies to Combat Gray Market Activity

Type of Strategy	*Implemented by*	*Cost of Implementation*	*Difficulty of Implementation*	*Does It Curtail Gray Market Activity at Source?*	*What Relief Does It Provide Authorized Dealers?*	*Long-Term Effectiveness*	*Legal Risks to Manufacturers or Dealers*	*Company Examples*
Product/service differentiation and availability	Jointly, with manufacturer leadership	Moderate to high	Not difficult	Yes	Medium to long term	Very effective	Very low	General Motors, Ford, Porsche, Kodak
Strategic pricing	Manufacturer	Moderate to high	Complex; impact on overall profitability needs monitoring	Yes	Slightly delayed	Very effective	Low	Porsche
Dealer development	Jointly, with manufacturer leadership	Moderate to high	Not difficult; requires close dealer participation	No	Long term	Very effective	None	Caterpillar, Canon
Marketing information systems	Jointly, with manufacturer leadership	Moderate to high	Not difficult; requires dealer participation	No	After implementation	Effective	None	IBM, Caterpillar, Yamaha, Hitachi, Komatsu, Lotus Development, Insurance companies
Long-term image reinforcement	Jointly	Moderate	Not difficult	No	Long term	Effective	None	Most manufacturers with strong dealer networks
Establishing legal precedence	Manufacturer	High	Difficult	Yes, if fruitful	No	Uncertain	Low	COPIAT, Coleco, Charles of the Ritz Group, Ltd.
Lobbying	Jointly	Moderate	Difficult	Yes, if fruitful	No	Uncertain	Low	COPIAT, Duracell, Porsche

Note: Company strategies include, but are not limited to, those mentioned here.

Source: S. Tamer Cavusgil and Ed Sikora, ''How Multinationals Can Counter Gray Market Imports,'' *Columbia Journal of World Business*, 23 (Winter 1988), pp. 75–85.

goods to negligible levels. As rule of thumb, firms using independent distributors (e.g., commission agents and merchant distributors) tend to suffer most from gray market activity while firms with ownership-based control over distribution channels (e.g., joint venture partners, wholly owned subsidiaries, and direct sale of exports to end users) offer more control over the final sale of the product.[50] As presented in Exhibit 17-8, international marketers not only try to confront existing gray markets reactively but also are increasingly developing more proactive approaches to gray market problems before they arise.

Gray marketing is a legal trading transaction. On the other hand, *smuggling* and *black market* refer to the illegal importation and sales of either otherwise legal goods or illegal products. Although such illegal transactions are outside the scope of this book, we address these issues in Global Perspective 17-3 to introduce you to some ethical dilemma that multinational companies can face concerning the smuggling and black market activities by independent distributors of what would otherwise be legal products.

---

[50]Ibid.

SUMMARY ✦

The national government has a variety of programs to support exports, although many government policies—which are sometimes dictated by political compulsions—also hinder exports. Export markets provide a unique opportunity for growth, but competition in these markets is usually fierce. With the rise of the big emerging markets (Brazil, China, and India), competition is likely to intensify even more.

Procedurally, exporting requires locating customers, obtaining an export license from the federal government (a general or validated license), collecting export documents (such as the bill of lading, commercial invoice, export packing list, insurance certificate), packing and marketing, shipping abroad, and receiving payment—most of the time through a bank. Conversely, importing requires locating a seller, obtaining an import license, usually establishing a letter of credit, turning over import documents (bill of lading, etc.) to indicate receipt of goods, and making payment through the banking system. Methods of payment include advance payment, open account, consignment sale, documents against payment (D/P), documents against acceptance (D/A), and letter of credit. Of these, the last two are the most popular. Depending on the nature of the payment terms and the currency of payment, the

exporter could need to make foreign exchange hedging transactions. The U.S. government is now taking a more active role in promoting the exports of U.S. firms as they bid for big-ticket items in the emerging markets.

Imports are the obverse of exports. A U.S. importer can make payments in U.S. dollars unlike an importer in many other countries. Any good coming in through a U.S. port must pass through customs and pay the appropriate duty and be authorized by customs at the port of entry or the port of destination for entry. Unlike an exporter who faces a payment risk, the importer's risks are associated with delivery schedules and product quality. Foreign exchange risk is common to both imports and exports. Entry of some goods into a country is restricted by bilateral and multilateral quotas as well as by political considerations.

Finally, globalization of markets has spawned gray marketing activities by unauthorized distributors taking advantage of price differences that exist among various countries due to currency exchange rate fluctuations, different market demand conditions, and price discrimination, among other factors. For companies marketing well-known branded products, gray markets have become a serious issue to be confronted proactively as well as reactively.

KEY TERMS ✦

Ad valorem duty

American Export Trading company of 1982

Antidumping import duty

Automated Export System (AES)

Bill of lading

Bond

Combination export manager (CEM)

Commercial invoice

Compound duty

Confirmed irrevocable letter of credit

Counterveiling duty

Credit risk

Customs receipt

Direct exporting

Documents against acceptance (D/A)

Documents against payment (D/P)

Duty drawback

Export broker

Export commission house

Export department

Export Enhancement Act of 1992

Export–Import Bank (Ex–Im Bank)

Export license

Export merchant

Export sales subsidiary

Foreign exchange risk

Foreign sales branch

Foreign sales corporation

Foreign trade zone

Freight forwarder

General license

Gray market (parallel
   import)
Import duty
INCOTERMS 2000
Indirect exporting

Open account
Piggyback exporting
Political risk
Shipper's order bill of lading

Special Permit for
   Immediate delivery
Specific duty
Straight bill of lading
Trading company

Transfer risk
Unconfirmed letter of credit
Validated license

REVIEW QUESTIONS

1. How does a prospective exporter choose an export market?

2. What are the factors that influence the decision of the exporter to use a standardized product strategy across countries and regions?

3. What are the direct and indirect channels of distribution available to exporters? Under what conditions would the use of each be the most appropriate?

4. Terms of payment represent an extremely important facet of export transactions. Describe the various terms of payments in increasing order of risk.

5. Describe the various terms of shipment and sale.

6. What is the role of government (home country) in export activities? Explain in the context of U.S. exporters.

7. Managing imports in the United States is by and large easier and less risky than managing exports. Give reasons why this is true.

8. What are gray markets? What factors led to the development of gray markets?

DISCUSSION QUESTIONS

1. A friend of yours who owns a small firm manufacturing and selling CD-ROM–based computer games would like to market the company's products abroad. Your friend seeks information from you on the following:

   a. Which markets should the firm target (what sources of information to tap)?

   b. How should it tap these markets (what are the steps you would advise)?

   c. What are the direct and indirect costs involved in exporting?

   d. What kind of assistance can your friend get from governmental and nongovernmental agencies at any of the stages involved? What would your advice be?

2. General trading companies have played and continue to play a leading role in the exports and imports of products from and to Japan. The effectiveness of these companies is evident from the fact that in the recent Fortune 500 list of the world's largest corporations, 5 of the top 10 corporations (including the top three) are Japanese trading firms. Although there is little question about the effectiveness of these firms, various business executives, especially outside Japan, interpret the directing of exports and imports through such firms as adding to significant inefficiencies in terms of higher costs and lost opportunities. Do you agree with this contention? Why or why not? The top three trading houses, Mitsubishi, Mitsui, and Itochu, had profitability ratios (profits after taxes/total revenues) of 0.18 percent, 0.17 percent, and 0.07 percent, respectively. Would this information have any bearing on your answer?

3. You are the manager for international operations of a manufacturer of steel in the United States. You have received an offer to purchase at a very attractive price 5,000 metric tons of wire rods (used to draw wires for the manufacture of nails) from a large nail manufacturer located in a developing country

X. What would you deem to be the most appropriate choice of export terms of payment and terms of shipment, given the following information (include any precautions that you would take to ensure the successful execution of the order):

   a. The prospective importer has its account at a local bank. Local government rules stipulate making payments only through this bank.

   b. The local bank does not have any international operations/branches.

   c. The currency of country X has been extremely unstable, with its value having depreciated by more than 20 percent recently.

   d. The interest rates are extremely high in this country.

   e. The legal system in this country is weak, but the firm that is willing to place the order has a good reputation based on past experience with other international manufacturers.

   f. Rain and summer heat can cause the product to deteriorate if kept unused for a time longer than necessary.

   g. This country exports a larger amount by sea than it imports. Hence, many ships have to go empty to get cargo from this country to the United States.

4. Nontariff barriers to international trade have significant implications for both exporters and importers. One of the most prevalent nontariff barriers used is antidumping duties or the threat of initiating antidumping investigations. The use of antidumping duties has recently received some criticisms as affecting certain high-growth industries adversely while protecting some smaller inefficient (as claimed) industries. One typical example quoted is the manufacture of laptop computers. Antidumping duties were levied against Japanese manufacturers of flat-panel screens (used in the manufacture of laptop computers) at the behest of would-be flat-panel manufacturers in the United States. It was the contention of

these U.S. producers that if the flat panels were not dumped by Japanese manufacturers, the U.S. producers would be able to raise capital to initiate production of this product. As a result of the duties levied, which would have added significant costs to the computers manufactured in the United States, most U.S. manufacturers (many of whom had plans to manufacture laptop computers within the United States) shifted to sites abroad. According to the computer manufacturers, the antidumping decision sacrificed the fastest-growing segment of the computer industry to a nonexistent domestic flat-panel industry. The proponents of antidumping legislation, however, contend that the threat of predatory practices is real and antidumping procedures take care of this threat. Whom would you side with, the proponents or the critics of antidumping actions?

5. The Internet has become a powerful place for products, information—everything you can think of today. Internet retailing has become increasingly accepted by most consumers. While consumers are surfing for the best prices, it is difficult for them to tell a legitimate, authorized dealer from a gray marketer. Assuming that you are a consultant of a famous computer company, what are your recommendations for the firm to be able to combat gray market activities? Could the company continuously attract bargain-seeking consumers by informing consumers of the dark side of gray market retailing?

♦ ♦ ♦ ♦ ♦ ♦ ♦ ♦ ♦ SHORT CASES

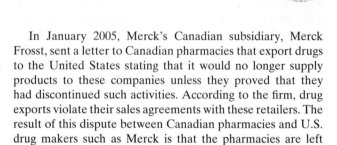

*C*ASE 17-1

AN UPSET MERCK

Purchasing medicines through Internet pharmacies is the latest trend to hit the drug industry. This channel of distribution has existed for years but drew attention to itself when Pfizer's popular drug for erectile dysfunction was released and consumers who were too embarrassed to buy this drug offline, resorted to buying it online. At the time, drug companies were not too distressed at this trend because it added one more channel of distribution of their products, and drug companies willingly supplied pharmacies with drugs to sell over the Internet.

However, during the past several years, major U.S. pharmaceutical companies have cut off drug supplies to some Canadian pharmacies, and Merck, the second largest U.S. drug company with sales of over $20 billion worldwide, has joined the bandwagon. The reason for this move is that Canadian pharmacies operating through mail-order or online channels provide drugs not only to Canadian consumers but also to those in the United States who demand drugs at lower prices are offered in the U.S. The Canadian government, unlike the U.S. government, controls prices of pharmaceuticals in Canada and therefore prices of drugs there tend to be less expensive than the same ones in the United States.

According to U.S. pharmaceuticals companies, this export-import practice affects Canadian consumers on one hand because drug exports to the United States result in a shortage of medicines for Canadian patients. On the other hand, firms such as Merck argue that these drug exports to patients are essentially risky due to the lack of stringent controls in manufacturing. Furthermore, the emergence of Internet pharmacies that sell counterfeit medicines has increased the possibility of health hazards to patients who expect to get genuine products but do not. Merck also argued that some of its drugs provided under the U.S. Medicaid program are affordably priced and should preclude drug exports by Canadian pharmacies.

Source: "Pain of the Pill Market," *Maclean's,* (February 21, 2005), pp. 28-29.

In January 2005, Merck's Canadian subsidiary, Merck Frosst, sent a letter to Canadian pharmacies that export drugs to the United States stating that it would no longer supply products to these companies unless they proved that they had discontinued such activities. According to the firm, drug exports violate their sales agreements with these retailers. The result of this dispute between Canadian pharmacies and U.S. drug makers such as Merck is that the pharmacies are left struggling to fill orders from consumers in the United States.

Drug exportation has proved to be extremely attractive for the pharmacies. Sale of prescription and other drugs over the Internet started on a small scale but over the years, due to the high demand for this method of sale, these firms have grown so much that drug companies are becoming more vigilant and defensive against them. Nevertheless, such moves by Merck and others have managed to curb drug exports to a certain extent. Since Merck's decision to boycott these pharmacies, Internet pharmacies have reduced their workforce. Some, however, are still obtaining drugs from wholesalers and retailers behind closed doors. Still others are now looking to foreign countries, mainly in Europe, to supply drugs.

It will be interesting to see whether drug exports will cease in the future. This could require strict regulation and governmental interference. In response to complaints by pharmaceutical giants, the Canadian government has considered passing a law to shut down Internet pharmacies, but the talks are still on....

DISCUSSION QUESTIONS

1. What else can Merck do to reduce the exports of its drugs into the United States by Canadian pharmacies?

2. Should the U.S. and Canadian governments step in to solve this problem? If so, what can they do?

3. Will Merck's recent move prevent further exports by Canadian pharmacies?

4. What does the future likely hold for this retail method for drugs in particular?

*C*ASE 17-2

SONY—COMBATING GRAY MARKETS FOR PSPS

Sony Corp., the famous Japanese consumer electronics company recently launched its (Playstation Portable) PSP product, a handheld media system, amid much hype and publicity. The product is the latest addition to its popular PS (Playstation)

line of products. The company planned to introduce the product in major world markets. However, even before its launch everywhere, the much awaited PSP gadgets were already available in some target markets via the gray market channel.

Sony, along with its subsidiary Sony Computer Entertainment Europe, is fighting tooth and nail to prevent retailers worldwide from biting into its revenues.

Although multinational firms have recently introduced their innovations in the Triad markets almost simultaneously, Sony launched the PSP system in Japan late 2004, in the United States in March 2005, and in the U.K. market and the rest of Europe in September 2005. The delay was partly due to the multicultural requirements for software for European consumers and Europe's stringent safety and standard compliances. Another reason for the deferred European launch was that Sony wanted to ensure that there was sufficient supply to meet demand in the United States. The company, however, did not offer any apologies for the late launch, stating that Europeans would eventually benefit from a better version of the product after Sony corrected the "bugs."

Even before the launch, however, retailers in the United Kingdom were importing PSPs from Japan and the United States and selling them in Europe. To keep retailers from selling PSPs, Sony finally brought legal action against these parties in the United Kingdom in June 2005. Sony sent more than 500 letters to importers who were selling gray market PSPs in Europe, including some who sold their products on the popular online auctioneer eBay. Sony claimed that it wanted confiscation of PSPs and sought compensation for damages. Pushed to the edge by these sales, Sony also demanded that it be given the identities of retailers and consumers who had indulged in these transactions.

One of the main adversaries in this legal battle in the United Kingdom was the online retail firm ElectricBirdLand (EBL), which decided to stand up against Sony and fight the charges. Moreover, EBL argued that Sony did not have appropriate trademarks for its PSP product and related technologies in Europe. EBL also claimed that Sony was pursuing action against smaller firms while ignoring larger firms such as music company HMV, which sold PSP add-ons to parties who were importing Sony PSPs. However, HMV was advertising only the product's presales and would make them available to consumers after the formal launch in September. This controversy surrounding the PSP's launch gave rise to doubts as to whether Sony would in fact be able to stick to its schedule to present the PSP to Europeans on time. In June 2005, Sony won the case against EBL but had similar ongoing cases against retailers such as Nuplayer. Nevertheless, some retailers responded by pulling the products off their real and virtual shelves. Still others pushed Sony's buttons by continuing to sell PSPs because the lucrative margins of over 60 percent made it worthwhile. Sony's headaches were not restricted to the United Kingdom only. Gray markets for PSPs exist all over Europe.

Even before the unveiling of the PSP in Europe, it created a buzz, and Sony is not the only one benefiting from its popularity. Gray market sellers have made sizable incomes. Meanwhile, hackers all over the world busied themselves trying to run unauthorized games and other software on Sony's PSPs. Sony, meanwhile, worked to continuously develop new versions of the PSP to keep hackers at bay. As Sony awaited the U.K. High Court's decision, gray marketers continued to sell PSPs through their Web sites.

Technology geeks as end consumers are the happiest. Even though they pay a higher price for the gray market product than in Japan, which comes with no warranties, they get to keep up with the latest advances in electronics. Some believe that there is a difference in the PSPs sold in Japan and the rest of the world because the products sold at home are superior in terms of their hardware and software.

DISCUSSION QUESTIONS

1. What can firms like Sony do to prevent sale of new products in gray markets?

2. Do you think Sony launched the PSP too early and should instead have waited to launch it in the Triad simultaneously? Why did the company then rush to introduce its product?

3. How did the sale of PSPs in Europe through gray markets threaten Sony?

4. How does the sale of PSPs in Europe through gray markets affect the future of the product itself?

FURTHER READING ◆

Anckar, Patrik, and Saeed Samiee. "Customer-Oriented Invoicing in Exporting." *Industrial Marketing Management,* 29 (November 2000), pp. 507–20.

Antia, Kersi D., Mark Bergen, and Shantanu Dutta. "Competing with Gray Markets," *Sloan Management Review,* 46 (Fall 2004), pp. 63–69.

Bello, Daniel C., and Ritu Lohtia. "Export Channel Design: The Use of Foreign Distributors and Agents." *Journal of Academy of Marketing Science,* 23(2), 1995, pp. 83–93.

Katsikea, Evangelia S., Marios Theodosiou, Robert E. Morgan, and Nikolaos Papavassiliou. "Export Market Expansion Strategies of Direct-Selling Small and Medium-Sized Firms: Implications for Export Sales Management Activities." *Journal of International Marketing,* 13 (2), 2005, pp. 57–92.

Lages, Luis Filipe, Carmen Lages, and Cristiana Raquel Larges. "Bringing Export Performance Metrics into Annual Reports: The APEV Scale and the PERFEX Scorecard." *Journal of International Marketing,* 13 (3), 2005, pp. 79–104.

Leonidou, Leonidas C., Constantine S. Katsikeas, and John Hadjimarcou. "Building Successful Export Business Relationships: A Behavioral Perspective." *Journal of International Marketing,* 10 (3), 2002, pp. 96–115.

Liang, Neng, and Arvind Parkhe. "Importer Behavior: The Neglected Counterpart of International Exchange." *Journal of International Business Studies,* 28 (Third Quarter 1997), pp. 495–530.

Michael, James. "A Supplemental Distribution Channel? The Case of U.S. Parallel Export Channels." *Multinational Business Review,* 6 (Spring 1998), pp. 24–35.

Moen, Oystein, and Per Servais. "Born Global or Gradual Global? Examining the Export Behavior of Small and Medium-Sized Enterprises." *Journal of International Marketing,* 10 (3), 2002, pp. 49–72.

Moini, A. H. "Small Firms Exporting: How Effective Are Government Export Assistance Programs?" *Journal of Small Business Management,* 36 (January 1998), pp. 1–15.

Mullen, Michael R., C. M. Sashi, and Patricia M. Doney. "Gray Markets: Threats or Opportunity? The Case of Herman Miler vs. Asal GMBH." In *Advances in International Marketing,* ed. Tiger Li and Tamer S. Cavusgi. (Greenwich, CT: JAI Press, 2003.)

Myers, Matthew B., and David A. Griffith. "Strategies for Combating Gray Market Activity." *Business Horizons,* 42 (November–December 1999), pp. 2–8.

Wilkinson, Timothy J. "The Effect of State Appropriations on Export-Related Employment in Manufacturing." *Economic Development Quarterly,* 13 (May 1999), pp. 172–82.

PLANNING, ORGANIZATION, AND CONTROL OF GLOBAL MARKETING OPERATIONS

HAPTER OVERVIEW

1. GLOBAL STRATEGIC MARKETING PLANNING

2. KEY CRITERIA IN GLOBAL ORGANIZATIONAL DESIGN

3. ORGANIZATIONAL DESIGN OPTIONS

4. ORGANIZING FOR GLOBAL BRAND MANAGEMENT

5. LIFE CYCLE OF ORGANIZATION STRUCTURES

6. CENTRALIZATION OR DECENTRALIZATION

7. CONTROL OF GLOBAL MARKETING EFFORTS

The capstone of a company's global marketing activities will be its strategic marketing plan. To implement its global plans effectively, a company needs to reflect on the best organizational setup that enables it to successfully meet the threats and opportunities posed by the global marketing arena. Organizational issues that the global marketer must confront cover questions like: What is the proper communication and reporting structure? Who within our organization should bear responsibility for each of the functions that need to be carried out? How can we as an organization leverage the competencies and skills of our individual subsidiaries? Where should the decision-making authority belong for the various areas?

We consider the major factors that influence the design of a global organizational structure. Multinational corporations (MNCs) can choose from a wide variety of organizational structures. In this chapter, we discuss the major alternative configurations. We also highlight the central role played by country managers within the MNC's organization. More and more companies try to build up and nurture global brands. We look at several organizational mechanisms that firms can adopt to facilitate such efforts. Because change requires flexibility, this chapter investigates different ways that MNCs can handle environmental changes. MNCs must also decide where the decision-making locus belongs. The challenge is to create a structure that bridges the gap between two forces: being responsive to local conditions and integrating global marketing efforts.

The final section focuses on control mechanisms companies can utilize to achieve their strategic goals.

◆ ◆ ◆ ◆ ◆ ◆ ◆ ◆ GLOBAL STRATEGIC MARKETING PLANNING

The vast majority of multinational companies prepare a **global strategic marketing plan** to guide and implement their strategic and tactical marketing decisions. Such plans are usually developed on an annual basis and look at policies over multiple years. The content of a global strategic marketing plan can be very broad in scope but usually covers four areas:[1]

1. Market situation analysis. A situation analysis of the company's customers (market segments, demand trends, etc.) on a global basis, the competition (SWOT analysis), the company itself, and the collaborators (e.g., suppliers, distribution channels, alliance partners).

2. Objectives. For each country, management states goals that are achievable and challenging at the same time.

3. Strategies. Once the objectives have been determined, management needs to formulate marketing strategies for each country to achieve the set goals, including resource allocation.

4. Action plans. Strategies need to be translated into concrete actions that will implement those strategies. Specific actions are to be spelled out for each marketing mix element.

Although these are the core areas of a global strategic marketing plan, such a plan will also discuss anticipated results and include contingency plans.

Bottom-Up versus Top-Down Strategic Planning

International planning can be top-down (centralized) or bottom-up (decentralized). Obviously, hybrid forms that combine both options are also possible. With **top-down planning,** corporate headquarters guides the planning process. **Bottom-up planning** is the opposite. The planning process starts with the local subsidiaries and is then consolidated at headquarters level. The bottom-up approach has the advantage of embracing local responsiveness. Top-down planning, on the other hand, facilitates performance monitoring. A centralized approach also makes it easier to market products with a global perspective. A recent survey of large multinational corporations found that pure bottom-up planning was most popular (used by 66 percent of the companies surveyed). Only 10 percent of the interviewed companies, on the other hand, relied on a pure top-down planning process. The balance used a hybrid format (11 percent) or no planning at all (12 percent).[2]

Pitfalls

Marketing plans can go awry. Exhibit 18-1 is a listing of the internal obstacles that can undermine the global strategic marketing plan preparation. As you can see, the top-three stumbling blocks are lack of proper information, too little emphasis on the development of alternative strategic options, and unrealistic strategic objectives. Obviously, external factors can also interfere. Changes in the political and economic environment can upset the finest strategic plans. China's sudden clampdown on direct selling created upheaval for Avon, Amway, and Mary Kay, among other companies. The suddenness and severity of the recent Asian financial crisis wreaked havoc for the plans of most Western MNCs. Other external factors include changes in the

---

[1] See, for instance, Douglas J. Dalrymple and Leonard J. Parsons, *Marketing Management* (New York: Wiley, 1995), Chapter 17.

[2] Myung-Su Chae and John S. Hill, "The Hazards of Strategic Planning for Global Markets," *Long Range Planning*, 29 (6), 1996, pp. 880–91.

EXHIBIT 18-1
INTERNAL OBSTACLES TO GLOBAL STRATEGIC MARKETING
PLAN PREPARTION

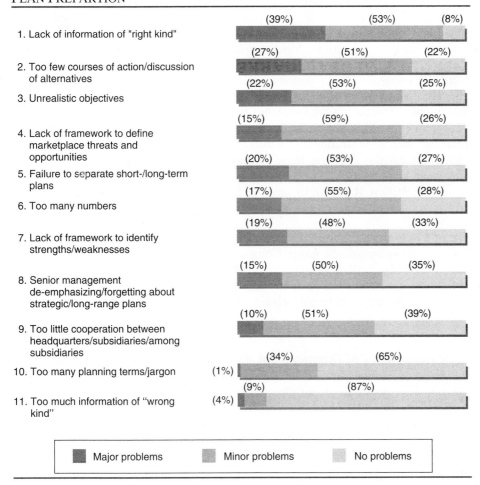

1. Lack of information of "right kind" (39%) (53%) (8%)

2. Too few courses of action/discussion of alternatives (27%) (51%) (22%)

3. Unrealistic objectives (22%) (53%) (25%)

4. Lack of framework to define marketplace threats and opportunities (15%) (59%) (26%)

5. Failure to separate short-/long-term plans (20%) (53%) (27%)

6. Too many numbers (17%) (55%) (28%)

7. Lack of framework to identify strengths/weaknesses (19%) (48%) (33%)

8. Senior management de-emphasizing/forgetting about strategic/long-range plans (15%) (50%) (35%)

9. Too little cooperation between headquarters/subsidiaries/among subsidiaries (10%) (51%) (39%)

10. Too many planning terms/jargon (1%) (34%) (65%)

11. Too much information of "wrong kind" (4%) (9%) (87%)

■ Major problems ▨ Minor problems ▨ No problems

Source: Myung-Su Chae and John S. Hill, "The Hazards of Strategic Planning for Global Markets," *Long Range Planning,* 29 (1996), pp. 880–91, Copyright (1996), with permission from Elsevier.

competitive climate (e.g., deregulation), spread of diseases (e.g., SARS), technological developments, and consumer-related factors.[3]

KEY CRITERIA IN GLOBAL ORGANIZATIONAL DESIGN ◆ ◆ ◆ ◆ ◆ ◆ ◆ ◆

As is true of most other global managerial issues, there is no magical formula that prescribes the "ideal" organizational setup under a given set of circumstances. Yet, companies should consider certain factors when engineering their global organizational structure. In the following discussion, we make a distinction between environmental and firm-specific factors. Let us start with a look at the major environmental factors.

Competitive Environment. Global competitive pressures force MNCs to implement structures that facilitate quick decision making and alertness. In industries where competition is highly localized, a decentralized structure where most of the decisions are made at the country level is often appropriate. Nevertheless, even in such situations, MNCs can often benefit substantially from mechanisms that allow the company to leverage its global knowledge base.

Environmental Factors

---

[3] Ibid.

Rate of Environmental Change. Drastic environmental change is a way of life in scores of industries. New competitors or substitutes for a product emerge. Existing competitors form or disband strategic alliances. Consumer needs worldwide constantly change. Businesses that are subject to rapid change require an organizational design that facilitates continuously scanning of the firm's global environment and swift responsiveness to opportunities or threats posed by that environment.

Regional Trading Blocs. Companies that operate within a regional trading bloc (e.g., the European Union, NAFTA, MERCOSUR) usually integrate their marketing efforts to some extent across the affiliates within the block area. A case in point is the European Union. In light of the European integration, numerous MNCs decided to streamline their organizational structure. Many of these companies still maintain their local subsidiaries, but the locus of most decision making now lies with the pan-European headquarters. As other trading blocs such as Asia's APEC and South America's MERCOSUR evolve toward the European model, one can expect similar makeovers in other regions.

Nature of Customers. The company's customer base also has a great impact on the MNC's desired organizational setup. Companies such as DHL, IBM, and Citigroup, which have a "global" clientele, need to develop structures that permit a global reach and at the same time allow the company to stay "close" to its customers.

These are the major external drivers. We now turn to the prime firm-specific determinants.

Firm-Specific Factors

Strategic Importance of International Business. Typically, when overseas sales account for a very small fraction of the company's overall sales revenues, simple organizational structures (e.g., an export department) can easily handle the firm's global activities. As international sales increase, the organizational structure will evolve to mirror the growing importance of the firm's global activities. For instance, a company may start with an international division when it tests the international waters. Once its overseas activities expand, it is likely to adopt an area-type (country- and/or region-based) structure.

Product Diversity. The diversity of the company's foreign product line is another key factor in shaping the company's organization. Companies with substantial product diversity tend to go for a global product division configuration.

Company Heritage. Differences in organizational structures within the same industry can also be explained via corporate culture. Nestlé and Unilever, for example, have always been highly decentralized MNCs. A lot of the decision-making authority has always been at the local level. When Unilever realized that its marketing efforts required a more pan-European approach to compete with the likes of Procter & Gamble, the company transformed its organization and revised its performance measures to provide incentives for a European focus. One of Unilever's senior executives, however, noted that the changeover "comes hard to people who for years have been in an environment where total business power was delegated to them."[4] As long as a given formula works, companies have little incentive to tinker with it. Revamping an organization to make the structure more responsive to new environmental realities can be a daunting challenge.

Quality of Local Managerial Skills. Decentralization could become a problem when local managerial talents are missing. Granted, companies can bring in expatriates, but this is typically an extremely expensive remedy that does not always work out. For instance, expatriate managers could find it difficult to adjust to the local environment.

[4]"Unilever Adopts Clean Sheet Approach," *Financial Times,* October 21, 1991.

ORGANIZATIONAL DESIGN OPTIONS ◆ ◆ ◆ ◆ ◆ ◆ ◆ ◆ ◆

The principal designs that firms can adopt to organize their global activities are:

- **International division.** Under this design, the company basically has two entities: the domestic division, which is responsible for the firm's domestic activities, and the international division, which is in charge of the company's international operations.
- **Product-based structure.** With a product structure, the company's global activities are organized along its various product divisions.
- **Geographic structure.** This is a setup where the company configures its organization along geographic areas: countries, regions, or some combination of these two levels.
- **Matrix structure.** This is an option where the company integrates two approaches—for instance, the product and geographic dimensions—so, there is a dual chain of command.

We now consider each of these options in more detail. At the end of this section, we also discuss the so-called **networked organization model.**

International Division Structure

Most companies that engage in global marketing initially start by establishing an export department. Once international sales reach a threshold, the company could set up a full-blown international division. The charter of the international division is to develop and coordinate the firm's global operations. The unit also scans market opportunities in the global marketplace. In most cases, the division has equal standing with the other divisions within the company.

This option is most suitable for companies that have a product line that is not too diverse and does not require a large amount of adaptation to local country needs. It is also a viable alternative for companies whose business is still primarily focused on the domestic market. Over time, as international marketing efforts become more important to the firm, most companies tend to switch to a more globally oriented organizational structure.

Global Product Division Structure

The second option centers around the company's different product lines or strategic business units (SBUs). Each product division, being a separate profit center, is responsible for managing worldwide the activities for its product line. This alternative is especially popular among high-tech companies with highly complex products or MNCs with a very diversified product portfolio. The approach is adopted by companies such as Ericsson, John Deere, and Sun Microsystems (see Exhibit 18-2).

Several benefits are associated with a global product structure. The product focus offers the company a large degree of flexibility in terms of cross-country resource allocation and strategic planning. For instance, market penetration efforts in recently entered markets can be cross-subsidized by profits generated in developed markets. In many companies, a global product structure goes in tandem with consolidated manufacturing and distribution operations. This approach is exemplified by Honeywell, the U.S. maker of control tools, which has set up centers of excellence that span the globe.[5] That way, an MNC can achieve substantial scale economies in the area of production and logistics, thereby improving the firm's competitive cost position. Another appeal is that global product structures facilitate the development of a global strategic focus to cope with challenges posed by global players.[6]

---

[5] Honeywell *1995 Annual Report.*

[6] W. H. Davidson and P. Haspeslagh, "Shaping a Global Product Organization," *Harvard Business Review,* July–August 1982, pp. 125–32.

EXHIBIT 18-2
THREE EXAMPLES OF A GLOBAL PRODUCT STRUCTURE

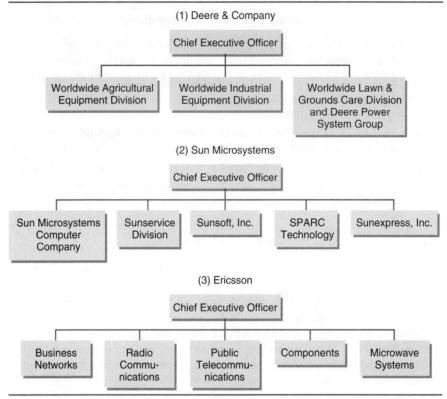

The shortcomings of a product division are not insignificant. Lack of communication and coordination among the various product divisions could lead to needless duplication of tasks. A relentless product-driven orientation can distract the company from local market needs. The global product division system has also been criticized for scattering the company's global resources.[7] Instead of sharing resources and creating a global know-how pool, international resources and expertise become fragmented. A too narrow focus on the product area will lead to a climate where companies fail to grasp the synergies that might exist between global product divisions.

Geographic Structure

The third option is the geographic structure that organizes the MNC along geographic units, which could be individual countries or regions. In many cases, MNCs use a combination of country-based subsidiaries and regional headquarters. There are other variants. Coca-Cola, for instance, has five different regions, each one further divided into subregions, as is shown in Exhibit 18-3. Area structures are especially appealing to companies that market closely related product lines with very similar end users and applications around the world.

Country-Based Subsidiaries. Scores of MNCs set up subsidiaries on a country-by-country basis. To some degree, such an organization reflects the marketing concept. By setting up country affiliates, the MNC can stay in close touch with local market conditions. The firm can thereby easily spot new trends and swiftly respond to local market developments.

---

[7]Ibid., p. 129.

EXHIBIT 18-3
THE COCA-COLA COMPANY: EXAMPLE OF A GEOGRAPHIC STRUCTURE

Operations

Africa	*Latin America*
President	President
East and Central Africa	Brazil
Nigeria and Equatorial Africa	Latin Center Division
North and West Africa	Mexico
South Africa	South Latin Division
East, South Asia and Pacific Rim	*North Asia, Eurasia and Middle East*
President	President
India	China
Philippines	Eurasia and Middle East
South Pacific and Korea	Russia/Ukraine/Belarus
Southeast Asia and West Asia	Japan
European Union	*North America*
President	President
Central Europe	Canada
Germany and Nordic Division	Foodservice and Hospitality Division
Iberian Division	
Mediterranean Division	
Northwest Europe	

Source: The Coca-Cola Company, 2005 Annual Report

Country-based organizations have several serious handicaps, however. They tend to be costly. Coordination with corporate headquarters and among subsidiaries can easily become extremely cumbersome. A country focus often leads to a "not-invented-here" mentality that hinders cross-fertilization. Some critics of the country model derisively refer to it as a mini-United Nations with a multitude of local fiefs run by scores of country managers.[8] Kenichi Ohmae sums up the weaknesses of the country-structure as follows:

> One of the prime difficulties of organizing a company for global operations is the psychology of managers who are used to thinking by country-based line of authority rather than by line of opportunity. Lots of creative ideas for generating value are overlooked because such managers are captive to nation state-conditioned habits of mind. Once that constraint is relaxed.... a nearly infinite range of new opportunities comes into focus: building cross-border alliances, establishing virtual companies, arbitraging differential costs of labor or even services.... I strongly believe that, as head-to-head battles within established geographies yield less and less incremental value, changing the battleground from nation to cross-border region will be at the core of 21st-century corporate strategy.[9]

New Role of Country Managers. Corporate strategy gurus such as Ohmae foresee the demise of the country manager. Some major companies have already downgraded the role of their country managers within the organization and have transferred power to a new breed, the "product champion." Often these days, country managers fulfill administrative duties and are described as "hotel managers." Companies such as P&G and Dow Chemical have created global business divisions to handle investment strategic decisions. Oracle cut its country managers down to size when it realized that

---

[8]Some of the major MNCs operate in more countries than the number of U.N. member states.
[9]Kenichi Ohmae, *The End of the Nation State. The Rise of Regional Economies,* (New York: The Free Press, 1995), p. 112.

its country-based organization had become a patchwork of local fiefs that did not communicate with each other: Oracle's logo in France differed from the one in the United Kingdom, global accounts such as Michelin were treated as different customers, and so forth.[10] Several forces are held responsible for this change.[11]

- The threats posed by global competitors who turn the global marketplace into a global chess-game.
- The growing prominence of global customers who often develop their sourcing strategies and make their purchase decisions on a global (or pan-regional) basis.
- The rise of regional trading blocs that facilitate the integration of manufacturing and logistics facilities but also open up arbitrage opportunities for gray marketers.
- Knowledge transparency. The Internet and other information technologies allow customers and suppliers to become more knowledgeable about products and prices across the globe.

At the same time, several developments create a need for strong country managers.[12] Nurturing good links with local governments and other entities (e.g., the European Union) becomes increasingly crucial. Local customers still represent the lion's share of most companies' clientele. Local competitors sometimes pose a far bigger threat than global rivals. In many emerging markets, strong local brands (e.g., Lenovo in China; Jollibee, a McDonald's copycat, in the Philippines) often have a much more loyal following than regional or global brands. Many winning new-product or communication ideas come from local markets rather than regional or corporate headquarters. Also, if the role of local management is reduced to pen-pushing and paperwork, it becomes more difficult to hire talented people. For these reasons, several firms have increased the clout of their country managers. A good example is 3M, which set up 30 product-based units in 1991. To cut costs, 3M centralized procurement, production, distribution, and service centers (e.g., human resources). However, a decade later, 3M decided to hand power back to its country managers who can provide a local perspective on group policies. They also play a valuable role in establishing contacts with local customers and spotting opportunities for new businesses.[13]

To strike the balance between these countervailing forces, country managers of the 21st century should fit any of the following five profiles depending on the nature of the local market.[14]

- The **trader** who establishes a beachhead in a new market or heads a recently acquired local distributor. Traders should have an entrepreneurial spirit. Their roles include sales and marketing, scanning the environment for new ideas, and gathering intelligence on the competition.
- The **builder** who develops local markets. Builders are entrepreneurs who are willing to be part of regional or global strategy teams.
- The **cabinet member** who is a team player with profit and loss responsibility for a small- to medium-size country. Teamwork is key here, since marketing efforts may require a great deal of cross-border coordination, especially for global and pan-regional brands. Major strategic decisions are often made at the regional level rather than by the country subsidiary.
- The **ambassador** is in charge of large and/or strategic markets. His responsibilities include handling government relations, integrating acquisitions and strategic

---

[10]"From Baron to Hotelier," *Economist,* May 11, 2002, pp. 57–58.

[11]John A. Quelch, "The New Country Managers," *McKinsey Quarterly,* 4 (1992), pp. 155–65.

[12]John A. Quelch and Helen Bloom, "The Return of the Country Manager," *McKinsey Quarterly,* 2 (1996), pp. 30–43.

[13]"Country Managers Come Back in from the Cold," *Financial Times,* September 24, 2002.

[14]Quelch and Bloom, "The Return of the Country Manager," pp. 38–39; and Michael Goold and Andrew Campbell, *Designing Effective Organizations* (San Francisco, CA: Jossey-Bass, 2002).

alliances, and coordinating activities across SBUs. In this role, the country manager can provide hands-on parenting for local markets that need more attention than they can get from the global product division. Ideally a seasoned manager, the ambassador should be somebody who is able to manage a large staff. For instance, Asea Brown Boveri, the Swiss/Swedish engineering, views the tasks of its Asia-based country managers as "to exploit fully the synergies between our businesses in the countries, to develop customer based strategies, to build and strengthen relationships with local customers, governments, and communities."[15]

- The **representative** in large, mature markets whose tasks include handling government relations and legal compliance and maintaining good relations with large, local customers. Dow Chemical, for example, realized that it needed to have strong local management in Germany, able to talk shop with the German government authorities.

Whatever role is determined for the country manager, the main requirement is to clearly define the scope of the job. Some companies are now combining the two jobs of country manager and product champion. This new breed of hybrid manager, referred to as a country prince by some, is based in a country that is seen as strategically important for the product category. Paris-based Nexans, the world's biggest maker of electric cables, adopted this approach with three country princes. For instance, one heads the global product division for ship cables and is country manager for South Korea.

Regional Structures. Many MNCs that do not feel entirely comfortable with a pure country-based organization opt for a region-based structure with regional headquarters. To some extent, a regional structure offers a compromise between a completely centralized organization and the country-focused organization. The intent behind most region-based structures is to address two concerns: lack of responsiveness of headquarters to local market conditions and parochialism among local country managers. In more and more industries, markets tend to cluster around regions rather than national boundaries. In some cases, the regions are formal trading blocs such as the European Union or NAFTA that allow almost completely free movement of goods across borders. In other cases, the clusters tend to be more culture driven.

A survey done in the Asia-Pacific region identified five distinct roles for regional headquarters (RHQs):[16]

- **Scouting.** The RHQ serves as a listening post to scan new opportunities and initiate new ventures.
- **Strategic stimulation.** The RHQ functions as a "switchboard" between the product divisions and the country managers. It helps the SBUs in understanding the regional environment.
- **Signaling commitment.** By establishing an RHQ, the MNC signals a commitment to the region that the company is serious about doing business in that region.
- **Coordination.** Often the RHQ's most important role is to coordinate strategic and tactical decisions across the region. Areas of cohesion include developing pan-regional campaigns in regions with a lot of media overlap, price coordination, especially in markets where parallel imports pose a threat, and consolidation of manufacturing and logistics operations.
- **Pooling resources.** Certain support and administrative tasks are often done more efficiently at the regional level instead of locally. The RQH might fulfill support functions such as after-sales services, product development, and market research.[17]

---

[15]Gordon Redding, "ABB—The Battle for the Pacific," *Long Range Planning,* 28 (1) 1995, pp. 92–94.

[16]"The Country Prince Comes of Age," *Financial Times,* August 9, 2005, p. 7.

[17]Philippe Lasserre, "Regional Headquarters: The Spearhead for Asia Pacific Markets," *Long Range Planning,* 29 (February 1996), pp. 30–37.

Matrix Structure   Imposing a single-dimensional (product, country, or function-based) management structure on complex global issues is often a recipe for disaster. In the wake of the serious shortcomings of the geographic and product-based structures, several MNCs have opted for a matrix organization. The matrix structure explicitly recognizes the multidimensional nature of global strategic decision making. With a matrix organization, two dimensions are integrated in the organization. For instance, the matrix could consist of geographic areas and business divisions. The geographic units are in charge for all product lines within their area. The product divisions have worldwide responsibility for their product line. So there is a dual chain of command, with managers reporting to two superiors.

A somewhat unorthodox example of a matrix organization was the initial marketing organization of DaimlerChrysler's automotive businesses created after the company was formed in 1998 (see Exhibit 18-4).[18] Along geographic lines, the organization was divided into three regions (North America, Latin America, and the rest of the world). Along product-lines, the organization was split into three areas: Chrysler car brands (Chrysler, Dodge, Plymouth, and Jeep), Mercedes-Benz car brands, and the commercial vehicle brands.

Sometimes the MNC might even set up a three-dimensional structure (geography, function, and business area). The various dimensions do not always carry equal weight. For instance, at Siemens, the locus of control is shifting more and more toward the business areas, away from the geographic areas.

The matrix structure has two major advantages.[19] First, matrices reflect the growing complexities of the global market arena. In most industries, MNCs face global *and* local competitors; global *and* local customers; and global *and* local distributors. In that sense, the matrix structure facilitates the MNC's need to "think globally and act locally"—to be *glocal*—or, in Unilever's terminology, to be a *multilocal multinational*. The other appeal of the matrix organization is that, in principle at least, it fosters a team spirit and cooperation among business area managers, country managers, and/or functional managers on a global basis.

EXHIBIT 18-4
DAIMLERCHRYSLER'S MATRIX ORGANIZATION FOR
PASSENGER CARS AND COMMERCIAL VEHICLES

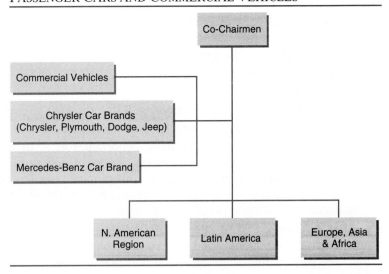

Source: www.daimlerchrysler.com

---

[18]"DaimlerChrysler Decides on New Global Sales and Marketing Organization for Passenger Cars and Commercial Vehicles," Press-wire, December 15, 1998.

[19]Thomas H. Naylor, "The International Strategy Matrix," *Columbia Journal of World Business,* Summer 1985, pp. 11–19.

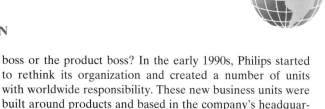

◆ ◆

𝒢LOBAL PERSPECTIVE 18-1

PHILIPS'S QUEST FOR THE RIGHT ORGANIZATION

The Dutch company Philips is one of the world's biggest electronics companies with 159,000 employees in 60 countries. Its was one of the earliest adopters of the matrix structure. After World War II, it set up both national units and product divisions. The head of, say, the lighting division in France would report to two superiors: the French country manager and the global head of the lighting unit. Conflicts between the two lines of command were resolved via committees.

Philips's matrix was plagued by numerous problems. One major issue was accountability: Who was to be held responsible for the profit and loss account? Should it be the country

Source: "The Matrix Master," "The New Organization. A Survey of the Company," *Economist,* January 21, 2006, p. 4.

boss or the product boss? In the early 1990s, Philips started to rethink its organization and created a number of units with worldwide responsibility. These new business units were built around products and based in the company's headquarters. Local country offices became subservient to the new units.

More recently, Philips has tinkered further with its organization. To become more customer driven, Philips appointed a chief marketing officer. Under the motto "One Philips," it has launched several low-key changes. Employees are encouraged to work across different business units. They are also expected to rotate in their careers across geographical boundaries and product divisions.

Despite these benefits, companies such as BP and Philips (see Global Perspective 18-1), have disbanded their matrix structure. Others, such as IBM and Dow Chemical, have streamlined their matrix setup.[20] Matrix structures have lost their appeal among many MNCs for several reasons. Dual (or triple) reporting and profit responsibilities frequently lead to conflicts or confusion. For instance, a product division could concentrate its resources and attention on a few major markets, thereby upsetting the country managers of the MNC's smaller markets. Another shortcoming of the matrix is bureaucratic bloat. Very often, the decision-making process gets bogged down, thereby discouraging swift responsiveness toward competitive attacks in the local markets. Overlap among divisions often triggers tensions, power clashes, and turf battles.[21]

The four organizational structures that we covered so far are the standard structures adopted by most MNCs. The simplicity of the one-dimensional structures and the shortcomings of the matrix model have led several companies to look for better solutions. Below, we discuss one of the more popular forms: the *networked organization.*

Global networking has been suggested as one solution to cope with the shortcomings associated with the classical hierarchical organization structures. The network model is an attempt to reconcile the tension between two opposing forces: the need for local responsiveness and the wish to be an integrated whole.[22] Strictly speaking, the network approach is not a formal structure but a mindset. That is, a company might still formally adopt, say, a *matrix* structure but at the same time develop a global network. The networked global organization is sometimes also referred to as a **transnational.**[23]

According to advocates of the network model, MNCs should develop processes and linkages that allow each unit to tap into a global knowledge pool. A good metaphor for the global network is the atom (see Exhibit 18-5). At the center is a common knowledge

The Global Network Solution

---

[20]"End of a Corporate Era," *Financial Times,* March 30, 1995, p. 15.

[21]Christopher A. Bartlett and Sumantra Ghoshal, "Matrix Management, not a Structure, a Frame of Mind," *Harvard Business Review,* July–August 1990, pp.138–45.

[22]Christopher A. Bartlett and Sumantra Ghoshal, "Organizing for Worldwide Effectiveness: The Transnational Solution," *California Management Review,* Fall 1988, pp. 54–74.

[23]Ibid.

EXHIBIT 18-5
NEW ORGANIZATIONAL METAPHOR

OLD HIERARCHICAL PYRAMID   NEW SPHERICAL STRUCTURE

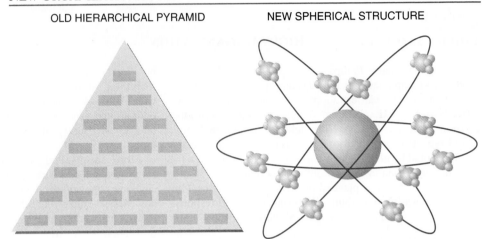

Source: Raymond E. Miles and Charles C. Snow, "The New Network Firm: A Spherical Structure Built on a Human Investment Philosophy." Reprinted by permission of the publisher, from ORGANIZATIONAL DYNAMICS SPRING 1995 © 1995. American Management Organization, New York. All rights reserved.

base. Each national unit can be viewed as a source of ideas, skills, capabilities, and knowledge that can be harnessed for the benefit of the total organization.[24]

Ideally, the entire global organization functions as a sphere. When one unit within the organization anywhere around the world faces a problem or an opportunity, the sphere rotates, thereby giving the unit immediate access to the company's global resource and expertise pool.[25]

Asea Brown Boveri (ABB) is often touted as a prime example of a global networking.[26] Percy Barnevik, former CEO and one of the major forces behind ABB's reorganization, describes the vision as follows:

> Our vision was to create a truly global company that knows no borders, has many home countries and offers opportunities for all nationalities. While we strived for size to benefit from economies of scale and scope, our vision was also to avoid the stigma of the big company with a large headquarters and stifling bureaucracy, countless volumes of instructions, turf defenders and people working far from their customers. With our thousands of profit centers close to customers we wanted to create a small company culture with its huge advantages of flexibility, speed and the power to free up the creative potential of each employee.[27]

Several mechanisms can help develop the required vision and cement the necessary linkages. One approach is the *international teaming concept.* The charter of the international management team may cover areas such as communicating the overall corporate vision ("missionary" work, so to speak), new product development, technology transfer, strategy development, and so forth. In the wake of new technology development, more and more companies are moving toward "virtual teams." Spread around the world, these teams communicate through e-mail or videoconferences rather than on a face-to-face basis. Exhibit 18-6 lists guidelines for global virtual teams to be successful. ABB uses a company "bible" to tie together the different companies within

---

[24]Christopher A. Bartlett, "Building and Managing the Transnational: The New Organizational Challenge," in *Competition in Global Industries,* ed. Michael E. Porter (Boston, MA: Harvard Business School Press, 1986), pp. 367–401.

[25]Raymond E. Miles and Charles C. Snow, "The New Network Firm: A Spherical Structure Built on a Human Investment Philosophy," *Organizational Dynamics,* pp. 5–18.

[26]William Taylor, "The Logic of Global Business: An Interview with ABB's Percy Barnevik," *Harvard Business Review,* March–April 1991, pp. 91–105.

[27]Asea Brown Boveri 1995 Annual Report, p. 5.

EXHIBIT 18-6
GUIDELINES ON GLOBAL VIRTUAL TEAMWORK

Tips for Top Performance

- Start with a face-to-face meeting to kick off trust building.
- Keep the team as small as practical.
- Have a code of practice including how to communicate and behave (e.g., how to respond to e-mails).
- Communicate regularly, but do not overdo it.
- Ensure that everyone understands each other's role.
- Have a supportive sponsor who represents his or her interests at a senior level within the organization.
- Keep strong links with the parent organization.
- Reward results, not how people work.

Source: " 'Virtual Teams' Endeavor to Build Trust," *Financial Times,* September 9, 2004, p. 8.

its organization. Its bible describes the firm's mission and values, long-term objectives, and guidelines on how to behave internally.[28]

Another well-known network example is Toyota. Toyota has 580 different companies spread around the world and sells its cars in more than 170 countries. What holds these operations together is "The Toyota Way." This vision embraces five distinct values:[29]

- *Kaizen. Kaizen* is the mindset of continuous improvement. Toyota employees are driven to become a little better at whatever they are working on than they were the day before.
- *Genchi genbutsu (GG).* This concept roughly translates as "go to the source." GG means go to the source of the problem rather than relying on hearsay. Spend more time defining a problem before trying to come up with solutions.
- *Challenge.* Toyota employees are expected to look at each problem positively as a way to improve their performance further. Problems should not be seen as undesirable.
- *Teamwork.* Put the company's interest ahead of the individual's and share knowledge with the team.
- *Respect for other people.* If two people always agree, one of them is redundant. Different opinions must be expressed but in a respectful way.

ORGANIZING FOR GLOBAL BRAND MANAGEMENT ◆ ◆ ◆ ◆ ◆ ◆ ◆ ◆ ◆

Global branding is the rage for more and more companies. However, to foster and nurture global brands, companies often find it useful to put organizational mechanisms in place. This is especially so for decentralized companies in which local decisions compromise the global branding strategies. Several options exist: (1) a global branding committee, (2) a brand champion, (3) a global brand manager, and (4) informal, ad hoc brand meetings. Let us look each of these in detail.

Global branding committees are usually made up of top-line executives from headquarters and regional and/or local offices. Their charter is to integrate and steer global and local branding strategies. Visa International's "Global Branding Marketing Group"

Global Branding Committee

---

[28]Manfred F.R. Kets de Vries, "Making a Giant Dance," *Across the Board,* October 1994, pp. 27–32.

[29]"Inculcating Culture," in "The New Organization. A Survey of the Company," *Economist,* (January 21, 2006), p. 10 Publication title & part of article title'.

exemplifies this approach.[30] The group's goal is to establish better communications among regions and to leverage global media buying power. It is made up of the heads of marketing from each region. HP created to Global Brand Steering Committee in 1998. Its primary tasks include brand positioning and vision development.[31]

Brand Champion

This is a top-line executive (sometimes the CEO) who serves as the brand's advocate.[32] The approach works well for companies whose senior executives have a passion and expertise for branding. One practitioner of brand championship is Nestlé, which has a brand champion for each of its 12 corporate strategic brands. The brand champion approves all brand and line extension decisions,[33] monitors the presentation of the brand worldwide, and spreads insights on best practices within the organization.[34]

Global Brand Manager

This is a steward of the brand whose main responsibility is to integrate branding efforts across countries and combat local biases. In the corporate hierarchy, the position is usually just below top-line executives. The position is most suitable for organizations whose top management lacks marketing expertise, as do many high-tech firms. For the global brand manager to be effective, the following conditions should hold:[35]

- Commitment to branding at the top of the organization. Top-line executives—although most likely lacking a marketing background—should share the vision and a belief in strong branding.

- Need to create and manage a solid strategic planning process. Country managers should adopt the same format, vocabulary, and planning cycle.

- Need to travel to learn about local management and best practices and to meet local customers and/or distributors.

- Need for a system to identify, mentor, and train prospects who can fill the role.

Informal, Ad Hoc Branding Meetings

Even if for some reason a company decides against a formal structure, it could still find it worthwhile to have informal mechanisms to guide global branding decisions. This usually takes the form of ad-hoc branding meetings. A good example of this organizational method is Abbott International, a U.S.-based pharmaceutical company. Whenever it plans a new product, international executives meet with local staff to discuss the global brand. The ad hoc committee reviews patents and trademarks for each country to decide whether or not to use the U.S. name in the other countries.[36]

◆ ◆ ◆ ◆ ◆ ◆ ◆ ◆ **LIFE CYCLE OF ORGANIZATION STRUCTURES**

Organization structures are not set in stone. Change occurs and is not always welcomed by the local staff. Companies need to adapt their organization for several reasons.[37] First, existing structures could have become too rigid or complex with too

[30] "U.S. Multinationals," *Advertising Age International,* June 1999, p. 44.

[31] Ibid.

[32] "David A. Aaker and Erich Joachimsthaler, "The Lure of Global Branding," *Harvard Business Review,* (November–December 1999), p. 142.

[33] A *brand extension* uses the same brand for a new product in another product category; a *line extension* launches new varieties (e.g., a new flavor, a new package format) of the brand within the same product category.

[34] Aaker and Joachimsthaler, p. 142.

[35] Ibid.

[36] "U.S. Multinationals," p. 44.

[37] Michael Goold and Andrew Campbell, *Designing Effective Organizations* (San Francisco: Jossey-Bass, 2002), pp. 88–89.

many divisions and management layers. A second reason is that the environment changes. To cope with these dynamics, the organization may need an overhaul. Third, managers learn new skills, or new senior management is brought in from outside the firm. Fad-prone managers are often attracted to new theories regardless of whether they actually serve the organization's purpose. Finally, the pursuit of new strategic opportunities or directions often demands a change in the organization.

Regardless of the reasons, successful restructuring takes time, planning, and resources. Change can imply new relationships, new responsibilities, and even downsizing. Not surprisingly, employees who think they "know better" often resist it. Hence, in addition to the physical changes, restructuring often requires a fundamental cultural change.[38]

In some cases, companies have moved from one extreme to another before finding a suitable configuration. A case in point is Kraft General Foods Europe (KGFE).[39] In the early 1980s, KGFE tried to impose a centralized system of uniform marketing strategies across Europe. This attempt led to so much ill-will among KGFE's local units that Kraft soon abandoned its centralized system. It was replaced by a loose system in which country managers developed their own marketing strategies for all Kraft brands, including the regional (e.g., Miracoli pasta) and global (e.g., Philadelphia cream cheese) brands. Not surprisingly, this system created a great deal of inconsistency in marketing strategies. In 1990 Kraft was split into North American and international divisions with two chief executives, although the largest product categories had global councils to cover best practices. Still, Kraft struggled. In 2004, the dual structure was swept away to make Kraft truly global, cut costs, and ramp up innovation. The overhaul led to the creation of five global product units (beverages, snacks, cheese and dairy, convenient meals, and grocery) backed by two regional commercial units (one for North America, one for elsewhere). Kraft also set up global units to handle support functions such as supply chain and product development.[40]

Several management theorists have made an attempt to come up with the "right" fit between an MNC's environment (internal and external) and its organization setup. One of the more popular schemas is the stages model in Exhibit 18-7, which Stopford and Wells developed.[41] The schema shows the relationship between the organizational structure, foreign product diversity, and the importance of foreign sales to the company (as a share of total sales). According to their model, when companies first explore the global marketplace, they start with an international division. As foreign sales expand without an increase in the firm's foreign product assortment diversity, the company is most likely to switch to a geographic area structure. If instead the diversity of the firm's foreign product line substantially increases, it could organize itself along global product lines. Finally, when both product diversity and international sales grow significantly, MNCs tend to adopt a two-dimensional matrix structure.

Several scholars have criticized the Stopford-Wells model for several reasons. First, it is a purely descriptive representation of how MNCs develop over time based on an analysis of U.S.-based MNCs. Therefore, it would be misleading to apply the framework in a prescriptive manner, as several people have done.[42] Second, the structure of the organization is only one aspect of a global organization. Other, equally important, components are the mindsets of the managers and managerial processes. The MNC's environment is dynamic; it changes all of the time. Thus, a fit between the environment and the MNC's organizational structure is not enough. Global organizations also need flexibility.[43]

---

[38]"Be Principled for a Change," *Financial Times,* August 23, 2004, p. 9.

[39]"Cross-border Kraftsmen," *Financial Times,* June 17, 1993.

[40]"Search for the Right Ingredients," *Financial Times,* October 7, 2004, p. 8.

[41]John M. Stopford and Louis T. Wells, Jr.; *Managing the Multinational Enterprise: Organization of the Firm and Ownership of the Subsidiary,* (New York: Basic Books, 1972).

[42]Bartlett, "Building and Managing the Transnational," pp. 367–401.

[43]Sumantra Ghoshal and Nitin Nohria, "Horses for Courses: Organizational Forms for Multinational Corporations," *Sloan Management Review,* Winter 1993, pp. 23–35.

EXHIBIT 18-7
STOPFORD-WELLS INTERNATIONAL STRUCTURAL STAGES MODEL

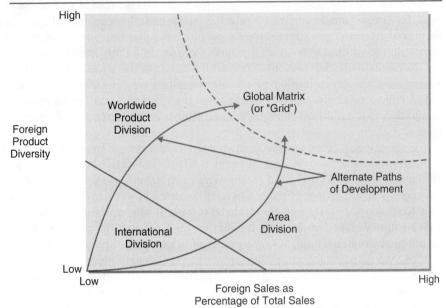

Source: Reprinted by permission of Harvard Business School Press. From Christopher A. Barlett, "Building and Managing the Transnational: The New Organizational Challenge," in *Competition in Global Industries,* ed. M.E. Porter (Boston, MA: Harvard University Press, 1987), p. 368. Copyright © 1986 by the President and Fellows of Harvard College.

An in-depth study of a sample of 10 successful U.S.-based MNCs shows that the key challenge for MNCs is to build and sustain the right management process instead of looking for the proper organizational structure.[44] According to the study, the installation of such a process moves through three stages. The first step is to recognize the complexity of the MNC's environment. Country and regional managers must look at strategic issues from multiple perspectives—a **glocal mindset,** so to speak. During the second stage, the company introduces communication channels and decision-making platforms to facilitate more flexibility. In the final stage, the MNC develops a corporate culture that fosters collaborative thinking and decision making. Such an agenda could include activities such as formulating common goals and values, developing reward systems and evaluation criteria that encourage a cooperative spirit, and providing role models.

◆ ◆ ◆ ◆ ◆ ◆ ◆ ◆ CENTRALIZATION OR DECENTRALIZATION?

Power sharing between headquarters and local business units is a delicate but extremely important matter. Roughly speaking, companies can move into two opposite directions. Within decentralized organizations, the national operating companies are highly autonomous. Each local unit represents a profit center. Corporate headquarters can provide guidance and advice, but when push comes to shove, the local subsidiary makes the decisions. Peter Brabeck-Letmathe, Nestlé's CEO, describes the decision-making process within his company as follows:

> We respond to what the local market says, and they may take another look and change their mind. But if they don't want something, we don't force them. We might send a couple of people to offer encouragement, but that's as far as it goes.[45]

Centralized organizations, on the other hand, consolidate most decision-making power at corporate headquarters. They have a strict command-and-control culture.

[44]Christopher A. Bartlett, "MNCs: Get Off the Reorganization Merry-Go-Round," *Harvard Business Review,* March–April 1983, pp. 138–46.

[45]Andrew J. Parsons, "Nestlé: The Visions of Local Managers," *McKinsey Quarterly,* 2 (1996), pp. 5–29.

In practice, most MNCs are somewhere between these two extremes: certain tasks (e.g., finance and R&D) are typically centralized while other tasks (e.g., pricing and advertising) are the realm of the local subsidiaries. Forces for global integration such as global brands, global customers, and scale economies push companies toward globalized decision making. Drivers towards local responsiveness favor a local autonomy approach. The two forces can jointly have a high impact. Under such conditions, a transnational solution is called for where companies strike a delicate balance between centralization and decentralization.

In recent years, several management theorists have offered **federalism** as a way to combine the autonomy of the local units with the benefits of coordination.[46] MNCs that follow this model share the following characteristics[47]:

- **Noncentralization.** Power is diffused. It belongs to the local units. Power cannot be taken away unilaterally by corporate headquarters. Charles Handy, a long-time preacher of federalism, notes that federal organizations are decentralized *and* centralized.[48]

- **Negotianalism.** Decisions are made via a bargaining process. Each local unit has a voice. Each local unit is listened to.

- **Constitutionalism.** Another feature is that many of these companies often have a ''constitution'' such as Asea Brown Boveri's company bible mentioned earlier.

- **Territoriality.** There are clear boundary markers based on geography or business areas.

EXHIBIT 18-8
INITIATIVES TAKEN BY MNCS TO COORDINATE GLOBAL ACTIVITIES

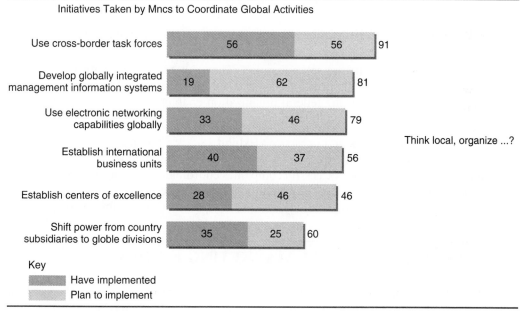

Source: Ingo Theuerkauf, David Ernst, and Amir Mahini, ''Think Local, Organize. . .?'' *International Marketing Review,* 13 (3), 1996, p. 11.

---

[46]See, for instance, Charles Handy, ''Balancing Corporate Power: A New Federalist Paper,'' *Harvard Business Review,* November–December 1992, pp. 59–72.

[47]James O'Toole and Warren Bennis, ''Our Federalist Future: The Leadership Imperative,'' *California Management Review,* Summer 1992, pp. 73–90.

[48]Barbara Ettorre, ''A Conversation with Charles Handy: On the Future of Work and an End to the 'Century of the Organization,''' *Organizational Dynamics,* Summer 1996, pp. 15–26.

EXHIBIT 18-9
INTERNATIONAL DECISION MAKING: MORE VERSUS LESS
SUCCESSFUL COMPANIES

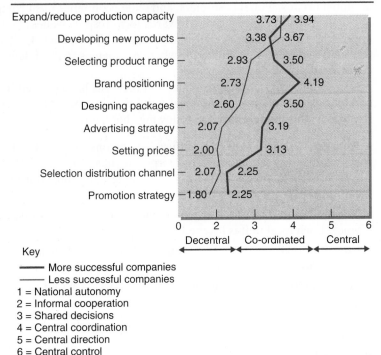

	Decentral	Co-ordinated	Central
Expand/reduce production capacity		3.73	3.94
Developing new products		3.38	3.67
Selecting product range	2.93	3.50	
Brand positioning	2.73		4.19
Designing packages	2.60	3.50	
Advertising strategy	2.07	3.19	
Setting prices	2.00	3.13	
Selection distribution channel	2.07	2.25	
Promotion strategy	1.80	2.25	

Key
— More successful companies
— Less successful companies
1 = National autonomy
2 = Informal cooperation
3 = Shared decisions
4 = Central coordination
5 = Central direction
6 = Central control

Source: Ingo Theuerkauf, David Ernst, and Amir Mahini,
"Think Local, Organize. . .?" *International Marketing Review,*
13 (3), 1996, p. 11.

- **Balance of power.** Federations seek balance of power between headquarters and units and among units.
- **Autonomy.** The units are self-governing. They can experiment with new ideas as long as they respect the principles spelled out in the company's constitution. As a result, a properly working federal organization enables the company to gather the benefits of "big" and "small" companies.

What do companies do in practice? Exhibit 18-8 is a ranking of the most popular initiatives based on a survey of CEOs of leading U.S.-based consumer goods companies. In general, the more successful companies coordinate their international decision making on a worldwide basis. Coordination is especially crucial for brand positioning, package design, advertising strategy, and pricing policies (see Exhibit 18-9).

◆ ◆ ◆ ◆ ◆ ◆ ◆ ◆ **CONTROL OF GLOBAL MARKETING EFFORTS**

To make global marketing strategies work, companies need to establish a control system. The main purpose of controls is to ensure that the behaviors of the various parties within the organization are in line with the company's strategic goals. We will first concentrate on formal control methods. We will then turn to less formal means to implement control: establishment of a corporate culture and management development.

**Formal
("Bureaucratic")
Control Systems**

Any formal control system consists of basically three building blocks: (1) the establishment of performance standards, (2) the measurement and evaluation of performance against standards, and (3) the analysis and correction of deviations from standards.

Establishing Standards (Metrics). The first step of the control process is to set standards (metrics). These standards should be driven by the company's corporate goals. There are essentially two types of standards: behavior and outcome based. Behavior-based control involves specifying the actions that are necessary to achieve good performance. Managers are told through manuals/policies how to respond to various scenarios. Rewards are based on whether the observed behavior matches the prescribed behavior. Examples of behavior-based standards include distribution coverage, branding policies, pricing rules, and R&D spending. Output-based control depends on specific standards that are objective, reliable, and easy to measure. Outcome standards focus on very specific outcome-oriented measures such as profit-loss statements, ROI, market share, sales, and customer satisfaction.

When applied too rigorously, behavior-based standards restrain local management's ability to respond effectively to local market conditions. An example is Johnson & Johnson's experience in the Philippines.[49] In the early 1990s, J&J's managers learned that young Philippine women used J&J's baby talcum to freshen their makeup. To cater to their needs, local management developed a compact holder for the talcum powder. However, a few days before the planned launch of the new product, corporate headquarters asked the local managers to drop the product, claiming that the cosmetics business is not a core business for J&J. Only after the local marketing head made a personal plea for the product at J&J's headquarters was the subsidiary given the green light. The product became a big hit, although it was never launched in other markets because J&J does not want to run the risk of being perceived as a cosmetics maker.

Output-based standards could also create problems, especially when internal and external factors undermine the validity of the output norm as a performance measure. For instance, profits of the local subsidiary could be distorted by the firm's transfer pricing rules.[50]

For most companies, the two types of standards matter. Let us show you why with a simple illustration. Imagine that headquarters wants country A to increase its market share by 3 percentage points over a one-year period. Country A could take different approaches to achieve this target. One path is to do many promotional activities: couponing, price promotions, trade deals, and so on. Another route is to spend more on advertising. Both paths could achieve the outcome. However, with the first option—heavy dealing—the company risks tarnishing its brand image. With the second option, the subsidiary would invest in brand equity. Thus, the same outcome can be realized through two totally different behaviors, one of which can ruin the long-term viability of the company's brand assets.

Ideally, standards are developed via a bottom-up and top-down planning process of listening, reflecting, dialoging, and debating between headquarters and the local units. Standards should also strike a delicate balance between long- and short-term priorities.[51]

Measuring and Evaluating Performance. Formal control systems also need mechanisms to monitor and evaluate performance. The actual performance is compared against the established standards. In many instances, it is fairly straightforward to measure performance, especially when the standards are based on within-country results. To make global or pan-regional strategies work, however, MNCs also need to assess and reward individual managers' contributions to the "common good." For example, two-thirds of the bonuses payable to Unilever's senior executives in Europe are now driven by Unilever's performance in that region.[52] In practice, however,

[49]Niraj Dawar and Tony Frost, "Competing with Giants: Survival Strategies for Local Companies in Emerging Markets," *Harvard Business Review,* March–April 1999, pp. 119–129.
[50]Robert D. Hamilton III, Virginia A. Taylor, and Roger J. Kashlak, "Designing a Control System for a Multinational Subsidiary," *Long Range Planning,* 29 (6) 1996, pp. 857–68.
[51]Guy R. Jillings, "Think Globally, Act Locally," *Executive Excellence,* October 1993, p. 15.
[52]"Unilever Adopts Clean Sheet Approach," *Financial Times,* October 21, 1991.

it is tremendously hard to gauge managers' contributions to the regional or global well-being of the firm.

Analyzing and Correcting Deviations. The third element is to analyze deviations from the standards and, if necessary, make the necessary corrections. If actual performance does not meet the set standard, the company needs to analyze the cause behind the divergence. If necessary, corrective measures will be taken. This part of the control system also involves devising the right incentive mechanisms—checks and balances—that make subsidiary managers "tick." While proper reward systems are crucial to motivate subsidiary managers, one study has shown the key role played by the presence of **due process**.[53] Due process encompasses five features: (1) the head office should be familiar with the subsidiaries' local situation; (2) the global strategy-making decision processes should involve two-way communication; (3) the head office is relatively consistent in making decisions across local units; (4) local units can legitimately challenge headquarters' strategic views and decisions; and (5) subsidiary units receive explanations for final strategic decisions.

Informal Control Methods

Aside from formal control mechanisms, most MNCs establish informal control methods. In the following sections, we cover the two most common informal control tools: corporate culture and human resource development.

Corporate Culture. For many MNCs with operations scattered all over the globe, shared cultural values are often a far more effective "glue" to bond subsidiaries than formal bureaucratic control tools. Corporate cultures can be *clan based* or *market based*.[54] **Clan cultures** have the following distinguishing features: they embody a long socialization process; strong, powerful norms; and a defined set of internalized controls. **Market cultures** are the opposite: norms are loose or absent, socialization processes are limited, and control systems are purely based on performance measures. In most global organizations for which integration is an overriding concern, a clanlike culture is instrumental in creating a shared vision.

Corporate values are more than slogans that embellish the company's annual report. To shape a shared vision, cultural values should have three properties:[55]

1. **Clarity.** The stated values should be simple, relevant, and concrete.
2. **Continuity.** Values should be stable over time, long-term oriented, not flavor-of-the-month-type values.
3. **Consistency.** To avoid confusion, everyone within the organization should share the same vision. Everybody should speak the same language. Everyone should pursue the same agenda.

Human Resource Development. The company's management development programs are another major informal control tool. Their role is critical in at least three regards.[56] First and foremost, training programs can help managers worldwide to understand the MNC's mission and vision and their part in pursuing them. Second, such programs can speed up the transfer of new values when changes in the company's environment dictate a "new" corporate mentality. Finally, they can also prove fruitful in allowing managers from all over the world to share their best practices and success stories.

[53]W. Chan Kim and Renée A. Mauborgne, "Making Global Strategies Work," *Sloan Management Review,* Spring 1993, pp. 11–24.

[54]David Lei, John W. Slocum, Jr., and Robert W. Slater, "Global Strategy and Reward Systems: The Key Roles of Management Development and Corporate Culture," *Organizational Dynamics,* Winter 1989, pp. 27–41.

[55]Christopher A. Bartlett and Sumantra Ghoshal, "Matrix Management," pp. 138–45.

[56]David Lei et al., "Global Strategy and Reward Systems, p. 39.

A joint research project conducted by the Stanford Business School and McKinsey sought to uncover the tools that multinationals rely on to resolve global versus local tensions.[57] Dubbed the "Globe Project," it studied 16 multinational companies through in-depth interviews, questionnaires, and network analysis. Based on company interviews, the researchers identified seven management tools or "levers" that companies use to resolve the global/local tradeoffs:

"Soft" versus "Hard" Levers

- *Organizational structure.* Creating formal positions and lines of authority.
- *Process.* Defining work flows and procedures.
- *Incentives.* Reward systems that encourage outcomes in line with the desired balance between global and local priorities.
- *Metrics.* Measurement systems that focus on desired outcomes.
- *Strategy.* The extent to which the central strategy guides local decisions.
- *Networks.* Building personal relationships that help resolve disputes and encourage sharing of knowledge and resources.
- *Culture.* Shared values that encourage a common approach among all members of the organization.

As you can see, there is some overlap between these levers and the control methods discussed earlier. Three of the tools—process, incentives, and metrics—are *hard levers*; three other tools—strategy, networks, and culture—are *soft levers* (formal versus informal methods). Structure is a hybrid. The study scored each company that participated in the project on each of these levers. Depending on the score, companies could be classified as a "hard" or "soft" firm. 3M, the conglomerate with its unique innovation culture, leans very heavily toward soft levers. Toyota, on the other hand, with its heavy focus on quality control is a prototypical "hard" company.

---

[57]"Corporations with Hard and Soft Centres," *Financial Times,* February 20, 2002, p. 11.

SUMMARY ◆

Running a multinational organization is a tremendous challenge. Local managers need empowerment so that the local unit is able to respond rapidly and effectively to local market threats, grab opportunities, and stay in tune with local market developments. A laissez-faire situation, in contrast, can easily evolve into a patchwork of local barons who will inevitably jeopardize the interests of the group as a whole. Too much centralization, however, will strait-jacket the country manager, create resentment, and stifle local creativity and responsiveness. This global versus local tension needs to be addressed. In this chapter, we discussed the structures and control mechanisms that MNCs can use to shape a global organization. Companies can pick from a variety of structures, ranging from a single international division to a global network operation. Formal and informal (culture, management development) control mechanisms are available to run global operations. However, the dynamics of the global marketing arena means that building a global organization is much more than just choosing the "right" organizational configuration and control systems. Global players constantly need to reflect on how to strike the balance between centralization *and* decentralization, local responsiveness *and* global integration, center *and* the periphery. As with many other challenges in global marketing, there are no one-size-fits-all solutions. In their search for the proper structure and strategic coherence,

countless MNCs developed schemes that led to confusion, frustration, and ill-will among subsidiary managers. We can, however, offer some pieces of advice:

- **Recognize the need for business asymmetry.** Due to relentless environmental changes, power sharing between the center and the periphery will vary over time, over business units, and even across activities (product development, advertising, pricing) within business units. Different SBUs within the organization have different needs for responsiveness and global coordination.[58] Widely diversified companies especially should recognize that each business unit needs a different format, depending on its particular circumstances and needs. For instance, Asea Brown Boveri has businesses that are *superlocal* (e.g., electrical installation) and *superglobal* (e.g., power plant projects). P&G's model treats countries differently based on their income. In high-income countries, the business unit is in charge of resource allocation; in low-income countries (e.g., China, Eastern Europe) the region is responsible. The reason for this is that low-income countries are more challenging and less familiar business environments. However, the global product unit makes production and marketing decisions for products such as Pantene shampoo, which are global in

---

[58]"Fashionable Federalism," *Financial Times,* December 18, 1992.

EXHIBIT 18-10
GOODYEAR: EXAMPLE OF "BUSINESS ASYMMETRY"

Strategic Business Unit	Products and Markets	Geographic Markets Served
North American Tire	Original equipment, replacement tires for autos, trucks, farm, aircraft, construction	United States, Canada, Export
Kelly-Springfield	Replacement tires for autos, trucks, tractors	United States, Canada, Export
Goodyear Europe	Original equipment, replacement tires for autos, trucks, farm, construction	Europe, Africa, Middle East, Export
Goodyear Latin America	Original equipment, replacement tires for autos, trucks, tractors	Central, South America, Export
Goodyear Asia	Original equipment, replacement tires for autos, trucks, farm, aircraft, construction	Southeast, Western Asia, North Pacific Rim, Export
Engineered Products	Auto belts, hose, body components, industrial products	Worldwide
Chemicals	Synthetic and natural rubber, chemicals for internal, external customers	Worldwide
Celeron	Crude oil transportation, related services	Operates only pipeline from U.S. West Coast to Texas
Goodyear Racing	Tires for all major motor racing series	Worldwide

Source: The Goodyear Tire & Rubber Company 1994 Annual Report.

nature in terms of consumer buying habits and usage.[59] The principle of **business asymmetry** is illustrated in Exhibit 18-10 for Goodyear, the world's leading tire maker. Depending on the business area, units are structured on a regional or global basis.

- **Democracy is a must.** Getting the balance right also requires democracy. When building a global organization, make sure that every country subsidiary has a "voice." Subsidiaries of small countries should not be concerned about getting pushed over by their larger counterparts. As we discussed earlier, **global team-work** is one tool MNCs can use to establish a democratic forum.

- **Importance of a shared vision.** Getting the organizational structure right—the "arrows" and "boxes," so to speak—is important. Far more critical, though, is the organizational "psychology."[60] People are key in building an organization. Having a clear and consistent corporate vision is a major ingredient in getting people excited about the organization. To instill and communicate corporate values, companies should also have human resource development mechanisms in place that will facilitate the learning process.

- **Recognize the need for a good mix of specialists of three types: country, functional, and business.** There is no such thing as a *transnational manager.* Companies should breed specialists of three different kinds: country, functional, and global business (SBU). In particular, country managers—once feared to become part of the endangered species list—play a key role. As we discussed earlier in this chapter, the country manager's skills and role will differ from country to country. Some subsidiaries need a "trader"; others need an "ambassador."

- **Understand that moving unit headquarters abroad seldom solves the organization's problems.** In recent years, some companies (IBM, HP, Siemens) have moved business unit headquarters abroad. Several of these moves were for very sensible reasons: getting closer to the customer or supplier, being in the big guys' backyard, cutting costs. For instance, the Japanese company Hoya, one of the world's largest makers of spectacle lenses, moved the headquarters of its vision care business to the Netherlands. The move was prompted by Europe's technological prowess in this sector.[61] Unfortunately, in numerous cases, the relocation typically turns out to be mere window dressing in a drive to become more globally oriented. Sometimes transfers can even be counterproductive, weakening the corporate identity or the "authenticity" of the brand when it is strongly linked to the firm's home country.[62]

[59]"From Baron to Hotelier," pp. 57–58.
[60]Bartlett and Ghoshal, "Matrix Management," pp. 138–45.
[61]"A European Move with Global Vision," *Financial Times,* January 12, 2006, p. 10.
[62]"Home Is not Always Where the Heart Is," *Financial Times,* January 10, 2005, p. 6.

KEY TERMS ✦

Ambassador
Bottom-up (top-down) planning
Builder
Business asymmetry
Cabinet member
Clan culture
Country prince
Due process

Federalism
Geographic structure
Global networking
Global strategic marketing plan
Global team-work
Glocal mindset
International division
Market culture

Matrix structure
Networked organization model
Product-based structure
Representative
Trader
Transnational

REVIEW QUESTIONS ✦

1. How does a globally networked organization differ from one using the matrix structure?

2. Describe how external environmental drivers influence the organizational design decision.

3. What are the pros and cons of a regional organization structure?

4. What mechanisms can companies use to foster a global corporate culture?

5. What does it take for an MNC to be a "multilocal multi-national"?

◆ ◆ ◆ ◆ ◆ ◆ ◆ ◆   **SHORT CASES**

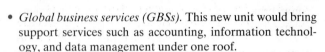

ASE 18-1

REVAMPING PROCTER & GAMBLE: ORGANIZATION 2005

Until the late 1990s, Procter & Gamble was split into four regional divisions: North America; Europe, Middle East, and Africa; Asia; and Latin America. Each division was responsible for its profits and losses. Despite heavy R&D spending, P&G failed through the 1990s to develop and successfully launch innovative products. After a lackluster sales performance during the mid-90s, P&G decided to embark on a self-improvement plan. Top executives of the firm traveled around the country, visiting the CEOs of a dozen major companies such as Kellogg, Hewlett-Packard, and 3M in search of advice. The result of the whole exercise was Organization 2005 a new bold plan to revamp the P&G organization. The goal of the restructuring exercise was to boost sales and profits by launching an array of new products, closing plants, and cutting jobs. The plan was spearheaded by then CEO Durk Jager. According to Jager, P&G's management had become too conservative: "Speed builds sales. But speed has been an issue for us."

Under Organization 2005, P&G was to be remolded from a geographically based organization to one based on global product lines. The key elements of the program were:

- *Global business units (GBUs).* P&G moved from four geographic units to seven GBUs based on product lines. Each GBU would have all of the resources it needs to understand consumer needs in its product area and to do product innovation. By shifting the focus to products, P&G hoped to boost innovation and speed. The GBUs were to develop and sell products on a worldwide basis. They would replace a system in which country managers ruled their local fiefs, setting prices and devising product policies as they saw fit. By 2000, P&G had consolidated into five GBUs: paper ($12 billion in net sales in FY 2001), fabric and home care ($11.7 billion), beauty care ($7.3 billion), health care ($4.4 billion), and food and beverage ($4.1 billion).

Sources: "P&G's Hottest New Product: P&G," *Business Week,* October 5, 1998, pp. 58–59: "The What, not the Where, to Drive P&G," *Financial Times,* September 3, 1998, p. 18; http://www.pg.com/investor/news/recentnews_newsrel.html; and http://www.indiainfoline.com/fmcg/feat/pgga.html.

- *Global business services (GBSs).* This new unit would bring support services such as accounting, information technology, and data management under one roof.

- *Market development organizations (MDOs).* The MDOs were created to tailor global marketing programs to local markets.

- *Corporate functions.* Corporate functions were streamlined, and most of the corporate staff was transferred to one of the new business units.

- *Overhaul of reward systems and training programs.*

P&G saw the revamped organization as a continuation of the strategy it started in the 1980s when it moved from brand management to category management. With the new setup, category management would be run on a global basis. Durk Jager, P&G's CEO, made the case for Organization 2005 as follows: "Organization 2005 is focused on one thing: leveraging P&G's innovative capability. Because the single best way our growth ... is to innovate bigger and move faster consistently and across the entire company. The cultural changes we are making will also create an environment that produces bolder, more stretching goals and plans, bigger innovations and greater speed."

However, in FY 2000, P&G was struggling. Results were below plan. Core earnings (earnings excluding restructuring charges) grew a modest 2.0 percent. Jager commented, "I am proud of our vision of Organization 2005, and we've made important progress. It's unfortunate our progress in stepping up top-line sales growth resulted in earnings disappointments." Jager resigned in June 2000, after less than two years on the job. A.G. Laffey, the new CEO, said: "In hindsight, it is clear that we have changed too much too fast, all with the right intent of accelerating growth—but still, too much change too fast."

DISCUSSION QUESTIONS

1. What went wrong with Organization 2005? Do you agree with Laffey's comments of "too much too fast"?

2. Is Organization 2005 fundamentally right for P&G, or should P&G nip it in the bud? Explain.

FURTHER READING   ◆ ◆ ◆ ◆ ◆ ◆ ◆ ◆ ◆ ◆ ◆ ◆ ◆ ◆ ◆ ◆ ◆ ◆ ◆

Bartlett, Christopher A. "Building and Managing the Transnational: The New Organizational Challenge," In *Competition in Global Industries,* ed. M. E. Porter. Boston, MA: Harvard University Press, 1986, pp. 367–401.

Bartlett, Christopher A., and Sumantra Ghoshal. "Organizing for Worldwide Effectiveness: The Transnational Solution." *California Management Review,* Fall 1988, pp. 54–74.

Corstjens, Marcel, and Jeffrey Merrihue. "Optimal Marketing." *Harvard Business Review,* October 2003, pp. 114–21.

Davidson, W. H., and P. Haspeslagh. "Shaping a Global Product Organization." *Harvard Business Review,* July–August 1982, pp. 125–32.

Goold, Michael, and Andrew Campbell. *Designing Effective Organizations.* San Francisco: Jossey-Bass, 2002.

Hamilton, Robert D. III, Virginia A. Taylor, and Roger J. Kashlak. "Designing a Control System for a Multinational Subsidiary." *Long Range Planning,* 29 (6), pp. 857–68.

Lasserre, Philippe. "Regional Headquarters: The Spearhead for Asia Pacific Markets." *Long Range Planning,* 29 (February 1996) pp. 30–37.

Naylor, Thomas H. "The International Strategy Matrix." *Columbia Journal of World Business,* Summer 1985, pp. 11–19.

Quelch, John A. "The New Country Managers." *McKinsey Quarterly,* 4 (1992), pp. 155–165.

Quelch, John A., and Helen Bloom. "The Return of the Country Manager." *McKinsey Quarterly,* 2 (1996), pp. 30–43.

Roberts, John. *The Modern Firm.* Oxford: Oxford University Press, 2004.

Snow, Charles C., Sue C. Davison, Scott A. Snell, and Donald C. Hambrick. "Use Transnational Teams to Globalize Your Company." *Organizational Dynamics,* Spring 1996, pp. 50–67.

Solberg, Carl Arthur. "Standardization or Adaptation of the International Marketing Mix: The Role of the Local Subsidiary/Representative." *Journal of International Marketing,* 8 (1), 2000 pp. 78–98.

"The New Organization: A Survey of the Company." *Economist,* January 21, 2006.

Tennant, Nancy, and Deborah L. Duarte. *Strategic Innovation.* San Francisco: Jossey-Bass, 2003.

Theuerkauf, Ingo, David Ernst, and Amir Mahini. "Think local, organize…?" *International Marketing Review,* 13 (3), 1996 pp. 7–12.

GLOBAL MARKETING AND THE INTERNET

19

CHAPTER OVERVIEW

1. THE INTERNET AND THE GLOBAL MARKETPLACE
2. STRUCTURAL BARRIERS TO GLOBAL E-COMMERCE
3. USE OF THE INTERNET FOR UNDERSTANDING GLOBAL BUYERS
4. COMPETITIVE ADVANTAGE AND CYBERSPACE
5. GLOBAL INTERNET CONSUMERS
6. INTERNET RAMIFICATIONS FOR GLOBAL MARKETING STRATEGIES

Although the obituaries of numerous dot.com companies were written during the dot.com bust, the Internet remains a technological marvel for global marketers. The Web clearly provides a unique distribution and communication channel to marketers across the globe. It is the ultimate marketplace to buy and to sell goods and services. The challenge for many global multinationals is to wring out the benefits that the Web offers. For scores of dot.com startups that initially focused on their home market, going global is likely to provide an avenue for further growth. Amazon.com foresees that Europe could ultimately prove to be a better place for doing **e-commerce** than the United States for two reasons: with Europe's high population density, (1) delivery is faster and (2) real estate prices are high in high-traffic city areas, leading to a cost advantage to virtual retailers over brick-and-mortar competitors.[1] eBay has already planted its foot in around 20 countries across the globe. Other Web firms are following suit. Small- and medium-size enterprises (SMEs) are also participating in the flurry. In fact, for many SMEs, the Internet has proven to be a welcome opportunity for overseas expansion.

Roughly speaking, the Internet is a network of computers interconnected throughout the world operating on a standard protocol that allows data to be transmitted. Participants in the network include universities, governments, companies, and research organizations, among others.[2] The Internet has been around for more than three

---

[1] "Jeff Bezos' Amazon Adventure," *Ad Age Global,* February 2002, pp. 16–17.
[2] Jim Hamill, "The Internet and International Marketing," *International Marketing Review,* 14 (5), 1997, pp. 300–323.

decades. The launch of the Sputnik in 1957 spurred the foundation of the Advanced Research Projects Agency (ARPA). One of ARPA's major achievements was the development of a standard protocol which allowed otherwise incompatible computers to communicate with one another. This protocol was basically the umbilical cord for the Internet. Until the early 1990s, the Internet was primarily the preserve of the military and academic researchers. However, the development of new software (e.g., Java, Netscape) during the early 1990s has turned the Internet into a commercial medium that has transformed businesses worldwide. In the advent of the forces unleashed by this new technology, this final chapter focuses on the impact of the Internet on global marketing. We first explore Internet developments in three regions: Asia, Europe, and Latin America. We will then turn to the major challenges that the use of the Internet poses for global marketers. The final part of the chapter considers the impact of the Web on global marketing strategies.

THE INTERNET AND THE GLOBAL MARKETPLACE ◆ ◆ ◆ ◆ ◆ ◆ ◆ ◆

Internet usage worldwide is growing rapidly. Although the Internet originated in the United States, it has rapidly turned into a global phenomenon. The worldwide Internet population surpassed 1 billion in 2005—up from only 45 million 10 years ago and 420 million in 2000.[3] Of these users, 80 percent live outside the United States. Current estimates foresee a global Internet population of 1.8 billion by 2010. Exhibit 19-1 presents a geographic breakdown of Internet usage worldwide. As you can see, the Internet population in China ranks second. By the year 2010, analysts estimate that China's Internet population will equal the entire U.S. population.[4] These projections underscore the growing importance of the Internet for marketers around the world. In this section, we explore the spread of the Web in three continents: Asia–Pacific, Europe, and Latin America.

Internet use in the Asia–Pacific region is growing rapidly. In fact, as you can see from Exhibit 19-1, Internet penetration in Japan and South Korea is higher now than in the United States. Most of the action in the region is in the business-to-business (B2B) area, which is the fastest growing segment of e-commerce. There seem to be two key-drivers behind the region's booming e-commerce. First, scores of government initiatives entice Asian companies to move online. Thailand passed a law that required all export and import documents to go online by the year 2000. Hong Kong established a "cyberport" and Singapore a "wired island." Likewise, the Chinese government has boosted the spread of e-commerce by cutting access charges and encouraging government departments to put up their own Web sites.

Asia–Pacific

The second factor is competitive pressure. In many industries, response time—the time to take orders and ship products—is often at least as critical as the cost factor. Asian manufacturers that are not able to slash their response times risk losing foreign customer accounts. Digital links between customers and suppliers offer a solution for Asian businesses that want to stay ahead of their competitors.[5] Some overseas customers such as Kmart and J.C. Penney now do business only with suppliers that know how to handle orders online.

Online shopping, on the other hand, is still a relatively modest phenomenon. There are about 1,400 Asian Internet retailers. Of those, more than half are located in South Korea (409) and Greater China (405)—China, Taiwan, and Hong Kong—combined.[6]

---

[3] http://www.c-i-a.com/pr0106.htm.
[4] http://news.bbc.co.uk/2/hi/business/4237122.stm.
[5] "Racing to Get Globally Wired," *Business Week,* April 20, 1998, pp. 24–25.
[6] "E-Commerce Takes Root in the Biggest Continent," *Asian Wall Street Journal,* October 27, 1999, pp. 1, 8.

EXHIBIT 19-1

TOP 15 COUNTRIES IN INTERNET USAGE

Country	Internet Users (in millions)	Active Users (in millions)	Worldwide Internet Population (as % of share)	Penetration (as % of country's population)
1. United States	197.8	142.7	18.3%	66.9%
2. China	119.5	NA	11.1	9.1
3. Japan	86.3	39.1	8.0	67.7
4. India	50.6	NA	4.7	4.7
5. Germany	46.3	31.8	4.3	56.0
6. United Kingdom	35.8	23.6	3.3	59.2
7. South Korea	33.9	NA	3.1	70.0
8. Italy	28.8	16.9	2.7	49.6
9. France	28.8	16.9	2.7	47.5
10. Brazil	25.9	12.5	2.4	13.9
11. Russia	23.7	NA	2.2	16.5
12. Canada	21.9	8.8	2.0	66.8
13. Indonesia	18.0	NA	1.7	7.4
14. Mexico	16.9	NA	1.6	15.9
15. Spain	15.8	11.1	1.5	39.2
Worldwide total	1,081.0	NA	100.0	16.8

Sources: http://www.c-i-a.com/pr0106.htm; and http://www.cia.gov/cia/publications/factbook/, accessed February 11, 2006. The term *active users* applies to people who go online at least once a month.

The most common products bought online by Asian users include books, magazines, and computer software.[7]

Although Web mania has taken hold of the region, several obstacles hinder the spread of B2B e-commerce in Asia. In many countries, businesspeople prefer to do business on a face-to-face basis instead of via anonymous channels. Cultivating relationships and networking is what really matters. Over time, this mindset will most likely change, but this may take a while. Another stumbling block for B2B e-commerce is the deeply rooted secrecy to which many Asian businesses, especially family-owned ones, adhere. Because of that mindset, companies are reluctant to share information with their suppliers. Another formidable hurdle to e-commerce growth is the knowledge barrier.[8] Talent to create and maintain Web sites is rare.

Likewise, B2C e-commerce is hampered by numerous barriers in Asia. In Asia's big metropolitan cities such as Hong Kong and Singapore, most consumers see no reason to buy merchandise online when most things can be easily bought in a nearby store. Shopping is often seen as an enjoyable pastime.[9] The credit card culture common in most Western countries has not taken off yet in Asia. Asian consumers are skittish about revealing their credit card numbers and other personal data to online retailers. Instead, they prefer to put a check in the mail or fax credit card information. There are other major structural barriers for B2C e-commerce in Asia. Apart from a polyglot of languages, e-tailers in Asia must cope with currency conversion, high shipping costs, and delivery delays. Finally, there is also a chicken-and-egg problem: Asian consumers find few compelling Web sites and Asian companies are reluctant to heavily invest when the critical mass is missing. With high broadband penetration, online shopping is more attractive in South Korea than in the rest of the region. In China, Web surfers

---

[7]"More Asians Shop Online but on Non-Asian Sites," *Asian Wall Street Journal,* November 1, 1999, p. 8.

[8]"Report for APEC Cites Barriers to E-Commerce Growth," *International Herald Tribune,* September 8, 1999, p. 15.

[9]"Shoppers Lost in Cyberspace," *Far Eastern Economic Review,* February 22, 2001, pp. 34–36.

◆ ◆

$\mathcal{G}$LOBAL PERSPECTIVE 19-1

SELLING VIA THE INTERNET IN CHINA

The number of Internet users in China was around 120 million at the end of 2005 according to a market research report compiled by *Computer Industry Almanac*. In terms of Internet usage, China now ranks second behind the United States but ahead of Japan, Germany, and the United Kingdom. However, industry research shows that most Chinese users go online for information (e.g., news) rather than for e-shopping. The Chinese government is eager to develop e-commerce, both B2C and B2B.

The Chinese e-commerce market was expected to be around US$76.5 billion by the end of 2005, although businesses face numerous hurdles:

- *Lack of payment options.* The Chinese credit card market is still underdeveloped, even though it is growing rapidly. Most online buyers have no access to electronic payment options. As a result, they must pay either on delivery or at their local post office. Companies often need to come up with creative solutions to address the payment problem. Dell China, for

Source: "China Hand" (September 2005), *Economist Intelligence Unit:* Chapter 9.

instance, offers its urban customers the option to pay for their order at local bank branches.

- *Shady operators.* According to one study, one of eight online buyers have ordered goods that never arrived. Not surprisingly, such shady practices have created a culture of mistrust.
- *Unreliable distribution channels.* Distribution is also a big obstacle. This is changing rapidly as some local companies are specializing in shipping goods ordered online.

The outlook for online shopping is bright. iResearch estimates that the B2C market in China will grow from $555 million in 2004 to $3.6 billion in 2007 as Chinese consumers grow more comfortable with online buying. eBay plans to turn China into its biggest market within a decade. It currently has 11.6 million registered users in China but faces a strong challenge from Taobao.com. Alibaba, the parent company of Taobao.com, sold a 40 percent stake in the firm to Yahoo! According to iResearch, China's online auction market could grow to $2.6 billion by 2007.

---

apparently have a positive attitude toward online shopping (see Global Perspective 19-1 for further information on China's Internet sector).[10]

After a slow start, Web usage in Europe is rapidly expanding. The largest growth is occurring in southern Europe, although Internet penetration is still far below the levels observed in northern Europe. Consumer spending at European Web sites has been growing at an amazing rate. The most popular items are computer hardware (44 percent), air travel (23 percent), books (14 percent), and music and software (5 percent each).[11] Travel companies such as SNCF, the French railroad company, and easyJet Airline, Europe's biggest discount carrier, saw their online sales revenues soar by 65 to 70 percent in 2002.[12] Small- and medium-size European companies are finding the Internet a low-cost way to broaden their geographic scope. As in Asia, their vendors become wired in order sustain a business relationship. One major catalyst in Europe for e-commerce is the launch of the euro. The euro makes it much easier for online European retailers to sell across borders. Other drivers behind the rise in e-commerce include: the rise of broadband, a drop in security concerns, and word of mouth.

Europe

Several challenges to e-commerce in Europe persist though. One major stumbling block is government red tape. An incredible maze of rules, laws, and regulations burden the development of e-commerce in the region, especially in Germany. For example, Germany's discount law ("Rabattgesetz") forbids special price offers to individual customers. The price of the product or service must be identical for everybody. Therefore, it is illegal in Germany to operate a reverse auction of the type that

---

[10]Ibid.

[11]"E-Shop Till You Drop," *Business Week,* February 9, 1998, pp. 18–19.

[12]"E-Commerce Is Starting to Click," *Business Week* (Asian Edition), August 26, 2002, pp. 24–25.

Priceline.com uses in which customers state the price they are willing to pay for a certain item. European firms, like their Asian counterparts, also face a knowledge barrier. Another hurdle in Europe is the lack of a credit card culture. Unlike Americans, Europeans are reluctant to reveal credit card numbers on the Internet. In addition, European Internet users also face higher costs of going online. Penetration of personal computers in southern Europe is still very low. This partly explains the digital divide between southern and northern Europe. The EU's rigid privacy constraints represent another barrier to e-commerce. The EU's privacy regulations to protect consumers are among the strictest in the world now. Consumers have the right to access their records. Web sites are also required to give consumers an option to opt out of having their records shared with third parties.

Latin America   Net fever is spreading rapidly in Latin America, although Internet penetration is still far lower than in other regions. Brazil has been one of the strongest e-commerce markets in the region, although Internet penetration is still fairly low. The country boasts almost 50 Internet service providers (ISPs), including local players such as Universo Online and global players such as AOL. Brazil also has the largest number of online retailers in the region. Two factors set Brazil apart from other Latin American markets: the high use of PCs and its technically sophisticated banking system. Online shopping habits of Latin American Internet users are similar to those of the rest of the world except for grocery shopping, which is far more popular in the area than elsewhere.

E-commerce in Latin America has been spurred by several factors. The Internet helps to level the playing field for companies bidding for contracts by offering fewer opportunities for corruption. Companies are also be able to slash their costs and increase productivity by linking up with their supply chain members. Cultural factors also affect e-commerce. People in Latin America do not enjoy shopping in person as much as their U.S. counterparts. Most would rather stay at home and shop.[13]

E-commerce in Latin America faces a number of obstacles, however. One is the high cost of Internet access; another is the maze of customs regulations and import duties that delay the arrival of goods and increase costs. For example, Dell's online customers in Brazil and Argentina must go to the main international airport to clear their purchases through customs.[14] Like their Asian and European counterparts, online shoppers in Latin America are reluctant to release their credit card number.[15]

♦ ♦ ♦ ♦ ♦ ♦ ♦ ♦   **STRUCTURAL BARRIERS TO GLOBAL E-COMMERCE**

Although most forecasts about the future of global e-commerce are rosy, several structural barriers might slow down its expansion. In particular, the following obstacles might interfere: (1) language barriers, (2) cultural barriers, (3) infrastructure (penetration of personal computers, broadband), (4) knowledge barriers, (5) access charges, and (6) government regulations. Let us look at each one of these in turn.

**Language   When Avis Europe PLC set up its global car-rental Web site in 1997, clients could
Barriers**   rent a car almost anywhere in the world—as long as they spoke English. Avis soon found that its English-only Web site was not enticing to non-English speakers. To win customers, it rolled out localized sites with the client's language.[16] The multilingual sites were also customized in other ways. For instance, the German site targets the business segment whereas the Spanish site focuses on leisure bookings. Because of the

---

[13] Ibid.

[14] Ibid.

[15] Check out the Internet surveys on www.nua.ie for updates on Internet developments in these and other regions.

[16] "Learning Local Languages Pays Off for Online Sellers," *Asian Wall Street Journal,* November 24–26, 2000, p. 12.

Internet's origins in the United States, it is not surprising that much of the content has a U.S. focus and that the English language has dominated the Web so far.

One recent survey of 186 U.S. online merchants found that 74 percent use English only on their sites and 79 percent present prices in U.S. dollars only.[17] However, the majority of Internet users now live outside English-speaking countries. One report anticipated that 57 percent of the Internet audience would speak a language other than English by the year 2005.[18] A study by Forrester Research found that business users on the Web are three times more likely to purchase when the Web site "speaks" their native language.[19] Hence, a company that plans to become a global e-business player may need to localize its Web sites to communicate with target customers in their native tongue. As Willy Brandt, a former German Chancellor, once put it, "If I'm selling to you, I speak your language. If I'm buying, *dann muessen Sie Deutsch sprechen"*—then you must speak German.

The demand for Web site localization services has boosted a new Web-oriented translation industry. For instance, WorldPoint (http://www.worldpoint.com) is a Honolulu-based firm with a network of 10,000 translators. The company offers a Web-based "localization" service that translates and edits documents such as annual reports, manuals, and marketing materials into a host of different languages, and not just text but also currencies, dates, and even color and image conventions. Translation fees range between 20 and 30 cents a word, depending on the languages involved. DaimlerChrysler hired WorldPoint to expand its Web presence into 65 markets.

Global Web marketers need to strike a balance between a multilingual polyglot approach and a single-language Web site. Obviously, the latter is much less costly to maintain, but the company can lose sales to sites that communicate in the client's language. Generally speaking, companies that want to localize their Web sites by translating the content into other languages have three options. The first is to hire a firm such as WorldPoint or use local people to do the translation job. This is a very time-consuming job and has huge operating costs. Another alternative is to use software that offers instantaneous translations. Although this option is less costly and time consuming than the first one, the results can be very imprecise. A third method is to pick a few key languages. Gillette, for example, set up a Web site for its Mach3 razor blade in Japanese and German after studying the number of Internet users in these countries.[20]

Cultural Barriers

Cultural norms and traditions can also hinder the spread of the Internet. In Confucian-based cultures (most East Asian nations), business is conducted on a personal basis. Networking and personal relationships play a major role in business transactions. Nonetheless, Dell was able to gain a foothold in markets in China and Hong Kong with its Dell Online business concept. Another impediment is the lack of a credit card culture and security concerns, as previously mentioned. Even where credit card penetration is high, online shoppers could be wary about releasing their credit card number and other personal data. Instead, Internet users end up giving the information through fax or over the phone to the online merchant. Advances in encryption and smart card technology may provide a solution on this front. However, even with enhanced security features, many Internet users still prefer to pay for their transactions offline.

Culture sensitivity also matters in Web site design.[21] On the U.S. site of Amazon .com, book delivery is promised with "Usually ships within 24 hours." On the U.K. site, the wording is "Usually dispatched within 24 hours." Books chosen go into a "shopping

---

[17]www.imediaconnection.com/global/5728.asp?ref = http://www.imediaconnection.com/content/6090.asp.

[18]"Majority of Users Will Be Non-English Speakers," www.nua.ie, accessed June 10, 1999.

[19]www.internetindicators.com/global.html.

[20]"the Internet," *Advertising Age International,* June 1999, pp. 42, 44.

[21]"Global Web site Design: It's All in the Translation," *International Herald Tribune,* March 22, 2001, p. 17.

cart'' on Amazon.com's U.S. site and into a ''shopping basket'' on the U.K. site. These are subtle distinctions, but they can be very important if a global Web marketer wants to lure foreign customers. By failing to respect the local cultural norms, companies run the risk of antagonizing the customers they are trying to attract. For instance, in the male-dominated Arab world, Web sites should avoid portraying women in roles of authority. In countries with strong individualism (e.g., the United States), Web sites should show how the product can improve the individual's life; in countries with a strong group sense (e.g., many Asian countries), a sales pitch should reveal how the product can benefit the group as a whole.

Symbols familiar in the home market do not necessarily have a universal meaning or may even offend foreign customers. A thumbs-up icon would indicate something good to U.S. consumers but would be insulting in Italy. Web site colors also convey different meanings. In Japan, soft pastels are effective, whereas in the United States bold and sharp tones work better in connecting with consumers.

One concern is that managers may overlook the need for cultural alertness when setting up a global online business operation. Traditionally, managers scouted local markets and communicated with local partners to become familiar with the local culture. With a virtual business, face-to-face contacts are minimal, especially for SMEs. One suggestion here is for managers to join Internet discussion groups and bulletin boards to learn about cultural norms and values in the foreign market.[22] Global Perspective 19-2 discusses how Dell surmounted cultural sensitive issues.

Infrastructure

In many countries, the local information technology (IT) infrastructure is a major obstacle that lessens the appeal of various markets for electronic commerce. One measure of interest here is Economist Intelligence Unit's annual ranking of e-readiness.[23] A country's e-readiness measures the extent of its Internet connectivity and technology (ICT) infrastructure and the ability of its consumers, businesses, and governments to use ICT to their benefit. Obviously, a key component of the measure relates to the hardware infrastructure: number of servers, Web sites, and mobile phones in the country. The index also captures other elements such as citizens' ability to utilize technology skillfully, the transparency of the country's business and legal environments, and the extent to which the government encourages the use of digital technologies. Exhibit 19-2 shows the e-readiness rankings and scores for 2006. Note that only one Asian market (Hong Kong) joined the top 10.

Most emerging markets rank very low in terms of e-readiness. This phenomenon is often referred to as the **digital divide** between rich and poor nations.[24] India (53rd) and China (57th), the two economic giants, actually dropped a few places in terms of overall e-readiness (four places down for India compared to 2005, three places down for China). This is in spite of the fact that these two countries together absorb nearly one-third of the world's investment in information and communications technology.

Knowledge Barrier

A report prepared for an APEC[25] meeting warned that none of the promises of the Internet can be exploited unless the **knowledge barrier** is dismantled.[26] Setting up an e-business requires certain knowledge skills that are usually not readily available. The hardware infrastructure problems and software-related challenges flowing from e-commerce burden small and large companies alike. Although the Internet has been touted as a level playing field for smaller businesses, such companies can have difficulty

---

[22] John Q. Quelch and Lisa R. Klein, ''The Internet and International Marketing,'' *Sloan Management Review*, Spring 1996, pp. 60–75.

[23] http://www.eiu.com/2006eReadinessRankings.

[24] http://news.bbc.co.uk/2/hi/technology/4296919.stm.

[25] Asia-Pacific Economic Cooperation.

[26] ''Report for APEC Cites Barriers to E-Commerce Growth,'' *International Herald Tribune*, September 8, 1999, p. 15.

GLOBAL PERSPECTIVE 19-2

LESSONS FROM DELL'S WEB GLOBALIZATION PROJECT

In October 2003, Dell Inc (www.dell.com) launched an enhanced global e-commerce site, followed by an upgraded service and support site in July 2004. The project had taken 3 years to complete and involved the joint efforts of 30 business teams. A key challenge of the web globalization project was the creation of a global online brand communication. To implement this task, Dell formed a core team, Global Brand Management (GBM), in spring 2002 with participants from the Americas, Asia, and Europe/Middle East. The main goal of their assignment was to develop a coherent visual interface design (VID) standard for Dell's Web sites balanced with local adaptations if necessary. The key issues in this endeavor centered around five VID components: corporate logotype and brand tagline; country names; national flags and country selection menu; language selection.

CORPORATE LOGOTYPE AND TAGLINE

The first VID issue dealt with the degree of localization of Dell's corporate icon. For regions not using Latin alphabets, westernized corporate names are typically phonetically transcribed for legal registration and to ease customer pronunciation. For some languages, choosing a proper phonetic equivalent is rarely easy. For instance, picking Chinese characters purely based on phonetics might lead to meaningless or even bizarre combinations. For the Dell brand name, the following character groupings all have a similar *dai er* sound: 怠饵 (*idle pastry*), 歹儿 (*evil child*), and 呆二 (*imbecile two*). In the case of Dell China, the corporate name in local script was rendered by 戴尔 *dai er* (*honor thus*), which projects a positive corporate image.

Although localizing the corporate icon could have benefits, it violates the spirit of a coherent imagery in terms of geometric dimensions, color schema, and typeface. A well-recognized and valued logotype can communicate a range of positive marketing messages (e.g., trust, product quality, prestige). For that reason, local Dell Web sites incorporate the blue corporate logotype with an angled E character even in regions not using Latin alphabets.

Another important brand element is the brand tagline. In October 2001, Dell had introduced the *Easy as Dell* slogan. For the homepages of many countries, Dell simply settled on the English tagline. However, for some countries, Dell opted to create an equivalent localized tagline. This was not always an easy task. For example, for the Japanese tagline, Dell's team came up with a pool of 60 candidates. In the end, the localized tagline became シンプルをあなたにデル *Sinpuru Anata ni Deru (Simple for you, Dell)*.

COUNTRY NAMES

Choosing the right country name for Dell's web sites was far less trivial than it sounds. Part of the discussion centered around using a country's official name or its short-form equivalent. The short form was chosen as the standard (e.g., *Mexico* instead of *Estados Unidos Méxicanos*). For some regions, Dell also needed to navigate around delicate political issues. For instance, to avoid controversy with mainland China, Dell chose for Taiwan the provincial name 台灣 *tai wan* instead of the Republic of China. The name was written in traditional Chinese characters, not the simplified script used in mainland China.

FLAG IDENTIFIERS AND COUNTRY SELECTOR MENU

Another delicate issue is the usage of flag identifiers. Flags carry many meanings. While for most countries flag identifiers are not controversial, Greater China poses obstacles. Focus group research showed that mainland Chinese might lodge objections over the display of the Taiwanese flag. As a result, no flag identifier is used for the Taiwan Web site. Likewise, the Korean Web site does not display any flag. A similar issue arose with the design of the country selector menu. For markets like Taiwan or Canada, the team inserted the phrase "Choose a country/region" to take a neutral stance. For other regions, it kept the original "Choose a country" phrase.

LANGUAGE SELECTION

Countries with multiple languages also needed a language toggle. Toggle options were decided for the respective regions based on socioeconomic factors. For instance, the Dell-Canada website displays the "English/Français" toggle, the Dell-Belgium website contains a "Nederlands/Français" toggle. Given the significance of English as a language of commerce, websites for markets such as Hong Kong, Taiwan, and Switzerland also include "English" as an option for the language toggle.

Sources: Leon Z. Lee, "Creating Worldwide Brand Recognition," *Multilingual Computing & Technology* 16 (1): 41–46 and Leon Z. Lee, "Virtual Teams: Formation, Flexibility, and Foresight in the Global Realm," *The Globalization Insider,* www.localization.org, accessed on April 16, 2005.

finding and hiring the talent needed to assist them in running an electronic storefront. Especially in emerging markets, the scarcity of proper talent and skills will restrain the development of a digital economy.

Computer illiteracy in some countries will also slow the adoption of the Internet. This obstacle, however, will likely be removed as training and education improves.

EXHIBIT 19-2
EIU E-READINESS RANKINGS 2006

Country	2006 E-Readiness Rank	2005 Rank	2006 E-Readiness Score (max. = 10)
Denmark	1	1	9.00
USA	2	2	8.81
Switzerland	3	4	8.64
Sweden	4	3	8.74
UK	5	5	8.64
Netherlands	6	8	8.60
Finland	7	6	8.55
Australia	8	10	8.50
Canada	9	12	8.37
Hong Kong	10	6	8.36
Norway	11	9	8.35
Germany	12	12	8.34
Singapore	13	11	8.24
Austria	14 (tie)	14	8.19
New Zealand	14 (tie)	16	8.19
Ireland	16	15	8.09
Belgium	17	17	7.99
South Korea	18	18	7.90
France	19	19	7.86
Bermuda	20	NA	7.81
Japan	21	21	7.77
Israel	22	20	7.59
Taiwan	23	22	7.51
Spain	24	23	7.34
Italy	25	24	7.14

EXHIBIT 19-2B
REGION 2006

Region	2006 Rank	E-Readiness Score (max. = 10)
North America	1	8.62
Western Europe	2	8.07
Asia–Pacific	3	5.77
Central and Eastern Europe	4	5.07
Latin America	5	4.91
Middle East and Africa	6	4.76

Source: Economist Intelligence Unit, 2006.

Also, new user-friendly devices and software products will sooner or later bridge the computer illiteracy gap for even the most computer-anxious consumers.

Access Charges Early in 1999, the Campaign for Unmetered Telecommunications (CUT) organized a Web boycott in several European countries. Internet users in Belgium, France, Italy, Poland, Portugal, Spain, and Switzerland were asked to go offline for 24 hours to protest high access charges. In October 1998, Italian Internet users repeatedly downloaded information from the Web site of Telecom Italia, thereby blocking access to the site for other users. The move was organized to protest an increase in local telephone rates. Similar campaigns have occurred in other countries as protest against high telecommunication charges.

In numerous countries, high Internet access charges are a sore point. Until March 1999, the cost to Chinese Internet users was 30 times higher than in the United States. The cost of surfing the Web typically consists of two parts: Internet subscription rates and telephone charges. While Internet subscription fees are often low or free of charge, telephone charges can be prohibitive. In markets with excessive access charges, comparison shopping becomes very costly. For instance, while eBay's U.S. customers may spend hours browsing the auction site, this is less likely in Europe where most people pay per minute phone charges for Internet access.[27] Furthermore, shoppers are less likely to complete a purchase transaction.

Government deregulation, increased competition, and new access alternatives (e.g., through cable TV) should put downward pressure on the cost of going online. Internet users in Germany used to pay between $6 and $28 per month for ISPs and then paid Deutsche Telekom 4 cents for each minute on the phone to their ISP. Even for moderate users, these charges easily led to bills of over $50 per month. New competitors now offer Internet access at much lower rates. Access to the Web in Japan used to be dominated by NTT, which charged sky-high fees. However, as new rivals such as Sony and SpeedNet (a joint venture between Softbank, Microsoft, and Tokyo Electric Power) enter the Web access market in Japan, access rates are falling rapidly.[28]

Legal Constraints and Government Regulations

Most governments are very enthusiastic about the Internet and the opportunities that e-commerce offers. Yet red tape and government regulations stall e-commerce in dozens of countries. Regulations on issues such as data protection, intellectual property rights, taxation, customs, and import duties vary across countries.

E-commerce is global; the law, on the other hand, is mostly national. Hence, one of the fundamental issues is the question of jurisdiction: Whose contract and consumer laws apply? These issues remain largely unsolved. Problems related to national laws are compounded by a shortage of legal precedents and experts who can interpret existing legislation. The European Union recently drafted legislation that states that the consumer's home jurisdiction applies to e-commerce purchases. In general, companies have two alternatives to handle legal concerns. They can either set up separate Web sites that comply with local laws or one mega-site that copes with every conceivable local legal requirement.[29]

To see how fragmented government regulations and laws affect e-commerce, consider the experience in Europe of Gateway, the U.S.-based PC-maker. When Gateway wanted to sell computers in Europe online, it initially planned to set up a single electronic storefront with different views for each separate market listing a different price. However, differences in value-added tax rates, currencies, and culture in the end forced Gateway to create separate Web sites for each individual European market.[30]

Several governments have been trying to come to terms with global e-commerce issues by issuing legislation that covers the various areas of concern. One area involves legal conflicts about domain names. AOL, for example, was engaged in a lengthy legal battle over the use of the "aol.com.br" domain name in Brazil with Curitiba America, a small local Internet concern.[31] One attempt to resolve such domain disputes was

[27]"EBay Steams into Europe," *Business Week* (Asian Edition), October 16, 2000, p. 32.

[28]"Finally, Japan's Netizens May Be Able to Afford the Net," *Business Week,* November 22, 1999.

[29]"Global E-commerce Law Comes under the Spotlight," *Financial Times,* December 23, 1999, p. 4. Gateway pulled out of Europe in the late 1990s.

[30]"Net Marketers Face Hurdles Abroad," *Advertising Age International,* June, 1999, p. 42.

[31]"AOL Waltzes into Brazil, Unprepared for the Samba," *New York Times,* December 11, 1999, p. B2.

the establishment of ICANN,[32] a nongovernmental body that handles such disputes through a process of mandatory arbitration.[33]

Aside from the barriers we discussed above there are others. Geographical distances can be a major constraint when goods need to be stocked and shipped. Shipping costs easily become a major hurdle for many e-shoppers, especially for bulky items. Delivery delays also increase with distance. Getting paid is another complicating factor. In many developing countries, credit card usage is still in its infancy. MNCs that engage in B2C[34] e-commerce in developing countries are usually forced to offer a range of payment options such as cash on delivery, wire transfers, and e-money.[35] Credit card fraud and lack of trust in general are other challenges. Several e-tailers have a black list of countries to which they refuse to ship because of past fraud problems. Currency conversion is also a headache.

◆ ◆ ◆ ◆ ◆ ◆ ◆ ◆ ◆ USE OF THE INTERNET FOR UNDERSTANDING GLOBAL BUYERS

The Internet has opened up new avenues for gathering market intelligence about consumers and competitors worldwide. It is without doubt one of the richest resources of secondary data available. One shortcoming is that the sheer wealth of data has led to an embarrassment of riches: How does one separate out the useful from the not-so-useful information? Advances in search engine technology will hopefully provide a solution.

In terms of primary research, the Internet has created some stunning possibilities.[36] Marketers can get instant feedback on new product concept or advertising copy. They can also set up worldwide consumer panels that can be used to track buying behavior and test out marketing mix programs. Other new measurement tools that are available include the following.[37]

- **Online surveys.** These could simply be surveys that are sent as attachments to e-mails to be filled out and sent back by the respondent. An alternative is a Web site survey that invites visitors to fill out a questionnaire on the Web site in question. A third possibility is the panel Web site survey. A panel is set up and each panel member has a password. When eligible for a survey, members are e-mailed a request to visit the Web site and fill out the survey.[38]

- **Bulletin boards and chat groups.** Online bulletin boards are virtual cork boards where visitors can post questions and responses. Chat groups are virtual discussion groups that hold online conversations on a topic of their choice. Companies can monitor and participate in bulletin board and chat group discussions in many countries simultaneously.

- **Web visitor tracking.** Servers automatically collect a tremendous amount of information on the surfing behavior of visitors such as the time spent on each page. Marketers can access and analyze this information to see how observed patterns relate to purchase transactions.

- **Virtual panels.** Web sites often require visitors to register. Visitor profiles can be used to run global **virtual panels.** Obviously, such panels will not be as reliable as traditional panels as the information thus collected may be inaccurate or incomplete.

---

[32] Internet Corporation for Assigned Names and Numbers (www.icann.org).

[33] "Global E-commerce," p. 4.

[34] Business to consumer.

[35] Stephen Hawk, "A Comparison of B2C E-Commerce in Developing Countries," *Electronic Commerce Research*, 4 (3), July 2004 181–199.

[36] Quelch and Klein, "The Internet and International Marketing," pp. 60–75.

[37] Ibid.

[38] Jonathan Dodd, "Market Research on the Internet—Threat or Opportunity," *Marketing and Research Today*, February 1998, pp. 60–66.

- **Focus groups.** An online focus group is set up by selecting participants who meet certain criteria. Subjects are told which chatroom to enter and when. They are run like ordinary focus groups. Not only can they be run worldwide, but transcripts are immediately available.[39]

Although online research can produce high-quality intelligence, it is imperative that one is aware of its shortcomings.[40] Sample representativeness could be a major issue when Internet users are not representative of the target population as a whole. This is especially a concern in countries where Internet access is still very low. When a sample is to be drawn, online research could be hampered through incorrect or outdated e-mail addresses.

With some of the survey methods described (e.g., Web site surveys), there could also be a self-selection bias. Web site visitors might also fill out the same questionnaire multiple times. It is also difficult to find out whether or not respondents are honest. Identity validation can also be a problem, especially when multiple people use the same e-mail address.

COMPETITIVE ADVANTAGE AND CYBERSPACE   ◆ ◆ ◆ ◆ ◆ ◆ ◆ ◆

The Internet offers two major benefits to companies that use the tool as a gateway to global marketing: cost/efficiency savings and accessibility ("connectivity"). Compared to traditional communication tools (e.g., media advertising, catalogs) and distribution channels, the costs of the Internet as a delivery channel are far lower. It also offers access to customers around the world. As a result, the value of some of the pre-Internet sources of competitive advantage has been deflated. One of these sources is scale. Some observers have argued that one of the major consequences of the Internet is that small and large firms are on an equal footing as far as global competition is concerned. Barriers to entry due to size have been dismantled. The advantages of size will disappear.[41] Barriers due to geographical space and time zones are no longer relevant.[42]

Although size-related advantages will probably lessen, claims that the Internet provides a level playing field for small and large global players alike are somewhat overblown. Large multinationals will still maintain an edge in most industries over their smaller competitors, especially in the global arena. Large firms still enjoy a substantial competitive advantage because of larger resources and more visibility among prospective customers worldwide. Deep pockets allow them to hire the best talent and buy the latest technologies in the area. Large multinationals can also tap into their global expertise to cope with the countless challenges that going international poses: the logistics of getting tangible goods to the customers, the different payment methods and currencies, the maze of rules and regulations, the need to cope with customs, and so forth. It is also more likely that target customers will find the Web site of a well-known large multinational rather than of a smaller company.[43]

Instead of size, technology is now being touted as a key source for competitive advantage. Although technology matters, marketing skills still play a major role in global marketing: "A site with the latest technologies but one that doesn't meet customer expectations will not make the cut."[44]

---

[39] Ibid.

[40] Ibid.

[41] "The Internet and International Marketing," p. 71.

[42] "The Integration of Internet Marketing," p. 13–14.

[43] Saeed Samiee, "The Internet and International Marketing: Is There a Fit?" *Journal of Interactive Marketing,* 12 (Autumn 1998), pp. 5–21.

[44] Howie Lau How Sin, "The Integration of Internet Marketing," *Economic Bulletin,* May 1998, p. 15.

EXHIBIT 19-3
WEB USAGE DECEMBER 2005

Country	Session/Visit per Person	Domains Visited per Person	PC Time per Person (hours : minutes)	Time to View of a Web Page (in seconds)
Australia	35	59	30:37	50
Brazil	28	53	29:37	44
France	41	87	35:17	38
Germany	34	77	30:33	36
Japan	25	76	14:57	31
Spain	36	71	30:43	45
Sweden	29	52	24:02	33
Switzerland	36	71	28:46	36
United Kingdom	31	69	25:14	40
United State of America	35	65	32:34	47

Note: Data for Japan were obtained for November 2004.

Source: http://www.nielsennetratings.com.

◆ ◆ ◆ ◆ ◆ ◆ ◆ ◆ **GLOBAL INTERNET CONSUMERS**

One of the tasks facing global marketers who plan e-commerce endeavors is to gain a solid understanding of their prospective customers. One question that arises is to what extent online customers differ from offline ones. A second issue is to what degree Internet buyers differ across cultures or countries: Do their preferences and buying motivations overlap, or do they differ and how? If they are indeed similar, companies can standardize their e-commerce strategies on a global or pan-regional basis, except for a few minor changes, such as language or shipping policies. If, on the other hand, there are significant differences, then a standardized Internet strategy might be a recipe for disaster.

So are there differences in the profile of Internet buyers across the globe or is there a prototype global Internet consumer? Do Web buyers worldwide have more in common with one another than consumers in the same country? The data reported in Exhibit 19-3 indicate clear differences in surfing behavior. Differences across countries are due to factors such as access charges and the availability of other entertainment options. What about variations in buying behavior among Internet users? One study organized by Accenture, an international management consulting firm, provides some answers.[45] The study sampled 515 individuals from 20 countries. The key finding of the study was that there are enormous regional differences. However, differences between countries *within* the same region were few. North Americans have a greater affinity for the Web, more trust, less anxiety, enjoy shopping more, and look for branded products more than in most other regions. They also showed the highest commitment to return to Web sites for purchases. Asians had the least favorable attitude toward the Web with the greatest fear about Internet shopping. Their intent to purchase through the Web and to return to Web sites was fairly low, despite their affinity for technology.

◆ ◆ ◆ ◆ ◆ ◆ ◆ ◆ **INTERNET RAMIFICATIONS FOR GLOBAL MARKETING STRATEGIES**

The Internet has been hyped as one of the most important marketing tools for the global marketers. Companies can use the Web to contact internal users (e.g., staff,

[45]Patrick D. Lynch and John C. Beck, "Profiles of Internet Buyers in 20 Countries: Evidence for Region-Specific Strategies," *Journal of International Business Studies,* 32 (4), 2001, pp. 725–48.

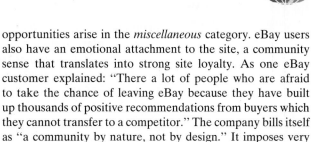

$\mathcal{G}$LOBAL PERSPECTIVE 19-3

EBAY: A GLOBAL FLEA MARKET

A *New Yorker* cartoon shows a woman driving a huge tractor into her living room to show it to friends. Its caption: "I got it from eBay." An eBay search on the magazine's cartoon-bank produces five other cartoons. Clearly, eBay has become part of the cultural landscape. eBay, the online auction group, was founded in the mid-90s by Pierre Omidyar, a young French computer programmer. To most venture capitalists, the idea of an online flea market was not exactly captivating. And yet, eBay managed to do something that very few other dotcoms were able to: it always made a profit. Its business model is basically very simple: match individual buyers and sellers online and take a cut of the transaction. What is behind eBay's profit potential? A mixture of no cost of goods, no inventories, low marketing costs, and no huge capital investments. eBay has turned into one of the world's most successful Internet enterprises with 38 million customers making deals of about $9.4 billion a year. Meg Whitman, eBay's current CEO, managed to turn the firm from a purely domestic company with auctions in 300 categories into a global empire spanning 21 countries and 16,000 categories. Categories now include computers, used cars, and time-share holidays. eBay has truly become a global trading platform.

eBay's biggest strength has been its willingness to listen and respond to its customers incessantly. Early on, it introduced buyer and seller feedback ratings and showed pictures of the goods being sold. When the firm launched Billpoint, many customers resented the new payment service. eBay quickly redesigned the site and explained that Billpoint was optional. eBay also constantly scans the site to see whether any new

opportunities arise in the *miscellaneous* category. eBay users also have an emotional attachment to the site, a community sense that translates into strong site loyalty. As one eBay customer explained: "There a lot of people who are afraid to take the chance of leaving eBay because they have built up thousands of positive recommendations from buyers which they cannot transfer to a competitor." The company bills itself as "a community by nature, not by design." It imposes very few restrictions on the merchandise being traded, although it stopped the auction of a human kidney and bans the sales of guns, alcohol, and tobacco.

eBay has patched together a global empire via a string of acquisitions (e.g., Alando in Germany, France) and start-ups (e.g., Japan, the U.K.). It dominates most of its markets. One notable exception is Japan where Yahoo! pre-empted eBay and has claimed leadership. eBay made two mistakes in Japan: It came in late (5 months after Yahoo! Japan launched its auction site) and it charged a commission for every transaction (Yahoo! Japan did not). The company claims that as a whole, its international business is profitable. China is the group's big ambition. In March 2002, the firm took a cautious first step by investing $30 million for a one-third stake in EachNet, a Shanghai company that runs the leading Internet auction Web site in China. It acquired the company fully in June 2003. eBay's aim is to turn China into its biggest market within a decade. In 2005, eBay dominated China's online auction market. It had some 11.6 million registered users. However, eBay now faces a strong challenge from Taobao.com, in which Yahoo! holds a major stake. Although eBay still dominates China's online auction market with a 65 percent market share (2004), Taobao.com (with a 29 percent market share) is growing fast. In the fourth quarter of 2005, Taobao registered an increase of 3.85 million new users compared to 2.8 million new users for eBay's Eachnet. eBay scrapped all sellers' transaction fees in China to meet local competitors' (including Yahoo!'s Taobao) free services.

Sources: "EBay, the Flea Market That Spanned the Globe," *Financial Times,* January 11, 2002, p. 18; "The Community That Listens to Customers," *Financial Times,* January 11, 2002, p. 18; "Success Depends on Rapid Growth Abroad," *Financial Times,* January 11, 2002, p. 18; "EBay Bids for a Piece of China," *Asian Wall Street Journal,* March 18, 2002, p. A12; "Auction Brawl," *Business Week* (Asian edition), June 4, 2001, pp. 18–19; http://www.ecommerce-guide .com/essentials/ebay/article.php/3578921.

---

salespeople) or external users (e.g., customers, suppliers, distributors) around the globe. Regardless of the target, the medium can be used effectively as a business model to generate revenues and/or cut costs. Indeed, quite a few entrepreneurs have been able to transform their Internet start-up into a global empire. Global Perspective 19-3 discusses one success story. We now consider in more detail how the Internet affects the various areas of international marketing.

Globally Integrated versus Locally Responsive Web Marketing Strategies[46]

At the core of any global web marketing strategy is the conflict between local responsiveness and global integration. By being in tune with the local market's demands, the MNC does a better job in satisfying its foreign customers. However, localization comes at a high price. By global or regional integration, the global Web marketer can achieve operational efficiencies in terms of setup, learning, and maintenance costs. MNCs can leverage these efficiencies to gain a competitive edge over local players or global rivals that use a different business model. These cost savings can be passed on to the distributors and end customers.

To a large extent, the type of strategy that is most appropriate will be driven by the nature of the product or service. Exhibit 19-4 provides a useful framework. The first class of goods covers "Look and feel" products. These are products where no gains can be made from global integration (e.g., because the local markets are large enough to get economies of scale). MNCs pursue a strategy of national differentiation for this class of products (Cell 1). A competitive edge is developed by adapting to unique characteristics of each individual country. Adaptations may be in terms of Web site design, language, shipping policies, assortment, and so forth. Given that such strategy can easily become expensive, MNCs should carefully deliberate whether market presence is really justified. The second class covers goods where neither local sensitivity nor global integration offers a competitive edge. A typical example is commodity-like products that are very local in nature because of perishability or bulkiness. Cell 3 involves goods where there is no need for localization but there are opportunities for global integration. As with the previous case, these are mostly commodity-like products. However, here a competitive advantage is achievable via global scale efficiencies. The last category is products or services that require both global integration and local sensitivity. A global Web marketing strategy for these goods demands a balancing act that allows the company to achieve scale economies while coping with local peculiarities. On the product side, a transnational strategy could be accomplished via mass customization.

One recent empirical study investigated 206 Web sites to explore how U.S. brands standardize their Web sites in four European countries (the United Kingdom, France, Germany, and Spain).[47] Most U.S. MNCs tailored the specific content of their country Web sites, especially textual information and visual images. However, a minimum level

EXHIBIT 19-4

GLOBAL INTERNET STRATEGIES ACCORDING TO NATURE OF GOOD OR SERVICE BEING SOLD

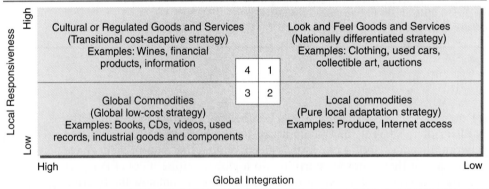

Source: Reprinted with permission from *Business Horizons,* May–June 2002. Copyright (2002) by the Trustees at Indiana University, Kelley School of Business.

---

[46]This section is based on Mauro F. Guillèn, "What Is the Best Global Strategy for the Internet?" *Business Horizons,* 45 (3), 2002, pp. 39–46.

[47]Shintaro Okazaki, "Searching the Web for Global Brands: How American Brands Standardise Their Web Sites in Europe," *European Journal of Marketing,* 39 (1/2), 2005, pp. 87–109.

of standardization was found for logos, colors, and layouts. Furthermore, the amount of Web standardization was larger for durable goods than for nondurables.

One-on-One Marketing

EZface (www.ezface.com) allows visitors to its Web site to get a free makeover. After registering, you can upload a digital photo of yourself and then experiment with skin color cosmetics, nail polish, eyewear, and other fashion accessories to create a new look. The results are displayed on the screen using proprietary software. Once you are satisfied with the results, you are ready to buy the products. Companies such as L'Oréal have integrated the service with their Web sites.

The interactive nature of the Internet has turned the medium into the "holy grail" for global marketers. Mass customization—both in terms of product offerings and promotion—on a global scale is now much easier because of the Internet. The mantra—target, aim, personalize, sell—is now much more than just a catchphrase. With traditional marketing, one-way communication was the norm. The Web, however, allows buyers and sellers worldwide to develop close relationships. Customers can get the information, products, and services that match their needs. Companies can communicate with their customers and prospects in a personalized and interactive manner through e-mail or other Internet tools.[48] By analyzing past buying patterns and conversing online with their consumers, firms such as Amazon.com are able to build customer profiles. Amazon sends book recommendations to its customers based on previous purchases and books bought by readers with similar tastes. Buyers are also invited to submit book reviews.

Product Policy

From a product policy perspective, the Internet offers rich opportunities. Given its intrinsic nature, the medium can be used to foster global brand building. The Internet also enables firms to develope new Internet-based products that can be rolled out globally.

Global Branding. One of the challenges that global Internet marketers face is the management of global brands on the Web.[49] Many MNCs allow their local subsidiaries to set up their own Web sites. Cultural fragmentation is often the main driver behind customization. Yahoo! deliberately puts its country managers in charge of the local Web site's content.[50] Yahoo! portals around the world carry the Yahoo! logo on top and offer standard services, but differences exist. In India (see in.yahoo.com), for instance, online auctions and online shopping are not offered because few people have credit cards. On the other hand, the India Yahoo! portal has features such as an astrology and a cricket channel that portals in other countries do not provide. By granting autonomy to its country managers, Yahoo! hopes to capitalize on its technology and global brand while catering to local customers.

Often, however, Web sites lack coordination and oversight. As a result, they are a collage projecting different images, visuals, content, and messages for the brand and/or company. Consequently, consumers who visit sites associated with the brand or the company can become confused. With global cult brands (e.g., Land Rover, Harley Davidson), the issue of multiple sites becomes further compounded as individual distributors and brand enthusiasts set up their own Web sites featuring the brand. This problem becomes especially thorny when the company tries to broadcast a single brand or corporate image. Therefore, just as with more traditional communication media such as advertising, some amount of coordination of the content and tone of Web sites under the MNC's control is a must when a consistent brand or company image is desirable.

---

[48] Howie Lau How Sin, "The Integration of Internet Marketing," *Economic Bulletin,* May 1998, pp. 13–15.

[49] Qucleh Klin "The Internet and International Marketing," p. 70.

[50] "Yahoo Uses Local Road in Drive to Expand Its Brand Across Asia," *Asian Wall Street Journal,* March 1, 2001, p. N1.

*G*LOBAL PERSPECTIVE 19-4

WHIRLPOOL: INNOVATION E-SPACE

In the late 1990s, Whirlpool Corp., the top U.S. appliance maker, launched a far-reaching effort to spark innovation spearheaded by its CEO Dave Whitwam. His goal was to turn the company into a customer-focused innovator whose products would breed consumer loyalty. To get innovative ideas, Whitwam realized that innovation could not come from some central product development team. Instead, he wanted to embed innovation as a core competency. Ideas should come from "everywhere and everyone": 60,000 employees across four continents, retail partners, and end customers. In other words, innovation should become a democratic process.

To get started, Whirlpool transformed its organization. It named a global vice president of innovation, reporting directly to the CEO. Whirlpool also appointed three vice presidents

Sources: "Innovation Democracy," *Computerworld,* February 16, 2004; and Nancy Tennant Snyder and Deborah L. Duarte, *Strategic Innovation* (San Francisco: Jossey-Bass, 2003).

of innovation and formed so-called I-teams of 25 each for its three largest regions: North America, Europe, and Latin America.

To facilitate the new innovation process, Whirlpool developed a new IT infrastructure. The goal of the new system was to track innovation efforts and disseminate the knowledge the I-teams generated. The first tracking system was the I-Pipe, which displayed the number of projects in each NPD stage and the incremental revenue each project could produce. Access was open to any Whirlpool employee via the company's intranet.

A package of online modules, dubbed the Innovation E-Space, was soon added to the original I-Pipe. E-Space is a place where Whirlpool employees can input suggestions and ideas, get feedback, volunteer for innovation projects, and track ideas as they move through the innovation pipeline. Any Whirlpool employee with intranet access can use the site.

Internet-Based New Product Development. MNCs increasingly use the Web to support different activities of the new product development (NPD) process.[51] The Internet provides a range of features that firms can leverage to bolster their NPD efforts: global coverage, speed, interactivity, and cost efficiencies. Companies such as Procter & Gamble rely on the Internet to solicit new product ideas from their customers worldwide. One concern, however, is that the people who take part in online idea generation may not represent target customers. MNCs can also employ the Web to coordinate their NPD activities. New product team members can communicate with one another and exchange product designs via the Internet. Global Perspective 19-4 discusses how Whirlpool Corporation used the Web to revamp its NPD process.

Marketing of Services The Internet heralds changes in the marketing of international services. Services differ from goods in four respects: (1) intangibility, (2) simultaneity, (3) heterogeneity, and (4) perishability. *Intangibility* means that services cannot be stored, protected through patents, or displayed. *Simultaneity* refers to the fact that services are typically produced and consumed at the same time. Service delivery is also *heterogeneous,* meaning that it depends on many uncontrollable factors. There is no guarantee that the service delivered will match the service that was promised. The final characteristic, *perishability,* refers to the fact that services usually cannot be saved, stored, resold, or returned. In the global marketplace, these issues become even more taxing because of environmental differences between foreign markets and the domestic market.

The Internet allows global service marketers to break the logjam posed by these challenges.[52] Consider the tangibility issue first. International service providers can use the Web to substantiate the service promises they make. For instance, international travelers who rent a car or book a hotel online can print out the confirmation note. Thereby they get instant tangible evidence of the transaction. Another way to manage

---

[51] Muammer Ozer, "Using the Internet in New Product Development," *Research Technology Management,* 46 (1), January/February 2003, pp. 10–16.

[52] Pierre Berthon, Leyland Pitt, Constantine S. Katsikeas, and Jean Paul Berthon, "Virtual Services Go International: International Services in the Marketspace," *Journal of International Marketing,* 7 (3), 1999, pp. 84–105.

intangibility is to offer samples of the service online. Visitors of the Amazon.com Web site can sample music or read book extracts before placing their order.

The Web also offers solutions to overcome the simultaneity issue. The fact that services in general need to be "manufactured" so to speak at the point of sale makes mass production difficult. However, simultaneity becomes less of an issue with the Internet. Indeed, mass customization is one of the major pluses of the Web based on information technology, data storage, and data processing capabilities. Services can be tailored easily via the Internet to the individual needs of the customer.

The Web also makes it easier for international service marketers to deal with the heterogeneity issue. The medium offers opportunities to standardize many aspects of the service provision, thereby making service transactions less unpredictable and more consistent. Elements such as greetings, reminders, and thank-you expressions can easily be standardized. Obviously, one risk here is that in some cultures customers could resent having the human element removed from service encounters. Therefore, one of the dilemmas that international service firms face is identifying the elements of the service provision that can be standardized. Because of cultural differences, these choices could differ across countries.

Finally, the Web also enables companies to manage perishability. Marketers can use their Web site to balance demand and supply.[53] A Web site gives service marketers the ability to offer 24-hour service to customers around the world. Geographic boundaries and time zones no longer matter. Marketers can also use their site to manage demand. Airlines occasionally use their Web site to sell seats via online auctions.

Global Pricing

Many MNCs that have set up a Web presence find that a downside of the Internet is that it makes global pricing decisions less flexible. The Web provides a window to customers and distributors alike on price levels for competing brands. Prospective customers around the world have access to an incredible wealth of price- and product-related information. Most European retailers that set up an electronic storefront have failed miserably to attract buyers. A key reason is that European Internet users quickly found out that they could order identical items from competing U.S.-based Web sites at a fraction of the European prices, even after shipping costs and other charges.

The Internet creates **cost transparency** for customers and distributors alike around the world. It now takes only a few clicks of a mouse to gather and compare price and product attribute information for a given product from the different markets where the product is sold. Various Web sites (e.g., Germany's DealPilot.com or Britain's shopguide.co.uk) offer price comparisons of different shopping sites, thereby lowering the search effort for e-shoppers. Customers can also sample the "price floor" through various auction sites sponsored by firms such as eBay.com or qxl.com. The information advantage that sellers traditionally enjoyed over buyers has dissipated due to the very nature of the Internet technology.

For global marketers, cost transparency creates several issues.[54] First and foremost, it severely impairs the firm's ability to sustain high margins for its products. In Europe, for example, powerful mega-retailers increasingly press their suppliers to charge one single price throughout the region. Transparency may also transform differentiated products into commodity-like goods, where the only point of difference is price. A third consequence, coupled to the previous one, is that cost transparency might undermine consumers' brand loyalties and make them more price conscious. The number-one purchase criterion becomes price. Rather than being loyal to a particular brand, consumers become more and more deal prone, buying the cheapest brand available within their consideration set of acceptable brands. Finally, cost transparency

[53] Leyland Pitt, Pierre Berthon, and Richard T. Watson, "Cyberservice: Taming Service Marketing Problems with the World Wide Web," *Business Horizons,* Jan/Feb. 1999, pp. 11–18.

[54] Indrajit Sinha, "Cost transparency and the Net," *Harvard Business Review,* 78, March/April 2000, 43–49. Iss. 2; p. 43.

may also raise questions among consumers about price unfairness. Because of various restrictions, customers in one country may not be unable to order the same product via the Internet at a lower price from another country. When they realize the product is much cheaper outside their country, consumers in high-price markets may feel that they are being taken for a ride unless the price gaps can be fully justified.

To cope with cost transparency due to the Internet, companies can pursue various routes. First, as we discussed in Chapter 13, firms can align their prices by, for instance, cutting prices in high-price countries and raising them in low-price markets. Second, firms can also "localize" their products so that they differ across countries, making comparison shopping less feasible. In some industries (e.g., pharmaceuticals, consumer electronics), manufacturers can also alert buyers to the adverse consequences of buying from low-price overseas suppliers. Risks that consumers could encounter include limited or no warranty coverage, lack of service support, and purchase of products that are not suitable (e.g., wrong technology standard) or that turn out to be counterfeit. Finally, outright refusal to handle orders from overseas buyers is another tactic.

Distribution

The Internet has also brought momentous changes for international distribution strategies. Firms that plan to make the Internet an integral part of their international distribution channel need to reflect on issues such as these: Should Internet distribution complement or replace our existing channels? Will the role of our current distributors change as a result of having the Internet as an additional channel medium? Should we allow our distributors to set up their own Internet channels? Global retailers, facing the onslaught of online sellers, need to decide whether they should remain a brick-and-mortar business or transform themselves into a **click-and-mortar** business by setting up a Web presence.

Role of Existing Channels.

Connectivity means that in many industries buyers can now hook up directly with manufacturers through the Internet, thereby bypassing existing channels. Some observers have gone so far as to claim that the Internet heralds the end of the middleman. Especially in Japan, where there are sometimes up to seven layers of distribution between the manufacturer and the end user, the Internet is likely to cut out many middlemen. Because of this redundancy process, some people foresee that the business-to-business e-commerce will grow more rapidly in Japan than in the United States.[55]

Although the Internet could diminish the role of intermediaries in certain businesses, distributors in most industries will still play a key role. Manufacturers that plan to add the Internet to their existing international channels need to ponder the effects of this new medium on the incumbent channels. In general, there are two possibilities: a **replacement effect** and a **complementary effect.** With the former, the Internet primarily cannibalizes existing distribution channels. With the latter, on the other hand, the Internet expands the overall business by offering a more attractive value proposition to prospective buyers. The extent to which the Internet has mostly a replacement or complementary impact will depend on the nature of the industry (see Exhibit 19-5).[56] Most likely, the effects also depend on the country. Manufacturers could have different distribution channels in place in the various countries where they operate. Also, when the product life cycle stage varies across markets, the effect of the Internet on incumbent channels will probably differ.

The most successful distributors will be those who are able to build new competences that leverage the Internet. The reason for having a distribution channel in the first place is the added value that the middleman offers. Traditionally, sources of added value have been scale, inventory, assortment, and so forth. With the rise of the Internet,

[55]"Web Cuts Out an Entire Order of Middlemen," *Financial Times,* January 5, 2000, p. 14.

[56]"Internet Distribution Strategies: Dilemmas for the Incumbent," *Mastering Information Management. Part Seven—Electronic Commerce, Financial Times,* supplement, March 15, 1999, pp. 6–7.

EXHIBIT 19-5
COMPLEMENTARY VERSUS REPLACEMENT
EFFECT OF THE INTERNET

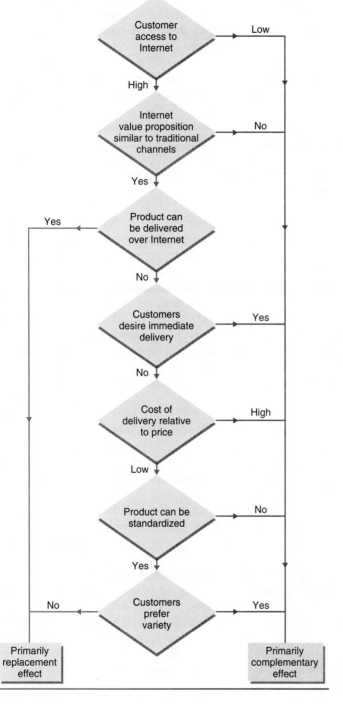

Source: Courtesy of Professor Nirmayal Kumar, London Business School.

distributors will need to look into novel ways to build competencies. For instance, one potential downside of the Internet is "information overload." Intermediaries can add value for their customers by collecting, interpreting, and disseminating information.[57]

Manufacturers who decide to incorporate the Web into their international distribution strategy also need to decide what approach to adopt.[58] One choice is not to

---

[57]"The Internet and International Marketing," p. 66.

[58]"Internet Distribution Strategies: Dilemmas for the Incumbent," p. 7.

use the Internet for purchase transactions and forbid distributors also from using it as a sales medium. In that case, Web sites accessible to outsiders would merely function as a product information tool. Another approach consists of allowing middlemen to sell goods over the Internet. However, the manufacturer itself would not sell directly via the Internet. One downside with this strategy is that sales from middlemen via the Internet may impinge on existing pricing policies and territorial restrictions. In the worst-case scenario, Internet sales could spur gray market activity. Another strategy is the complete opposite of the previous one. Internet sales are restricted to the manufacturer. A major risk here is that sales thus generated simply cannibalize incumbent resellers, thereby leading to channel conflicts. One way to counter such a risk is to sell different product lines through the various channels. However, resellers could dislike such differentiation strategy if it turns out that the product lines sold directly over the Internet are more popular than the ones allocated to them. Finally, companies can also pursue a free-for-all strategy where goods are sold directly through the Internet and manufacturers allow their resellers to sell online. It is then up to the market to settle on the ultimate winning combination.

E-Tailing Landscape. Some people have seen the battle between conventional bricks-and-mortar retailers and Internet retailers as a beauty contest with the cards stacked in favor of the latter. Consumers enjoy the convenience, the broad product assortment, and the product information provided by shopping Web sites. There are three e-tailing business models. First, there is the manufacturer's direct Web site by which it sells directly to the end customer. Second, there are the pure Web or virtual-only retailers. Pure Web retailers often have a price advantage over traditional retailers because they have lower property and warehousing costs. The third possibility is the **click-and-retailing model** in which the online presence becomes an extension of the traditional channel. Dozens of large retail chains have been trying to meet the challenge posed by pure Web retailers by setting up a Web site presence. By going online, these chains are able to combine the advantages of having a Web site presence with those of a physical presence.[59] Click-and-mortar retailers can cross-market between their Web site and their store outlets, thereby adding value for their clients. Customers have the advantage of being able to touch the goods or even try them on (clothing) before buying them online. They can pick up the goods ordered online at the local retail outlet to save shipping costs. Click-and-mortar retailers also often enjoy substantial brand equity whereas most pure Web retailers still need to invest a lot to build up a brand. As a result, their customer acquisition costs are generally much higher than for their click-and-mortar competitors. Most of them also have a financial advantage. Whereas retailers such as Wal-Mart, FNAC, and Bertelsmann have plenty of cash available, most pure cyber-retailers (e.g., Amazon) have only seen huge losses or minuscule profits so far. One final benefit is that local chains often have a better feel for the local culture. Most of the well-known brands in pure Web retailing (e.g., E-trade, Amazon.com) still have rather limited international expertise.

A good example of the clash between click-and-mortar and pure Internet retailers was the rivalry in France between FNAC, a leading French music and bookstore chain, and CDNOW, a U.S.-based online music vendor.[60] When CDNOW entered France and Germany, it added local language "gateways" to its U.S. Web site. For instance, French shoppers could place orders in French and pay in their local currency. FNAC launched a pre-emptive strike by setting up a music Web site to compete with CDNOW, but the latter enjoyed several competitive advantages. Sony and AOL Time Warner, two leading music content companies, had a major stake in CDNOW (37 percent each). This enabled CDNOW to offer international Internet shoppers the latest releases at bargain prices. As one of the pioneers in online retailing, CDNOW also enjoyed a technology advantage over FNAC. FNAC, on the other hand, also had

---

[59]"The Real Internet Revolution," *Economist,* August 21, 1999, pp. 53–54.

[60]"Storming a CD Bastille," *Business Week,* November 15, 1999, pp. 46–47.

several competitive advantages. It was able to use its Web site as an extension of its store network and vice versa. In France and other European countries, the FNAC brand name is a trusted brand with much more familiarity among consumers than the CDNOW brand name.

Whether the e-tailing business model will succeed in a particular country depends on a wide range of factors:[61]

- **Consumer behavior.** Will consumers value a Web site component? Does it add value (e.g., customization, information, larger selection, price)? Are there any valuable benefits of being part of an online community (e.g., eBay)? Are there concerns about releasing personal data or paying via a credit card online?

- **Cost structure.** Are the costs of distribution (shipping, logistics) and marketing acceptable?

- **Government policies.** What are the tax rules for buying online? Are they likely to change? Is there (or will there be) any restrictive privacy legislation or customs policies?

Global Communication and the Web

From a communication perspective, global marketers can leverage the Internet in two ways. The first is as a pure advertising medium. This can be done by using banner ads or more sophisticated forms. The second—and probably far more crucial—role is as a communication vehicle that allows the company to build customer ties.

Online Advertising. One use of the Web is as an advertising tool. In that function, Internet advertising complements other forms of promotion such as TV, radio, and outdoor displays. Online advertising spending, although still marginal, is growing rapidly. JupiterResearch forecasts that by 2009 advertising spending will grow to about $16.1 billion in the United States and $3.9 billion in Europe.[62] Overall, in almost all countries, Internet advertising is still a tiny slice of the global advertising pie, even in the developed world.

As a global, interactive broadcast medium, the Internet offers several advantages to international advertisers. One potent quality is the Internet's global reach. In principle, customers anywhere around the world can be targeted via Web advertisements. Online advertising is also far less expensive than more traditional forms of advertising, even though its rates are rising rapidly. The Internet also allows precision. The creative message can be replaced very easily. Online marketers can get precise information about Web site visitors based on visitor feedback, browsing behavior, and historical buying patterns. Interactivity and precision offer a potent mix to international Internet advertisers. Advertising messages can be customized to individual prospects. Advertisers can save money by sending the right message to the right people.[63] One more useful characteristic that sets the Internet apart from conventional advertising media is the fact that advertisers can instantly assess whether particular advertisement is working.

Internet advertising uses a wide spectrum of techniques. One form that is still popular is banner advertising. By clicking on the **banner ad,** users are taken to the advertiser's Web site where they can have more product information. Banners combined with buttons comprise about 60 percent of all online advertising.[64] Unfortunately, it is also the least effective technique. One form of online advertising, which is gaining increasing popularity, is search engine advertising based either on keyword search or Web site context. Keyword search advertising allows the company to have a link to its Web site when people are looking for product-related information. Advertisers pay a fee to the search engine provider only when users click on the link. Web site publishers

---

[61] Diane D. Wilson, "The Future of Internet Retailing: Bigger than Catalogs? Bigger than Bricks and Mortar?" *The World According to E: E-Commerce and E-Customers,* MSI Report No. 00–102, pp. 5–8.

[62] http://news.bbc.co.uk/2/hi/business/4203805.stm.

[63] "Advertising that Clicks," *Economist,* October 9, 1999, pp. 75–81.

[64] Ibid., p. 76.

can also earn advertising money by allowing the search engine company to display targeted advertising on its Web site related to its content.

A very effective form of online campaigns is the microsite that marketers often create to promote a particular brand. Such campaigns are often integrated with other communication tools. Dockers India created a new microsite (www.dockersindia.com) to promote a new range of Never-Iron 100% cotton pants in India. The site targeted 25 to 35-years old urban males. To drive visitors to the site, Dockers did online advertising on Web sites such as Yahoo! India, Rediff.com, and tech-oriented Zdnetindia.com. The campaign also had a viral marketing element by encouraging visitors via a lucky drawing to spread information about the site to their friends by word of mouth.[65]

Despite the appeal of Internet advertising as a medium, many advertisers are still quite wary about its potential as a global promotion tool. For one thing, there is the annoyance factor: Most people find online ads irritating. Audience measurement is still a major issue. To monitor the effectiveness of an online campaign, what should be the right metric? Should it be the number of views of the page that contains the ad or should it be the *click-through rate,* that is, the number of times that surfers click on the ad?[66] Too often, advertisers simply look at the click-through rate to determine whether an online ad campaign is working. The choice of metric to use depends on the purpose of the campaign.[67] If the goal is to sell or to gather a database, click-through rates, cost per acquisition, or cost per sale are possible metrics. However, if the campaign's purpose is to build the brand, gross impressions are more appropriate.

Several forms of online advertising take a long time to download. This can be irritating to users in countries where access and/or phone charges are high, especially in places where Internet access is slow. In many countries, access to the Internet is still quite limited. Therefore, the scope of Internet advertising could be restricted to a narrow segment of the target population. Also, the agency talent to create attractive Internet advertisements is lacking in many countries. Finally, international marketers that plan to use the Web as an advertising tool should familiarize themselves with advertising regulations and restrictions that apply in the foreign markets.[68] The ultimate success of an online campaign hinges on four factors:

- **The nature of the product.** Online advertising for some products is much more suitable than for others. For example, online campaigns would work for high-involvement goods whose buyers engage in product research and price comparisons (e.g., mortgages, travel).

- **The target.** Whether a campaign will work also depends on how well the target markets have been chosen. For mass-market campaigns, the Web is usually not the right medium.

- **Choice of site.** Picking the right sites is also vital. Ads on low-traffic niche sites are often more effective than ads on high-traffic general portals (e.g., Yahoo!).

- **Execution of the ad.** The quality of the production is also an important variable. No matter how many sites the banner ads appears on, if the banner is boring, it will fail to grab viewers' attention or build strong brand impressions.[69]

Apart from online advertising, global online marketers can use the Web for non-traditional communication campaigns. BMW lures potential clients with a virtual test drive on its Web site. It also set up a Web site—www.bmwfilms.com ⟨http://www.bmwfilms.com⟩—that showcases specially made short movies featuring BMW cars and starring Clive Owen. Each short movie was directed by an acclaimed Hollywood director (e.g., Ang Lee, Guy Richie).

---

[65]"Dockers Goes Online to Hit Target," *Media,* August 12, 2005, p. 16.

[66]"Caught in a Tangled "Web of Confusion,'" *Financial Times,* January 21, 2000.

[67]"Clients Must Look at Available Tools for Better Online Results," *Media,* August 9, 2002, p. 9.

[68]Richard C. Balough, "Websites Shouldn't Advertise Trouble," *Marketing News,* August 16, 1999, p. 15.

[69]"Netting Gains as Hype Dies Down," *Media,* August 23, 2002, pp. 16–17.

SUMMARY ◆

The Internet offers international marketers many promises. It can be leveraged to save costs and time and to generate revenues. Customers previously outside the marketer's reach now become easily accessible. The medium can be used to build brand equity or to showcase new products or services. For scores of businesses around the world, it has proven to be a cost-efficient distribution channel. It offers great potential as a global interactive advertising channel. One-to-one marketing to customers anywhere in the world is no longer a pipe dream.

Despite these advantages, marketers should not overlook the challenges that international Internet marketing poses. Some of those barriers are structural and can be difficult to overcome: government regulations, cultural barriers, lack of Internet access, the knowledge barrier, and so forth. Other challenges are strategic. Companies that want to embrace the Internet have to think about the implications of this medium for their global marketing strategy. Building a Web site does not automatically mean that consumers worldwide will beat a path to your door; they need to be lured to the site. Also, the site should be continuously updated and refreshed to entice first-time visitors to come back. Global marketers also need to balance the advantages of customized content versus the rewards of having a consistent worldwide image.

The Internet has brought profound changes for businesses around the world. It has created a new business paradigm: e-commerce. In a cover article in *The Atlantic* magazine, the late Peter Drucker wrote, "In the mental geography of e-commerce, distance has been eliminated. There is only one economy and only one market . . . every business must be globally competitive . . . the competition is not local anymore—in fact, it knows no boundaries."[70] For marketers, probably the most significant consequence of the Web is indeed that competition is no longer local. Any firm can set up a global business on the Internet from day one. Having an Internet presence has become a matter of survival for scores of companies. Suppliers who are reluctant to go online risk losing out to those who are not. Companies that do not develop a Web site presence soon risk having their customers browsing their competitors' sites for information.

[70]Peter Drucker, "Beyond the Information Revolution," *The Atlantic,* October 1999, pp. 47–57.

KEY TERMS ◆

Banner ad
Click-and-mortar retailer
Complementary effect

Cost transparency
Digital divide
E-commerce

Knowledge barrier
Online survey
Replacement effect

Virtual panel

REVIEW QUESTIONS ◆

1. What structural barriers impact the use of the Internet as an international marketing medium?

2. What advantages do click-and-mortar retailers have over pure Web retailers? What are the disadvantages?

3. Explain the notion of cost transparency in the context of the Internet. What are the possible solutions that marketers can use to cope with the problem?

4. In many countries, Internet infrastructure is far less sophisticated than in the United States. For example, phone lines are of poor quality and transmission rates are slow. What does poor infrastructure imply for "internationalizing" e-commerce?

5. One major dilemma for international Web marketers is the degree to which they should localize their Web sites. What forces favor centralization? Which factors could tilt the balance toward localization?

DISCUSSION QUESTIONS ◆ ◆ ◆ ◆ ◆ ◆ ◆ ◆ ◆ ◆ ◆ ◆ ◆ ◆ ◆ ◆ ◆ ◆ ◆

1. Some observers claim that the Internet is revolutionizing the way small- and medium-size companies (SMEs) can compete in the global market place. In essence, the Internet has created a level playing field for them. Before the Internet, SMEs had difficulty internationalizing, but now any mom-and-pop outfit can open an electronic storefront with a global reach. Do you agree? What downsides do small e-businesses face vis-à-vis large companies?

2. Dozens of Internet research firms such as Forrester Research and International Data Corp. issue projections and studies about the future of e-commerce and the Internet market in general. The figures usually vary wildly. For instance, when forecasts were made for the number of Internet users worldwide during 2000, predictions ranged from a low of 157 million (Morgan Stanley) to a high of 327 million users (Internet Industry Almanac). What explains this huge data disparity?

3. Go to the listing of Yahoo!'s international Web sites at world.yahoo.com. Pick three different countries (e.g., India, the United Kingdom, and Australia) and contrast the portals. How does the Web site design differ across these countries? What are the similarities? Discuss possible reasons behind these differences.

SHORT CASES

CASE 19-1

YAHOO! AND ALIBABA: SEEKING DOMINANCE IN CHINESE CYBERSPACE

People who thought that the Internet craze died during the dot.com bust of the late 1990s may have had groundhog day feelings in the summer of 2005. Early in August 2005, the share price of Baidu, a search engine company heralded as China's answer to Google, went up some 350 percent on the day of its US$4 billion initial public offering (IPO). Then, on August 11, 2005, Yahoo!, the U.S. portal, announced it would pay $1 billion for a 40 percent stake in Alibaba, a Chinese B2B portal, owned by Jack Ma. With 15 million registered users, Alibaba clearly offers great reach. Its two B2B Web sites generated around $5 billion worth of transactions in 2005. However, the portal had revenues of only $46 million in 2004. Taobao, its online auction Web site, rapidly became China's no. 2 consumer auction Web site behind Eachnet, the auction site owned by eBay. The quick market share increase, though, was partly due to Taobao's free services.

Jack Ma once compared local e-commerce companies such as Alibaba to crocodiles in the Yangtze River. He claimed that foreign "sharks" who swim up from the sea would have a hard time fighting the local crocodiles lurking in the river because "the smell of the water is different." Such logic must have resonated with Yahoo!. So far, foreign Internet players have had little success with their stand alone operations. Most of the top players in China's Internet market are home grown: Sina is the top portal; Baidu dominates the search engine market; and Shanda Interactive is the largest gaming company.

Jerry Yang, Yahoo!'s co-founder, said, "We are playing for the long term. We believe the prize is huge." No doubt, the Chinese Internet sector offers great promise. The value of all e-commerce transactions is expected to rise to around $217.5 billion by 2007. Online advertising is predicted to go up from $208 million in 2004 to $1 billion by 2009. China's online auction market could rise from $425 million in 2004 to $2.7 billion in 2007. However, riches are not guaranteed. Credit card usage, although on the rise, is still very limited. Foreign companies also need to cope with the challenges of

cultural and linguistic differences. Also, the Beijing government exercises strict control over the Internet. Policy or regulatory changes are a constant hazard for China's Internet companies. For instance, Communist party officials recently expressed unease over the spread of multiplayer role-playing games.

The Alibaba/Yahoo! deal closely resembles the cooperation model that Yahoo! used in Japan and that worked out very well in that market. According to the deal, Alibaba would take control of Yahoo's assets in China. The diversity of Alibaba's business could prove a clear strength. The company commands a strong position in B2B e-commerce. Other assets include Alipay, an online payment facility similar to eBay's Paypal, and Taobao, an eBaylike auction site. The assets thrown in by Yahoo! included its Internet portal, its e-mail service, a search engine (3721), and an online auction site (1Pai). The new operation covers almost all major Internet areas except for online gaming.

Skeptics view the diversity as a lack of focus. Some analysts have suggested that Yahoo! overpaid for its 40 percent share of Alibaba. Rival eBay's aspirations for China most likely triggered the deal. Meg Whitman, eBay's CEO, declared that China is a "must win" for the company. Rumor had it that eBay was courting Jack Ma.

There are immediate branding considerations on the horizon for the newly formed entity. The combination owns a mishmash of brands. Whether the Sino–U.S. marriage will be a success remains to be seen. Yahoo! offered a huge pile of cash and its Chinese brand portfolio. Alibaba already has a critical mass of 15 million registered users. The task for Jack Ma is to turn those eyeballs into profits.

DISCUSSION QUESTIONS

1. Was Yahoo! right to outsource its future in China to Alibaba?

2. The case points out that the Alibaba/Yahoo! combination led to a mishmash of Internet brands. How should Alibaba manage this mix of brands?

3. What other marketing actions would you prescribe for the Alibaba/Yahoo! combination to succeed?

4. Do you agree with some of the critics that the new entity lacks focus? What could be some of the advantages that diversity offers to Internet players in China?

Source: "Yahoo Search Is Complete: Alibaba Finds a Way to Reap the Riches of Online China," *Financial Times,* August 12, 2005, p. 9; "Crocodile Amid the Pebbles," *Financial Times,* August 12, 2005, p. 9; China Hand, Chapter 12, *Economist Intelligence,* (December 1, 2005) and "Seeking to Dominate Chinese Cyberspace," *Media,* December 2, 2005, p. 20.

ASE 19-2

NET-A-PORTER: SELLING DESIGNER CLOTHING TO NETIZENS

Few people have so far associated online B2C e-commerce with selling luxury brands or high-end fashion. However, Net-a-Porter, the U.K.-based high-end fashion e-tailer, does exactly that. Net-a-Porter is the brainchild of Natalie Massenet, a former fashion editor with *Tatler* magazine. Having worked in the industry on both sides of the Atlantic, Massenet realized that although women around the world want the latest designer clothes, few of them live near the trendy boutiques that sell the "in" look. She explains, "It was an obvious problem in the fashion industry. All the various media were telling women about what this season's look is but when it came to distribution, not everyone can get to a designer's boutique. Even those who do live in a major city don't always have the time to go out shopping, much as they'd love to. So, Net-a-Porter was formed because the media was creating a thirst for designer clothing that we didn't think was being met." As the *London Times* newspaper put it, "Women who live in Riyadh, Portofino, Monaco, Honolulu, and Gstaad use Net-a-Porter as they would a local boutique—if only they had one that stocked Jimmy Choo, Marc Jacobs, Diane von Furstenberg, ... "

Massenet insisted that the site should have the look and feel of an online magazine. The homepage (www.net-a -porter.com) is laid out in the style of a glossy fashion magazine cover. The Web site targets an international audience and can be viewed in English and Japanese. Web site visitors can read fashion articles, get fashion tips or gift advice, find out what is "new" in the fashion world, and, click on an item they want to order. The site adheres to designers' recommended retail prices. Massenet explains, "There's a real misperception that

Source: "Net-a-Porter: Designer Solutions," *NewMediaAge,* September 18, 2003, p. 22, "Profits in the Laptop of Luxury," *Financial Times,* May 13, 2004, p. 11: "Looking Good: Designer Clothing is starting to Find its Fit," *Wall Street Journal,* December 19, 2005, p. R11; and http://www.brandchannel.com/features_webwatch.asp?ww_id=205.

the Internet is just about consumers saving money or buying an unplanned last minute gift. There's now a significant body of consumers online who are willing to pay good money for luxury items. What we've always found is that people will buy for brands, so if they trust those brands then they don't mind spending online for them, even if it is sight unseen." With the high prices comes excellent service. Natalie Massenet says, "If a customer asks us to delay delivery until after her holiday, we offer to deliver to her resort." Purchases arrive wrapped "like a hat box carried by a hotel porter in a 1950s film set."

Clearly, consumers are more willing to buy fashion online. Online apparel sales in the U.S. were expected to grow to $12.5 billion in 2005. The percentage of Europeans who have bought clothes online tripled to 16 percent by mid-2005. Net-a-Porter's revenues doubled to about $21 million in 2005. What is behind the rise of online fashion buying? More shoppers have broadband access, making it easier for fashion Web sites to use data-rich applications and visuals. Another factor is celebrity mania. Celebrity watchers can use the Web to shop for the same fashion apparel their stars are wearing.

Still, there are major challenges for an e-tailer like Net-a-Porter. Several luxury and designer brands such as Tiffany, Gucci, and Armani are now selling online. Whether Net-a-Porter will become an e-tailer success story or another dot.com has-been remains to be seen.

DISCUSSION QUESTIONS

1. Visit the Net-a-Porter Web site (www.net-a-porter.com). How do you assess Net-a-Porter's business model? What are its key strengths? What are some potential vulnerabilities?

2. Why would luxury brands be hesitant to sell their clothes via Net-a-Porter?

3. Prepare a marketing action plan for Net-a-Porter to continue maintaining its growth momentum in the coming five years.

FURTHER READING

Berthon, Pierre, Leyland Pitt, Constantine S. Katsikeas, and Jean Paul Berthon. "Virtual Services Go International: International Services in the Marketspace". *Journal of International Marketing,* 7 (3), 1999, pp. 84–105.

Cronin, Mary J. *Global Advantage on the Internet: From Corporate Connectivity to International Competitiveness.* New York: Van Nostrand Reinhold, 1996.

Dodd, Jonathan. "Market Research on the Internet—Threat or Opportunity?" *Marketing and Research Today,* February 1998, pp. 60–67.

Garton, Steve. "An Assessment of Internet Users across and within Regions of the World". *Marketing and Research Today,* May 1999, 77–83.

Hamill, Jim. "The Internet and International Marketing". *International Marketing Review,* 14 (5), 1997, pp. 300–23.

Okazaki, Shintaro. "Searching the Web for Global Brands: How American Brands Standardise Their Web Sites in Europe". *European Journal of Marketing,* 39 (1/2), 2005, pp. 87–109.

Pitt, Leyland, Pierre Berthon, and Richard T. Watson. "Cyberservice: Taming Service Marketing Problems with the World Wide Web". *Business Horizons,* January–February 1999, 11–18.

Quelch, John A., and Lisa R. Klein. "The Internet and International Marketing". *Sloan Management Review*, Spring 1996, pp. 60–75.

Samiee, Saeed. "The Internet and International Marketing: Is There a Fit?" *Journal of Interactive Marketing*, 12 (4), Autumn 1998, pp. 5–21.

Samli, A. Coskun, James R. Wills, Jr., and Paul Herbig. "The Information Superhighway Goes International: Implications for Industrial Sales Transactions". *Industrial Marketing Management*, 26 (1997), pp. 51–58.

CASES

CASE OUTLINE

*Indicates available on the Web at: www.wiley.com/college/kotabe

CASE 1

CLUB MED: MAKING A COMEBACK

Club Méditerranée (Club Med), a corporation in the all-inclusive resort market, manages over 140 resort villages in Mediterranean, snow, inland, and tropical locales in over 40 countries. Its resorts do business under the Club Med, Valtur, Club Med Affaires (for business travelers), and Club Aquarius brand names. Club Med also operates tours and two cruise liners: *Club Med 1* cruises the Caribbean and the Mediterranean, and *Club Med 2* sails the Pacific. The company also arranges specialized sports facilities. Club Méditerranée's clientele is about one-third French, with the rest being mainly from North America and Japan.

Club Med found that its all-inclusive price is not as widely accepted today as it was in the past and that consumers' preferences have changed. Vacationers are not willing to spend large amounts of money for vacations that include many activities they are not using as much as they had been in the past. This change in preference poses a problem for the company because Club Med's competition has been able to customize travel packages for each consumer at prices that vacationers feel more comfortable with.

Although it appears easy for Club Med to customize travel packages, the company is at a disadvantage compared to its competition. Most of the competitors are found in a small number of locations, whereas Club Med has resorts scattered all over the world. Currency devaluation and political boycotts are some of the situations that Club Med faces worldwide on an ongoing basis. These external factors are reducing the company's ability to increase sales and gain new customers.

BACKGROUND AND HISTORY

Club Méditerranée, otherwise known as "Club Med," was originally founded by a group of travelers, headed by Gerald Blitz, in 1950. However, through the years, as this group was increasing in size, it was becoming increasingly more difficult to manage. Blitz, therefore, took the opportunity to turn this "association" into a business, with the aid of Gilbert Trigano, in 1954. Trigano sought to establish this organization, and by 1985, Club Méditerranée S.A. was transformed into a publicly traded company on the Paris Stock Exchange. Club Med Inc. became the U.S.-based subsidiary of Club Méditerranée, headed by Trigano's son Serge. Today, Club Med encompasses over 114 villages, on six continents, and 33 countries (see Exhibit 1). In addition, Club Med has two cruise ships.

The Club Med style can be best described by the sense of closeness found among the managers. All managers are former village chiefs and are therefore knowledgeable of the

This case was prepared by Karen Bartoletti, Alexandra Doiranlis, Steven Kustin, and Sharon Salamon of New York University's Stern School of Business and updated by Sonia Ketkar of Temple University under the supervision of Professor Masaaki Kotabe for class discussion rather than to illustrate either effective or ineffective management of a situation described (2006).

company's everyday operations. This immediately reflects on the "friendly" relationships that the GOs (Club Med-speak for assistants or gracious organizers) and GMs (Club Med-speak for guests or gracious members) have with each other, making every vacationer's experience a memorable one. A distinguishing feature of a Club Med resort is the living area, which is much simpler than that of a typical hotel chain. Rooms are sparsely decorated (i.e., no phones, televisions, etc.). Unlike typical hotel chains, Club Med measures its capacity in each resort by the number of beds, not the number of rooms, because singles have roommates. This simpler approach has made Club Med very successful. Another key to success was Club Med's image as a place to go when you want to escape. However, in the year 2004, after years of trying to make higher profits, the company altered its strategy hoping to make a comeback. The new strategy aimed at giving consumers a differentiated product that was more upscale and luxurious, especially in the Americas.

INDUSTRY STRUCTURE

Until 1986, Club Med had a very strong position in the all-inclusive resort market. The corporation's level of bargaining power with buyers, suppliers, and labor was high (see Exhibit 2). During that time period, a client interested in duplicating "the Club Med experience" would have had to pay an additional 50 percent to 100 percent to have an identical experience at other resorts (see Exhibit 3). With regard to suppliers, companies that provided vacation-related services, such as airlines, were willing to give Club Med significant discounts in exchange for mass bookings. In keeping with the advance in information technology and the value of the Web, Club Med launched a Web site www.clubmed.com at the end of 2003. The Internet now accounts for around 20 percent of its sales. This proved to be a huge boon to travel agents who check availability, prices, air fares, and even make bookings online. The Web site also allows travel agents to block reservations rather than book and confirm them for up to 48 hours. In 2004 Club Med developed a specialist program for travel agents. Under the program, the company certified 12,000 travel agents and apparently the certification has enabled the agents to increase bookings significantly. Finding labor was not a problem for this resort chain because thousands of people were interested in working at such a pleasurable location.

COMPETITION

As of 1986, Club Med began facing competition. This company was no longer the only all-inclusive resort. Many of the firm's competitors were realizing similar success. In 1986, most of the all-inclusive competitors had adopted Club Med's style of recreational activities, with staff members acting as directors of these organized games. By then, the only major difference that Club Med maintained was the fact that their price did not include drinks. At the start of the year 2004, after several years of listening to agents complain that vacationers

EXHIBIT 1

THE CLUB MEDITERRANEE GROUP VILLAGES WORLDWIDE

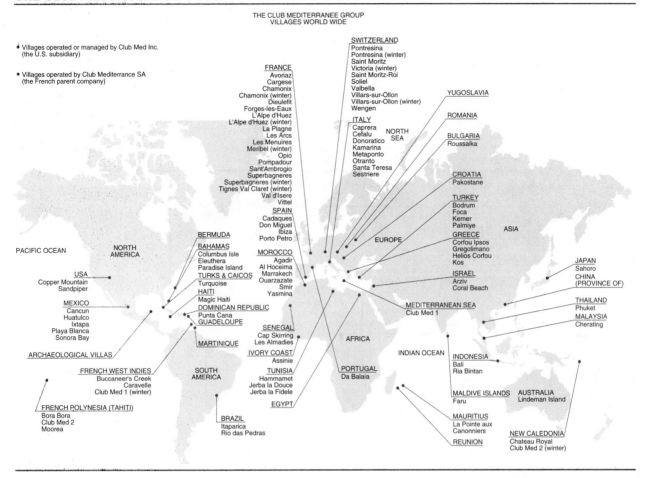

THE CLUB MEDITERRANEE GROUP
VILLAGES WORLD WIDE

♦ Villages operated or managed by Club Med Inc.
(the U.S. subsidiary)

• Villages operated by Club Mediterrance SA
(the French parent company)

SWITZERLAND
Pontresina
Pontresina (winter)
Saint Moritz
Victoria (winter)
Saint Moritz-Roi
Soliel
Valbella
Villars-sur-Ollon
Villars-sur-Ollon (winter)
Wengen

FRANCE
Avoriaz
Cargese
Chamonix
Chamonix (winter)
Dieulefit
Forges-les-Eaux
L'Alpe d'Huez
L'Alpe d'Huez (winter)
La Plagne
Les Arcs
Les Menuires
Meribel (winter)
Opio
Pompadour
Sant'Ambrogio
Superbagneres
Superbagneres (winter)
Tignes Val Claret (winter)
Val d'Isere
Vittel

SPAIN
Cadaques
Don Miguel
Ibiza
Porto Petro

ITALY
Caprera
Cefalu
Donoratico
Kamarina
Metaponto
Otranto
Santa Teresa
Sestriere

NORTH SEA

YUGOSLAVIA

ROMANIA

BULGARIA
Roussalka

CROATIA
Pakostane

TURKEY
Bodrum
Foca
Kemer
Palmiye

GREECE
Corfou Ipsos
Gregolimano
Helios Corfou
Kos

ISRAEL
Arziv
Coral Beach

ASIA

JAPAN
Sahoro
CHINA
(PROVINCE OF)

THAILAND
Phuket
MALAYSIA
Cherating

EUROPE

PACIFIC OCEAN

NORTH AMERICA

USA
Copper Mountain
Sandpiper

MEXICO
Cancun
Huatulco
Ixtapa
Playa Blanca
Sonora Bay

ARCHAEOLOGICAL VILLAS

BERMUDA

BAHAMAS
Columbus Isle
Eleuthera
Paradise Island

TURKS & CAICOS
Turquoise

HAITI
Magic Haiti

DOMINICAN REPUBLIC
Punta Cana
GUADELOUPE

MOROCCO
Agadir
Al Hoceima
Marrakech
Ouarzazate
Smir
Yasmina

MARTINIQUE

FRENCH WEST INDIES
Buccaneer's Creek
Caravelle
Club Med 1 (winter)

FRENCH POLYNESIA (TAHITI)
Bora Bora
Club Med 2
Moorea

SOUTH AMERICA

SENEGAL
Cap Skirring
Les Almadies

IVORY COAST
Assinie

TUNISIA
Hammamet
Jerba la Douce
Jerba la Fidele

EGYPT

BRAZIL
Itaparica
Rio das Pedras

AFRICA

PORTUGAL
Da Balaia

MEDITERRANEAN SEA
Club Med 1

INDIAN OCEAN

INDONESIA
Bali
Ria Bintan

MALDIVE ISLANDS
Faru

MAURITIUS
La Pointe aux
Canonniers

REUNION

AUSTRALIA
Lindeman Island

NEW CALEDONIA
Chateau Royal
Club Med 2 (winter)

were skeptical above booking Club Med resorts due to its exclusive prices, Club Med reverted to an all-inclusive deal and launched its "total" all-inclusive package in most of its villages. In the first part of 2005, the company declared the Alps area, in which it operates 22 villages, a cash-free zone, meaning that an all-inclusive package with snacks and drinks around the clock. That area of the world being a major ski locale, it attracts thousands of people every year. Therefore, Club Med has also launched ski programs for its members at its resorts around the Alps.

One competitor, Jack Tar Village, the Jamaica-based company, operates resorts located mostly in the Caribbean. Jack Tar positions the resorts as more glamorous and modern than those of Club Med. This can be seen in advertisements where the company implicitly criticizes the spartan rooms and methods of Club Med. Jack Tar's claim to fame in relation to Club Med is its open-bar policy.

Another competitor that the firm must consider is the SuperClubs Organization, which operates four resorts in Jamaica. These resorts have reputations for being the most uninhibited and sexually oriented resorts. SuperClubs also follow a system of having drinks included in their price, but the other distinction from Club Med is the vacation's packaging and distribution. Club Med bundles the ground transportation with the rest of their packages while air transportation was

to be distributed directly to consumers or travel agencies. SuperClubs, on the other hand, bundled ground transportation packages to be sold through large tour wholesalers, who in turn grouped these packages to be sold to the travel agencies.

Activities that Club Med and their competition offer are similar, but the way they are offered is somewhat different. Club Med's competitors offer the same activities but do not include them in the initial price of the vacation. A few of SuperClubs' activities that were included were tennis, basketball, and exercise rooms, but jet-skiing and parasailing were available for an additional fee. This allowed Club Med's competitors to offer lower prices and take away potential clients from Club Med. This concept has worked for the competition because consumers find that they are not using all the activities offered. Therefore, there is no reason to pay an all-inclusive price. Club Med, on the other hand, suffers from ecological, economic, and political constraints that prevent the firm from using this individual pricing method, which could lead to customized packages for vacationers.

THE SERVICE CONCEPT

Club Med has a worldwide presence in the resort vacation business that has allowed the firm to grow and dominate this industry. The original mission statement includes the idea that the company's goal is to take a group of strangers away from

EXHIBIT 2
FORCES DRIVING INDUSTRY COMPETITION

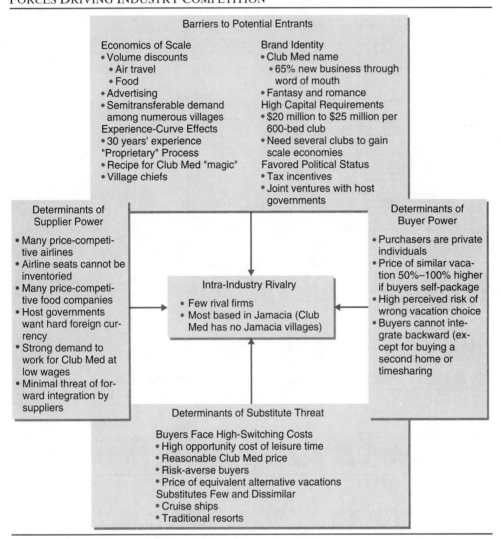

Barriers to Potential Entrants

Economics of Scale
- Volume discounts
  - Air travel
  - Food
- Advertising
- Semitransferable demand among numerous villages

Experience-Curve Effects
- 30 years' experience

"Proprietary" Process
- Recipe for Club Med "magic"
- Village chiefs

Brand Identity
- Club Med name
  - 65% new business through word of mouth
- Fantasy and romance

High Capital Requirements
- $20 million to $25 million per 600-bed club
- Need several clubs to gain scale economies

Favored Political Status
- Tax incentives
- Joint ventures with host governments

Determinants of Supplier Power
- Many price-competitive airlines
- Airline seats cannot be inventoried
- Many price-competitive food companies
- Host governments want hard foreign currency
- Strong demand to work for Club Med at low wages
- Minimal threat of forward integration by suppliers

Intra-Industry Rivalry
- Few rival firms
- Most based in Jamacia (Club Med has no Jamacia villages)

Determinants of Buyer Power
- Purchasers are private individuals
- Price of similar vacation 50%–100% higher if buyers self-package
- High perceived risk of wrong vacation choice
- Buyers cannot integrate backward (except for buying a second home or timesharing)

Determinants of Substitute Threat

Buyers Face High-Switching Costs
- High opportunity cost of leisure time
- Reasonable Club Med price
- Risk-averse buyers
- Price of equivalent alternative vacations

Substitutes Few and Dissimilar
- Cruise ships
- Traditional resorts

EXHIBIT 3
COST COMPARISON

Average Costing of a 7-day holiday in Don Miguel	*Normal Marbella Prices*	*Typical Club Med Holiday*
Return airfare London/Málaga	£199	Included
Coach transfer to resort	£20	Included
U.K. government departure taxes	£5	Included
Hotel (3-star equivalent) & breakfast	£300	Included
Seven three-course lunches (@ £15)	£105	Included
Wine with lunch and dinner (7 bottles @ £5)	£35	Included
Seven three-course dinners (@ £17)	£119	Included
Cycling (6 days @ £5/hr)	£30	Included
Tennis lessons (6 days @ £8/hr)	£48	Included
Night club entrance (6 × £5)	£30	Included
Tips to staff (7 × £2)	£14	Included
Child care facilities (6 × 4 hrs @ £5/hr)	£120	Included
Total	£1,025	From £569

Other activities/facilities included in the price at Club Med Don Miguel: Swimming Pool, Circus School, Archery, Weights Room, Keepfit Classes, Specialty Restaurant, Bridge, Evening Entertainment/Shows, Ping Pong, Jacuzzi, Sauna, Hamman. Other on-site conveniences at Club Med: Bank, Boutique, Medical Center, Bars (bar drinks extra cost), Car Rental, and Laundry Service.

their everyday lives and bring them together in a relaxing and fun atmosphere in different parts of the world. This feeling can be expected in any of the 110 resorts. This mission is the key to Club Med's competitive advantage. Consumers anywhere in the world know they will get the same preferential treatment while they are in the Club Med villages.

The company's strategy of keeping members coming back is carried out by having their guests join a club as members with an initiation fee as well as annual dues. With the membership, they receive newsletters, catalogs featuring their resorts, and discounts on future Club Med vacations. This makes people feel more like a part of the Club Med and creates strong brand loyalty. In fact, an average Club Med vacationer revisits four times after their initial stay at one of its resorts.

All Club Med villages are similar in their setup regardless of what part of the world they are located. The resort sites are carefully chosen by taking into consideration the natural beauty (i.e., scenic views, beachfront, woodland, no swampland, etc.), good weather, and recreational potential. Each resort has approximately 40 acres to accommodate all the planned activities: windsurfing, sailing, basketball, volleyball, tennis, and so on. The resorts' secluded atmosphere is further exemplified by the lack of daily "conveniences" such as: TV, clocks, radios, even writing paper. This is done to separate individuals from civilization so they can relax as much as possible. However, under the new luxury experience model, Club Med is in fact adding room facilities in some of its resorts.

Club Med organizes everything in a manner that encourages social interaction between guests. The rooms are built around core facilities such as the pool. Meals are done buffet style, and the tables seat six to eight people so guests can sit and meet with many different people at every meal.

All activities and meals are included in the fee paid before the vacation begins. The only exceptions are bar drinks and items purchased in the small shops; those items are put on a tab and paid for at the end of the vacation as guests check out. The goal behind this all-inclusive price is to limit the number of financial decisions made by the guests so that, once again, they do not have to think of the pressures of the "real world."

Each day the guests have a choice of participating in a variety of activities. As evening sets in, there are choices for after-dinner activities such as dancing and shows. All activities are designed to encourage guests to join in. Even the shows allow for audience participation.

PROBLEMS

Until 1996, Club Mediterranée was predicted to have strong sales growth due to successful market penetration in other countries (see Exhibit 4). However, the same expansion that helped the firm become famous may be the cause of the firm's disadvantage in relation to its competitors. Club Med does not have as large of a sales increase as it had anticipated. This is due to economic and ecological disasters in countries where Club Med resorts are located. This makes it difficult for Club Med to maintain its beautiful resorts in countries that suffer from such disasters.

With this knowledge taken into consideration, contracts are drawn up between Club Med and the government of the corresponding country. The key clause in these contracts states that if Club Med is allowed to enter the country, the firm

will increase tourism in the area. In turn, the government will provide financial aid to help pay for the costs of maintaining the new resort facilities.

EXHIBIT 4
REVENUES BY REGION (2002)

France	32%
Europe (excluding France)	20%
America	17.7%
Asia	10.2%

Joint ventures with host governments have not proven to be as profitable as expected. An example of such a disappointment occurred when the Mexican government agreed to maintain Club Med's facilities if the corporation would increase Mexico's tourism level. However, unexpected occurrences, such as depreciation in the country's currency, limited the amount of capital the Mexican government could allocate to maintain the resort's facilities. This put Club Med in a difficult situation when the firm had to suddenly maintain its facilities with less government funds than expected. Although Club Med's resorts are very profitable in Mexico, the devaluation of the peso has caused Club Med's maintenance costs to rise dramatically. This in turn prevents Club Med from reducing its prices and offering customized packages to its vacationers.

A second example of how international resorts reduce the firm's ability to compete effectively is Club Med's penetration into France. The resorts in the area had been doing well until March 1996. At that time, it became known that France had been conducting nuclear tests in the South Pacific. This caused Club Mediterranée to receive fewer bookings than expected in its Tahiti-based resorts. Tourists avoided these resorts because of riots among residents concerned about the testing; this resulted in negative publicity in this part of the world. The riots, which often occurred in airports, deterred potential tourists from flying into this region.

Another significant event in the history of Club Med was September 11, 2001, in the United States, which caused a considerable reduction in travel the world over. For Club Med, however, it was followed by the closing of 15 of its villages. Since then, it has reopened six and opened four new villages.

The hurricanes in the Caribbean in 2004 also caused some serious damage to Club Med's resorts in those regions. The company had to rebuild its Punta Cana village and at the time it gave out hurricane protection certificates that allowed guests who had lost out on vacation days due to the category 1 hurricane. Guests can exchange those certificates for travel to that destination in the future.

Worse still, the terrible tsunami disaster in South East Asia devoured most of its coastline and Club Med's properties in Malaysia, Phuket, and the Maldives. Furthermore, the region has experienced a huge reduction in tourism.

Happenings in one area where Club Med is based often indirectly affect other Club Med resorts as well. With a lower clientele in its Tahiti-based resorts, and in the surrounding territories, Club Med experiences lower revenues and, therefore, acquires less money to maintain these resorts. As a result, the firm compensates for such losses by using the profits from other resorts that have not suffered from similar disasters. Problems such as these prevent Club Med from reducing prices by implementing a customized travel package, which would enable the firm to compete more effectively in the vacation resort market.

WHAT LIES AHEAD?

Club Med fell on hard financial times through much of the 1990s, as a result of rundown properties, a reputation for mediocre food and amenities, the aging of the baby boomers, a backlash against the sexual revolution, and an inconsistent message that was filtered through eight advertising agencies in different countries.

In 1998, Philippe Bourguignon, who is credited with turning around Euro Disney, was brought in as the new chairman to stem the decline. He immediately instigated a $500-million, three-year rescue program. Unprofitable villages and some sales offices were closed, and older resorts are being refurbished. Thanks to the new chairman's leadership, Club Med is making a comeback. Attendance is rising, the company turned a modest profit last year, and 74 villages are undergoing a $350 million restructuring. In April 1999, after the growth strategy was put into action, the stock bounced back from a 12-month low of $63.67 to close at $84.17. Occupancy rose to 72.3 percent last year, up from 69.1 percent in the 1997 fiscal year and 66.9 percent in the 1996 fiscal year to 73.7 percent in 2000. In fiscal 1998, attendance at Club Med rose 5 percent to almost 1.6 million, although it is still well below the record 1.8 million set in 1989. Equally important, after huge losses in both 1997 ($215 million) and 1996 ($130 million), the company earned $30 million in revenue of $1.5 billion in sales. In 2001, revenues were up 5.1 percent, to 1.985 billion euros. Although many problems still confront the resort club, such as a 10 percent loss of room space because of renovations, Club Med appears to be back on track to success.

The company finally reported a net profit of 3 million euros for the six months ended April 2005 compared with a loss of 4 million euros the previous year, its first time in four years, despite calamities such as the devastating tsunami in the Indian Ocean and the continuous storms in the Caribbean, which caused a drop of 4.3 percent in sales. The company also attributed this positive profitability to a slight change in its strategy away from "two-trident" properties to a more upscale position. Boosted by these results, the company is aiming at an operating profit of 100 million euros in the year 2006.

After serious losses and cash problems in 2002, former chairman Bourguignon resigned and Henri Giscard d'Estaing was appointed as the new chairman. With this new appointment, the company started looking toward a change in strategy and a brighter future. Current management is well aware of the strong brand recognition that Club Med holds. It is synonymous with the pursuit of pleasure. However, management would like to alter this perception. It would like to eliminate the perception of Club Med as a "swingers" paradise. Even if Club Med wanted it to be such a resort, it would be virtually impossible to compete with resorts that have sprung up in Europe, Asia and the Caribbean in recent years catering exclusively to hedonistic life styles. But Club Med has not just been renovating properties. A big change is the decision to concentrate its sales and marketing efforts on France, the United States, Canada, Belgium, Japan, Italy, Germany and Switzerland. These countries account for 74 percent of visitors. Club Med also plans to enter the Chinese market once again. It tried to enter China a few times before but the effort was largely unsuccessful. Therefore, this time it will not open a resort until it has developed brand familiarity in China by opening a sales office first. The company intends to follow this similar strategy it adopted while entering the South Korean market, which has been growing every year. In January 2005, the company announced that it was opening its first report in Albania. The company's next step is opening villages in Italy and Brazil.

The U.S. is Club Med's No. 1 target. To increase U.S. visitors, Club Med is considering opening three new resorts around the U.S., one of them being a resort for couples in the Dominican Republic, another being a family report in the Yucatan Peninsula near Mexico, and the third being a family resort in Brazil. It has invested over $350 million from 1998 to 2004, in advertising to rejuvenate their strong brand name in the U.S., which has been misunderstood because of poor advertising campaigns. Each village is now ranked with two, three, or four tridents, based on amenities and comfort level, with the result that the 13 budget Club Aquarius villages are being folded into the two-trident category. A major expansion is under way around the Pacific Rim, including new resorts in Indonesia, China, the Philippines, and Vietnam. As part of its agenda to promote itself and leverage occupancy, Club Med has started entering strategic alliances with firms all over the world. In November 2002, it signed a deal with match.com, an online dating company and a part of USA interactive, to offer vacation packages for singles who could 'casually' meet people in a different setting. This was part of its focus on the American customer.

In the year 2004, Club Med executed its new upmarket strategy. Prior to that, French hospitality group Accor had acquired a 28.9 percent stake in Club Med, which provided it with the much needed financial assistance and association with a powerful ally. To start with, it changed its brand identity and logo with a makeover expenditure of more than 500 million euros. The company believed that with consumers' changing preferences, these were looking for a different vacation experience and it launched its New Luxury product. This included major renovations at its U.S. locations, namely Club Med Columbus Isle, Club Med Buccaneer's Creek and Club Med Turkoise. Club Med Columbus Isle went through a $5 million upgrade to include more luxury features that include king sized beds, flat screen TVs and well-stocked minifridges among many other such facilities. Add to that three new dining options and a poolside with eclectic music, daybeds, and lounges that it hopes to offer an experience like no other. The company also spent $50 million on refurbishing its resorts at Buccaneer's Creek and $6 million on the one at Turkoise.

Among the new experiences that Club Med is trying to bring to its members are the unique gym facilities in some of its resorts and the 'Seven Senses of Summer Program' offering a different activity every day of the week (including art classes, movie nights, dancing, and meditation). In early 2005, the company launched its first flagship store in London, UK, known as the 'The Travel Boutique.'

For the future, Club Med is scanning for new properties in the Americas that it can convert into boutique style luxury properties like the one on Columbus Isle.

DISCUSSION QUESTIONS

1. Given Club Med's current problems, do you feel the company could have avoided its pricing scheme problems through different expansion plans?

2. Why is Club Med unable to offer competitive prices?

3. Given Club Med's current problems, do you think that "the Club" will be able to survive by keeping its current pricing strategy, or do you think a new strategy should be implemented?

4. How can Club Med continue to differentiate itself in order to sustain its competitive advantage against its competitors who seem to be imitating its service concepts?

ASE 2

HONDA IN EUROPE

INTRODUCTION

The Honda Motor Company first entered the European market in the early 1960s through the sale of its motorcycles. The company's motor vehicles were introduced into Europe at a much later date. Honda's motor vehicle sales in Europe have been relatively poor, especially in the previous five years. Despite its huge success in the North American market, Honda is struggling to gain a significant foothold in the European market. Honda executives wonder why their global strategy is sputtering. Is global strategy just a pipedream, or is something wrong with Honda's European strategy?

HISTORY OF HONDA

In 1946, Souichiro Honda founded the Honda Technology Institute. The company started as a motorcycle producer and by the 1950s had become extremely successful in Japan. In 1956, Honda entered the U.S. market and was able to position itself effectively, selling small-sized motorcycles. In the early 1960s, the company commenced automobile manufacturing and participated in Formula-1 racing (F-1) to assist its technology development. Thanks mainly to its F-1 efforts, Honda became recognized as a technologically savvy company not only in Japan but in the rest of the world as well.

Until the early 1990s, the company experienced serious organizational mismanagement resulting from tension between the technology side and the marketing-sales side. The situation became so dire that the technology-biased president and founder, Souichiro Honda, was forced out, as a result of his neglect in important marketing decisions. After Souichiro Honda's departure, the company became more marketing-technology balanced, and by 1999 it was second in sales only to Toyota in the Japanese market. The company's underlying success is best summarized in its mission statement, "pleasure in buying, selling and producing," and "Beat GM, not Toyota." Honda currently has 25 separate factories in the world, and its operations cover automobiles, motorcycles, financial services, power products, and power tools. In fiscal 2004, 83

percent of Honda's revenues came from its automobile sector, as outlined in the accompanying table.

HONDA'S BUSINESS PORTFOLIO (IN MILLION YEN)

Motor cycle	446,622
Automobile	**2,918,750**
Others	123,733
Total	**3,489,105**

AUTOMOBILE INDUSTRY

The automobile industry worldwide is in the mature stage of its life cycle. By the 1990s, an oversupply of motor vehicles became such a problem to the industry that a number of mergers and acquisitions (M&A) and alliances took place. In the late 1990s, industry experts stated that only six or seven companies would remain global players, while other companies would be forced to sell in niche markets. In the last decade, DaimlerChrysler acquired a major share of Mitsubishi, GM became the controlling shareholder of Fiat and Saab, Ford acquired Volvo, Jaguar, and a major share of Mazda, and Renault became the controlling shareholder of

WORLD AUTOMOBILE PRODUCTION RANKING IN SALES

Ranking	Name	Number (million)
1	GM	8.303
2	Toyota	6.768
3	Ford	6.459
4	Volkswagen	4.881
5	Daimler-Chrysler	3.995
6	Peugeot(Citoreng)	3.013
7	**Honda**	**2.904**
8	Nissan	2.901
9	Hyundai-Kia	2.777
10	Renault	2.282

This case was prepared by Jong Won Ko, Peter Wirtz, Mike Rhee, and Vincent Chan of the University of Hawaii at Manoa and updated by Sonia Ketkar of Temple University under the supervision of Professor Masaaki Kotabe for class discussion rather than to illustrate either effective or ineffective management of a situation described (2006).

Nissan. Global scale production and sales became important as a way to cut cost through developing a common platform or engines as well as global procurement. Unlike their European and American counterparts, Japanese automobile companies, including Honda, did not adopt the M&A strategy for expansion. To remain a global competitor, Honda instead expanded its operations by setting up plants in regional markets. The following table shows that Honda is currently ranked seventh in the world in auto production.

HONDA IN EUROPE

Currently, Honda has five regional operations: North America, South America, Japan, Asia-Oceania, and Europe. The European operation covers Europe, the Middle East, and Africa. Honda entered the European market in 1961 as a motorcycle manufacturer, with its automobile operations following several years later. In 1986, Honda started engine production in the UK, and six years later it launched its European production at Swindon in Somerset, UK. Honda opened production facilities in Turkey in 1999 to target the Middle East and Eastern European markets. The European operation accounts for a small portion of Honda's global operation, as shown in the following table.

players in the market. The company needs to expand its sales and production in order to survive in global scale competition.

BRAND IMAGE IN EUROPE

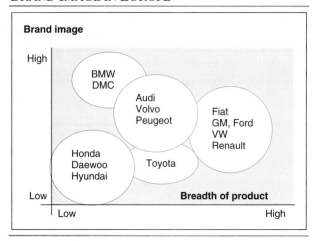

HONDA'S EUROPEAN MARKETING

The four largest markets within the European market are those of Germany, the UK, Italy, and France.

HONDA'S GLOBAL SALES BY REGION

Net Sales (in billion Yen)	Year 2004	Year 2005	Unit Sales (in thousands)	Year 2004	Year 2005
Japan	3930	4138	Japan	716	712
United States	4673	4705	United States	1558	1575
Europe	**948**	**1043**	**Europe**	**231**	**267**
Other	348	465	Other	137	176
			Year ended March 31		

There are a number of reasons for the low sales in Europe. Honda entered the European market rather late, and its first production facility in the region was built in 1992, at a time when Honda was still only a minor player in the Japanese market. Prior to 1992, Honda Europe was forced to import its vehicles from the United States, making it impossible for the company to aggressively attack the European market. One of the most important reasons for the lack of success was that the European market was highly saturated with locally owned car manufacturers. Companies such as Saab, Volvo, BMW, Audi, Volkswagen, DM, Opel, Renault, Peugeot, and Fiat have been dominating the European market for a considerable number of years. In addition, other foreign companies, such as Toyota, Nissan, Ford, and Hyundai make the European market extremely competitive.

In 2001, Volkswagen was ranked number one in Europe with 17.6 percent of the market and Peugeot number 2 with 15.8 percent. Renault, Ford, Fiat, and GM had approximately 10 percent of the market each, and Toyota, BMW, and Audi had a market share in the region of 5 percent. Honda captured only 2.4 percent of the European market. The competitive industry map below shows Honda's current position in the European automobile market.

The Honda brand image in Europe is relatively weak, and the product line is narrow compared to the other major

Product. Honda's European manufacturing plant is located in the UK, and as a result, the country has more Honda models than any other country in Europe, with a total of 20. Germany, the country with the highest number of vehicle registrations, has the next largest number of models, 16. Italy and France, both similar in size to the UK, have 11 and 9 models, respectively. The products found in Italy and France are found in Germany and the UK. The UK has a number of automobiles that cannot be found in the other three countries, including diesel-powered cars.

Price. The prices of Honda's vehicles in Europe are comparable to those of similar cars produced by local manufacturers.

AUTOMOBILE PRICES

Vehicle	Price (euro)
Honda Jazz	13,800
Peugeot 307	13,250
VW Polo	13,930
Renault Clio	13,650
Opel Astra	13,400
Fiat Stilo	13,500

The following table compares the price in euro of Honda's new 1.4-liter Jazz with similar cars offered in the European market.

The table clearly implies that Honda is attempting to price its product at a similar level to that of the competition.

HONDA'S UNIT SALES IN EUROPE: 1996–2001

Year	Civic	Accord	Shuttle	CR-V	HR-V	Logo	S2000	Stream	Total
1996	150,783	44,248	3,255	11					203,276
1997	160,530	39,410	3,278	16,502					232,242
1998	151,270	31,536	4,670	41,886	88				240,489
1999	99,156	48,835	4,261	35,923	26,257	12,856	1,179		234,942
2000	74,653	46,579	2,956	29,751	28,537	10,593	3,948		201,284
2001	83,024	28,822	320	24,381	17,726	4,145	2,195	7,283	169,922

Distribution. The image of Honda's vehicles and motorcycles in Europe is aligned together. Consequently, Honda vehicles throughout Europe are distributed at the same locations that their motorcycles are. Vehicles produced in the UK

HONDA'S UNIT SALES IN EUROPE BY COUNTRY: 1994–2003

Country	1994	1995	1996	1997	1998	1999	2000	2001	2002	2003
UK	38,187	45,772	50,075	55,611	61,044	65,290	68,736	63,459	77,842	81,858
Germany	53,687	52,614	54,550	55,918	48,247	43,610	33,536	31,868	32,580	34,251
France	14,411	11,848	13,260	12,585	14,095	15,270	8,717	6,495	6,392	5,547
Italy	12,063	14,101	15,014	25,406	24,532	22,031	18,570	13,732	15,509	18,887

and Turkey are distributed throughout Europe, the Middle East, and Africa. Recently, because of the depreciating euro vis-à-vis the U.S. dollar, cars manufactured in the UK have also been exported to the United States.

Promotion. The promotion of Honda's motor vehicles is essentially the same throughout Europe, whether in France, Germany, Italy, or the UK. The company spends very little time and money in promotion, however. It believes that its success in Formula-1 racing, together with its ability to produce high-mileage fuel-efficient products that exhibit great engineering, is enough to make it popular in the European market. It relies on word of mouth by its customers to potential customers and, to a lesser extent, on the Internet and the company's various Web sites.

In the recent 2002 launch of the Jazz (known as the Fit in Japan), the company relied heavily on word of mouth and on a Web site created especially for the occasion. The Web site, using the same design for all European countries, promoted the car as suitable for young working women. The Web site attempted to give the car a cool, young image by associating it with Feng Shui, Yoga, and other relatively hip activities. A sense of fun was also attached to the Web site in an attempt to draw in young women. Once inside the Jazz Web site, the user could easily find the nearest dealership to purchase the vehicle.

EUROPEAN SALES

The following table shows the sales figures for Honda's eight most popular motor vehicles through 2002. Honda's most successful year was in 1998; since then, however, sales have been decreasing dramatically.

Honda's motor vehicles have been relatively unpopular in the majority of Europe, in particular Italy and France. The company's best sales have occurred in the UK and Germany as shown in the accompanying table.

EUROPEAN CULTURE

Honda's relatively poor showing in Europe may be explained by a number of reasons. The main problem was that the company failed to truly understand the culture of Europe, and, more importantly, it treated Europe as one giant single market. Although France, Germany, the UK, and Italy are all European, cultural differences abound among them. One theory that explains the differences between the four nations is that of high-context versus low-context cultures. In a high-context culture, the interpretation of messages depends on contextual cues like gender, age, and balance of power, and not on physical written text. In a high-context culture things may be understood, rather than said. High-context cultures include those of China, Japan, Italy, France, Spain, and Latin America.

Conversely, a low-context culture emphasizes a distinctive written text or spoken words, where ideas are communicated explicitly. Low-context cultures expect others to say what they mean and do what they say. There is far less emphasis on contextual cues, such as ranking and balance of power. Examples of countries that fall within this category are the United States, the Scandinavian nations, and Germany. The accompanying figure presents a graphical view of high-context and low-context countries.

CULTURAL CONTEXT

Cultural Context

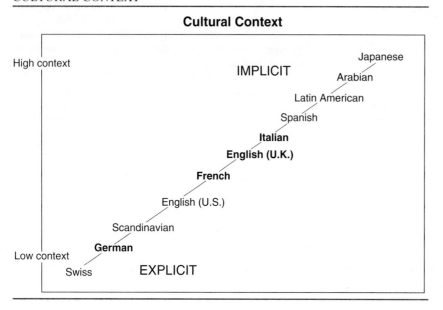

CULTURAL CONTEXT

Successful advertising in low-context cultures differs from that in high-context cultures. An advertisement for a high-context culture is based on an implicit style where the emphasis is on the overall feel and outlook rather than on the feeding of pure information. In this type of advertisement, the actual product may not even be shown. The audience may only be given implied images and subliminal messages. Honda's Jazz Web site contained a large amount of information which would have been too much for high-context cultures such as the French and the Italians. In addition, high-context cultures have been much slower than their low-context counterparts in adopting the Internet.

On the other hand, the advertisement for a low-context culture includes the actual product, together with a large amount of information. Low-context nations such as Germany would have most likely been able to appreciate Honda's Jazz Web site. It is therefore unlikely that an advertisement/promotion campaign created for a high-context culture will be effective in a low-context culture country and vice versa. Since Europe consists of both high-context and low-context culture countries, companies such as Honda, intending to expand its business, should take into consideration two separate market segments when planning its marketing strategy. Honda's situation in France, Italy, Germany, and the UK in regard to their culture is outlined in the following sections.

France. France is a high-context culture where style and image are of the utmost importance. The perceived quality of a product means that the French have a bias toward the style and image of a product. The image of Japanese cars in France is relatively poor, dating back to the 1930s when Japanese manufacturers entered the European market with low-quality

products. Since that time, Japanese carmakers, in particular Honda, have not understood the concept of style and image in marketing. They appear to show a car only in a factual way, which is extremely low-context. Japanese carmakers in France have recently tried to alter their image, though with limited success.

Today France's image of Japanese cars, and in particular that of Honda, is that of a small, low-quality car, suitable only for a second car. Most buyers of Japanese cars are young career women who have just entered the workforce and housewives with limited cash. The main family car is likely to be a Renault or Peugeot and is driven by the man in the family. In addition, the French are risk-averse people, who dislike trying new things. They are also highly patriotic, supporting and purchasing their national products, such as Renault and Peugeot cars.

The patriotism and risk averseness of the French, together with their low image of Japanese cars and the large number of other European automobiles available in the market, makes it extremely difficult for Honda to be successful in this market.

Italy. Italy, like France, is a high-context culture where a great deal of emphasis is placed on feeling and style. The Italian culture is reflected in their daily lifestyle, which gives a sense of romance to the people living there. As in France, the Italians view Japanese cars as small, low-quality vehicles, suitable only as a second family car. The most popular automobile in Italy, especially for families, is the Fiat. The Fiat is dominant because the Italians, like their high-context cousins the French, are very patriotic.

Italians are also risk-averse and are not adventurous in sampling products outside of Europe. Italians, like the majority of Europeans, love to drive diesel automobiles. Only the French enjoy driving diesel cars more than the Italians.

However, Honda produces very few diesel cars, and the only country in which they are offered is the UK, where they are relatively unpopular. The following table shows the five-year diesel car market share percentages in the UK, Germany, France, and Italy.

MARKET SHARE OF DIESEL CARS BY COUNTRY

Year	UK	Germany	France	Italy	Euro Avg.
1997	16.17	14.9	41.8	16.9	25.2
1998	15.28	17.6	40.2	22.3	27.7
1999	13.8	22.4	44.1	32.1	33.1
2000	14.1	30.3	49.1	33.3	33.3
2001	17.7	N.A.	N.A.	N.A.	N.A.

The table shows that diesel cars account for 30 to 50 percent of vehicles in France, Italy, and Germany. Diesel cars are hugely popular because of the high gasoline prices in those countries. Diesel engine cars are cheaper to maintain in the long run, compared to gasoline engine cars.

A large number of European cars compete in Europe, particularly at the luxury end. BMW, Mercedes, and Audi are very popular for the very rich, as are Ferrari, Lamborghini, and Porsche. It is difficult for Japanese cars to enter the European market, especially at the higher end. The only Japanese cars that are selling reasonably well are Toyota's Yaris, Nissan's Micra, and Jazz from Honda. All three models compete in the 1.4 liter and under segment.

Germany. Of the four main European countries in which Honda is sold, Germany has had the second highest sales volume. Germany is a low-context culture where practicality and durability are two of the main concerns of a product. Consumers are concerned with every detail regarding a product and wish to know all relevant information before making a purchase. The promotion style used by Honda on the Internet, bursting with information on their automobiles, seems to be an appropriate form of promotion for the low-context nature of the Germans.

Another factor that should place Honda's products in a better position in Germany is the Germans' greater willingness to take risks and to purchase new products. As a result, Honda would not have to spend additional resources to change the image of their vehicles in Germany, as it should probably do in France and Italy. In reality, however, Honda's sales have been dropping rapidly in the past five years—50 percent of what they were five years ago. If Honda's promotion is in line with the German's low-context nature, there must be another reason for the decrease in sales. The most logical is the perceived nature of Honda's quality. The company needs to use its marketing to promote quality because competitors such as Mercedes (under DaimlerChrysler), Audi, Volvo, Jaguar (under Ford), and Volkswagen, to name a few, are seen as high-quality carmakers.

The United Kingdom. The English are a moderately high-context culture, who focus on tradition and class. Accordingly, the type of advertising and marketing promotion that will appeal to the English is similar to that popular in France and

Italy but is more conservative in nature. On the other hand, the English are more individualistic and less risk averse than the French and Italians. Hence, it should be easier for Honda to introduce its range of cars in the UK and to improve sales. The fact that the manufacturing plant is located in the UK helps in the promotion of the cars. The construction of a second assembly plant should also help Honda's position in the UK.

The existence of the assembly plant, together with the risk-taking nature of the English, has increased the number of Hondas sold in the UK in the last five years to such a level that it is easily Honda's best market. The number sold in the UK as of 2001 was twice that of Germany, which only five years before had recorded more sales than the UK. However, no Honda vehicle has entered the list of the top ten cars sold in the UK, as shown in the following table for 2001.

TOP 10 CARS SOLD IN EUROPE

1. Ford Focus
2. Vauxhall Astra
3. Ford Fiesta
4. Peugeot 206
5. Vauxhall Corsa
6. Ford Mondeo
7. Renault Clio
8. Renault Megane
9. Volkswagen Golf
10. Citroen Xsara

POSSIBLE ENTRY WEDGE

A possible entry wedge exists in Europe that could help Honda recover some of its lost ground. The European automotive industry is committed to a voluntary agreement to reduce CO_2 emissions by 25 percent from the 1995 levels by 2008 for all new cars. As an incentive for individuals to drive low-emission cars, special tax brackets will be given to drivers of low-emission cars.

In 2001, Honda's Insight produced the lowest levels of CO_2 emission of any car in Europe. The following table shows the five cars with the lowest CO_2 emission.

TOP 5 CARS WITH THE LOWEST CO_2 EMISSION

Rank	Car	Engine	Gas Type	CO_2 g/km
1.	Honda Insight	1 liter	Gasoline	80
2	Peugeot 206	1.4 liter	Diesel	113
3	Toyota Prius	1.5 liter	Gasoline	114
4	Renault Clio	1.5 liter	Diesel	115
5	Audi A2	1.4 liter	Diesel	116

The ranking is an excellent opportunity for Honda to promote its cars in Europe, where people (especially in Germany) are obsessed with the environment and are burdened with high taxes. In addition, Honda is introducing the Civic Hybrid in 2003. It is a gasoline-electric power train, fuel-efficient car with a low CO_2 emission level. Although the car has an electric engine, it does not need to be plugged in and recharged. The battery pack recharges itself automatically as the car is running.

THE ISSUE

Honda is currently at the crossroads of its European expansion in the automobile market. It has been successful in managing to market essentially the same cars in many parts of the world, particularly in the North American and Japanese markets. Honda executives are wondering whether or not they should adopt more localized product development in Europe.

DISCUSSION QUESTIONS

1. Does adapting the promotion of its motor vehicles to suit each country's culture make sense for Honda?

2. Is it wise for Honda to market its products the same way in every country?

3. Is pricing its vehicles similar to the competition a good strategy for Honda?

4. Should Honda change its product mix from country to country?

5. Is distributing its motor vehicles together with its motorcycles a good strategy for Honda?

6. Is the European market too competitive for Honda?

◆ ◆

$\mathcal{C}$ASE 3

ANHEUSER-BUSCH INTERNATIONAL, INC.: MAKING INROADS INTO BRAZIL AND MEXICO

HISTORY

In 1852 George Schneider started a small brewery in St. Louis. Five years later the brewery faced insolvency. Several St. Louis businessmen purchased the brewery, launching an expansion financed largely by a loan from Eberhard Anheuser. By 1860 the enterprise had run into trouble again. Anheuser, with money already earned from a successful soap-manufacturing business, bought up the interest of minority creditors and became a brewery owner. In 1864 he joined forces with his new son-in-law, Adolphus Busch, a brewery supplier, and eventually Busch became president of the company. Busch is credited with transforming it into an industry giant and is therefore considered the founder of the company.

Busch wanted to break the barriers of all local beers and breweries, so he created a network of railside ice-houses to cool cars of beer being shipped long distances. This moved the company that much closer to becoming one of the first national beers. In the late 1870s, Busch launched the industry's first fleet of refrigerated cars but needed more to ensure the beer's freshness over long distances. In response, Busch pioneered the use of a new pasteurization process.

In 1876 Busch created Budweiser, and today the company brews Bud the same way it did in 1876. In 1896 the company introduced Michelob as its first premium beer. By 1879 annual sales rose to more than 105,000 barrels, and in 1901 the company reached the one-million barrel mark.

In 1913, after his father's death, August A. Busch Sr. took charge of the company, and with the new leadership came new problems: World War I, Prohibition, and the Great Depression. To keep the company running, Anheuser-Busch switched its emphasis to the production of corn products, baker's yeast, ice cream, soft drinks, commercial refrigeration units, and truck bodies. They stopped most of these activities when

Prohibition ended. However, the yeast production was kept and even expanded to the point that Anheuser-Busch became the nation's leading producer of compressed baker's yeast through the encouragement of the company's new president in 1934, Adolphus Busch III.

August A. Busch Jr. succeeded his brother as president in 1946 and served as the company's CEO until 1975. During this time eight branch breweries were constructed, and annual sales increased from 3 million barrels in 1946 to more than 34 million in 1974. The company was extended to include family entertainment, real estate, can manufacturing, transportation, and major league baseball.

August A. Busch III became president in 1974 and was named CEO in 1975. From that time to the present, the company opened three new breweries and acquired one. Other acquisitions included the nation's second-largest baking company and Sea World. The company also increased vertical integration capabilities with the addition of new can manufacturing and malt production facilities, container recovery, metalized label printing, snack foods, and international marketing and creative services.

CORPORATE MISSION STATEMENT

Anheuser-Busch's corporate mission statement provides the foundation for strategic planning for the company's businesses:

> The fundamental premise of the mission statement is that beer is and always will be Anheuser-Busch's core business. In the brewing industry, Anheuser-Busch's goals are to extend its position as the world's leading brewer of quality products; increase its share of the domestic beer market 50% by the late 1990s; and extend its presence in the international beer market. In non-beer areas, Anheuser-Busch's existing food products, packaging, and entertainment will continue to be developed.

The mission statement also sets forth Anheuser-Busch's belief that the cornerstones of its success are a commitment to quality and adherence to the highest standards of honesty and integrity in its dealings with all stakeholders.

This case was prepared and updated by Masaaki Kotabe with the assistance of Sonia Ketkar of Temple University for class discussion rather than to illustrate either effective or ineffective management of a situation described (2006).

ANHEUSER-BUSCH INTERNATIONAL PARTNERSHIPS

Country	Partner	Investment	Date
Argentina	Compañía Cervecerías Unidas S.A.-Argentina (CCU—Argentina)	Equity investment (of which 28.6% is direct and indirect); licensed brewing and joint marketing	Dec. 1995
Central America (Costa Rica, El Salvador, Guatemala, Honduras, Nicaragua, Panama)	(Cervecería Costa Rica –La Constancia –Cervecería Centroamericana –Cervecería Hondureña –Compañía de Nicaragua –Cervecería Nacional)	Import, distribution	Apr. 1994
Chile	Compañía Cervecerías Unidas (CCU)	20% equity investment	Jan. 2001
China	Budweiser Wuhan International Brewing Co.	98% A-B owned brewery, A-B sales, marketing, distribution	Feb. 1995
China	Tsingtao Brewery Co. Ltd.	4.5% Equity investment	June 1993
Denmark	Carlsberg Breweries A/S	Import, distribution	May 1998
France	Brasseries Kronenbourg	Import, distribution, packaging	Jan. 1996
Ireland	Guinness Ireland Ltd.	Licensed brewing; joint marketing	June 1986
Italy	Birra Peroni Industrial S.p.A.	Licensed brewing; joint marketing	Apr. 1993
Japan	Kirin Brewery Co. Ltd.	Licensed brewing; joint marketing Kirin sales, distribution	Jan. 2000
Mexico	Grupo Modelo	Import, distribution	July 1989
		Equity investment (of which 50% is direct and indirect)	Jan. 1993
South Korea	Oriental Brewery Co. Ltd.	Licensed brewing; joint marketing	Dec. 1986

BEER AND BEER-RELATED OPERATIONS

Anheuser-Busch, which began operations in 1852 as the Bavarian Brewery, ranks as the world's largest brewer and has held the position of industry leader in the United States since 1957. More than four out of every ten beers sold in the United States are Anheuser-Busch products. In 2004, when the world's third largest brewing company, Brazil's Companhia de Bebidas das Americas (AmBer) joined hands with Belgium's Interbrew, the combined firm InterbrewAmBer became the world's largest Brewer with a global market share of 14 percent and revenues of over $12 billion.

Anheuser-Busch's principal product is beer, produced and distributed by its subsidiary, Anheuser-Busch, Inc. (ABI), in a variety of containers primarily under the brand names Budweiser, Bud Light, Bud Dry Draft, Michelob, Michelob Light, Michelob Dry, Michelob Golden Draft, Michelob Gold, Draft Light, Busch Light, Natural Light, and King Cobra, to name just a few. In 1993 Anheuser-Busch introduced a new brand, Ice Draft from Budweiser, which is marketed in the United States and abroad as the preferred beer because it is lighter and less bitter than beer produced in foreign countries. Bud Draft from Budweiser was first introduced in the United States in late 1993 in 14 states, with a full national rollout in 1994 in the United States and abroad.

SALES

Anheuser-Busch's sales grew slowly after a sales decline in 1994. Net sales increased consistently from 1993 to almost $13.3 billion in 1998 but fell again to $11.8 billion in 1999. Net sales were up again in the next five years to $14.9 billion in 2004.

ANHEUSER-BUSCH INTERNATIONAL, INC

Anheuser-Busch International, Inc. (A-BII), was formed in 1981 to explore and develop the international beer market. A-BII is responsible for handling the company foreign beer operations and for exploring and developing beer markets outside the United States. Its activities include contract and license brewing, export sales, marketing and distribution of the company's beer in foreign markets, and equity partnerships with foreign brewers.

A-BII has a two-pronged strategy: (1) build Budweiser into an international brand and (2) build an international business through equity investments and creating partnerships with, or leading foreign brewers. In seeking growth, Anheuser-Busch International emphasizes part-ownership in foreign brewers, joint ventures, and contract-brewing arrangements. These elements give the company opportunities to use its marketing expertise and its management practices in foreign markets. The success of these growth opportunities depends largely on finding the right partnerships that create a net gain for both companies. Other options for international expansion include license-brewing arrangements and exporting. In addition to its domestic breweries in the United States, the company operates two international breweries in China and the United Kingdom, respectively. Budweiser beer is locally brewed through partnerships in seven other countries, Argentina, Canada, Italy, Ireland, Spain, Japan, and South Korea.

A-BII is currently pursuing the dual objectives of building Budweiser's worldwide presence and establishing a significant international business operation through joint ventures and equity investments in foreign brewers. Anheuser-Busch brands are exported to more than 60 countries and are brewed under Anheuser-Busch's supervision in five countries. A-BII has experienced international growth in all operating regions, with a 9-percent market share worldwide, and has the largest export volume of any U.S. brewer. Anheuser-Busch had more than 45 percent of all U.S. beer exports and exported a record volume of more than 3.4 million barrels of beer in 1998. From 2002 to 2003, Anheuser-Busch's international sales volume increased by 5 percent to 8.4 million barrels. The company now sells beer in over 80 countries worldwide.

MARKET SHARE

The top 10 beer brands worldwide for 2000 in worldwide market share are shown in Exhibit 1. Most recently, Anheuser-Busch has announced several agreements with other leading brewers around the world, including Modelo in Mexico, Antarctica in Brazil, and Tsingtao Brewery in China. These agreements are part of A-BII's two-pronged strategy of investing internationally through both brand and partnership development. Through partnerships, A-BII will continue to identify, execute, and manage significant brewing acquisitions and joint ventures, partnering with the number-one or number-two brewers in growing markets. This strategy will allow A-BII to participate in beer industries around the world by investing in leading foreign brands, such as Corona in Mexico through Modelo. A-BII's goal is to share the best practices with its partners, allowing an open interchange of ideas that will benefit both partners.

LATIN AMERICA

The development of Budweiser in Latin America is one of the keys to long-term growth in the international beer business, for it is one of the world's fastest growing beer markets and is a region with a growing consumer demand for beer. Anheuser-Busch products are sold in 11 Latin American countries—Argentina, Belize, Brazil, Chile, Ecuador, Mexico, Nicaragua, Panama, Paraguay, Uruguay, and Venezuela—with a total population of over 380 million consumers. In particular, the three countries showing the fastest growth in total beer consumption in the 1990–2000 period are Brazil (+200 percent), Colombia (+130 percent), and Mexico (+100 percent). In Brazil and Mexico—the two largest beer markets in Latin America—Anheuser-Busch International acquired an equity position in their major local breweries.

Brazil. Anheuser-Busch International recently made an initial investment of 10 percent in a new Antarctica subsidiary in Brazil that consolidates all of Antarctica's holdings in affiliated companies and controls 75 percent of Antarctica's operations. Anheuser-Busch will have an option to increase its investment to approximately 30 percent in the new company in the future. The amount of the initial investment was approximately $105 million. The investment has established a partnership that gives Antarctica a seat on the board of Anheuser-Busch, Inc. and gives Anheuser-Busch International proportionate representation on the board of the new Antarctica subsidiary. The two brewers will also explore joint distribution opportunities in the fast-growing South American beer market.

According to Scott Bussen (South American representative for A-BII), A-BII is currently in the process of signing a deal that calls for establishing an Anheuser-Busch–controlled marketing and distribution agreement between the two brewers to support sales of Budweiser in Brazil.

The deal makes Anheuser-Busch the first American brewer to hold an equity stake in the Brazilian beer market, which is the largest in Latin America and the sixth-largest in the world. Last year the Brazilian beer market grew by more than 15 percent. Its potential for future growth markets is one of the most important global beer markets.

The second component of the partnership will be a licensing agreement in which Antarctica will brew Budweiser in Brazil. The joint venture will be 51 percent owned and controlled by Anheuser-Busch and 49 percent by Antarctica. Antarctica's production plants will produce Budweiser according to the brand's quality requirements. Local sourcing of Budweiser will allow more competitive pricing and increased sales of the brand in Brazil.

EXHIBIT 1
TOP TEN BEER BRANDS WORLDWIDE, 2000

Brand	Company	Share of World Beer Market
Budweiser	ABI	4.4%
Miller Lite	Miller Brewing Co.	1.7%
Kirin Lager	Kirin Brewery	1.7%
Bud Light	ABI	1.5%
Brahma Chopp	Companhia Cervejaria	1.4%
Coors Light	Coors Brewing Co.	1.4%
Heineken	Heineken NV	1.3%
Antarctica	Antarctica Paulista	1.3%
Polar	Cerveceria Polar SA	1.2%
Asahi Super Dry	Asahi Breweries	1.2%

Antarctica, based in São Paulo, controls 35 percent of the Brazilian beer market. Its annual production in 1998 was about 20 million barrels of beer. Antarctica has a network of nearly 1000 Brazilian wholesalers. Prior to its investment in Antarctica, Budweiser had achieved a distribution foothold in the Brazilian beer market in cooperation with its distributor, Arisco. Brazil has a population of 175 million people, with per capita beer consumption in Brazil estimated to be 40 liters per year. With Brazil's population growing by 1.7 percent a year, reduced import duties, and free market reforms, Anheuser-Busch is expected to do well in the Brazilian market over the next decade.

The combined strengths of Anheuser-Busch and Antarctica in the booming Brazilian environment will lead to increased sales for both companies' products, resulting in a more competitive beer market, which benefits consumers, suppliers, and distribution in Brazil over the long term. Since 2003 the company has not significantly increased its investment in Brazil.

Mexico. In a further move to strengthen its international capabilities, Anheuser-Busch companies purchased a 37 percent direct and indirect equity interest for $980 million in Grupo Modelo (located in Mexico City) and its subsidiaries, which thus far are privately held. Modelo is Mexico's largest brewer and the producer of Corona, that country's best-selling beer. The brewer has a 51 percent market share and exports to 56 countries. In connection with the purchases, three Anheuser-Busch representatives have been elected to the Modelo board, and a Modelo representative has been elected to serve on the Anheuser-Busch board. As of 2002, Anheuser Busch owned approximately 50 percent of Grupo Modelo (directly and indirectly). Its brands Budweiser and Bud Light sales volume grew 25 percent in Mexico in 2003. Mexico is now the company's largest export market as well. In 2003, Anheuser-Busch's sales volume in Mexico saw double-digit growth for the fifth consecutive year.

In addition, the agreement includes the planned implementation of a program for the exchange of executives and management personnel between Modelo and Anheuser-Busch in key areas, including accounting/auditing, marketing, operations, planning, and finance. Modelo will remain Mexico's exclusive importer and distributor of Budweiser and other Anheuser-Busch brands, which have achieved a leadership position in imported beers sold in Mexico. These brands will continue to be brewed exclusively by Anheuser-Busch breweries in the United States. Currently, Anheuser-Busch brews beer for Mexico at its Houston and Los Angeles breweries, which are not very far away from Mexico but add to the markup of A-BII brands.

All of Modelo's brands will continue to be brewed exclusively in its seven existing Mexican breweries and a new brewery in North Central Mexico. U.S. distribution rights for the Modelo products are not involved in the arrangement. Corona and other Modelo brands will continue to be imported into the United States by Barton Beers and Gambrinus Company and distributed by those importers to beer wholesalers.

Modelo is the world's tenth-largest brewer and, through sales of Corona Modelo Especial, Pacifico, Negra Modelo, and other regional brands, holds more than 51 percent of

the Mexican beer market. Its beer exports to 56 countries in North and South America, Asia, Australia, Europe, and Africa account for more than 69 percent of Mexico's total beer exports.

Modelo is one of several companies that distribute Budweiser besides Antarctica in Brazil and other local import-export companies in other Latin American countries. Modelo is the exclusive importer and distributor of Anheuser-Busch beers in Mexico. The newest brand, Ice Draft, will be the fourth ABl brand distributed in Mexico by Modelo, joining Budweiser, Bud Light, and O'Douls.

The Modelo agreement is significant because beer consumption has grown 6.5 percent annually in Mexico in the past few years. Mexico's beer consumption is the eighth-largest in the world but still only half of U.S. consumption. The per capita beer consumption rate in Mexico is estimated at 44 liters, compared to 87 liters per person in the United States, which is high given that Mexico's per capita income is one-tenth that of the United States. The Mexican market is expected to grow at a rapid rate.

Anheuser-Busch does not have control over pricing. The local wholesalers and retailers set prices for Budweiser. A-BII also does not have plans to set up a full-scale production facility in Mexico at this time. At present Budweiser is imported, which makes it two to three times higher in price than local beers, so it is largely an upscale, niche market brand at this time. An equity arrangement in another brewery or an agreement with Modelo could lead to local production and make A-BII brands more competitive with the local beer brands. In 2002, Budweiser brands made up 34 percent of the beer imports in Mexico. In 2002, net income for the company's international beer operations rose 6.3 percent in the third quarter, which the company claimed was due to the performance of Grupo Modelo.

Besides the 11 Latin American countries mentioned, Anheuser-Busch has signed agreements with the largest brewers in Costa Rica, El Salvador, Guatemala, and Honduras to distribute and market Budweiser in their respective countries. Local breweries (Cervecería Costa Rica in Costa Rica, La Constancia in El Salvador, Cervecería Centroamericana in Guatemala, and Cervecería Hondureña in Honduras) distribute Budweiser in 12-ounce bottles and 12-ounce aluminum cans.

These distribution agreements will allow Budweiser to expand its distribution throughout the rest of Central America. These countries have an extensive national distribution network and, more important, have local market expertise to develop Budweiser throughout the region. Under the agreements, the Central American brewers will import Budweiser from Anheuser-Busch plants in Houston, Texas, and Williamsburg, Virginia. Anheuser-Busch will share responsibility for Budweiser's marketing with each of its Central American partners, supported by nationwide advertising and promotional campaigns.

ADVERTISING

Event Sponsorship. Given Budweiser's advertising approach, which is traditionally built around sports, the decision to hold the 1994 World Cup tournament in the United States gave A-BII a perfect venue to pitch Budweiser to Latin Americans. The company signed a multimillion-dollar sponsorship deal with the World Cup Organizing Committee, making Budweiser the only beer authorized to use the World Cup logo. "The World Cup has become a vehicle for us to reach Latin America," said Charlie Acevedo, director of Latin American marketing for Anheuser-Busch International.

For 10 months, soccer fans in South America saw the Bud logo on everything from soccer balls to beer glasses. Soccer fans collected a World Cup bumper sticker when they purchased a 12-pack of Bud. When they watched the game on television, they saw Budweiser signs decorating the stadiums and a glimpse of the Bud blimp hovering overhead. According to Charlie Acevedo, the goal is to make Budweiser a global icon like McDonald's golden arches or Coca-Cola.

Anheuser-Busch just signed its second two-year agreement with ESPN Latin America. "Being able to buy on a regional basis gives a consistent message that is very reasonable in terms of cost," said Steve Burrows, A-BII's executive vice president of marketing.

Latin America offers promise with its youthful population and rising personal income. Half of Mexico's population is under 21, and other Latin American countries have similar profiles, offering opportunities for advertisers to reach the region's 450 million population.

The biggest new advertising opportunities in the Latin American market are Fox Latin America, MTV Latino, Cinemax Ole (a premium channel venture with Caracas cable operator Omnivision Latin American Entertainment), USA Network, and Telemundo (a 24-hour Spanish-language news channel). Marketers will have yet another pan-regional advertising option. Hughes (the U.S. aerospace company) and three Latin American partners—Multivision in Mexico, Televisao Abril in Brazil, and the Cisneros Group in Venezuela—launched a $700 million satellite that will beam programs in Spanish and Portuguese into homes across the continent. The service is called DirectTV. Because of this satellite, Central and South America have added 24 new channels; with digital compression technology, its capability could reach 144 cable channels.

In the past, Anheuser-Busch used CNN International as its only ad vehicle, but with all the new opportunities, "The company will begin adding a local media presence throughout

EXHIBIT 2

PENETRATION OF PAID CABLE TV CHANNELS

Location	TV Households (in millions)	Paid Subscribers	Penetration Rate
Brazil	30.0	3,300,000	15%
Mexico	14.0	1,700,000	12
Argentina	9.0	4,300,000	47
Chile	3.4	200,000	6
Venezuela	3.3	90,000	3
Uruguay	0.7	35,000	5
Ecuador	0.5	25,000	5
Paraguay	0.5	45,000	9

Latin America," said Robert Gunthner, A-BII's vice president of the Americans region (see Exhibit 2).

Anheuser-Busch will be using ads originally aimed at U.S. Hispanics, most of which were created by Carter Advertising of New York. A-BII will let the local agencies pick its messages, customize advertising, and do local media planning. In the past, there has been much criticism of ABI's ethnocentric approach to marketing Budweiser; however, because of the world obsession with American pop culture, they feel they don't need to tone down their American image. In Costa Rica, A-BII will use JBQ, San Jose; in El Salvador, Apex/BBDO, San Salvador; in Guatemala, Cerveceria's in-house media department; and in Honduras, McCann-Erickson Centroamericana, San Pedro.

Imported beers cost two or three times as much as locally brewed beers in South America, but thanks to cable television and product positioning in U.S. movies, Budweiser was already a well-known brand in South America when the company began exporting to the continent.

Strategy. According to Charlie Acevedo, Anheuser-Busch has seen double-digit increases in Latin American sales in the past five years. The gains came from both an increase in disposable income and increasingly favorable attitudes

EXHIBIT 3

GDP PER CAPITA IN SELECTED LATIN AMERICAN COUNTRIES (2005)

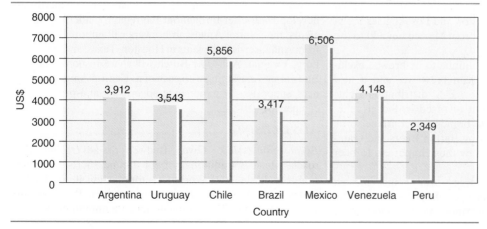

toward U.S. products, especially in Argentina, Brazil, Chile, and Venezuela. Because Latin America has a very young population, Anheuser-Busch expects this market to grow at 4 percent annually. Furthermore, with NAFTA and a free trade zone, the company expects to see a significant rise in personal income in Latin American countries, which translates to great growth potential for Anheuser-Busch brands. The GDP (gross domestic product) per capita in 2005 is presented in Exhibit 3.

North American products and lifestyles are very much accepted in South America, but beer consumption still lags far behind U.S. levels. Argentines consume about 30 liters annually per capita. Brazilians 40 liters, Chileans 50 liters, and Venezuelans 65 liters, compared to 87 liters per person annually in the United States.

"The international focus will be almost completely on Budweiser because there is a worldwide trend toward less-heavy, less-bitter beers," and Jack Purnell, chair and chief executive officer of Anheuser-Busch International. They're counting on the American image to carry their beer, therefore opting for a universal campaign with American themes as opposed to tailoring Budweiser's image for local markets.

In the past, A-BII has tinkered with its formula and marketed Budweiser under different names to give a local flavor to their beer but had absolutely no success. Purnell said, "What the market does not need is an American brewery trying to make up from scratch, new European-style beers. Bud should be Bud wherever you get it."

OPPORTUNITIES

Mexico offers the U.S. exporter a variety of opportunities encompassing most product categories. Mexico is continuing to open its borders to imported products. Mexico's population of approximately 105 million is the eleventh-largest in the world and the second largest in Latin America (after Brazil and Argentina). Mexico is a young country, with 69 percent of its population under 30 years of age. In addition, the Mexican government has adopted new privatization policies decreasing its involvement in the country's economy. As a result, private resources, both local and foreign, are playing a greater role in all areas of the Mexican economy. NAFTA, which aims to eliminate all tariffs on goods originating from Canada and the United States, is expected to create a massive market, with more than 360 million people and $6 trillion in annual output.

DEMOGRAPHICS

Mexico's overall population in 2004 was estimated at 105 million people. Based on 2000 statistics, the age breakdown is as follows: under 15, 38 percent; 15–29, 29 percent; 30–44, 17 percent; 45–59, 9 percent; 60–74, 5 percent; 75 and over, 2 percent. The average age of the Mexican population was 23.3 years.

Between 1970 and 1990, the ratio of the population living in localities with between 100,000 and 500,000 inhabitants grew from 12 to 22 percent. This was largely due to rural–urban migration. More than 71 percent of the population lives in urban areas of Mexico. In 1990, 22 percent of the national population lived in Mexico City and the State of Mexico. The Mexican population is expected to rise to 112 million in the year 2010.

 CASE 4

VOLKSWAGEN AG NAVIGATES CHINA

On December 11, 2001, China joined the World Trade Organization. This was a momentous occasion for many. To any large, small, or mid-sized global entrepreneur, the idea of the additional demand of over one billion people is very attractive. After all, there are not many countries in the world that have populations even near the size of China's. WTO press release archives contain the excitement and anticipation of China's accession. In order to be approved for accession, China committed to economic language like "opening, liberalizing, stabilizing, integrating, cooperative," which is like fresh blood in the shark tank of world economics. The WTO Director-General, Mike Moore, voiced a healthy outlook by saying, "Now this economy will be subjected to the rules-based system of the WTO, something which is bound to enhance global economic cooperation."

Similar to many other industries, hopes of a freer market had automobile manufacturers practically salivating, because the Chinese auto market held much potential. In 2001, China had only 1.5 cars per 1,000 people, which is well below the global average of 90 cars per 1,000 people. Although it would not be wise to assume that Chinese demand for automobiles will grow by 5,900% and catch up to the global average for cars/per 1,000 people, production outputs continue to reflect positive growth for Chinese automakers. For the 12-month period ending July 2003, motor vehicle output was up over 33%. Thirty-three percent growth is impressive regardless of the industry, but can automakers really expect to sustain growth in China, a country whose government can be viewed as controlling, yet influential?

Peering into the Chinese automobile market might leave an analyst somewhat puzzled. For some, they may be overwhelmed and encouraged by the tremendous upside potential (large population for demand and production), but others may not be able to "see the trees through the forest" (a confusing maze of bureaucratic regulations and low-skilled workforce).

This case was prepared by Elizabeth Eckhardt, Asaad Faquir, Neeraj Kulkarni, Keith Mandia, Manoj Raghunandanan of the Fox School of Business and Management at Temple University under the supervision of Professor Masaaki Kotabe for class discussion rather than to illustrate either effective or ineffective management of a situation described (2004).

Regardless of whether you are an adventurous risk-taking, first-to-market type, or the conservative, mainstream-adopter type, the Chinese auto market offers an abundant supply of evidence for your case to justify your market globalization recommendation to senior management.

CHINESE AUTOMOBILE MARKET

For adventure seekers, the upside potential seems blinding. According to the China Automobile Industry Association, China's automobile industry has hit a ten-year record high for vehicle production. The 3.25 million vehicles produced in 2002 represented a 38.5% increase over 2001. Sales reached 3.24 million, a 36.7% increase over 2001. The increase in demand for private cars has been the main factor stimulating growth. China's GDP per capita reach $900 in 2002 and in some areas of the coastal areas it topped $3,000. The fervor of the Chinese auto market has been well publicized internationally.

- In the Japanese press, a staff writer for the Nikkei Weekly reported, "The Chinese automobile industry is about to enter an era of all-out battle for market share, where all aspects of an operation, ranging from raising cash to financing to the release of new models to flexible production systems that can turn out a number of models at the same time, to sales networks, are tested."[1]

- In the United States press, a Fortune magazine reporter wrote, "After nearly a quarter century of economic liberalization, car ownership is suddenly within reach of millions of ordinary Chinese. An economic rise, new car prices plummet, and the government adds new roadways. In 2002 passenger car sales topped one million for the first time. In the first six months of this year, China's new car sales surged 85% over the same period last year."[2]

With mounting upside potential many of the world's largest automotive manufacturers are stepping up their efforts in China. For example, GM plans to build Cadillacs in China for the luxury car market, Ford and partner Mazda announce a $500 million investment plan, Nissan plans to launch 5 new models in China by 2006, and BMW has founded a 50-50 joint venture with Brilliance China Automotive Holdings. The surge in the Chinese automobile market can be seen in Exhibit 1 below. According to CSM Worldwide projections, there will be over 6.3 million vehicles produced in China by the year 2007. That represents 133% growth over the 2.7 million produced in 2002.

Not only is substantial domestic production expected, but supply will also be bolstered by foreign car imports. For example, GM, Ford, and DaimlerChrysler have all recently announced plans to increase automobile exports to China. The recently announced agreement is worth over $1.3 billion to GM over the next few years. GM plans to send mostly luxury models to China and Ford will send mostly SUVs. The European Union is also hoping to export more cars to China. According to the EU Chamber of Commerce in China, as of April 2002 EU car makers had cumulatively invested more than $3.3 billion in China and commanded an overall market share of 65% of domestically made car sales, but were limited to just a 40-45% share of China's auto imports.

EXHIBIT 1
PASSENGER VEHICLE PRODUCTION IN CHINA

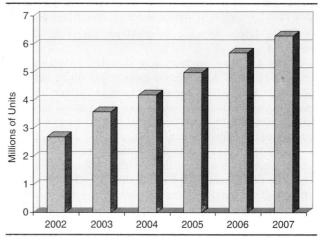

Regardless of the political and economic maneuvering by American, European or any other auto makers, China's car imports rose over 76% in 2002, and China has already promised to abolish their import quota system in 2006, which opens the supply ceiling even further. An official of Beijing Asian Games Village Auto Exchange predicted that prices will fall by an average of 8%-10% by the end of the 2003.

Tariff decreases are the other factor expected to increase the supply of cars in China, because foreign firms will find it cheaper to export vehicles and parts into the country. By July 2006, small-engined automobile tariffs are scheduled to fall to 25%, as compared to their 2000 level of 63.5% (see Exhibit 2 below).

Over the next 3–5 years, the combination of increased domestic production, increased imports, and lowered tariffs means that there will be many global entrepreneurs vying for their own respective share of the percolating Chinese auto market.

Stimulating the positive growth in the automobile market, as well as others, has been the Chinese government's public demonstration of meaningful policy adjustments in order to integrate its economy with the global economy. Policy moves ranging from loosening its regulations pertaining to Wholly Foreign Owned Enterprises selling their goods in China, to establishing Special Economic Zones, which offer many incentives to foreign enterprises including tax benefits such as a 5-year gradual taxation scale on profits. Clearly, there are many positive overtures by China's Communist regime to adhere to the agreed upon terms of their WTO accession and to elevate China into a global economic powerhouse. Yet despite the encouraging regulatory beacons from China, there still seems to be enough regulatory fodder for skeptics to question whether or not the Chinese government is fully committed to facilitating an "open-door" automobile industry.

One example of the Chinese government's conservative-growth approach was published when the Chinese State Development and Reform Commission recently circulated policy on

---

[1]"Shanghai GM Gaining Momentum". *Nikkei Weekly*, December 24, 2002.

[2]"China Goes Car Crazy," *Fortune*, August 2003.

EXHIBIT 2
CHINA'S WTO AUTOMOBILE TARIFF REDUCTION SCHEDULE (%)

Engine Size	2000	2001	2002	2003	2004	2005	1/2006	7/2006
Large	77.5%	61.7%	50.7%	43.0%	37.6%	30.0%	28.0%	25.0%
Small	63.5%	51.9%	43.8%	38.2%	34.2%	30.0%	28.0%	25.0%

auto import distribution. The July 2003 announcement would require foreign automakers to maintain separate distribution outlets for imported and domestically produced cars. Bernd Leissner, President of VW's AG Asia-Pacific operations, criticized the policy as "stupid and old-fashioned," because it will require international auto manufacturers to build separate showrooms for their imported vehicles, thus increasing operational costs.

The other point of discontent for international automobile manufacturers is financing. Pursuant to China's WTO accession, non-bank financial institutions are supposed to be permitted to provide auto financing without any market access or national treatment limitations. To date, the Chinese government has curtailed financial service competition. Currently only 10%–15% of purchasers in China have auto loans, and any loans have had to have been written by one of four Chinese Banks: the Industrial and Commercial Bank of China, China Construction Bank, Agricultural Bank of China or the Bank of China. Industry pundits are arguing that the Chinese banks have already substantially benefited from the increase in car financing, with the volume of car loans increasing over 286% between 1998 and 2002. In essence, this could negatively impact purchasing power of the Chinese consumers (especially the middle and lower classes) if there is lack of competition between financial institutions. The Chinese middle class is expected to balloon to 200 million in 2004. Since many of the manufacturers are putting forth affordable models aimed at the middle class, the lack of financing competition and the inability to facilitate loans for its middle class consumers could impede sales.

VOLKSWAGEN GROUP

The Volkswagen Group did not wait until the Chinese WTO in December 2001 or the well-publicized potential before entering the Chinese car market. VW forged established themselves in China in 1985. As an organization, they have the following mission statement:

> It is the goal of the Group to offer attractive, safe, and environmentally friendly vehicles which are competitive on an increasingly tough market and which set world standards in their respective classes.

Company Overview

The Volkswagen Group with its headquarters in Wolfsburg is one of the world's leading automobile manufacturers and the largest car producer in Europe. In 2002, the Volkswagen Group achieved the second-highest profit before tax in the company's history at 4.0 billion and attained a global market share of 12.1 percent. It is the parent company of all other companies in the Volkswagen Group, which are either wholly owned subsidiaries or companies of which Volkswagen AG has majority ownership.

The Group operates 44 production plants in eleven European countries and seven countries in the Americas, Asia, and Africa. Around the world more than 320,000 employees produce over 21,500 vehicles or are involved in vehicle-related services. The Volkswagen Group sells its vehicles in more than 150 countries.

Key Numbers:	
2002 Sales (mil.)	$91,130.2
1-Year Sales Growth	16.2%
2002 Net Income (mil.)	$2,708.3
1-Year Net Income Growth	4.9%
2002 Employees	324,892
1-Year Employee Growth	0.9%

Brand Groups

The Volkswagen Auto Group is comprised of the Audi, the Volkswagen and the Volkswagen Commercial Vehicle Brand Groups. The Audi and Volkswagen Groups encompass the company's passenger car business and are responsible for the results of their respective Brand Group worldwide. Audi's Brand Group is made up of the Audi, Seat and Lamborghini brands and places an emphasis on sporty values. The Volkswagen Brand Group is made up of the Volkswagen, Škoda Auto, Bentley and Bugatti brands and stands for more classic values. Each brand retains its differentiated brand-image and operates as an independent entity on the market. Together, the product ranges extend from the low-consumption 3-liter vehicle to luxury class vehicles.

The Group's commercial vehicle products are the responsibility of the Volkswagen Commercial Vehicles brand.

Sustainable Development & Corporate Responsibility

As the presence of Volkswagen AG expands around the globe, so too does the company's commitment to social responsibility. Volkswagen AG has identified that a company can only practice sustainable development if it is constantly aware of the social, economic and ecological dimensions and consequences of its corporate activities.

For Volkswagen, sustainability and responsibility to society mean the ability to develop solutions for economic, environmental and social problems. Dialogue and cooperation are important principles in this process. The Volkswagen Group is a founding member of the World Business Council for Sustainable Development (WBCSD) and the business-to-business network for Corporate Social Responsibility (CSR Europe).

GERMAN TRACTION: VOLKSWAGEN IN CHINA

Volkswagen realized the potential for the Chinese market for automobiles some 19 years earlier, and from this vision sought out to establish a joint venture that would make them the first major foreign car company in China. Although this relationship had humble beginnings, the fact is that the immense growth and increased demand in automotive industry have led Volkswagen to be the most established foreign car brand in China.

Looking back, VW's efforts in China may have been susceptible to criticism, because getting in first in China has often proved foolish. Many early joint ventures were ill-advised partnerships between overconfident foreigners and inexperienced, often greedy locals. VW, however, played its cards right and enjoyed a bit of luck. Volkswagen has been able to position itself as the primary brand in the passenger vehicle market. In 1999, it was believed that VW controlled 60% of the passenger-car market. As recently as August 2003, Volkswagen was still recognized as China's biggest foreign automaker and currently holds a 37% market share in China.

Clearly, Volkswagen was "ahead of the curve" in China since much of the recent press depicts many of the other foreign automakers are still quickly trying to establish themselves in a market that is booming. Major players in this industry like GM and BMW are still no where near as established as VW. So much so, that GM has now established a joint venture with the same production company as VW used 19 years ago. The fact is that although many companies see the benefit of entrance in the automotive market in China few have the same established brand, and brand equity that VW has in the market.

VOLKSWAGEN'S ENTRY STRATEGY

A major reason why VW has been able to dominate in China is due to their joint ventures established with prominent players in China's automotive industry. VW co-owns Shanghai VW with Shanghai Automotive and FAW-VW with First Automotive Works Corp. VW was the first foreign carmaker to set up a joint venture in China back in 1985, in Shanghai. VW established ties with powerful local partners at a time when there was little competition but a surging demand for cars. Better yet, the government in Shanghai shielded VW from central government meddling and gave the joint venture quite a bit of business at a time when institutions rather than individuals bought most cars. Now, for 2001, VW's two joint ventures will turn out more than 400,000 Audis, Jettas, Passats, Santanas, and Polos. "Everybody in China knows Volkswagen," says Credit Suisse First Boston analyst Catherine Zhu.

These partnerships have allowed VW to localize production, which in turn minimizes production costs, and creates a more efficient method of distribution. VW can expect to remain the market leader in China for a few more years. Other carmakers will find it hard to beat VW's prices, kept lower by the fact that 90% of its cars' parts are locally produced. Competitor General Motors Corp.'s new $44,000 Buick GS sedan has only 60% of its components made in China, and its sales have been disappointing. SAIC is "the largest and most successful automotive manufacturer in China" and when VW established a relationship with them, they established a relationship with a trusted brand amongst the Chinese market, and a powerhouse within the industry.

Shanghai VW formed in 1985 boasting brand names like Polo, Passat and Santana 2000 series. Shanghai Volkswagen has won the confidence of Chinese consumers with its high quality and good after-sale service, said the official, stating that apart from weighing up between price and high quality, Chinese consumers are now paying more attention to brand and service. FAW-VW, formed in 1991, makes the Jetta, Bora and Golf sedans, plus the Audi A4 and A6.

CURRENT LANDSCAPE OF VW'S POSITION

Volkswagen has suffered a decreasing market share over the past few years, but as noted in Exhibit 3 below, VW's sales have increased during that same time period. Increased competition from Honda, Toyota, GM, Ford, and Mitsubishi has eroded VW's market share.

China has become an integral part of Volkswagen's earnings. In fact, investment firm Goldman Sachs believes that because VW's profitability in China is slipping the German car maker's overall performance could be hurt. The investment firm believes that China represented over 80% of Volkswagens 2003 first-half earnings. Proof of China's importance to VW was evident in April 2003 when Volkswagen CEO Bernd Pischetsrieder announced that VW sold more new vehicles in China than it did in Germany. This is the first time in its 65-year history that VW sold more cars in a foreign country than in Germany in a given period.

VW PRODUCTION

While their competitors, like GM, are attempting to establish their first production facility in China, VW has already established two, with plans to open a third facility to manufacture engines for domestic use and export. Volkswagen believes this plant will help them reach their goal of doubling annual production by 2007. A Volkswagen official said the company plans on investing more than EUR 6 billion in China region over the next five years. The main reason why this is possible,

EXHIBIT 3
VW'S FALLING MARKET SHARE IN CHINA

Manufacturer	Projected 2003 Unit Sales %)	2002 Unit Sales (share %)	2001 Unit Sales (share %)
TOTAL MARKET	**1,680,000 (100%)**	**1,266,000 (100%)**	**717,945 (100%)**
Shanghai VW	359,000 (21.3%)	308,000 units (24.3%)	230,050 units (32.1%)
FAW-VW	241,000 (14.3%)	205,000 (16.1%)	124,399 (17.3%)

and why it can happen so expeditiously, is because the relationships and financial stability of these joint ventures, which have been in place for a combined 30 years.

Another aspect of the Chinese market from which VW, and other foreign carmakers, have benefited is the low-cost manufacturing. Unfortunately for carmakers there is a reason for the low cost, and that is low skills. The Chinese government is probably aware of this and is enthusiastic about the flourishing auto industry, which requires above average workforce skills. One instance of poor manufacturing has already

been identified, and it involved ignition coils on VW China's Bora model. Although this is only one instance of poor manufacturing, this is an inherent weakness of the current Chinese workforce.

Infrastructure also remains a challenge, because the market seems to be growing faster than the roads and highways to support it, more roads are necessary to handle the booming auto sales. Major traffic jams on the roads in cities have been cited.

Who Makes What Where? Existing/Planned Major Assembly Operations in China

Auto Maker	Chinese Partner	Products	Plant Location
BMW	Brilliance China	3-, 5-Series	Shenyang
DaimlerChrysler	Beijing Automotive	Jeep Cherokee and Grand Cherokee; Mitsubishi Pajero Sport, Outlander, Lancer and Cedia; Mercedes C- and E-Class	Beijing
Fiat	Yuejin Automotive	Palio, Palio Weekend, Siena, Ducato	Nanjing
Ford	Chongqing Changan Auto	Fiesta, Mondeo, Ikon	Chongqing
Ford	Jiangling Motors	Transit	Nanchang
GM	Shanghai Automotive	Buick Century, Sail, GL8 and Excelle; Opel Corsa, Zafira and Combo	Shanghai
GM	Brilliance China	Chevrolet Blazer, Tahoe, TrailBlazer	Shenyang
GM	Shanghai Automotive, Wuling Automotive	Chevrolet Spark	Liuzhou
Honda	Guangzhou Automotive	Accord, Odyssey, Fit, Civic, CR-V, Mobilio	Guangzhou
Honda	Guangzhou Automotive/Dongfeng Motor	1L-1.5L cars	Guangzhou
Hyundai	Beijing Automotive	EF Sonata, Elantra, XD, Click/Getz, Lavita, Matrix, Trajet XG	Beijing
Isuzu	Changfeng Motor	Rodeo	Younghou
Isuzu	Qingling Motors/ Jianxi Motors	Rodeo	Nanchang
Mazda	First Auto	Mazda6	Changchun
Mazda	First Auto	Premacy, 323, Familia	Haikou
Mitsubishi	Changfeng Motor	Pajero	Younghou
Nissan	Dongfeng Motor/Fengshen	Bluebird, March, Sunny, Cefiro,	Guangzhou
Nissan	Zhengzhou	Paladin, Navara, March, pickups	Zhengzhou
PSA Peugeot Citroen	Dongfeng Motor	Citroen Elysee, Xsara Picasso, ZX, Saxo and Berlingo; Peugeot 307, Platform 2	Wuhan
Suzuki	Chongqing Changan Auto	Alto, City Baby, Gazelle, Happy Prince, Cultus	Chongqing
Suzuki	Jiangxi Changhe Automobile	Swift	Jingdezhen
Toyota	First Auto	Land Cruiser	Changchun
Toyota	First Auto	Crown/Camry	Tianjin
Toyota	Sichuan Motor	Land Cruiser	Chengdu
Toyota	First Auto/Tianjin Motor	Vios, Corolla, Crown, Vitz	Tianjin

Source: Wards Auto, November 1, 2003.

VW'S COMPETITION

Every carmaker wants to be in China. With a population of over 1.2 billion and with the second largest in terms of purchasing power parity, China presents a highly attractive market. The Chinese accession into the WTO, coupled with falling car prices in China and rising incomes seems to have fueled an unprecedented boom in the Chinese market. It is predicted that the Chinese auto market will grow 9% annually for the next five years and 15% a year after that. That would mean Chinese consumers will be buying 2 million cars annually, three times the current total. Foreign carmakers have rushed to take advantage of the market, teaming up the local car manufacturers in China.

General Motors

The world's biggest car manufacturer started with a local alliance with the Shanghai Automotive industry in 1997. It introduced the Buick in the Chinese market in 1998 with manufacturing done locally in Shanghai. Subsequently it also introduced the Chevrolet in the market. Their current manufacturing capacity in Shanghai is around 150,000 units of which about 75% is dedicated to manufacturing Buicks while the rest is utilized for the manufacture of the Chevrolet. The Buick Regal is currently priced at $29,455 (RMB 243,800) while the Buick GL2.5 is priced at $31,871(RMB 263,800). GM currently has an 8.2% share of the China car market and ranks second to VW in terms of overall market share. About 1/3 of its cars have an average selling price of around $30,000. This suggests that the Chinese consumer perceives GM to be a premium carmaker. Understanding these current aspirations of the Chinese consumers to own upscale cars, GM is planning to introduce Cadillacs in China. Cadillacs will be assembled alongside Buicks at GM's Shanghai plant, which will hike capacity by 50 percent to 300,000 vehicles by the end of 2005.

Ford

Though the Ford T model was first launched in China in 1914, Ford hasn't made any major inroads in China till date. Infact, it only entered China through a local alliance with Changan Automobile group in 2001. Ford has pledged to invest more than $1 billion over the next two years in China and intends to be the second biggest player in China by 2007 with about 10% market share. Its current car manufacturing capacity is around 50,000 units and it plans to raise that to about 150,000 units by next year. The "Fiesta," their present offering in China is a four-door sedan and is targeted to the middle class price conscious consumers. However, they have been outclassed in the market by the VW Golf and Bora, and the GM Buick, which also caters to the same consumer. Ford actually suffered a loss of $25.3 million in the third quarter this year. However it still is extremely optimistic about its future in China and now plans to shift its focus to the luxury car market segment. Ford plans to sell its premium brands like Mondeo and Maverick and also plans to introduce the Volvo, Aston Martin, Land Rover and Jaguar in this market. This is a strategic move to strengthen the company's brand position in the increasingly competitive Chinese market. However competition is intense in the luxury market with the likes of the Audi, Mercedes, and BMWs with GM and Nissan planning to introduce its own luxury brands in this market. Ford will have to continuously invest in product quality and service networks if it wants to be a leading player in this market.

Toyota

In a car market that is dominated by European and US car manufacturers, Toyota is the one of the first Japanese companies to lead the charge for Japanese car entry in this market. However, Toyota the world's third largest car manufacturer entered the Chinese car market only recently in the year 2002 through a local alliance with FAW. From almost a standing start in 2001, Toyota has built up a significant presence and charted massive expansion plans in China. By 2005, it expects to have plants from the country's northeast to its deep interior, producing 250,000 vehicles a year—about 10% of the vehicles Toyota and its affiliates produce outside Japan today. By 2010, Toyota executives hope to sell a million vehicles in China, an important piece of Toyota's broader strategy to grab 15% of the world market and be the no.1 auto manufacturer in the world. "I'd resign from Toyota if I couldn't pull it all off in China," said Mr. Akio Toyoda, the grandson of the founder of Toyota motors in a recent interview with Wall Street Journal reporter.[3] Currently the company makes "Vios"—small cars for the middle class private consumers in China. Its current selling price is around $17,000. However Toyota and its FAW plan to invest around 3 billion Yuan (US$360 million) to produce four new models at their local joint ventures (JVs) in the economy and the luxury SUV segments by the end of 2005. The new models, to be produced within two years, will be the Crown, Corolla, Land Cruiser, and Land Cruiser Prado. The company is also in negotiations with Guangzhou Automobile group to produce Camry Sedans for the upscale consumers. The company is currently in negotiations with several local car manufacturers, and also intends to expand its current dealer network to penetrate throughout China.

PRICING

From a pricing perspective, the combination of increased imports and increased localized production by foreign carmakers is driving down prices. Manufacturers such as Volkswagen, GM, Honda and Dongfeng Peugeot had to cut prices in 2003 due to the increasing supply of cars across all market segments. For example, GM has dropped the price of its 2.5 liter Buick sedan and its compact Sail model, and VW has dropped the price on its upscale Passat as well as its mid-sized Bora. Overall, Chinese car prices are expected to fall by an average of 8 to 10% by the end of 2003. With the current pricing strategy, VW is attempting to address all the consumer markets in the China. The Golf and the economy versions of the Polo are priced to attract the mass markets that aspire to own a car but can't really afford to buy an expensive car. With the Santana, a taxi like car, and the high end Passats VW has targeted the niche fast growing luxury car market currently targeting state-owned enterprises and the affluent class in China. The Bora is actually targeting a completely a new segment in the Chinese market—the private consumers. According to the National Bureau of Statistics latest report in May' 2003, 360,000 cars were sold in China during the first four months this year, with about 60% bought by individuals.

---

[3]http://uk.biz.yahoo.com/031119/241/eefny.html

VW Pricing

Model	Price($)	Price(RMB)	Model Type	Capacity
Golf	$12,500	100000 RMB	Automatic economy model	1.4 lts
Bora	$19,500	161300 RMB	Automatic compact model	1.5 lts
Bora	$27,448	227000 RMB	Automatic compact model	1.5 lts
Passat	$25,300	209500 RMB	Automatic luxury model	1.8 lts
Passat	$39,750	329000 RMB	Automatic economy model	2.8 lts
Santana	$21,687	180000 RMB	Automatic economy model	1.4 lts
Polo	$15,400	127500 RMB	Manual economy model	1.4 lts
Polo	$15,471	128100 RMB	Manual economy model	1.4 lts
Polo	$16,908	140000 RMB	Manual luxury model	1.4 lts
Polo	$16,304	135500 RMB	Automatic economic model	1.4 lts
Polo	$16,437	136100 RMB	Automatic economic model	1.4 lts
Polo	$17,874	148000 RMB	Automatic luxury model	1.4 lts

The idea of supply increasing and prices falling is basic macroeconomics, but the Volkswagen Group is expected to withstand the market's move to cut prices better than its competition. VW has already established strong local production and offers a wide range of models to the Chinese shoppers (currently offers 11 models with an additional 4 planned to hit the market in 2004).

LOOKING DOWN THE ROAD

Simply stated, VW has more positioning and production leverage. For example, with so many models, VW can be very versatile when it comes to continuing and discontinuing models as necessary based on competition and consumer purchasing power. Also, with such a large portfolio, VW can adjust the positioning of its models to keep the competition off balance.

As Volkswagen attempts to slow their market share erosion, they have expanded their marketing efforts on sponsorships. They are focusing their efforts on social awareness in the form of one million Yuan to help fight SARS and its third annual tree planting day, music events, and Chinese auto shows.

Volkswagen's 50% market share in 2001 is already down to around 36% in 2003, and the likes of the Japanese, North Americans, South Koreans, other Europeans, and Vietnamese are waking up to the potential VW acted upon years ago. Even though Volkswagen China's general manager, Zhang Suixin, has admitted "It is an unrealistic goal for us to control 50% of China's car market according to the current market development," VW will undoubtedly attempt to hold onto as much market share as possible.

CASE 5

WAL-MART OPERATIONS IN BRAZIL: AN EMERGING GIANT

INTRODUCTION

In September 1994, Brazil was experiencing a new thrust in its economy. After several years of hyperinflation, the "Real Plan," implemented in March 1994, an economic stabilization program that indexed the Brazilian currency to the U.S. dollar, began to reduce inflation to reasonable levels. In February 1994, the annual inflation rate was 40 percent, whereas by September of that same year, it was a relatively low 3 percent. A lower inflation rate was viewed as a viable step in improving the purchasing power of the Brazilian people, particularly those in the lower socioeconomic stratum.

Professor Masaaki Kotabe, Louie Pranic, and Richard Smith of the Fox School of Business and Management at Temple University and Kleber G. de Godoy and Moacir Salzstein of Fundação Getúlio Vargas, São Paulo, Brazil, prepared this case as the basis for class discussion rather than to illustrate either effective or ineffective management of a situation described, (2006).

The optimistic scenario encouraged many foreign companies to make new investments in Brazil. If Brazil is the leading economy in Latin America with a population of more than 170 million, why not invest there, now that a better business horizon lies ahead in this continental country? Wal-Mart Stores, the world leader in retailing, announced on May 9, 1994, that it had decided to invest heavily in Brazil through a partnership with Lojas Americanas, Brazil's leading department store chain.

Following the implementation of "Real Plan" in 1994, and subsequent stabilization of Brazil's economy, appreciation of the U.S. dollar in the late 1990s and a global economic slowdown due to the Asian crisis forced the country to float its currency in January 1999. As a result, inflation increased moderately from 3 percent to 8.9 percent but has steadily declined since, with a 8 percent inflation rate at the end of 2005. In addition, with estimated economic growth of 5 percent for 2005, Brazil was viewed as a viable investment opportunity by foreign investors. As an illustration of Brazil's economic prospects, it must be pointed that the year 2000 showed a record amount of direct foreign investment in Brazil from abroad, amounting to US$30 billion. However, a recent energy crisis presents significant problems to Brazil's economy and its retail industry, in lieu of changes in consumers' purchase behavior and income allocation.

WAL-MART OPERATIONS

Sam Walton entered the retail business through a small store in Newport, Arkansas, in 1945, as a variety store franchisee. Six years later, he decided to open his own stores with the name "Walton's Five and Dime," referring to the coins that could have value to the customers.

As of 2005, there were 5,379 Wal-Mart units around the world, with 3,752 located in the United States, 706 in Mexico, 291 in the United Kingdom, 261 in Canada, 89 in Germany, 152 in Brazil, 54 in Puerto Rico, 47 in China, 11 in Argentina, and 16 in Korea. Net sales for the year 2004 totaled $287 billion (see Exhibits 1 and 2). Wal-Mart also owns a 37.8 percent interest in Japan's Seiyu Ltd., which operates 403 stores in Japan.

Wal-Mart operates with five different divisions within the United States: Wal-Mart Stores, Wal-Mart Supercenters, Sam's Club, McLane's Company, and Wal-Mart International. Wal-Mart Stores is the division accounting for about 55 percent of total company revenues. Wal-Mart Supercenters generates 10 percent of total company revenues and is the fastest growing division. In the United States, there are three different Supercenters: Wal-Mart Supercenters, Hypermart USA's, and Bud's Warehouse Outlets. Supercenters are stores with more than 10,000 m^2 of area and a minimum of 40,000 items. Sam's Club is the division responsible for 25 percent of revenues. The first Sam's Club—a "buyers' club," namely, a store where the consumer pays an annual fee to have access—was opened in 1976. By the end of 2005, there were already more than 500 Sam's Clubs in the United States. McLane's Company is Wal-Mart's distribution company. Wal-Mart acquired this company, a leading distribution company, in 1990. In 1995, McLane's represented 6 percent of Wal-Mart's total revenues. McLane's has 14 distribution centers in the United States and caters not only to Wal-Mart needs but also to 25,000 other retailing stores in the United States.

EXHIBIT 1
WAL-MART STORES (2005)

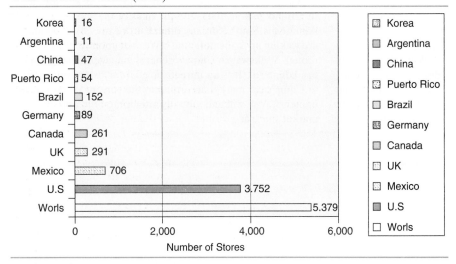

EXHIBIT 2
WAL-MART NET SALES

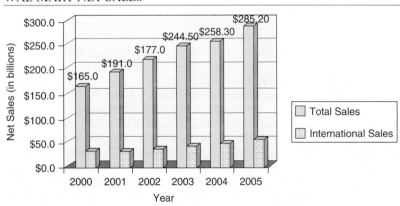

Wal-Mart International, the fifth division, accounts for 17 percent of Wal-Mart's total revenues, with net sales of $35 billion for the year 2002. The international division is the fastest growing, with over 41 percent increase in net sales from the year 2000.

INTERNATIONAL EXPANSION

In the second half of the 1980s, Wal-Mart began its international expansion in Mexico, Canada, Argentina, Hong Kong, and Brazil, among others. The company expected that all its strengths and retailing knowledge could leverage operations abroad as well as the efficient logistics and communication systems. The company considered that with a prospective of market globalization, the brand "Wal-Mart" could be a competitive advantage in many countries where it would operate. The company also decided that the entry strategy in each country should be through a partnership with local companies. A brief summary of Wal-Mart's international operations in Mexico and Canada is provided in order to ensure better understanding of Wal-Mart's operation in Brazil.

Mexico

Mexico was the first country in which Wal-Mart initiated its international expansion. The first store was opened in 1991. The local partner was Cifra, a Mexican retailing leader. It is undeniable that Wal-Mart has had some difficulties adapting to and understanding Mexican culture and consumer habits. For example, Mexican consumers prefer to buy Mexican food and other goods rather than American products. Wal-Mart insisted on prioritizing imported goods from the United States for a long time. Another problem in Mexico is related to the Mexican habit of buying food in small stores rather than in supermarkets.

Despite its initially disappointing performance, Wal-Mart is currently Mexico's largest retailer. This success was achieved only after the company changed its name from Cifra to Wal-Mart de Mexico, and spread its operations into six different retail formats and the country's largest sit-down restaurant chain. Wal-Mart de Mexico's six retail formats allowed the company to meet the needs and purchase behaviors of various customer segments. In November 2004, Wal-Mart opened a massive 7.5 acre Superstore a mile from Mexico's holy area, Teotihuaćan, just outside of Mexico City.

Canada

In Canada, Wal-Mart preferred to acquire a local chain— Woolco—instead of having a local partner. Due to the maturity of the Canadian retail market, and due to significant income and cultural similarities between the United States and Canadian markets, acquisition was arguably the easiest way for Wal-Mart to tap into Canada. Since most Canadians live near the U.S. border, they were already familiar with the company. Hence, Wal-Mart leveraged this high brand recognition into customer acceptance and loyalty by introducing its "Everyday Low Prices" approach to a market accustomed to high/low retail pricing. Coincidence or not, Canada is the most successful Wal-Mart operation abroad. Nevertheless, out of the 196 stores in Canada, 122 were originally Woolco stores. By the year 2002, Wal-Mart was Canada's number one retailer with revenues of approximately $8.75 billion, just eight years after its entry into Canada. In early 2005 Wal-Mart shut down its only unionized store in Canada, claiming it was due to dropping sales and the problem of dealing with a union.

ENTRY INTO BRAZIL

Wal-Mart's original intention was to achieve the number one retailer position in the Brazilian retail market through a partnership with a local "player" in a very short period of time. In order to achieve this ambitious goal, Bentonville headquarters planned a logistics and communication infrastructure capable of supporting no fewer than 80 stores in the Brazilian market. In addition, the headquarters' intention was to export its expertise and practices in the form of an extensive set of operational manuals that proved successful in the United States, including product assortment and internal space utilization as well as its product mix.

Wal-Mart began its operation in Brazil in spectacular fashion. The first five stores were opened in a few months and, through a very aggressive pricing strategy, attracted thousands of enthusiastic consumers ready to empty the shelves. Another attraction was employees' disposition to help consumers, as well as wide product offering. Overall, during its initial periods of operation in the Brazilian market, Wal-Mart had captured a very favorable image from consumers and, subsequently, had painted a dark picture for its competitors' future.

The initially aggressive and promising entry strategy came to a halt after Wal-Mart immediately encountered severe unexpected operational problems. Long checkout lines, a high stockout rate (40 percent), unreliable supply lines, faulty management-performance measures, traffic congestion, competitors' reactions, and governmental forces were responsible for Wal-Mart's initial failure in the Brazilian retail market.

Following Wal-Mart's disappointing performance in the Brazilian retail market, the company had to revise its originally aggressive strategy. To accomplish this, some valuable lessons learned from Wal-Mart's international expansion into Mexico and Canada had to be incorporated into the redesigned strategy for Brazil. Consequently, Wal-Mart's strategy revision planned for adoption of a more conservative and controlled expansion, consolidation of distribution lines, and improved assimilation into the Brazilian culture. An example of Wal-Mart's revised strategy included the opening of only 10 stores from 1995 to 1997, down from the initial 80-plus stores. Furthermore, Wal-Mart intended to acquire an existing retail chain instead of exploring other partnerships, as was originally planned. In addition, the company wanted to acquire experienced managers from other competitors.

CHALLENGES IN BRAZIL

The challenges that Wal-Mart has experienced in Brazil may be grouped into six categories: state of the economy, cultural differences, management, advertising, logistics and distribution, and competition.

Economy

Since Wal-Mart's entry into the Brazilian retail market in 1994 until the end of 2001, Brazil's economy has been all but stable. The "Real Plan," implemented in 1994 to curb the currency hyperinflation brought the inflation rate from 40 percent in the year it was instituted to 3 percent in 1999. Thanks to the appreciation of the U.S. dollar, the Asian financial crisis, and a resulting global economic slowdown, Brazil floated its currency in 1999, as was the case prior to the Real Plan of 1994. This caused the inflation to increase moderately to 8.9 percent in 1999, but it was brought down to 5.3 percent at the end of 2001. However, triggered by the national currency depreciation, inflation increased again in 2002 and had crossed 8 percent by 2005.

The Brazilian economy was recently struck with the energy crisis. The crisis was the result of Brazil's electricity consumption exceeding its production, thus forcing the import of electricity from Paraguay. Although the current state of the Brazilian economy could be characterized as somewhat stable as compared to that before 1994, the future outlook of the economy does not provide any guarantees on a long-term basis.

Cultural Differences

Brazilian retail consumers consider product quality the most important factor in the decision-making process of purchasing, followed by product price, customer service, store cleanliness, and store distance.

Most Brazilians prefer shopping in small- to medium-sized neighborhood stores. Nevertheless, they also enjoy the occasional shopping trip to a big discount supercenter. This trip, however, occurs only once a month, and thus making so-called monthly purchases, instead of weekly as in the United States. Yet the current energy crisis has forced most Brazilians to turn off their freezers and to adjust their shopping habits accordingly. Namely, food-related trips to the store in Brazil have increased in frequency but decreased in the quantity of food purchased, especially in perishable goods.

Despite the unbelievably bad traffic jams, the average São Paulo residents are willing to take the long trip to a specific Supercenter if they perceive it as cost efficient and need satisfying. Similarly, Brazilian consumers do not greatly appreciate the notion of having to pay a membership fee in order to shop at Sam's Club, especially when shopping at a "buyer's club" is not perceived as providing greater savings and overall extra benefit to the end-consumer.

The product mix in Wal-Mart's supercenters should reflect the needs of Brazilian consumers as closely as possible. Offering products popular in the United States such as golf equipment, vacuum cleaners for garden leaves, American footballs, and food grinders shows complete ignorance to Brazilian consumers since they have little or no use for these items. Assigning 25 percent of supercenter space for food in a country where food represents 60 percent of supermarket sales is another example of Wal-Mart's cultural ignorance.

Management

Because of dissimilarities in income and culture between U.S. and Brazilian markets, a greater degree of managerial autonomy may be desirable for Wal-Mart in Brazil. In addition, Wal-Mart in Brazil has not made full use of the concept of getting back to the basics, or in other words, implementing Sam Walton's "Management by Walking Around" concept. A faulty product mix and store-space misallocation present examples of bad management policies. Moreover, Wal-Mart's overall corporate grip on its subsidiary in Brazil can best be exemplified by the fact that performance of the local managers in Brazil was based primarily on store sales volume.

Thus, managers set prices below cost to artificially stimulate demand and inflate sales volume numbers. Managers should have greater freedom in managing on a micro level. Wal-Mart, recognizing the need to hire professionals, has recently started a head-hunting campaign to acquire proven professionals from local competitors. This move should reduce Wal-Mart's need to micromanage the Brazilian effort.

Advertising

Many Brazilian consumers, housewives in particular, listen to the radio during the day while cooking and/or cleaning the house. Radio advertisements, therefore, should be used to reach and attract potential shoppers. Contrary to logic, however, Wal-Mart did not use radio as a medium for communicating to its customers. The company uses some television and newspaper advertising, but the resources allocated to the overall advertising campaign amount roughly to only 2 percent of Wal-Mart's revenues. Although Wal-Mart has hired a Brazilian advertising agency, the lack of autonomy given to the agency defeats the whole purpose of "going local" through advertising.

Logistics and Distribution

Initially, Wal-Mart experienced an alarming 40 percent stockout rate in Brazil, as compared to 5 percent in the United States. Although the stockout rate has decreased since then, the problem is far from being completely eliminated. Namely, Brazilian suppliers are lagging behind their U.S. counterparts in logistics technology, thus making computerized inventory management systems useless. In addition, constant traffic jams present another major obstacle to consistency and predictability in supply of both Wal-Mart stores and distribution center(s).

Competition

Since Wal-Mart entered the Brazilian retail market in 1994, competition has been ever increasing, and all to the benefit of end-consumers. Many retailers are focused on expansion into different retail formats, with the purpose of targeting different customer segments. Increasing the number of stores across the country is another way retailers compete in Brazil. Thanks to Wal-Mart, "price wars" are the most visible effects of fierce competition.

According to 1995 data, Brazil's entire retail industry accounts for 6.6 percent of GNP, with total consolidated sales of US$43.7 billion. The top five retailers in the Brazilian retail market account for roughly US$11.2 billion. The 1997 data show that Wal-Mart's major competitors are Carrefour, Companhia Brasileira de Distrubuição (Pão de Açucar), Royal Ahold, and Makro Atacadista. In addition, some smaller retail chains and a large number of individually owned stores account for the remaining portion of the Brazilian retail market.

Carrefour. Carrefour, a giant French retailer that entered the Brazilian retail market in 1974, is the oldest and most established foreign competitor. This company has fully adapted to Brazilian culture and thus is not viewed as a foreign company. Carrefour currently controls 20 percent of the Brazilian market, with 229 stores total. Interestingly enough, the French retailer purchased 23 supermarkets from Wal-Mart's entry partner, Lojas Americanas, in 1998 when that company exited the grocery business.

In addition, Carrefour merged with Promodes SA, the rival Brazilian retailer, in 1999 in an attempt to achieve an even stronger position in that market. Decentralized management style and effective advertising campaigns continue being Carrefour's competitive strengths.

Companhia Brasileira de Distrubuição (CBD).   CBD, the second largest food retailer in Brazil, currently operates more than 500 stores in Brazil with over US$4.7 billion in total sales for 2004. The company is grouped into hypermarkets, supermarkets, an electronics and home appliances division, and an e-commerce division. The supermarket division consists of two retail formats: Pão de Açucar and Barateiro Supermercados. Pão de Açucar's total 2000 sales were similar to those of Carrefour. When adding the sales of Barateiro Supermercados, the division that caters to the lower class, CBD's total sales make it the number one competitor within Brazil. With regard to the ownership of the company, France's Casino Group currently owns minority share (40 percent) in CBD. Use of Sam Walton's "Management by Walking Around" concept continues to be one of CBD's advantages.

Royal Ahold.   Royal Ahold is a Dutch firm specializing in supermarket retailing. Surprisingly enough, the company entered the Brazilian retail market through a joint venture with Brazil's fourth largest retailer, Bompreco, in 1996. The company has since purchased Bompreco and is currently the leading food retailer in the northeast region of Brazil, with 108 hypermarkets and supermarkets. Royal Ahold's 2002 sales totaled 16.4 billion euros (approximately US$17 billion). Local retailer flexibility and rich product mix present the company's source of advantage.

Makro Atacadista.   Makro Atacadista is another Dutch retailer whose wholesale outlets represent direct competition to Wal-Mart's Sam's Club. Established in 1972, the company currently operates more than 30 stores across most of the country. It has over 1.3 million registered users, of which 80 percent are small business owners and the remaining 20 percent are individual customers. Unlike Sam's Club, Makro Atacadista charges no annual fee to its members. Selling third-party products under its own brand name (thus achieving economies of scale in advertising) continues to be a major advantage for the company.

WAL-MART NOW

Since originally entering the Brazilian retail market in 1995, Wal-Mart has revised its strategy and has consequently gained a substantial share of the marketplace. Although Wal-Mart is currently the sixth largest retailer in Brazil, it still holds a relatively small share of the retail market, which is dominated by the French retailer Carrefour. Still, future prospects are looking good for Wal-Mart in Brazil.

As of 2005, Wal-Mart had a total of 152 stores in operation (see Exhibit 3) and 7 percent of the market. Out of 152 Wal-Mart stores in Brazil today, it operates under three different formats: 16 Supercenters, 11 Sam's Clubs, and 2 Wal-Mart Todo Dia stores in the states of São Paulo, Rio de Janeiro, Minas Gerais, and Parana (AOL Latin America Announces Marketing Alliance with Wal-Mart Brazil, 2001). To add to that is the newly acquired 118 Bompreço unit formats. Bompreço stores are operated under various formats. Bompreço stores sell apparel, food, and general merchandize. Prior to this acquisition, some industry analysts believed that Wal-Mart was facing problems succeeding in Brazil because it had not made an acquisition.

As previously stated, Wal-Mart's first revised strategy called for the opening of only 10 stores from 1995 to 1997, down from initial plans of over 80 stores. Looking back, Wal-Mart actually opened only three stores over that same time period. Most of the expansion occurred within the two years until 2001 (see Exhibit 4 for store openings). Wal-Mart revealed its

EXHIBIT 3
NUMBER OF WAL-MART STORES IN BRAZIL (2004)

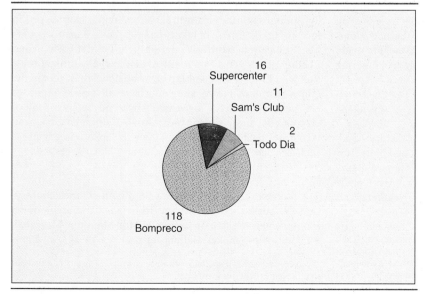

EXHIBIT 4
BRAZIL STORE OPENINGS

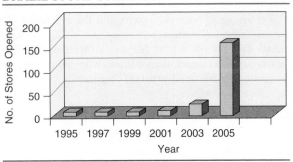

revised plan for expansion in Brazil in July 2002. According to the plan, the company would inaugurate five stores in Brazil. However, by the end of 2002, the total number of stores in operation continued to be 22. But, in the next few years until 2005, Wal-Mart added a whopping 130 stores to bring the total to 152. Most of these stores (118) were acquired from Royal Ahold in 2004.

In May of 2001, Wal-Mart opened the Barueri distribution center in São Paulo. Wal-Mart previously had three rented, limited-capacity distribution centers. The new distribution center has 35,000 square meters of storage space and is built on a 200,000 square meter lot owned by Wal-Mart. This new facility is designed to easily supply 20 local stores at its current size; it gives Wal-Mart better control over supply lines and allows for future building expansion.

In May of 2001, Wal-Mart also opened its first Todo Dia store in the eastern São Paulo section, Sapopemba. Since the Sapopemba section of São Paulo is inhabited mostly by a lower income segment of the population, this move signals that Wal-Mart is looking to increase its market share through catering to different market segments. Another Todo Dia store opened on October 10, 2001, in the Taboao de Serra region of São Paulo, with a third store scheduled for opening by the end of the fiscal year 2001. As opposed to a Wal-Mart Supercenter which carries 60,000 items, Wal-Mart's Todo Dia carries only 12,000 items. Besides being a smaller format store, Todo Dia's inventory is stored directly above display shelves. It is reasonable to suspect that Wal-Mart's introduction of the Todo Dia store format is being used to test the market in Brazil for future expansion into local and extremely value-conscious neighborhoods. This strategy is similar to that of Wal-Mart de Mexico where the company currently dominates the retail market with six retail formats.

In line with Wal-Mart's revised strategy which called for improved assimilation into Brazilian culture, the company is currently involved with local communities, supporting social programs such as Special Olympics Brazil and Mesa São Paulo.

Wal-Mart's latest move is the announcement of the marketing alliance with AOL Latin America whereby AOL Brazil will be promoted in all Wal-Mart and Sam's Club units in Brazil. This marketing partnership is a logical strategic response to the current growth of the e-commerce sector. The value of business-to-consumer (B2C) e-commerce sales is forecasted to reach $4.3 billion in 2005. The number of Internet users in Brazil is expected to jump to 29 million in 2005.

The Wal-Mart executive team in Brazil will be meeting with business consultants in a few weeks. In the meantime, they are wondering whether they have made the right moves for further expansion in the Brazilian market.

CASE 6

LOUIS VUITTON IN JAPAN: THE MAGIC TOUCH

It was a hot August night on the streets of the swank Omotesando district, but that did not deter 1,400 people from waiting in a mile-long line for the grand opening of the new Louis Vuitton store. As Japanese movie star Ryoko Yonekura made her appearance, the crowd cheered in anticipation of entering the store for an early opportunity to pay $700 for a knapsack or above $1,500 for a suitcase stamped with the LV trademark initials. Opening day sales were $1.04 million, setting the company's single day sales record.

Louis Vuitton is a classic French brand of luxury handbags, luggage, and accessories such as scarves and belts. It is the star brand of the LVMH group, the world's largest luxury goods producer. Some other brands carried by LVMH include Fendi, Celine, and Marc Jacobs. The fashion and leather goods division of LVMH has seen its sales driven by Louis Vuitton's dynamic growth, especially in Japan where it is number one in terms of market share of luxury handbag sales. Japan accounts for 31 percent of worldwide net sales for LVMH Fashion and Leather goods. This can be attributed to the cult like obsession with Louis Vuitton in Japan. Walk down the street in the Ginza district of Tokyo, and you will see dozens of handbags bearing the golden LV logo carried by trendy women. Half of all young Japanese women own a Louis Vuitton handbag, and 90 percent own a Louis Vuitton item. In Japan status symbols such as Louis Vuitton are treated almost like a necessity.

HISTORY OF LOUIS VUITTON

The founder, Louis Vuitton, was born in the French countryside on August 4, 1821. At age 16 he went to Paris looking for work and became an apprentice for Monsieur Marèchal, a famous trunk maker and master packer.[1] By age 30, Louis

Melanie Neault, Philip C H Lee and Philippe Nivelle from the Japan-focused MBA program at University of Hawaii at Manoa prepared this case under the supervision of Professor Masaaki Kotabe, solely as the basis for class discussion (2005). The case is not intended to serve as endorsement, sources of primary data, or illustration of effective or ineffective management.

[1] A master packer is a specialist who packs gowns and suits in a manner that prevents them from wrinkling.

EXHIBIT 1

COMPARISON BETWEEN SALES OF LVMH IN JAPAN AND JAPAN'S GDP

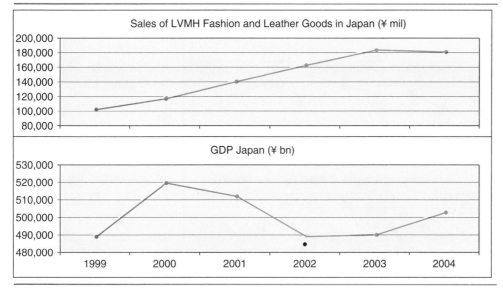

Vuitton became a dress packer for Empress Eugenie, wife of Napoleon III. A few years later, in 1854, he started making trunks and opened his first luggage store. Louis Vuitton soon became the leading luggage maker for aristocracy. He made luggage not only for Empress Eugene but also Pasha of Egypt, and French explorer Pierre Savorgnan. In 1892 Louis Vuitton started selling handbags. He also died that same year and his son Georges Vuitton took over the company.

Georges Vuitton can be credited for expanding the company overseas, turning it into a world recognized brand, masterminding over 700 LV designs, and designing the "Monogram Canvas" pattern. The Monogram Canvas pattern was inspired by Japanese floral print, reflecting that era's fascination with Japan. The four-petal pattern on the LV logo is seen today on many Louis Vuitton bags. The new intricate pattern was designed not only to update LV's image but to thwart competitors from copying Louis Vuitton handbags. When George died in the 1930s, his son Gaston took over. His creativity and love for the arts spurned many new products. Throughout the years that George and then Gaston ran the company, Louis Vuitton items became increasingly popular among the elite of society, such as Charles Lindbergh, opera singer Marthe Chenal, the Duke and Duchess of Windsor, Ernest Hemingway, and Prince Borghese.

In 1977, Henry Racamier married a Louis Vuitton descendant and was named to run the family business. He was a savvy marketer who expanded the business, broadened the product mix and promoted the brand via advertisements. In 1987 with ambitions to further grow the company, Louis Vuitton merged with a financially strong business partner Moët Hennessy. LVMH was born. Louis Vuitton was to remain independently managed by Racamier, however disputes erupted between him and other executives. The dispute ended in 1990 with Racamier being forced out of the company and the Vuitton family selling its 27 percent ownership in LVMH.

THE JAPANESE MARKET

When a sales office first opened in Japan, Gaston's intentions were not for Louis Vuitton to become Japan's most popular luxury brand, rather he was trying to curb the production and sales of counterfeit goods in the Asia region. In the 1960's, Louis Vuitton experienced a high number of fakes being made, especially overseas. Gaston Vuitton decided that a good way to combat the production of these fakes would be to open a sales office in Asia, the very place where these fakes were being made. In 1968 Asia's first Louis Vuitton sales office was opened in Tokyo Japan. Ten years later with increasing popularity of LV products, two stores were opened in Tokyo and Osaka. This was just one year after the Louis Vuitton SA holding company was created to assist with a new international development strategy to control and integrate distribution. Since the opening of the two stores in Japan, the company had rapidly continued to expand its international market. By 1981 Louis Vuitton Japan KK was incorporated.

Today, Louis Vuitton is the most popular luxury brand in Japan and enjoys a 28 percent share of the Japanese market. Sales from Japan account for about 30 percent of Louis Vuitton's worldwide sales in 2004. In spite of the hefty price tag on a Louis Vuitton bag, around $500-$5000, Japanese women cannot get enough of it.

THE TWO TIERED ECONOMY IN JAPAN

Japan's economy has been shaky since the burst of the economic bubble that formed in the 1980s. Over the past decade, Japan has been faced with rising unemployment, numerous bankruptcies, deflation, drops in consumer spending, and declining income (refer to Exhibit 2–3). In a time when people are feeling less economically secure, 100-yen shops[2] and discount brands such as Uniqlo have become increasingly popular. One would expect that in such dire

---

[2]Japan's equivalent of a Dollar store in USA.

EXHIBIT 2

JAPAN UNEMPLOYMENT RATE STATISTIC BUREAU OF THE MINISTRY
OF INTERNAL AFFAIRS AND COMMUNICATIONS

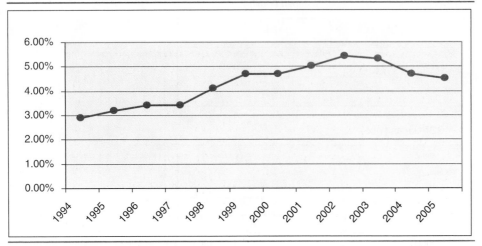

EXHIBIT 3

ANNUAL AVERAGE OF MONTHLY HOUSEHOLD
INCOME AND EXPENDITURE BY YEARLY INCOME QUINTILE
GROUP STATISTIC BUREAU MINISTRY OF INTERNAL
AFFAIRS AND COMMUNICATIONS
(Workers' Household—Values in Yen)

Year	Persons per Household	Income	Living Expenditure	Disposable Income
1994	3.63	567,174	353,116	481,178
1995	3.58	570,817	349,663	482,174
1996	3.53	579,461	351,755	488,537
1997	3.53	595,214	357,636	497,036
1998	3.50	588,916	353,552	495,887
1999	3.52	574,676	346,177	483,910
2000	3.46	560,954	340,977	472,823
2001	3.47	551,160	335,042	464,723
2002	3.46	538,277	330,651	452,501
2003	3.49	524,542	325,823	440,461
2004	3.48	530,028	330,836	444,966
2005	3.48	457,317	331,064	388,185

times, consumption of luxury goods would decline. However, the opposite has been the case in Japan. The luxury business continues to boom and over the past five years, Louis Vuitton and its competitors Hermes, Gucci, Burberry, Versace, Chanel, and Rolex, have all opened lavish boutiques in Tokyo. In 2002, European luxury brands rang up record sales in Japan in spite of its negative GDP growth and an unemployment rate that was climbing towards a record high.

THE COMPETITION

While Louis Vuitton enjoyed a great sales performance in Japan, so have the luxury brand competitors. Some of Louis Vuitton's key competitors in Japan include, Gucci, Prada,

Coach, Hermes, and Chanel to name a few. Recession or no recession, a stunning 94.3 percent of Tokyo women in their 20s own something made by Louis Vuitton, according to Saison Research Institute. Goods made by Gucci sit in the closets of 92.2 percent of Tokyo twentysomethings; 57.5 percent own Prada and 51.7 percent Chanel.

GUCCI

Gucci was founded during the roaring 1920s in Florence Italy as a saddle and luggage maker. In the 1960s Gucci opened stores worldwide and became a popular brand among high profile people such as Princess Grace of Monaco and Jacqueline Kennedy. A decade later Gucci opened its first store in Japan. Today Gucci is owned by Gucci Group, one the world's

EXHIBIT 4

LV AND COMPETITION IN 2003: HOW LOUIS VUITTON MATCHES UP

The century and a half old company is not only the number 1 luxury brand in Japan. It is bigger, richer, and faster growing than most competitors worldwide

Brand	2003 Sales in Billions	Percent Change	Operating Margin
Louis Vuitton	**$3.80**	**+16%**	**45.0%**
Prada	1.95	0.0	13.0
Gucci	1.85	−1.0	27.0
Hermès	1.57	+7.7	25.4
Coach	1.20	+34.0	29.9

Source: Business Week, March 22, 2004

EXHIBIT 5

A GRAPHICAL ILLUSTRATION OF LOUIS VUITTON'S SUCCESS BY BUSINESS WEEK, MARCH 22, 2004)

Attention to Detail...And Cost

ZIPPER
Laboratory equipment randomly tests zippers by opening and closing them 5,000 times.

PRODUCTION
Manufacturing methods adopted from automakers and other industries are boosting productivity by 5% a year.

HANDLE METAL RING
To cut costs, Vuitton pressured supplier of metal rings to improve production efficiency.

LEATHER TRIM
Vuitton uses hides from Northern European cattle, which have relatively few blemishes from insect bites.

PRICE TAG
Forget bargains: Vuitton never holds sales, and prices rose 10% to 12% in United States and Japan last year as the euro strengthened.

Data: Company, Business Week

leading multi-brand luxury goods companies, which includes brands such as Stella McCartney and Yves Saint Laurent. Japan accounts for 20 percent of the Gucci Groups total worldwide sales. Gucci's image is very sexy and provocative. This image is portrayed in Gucci's controversial advertisements that contain sexual innuendos (refer to Exhibit 6). The price range for a Gucci bag is in the $600-$8500 range, similar to LV.

PRADA

In 1913 Mario Prada founded a luxury leather goods boutique. Although an Italian brand, Mario Prada started making Luxury leather goods in the USA and other parts of Europe before moving to Milan. Today Prada remains a family ran company and is currently managed by Mario Prada's daughter Muccia and her husband. Prada's image portrayed in ads is very mod,

EXHIBIT 6

ADVERTISEMENTS SHOWING DIFFERENT IMAGES OF THE BRANDS

Louis Vuitton

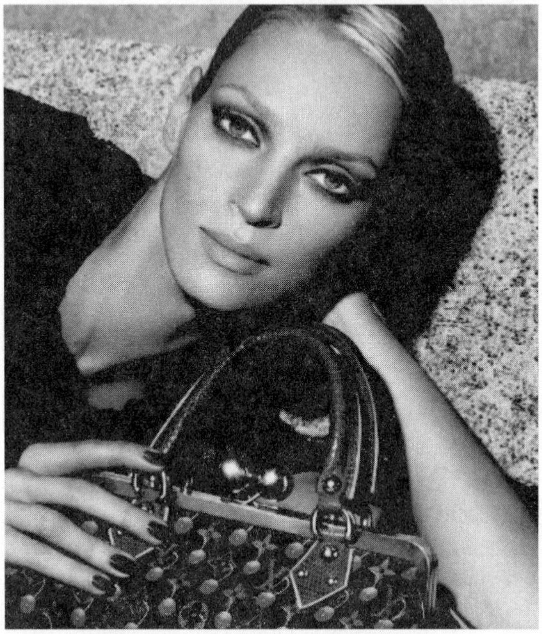

HERMÈS
PARIS

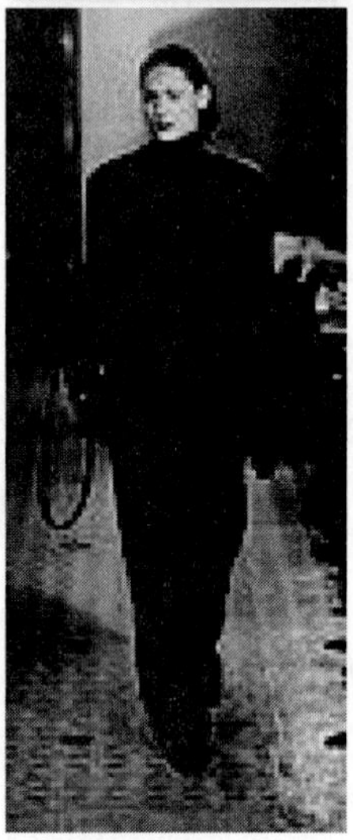

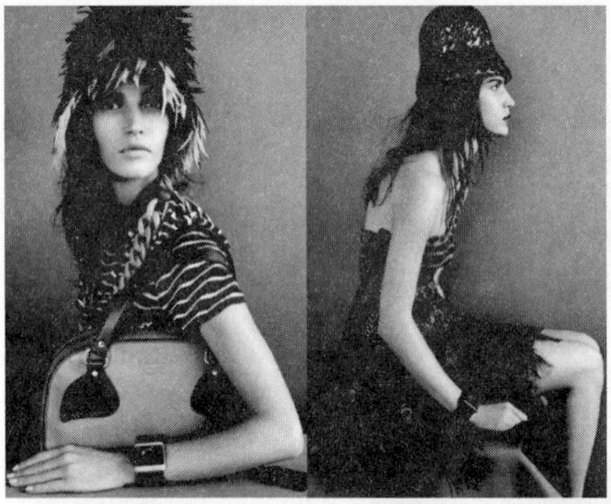

Prada

CHANEL

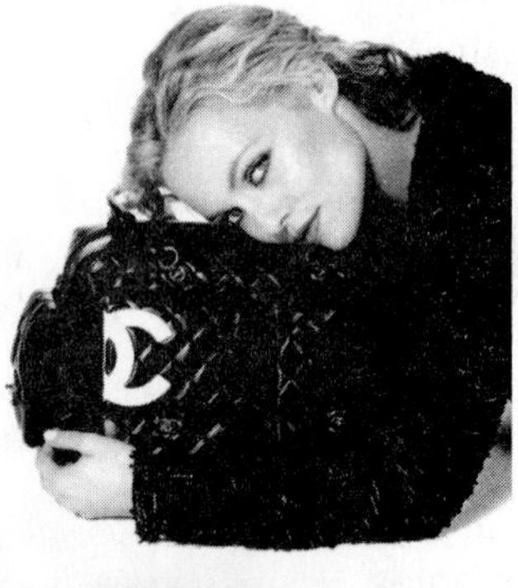

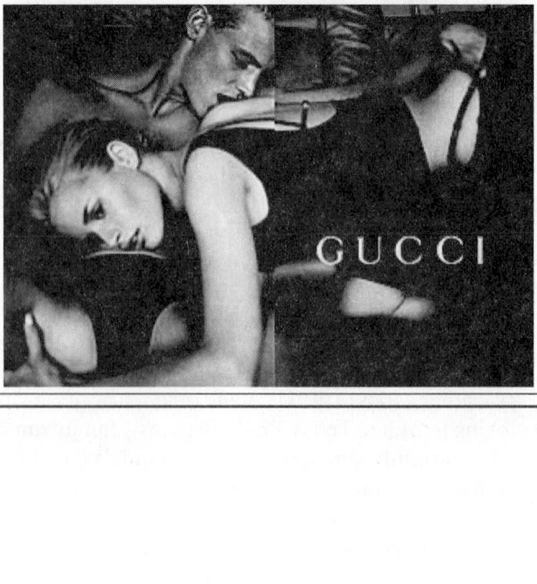

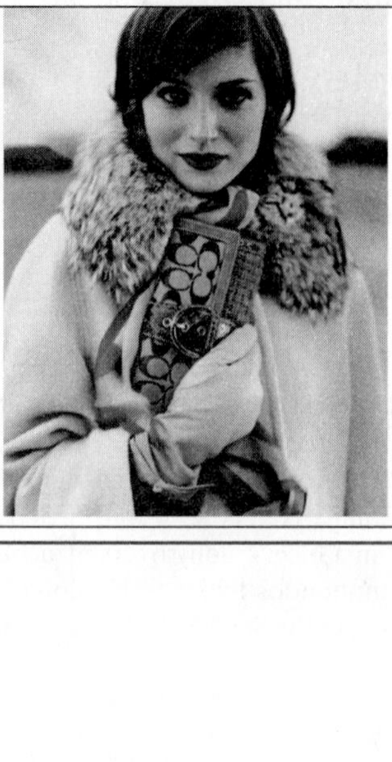

Coach

in contrast to Louis Vuitton's sexy sleak advertisements. The price range for a Prada bag is less than Louis Vuitton at about $150–$3000.

COACH

In 1940 Coach was founded in New York as a quality leather goods company. Today, 21 percent of Coach's total worldwide revenue comes from Japan. Coach is one of Louis Vuitton's fiercest competitors at number two below Louis Vuitton, in terms of market share of luxury handbags in Japan. Recently, Coach submitted a complaint to the Japanese Fair Trade Commission (JFTC) stating that LVMH is threatening to pull bags from Japanese department stores that sell Coach brand items. Currently the JFTC is investigating whether or not Louis Vuitton really has been involved in predatory business practices. In contrast to LV, Coach has a softer image. Their bags are also more affordable than Louis Vuitton. A small Coach bag averages about $275 whereas a small Louis Vuitton bag averages about $875.

HERMES

Hermes is a French-based company and the oldest of Louis Vuitton's competitors. It was originally founded in 1837 as a saddle making company and has evolved into an international producer of luxury fashion accessories. Hermes image is very classic and conservative.

CHANEL

Chanel is a privately held French company. It all began in 1908 when Gabriel Chanel started selling hats in Paris. Two years later she opened up a storefront and later began selling clothing that revolutionized the fashion industry. Gabriel Chanel saw beauty in simplicity and detested frills, big hats and tight corsets. Her clothing line was simple yet sexy, because it clung to the body and hemlines revealed the ankle. Her fashion roared through the twenties and Gabriel Chanel enjoyed great fame. Today, the Chanel brand accessories are very popular in Japan and 35 of Chanel's 100 worldwide boutiques are located in Japan.

LOUIS VUITTON'S ATTENTION TO QUALITY

So what sets Louis Vuitton apart from its competitor, placing it first place in Japan? The answer is found behind a locked door in the basement of Louis Vuitton's elegant Paris headquarters. Mechanical arms would hold handbags loaded with weights half a meter off the floor then drops it. Another machine would bombard the handbags with ultraviolet rays to test resistance to fading. Still another would tests zippers by opening and shutting them 5000 times. Quality is the most important priority for Louis Vuitton and making sure that each product must pass a rigorous control to check for default and consistency. Any bags or wallets that do not conform to the standard are destroyed.

Another way Louis Vuitton keeps its quality under tight control is by manufacturing most of its products in France. Of the 13 factories operated by the firm, 11 are located in France. Despite the high cost of labor, the management feels that it is a price to pay in order to monitor quality.

Behind the commitment to quality lies Louis Vuitton's work process that is unique and not easily imitated. In a Vuitton's factory in Ducey, employees work in teams of 20 to 30 to produce about 120 handbags a day. Each team works on one product at a time and the teams are encouraged to suggest improvements. Each employee would be performing a different task such as stitching in line. Every employee is briefed on the performance of Louis Vuitton's products such as its retail price and how well it is selling to promote continuous improvement. This in turn makes the employees autonomous for their work and responsible for the quality demanded by the luxury market. Louis Vuitton has adopted a very unique process for a French company, one that resembles the ones found in Japanese corporations.

For instance, during a test production, it was discovered that certain decorative metal studs were causing the zipper to bunch up, adding time and effort to the assembly process. The factory managers were alerted, and within a day, technicians had moved the studs further away from the zipper. The teamwork has paid off. An analyst who covered LVMH visited the factories of Vuitton and competitor Hermes, says that "Vuitton has achieved pretty close to the perfect balance between mechanization and handmade. At Hermes, it looks like you stepped into the 14th century, just rows and rows of people stitching." Hermes bags cost more, but its operating margins are only about 25 percent.

The teamwork model in Vuitton's factories was modeled on the quality circles pioneered by Japan's auto-makers and introduced by Emmanuel Mathieu who's headed industrial operations since 2000. With more efficient equipment, manufacturing productivity was boosted by 5 percent a year. The time to launch a new product until the item hit the stores was reduced from 12 months to six months in 2000.

Louis Vuitton has recently invested in i2 solutions to launch a global supply chain project focused firmly on improving the way it meets the needs of its international clientele. Supported by consultants from Cap Gemini Consulting, it improved its business processes and adopted sales forecasting and demand planning technologies to close the lead time on the products. It has significantly shrunk down the lead time to just three weeks. An overgrown cottage industry has now been transformed into a 21st-century business.

DESIGNING A TRENDY IMAGE

When Yvees Carcelle took over as president of the LVMH fashion group in 1990, he made many changes to make LV a trendy brand name. In 1997, he hired Marc Jacobs, a young hip designer from New York as creative director. Jacobs studied Vuitton's history and developed a series of modern twists on it. The first was the graffiti bag, which bore a scrawled Louis Vuitton signature. The second was the Murakami bag, designed in collaboration with Japanese artist Takashi Murakami, who rendered the famous LV initials in a kaleidoscope of colors on a white background.

The French see both the importance of keeping up with the trends with originality and flamboyance, as well as maintaining enduring prestige. Louis Vuitton invites name designers to stitch its monogram canvas into unexpected shapes and places. Young designers with short contracts are also brought in to introduce creative ideas to designs.

Many of Louis Vuitton stores are also designed with sleek and modern interior design. In 2003, a flashy, 2970-square foot store was opened in Tokyo's upscale Roppongi Hills. It has a façade built of 30,000 glass tubes and dramatic spatial interior to reinforce its brand identity. Its furnishings and innovative lighting treatment reflect the need to address the modern generation who are predisposed to DVD reruns of Sex and the City. According to a review, "Louis Vuitton Roppongi Hills delivers to its customers a sanitized yet amplified milieu." Besides high quality handbags, Louis Vuitton pampers its customers with a unique handbag shopping experience.

MARKETING

While many of the company's designs come from Marc Jacob's high-profile design team, the management values the input from its marketing team as well. One example is the Boulogne Multicolor, Louis Vuitton's shoulder bag, that went on sale in 2004 for about $1,500. It was created from a market need when marketing executives shadowed the store managers. With the success of the Murakami line in 2003, they learned that customers were asking for a Murakami shoulder bag. In a workshop attached to the marketing department, technicians modified an existing bag, the Boulogne. They added metal studs and other touches and the prototype bypassed the designers. It was approved by top executives who later sent it to production who could utilize existing templates quickly.

In terms of advertising, Louis Vuitton has outpaced its competitors by signing up superstars like Jennifer Lopez, Naomi Campbell, Kate Moss, and more recently Uma Thurman for their ad campaigns. Yet, its advertising budget is still a small portion of Louis Vuitton's annual revenues. Because of its huge revenue, it is speculated to be merely 5 percent of its revenues, half the industry average.

The distribution network is also rigidly controlled. No Vuitton bag is ever marked down. It maintains its high price points despite any marketing campaign it organizes. Louis Vuitton products are sold in Japan at an average 25 percent premium to prices in Paris. Analyst applauded Louis Vuitton's strategy of constantly building its luxury brand equity even when the economy outlook is not favorable. Market experts also approve of its insistence to own its distribution channels and to protect brand image.

CULTURAL FACTORS

It is intriguing: Why is Louis Vuitton so sought after by young Japanese women? Several experts tried to answer the question including sociologist and fashion experts. One Japanese sociologist named Masahiro Yamada coined the term "parasite singles" to define unmarried Japanese women who still live with their parents. The latter, provide for room and board, leaving their daughters with a huge disposable income to spend. According to Yamada, these young women, in their 20s and 30s are estimated to be numbering 10 million and account for the greatest part of Louis Vuitton regular customers.

However, there is another theorist named Jerry Colonna who argues that only 40 percent of sales can be attributed to the "parasite singles." As he put it himself, he sees "a wave of hedonism tinged with despair." Colonna believes that young Japanese women are "living it up" because they have no faith in the future. This would probably fit in the current economic context of Japan. For over a decade, the country has been in

an economic slump, and it might be difficult for the younger generation who has been in this environment half of their lives to be upbeat about their future.

Masanobu Sugasuke, editor of *Invitation,* a Tokyo lifestyle magazine, argues that Japanese people are more inclined to buy things that are extravagant instead of buying "regular" goods like a car or food as their level of income remains stagnant. This is the most unrealistic of all explanations so far. Why would someone, with no hopes of future income, splurge on superfluous purchases? At the extreme end, madness due to the bad economy had pushed some to get obsessed with owning luxury items.

Another consideration for Louis Vuitton's success in Japan comes from the company products' track record for high quality which appeals to the Japanese shoppers' quest for perfection. Obviously, culture has an important role when it comes to behaviors in general. Japanese people strive to maintain *wa* (harmony) and standing out in the crowd would be rude. Therefore the need to conform to a group might also explain why most women in Japan own a Louis Vuitton item.

THREATS

Like many other luxury manufacturers, Louis Vuitton has to fight against counterfeiting which has been rising in the past 2 years. Recently, Louis Vuitton closed a huge factory in Guangzhou as part of their efforts to crack down on the Chinese fake industry.

Louis Vuitton's reputation also comes from the designs of its products from its reputable lead designers. The loss of lead designers would be felt deeply and Louis Vuitton needs to address this issue seriously, especially at times when the competitions are trying to steal key personnel from top companies.

One of the biggest challenges though will be to keep the corporate machine under control. Because of the tremendous growth under which the firm operates, it is easy to expand too fast, create too many new brands, and open too many stores. Louis Vuitton managed to maintain a balance between protecting the products' exclusive aura and offering luxury for the masses. One analyst asserted, "LV has to be careful not to become a retailer and forget about the products." Louis Vuitton has shown that they are much disciplined and the company's president is fully aware of the negative consequences of loosing this discipline.

DISCUSSION QUESTIONS:

1. What are the key success factors of LV in Japan?

2. What accounts for the two tiered economy? Why are Japanese consumers (especially women) purchasing luxury goods during economically instable times?

3. What stimulates such a high demand for LV in Japan? What puts Louis Vuitton over its competitors in Japan?

4. Was there any strategy undertaken by LV to enter the Japanese market?

5. What are the challenges facing LV? And how should LV address them?

SUBJECT INDEX

Note: Page numbers followed by "e" indicate an Exhibit; page numbers followed by "gp" indicate Global Perspective.

AUTHOR INDEX

COMPANY INDEX

A

Acer, 1, 3, 263
ACNielsen, 199, 202, 209, 214, 215
    omnibus survey, China, 199e
Adams, 303
AES Corp, 162
Agfa-Gevaert, 387
Ahold, 104, 140, 380, 386
AIG, 402
Air France, 163
Alcoa, 185
    new investments, Russia, 55
Aldi, 386
Allianz, 102
Allied Domecq, 118
Altoids, and national personality
    perception, case study, 404–5
Altria, 379, 397
Amazon.com, 4, 63, 75, 143, 174, 250
    and e-commerce, 63, 250
    and euro-dominated debt, 75
    logistics management, 515
    third-party logistics (3PL)
        management, 517
AMD, 263
    global sourcing on the Web, case
        study, 346
American Export Trading Company,
    552
American Express, 99
Amway, direct selling, Chinese
    crackdown on, 570
Andean Group, 64
Anheuser-Busch
    Brazil and Mexico, expansion into,
        case study, 633–38
    Budweiser global positioning, 237e
    vs. Budweiser Budvar, Czech
        Republic, case study, 194e–195e
AOL, 63
    in China, 262gp
    and e-commerce, 63
Apple Computer, 8, 13, 335
Armani, 44
    as luxury brand in China, 44
Asea Brown Boveri (ABB), global
    networking and, 580, 580e
AT&T Wireless, 357
Audi, 143
Autolatina, 300

Avon, 135, 137, 241
    direct selling, Chinese crackdown on,
        570

B

Bajaj, 275
Barilla, 69
BarnesandNoble.com, 250
    e-commerce and, 250
BASF, entrance to gas field, Russia, 55
Bayer, 181
Behr, 353
Beiersdorf, 135
Benetton, 51
    franchising in India, 51
BenQ, acquisition of Siemens division,
    challenges of, case study, 315
Beseda, small packaging, Russian
    markets, 54
Billabong, 19
Black & Decker, 17, 261, 353, 360
    gaining competitive advantage,
        259
    product invention, 353
    Worldwide Household Board, 353
Blistex, 351, 389
Blockbuster Video, 295
    product piracy in China, 393
BMW, 3, 8, 16, 142, 198, 218, 231, 257,
    354
    and test marketing, 366
The Body Shop, 268
Boeing, 155, 291
    lobby by U.S. government for
        international orders for, 551
    vs. European Airbus, WTO and,
        72–73
Borden, and Meiji Milk, problems with
    licensing, 294gp
BP, global corporate makeover of,
    385gp
Bridgestone, 289
British Airways, 163
Brooke Bond, 54
Brown-Forman, 377
Burberry's, 98, 118
Burger King, 9
Business Monitor International (BMI),
    164
Buyback, 431

C

Cadbury, 303, 438
    and acquisitions, 303, 304
Cadbury-Schweppes, 224
Campbell Soup, 391
Canon, 19, 230, 331, 374
    and market segments, 230
    universal product with all features,
        331
Carlsberg, 188
Carrefour, 140, 249, 274–75, 386
    in Canada, 523
    e-commerce and, 249
    global account management (GAM),
        140
    retail operations, case study, 533
    SWOT analysis, 524e
Caterpillar, 289, 291
    and control, avoidance of joint
        ventures, 289–90
Cathay Pacific, 224–25
CDNOW, 614
Cemex, 1, 2
Cereal Partners Worldwide, 306
Cerveceria Cuauhtemoc Moctezuma,
    272
Champion, pricing strategy, 409
Chery, and affordable small cars in
    China, 45
Chongqing Lifan Industry Group, 179
Chrysler, 3, 91, 151, 158. *See also*
    DaimlerChrysler
    and trade restrictions, Brazil, 158
Cisco, 298
Citibank Malaysia, 401
Citigroup, 259–60
    operations in India, 48
Clan McGregor, 98
Clinique, 258
Clover, 383
Club Med, making a comeback, case
    study, 623–28
CNN, 3, 248
Coca-Cola, 16, 49, 50, 54, 55, 87, 113,
    114, 123, 153, 263, 305, 308, 366,
    374, 377, 378, 388, 389–90, 391, 411
    and currency hedging, 87
    effects of single-party-dominant
        system on, Russia and Hungary
        (1991), 153